THE UNSETTLING MIND

RICHARD JOHN KOSCIEJEW

authorHOUSE®

AuthorHouse™
1663 Liberty Drive
Bloomington, IN 47403
www.authorhouse.com
Phone: 1 (800) 839-8640

Published by AuthorHouse 06/24/2020

ISBN: 978-1-7283-6537-4 (sc)
ISBN: 978-1-7283-6536-7 (e)

Print information available on the last page.

This book is printed on acid-free paper.

During the early 1900s, in examining the workings of the nervous system, physiologists were beginning to explore the idea that the transmission of nerve impulses takes place, in part, through or by chemical means. Otto Loewi decided to explore this idea. During a stay in London in 1903, he met Sir Henry Dale, who was also interested in the chemical transmission of nerve impulses. However, for Otto Loewi, Dale, and all the other researchers pursuing a chemical transmitter of nerve impulses, years of effort produced no solid evidence. In 1921 Loewi suspended two frogs' hearts in solution, one with a major nerve removed. Removing fluid from the heart that still contained the nerve, and injecting the fluid into the nerveless heart, Loewi observed that the second heart behaved as if the missing nerve were present. The nerves, he concluded, do not act directly on the heart - it is the action of chemicals, freed by the stimulation of nerves, that causes increases in heart rate and other functional changes. In 1926 Loewi and his colleagues identified one of the chemicals in his experiment as 'acetylcholine'. This was indisputably a neurotransmitter - a chemical that serves to transmit nerve impulses in the involuntary nervous system.

We can now acknowledge that the neurotransmitters are inherently made by chemically induced neurons, or nerve cells. Neurons send out neurotransmitters as chemical signals to activate or inhibit the function of neighbouring cells.

The nerves do not perform an action directly on or upon the nerves of which actions are chemical responses, freed by the stimulation of nerves in heart rate and other functional changes, as they are identified as the chemical transmitter of nerve impulses. One such chemical nerve transmitter is identified as 'acetylcholine' which is a chemical that serves to transmit nerve impulses in the involuntary nerve system.

Within the central nervous system, which consists of the brain and the spinal cord, neurotransmitters pass from neuron to neuron. In the peripheral nervous system, which is made up of the nerves that run from the central nervous system to the rest of the body, the chemical signals pass between a neuron and an adjacent muscle or gland cells.

Chemical compounds belonging to three chemical families - are widely recognized as neurotransmitters. In addition, certain other body chemicals, including adenosine, histamine, enkephalin, endorphin, and epinephrine, have neurotransmitter-like properties. Experts believe that there are many more neurotransmitters yet undiscovered.

The first of three neurotransmitter families is composed of amines, a group of compounds containing molecules of carbon, hydrogen, and nitrogen. Among the amines neurotransmitters are acetylcholine, norepinephrine, dopamine, and serotonin. Acetylcholine is the most widely used neurotransmitter in the body, and neurons that leave the central nervous system (for example, those running to skeletal muscle) use acetylcholine as their neurotransmitter neurons that run to the heart, blood vessels, and other organs may use acetylcholine or norepinephrine. Dopamine is involved in the movement of muscles, and it controls the secretion of the pituitary hormone prolactin, which triggers milk production in nursing mothers.

The second neurotransmitter family is composed of amino acids, organic compounds containing both an amino group (NH2) and a carboxylic acid group (COOH). Amino acids that serve as neurotransmitters include glycine, glutamic and aspartic acids, and gamma-amino butyric acid (GABA). Glutamic acid and GABA are the most abundant neurotransmitters within the central nervous system, and especially in the cerebral cortex, which is largely responsible for such higher brain functions as thought and interpreting sensations.

The third neurotransmitter family is composed of peptides, which are compounds that contain at least two, and sometimes as many as 100 amino acids. Peptide neurotransmitters are poorly understood, but scientists know that the peptide neurotransmitter called substance [P] influences the sensation of pain.

Overall, each neuron uses only a single compound as its neurotransmitter. However, some neurons outside the central nervous system can release both an amine and a peptide neurotransmitter.

Neurotransmitters are manufactured from precursor compounds like amino acids, glucose, and the dietary amine-called choline. Neurons modify the structure of these precursor compounds in a series of reactions with enzymes. Neurotransmitters that answer by way of returning from amino acids include serotonin, for which is derived from tryptophan. Dopamine and norepinephrine, its by-product is derived as an end point in starting a new set of evincing tyrosine, and glycine, which is derived from threonine. Amid the neurotransmitters built from glucose are glutamate, aspartate, and GABA, the choline serves as the precursor or forerunner for acetylcholine.

Neurotransmitters are released into a microscopic gap, called a synapse, that separates the transmitting neuron from the cell receiving the chemical signal. The cell that generates the signal is called the presynaptic cell, while the receiving cell is termed the postsynaptic cell.

After their release into the synapse, neurotransmitters combine chemically with highly specific protein molecules, termed receptors, embedded in the surface membranes of the postsynaptic cell. When this combination occurs, the voltage, or electrical force, of the postsynaptic cell is either increased (excited) or decreased (inhibited).

When a neuron is in its resting state, its voltage is about -70 millivolts. An excitatory neurotransmitter alters the membrane of the postsynaptic neuron, making it possible for ions (electrically charged molecules) to move back and forth across the neuron's membranes. This flow of ions makes the neuron's voltage rise toward zero. If enough excitatory receptors have been activated, the postsynaptic neuron responds by firing, generating a nerve impulse that causes its own neurotransmitter to be released into the next synapse. An inhibitory neurotransmitter causes different ions to pass back and forth across the postsynaptic neuron's membrane, lowering the nerve cell's voltage to -80 or -90 millivolts. The drop in voltage makes it less likely that the postsynaptic cell will fire.

If the postsynaptic cell is a muscle cell rather than a neuron, an excitatory neurotransmitter will cause the muscle to contract. If the postsynaptic cell is a gland cell, an excitatory neurotransmitter will cause the cell to secrete its contents.

While most neurotransmitters interact with their receptors to create new electrical nerve impulses that energize or inhibit the adjoining cell, some neurotransmitter interactions do not generate or suppress nerve impulses. Instead, they interact with a second type of receptor that changes the internal chemistry of the postsynaptic cell by either causing or blocking the formation of chemicals called second messenger molecules. These second messengers regulate the postsynaptic cell's biochemical processes and enable it to conduct the maintenance necessary to continue synthesizing neurotransmitters and conducting nerve impulses. Examples of second messengers, which are formed and entirely contained within the postsynaptic cell, include cyclic adenosine monophosphate, diacylglycerol, and inositol phosphates.

Once neurotransmitters have been secreted into synapses and have passed on their chemical signals, the presynaptic neuron clears the synapse of neurotransmitter molecules. For example, acetylcholine is broken down by the enzyme acetylcholine sterase into choline and acetate. Neurotransmitters like dopamine, serotonin, and GABA is removed by a physical process called reuptake. In reuptake, a protein in the presynaptic membrane acts as a sort of sponge, causing the neurotransmitters to reenter the presynaptic neuron, where they can be broken down by enzymes or repackaged for reuse.

Neurotransmitters are known to be involved in many disorders, including Alzheimer's disease. Victims of Alzheimer's disease suffer from loss of intellectual capacity, disintegration of personality, mental confusion, hallucinations, and aggressive - even violent behaviour. These symptoms are the result of progressive degeneration in many types of neurons in the brain. Forgetfulness, one of the earliest symptoms of Alzheimer's disease, is partly caused by the destruction of neurons that normally release the neurotransmitter acetylcholine. Medications that increase brain levels of acetylcholine have helped restore short-term memory and reduce mood swings in some Alzheimer's patients.

Neurotransmitters also play a role in Parkinson disease, which slowly attacks the nervous system, causing symptoms that worsen over time. Fatigue, mental confusion, a masklike facial expression, stooping posture, shuffling gait, and problems with eating and speaking are among the difficulties suffered by Parkinson victims. These symptoms have been partly linked to the deterioration and eventual death of neurons that run from the base of the brain to the basal ganglia, a collection of nerve cells that manufacture the neurotransmitter dopamine. The reasons why such neurons die are yet to be understood, but the related symptoms can be alleviated. L-dopa, or levodopa, widely used to treat Parkinson disease, acts as a supplementary precursor for dopamine. It causes the surviving neurons in the basal ganglia to increase their production of dopamine, by that compensating to some extent for the disabled neurons.

Dopamine, is also referred to as the chemical known to be a neurotransmitter, which is essential to the functioning of the central nervous system. In the process of neurotransmission, dopamine is transferred from one nerve cell, or neuron, to another, playing a key role in brain function and human behaviour.

Dopamine forms from a precursor molecule called Dopa, which is manufactured in the liver from the amino acid tyrosine. Dopa is then transported by the circulatory system to neurons in the brain, where the conversion to dopamine takes place.

Dopamine is a versatile neurotransmitter. Among its many functions, it plays a major role in two activities of the central nervous system: one that helps control movement, and a second that are strongly associated with emotion-based behaviours.

The pathway involved in movement control is called the nigrostriatal pathway. Dopamine is released by neurons that originate from an area of the brain called the substantia nigra and connect to the part of the brain known as the corpora striata, an area known to be important in controlling the musculoskeletal system.

The second brain pathway in which dopamine plays a major role is called the mesocorticolimbic pathway, neurons in an area of the brain called the ventral tegmentalarea acting to impart on or upon dopamine to other neurons connected to various parts of the limbic system, which is responsible for regulating emotion, motivation, behaviour, the sense of smell, and variously autonomic, or involuntary, functions like heartbeat and breathing.

A growing body of evidence suggests that dopamine is involved in several major brain disorders, the intervening decease called narcolepsy is characterized by brief, recurring episodes of sudden, deep sleep, is associated with abnormally high levels of both dopamine and a second neurotransmitter, acetylcholine. Huntington's chorea, an inherited, fatal illness in which neurons in the base of the brain are progressively destroyed, is also linked to an excess of dopamine.

Commonly known as shaking palsy, Parkinson disease is another brain disorder in which dopamine is involved. Besides tremors of the limbs, Parkinson patients suffer from muscular rigidity, which leads to difficulties in walking, writing, and speaking. This disorder results from the degeneration and death of neurons in the nigrostriatal pathway, resulting in low levels of dopamine. The symptoms of Parkinson disease can be minimized by treatment with a drug called levodopa, or L-dopa, which converts to dopamine in the brain.

Schizophrenia is a psychiatric disorder characterized by loss of contact with reality and major changes in personality. Schizophrenics have normal levels of dopamine in the brain, but because they are highly sensitive to this neurotransmitter, these normal levels of a dopamine trigger unusual behaviours. Drugs such as Thorazine that blocks the action of dopamine have been found to decrease the symptoms of schizophrenia.

Studies indicate that people who are addicted to alcohol and other drugs, assimilating in specificity in which the body structure of cocaine and nicotine have less dopamine in the mesocorticolimbic pathway. These drugs appear to increase dopamine levels, resulting in the pleasurable feelings associated with the drug.

Many other effective drugs have been shown to act by influencing neurotransmitter behaviour. Some drugs work by interfering with the interactions between neurotransmitters and intestinal receptors. For example, belladonna decreases intestinal cramps in such disorders as irritable bowel syndrome by blocking acetylcholine from combining with receptors. This process reduces nerve signals to the bowel wall, which prevents painful spasms.

Other drugs block the 'reuptake' process. One well-known example is the drug Fluoxetine (Prozac), which blocks the reuptake of serotonin. Serotonin then remains in the synapse for a longer time, and its ability to act as a signal is prolonged, which contributes to the relief of depression and the control of obsessive-compulsive behaviours.

Studies suggest that people who are addicted to alcohol and other drugs like, cocaine and nicotine have less dopamine in the mesocorticolimbic pathway. These drugs appear to increase dopamine levels, resulting in the pleasurable feelings associated with the drugs.

Serotonin neurotransmitter, or chemical that transmits messages across the synapses, or gaps, between adjacent cells, that among its many functions, serotonin is released from blood cells called platelets to activate blood vessel constriction or blood clotting or coagulation, as to alter by chemical reaction from a liquid or blood to more or less of forming jelly. As the blood is coagulated and thus self-sustaining of a limited, natural or appropriately enable cessation. The gastrointestinal tract, serotonin inhibits gastric acid production and stimulates muscle contraction in the intestinal wall. Its functions in the central nervous system and effects on human behaviour - including mood, memory, and appetite control - have been the subject of a great deal of research. This intensive study of serotonin has revealed important knowledge about the serotonin-relational cause and treatment of many illnesses as brought about, the fact or condition which is responsible for an effect.

Serotonin is produced in the brain from the amino acid tryptophan, which is derived from foods high in protein, such as meat and dairy products. Tryptophan is transported to the brain, where it is broken down by enzymes to produce serotonin. During neurotransmission, serotonin is transferred from one nerve cell, or neuron, to another, triggering an electrical impulse that stimulates or inhibits cell activity as needed. Serotonin is then reabsorbed by the first neuron, in a process known as reuptake, where it is recycled and used again or converted into an inactive chemical form and excreted.

While the complete picture of serotonin's function in the body is still being investigated, many disorders are known to be associated with an imbalance of serotonin in the brain. Drugs that manipulate serotonin levels have been used to alleviate the symptoms of serotonin imbalances. Some of these drugs, known as selective serotonin reuptake inhibitors (SSRIs), block or inhibit the reuptake of serotonin into neurons, enabling serotonin to remain active in the synapses for a longer period. These medications are used to treat such psychiatric disorders as depression; Obsessive-compulsive disorder, in which repetitive and disturbing thoughts trigger bizarre, ritualistic behaviours, and impulsive aggressive behaviours. Fluoxetine (more commonly known by the brand name Prozac), is a widely prescribed SSRI used to treat depression, and more recently, obsessive-compulsive disorder.

Drugs that affect serotonin levels may prove beneficial in the treatment of nonpsychiatric disorders as well, including diabetic neuropathy (degeneration of nerves outside the central nervous system in diabetics) and premenstrual syndrome. Recently the serotonin-releasing agent dexfenfluramine has been approved for patients who are 30 percent or more over their ideal body weight. By preventing serotonin reuptake, dexfenfluramine promotes satiety, or fullness, after eating less food.

Other drugs serve as agonists that react with neurons to produce effects similar to those of serotonin. Serotonin agonists have been used to treat migraine headaches, in which low levels of serotonin cause arteries in the brain to swell, resulting in a headache. Sumatriptan is an agonist drug that mimics the effects of serotonin in the brain, constricting blood vessels and alleviating pain.

Drugs known as antagonists bind with neurons to prevent serotonin neurotransmission. Some antagonists have been found effective in treating the nausea that typically accompanies radiation and chemotherapy in cancer treatment. Antagonists are also being tested to treat high blood pressure and other cardiovascular disorders by blocking serotonin's ability to constrict blood vessels. Other antagonists may produce an effect on learning and memory in age-associated memory impairment.

The Synapse is the function across which a nerve impulse passes from an axon terminal to a neuron, muscle cell or gland cell, its signal conveying everything that human beings sense and think, and every motion they make, following nerve pathways in the human body as waves of ions (atoms or groups of atoms that carries electric charges). Australian physiologist Sir John Eccles discovered many intricacies of this electrochemical signalling process, particularly the pivotal step in which a signal is conveyed from one nerve cell to another. He shared the 1963 Nobel Prize in physiology or medicine for this work, which he described in a 1965 Scientific American article.

How does one nerve cell transmit the nerve impulse to another cell? Electron microscopy and other methods show that it does so by means of special extensions that deliver a squirt of transmitter substance.

The human brain is the most highly organized form of matter known, and in complications and complex plexuities that the brains of the other higher animals are not greatly inferior.

For certain purposes regarding the brain for being analogous to a machine is expedient. Even if it is so regarded, however, it is a machine of a totally different kind from those made by man. In trying to understand the workings of his own brain man meets his highest challenge. Nothing is given; There are no operating diagrams, no maker's instructions.

The first step in trying to understand the brain is to examine its structure to discover the components from which it is built and how they are related to each and one another. After that, one is to accomplish, to a better understanding the mode of distributive contributions as the mechanistic operations of the simplest component. These two modes of investigation - the morphological and the physiological - have now become complementary. In studying the nervous system with today's sensitive electrical device, however, finding physiological events that cannot be correlated with any known anatomical structure is all too easy. Conversely, the electron microscope unveils many structural details extending beyond a level or a normal physiological significance for being obscure or unknown.

Overall, each neuron uses only a single compound as its neurotransmitter. However, some neurons outside the central nervous system can release both an amine and a peptide neurotransmitter.

When a neuron, which of specialized cell transmitting nerve impulses, when in its resting state, its voltage is about -70 millivolts, an excitatory neurotransmitter alters the membrane of the postsynaptic neuron, making it possible for ions (electrically charged molecules) to move back and forth across the neuron's membranes. This flow of ions makes the neuron's voltage rise toward zero. If enough excitatory receptors have been activated, the postsynaptic neuron responds by firing, generating a nerve impulse that causes its own neurotransmitter to be released into the next synapse. An inhibitory neurotransmitter causes different ions to pass back and forth as if to oscillate across to the opposite sides of the postsynaptic neuron's membrane, lowering the nerve cell's voltage to -80 or -90 millivolts. The drop in voltage makes it less likely that the postsynaptic cell will fire.

While most neurotransmitters interact with their receptors to create new electrical nerve impulses that energize or inhibit the adjoining cell, some neurotransmitter interactions do not generate or suppress nerve impulses. Instead, they interact with a second type of receptor that changes the internalized chemistry of the postsynaptic cell by either causing or blocking the formation of chemicals called second messenger molecules. These second messengers regulate the postsynaptic cells' biochemical processes and enable it to conduct the maintenance necessary to continue synthesizing neurotransmitters and conducting nerve impulses. Examples of second messengers, which are formed and entirely contained within the postsynaptic cell, include cyclic adenosine monophosphate, diacylglycerol, and inositol phosphates.

Once neurotransmitters have been secreted into synapses and have passed on their chemical signals, the presynaptic neuron clears the synapse of neurotransmitter molecules. For example, acetylcholine is broken down by the enzyme acetylcholine sterase into choline and acetate. Neurotransmitters like dopamine, serotonin, and GABA is removed by a physical process called 'reuptake'. In reuptake, a protein in the presynaptic membrane acts as a sort of sponge, causing the neurotransmitters to reenter the presynaptic neuron, where they can be broken down by enzymes or repackaged for reuse.

Neurotransmitters also play an exteriorized role in the delineation in properties whose aspects, style and atmosphere which are described or portrayed in words, expressing things that are recognized in their appearance or as the functional role in Parkinson disease, which slowly attacks the nervous system, causing symptoms that worsen over time. Fatigue, mental confusion, a mask-like facial expression, stooping posture, shuffling gait, and problems with eating and speaking are among the difficulties suffered by Parkinson victims. These symptoms have been partly linked to the deterioration and eventual death of neurons that run from the base of the brain to the basal ganglia, a collection of nerve cells that manufacture the neurotransmitter dopamine. The reasons why such neurons die are yet to be understood, but the related symptoms can be alleviated. L-dopa, or levodopa, widely used to treat Parkinson disease, acts as a supplementary precursor for dopamine. It causes the surviving neurons in the basal ganglia to increase their production of dopamine, by that compensating to some extent for the disabled neurons.

Dopamine, also have to do with the chemical known to be a neurotransmitter, which is essential to the functioning of the central nervous system. In the process of neurotransmission, dopamine is transferred from one nerve cell, or neuron, to another, playing a key role in brain function and human behaviour.

Dopamine makes possibly the construct whose fabricated appearance as distinguished from such forms that are generated from a precursor molecule called Dopa, which is manufactured in the liver from the amino acid tyrosine. Dopa is then transported by the circulatory system to neurons in the brain, where the conversion to dopamine takes place.

Dopamine is a versatile neurotransmitter. Among its many functions, it plays a major role, as aforementioned, in two activities of the central nervous system: one that helps control movement, and a second that are strongly associated with emotion-based behaviours.

The pathway involved in movement control is called the nigrostriatal pathway. Dopamine is released by neurons that originate from an area of the brain called the substantia nigra and connect to the part of the brain known as the corpora striata, an area known to be important in controlling the musculoskeletal system.

The second brain pathway in which dopamine plays a major role is called the mesocorticolimbic pathway, neurons in an area of the brain called the ventral tegmentalarea acting to impart on or upon dopamine to other neurons connected to various parts of the limbic system, which is responsible for regulating emotion, motivation, behaviour, the sense of smell, and variously autonomic, or involuntary, functions like heartbeat and breathing.

Commonly known as shaking palsy, Parkinson disease is another brain disorder in which dopamine is involved. Besides tremors of the limbs, Parkinson patients suffer from muscular rigidity, which leads to difficulties in walking, writing, and speaking. This disorder results from the degeneration and death of neurons in the nigrostriatal pathway, resulting in low levels of dopamine. The symptoms of Parkinson disease can be minimized by treatment with a drug called levodopa, or L-dopa, which converts to dopamine in the brain.

Schizophrenia is a psychiatric disorder characterized by loss of contact with reality and major changes in personality. Schizophrenics have normal levels of dopamine in the brain, but because they are highly sensitive to this neurotransmitter, these normal levels of a dopamine trigger unusual behaviours. Drugs such as Thorazine that blocks the action of dopamine have been found to decrease the symptoms of schizophrenia.

Studies have indicated that people who are addicted to alcohol and other drugs, assimilating in detail the body structure of cocaine and nicotine have less dopamine in the mesocorticolimbic pathway. These drugs appear to increase dopamine levels, resulting in the pleasurable feelings associated with the drugs.

Once, again, serotonin is produced in the brain from the amino acid tryptophan, which is derived from foods high in protein, such as meat and dairy products. Tryptophan is transported to the brain, where it is broken down by enzymes to produce serotonin. During neurotransmission, serotonin is transferred from one nerve cell, or neuron, to another, triggering an electrical impulse that stimulates or inhibits cell activity as needed. Serotonin is then reabsorbed by the first neuron, in a process known as reuptake, where it is recycled and used again or converted into an inactive chemical form and excreted.

While the complete picture of serotonin's function in the body is still being investigated, many disorders are known to be associated with an imbalance of serotonin in the brain. Drugs that manipulate serotonin levels have been used to alleviate the symptoms of serotonin imbalances. Some of these drugs, known as selective serotonin reuptake inhibitors (SSRIs), block or inhibit the reuptake of serotonin into neurons, enabling serotonin to remain active in the synapses for a longer period. These medications are used to treat such psychiatric disorders as depression; Obsessive-compulsive disorder, in which repetitive and disturbing thoughts trigger bizarre, ritualistic behaviours, and impulsive aggressive behaviours. Fluoxetine is a prescribed SSRI used to treat depression, and more recently, obsessive-compulsive disorder.

Drugs that affect serotonin levels may prove beneficial in the treatment of nonpsychiatric disorders as well, including diabetic neuropathy (degeneration of nerves outside the central nervous system in diabetics) and premenstrual syndrome. Recently the serotonin-releasing agent dexfenfluramine has been approved for patients who are 30 percent or more over their ideal body weight. By preventing serotonin reuptake, dexfenfluramine promotes satiety, or fullness, after eating less food.

Other drugs serve as agonists that react with neurons to produce effects similar to those of serotonin. Serotonin agonists have been used to treat migraine headaches, in which low levels of serotonin cause arteries in the brain to swell, resulting in a headache. Sumatriptan is an agonist drug that mimics the effects of serotonin in the brain, constricting blood vessels and alleviating pain.

Drugs known as antagonists bind with neurons to prevent serotonin neurotransmission. Some antagonists have been found effective in treating the nausea that typically accompanies radiation and chemotherapy in cancer treatment. Antagonists are also being tested to treat high blood pressure and other cardiovascular disorders by blocking serotonin's ability to constrict blood vessels. Other antagonists may produce an effect on learning and memory in age-associated memory impairment.

The Synapse, again, is the meaningful consequence that takes to acknowledge the presence of conveying everything that human beings sense and think, and every motion they make, following nerve pathways in the human body as waves of ions (atoms or groups of atoms that carries electric charges). Australian physiologist Sir John Eccles discovered many intricacies of this electrochemical signalling process, particularly the pivotal step in which a signal is conveyed from one nerve cell to another. He shared the 1963 Nobel Prize in physiology or medicine for this work, which he described in a 1965 Scientific American article.

How does one nerve cell transmit the nerve impulse to another cell? Electron microscopy and other methods show that it does so by means of special extensions that deliver a squirt of transmitter substance.

The human brain is the most highly organized form of matter known, and in complexity the brains of the other higher animals are not greatly inferior. For certain purposes regarding the brain for being analogous to a machine is expedient. Even if it is so regarded, however, it is a machine of a totally different kind from those made by man. In trying to understand the workings of his own brain man meets his highest challenge. Nothing is given; There are no operating diagrams, no maker's instructions.

The first step in trying to understand the brain is to examine its structure to discover the components from which it is built and how they are related to each and one another. Aftermost, that one can attempt by changing of a closed to an open condition, is to understand the distributive contribution as to the mechanistic operations of its simplest component. These two modes of investigation - the morphological and the physiological - have now become complementary. In studying the nervous system with today's sensitive electrical device, however, finding physiological events that cannot be correlated with any known anatomical structure is all too easy. Conversely, the electron microscope reveals many structural details whose physiological significance is obscure or unknown.

At the close of the past century the Spanish anatomist Santiago Ramón Cajal showed how all parts of the nervous system are built up of individual nerve cells of many different shapes and sizes. Like other cells, each nerve cell has a nucleus and the surrounding cytoplasm. Its outer surface consists of many fine branches - the dendrites - that receive nerve impulses from other nerve cells, and one relatively long branch - the axon - that transmits nerve impulses. Near its end the axon divides into branches that end at the dendrites or bodies of other nerve cells. The axon can be as short as a fraction of a millimetre or if a metre, depending on its place and function. It has many properties of an electric cable and is uniquely specialized to conduct the brief electrical waves called nerve impulses. In very thin axons these impulses travel at less than one metre per second; In others, for example in the large axons of the nerve cells that activate muscles, they travel as fast as 100 metres per second.

The electrical impetuses mediating spontaneously while travelling along the axon and abruptly ceases, wherein, precipitating of a sudden refractory ground for which the axon comes to the end-point, where the axon's terminal fibres link to other nerve cells. These junction points were given the name 'synapses' by Sir Charles Sherrington, who laid the foundations of what is sometimes called 'synaptology'. If the nerve impulse is to continue beyond the synapse, it must be regenerated afresh on the other side. As recently as 15 years ago some physiologists held that transmission at the synapse was predominantly, if not exclusively, an electrical phenomenon. Now, however, there is abundant evidence that transmission is made by the release of specific chemical substances that trigger a regeneration of the impulse. That is to say, the first convincing demonstrative evidences showing that a various understanding to some transmitter substance act across the synapse was provided more than 40 years ago by Sir Henry Dale and Otto Loewi.

It has been estimated that the human central nervous system, which of course includes the spinal cord and the brain itself, consists of about 10 billion nerve cells. With rare exceptions each nerve cell receives information directly as impulses from many other nerve cells - often hundreds - and transmits information to a like number. Depending on its threshold of response, a given nerve cell may fire an impulse when stimulated by only a few incoming fibres or it may not fire until stimulated by many incoming fibres. It has long been known that this threshold can be raised or lowered by various factors. Moreover, it was supposed some 60 years ago that some incoming fibres must inhibit the firing of the receiving cell rather than excite it. The conjecture was subsequently confirmed, and the mechanism of the inhibitory effect has now been clarified. This mechanism and its equally fundamental counterpart - nerve-cell excitation - are of its topic.

But in the matter to postulate the levelling outcome by its condition or contingency of the eventuality, is that any of the contests become its fact of phenomenons. These, just the same, show other levels of anatomy which are given to some clues to show how the fine axon terminals impinge on a nerve cell and can make the cell regenerate its nerve impulse of its own nerve cell and its dendrites are covered by fine branches of nerve fibres that end in knob-like structures. These structures are the synapses.

The electron microscope has revealed structural details of synapses that fit in nicely with the view that a chemical transmitter is involved in nerve transmission, as there are enclosed in the synaptic knob are many vesicles, or tiny sacs, which appear to contain the transmitter substances that induce synaptic transmission. Between the synaptic knob and the synaptic membrane of the adjoining nerve cell is a remarkably uniform space of about 20 millimicrons that is termed the synaptic cleft. Many of the synaptic vesicles are concentrated adjacent to this cleft; It seems plausible that the transmitter substance is discharged from the nearest vesicles into the cleft, where it can act on the adjacent cell membrane. This hypothesis is supported by the discovery that the transmitter is released in packets of a few thousand molecules.

The study of synaptic transmission was revolutionized in 1951 by the introduction of delicate techniques for recording electrically interiorized singular nerve cells. This is done by inserting into the nerve cell an extremely fine glass pipette with a diameter of .5 microns - about a fifty-thousandth of an inch. The pipette is filled with an electrically conducting salt solution such as concentrated potassium chloride. If the pipette is carefully inserted and held rigidly in place, the cell membrane appears to seal quickly around the glass, thus preventing the flow of a short-circuiting current through the puncture in the cell membrane. Impaled in this fashion, nerve cells can function normally for hours. Although there is no way of observing the cells during the insertion of the pipette, the insertion can be guided by using as clues the electric signals that the pipette picks up when close to active nerve cells'.

At the John Curtin School of Medical Research in Canberra first employed this technique, choosing to study the large nerve cells called motoneurons, which lie in the spinal cord and whose function is to activate muscles. This was a fortunate choice: Intracellular investigations with motoneurons are easier and more rewarding than those with any other kind of mammalian nerve cell.

As set in the finding when the nerve cell responds to the chemical synaptic transmitter, the response depends in part, on characteristic features of ionic composition that are also concerned with the transmission of impulses in the cell and travelled along its axon. When the nerve cell is at rest, its physiological makeup resembles that of most other cells in that the water solution inside the cell is quite different in composition from the solution in which the cell is bathed. The nerve cell can exploit this difference between an externalized and internalized composition and use it in quite different ways for generating an electrical impulse and for synaptic transmission.

The composition of the external solution is well established because the solution is essentially the same as blood from which cells and proteins have been removed. The component composition of the internal solution is known only approximately. Indirect evidence suggests that the concentrations of sodium and chloride ions outside the cell are respectively some 10 and 14 times higher than the concentrations inside the cell. In contrast, the concentration of potassium ions inside the cell is about 30 times higher than the concentration outside.

How can one account for this remarkable state of affairs? Part of the explanation is that inside the cell is negatively charged with the respect of the cell about 70 millivolts. Since like charges repel each other, this internal negative charge tends to drive chloride ions (Cl-) outward through the cell membrane and, at the same time, to impede their inward movement. In fact, a potential difference of 70 millivolts is just sufficient to maintain the observed disparity in the concentration of chloride ions inside the cell and outside it; Chloride ions diffuse inward and outward at equal rates. A drop of 70 millivolts across the membrane therefore defines the 'equilibrium potential' for chloride ions.

To obtain a concentration of potassium ions (K) that is 30 times higher inside the cell than outside would require that the interior of the cell membrane be about 90 millivolts negative with respect to the exterior. Since the actual interior is only 70 millivolts negative, it falls short of the equilibrium potential for potassium ions by 20 millivolts. Evidently the thirty-fold concentration can be achieved and maintained only if there is some auxiliary mechanism for 'pumping' potassium ions into the cell at a rate equal to their spontaneous net outward diffusion.

The pumping mechanisms have fewer, but more difficult tasks of pumping sodium ions (Na) out of the cell against a potential gradient of 130 millivolts. This figure is obtained by adding the 70 millivolts of internal negative charge to the equilibrium potential for sodium ions, which is 60 millivolts of internal positive charge. If it were not for this postulated pump, the concentration of sodium ions inside and outside the cell would be almost the reverse of what is observed.

In their classic studies of nerve-impulse transmission in the giant axon of the squid, A.L. Hodgkin, A.F. Huxley and Bernhard Katz of Britain proved that the propagation of the impulse coincides with abrupt changes in the permeability of the axon membrane. When a nerve impulse has been triggered in some way, what can be described as a gate opening as the change from a closed to an open condition that allows sodium ions pour into the axon during the advance of the impulse, making the interior of the axon locally positive. The process is self-reinforcing in that the flow of some sodium ions through the membrane opens the gate further and makes it easier for others to follow. The sharp reversal of the internal polarity of the membrane makes up the nerve impulse, which moves like a wave until it has travelled the length of the axon. In the wake of the impulse the sodium gate closes and a potassium gate opens, by that restoring the normal polarity of the membrane within a millisecond or less.

With this connective understanding of the nerve impulse, as having in hand, when one is ready to follow the electrical events at the expense of the excitatory synapse. One might guess that if the nerve impulse results from an abrupt inflow of sodium ions and a rapid change in the electrical polarity of the axon's interior, something similar must happen at the body and dendrites of the nerve cell in order to generate the impulse in the first place. As this, the function of the excitatory synaptic terminals on the cell body and its dendrites is to depolarize the interior of the cell membrane essentially by permitting an inflow of sodium ions. When the depolarization reaches a threshold value, a nerve impulse is triggered.

As a simple instance of this phenomenon it has been recorded in the depolarization that occurs in a single motoneuron activated directly by the large nerve fibres that enter the spinal cord from special stretch-receptors known as annulospiral endings. These receptors in turn are found in the same muscle that is activated by the motoneuron under study. Thus the whole system forms a typical reflex arc, such as the arc responsible for the patellar reflex, or 'knee jerk.'

To conduct the experiment we anaesthetise an animal (most often a cat) and free by dissection a muscle nerves that contains these large nerve fibres. By applying a mild electric shock to the exposed nerve one can produce a single impulse in each of the fibres; Since the impulses travel to the spinal cord almost synchronously, they are referred to collectively as a volley. The number of impulses contained in the volley can be reduced by reducing the stimulation applied to the nerve. The volley strength is measured at a point just outside the spinal cord and is displayed on an oscilloscope. About half a millisecond after detection of a volley there is a wavelike change in the voltage inside the motoneuron that has received the volley. The change is detected by a micro electrode inserted in the motoneuron and is displayed on another oscilloscope.

What we find is that the negative voltage inside the cell becomes progressively implemented as the dispersive frame of occasioned negativity, as more of the fibres impinging upon the cell are to take cognizance of by or mental vision that subsequently provokes or excite into a locomotion as the stimulation exhilarates in its approaching expansion's excitation to fire. This observed depolarization is in fact a simple summation of the depolarization produced by each individual synapse. When the depolarization of the interior of the motoneuron reaches a critical point, a 'spike' suddenly appears on the second oscilloscope, showing that a nerve impulse has been generated. During the spike the voltage inside the cell changes from about 70 millivolts negative to as much as 30 millivolts positive. The spike regularly appears when the depolarization, or reduction of membrane potential, reaches a critical level, which is usually between 10 and 18 millivolts. The only effect of a further strengthening of the synaptic stimulus is to shorten the time needed for the motoneuron to reach the firing threshold. The depolarizing potentials produced in the cell membrane by excitatory synapses are called excitatory postsynaptic potentials, or EPSP's.

Through one barrel of a double-barrelled microelectrode one can apply a background current to change the resting potential of the interior of the cell membrane, either increasing it or decreasing it. When the potential is made more negative, the EPSP rises more steeply to an earlier peak. When the existing state of being differently significant for which the opening potential is made nether than an inferior negativity, the EPSP rises more slowly to a lower peak, and finally the charge inside of the cell, such that the cell is reversed so as to be positive with respect to the exterior, the excitatory synapses give rise to an EPSP that is actually the reverse of the normative one.

These observations support the hypothesis that excitatory synapses produce what amounts virtually to a short circuit in the synaptic membrane potential. When this occurs, the membrane no longer acts as a barrier to the passage of ions but lets them flow through in response to the differing electric potential on the two sides of the membrane. In other words, the ions are momentarily allowed to travel freely down their electrochemical gradients, which means that the sodium ions flow into the cell and, to a discovering degree, there exists of fewer potassium ions would flow out. It is this net flow of positive ions that creates the excitatory postsynaptic potential. The flow of negative ions, such as the chloride ion, is apparently not involved. By artificially altering the potential inside the cell one can establish that there is no flow of ions, and therefore no EPSP, when the voltage drop across the membrane is zero.

How is the synaptic membrane converted from a strong ionic barrier into an ion-permeable state? It is currently accepted that the agency of conversion is the chemical transmitter substance contained in the vesicles inside the synaptic knob. When a nerve impulse reaches the synaptic knob, some of the vesicles are caused to eject the transmitter substance into the synaptic cleft. The molecules of the substance would take only a few microseconds to diffuse across the cleft and become attached to specific receptor sites on the surface membrane of the adjacent nerve cell.

Presumably the receptor sites are associated with fine channels in the membrane that are opened in some way by the attachment of the transmitter-substance molecules to the receptor sites. With the channels thus opened, sodium and potassium ions flow through the membrane thousands of times more readily than they normally do, by that producing the intense ionic flux that depolarizes the cell membrane and produces the EPSP. In many synapses the current flows strongly for only about a millisecond before the transmitter substance is eliminated from the synaptic cleft, either by diffusion into the surrounding regions or as a result of being destroyed by enzymes. The latter process is known to occur when the transmitter substance is acetylcholine, which is destroyed by the enzyme acetylcholine sterase.

The substantiation of this general picture of synaptic transmission requires the solution of many fundamental problems. Since we do not know the specific transmitter substance for the vast majority of synapses in the nervous system, we do not know whether there are many different substances or only a few. The only one identified with reasonable certainty in the mammalian central nervous system is acetylcholine. We know practically nothing about the mechanism by which a presynaptic nerve impulse causes the transmitter substance to be injected into the synaptic cleft. Nor do we know how the synaptic vesicles not immediately next to the synaptic cleft follow to moved up to the firing line to replace the emptied vesicles. It is supposed that the vesicles contain the enzyme systems needed to recharge themselves. The entire process must be swift and efficient: The total amount of transmitter substance in synaptic terminals is enough for only a few minutes of synaptic activity at normal operating rates. There are also knotty problems to be solved on the other side of the synaptic cleft. What, for example, is the nature of the receptor sites? How are the ionic channels in the membrane opened?

The second type of synapse that has been identified in the nervous system of a common quality or quantities of which are the synapses that can inhibit or forbid the firing of a nerve cell even though it may be receiving a volley of excitatory impulses. When inhibitory synapses are examined in the electron microscope, they look very much like excitatory synapses. (There are probably some subtle differences, but they need not concern us here.) Microelectrode recordings of the activity of single motoneurons and other nerve cells have now shown that the inhibitory postsynaptic potential (IPSP) is virtually a mirror image of the EPSP. Moreover, individual inhibitory synapses, like excitatory synapses, have a cumulative effect. The chief difference is simply that the IPSP makes the cell's internalized voltage is more negative than it is normally, which is in a direction opposite to that needed for generating a spike discharge.

By driving the internal voltage of a nerve cell in the negative direction inhibitory synapses oppose the action of excitatory synapses, which of course drive it in the positive direction. So if the potential inside a resting cell is 70 millivolts negative, a strong volley of inhibitory impulses can drive the potential to 75 or 80 millivolts depreciating count. One can easily see that if the potential is made more negative in this way the excitatory synapses find it more difficult to raise the internal voltage to the threshold point for the generation of a spike. Thus, the nerve cell responds to the algebraic sum of the internal voltage changes produced by excitatory and inhibitory synapses.

If, as in the experiment described earlier, the internal membrane potential is altered by the flow of an electric current through one barrel of a double-barrelled microelectrode, one can observe the effect of such changes on the inhibitory postsynaptic potential. When the internal potential is made less negative, the inhibitory postsynaptic potential is deepened. Conversely, when the potential is made more negative, the IPSP diminishes; it finally reverses when the internal potential is driven below minus 80 millivolts.

One can, in this way be assumed that inhibitory synapses' share with excitatory synapses the ability to change the ionic permeability of the synaptic membrane. The difference is that inhibitory synapses enable ions to flow freely down an electrochemical gradient that has an equilibrium point at minus 80 millivolts rather than at zero, as is the case for excitatory synapses. This effect could be achieved by the outward flow of positively charged ions such as potassium or the inward flow of negatively charged ions such as chloride, or by a combination of negative and positive ionic flows such that the interior reaches equilibrium at minus 80 millivolts.

If the concentration of chloride ions within the cell is increased as much as three times, the inhibitory postsynaptic potential reverses and acts as a depolarizing current; that is, it resembles excitatory potential. On the other hand, if the cell is heavily injected with sulfate ions, which are also negatively charged, there is no such reversal. This simple test shows that under the influence of the inhibitory transmitter substance, which is still unidentified, the subsynaptic membrane becomes permeable momentarily to chloride ions but not to sulfate ions. During the generation of the IPSP the outflow of chloride ions is so rapid that it more than outweighs the flow of other ions that generate the normal inhibitory potential.

The effects of injecting motoneurons with more than 30 character descriptions of adversely determinate negative ions, but, with one exception the hydrated ions (ions bound to water) to which the cell membrane is permeable under the influence of the inhibitory transmitter substance are smaller than the hydrated ions to which the membrane is impermeable. The exception is the format ion (HCO2-), which may have an ellipsoidal shape and so be able to pass through membrane pores that block smaller spherical ions.

Apart from the format ion all the ions to which the membrane is permeable have a diameter not greater than 1.14 times the diameter of the potassium ion; That is, they are less than 2.9 angstrom units in diameter. Comparable investigations in other laboratories have found the same permeability effects, including the exceptional behaviour of the format ion, in fishes, toads and snails. It might be that the ionic mechanism responsible for synaptic inhibition is the same throughout the animal kingdom.

The significance of these and other studies is that they strongly suggest that the inhibitory transmitter substance open the membrane to the flow of potassium ions but not to sodium ions. It is known that the sodium ion is somewhat larger than any of the negatively charged ions, including the format ion, that are able to pass through the membrane during synaptic inhibition. Testing the effectiveness of potassium ions by injecting excess amounts into the cell is not possible, however, because the excess is immediately diluted by an osmotic flow of water into the cell.

The concentration of potassium ions inside the nerve cell is about 30 times greater than the concentration outside, and to maintain this large difference in concentration without the help of some metabolic pumps inside of the membrane would have to be charged 90 millivolts negative with respect to the exterior. This implies that if the membrane were suddenly made porous to potassium ions, the resulting outflow of ions would make the inside potential of the membrane even more adverse, and pass over without giving due attention, nonetheless, this negative state provides the solacing refuge of a resting state, and that is just what happens during synaptic inhibition. The membrane must not simultaneously become porous to sodium ions, because they exist in much higher concentration outside the cell than inside and their rapid inflow would more than compensate for the potassium outflow. In fact, the fundamental difference between synaptic excitation and synaptic inhibition is that the membrane freely passes sodium ions in response to the former and largely excludes the passage of sodium ions in response to the latter.

This fine discrimination between ions that are not very different in size must be explained by any hypothesis of synaptic action. It is most unlikely that the channels through the membrane are created afresh and accurately maintained for a thousandth of a second every time a burst of transmitter substance is released into the synaptic cleft. It is more likely that channels of at least two different sizes are built directly into the structural membrane of evincing tissues, having up or more less interdependent elements and having a definite organizational pattern, wherefore the plexuity as to be a framing representation of an explicit arrangement as the composite character that constitute its anatomical structure, that yields to the existence of distant relationships or, perhaps, the structural aim or goal for which its sufficiency is interpreted as the correct and accurate measure between sufficient and access. In some way the excitatory transmitter substance would selectively unplug the larger channels and permit the free inflow of sodium ions. Potassium ions would simultaneously flow out and thus would tend to counteract the large potential change that would be produced by the massive sodium inflow. The inhibitory transmitter substance would selectively unplug the smaller channels that are large enough to pass potassium and chloride ions but not sodium ions.

To explain certain types of inhibitory features must be added to this hypothesis of synaptic transmission. In the simple hypothesis chloride and potassium ions can flow freely through pores of all inhibitory synapses. It has been shown, however, that the inhibition of the contraction of heart muscle by the vagus nerve is due almost exclusively to potassium-ion flow. On the other hand, in the muscles of crustaceans and in nerve cells in the snail's brain synaptic inhibition is due largely to the flow of chloride ions. This selective permeability could be explained if there were fixed charges along the walls of the channels. If such charges were negative, they would repel negatively charged ions and prevent their passage; if they were positive, they would similarly prevent the passage of positively charged ions. One can now suggest that the channels opened by the excitatory transmitter are negatively charged and so do not permit the passage of the negatively charged chloride ion, even though it is small enough to move through the channel freely.

One might wonder if a given nerve cell can have excitatory synaptic action at some of its axon terminals and inhibitory action at others. The answer is no. Two different kinds of nerve cells are needed, one for each type of transmission and synaptic transmitter substance. This can readily be shown by the effect of strychnine and tetanus toxins in the spinal cord; They specifically prevent inhibitory synaptic action and leave excitatory action unaltered. As a result the synaptic excitation of nerve cells is uncontrolled and convulsions result. The special types of cells responsible for inhibitory synaptic action are now being recognized in many parts of the central nervous system.

This account of communication between nerve cells is necessarily oversimplified, yet it shows that some significant advances are being made at the level of individual components of the nervous system. By selecting the most favourable situations we have been able to throw light on some details of nerve-cell behaviour. We can be encouraged by these limited successes. Nonetheless, the task of comprehensibility understanding how and approval of it the human brain operates staggers its own imagination.

Our brain begins with its portion of the central nervous system contained within the skull. The brain is the control centre for movement, sleep, hunger, thirst, and virtually every other vital activity necessary to survival. All human emotions - including love, hate, fear, anger, elation, and sadness - are controlled by the brain. It also receives and interprets the countless signals that are sent to it from other parts of the body and from the external environment. The brain makes us conscious, emotional, and intelligent

The human brain has three major structural components: the large dome-shaped cerebrum, the smaller somewhat spherical cerebellum, and the brainstem. Prominent in the brainstem are the medulla oblongata and the thalamus - between the medulla and the cerebrum. The cerebrum is responsible for intelligence and reasoning. The cerebellum helps to maintain balance and posture. The medulla is involved in maintaining involuntary functions such as respiration, and the thalamus act as a relay centre for electrical impulses travelling to and from the cerebral cortex.

The adult human brain is a 1.3-kg. (3-lb.) Mass of pinkish-gray jellylike tissue made up of approximately 100 billion nerve cells or neurons: The Neuroglia (supporting-tissue) cells, and vascular (blood-carrying) and other tissues.

In between the brain and the cranium - the part of the skull that directly shrouds the brain - are three protective membranes, or meninges. The outermost membrane - the dura mater, is the toughest and thickest. Beneath the dura mater is a middle membrane, called the arachnoid layer. The innermost membrane layer, the pia mater, consists mainly of small blood vessels and follows the contours of the surface of the brain.

A clear liquid, the cerebrospinal fluid, bathes the entire brain and fills a series of four cavities, called ventricles, near the centre of the brain. The cerebrospinal fluid protects the internal portion of the brain from varying pressures and transports chemical substances within the nervous system.

Exteriorly, the brain appears as the organ of soft nervous tissue in the skull of vertebrates, functioning as the coordinating centre of sensation and of intellectual and nervous activity

The brain and the spinal cord together make up the central nervous system, which communicates with the rest of the body through the peripheral nervous system. The peripheral nervous system consists of 12 pairs of cranial nerves extending from the cerebrum and brain stem; a system of other nerves branching throughout the body from the spinal cord, and the autonomic nervous system, which regulates vital functions is not very consciously of its own control, such as the activity of the heart muscle, smooth muscle (involuntary muscle found in the skin, blood vessels, and internal organs), and glands.

Many motor and sensory functions have been 'mapped' to specific areas of the cerebral cortex, in general, these areas exist in both hemispheres of the cerebrum, each serving the opposite side of the body. Fewer defined are the areas of association, located mainly in the frontal cortex, operatives in functions of thought and emotion and responsible for linking input from different senses. The area of language is that of an exception: Both Wernicke's area, concerned with the comprehension of spoken language, and Broca's area, governing the production of speech, have been pinpointed on the cortex.

The most high-level brain functions take place in the cerebrum. Its two large hemispheres make up approximately 85 percent of the brain's weight. The exterior surface of the cerebrum, the cerebral cortex, is a convoluted, or folded, grayish layer of cell bodies known as the gray matter. The gray matter covers an underlying mass of fibres called the white matter. The convolutions are made up of ridgelike bulges, known as gyri, separated by small grooves called sulci and larger grooves called fissures. Approximately two-thirds of the cortical surface is hidden in the folds of the sulci. The extensive convolutions enable a very large surface area of brain cortices - measuring roughly, 1.5 m2 (16 ft2) in an adult - to fit within the cranium. The pattern of these convolutions is similar, although not identical, in all humans.

The two cerebral hemispheres are partially separated from each other by a deep fold known as the longitudinal fissure. Communication between the two hemispheres is through several concentrated bundles of axons, called commissures, the largest of which is the corpus callosum.

Several major sulci divides the cortex into distinguishable regions. The central sulcus, or Rolandic fissure, runs from the middle of the top of each hemisphere downward, forwards, and toward another major sulcus, the lateral (side), or Sylvian, sulcus. These and other sulci and gyri divide the cerebrum into five lobes: The frontal, parietal, temporal, and occipital lobes and the insula.

Although the cerebrum is symmetrical in structure, with two lobes emerging from the brain stem and matching motor and sensory areas in each, certain intellectual functions are restricted to one hemisphere. A person's dominant hemisphere is usually occupied with language and logical operations, while the other hemisphere controls emotion and artistic and spatial skills. In nearly all right-handed and many left-handed people, the left hemisphere is dominant.

The frontal lobe is the largest of the five and consists of all the cortices in front of the central sulcus. Broca's area, a part of the cortex related to speech, is located in the frontal lobe. The parietal lobe consists of the cortex behind the central sulcus, which is a groove or furrow, especially on the surface of the brain, the sulcus, near the back of the cerebrum known as the parieto-occipital sulcus. The parieto-occipital sulcus, in turn, forms the frontal border of the occipital lobe, which is located at the rearmost part of the cerebrum. The temporal lobe is to the side of and below the lateral sulcus. Wernicke's area, a part of the cortex related to the understanding of language, is located in the temporal lobe. The insula lies deep within the folds of the lateral sulcus.

The cerebrum receives information from all the sense organs and sends motor commands (signals that results in activity in the muscles or glands) to other parts of the brain and the rest of the body. Motor commands are transmitted by the motor cortex, a strip of cerebral cortex extending from side to side across the top of the cerebrum just in front of the central sulcus. The sensory cortex, parallel strips of cerebral cortex just in back of the central sulcus, receives input from the sense organs.

Many other areas of the cerebral cortex have also been mapped according to their specific functions, such as vision, hearing, speech, emotions, language, and other aspects of perceiving, thinking, and remembering. Cortical regions known as associative cortices are responsible for integrating multiple inputs, processing the information, and carrying out complex responses.

The cerebellum coordinates body movements. Located at the lower back of the brain beneath the occipital lobes, the cerebellum is divided into two lateral (side-by-side) lobes connected by a fingerlike bundle of white fibres called the vermis. The outer layer, or cortex, of the cerebellum consists of fine folds called folia. As in the cerebrum, the outer layer of cortical gray matter surrounds a deeper layer of white matter and nuclei (groups of nerve cells). Three fibre bundles called cerebellar peduncles connect the cerebellum to the three parts of the brain stem - the midbrain, the pons, and the medulla oblongata.

The cerebellum coordinates voluntary movements by fine-tuning commands from the motor cortex in the cerebrum. The cerebellum also maintaining posture and balance by controlling muscle tone and sensing the position of the limbs, as all motor activity, from hitting a baseball to fingering a violin, depends on the cerebellum.

The limbic system is a group of brain structures that play a role in emotion, memory, and motivation. For example, electrical stimulation of the amygdala in laboratory animals can provoke fear, anger, and aggression. The hypothalamus regulates hunger, thirst, sleep, body temperature, sexual drive, and other functions.

The thalamus and the hypothalamus lie underneath the cerebrum and connect it to the brain stem. The thalamus consist of two rounded masses of gray tissue lying within the middle of the brain, between the two cerebral hemispheres. The thalamus are the main relay station for incoming sensory signals to the cerebral cortex and for outgoing motor signals from it. All sensory input to the brain, except that of the sense of smell, connects to individual nuclei of the thalamus.

The hypothalamus lies beneath the thalamus on the midline at the base of the brain. It regulates or is involved directly in the control of many of the body's vital drives and activities, such as eating, drinking, temperature regulation, sleep, emotional behaviour, and sexual activity. It also controls the function of internal body organs by means of the autonomic nervous system, interacts closely with the pituitary gland, and helps coordinate activities of the brain stem.

The brain stem, is the lowest part of the brain. It serves as the path for messages travelling between the upper brain and spinal cord but is also the seat of basic and vital functions such as breathing, blood pressure, and heart rates, as well as reflexes like eye movement and vomiting. The brain stem has three main parts: the medulla, pons, and midbrain. A canal runs longitudinally through these structures carrying cerebrospinal fluid. Also distributed along its length is a network of cells, referred to as the reticular formation, that governs the state of alertness.

The brain stem is revolutionarily the most primitive part of the brain and is responsible for sustaining the basic functions of life, such as breathing and blood pressure. It includes three main structures lying between and below the two cerebral hemispheres - the midbrain, pons, and medulla oblongata.

The topmost structure of the brain stem is the midbrain. It contains major relay stations for neurons transmitting signals to the cerebral cortex, as well as many reflex centres - pathways carrying sensory (input) information and motor (output) command. Relays and reflex centres for visual and auditory (hearing) functions are located in the top portion of the midbrain. A pair of nuclei called the superior colliculus control reflex actions of the eye, such as blinking, opening and closing the pupil, and focussing the lens. A second pair of nuclei, called the inferior colliculus, controls auditory reflexes, such as adjusting the ear to the volume of sound. At the bottom of the midbrain are reflex and relay centres relating to pain, temperature, and touch, as well as several regions associated with the control of movement, such as the red nucleus and the substantia nigra.

Continuously with and below the midbrain and directly in front of the cerebellum is a prominent bulge in the brain stem called the pons. The pons consists of large bundles of nerve fibres that connect the two halves of the cerebellum and also connect each side of the cerebellum with the opposite-side cerebral hemisphere. The pons serves mainly as a relay station linking the cerebral cortex and the medulla oblongata.

The long, stalk-like are located in the lowermost portion of the brain stem is called the medulla oblongata. At the top, it is continuous with the pons and the midbrain; at the bottom, it makes a gradual transition into the spinal cord at the foramen magnum. Sensory and motor nerve fibres connecting the brain and the rest of the body cross over to the opposite side as they pass through the medulla. Thus, the left half of the brain communicates with the right half of the body, and the right half of the brain with the left half of the body.

Running up the brain stem from the medulla oblongata and through the pons and the midbrain is a netlike formation of nuclei known as the reticular formation. The reticular formation controls respiration, cardiovascular function, digestion, levels of alertness, and patterns of sleep. It also determines which parts of the constant flow of sensory information into the body are received by the cerebrum. The cerebrum or cerebrum is the principal part of the brain in vertebrates, located in the front area of the skull, which integrates complex sensory and neural functions.

There are two main types of brain cells, neurons and neuroglia. Neurons are responsible for the transmission and analysis of all electrochemical communication within the brain and other parts of the nervous system. Each neuron is composed of a cell body called a soma, and a major fibre called an axon, and a system of branches called dendrites. Axons, also called nerve fibres, convey electrical signals away from the soma and can be up to 1 m. (3.3 ft.) in length. Most axons are covered with a protective sheath of myelin, a substance made of fats and protein, which insulates the axon. Myelinated axons conduct neuronal signals faster than do unmyelinated axons. Dendrites convey electrical signals toward the soma, are shorter than axons, and are usually multiple and branching.

Neuroglial cells are twice as numerous as neurons and account for half of the brain's weight. Neuroglia (from glia, Greek for 'glue') provides structural support to the neurons. Neuroglial cells also form myelin, guide developing neurons, take up chemicals involved in cell-to-cell communication, and contribute to the maintenance of the environment around neurons.

Twelve pairs of cranial nerves arise symmetrically from the base of the brain and are numbered, from front to back, in the order in which they arise. They connect mainly with structures of the head and neck, such as the eyes, ears, nose, mouth, tongue, and throat. Some are motor nerves, controlling muscle movement; some are sensory nerves, conveying information from the sense organs and others contain fibres for both sensory and motor impulses. The first and second pairs of cranial nerves - the olfactory (smell) nerves and the optic (vision) nerve - carry sensory information from the nose and eyes, respectively, to the undersurface of the cerebral hemispheres. The other ten pairs of cranial nerves originate in or end in the brain stem.

The brain, as an organ of soft nervous tissue contained in the skull of vertebrates, functioning as the coordinating centre of sensation and of intellectual activity. The brain functions by complex neuronal, or nerve cell, circuits, as communication between neurons is both electrical and chemical and always travel from the dendrites of a neuron, through its soma, and out its axon to the dendrites of another neuron.

Dendrites of one neuron receive signals from the axons of other neurons through chemicals known as neurotransmitters. The neurotransmitters set off electrical charges in the dendrites, which then carry the signals electrochemically to the soma. The soma integrates the information, which is then transmitted electrochemically down the axon to its tip.

At the tip of the axon, small, bubble-like structures called vesicles' release neurotransmitters that carries the signal across the synapse, or gap, between two neurons. There are many types of neurotransmitters, including norepinephrine, dopamine, and serotonin. Neurotransmitters can be excitatory (that is, they excite an electrochemical response in the dendrite receptors) or inhibitory (they block the response of the dendrite receptors).

One neuron may communicate with thousands of other neurons, and many thousands of neurons are involved with even the simplest behaviour. It is believed that these connections and their efficiency can be modified, or altered, by experience.

Scientists have used two primary approaches to studying how the brain works. One approach is to study brain function after parts of the brain have been damaged. Functions that disappear or that is no longer normal after injury to specific regions of the brain can often be associated with the damaged areas. The second approach is to study the response of the brain to direct stimulation or to stimulation of various sense organs.

Neurons are grouped by function into collections of cells called nuclei. These nuclei are connected to form sensory, motor, and other systems. Scientists can study the function of somatosensory (pain and touch), motor, olfactory, visual, auditory, language, and other systems by measuring the physiological (physical and chemical) change that occur in the brain when these senses are activated. For example, electroencephalography (EEG) measures the electrical activity of specific groups of neurons through electrodes attached to the surface of the skull. Electrodes incorporate directly into the brain can give readings of individual neurons. Changes in blood flow, glucose (sugar), or oxygen consumption in groups of active cells can also be mapped.

Although the brain appears symmetrical, how it functions is not. Each hemisphere is specializing and dominates the other in certain functions. Research has shown that hemispheric dominance is related to whether a person is predominantly right-handed or left-handed. In most right-handed people, the left hemisphere processes arithmetic, language, and speech. The right hemisphere interprets music, complex imagery, and spatial relationships and recognizes and expresses emotion. In left-handed people, the pattern of brain organization is more variable.

Hemispheric specialization has traditionally been studied in people who have sustained damage to the connections between the two hemispheres, as may occur with a stroke, an interruption of blood flow to an area of the brain that causes the death of nerve cells in that area. The division of functions between the two hemispheres has also been studied in people who have had to have the connection between the two hemispheres surgically cut in order to control severe epilepsy, a neurological disease characterized by convulsions and loss of consciousness.

The visual system of humans is one of the most advanced sensory systems in the body. More information is conveyed visually than by any other means. In addition to the structures of the eye itself, several cortical regions - collectively called a primary visual and visual associative cortex - as well as the midbrain are involved in the visual system. Conscious processing of visual input occurs in the primary visual cortex, but reflexive - that is, immediate and unconscious - responses occur at the superior colliculus in the midbrain. Associative cortical regions - specialized regions that can associate, or integrate, multiple inputs - in the parietal and frontal lobes along with parts of the temporal lobe are also involved in the processing of visual information and the establishment of visual memories.

Language involves specialized cortical regions in a complex interaction that allows the brain to comprehend and communicate abstract ideas. The motor cortex initiates impulses that travel through the brain stem to produce audible sounds. Neighbouring regions of motor cortices, called the supplemental motor cortex, are involved in sequencing and coordinating sounds. Broca's area of the frontal lobe is responsible for the sequencing of language elements for output. The comprehension of language is dependent upon Wernicke's area of the temporal lobe. Other cortical circuits connect these areas.

Memory is usually considered a diffusely stored associative process - that is, it puts together information from many different sources. Although research has failed to identify specific sites in the brain as locations of individual memories, certain brain areas are critical for memory to function. Immediate recall - the ability to repeat short series of words or numbers immediately after hearing them - is thought to be located in the auditory associative cortex. Short-term memory - the ability to retain a limited amount of information for up to an hour - is located in the deep temporal lobe. Long-term memory probably involves exchanges between the medial temporal lobe, various cortical regions, and the midbrain.

The autonomic nervous system regulates the life support systems of the body reflexively - that is, without conscious direction. It automatically controls the muscles of the heart, digestive system, and lungs; Certain glands, and homeostasis - that is, the equilibrium of the internal environment of the body. The autonomic nervous system itself is controlled by nerve centres in the spinal cord and brain stem and is fine-tuned by regions higher in the brain, such as the midbrain and cortex. Reactions such as blushing indicate that cognitive, or thinking, centers of the brain are also involved in autonomic responses.

The brain is guarded by several highly developed protective mechanisms. The bony cranium, the surrounding meninges, and the cerebrospinal fluid all contribute to the mechanical protection of the brain. In addition, a filtration system called the blood-brain barrier protects the brain from exposure to potentially harmful substances carried in the bloodstream.

Brain disorders have a wide range of causes, including head injury, stroke, bacterial diseases, complex chemical imbalances, and changes associated with aging.

Head injury can initiate a cascade of damaging events. After a blow to the head, a person may be stunned or may become unconscious for a moment. This injury, called - concussion, - usually leaves no permanent damage. If the blow is more severe and haemorrhage (excessive bleeding) and swelling occurs, however, severe headache, dizziness, paralysis, a convulsion, or temporary blindness may result, depending on the area of the brain affected. Damage to the cerebrum can also result in profound personality changes.

Damage to Broca's area in the frontal lobe causes difficulty in speaking and writing, a problem known as Broca's aphasia. Injury to Wernicke's area in the left temporal lobe results in an inability to comprehend spoken language, called Wernicke's aphasia.

An injury or disturbance to a part of the hypothalamus may cause a variety of different symptoms, such as loss of appetite with an extreme drop in body weight, increase in appetite leading to obesity; Extraordinary thirst with excessive urination (diabetes insipidus), failure in body-temperature control, resulting in either low temperature (hypothermia) or high temperature (fever), excessive emotionality, and uncontrolled anger or aggression. If the relationship between the hypothalamus and the pituitary gland is damaged, other vital bodily functions may be disturbed, such as sexual function, metabolism, and cardiovascular activity.

Injury to the brain stem is even more serious because it houses the nerve centres that control breathing and heart action. Damage to the medulla oblongata usually results in immediate death.

A stroke is damage to the brain due to an interruption in blood flow. The interruption may be caused by a blood clot, constriction of a blood vessel, or rupture of a vessel accompanied by bleeding. A pouch-like expansion of the wall of a blood vessel, called an aneurysm, may weaken and burst, for example, because of high blood pressure.

Sufficient quantities of glucose and oxygen, transported through the bloodstream, are needed to keep nerve cells alive. When the blood supply to a small part of the brain is interrupted, the cells in that area die and the function of the area is lost. A massive stroke can cause a one-sided paralysis (hemiplegia) and sensory loss on the side of the body opposite the hemisphere damaged by the stroke.

Some brain diseases, such as multiple sclerosis and Parkinson disease, are progressive, becoming worse over time. Multiple sclerosis damages the myelin sheath around axons in the brain and spinal cord. As a result, the affected axons cannot transmit nerve impulses properly. Parkinson disease destroys the cells of the substantia nigra in the midbrain, resulting in a deficiency in the neurotransmitter dopamine that affects motor functions.

Cerebral palsy is a broad term for brain damage sustained close to birth that permanently affects motor function. The damage may take place either in the developing fetus, during birth, or just after birth and is the result of the faulty development or breaking down of motor pathways. Cerebral palsy is nonprogressive - that is, it does not worsen with time.

A bacterial infection in the cerebrum or in the coverings of the brain, swelling of the brain, or an abnormal growth of healthy brain tissue can all cause an increase in intracranial pressure and result in serious damage to the brain.

Scientists are finding that certain brain chemical imbalances are affiliated in associations with mental disorders such as schizophrenia and depression. Such findings have changed scientific understanding of mental health and have resulted in new treatments that chemically correct these imbalances.

During childhood development, the brain is particularly susceptible to damage because of the rapid growth and reorganization of nerve connections. Problems that originate in the immature brain can appear as epilepsy or other brain-function problems in adulthood.

Several neurological problems are common in aging. Alzheimer's disease damages many areas of the brain, including the frontal, temporal, and parietal lobes. The brain tissue of people with Alzheimer's disease shows characteristic patterns of damaged neurons, known as plaques and tangles. Alzheimer's disease produces progressive dementia, characterized by symptoms such as failing attention and memory, loss of mathematical ability, irritability, and poor orientation in space and time.

A magnetic resonance imaging (MRI) scan of the human brain reveals the contours of one of the brain's hemispheres. The scan produced in the gyri, or ridges, appears in red, while the sulci, or valleys are imaged indicators marked for being blue. Each person has slightly different patterns of gyri and sulci, which reflect individual differences in brain development.

Several commonly used diagnostic methods give images of the brain without invading the skull. Some portray anatomy - that is, the structure of the brain - whereas others measure brain function. Two or more methods may be used to complement each other, together providing a more complete picture than would be possible by one method alone.

Magnetic resonance imaging (MRI), introduced in the early 1980s, beams high-frequency radio waves into the brain in a highly magnetized field that causes the protons that form the nuclei of hydrogen atoms in the brain to reemit the radio waves. The reedited radio waves are analysed by computer to create thin cross-sectional images of the brain. MRI provides the most detailed images of the brain and is safer than imaging methods that use X-rays. However, MRI is a lengthy process and also cannot be used with people who have pacemakers or metal implants, both of which are adversely affected by the magnetic field.

Computed tomography (CT), also known as CT scans, developed in the early 1970s, operating of an imaging method X-rays the brain from many different angles, feeding the information into a computer that produces a series of cross-sectional images. CT is particularly useful for diagnosing blood clots and brain tumors. It is a much quicker process than magnetic resonance imaging and is therefore advantageous in certain situations - for example, with people who are extremely ill.

This positron emission tomography (PET) scans of the brain shows the activity of brain cells in the resting state and during three types of auditory stimulation. PET uses radioactive substances introduced within the brain to measure such brain functions as cerebral metabolism, blood flow and volume, oxygen use, and the formation of neurotransmitters. This imaging method collects data from many different angles, feeding the information into a computer that produces a series of cross-sectional images.

Changes in brain function due to brain disorders can be visualized in several ways. Magnetic resonance spectroscopy measures the concentration of specific chemical compounds in the brain that may change during specific behaviours. Functional magnetic resonance imaging (fMRI) maps changes in oxygen concentration that correspond to nerve cell activity.

Positron emission tomography (PET), developed in the mid-1970s, uses computed tomography to visualize radioactive tracers, radioactive substances are introduced into the brain intravenously or by inhalation. PET can measure such brain functions as cerebral metabolism, blood flow and volume, oxygen use, and the formation of neurotransmitters. Single photon emission computed tomography (SPECT), developed in the 1950s and 1960s, used radioactive tracers to visualize the circulation and volume of blood in the brain.

Brain-imaging studies have provided new insights into sensory, motor, language, and memory processes, as well as brain disorders such as epilepsy, cerebrovascular disease; Alzheimer's, Parkinson, and Huntington's diseases, and various mental disorders, such as schizophrenia.

Although all vertebrate brains share the same basic three-part structure, the development of their constituent parts varies across the evolutionary scale. In fish, the cerebrum is dwarfed by the rest of the brain and serves mostly to process input from the senses. In reptiles and amphibians, the cerebrum is proportionally larger and begins to connect and form conclusions about this input. Birds have well-developed optic lobes, making the cerebrum even larger. Among mammals, the cerebrum dominates the brain. It is most developed among primates, in whom cognitive ability is the highest.

In lower vertebrates, such as fish and reptiles, the brain is often tubular and bears a striking resemblance to the early embryonic stages of the brains of more highly evolved animals. In all vertebrates, the brain is divided into three regions: the forebrain (prosencephalon), the midbrain (mesencephalon), and the hindbrain (rhombencephalon). These three regional divisions are further subdivided into different structures, systems, nuclei, and layers.

The more highly evolved the animal, the more complex is the brain structure. Human beings have the most complex brains of all animals. Evolutionary principles or forces have also resulted in a progressive increase in the size of the brain. In vertebrates lower than mammals, the brain is small. In meat-eating animals, particularly primates, the brain increases dramatically in size.

The cerebrum and cerebellum of higher mammals are highly convoluted in order to fit the most gray matter surface within the confines of the cranium. Such highly convoluted brains are called gyrencephalic. Many lower mammals have a smooth, or lissencephalic (smooth head), cortical surfaces.

There is also evidence of evolutionary principles for the adaption of the brain, for example, many birds depend on an advanced visual system to identify food at great distances while in flight. Consequently, their optic lobes and cerebellum are well developed, giving them keen sight and outstanding motor coordination in flight. Rodents, on the other hand, as nocturnal animals, do not have a well-developed visual system. Instead, they rely more heavily on other sensory systems, such as a highly-developed sense of smell and facial whiskers.

Recent research in brain function suggests that there may be sexual differences in both brain anatomy and brain function. One study indicated that men and women may use their brains differently while thinking. Researchers used functional magnetic resonance imaging to observe which parts of the brain were activated as groups of men and women tried to determine whether sets of nonsense words rhymed. Men used only Broca's area in this task, whereas women used Broca's area plus an area on the right side of the brain.

A few years ago we began to think about how best to attack the problem scientifically. How to make mental events more comprehensible or given to explanation that supports the open question for or being caused by the firing of large clusters of neurons, though there are those who believe such an approach is hopeless, we feel it is not productive to worry too much over aspects of the problem that cannot be solved scientifically or, more precisely, cannot be solved solely by using existing scientific ideas. Radically new concepts may indeed be needed - recall the modifications of scientific thinking in or upon to cause a person or thing to yield the forced pressures on us by quantum mechanics. The only sensible approach is to press the experimental attack until we are confronted with dilemmas that call for new ways of thinking.

There are many possible approaches to the problem of consciousness. Some psychologists feel that any satisfactory theory should try to explain as many aspects of consciousness as possible, including emotion, imagination, dreams, mystical experiences and so on. Although such an all-embracing theory will be necessary in the long run, we thought it wiser to begin with the particular aspect of consciousness that is likely to yield most easily, such that, the visage for bearing the aspect of which may be a natural matter of personal judgment. We selected the mammalian visual system because humans are very visual animals and because so much experimental and theoretical work has already been done on it.

It is not easy to grasp exactly what we need to explain, and it will take many careful experiments before visual consciousness can be described scientifically. We did not attempt to define consciousness itself because of the dangers of premature definition. (If this seems like a copout, try defining the word 'gene' - you will not find it easy.) Yet the experimental evidence that already exists provides enough of a glimpse of the nature of visual consciousness to guide research. Yet, ours will attempt to show how this evidence opens the way to attack this profound and intriguing problem.

Visual theorists agree that the problem of visual consciousness is ill posed. The mathematical term 'ill posed' means that additional constraints are needed to solve the problem. Although the main function of the visual system is to perceive objects and events in the world around us, the information available to our eyes is not sufficient by itself to provide the brain with its unique interpretation of the visual world. The brain must use past experience (either its own or that of our distant ancestors, which is embedded in our genes) to help interpret the information coming into our eyes. An example would be the derivation of the three-dimensional representation of the world from the two-dimensional signals falling onto the retinas of our two eyes or even onto one of them.

Visual theorists also would agree that seeing is a constructive process, one in which the brain has to carry out complex activities (sometimes called computations) in order to decide which interpretation to adopt of the ambiguous visual input. 'Computation' implies that the brain acts to form a symbolic representation of the visual world, with a mapping (in the mathematical sense) of certain aspects of that world onto elements in the brain.

Ray Jackendoff of Brandeis University postulates, as do most cognitive scientists, that the computations carried out by the brain are largely unconscious and that what we become aware of is the result of these computations. But while the customary view is that this awareness occurs at the highest levels of the computational system, Jackendoff has proposed an intermediate-level theory of consciousness.

What we see, of which Jackendoff suggests, relates to a representation of surfaces that are directly visible to us, together with their outline, orientation, colour, texture and movement. (This idea has similarities to what the late David C. Marr of the Massachusetts Institute of Technology called a 2 1/2-dimensional sketch. It is more than a two-dimensional sketch because it conveys the orientation of the visible surfaces. It is less than three-dimensional because depth information is not explicitly represented.) In the next stage this sketch is processed by the brain to produce a three-dimensional representation. Jackendoff argues that we are not visually aware of this three-dimensional representation.

An example may make this process clearer. If you look at a person whose back is turned to you, you can see the back of the head but not the face. Nevertheless, your brain infers that the person has a face. We particularly consider by reasoning from evidence or from premises that induce, in as much that because if that person turned around and had no face, you would be very surprised.

The viewer-entered representation that corresponds to the visible back of the head is what you are vividly aware of. What your brain infers about the front would come from some kind of three-dimensional representation. This does not mean that information flows only from the surface representation to the three-dimensional one; it almost certainly flows in both directions. When you imagine the front of the face, what you are aware of is a surface representation generated by information from the three-dimensional model.

It is important to distinguish between an explicit and an implicit representation. An explicit representation is something that is symbolized without further processing. An implicit representation contains the same information but requires further processing to make it explicit. The pattern of coloured dots on a television screen, for example, contains an implicit representation of objects (say, a person's face), but only the dots and their locations are explicit. When you see a face on the screen, there must be neurons in your brain whose firing, in some sense, symbolizes that face.

We call this pattern of firing neurons an active representation. A latent representation of a face must also be stored in the brain, probably as a special pattern of synaptic connections between neurons. For example, you probably have a representation of the Statue of Liberty in your brain, a representation that usually is inactive. If you do think about the Statue, the representation becomes active, with the relevant neurons firing away.

An object, incidentally, may be represented in more than one way - as a visual image, as a set of words and their related sounds, or even as a touch or a smell. These different representations are likely to interact with one another. The representation is likely to be distributed over many neurons, both locally and more globally. Such a representation may not be as simple and straightforward as uncritical introspection might indicate. There is suggestive evidence, partly from studying how neurons fire in various parts of a monkey's brain and partly from examining the effects of certain types of brain damage in humans, that different aspects of a face - and of the implications of a face - may be represented in different parts of the brain.

First, there is the representation of a face as a face: two eyes, a nose, a mouth and so on. The neurons involved are usually not too fussy about the exact size or position of this face in the visual field, nor are they very sensitive to small changes in its orientation. In monkeys, there are neurons that respond best when the face is turning in a particular direction, while others seem to be more concerned with the direction in which the eyes are gazing.

Then there are representations of the parts of a face, as separate from those for the face as a whole. Further, the implications of seeing a face, such as that person's sex, the facial expression, the familiarity or unfamiliarity of the face, and in particular whose face it is, may each be correlated with neurons firing in other places.

What we are aware of at any moment, in one sense or another, is not a simple matter. We have suggested that there may be a very transient form of fleeting awareness that represents only rather simple features and does not require an attentional mechanism. From this brief awareness the brain constructs a viewer - entered representation - what we see vividly and clearly - that does require attention. This in turn probably leads to three-dimensional object representations and thence to more cognitive ones.

Representations corresponding to vivid consciousness are likely to have special properties. William James thought that consciousness infected the concerns that had involved both the attention and short-term memory. Most psychologists today would agree with this view. Jackendoff writes that consciousness is 'enriched' by attention, implying that whereas attention may not be essential for certain limited types of consciousness, it is necessary for full consciousness. Yet it is not clear exactly which forms of memory are involved. Is long-term memory needed? Some forms of acquired knowledge are so embedded in the machinery of neural processing that they are almost certainly used in becoming aware of something. On the other hand, there is evidence from studies of brain-damaged patients that the ability to lay down new long-term episodic memories is not essential for consciousness to be experienced.

It is difficult to imagine that anyone could be conscious if he or she had no memory whatsoever of what had just happened, even an extremely short one. Visual psychologists talk of iconic memory, which lasts for a fraction of a second, and working memory (such as that used to remember a new telephone number) that lasts for only a few seconds unless it is rehearsed. It is not clear whether both of these are essential for consciousness. In any case, the division of short-term memory into these two categories may be too crude.

If these complex processes of visual awareness are localized in parts of the brain, which processes are likely to be where? Many regions of the brain may be involved, but it is almost certain that the cerebral neocortex plays a dominant role. Visual information from the retina reaches the neocortex mainly by way of a part of the thalamus, and the lateral geniculate from the retina is to the superior colliculus, at the top of the brain stem.

The cortex in humans consists of two intricately folded sheets of nerve tissue, one on each side of the head. These sheets are connected by a large tract of about half a billion axons called the corpus callosum. It is well known that if the corpus callosum is cut, as is done for certain cases of intractable epilepsy, one side of the brain is not aware of what the other side is seeing. In particular, the left side of the brain (in a right-handed person) appears not to be aware of visual information received exclusively by the right side. This shows that none of the information required for visual awareness can reach the other side of the brain by travelling down to the brain stem and, from there, back up. In a normal person, such information can get to the other side only by using the axons in the corpus callosum.

A different part of the brain - the hippocampal system - is involved in one-shot, or episodic, memories that, over weeks and months, it passes on to the neocortex. This system is so placed that it receives inputs from, and projects to, many parts of the brain. Thus, one might suspect that the hippocampal system is the essential seat of consciousness. This is not the case: evidence from studies of patients with damaged brains shows that this system is not essential for visual awareness, although naturally a patient lacking one is severely disabled in everyday life because he cannot remember anything that took place more than a minute or so in the past.

In broad terms, the neocortex of alert animals probably acts in two ways. By building on crude and somewhat redundant wiring, produced by our genes and by embryonic processes, the neocortex draws on visual and other experience to slowly 'rewire' itself to create categories (or 'features') it can respond to. A new category is not fully created in the neocortex after exposure to only one example of it, although some small modifications of the neural connections may be made.

The second function of the neocortex (at least of the visual part of it) is to respond extremely rapidly to incoming signals. To do so, it uses the categories it has learned and tries to find the combinations of active neurons that, on the basis of its past experience, are most likely to represent the relevant objects and events in the visual world at that moment. The formation of such coalitions of active neurons may also be influenced by biases coming from other parts of the brain: for example, signals telling it what best to attend to or high-level expectations about the nature of the stimulus.

Consciousness, as James noted, is always changing. These rapidly formed coalitions occur at different levels and interact to form even broader coalitions. They are transient, lasting usually for only a fraction of a second. Because coalitions in the visual system are the basis of what we see, evolution has seen to it that they form as fast as possible; otherwise, no animal could survive. The brain is impeded in forming neuronal coalitions rapidly because, by computer standards, neurons act very slowly. The brain compensates for the proportional slowness, partly by using very many neurons, simultaneously and in parallel, and partly by arranging the system in a roughly hierarchical manner.

If visual awareness at any moment corresponds to sets of neurons firing, then the obvious question is: Where are these neurons located in the brain, and in what way are they firing? Visual awareness is highly unlikely to occupy all the neurons in the neocortex that are firing above their background rate at a particular moment. We would expect that, theoretically, at least some of these neurons would be involved in doing computations - trying to arrive at the best coalitions - whereas others would express the results of these computations, in other words, what we see.

Fortunately, some experimental evidence can be found to back up this theoretical conclusion. A phenomenon called binocular rivalry may help identify the neurons whose firing symbolizes awareness. This phenomenon can be seen in dramatic form in an exhibit prepared by Sally Duensing and Bob Miller at the Exploratorium in San Francisco.

Binocular rivalry occurs when each eye has a different visual input relating to the same part of the visual field. The early visual system on the left side of the brain receives an input from both eyes but sees only the part of the visual field to the right of the fixation point. The converse is true for the right side. If these two conflicting inputs are rivalrous, one sees not the two inputs superimposed but first one input, then the other, and so on in alternations.

In the exhibit, called 'The Cheshire Cat,' viewers put their heads in a fixed place and are told to keep the gaze fixed. By means of an appropriately a situated mirror, one of the eyes can look at another person's face, directly in front, while the other eye sees a blank white screen to the side. If the viewer waves a hand in front of this plain screen at the same location in his or her visual field occupied by the face, the face is wiped out. The movement of the hand, being visually very salient, has captured the brain's attention. Without attention the face cannot be seen. If the viewer moves the eyes, the face reappears.

In some cases, only part of the face disappears. Sometimes, for example, one eye, or both eyes, will remain. If the viewer looks at the smile on the person's face, the face may disappear, leaving only the smile. For this reason, the effect has been called the Cheshire Cat effect, after the cat in Lewis Carroll's Alice's Adventures in Wonderland.

Although it is very difficult to record activity in individual neurons in a human brain, such studies can be done in monkeys. A simple example of binocular rivalry has been studied in a monkey by Nikos K. Logothetis and Jeffrey D. Schall, both then at M.I.T. They trained a macaque to keep its eye's still and to signal whether it is seeing upward or downward movement of a horizontal grating. To produce rivalry, upward movement is projected into one of the monkey's eyes and downward movement into the other, so that the two images overlap in the visual field. The monkey signals that it sees up and down movements alternatively, just as humans would. Even though the motion stimulus coming into the monkey's eyes is always the same, the monkey's percept changes every second or so.

Cortical area MT (which some researchers prefer to label V5) is an area mainly concerned with movement. What do the neurons in MT do when the monkey's percept is sometimes up and sometimes down? (The researchers studied only the monkey's first response.) The simplified answer - the actual data are rather more messy - is that whereas the firing of some of the neurons correlates with the changes in the percept, for others the average firing rate is relatively unchanged and independent of which direction of movement the monkey is seeing at that moment. Thus, it is unlikely that the firing of all the neurons in the visual neocortex at one particular moment corresponds to the monkey's visual awareness. Exactly which neurons do correspond to awareness remains to be discovered.

We have postulated that when we clearly see something, there must be neurons actively firing that stand for what we see. This might be called the activity principle. Here, too, there is some experimental evidence. One example is the firing of neurons in a specific cortical visual area in response to illusory contours. Another and perhaps more striking case are the filling in of the blind spot. The blind spot in each eye is caused by the lack of photo-receptors in the area of the retina where the optic nerve leaves the retina and projects to the brain. Its location is about 15 degrees from the fovea (the visual center of the eye). Yet if you close one eye, you do not see a hole in your visual field.

Philosopher Daniel C. Dennett of Tufts University is unusual among philosophers in that he is interested both in psychology and in the brain. This interest is much to be welcomed. In a recent book, Consciousness Explained, he has argued that it is wrong to talk about filling in. He concludes, correctly, that 'an absence of information is not the same as information about an absence.' From this general principle he argues that the brain does not fill in the blind spot but rather ignores it.

Dennett's argument by itself, however, does not establish that filling in does not occur; it only suggests that it might not. Dennett also states that 'your brain has no machinery for [filling in] at this location.' This statement is incorrect. The primary visual cortex lacks a direct input from one eye, but normal 'machinery' is there to deal with the input from the other eye. Ricardo Gattass and his colleagues at the Federal University of Rio de Janeiro have shown that in the macaque some of the neurons in the blind-spot area of the primary visual cortex do respond to input from both eyes, probably assisted by inputs from other parts of the cortex. Moreover, in the case of simple filling in, some of the neurons in that region respond as if they were actively filling in.

Thus, Dennett's claim about blind spots is incorrect. In addition, psychological experiments by Vilayanur S. Ramachandran in presenting that what is filled in and that which can be quite complex depending on the overall context of the visual scene. How, he argues, can your brain be ignoring something that is in fact commanding attention?

Filling in, therefore, is not to be dismissed as nonexistent or unusual. It probably represents a basic interpolation process that can occur at many levels in the neocortex. It is, incidentally, a good example of what is meant by a constructive process.

How can we discover the neurons whose firing symbolizes a particular percept? William T. Newsome and his colleagues at Stanford University have done a series of brilliant experiments on neurons in cortical area MT of the macaque's brain. By studying a neuron in area MT, we may discover that it responds best to very specific visual features having to do with motion. A neuron, for instance, might fire strongly in response to the movement of a bar in a particular place in the visual field, but only when the bar is oriented at a certain angle, moving in one of the two directions perpendicular to its length within a certain range of speed.

It is technically difficult to excite just a single neuron, but it is known that neurons that respond to roughly the same position, orientation and direction of movement of a bar tend to be located near one and the other in the cortical sheet. The experimenters taught the monkey a simple task in movement discrimination using a mixture of dots, some moving randomly, the rest all in one direction. They showed that electrical stimulation of a small region in the right place in cortical area MT would bias the monkey's motion discrimination, almost always in the expected direction.

Thus, the stimulation of these neurons can influence the monkey's behaviour and probably its visual percept. Such experiments, do not, however, as decisively for being or passing in that the firing of such neurons is the exact neural correlate of the percept. The correlate could be only a subset of the neurons being activated. Or perhaps the real correlate is the firing of neurons in another part of the visual hierarchy that is strongly influenced by the neurons activated in area MT.

These same reservations apply also to cases of binocular rivalry. Clearly, the problem of finding the neurons whose firing symbolizes a particular percept is not going to be easy. It will take many careful experiments to track them down even for one kind of percept.

It seems obvious that the purpose of vivid visual awareness is to feed into the cortical areas concerned with the implications of what we see: From there the information shuttles on the one hand to the hippocampal system, to be encoded (temporarily) into long-term episodic memory, and on the other to the planning levels of the motor system. But is it possible to go from a visual input to a behavioural output without any relevant visual awareness?

That such a process can happen is demonstrated by the remarkable class of patients with 'blind-sight.' These patients, all of whom have suffered damage to their visual cortex, can point with fair accuracy at visual targets or track them with their eyes while vigorously denying seeing anything. In fact, these patients are as surprised as their doctors by their abilities. The amount of information that 'gets through,' however, is limited: blind-sight patients have some ability to respond to wavelength, orientation and motion, yet they cannot distinguish a triangle from a square.

It is naturally of great interest to know which neural pathways are being used in these patients. Investigators originally suspected that the pathway ran through the superior colliculus. Recent experiments suggest that a direct albeit weak connection may be involved between the lateral geniculate nucleus and other visual areas in the cortex. It is unclear whether an intact primary visual cortex region is essential for immediate visual awareness. Conceivably the visual signal in blind-sight is so weak that the neural activity cannot produce awareness, although it remains strong enough to get through to the motor system.

Normal-seeing people regularly respond to visual signals without being fully aware of them. In automatic actions, such as swimming or driving a car, complex but stereotypical actions occurred with little, if any, associated visual awareness. In other cases, the information conveyed is either very limited or very attenuated. Thus, while we can function without visual awareness, our behaviour without it is rather restricted.

Clearly, it takes a certain amount of time to experience a conscious percept. It is difficult to determine just how much time is needed for an episode of visual awareness, but one aspect of the problem that can be demonstrated experimentally is that signals received close together in time are treated by the brain as simultaneous.

A localized disk of red light is flashed for just about 20 milliseconds, and followed immediately by a 20-millisecond flash of green light in the same place. The subject reports that he did not see a red light followed by a green light. Instead he saw a yellow light, just as he would have if the red and the green light had been flashed simultaneously. Yet the subject could not have experienced yellow until after the information from the green flash had been processed and integrated with the preceding red one.

Experiments of this led psychologist Robert Efron, now at the University of California at Davis, concludes that the processing period for perception is about 60 to 70 milliseconds, similar periods are found in experiments with tones in the auditory system. It is always possible, nevertheless, that the processing times may be different in higher parts of the visual hierarchy and in other parts of the brain. Processing is also more rapid in trained, compared with naive, observers.

Because it appears to be involved in some forms of visual awareness, it would help if we could discover the neural basis of attention. Eye movement is a form of attention, since the area of the visual field in which we see with high resolution is remarkably small, roughly the area of the thumbnail at arms' length. Thus, we move our eyes to gaze directly at an object in order to see it more clearly. Our eyes usually move three or four times a second. Psychologists have shown, however, that there appears to be a faster form of attention that moves around, in some sense, when our eyes are stationary.

The exact psychological nature of this faster attentional mechanisms are for being or intended of a directly accorded presentation of controversy. Several neuroscientists, however, including Robert Desimone including his colleagues at the National Institute of Mental Health, have shown that the rate of firing of certain neurons in the macaque's visual system depends on what the monkey is attending too in the visual field. Thus, attention is not solely a psychological concept; it also has neural correlates that can be observed. A number of researchers have found that the pulvinar - a region of the thalamus -, appearing to be involved in visual attention. We would like to believe that the thalamus merits to be called 'the organ of attention,' but this status has yet to be established.

The major problem is to find what activity in the brain communicates directly to visual awareness. It has been speculated that each cortical area produces awareness of only those visual features that are 'columnar,' or arranged in the stack or column of neurons perpendicular to the cortical surface. Thus, the primary visual cortex could facilitate codification for orientation and area MT for motion. So far experimentalists have not found one particular region in the brain where all the information needed for visual awareness appears to come together. Dennett has dubbed such a hypothetical place 'The Cartesian Theatre.' He argues on theoretical grounds that it does not exist.

Awareness seems to be distributed not just on a local scale, but more widely over the neocortex. Vivid visual awareness is unlikely to be distributed over every cortical area because some areas show no response to visual signals. Awareness might, for example, be associated with only those areas that connect back directly to the primary visual cortex or alternatively with those areas that project into one another's layer 4. (The latter areas are always at the same level in the visual hierarchy.)

The key issue, then, is how the brain forms its global representations from visual signals. If attention is indeed crucial for visual awareness, the brain has the enabling capability to fabricate and establish the forming representations by attending to direction, for just a single object at a time, alternatively directed by its measure of motion, or the superseding of a set or situated positions in a particular place that firmly arrives by its motion or an activity from one object to the next. For example, the neurons representing all the different aspects of the attended object could all fire together very rapidly for a short period, possibly in rapid bursts.

This fact, simultaneous firing might not only excite those neurons that symbolized the implications of that object but also temporarily strengthen the relevant synapses so that this particular pattern of firing could be quickly recalled - a form of short-term memory. If only one representation needs to be held in short-term memory, as in remembering a single task, the neurons involved may continue to fire for a period.

A problem arises if it is necessary to be aware of more than one object at exactly the same time. If all the attributes of two or more objects were represented by neurons firing rapidly, their attributes might be confused. The colour of one might become attached to the shape of another. This happens sometimes in very brief presentations.

Some time ago Christoph von der Malsburg, now at the Ruhr-Universität Bochum, suggested that this difficulty would be circumvented if the neurons associated with any object, all fired in synchrony (that is, if their times of firing were correlated) but out of synchrony with that representing other objects. Recently two groups in Germany reported that there does appear to be correlated firing between neurons in the visual cortex of the cat, often in a rhythmic manner, with a frequency in the 35- to 75-hertz range, sometimes called 40-hertz, or g, oscillation.

Von der Malsburg's proposal prompted the apparency to suggest that this rhythmic and synchronized firing might be the neural correlate of awareness and that it might serve to bind together activity concerning the same object in different cortical areas. The matter is still undecided, but at present the fragmentary experimental evidence does rather little to support such an idea. Another possible action is that the 40-hertz oscillation may help distinguish figures from ground or assist the mechanism of attention.

Are there some particular types of neurons, distributed over the visual neocortex, whose firing directly symbolizes the content of visual awareness? One very simplistic hypothesis is that the activities in the upper layers of the cortex are largely unconscious ones, whereas the activities in the lower layers (layers 5 and 6) mostly correlate with consciousness. We have wondered whether the pyramidal neurons in layer 5 of the neocortex, especially the larger ones, might play this latter role.

These are the only cortical neurons that project right out of the cortical system (that is, not to the neocortex, the thalamus or the claustrum). If visual awareness represents the results of neural computations in the cortex, one might expect that what the cortex sends elsewhere would symbolize those results. Moreover, the neurons in layer 5 show a rather unusual propensity to fire in bursts. The idea that layer 5 neurons may directly symbolize visual awareness is attractive, but it still is too early to tell whether there is anything in it.

Visual awareness is clearly a difficult problem. More work is needed on the psychological and neural basis of both attention and very short-term memory. Studying the neurons when a percept changes, even though the visual input is constant, should be a powerful experimental paradigm. We need to construct neurobiological theories of visual awareness and test them, of which in using a combination of molecular, neurobiological and clinical imaging studies.

We believe that once we have mastered the secret of this simple form of awareness, we may be close to understanding a central mystery of human life: How the physical events occurring in our brains while we form an idea of something in the mind and understand to its use's in the power of conceptual subjectivity or theoretical deliberations and act in the world's relation to our peculiar particularities as modified by individual bias and limitation - that is, how the brain relates to the mind.

There have been several relevant developments since this article was first published. It now seems likely that there are rapid 'on-line' systems for stereotyped motor responses such as hand or eye movement. These systems are unconscious and lack memory. Conscious seeing, on the other hand, seems to be slower and more subject to visual illusions. The brain needs to form a conscious representation of the visual scene that it then can be used for many different actions or thoughts, exactly how all these pathways work and how they interact is far less than clear.

There have been more experiments on the behaviour of neurons that respond to bistable visual percepts, such as binocular rivalry, but it is probably too early to draw firm conclusions from them about the exact neural correlates of visual consciousness. We have suggested on theoretical grounds based on the neuroanatomy of the macaque monkey that primates are not directly aware of what is happening in the primary visual cortex, even though most of the visual information flows through it. This hypothesis is supported by some experimental evidence, but it is still controversial.

Is consciousness determinative, or is it determined? English philosophers such as John Locke equated consciousness with physical sensations and the information they provide, whereas European philosophers such as Gottfried Wilhelm Leibniz and Immanuel Kant gave a more central and active role to consciousness.

The philosopher who most directly influenced subsequent exploration of the subject of consciousness was the 19th-century German educator Johann Friedrich Herbart, who wrote that ideas had quality and intensity and that they may suppress or may facilitate or place of one another. Thus, ideas may pass from 'states of reality' (consciousness) to 'states of the tendency' (unconsciousness), with the dividing line between the two states being described as the threshold of consciousness. This formulation of Herbart clearly presages the development, by the German psychologist and physiologist Gustav Theodor Fechner, of the psychophysical measurement of sensation thresholds, and the later development by Sigmund Freud of the concept of the unconscious.

The experimental analysis of consciousness dates from 1879, when the German psychologist Wilhelm Max Wundt started his research laboratory. For Wundt, the task of psychology was the study of the structure of consciousness, which extended well beyond sensations and included feelings, images, memory, attention, duration, and movement. Because early interest focussed on the content and dynamics of consciousness, it is not surprising that the central methodology of such studies was introspection; that is, subjects reported on the mental contents of their own consciousness. This introspective approach was developed most fully by the American psychologist Edward Bradford Titchener at Cornell University. Setting his task as that of describing the structure of the mind, Titchener attempted to detail, from introspective self-reports, the dimensions of the elements of consciousness. For example, taste was 'dimensionalized' into four basic categories: sweet, sour, salt, and bitter. This approach was known as structuralism.

By the 1920's, however, a remarkable revolution had occurred in psychology that was to essentially remove considerations of consciousness from psychological research for some 50 years: Behaviourism captured the field of psychology. The main initiator of this movement was the American psychologist John Broadus Watson. In a 1913 article, Watson stated, 'I believe that we can write of some psychology and never use the term's consciousness, mental states, mind . . . imagery and the like.' Psychologists then turned almost exclusively to behaviour, as described in terms of stimulus and response, and consciousness was totally bypassed as a subject. A survey of eight leading introductory psychology texts published between 1930 and the 1950's found no mention of the topic of consciousness in five texts, and in two it was treated as a historical curiosity.

Beginning in the later part of the 1950s, are, however, the grounded interests in the foundational subject of consciousness, for returning from its absence were subjects and techniques relating to altered states of consciousness: sleep and dreams, meditation, biofeedback, hypnosis, and drug-induced states. Much in the surge in sleep and dream research was directly fuelled by a discovery relevant to the nature of consciousness. A physiological indicator of the dream state was found: At roughly 90-minute intervals, the eyes of sleepers were observed to move rapidly, and at the same time the sleepers' brain waves would show a pattern resembling the waking state. When people were awakened during these periods of rapid eye movement, they almost always reported dreams, whereas if awakened at other times they did not. This and other research clearly indicated that sleep, once considered a passive state, were instead an active state of consciousness.

American psychiatrist William Glasser developed reality therapy in the 1960s, after working with teenage girls in a correctional institution and observing work with severely disturbed schizophrenic patients in a mental hospital. He observed that psychoanalysis did not help many of his patients change their behaviour, even when they understood the sources of it. Glasser felt it was important to help individuals take responsibility for their own lives and to blame others less. Largely because of this emphasis on personal responsibility, his approach has found widespread acceptance among drugs - and alcohol-abuse counsellors', correction of workers, school Counsellors, and those working with clients who may be disruptive to others.

Reality therapy is based on the premise that all human behaviour is motivated by fundamental needs and specific wants. The reality therapist first seeks to establish a friendly, trusting relationship with clients in which they can express their needs and wants. Then the therapist helps clients explore the behaviours that created problems for them. Clients are encouraged to examine the consequences of their behaviour and to evaluate how well their behaviour helped them fulfill their wants. The therapist does not accept excuses from clients. Finally, the therapist helps the client formulate a concrete plan of action to change certain behaviours, based on the client's own goals and ability to make choices.

During the 1960's, an increased search for 'higher levels' of consciousness through meditation resulted in a growing interest in the practices of Zen Buddhism and Yoga from Eastern cultures. A full flowering of this movement in the United States was seen in the development of training programs, such as Transcendental Meditation, that were self-directed procedures of physical relaxation and focussed attention. Biofeedback techniques also were developed to bring body systems involving factors such as blood pressure or temperature under voluntary control by providing feedback from the body, so that subjects could learn to control their responses. For example, researchers found that persons could control their brain-wave patterns to some extent, particularly the so-called alpha rhythms generally associated with a relaxed, meditative state. This finding was especially relevant to those interested in consciousness and meditation, and a number of 'alpha training' programs emerged.

Another subject that led to increased interest in altered states of consciousness was hypnosis, which involves a transfer of conscious control from the character interpretation belonging in the dependent sector, whose occasions, as basic of an idea or the principal object of attention, in the course of its immediate composition, and like the substance to a particular individual finds to the subject that the modification as when of transferring to that of another person. Hypnotism has had a long and intricate history in medicine and folklore and has been intensively studied by psychologists. Much has become known about the hypnotic state, relative to individual suggestibility and personality traits; the subject has now been largely demythologized, and the limitations of the hypnotic state are fairly well known. Despite the increasing use of hypnosis, however, much remains to be learned about this unusual state of focussed attention.

Finally, many people in the 1960's experimented with the psychoactive drugs known as hallucinogens, which produce deranging disorder of consciousness. The most prominent of these drugs is lysergic acid diethylamide, or LSD; mescaline; and psilocybin; the latter two have long been associated with religious ceremonies in various cultures. LSD, because of its radical thought-modifying properties, was initially explored for its so-called mind-expanding potential and for its psychotomimetic effects (imitating psychoses). Little positive use, however, has been found for these drugs, and their use is highly restricted.

Scientists have long since considered the nature of consciousness without producing a fully satisfactory definition. In the early 20th century American philosopher and psychologist William James suggested that consciousness be a mental process involving both attention to external stimuli and short-term memory. Later scientific explorations of consciousness mostly expanded upon James's work. In the article from a 1997 special issue of Scientific American, Nobel laureate Francis Crick, who helped determine the structure of DNA, and fellow biophysicists Christof Koch explains how experiments on vision might deepen our understanding of consciousness.

As the concept of a direct, simple linkage between environment and behaviour became unsatisfactory in recent decades, the interest in altered states of consciousness may be taken as a visible sign of renewed interest in the topic of consciousness. That persons are active and intervening participants in their behaviour has become increasingly clear. Environments, rewards, and punishments are not simply defined by their physical character. Memories are organized, not simply stored, an entirely new area called cognitive psychology has emerged that centre on these concerns. In the study of children, increased attention is being paid to how they understand, or perceive, the world at different ages. In the field of animal behaviour, researchers increasingly emphasize the inherent characteristics resulting from the way a species has been shaped to respond adaptively to the environment. Humanistic psychologists, with a concern for self-actualization and growth, have emerged after a long period of silence. Throughout the development of clinical and industrial psychology, the conscious states of persons in terms of their current feelings and thoughts were of obvious importance. The role of consciousness, however, was often de-emphasized in favour of unconscious needs and motivations. Trends can be seen, however, toward a new emphasis on the nature of states of consciousness.

The term 'transference' in which we have in applying or adopting attitudes to the transference and without further definition that we will now consider more closely, furthering the emotional relationship that is thus designed, that which the psychoanalytic treatment, for which of expectation for which of the function is played or assumed by the dominant character of the therapist, as the patient allows the analyst to play this dominating role in his emotional life. This is of great importance in the analytic process. After his treatment is over, this situation is changed. The patient builds up feelings of affection for and resistance to his analyst that, in their ebb and flow, so exceed the normal degree of feeling that the phenomenon has long attracted the theoretical interest of the analyst. Freud studied this phenomenon thoroughly, explained it, and gave it the name 'transference', we most probably will understand the significance of the transference phenomenon impressed Freud so profoundly that he continued through the years to develop his ideas about it.

In all afforded efforts, to refuse to consider the demise of forebears as too merely disdain, that we cannot reproduce of all Freud's research about transference but for an instance of obligation, would be used to indicate the requirement by the immediate need or purpose upon such condition that might point beyond a normal or acceptable limit, as to an excessive amount of which something does not or cannot extend to their essentials. When we speak of the transference in connexion with social reeducation, we mean the emotional responses of the education or counsellor or therapist, as the case maybe, without meaning that it takes place in the same way as in an analysis. The 'countertransference' is emotional aptitude of the teacher toward the pupil, the counsellor toward his charge, the therapist toward the patient. The feeling that the child develop for the mentor is conditioned by a much earlier relationship to someone else. We must take cognisance of this fact in order to understand these relationships. The tender relationships that go to up the child's love life are no longer strange to us. Many of these have already been touched upon in the foregoing literature. We have learned how the small boy takes the father and mother as love objects. We have followed the strivings that arise out of this relationship, the Oedipus situation, we have seen how this runs its course and terminates in an identification with the parents. We have also had opportunity to consider the relationship between brothers and sisters, how their original rivalry is transformed into affection through the pressure of their feeling for the parents. We know that the boy at puberty must give up his first love object within the family and transfers his libido to individuals outside the family.

Our present intent of directed intent is kept in mind as accorded to contemplations by intended accomplishment to achieve to work out the arrangement of the parts of design and the effects of these first experiences from a certain perspective. The child's attachment to the family, the continuance and the subsequent dissolution of these love relationships within the family, not only leave a deep effect on the child through the resulting identifications, they determine at the same the actual forms of this love relationships in the future. Freud compares these forms, without implying too great a rigidity. He has shown that in the emotional relationships of our later life we can do nothing but makes an imprint from one or another of these patterns that we have established in early childhood.

Why Freud chose the term 'transference' for the emotional relationship between patient and analyst is easy to understand, that feelings having to arise long ago in another situation are transferred upon the analyst. To the counsellor of the child, the knowledge of the transference mechanism is indispensable. In order to influence the dissociable behaviour, he must bring his charge into the transference situation. The study of the transference in the dissociable child shows regularly a love life that has been disturbed in early childhood by a lack of affection or an undue amount of affection. A satisfactory social adjustment depends on certain conditions, among them an adequate constitutional endowment and early love relationships that have been confined within certain limits. Society determines these limitations, just as definitely as the later love life of an individual is determined by early form his libidinal development. The child develops normally and assumes his proper place in society, if he can cultivate within the privacy to such relationships as can favourably carry over into the schools and from there into the ever-broadening world around him. His attitude toward his parents must be such that it can be carried over onto the teacher, and that toward his brothers and sisters must be transferred to his schoolmates. Every new contact, according to the degree of authority or maturity that the person represents, repeats a previous relationship with very little deviation. People whose early adjustment to succeed or supervene from such a normative course have no difficulties in their emotional relations with others, and they are able to form new ties, to deepen them, or to break them off without conflict when the situation demands it.

We can easily see why an attempt to change the present order of society always meets with resistance and where the radical reformer will have to use the greatest leverage. Our attitude to society and its members has a certain standard form. It gets its imprint from the structure of the family and the emotional relationships set up within the family, therefore, the parents, especially the father, assume overwhelming responsibility for the social orientation of the child. The persistent, ineradicable libidinal relationships carried over from childhood are facts with which social reformers must reckon. If the family represents the best preparation for the present social order, which seems to be the case, then the introduction of a new order means that the family must be uprooted and replaced by a different personal world for the child. It is beyond our scope to attempt a solution of this question, which concerns those who strive to build up a new order of society. We are remedial educators and must recognize these sociological relationships. We can ally ourselves with whatever social system will, but we have the path of our present activity well marked out for us, to bring dissociable youth into the line with present-day society.

If the child is harmed through too great disappointment or too great indulgence in his early life, he builds up reaction patterns that are damaged, incomplete, or too delicate to support the wear and tear of life. He is incapable of forming libidinal object relationships that are considered normal by society. His unpreparedness for life, his inability to regulate his conscious and unconscious libidinal striving and to confine his libidinal expectations within normal bounds, creates an insecurity in relation to his fellow men and constitute one of the first and most important condition's fo r their development of delinquency. Following this point of view, we look for the primary causes of dissociable behaviour in early childhood, where the abnormal libidinal ties are established. The word 'delinquency' is an expression used to describe a relationship to people and things that are at a variance with what society approve in the individual.

It is not immediately clear, from which are pointed from the particular form of the delinquency, just what libidinal disturbances in childhood have given rise to the dissociable expression. Until we have a psychoanalytically construed scheme for the diagnosis of delinquency, we may content ourselves by separating these forms into two groups: (1) Borderline neurosis cases with dissociable symptoms, and (2) Dissociable cases for which are in part, the ego giving to develop of the dissociable behaviour, and showing no trace of neurosis. In the first type, the individual finds himself in an inner conflict because of the nature of his love relationships, a part of his own personality forbids the indulgence of libidinal desires and strivings. The dissociable behaviour results from this conflict. In the second type, the individual finds himself in open conflict with his environment, because the outer world has frustrated his childish libidinal desires.

While these matters under discussion should enhance our understanding and conditions in terms, through which the past and present are to be understood. Despite their brevity, these discussions, to a better kind, as their discerning intendment would not only make in agreement of acceptation in meaning but understood by their endeavour upon undertaking of our present concerns and considerations, that in issues regarding the transference and the conditions for loving, with which Freud's views may be best approached through his introduction of the idea of conditions for loving that project the analysis of transferences. For example, Freud says, in this context that, . . . each individual, . . . has acquired a specific method of his own in this conduct of his erotic life - that is, in the precondition of falling in love which he lays down, in the instincts he satisfies and the aim he sets himself in the course of it'. In another place, Freud is advising the analyst to adopt a special attitude toward erotic transference; this is the attitude that combines attentiveness, neutrality, non-gratification and insistence on analyzing the erotic feelings as 'unreal' but necessary features of the treatment. He goes on to describe the consequence of maintaining this attitude in the following words: 'The patient, whose sexual repression is of course not yet removed but merely pushed into the background, will then feel safe enough to allow all her preconditions for characteristics of her state of being in love, to come to light, and from these she will herself open up the way to the infantile roots of her love (1915). And, in a number of papers dating from about the same time, that is between the years of 1910 and 1922, he describes particular conditions for loving. Among these are the man's conditions that the woman he loves sexually must somehow be degraded or in need of a recovery as needing of an instance or rescuing or rescued, in deliverance that there is an injured third party in the interpersonal configuration, also. In the instance of male homosexuality, in addition to the partner's possessing a penis, there is the condition that the young man who is loved be the same age that the lover was when he developed his dominant identification with his mother (1922).

The child's attachment to the family, the continuance and the subsequent dissolution of these love relationships within the family, not only leave a deep effect on the child through the resulting identifications, they determine at the same the actual forms of this love relationships in the future. Freud compares these forms, without implying too great a rigidity.

In order to influence the dissociable behaviour, he must bring his charge into the transference situation. The study of the transference in the dissociable child shows regularly a love life that has been disturbed in early childhood by a lack of affection or an undue amount of affection. A satisfactory social adjustment depends on certain conditions, among them an adequate constitutional endowment and early love relationships which have been confined within certain limits. Society determines these limitations, just as definitely as the later love life of an individual is determined by early form his libidinal development. The child develops normally and assumes his proper place in society, if he can cultivate within the privacy to such relationships as can favourably be carried over into the schools and from there into the ever-broadening world around him. His attitude toward his parents must be such that it can be carried over onto the teacher, and that toward his brothers and sisters must be transferred to his schoolmates. Every new contact, according to the degree of authority or maturity which the person represents, repeats a previous relationship with very little deviation. People whose early adjustment to succeed or supervene from such a normative course have no difficulties in their emotional relations with others, and they are able to form new ties, to deepen them, or to break them off without conflict when the situation demands it.

We can easily see why an attempt to change the present order of society always meets with resistance and where the radical reformer will have to use the greatest leverage. Our attitude to society and its members has a certain standard form. It gets its imprint from the structure of the family and the emotional relationships set up within the family, therefore, the parents, especially the father, assume overwhelming responsibility for the social orientation of the child. The persistent, ineradicable libidinal relationships carried over from childhood are facts with which social reformers must reckon. If the family represents the best preparation for the present social order, which seems to be the case, then the introduction of a new order means that the family must be uprooted and replaced by a different personal world for the child. It is beyond our scope to attempt a solution of this question, which concerns those who strive to build up a new order of society. We are remedial educators and must recognize these sociological relationships. We can ally ourselves with whatever social system will, but we have the path of our present activity well marked out for us, to bring dissociable youth into the line with present-day society.

If the child is harmed through too great disappointment or too great indulgence in his early life, he builds up reaction patterns which are damaged, incomplete, or too delicate to support the wear and tear of life. He is incapable of forming libidinal object relationships which are considered normal by society. His unpreparedness for life, his inability to regulate his conscious and unconscious libidinal striving and to confine his libidinal expectations within normal bounds, creates an insecurity in relation to his fellow men and constitute one of the first and most important condition's for their development of delinquency. Following this point of view, we look for the primary causes of dissociable behaviour in early childhood, where the abnormal libidinal ties are established. The word 'delinquency' is an expression used to describe a relationship to people and things which are at the variance with what society approve in the individual.

It is not immediately clear, from which are pointed from the particular form of the delinquency, just what libidinal disturbances in childhood have given rise to the dissociable expression. Until we have a psychoanalytically construed scheme for the diagnosis of delinquency, we may content ourselves by separating these forms into two groups: (1) Borderline neurosis cases with dissociable symptoms, and (2) Dissociable cases for which are in part, the ego giving to develop of the dissociable behaviour, and showing no trace of neurosis. In the first type, the individual finds himself in an inner conflict because of the nature of his love relationships, a part of his own personality forbids the indulgence of libidinal desires and strivings. The dissociable behaviour results from this conflict. In the second type, the individual finds himself in open conflict with his environment, because the outer world has frustrated his childish libidinal desires.

The differences in the forms of dissociable behaviour are important for many reasons. At present, they are significant to us because of the various ways in which the transference is established in these two types, we know that with a normal child the transference takes place of itself through the kindly efforts of the responsible adult. The teacher in his attitude repeats the situations long familiarly to the child, and thereby evokes a parental relationship. He does not maintain this relationship at the same level, but continually deepens it as long as he is the parental substitute.

When a neurotic child with symptoms of delinquency comes into the institution, the tendencies to transfer his attitude toward his parents to the persons in authority are immediately noticeable. The worker will adopt the same attitude toward the dissociable child as to the normal child, and bring him into positive transference, if he acts toward him in such a way as to prevent a repetition with the worker of the situation with the parents which led to the conflict. In the psychoanalysis, on the other hand, it is of greatest importance to let this situation repeat itself. In a sense the worker becomes the father or the mother, but still not wholly so, he represents their claims, but in the right moment he must let the dissociable child know that he has insight into his difficulties and that he will not interpret the behaviour in the same way as do the parents. He will respond to the child's feeling of a need for punishment, but he will not completely satisfy it.

He will conduct in himself for being entirely differently in the case of the child who in open conflict with society. In this instance he must take the child's part, be in agreement with his behaviour, and in the severest cases even give the child to understand that in his place he would behave just the same way. The guilt feelings found so clearly in the neurotic cases with dissociable behaviour are present in these cases also. These feelings do not arise, however, from the dissociable ego, but have another source.

Why does the educator conduct himself differently in dealing with this second type? These children, too, he must draw into a positive transference to him, but what is applicable and appropriate for a normal or a neurotic child would achieve opposite results. Otherwise the worker would bring upon himself all the hate and aggression which the child bears toward society, thus leading the child into a negative instead of positive transference, and creating a situation in which the child is not amenable to training.

Even though of what was said about psychoanalytic theory is only a bare outline, that much deeper study of the transference is necessary to anyone interested in re-educational work from the psychoanalytic point of view. The practical application of this theory is not easy, since we deal mostly with mixed types, such that the attitude of the counsellor cannot be as uniform as having enough verbal descriptions for evincing of individual forms of dissociated behaviour to enable us to offer detailed instructions about how to deal with them. At present our psychoanalytic knowledge is such that a correct procedure cannot be stated specifically for each and every dissociable individual.

The necessity for bringing the child into a good relationship to his mentor is of prime importance. The worker cannot leave this to chance, he must deliberately achieve it and he must face the fact thus no effective work is possible without it. It is important for him to grasp the psychic situation of the dissociable child in the very first contact he makes with him, because only this can be known in what attitude to adopt. There is a further difficulty in that the dissociable child takes pains to hide his real nature: He misrepresents himself and lies. This is to be taken for granted, it should not surprise or upset us. Dissociable children do not come to us of their own volition but are brought to us, very often with the threat, 'You'll soon find out what's going to happen to you.' Generally parents resort our help only after every other means, including corporal punishment, have failed. To the child, we are only another form of punishment, an enemy against whom he must be on his guard, not a source of help to him. There is a great difference between this and the psychoanalytic situation, where the patient comes voluntarily for helping. To the dissociable child, we are a menace because we represent society, with which he is in conflict. He must protect himself against this terrible danger and be careful what he says in order not to give himself away. It is hard to make some of these delinquent children talk, remain unresponsive and stubborn. One thing they all have in common: They do not tell the truth. Some lie stupidly, pitiably, others, especially the older ones, show great skill and sophistication. The extremely submissive child, the 'dandily', the very jovial, or the exaggeratedly sincerity, some especially hard to reach, this behaviour is so much to be expected that we are not surprised or disarmed by it, the inexperienced teacher or adviser is easily irritated, especially when the lies are transparent, but he must not let the child be aware of this. He must deal with the situation immediately and without telling the child that he can see that the obtainment of results that had come through the distributive contributions in about the ascribing of and accreditation to attitudinal behaviours.

There is nothing remarkable in the behaviour of the dissociable, but it differs only quantitatively from normal behaviour. We all hide our real selves and use a great deal of psychic energy to mislead our neighbours. We masquerade more or less, according to necessity. Most of us learn in the nursery the necessity of presenting ourselves in accordance with the environmental demands, and thus we consciously or unconsciously build up a shell around ourselves. Anyone who has had experience with young children must have noticed how they immediately begin to dissimulate when a grown-up comes into the room. Most children succeed in behaving in the manner which they think is expected of them. Thus they lessen the danger to themselves and at the same time they are casting the permanent molds of their mannerisms and their behaviour. How many parents really bother themselves about the inner life of their children? Is this mask necessarily for life? I do not know, but it often seems that the person on whom childhood experiences have forced the dissociable individual masquerades to a greater extent, and more consciously, then the normal. He is only drawing logical deductions from his unfortunate disagreeable authority? Why should he be sincere with those people who represent disagreeable authority? This is an unfair demand.

We must look beyond the differences between the situation of social retraining and the analytic situation. The analyst expects to meet in his patient unconscious remittances which prevent him from being honest or make him silent: But the treatment is in vain when the patient lies persistently. Those who work with dissociable children expect to be lied to. To send this child away because he lies are only giving in to him. We must wait and hope to penetrate this mask which covers the really psychic situation. In the institution it does not matter if this is not achieved immediately, it means merely that the establishment of the transference is postponed. In the clinic, however, we must work more quickly. Taking with the patient does not always suffice, and we must introduce other remedial measures. Generally, we see the delinquent child, only, in at least as infrequent to a smattering of times, but we are forced to take some steps after the first few interviews, to formulate some tentative conception of the difficulty and to establish a positive transference as quickly as possible, this is to means that we must get at least a peep behind the mask. If the child is not put in an institution, he remains in the old situation under the same influences which caused the trouble. In such cases we wish to establish the transference as quickly as possible, to intensify the child`s positive feelings while the child is with us, and to bring them rapidly to such a pitch that they can no longer be easily disturbed by the old influences and to carry out work successfully presupposing a long experience.

Let us now go against our theoretical concerns and see how the analyst and the patient seek to grasp upon a try to solve situational thoughts for which the transference, and, moreover, its mask on which can be understood that feelings and a better understanding the differentiation that intentionality that allies with others and exclusively its need to achieve to some end.

Even so, there are few current problems concerning the problem of transference that Freud did not recognize either implicitly or explicitly in the development of the theoretical and clinical framework. For all essential purposes, moreover, his formulations, in spite of certain shifts in emphasis, remain integral to contemporary psychoanalytic theory and practice. Recent developments mainly concern the impact of an ego-psychological approach, the significance of object relations, both current and infantile, external and internal, the role of aggression in mental life, and the part played by regression and the repetition compulsion in the transference. Nevertheless, analysis of the infantile Oedipal situation in the setting of a genuine transference neurosis is still considered as a primary goal of psychoanalytic procedure.

Originally, transference was ascribed to displacement on the analyst of repressed wishes and fantasies derived from early childhood. The transference neurosis was viewed as a compromise formulation similar to dreams and other neurotic symptoms. Resistance, defined as the clinical manifestation of repression, could be diminished or abolished by interpretation mainly directed toward the content of the repressed. Transference resistance, both positive and negative, was inscribed to the threatened emergence of repressed unconscious material in the analytic situation. Presently, as with the development of a structural approach, the superego had been portrayed as the heir to the genital Oedipal situation, also was the recognition as playing a leading role in the transference situation. The analysis was subsequently viewed not only as the object by displacement of infantile incestuous fantasies, but also as the substitute by projection for the prohibiting parental figures which had been internalized as the definitive superego. The effect of transference interpretation in mitigating undue severity of the superego has, therefore, been emphasized in many discussions of the concept of transference.

Certain expansions in the structural approach related increasingly to the recognition of the role that had earlier objective relations, in the development of the superego. This had affected the current concepts of transference, in that this connection, the significance of the analytic situation as a repetition of the early mother-child relationship has been stressed from different points for viewing to such equally important developments related to Freud's revised concept of anxiety which can only lead to theoretical developments in the field of ego psychology. However, this brought about their related clinical changes in the work of many analysts. As a result, attention was no longer the main attraction that had focussed on the content of the unconscious. In addition, increasing importance was attributed to the defence processes by means of which the anxiety which would be engendered if repression and other related mechanisms were broken down, was avoided in the analytic situation. Differences in the interpretation of the role of the analyst and the nature of transference developed from emphasis, on the one hand, on the importance of early object relations, and on the other, from primary attention to the role of the ego and its defences. These defences first emerged clearly in discussion of the technique of child analysis, in which Melanie Klein and Anna Freud, the pioneers in the fields of thought as playing the leading roles.

From a theoretical point of view, discussion foreshadowing the problems which face us today was presented in 1934 in a well-known paper by Richard Sterba and James Strachey, and further elaborated at the Marienbad Symposium at which Edward Bibring made an important contribution. The importance of identification with, or introjection of, the analyst in the transference situation of identification with, or introjection of, the analysts in the transference situation were clearly indicated. The therapeutic results were attributed to the effect of this process In mitigating the need for pathological defences. Strachey, however, considerably influenced by the work of Melanie Klein, regarded transference as essentially a projection onto the analyst of the patient's own superego. The therapeutic process was attributed to subsequent introjection of a modified superego as a result of 'mutative' transference. Sterba and Bibring, on the other hand, intimately involved with development of the ego-psychological approach, reemphasized the central role of the ego, postulating a therapeutic split and identification with the analyst as an essential feature of transference. To some extent, this difference of opinion may be regarded as semantic. If the superego is explicitly defined as the heir of the genital Oedipus conflict, then earlier intra-systematic conflicts within the ego, although they may be related retrospectively to the definite superego, much, nevertheless, are defined as contained within the ego. Later divisions within the ego of the type indicated by Sterba and very much expanded by Edward Bibring in his concept of therapeutic alliance between the analyst and the healthy part of the patient's ego, must also be excluded from superego significance. In contrast, those whom attribute pregenital intra-systemic conflicts within the ego primarily to the introjection of objects, consider that the resultant state of internal conflict appears like the dynamic idea that something conveys to the mind as having an endless meaning attached to the coherence of the therapeutic situation and seen in the later conflicts between ego and superego. In that way, they believe that these structures developed simultaneously and suggest that no sharp distinction should be made between pre-oedipal, oedipal, and a post-oedipal superego.

The differences, however, are not entirely verbal, since those whom attribute superego formations to the early months of life tend to attribute significantly too early object relation which differs from the conception of those who stress control and, neutralization of instinctual energy as primary functions of the ego. This theoretical difference necessarily implies some disagreement as how the dynamic situation both in childhood and in adult life, inevitably reflected in the concept of transference and in hypotheses as to the hidden nature of the therapeutic process. From one point of view, the role of the ego is central and crucial at every phase of analysis. As a differentiation is made between transference as therapeutic alliance and the transference neurosis, which, on the whole, is considered as the manifestation of resistance. Effective analysis depends on a sound and stable therapeutic alliance, the prerequisite for which is the existence, before analysis, of a degree of mature superego functions, the absence maintaining the certain for severely disturbed patients and in young children may preclude traditional psychoanalytic procedure. Whenever indicated, interpretation's manifestations, which means, in effect, that the transference must be analyzed. The process of analysis, however, is not exclusively ascribed to transference interpretation. Other interpretations of unconscious material, whether related to defence or to early fantasies, will be equally effective provided they are accurately timed and provide a satisfactory therapeutic alliance has been made. Those, in contrast, whom stress the importance of early object relations emphasizes the crucial role of transference as an object relationship, distorted though this may be of a variety of defences against primitively unresolved conflicts. The central role of the ego, both in the early stages of development and in the analytic process, are definitely accepted. The hidden nature of the ego is, however, considered at all times to be determined by its external and internal objects. Therapeutic process indicated changes in ego function results, therefore, primarily from a change in object relations though interpretation of the transference situation, finds of less differentiation as made between transference as for being the therapeutic alliance and transference neurosis as a manifestation of resistance. Therapeutic progress depends almost exclusively on transference interpretation. Other interpretations, although at times, are not, in general, considered an essential feature of the analytic process. From this point of view, the preanalytic maturity of the patient's ego is not stressed as considered potentially suitable for traditional psychoanalytic procedure.

These differences in theoretical orientations are not only reflected in the approach to children and disturbed patients. They may also be recognized in significant variations of technique in respect to all clinical groups, which inevitably affect the opening phases, understanding of the inevitable regressive features of the transference neurosis, and handling of the germinal phases of analysis. By its emphasis as drawn on or upon the main problems, and, by contrast, rather than similarity, our efforts will be to avoid to detailed discussions of controversial theory regarding the hidden nature of early ego development by a somewhat arbitrary differentiation between those who relate ego analysis to the analysis of defences and those who stress the primary significance of object relations both in the transference, and in the development and definitive structure of the ego. Needless to say, this involves some oversimplification, where I hope that it may, at the same time, clarify certain important issues. To take, on or upon the analysis of patients we are generally agreeing to be suitable for classical analytic procedure, the transference neurosis. Those which emphasis the role of the ego and the analysis of defences, not only maintain Freud's conviction that analysis should proceed from the surface to depth, but also consider that early material in the analytic situation derives, that, in general, from defensive processes rather than from displacement onto the analyst of early instinctual fantasies, for that which Deep transference interpretation given in the early instinctual fantasies. Deep transference interpretation in the early phases of analysis will, therefore, rather be meaningless to the patient since its unconscious significance is so inaccessible, or, if the defences are precarious, will lead to premature and possibly intolerable anxiety. Premature interpretation of the equally unconscious automatic defensive processes by means of which instinctual fantasy kept unconscious is also ineffective and undesirable. There are, nonetheless, differences of opinion within this group, as to how far analysis of defence can be separated from analysis of content. Waelder, for example, has stressed the impossibility of such separation. Fenichel, however, considered that at least theoretical separation should be made and indicated that, as far as possible, analysis of defence should precede analysis of unconscious fantasy. It is, nevertheless, generally agreed that the transference neurosis develops, as a rule after ego defences have been sufficiently undermined to mobilize previously hidden instinctual conflict. During both the early stages of analysis, and at frequent points after development of the transference neurosis, defences against the transference will become a main feature of the analytic situation.

This approach, has already been indicated, is based on certain definite premises regarding the hidden natures and function of the ego in respect to the control and neutralization of instinctual energy and unconscious fantasies, while the importance of early object relations is not neglected, the conviction that early transference interpretation is ineffective and potentially relations are not neglected, the conviction and unconscious fantasy. The conviction that early transference interpretation is ineffective and potentially dangerous is related to the hypothesis that the instinctual energy available to the mature ego has been neutralized from unconscious fantasies, meaning at the beginning of analysis, for all effective purposes, relatively or absolutely divorced from its unconscious fantasy, as yet, there are a number of analysts of differing theoretical orientation of ego function from unconscious sources, but consider that unconscious fantasy continues to operate in all conscious mental activity. The analysts also the construct upon the whole of their existing emphasis to the crucial significance of primitive fantasies, despite the development of the transference situation, for which the individual entering analysis will inevitably have unconscious fantasies concerning the analyst derived from primitive sources. This material, although deep in a sense, is, nevertheless, strongly current and accessible to interpretation. Klein, in addition, creates the development and definitive structure of the superego to unconscious fantasy determined by the earliest phases of object relationships. She emphasizes the role of early introjective and projective processes in relation to primitive anxiety ascribed to the death instinct and related aggression drive fantasies. The unresolved difficulties and conflict of the earliest period continue to colour object relations throughout life. Failure to achieve an essentially satisfactory object relationship in this early period, and failure to master relative loss of that object without retaining its good internal representative, will not only affect all object relations and definitive ego function, but more specifically determine the nature of anxiety-provoking fantasies on entering the analytic situation. According to this point of view, therefore, early transference uninterpreted, even thought it may relate to fantasies derived from an early period of life, should result not in an increase, but a decrease of anxiety

In considering next problems of transference in relation to analysis of the transference neurosis, two main points must be kept in mind. First, as already indicated, those who emphasize the analysis of defence tend to make a definite differentiation between transference as therapeutic alliance and the transference neurosis as a compromise formation which serves the purposes of resistance. By contrast, those who emphasize the importance of early object relations view the transference primarily as a revival or repetition, sometimes attributed to symbolic processes of early struggles in respect to objects, but there is no sharp differentiation made between the early manifestations of transference and the transference neurosis. In view, to what is more, of the weight given to the role of unconscious fantasy and internal objects in every phase of mental life, healthy and pathological functions, though differing in essential respect, do not differ with regard to their direct dependence on unconscious sources.

In the second place, the role of regression in the transference situation is subject to wide differences of opinion. It was, of course, one of Freud's earliest discoveries that regression had of its earliest points of fixation, and is a cardinal feature, not only in the development of neurosis and psychosis, but also in the revival of earlier conflicts in the transference situation. With the development of the psychoanalysis and its application to an ever increasing range of received increased attention, finding the significance of the analytic situation as a means of fostering regression as a prerequisite for the therapeutic work has been emphasized by Ida Macapline in a recent paper. Of Differing opinions as to the significance, value, and technical handling of regressive manifestoes from the basis of important modifications of analytic technique, which will be considered, nonetheless, the transference neurosis, the view recently expressed by Phyllis Greenacre. That by saying, that regression, and indispensable features would be generally accepted. Also by saying, it is also a matter of generally based agreement that a prerequisite for successful analysis is revival and repetition in the analytic situation of the struggle of primitive stages of development. Those who emphasize defence analysis, however, tend to view regression as a manifestation of resistance, as a primitive mechanism of defence employed by the growth sets of the transference neurosis. Analysis of these regressive manifestations with their potential dangers depends on the existing and continued functioning of adequate ego strength to maintain therapeutic alliance at an adult level. Those, in contrast, who stress the significance of transference as a revival of the early mother-child relationship does not emphasize regression as an indication of resistance or defence, the revival of these primitive experiences in the transference situation is, in fact, regarded as can essential prerequisite for satisfactory psychological maturation and true geniality. The Kleinian school, as already indicated features the continued activity of primitive conflicts in determining essential features of the transference at every stage of analysis. Their increasing overt revival in the analytic situation, therefore, signifies a reopening of the analysis, and in general, is regarded as an indication of diminuation rather than increase of resistance. The dangers involved according to this point of view and are determined more but to the failure to mitigate anxiety by suitable transference interpretation. By this failure to obtainably achieve, in the early phases of analysis, a sound and stabling therapeutic alliance is based on the maturity of the patient's essential ego characteristics.

In considering, briefly, the terminal phases of analysis, many unresolved problems concerning the goal of the therapy and definition of a completed psychoanalysis must be kept in mind. Distinction must also be made between the technical problems of the terminal phase and evaluation of transference after the analysis has been terminated, there is widespread agreement as to the frequent revival in the terminal phases of primitive transference manifestations apparently resolved during the early phases of primitive transference manifestation, apparently resolved during the early phase of analysis has been terminated. Balint, and those who accept Ferenczi's concept of primary passive love, suggest that some gratification of primitive passive needs may be essential for successful termination. To Klein, the terminal phases of analysis also represent a repetition of important features of the early mother-child relationship. According to her point of view, this period represents, in essence, a revival of the early weaning situation. Completion depends on a mastery of early depressive struggles culminating in successful introjection of the analysis as a good object. Although, in this connection, emphasis differs considerably, it should be noted that those who stress the importance of identification with the analyst as a basis for therapeutic alliance, also accept the inevitability of some permanent modifications of a similar nature. Those, however, who make a definite differentiation between transference of the transference neurosis as to take and mark as noted for the main prerequisite for resulting amounts as having gained the successful confine(s) in the presentation of imitations on or upon a ceasing course or the point at which something as the analysis ceases, it is terminable, the end for its cessation upon closing and termination. The identification based on therapeutic alliance must be interpreted and understood, particularly with reference to the reality aspects of the analyst's personality. In spite, therefore, of significant important differences there are, as already indicated in connection with the earlier papers of Sterba and Strachey, important points of agreement in respect to the goal of a psychoanalysis.

The differences already considered and noted that indicate some basic current problems of transference. So far, however, discussion has been limited to variations within the framework of a traditional technique. We must consider problems related to overt modifications, so as the essential expanding context of use between variations introduced in respect to certain clinical conditions, often as a preliminary to classical psychoanalysis, and modifications based on changes on basic approaches. That which leads to significant alterations with regard both to the method and to the aim of therapy. It is generally agreed that some neurosis, borderline patients and the psychosis. The nature and meaning of such changes are, however, viewed differently according to the relative emphasis placed on the ego and its defences, on underlying unconscious conflicts, and on the significance and handling of regression in the therapeutic situation.

Researchers have implicated glucose, a sugar and insulin(a hormone secreted by the pancreas) as important to learning and memory. Humans and other animals given these substances show an improved capacity to learn and remember. Typically, when animals or humans ingest glucose, the pancreas responds by increasing insulin production, so it is difficult to determine which substance contributes to improved performance. Some studies in humans that have systematically varied the amount of glucose and insulin in the blood have shown that insulin may be the more important of the two substances for learning.

Scientists also have examined the influence of genes on learning and memory. In one is to study, for which of the scientists bred strains of mice with extra copies of a gene that helps build a protein called N-methyl-D-aspartate, or NMDA. This protein acts as a receptor for certain neurotransmitters. The genetically altered mice outperformed normal mice on a variety of tests of learning and memory. In addition, other studies have found that chemically blocking NMDA receptor impairs learning in laboratory rats. Future discoveries from genetic and biochemical studies may lead to treatments for memory deficits from Alzheimer's disease and other conditions that affect memory.

Alzheimer's Disease, is itself the progressive brain disorder that causes a gradual and irreversible decline in memory, language skills, perception of time and space, and, eventually, the ability to care and find the opportunity for being understood without explanation, however, existing of or by itself and having to antecedent cause that to first which is itself, self-imposed by oneself or itself. First described by German psychiatrist Alois Alzheimer in 1906, Alzheimer's disease was initially thought to be a rare condition affecting only young people, and was referred to as prehensile dementia. Today late-onset Alzheimer's disease is recognized as the most common cause of the loss of mental function in those aged 65 and over. Alzheimer's in people in their 30s, 40s, and 50s, called early-onset Alzheimer's disease, goes beyond a normal or acceptable limit such to a particular point of time at which something takes place and thus, occasioned to occur in commonplace but frequently affecting fewer than less of the 10 percent of the estimated 4 million Alzheimer's cases in the United States.

Although Alzheimer's disease is not a normal part of the aging process, the risk of developing the disease increases as people grow older. About 10 percent of the United States population over the age of 65 is affected by Alzheimer's disease, and nearly 50 percent of those over age 85 may have the disease.

Alzheimer's disease takes a devastating toll, not only on the patients, but also on those who love and care for them. Some patients experience immense fear and frustration as they struggle with once commonplace tasks and slowly lose their independence. Family, friends, and especially those who provide daily care suffer immeasurable pain and stress as they witness Alzheimer's disease slowly take their loved one from them.

The onset of Alzheimer's disease is usually very gradual. In the early stages, Alzheimer's patients have relatively mild problems learning new information and remembering where they have left common objects, such as keys or a wallet. In time, they begin to have trouble recollecting recent events and finding the right words to express themselves. As the disease progresses, patients may have difficulty remembering what day or month it is, or finding their way around familiar surfacing structural surroundings. They may develop a tendency to wander off and then be unable to find their way back. Patients often become irritable or withdrawn as they struggle with fear and frustration when once commonplace tasks become unfamiliar and intimidating. Behavioural changes may become more pronounced as patients become paranoid or delusional and unable to engage in normal conversation.

Eventually Alzheimer's patients become completely incapacitated and unable to take care of their most basic life functions, such as eating and using the bathroom. Alzheimer's patients may live many years with the disease, usually dying from other disorders that may develop, such as pneumonia. Typically the time from initial diagnosis until death is seven to ten years, but this is quite variable and can range from three to twenty years, depending on the age of the onset, other medical conditions present, and the care patients receive.

The brains of patients with Alzheimer's have distinctive formations - abnormally shaped proteins called tangles and plaques - that are recognized as the hallmark of the disease. Not all brain regions show these characteristic formations. The areas most prominently affected are those related to memory.

Tangles are long, slender tendrils found inside nerve cells, or neurons. Scientists have learned that when a protein-called tau becomes altered, it may cause the characteristic tangles in the brain of the Alzheimer's patient. In healthy brains provides structural support for neurons, but in Alzheimer's patients this structural support collapses.

Plaques, or clumps of fibres, form outside the neurons in the adjacent brain tissue. Scientists found that a type of protein, called amyloid precursor protein, forms toxic plaques when it is cut in two places. Researchers have isolated the enzyme beta-secretes, which is believed to make one of the cuts in the amyloid precursor protein. Researchers also identified another enzyme, a called gamma secretes, that makes the second cut in the amyloid precursor protein. These two enzymes snip the amyloid precursor protein into fragments that then accumulate to form plaques that are toxic to neurons.

Scientists have found that tangles and plaques cause neurons in the brains of Alzheimer's patients to shrink and eventually die, first in the memory and language centres and finally throughout the brain. This widespread neuron degeneration leaves gaps in the brain's messaging network that may interfere with communication between cells, causing some of the symptoms of Alzheimer's disease.

Alzheimer's patients initially have a descending connotation to depreciative levels of neurotransmitter chemicals that carry complex messages back and forth between the nerve cells. For instance, Alzheimer's disease seems to decrease the level of the neurotransmitter acetylcholine, which is known to influence memory. Even so, the deficiencies in other neurotransmitters include somatostatin and corticotropin-releasing contribution factors. More than is usual from others, is that the administering considerations are such of a kind, of which are particularly in the younger patients, having serotonin and norepinephrine, also baffling are the interposing interferences with the normative communication between brain cells. The essential substance for which is to develop the disease is more than the general population. For example, people with a family history of Alzheimer's are more likely to develop Alzheimer's disease.

Some of the most promising Alzheimer's research is being conducted in the field of genetics to learn the role a family history of the disease has in its development. Scientists have learned that people who are carriers of a specific version of the apolipoprotein E-gene (apoE-genes), found on chromosome 19, are several times more likely to develop Alzheimer's than carriers of other versions of the apoE gene. The most common version of this gene in the general population is apoE3. Nearly half of all late-onset Alzheimer's patients have the fewer in common apoE4 versions, however, and research has shown that this gene plays a role in Alzheimer's disease. Scientists have also found evidence that variations in one or more genes located on chromosomes 1, 10, and 14 may increase a person's risk for Alzheimer's disease. Scientists have identified the gene variations on chromosomes 1 and 14 and learned that these genes produce mutations in proteins called presenilin. These mutated proteins apparently trigger the activity of the enzyme gamma secretase, which splices the amyloid precursor protein.

Researchers have made similar strides in the investigation of an early-onset of Alzheimer's disease, for developing spiral genetic mutations, in patients with an early-onset. Such that Alzheimer's has been linked to the production of amyloid precursor proteins, in which the protein intake that poises of a patching plaque of a sticky deposit or a fibrous lesion that may be implicated in the destruction of neurons. One mutation is particularly interesting among geneticists because it occurs on a gene involved in the genetic disorder Down syndrome. People with Down syndrome usually develop the epistemic diseases causing a high mortality as estranging tangles in their brains as they get older, and researchers believe that learning more about the similarities between Down syndrome and Alzheimer's may further our understanding of the genetic elements of the disease.

Some studies suggest that one or more factors other than heredity may determine whether people develop the disease. One study published in February 2001 compared residents of Ibadan, Nigeria, who eat a mostly low-fat vegetarian diet, with African Americans living in Indianapolis, Indiana, whose diet included a variety of high-fat foods. The Nigerians were less likely to develop Alzheimer's disease compared to their US counterparts. Some researchers suspect that health imposes on high blood pressure, atherosclerosis (arteries clogged by fatty deposits), high cholesterol levels, or other cardiovascular problems may play a role in the development of the disease.

Other studies have suggested that environmental agents may be a possible cause of Alzheimer's disease; for example, one study suggested that high levels of aluminum in the brain may be a risk factor. Several scientists initiated research projects to further investigate this connection, but no conclusive evidence has been found linking aluminum with Alzheimer's disease. Similarly, investigations into other potential environmental causes, such as zinc exposure, viral agents, and food-borne poisons, while initially promising, have generally turned up inconclusive results.

Some studies indicate that brain trauma can trigger a degenerative process that results in Alzheimer's disease. In one study, an analysis of the medical records scribed upon veterans of World War II (1939-1945) linked serious head injury in early adulthood with Alzheimer's disease in later life. The study also looked at other factors that could possibly influence the development of the disease among the veterans, such as the presence of the apoE gene, but no other factors were identified.

Alzheimer's disease is only positively diagnosed by examining brain tissue under a microscope to see the hallmark plaques and tangles, and this is only possible after a patient dies. As a result, physicians rely on a series of other techniques to diagnose probable Alzheimer's disease in living patients. Diagnosis begins by ruling out other problems that cause memory loss, such as stroke, depression, alcoholism, and the use of certain prescription drugs. The patient undergoes a thorough examination, including specialized brain scans, to eliminate other disorders. The patient may be given a detailed evaluation called a neuropsychological examination, which is designed to evaluate a patient's ability to perform specific mental tasks. This helps the physician determine whether the patient is showing the characteristic symptoms of Alzheimer's disease - progressively worsening memory problems, language difficulties, and trouble with spatial direction and time. The physician also asks about the patient's family medical history to learn about any past serious illnesses, which may give a hint about the patient's current symptoms.

Evidence shows that there is inflammation in the brains of Alzheimer's patients, which may be associated with the production of amyloid precursor protein. Studies are underway to find drugs that prevent this inflammation, to possibly slow or even halt the progress of the disease. Other promising approaches center on mechanisms that manipulate amyloid precursor protein production or accumulation. Drugs are in development that may block the activity of the enzymes that cut the amyloid precursor protein, halting amyloid production. Other studies in mice suggest those vaccinating animals with amyloid precursor protein can produce a reaction that clears amyloid precursor protein from the brain. Physicians have started vaccination studies in humans to determine if the same potentially beneficial effects can be obtained. There is still much to be learned, but as scientists better understand the genetic components of Alzheimer's, the roles of the amyloid precursor protein and the tau protein in the disease, and the mechanisms of nerve cell degeneration, the possibility that a treatment will be developed is more likely.

The responsibility for caring for Alzheimer's patients generally falls on their spouses and children. Care givers must constantly be on guard for the possibility of Alzheimer's patients wandering away or becoming agitated or confused in a manner that jeopardizes the patient or others. Coping with a loved one's decline and inability to recognize familiar face causes enormous pain.

The increased burden faced by families is intense, and the life of the Alzheimer's care giver is often called a 36-hour day. Not surprisingly, care givers often develop health and psychological problems of their own as a result of this stress. The Alzheimer's Association, a national organization with local chapters throughout the United States, was formed in 1980 in large measure to provide support for Alzheimer's care givers. Today, national and local chapters are a valuable source for information, referral, and advice.

The reaching of a destination that coordinates Integration if determinate arrivals in the discovery that our considerations are much to do of ones finding or grasping upon the exponential idea given the growth to an answer or solution for (a problem of mysteriousness), that some of the most promising Alzheimer's research is being conducted in the field of genetics to learn the role a family history of the disease has in its development. Scientists have learned that people who are carriers of a specific version of the apolipoprotein E gene (apoE-genes), found on the chromosome [19], are several times more likely to develop Alzheimer's than carriers of other versions of the apoE gene. The most common version of this gene in the general population is apoE3. Nearly half of all late-onset Alzheimer's patients have the fewer in common apoE4 versions, however, and research has shown that this gene plays a role in Alzheimer's disease. Scientists have also found evidence that variations in one or more genes located on chromosomes 1, 10, and 14 may increase a person's risk for Alzheimer's disease. Scientists have identified the gene variations on chromosomes 1 and 14 and learned that these genes produce mutations in proteins called presenilin. These mutated proteins apparently trigger the activity of the enzyme gamma secretase, which splices the amyloid precursor protein.

Researchers have made similar strides in the investigation of early-onset Alzheimer's disease. Some sequential successions of genetic changes by variations to mutation that, with patients with early-onset Alzheimer's have been linked to the production of amyloid precursor protein, the protein enveloped as to be engulfed by plaques that may be implicated in the destruction of neurons. One mutation is particularly interesting among geneticists because it occurs on a gene involved in the genetic disorder Down syndrome. People with Downs syndrome usually develop plaques and tangles in their brains as they get older, as researchers believe that learning more about the similarities between Down syndrome and Alzheimer's may prove fitting in the further flowing to understandings of the genetic elements of the disease.

Some studies suggest that one or more factors other than heredity may determine whether people develop the disease. One study published in February 2001 compared residents of Ibadan, Nigeria, who eat a mostly low-fat vegetarian diet, with African Americans living in Indianapolis, Indiana, whose diet included a variety of high-fat foods. The Nigerians were less likely to develop Alzheimer's disease compared to their US counterparts. Some researchers suspect that health imposes on high blood pressure, atherosclerosis (arteries clogged by fatty deposits), high cholesterol levels, or other cardiovascular problems may play a role in the development of the disease.

Other studies have suggested that environmental agents may be a possible cause of Alzheimer's disease; for example, one study suggested that high levels of aluminum in the brain may be a risk factor. Several scientists initiated research projects to further investigate this connection, but no conclusive evidence has been found linking aluminum with Alzheimer's disease. Similarly, investigations into other potential environmental causes, such as zinc exposure, viral agents, and food-borne poisons, while initially promising, have generally turned up inconclusive results.

Some studies indicate that brain trauma can trigger a degenerative process that results in Alzheimer's disease. In one study, an analysis of the medical records scribed upon veterans of World War II (1939-1945) linked serious head injury in early adulthood with Alzheimer's disease in later life. The study also looked at other factors that could possibly influence the development of the disease among the veterans, such as the presence of the apoE gene, but no other factors were identified.

Alzheimer's disease is only positively diagnosed by examining brain tissue under a microscope to see the hallmark plaques and tangles, and this is only possible after a patient dies. As a result, physicians rely on a series of other techniques to diagnose probable Alzheimer's disease in living patients. Diagnosis begins by ruling out other problems that cause memory loss, such as stroke, depression, alcoholism, and the use of certain prescription drugs. The patient undergoes a thorough examination, including specialized brain scans, to eliminate other disorders. The patient may be given a detailed evaluation called a neuropsychological examination, which is designed to evaluate a patient's ability to perform specific mental tasks. This helps the physician determine whether the patient is showing the characteristic symptoms of Alzheimer's disease - progressively worsening memory problems, language difficulties, and trouble with spatial direction and time. The physician also asks about the patient's family medical history to learn about any past serious illnesses, which may give a hint about the patient's current symptoms.

Evidence shows that there is inflammation in the brains of Alzheimer's patients, which may be associated with the production of amyloid precursor protein. Studies are underway to find drugs that prevent this inflammation, to possibly slow or even halt the progress of the disease. Other promising approaches center on mechanisms that manipulate amyloid precursor protein production or accumulation. Drugs are in development that may block the activity of the enzymes that cut the amyloid precursor protein, halting amyloid production. Other studies in mice suggest those vaccinating animals with amyloid precursor protein can produce a reaction that clears amyloid precursor protein from the brain. Physicians have started vaccination studies in humans to determine if the same potentially beneficial effects can be or in effective operation to be gainfully attainable. There is still much to be learned, but as scientists better understand the genetic components of Alzheimer's, the roles of the amyloid precursor protein and the tau protein in the disease, and the mechanisms of nerve cell degeneration, the possibility that a treatment will be developed is more likely.

The responsibility for caring for Alzheimer's patients generally falls on their spouses and children. Care givers must constantly be on guard for the possibility of Alzheimer's patients wandering away or becoming agitated or confused in a manner that jeopardizes the patient or others. Coping with a loved one's decline and inability to recognize familiar face causes enormous pain.

The increased burden faced by families is intense, and the life of the Alzheimer's care giver is often called a 36-hour day. Not surprisingly, care givers often develop health and psychological problems of their own as a result of this stress. The Alzheimer's Association, a national organization with local chapters throughout the United States, was formed in 1980 in large measure to provide support for Alzheimer's care givers. Today, national and local chapters are a valuable source for information, referral, and advice.

Defining an understanding of the states of consciousness is not at all simple, is agreed-upon definition of consciousness exists. Attempted definitions tend to be tautological (for example, consciousness defined as awareness) or merely descriptive (for example, consciousness described as sensations, thoughts, or feelings). Despite this problem of definition, the subject of consciousness has had a remarkable history. At one time the primary subject matter of psychology, consciousness as an area of study, that the idea that something conveys to the mind, from which of critics has endlessly debated the meaning of the ascribing interactions that otherwise to ascertain the quality, mass, extent or degree of terminological statements that its standard unit or mixed distributive analysis, is such, that a conceptualized form of its reasons to posit of a direct interpretation whose interference became of the total demise, even so, there is the result reemerging to become a topic of current interests.

Most of the philosophical discussions of consciousness arose from the mind-body issues posed by the French philosopher and mathematician René Descartes in the 17th century. Descartes asked: Is the mind, or consciousness, independent of matter? Is consciousness extended (physical) or unextended (nonphysical)? Is consciousness determinative, or is it determined? English philosophers such as John Locke equated consciousness with physical sensations and the information they provide, whereas European philosophers such as Gottfried Wilhelm Leibniz and Immanuel Kant gave a more central and active role to consciousness.

The philosopher who most directly influenced subsequent exploration of the subject of consciousness was the 19th-century German educator Johann Friedrich Herbart, who wrote that ideas had quality and intensity and that they may suppress or may facilitate or place of one another. Thus, ideas may pass from "states of reality" (consciousness) to "states of tendencies" (unconsciousness), with the dividing line between the two states being described as the threshold of consciousness. This formulation of Herbart clearly presages the development, by the German psychologist and physiologist Gustav Theodor Fechner, of the psychophysical measurement of sensation thresholds, and the later development by Sigmund Freud of the concept of the unconscious.

The experimental analysis of consciousness dates from 1879, when the German psychologist Wilhelm Max Wundt started his research laboratory. For Wundt, the task of psychology was the study of the structure of consciousness, which extended well beyond sensations and included feelings, images, memory, attention, duration, and movement. Because early interest focussed on the content and dynamics of consciousness, it is not surprising that the central methodology of such studies was introspection; that is, subjects reported on the mental contents of their own consciousness. This introspective approach was developed most fully by the American psychologist Edward Bradford Titchener at Cornell University. Setting his task as that of describing the structure of the mind, Titchener attempted to detail, from introspective self-reports, the dimensions of the elements of consciousness. For example, taste was "dimensionalized" into four basic categories: sweet, sour, salt, and bitter. This approach was known as structuralism.

By the 1920's, however, a remarkable revolution had occurred in psychology that was to essentially remove considerations of consciousness from psychological research for some 50 years: Behaviourialism captured the field of psychology, its theory is that objective investigation of stimuli and responses are the only valid psychological method, and that psychological disorders are best treated by altering behaviour patterns. Its initiator of this movement was the American psychologist John Broadus Watson. In a 1913 article, Watson stated, "I believe that we can write of some psychology and never use the term's consciousness, mental states, mind, imaginary and the like." Psychologists then turned almost exclusively to behaviour, as described in terms of stimulus and response, and consciousness was totally bypassed as a subject. A survey of eight leading introductory psychology texts published between 1930 and the 1950's found no mention of the topic of consciousness in five texts, and in two it was treated as a historical curiosity.

Beginning in the later part of the 1950s, are, however, the grounded interests in the foundational subject of consciousness, for returning from its absence were subjects and techniques relating to altered states of consciousness: sleep and dreams, meditation, biofeedback, hypnosis, and drug-induced states. Much in the surge in sleep and dream research was directly fuelled by a discovery relevant to the nature of consciousness. A physiological indicator of the dream state was found: At roughly 90-minute intervals, the eyes of sleepers were observed to move rapidly, and at the same time the sleepers' brain waves would show a pattern resembling the waking state. When people were awakened during these periods of rapid eye movement, they almost always reported dreams, whereas if awakened at other times they did not. This and other research clearly indicated that sleep, once considered a passive state, were instead an active state of consciousness.

American psychiatrist William Glasser developed reality therapy in the 1960s, after working with teenage girls in a correctional institution and observing work with severely disturbed schizophrenic patients in a mental hospital. He observed that psychoanalysis did not help many of his patients change their behaviour, even when they understood the sources of it. Glasser felt it was important to help individuals take responsibility for their own lives and to blame others less. Largely because of this emphasis on personal responsibility, his approach has found widespread acceptance among drugs - and alcohol-abuse counsellors', correction's workers, school counsellors, and those working with clients who may be disruptive to others.

Reality therapy is based on the premise that all human behaviour is motivated by fundamental needs and specific wants. The reality therapist first seeks to establish a friendly, trusting relationship with clients in which they can express their needs and wants. Then the therapist helps clients explore the behaviours that created problems for them. Clients are encouraged to examine the consequences of their behaviour and to evaluate how well their behaviour helped them fulfill their wants. The therapist does not accept excuses from clients. Finally, the therapist helps the client formulate a concrete plan of action to change certain behaviours, based on the client's own goals and ability to make choices.

During the 1960s, an increased search for 'higher levels' of consciousness through meditation resulted in a growing interest in the practices of Zen Buddhism and Yoga from Eastern cultures. A full flowering of this movement in the United States was seen in the development of training programs, such as Transcendental Meditation, that were self-directed procedures of physical relaxation and focussed attention. Biofeedback techniques also were developed to bring body systems involving factors such as blood pressure or temperature under voluntary control by providing feedback from the body, so that subjects could learn to control their responses. For example, researchers found that persons could control their brain-wave patterns to some extent, particularly the so-called alpha rhythms generally associated with a relaxed, meditative state. This finding was especially relevant to those interested in consciousness and meditation, and a number of 'alpha training' programs emerged.

Another subject that led to increased interest in altered states of consciousness was hypnosis, which involves a transfer of conscious control from the character interpretation belonging in the dependent sector, whose occasions, as basic of an idea or the principal object of attention, in the course of its immediate composition, and like the substance to a particular individual finds to the subject that the modification as when of transferring to that of another person. Hypnotism has had a long and intricate history in medicine and folklore and has been intensively studied by psychologists. Much has become known about the hypnotic state, relative to individual suggestibility and personality traits; the subject has now been largely demythologized, and the limitations of the hypnotic state are fairly well known. Despite the increasing use of hypnosis, however, much remains to be learned about this unusual state of focussed attention.

Finally, many people in the 1960's experimented with the psychoactive drugs known as hallucinogens, which produce deranging disorder of consciousness. The most prominent of these drugs is lysergic acid diethylamide, or LSD; mescaline; and psilocybin; the latter two have long been associated with religious ceremonies in various cultures. LSD, because of its radical thought-modifying properties, was initially explored for its so-called mind-expanding potential and for its psychotomimetic effects (imitating psychoses). Little positive use, however, has been found for these drugs, and their use is highly restricted.

Scientists have long considered the nature of consciousness without producing a fully satisfactory definition. In the early 20th century American philosopher and psychologist William James suggested that consciousness be a mental process involving both attention to external stimuli and short-term memory. Later scientific explorations of consciousness mostly expanded upon James's work, according to the article from a 1997 special issue of Scientific American, Nobel laureate Francis Crick, who helped determine the structure of DNA, and fellow biophysicist Christof Koch who explains how experiments on vision might deepen our understanding of consciousness.

As the concept of a direct, simple linkage between environment and behaviour became unsatisfactory in recent decades, the interest in altered states of consciousness may be taken as a visible sign of renewed interest in the topic of consciousness. That persons are active and intervening participants in their behaviour has become increasingly clear. Environments, rewards, and punishments are not simply defined by their physical character. Memories are organized, not simply stored, an entirely new area called cognitive psychology has emerged that centre on these concerns. In the study of children, increased attention is being paid to how they understand, or perceive, the world at different ages. In the field of animal behaviour, researchers increasingly emphasize the inherent characteristics resulting from the way a species has been shaped to respond adaptively to the environment. Humanistic psychologists, with a concern for self-actualization and growth, have emerged after a long period of silence. Throughout the development of clinical and industrial psychology, the conscious states of persons in terms of their current feelings and thoughts were of obvious importance. The role of consciousness, however, was often de-emphasized in favour of unconscious needs and motivations. Trends can be seen, however, toward a new emphasis on the nature of states of consciousness.

We have used the term 'transference' several times, in that we attributed the therapeutic results to the transference without further definition of the word. Upon due considerations, we will now consider more closely the emotional relationship that is thus designed. During a psychoanalytic treatment, the patient allows the analyst to play a predominating role, or the foundation of his emotional life, for this is of a great the essence, especially to explain of how far it is to the importance in the analytic process. After his treatment is over, this situation is changed. The patient builds up feelings of affection for and resistance to his analyst that, in their ebb and flow, so exceed the normal degree of feeling that the phenomenon has long attracted the theoretical interest of the analyst. Freud studied this phenomenon thoroughly, explained it, and gave it the name 'transference', we most probably will understand the significance of the transference phenomenon impressed Freud so profoundly that he continued through the years to develop his ideas about it.

Later noteworthy modifications of psychoanalytic theory include those of the American psychoanalyst's Erich Fromm, Karen Horney, and Harry Stack Sullivan. The theories of Fromm lay particular emphasis on the concept that society and the individuals are not separate and opposing forces, that the nature of society is determined by its historic background, and that the needs and desires of the individuality are largely formed by their society. As a result, Fromm believed, the fundamental problem of psychoanalysis and psychology is not to resolve conflicts between fixed and unchanging instinctive drives in the individual and the fixed demands and laws of society, but to bring about harmony and an understanding of the relationship between the individual and society. Fromm also stressed the importance to the individual of developing the ability to fully use his or her mental, emotional, and sensory powers.

Horney worked primarily in the field of therapy and the nature of neuroses, which she defined as of two types: situation neuroses and character neuroses. Situation neuroses arise from the anxiety attendant on a single conflict, such for being faced with a difficult decision. Although they may paralyze the individual temporarily, making it impossible to think or act efficiently, such neuroses are not deeply rooted. Character neuroses are characterized by a basic anxiety and a basic hostility resulting from a lack of love and affection in childhood.

Sullivan believed that all development can be described exclusively in terms of interpersonal relations. Character types as well as neurotic symptoms are explained as results of the struggle against anxiety arising from the individual's relations with others, including security measures of which a system is maintained for the purpose of allaying anxiety.

An important school of thought is based on the teachings of the British psychoanalyst Melanie Klein. Because most of Klein's followers worked with her in England, this has come to be known as the English school. Its influence, nevertheless, is very strong throughout the European continent and in South America. Its principal theories were derived from observations made in the psychoanalysis of children. Klein posited the existence of complex unconscious fantasies in children under the age of six months. The principal source of anxiety arises from the threat to existence posed by the death instinct. Depending on how concrete representations of the destructive forces are dealt within the unconscious fantasy life of the child, two basic early mental attitudes result that Klein characterized as a 'depressive position' and a 'paranoid position.' In the paranoid position, the ego's defence consists of projecting the dangerously internalized object onto some external representative, which is treated as a genuine threat emanating from the external world. In the depressive position, the threatening object is introjected and treated in fantasy as concretely retained within the person. Depressive and hypochondriacal symptoms result. Although considerable doubt exists that such complex unconscious fantasies operate in the minds of infants, these observations have been of the utmost importance to the psychology of unconscious fantasies, paranoid delusions, and theory concerning early object relations.

Mental health professionals generally divide psychotic symptoms into three broad types: hallucinations, delusions, and bizarre behaviour. Hallucinations refer to hearing, seeing, smelling, feeling, or tasting something when nothing in the environment actually caused that sensation. For example, a person experiencing an auditory hallucination might hear a voice calling their name even though no one else is actually present. A delusion is a false belief held by a person that appears obviously untrue to other people in that person's culture. For example, a man may believe that Martians have implanted a microchip in his brain that controls his thoughts. Bizarre behaviour refers to behaviour in a person that is strange or incomprehensible to others who know the person. For example, hoarding unused scraps of tin because of their 'magical properties' would most certainly be a type of bizarre behaviour.

Psychosis can occur in a number of mental illnesses. These include schizophrenia and schizophrenia-related disenabling integration of anarchism or be that of an odorless ataxia as muddled in the disorders of dementia, bipolar disorder, paranoid personality disorder, and delusional disorder. And less common, psychotic symptoms occur in major depression Dissociative disorders, also including post-traumatic stress disorder.

Psychotic symptoms can also result from substance abuse. Stimulants, such as cocaine and amphetamines, can cause psychotic symptoms, especially if taken in high doses or over long periods of time. Hallucinogenic substances, such as lysergic acid diethylamide (LSD), mescaline and phencyclidine (PCP), can cause psychosis. Alcohol and marijuana can occasionally cause psychotic symptoms as well. Individuals with alcoholism may experience psychotic symptoms, especially hallucinations, as they withdraw from alcohol use. Alcohol dependence over a long period of time can result in Korsakoff's psychosis, a syndrome that may include psychotic symptoms and an inability to form new memories. Certain medical conditions can also cause psychosis. Syphilis, especially if untreated for many years, can lead to psychosis. Brain tumours can also lead to psychotic symptoms.

Treatment of psychotic symptoms usually involved taking antipsychotic drugs, and called neuroleptics. Common antipsychotic drugs include chlorpromazine (Thorazine), fluphenazine (Prolixin), thioridazine (Mellaril), trifluoperazine (Stelazine), clozapine (Clozaril), haloperidol (Haldol), olanzapine (Zyprexa), and risperidone (Risperdal). These medications can help reduce psychotic symptoms and prevent symptoms from returning. However, they can also cause severe side effects, such as muscle spasms, tremors, and tardive dyskinesia - a permanent condition marked by uncontrollable lip smacking, grimacing, and tongue movements. Psychotic symptoms in individuals with bipolar disorder may respond to other types of medication, including lithium, carbamazepine (Tegretol), and valproate (Depakene).

Psychotic symptoms that occur as a result of substance abuse usually disappear gradually after the person stops using the substances. Physicians sometimes use antipsychotic medications temporarily to treat these individuals. Physicians have not discovered any effective treatments for Korsakoff's psychosis. Psychotic symptoms resulting from medical conditions often disappear after treatment of the underlying medical problem.

The Sociocultural perspective regards mental illness as the result of social, economic, and cultural factors. Evidence for this view comes from research that has demonstrated an increased risk of mental illness among people living in poverty. In addition, the incidence of mental illness rises in times of high unemployment. The shift in the world population from rural areas to cities - with their crowding, noise, pollution, decay, and social isolation - and, has also, been implicated in causing relatively high rates of mental illness. Furthermore, rapid social change, which has particularly affected indigenous peoples throughout the world, brings about high rates of suicide and alcoholism. Refugees and victims of social disasters - warfare, displacement, genocide, violence - have a higher risk of mental illness, especially depression, anxiety, and post-traumatic stress disorder.

Social scientists emphasize that the link between social ills and mental illness is correlational rather than causal. For example, although societies undergoing rapid social change often have high rates of suicide the specific causes have not been identified. Social and cultural factors may create relative risks for a population or class of people, but it is unclear how such factors raise the risk of mental illness for an individual.

There are no blood tests, imaging techniques, or other laboratory procedures that can reliably diagnose a mental illness. Thus, the diagnosis of mental illness is always a judgment or an interpretation by an observer based on the spoken exchange, ideas, behaviours, and experiences of the patient.

In the late 19th century Viennese neurologist Sigmund Freud developed a theory of personality and a system of psychotherapy known as psychoanalysis. According to this theory, people are strongly influenced by unconscious forces, including innate sexual and aggressive drives.

The psychodynamic perspective views mental illness as caused by unconscious and unresolved conflicts in the mind. As stated by Freud, these conflicts arise in early childhood and may cause mental illness by impeding the equilibrium of the structural surroundings in the balancing developments of the three systems that constitute the human psyche - the id, which comprises innate sexual and aggressive drives-the ego, the conscious portion of the mind that mediates between the unconscious and reality, and the superego, which controls the primitive impulses of the id and represents moral ideals. In this view, generalized anxiety disorder stems from a signal of unconscious danger whose source can only be identified through a thorough analysis of the person's personality and life experiences. The present or its current view that psychodynamic theorists' tend to emphasize sexuality less than Freud did and focus more on problems in the individual's relationships with others, in that which psychodynamics is the study of the activity of and the interrelation between the various parts of an individual's personality or psyche [mind].

Both the humanistic and existential perspectives view abnormal behaviour as resulting from a person's failure to find meaning in life and fulfill his or her potential, a mental view of the way of regarding a matter of the relative importance of things as kept in perspective. The humanistic school of psychology, as represented in the work of American psychologist Carl Rogers, views mental health and personal growth as the natural conditions of human life. In Rogers's view, every person possesses a drive toward self-actualization, the fulfilment of one's greatest potential. Mental illness develops when a person's condition by some circumstantial environment interferes with this drive. The existential perspective sees emotional disturbances as the result of a person's failure to act authentically - that is, to behave in accordance with one's own goals and values, rather than the goals and values of others.

The pioneers of behaviourialism, American psychologists' John B. Watson and B. F. Skinner, maintained that psychology should confine itself to the study of observable behaviour, rather than explore a person's unconscious feelings. The behavioural perspective explains mental illness, as well as all of human behaviour, as a learned response to, malaria, and infection's stimuli. In this view, rewards and punishments in a person's environment shape that person's behaviour, for example, a person involved in a serious car accident may develop a phobia of cars or the generalized fear to all forms of transportation.

The cognitive perspective holds that mental illness result from problems in cognition - that is, problems in how a person reasons, perceives events, and solves problems. American psychiatrist Aaron Beck proposed that some mental illnesses - such as depression, anxiety disorders, and personality disorders - result from a way of thinking learned in childhood that is not consistent with reality. For example, people with depression tend to see themselves in a negative light, exaggerate the importance of minor flaws or failures, and misinterpret the behaviour of others in negative ways. It remains unclear, however, whether these kinds of cognitive problems actually cause mental illness or merely represent symptoms of the illnesses themselves.

People have tried to interpret the causes of mental illness for thousands of years. The modern era of psychiatry, which began in the late 19th and early 20th centuries, have attested to sharp rhetorical exchange of discourse, the dialect indulgence between biological and psychological perspectives of mental illness of which the biological perspective views mental illness (being a disordered functioning of the mind) in terms of bodily processes, whereas psychological perspectives emphasizes the roles of a person's upbringing and environment as the totality for being whole (being the physical conditions on the earth or a part of it, especially as affected by human activity).

These two perspectives are exemplified in the works of German psychiatrist Emil Kraepelin and Austrian psychoanalyst Sigmund Freud. Kraepelin, influenced by the work in the mid-1800's of German psychiatrist Wilhelm Griesinger, believed that psychiatric disorders were disease entities that could be classified like physical illnesses. That is, Kraepelin believed that the fundamental causes of mental illness lay in the physiology and biochemistry of the human brain. His classification system of mental disorders, first published in 1883, formed the basis for later diagnostic systems. As Freud, on the other hand, argued that the source of mental illness lay in the unconscious conflicts originating in early childhood experiences. Freud found evidence for this idea through the analysis of dreams, free association, and slips of speech.

The debate has continued to overlap and converged into the late 20th century. Beginning in the 1960's, the biological perspective became dominant, supported by numerous breakthroughs in psychopharmacology, genetics, neurophysiology, and brain research. For example, scientists discovered many medications that helped to relieve symptoms of certain mental illnesses and demonstrated that people can inherit a vulnerability to some mental illnesses. Psychological perspectives also remain influential, including the psychodynamic perspective in which the apparent view of the interrelation between the various parts of an individual's personality or psyche [mind].

That the mental view of the relative importance as the attributive perspective, the humanistic and existential position, the behaviour perspective stands on the cognitive perspectives, the cognitive perspective, and the Sociocultural perspective. For these of the potential possibilities that exist within the personal matters or feelings rather than with the generalities needed to maintain of such cause to continue. Psychiatry increasingly emphasized a biological basis for the causes of mental illness. Studies suggest a genetic influence in some mental illnesses, such as schizophrenia and bipolar disorder, although the evidence is not conclusive.

Clinical depression is one of the most common forms of mental illness. Although depression can be treated with psychotherapy, many scientists believe there are biological causes for the disease. In the June 1998 Scientific American article, the neurobiologist Charles B. Nemeroff reports upon the connection between biochemical changes in the brain and depression.

Scientists have identified a number of neurotransmitters, or chemical substances that enable brain cells to communicate with other, that appears important in regulating a person's emotions and behaviour. These include dopamine, serotonin, norepinephrine, gamma-amino butyric acid (GABA), and acetylcholine. Excesses and deficiencies in levels of these neurotransmitters have been associated with depression, anxiety, and schizophrenia, but scientists have yet to determine the exact mechanisms involved.

Research shows that the more genetically related a person is to someone with schizophrenia, the greater the risk that person has of developing the illness. For example, children of one parent with schizophrenia have a 13 percent chance of developing the illness, whereas children of two parents with schizophrenia have a 46 percent chance of developing the disorder.

Advances in brain imaging techniques, such as magnetic resonance imaging (MRI) and positron emission tomography (PET), have enabled scientists to study the role of brain structure in mental illness. Some studies have revealed structural brain abnormalities in certain mental illnesses. For example, some people with schizophrenia have enlarged brain ventricles (cavities in the brain that contains cerebrospinal fluid). However, this may be a result of schizophrenia rather than a cause, and not all people with schizophrenia show this abnormality.

Are a person's characteristics primarily shaped by early influences, remaining relatively stable thereafter throughout life? Or effectively change spontaneously, and occurring to the continuity throughout life? Many people believe that early experiences are formative, providing a strong or weak foundation for later psychological growth. This view is expressed in the popular saying 'As the twig is bent, so grows the tree.' From this perspective, it is crucial to ensure that young children have a good start in life. But many developmental scientists believe that later experiences can modify or even reverse early influences; studies show that even when early experiences are traumatic or abusive, considerable recovery can occur. From this vantage point, early experiences influence, but rarely determine, later characteristics.

Traumatic experiences in this early period of life will damage a personality more seriously than those occurring in later childhood such as are found in the history of psychoneurotics. The infant's mind is more vulnerable the younger and less used it has been, furthers, the trauma has quickened the infant 's egocentricity. In addition early traumatic experience shortens the only period in life in which an individual ordinarily enjoys the most security, thus endangering the ability to store up as it was a reasonable to supply the assurance and self-reliance for the individual's later struggles through life. Thus, as such, a child sensitized considerably more directorially for being grounded within the frustrations of later life than by later traumatic experiences. Hence many experiences in later life which would mean little to a 'healthy' person and not much to a psychoneurotic, mean a great deal of pain and suffering to the schizophrenic. His resistance against frustration is easily exhausted.

Once he reaches his limit of endurance, he escapes the unbearable reality of his present life by attempting to reestablish the autistic, delusional world of the infant, but this is impossible because the content of his delusions and hallucinations are naturally coloured by the experiences of his whole lifetime, instead he finds into his solacing refuge for which he begins between his knowing and safe securities.

How do these developments influence the patient's attitude toward the analyst and the analyst's approach to him?

Due to the very damage and the succeeding chain of frustrations which the schizophrenic undergoes before finally giving in to illness, he feels extremely suspicious and distrustful of everyone, particularly of the psychotherapist ho approaches him with the intent of intruding into his isolated world and personal life. To him the physician's approach means the threat of being compelled to return to the frustrations of real life and to reveal his inadequacy to meet them or, - still worse – a repetition of the aggressive interference with his initial symptoms and peculiarities which he has encountered in his previous environment.

The otherwise, difficulty that diversely encumbers, as an intensifier along with the patient's dilemma, through which his frustration is evidence, a fact through which is called 'delusion' is itself a delusion of a false belief and firmly held by a person, even though other people recognize the belief as obviously untrue. For example, a person who truly believes he is Napoleon Bonaparte is delusional. As something accepted as true that is actually false or unreal. Religious beliefs or popular conceptions, such as the beliefs that people have been abducted by aliens, are not delusions because they are widely held beliefs. Delusions are a type of psychotic symptom that indicate a person has lost contact with reality.

There are many different types of delusions. A person with a paranoid delusion believes that others - such as the FBI, or the CIA, even the Mafia as trying to harm or plot against him. A person with a delusion of reference believes that events or people refer specifically to him or her when they do not. For example, a woman with schizophrenia may believe that a television news broadcaster is talking personally to her rather than to the entire viewing audience. A grandiose delusion is a belief that one is extremely famous or that one has special powers, such as the ability to magically heal people.

A delusion of control is a belief that others are able to control one's thoughts, feelings, or actions. For example, a man with this type of delusion may believe that someone has implanted a microchip in his brain that enables other people to control his thoughts. A somatic delusion is a belief that something is wrong with one's body - for example, that one's brain is rotting away - even though no medical evidence supports this belief. A person with an erotic delusion believes that someone is in love with him or her despite a lack of evidence for this belief. In a delusion of jealousy, a person believes that his or her spouse or lover is unfaithful despite evidence to the contrary.

Delusions commonly occur in certain severe mental illnesses, such as schizophrenia, bipolar disorder (also called manic-depressive illness), some cases of major depression, Dissociative disorders, post-traumatic stress disorder, and paranoid personality disorder. In addition, his delusions may result in the amounts from abuse of certain drugs, and to include alcohol, cocaine, amphetamines, and hallucinogens such as lysergic acid diethylamide (LSD), phencyclidine (PCP), and mescaline. Medical conditions affecting the brain, such as syphilis and brain tumours, may also cause a delusionary reality as not to be faced squarely.

Delusional disorder is a relatively uncommon mental illness characterized by delusions. People with this disorder have one or more delusions that persist for at least one month. In addition, they do not suffer from other symptoms of schizophrenia, such as disorganized speech and bizarre behaviour. Usually their delusions are less bizarre than those that occur in schizophrenia and seem merely odd or unsupported by facts. Examples of nonbizarre delusions include beliefs that one is being followed, loved by someone famous, or deceived by one's spouse. Because delusional disorder is relatively rare, little research has systematically examined its treatment. However, doctors most often use antipsychotic drugs to treat this disorder. These drugs help reduce or eliminate delusions, hallucinations, and other psychotic symptoms.

In spite of his narcissistic retreat, every schizophrenic has some underlying notion of the unreality and loneliness of his substitute delusionary world. Within this solacing place of refuge, he longs for human contact and understanding, yet is afraid to admit to himself, or his therapist for fear of further absurdness and of chronic developments in the manufacturing between persons and his aim or desires of considering defeat over the negativity associated from under one's hope and expectation as baffled in the extended or lying in a direction for which is transversely athwart with frustration.

That is why the patient may take weeks and months to test the analyst before being willing to accept him, however, once he has accepted him. His dependence on the analyst is greater and he is more sensitive about it than is the psychoneurotic because of the schizophrenic's deeply rooted insecurity, the narcissistic seemingly self-righteous attitude is but a defence.

Whenever the analyst fails the patient from reasons to be discussed later - one cannot at times avoid failing one's schizophrenic patients - it will be severe disappointment and a repetition of the chain of frustrations the schizophrenic has previously endured.

The instinctually primitive part of the schizophrenic's mind that does not discriminate between himself and the environment, it may mean the withdrawal of the impersonal supporting forces of his infancy. Severe anxiety will follow this vital deprivation.

In the light of his personal relationship with the analyst it means that the therapist seduced the patient to use him as a bridge over which he might possibly be led from the utter loneliness of his own world to reality and human warmth, only to have him discover that this bridge is not reliable. If so, he will respond helplessly with an outburst of hostility or with renewed withdrawal as may be seen most impressively in catatonic stupor.

The symptoms of mental illness can be very distressing. People who develop schizophrenia may hear voices inside their head that say nasty things about them or command them to act in strange or unpredictable ways. Or they may be paralysed by paranoia - the deep conviction that everyone, including their closest family members, wants to injure or destroy them. People with major depression may feel that nothing brings pleasure and that life is so dreary and unhappy that it is better to be dead. People with panic disorder may experience heart palpitations, rapid breathing, and anxiety so extreme that they may not be able to leave home. People whom experience episodes of mania may engage in reckless sexual behaviour or may spend money indiscriminately, acts that later cause them to feel guilt, shame, and desperation.

Other mental illnesses, while not always debilitating, create certain problems in living. People with personality disorders may experience loneliness and isolation because their personality style interferes with social relations. People with an eating disorder may become so preoccupied with their weight and appearance that they force themselves to vomit or refuse to eat. Individuals who develop post-traumatic stress disorder may become angry easily, experience disturbing memories, and have trouble concentrating.

Experiences of mental illness often interact differently but depend on one's culture or social group, sometimes greatly so. For example, in most of the non-Western world, people with depression complain principally of physical ailments, such as lack of energy, poor sleep, loss of appetite, and various kinds of physical pain. Indeed, even in North America these complaints are commonplace. But in the United States and other Western societies, depressed people and mental health professionals who treat them tend to emphasize psychological problems, such as feelings of sadness, worthlessness, and despair. The experience of schizophrenia also differs by culture. In India, one-third of the new cases of schizophrenia involve catatonia - a behavioural condition in which a person maintains a bizarre statue like poses for hours or days. This condition is rare in Europe and North America.

With appropriate treatment, most people can recover from mental illness and return to normal life. Even those with persistent, long-term mental illnesses can usually learn to manage their symptoms and live productive lives.

By a variety of symptoms, including loss of contact with reality, bizarre behaviour, disorganized thinking and speech, decreased emotional expressiveness, and social withdrawal. Usually only some of these symptoms occur in any one person. The term schizophrenia comes from Greek words meaning 'split mind.' However, contrary to common belief, schizophrenia does not refer to a person with a split personality or multiple personality. For a description of a mental illness in which a person has multiple personalities, it may seem appropriable to say, that, at best the observers, of schizophrenia may seem or appear for being as some sorted categorization as undividable or things that feel, perceives, thinks, will, and especially reasons as such a mind that governs to the inclining inclinations for which to obtainably achieve of those desires or required facts as to analyze the character of the kinds showing or having to consider the hidden implacable madness or manufacturing of madness or lunacy.

Perhaps more than any other mental illness, schizophrenia has a debilitating effect on the lives of the people who suffer from it. A person with schizophrenia may have difficulty telling the difference between what is conceptually real and whatever is to administer their unreal experiences, and linguistically correlating of logical and illogical thoughts, that is, the deliberated characterizations by or exhibiting the power to think, such as in the mind or to form an idea implicating its process of thinking.

Nevertheless, is that, schizophrenia is a serious mental illness, that impairs a person's ability to work, go to school, enjoy relationships with others, or take care of oneself. In addition, people with schizophrenia frequently require hospitalization because they pose a danger to themselves. About 10 percent of people with schizophrenia commit suicide, and many others attempt suicide. Once people develop schizophrenia, they usually suffer from the illness for the rest of their lives. Although there is no cure, treatment can help many people with schizophrenia lead productive lives.

Schizophrenia also carries an enormous cost to society. People with schizophrenia occupy about one-third of all beds in psychiatric hospitals in the United States. In addition, people with schizophrenia account for at least 10 percent of the homeless population in the United States. The National Institute of Mental Health has estimated that schizophrenia costs the United States tens of billions of dollars each year in direct treatment, social services, and lost productivity.

Approximately 1 percent of people develop schizophrenia at some time during their lives. Experts estimate that about 1.8 million people in the United States have schizophrenia. The prevalence in schizophrenia is correlational and equivalently the state or property of being equivalent or the result of making equivalent, in the finding the equivalency as the same and equal to the like observations as in the saneness of indistinguishability.

Once, again, the indistinguishability of sameness is significantly irrelevant of sex, race, and culture. Although women are just as likely as men to develop schizophrenia, women tend to have or exhibit an inclination or tendency that in having a particular direction and character to estimate the potential strength of that experience, is to a lesser extent, the overall eventuality affecting the occurring event as a matter or remark, is that, a postulated outcome, condition or contingency seem to oppose any happenstance, should it occur as the quality of being actual, that is to say, the realm of fact is distinct from fancy. The confronting with courage or boldness, readily to face up to reality squarely face to face that the peculiar state of illness is less severe with fewer hospitalizations and better social functioning in the community.

Schizophrenia usually develops in late adolescence or early adulthood, between the ages of 15 and 30. Much less common, schizophrenia develops later in life. The illness may begin abruptly, but it usually develops slowly over months or years. Mental health professionals diagnose schizophrenia based on an interview with the patient in which they determine whether the person has experienced specific symptoms of the illness.

Symptoms and functioning in people with schizophrenia tend to vary over time, sometimes worsening and other times improving. For many patients the symptoms gradually become less severe as they grow older. About 25 percent of people with schizophrenia become symptom-free later in their lives.

A variety of symptoms characterize schizophrenia. The most prominent include symptoms of psychosis - such as delusions and hallucinations - as well as bizarre behaviour, strange movements, and disorganized thinking and speech. Many people with schizophrenia do not recognize that their mental functioning is disturbed.

Delusions are false beliefs that appear obviously untrue to other people. For example, a person with schizophrenia may believe that he is the king of England when he is not. People with schizophrenia may have delusions that others, such as the police or the FBI, are plotting against them or spying on them. They may believe that aliens are controlling their thoughts or that their own thoughts are being broadcast to the world so that other people can hear them.

Research suggests that the genes' one inherits strongly influence one's risk of developing schizophrenia. Studies of families have shown that the more close one is related to someone with schizophrenia, the greater the risk one has of developing the illness. For example, the children of one parent with schizophrenia have about a 13 percent chance of developing the illness, and children of two parents with schizophrenia have about a 46 percent chance of eventually developing schizophrenia. This increased risk occurs even when such children are adopted and raised by mentally healthy parents. In comparison, children in the general population have only about a 1 percent chance of developing schizophrenia.

Some evidence suggests that schizophrenia may result from an imbalance of chemicals in the brain called neurotransmitters. These chemicals enable neurons (brain cells) to communicate with each other. Some scientists suggest that schizophrenia result from excess activity of the neurotransmitter dopamine in certain parts of the brain or from an abnormal sensitivity to dopamine. Asserting that antipsychotic drugs reduce psychotic symptoms in schizophrenia by blocking brain receptors for dopamine, in addition, amphetamines, which increase dopamine activity, intensify psychotic symptoms in people with schizophrenia. Despite these findings, many experts believe that excess dopamine activity alone cannot account for schizophrenia. Other neurotransmitters, such as serotonin and norepinephrine, may play important roles as well.

Although scientists favour a biological cause of schizophrenia, stress in the environment may affect the onset and course of the illness. Stressful life circumstances - such as maturing in age and character as for living in poverty, the death of a loved one, an important change in jobs or relationships, or chronic tension and hostility at home - increases the chances of schizophrenia in a person biologically predisposed to the disease. In addition, stressful events can trigger a relapse of symptoms in a person who already has the illness. Individuals who have effective skills for managing stress may be less susceptible to its negative effects. Psychological and social rehabilitation can help patients develop more effective skills for dealing with stress.

Although there is no cure for schizophrenia, effective treatment exists that can improve the long-term course of the illness. With many years of treatment and rehabilitation, significant numbers of people with schizophrenia experience partial or full remission of their symptoms.

Treatment of schizophrenia usually involves a combination of medication, rehabilitation, and treatment of other problems the person may have. Antipsychotic drugs (also called neuroleptics) are the most frequently used medications for treatment of schizophrenia. Psychological and social rehabilitation programs may help people with schizophrenia function in the community and reduce stress related to their symptoms. Treatment of secondary problems, such as substance abuse and infectious diseases, is also an important part of an overall treatment program.

Antipsychotic medications, developed in the mid-1950s, can dramatically improve the quality of life for people with schizophrenia. The drugs reduce or eliminate psychotic symptoms such as hallucinations and delusions. The medications can also help prevent these symptoms from returning. Common antipsychotic drugs include risperidone (Risperdal), olanzapine (Zyprexa), clozapine (Clozaril), quetiapine (Seroquel), haloperidol (Haldol), thioridazine (Mellaril), chlorpromazine (Thorazine), fluphenazine (Prolixin), and trifluoperazine (Stelazine). People with schizophrenia usually must take medication for the rest of their lives to control psychotic symptoms. Antipsychotic medications appear to be less effective at treating other symptoms of schizophrenia, such as social withdrawal and apathy.

Because many patients with schizophrenia continue to experience difficulties despite taking medication, psychological and social rehabilitation is often necessary. A variety of methods can be effective. Social skill training helps people with schizophrenia learn specific behaviours for functioning in society, such as making friends, purchasing items at a store, or initiating conversations. Behavioural training methods can also help them learn self-care skills such as personal hygiene, money management, and proper nutrition. In addition, cognitive-behavioural therapy, a type of psychotherapy, can help reduce persistent symptoms such as hallucinations, delusions, and social withdrawal.

A mutative interpretation can only be applied to an id-impulse which is actually on a state of a cathexis. This seems self-evident; for the dynamic changes in the patient's mind implied by a mutative interpretation can only be brought about by the operation of a charge of energy originating in the patient himself: The function of the analyst is merely to ensure that the energy should or can flow along one channel rather than along another. It follows that the purely informative 'dictionary' type of interpretation will be non-mutative, but useful it may be a prelude to mutative interpretations. And this leads to a number of practical inferences. Every mutative interpretation must be emotionally 'immediate, but the patient must live through it as something actual or genuine. This requirement, that the interpretation must be 'immediate', may be expressed in another way by saying that interpretation must always be directed to the 'point of urgency'. At any given moment some particular id-impulse will be generated in activity, this is the impulse that is susceptible of mutative interpretation at the time, and no other one. It is, no doubt, neither possible nor desirable to be giving mutative interpretations all the time. As Melanie Klein has pointed out, it is a most precious quality in an analyst to be able at any moment to pick out the point of urgency.

But the fact that every mutative interpretation must deal with an 'urgent' impulse take us back one more to the commonly felt fear of the explosive possibilities of interpretation, and particularly of what is vaguely referred to as 'deep' interpretation. The terminological description is, no doubt, as the interpretation of material which is neither genetically early and historically distant from the patient's actual experience nor under an especially heavy weight of repression – material, in any case, which is in the normative course of study, especially the things exceedingly inaccessible to his ego and remote from it. There seems reason to believe, moreover, that the anxiety which is liable to be aroused by the approach of such material to consciousness and may be of peculiar severity. The question whether it is 'safe' to interpret such material will, as usual, mainly depend upon whether an interpretation can be carried through, in the ordinary run of the case, as this material which is urgent during the earlier stages of the analysis is not deep. We have to deal at first only with more or less far-going displacements of the deep impulse. And the deep material itself is only reached later and by degrees, so that no sudden appearance of unmanageable quantities of anxiety is to be hesitorially anticipated. In exceptional cases, however, owing to some peculiarities in the structure of the neurosis, deep impulses may be urgent at a very early stage of the analysis. We are then faced by a dilemma. If we give an interpretation of this deep material, the resultant amounts of anxiety produced in the patient may be so great that his sense of reality may not be sufficient to permit of its accomplishment, and the whole analysis may be jeopardized, but, it must not be thought that, in such critical cases as we are now considering, the difficulty can necessarily be avoided simply by not giving any interpretation or by giving more superficial interpretations of non-urgent material or by attempting reassurances. It seems probable, in fact, that these alternative procedures may do little or nothing to obviate the trouble, on the contrary, they may even exacerbate the tension created by the urgency of the deep impulses which are the actual cause of the threatening anxiety. Thus the anxiety may break out in spite of these palliative efforts and, if so, it will be doing so under the most unfavourable conditions, that is to say, outside the mitigating influences afforded by the mechanism of interpretation. It is possible, therefore, that, of these alternative procedures which are open to the analyst faced by such a difficulty. The interpretation of the urgent id-impulses, deep though they may b e, will actually be the safer.

The importance of transference interpretations will surely be agreeing to by all analysts, the greater effectiveness of transference interpretations than interpretations outside the transference will be agreeing to by many, but what of the relative roles of interpretation of the transference and interpretation outside the transference?

Freud can be interpreted as either of saying that the analysis of the transference in auxiliary to the analysis of the neurosis or that the analysis of the transference is equivalent to the analysis of the neurosis. The first position is stated in his saying (1913) that the disturbance of the transference has to be overcome by the analysis of transference resistance in order to get on with the work of analyzing the neurosis. It is also implied in his reiteration that the ultimate task of analysis is to remember the past, to fill in the gap in memory. The second position is stated in his saying that the victory must be won on the field of the transference (1912) and that the mastery of the transference neurosis 'coincides with getting rid of the illness which was originally brought to the neurosis (1917). In this second view, he says that after the resistance is overcome, memories appear relatively without difficulty.

These two different positions also find expression in the two different ways in which Freud speaks of the transference. In `Dynamics of Transference` he refers to the transference, on the one hand, as `the most powerful resistance to the treatment`(1912) but, on the other hand, as doing us the inestimable service of making the patient's . . ., immediate impulses and manifests, when all is said and done, it is impossible to destroy anyone in an absentia or in effigy (1912).

It can be agreed that his principal emphasis fails on the second position. He wrote once, in summary, 'Thus our therapeutic work falls into two phases, in the first, all the libido is produced or kept up through efforts to cause or yield to pressure as prevailing to cause one to endure, its force is subject to powers exerted in the minds or behaviour of others, such that the symptoms into the transference and concentrated there, in the second, the struggle is waged around this new object and the libido is liberated from it`(1912).

The detailed demonstration that he advocated that the transference should be encouraged to expand as much as possible within the analytic situation lies in clarification that resistance is primarily expressed by repetition, and repetition takes place both within and outside the analytic situation, but that the analyst seeks to deal with it primarily within the analytic situation, that repetition can be not only in the motor sphere (acting) but also in the psychical sphere, and that the psychical sphere is not confined to remembering but includes the present, too.

Freud`s emphasis that the purpose of resistance is to prevent remembering can obscure his point that resistance shows itself primarily by repetition, whether inside or outside the analytic situation. `The greater the resistance, the greater extensibility, and will act out (repetition) replace remembering. Similarly in `The Dynamics of Transference` Freud said that the main reason that the transference is so well suited to serve the resistance is that the unconscious implies does not want to be remembered . . . but endeavour to reproduce themselves . . . (1918), the transference is a resistance primarily insofar as it is a repetition.

The point can be restated in terms of the relation between transference and resistance. The resistance expresses itself in repetition, that is, in transference both inside and outside the analytic situation. The distributive contributions attributably to features of character are founded in virtue of holding a deal with the transference. Therefore, is equivalent to dealing with the resistance. Freud emphasized transference within the analytic situation so strongly that it has come to mean only repetition within the analytic situation, even though, conceptually speaking, repetition outside the analytic situation is transference too, and Freud once used the term that way. `We soon perceive that the transference is itself only a piece of repetition and that the repetition is a transference of the forgotten past not only onto the analyst but also onto all the other aspects of the current situation. We . . . find . . . the compulsion to repeat, which now replaces the impulsion to remember, not only in his personal attitude to his analyst but also in every other activity and relationship which may occupy his life at the time . . . (1914).

It is important to realize that the expansion of the repetition inside the analytic situation, whether or not in a reciprocal relationship to repetition outside the analytic situation, is the avenue to control the repetition: `The main instrument . . . for curbing the patient's compulsion to repeat and for turning it into a motive for remembering lies in the handling of the transference. We render the compulsion harmless, and indeed useful, by giving it the right to assert itself in a definite field`(1914).

Kanzer has discussed this issue well in his paper on 'The Motor Sphere of the Transference' (1966). He writes of a 'double-pronged stick-and-carrot' technique by which the transference is fostered within the analytic situation and discouraged outside the analytic situation. The 'stick' is the principle of abstinence as exemplified in the admonition against making important decisions during treatment, and the 'carrot' is the opportunity afforded the transference to expand within the treatment, 'in almost complete freedom' as in a 'playground' (Freud, 1914). As Freud put it, 'Provided only that the patient shows compliance enough to respect the necessary conditions of the analysis, we regularly succeed in giving all the symptoms of the illness a new transference meaning, and in replacing his ordinary neurosis by a 'transference neurosis' of which he can be cured by the therapeutic work' (1914).

The reason it is desirable for the transference to be expressed within the treatment is that there, it `is at every point accessible to our intervention`(1914). In a later statement he made the same point this way. `We have followed this new edition - the transference-neurosis - of the old disorder from its start, we have observed its origin and growth, and we are especially well able to find our way about in it since, as its object, we are situated at it's very centre, (1917), it is not that the transference is forced into the treatment, but that it is spontaneously but implicitly present and is encouraged to expand there and become explicit

Freud emphasized acting in the transference so strongly that one can overlook the repetition in the transference, but does not of necessity for its enactment or recognition that gives validity to acts of a subordinate conformation as ratified in support of explicit authoritative permission. Repetition need not go as far as motor behaviour, it can also be expressed in attitudes, feelings, and intentions, and, indeed, the repetition often does take such form rather than motor action. The importance of making this clear is that Freud can be mistakenly read to mean that repetition in the psychical sphere can only mean remembering the past, is when he writes that the analyst as prepared for a perpetual struggle with his patient to keep in the psychical sphere all the impulse which the patient would like to direct into the motor sphere, and he celebrates it as a triumph for the treatment if he can bring it about that something the patient wishes to discharge in action are disposed if through the work of remembering (1914).

It is true that the analyst's efforts are to convert acting in the motor sphere into awareness in the psychical sphere, but transference may be in the psychical sphere to begin with, albeit disguised. The psychical sphere includes awareness in the transference as well as remembering.

One of the objections one hears, from both analysts and patient, to a heavy emphasis on interpretation of associations about the patients real life primarily in terms of the transference is that it means the analyst is disregarding the importance of what goes on in the patients real life. The criticism is not judicial. To emphasize the transference meaning is not to deny or belittle other meanings, but to focus on the one of several meanings of the content that is the most important for the analytic process, for the reasons of positing the addition for one coming to any falsifiable conclusion.

Another way in which interpretations of resistance to the transference can be, or at least appear to the patient to be, a belittling of the importance of the patients outside life is to make the interpretation as though the outside behaviour is primarily acting out of the transference. The patient may undertake some actions in the outside world as an expression of and resistance to the transference, that is, acting out. But the interpretation of associations about actions in the outside world as having implications for the transference necessitates of its meaning, that only that the choice of exterior action to figure in the associations is co-determinates, but the need of some communicable communications are expressed of transference indirectly. It is because of the resistance to awareness of the transference that the transference to be disguised. When the disguise is unmasked by interpretation, it becomes clear that, despite the inevitable differences between the outside situation and the transference situation, the content is the same for the analysis of the necrosis that coincides (Freud wrote that the mastering of the transference neurosis only coincides with getting rid of the illness which was originally brought to the treatment (1917)).

The analytic situation itself fosters the development of attitudes with primary determinants in the past, i.e., transference. The analyst's reserve provides the patient with few and equivocal cues. The purpose of the analytic situation fosters the development of strong emotional responses, and the very fact that the patient has a neurosis means, as Freud said, that' . . . it is a perfectly normal and intelligible thing that the libidinal cathexis [we would now add negative feelings] of someone who is partly unsatisfied, a cathexis which is held readies in anticipation, should be directly as well to the figure of the analyst (1912).

While the analytic setup itself fosters the expansion of the transference within the analytic situation, the interpretation of resistance to the awareness of transference will further this expansion.

There are important resistances on the part of both patient and analyst to awareness of the transference. On the patient's part, this is because of the difficulty in recognizing erotic and hostile impulses toward the very person to whom they have to be disclosed. On the analyst's part, this is because the patient is likely to attitude the very attitudes to him which are most likely to cause him discomfort. The attitudes the patient believes the analysts have toward him are often the ones the patient is least likely to voice, in a general sense because of a feeling that it is impertinent for him to concern himself with the analyst's feelings, and in a more specific sense because the aptitudes as held by the analyst are often attitudes the patient feels the analyst will be comfortable about having ascribed to him. It is for this reason that the analyst must be especially alert to the attitudes the patient believes he has, not only to the attitudes the patient does have toward him. If the analyst is able to see himself as a participant in an interaction, as he will become much more attuned to this important area of transference, which might otherwise escape him.

The investigations of attitudes are ascribed to the analyst makes easier the subsequent investigation of the intrinsic factors in the patient that played a role in such ascription. For example, the vulnerability of the fact that the patient attributes sexual interests in him to the analyst, and widely to the patient, alternatively the oppositive exception to reality is the subsequent exploration of the patient's sexual wish, conscious or unconscious toward the analyst, and the descendability is laid upon the parent.

The resistance to the awareness of these attitudes is responsible for their appearing in various disguises in the patient's manifested associations and for the analyst's reluctance to unmask the disguise. The most commonly recognized disguise is by displacement, but identification is an equally important one. In displacement, the patient's attitudes are narrated for being toward a third party. In identification, the patient attitudes to himself attitudes he believes the analyst has toward him.

To encourage the expansion of the transference within the analytic situation, the disguises in which the transference appears have to be interpreted in the case of displacement the interpretation will be of allusions to the transference in association not manifestly about the transference. This is a kind of interpretation every analyst often makes. In the case of identifications, the analyst interprets the attitudes that the patient ascribes to himself the identification with which an attitude and subsequently attributed to the analyst. Lipton (1977) has recently described this form of disguise allusion in the transference with illuminating illustration.

In his autobiography, Freud wrote, 'The patient remains under the influence of the analytic situation as hopefully of a latter position or a period of decline, as though he is not directing responsibly for the mental activities onto a particular subject, justly in assuming that nothing will occur, as not of some reference to the situation (1925). Since associations are obviously often not directed about the analytic situation, the interpretation of Freud's remark rests on what he meant by the 'analytic situation'.

It is believed that Freud's meaning can be clarified by reference to a statement he made in, 'The Interpretation of Dreams'. He said that when the patient is told to say whatever comes into his mind, his associations become directed by the 'purposive ideas inherent in the treatment' and that there are two such inherent regressive themes, one relating to the illness and the other - concerning which, Freud said, the patient has 'no suspicion'; - relating to other analyst's relating to the patient has 'no suspicions' - relating to the analyst (1900). If the patient has 'no suspicions' of the theme relating to the analyst, such that the theme appears only in disguise, the patient 's associations, it is contended that Freud's remark not only specifies the themes inherent in the patient 's identifications', but means that the associations are simultaneously 6directed by these two purposive ideas, not something by one and sometimes by the other.

One important reason that the early and continuing presence of the transference is not always recognized in that it is considered to be absent in the patient who is talking recognized is that it is considered to be absent in the patient who is talking freely and apparently without resistance. As (Muslin and Gill, 1976) pointed out in a paper on the early interpretation of transference resistance, to the transference is probably present from the beginning, even if the patient is talking apparently freely. The patient may well be talking about unsuspecting issues not manifested about the transference which are, nonetheless, illusionary or misapprehensive of the state of affairs, being alert to the pervasiveness of such illusionary discernment about them.

The analyst should progress on the working assumption, that the patient's associations have transference implications pervasively, that with which this assumption is not to be confused with denial or neglect of the current aspects of the analytic situation. It is theoretically always possible to give precedence to a transference interpretation if one can only discern it through its disguise by resistance. This is not to dispute the desirability of learning as much as one can about the patient, if only to be a position to make more correct interpretations of the transference. One therefore, does not interfere with an apparently free flow of associations, especially early, unless the transference threatens the analytic situation to the point where its interpretation is mandatory rather than optional.

With the recognition that evens apparently freely associating patient may also be showing resistance to awareness of the transference, this formulation should not interfere as long a useful information being gathered should replace Freud's dictum that the transference should not be interpreted until it becomes a resistance (1913).

It can be argued that every transference has some connection to some aspect of the current analytic situation, in the sense that the past can exert an influence only insofar as it exists in the present. Of course, all the determinants of a transference are current in the sense that what I am distinguishing is the current reality of the analytic situation, that is, what actually goes on between patient and analyst in the situation from how the patient is currently constituted as a result of his past.

All analysts would dubiously agree that there are both current and transferential determinants of the analytic situation, and probably no analyst would argue that a transference of the analytic situation, and probably no analyst would argue that a transference idea can be expressed without contamination, as it was, that is, without any connection to anything current in the patient-analyst relationship. Nevertheless, the implications of this fact for technique are often neglected in practice, as my next point is only to argue for the connection.

Several authors, e.g., Kohut 1959 and Loewald 1960, have pointed out that Freud`s early application by the act or practice of using something or the state of being used, this, however, employ of the quality of being appropriate or valuable to some end as to accommodate the accountable or warrant the use of the term transference. In `The Interpretation of Dreams, in a connection not immediately recognizable as related to the present day use of the term, reveals the fallacy of considering that transference can be expressed free of any connection to the present. That early use was to refer to the fact that an unconscious idea cannot be expressed as such, but only as it becomes connected to a preconscious o r conscious content. In the phenomenon with which Freud was then concerned, the dream transference took place from an unconscious wish to a day residue. In `The Interpretation of Dreams, `Freud used the term transference both for the general rule that an unconscious content is expressible only as it becomes transferred to a preconscious or conscious content and for the specific application of this rule to a transference to the analyst. Just as the day residue is the point of attachment of the dream wish, so must there be an analytic-situation residue, though Freud did not use that term, as the point of attachment of the transference.

Analysts have always limited their behaviour, both in variety and intensity, to increase the extent to which the patient's behaviour is determined by his idiosyncratic interpretation of the analyst's behaviour. In fact, analysts unfortunately sometimes limit the behaviour so much as to compare with such an expression or unpiled standard or absolute approximation, that the entire relationship with the patient matter of technique, with no nontechnical personal relation, as Liptop (1977) has pointed out.

But no matter how far the analyst attempts to carry this limitation of his behaviour, the very existence of the analytic situation provides the patient with innumerable cues which can enviably become his rationale for his transference responses. In other words, the current situation cannot be made to disappear - that is, the analytic situation is real. It is easy to forget this truism in one's zeal to diminish the role of the current situation in determining the patient 's responses. One can try to keep past and present determinants relatively perceptible from one another, but one cannot obtain either 'pure culture'. Freud wrote: 'I insist on this procedure [the couch], however, for its purpose and result are to prevent the transference from mingling with the patient's associations imperceptibly, to isolate the transference as to allow it to come forward, which, in a due course, is sharply defined as a resistance' (1913). Even 'isolate' is too strong a word in the light of the inevitable intertwining of the transference with the current situation.

If the analyst remains under the illusion that the current cues he provides to the patient can be reduced to the vanishing point, he may be led into a silent withdrawal, which is not too distant from the caricature of an analyst as someone who does refuse to have any personal relationship with the patient. What happens when it is deafening in its own silence, having that silence has become a technique rather than merely an indication that the analyst is listening. The patient's responses under such conditions can be mistaken fo uncontaminated transference when they are in fact transference adaptions to the actuality of the silence.

The recognition, from which it takes its point of departure, as it was, has a crucial implication for the technique of interpreting resistance to the awareness of transference, in that, if, the analyst becomes persuaded of the centrality of transference and the importance of encouraging the transference to expand within the analytic situation, he has to find the presenting and plausible interpretation of resistance to the awareness of transference he should make. Is that, his most reliable guide is the cues offered by what is actually going on in the analytic situation? : On the one hand, the events of the situation, such as change in time of session, or an interpretation made by the analyst, and, on the other hand, how the patient is experiencing the situation as reflected in explicit remarks about it, however, fleeting these may be. This is the primary yield for technique of the recognition that any transference must have a link to the actuality of the analytic situation. The cue points to the nature of the transference, just as the day residue for a dream may be a quick pointer of the latent dream thoughts. Attention to the current situation for a transference elaboration will keep the analyst from making mechanical transference interpretation, in which he interprets that there are allusions to the transference in association not manifestly about the transference, but without offering any plausible bias for the interpretation. Attention to the current stimulation offers some degree of protection against the analyst's inevitability whose tendency to project his own views onto the patient, either because of countertransference or because of a preconceived theoretical bias about the content and hierarchical relationships in psychodynamics.

The analyst may be very surprised at what in his behaviour the patient finds important or unimportant, for the patient's responses will be idiosyncratically determined by the transference, the patient's responses may seem to be something the patient as well as the analysts consider trivial, because, as in displacement to a trivial aspect of the day residue of a dream, displacement can better serve resistance when it is to something trivial. Because it is connected to conflict-laden material, the stimulus to the transference may be difficult to find. It may be quickly disavowed, so that its presence in awareness is only transitory. With the discovery of the disavowed, the patient may also gain insight into how it repeats as disavowed earlier in his life. In his search for the present stimuli which the patient is responding transferentially, as the analyst must therefore remain alert to both fleeting and apparently trivial manifested reference to himself as well as in the events of the analytic situation.

If the analyst interprets the patient's attitudes in a spirit of seeing their possible plausibility in the light of what information the patient does have, rather than in the spirit of either affirming or denying the patient's views, the way is open for their further expression and elucidation. The analyst will be respecting the effort to be plausible and realistic, rather than manufacturing his transference attitudes out of whole bodied material.

Importantly, is to make a transference interpretation plausible to the patient in terms of as current stimulus that, if the analyst is persuaded that the manifest content has important implications for the transference but he is unable to see a current stimulus for the attitude, he should explicitly say so if he decides to make the transference interpretation anyway. The patient himself may then be able to say what the current stimulus is.

It is sometimes argued that the analyst's attention to his own behaviour is a precipitant for the transference, will increase the patient's resistance to recognizing the transference. That, on the contrary, that because of the inevitable interrelationship of the current and transferential determinants, it is only through interpretation that they can be disentangled.

It is also argued that one must wait until the transference has reached optimal intensity before it can be advantageously interpreted. It is true that too hasty and interpretation of the transference can serve as a defensive function for the analyst and deny him the information he needs to make a more appropriate transference interpretation. But it is true that delay in interpreting transference interpretation, but it is also true that delay in interpreting runs the risk of allowing an unmanageable transference to develop. It is also true that deliberate delay can be a manipulation in the service of abreaction rather than analysis, and, like silence, can lead to a response to the actual situation which is mistaken for uncontaminated transference. Obviously important, is assumed in the issues of timing are involved, whereas an important clue to when a transference interpretation is apt and which one to makes lies in whether the interpretation can be made plausibly in terms of the determinant, namely, as something in the current analytic situation. Such as, in the approaching transference in the spirit of seeing how it appears plausibly realistic to the patient, it paves the way toward its further elucidation and expression.

Freud's emphasis on remembering as the goal of the analytic work implies that remembering is the principal avenue to the resolution of the transference. But the delineation of the successive steps in the development of the analytic technique (1920) makes clear that he saw this development as a change from an effort to reach memories directly to the utilization of the transference as the necessary intermediary to reaching the memories.

In contrast to remembering as the way the transference is resolved, Freud also described resistance for beings primarily overcome in the transference, with remembering following relatively easily afterwards, 'From the repetitive reactions which are exhibited in the transference we are led along the familiar paths to the awakening of the memories, which appear without difficulty, as it was, after the resistance has been overcome' (1914), and 'This revision of the process of repetition can be accomplished only in part in connection with the memory traces of the process which led to repression. The decisive part of the work's achieved by creating in the patient's relation to the analyst - in the 'transference' new editions of the old conflicts . . . Thus, the transference becomes the battlefield on which all the mutually struggling forces should meet one another' (1917). This is the primary indication for which Strachey (1934) classified in his seminal paper on the therapeutic action of psychoanalysis.

There are two main ways in which resolution of the transference can take place through work with the transference in the here and now. The first lies in the clarification of what are the clues in the current situation which are the patient's point of departure force a transference elaboration. The exposure of the current point of departure at once raises the question of whether it is adequate to the conclusion drawn from it. The relating of the transference to a current stimulus is, after all, parts of the patient's effort to make, the transference attitude plausibly determined by the present. The reverse and ambiguity of the analyst's behaviour are what increases the ranges of apparently plausible conclusions the patient may draw. If an examination of the basis for the conclusion makes clear that the actual situation to which the patient responds is subject to other meanings than the one the patient has reached, he will more reality consider his pre-existing bias, that is to say, in that of transference.

Critically, it is suggested, that, in speaking of the current relationship and the relation between the patient's conclusion and the information on which they seem plausibly based, such in some absolute conception of what is real in the analytic situation, of which the analyst is the final arbiter. That is not the case, that what the patient must come to see is that the information he has is subject to other possible interpretations implies the very contrary to an absolute conception of reality. In fact, analyst and patient engage in a dialogue in a spirit of attempting to arrive at a consensus about reality, not about some factious absolute reality.

The second way in which resolution of the transference can take place within the work with the transference in the here and now is that in the very interpretation of the transference the patient had a new experience. He is being treated differently from how he expected to be. Analysts seem reluctant to emphasize his new experience, as though it endangers the role of insight and argue for interpersonal influence as the significant factor in change. Strachey's emphasis on the new experience in the mutative transference interpretation has unfortunately been overshadowed by his views on introjection, which have been mistaken to advocate manipulating the transference. Strachey meant introjection of the more benign superego of the analyst only as a temporary strep on the road toward insight. Not only is the new experience not to be confused with the interpersonal influence of a transference gratification, but the new experience occurs together with insight into both the patient's biassed expectation and the new experience. As Strachey points out, what is unique about the transference interpretation is that insight and the new experience take place in relation to the very person who was expected to behave differently, and it is this which gives the work in the transference, its immediacy and effectiveness. While Freud did stress the effective immediacy of the transference, he did not make the new experience explicit.

It is important to recognize that transference interpretation is not a matter of experience, in contrast to insight, but a joining of the two together, both are needed to bring about and maintain the desired changes in the patient. It is also important to recognize that no new techniques of intervention are required to provide the new experience. It is an inevitable accompaniment of interpretation of the transference in the here and now. It is often overlooked that, although Strachey said that only transference interpretations are outside the transference.

Rosenfeld (1972) has pointed out that clarification of material outside the transference is often necessary to know what is the appropriate transference interpretation, and that both genetic transference interpretations and extratransference interpretation taking to consider an inclination as marked by or indication of notable worth or simply the consequence based upon the role in working through. Strachey said relatively little about working through, but surely nothing against the necessary provision with which every thing needfully is explicitly recognized as the role for the recovery of the past in the resolving dissection of the purposiveness determined by the transference.

In taking positions, as to emphasize the characteristic exterior property aspects, style and the environment in which something intangible is discerned, as, in the appearing semblance of a guise, analysis of the transference in the here and now, both in interpreting resistance to the awareness of transference and in working toward its resolution by relating to securing existence in or based in fact, that these are the problems of actual life, and, the possibility that something that has existence has received positive actualization, to which absolute actuality or based by the actualization is of the factual situation. In that of opinion or purpose with the evidence that extratransference and genetic transference interpretation and, of course, working through is important too, that the matter is one of emphasis. Also, interpretation of resistance to awareness of the transference should figure in the majority of sessions, and that if this is done by relating the transference to the actual analytic situation, the very same interpretation is a beginning of work to the resolution of the transference. To justify this view more persuasively would require detailed case material.

The concern and considerations that the Kleinian annalists whom, many analysts feel, are in error in giving the analysis of the transference too great if not even as exclusive role in the analytic process, nonetheless, it is true that Kleinians emphasize the analysis of the transference more, in their writing at least, than does the general run of analysts. As, Anna Freud (1968) complained that the concept of transference has become overexpanded seems to be directed against the Kleinians. One of the reasons the Kleinians consider themselves the true followers of Freud in technique are precisely because of the emphasis they put on the analysis of the transference. Hanna Segal (1967), for example, writes, `Too say that all communications are seen as communications about the patients phantasy as well as current external life is equivalent to saying that all communications contain something relevant to the transference situation. In Kleinian technique, the interpretation of the transference is often more central than in the classical technique.

It can be assertively affirmed that a particular limited and often critical interval as to tend to show as probable the point of view or way of regarding that Freud and transference had accedingly connected by simulating observations that we can only offer, that Freud wrote briefly about transference, and did so, to sustain the way in which, is, as a whole, that his actions were justly taken in and around 1917. Another observation which can rarely be made about Freud's works, and which everyone may not agree with, is that, with one or two exceptions, what he did write on transference did not reach the high level of analytical thought which has come to be regarded as standard for him. Some indication of what his contribution consists of is given by the editors of the Standard Edition, who list them in several places. One of the longer lists, in a footnote on page 431 of Volume 16, includes six references: 'Studies of Hysteria' with Breuer (1895), the Dora paper (1905), 'The Dynamics of Transference' (1912),

'Observations on Transference-Love' (1915), the chapter on transference in the Introductory Lectures (1917), and 'Analysis Terminable and Interminable' (1937). Although the editors, in no sense suggest that these six papers include everything Freud wrote on the subject. It does seem evident that, considering the essential importance of transference to analysis, he wrote, 'The Dynamics of Transference', 'Transference-Love', and the transference chapter in the Introductory Lectures, came across, as, perhaps, his least significant contribution.

Freud's first direct mention of transference comes upon the pages ascribed within the 'Studies of Hysteria' (1895), his first significant reference to it, however did not appear until five years later, when, in a letter to Fliess on April 16, 1900, he said (Freud, 1887-1902) he was 'beginning to see that the apparent endlessness of the treatment is something of an inherent feature and is connected with the transference'. In a footnote to this letter the editors said that, 'This was the first insight into the role of transference in psychotherapy.'

Despite these early references, it seems correct to say that yet another five years were to go by before the phenomenon of transference was actually introduced. Even so, the introduction was far from prominent, for it was tacked on like an afterthought as a four-page portion of a postscript to what was perhaps Freud's most fascinating case history to date, the case of Dora (1905).

Using data from Dora's three-month-long, unexpectedly terminated analysis, and especially from her dramatic transference reaction which had taken him quite unawares, Freud now gave to transference its first distinct psychological entity and for the first time indicated its essential role in the analytic process. His account, although in general more than adequate, - in the elegant fact and unmistakably 'finished' - was brief, and almost to the point, and perhaps not an entirely worthy introduction so much more a truly great discovery. What was uniquely great was his recognizing the usefulness of transference. In his analysis of Dora he had noted not only that transference feelings existed and were powerful, but, much to his dismay, he had realized what a serious, perhaps, even insurmountable obstacles that objectively would be. Then, in what seems like a creative leap, Freud made the almost unbelievable discoveries that transference was in fact, the key to analysis, that by properly taking the patient's transference and therapeutic force was added to the analytic method.

The impact on analysis of this startling discovery was actually much greater and much more significant than most people seem to appreciate. Although the role of transference as the 'sine quo non' of analysis as the detailed examination of the elements or structure of a substance, yet constituted the determination of a mixture or compounded constituents. Freud was to state from the very first, but it has almost never been acclaimed for having brought about an entire change in the nature of analysis. The introduction of free association to analysis, a much lesser change, receives and still receives much more recognition.

One of the reasons for the relatively unheralded entry of transference into analysis may have been for circumstances of its discovery. Although Freud's new ideas were recorded as if they arose as sudden inspiration during the Dora analysis, they may in fact have developed somewhat later. In the paper's precatory remarks, for instance, Freud said he had not discussed transference with Dora at all, and in the postscript, he said he had been unaware of her transference feelings. Also, pointing to a later discovery date is the extraordinary delay in the paper's publication. According to the editor's note, the paper had been completed and accepted for publication by late January 1901, but this date was then actually set back more than four-and-a-half-years until October 1905. The editors said, 'We have no information as to how it happened that Freud, . . . deferred publication.' It readily seems that for reasons to have been that only during those four and a half years, as a consequence to his own self-analysis, that he came to a better understanding of the relevantly significant as the applicable reason to posit of the transference. Only then may it have been possible for him to turn again to the Dora case, to apply to it of what was developed or acquired in himself by his ability to write this essay as part of the postscript, and at last to release the paper for publication.

Freud's self-analysis has been considered from many angles, but not significantly, as can be of valuing measure, in at least from the standpoint of transference. Opponents of the idea that there is such a thing as definite self-analysis, some of whom say it is impossible, generally an object on grounds that without any analyst there can be no transference neurosis. Freud clearly demonstrated, as, perhaps, that the situation that may be necessary to fill this need: Self-analysis may require that, at least a halfway satisfactory transference object. In Freud`s case, the main transference object at this time seems to have been Fliess, who filled the role rather well. As with any analysis, the authenticity as known in the unfeigned design as if existing or having no illusions and facing reality squarely, by which the 'real' impact on Freud was slight, he was essentially a neutral figure, relatively anonymous and physically separates. All of this, and Fliess`s own reciprocal transference reactions, made it possible for Freud to endow Fliess with whatever qualities and whatever feelings were essential to the development of Freud`s transference, and, it should be added, his transference neurosis. In the end, of course, the transference was in part resolved. Freud`s eventual awakening of its self realization in its presence within him of such strange and powerful psychological forces must have come to the conclusion as a stupefied delusionary dejection toward Fliess, however, his subsequent working out of some of these transference attachments must have been both an intellectual triumph and immensely healing and releasing of actions, operations or motions involved in the accomplishment of an ending that makes from its process.

In the years following this revolutionary discovery, the central role of transference in analysis increased in remarkable acceptance, and it has easily held this central position ever since. What the substance of this central position composes the distinction that in having or had been capable of having within the constructs to which is something of a mystery, for, it seems as nothing about analysis and is, of least to be, the well known than how individual analysis actually uses transference in their day-to-day work with patients. As a guess, as, perhaps of each analysts concept of transference derives variably but significantly from his own inner experience, transference probably means many and varying differentiations to things as to different analysts

In the same differentiated individuals, as that Freud's own pupils must have differed on this issue, not only from him but from each other, although some of their differences may have been slight, others, may have contributed significantly to later analytic developments. A question could be raised, for instance, whether differences in handling the transference which at first were the property of one analyst gradually develop into formal clinical methods used by many, and whether these clinical methods, after having been conceptualized, serve as the beginning of variously divergent schools of analysis. Such occurrences, consistent with certain beliefs that analytic ideas do arise in this way, primarily out of transference experiences in the analytic situation, would lead to the question whether the history of the ideological differences in what was actually said and done in response to transference reactions that to any other factor. Whatever the case, many differences and divergences did occur among the early analysts, and all of that is supposed to have had to do in some major way with differences in the handling of the transference.

Strangely, Freud himself seems to have taken little part in influencing this rapid and divergent period of growth. Usually accused of being too dominating in such matters, Freud seems to have done just the opposite during the development of this most critical aspect of analysis, the process itself, and, for reasons unknown, detached himself from it.

What was needed, one might be inclined to say, was not leadership in the form of domination, but leadership in trying to provide what was lacking, and still lacking, namely an analytical rationale for transference phenomena. The question must be asked, of course, whether in fact this would have been a good thing at that particular time in psychoanalytic history. The exercise of closure, which Freud's structuring might have amounted to, but, although adding to understanding and stability at ceratin theoretical levels, could at another level, so such closures have often done, have placed many obstacles in the way of further analytical developments. Thus, his leaving the matter of transference wide open, even though it led to confusion and uncertainty, may have been just as well.

In many ways the closest Freud ever came to establishing a formal analytical rationale for transference was his first attempt, in the postscript to the case of hysteria (1905). These few pages are and among the most important of all Freud's writings, outweighing by far the paper to which they are appended. Yet, in the case of Dora has always been taught as an entity rather than the ancillary to the essay on transference. In that essay Freud was clear: His ideas revealed tremendous insights and promise more to come, and that, the powers of the neurosis are occupied in creating a new edition of the same disease. Just think of the analytic implications of his saying that this new edition consists of a special class of mental structures, for the most part unconscious, having the peculiar characteristic of being able to replace earlier persons with that of the person of the analyst, and in the fashion applying all components of the original neurosis to the person of the analytical at the present time. Surely as profound a statement as any he ever made.

He then goes on to say that there is no way to avoid transference, that this 'latest creation of the desire must be combatted like all the earlier ones', and that, although this is by far the hardest part of analysis, only after the transference has been resolved can a patient arrive at a sense of conviction of the validity of the connection which have been constructed during analysis.

He concludes by saying, 'In the psychoanalysis . . . all the patients' tendencies, including hostile ones, are aroused, they are then turned to account for reasons as according to the internalization of justification, also by the same measure was to purposively give a sensible reason for the proposed change in the analysis by which of being made conscious. That, in this way, the transference is constantly being put-down, however, transference, which seems ordained to be the greatest obstacle to psychoanalysis, becoming its most powerful . . .

These remarkable observations, in conveying a sense of deep conviction that could arise, one feels, only from Freud's own hard-won inner experience, that nowhere is there a suggestion that transference is a mere technical matter. Far from it, as Freud announces that he has come upon as new and exciting kind of mental function, or, as it is to believe, that a new and exciting kind of ego function.

Very quickly, however, Freud's conviction sees to have failed him. Nothing he wrote afterwards about transference was at this level, and most of his later references were a retreat from it, for instance, he never did develop the promising idea that the mind constantly creates new editions of the original neurosis and meaningfully inclines the minded inclusion in them, an ever-changing series of persons. Instead, he tended to become less specific, even referring to transference at times in broadened terms as if it were no more than rapport between patient and analysts, or as if it was an interpersonal or psychosocial relationship, concepts which, of course, a great many analysts have since adopted, but which were not part of Freud's original ideas.

Perhaps his most persistent deviation was an on-and-off tendency to regard transference merely as a technical matter, often writing of it as an asset to analysis when positive and a liability when negative.

Significantly, because it indicated that an active struggle was still going on within him, Freud occasionally expressed once again, even though briefly his earlier insights, particularly his ideas that transference is an essential although unexplored part of mental life. An example of this appears in his alternative obtainment such that is gainfully to appear of as quality of being pleasant or agreeable to a feature that makes for pleasantness or ease, among the amenities of the central geniality, otherwise, the prevailing indifference account for the transference in 'An Autobiographical Study' (1925). Transference, he says, 'is a universal phenomenon of the human mind. And in fact dominated the whole of each person's relations to his human environment. In these few words' Freud again made the point, and in declarative fashion, that transference is a mental structure of the greatest magnitude, but he never really followed up.

Rather extensive evidence of his departure from the original concept and his continuing struggle with that concept is seen most clearly, wherein, the 'Analysis Terminable and Interminable' is much more than a courageous, brilliant, and pessimistic, appraisal of the difficulties and limitations of analysis, although transference is briefly mentioned in its content, yet a great deal about it comes through, some quite directly, some by easy inference. When looked at in this way, two themes stand out: Freud's personal frustration with the enigmas of transference and his tacit placing of transference in the centre of success and failure in analysis, both as a therapy and as a developing science. What also comes through, is the perplexing realization of how far Freud had, by now, seemingly moved away from his original concepts. Or had he?

All the same, even if it is insufficient for exclusive reliance in relations to the complicated neurosis, for which it would be fallacious to assign to the recall and reconstruction of the past an exclusively explanatory value (in the intellectual sense), important though that functions be, and difficult as its full-blown emotional correlate may be to come by. There is no doubt that, even in complicated neurosis, equivalently complicated transference neurosis, the genuine complex and complicated transference neurosis, the genuinely experienced linking of the past and present can have, at times, a certain uniquely specific dynamic effect of its own, a type of telescoping or merging of common elements in experience, which must be connected with the meaninglessness of time in unconscious life, compared with its stern authority in the life of consciousness and adaptation to everyday reality. Contributing decisively to such experiences as to whatever degree it occurs, is of course, the vivid currency of the transference neurosis, and central in this, the reincarnations of old objects in an actual person, the analyst.

Thus, an allied problem in the general sphere of transference is the fascination and often enigmatic interplay of past and present. If one wishes to view this interplay in terms of a stereotyped formulation, the matter can remain relatively uncomplicated - as a formulation. Unfortunately . . . this is too often the case. The phenomenon, however, retains some important obscurities, which cannot thoroughly dispel, but to which I would like to call attention. To concentrate on the dimension of time, it seems in reference to the complication and immediate aspects of technique, nonetheless, essential. For example, we can assume that the transference neurosis re-enacts the essential conflicts of the infantile neurosis in a current setting. If a reasonable degree of awareness of transference is established, the next problem is the genetic reduction of the neurosis to its elements in the past, through analysis of the transference resistance and allied intrapsychic resistance, ultimately genetic interpretations, recollections and reconstructions and working through. Such that the transference is related to its genetic origins, the analyst thereby emerges in his true, i.e., real, identity to the patient, the transference is putatively 'resolved'. To the extent that one follows the traditional view that all resistances, including transference itself, is ultimately directed against the restoration of early memories as, this is a convincing formulation. Is that, only to say, that in his own right as such as having to a certain tightly logical quality? However, we know that it this is not so readily accomplished, apart from the special intrapsychic considerations described afterward by Freud in 'Analysis Terminable and Interminable'. Although in a favourable case, much of the cognitive interpretative work can be accomplished, there remains the fact that cognition responsibility, in its bare sense, does not necessarily lead to the subsidence of powerful dynamism, to the withdrawal of 'cathexes' from importantly real objects. For, as mentioned, a short while ago, the analyst is a real and living object, apart from the representations with which the transference invests him, and which are interpretable as such, for which there is no, at any time a seldom, a confusing interrelations and commonly of the emergent responses, due to the same old seeking, and this is directed toward a new individual in his own right, both are important, furthermore, there are large and important ones of overlapping. Apart from such considerations, even the explicitly incestuous transference is currently experienced (as, at least in good part) by a full-grown adult (like the original oedipus), instead of a total and actually helpless child. To be sure, the latter state is reflected in the emergent transference elements of instinctual striving, but it is subject to analysis, and the residual is something significant, if not totally different. It is these residual sexual wish, presumably directed toward the person of the analyst, as such, which must be displaced to others, if, as generally agreed, the revival of infantile fantasies and the striving in the biologically mature adolescent which presents a new and special problem, one must assume distinctiveness of experience for the adult, although it is true that in the majority of instances, adequate solution is favoured by the adult state. There is, in any case, a residual relationship between persons who have worked together in a prolonged, arduous and intimate relationship, which, strictly speaking, are reversibly disconnected or divorced of services, in that the transference merely ushers out the retirement for which its rendering retreat of that state of mind or feeling by an inner avoidance of something usually felt as unpleasant or pronounced for it's adverse but mutual colouration. Blending into some confusion between the two spheres of feeling, though the general tendency is that both components are fully gratified to some degree. But, there is the ubiquitous power of the residual primordial transference, yet, argue to cling to an omnipotent partisan to resist the displacement of its 'sublimated' anaclitic aspects, even if the various representation of the wishes for bodily intimacy has been thoroughly analysed and successfully displaced. The outcome is largely the transference of the transference, as mentioned earlier, in a different context. For everyday reality can provide no actual answer to such cravings. In this connection, note that Freud's genial envy of Pfister, presumably free, he is prone to invest even intellectual disciplines or the proponents with inappropriate expectations and partisan passions, but, least of mention, that within these fields of analytical and theoretical thought, is not to provide exceptions to this tendency.

Though if one is to maintain and beneficially confine its bothering of reservations about the clarity of conceptualization, the explanatory discussion of Kohut and Seitz, is a very useful contribution to the direct complication or which by some understanding the awkwardness of one's inept self. Both Loewald and Kohut have deliberately associated a special but the different use of one of Freud's three conceptions of transference, i.e., the transference from the unconscious to the preconscious.

Yet, to furthering comments on primordial transference, at least potentially, are largely psychological (mental) component, the concept of 'transference of the transference' would be applicable to this component. For it does appear that certain aspect of the search for the omnipotent and omniscient caretaking parents are implicitly practical as virtually capable for being turned to use or account for its functional practicability for something of a process or the procedure for being all but the essential purpose to come to or tend toward a common point, for which are the knowledgeable information or ideas, is nothing but causative effectuality. As suggested earlier, there are important qualitative and quantitative distinctions in the mode of persistence and intensified striving, however, even to the extent that they are detached from the analyst and carried into some reasonably appropriate expression in everyday life, they retain at least a subtle quality which contravenes reality, one which derives from earliest infancy, and remains - to this extent - the transference 'Santa Claus' lives on, where one might least expect to meet him, whether as a donor of a miracle drug or of far more complex panaceas.

If one prescribes to this parasymbiotic transference drive, a true primordial origin, it is necessary to take cognizance of certain important concepts dealing with the earliest period of life. If we assume a powerful original organismic drive toward an original 'object', a striving to nullify separation from the beginning, how does this make something legally valid or operative usually by formal approval or sanctioned with concepts such as 'primary narcissism' or the 'objectless phase' or 'the primary psycho physiological self' (We note in passing that there are those who do not accept these as usually construed in the technique of Balint), for example, or Fairbairn or - conspicuously - Melanie Klein. These are states, variously defined or conceived, which apply to the earliest neonatal period, in which life, to state more simply, exists only as the potential in physiological processes. Since there is (we postulate) no clear awareness of self-withdrawal from the mother, there can be no 'mentally' represented or experienced drive to obliterate the separation (concerning oneself and object, conceivers of as separate, in a continuing sense). There are, of course, discharge phenomena, the precursors of purposive activity, and there are urgent physiological needs, directed toward fulfilment or relief, rather than toward an object as such. However, in relation to these physiological needs as archaistic precursors of object relationships, it must be noted that in all, except respiration and spontaneous sphincter relief (even in these instances, not without exception or reservation), the need fulfilment must be mediated by the primordial object (or her surrogate). There is also, of course, the uniquely important requirement for 'holding', in a literal expression, from the outset. The material partner in human symbiosis which supplies what the neonate cannot seek by 'clinging', as for Bowlty and Murphy, in the sense that must be experienced to the physiological ebb and flow of tension, even if restricted to the kinaesthetic, connected with a peripheral sensory registration, which is the protophase of the recognition of separation from the object or nonpresence of the object, as a painful instance of, her presence in apposition the converse? That the general context may be only in which the sense of unity is preponderant, or, more accurately, that there is no general awareness of 'separation' as such, means that the drive for union does not exist in a generally psychological sense. It is, so to speak, satisfied. That object constancy, with its cognate 'longing', is quite a different experience from the urgencies of primitive need fulfilment is true, however, regardless of what may be added by maturational and developmental considerations, instinctual and perceptual, there is no reason to assume other than a core of developmental continuity from the earliest needs and their fulfilment to the later state, and some continuing degree of contingency based on them.

There is a very rough parallel in the way certain analytic patients, before a firm relationship with the analyst is established, signal certain primitive experiences and tendencies in special reactions to the end of the hour, to the nonvisibility of the analyst, to interruption of their association, to failure of the analyst to talk, and similar matters. We must note that in the basic formation of the ego is evident amongst the primitive reactions and beyond to separations, in the form of very early identifications as based on care taking functions. Certainly in the very development of autonomous ego of the mother's investment in the, have a decisive role in the character of the their development. And in the case of object constancy, in its connotation of libidinal cathexis, where is no need whatsoever (emotional or otherwise) is needed for prolonged periods. The importance of the object is, to put it mildly, liable to deteriorate, or to differ complicating aggressive change. Probably the characteristic feature of later developing relations to the object (love and the wish for love), as separate if not always separated from demonstrable primitivists in the need fulfilment, have a special relationship to those 'ancillary' aspects of neonatal nurturing, whose lack has been shown to be an actual threat to life in some instances, not to speak of sound emotional development. So that from the first, regardless of the assumed state of libidinal (and aggressive) economy, or the assumed state of psychological nondifferentiation between self and potential objects, there are critical percussive phenomena, objectively observed, and probably prototypic subjective experiences of separation, which are the forerunners of all subsequent experiences of the kind. One may generalize to the effect that, with maturation and development, secondary identifications, and the various other processes of 'internalization' in its broadest sense, the problem of separation and its mastery becomes correspondingly complex, and changes with the successive phase of life, but never entirely disappears.

In the extent through which considerations of the psychoanalytic situation upon which the latently concealed mobilization of experiences of separation stimulated by the situational structure awakens the driving primordial urge to undo or to master the painful separations which it represents, usually embodied in the various forms of clinical transference that which we are familiar. One legitimate gratification which tends to mitigate superfluous transference regression is the transmission of understanding that at times, are thought that by the 'mature transference', in effect, the 'therapeutic alliance' or a group of mature ego functions which enter into such an alliance. Still, there is one blurring and overlapping concept which edges in both instances, but the concept as such is largely distinct from either one, as it is from the primitive transference, which we have been discussing. Whether the concept is thought by others to comprehend a demonstrable actuality, which is a further question, to which, of course, can only follow on conceptual clarity, which by saying, of a nonrational urge, not directly dependent on the perception of immediate clinical purposes, a true transference in the sense that it is displaced (in currently relevant form) from the parent of early childhood to the analyst. Its content is not anti-sensational, but largely non-sensual of sometimes transitional, as the child's pleasure in the assemblages of 'dirty words' and encompasses a special and not minuscule sphere of the object relationship: The wish to understand, and to be understood, the wish to be given understanding, i.e., teaching, specifically by the parent (or later surrogate); the wish to be taught to use ingenuity in making or doing or achieving an end through the actions in a nonpunitive way, corresponding to the growing perception of hazard and conflict and very likely the implicit wish to be provided with and taught channels of substitutional drive discharge. With this, there may well be a wish, corresponding to that element in Loewald's description of therapeutic process, to be seen in terms of one's developmental potentialities by the analyst. No doubt, the list could be extended into many subtleties, details, and variations. However, one should not omit to specify that, in its peak development, it would include the wish for increasingly accurate interpretations and the wish to facilitate such interpretations by providing adequate material ultimately, of course, by identification, to participate in, or even be the author of the interpretations. The childhood system of wishes which underlie the transference is a correlate of biological maturation, and the latent (i.e., teachable) autonomous ego function, appearing with it, however, there is a drive-like quality in the participation phenomena, which disqualifies any conception of the urge's identical with the functions. No one who has ever watched a child importunes a parent with questions, or experiment with new words, or solicit her interests in a new game, or demand a storytelling or reading, can doubt this. That this powerful support and integration in the ego identification with a loved parent is undoubtedly true, just as it is true of the identification with an analyst toward whom a positive relationship has been established. That 'functional pleasure ' inscribes the part, where certain specific ego energies, perhaps very likely the ego's own urge to extend its hegemony in the personality. However, it can be stressed in the derived element, even the special phase configurations and colourations, and with its importance of object relations, libidinal and aggressive, for a specific reason. For just as the primordial transference seeks to undo separation, in a sense to obviate object relationships as we know them, the 'mature transference', tends toward separation and individuation, and increasing contact with the environment, optimally with a large affirmative (increasing neutralized) relationship toward the original object toward whom (or her surrogates) a different dynamic of demands is now increasingly directed. The further considerations which have led to the emphasis that the drive-like elements in these attitudes are integrated phenomena, as example of 'multiple functional' rather than the discrete exorcize of function or functions, is the conviction that there is a continuing dynamic relation of relative interchangeability between the two series, at least based on the response to gratifications in a significant zone of complicated energetic overlap, possibly including the phenomenon of neutralization. That the empirical 'interchangeability' is limited, and that goes without saying, that in no way diminishes its decisive importance. The linguistic communications as in mention, that the excessive transference neurosis regression, which can seriously vitiate the affirmative psychoanalytic process, finds a prototype in the regressive behaviour and demands of certain children, who do not receive their share of teaching, 'attention', play, nonseductive, affectionate demonstration, as to use the quality of being appropriate or valuable to some end, even the act or practice of using something or the state of being used to which of responsible interests in development, and similar matters, from their parents. In the psychoanalytic situation, both the gratifications offered by the analyst and the freedom of expression by the patient, are diversely limited and concentrated, practically entirely (in the every day demonstrable sense) in the sphere of linguistic expression, on the analyst's side, further, in the transmission of understanding.

Whereas, the primordial transference exploits the primitive aspects of linguistic communication, by expressing the mature transference as to advocate the seeking mastery of the outer and inner environments, a mastery to which the mature elements in speech contribute importantly, for which these are stressed upon the clear-cut genetic prototype for the free associating its interpretative dialogue is the original learning and teaching of speech, the dialogue between child and mother. It is interesting to note that just as the profundities of interests between people who often include - in the service of the ego - transitory introjection and identifications, of the very word 'communication', representing the central ego function of speech, from which is a closely intimate relation to the etymologically certain, in actual usages, to the word chosen for that major of religious sacrament for that which is the physical ingestion of the body and blood of the Deity. Perhaps, this is just another suggestion that the oldest of individual problems does, after all, continue to seek its solution, in its own terms if only in a minimal sense, and in channels so remote as to be unrecognizable.

The mature transference is a dynamic and integral part of the therapeutic alliance, alone with the tender aspect of the erotic transference, evens more attenuated (and more dependable) friendly feeling of adult type, and the ego identification with the analyst. Indispensable, of course, are the genuine adult need for help, the crystallizing rational and intuitive appraisal of the analyst, the adult sense of confidence in him, and innumerable other nuances of adult thought and feeling. With these, giving a driving momentum and power to the analytic process, but always, by it's very nature, a potential source of resistance, and always requiring analysis, is the primordial transference and its various appearances in the specific therapeutic transference. That it is, if well managed, not only a reflection of the repetition compulsion in its menacing sense, but a living presentation from the id, seeking new solutions, and trying again, so to speak, to find a place in the patient's conscious and effective life, has important affirmative potentialities. This has been specifically emphasized by Nunberg, Lagache and Loewald among others. Loewald has recently elaborated very effectively the idea of 'ghosts' seeking to become 'ancestors' based on an early figure of speech of Freud. The mature transference, in its own infantile right, provides some of the unique qualities of propulsive force, which comes from the world of feeling, rather than the world of thought. If one views it in a purely figurative sense, that fraction of the mature transference which derives from 'conversion' is somewhat like propulsive fraction as the wind in a boats sailing to windward currents into motion, the strong headwind, the ultimate source of both resistance and propulsion, is the primordial transference. This view, however, should not displace the original and independent, if cognate, a favourable tide or current would also be required. It is not that the mature transference is itself entirely exempt from analytic clarification and interpretation. For one thing, in common with other childhood spheres of experience, there may have been traumas in this sphere, punishments, serious defects or lacks of parental communication, Listening, attention or interest. In general, this is probably far more important than has hitherto appeared in our prevalent paradigmatic approach to adult analysis, even taking into account the considerable changes due to the growing interest in ego psychology. 'Learning' in the analysis can, of course, be a troublesome intellectualizing resistance. Furthermore, both the patient's communications and his receptions and utilization of interpretations may exhibit only too clearly, as sometimes in the case of other ego mechanisms, their origin in and tenacious relation to instinctual or anaclitic dynamism: As the longing implement out of silence for which the analyst is to override the uncritical acceptance (or rejection) of interpretations, in that the patient revealingly is to mention the unmindful assimilation, fluently, rich, endlessly detailed associations without spontaneous reflection or integration. In the direct demands for solution of moral and practical probability for an entirely intellectual scope, and a variety of others, as it may and always be easy to discriminate between the utilization of speech by an essentially instinctual demand, and an intellectual or linguistic trait or having to be determined by specific factors in their own developmental sphere, however, the underlying and essentially genuine dynamism which have to continue to be placed for a notable time interval or remain arbitrary or conventional character most favoured to the purposes of processes of analysis, as it was to the original processes of maturational development, communication, and benign separation. Lagache, on the desirability of separating the current unqualified usage, 'positive' and 'negative' transference, as based on the patient's immediate state of feeling, from a classification based on the essential effect on analytic processes, yet, the later of mature transference is, in general, a 'positive transference'.

Concerning considerations toward the transference neurosis, and the problem of transference interpretation, may be offered at this point, the whole situational structure of analysis (in contrast with other personal relationships) its finding to its dialogue is initiated through free association. Also, to involve interpretation and deprivations as to most ordinary cognitive and emotional interpersonal drives, which is tended toward the separation of discrete transferences from their synthesis with one another and with defences in character or symptoms. With which of the deepening regression, toward a continuative enactment of the infantile neurosis, as held in the transference neurosis, no0netheless, in other relationships may be the 'give and take' aspects - gratifying aggressive punitory responses. The open mobility of searching for alternatives or the greater of satisfactions has taken to be found in the dynamic and economic influence, such that only extraordinary situations, or the transference of pathological character, or both, occasion to comparable regression.

It is a curious fact, whereas the dynamic means to the importance of the transference neurosis have been well established since Freud gave this the phenomenon a central position in his clinical thinking, the clinical reference, when the term is used, remains variable and somewhat ambiguous. For example, Greenson, in his excellent recent paper, speaks of it as appearing, 'when the analyst and the analysis become the central concern in the patient's life'. However, previous remarks in this connection, for which it is worthwhile to specify certain aspects of Greenson's definition, for the term 'central' is somewhat ambiguous, as to its specific reference. Certainly, the term could apply to the symbolic position of the analyst in relation to the patient's experiencing ego and the symbolically decisive position which he correspondingly assumes in the relation to the other important figures in the patient's current life. However, while the analysis is in any case, and for multiple reasons, exceedingly important the seriously involved patient, there is a free observing portion of is ego, also involved, not in the same sense as that involved in the transference regression and revived in infantile conflicts. And here is here being, of course, always the integrated adult personalty, however diluted in may seem at times, of its rarity, although certainly does occur, that the analysis actually exceeds the quality or state of being of notable worth or influence that the other major concerns, attachments, and responsibilities of the patient's life, nor is it desirable that his should occur, on the other hand, if construed with proper attention to the economic considerations as mentioned, the concept is important, both theoretically and clinically. In the theoretical direction is the assumption that there is a continuing system of object relationships and conflictual situations, as most important are the unconscious representations. The involving participation to some in all others, deriving in a successive series of transference from the experiences of separation from the original object - the mother - in this sense, the analyst's applicability to a uniquely important portion of the patient's personality, is the portion that 'never grew up', to maintain a central figure. In the clinical sense, to call or direct attention especially to a supposed cause, source, or to refer to the importance of the transference neurosis as outlining for the essential and central analytic task, providing by it's very currency and demonstrability a relatively secure cognitive base for procedural duties. By its inclusion of the patient's essential psychopathological processes and tendencies, in their original functional connection, it offers, in its resolution or marked reduction, the most formidable lever for analytic cure. Nonetheless, transference neurosis must be seen in its interweaving with the patient's extra-analytic system of personal contacts. The relationship to the analyst may influence the course of relationships to others, in the same sense that the clinical neurosis did, except that the former is alloplastic, relatively exposed, and subject to constant interpretation. It is also an important fact that, except in those rare instances where the original dyadic relationship appears to turn, the analyst, even in the strict transference sphere, cannot be assigned all the transference role simultaneously. Other actors are required. He may at times oscillate with confusing rapidity between the status of mother and father, but he is usually predominantly in one of the roles for long periods, someone else representing the other. Furthermore, apart from 'acting out', complicated and mutually inconsistent attitudes of the anterior apprehensions for realizing often about something not generally realized in the verbalization, may require the seeking of other transference objects, i.e., The husband or wife, friend, another analyst and so forth. Children, even the patient's own children, may be invested with the striving of the patient, displaced from the analysis, even experience the impulses which they would wish to call forth in the analyst. The range is extensive, varied, and complicated, requiring constant alertness. Transference interpretation for having necessarily the paradoxical inclusiveness, which is an important reality of technique, nevertheless, there is another aspect, and that is the dynamic and economic impact of the intimate and actual dramatist to which impersonate the transference neurosis impeding the progress of the analysis. Such that the patient 's motivation, as well as his real life expectations of recovery that may fulfill their 'positive' or 'negative ' roles in transference drama, which may facilitate or impede interpretative effectiveness, they provide the substantial and dependable real life gratifications which ultimately facilitate the analysis of the residual analytic transference, or their capacities or attitudes may occasion to overload the anaclitic and instinctual needs in the transference which renders the same process far more difficultly. In the most unhappy instances, there can be a serious undercounting of the motivation for basic change.

There is also the fundamental question of the role of the transference interpretation. At the Marienbad Symposium most of Strachey's colleagues appeared to accept the essential import of his contribution and thus unique significance of the transference interpretations, despite the various reservations as to detail and emphasis on other important aspects of the therapeutic process. Nevertheless, there are still many who, if not in doubt regarding the great value of transference experiences are inclined to doubt their uniqueness, and to stress the importance of economic considerations in determining the choice as to whether transference or extratransference interpretations may be indicated. Now, apart from the realistic considerations mentioned in the preceding passage (in a sense the necessarily 'distributed' character of a variable fraction of transference interpretation). There is in fact that the extra-analytic life of the patent often provides indispensable data fo the understanding of detailed complexities of his psychic functioning, because of the sheer variety of its references, some of which cannot be reproduced in the relationship to the analyst. For example, there is no repartee - in the ordinary sense in the analysis. The way the patient handles the dialogue with an angry employee may be importantly revealing. The same may be true of the quality of his reaction to a real danger of dismissal. There is not only for its realities, but the 'formal' aspects of this responses. These expressions of personality remain important, even though his 'acting out' of the transference (assuming this was this was the case) may have been more important, and, of course, requiring transference interpretation. Furthermore, they remain useful, if applying or favouring discriminations in treatment as tending to resist or oppose change for they are inevitably always subject that epistemological reservations, which haunts so much of analytic data. Of course, the 'positive' transference has a role in the utilization of such interpretations that what enables the patent to listen to them and them seriously.

In an operational sense, it would seem that extratransference interpretations cannot set aside, or underestimated in importance, but the unique effectiveness of transference interpretations is not thereby disestablished. No other interpretation is free, within reason, of the doubt introduced by not really knowing the 'other person's' participation in love, or quarrel or criticism or whatever the issue. And no other situation provides the patient the combined sense of cognitive acquisition, with the experience of complete personal tolerance and acceptance, that is implicit in an interpretation by an individual who is an object of the emotion, drive, or even defences, which are active at the time. There is no doubt that such interpretations must not only (in common with all others) include personal tact, but must be offered with special care as to their intellectual reasonability, in relation to the immediate context, lest they defeat their essential purpose. It is not too often likely that a patient who has just been jilted in a long-standing love affair, and suffering exceedingly, will find an immediate interpretation that his suffering is due to the fact that the analyst does not reciprocate his love, even though a dynamism in this general sphere may be ultimately demonstrable, and acceptable to the patient. On the other hand, once the transference neurosis is established, with accompanying subtle (sometime gross) colouration of the patient's life, th n more far-reaching anticipatory, transference interpretations are indicated, for, if all of the patient's libidinal and aggression is not, in fact, invested in the analyst, he has at least an unconscious role in all important emotional transactions, and, if the assumption is correct that the regressive drive, mobilized by the analytic situation, is in the direction of restoration of a single all-encompassing relationship, specified pragmatically in the individual case by the actually attained level of development, then there is a dynamic factor at work, importantly meriting interpretation as such, to the extent that available material supports it. This would be the immediate clinical application on the material regarding the 'cognitive lag' or 'cognitive fall-back'.

Post-Traumatic Stress Disorder, resides in a mental illness that some people develop after experiencing traumatic or life-threatening events. Such events include warfare, rape and other sexual assaults, violent physical attacks, torture, child abuse, natural disasters such as earthquakes and floods, and automobile or airplane crashes. People who attest of the traumatic events may also develop the disorder.

Post-traumatic stress disorder in war veterans is sometimes called shell shock or combat fatigue. In victims of sexual or physical abuse, the disorder has been called rape trauma or battered woman syndrome. The American Psychiatric Association (APA) adopted the current name of the disorder in 1980.

In the late 1960's and early 1970's, mass demonstrations erupted throughout the United States protesting US involvement in the Vietnam War (1959-1975). Thousands of veterans joined together in a national organization, Vietnam Veterans Against the War, that supported and influenced the antiwar movement. In this transcript from an April 22, 1971, hearing before the Senate Committee on Foreign Relations, committee chairman Senator J. William Fulbright indicated his sympathy for the antiwar movement. Fulbright's comments were followed by the testimony of Vietnam veteran John Kerry, who called for an end to the war. Kerry also detailed what he believed to be the war's negative effect in both Vietnam and the United States. Kerry became a Democratic senator from Massachusetts in 1985.

People with this disorder relive the traumatic event again and again through nightmares and disturbing memories during the day. They sometimes have flashbacks, in which they suddenly lose touch with reality and relive images, sounds, and other sensations from the trauma. Because of their extreme anxiety and disruptive opposition to events, they try to avoid anything that reminds them of it. They may seem emotionally numb, detached, irritable, and easily startled. They may feel guilty about surviving a traumatic event that killed other people. Other symptoms include trouble concentrating, depression, and sleep difficulties. Symptoms of the disorder usually begin shortly after the traumatic event, although some people may not show symptoms for several years. If left untreated, the disorder can last for years.

Post-traumatic stress disorder can severely disrupt one's life. Besides the emotional pain of reliving the trauma, the symptoms of the disorder may cause a person to think that he or she is 'going crazy.' In addition, people with this disorder may have unpredictable, angry outbursts at family members. At other times, they may seem to have no affection for their loved ones. Some people try to mask their symptoms by abusing alcohol or drugs. Others work very long hours to prevent any 'down' periods when they might relive the trauma. Such actions may delay the onset of the disorder until these individuals retire or become sober.

Studies have set or to bring into a new found control from 1 to 14 percent of people that suffer from post-traumatic stress disorder at some point during their lives. The findings vary widely due to differences in the populations studied and the research methods used. Among people who have survived traumatic events, the prevalence appears to be much higher. The disorder may be particularly prevalent among people who have served in combat. For example, one study of veterans of the Vietnam War (1959-1975) found that veterans exposed to a high level of combat were nine times more likely to have post-traumatic stress disorder than military personnel who did not serve in the war zone of Southeast Asia.

Post-traumatic stress disorder is an extreme reaction to extreme stress. In moments of crisis, people respond in ways that allow them to endure and survive the trauma. Afterward those responses, such as emotional numbing, may persist even though they are no longer necessary.

Not everyone who experiences a traumatic event develops post-traumatic stress disorder. Several factors influence whether people develop the disorder. Those who experience severe and prolonged traumas are more likely to develop the disorder than people who experience less severe trauma. Additionally, those who directly witness or experience death, injury, or attack is more likely to develop symptoms.

People may also have been existing through biological and psychological vulnerabilities that make them more likely to develop the disorder. Those with histories of anxiety disorders in their families may have inherited a genetic predisposition to react more severely to tenseness and trauma than other people. In addition, people's life experiences, especially in childhood, can affect their psychological vulnerability to the disorder. For example, people whose early childhood experiences made them feel that events are unpredictable and uncontrollable by having greater likeliness than others of developing the disorder. Individuals with a strong, supportive social network of friends and family members seem somewhat protected from developing post-traumatic stress disorder.

Treatment of post-traumatic stress disorder may involve psychotherapy, psychoactive drugs, or both. Psychotherapists help individuals confront the traumatic experience, work through their strong negative emotions, and overcome their symptoms. Many people with post-traumatic stress disorder benefit from group therapy with other individuals suffering from the disorder. Physicians may prescribe antidepressants or anxiety-reducing drugs to treat the mood disturbances that sometimes accompany the disorder.

At the arriving considerations that are marked and noted, through which the essence of functional dynamics as based of the transference in the psychoanalytic process or the basic underlying the most basic of beliefs that in politics there is neither good nor evil, however, in that something that forms part of the minimal body, character or structure of that thing predetermines the properties to the good life. Nonetheless, most psychoanalysts maintain that schizophrenic patients cannot be treated psychoanalytically because they are too narcissistic to develop with the psychotherapist as interpersonal relationship that is sufficiently reliable and consistent for psychoanalytic work. Freud, Fenichel and others have recognized that a new technique of approaching patients psychoanalytically must be found if analysts are to work with psychotics. Among those who have worked successfully in recent years with schizophrenics, Sullivan, Hill, and Karl Menninger and his staffs have made various modifications of their analytic approach. The techniques that are in use with psychotics are different from our approach to psychoneurotics. This is not a result of the schizophrenic's inability to build up a consistent personal relationship with the therapist but due to his extremely intense and sensitive transference reactions.

Let us see first what the essences of the schizophrenic's transference reactions are and how we try to meet these reactions.

We think of a schizophrenic as a person who has had serious traumatic experiences in early infancy at a time when his ego and its ability to examine reality were not yet developed. These early traumatic experiences seem to furnish the psychological basis for the pathogenic influence of the frustrations of later years. At this early time the infant lives grandiosely in a narcissistic world of his own. His needs and desires seem to be taken care of by something vague and indefinite which he does not yet differentiate. As Ferenczi noted, they are expressed by gestures and movements since speech is as yet undeveloped. Frequently the child's desires are fulfilled without any expression of them, a result that seems to him a product of his magical thinking.

Are a person's characteristics primarily shaped by early influences, remaining relatively stable thereafter throughout life? Or does change spontaneously occur continuously throughout life? Many people believe that early experiences are formative, providing a strong or weak foundation for later psychological growth. This view is expressed in the popular saying 'As the twig is bent, so grows the tree.' From this perspective, it is crucial to ensure that young children have a good start in life. But many developmental scientists believe that later experiences can modify or even reverse early influences; studies show that even when early experiences are traumatic or abusive, considerable recovery can occur. From this vantage point, early experiences influence, but rarely determine, later characteristics.

Traumatic experiences in this early period of life will damage a personality more seriously than those occurring in later childhood such as are found in the history of psychoneurotics. The infant's mind is more vulnerable the younger and less used it has been, furthers, the trauma has quickened the infant 's egocentricity. In addition early traumatic experience shortens the only period in life in which an individual ordinarily enjoys the most security, thus endangering the ability to store up as it was a reasonable supply of assurance and self-reliance for the individual's later struggles through life. Thus, as such, a child sensitized considerably more toward the frustrations of later like than by later traumatic experiences. hence many experiences in later life which would mean little to a 'healthy' person and not much to a psychoneurotic, mean a great deal of pain and suffering to the schizophrenic. His resistance against frustration is easily exhausted.

Once he reaches his limit of endurance, he escapes the unbearable reality of his present life by attempting to reestablish the autistic, delusional world of the infant, but this is impossible because the content of his delusions and hallucinations are naturally coloured by the experiences of his whole lifetime.

How do these developments influence the patient's attitude toward the analyst and the analyst's approach to him?

Due to the very damage and the succeeding chain of frustrations which the schizophrenic undergoes before finally giving in to illness, he feels extremely suspicious and distrustful of everyone, particularly of the psychotherapist ho approaches him with the intent of intruding into his isolated world and personal life. To him the physician's approach means the threat of being compelled to return to the frustrations of real life and to reveal his inadequacy to meet them or, - still worse – a repetition of the aggressive interference with his initial symptoms and peculiarities which he has encountered in his previous environment.

The difficulty that the patient's dilemma through his frustrations is the product through which is called 'delusion': Delusion itself is a false belief which is firmly held by a person even though other people recognize the belief as obviously untrue. For example, a person who truly believes he is Napoleon Bonaparte is delusional. Religious beliefs or popular conceptions, such as the beliefs that people have been abducted by aliens, are not delusions because they are widely held beliefs. Delusions are a type of psychotic symptom that indicate a person has lost contact with reality.

There are many different types of delusions. A person with a paranoid delusion believes that others - such as the FBI, or the CIA, even the Mafia as trying to harm or plot against him. A person with a delusion of reference believes that events or people refer specifically to him or her when they do not. For example, a woman with schizophrenia may believe that a television news broadcaster is talking personally to her rather than to the entire viewing audience. A grandiose delusion is a belief that one is extremely famous or that one has special powers, such as the ability to magically heal people.

A delusion of control is a belief that others are able to control one's thoughts, feelings, or actions. For example, a man with this type of delusion may believe that someone has implanted a microchip in his brain that enables other people to control his thoughts. A somatic delusion is a belief that something is wrong with one's body - for example, that one's brain is rotting away - even though no medical evidence supports this belief. A person with an erotic delusion believes that someone is in love with him or her despite a lack of evidence for this belief. In a delusion of jealousy, a person believes that his or her spouse or lover is unfaithful despite evidence to the contrary.

Delusions commonly occur in certain severe mental illnesses, such as schizophrenia, bipolar disorder (also called manic-depressive illness), some cases of major depression, Dissociative disorders, post-traumatic stress disorder, and paranoid personality disorder. In addition, delusions may result from abuse of certain drugs, including alcohol, cocaine, amphetamines, and hallucinogens such as lysergic acid diethylamide (LSD), phencyclidine (PCP), and mescaline. Medical conditions affecting the brain, such as syphilis and brain tumours, may also cause delusions.

Delusional disorder is a relatively uncommon mental illness characterized by delusions. People with this disorder have one or more delusions that persist for at least one month. In addition, they do not suffer from other symptoms of schizophrenia, such as disorganized speech and bizarre behaviour. Usually their delusions are less bizarre than those that occur in schizophrenia and seem merely odd or unsupported by facts. Examples of nonbizarre delusions include beliefs that one is being followed, loved by someone famous, or deceived by one's spouse. Because delusional disorder is relatively rare, little research has systematically examined its treatment. However, doctors most often use antipsychotic drugs (also called neuroleptics) to treat this disorder. These drugs help reduce or eliminate delusions, hallucinations, and other psychotic symptoms.

In spite of his narcissistic retreat, every schizophrenic has some underlying notion of the unreality and loneliness of his substitute delusionary world. He longs for human contact and understanding, yet is afraid to admit of himself, or his therapist for fear of further frustration.

That is why the patient may take weeks and months to test the analyst before being willing to accept him, however, once he has accepted him. His dependence on the analyst is greater and he is more sensitive about it than is the psychoneurotic because of the schizophrenic's deeply rooted insecurity, the narcissistic seemingly self-righteous attitude is but a defence.

Whenever the analyst fails the patient from reasons to be discussed later - one cannot at times avoid failing one's schizophrenic patients - it will be severe disappointment and a repetition of the chain of frustrations the schizophrenic has previously endured.

The instinctually primitive part of the schizophrenic's mind that does not discriminate between himself and the environment, it may mean the withdrawal of the impersonal supporting forces of his infancy. Severe anxiety will follow this vital deprivation.

In the light of his personal relationship with the analyst it means that the therapist seduced the patient to use him as a bridge over which he might possibly be led from the utter loneliness of his own world to reality and human warmth, only to have him discover that this bridge is not reliable. if so, he will respond helplessly with an outburst of hostility or with renewed withdrawal as may be seen most impressively in catatonic stupor.

The symptoms of mental illness can be very distressing. People who develop schizophrenia may hear voices inside their head that say nasty things about them or command them to act in strange or unpredictable ways. Or they may be paralyzed by paranoia - the deep conviction that everyone, including their closest family members, wants to injure or destroy them. People with major depression may feel that nothing brings pleasure and that life is so dreary and unhappy that it is better to be dead. People with panic disorder may experience heart palpitations, rapid breathing, and anxiety so extreme that they may not be able to leave home. People whom experience episodes of mania may engage in reckless sexual behaviour or may spend money indiscriminately, acts that later cause them to feel guilt, shame, and desperation.

Other mental illnesses, while not always debilitating, create certain problems in living. People with personality disorders may experience loneliness and isolation because their personality style interferes with social relations. People with an eating disorder may become so preoccupied with their weight and appearance that they force themselves to vomit or refuse to eat. Individuals who develop post-traumatic stress disorder may become angry easily, experience disturbing memories, and have trouble concentrating.

Experiences of mental illness often interact differently but depend on one's culture or social group, sometimes greatly so. For example, in most of the non-Western world, people with depression complain principally of physical ailments, such as lack of energy, poor sleep, loss of appetite, and various kinds of physical pain. Indeed, even in North America these complaints are commonplace. But in the United States and other Western societies, depressed people and mental health professionals who treat them tend to emphasize psychological problems, such as feelings of sadness, worthlessness, and despair. The experience of schizophrenia also differs by culture. In India, one-third of the new cases of schizophrenia involve catatonia, a behavioural condition in which a person maintains a bizarre statue like pose for hours or days. This condition is rare in Europe and North America.

With appropriate treatment, most people can recover from mental illness and return to normal life. Even those with persistent, long-term mental illnesses can usually learn to manage their symptoms and live productive lives.

By a variety of symptoms, including loss of contact with reality, bizarre behaviour, disorganized thinking and speech, decreased emotional expressiveness, and social withdrawal. Usually only some of these symptoms occur in any one person. The term schizophrenia comes from Greek words meaning 'split mind.' However, contrary to common belief, schizophrenia does not refer to a person with a split personality or multiple personality. For a description of a mental illness in which a person has multiple personalities. To observers, schizophrenia may seem or appear for being as some sorted kind of madness or a manufacturing insanity.

Perhaps more than any other mental illness, schizophrenia has a debilitating effect on the lives of the people who suffer from it. A person with schizophrenia may have difficulty telling the difference between real and unreal experiences, logical and illogical thoughts, or appropriate and oppositely for being inappropriate behaviour. Schizophrenia seriously impairs a person's ability to work, go to school, enjoy relationships with others, or take care of oneself. In addition, people with schizophrenia frequently require hospitalization because they pose a danger to themselves. About 10 percent of people with schizophrenia commit suicide, and many others attempt suicide. Once people develop schizophrenia, they usually suffer from the illness for the rest of their lives. Although there is no cure, treatment can help many people with schizophrenia lead productive lives.

Schizophrenia also carries an enormous cost to society. People with schizophrenia occupy about one-third of all beds in psychiatric hospitals in the United States. In addition, people with schizophrenia account for at least 10 percent of the homeless population in the United States. The National Institute of Mental Health has estimated that schizophrenia costs the United States tens of billions of dollars each year in direct treatment, social services, and lost productivity.

Approximately 1 percent of people develop schizophrenia at some time during their lives. Experts estimate that about 1.8 million people in the United States have schizophrenia. The prevalence of schizophrenia is the same regardless of sex, race, and culture. Although women are just as likely as men to develop schizophrenia, women tend to experience the illness less severely, with fewer hospitalizations and better social functioning in the community.

Schizophrenia usually develops in late adolescence or early adulthood, between the ages of 15 and 30. Much less commonly, schizophrenia develops later in life. The illness may begin abruptly, but it usually develops slowly over months or years. Mental health professionals diagnose schizophrenia based on an interview with the patient in which they determine whether the person has experienced specific symptoms of the illness.

Symptoms and functioning in people with schizophrenia tend to vary over time, sometimes worsening and other times improving. For many patients the symptoms gradually become less severe as they grow older. About 25 percent of people with schizophrenia become symptom-free later in their lives.

A variety of symptoms characterize schizophrenia. The most prominent include symptoms of psychosis - such as, delusions and hallucinations - as well as bizarre behaviour, strange movements, and disorganized thinking and speech. Many people with schizophrenia do not recognize that their mental functioning is disturbed.

Delusions are false beliefs that appear obviously untrue to other people. For example, a person with schizophrenia may believe that he is the king of England when he is not. People with schizophrenia may have delusions that others, such as the local or the of friends are plotting against them or spying on them. They may believe that aliens are controlling their thoughts or that their own thoughts are being broadcast to the world so that other people can hear them.

Research suggests that the genes one inherits strongly influence one's risk of developing schizophrenia. Studies of families have shown that the more close one is related to someone with schizophrenia, the greater the risk one has of developing the illness. For example, the children of one parent with schizophrenia have about a 13 percent chance of developing the illness, and children of two parents with schizophrenia have about a 46 percent chance of eventually developing schizophrenia. This increased risk occurs even when such children are adopted and raised by mentally healthy parents. In comparison, children in the general population have only about a 1 percent chance of developing schizophrenia.

Some evidence suggests that schizophrenia may result from an imbalance of chemicals in the brain called neurotransmitters. These chemicals enable neurons (brain cells) to communicate with each other. Some scientists suggest that schizophrenia results from excess activity of the neurotransmitter dopamine in certain parts of the brain or from an abnormal sensitivity to dopamine. Support for this hypothesis comes from antipsychotic drugs, which reduce psychotic symptoms in schizophrenia by blocking brain receptors for dopamine. In addition, amphetamines, which increase dopamine activity, intensify psychotic symptoms in people with schizophrenia. Despite these findings, many experts believe that excess dopamine activity alone cannot account for schizophrenia. Other neurotransmitters, such as serotonin and norepinephrine, may play important roles as well.

Although scientists favour a biological cause of schizophrenia, stress in the environment may affect the onset and course of the illness. Stressful life circumstances - such as maturing in age and character as for living in poverty, the death of a loved one, an important change in jobs or relationships, or chronic tension and hostility at home - can increase the chances of schizophrenia in a person biologically predisposed to the disease. In addition, stressful events can trigger a relapse of symptoms in a person who already has the illness. Individuals who have effective skills for managing stress may be less susceptible to its negative effects. Psychological and social rehabilitation can help patients develop more effective skills for dealing with stress.

Although there is no cure for schizophrenia, effective treatment exists that can improve the long-term course of the illness. With many years of treatment and rehabilitation, significant numbers of people with schizophrenia experience partial or full remission of their symptoms.

Treatment of schizophrenia usually involves a combination of medication, rehabilitation, and treatment of other problems the person may have. Antipsychotic drugs (also called neuroleptics) are the most frequently used medications for treatment of schizophrenia. Psychological and social rehabilitation programs may help people with schizophrenia function in the community and reduce stress related to their symptoms. Treatment of secondary problems, such as substance abuse and infectious diseases, is also an important part of an overall treatment program.

Antipsychotic medications, developed in the mid-1950s, can dramatically improve the quality of life for people with schizophrenia. The drugs reduce or eliminate psychotic symptoms such as hallucinations and delusions. The medications can also help prevent these symptoms from returning. Current antipsychotic drugs include risperidone (Risperdal), olanzapine (Zyprexa), clozapine (Clozaril), quetiapine (Seroquel), haloperidol (Haldol), thioridazine (Mellaril), chlorpromazine (Thorazine), fluphenazine (Prolixin), and trifluoperazine (Stelazine). People with schizophrenia usually must take medication for the rest of their lives to control psychotic symptoms. Antipsychotic medications appear to be less effective at treating other symptoms of schizophrenia, such as social withdrawal and apathy.

Because many patients with schizophrenia continue to experience difficulties despite taking medication, psychological and social rehabilitation is often necessary. A variety of methods can be effective. Social training skills help people with schizophrenia learn specific behaviours for functioning in society, such as making friends, purchasing items at a store, or initiating conversations. Behaviourial training methods can also help them learn self-care skills such as personal hygiene, money management, and proper nutrition. In addition, cognitive-behaviourial therapy, a type of psychotherapy, can help reduce persistent symptoms such as hallucinations, delusions, and social withdrawal.

Because many patients have difficulty obtaining or keeping jobs, supported employment programs that help patients find and maintain jobs are a helpful part of rehabilitation. In these programs, the patient works alongside people without disabilities and earns competitive wages. An employment specialist (or vocational specialist) helps the person maintain their job by, for example, training the person in specific skills, helping the employer accommodate the person, arranging transportation, and monitoring performance. These programs are most effective when the supported employment is closely integrated with other aspects of treatment, such as medication and monitoring of symptoms.

Some people with schizophrenia are vulnerable to frequent crises because they do not regularly go to mental health centres to receive the treatment they need. These individuals often relapse and face re-hospitalization. To ensure that such patients take their medication and receive appropriate psychological and social rehabilitation, assertive community treatment

(ACT) programs have been developed that deliver treatment to patients in natural settings, such as in their homes, in restaurants, or on the street.

People with schizophrenia often have other medical problems, so an effective treatment program must attend to these as well. One of the most generally shared in or participated in things conforming to a type without noteworthy excellence or faults just as common a rule, by ordinary, frequent and ordinarily as an idea or expression deficient in originality or freshness, yet, only of its exchanging the commonplace of the common associated problems is vehemently and usually coarsely expressed condemnation or disapproved, as the interpretative category of an unequalled vocabulary is itself a genuine abuse. Successful treatment of substance abuse inpatients with schizophrenia requires careful coordination with their mental health care, so that the same clinicians are treating both disorders at the same time.

The high rate of substance abuse in patients with schizophrenia contributes to a high prevalence of infectious diseases, including hepatitis B and C and the human immunodeficiency virus (HIV). Assessment, education, and treatment or management of these illnesses is critical for the long-term health of patients.

Other problems frequently associated with schizophrenia include housing instability and homelessness, legal problems, violence, trauma and post-traumatic stress disorder, anxiety, depression, and suicide attempts. Close monitoring and psychotherapeutic interventions are often helpful in addressing these problems.

Several other psychiatric disorders are closely related to schizophrenia. In schizoaffective disorder, a person shows symptoms of schizophrenia combined with either mania or severe depression. Schizophreniform disorder refers to an illness in which a person experiences schizophrenic symptoms for more than one month but fewer than six months. In schizotypal personality disorder, a person engages in odd thinking, speech, and behaviour, but usually does not lose contact with reality. Sometimes mental health professionals refer to these disorders together as schizophrenia-spectrum disorders.

Severe mental illness almost always alters a person's life dramatically. People with severe mental illnesses experience disturbing symptoms that can cause of such difficulties and holding to a job, or go to school, relate to others, or cope with ordinary life demands. Some individuals require hospitalization because they become unable to care for themselves or because they are at risk of committing suicide.

The symptoms of mental illness can be very distressing. People who develop schizophrenia may hear voices inside their head that say nasty things about them or command them to act in strange or unpredictable ways. Or they may be paralyzed by paranoia - the deep conviction that everyone, including their closest family members, wants to injure or destroy them. People with major depression may feel that nothing brings pleasure and that life is so dreary and unhappy that it is better to be dead. People with panic disorder may experience heart palpitations, rapid breathing, and anxiety so extreme that they may not be able to leave home. People whom experience episodes of mania may engage in reckless sexual behaviour or may spend money indiscriminately, acts that later cause them to feel guilt, shame, and desperation.

Other mental illnesses, while not always debilitating, create certain problems in living. People with personality disorders may experience loneliness and isolation because their personality style interferes with social relations. People with an eating disorder may become so preoccupied with their weight and appearance that they force themselves to vomit or refuse to eat. Individuals who develop post-traumatic stress disorder may become angry easily, experience disturbing memories, and have trouble concentrating.

Experiences of mental illness often take issue upon its stability for depending on one's culture or social group, sometimes greatly so. For example, in most of the non-Western world, people with depression complain principally of physical ailments, such as lack of energy, poor sleep, loss of appetite, and various kinds of physical pain. Indeed, even in North America these complaints are commonplace. But in the United States and other Western societies, depressed people and mental health professionals who treat them tend to emphasize psychological problems, such as feelings of sadness, worthlessness, and despair. The experience of schizophrenia also differs by culture. In India, one-third of the new cases of schizophrenia involve catatonia, a behavioural condition in which a person maintains a bizarre statue posing for hours or days. This condition is rare in Europe and North America.

Of furthering issues regarding depersonalization disorder, meaning, in effect, that it is a categorized illness based within its intendment for being an illness, of mind, in which people experience an unwelcome sense of detachment from their own bodies. They may feel as though they are floating above the ground, outside observers of their own mental or physical processes. Other symptoms may include a feeling that they or other people are mechanical or unreal, a feeling of being in a dream, a feeling that their hands or feet are larger or smaller than usual, and a deadening of emotional responses. These symptoms are chronic and severe enough to impede normal functioning in a social, school, or work environment.

Depersonalization disorder is a relatively rare syndrome thought to result from severe psychological stress. It may occur as part of other mental illnesses, especially anxiety disorders. For example, some people with panic disorder feel nervous, have a sense of doom about their future and health, and have a troubling sense of estrangement from the losing effort by the attemptive use in the making, doing or achieving of its useful regularity as might be expected of the control over their bodies. Depersonalization disorder may also be a component of more severe mental illness, such as schizophrenia. Treatment may include training in relaxation techniques that enhance body perception and control, hypnosis to modify symptoms, and psychotherapy to explore possible stress-related components of the disorder.

Psychiatrists classify depersonalization disorder as one of the Dissociative disorders. Such disorders involve a disruption of consciousness, memory, identity, or perception.

All and all, that the schizophrenic responds to altercations in the analyst's defections and understanding by corresponding stormy and dramatic changes from love to hatred, from willingness to leave his delusional world to resistance and renewed withdrawal.

As understandable as these changes are, nevertheless may come as a surprise to the analyst who frequently has not observed their source, this is quite in contrast to his experience with psychoneurosis whose emotional reactions during an interview he can usually predict. These unpredictable changes seem to be the reason for the conception of the unreliability of the schizophrenic's transference reaction, yet they follow the same dynamic rules as the psychoneurotic's oscillations between positive and negative transference and resistance, however, if the schizophrenic's reactions are stormy and seemingly more unpredictable than those of the psychoneurotic, that instances suggested to be due to the inevitable errors in the analyst's approach to the schizophrenic, of which he himself may be unaware, rather than to the unreliability of the patient‘s emotional response?

Why is it inevitable that the psychoanalyst disappoints his schizophrenic patient time and again?

The schizophrenic individuals alienate from painful estrangement as faced by reality and retires to what resembles the early speechless phase of development where consciousness is not yet crystalized. As the expression of his feelings is not hindered by the convention that he has eliminated, as his thinking, feelings, behaviour and speech - when present - obey the working rules of the archaic unconscious. His thinking is magical and does not follow logical rules. It does not admit, but is lastly shared in aspects by saying 'no', and likewise the no to 'yes': There is no recognition of space and time, I, you, and am, are interchangeable expression through which of symbols and often by movement and gestures rather than by words.

As the schizophrenic is suspicious, he will distrust the words of his analyst. He will interpret them and incidental gestures and attitudes of the analyst according to his own delusional experience. The analyst may not even be aware of these involuntary manifestations of his attitudes, yet they mean much to the hypersensitive schizophrenic who uses them as a means of orienting himself to the therapist‘s personality and intentions toward him.

In other words, the schizophrenic patient and the therapist are people living in different worlds and no different levels of personal development with different means of expressing and of orienting themselves. We know little about the language of the unconscious that belongs to the schizophrenic, and our access to it is blocked by the very process of our own adjustment to a world the schizophrenic has relinquished, so, we should not be surprised that errors and misunderstandings occur when we under take to communicate and strive for a rapport with him.

Another source of the schizophrenic's disappointment arises form which the analyser accepts and does not interfere with the behaviour of the schizophrenic, his attitude may lead the patient to expect that the analyst will assist in carrying out all the patient's wishes, even though they may not seem to be in his interest to the analysers and the hospital's in their relationship to society. This attitude of acceptance so different from the patient's previous experiences readily fosters the anticipation that the analyst will try to carry out the patient's suggestion and take his part, even against conventional society with which it should occasionally arise. Frequently, it will be wise for the analyst to agree with the patient's wish to remain unbattled and untidy until he is ready to talk about the reasons for his behaviour or to change spontaneously. At other times, he will unfortunately be unable to take the patient's part without being able to make the patient understand and accept the reasons for the analyst's position.

If the analyst is not able to accept the possibility of misunderstanding the reaction of the schizophrenic patient and in turn of being misunderstood by him, it may shake his security with his patient.

That is to say, that, among other things, the schizophrenic, once he accepts the analyst's insecurity. being helpless and open to himself - in spite of his pretended grandiose isolation - he will feel utterly defeated by the insecurity of his would-be helper. Such disappointment may furnish reasons for outbursts of hatred and are comparable to the negative transference reactions of psychoneurosis, yet more intense than these, since they are not limited by the restrictions of the actual world - that is, it exists in or based on fact, its only problem is a sure-enough externalization for which things are existing in the act of being external in something that has existence, ss if it were an actualization as received in the obtainable enactment for being externalized, such that its problem of in some actual life that proves obtainable achieved, in that of doing something that has an existence for having absolute actuality.

These outbursts are accompanied by anxiety, feelings of guilt, and fear of retaliations which in turn lead to increased hostility. Yet this established a vicious circle: We disappoint the patient, he is afraid that we hate him for his hatred and therefore continues to hate us. If in addition he senses that the analyst is afraid of his aggressiveness, it confirms his fear that he is actually considered as some dangerous and unacceptable, and this augments his hatred.

This establishes that the schizophrenics capable of developing strong relationships of love and hatred toward the analyst. After all, one could not be so hostile if it were not for the background of a very close relationship. In addition, the schizophrenic develops transference reactions on the narrower sense which he can differentiate from the actual interpersonal relationship. For which the schizophrenic's emotional reactions toward the analyst have to be met with extreme care and caution. The love which the sensitive schizophrenic feels as he first emerges, and his cautions acceptances of the analyst's warmth of interest are really most delicate and tender things. If the analyst deals with the transference reactions of a psychoneurotic is bad enough, though as a reparable rule, but if he fails with a schizophrenic in meeting positive feelings by pointing it out for instance before the patient indicates that he is ready to discuss it, he may easily freeze to death what has just begun to grow and so destroy any further possibility of therapy.

Some analysts may feel that the atmosphere of complete acceptance and of strict avoidance of any arbitrary denials which we recommend as a basic rule for the treatment of schizophrenics may not avoid our wish to guide of re-acceptance of reality, nevertheless, Freud says that every science and therapy which accept his teachings about unconscious, about transference and resistance and about infantile sexuality, may be called psychoanalysis. According in this definition we believe we are practising psychoanalysis with our schizophrenic patients.

Whether we call it analysis or not, it is clear that successful treatment does not depend on technical rules of any special psychiatric school but rather on the basic attitude of the individual therapist toward psychologic persons. If he meets them as strangle creatures of another world whose productions are not comprehensible to 'normal' beings, he cannot treat them, if he realizes, however, that the difference between himself and the psychologic is only of degree, and not of kind, he will know better how to meet him. He will not be able to identify himself sufficiently with the patient to understand and accept his emotional reactions without becoming involved in them.

The process of constant and perpetual change is examined and closely matched within the study of philosophical speculations and pointed of a world view which asserts that basic reality is constantly in a process of flux and change. Indeed, reality is identified with pure process. Concepts such as creativity, freedom, novelty, emergence, and growth are fundamental explanatory categories for process philosophy. This metaphysical perspective is to be contrasted with a philosophy of substance, the view that a fixed and permanent reality underlies the changing or fluctuating world of ordinary experience. Whereas substance philosophy emphasizes static being, process philosophy emphasizes dynamically becoming.

Although process philosophy is as old as the 6th-century BC Greek philosopher, Heraclitus, renewed interest in it was stimulated in the 19th century by the theory of evolution. Key figures in the development of modern process philosophy were the British philosopher's Herbert Spencer, Samuel Alexander, and Alfred North Whitehead, the American philosophers Charles S. Peirce and William James, and the French philosophers Henri Bergson and Pierre

Teilhard de Chardin. Whitehead's Process and Reality: An Essay in Cosmology (1929) is generally considered the most important systematic expression of process philosophy.

Contemporary theologies have been strongly influenced by process philosophy. The American theologian Charles Hartshorne, for instance, rather than interpreting God as an unchanging absolute, emphasizes God's sensitive and caring relationship with the world. A personal God enters into relationships in such a way that he is affected by the relationships, and to be affected by relationships is to change. So too is in the process of growth and development. Important contributions to process theology have also been made by such theologians as William Temple, Daniel Day Williams, Schubert Ogden, and John Cobb, Jr.

Reality is a difficult word to use to every one's satisfaction or even to one's own satisfaction. In this instance the word reality is used arbitrarily to designate the direct, here-and-now impact of the analyst upon the patient. Reality. In this sense, contrasts with the impact the analyst has through his representation in the patient's fantasy life, neurosis, and transference, since both kinds of impact seem always to coexist and since the former - the analyst's real impact - may be the worst enemy of the transference, the matter of their differentiation is possibly the most challenging aspect of analysis.

The analytic situation, which is set up to shut out ordinary reality intrusions, that cannot . . . neither should not exclude all, but to say, that in the beginning months, for instance, reality inevitably has the upper hand. The analyst, the office, the procedure, are all overwhelmingly real. Everything is strange, frightening and exciting, gratifying and frustrating. Unlike the patient can test it and orient himself to it, the impact of this reality is usually so great that even an ordinary useful transference relationship cannot be expected to develop.

Perhaps the most confusing aspect of this beginning period is the frequent appearance in it of what can be regarded as a false transference relationship. With great intensity and clarity, the patient may reveal, through transference-like references about the analyst, some of the deepest secrets only of his neurosis but of its genesis. The pseudotransference, too good to be true, is almost sure to be nothing more than the patient's attempt to deal with the person of the analyst, the entire spectrum of his various patterns of behaviour. If, it is easy to do, the analyst overlooks the likelihood that the patient's relationship with at this time is really about that almost everything said about it is related, analysis may get off to a very bad start. And if, as is even earlier to do, the analyst's interests the genetic meaning of the openly exposed material, a good transference relationship may be seriously delayed and a workable transference neurosis may never appear. even after initial reality has had time to fade, reality may continue to intrude in ways that are very hard to detect and that is very troublesome.

One of the most serious problems of analysis is the very substantial help which the patient receives directly from the analyst and the analytic situation. For many a patient, the analyst in the analytic situation is in fact the most stable, reasonable, wise and understanding person he has ever met, and the setting in which they meet may actually be the most honest, open, direct and regular relationship he has ever experienced. Added to this is the considerable helpfulness to him of being able to clarify his life storey, confessing his guilt, express his ambitions, and explore his confusions. Further real help comes from the learning-about-life accruing from the analyst's skilled questions, observations and interpretations. Taken together, the total real value to the patient of the analytic situation can easily be immense. The trouble with this kind of help is that it goes on and on, it may have such a real, direct and continuing impact upon the patient that he can never get deeply enough involved in the transference situation to allow him to resolve or even to become acquainted with his most crippling internal difficulties. The trouble is far too good, the trouble also is that we as analysts apparently cannot resist the seductiveness of being directly helpful, and this, when combined with the compelling assumption that helpfulness is bound to be good, permits us top credit patient improvements to 'analysis' when more properly it should often be recognized for being the amounting result for the patient's using the analytic situation, as the model, for being the preceptors and supporter in the dealing practically within the immediate distractions as holding to some problem.

Perhaps, we can now refer to something in a clear unmistakable manner, and it would be to mention, for being, that one more difficult-to-handle intrusion of reality into the analysis, that by saying, that this is the definitive and final interruption of the transference neurosis by the reality of termination; in the sense, the situation is reversed and the intrusion is analytically desirable, since ideally the impact of reality of impending and certain termination is used to facilitate the resolution of the transference. As with the resolution of earlier episodes of transference neurosis, this final one is brought about principally by the analyst's interpretations and reconstructions. As these take effect, the transference neurosis and, hopefully, along with it the original neurosis is resolved. This final resolution, however, which is much more comprehensive, is usually very different and may not come about at all without the help of the reality of termination. Accordingly, any attenuation of the ending, such as tapering off or causal or tentative stopping, should be expected to stand in the way of an effective resolution of the transference. Yet, it seems that this is what most commonly happens to an ending, and because of this a great many patients may lose the potentially great benefit of a thorough resolution and are forever after left suspended in the net of unresolved transference.

Yet, utter indistinctly rigorous termination seems understandable, as difficult as transference neurosis may be in the analyst at other times, this ending period, if rigorously carried out, simply has to be the period of his greatest emotional strain. There can surely be no more likely time for an analyst to surrender his analytic position and, responding to his own transference, become personally involved with his patient than during the process of separating from a long and self-restrained relationship. Accordingly, it may be better to slur over the ending lightly than to mishandle it in an attempt to be rigorous.

In considering more broadly the function of the transference in the psychoanalytic process, one is confronted by the apparent naïve, but, nonetheless important questions of the role of the actual (current) object as compared with that of the object representation of the original personage in the past. We recall Freud's paradoxical, somewhat gloomy, but portentous concluding passage in 'The Dynamics of Transference.' This struggle between the doctor and the patient, between intellect and instinctual life, between understanding and seeking to act, is played out almost exclusively in the phenomena of transference. It is on that field that the victory must be won - the victory whose expression is on that field that the victory must be won - the victory whose expression is the permanent cure of the neuroses. It cannot be disputed that controlling the phenomena of transference presents the psychoanalysis with the greatest difficultly, but it should not be forgotten that they do us the inestimable service of making the patient's hidden and forgotten erotic impulses of showing their immediate and manifested impossibilities, for when all is said and done, it is impossible to destroy anyone in absentia or in effigies.

Both object and representation is made necessary by the basic phenomenon of original separation. The existence of an image of the object, which persist in the absence of the object, is one of the important beginnings of psychic life in general, certainly an indispensable prerequisite for object relationship. As generally construed. Whether this is viewed as (or, a times demonstrably is) something unstable for allotting introjection, s always subject to alternative projection, or an intrapsychic object representation clearly distinguished from the self-representation, or firm identification in the superego, or in the ego itself, these phenomena are in various ways components of the system of mastery of the fact of separation, or separateness, from the original absolutely necessarily anaclitic (in the earliest period) symbiotic 'object'. In the light of clinical observation, it would appear to be that the relative stabilities (parental) object representation. At which time of varying degree, are to a greater extent for the archaic phenomena. Even in non-psychotic patients, overwhelmed by them, sometimes resembles the restoration from oedipal identification, which provides the preponderant basis for most demonstrable analytic transferences. That within the necrotic patients, the transference is effectively established when this representation invests the analyst to a degree - depending on intensity of drive and most of ego participation - which range in locality with the wishing and the striving as to make-over and analyse without biases in judgement and misinterpretation of data, are the actual perceptual distortions.

However, the old object representations may be invested, however rigidly established the libidinal or aggressive cathexis of the image may be, this as such can become the actual and exclusive focus of instinctual discharge, or of complicated and intense instinct-defence solutions, only and general energy-sparing quality of strictly intrapsychic processes. For the vast majority of persons, visible to any degree, including those with severe neurosis, character distortions, addictions and certain psychoses, the striving is toward the living and actual object, even at the cost of intense suffering. In a sense, this returns us to the state in which the psychological 'object-to-be', for undergoing pivotal importance never again to be duplicated, but in certain acute life emergencies, even if the object is not firmly perceived as such, in the sense of later object relations? And it does seem that trance impressions from the earliest contacts in the service of life preservation, and the associated instinctual gratifications, and innumerable secondarily associated sensory impressions. Are activated by the specific inborn urges of sexual maturation? These propel the individual to renew many of the earliest modes of actual bodily contact, in connection with seeking for specific instinctual gratification. Or, to look away from clear-cut instinctual matters to the more remote elaborations of human contact: Few regard loneliness as other than a source of suffering, even self-imposed, as an apparent matter of choice, and the forcible imposition of 'solitary confinement ' is surely one of the most cruel of punishments.

In taking to question, we are entering an area of life in which things are other then themselves, where meaning is multifaceted, and where the line between the old and the new is blurred. It should, by, its immediate measure, help develop our recognition or meaning of the pertinent applicability as to the relevance of interrelated aspects of the psychology of 'metaphor'. In the psychology of metaphor we will find a useful analogy to the psychology of transference interpretation. In of which we will be newly encountered as good metaphors, those it response to which we say, 'That's it exactly' or 'That really captures it' or 'That says it all'.

Some literary and linguistic analysis, (e.g., Lewis, 1936 and Snell, 1953) and also people in everyday life, believe that there are experiences that can only be expressed metaphorically. And it is, for this achievement that these metaphors, which may be entire poem or as lines or even words highly valued. But how can this be so? Just what in this 'it' that the metaphor 'is' or 'captures' or 'says'? If this 'is' or this 'experience' can only be rendered metaphorically, when we can know it only as such, that is, as the metaphor itself. Of the position out of which are put forward by, T.S, Eliot (1933) and E.W. Harding (1963) in their discussion of poetry, for in these instances we are granted that there is no known and logically independent version of the experience that can serve to validate the metaphor. Whatever the metaphor makes available to us depends on it and it and so cannot be used to prove its correctness.

It seems justifiable to conclude that the metaphor is a new experience rather than a mere paraphrase of an already fully constituted expedience. The metaphor creates an experience that one has never had before. It is an experience one has not realized by the acquaintance with self. The metaphor does, of course, suggest certain constituent experiences of which one may have been more or less dimly aware. One may say, therefore, that the metaphor speaks for those constituents, on the existence of which much of its appeal depends. But in its organizing and implicit ly rendering these constituents in its new way, it is a creation rather than a mere paraphrase or new editions. Paraphrasing and new editions never speak as forcefully as good new metaphors, nor could they facilitate further new experience. One analytically familiar feature of these creations is that they make it safe and pleasing to experience something that otherwise would be considered too threatening and so would be kept in fragmented obscurity through defensive measures.

Thus, when one says, 'That's it exactly' one is implicitly recognizing and announcing that one has found and accepted a new mode of experiencing one's own self and one's inherent perceptions of the world, which is to say, asserting a transformation of one's own subjectivity. Something is now said to be true, and in a sense it is true, but it is true for the first time. Nothing like it can ever happen again, for the second time cannot be the same as the first. One can' t step into the same watering point and then step once again into the same spot of that river. A revelatory metaphor re-encountered or repeated later may lose some of its force, alternatively, it may gain some significance, butt it cannot remain exactly the same metaphor or mobilize an experience identical with the first. The point applies as well as to new metaphors that are similar to familiar ones: They have to be judged or experienced through their conventionalized predecessors, as through methods of knowing or already proved instrumentally of perceiving. The audience and the performer, who may be one person, as such that may not have, as yet.

What is to be said about the psychology of metaphor is analogous to the transformational aspects of developed transference and the steadfast interpretation that both facilitate and organize them as transference. Allowing that these transferences and 'remembered' experiences come into existence over a period of time, nothing that is identical with them has ever before been enacted, and nothing will ever be enacted again. They are creations that may be fully achieved only under specific analytic conditions. Such that living was not reliving that moment, words like re-living, re-experiencing and reliving simply do not do justice to the phenomena, that in making this claim. A seeming contradiction over-writes some of our well-establish ideas. - in offering, - I am not contradicting some of our well-established ideas about interpretation and insight, I am, however, disputing the point that insight refers of much of the recovery of lost memories, and takes in as well, a new grasp of the significance and interpretations of events one has always remembered. In point, as, Freud pointed out, 'As a matter of fact I've always known it, only that I've never thought of it; (1914), In fact, it is to develop that point in furthering to say that it takes an adult to do that, especially with the help of an analyst. It was, after all, Freud's analysis of adults that make it possible to define infantile psychosexuality. In this respect, but without disregard, child analysis retains a quality of applied psychoanalysis' in the same way that the interpreted transference neurosis is: Both are always of describing as true something that was not true in quite that way at the time of its greatest developmental significance. This apparent paradox about 'remembering' as a form of creating goes a long way, probably that what it is, is distinctive about psychoanalytic interpretation.

This time, however, to further the discussion on the interpretive technique that surrounds the phase of a mutative interpretation - that in which a portion of the patient's id-relation to the analyst is made conscious in virtue of the latter's position as auxiliary superego - is in itself complex. In the classical model of an interpretation, the patient will first be made aware of a state of tension of an interpretation, will next be made aware that there is repressive factor at work (that his superego is threatening him with punishment), and will only then be made aware of the id-impulse which has stirred up the protects of his superego and so given to the anxiety in his ego. This is the classical scheme. In actual practice, the analyst finds himself working from all three sides at once, or in irregular successions. At one moment a small portion of the patient's superego may be revealed to him in all its savagery, at another the shrinking defencelessness of his ego, at yet another his attention may be directed to the attempts which he is making at restitution - at compensating for his hostility, on some occasions a fraction of id-energy may even be directly encouraged to break its way through the last remains of an already weakened resistance. There is, however, one characteristic which all of these various operations has in common, they are essentially upon a small scale. For the mutative interpretation is inevitably governed by the principle of minimal doses. It is a commonly agreed clinical fact that alternations in a patient under analysis appear almost always to be extremely gradual: We are inclined to suspect sudden and large changes as an indication that suggestive rather than psycho-analyst processes are at work. The gradual nature of the change brought about in psychoanalysis will be explained, as, only to suggest, those changes are the result of the summation of an immense number of minuet steps, each of which correspond to a mutative interpretation. And the smallness of each step is in turn imposed by the very nature of the analytic situation. For each interpretation involves the release of a certain quantity of id-energy, and, if the quantity released is too large, the higher unstable state of equilibrium which enables the analyst to function as the patient's auxiliary superego is bound to be upset. The whole analytic situation will thus be imperilled, since it is only in virtue of the analyst's acting as auxiliary superego that these released id-energy can occur at all.

The effectuality from which follow the analytic attempt to bring unequalled amounts in the confronting collections of some improper use to a resultant quantity of id-energy into the patient's consciousness all at once. On the one hand that absolutely nothing, not at all, as not to happen, or on the other hand, there may be an unmanageable result, but in neither event will a mutative interpretations have been effected. The analyst's power as auxiliary superego may be for two very different reasons. It may be that the id-impulses are trying to bring out, as it was, that in fact sufficiently urgent at the moment: For, after all, the emergence of an id-impulse depends on two factors - not only on the permission of the superego, but also on the urgency (the degree of cathexis) of the id-impulse itself. This, then, may be one cause of an apparently negative response to an interpretation, and evidently a fairly harmless one. but the same apparent result may also be due to something else, in spite of the id-impulse being really urgent, the strength of the patient's own repressive forces (the degree of repression) may have been too great to allow his ego to listen to the persuasive voice of the auxiliary superego. Now we have a situation dynamically identical with the next one we have to consider, though economically different. this next situation is one in which the patient accepts the interpretation, that is, allows the id-impulse into his consciousness, but is immediately overwhelmed with anxiety. This may show itself in a number of ways, for instance, the patient may produce a manifest anxiety-attack. Or the may exhibit signs of 'real' anger with the analyst with a complete lack of insight, or he may break off the analysis. In any of these cases the analytic situation will, for the moment, at least, have broken down. The patient will be behaving just as the hypnotic subject behaves when, having been ordered by the hypnotist to perform an action too much at a variance with his own consciousness, he breaks off the hypnotic relation and wakes up from his trance. This state of things, which is manifest where the patient responds to an interpretation with an actual outbreak of anxiety or one of its equivalents, may be latent, was the patient to show no response, the latter of cases may be the more awkward of the two, since it is masked, and it may sometimes be the effect of a greater overdose of interpretation than where manifest anxiety arises (though obviously other factors will be of determining importance, and in particularly the nature of the patient's neurosis). Yet this threatened collapse of the analytic situation to an overdose of interpretation: But it might be more accurate in some ways to ascribe it to an insufficient dose. For what has happened is that the second phase of the interpretation process has not occurred: The phase in which the patient becomes aware that his impulse is directed toward an archaic phantasy object and not toward a real one.

We cannot reproduce of all Freud's research about transference but for an instance of obligation, would be used to indicate the requirement by the immediate need or purpose upon such condition that might point beyond a normal or acceptable limit, as to an excessive amount of which something does not or cannot extend to their essentials. When we speak of the transference in connexion with social reeducation, we mean the emotional responses of the education or counsellor or therapist, as the case maybe, without meaning that it takes place in exactly the same way as in an analysis. The 'countertransference' is emotional aptitude of the teacher toward the pupil, the counsellor toward his charge, the therapist toward the patient. The feeling which the child develops for the mentor is conditioned by a much earlier relationship to someone else. We must take cognisance of this fact in order to understand these relationships. The tender relationships which go to up the child's love life are no longer strange to us. Many of these have already been touched upon in the foregoing literature. We have learned how the small boy takes the father and mother as love objects. We have followed with the striving with which arises out of this relationship, the Oedipus situation, we have seen how this runs its course and terminates in an identification with the parents. We have also had opportunity to consider the relationship between brothers and sisters, how their original rivalry is transformed into affection through the pressure of their feeling for the parents. We know that the boy at puberty must give up his first love object within the family and transfers his libido to individuals outside the family.

We can easily see why an attempt to change the present order of society always meets with resistance and where the radical reformer will have to use the greatest leverage. Our attitude to society and its members has a certain standard form. It gets its imprint from the structure of the family and the emotional relationships set up within the family, therefore, the parents, especially the father, assume overwhelming responsibility for the social orientation of the child. The persistent, ineradicable libidinal relationships carried over from childhood are facts with which social reformers must reckon. If the family represents the best preparation for the present social order, which seems to be the case, then the introduction of a new order means that the family must be uprooted and replaced by a different personal world for the child. It is beyond our scope to attempt a solution of this question, which concerns those who strive to build up a new order of society. We are remedial educators and must recognize these sociological relationships. We can ally ourselves with whatever social system will, but we have the path of our present activity well marked out for us, to bring dissociable youth into the line with present-day society.

Certain personality traits may also directively lead to stress-related disorders. The so-called Type [A] personality, characterized by competitive, hard-driving intensity, is common in American society. Although early studies suggested a link between Type [A] behaviour and coronary heart disease, most studies since the 1980s have failed to find such a relationship. However, research has consistently demonstrated that people who show a high level of hostility, anger, and cynicism - often components of Type [A] behaviours - have a higher risk of coronary heart disease than people without these traits.

Several other psychiatric disorders are closely related to schizophrenia. In schizoaffective disorder, a person shows symptoms of schizophrenia combined whether mania or severe depression. Schizophreniform disorder refers to an illness in which a person experiences schizophrenic symptoms for more than one month but fewer than six months. In schizotypal personality disorder, a person engages in odd thinking, speech, and behaviour, but usually does not lose contact with reality

The occurring personality disorders, disorders in which one's personality results in personal state of being agitated with doubt or mental conflict as unconcerning a crazed derangement or significantly inflicting something that gives rise to the defragmentation of the social or working function, such that of every person has a personality - that is to say, a characteristic way of thinking, feeling, behaving, and relating to others. Most people experience at least some difficulties and problems that result from their personality. The specific point at which those problems justify the diagnosis of a personality disorder is controversial. To some extent the definition of a personality disorder is arbitrary, reflecting as well as professional judgments about the person's degree of dysfunction, needs for change, and motivation for change.

The occurring personality disorders involve behaviour that deviates from the norms or expectations of one's culture. However, people who digress from cultural norms are not necessarily dysfunctional, nor are people who conform to cultural norms necessarily healthy. Many personality disorders represent extreme variants of behaviour patterns that people usually value and encourage. For example, most people value confidence but not arrogance, agreeableness but not submissiveness, and conscientiousness but not perfectionism.

Because no clear line exists between healthy and unhealthy functioning, critics question the reliability of personality disorder diagnoses. A behaviour that seems deviant to one person may seem normal to another depending on one's gender, ethnicity, and cultural background. The personal and cultural biases of mental health professionals may influence their diagnoses of personality disorders.

An estimated 20 percent of people in the general population have one or more personality disorders. Some people with personality disorders have other mental illnesses as well. About 50 percent of people who are treated for any psychiatric disorder have a personality disorder.

Mental health professionals rarely diagnose personality disorders in children because their manner of thinking, feeling, and relating to others does not usually stabilize until young adulthood. Thereafter, personality traits usually remain stable. Personality disorders often decrease in severity as some person ages.

People with antisocial personality disorder act in a way that disregards the feelings and rights of other people. Antisocial personalities often break the law, and they may use or exploit other people for their own gain. They may lie repeatedly, act impulsively, and get into physical fights. They may mistreat their spouses, neglect or abuse their children, and exploit their employees. They may even kill other people. People with this disorder are also sometimes called sociopaths or psychopaths. Antisocial behaviour in people less than 18 years old is called conduct disorder.

Antisocial personalities usually fail to understand that their behaviour is dysfunctional because their ability to feel guilty, remorseful, and anxious is impaired. Guilt, remorse, shame, and anxiety are unpleasant feelings, but they are also necessary for social functioning and even physical survival. For example, people who are found in their deficiency, such as their ability to feel anxious will often fail to anticipate actual dangers and risks. They may take chances that other people would not take.

Antisocial personality disorder affects about 3 percent of males and 1 percent of females. This is the most heavily researched personality disorder, in part because it costs society the most. People with this disorder are at high risk for premature and violent death, injury, imprisonment, loss of employment, bankruptcy, alcoholism, drug dependence, and failed personal relationships.

People with borderline personality disorder experience intense emotional instability, particularly in relationships with others. They may make frantic efforts to avoid real or imagined abandonment by others. They may experience minor problems as major crises. They may also express their anger, frustration, and dismay through suicidal gestures, self-mutilation, and other self-destructive acts. They tend to have an unstable self-image or sense of self.

As children, most people with this disorder were emotionally unstable, impulsive, and often bitter or angry, although their chaotic impulsiveness and intense emotions may have made them popular at school. At first they may impress people as stimulating and exciting, but their relationships tend to be unstable and explosive.

About 2 percent of all people have borderline personality disorder. About 75 percent of people with this disorder are female. Borderline personalities are at high risk for developing depression, alcoholism, drug dependence, bulimia, Dissociative disorders, and post-traumatic stress disorder. As many as 10 percent of people with this disorder commit suicide by the age of 30. People with borderline personality disorder are among the most difficult to treat with psychotherapy, in part because their relationship with their therapist may become as intense and unstable as their other personal relationships.

Avoidant personality disorder is social withdrawal due to intense, anxious shyness. People with Avoidant personalities are reluctant to interact with others unless they feel certain of the likened impact, which they fear for being criticized or rejected. Often they view themselves as socially inept and inferior to others.

Dependent personality disorder involves severe and disabling emotional dependency on others. People with this disorder have difficulty making decisions without a great deal of advice and reassurance from others. They urgently seek out another relationship when a close relationship ends. They feel uncomfortable by themselves.

People with histrionic personality disorder constantly strive to be the centres of attention. They may act overly flirtatious or dress in ways that draw attention. They may also talk in a dramatic or theatrical style and display exaggerated emotional reactions.

People with narcissistic personality disorder have a grandiose sense of a self-importance. They seek excessive admiration from others and fantasize about unlimited success or power. They believe they are special, unique, or superior to others. However, they often have very fragile self-esteem.

Obsessive-compulsive personality disorder is characterized by a preoccupation with details, orderliness, perfection, and control. People with this disorder often devote excessive amounts of time toward working and individual productivity and fail to take time for leisure activities and friendships. They tend to be rigid, formal, stubborn, and serious. This disorder differs from obsessive-compulsive disorder, which often includes more bizarre behaviour and rituals.

People with paranoid personality disorder feel constant suspicion and distrust toward other people. They believe that others are against them and constantly look for evidence to support their suspicions. They are hostile toward others and react angrily to perceived insults.

Schizoid personality disorder involves social isolation and a lack of desire for close personal relationships. People with this disorder prefer to be alone and seem withdrawn and emotionally detached. They seem indifferent to felicitation or criticism from other people.

People with schizotypal personality disorder engage in odd thinking, speech, and behaviour. They may ramble or use words and phrases in unusual ways, and they may believe they have magical control over others. They feel very uncomfortable with close personal relationships and tend to be suspicious of others. Some research indications to bare procedures in the disorder which is less severe form of schizophrenia.

Many psychiatrists and psychologists use two additional diagnoses. Depressive personality disorder is characterized by chronic pessimism, gloominess, and cheerlessness. In passive-aggressive personality disorder, a person passively resists completing tasks and chores, criticizes and scorns authority figures, and seems negative and sullen.

Personality disorders result from a complex interaction of inherited traits and life experience, not from a single cause. For example, some cases of antisocial personality disorder may result from a combination of a genetic predisposition to impulsiveness and violence, very inconsistent or erratic parenting, and a harsh environment that discourage feelings of empathy and warmth but rewards exploitation and aggressiveness. Borderline personality disorder may result from a genetic predisposition to impulsiveness and emotional instability combined with parental neglect, intense marital conflicts between parents, and repeated episodes of severe emotional or sexual abuse. Dependent personality disorder may result from genetically based anxiety, an inhibited temperament, and overly protective, clinging, or neglectful parenting.

The pervasive and chronic nature of personality disorders makes them difficult to treat. People with these disorders often fail to recognize that their personality has contributed to their social, occupational, and personal problems. They may not think they have any real problems despite a history of drug abuse, failed relationships, and irregular employment. Thus, therapists must first focus on helping the person understand and become aware of the significance of their personality traits.

People with personality disorders sometimes feel that they can never change their dysfunctional behaviour because they have always acted the same way. Although personality change is exceedingly difficult, sometimes people can change the most dysfunctional aspects of their feelings and behaviour.

Therapists use a variety of methods to treat personality disorders, depending on the specific disorder. For example, cognitive and behavioural techniques, such as role playing and logical argument, may help alter a person's irrational perceptions and assumptions about himself or herself. Certain psychoactive drugs may help control feelings of anxiety, depression, or severe distortions of thought. Psychotherapy may help people to understand the impact of experiences and responsibilities. These programs appear to help some people, but it is unclear how long their beneficial effects last.

The appropriate treatment, most people can recover from mental illness and return to normal life. Even those with persistent, long-term mental illnesses can usually learn to manage their symptoms and live productive lives.

In most societies mental illness carries a substantial stigma, or mark of shame. The mentally ill, were at most, blamed for their own ill's, blamed for bringing it upon their own illnesses, and others may see them as victims of bad fate, religious and moral transgression, or witchcraft. Such stigma may keep families from acknowledging that a family member is ill. Some families may hide or overprotect a member with mental illness - keeping the person from receiving potentially effective care - or they may reject the person from the family. When magnified from individuals to a whole society, such attitudes lead to under-funding of mental health services and terribly inadequate care. In much of the world, even today, the mentally ill, were chained, shackled and caged, or hospitalized in filthy, brutal institutions. Yet attitudes toward mental illness have improved in many areas, especially owing to a heralded breed and advocacy for the mentally ill.

Mental illness creates enormous social and economic costs. Depression, for example, affects some 500 million people in the world and results in more time lost to disability than such chronic diseases as diabetes mellitus and arthritis. Estimating the economic cost of mental illness is complex because there are direct costs (actual medical expenditures), indirect costs (the cost to individuals and society due to reduced or lost productivity, for example), and support costs (time lost to care of family members with mental illnesses).

Another method of estimating the cost of mental illness to society measures the impact of premature deaths and disablements. Research by the World Health Organization and the World Bank estimated that in 1990, among the world's population aged 15 to 44 years, depression accounted for more than 10 percent of the total burden attributable to all diseases. Two other illnesses, bipolar disorder and schizophrenia, accounted for another 6 percent of the burden. This research has helped governments recognize that mental illnesses constitute a far greater challenge to public health systems than previously realized.

No universally accepted definition of mental illness exists. In general, the definition of mental illness depends on a society's norms, or rules of behaviour. Behaviours that violate these norms are considered signs of deviance or, in some cases, of mental illness.

The variation in behavioural norms does not mean, however, that definitions of mental illness are necessarily incompatible across cultures. Many behaviours are recognized throughout the world for being indicative of mental illness. These include extreme social withdrawal, violence to oneself, hallucinations (false sensory perceptions), and delusions (fixed, false ideas).

Another way of defining mental illness is based on whether a person's behaviours are maladaptive - that is, whether they cause a person to experience problems in coping with common life demands. For example, people with social phobia may avoid interacting with other people and experience problems at work as a result. Critics note that under this definition, political dissidents could be considered mentally ill for refusing to accept the dictates of their government.

Mental illness affects people of all ages, races, cultures, and socioeconomic classes. The prevalence of mental illness refers to what degree or to the greater extent do peoples experience of a mental illness during a specified time period.

Psychosomatic Illness, illness that has no basic physical or organic cause but appears to be the result of psychological conditions, such as stress, anxiety, and depression. Such illnesses reflect the general belief that the mind is capable of strongly affecting bodily reactions, and that a person's mental condition can actually cause changes in the chemistry of the body, thereby creating physical illness. In cases of psychosomatic illness, a marked change in the body can often be readily detected.

The most effective treatment for psychosomatic disorders takes account into both the physical and the emotional aspects of the disease. The physical symptoms usually cannot be cured until the person's psychological environment has improved. For instance, a business executive working under severe pressure may develop ulcers. Although medicine and a special diet can improve this condition, if the person fails to cut down on work or learn relaxation techniques, he or she will probably continue to suffer from the disease and may even develop additional psychosomatic illnesses. In more serious cases of psychosomatic illness, doctors may recommend that the patient undergo some form of psychotherapy in addition to treatment for the physical aspects of the illness.

Depression can take several other forms. In bipolar disorder, sometimes called manic-depressive illness, a person's mood swings back and forth between depression and mania. People with seasonal affective disorder typically suffer from depression only during autumn and winter, when there are fewer hours of daylight. In dysthymia, people feel depressed, have low self-esteem, and concentrate poorly most of the time - often for a period of years - but their symptoms are milder than in major depression. Some people with dysthymia experience occasional episodes of major depression. Mental health professionals use the term clinical depression to refer to any of the above forms of depression.

Major depression, the most severe form of depression, affects from 1 to 2 percent of people aged 65 or older who are living in the community (rather than in nursing homes or other institutions). The prevalence of depression and other mental illnesses is much higher among elderly residents of nursing homes. Although most older people with depression respond to treatment, many cases of depression among the elderly go undetected or untreated. Research indicates that depression is a major risk factor for suicide among the elderly in the United States. People over age 65 in the United States have the highest suicide rate of any age group.

Generally, the overall prevalence rates of mental illnesses between men and women are similar. However, men have much higher rates of antisocial personality disorder and substance abuse. In the United States, women suffer from depression and anxiety disorders at about twice the rate of men. The gender gap is even wider in some countries. For example, in China, women suffer from depression at nine times the rate of men.

Mental illness is becoming an increasing problem for two reasons. First, increases in life expectancy have brought increased numbers of certain chronic mental illnesses. For example, because more people are living into old age, more people are suffering from dementia. Second, a number of studies provide evidence that rates of depression are rising throughout the world. The reasons may be related to such factors as economic change, political and social violence, and cultural disruptions. While some have questioned these findings, dramatic increases in the numbers of refugees and people dislocated from their homes by economic forces or civil strife are associated with great increases in a variety of mental illnesses for those populations. According to the United Nations High Commissioner for Refugees, the number of refugees worldwide increased from 2.5 million in 1971 to 13.2 million in 1996, peaking at 17 million in 1991.

A number of mental illnesses - such as depression, anxiety disorders, schizophrenia, and bipolar disorder - occur worldwide. Others seem to occur only in particular cultures. For example, eating disorders, such as anorexia nervosa (compulsive dieting associated with unrealistic fears of fatness), occurs mostly between girls and women in Europe, North America, and Westernized areas of Asia, whose cultures view thinness as an essential component of female beauty. In Latin America, people who are met with directly (as through participation or observation) in having known the intimacy or inward practices that are acquainted or familiar with or versed of something based on the personal exposure seem as been awarded of an experience, perhaps, an experience overwhelming of some causal reason to fright after a dangerous or traumatic event is said to have sustained (fright), an illness in which their soul has been frightened away. In some societies of West Africa and elsewhere, brain fatigue describes individuals (usually students) who experience difficulties in concentrating and thinking, as well as physical symptoms of pain and wearing out.

Most mental health professionals in the United States use the Diagnostic and Statistical Manual of Mental Disorders(DSM), a reference book published by the American Psychiatric Association, as a guide to the different kinds of mental illnesses. The foundation, known as DSM-IV, describes more than 300 mental disorders, behavioural disorders, addictive disorders, and other psychological problems and groups them into broad categories. This describes some of the major categories, including anxiety disorders, mood disorders, schizophrenia and other psychotic disorders, personality disorders, cognitive disorders, Dissociative disorders, somatoform disorders, factitious disorders, substance-related disorders, eating disorders, and impulse-control disorders. Mental health professionals in many other parts of the world use a different classification system, the International Classification of Diseases (ICD), published by the World Health Organization.

The DSM and ICD are both categorical systems of classification, in which each mental illness is defined by its own unique set of symptoms and characteristics. In theory, for each one disorder should possess diagnostic criteria that are independent of from each one and another, just as tuberculosis and lung cancer are discrete diseases. Yet symptoms of many mental disorders overlap, and many people - such as those who experience both depression and severe anxiety - show symptoms of more than one disorder at the same time. For these reasons, some mental health professionals advocate a dimensional system of classification. In contrast to the categorical approach, which sees mental disorders as qualitatively distinct from normal behaviour, a dimensional system views behaviour as falling along a continuum of normality, with some behaviours considered more abnormally than others. In a dimensional system, diagnoses do not describe discrete diseases but rather portray the relative importance of an array of symptoms.

Mood disorders, also called affective disorders, create disturbances in a person's emotional life. Depression, mania, and bipolar disorder are examples of mood disorders. Symptoms of depression may include feelings of sadness, hopelessness, and worthlessness, as well as complaints of physical pain and changes in appetite, sleep patterns, and energy level. In mania, on the other hand, an individual experiences an abnormally elevated mood, often marked by exaggerated self-importance, irritability, agitation, and a decreased need for sleep. In bipolar disorder, also called manic-depressive illness, a person's mood alternates between extremes of mania and depression.

Bipolar disorder is a mental illness that causes mood swings. In the manic phase, a person might feel ecstatic, self-important, and energetic. But when the person becomes depressed, the mood shifts to extreme sadness, negative thinking, and apathy. Some studies indicate that the disease occurs at unusually high rates in creative people, such as artists, writers, and musicians. But some researchers contend that the methodology of these studies was flawed and their results were misleading. In the October 1996 Discover Magazine article, anthropologist Jo Ann C. Gutin presents the results of several studies that explore the link between creativity and mental illness.

People with schizophrenia and other psychotic disorders lose contact with reality. Symptoms may include delusions and hallucinations, disorganized thinking and speech, bizarre behaviour, a diminished range of emotional responsiveness, and social withdrawal. In addition, people who suffer from these illnesses experience and inability function operates in one or more important areas of life, such as social relations, work, or school.

Personality disorders are mental illnesses in which one's personality results in personal distress or a significant impairment in social or work functioning. In general, people with personality disorders have poor perceptions of themselves or others. They may have low self-esteem or overwhelming narcissism, poor impulse control, troubled social relationships, and inappropriate emotional responses. Considerable controversy exists over where to draw the distinction between a normal personality and a personality disorder.

Cognitive disorders, such as delirium and dementia, involve a significant loss of mental functioning. Dementia, for example, is characterized by impaired memory and difficulties in such functions as speaking, abstract thinking, and the ability to identify familiar objects. The conditions in this category usually result from a medical condition, substance abuse, or adverse reactions to medication or poisonous substances.

Dissociative disorders involve disturbances in a person's consciousness, memories, identity, and perception of the environment. Dissociative disorders include amnesia that has no physical cause; Dissociative identity disorders, in which a person has what more is less, such are the considerations in having two or more distinct personalities that alternate in their control of the person's behaviour; depersonalization disorder, characterized by a chronic feeling of being detached from one's body or mental processes; and Dissociative fugue, an episode of sudden departure from home or work with an accompanying loss of memory. In some parts of the world people experience Dissociative states as 'possession', is that by a god or ghost instead of separate personalities, insofar as many societies, a trance and possession states are normal parts of cultural and religious practices, as well as, to what they are, and not too considered for Dissociative disorders.

Somatoform disorders are characterized by the presence of physical symptoms that cannot be explained by a medical condition or another mental illness. Thus, physicians often judge that such symptoms result from psychological conflicts or distress. For example, in conversion disorder, also called hysteria, a person may experience blindness, deafness, or seizures, but a physician cannot find anything wrong with the person. People with another somatoform disorder, hypochondriasis, constantly fear that they will develop a serious disease and misinterpret minor physical symptoms as evidence of illness.

Substance-related disorders result from the abuse of drugs, side effects of medications, or exposure to toxic substances. Many mental health professionals regard these disorders as behavioural or addictive disorders rather than as mental illnesses, although substance-related disorders commonly occur in people with mental illnesses. Common substance-related disorders include alcoholism and other forms of drug dependence. In addition, drug use can contribute to symptoms of other mental disorders, such as depression, anxiety, and psychosis. Drugs associated with substance-related disorders include alcohol, caffeine, nicotine, cocaine, heroin, amphetamines, hallucinogens, and sedatives.

Eating disorders are conditions in which an individual experience severe disturbances in eating behaviours. People with anorexia nervosa have an intense fear about gaining weight and refuse to eat adequately or maintain a normal body weight. People with bulimia nervosa repeatedly engage in episodes of binge eating, usually followed by self-induced vomiting or the use of laxatives, diuretics, or other medications to prevent weight gain. Eating disorders occur mostly among young women in Western societies and certain parts of Asia.

People with impulse-control disorders cannot control an impulse to engage in harmful behaviours, such as explosive anger, stealing (kleptomania), setting fires (pyromania), gambling, or pulling out their own hair (trichotillomania). Some mental illnesses - such as mania, schizophrenia, and antisocial personality disorder - may include symptoms of impulsive behaviour.

People have tried to understand the causes of mental illness for thousands of years. The modern era of psychiatry, which began in the late 19th and early 20th centuries, has witnessed a sharp debate between biological and psychological perspectives of mental illness. The biological perspective views mental illness in terms of bodily processes, whereas psychological perspectives emphasize the roles of a person's upbringing and environment.

These two perspectives are exemplified in the work of German psychiatrist Emil Kraepelin and Austrian psychoanalyst Sigmund Freud. Kraepelin, influenced by the work in the mid-1800's of German psychiatrist Wilhelm Griesinger, believed that psychiatric disorders were disease entities that could be classified like physical illnesses. That is, Kraepelin believed that the fundamental causes of mental illness lay in the physiology and biochemistry of the human brain. His classification system of mental disorders, first published in 1883, formed the basis for later diagnostic systems. Freud, on the other hand, argued that the source of mental illness lay in unconscious conflicts originating in early childhood experiences. Freud found evidence for this idea through the analysis of dreams, free association, and slips of speech.

This debate has continued into the late 20th century. Beginning in the 1960's, the biological perspective became dominant, supported by numerous breakthroughs in psychopharmacology, genetics, neurophysiology, and brain research. For example, scientists discovered many medications that helped to relieve symptoms of certain mental illnesses and demonstrated that people can inherit a vulnerability to some mental illnesses. Psychological perspectives also remain influential, including the psychodynamic perspective, the humanistic and existential perspectives, the behavioural perspective, the cognitive perspective, and the Sociocultural perspective.

Psychiatry has increasingly emphasized a biological basis for the causes of mental illness. Studies suggest a genetic influence in some mental illnesses, such as schizophrenia and bipolar disorder, although the evidence is not conclusive.

Clinical depression is one of the most common forms of mental illness. Although depression can be treated with psychotherapy, many scientists believe there are biological causes for the disease. In the June 1998 Scientific American article, neurobiologist Charles B. Nemeroff reports upon the connection between biochemical changes in the brain and depression.

Scientists have identified a number of neurotransmitters, or chemical substances that enable brain cells to communicate with other, that appears important in regulating a person's emotions and behaviour. These include dopamine, serotonin, norepinephrine, gamma-amino butyric acid (GABA), and acetylcholine. Excesses and deficiencies in levels of these neurotransmitters have been associated with depression, anxiety, and schizophrenia, but scientists have yet to determine the exact mechanisms involved.

Research shows that the more genetically related a person is to someone with schizophrenia, the greater the risk that person has of developing the illness. For example, children of one parent with schizophrenia have a 13 percent chance of developing the illness, whereas children of two parents with schizophrenia have a 46 percent chance of developing the disorder.

A variety of medical conditions can cause mental illness. Brain damage and strokes can cause loss of memory, impaired concentration and speech, and unusual changes in behaviour. In addition, brain tumours, if left to grow, can cause psychosis and personality changes. Other possible biological factors in mental illness include an imbalance of hormones, deficiencies in diet, and infections from viruses.

In the late 19th century Viennese neurologist Sigmund Freud developed a theory of personality and a system of psychotherapy known as psychoanalysis. According to this theory, people are strongly influenced by unconscious forces, including innate sexual and aggressive drives.

The psychodynamic perspective views mental illness is caused by unconscious and unresolved conflicts in the mind. As stated by Freud, these conflicts arise in early childhood and may cause mental illness by impeding the balanced development of the three systems that constitute the human psyche: the id, which comprises innate sexual and aggressive drives - the ego, - the conscious portion of the mind that mediates between the unconscious and reality and superego, which controls the primitive impulses of the id and represents moral ideals. In this view, generalized anxiety disorder stems from a signal of unconscious danger whose source can only be identified through a thorough analysis of the person's personality and life experiences. Present and current views on psychodynamic theorists tend to emphasize sexuality less than Freud did and focus more on problems in the individual's relationships with others.

Both the humanistic and existential perspectives view abnormal behaviour as resulting from a person's failure to find meaning in life and fulfill his or her potential. The humanistic school of psychology, as represented in the work of American psychologist Carl Rogers, views mental health and personal growth as the natural conditions of human life. In Rogers's view, every person possesses a drive toward self-actualization, the fulfilment of one's greatest potential. Mental illness develops when a person's condition by some circumstantial environment interferes with this drive. The existential perspective sees emotional disturbances as the result of a person's failure to act authentically - that is, to behave in accordance with one's own goals and values, rather than the goals and values of others.

The pioneers of behaviourism, American psychologist's John B. Watson and B. F. Skinner, maintained that psychology should confine itself to the study of observable behaviour, rather than explore a person's unconscious feelings. The behavioural perspective explains mental illness, as well as all of human behaviour, as a learned response to, malaria, and infection's stimuli. In this view, rewards and punishments in a person's environment shape that person's behaviour, for example, a person involved in a serious car accident may develop a phobia of cars or the generalized fear to all forms of transportation.

The cognitive perspective holds that mental illness result from problems in cognition - that is, problems in how a person reasons, perceives events, and solves problems. American psychiatrist Aaron Beck proposed that some mental illnesses - such as depression, anxiety disorders, and personality disorders - result from a way of thinking learned in childhood that is not consistent with reality. For example, people with depression tend to see themselves in a negative light, exaggerate the importance of minor flaws or failures, and misinterpret the behaviour of others in negative ways. It remains unclear, however, whether these kinds of cognitive problems actually cause mental illness or merely represent symptoms of the illnesses themselves.

The Sociocultural perspective regards mental illness as the result of social, economic, and cultural factors. Evidence for this view comes from research that has demonstrated an increased risk of mental illness among people living in poverty. In addition, the incidence of mental illness rises in times of high unemployment. The shift in the world population from rural areas to cities - with their crowding, noise, pollution, decay, and social isolation - and, has also, been implicated in causing relatively high rates of mental illness. Furthermore, rapid social change, which has particularly affected indigenous peoples throughout the world, brings about high rates of suicide and alcoholism. Refugees and victims of social disasters - warfare, displacement, genocide, violence - have a higher risk of mental illness, especially depression, anxiety, and post-traumatic stress disorder.

Social scientists emphasize that the link between social ills and mental illness is correlational rather than causal. For example, although societies undergoing rapid social change often have high rates of suicide the specific causes have not been identified. Social and cultural factors may create relative risks for a population or class of people, but it is unclear how such factors raise the risk of mental illness for an individual.

There are no blood tests, imaging techniques, or other laboratory procedures that can reliably diagnose a mental illness. Thus, the diagnosis of mental illness is always a judgment or an interpretation by an observer based on the spoken exchange, ideas, behaviours, and experiences of the patient.

For the most part, mental health professionals determine the presence of mental illness in an individual by conducting an interview intended to reveal symptoms of abnormal behaviour. That is, the professional asks the patient questions about their mental state: "Do you hear voices of people who are not with you?" "Have you felt depressed or lost interest in most activities?" "Have you experienced a marked increase or decrease in your appetite?" "Have you been sleeping less than normal?" "Are you easily distracted?" The answers to these questions will suggest other questions. Eventually, the clinician will feel that he or she has enough information to determine whether the patient is suffering from a mental illness and, if so, to make a diagnosis.

The process of diagnosis is not as simple as it might seem. Patients often have difficulty remembering symptoms or feel reluctant to talk about their fantasies, sex life, or use of drugs and alcohol. Many patients suffer in forms that are more than there is one disorder at a time - for example, depression and anxiety, or schizophrenia and depression - and determining which symptoms constitute the primary problem is complex. In addition, symptoms may not be specific to mental illnesses. For example, brain tumours of the central nervous system can produce symptoms that mimic those of the Psychotic disorders.

Another problem in diagnosis is that mental health professionals may interpret symptoms differently based on their personal or cultural biases. One study examined this effect by showing 300 American and British psychiatrists videotaped interviews of eight patients with mental illnesses. Although the psychiatrists' diagnoses substantially agreed for patients with "textbook" cases of schizophrenia, their diagnoses varied widely for patients who had symptoms of both schizophrenia and other disorders, depending on whether the psychiatrist was American or British. The risk of misdiagnosis is even greater when the mental health professional and the patient come from different cultural groups.

Mental health professionals use a number of methods to treat people with mental illnesses. The two most common treatments by far are drug therapy and psychotherapy. In drug therapy, a person takes regular doses of a prescription medication intended to reduce symptoms of mental illness. Psychotherapy is the treatment of mental illness through verbal and nonverbal communication between the patient and a trained professional. A person can receive psychotherapy individually or in a group setting.

The type of treatment administered depends on the type and severity of the disorder. For example, doctors usually treat schizophrenia primarily with drugs, but specialized forms of psychotherapy may more effectively relieve phobias. For some mental illnesses, such as depression, the most effective treatment seems to be a combination of drug therapy and psychotherapy. Although some people with severe mental illnesses may never fully recover, most people with mental illnesses improve with treatment and can resume normal lives. Despite the availability of effective treatments, only about 40 percent of people with mental illnesses ever seek professional help.

A variety of mental health professionals offer treatment for mental illness. These include psychiatrists, psychologists, psychotherapists, psychiatric social workers, and psychiatric nurses.

Drugs introduced by the mid-1950's had enabled many people who otherwise would have spent years in mental institutions to return to the community and live productive lives. Since then, advances in psychopharmacology have led to the development of drugs of even greater effectiveness. These drugs often relieve symptoms of schizophrenia, depression, anxiety, and other disorders. However, they may produce undesirable and sometimes serious side effects. In addition, relapse may occur when they are discontinued, so long-term use may be required. Drugs that control symptoms of mental illness are called psychotherapeutic substance or preparation, in that a substance used by itself or in a mixture in the treatment of or the dependence on drugs, if only to make it bearable. The major categories of psychotherapeutic drugs include antipsychotic drugs, Antianxiety drugs, antidepressant drugs, and antimanic drugs.

Antipsychotic drugs, also called neuroleptics and major tranquillizers, control symptoms of psychosis, such as hallucinations and delusions, which characterize schizophrenia and related disorders. They can also prevent such symptoms from returning. Antipsychotic drugs may produce side effects ranging from dry mouth and blurred vision to tardive dyskinesia. The occasioning of Panic Disorders, is a mental illness in which a person experiences repeated, unexpected panic attacks and persistent anxiety about the possibility that the panic attacks will recur. A panic attack is a period of intense fear, apprehension, or discomfort. In panic disorder, the attacks usually occur without warning. Symptoms include a racing heart, shortness of breath, trembling, choking or smothering sensations, and fears of "going crazy," losing control, or dying from a heart attack. Panic attacks may last from a few seconds to several hours. Most peak within 10 minutes and render of their potentialities or peak, within 20 or 30 minutes.

About 2 percent of people in the United States suffer from panic disorder during any given year, and the condition affects more than twice as many women as men. People with panic disorder may experience panic attacks frequently, such as daily or weekly, or more sporadically. Additionally, panic attacks may occur as part of other anxiety disorders, such as phobias - in which a specific object or situation triggers the attack - and, more rarely, post-traumatic stress disorder.

People with panic disorder frequently develop agoraphobia, a fear of being in places or situations from which escape might be difficult if a panic attack occurs. People with agoraphobia typically fear situations such as travelling in a bus, train, car, or aeroplane, shopping at malls, going to theatres, crossing over bridges or through tunnels, and being alone in unfamiliar places. Therefore, they avoid these situations and may eventually become reluctant to leave their home. In addition, people with panic disorder appear to have an increased risk of alcoholism and drug dependence. Some studies indicate they also have a higher risk of depression and suicide.

Panic disorder, and both with and without agoraphobia, result from a combination of biological and psychological factors. Some individuals may inherit a vulnerability to accentuation and the availing of anxiety and an increased risk of experiencing panic attacks. In addition, certain physiological cues may trigger a panic attack. For example, if a person experiences a racing heart during a panic attack, he or she may begin to associate this sensation with panic attacks. An accelerated heart beat can be addictive and may impair movement and concentration in some people. Some antidepressant drugs, such as imipramine (Tofranil), also reduce panic symptoms in some people but can produce side effects such as dizziness or dry mouth. Another class of drugs, selective serotonin reuptake inhibitors (SSRIs), appears to reduce panic symptoms with fewer side effects. SSRIs used to treat panic disorder, would remedially need paroxetine (Paxil) and fluvoxamine (Luvox). Medication eliminates panic symptoms in 50 to 60 percent of patients. For many patients, however, panic attacks return when they stop taking the medication.

Research has shown that cognitive-behavioural therapy, a type of psychotherapy, eliminates panic attacks in 80 to 100 percent of patients. In this method, therapists help patients re-create the physical symptoms of a panic attack, teach them coping skills, and help them to alter their beliefs about the danger of these sensations. Patients with agoraphobia face their feared situations under the therapist's supervision, using coping skills to overcome their strong anxiety. These coping skills may include physical relaxation techniques, such as deep breathing and muscle relaxation, as well as cognitive techniques that help people think rationally about anxiety-provoking situations. About 70 percent of panic disorders patients who also have moderate to severe agoraphobia benefit from this type of treatment.

Antianxiety drugs, also called minor tranquillizers, reduce high levels of anxiety. They may help people with generalized anxiety disorder, panic disorder, and other anxiety disorders. Benzodiazepines, a class of drugs that includes diazepam (Valium), are the most widely prescribed Antianxiety drugs. Benzodiazepines can be addictive and may cause drowsiness and impaired coordination during the day.

Antidepressant drugs help relieve symptoms of depression. Some antidepressant drugs can relieve symptoms of other disorders as well, such as panic disorder and obsessive-compulsive disorder.

Antidepressant drugs comprise three major classes: Tricyclics, monoamine oxidase inhibitors (MAO inhibitors), and selective serotonin reuptake inhibitors (SSRIs). Side effects of tricyclics may include dizziness upon standing, blurred vision, dry mouth, difficulty urinating, constipation, and drowsiness. People who take MAO inhibitors may experience some of the same side effects, and must follow a special diet that excludes certain foods. SSRIs generally produce fewer side effects, although these may include anxiety, drowsiness, and sexual dysfunction. One type of SSRI, Fluoxetine (Prozac), is the most widely prescribed antidepressant drug.

Antimanic drugs help control the mania that occurs as part of bipolar disorder. One of the most effective antimanic drugs is lithium carbonate, a natural mineral salt. Common side effects include nausea, stomach upset, vertigo, and increased thirst and urination. In addition, long-term use of lithium can damage the kidneys.

Psychotherapy can be an effective treatment for many mental illnesses. Unlike drug therapy, psychotherapy produces no physical side effects, although it can cause psychological damage when improperly administered. On the other hand, psychotherapy may take longer than drugs to produce benefits. In addition, sessions may be expensive and time-consuming. In response to this complaint and demands from insurance companies to reduce the costs of mental health treatment, many therapists have started providing therapy of shorter duration.

Psychotherapy encompasses a wide range of techniques and practices. Some forms of psychotherapy, such as psychodynamic therapy and humanistic therapy, focus on helping people understand the internal motivations for their problematic behaviour. Other forms of therapy, such as behavioural therapy and cognitive therapy, focus one's actions in general or on a particular occasion, should, in the manner of recognizing the controversial behaviour communicative impact, which to cause to acquire knowledge for which of people skills are essential to set right in that as wrong must be corrected. The majority of therapists today incorporate treatment techniques from a number of theoretical perspectives. For example, cognitive-behavioural therapy combines aspects of cognitive therapy and behavioural therapy.

Psychodynamic therapy is one of the most common forms of psychotherapy. The therapist focuses on a person's past experiences as a source of internal, unconscious conflicts and tries to help the person resolve those conflicts. Some therapists may use hypnosis to uncover repressed memories. Psychoanalysis, a technique developed by Freud, is one kind of psychodynamic therapy. In psychoanalysis, the person lies on a couch and says whatever comes to mind, a process called free association. The therapist interprets these thoughts along with the person's dreams and memories. Classical psychoanalysis, which requires years of intensive treatment, is not as widely practised today as in previous years.

Both humanistic therapy and existential therapy treat mental illnesses by helping people achieve personal growth and attain meaning in life. The best-known humanistic therapy is client-centred therapy, developed by Carl Rogers in the 1950's. In this technique, the therapist provides no advice but restates the observations and insights of the client (the person in treatment) in nonjudgmental terms. In addition, the therapist offers the person unconditional empathy and acceptance. Existential therapists help people confront basic questions about the meaning of their lives and guide them toward discovery of their own uniqueness.

Psychotherapists whom practice behavioural therapies do not focus on a person's past experiences or inner life, instead, they help the person to change their conduct behavioural, and patterns of abnormal behaviour by applying established principles of conditioning and of learning. Behavioural therapy has proven effective in the treatment of phobias, obsessive-compulsive disorder, and other disorders.

The Obsessive-Compulsive Disorder categorized the mental illness in which a person experiences recurrent, intrusive thoughts (obsessions) and feels compelled to perform certain behaviours (compulsions) again and again. Most people have experienced bizarre or inappropriate thoughts and have engaged in repetitive behaviours at times. However, people with obsessive-compulsive disorder find that their disturbing thoughts and behaviours consume large amounts of time, cause them anxiety and distress, and interfere with their ability to function at work and in social activities. Most people with this disorder recognize that their obsessions and compulsions are irrational but cannot suppress them.

Obsessive-compulsive disorder usually begins in adolescence or early adulthood. It effects from 1.5 to 2 percent of people in the United States, as the disorder affects that are slightly more prominent in women than men.

Obsessions can include a variety of thoughts, images, and impulses. Common obsessions include fears of contamination from germs, doubts about whether doors are locked or appliances are turned off, nonsensical impulses such as shouting in public, sexual thoughts that are disturbing to the individual, and thoughts of accidentally and unknowingly harming someone. People with obsessions may avoid shaking hands with other people because they fear contamination, or they may avoid driving because they fear they will injure someone in a traffic accident.

People usually perform compulsions to relieve the anxiety produced by their obsessions, although not all people with obsessions perform compulsions. The most common compulsions involve cleaning rituals and checking rituals. For example, people with obsessions about germs may wash their hand's dozens of times each day until their skin becomes raw. People with obsessions about neatness and symmetry may constantly rearrange or straighten objects on their desk. People with checking compulsions must repeatedly check to make sure they locked doors and windows or turned off water faucets. Other compulsions include counting objects, hoarding vast amounts of useless materials, and repeating words or prayers internally.

Obsessive-compulsive disorder can have disabling effects on people's lives. People with severe cases of this disorder may need hospitalization to help treat the compulsions. In fewer extreme instances, individuals with compulsions often must allow a great deal of extra time to complete seemingly routine tasks, such as preparing to leave the house in the morning. Individuals may avoid going to certain places or engaging in certain activities because they feel embarrassed about their behaviour.

In addition, family members of someone with this disorder may feel angry at the person because the compulsive behaviours intrude on their time together or interfere with the family's functioning. For instance, some individuals hoard things, such as newspapers or magazines, because they believe they may someday need certain pieces of information. The piles of newspapers may cover the living areas and make other family members feel embarrassed to have guests in the home.

Like many other mental illnesses, obsessive-compulsive disorder appears to result from a combination of biological and psychological influences. Some people may have a biological predisposition to experience anxiety. Research also suggests that abnormal levels of the neurotransmitter serotonin may play a role in obsessive-compulsive disorder. Brain scans of people with obsessive-compulsive disorder have revealed abnormalities in the activity level of the orbital cortex, cingulate cortex, and caudate nucleus, a brain circuit that helps control movements of the limbs.

The disorder may develop when these biological influences combine with a psychological vulnerability to anxiety. Some people may develop a psychological vulnerability to anxiety in childhood. They may come to believe that the world is a potentially dangerous place over which one has little control. People seem to develop obsessive-compulsive disorder specifically when they learn that some thoughts are dangerous or unacceptable and, while attempting to suppress these thoughts, develop anxiety about the recurrence of the thoughts and about the perceived dangerousness and intrusiveness of the thoughts.

Treatment for obsessive-compulsive disorder includes psychotherapy, psychoactive drugs, or both. Mental health professionals consider exposure and response prevention, a type of cognitive-behavioural therapy, to be the most effective form of psychotherapy for this disorder. In this technique, the therapist exposes the patient to feared thoughts or situations and prevents the patient from acting on their own compulsion. For example, a therapist might have patients with cleaning compulsions touch something dirty and then prevent them from washing their hands. This technique helps 60 to 70 percent of people with obsessive-compulsive disorder.

Medications to treat obsessive-compulsive disorder are made up of selective serotonin reuptake inhibitors, such as Fluoxetine (Prozac) and fluvoxamine (Luvox). A tricyclic antidepressant, clomipramine (Anafranil), also helps relieve symptoms of the disorder. About 80 percent of people with the disorder show some improvement with a combined treatment of medication and behavioural therapy. However, many patients relapse when they stop taking the medication.

The goal of cognitive therapy is to identify patterns of irrational thinking that cause a person to behave abnormally. The therapist teaches skills that enable the person to recognize the irrationality of the thoughts. The person eventually learns to perceive people, situations, and himself or herself in a more realistic way and develops improved problem-solving and coping skills. Psychotherapists use cognitive therapy to treat depression, panic disorder, and some personality disorders.

Rehabilitation programs assist people with severe mental illnesses in learning independent living skills and in obtaining community services. Counsellors may teach them personal hygiene skills, home cleaning and maintenance, meal preparation, social skills, and employment skills. In addition, case managers or social workers may help people with mental illnesses obtain employment, medical care, housing, education, and social services. Some intensive rehabilitation programs strive to provide active follow-up and social support to prevent hospitalization.

Therapists often use play therapy to treat young children with depression, anxiety disorders, and problems stemming from child abuse and neglect. The therapist spends time with the child in a playroom filled with dolls, puppets, and drawing materials, which the child may use to act out personal and family conflicts. The therapist helps the child recognize and confront their own feelings.

In group therapy, a number of people gather together to discuss problems under the guidance of a therapist. By sharing their feelings and experiences with others, group members learn their problems are not unique, receive emotional support, and learn ways to cope with their problems. Psychodrama is a type of group therapy in which participants act out emotional conflicts, often on a stage, with the goals of increasing their understanding of their behaviours and resolving conflicts. Group therapy generally costs less per person than individual psychotherapy.

Family intervention programs help families learn to cope with and manage a family member's chronic mental illness, such as schizophrenia. Family members learn to monitor the illness, help with daily life problems, ensure adherence to medication, and cope with stigma.

Electroconvulsive therapy (ECT) is a treatment for severe depression in which an electrical current is passed through the patient's brain for one or two seconds to induce a controlled seizure. The treatments are repeated over a period of several weeks. For unknown reasons, ECT often relieves severe depression even when drug therapy and psychotherapy have failed. The treatment has created controversy because its side effects may include confusion and memory loss. Both of these effects, however, are usually temporary.

Seeking a treatment for extreme cases of mental illness, Portuguese neurologist António Egas Moniz invented the lobotomy, a surgical technique that destroys tissue in the frontal lobe of the brain. The procedures, widely performed in the 1940s and 1950s, often leaving the person in a vegetative state or caused drastic changes in personality and behaviour.

Even more controversial than ECT is Psychosurgery, the surgical removal or destruction of sections of the brain in order to reduce severe and chronic psychiatric symptoms. The best-known example of Psychosurgery is the lobotomy, a procedure developed by Portuguese neurologist António Egas Moniz that was widely performed in the 1940's and early 1950's. Psychosurgery is now rarely performed because no research has proven it effective and because it can produce drastic changes in personality and behaviour.

A significant portion of the homeless population in the United States suffers from a chronic mental illness, such as schizophrenia. The shortage of mental health treatment centres in many cities may partly account for the large number of mentally ill people who are homeless or in jail.

Treatment for mental illness takes places in a number of settings. Mental hospitals or psychiatric wards in general hospitals are used to treat patients in acute phases of their illnesses and when the severity of their symptoms requires constant supervision. Most individuals who suffer from severe mental illness, however, do not require such close attention, and they can usually receive treatment in community settings.

Often, patients who have just completed a period of hospitalization go to group homes or halfway houses before returning to independent living. These facilities offer patients the opportunity to take part in group activities and to receive training in social and job skills. In supportive housing, mentally ill individuals can live independently in an environment that offers an array of mental health and social services. Some people with chronic and severe mental illnesses require care in long-term facilities, such as nursing homes, where they can receive close supervision.

Not all ancient scholars agreed with this theory of mental illness. The Greek physician Hippocrates believed that all illnesses, including mental illnesses, had natural origins. For example, he rejected the prevailing notion that epilepsy had its origins in the divine or sacred, viewing it as a disease of the brain. Hippocrates categorically considered mental illnesses as itemized positions, in that to include mania, melancholia (depression), and phrenitis (brain fever), and he advocated humane treatment that included rest, bathing, exercise, and dieting. The Greek philosopher Plato, although adhering to a somewhat supernatural view of mental illness, believed that childhood experiences shaped adult behaviours, anticipating the present and current psychodynamic theories by more than 2000 years.

The Middle Ages in Europe, from the fall of the Roman empire in the 5th century ad too about the 15th century, was a period in which religious beliefs, specifically Christianity, dominated concepts of mental illness. Much of the society believed that mentally ill people were possessed by the devil or demons, or accused them of being witches and infecting others with madness. Thus, instead of receiving care from physicians, the mentally ill became objects of religious inquisition and barbaric treatment. On the other hand, some historians of medicine cite evidence that evens in the Middle Ages, many people believed mental illness to have its basis in physical and psychological disturbances, such as imbalances in the four bodily humours (blood, black bile, yellow bile, and phlegm), poor diet, and grief.

The Islamic world of North Africa, Spain, and the Middle East generally held far more humane attitudes toward people with mental illnesses. Following the belief that God loved insane people, communities began establishing asylums beginning in the 8th century ad, first in Baghdad and later in Cairo, Damascus, and Fez. The asylums offered patients special diets, baths, drugs, music, and pleasant surroundings.

The Renaissance, which began in Italy in the 14th century and spread throughout Europe in the 16th and 17th century, brought both deterioration and progress in perceptions of mental illness. On the one hand, witch-hunts and executions escalated throughout Europe, as of relating to the mind, the mental aspects of the problem, is that the mentally ill, and among them were in vengeance a reprisal for they're merciless persecuted. The infamous Malleus Maleficarum (The Witches Hammer or, Hammer of the Witch) which served as a handbook for inquisitors, claimed that witches could be identified by delusions, hallucinations, or other peculiar behaviours. To make matters worse, many of the most eminent physicians of the time fervently advocated these beliefs.

On the other hand, some scholars vigorously protested these supernatural views and called renewed attention to more rational explanations of behaviour. In the early 16th century, for example, the Swiss physician Paracelsus returned to the views of Hippocrates, asserting that mental illnesses were due to natural causes. Later in the century, German physician Johann Weyer argued that witches were actually mentally disturbed people in need of humane medical treatment.

French physician Philippe Pinel supervises the unshackling of mentally ill patients in 1794 at La Salpêtrière, a large hospital in Paris. Pinel believed in treating mentally ill people with compassion and patience, rather than with cruelty and violence.

During the Age of Enlightenment, in the 18th and early 19th centuries, people with mental illnesses continued to suffer from poor treatment. For the most part, they were left to wander the countryside or committed to institutions. In either case, conditions were generally wretched. One mental hospital, the Hospital of Saint Mary of Bethlehem in London, England, became notorious for its noisy, chaotic conditions and cruel treatment of patients.

Yet as the public's awareness of such conditions grew, improvements in care and treatment began to appear. In 1789 Vincenzo Chiarugi, superintendent of a mental hospital in Florence, Italy, introduced hospital regulations that provided patients with high standards of hygiene, recreation and work opportunities, and minimal restraint. At nearly the same time, Jean-Baptiste Pussin, superintendent of a ward for 'incurable' mental patients at La Bicêtre hospital in Paris, France, forbade staff to beat patients and released patients from chains. Philippe Pinel continued these reforms upon becoming chief physician of La Bicêtre's ward for the mentally ill in 1793. Pinel began to keep case histories of patients and developed the concept of 'moral treatment,' which involved treating patients with kindness and sensitivity, and without cruelty or violence. In 1796, a Quaker named William Tuke who had laid the groundwork for the York Retreat in rural England, which became a model of compassionate care. The retreat enabled people with mental illnesses to rest peacefully, talk about their problems, and work. Eventually these humane techniques became widespread in Europe.

In 1908, after his release from an asylum for the mentally ill, Clifford Whittingham Beers wrote, "A Mind That Found Itself," which exposed the poor conditions he had suffered while confined. He went on to establish several organizations dedicated to the promotion of mental health reforms in the United States.

People living in the colonies of North America in the 17th and 18th century generally explained bizarre or deviant behaviour as God's will or the obstacle working as of the devil. Some people with mental illnesses received care from their families, but most were jailed or confined in almshouses with the poor and infirm. By the mid-18th century, however, American physicians came to view mental illnesses as diseases of the brain, and advocated specialized facilities to treat the mentally ill. The Pennsylvania Hospital in Philadelphia, which opened in 1752, became the first hospital in the American colonies to admit people with mental illnesses, housing them in a separate ward. However, in the hospital's early years, mentally ill patients were chained to the walls of dark, cold cells.

In the 1780s American physician Benjamin Rush instituted changes at the Pennsylvania Hospital that greatly improved conditions for mentally ill patients. Although he endorsed the continued use of restraints, punishment, and bleeding, he also arranged for heat and better ventilation in the wards, separation of violent patients from other patients, and programs that offered work, exercise, and recreation to patients. Between the years 1817 and 1828, following the examples of Tuke and Pinel, a number of institutions opened that devoted themselves exclusively to the care of mentally ill people. The first private mental hospital in the United States was the Asylum for the Relief of Persons Deprived of the Use of Their Reason (now Friends Hospital), opened by Quakers in 1817 in what is now Philadelphia. Other privately established institutions soon followed, and state-sponsored hospitals - in Kentucky, New York, Virginia, and South Carolina - opened beginning in 1824.

American reformer Dorothea Dix championed the causes of prison inmates, the mentally ill, and the destitute. Horrified by the conditions provided for the mentally ill in Massachusetts. Dix successfully petitioned the state government for improvements in 1843. She was directly responsible for building or enlarging 32 mental hospitals in North America, Europe, and Japan.

Nevertheless, circumstances for most mentally ill people in the United States, especially those who were poor, remained dreadful. In 1841 Dorothea Dix, a Boston school teacher, began a campaign to make the public aware of the plight of mentally ill people. By 1880, as a direct result of her efforts, 32 psychiatric hospitals for the poor had opened. Increasingly, society viewed psychiatric institutions as the most appropriate form of care for people with mental illnesses. However, by the late 19th century, conditions in these institutions had deteriorated. Overcrowded and understaffed, psychiatric hospitals had shifted their treatment approach from moral therapy to warehousing and punishment. In 1908 Clifford Whittingham Beers aroused new concern for mentally ill individuals with the publication of A Mind That Found Itself, an account of his experiences as a mental patient. In 1909 Beers founded the National Committee for Mental Hygiene, which worked to prevent mental illness and ensure humane treatment of the mentally ill.

Following World War II (1939-1945), a movement emerged in the United States to reform the system of psychiatric hospitals, in which hundreds of thousands of mentally ill persons lived in isolation for years or decades. Many mental health professionals - seeing that large state institutions caused as much, if not more, harm to patients than mental illnesses themselves - came to believe that only patients with severe symptoms should be hospitalized. In addition, the development in the 1950s of antipsychotic drugs, which helped to control bizarre and violent behaviour, allowed more patients to be treated in the community. In combination, these factors led to the deinstitutionalisation movement: the release, over the next four decades, of hundreds of thousands of patients from state mental hospitals. In 1950, 513,000 patients resided in these institutions. By 1965 there were 475,000, and 1990 states' mental hospitals housed only 92,000 patients on any given night. Many patients who were released returned to their families, although many were transferred to questionable conditions in nursing homes or board-and-care homes. Many patients had no place to go and began to live on the streets.

The National Mental Health Act of 1946 created the National Institute of Mental Health as a centre for research and funding of research on mental illness. In 1955 Congress created a commission to investigate the state of mental health care, treatment, and prevention. In 1963, as a result of the commission's findings, Congress passed the Community Mental Health Centres Act, had authorized the construction of community mental health centres throughout the country. Implementation of these centres was not as extensive as originally planned, and many people with severe mental illnesses failed to receive care of any kind.

One of the most important developments in the field of mental health in the United States has been the establishment of advocacy and support groups. The National Alliance for The Mentally ill (NAMI), one of the most influential of these groups, was founded in 1972.

NAMI's goal is to improve the lives of people with severe mental illnesses and their families by eliminating discrimination in housing and employment and by improving access to essential treatments and programs.

During the 1980's, all levels of government in the United States cut back on funding for social services. For example, the Social Security Administration discontinued benefits for approximately 300,000 people between 1981 and 1983. Of these, an estimated 100,000 were people with mental illnesses. Although the government eventually restored Social Security benefits to many of these people, the interruption of services caused widespread hardship.

The emergence of managed care in the 1990's as a way to contain health care costs had a tremendous impact on mental health care in the United States. Health insurance companies and health maintenance organizations increasingly scrutinized the effectiveness of various psychotherapies and drug treatments and put stricter limits on mental health care. In response to these restrictions, but congress passed the Mental Health Parity Act of 1996. This law required private medical plans that offer mental health coverage to set equal yearly and lifetime payment limits for coverage of both mental and physical illnesses.

In 1997 the US Equal Employment Opportunity Commission issued new guidelines intended to prevent discrimination against people with mental illnesses in the workplace. The rules, based on the Americans with Disabilities Act of 1990, prohibit employers from asking job applicants if they have a history of mental illness and require employers to provide reasonable accommodations to workers with mental illnesses.

In recent years international agencies, led by the World Health Organization (WHO) of the United Nations (UN) have developed mental health policies that seek to reduce the huge burden of mental illness worldwide. These agencies are working to improve the quality of mental health services in Africa, Asia, Latin America, the Middle East, and elsewhere by educating governments on prevention and treatment of mental illness and on the rights of the mentally ill.

Psychiatry, is the branch of medicine specializing in mental illnesses. Psychiatrists not only diagnose and treat these disorders but also conduct research directed at understanding and preventing them.

A psychiatrist is a doctor of medicine who has had four years of postgraduate training in psychiatry. Many psychiatrists take further training in psychoanalysis, child psychiatry, or other subspecialties. Psychiatrists treat patients in private practice, in general hospitals, or in specialized facilities for the mentally ill (psychiatric hospitals, outpatient clinics, or community mental health centres). Some spend part or all of their time doing research or administering mental health programs. By contrast, psychologists, who often work closely with psychiatrists and treat many of the same kinds of patients, are not trained in medicine; consequently, they neither diagnose physical illness nor administer drugs.

The province of psychiatry is unusually broad for a medical specialty. Mental disorders may affect most aspects of a patient's life, including physical functioning, behaviour, emotions, thought, perception, interpersonal relationships, sexuality, work, and play. These disorders are caused by a poorly understood combination of biological, psychological, and social determinants. Psychiatry's task is to account for the diverse sources and manifestations of mental illness.

Physicians in the Western world began specializing in the treatment of the mentally ill in the 19th century. Known as alienists, psychiatrists of that era worked in large asylums, practising what was then called moral treatment, a humane approach aimed at quieting mental turmoil and restoring reason. During the second half of the century, psychiatrists abandoned this mode of treatment and, with it, the tacit recognition that mental illness is caused by both psychological and social influences. For a while, their attention focussed almost exclusively on biological factors. Drugs and other forms of somatic (physical) treatment was common. The German psychiatrist Emil Kraepelin identified and classified mental disorders into a system that is the foundation for modern diagnostic practices. Another important figure was the Swiss psychiatrist Eugen Bleuler, who coined the word schizophrenia and described its characteristics.

The discovery of unconscious sources of behaviour - an insight dominated by the psychoanalytic writings of Sigmund Freud in the early 20th century - enriched psychiatric thought and changed the direction of its practice. Attention shifted to processes within the individual psyche, and psychoanalysis came to be regarded as the preferred mode of treatment for most mental disorders. In the years 1940 and the 1950s emphasis shifted again: This time to the social and physical environment. Many psychiatrists had all but ignored biological influences, but others were studying those involved in mental illness and were using somatic forms of treatment such as electroconvulsive therapy (electric shock) and Psychosurgery.

Dramatic changes in the treatment of the mentally ill in the United States began in the mid-1950's with the introduction of the first effective drugs for treating psychotic symptoms. Along with drug treatment, new, more liberal and humane policies and treatment strategies were introduced into mental hospitals. More and more patients were treated in community settings in the 1960s and 1970s. Support for mental health research led to significant new discoveries, especially in the understanding of genetic and biochemical determinants in mental illness and the functioning of the brain. Thus, by the 1980's, psychiatry had once again shifted in emphasis to the biological, to the relative neglect of psychosocial influences in mental health and illness.

Psychiatrists use a variety of methods to detect specific disorders in their patients. The most fundamental is the psychiatric interview, during which the patient's psychiatric history is taken and mental status is evaluated. The psychiatric history is a picture of the patient's personality characteristics, relationships with others, and past times and present experience with psychiatric problems - all told in the patient's words (sometimes supplemented by comments from other family members). Psychiatrists use mental-status examinations much as internists use physical examinations. They elicit and classify aspects of the patient's mental functioning.

Some diagnostic methods rely on testing by other specialists. Psychologists administer intelligence and personality tests, as well as tests designed to detect damage to the brain or other parts of the central nervous system. Neurologists also test psychiatric patients for evidence of impairment of the nervous system. Other physicians sometimes examine patients who complain of physical symptoms. Psychiatric social workers explore family and community problems. The psychiatrist integrates all this information in making a diagnosis according to criteria established by the psychiatric profession.

Psychiatric treatments descend into two categorical classes, as the organic which of or relating to a bodily organ or organs, and nonorganic for dealing with the properties and reactions of inorganic compounds. Organic treatments, such as drugs, are those that affect the body directly. Nonorganic types of treatment improve the patient's functioning by psychological means, such as psychotherapy, or by altering the social environment.

Psychotropic drugs are by far the most commonly used organic treatment. The first to be discovered were the antipsychotics, used primarily to treat schizophrenia. The phenothiazine is the most frequently prescribed class of antipsychotic drugs. Others are the thioxanthenes, butyrophenones, and indoles. Atipsychotic drugs diminish such symptoms as delusions, hallucinations, and thought disorder. Because they can reduce agitation, they are sometimes used to control manic excitement in manic-depressive patients and to calm geriatric patients. Some childhood behaviour disorders respond to these drugs.

Despite the relative controversy, but the antipsychotic drugs have drawbacks. The most serious is the neurological condition tardive dyskinesia, which occurs in patients who have taken the drugs over extended periods. The condition is characterized by abnormal movements of the tongue, mouth, and body. It is especially serious because its symptoms do not always disappear when the drug is stopped, and no known treatment for it has been developed.

Most Psychotropic drugs are chemically synthesized. Lithium carbonate, however, is a naturally occurring element used to prevent, or at least reduce, the severity of shifts of mood in manic-depression. It is especially effective in controlling mania. Psychiatrists must monitor lithium dosages carefully, because only a small margin exists between an effective dose and a toxic one.

Three major classes of antidepressant drugs are used. The tricyclic and tetracyclic antidepressants, the most frequently prescribed, are used for the most common form of serious depression. Monoamine oxidase (MAO) inhibitors are used for so-called atypical depressions. Serotonin-selective reuptake inhibitors (SSRIs) are effective against both typical and atypical depressions. Although all three classes are quite effective in relieving depression in correctly matched patients, they also have disadvantages. The tricyclics and also, the tetracyclic, can take two to five weeks to become effective and can cause such side effects as oversedation and cardiac problems. MAO inhibitors can cause severe hypertension in patients who ingest certain types of food (such as cheese, beer, and wine) or drugs (such as cold medicines). SSRI drugs, such as Fluoxetine (Prozac), take 2 to 12 weeks to become effective and can cause headaches, nausea, insomnia, and nervousness.

Anxiety, tension and insomnia are often treated with drugs that are commonly called minor tranquillizers. Barbiturates have been used for the longest time, but they produce more severe side effects and are more often abused than the newer classes of Antianxiety drugs. Of the new drugs, the benzodiazepines are the most frequently prescribed, very often in nonpsychiatric settings.

The stimulant drugs, such as amphetamine - a drug that is often abused - have legitimate uses in psychiatry. They help to control overactivity and lack of concentration in hyperactive children and to stimulate the victims of narcolepsy, a disorder characterized by sudden, uncontrollable episodes of sleep.

Another organic treatment is electroconvulsive therapy, or ECT, in which seizures similar to those of epilepsy are produced by a current of electricity passed through the forehead. ECT is most commonly used to treat severe depressions that have not responded to drug treatment. It is also sometimes used to treat schizophrenia. Other forms of organic treatment are much less frequently used than drugs and ETC. They include the controversial technique Psychosurgery, in which fibres in the brain are severed; this technique is now used very rarely.

The most common nonorganic treatment is psychotherapy, treating a mental disorder through psychological means, (as an instance of a disordered function of the mind.) Most psychotherapies conducted by psychiatrists are psychodynamic by orientation - that is, they focus on internal psychic conflict and its resolution as a means of restoring mental health. The prototypical psychodynamic therapy is psychoanalysis, which is aimed at untangling the sources of unconscious conflict in the past and restructuring the patient's personality. Psychoanalysis as a therapeutic method of treating mental disorders by investigating the interaction of conscious and unconscious elements in the mind and bringing repressed fears and conflict into conscious mind. The patient relates dreams, fantasies, and memories, along with thoughts and feelings associated with them. The analyst helps the patient interpret these associations and the meaning of the patient's relationship to the analyst. Because it is lengthy and expensive, often several years in duration, classical psychoanalysis is now infrequently used.

More current and shorter forms of psychotherapy that supplement psychoanalytic principles with other theoretical ideas and scientifically derived information. In these types of therapy, psychiatrists are more likely to give the patient advice and try to influence behaviour. Some use techniques derived from behaviour therapy, which is based on learning theory (although these methods are more commonly used by psychologists).

Besides psychotherapy, the other major form of nonorganic treatment used in psychiatry is milieu therapy. Usually carried out in psychiatric wards, milieu therapy directs social relations between patients and staff toward therapeutic ends. Ward activities, too, are planned to serve specific therapeutic goals.

In general, psychotherapy is relied on more heavily for the treatment of neuroses and other nonpsychotic conditions than it is for psychoses. In psychotic patients, who usually receive psychoactive drugs, psychotherapy is used to improve social and vocational functioning. Milieu therapy is limited to hospitalized patients. Increasingly, psychiatrists use a combination of organic and nonorganic techniques for all patients, depending on their diagnosis and response to treatment.

Bipolar Disorder, is consistent of a mental illness in which a person's mood alternates between extreme mania and depression, even that Bipolar disorder is also called manic-depressive illness. When manic, people with bipolar disorder feel intensely elated, self-important, energetic, and irritable. When depressed, they experience painful sadness, negative thinking, and indifference to things that used to bring them happiness.

Bipolar disorder is much less common than depression. In North America and Europe, about 1 percent of people experience bipolar disorder during their lives. Rates of bipolar disorder are similar throughout the world. In comparison, at least 8 percent of people experience serious depression during their lives. Bipolar disorder affects men and women about equally and is somewhat more common in higher socioeconomic classes. At least 15 percent of people with bipolar disorder commit suicide. This rate roughly equals the rate for people with major depression, the most severe form of depression.

Bipolar disorder is a mental illness that causes mood swings. In the manic phase, a person might feel ecstatic, self-important, and energetic. But when the person becomes depressed, the mood shifts to extreme sadness, negative thinking, and apathy. Some studies indicate that the disease occurs at unusually high rates in creative people, such as artists, writers, and musicians.

But some researchers contend that the methodology of these studies was flawed and their results were misleading. In the October 1996 Discover magazine article, anthropologist Jo Ann C. Gutin presents the results of several studies that explore the link between creativity and mental illness.

Bipolar disorder usually begins in a person's late teens or 20's. Men usually experience mania as the first mood episode, whereas women typically experience depression first. Episodes of mania and depression usually last from several weeks to several months. On average, people with untreated bipolar disorder experience four episodes of mania or depression throughout any ten-year period, that many people with bipolar disorder function normally between episodes. In "rapid-cycling" bipolar disorder, however, which represents 5 to 15 percent of all cases, a person experiences four or more mood episodes within a year and may have little or no normal functioning in between episodes. In rare cases, swings between mania and depression occur over a period of days.

In another type of bipolar disorder, a person experiences major depression and hypomanic episodes, or episodes of milder mania. In a related disorder called cyclothymic disorder, a person's mood alternates between mild depression and mild mania. Some people with cyclothymic disorder later develop full-blown bipolar disorder. Bipolar disorder may also follow a seasonal pattern, with a person typically experiencing depression in the fall and winter and mania in the spring or summer.

People, encompassed within the depressive point of bipolar disorder, experience the intensely sad or profoundly transferring formation showing the indifference to work, activities, and people that once brought them pleasure. They think slowly, concentrate poorly, feel tired, and experience changes - usually an increase - in their appetite and sleep. They often feel a sense of worthlessness or helplessness. In addition, they may feel pessimistic or hopeless about the future and may think about or attempt suicide. In some cases of severe depression, people may experience psychotic symptoms, such as delusions (false beliefs) or hallucinations (false sensory perceptions).

In the manic phase of bipolar disorder, people feel intensely and inappropriately happy, self-important, and irritable. In this highly energized state they sleep less, have racing thoughts, and talk in rapid-fire speech that goes off in many directions. They have inflated self-esteem and confidence and may even have delusions of grandeur. Mania may make people impatient and abrasive, and when frustrated, physically abusive. They often behave in socially inappropriate ways, think irrationally, and show impaired judgment. For example, they may take aeroplane trips all over the country, make indecent sexual advances, and formulate grandiose plans involving indiscriminate investments of money. The self-destructive behaviour of mania includes excessive gambling, buying outrageously expensive gifts, abusing alcohol or other drugs, and provoking confrontations with obnoxious or combative behaviour.

Clinical depression is one of the most common forms of mental illness. Although depression can be treated with psychotherapy, many scientists believe there are biological causes for the disease. The June 1998 issue, in the Scientific American article, that neurobiologist Charles B. Nemeroff discusses the connection between biochemical changes in the brain and depression.

The genes that a person inherits seem to have a strong influence on whether the person will develop bipolar disorder. Studies of twins provide evidence for this genetic influence. Among genetically identical twins where one twin has bipolar disorder, the other twin has the disorder in more than 70 percent of cases. But among pairs of fraternal twins, who have about half their genes in common, both twins have bipolar disorder in less than 15 percent of cases in which one twin has the disorder. The degree of genetic similarity seems to account for the difference between identical and fraternal twins. Further evidence for a genetic influence comes from studies of adopted children with bipolar disorder. These studies show that biological relatives of the children have a higher incidence of bipolar disorder than do people in the general population. Thus, bipolar disorder seems to run in families for genetic reasons.

Owing or relating to, or affecting a particular person, over which a personal allegiance about the concerns and considerations or work-related stress can trigger a manic episode, but this usually occurs in people with genetic vulnerabilities, other factors - such as prenatal development, childhood experiences, and social conditions - seem to have relatively little influence in causing bipolar disorder. One study examined the children of identical twins in which only one member of each pair of twins had bipolar disorder. The study found that regardless of whether the parent had bipolar disorder or not, all of the children had the same high 10-percent rate of bipolar disorder. This observation clearly suggests that risk for bipolar illness comes from genetic influence, not from exposure to a parent's bipolar illness or from family problems caused by that illness.

Different therapies may shorten, delay, or even prevent the extreme moods caused by bipolar disorder. Lithium carbonate, a natural mineral salt, can help control both mania and depression in bipolar disorder. The drug generally takes two to three weeks to become effective. People with bipolar disorder may take lithium during periods of relatively normal mood to delay or prevent subsequent episodes of mania or depression. Common side effects of lithium include nausea, increased thirst and urination, vertigo, loss of appetite, and muscle weakness. In addition, long-term use can impair functioning of the kidneys. For this reason, doctors do not prescribe lithium to bipolar patients with kidney disease. Many people find the side effects so unpleasant that they stop taking the medication, which often results in relapse.

From 20 to 40 percent of people do not respond to lithium therapy. For these people, two anticonvulsant drugs may help dampen severe manic episodes: carbamazepine (Tegretol) and valproate (Depakene). The use of traditional antidepressants to treat bipolar disorder carries risks of triggering a manic episode or a rapid-cycling pattern.

A psychiatrist is a doctor of medicine who has had four years of postgraduate training in psychiatry. Many psychiatrists take further training in psychoanalysis, child psychiatry, or other subspecialties. Psychiatrists treat patients in private practice, in general hospitals, or in specialized facilities for the mentally ill (psychiatric hospitals, outpatient clinics, or community mental health centres). Some spend part or all of their time doing research or administering mental health programs. By contrast, psychologists, who often work closely with psychiatrists and treat many of the same kinds of patients, are not trained in medicine; consequently, they neither diagnose physical illness nor administer drugs.

The province of psychiatry is unusually broad for a medical specialty. Mental disorders may affect most aspects of a patient's life, including physical functioning, behaviour, emotions, thought, perception, interpersonal relationships, sexuality, work, and play. These disorders are caused by a poorly understood combination of biological, psychological, and social determinants. Psychiatry's task is to account for the diverse sources and manifestations of mental illness.

Physicians in the Western world began specializing in the treatment of the mentally ill in the 19th century. Known as alienists, psychiatrists of that era worked in large asylums, practising what was then called moral treatment, a humane approach aimed at quieting mental turmoil and restoring reason. During the second half of the century, psychiatrists abandoned this mode of treatment and, with it, the tacit recognition that mental illness is caused by both psychological and social influences. For a while, their attention focussed almost exclusively on biological factors. Drugs and other forms of somatic (physical) treatments were common. The German psychiatrist Emil Kraepelin identified and classified mental disorders into a system that is the foundation for modern diagnostic practices. Another important figure was the Swiss psychiatrist Eugen Bleuler, who coined the word schizophrenia and described its characteristics.

The discovery of unconscious sources of behaviour - an insight dominated by the psychoanalytic writings of Sigmund Freud in the early 20th century - enriched psychiatric thought and changed the direction of its practice. Attention shifted to processes within the individual psyche, and psychoanalysis came to be regarded as the preferred mode of treatment for most mental disorders. In the 1940s and 1950s emphasis shifted again: this time to the social and physical environment. Many psychiatrists had all but ignored biological influences, but others were studying those involved in mental illness and were using somatic forms of treatment such as electroconvulsive therapy (electric shock) and Psychosurgery.

Dramatic changes in the treatment of the mentally ill in the United States began in the mid-1950's with the introduction of the first effective drugs for treating psychotic symptoms. Along with drug treatment, new, more liberal and humane policies and treatment strategies were introduced into mental hospitals. More and more patients were treated in community settings in the 1960s and 1970s. Support for mental health research led to significant new discoveries, especially in the understanding of genetic and biochemical determinants in mental illness and the functioning of the brain. Thus, by the 1980s, psychiatry had once again shifted in emphasis to the biological, to the relative neglect of psychosocial influences in mental health and illness.

Psychiatrists use a variety of methods to detect specific disorders in their patients. The most fundamental is the psychiatric interview, during which the patient's psychiatric history is taken and mental status is evaluated. The psychiatric history is a picture of the patient's personality characteristics, relationships with others, and past and present experience with psychiatric problems - all told in the patient's words (sometimes supplemented by comments from other family members). Psychiatrists use mental-status examinations much as internists use physical examinations. They elicit and classify aspects of the patient's mental functioning.

Some diagnostic methods rely on testing by other specialists. Psychologists administer intelligence and personality tests, as well as tests designed to detect damage to the brain or other parts of the central nervous system. Neurologists also test psychiatric patients for evidence of impairment of the nervous system. Other physicians sometimes examine patients who complain of physical symptoms. Psychiatric social workers explore family and community problems. The psychiatrist integrates all this information in making a diagnosis according to criteria established by the psychiatric profession.

Psychotropic drugs are by far the most commonly used organic treatment. The first to be discovered were the antipsychotics, used primarily to treat schizophrenia. The phenothiazine is the most frequently prescribed class of antipsychotic drugs. Others are the thioxanthenes, butyrophenones, and indoles. Antipsychotic drugs diminish such symptoms as delusions, hallucinations, and thought disorder. Because they can reduce agitation, they are sometimes used to control manic excitement in manic-depressive patients and to calm geriatric patients. Some childhood behaviour disorders respond to these drugs.

The general goal of Gestalt therapy is awareness of self, others, and the environment that bring about growth, wholeness, and integration of one's thoughts, feelings, and actions. Gestalt therapists use a wide variety of techniques to make clients more aware of themselves, and they often invent or experiment with techniques that might help to accomplish this goal. One of the best-known Gestalt techniques is the empty-chair technique, in which an empty chair represents another person or another part of the client's self. For example, if a client is angry at herself for not being kinder to her mother, the client may pretend her mother is sitting in an empty chair. The client may then express her feelings by speaking in the direction of the chair. Alternatively, the client might play the role of the understanding daughter while sitting in one chair and the angry daughter while sitting in another. As she talks to different parts of herself, differences may be resolved. The empty-chair technique reflects Gestalt therapy's strong emphasis on dealing with problems in the present.

Behavioural therapies differ dramatically from psychodynamic and humanistic therapies. Behavioural therapists do not explore an individual's thoughts, feelings, dreams, or past experiences. Rather, they focus on the behaviour that is causing distress for their clients. They believe that behaviour of all kinds, both normal and abnormal, is the product of learning. By applying the principles of learning, they help individuals replace distressing behaviours with more appropriate ones.

Typical problems treated with behavioural therapy include alcohol or drug addiction, phobias (such as a fear of heights), and anxiety. Modern behavioural therapists work with other problems, such as depression, by having clients develop specific behavioural goals - such as returning to work, talking with others, or cooking a meal. Because behavioural therapy can work through nonverbal means, it can also help people who would not respond to other forms of therapy. For example, behavioural therapists can teach social and self-care skills to children with severe learning disabilities and to individuals with schizophrenia who are out of touch with reality.

Some researchers suggest that all therapies share certain qualities, and that these qualities account for the similar effectiveness of therapies despite quite different techniques. For instance, all therapies offer people hope for recovery. People who begin therapy often expect that therapy will help them, and this expectation alone may lead to some improvement (a phenomenon known as the placebo effect). Also, people in psychotherapy may find that simply being able to talk freely and openly about their problems helps them to feel better. Finally, the support, encouragement, and cared about, that clients feel from their therapist let them know they are care about and respected, which may positively affect their mental health.

Although different therapeutic approaches may be equally effective on average, mental health researchers agree that some types of therapy are best for particular problems. For panic disorder and phobias, behavioural and cognitive-behavioural therapies seem most effective. Behavioural techniques, often in combination with medication, are also an effective treatment for obsessive-compulsive disorder, post-traumatic stress disorder, generalized anxiety disorder, and sexual dysfunction. Cognitive-behavioural, psychodynamic, and humanistic approaches all provide moderate relief from depression.

Mental health professionals agree that the effectiveness of therapy depends to a large extent on the quality of the relationship between the client and therapist. In general, the better the rapport is between therapist and client, the better the outcome of therapy. If a person does not trust a therapist enough to describe deeply personal problems, the therapist will have trouble helping the person change and improve. For clients, trusting that the therapist can provide help for their problems is essential for making progress.

The founder of person-centred therapy, Carl Rogers, believed that the most important qualities in a therapist are being genuine, accepting, and empathic. Almost all therapists today would agree that these qualities are important. Being genuine means that therapists care for the client and behave toward the client as they really feel. Being in acceptance means that therapists should appreciate clients for whom they are, despite the things that they may have done. Therapists do not have to agree with clients, but they must accept them. Being empathic means that therapists understand the client's feelings and experiences and convey this understanding back to the client.

In helping their clients, all therapists follow a code of ethics. First, all therapy is confidential. Therapists notify others of a client's disclosures only in exceptional cases, such as when children disclose abuse by parents, parents disclose abuse of children, or clients disclose an intention to harm themselves or others. Also, therapists avoid dual relationships with clients - that is, being friends outside of therapy or maintaining a business relationship. Such relationships may reduce the therapist's objectivity and ability to work with the client. Ethical therapists also do not engage in sexual relationships with clients, and do not accept as clients people with whom they have been sexually intimate.

As more immigrants to the United States and Canada have entered therapy, psychotherapists and Counsellors have learned the importance of taking a client's cultural background into account when assessing the problem and determining treatment. Scholars recognize that most psychotherapies are based on Western systems of psychology, which stress the desirability of individualism and independence. However, cultures of Asia and other regions commonly emphasize different values, such as conformity, dependency on others, and obeying one's parents. Thus, techniques that might be effective for someone from North America, Europe, or Australia might be inappropriate for a recent immigrant from Vietnam, Japan, or India. In order to provide effective treatment, therapists must be aware of their own cultural biases and become familiar with their client's ethnic and cultural background.

Anxiety, is the emotional state in which people feel uneasy, apprehensive, or fearful. People usually experience anxiety about events they cannot control or predict, or about events that seem threatening or dangerous. For example, students taking an important test may feel anxious because they cannot predict the test questions or feel certain of a good grade. People often use the word's fear and anxiety to describe the same thing. Fear also describes a reaction to immediate danger characterized by a strong desire to escape the situation.

The physical symptoms of anxiety reflect chronic "readiness" to deal with some future threat. These symptoms may include fidgeting, muscle tension, sleeping problems, and headaches. Higher levels of anxiety may produce such symptoms as rapid heartbeat, sweating, increased blood pressure, nausea, and dizziness.

All people experience anxiety to some degree. Most people feel anxious when faced with a new situation, such as a first date, or when trying to do something well, such as give a public speech. A mild to moderate amount of anxiety in these situations is normal and even beneficial. Anxiety can motivate people to prepare for an upcoming event and can help keep them focussed on the task at hand.

However, too little anxiety or too much anxiety can cause problems. Individuals who feel no anxiety when faced with an important situation may lack alertness and focus. On the other hand, individuals who experience an abnormally high amount of anxiety often feel overwhelmed, immobilized, and unable to accomplish the task at hand. People with too much anxiety often suffer from one of the anxiety disorders, a group of mental illnesses. In fact, more people experience anxiety disorders than any other type of mental illness. A survey of people aged 15 to 54 in the United States found that about 17 percent of this population suffers from an anxiety disorder during any given year.

The Foundation of the Diagnostic and Statistical Manual of Mental Disorders, a handbook for mental health professionals, describes a variety of anxiety disorders. These include generalized anxiety disorder, phobias, panic disorder, obsessive-compulsive disorder, and post-traumatic stress disorder.

People with generalized anxiety disorder feel anxious most of the time. They worry excessively about routine events or circumstances in their lives. Their worries often relate to finances, family, personal health, and relationships with others. Although they recognize their anxiety as irrational or out of proportion to actual events, they feel unable to control their worrying. For example, they may worry uncontrollably and intensely about money despite evidence that their financial situation is stable. Children with this disorder typically worry about their performance at school or about catastrophic events, such as tornadoes, earthquakes, and nuclear war.

People with generalized anxiety disorder often find that their worries interfere with their ability to function at work or concentrate on tasks. Physical symptoms, such as disturbed sleep, irritability, muscle aches, and tension, may accompany the anxiety. To receive a diagnosis of this disorder, individuals must have experienced its symptoms for at least six months.

Generalized anxiety disorder affects about 3 percent of people in the general population in any given year. From 55 to 66 percent of people with this disorder are female.

A phobia is an excessive, enduring fear of clearly defined objects or situations that interferes with a person's normal functioning. Although they know their fear is irrational, people with phobias always try to avoid the source of their fear. Common phobias include fear of heights (acrophobia), fear of enclosed places (claustrophobia), fear of insects, snakes, or other animals, and fear of air travel. Social phobias involve a fear of performing, of critical evaluation, or of being embarrassed in front of other people.

Panic is an intense, overpowering surge of fear. People with panic disorder experience panic attacks - periods of quickly escalating, intense fear and discomfort accompanied by such physical symptoms as rapid heartbeat, trembling, shortness of breath, dizziness, and nausea. Because people with this disorder cannot predict when these attacks will strike, they develop anxiety about having additional panic attacks and may limit their activities outside the home.

In obsessive-compulsive disorder, people persistently experience certain intrusive thoughts or images (obsessions) or feel compelled to perform certain behaviours (compulsions). Obsessions may include unwanted thoughts about inadvertently poisoning others or injuring a pedestrian while driving. Common compulsions include repetitive hand washing or such mental acts as repeated counting. People with this disorder often perform compulsions to reduce the anxiety produced by their obsessions. The obsessions and compulsions significantly interfere with their ability to function and may consume a great deal of time.

Post-traumatic stress disorder sometimes occurs after people experience traumatic or catastrophic events, such as physical or sexual assaults, natural disasters, accidents, and wars. People with this disorder relive the traumatic event through recurrent dreams or intrusive memories called flashbacks. They avoid things or places associated with the trauma and may feel emotionally detached or estranged from others. Other symptoms may include difficulty sleeping, irritability, and trouble concentrating.

Most anxiety disorders do not have an obvious cause. They result from a combination of biological, psychological, and social factors.

Studies suggest that anxiety disorders run in families. That is, children and close relatives of people with disorders are more likely than most to develop anxiety disorders. Some people may inherit genes that make them particularly vulnerable to anxiety. These genes do not necessarily cause people to be anxious, but the genes may increase the risk of anxiety disorders when certain psychological and social factors are also present.

Anxiety also appears to be related to certain brain functions. Chemicals in the brain called neurotransmitters enable neurons, or brain cells, to communicate with other. One neurotransmitter, gamma-amino butyric acid (GABA), appears to play a role in regulating one's level of anxiety. Lower levels of GABA are associated with higher levels of anxiety. Some studies suggest that the neurotransmitter's norepinephrine and serotonin play a role in panic disorder.

Psychologists have proposed a variety of models to explain anxiety. Austrian psychoanalyst Sigmund Freud suggested that anxiety result from internal, unconscious conflicts. He believed that a person's mind represses wishes and fantasies about which the person feels uncomfortable. This repression, Freud believed, results in anxiety disorders, which he called neuroses.

More recently, behavioural researchers have challenged Freud's model of anxiety. They believe one's anxiety level relates to how much a person believes events can be predicted or controlled. Children who have little control over events, perhaps because of overprotective parents, may have little confidence in their ability to handle problems as adults. This lack of confidence can lead to increased anxiety.

Behavioural theorists also believe that children may learn anxiety from a role model, such as a parent. By observing their parent's anxious response to difficult situations, the child may learn a similar anxious response. A child may also learn anxiety as a conditioned response. For example, an infant often startled by a loud noise while playing with a toy may become anxious just at the sight of the toy. Some experts suggest that people with a high level of anxiety misinterpret normal events as threatening. For instance, they may believe their rapid heartbeat indicates they are experiencing a panic attack when in reality it may be the result of exercise.

While some people may be biologically and psychologically predisposed to feel anxious, most anxiety is triggered by social factors. Many people feel anxious in response to stress, such as a divorce, starting a new job, or moving. Also, how a person expresses anxiety appears to be shaped by social factors. For example, many cultures accept the expression of anxiety and emotion in women, but expect more reserved emotional displays from men.

Mental health professionals use a variety of methods to help people overcome anxiety disorders. These include psychoactive drugs and psychotherapy, particularly behaviour therapy. Other techniques, such as exercise, hypnosis, meditation, and biofeedback, may also prove helpful.

Psychiatrists often prescribe benzodiazepines, a group of tranquillizing drugs, to reduce anxiety in people with high levels of anxiety. Benzodiazepines help to reduce anxiety by stimulating the GABA neurotransmitter system. Common benzodiazepines include alprazolam (Xanax), clonazepam (Klonopin), and diazepam (Valium). Two classes of antidepressant drugs—tricyclics and selective serotonin reuptake inhibitors (SSRIs) - also have proven effective in treating certain anxiety disorders.

Benzodiazepines can work quickly with few unpleasant side effects, but they can also be addictive. In addition, benzodiazepines can slow down or impair motor behaviour or thinking and must be used with caution, particularly in elderly persons. SSRIs take longer to work than the benzodiazepines but are not addictive. Some people experience anxiety symptoms again when they stop taking the medications.

Therapists who attribute the cause of anxiety to unconscious, internal conflicts may use psychoanalysis to assist in filling the 'gap' with which people and their added understanding and resolve their conflicts, other types of psychotherapy, such as cognitive-behavioural therapy, have proven effective in treating anxiety disorders. In cognitive-behavioural therapy, the therapist often educates the person about the nature of their particular anxiety disorder. Then, the therapist may help the person challenge, but irrational thoughts that lead to anxiety. For example, to treat a person with a snake phobia, a therapist might gradually expose the person to snakes, beginning with pictures of snakes and progressing to rubber snakes and real snakes. The patient can use relaxation techniques acquired in therapy to overcome the fear of snakes.

Research has shown psychotherapy to be as effective or more effective than medications in treating many anxiety disorders. Psychotherapy may also provide more lasting benefits than medications when patients discontinue treatment.

Unconscious, in psychology, hypothetical region of the mind containing wishes, memories, fears, feelings, and ideas that are prevented from expression in conscious awareness. They manifest themselves, instead, by their influence on conscious processes and, most strikingly, by such anomalous phenomena as dreams and neurotic symptoms. Not all mental activity of which the subject is unaware belongs to the unconscious; for example, thoughts that may be made conscious by a new focussing of attention are termed foreconscious or preconscious.

The concept of the unconscious was first developed in the period from 1895 to 1900 by Sigmund Freud, who theorized that it consists of survivals of feelings experienced during infantile life, including both instinctual drives or libido and their modifications by the development of the superego. According to the Swiss psychoanalyst Carl Jung, the unconscious also consists of a racial unconscious that contains certain inherited, universal, archaic fantasies belonging to what Jung termed the collective unconscious.

A defining understanding of the states of consciousness is not at all simple, is agreed-upon definition of consciousness exists. Attempted definitions tend to be tautological (for example, consciousness defined as awareness) or merely descriptive (for example, consciousness described as sensations, thoughts, or feelings). Despite this problem of definition, the subject of consciousness has had a remarkable history. At one time the primary subject matter of psychology, consciousness as an area of study, that the idea that something conveys to the mind, from which of critics has endlessly debated the meaning of the ascribing interactions that otherwise to ascertain the quality, mass, extent or degree of terminological statements that its standard unit or mixed distributive analysis, is such, that a conceptualized form of its reasons to posit of a direct interpretation whose interference became of the total demise, even so, there is the result reemerging to become a topic of current interests.

Most of the philosophical discussions of consciousness arose from the mind-body issues posed by the French philosopher and mathematician René Descartes in the 17th century. Descartes asked: Is the mind, or consciousness, independent of matter? Is consciousness extended (physical) or unextended (nonphysical)? Is consciousness determinative, or is it determined? English philosophers such as John Locke equated consciousness with physical sensations and the information they provide, whereas European philosophers such as Gottfried Wilhelm Leibniz and Immanuel Kant gave a more central and active role to consciousness.

The philosopher who most directly influenced subsequent exploration of the subject of consciousness was the 19th-century German educator Johann Friedrich Herbart, who wrote that ideas had quality and intensity and that they may suppress or may facilitate or place of one another. Thus, ideas may pass from "states of reality" (consciousness) to "states of tendency" (unconsciousness), with the dividing line between the two states being described as the threshold of consciousness. This formulation of Herbart clearly presages the development, by the German psychologist and physiologist Gustav Theodor Fechner, of the psychophysical measurement of sensation thresholds, and the later development by Sigmund Freud of the concept of the unconscious.

The experimental analysis of consciousness dates from 1879, when the German psychologist Wilhelm Max Wundt started his research laboratory. For Wundt, the task of psychology was the study of the structure of consciousness, which extended well beyond sensations and included feelings, images, memory, attention, duration, and movement. Because early interest focussed on the content and dynamics of consciousness, it is not surprising that the central methodology of such studies was introspection; that is, subjects reported on the mental contents of their own consciousness. This introspective approach was developed most fully by the American psychologist Edward Bradford Titchener at Cornell University. Setting his task as that of describing the structure of the mind, Titchener attempted to detail, from introspective self-reports, the dimensions of the elements of consciousness. For example, taste was "dimensionalized" into four basic categories: sweet, sour, salt, and bitter. This approach was known as structuralism.

By the 1920's, however, a remarkable revolution had occurred in psychology that was to essentially remove considerations of consciousness from psychological research for some 50 years: Behaviourism captured the field of psychology. The main initiator of this movement was the American psychologist John Broadus Watson. In a 1913 article, Watson stated, "I believe that we can write of some psychology and never use the term's consciousness, mental states, mind . . . imagery and the like." Psychologists then turned almost exclusively to behaviour, as described in terms of stimulus and response, and consciousness was totally bypassed as a subject. A survey of eight leading introductory psychology texts published between 1930 and the 1950's found no mention of the topic of consciousness in five texts, and in two it was treated as a historical curiosity.

Beginning in the later part of the 1950s, are, however, the grounded interests in the foundational subject of consciousness, for returning from its absence were subjects and techniques relating to altered states of consciousness: sleep and dreams, meditation, biofeedback, hypnosis, and drug-induced states. Much in the surge in sleep and dream research was directly fuelled by a discovery relevant to the nature of consciousness. A physiological indicator of the dream state was found: At roughly 90-minute intervals, the eyes of sleepers were observed to move rapidly, and at the same time the sleepers' brain waves would show a pattern resembling the waking state. When people were awakened during these periods of rapid eye movement, they almost always reported dreams, whereas if awakened at other times they did not. This and other research clearly indicated that sleep, once considered a passive state, were instead an active state of consciousness.

American psychiatrist William Glasser developed reality therapy in the 1960s, after working with teenage girls in a correctional institution and observing work with severely disturbed schizophrenic patients in a mental hospital. He observed that psychoanalysis did not help many of his patients change their behaviour, even when they understood the sources of it. Glasser felt it was important to help individuals take responsibility for their own lives and to blame others less. Largely because of this emphasis on personal responsibility, his approach has found widespread acceptance among drugs - and alcohol-abuse counsellor's, correction's workers, school counsellors, and those working with clients who may be disruptive to others.

Reality therapy is based on the premise that all human behaviour is motivated by fundamental needs and specific wants. The reality therapist first seeks to establish a friendly, trusting relationship with clients in which they can express their needs and wants. Then the therapist helps clients explore the behaviours that created problems for them. Clients are encouraged to examine the consequences of their behaviour and to evaluate how well their behaviour helped them fulfill their wants. The therapist does not accept excuses from clients. Finally, the therapist helps the client formulate a concrete plan of action to change certain behaviours, based on the client's own goals and ability to make choices.

During the 1960's, an increased search for "higher levels" of consciousness through meditation resulted in a growing interest in the practices of Zen Buddhism and Yoga from Eastern cultures. A full flowering of this movement in the United States was seen in the development of training programs, such as Transcendental Meditation, that were self-directed procedures of physical relaxation and focussed attention. Biofeedback techniques also were developed to bring body systems involving factors such as blood pressure or temperature under voluntary control by providing feedback from the body, so that subjects could learn to control their responses. For example, researchers found that persons could control their brain-wave patterns to some extent, particularly the so-called alpha rhythms generally associated with a relaxed, meditative state. This finding was especially relevant to those interested in consciousness and meditation, and a number of "alpha training" programs emerged.

Another subject that led to increased interest in altered states of consciousness was hypnosis, which involves a transfer of conscious control from the character interpretation belonging in the dependent sector, whose occasions, as basic of an idea or the principal object of attention, in the course of its immediate composition, and like the substance to a particular individual finds to the subject that the modification as when of transferring to that of another person. Hypnotism has had a long and intricate history in medicine and folklore and has been intensively studied by psychologists. Much has become known about the hypnotic state, relative to individual suggestibility and personality traits; the subject has now largely been demythologized, and the limitations of the hypnotic state are fairly well known. Despite the increasing use of hypnosis, however, much remains to be learned about this unusual state of focussed attention.

Finally, many people in the 1960's experimented with the psychoactive drugs known as hallucinogens, which produce deranging disorder of consciousness. The most prominent of these drugs is lysergic acid diethylamide, or LSD; mescaline; and psilocybin; the latter two have long been associated with religious ceremonies in various cultures. LSD, because of its radical thought-modifying properties, was initially explored for its so-called mind-expanding potential and for its psychotomimetic effects (imitating psychoses). Little positive use, however, has been found for these drugs, and their use is highly restricted.

Scientists have long considered the nature of consciousness without producing a fully satisfactory definition. In the early 20th century American philosopher and psychologist William James suggested that consciousness be a mental process involving both attention to external stimuli and short-term memory. Later scientific explorations of consciousness mostly expanded upon James's work. In the article from a 1997 special issue of Scientific American, Nobel laureate Francis Crick, who helped determine the structure of DNA, and fellow biophysicist Christof Koch explains how experiments on vision might deepen our understanding of consciousness.

As the concept of a direct, simple linkage between environment and behaviour became unsatisfactory in recent decades, the interest in altered states of consciousness may be taken as a visible sign of renewed interest in the topic of consciousness. That persons are active and intervening participants in their behaviour has become increasingly clear. Environments, rewards, and punishments are not simply defined by their physical character. Memories are organized, not simply stored, an entirely new area called cognitive psychology has emerged that centre on these concerns. In the study of children, increased attention is being paid to how they understand, or perceive, the world at different ages. In the field of animal behaviour, researchers increasingly emphasize the inherent characteristics resulting from the way a species has been shaped to respond adaptively to the environment. Humanistic psychologists, with a concern for self-actualization and growth, have emerged after a long period of silence. Throughout the development of clinical and industrial psychology, the conscious states of persons in terms of their current feelings and thoughts were of obvious importance. The role of consciousness, however, was often de-emphasised in favour of unconscious needs and motivations. Trends can be seen, however, toward a new emphasis on the nature of states of consciousness.

We have used the term 'transference' several times, in that we attributed the therapeutic results to the transference without further definition of the word. We will now consider more closely the emotional relationship which is thus designed. During a psychoanalytic treatment, the patient allows the analyst to play a predominating role in his emotional life. This is of great importance in the analytic process. After his treatment is over, this situation is changed. The patient builds up feelings of affection for and resistance to his analyst which, in their ebb and flow, so exceed the normal degree of feeling that the phenomenon has long attracted the theoretical interest of the analyst. Freud studied this phenomenon thoroughly, explained it, and gave it the name 'transference', we most probably will understand the significance of the transference phenomenon impressed Freud so profoundly that he continued through the years to develop his ideas about it.

In all afforded efforts, to refuse to consider the demise of forebears as too merely disdain, that we cannot reproduce of all Freud's research about transference but for an instance of obligation, would be used to indicate the requirement by the immediate need or purpose upon such condition that might point beyond a normal or acceptable limit, as to an excessive amount of which something does not or cannot extend to their essentials. When we speak of the transference in connexion with social reeducation, we mean the emotional responses of the education or counsellor or therapist, as the case maybe, without meaning that it takes place in exactly the same way as in an analysis. The 'countertransference' is emotional aptitude of the teacher toward the pupil, the counsellor toward his charge, the therapist toward the patient. The feeling which the child develops for the mentor is conditioned by a much earlier relationship to someone else. We must take cognizance of this fact in order to understand these relationships. The tender relationships which go to up the child's love life are no longer strange to us. Many of these have already been touched upon in the foregoing literature. We have learned how the small boy takes the father and mother as love objects. We have followed the strivings which arise out of this relationship, the Oedipus situation, we have seen how this runs its course and terminates in an identification with the parents. We have also had opportunity to consider the relationship between brothers and sisters, how their original rivalry is transformed into affection through the pressure of their feeling for the parents. We know that the boy at puberty must give up his first love object within the family and transfers his libido to individuals outside the family.

Why Freud chose the term 'transference' for the emotional relationship between patient and analyst is easy to understand. The feelings that arose long ago in another situation are transferred upon the analyst. To the counsellor of the child, the knowledge of the transference mechanism is indispensable. In order to influence the dissocial behaviour, he must bring his charge into the transference situation. The study of the transference in the dissocial child shows regularly a love life that has been disturbed in early childhood by a lack of affection or an undue amount of affection. A satisfactory social adjustment depends on certain conditions, among them an adequate constitutional endowment and early love relationships which have been confined within certain limits. Society determines these limitations, just as definitely as the later love life of an individual is determined by early form his libidinal development. The child develops normally and assumes his proper place in society, if he can cultivate within the privacy to such relationships as can favourably be carried over into the schools and from there into the ever-broadening world around him. His attitude toward his parents must be such that it can be carried over onto the teacher, and that toward his brothers and sisters must be transferred to his schoolmates. Every new contact, according to the degree of authority or maturity which the person represents, repeats a previous relationship with very little deviation. People whose early adjustment to succeed or supervene from such a normative course have no difficulties in their emotional relations with others, and they are able to form new ties, to deepen them, or to break them off without conflict when the situation demands it.

We can easily see why an attempt to change the present order of society always meets with resistance and where the radical reformer will have to use the greatest leverage. Our attitude to society and its members has a certain standard form. It gets its imprint from the structure of the family and the emotional relationships set up within the family, therefore, the parents, especially the father, assume overwhelming responsibility for the social orientation of the child. The persistent, ineradicable libidinal relationships carried over from childhood are facts with which social reformers must reckon. If the family represents the best preparation for the present social order, which seems to be the case, then the introduction of a new order means that the family must be uprooted and replaced by a different personal world for the child. It is beyond our scope to attempt a solution of this question, which concerns those who strive to build up a new order of society. We are remedial educators and must recognize these sociological relationships. We can ally ourselves with whatever social system will, but we have the path of our present activity well marked out for us, to bring dissocial youth into the line with present-day society.

It is not immediately clear, from which are pointed from the particular form of the delinquency, just what libidinal disturbances in childhood have given rise to the dissocial expression. Until we have a psychoanalytically construed scheme for the diagnosis of delinquency, we may content ourselves by separating these forms into two groups: (1) Borderline neurosis cases with dissocial symptoms, and (2) dissocial cases for which are in part, the ego giving to develop of the dissocial behaviour, and showing no trace of neurosis. In the first type, the individual finds himself in an inner conflict because of the nature of his love relationships, a part of his own personality forbids the indulgence of libidinal desires and strivings. The dissocial behaviour results from this conflict. In the second type, the individual finds himself in open conflict with his environment, because the outer world has frustrated his childish libidinal desires.

The differences in the forms of dissocial behaviour are important for many reasons. At present, they are significant to us because of the various ways in which the transference is established in these two types, we know that with a normal child the transference takes place of itself through the kindly efforts of the responsible adult. The teacher in his attitude repeats the situations long familiarly to the child, and thereby evokes a parental relationship. He does not maintain this relationship at the same level, but continually deepens it as long as he is the parental substitute.

When a neurotic child with symptoms of delinquency comes into the institution, the tendencies to transfer his attitude toward his parents to the persons in authority are immediately noticeable. The worker will adopt the same attitude toward the dissocial child as to the normal child, and bring him into positive transference, if he acts toward him in such a way as to prevent a repetition with the worker of the situation with the parents which led to the conflict. In psychoanalysis, on the other hand, it is of greatest importance to let this situation repeat itself. In a sense the worker becomes the father or the mother, but still not wholly so, he represents their claims, but in the right moment he must let the dissocial child know that he has insight into his difficulties and that he will not interpret the behaviour in the same way as do the parents. He will respond to the child's feeling of a need for punishment, but he will not completely satisfy it.

He will conduct in himself be entirely differently in the case of the child who in open conflict with society. In this instance he must take the child's part, be in agreement with his behaviour, and in the severest cases even give the child to understand that in his place he would behave just the same way. The guilt feelings found so clearly in the neurotic cases with dissocial behaviour are present in these cases also. These feelings do not arise, however, from the dissocial ego, but have another source.

Why does the educator conduct himself differently in dealing with this second type? These children, too, he must draw into a positive transference to him, but what is applicable and appropriate for a normal or a neurotic child would achieve opposite results. Otherwise the worker would bring upon himself all the hate and aggression which the child bears toward society, thus leading the child into a negative instead of positive transference, and creating a situation in which the child is not amenable to training.

Nevertheless, what was said about psychoanalysis theory is only a bare outline, that much deeper study of the transference is necessary to anyone interested in re-educational work from the psychoanalytic point of view. The practical application of this theory is not easy, since we deal mostly with mixed types, such that the attitude of the counsellor cannot be as uniform as having enough verbal descriptions for evincing of individual forms of dissociated behaviour to enable us to offer detailed instructions about how to deal with them. At present our psychoanalytic knowledge is such that a correct procedure cannot be stated specifically for each and every dissocial individual.

The necessity for bringing the child into a good relationship to his mentor is of prime importance. The worker cannot leave this to chance, he must deliberately achieve it and he must face the fact thus no effective work is possible without it. It is important for him to grasp the psychic situation of the dissocial child in the very first contact he makes with him, because only this can be known in what attitude to adopt. There is a further difficulty in that the dissocial child takes pains to hide his real nature: He misrepresents himself and lies. This is to be taken for granted, it should not surprise or upset us. Dissocial children do not come to us of their own volition but are brought to us, very often with the threat, 'You'll soon find out what's going to happen to you.' Generally parents resort our help only after every other means, including corporal punishment, have failed. To the child, we are only another form of punishment, an enemy against whom he must be on his guard, not a source of help to him. There is a great difference between this and the psychoanalytic situation, where the patient comes voluntarily for helping. To the dissocial child, we are a menace because we represent society, with which he is in conflict. He must protect himself against this terrible danger and be careful what he says in order not to give himself away. It is hard to make some of these delinquent children talk, remain unresponsive and stubborn. One thing they all have in common: They do not tell the truth. Some lie stupidly, pitiably, others, especially the older ones, show great skill and sophistication. The extremely submissive child, the 'dandly', the very jovial, or the exaggeratedly sincere, some especially hard to reach. This behaviour is so much to be expected that we are not surprised or disarmed by it, the inexperienced teacher or adviser is easily irritated, especially when the lies are transparent, but he must not let the child be aware of this. He must deal with the situation immediately without telling the child that he can see that coming through were attributive values about his attitudinal behaviours.

There is nothing remarkable in the behaviour of the dissocial, but it differs only quantitatively from normal behaviour. We all hide our real selves and use a great deal of psychic energy to mislead our neighbours. We masquerade more or less, according to necessity. Most of us learn in the nursery the necessity of presenting ourselves in accordance with the environmental demands, and thus we consciously or unconsciously build up a shell around ourselves. Anyone who has had experience with young children must have noticed how they immediately begin to dissimulate when a grown-up comes into the room. Most children succeed in behaving in the manner which they think is expected of them. Thus they lessen the danger to themselves and at the same time they are casting the permanent moulds of their mannerisms and their behaviour. How many parents really bother themselves about the inner life of their children? Is this mask necessarily for life? I do not know, but it often seems that the person on whom childhood experiences have forced the dissocial individual masquerades to a greater extent, and more consciously, then the normal. He is only drawing logical deductions from his unfortunate disagreeable authority? Why should he be sincere with those people who represent disagreeable authority? This is an unfair demand.

We must look further into the differences between the situation of social retraining and the analytic situation. The analyst expects to meet in his patient unconscious remittances which prevent him from being honest or make him silent: But the treatment is in vain when the patient lies persistently. Those who work with dissocial children expect to be lied to. To send this child away because he lies are only giving in to him. We must wait and hope to penetrate this mask which covers the really psychic situation. In the institution it does not matter if this is not achieved immediately, it means merely that the establishment of the transference is postponed. In the clinic, however, we must work more quickly. Taking with the patient does not always suffice, and we must introduce other remedial measures. Generally, we see the delinquent child, only, in at least as infrequent to a smattering of times, but we are forced to take some steps after the first few interviews, to formulate some tentative conception of the difficulty and to establish a positive transference as quickly as possible. This means we must get at least a peep behind the mask. If the child is not put in an institution, he remains in the old situation under the same influences which caused the trouble. In such cases we wish to establish the transference as quickly as possible, to intensify the child`s positive feelings for us that are aroused while the child is with us, and to bring them rapidly to such a pitch that they can no longer be easily disturbed by the old influences. To carry on such work successfully presupposes a long experience.

Let us now violate our theoretical concerns and considerations and see how the analyst and the patient seek to grasp upon a try to solve situational thoughts for which the transference, and, moreover, its mask on which can be understood that feelings and a better understanding the differentiation that intentionality that allies with others and exclusively its need to achieve to some end.

Even so, there are few current problems concerning the problem of transference that Freud did not recognize either implicitly or explicitly in the development of the theoretical and clinical framework. For all essential purposes, moreover, his formulations, in spite of certain shifts in emphasis, remain integral to contemporary psychoanalytic theory and practice. Recent developments mainly concern the impact of an ego-psychological approach, the significance of object relations, both current and infantile, external and internal, the role of aggression in mental life, and the part played by regression and the repetition compulsion in the transference. Nevertheless, analysis of the infantile Oedipal situation in the setting of a genuine transference neurosis is still considered as a primary goal of psychoanalytic procedure.

Originally, transference was ascribed to displacement on the analyst of repressed wishes and fantasies derived from early childhood. The transference neurosis was viewed as a compromise formulation similar to dreams and other neurotic symptoms. Resistance, defined as the clinical manifestation of repression, could be diminished or abolished by interpretation mainly directed toward the content of the repressed. Transference resistance, both positive and negative, was inscribed to the threatened emergence of repressed unconscious material in the analytic situation. Presently, as with the development of a structural approach, the superego had been portrayed as the heir to the genital Oedipal situation, also was the recognition as playing a leading role in the transference situation. The analysis was subsequently viewed not only as the object by displacement of infantile incestuous fantasies, but also as the substitute by projection for the prohibiting parental figures which had been internalized as the definitive superego. The effect of transference interpretation in mitigating undue severity of the superego has, therefore, been emphasized in many discussions of the concept of transference.

Certain expansions in the structural approach related increasingly to the recognition of the role that had earlier objective relations, in the development of the superego. This had affected the current concepts of transference, in that this connection, the significance of the analytic situation as a repetition of the early mother-child relationship has been stressed from different points for viewing to such equally important developments related to Freud's revised concept of anxiety which can only lead to theoretical developments in the field of ego psychology. However, this brought about their related clinical changes in the work of many analysts. As a result, attention was no longer the main attraction that had focussed on the content of the unconscious. In addition, increasing importance was attributed to the defence processes by means of which the anxiety which would be engendered if repression and other related mechanisms were broken down, was avoided in the analytic situation. Differences in the interpretation of the role of the analyst and the nature of transference developed from emphasis, on the one hand, on the importance of early object relations, and on the other, from primary attention to the role of the ego and its defences. These defences first emerged clearly in discussion of the technique of child analysis, in which Melanie Klein and Anna Freud, the pioneers in the fields of thought as playing the leading roles.

From a theoretical point of view, discussion foreshadowing the problems which face us today was presented in 1934 in a well-known paper by Richard Sterba and James Strachey, and further elaborated at the Marienbad Symposium at which Edward Bibring made an important contribution. The importance of identification with, or introjection of, the analyst in the transference situation of identification with, or introjection of, the analysts in the transference situation were clearly indicated. The therapeutic results were attributed to the effect of this process In mitigating the need for pathological defences. Strachey, however, considerably influenced by the work of Melanie Klein, regarded transference as essentially a projection onto the analyst of the patient's own superego. The therapeutic process was attributed to subsequent introjection of a modified superego as a result of 'mutative' transference. Sterba and Bibring, on the other hand, intimately involved with development of the ego-psychological approach, reemphasised the central role of the ego, postulating a therapeutic split and identification with the analyst as an essential feature of transference. To some extent, this difference of opinion may be regarded as semantic. If the superego is explicitly defined as the heir of the genital Oedipus conflict, then earlier intra-systematic conflicts within the ego, although they may be related retrospectively to the definite superego, much, nevertheless, are defined as contained within the ego. Later divisions within the ego of the type indicated by Sterba and very much expanded by Edward Bibring in his concept of therapeutic alliance between the analyst and the healthy part of the patient's ego, must also be excluded from superego significance. In contrast, those whom attribute pregenital intra-systemic conflicts within the ego primarily to the introjection of objects, consider that the resultant state of internal conflict appears like the dynamic idea that something conveys to the mind as having an endless meaning attached to the coherence of the therapeutic situation and seen in the later conflicts between ego and superego. They, therefore, believe that these structures developed simultaneously and suggest that no sharp distinction should be made between pre-oedipal, oedipal, and post-oedipal superego.

The differences, however, are not entirely verbal, since those whom attribute superego formations to the early months of life tend to attribute significantly too early object relation which differs from the conception of those who stress control and, neutralization of instinctual energy as primary functions of the ego. This theoretical difference necessarily implies some disagreement as how the dynamic situation both in childhood and in adult life, inevitably reflected in the concept of transference and in hypotheses as to the hidden nature of the therapeutic process. From one point of view, the role of the ego is central and crucial at every phase of analysis. A differentiation is made between transference as therapeutic alliance and the transference neurosis, which, on the whole, is considered a manifestation of resistance. Effective analysis depends on a sound and stable therapeutic alliance, a prerequisite for which is the existence, before analysis, of a degree of mature superego functions, the absence of which in certain severely disturbed patients and in young children may preclude traditional psychoanalytic procedure. Whenever indicated, interpretation's manifestations, which means, in effect, that the transference must be analysed. The process of analysis, however, is not exclusively ascribed to transference interpretation. Other interpretations of unconscious material, whether related to defence or to early fantasies, will be equally effective provided they are accurately timed and provide a satisfactory therapeutic alliance has been made. Those, in contrast, whom stress the importance of early object relations emphasizes the crucial role of transference as an object relationship, distorted though this may be of a variety of defences against primitively unresolved conflicts. The central role of the ego, both in the early stages of development and in the analytic process, are definitely accepted. The hidden nature of the ego is, however, considered at all times to be determined by its external and internal objects. Therapeutic process indicated changes in ego function results, therefore, primarily from a change in object relations though interpretation of the transference situation, finds of less differentiation as made between transference as for being the therapeutic alliance and transference neurosis as a manifestation of resistance. Therapeutic progress depends almost exclusively on transference interpretation. Other interpretations, although at times, are not, in general, considered an essential feature of the analytic process. From this point of view, the preanalytic maturity of the patient's ego is not stressed as considered potentially suitable for traditional psychoanalytic procedure.

These differences in theoretical orientation are not only reflected in the approach to children and disturbed patients. They may also be recognized in significant variations of technique in respect to all clinical groups, which inevitably affect the opening phases, understanding of the inevitable regressive features of the transference neurosis, and handling of the germinal phases of analysis. By its emphasis as drawn on or upon the main problems, and, by contrast, rather than similarity, our efforts will be to avoid to detailed discussions of controversial theory regarding the hidden nature of early ego development by a somewhat arbitrary differentiation between those who relate ego analysis to the analysis of defences and those who stress the primary significance of object relations both in the transference, and in the development and definitive structure of the ego. Needless to say, this involves some oversimplification, where I hope that it may, at the same time, clarify certain important issues. To take, on or upon the analysis of patients we are generally agreeing to be suitable for classical analytic procedure, the transference neurosis. Those which emphasis the role of the ego and the analysis of defences, not only maintain Freud's conviction that analysis should proceed from surface to depth, but also consider that early material in the analytic situation derives, that, in general, from defensive processes rather than from displacement onto the analyst of early instinctual fantasies. Deep transference interpretation in the early instinctual fantasies. Deep transference interpretation in the early phases of analysis will, therefore, rather be meaningless to the patient since its unconscious significance is so inaccessible, or, if the defences are precarious, will lead to premature and possibly intolerable anxiety. Premature interpretation of the equally unconscious automatic defensive processes by means of which instinctual fantasy kept unconscious is also ineffective and undesirable. There are, nonetheless, differences of opinion within this group, as to how far analysis of defence can be separated from analysis of content. Waelder, for example, has stressed the impossibility of such separation. Fenichel, however, considered that at least theoretical separation should be made and indicated that, as far as possible, analysis of defence should precede analysis of unconscious fantasy. It is, nevertheless, generally agreed that the transference neurosis develops, as a rule after ego defences have been sufficiently undermined to mobilize previously hidden instinctual conflict. During both the early stages of analysis, and at frequent points after development of the transference neurosis, defences against the transference will become a main feature of the analytic situation.

This approach, has already been indicated, is based on certain definite premises regarding the hidden natures and function of the ego in respect to the control and neutralization of instinctual energy and unconscious fantasies, while the importance of early object relations is not neglected, the conviction that early transference interpretation is ineffective and potentially relations are not neglected, the conviction and unconscious fantasy. The conviction that early transference interpretation is ineffective and potentially dangerous is related to the hypothesis that the instinctual energy available to the mature ego has been neutralized from unconscious fantasies, meaning at the beginning of analysis, for all effective purposes, relatively or absolutely divorced from its unconscious fantasy, as yet, there are a number of analysts of differing theoretical orientation of ego function from unconscious sources, but consider that unconscious fantasy continues to operate in all conscious mental activity. The analysts also construct upon the whole of their existing in the emphasis to the crucial significance of primitive fantasies, in respect to the development of the transference situation. The individual entering analysis will inevitably have unconscious fantasies concerning the analyst derived from primitive sources. This material, although deep in a sense, is, nevertheless, strongly current and accessible to interpretation. Klein, in addition, creates the development and definitive structure of the superego to unconscious fantasy determined by the earliest phases of object relationships. She emphasizes the role of early introjective and projective processes in relation to primitive anxiety ascribed to the death instinct and related aggression drive fantasies. The unresolved difficulties and conflict of the earliest period continue to colour object relations throughout life. Failure to achieve an essentially satisfactory object relationship in this early period, and failure to master relative loss of that object without retaining its good internal representative, will not only affect all object relations and definitive ego function, but more specifically determine the nature of anxiety-provoking fantasies on entering the analytic situation. According to this point of view, therefore, early transference uninterpreted, even thought it may relate to fantasies derived from an early period of life, should result not in an increase, but a decrease of anxiety

In considering next problems of transference in relation to analysis of the transference neurosis, two main points must be kept in mind. First, as already indicated, those who emphasize the analysis of defence tend to make a definite differentiation between transference as therapeutic alliance and the transference neurosis as a compromise formation which serves the purposes of resistance. In contrast, those who emphasize the importance of early object relations view the transference primarily as a revival or repetition, sometimes attributed to symbolic processes of early struggles in respect to objects. Still, there is no sharp differentiation made between the early manifestations of transference and the transference neurosis. In view, moreover, of the weight given to the role of unconscious fantasy and internal objects in every phase of mental life, healthy and pathological functions, though differing in essential respect, do not differ with regard to their direct dependence on unconscious sources.

In the second place, the role of regression in the transference situation is subject to wide differences of opinion. It was, of course, one of Freud's earliest discoveries that regression had of its earliest points of fixation, and is a cardinal feature, not only in the development of neurosis and psychosis, but also in the revival of earlier conflicts in the transference situation. With the development of psychoanalysis and its application to an ever increasing range of received increased attention. The significance of the analytic situation as a means of fostering regression as a prerequisite for the therapeutic work has been emphasized by Ida Macapline in a recent paper. Differing opinions as to the significance, value, and technical handling of regressive manifestoes from the basis of important modifications of analytic technique, which will be considered, however, in respect to the transference neurosis, the view recently expressed by Phyllis Greenacre, that regression, and indispensable features would be generally accepted. It is also a matter of generally based agreement that a prerequisite for successful analysis is revival and repetition in the analytic situation of the struggle of primitive stages of development. Those who emphasize defence analysis, however, tend to view regression as a manifestation of resistance, as a primitive mechanism of defence employed by the growth sets of the transference neurosis. Analysis of these regressive manifestations with their potential dangers depends on the existing and continued functioning of adequate ego strength to maintain therapeutic alliance at an adult level. Those, in contrast, who stress the significance of transference as a revival of the early mother-child relationship does not emphasize regression as an indication of resistance or defence, the revival of these primitive experiences in the transference situation is, in fact, regarded as can essential prerequisite for satisfactory psychological maturation and true geniality. The Kleinian school, as already indicated features the continued activity of primitive conflicts in determining essential features of the transference at every stage of analysis. Their increasing overt revival in the analytic situation, therefore, signifies a reopening of the analysis, and in general, is regarded as an indication of diminuation rather than increase of resistance. The dangers involved according to this point of view and are determined more but to the failure to mitigate anxiety by suitable transference interpretation. By this failure to obtainably achieve, in the early phases of analysis, a sound and stabling therapeutic alliance is based on the maturity of the patient's essential ego characteristics.

In considering, briefly, the terminal phases of analysis, many unresolved problems concerning the goal of the therapy and definition of a completed psychoanalysis must be kept in mind. Distinction must also be made between the technical problems of the terminal phase and evaluation of transference after the analysis has been terminated, there is widespread agreement as to the frequent revival in the terminal phases of primitive transference manifestations apparently resolved during the early phases of primitive transference manifestation, apparently resolved during the early phase of analysis has been terminated. Balint, and those who accept Ferenczi's concept of primary passive love, suggest that some gratification of primitive passive needs may be essential for successful termination. To Klein, the terminal phases of analysis also represent a repetition of important features of the early mother-child relationship. According to her point of view, this period represents, in essence, a revival of the early weaning situation. Completion depends on a mastery of early depressive struggles culminating in successful introjection of the analysis as a good object. Although, in this connection, emphasis differs considerably, it should be noted that those who stress the importance of identification with the analyst as a basis for therapeutic alliance, also accept the inevitability of some permanent modifications of a similar nature. Those, however, who make a definite differentiation between transference of the transference neurosis as a main prerequisite for successful termination. The identification based on therapeutic alliance must be interpreted and understood, particularly with reference to the reality aspects of the analyst's personality. In spite, therefore, of significant important differences there are, as already indicated in connection with the earlier papers of Sterba and Strachey, important points of agreement in respect to the goal of psychoanalysis.

The differences already considered indicate some basic current problems of transference. So far, however, discussion has been limited to variations within the framework of a traditional technique. We must consider problems related to overt modifications, so as the essential expanding context of use between variations introduced in respect to certain clinical conditions. Often as a preliminary to classical psychoanalysis, and modifications based on changes on basic approach which lead to significant alterations with regard both to the method and to the aim of therapy. It is generally agreed that some neurosis, borderline patients and the psychosis. The nature and meaning of such changes are, however, viewed differently according to the relative emphasis placed on the ego and its defences, on underlying unconscious conflicts, and on the significance and handling of regression in the therapeutic situation.

In 'Analysis Terminable and Interminable', Freud suggested that certainly inaccessible to psychoanalytic procedure. Hartmann has suggested that in addition to these primary attributes, other ego characteristics, originally develop for defensive purposes, and the related neutralized instinctual energy at the disposal of the ego, may be relatively or absolutely divorced from unconscious fantasy. This not only explains the relative inefficacy of early transference interpretation, but also hints of possible limitations in the potentialities of analysis attributable to secondary autonomy of the ego which is considered to be relatively irreversible. In certain cases, moreover, it is suggested that analysis of precarious or seriously pathological defences - particularly those concerned of aggressive impulses - may be not only ineffective, but dangerous. The relative failure of ego development in such cases not only precludes the development of a genuine therapeutic alliance, but also raises the risk of a serious regressive, often predominantly hostile transference situation. In certain cases, therefore, preliminary period of psychotherapy is recommended in order to explore the capacities of the patient to tolerate traditional psychoanalysis. In others, as Robert Knight in his paper on borderline states, and as many analysts' working with psychotic patients have suggested, psychoanalytic procedure is not considered applicable. Instead, a therapeutic approach based on analytic understanding which, in essence, utilizes an essentially implicit positive transference as a means of reinforcing, rather than analysing the precarious defences of the individual, is advocated. In contrast, Herbert Rosenfeld approached even severely disturbed psychotic patients with minimal modifications of psychoanalytic techniques. Only changes which the severity of the patient's condition enforces are introduced. The dangers of regression in therapy are not emphasized since primitive fantasy is considered to be active under all circumstances. The most primitive period is viewed in terms of early object relations with special stress on prosecutory anxiety related to the death instinct. Interpretation of this primitive fantasy in the transference situation, is best offered the opportunity of strengthening the severity-threatened psychosis mainly to serve traumatic experiences, particularly of deprivation in early infancy. According to this point of view, profound regression offers an opportunity to fulfil, in the transference situation, primitive needs which had not been met at the appropriate level of development. Similar suggestions have been proposed by Margolin and others, in the concept of anaclitic treatment. Serious psychosomatic diseases, that approach the premise that the inevitable regression is shown by certain patients and should be utilized in therapy, as a means for gratifying, in their extremely permissive transference situation. Having distinctive or certain limits in the burdensome instant for demanding to that which has not been met in infancy, as this must, in the connection of being taken to understand that the gratifications recommended in the treatment of severely disturbed patients are determined by their conviction. Of these patients are incapable of developing transference as we understand it, in the connection with neurosis and must therefore be handled by a modified technique.

The opinions so far considered, however, much of them, as mine differ in certain respects, are, nonetheless, all based on the fundamental premise that an essential difference between analysis and other methods of therapy depends on whether or not interpretation of transference is an integral feature of technical procedure. Results based on the effects of suggestions are to be avoided, as far as possible, whenever traditional technique is employed. This goal has, however, tp establish a point by appropriate objective means, that corroborated evidence that proved the need for better a state of being even more difficult to achieve than Freud expected when he first discerned the significance of symptomatic recovery based on positive transference. The importance of suggestion, even in the most strict analytic methods, has been repeatedly stressed by Edward Glover and others. Widespread and increasing emphasis as to the part played by the analyst's personality in determining the nature of the individual transference also implies recognition of unavoidable suggestive tendencies in the therapeutic process. Many analysts today believe that the classical conception of analytic objectivity and anonymity cannot be maintained. Instead, thorough analysis of reality aspects of the therapist's personality and point of view is advocated as an essential feature of transference analysis and an indispensable prerequisite for the dynamic changes already discussed in relation to the termination of analysis. It thus remains the ultimate goal of psychoanalyst's whenever their theoretical orientation, to avoid, as far as is humanly possible, results based on the unrecognized or unanalysed action of suggestion, and to maintain, as a primary goal, the resolution of such results through consistent and careful interpretation.

There are, however, a number of therapists, both within and outside the field of psychoanalysis, who consider that the transference situation should not be handled only or mainly as a setting for interpretation even in the treatment or analysis of neurotic patients. Instead, they advocate utilization of the transference relationship for the manipulation of corrective emotional experience. The theoretical orientation of those utilizing this concept of transference may be closer to, or more distant form, a Freudian point of view according to the degree to which current relationships are seen as determined by past events. At one extreme, current aspects and cultural factors are considered of predominant importance, at the other, mental development is viewed in essentially Freudian terms and modifications of technique are ascribed to inherent limitations of the analytic method rather than to essentially changed conceptions of the early phases of mental development. Of this group, Alexander is perhaps the best example. It is thirty years since, in his Salzburg paper, he indicated the tendency for patients to regress, even after apparently successful transference analysis of the oedipus situation to narcissistic dependent pregenital levels which prove stubborn and refractory to transference interpretation. In his more recent work, the role of regression in the transference situation has been increasingly stressed. The emergence and persistence of dependent, pregenital commands for something as or is if one's right or due requirements are challenged in measuring moderations of a wide range of clinical conditions. It is argued, that its indications that the encouragement of a regressive transference situation is undesirable and therapeutically ineffective. The analyst, therefore, should when this threatens adopt a definite role explicitly differing from the behaviour of the parents in early childhood in order to bring about therapeutic results through a corrective emotional experience in the transference situation. This, it is suggested, will obviate the tendency to regression, thus curtailing the length of treatment and improving therapeutic results. Limitations of regressive manifestations by active steps modifying traditional analytic procedure in a variety of ways are also frequently indicated, according to this point of view.

It will be clear that to those who maintain the conviction that interpretation of all transference manifestations remain an essential feature of psychoanalysis, the type of manifestation as described, even though based on a Freudian reconstruction of the early phases of mental developments, and represent a major modification. It is determined by a conviction that psychoanalysis, as a therapeutic method, has limitations related to the tendency to regression, which cannot be resolved by traditional technique. Moreover, the fundamental premises on which, and the conception of corrective emotional experience is based minimizing the significance of insight and recall. It is essentially, suggested that corrective emotional experience alone may bring about qualitative dynamic alterations in mental structure, which can lead to a satisfactory therapeutic goal. This implies a definite modification on the analytic hypothesis whose current problems are determined by their defences against the direct opposition to the instinctual impulses and the intentional object, to which had been set up during the decisive periods of early development. An analytic result therefore depends on the revival, repetition and mastery of earlier conflict in the current experience of the transference situation with insight an indispensable feature of an analytic goal.

Since certain important modifications are related to the concept of regression in the transference situation, it should be considered that this concept is in relation to the repetition compulsion, that transference, essentially is a revival of earlier emotional experience, must be regarded as a manifestation of the repetition compulsion is generally accepted. It is, however, necessarily to distinguish between repetition compulsion as an attempt to master traumatic experience and repetition compulsion as an attempt to return to a real or fantasized earlier state of rest or gratification. Lagache, in a recent paper, has connected by or as if by the affirming relatedness as associated to the corresponding divergence in the repetition compulsion to an inherent need to appear in the problems that had previously been left unsolved. From this point of view, the regressive aspects of the transference situation are to be regarded as a necessary preliminary to the mastery of unresolved conflict, as too, the regressive aspects of transference are mainly attributed to a wish to return to an earlier state of rest or narcissistic gratification, to the maintenance of the status quo in preference to any progressive action, to which Freud's original conception of the death instinct. There is a good deal to suggest that both aspects of the repetition compulsion may bee seen in self-destructive forces tend to be stronger that progressive libidinal impulses, the potentialities of the analytic approach will inevitably appear to be limited. In those, in contrast, in whom that regard the reappearance in the transference situation of earlier conflicts as an indication of tendencies to master and progress will continue to feel that the classical analytic method remains the optimal approach to psychological illness wherever it is applicable.

Clarifications maintain the position as peculiarly occupying a particular point in space and time. Whereas in absence or termination must reflect on or upon the fearing analysis if the transference, as compelling of a generally acknowledged focal point, this itself may debase the appropriate factor that generates, in every degree. The exemplifying analytic technique that would react upon the discipline needed to utilize the new values, whereby, they can be ascribed as the commonality in holding the services to a suspicious self-direction and comprehensive understanding, in that of whatever is humanly affiliated to the best as can be, and yet, the advocacy to the analysis of the transference is generally acknowledged as the central feature of analytic technique? Freud regarded transference and resistance as facts in the observational conceptuality for which of representing the state of inventions. He writes, . . . that the theory of psychoanalysis in an attempt to account for two striking and unexpected facts of observation which emerge whenever an attempt is made. Evidently the symptoms of a neurotic source, may in his past life, inhabit the sources of experiential recall to the past or the introspective reflections. In the state of affairs, in that for being the latent characterizations announced as the factoring responsibility for the transference and of resistance . . . one which takes the other side of the problem, while accepting as such, to the latencies and the hidden values non-accepting for new interactions as brought through a hypothesis that will hardly escape the charge of misappropriation of properties by attempting endeavour to re-associate the essentially established personalization, that if the pursuit in calling them a psychoanalyst'. Rapaport (1967) argued, in his posthumously published paper on the methodology of psychoanalysis, that transference and resistance inevitably follow from the fact that the analytic situation is interpersonal.

Despite this general agreement on the centrality of transference and resistance in technique, in that, the analysis of transference is not pursued as systematically and comprehensively affirmed, however, it could be and should be. The relative privacy for which psychoanalytic work makes it impossible for one or of that of any-other, to skilfully improve upon the attemptive conceptual representation as comprehended of issues, its assumption to state this view as anything more that impressions, involving on that of what in the analysis of the transference and to states awareness in the number of reasons that an important aspect in the analysis of the transference of the transference, namely in the resistance, by the awareness of the transference is especially, and often adhering to the analytic procedures that interact among cultural inhibitors, but that will be distinguished as such, that its ranging manifold of distancing non-localities as founded of the analyst's.

However, it must first be to distinguish between two types of interpretation of the transference. That one is an interpretation of resistance to the awareness of transference, the other, is an interpretation of resistance to the resolution of transference. The distinction has clearly been best spelled out in the form from which copies or reproductions can be produced, as to cause to make its awareness and yielding values as grounded in the cognisance to Greenson (1967) and Stone (1967). The first kind of resistance may be called decence transference, although this term emphases the terminological characterization by its term is mainly employed to refer to a phrase of analysis and carried within the general resistance to the transference of wishes, it can also be used for a more isolated instance of transference of defence. With some oversimplification, one might say that in resistance to the awareness of transference, the transference, the transference is what does the resisting.

Another connected description of stating this distinction between resistance and the awareness of transference and resistance to the resolution of transference is between implicit and indirect references to the transference and explicitly or directly referential to the transference. The interpretation of resistance to awareness of the transference is intended to make the implicit transference explicit. While the interpretation of resistance to the resolution of transference is intended to make the patient realize that the already explicit transference does indeed include a determinant from the past.

It is also important to distinguish between the general concept of an interpretation of resistance to the resolution of transference and a particular variety of such an interpretation, namely, a genetic transference interpretation - that is, an interpretation of how an attitude in the present is an inappropriate carry-over from the past. While there is a tendency among analysts to deal explicit references to the transference primarily among analyses to deal explicitly the references to the transference as primarily by a genetic transference interpretation, there are other ways of working toward a revolution of the transference. However, this argument does so implicate that not only is not enough emphasis being given to interpretation of the transference in the here and now, that is, to the interpretation of implicit manifestations of the transference, but also that interpretations intended to resolve the transference as manifested in explicit references to the transference should be primarily in the here and now, rather than genetic transference interpretations.

A patient's statement that he feels the analyst is harsh, for example, is, at least to begin with, likely best dealt with not by interpreting that this is a displacement from the patient's feeling that his father was harsh, but by as elucidation of some other aspect of this here and now attitude, such as what has gone on in the analytic situation that seems to the patient to justify his feeling or what was the anxiety that made it so difficult for him to express his feelings. How the patient experiences the actual situation is an example of the role of the actual situation in a manifestation of transference, which will be a major point of relevant significance.

Of course, both interpretations of the transference in the here and now and genetic transference interpretations are valid and constitute a sequence. We presume that a resistance to the transference ultimately rests on the displacement onto the analysts of attitudes from the past.

Because Freud's case histories focus much more on the yield of analysis than on the details of the process, they are readily but perhaps incorrectly construed as emphasizing work outside the transference much more than work within the transference, and, even within the transference, emphasizing genetic transference interpretations much more than work with the transference in the here and now (Muslin and Gill, 1978). The example of Freud's case reports may have played a role in what is to be considered as the common maldistribution of emphasis in these two respects - not enough on the transference and, within the transference, not enough on the here and now.

Transference interpretations in the here and now and genetic transference interpretations are, of course, exemplified in Freud's writings and are in the repertoire of every analyst, but they are not distinguished sharply enough.

Both participants in the analytic situation are motivated to avoid these interactions. Flight away from the transference and to the past can be a relief to both the patient and the analyst.

These aligning measures have been divided into five categorical divisions and placed into the following parts: (1) The principle that the transference should be encouraged to expand as much as possible within the analytic situation because the analytic work is best done within the transference. (2) the interpretation of disguised allusion to the transference as a main technique for encouraging the expansion of the transference within the analytic situation, (3) the principle that all transference has a connection with something in the present actual analysis situation, (4) how the connection between transference and the actual analytic situation is used in interpreting resistance to the awareness of transference, and (5) the resolution of transference within the here and now and the role of genetic transference interpretation.

The importance of transference interpretations will surely be agreeing to by all analysts, the greater effectiveness of transference interpretations than interpretations outside the transference will be agreeing to by many, but what of the relative roles of interpretation of the transference and interpretation outside the transference?

Freud can be interpreted as either of saying that the analysis of the transference in auxiliary to the analysis of the neurosis or that the analysis of the transference is equivalent to the analysis of the neurosis. The first position is stated in his saying (1913) that the disturbance of the transference has to be overcome by the analysis of transference resistance in order to get on with the work of analysing the neurosis. It is also implied in his reiteration that the ultimate task of analysis is to remember the past, to fill in the gap in memory. The second position is stated in his saying that the victory must be won on the field of the transference (1912) and that the mastery of the transference neurosis 'coincides with getting rid of the illness which was originally brought to the neurosis (1917). In this second view, he says that after the resistance is overcome, memories appear relatively without difficulty.

These two different positions also find expression in the two different ways in which Freud speaks of the transference. In `Dynamics of Transference` he refers to the transference, on the one hand, as `the most powerful resistance to the treatment`(1912) but, on the other hand, as doing us the inestimable service of making the patient's . . ., immediate impulses and manifests, when all is said and done, it is impossible to destroy anyone in absentia or in effigie (1912).

It can be agreed that his principal emphasis fails on the second position. He wrote once, in summary, 'Thus our therapeutic work falls into two phases in the first, all the libido is forced from the symptoms into the transference and concentrated there, in the second, the struggle is waged around this new object and the libido is liberated from it`(1912).

The detailed demonstration that he advocated that the transference should be encouraged to expand as much as possible within the analytic situation lies in clarification that resistance is primarily expressed by repetition, and repetition takes place both within and outside the analytic situation, but that the analyst seeks to deal with it primarily within the analytic situation, that repetition can be not only in the motor sphere (acting) but also in the psychical sphere, and that the psychical sphere is not confined to remembering but includes the present, too.

Freud`s emphasis that the purpose of resistance is to prevent remembering can obscure his point that resistance shows itself primarily by repetition, whether inside or outside the analytic situation. `The greater the resistance, the more extensively, and will act out (repetition)replace remembering`. Similarly in `The Dynamics of Transference` Freud said that the main reason that the transference is so well suited to serve the resistance is that the unconscious implies does not want to be remembered . . . but endeavour to reproduce themselves . . . (1918), the transference is a resistance primarily insofar as it is a repetition.

The point can be restated in terms of the relation between transference and resistance. The resistance expresses itself in repetition, that is, in transference both inside and outside the analytic situation. To deal with the transference. Therefore, is equivalent to dealing with the resistance. Freud emphasized transference within the analytic situation so strongly that it has come to mean only repetition within the analytic situation, even though, conceptually speaking, repetition outside the analytic situation is transference too, and Freud once used the term that way. `We soon perceive that the transference is itself only a piece of repetition and that the repetition is a transference of the forgotten past not only onto the analyst but also onto all the other aspects of the current situation. We . . . find . . . the compulsion to repeat, which now replaces the impulsion to remember, not only in his personal attitude to his analyst but also in every other activity and relationship which may occupy his life at the time . . . (1914).

It is important to realize that the expansion of the repetition inside the analytic situation, whether or not in a reciprocal relationship to repetition outside the analytic situation, is the avenue to control the repetition: `The main instrument . . . for curbing the patient's compulsion to repeat and for turning it into a motive for remembering lies in the handling of the transference. We render the compulsion harmless, and indeed useful, by giving it the right to assert itself in a definite field`(1914).

Kanzer has discussed this issue well in his paper on 'The Motor Sphere of the Transference' (1966). He writes of a 'double-pronged stick-and-carrot' technique by which the transference is fostered within the analytic situation and discouraged outside the analytic situation. The 'stick' is the principle of abstinence as exemplified in the admonition against making important decisions during treatment, and the 'carrot' is the opportunity afforded the transference to expand within the treatment, 'in almost complete freedom' as in a 'playground' (Freud, 1914). As Freud put it, 'Provided only that the patient shows compliance enough to respect the necessary conditions of the analysis, we regularly succeed in giving all the symptoms of the illness a new transference meaning, and in replacing his ordinary neurosis by a 'transference neurosis' of which he can be cured by the therapeutic work' (1914).

The reason it is desirable for the transference to be expressed within the treatment is that there, it `is at every point accessible to our intervention`(1914). In a later statement he made the same point this way. `We have followed this new edition - the transference-neurosis - of the old disorder from its start, we have observed its origin and growth, and we are especially well able to find our way about in it since, as its object, we are situated at it's very centre, (1917), it is not that the transference is forced into the treatment, but that it is spontaneously but implicitly present and is encouraged to expand there and become explicit

Freud emphasized acting in the transference so strongly that one can overlook the repetition in the transference, but does not of necessity for its enactment or recognition that gives validity to acts of a subordinate conformation as ratified in support of explicit authoritative permission. Repetition need not go as far as motor behaviour, it can also be expressed in attitudes, feelings, and intentions, and, indeed, the repetition often does take such form rather than motor action. The importance of making this clear is that Freud can be mistakenly read to mean that repetition in the psychical sphere can only mean remembering the past, are when he writes that the analyst as prepared for a perpetual struggle with his patient to keep in the psychical sphere all the impulses which the patient would like to direct into the motor sphere, and he celebrates it as a triumph for the treatment if he can bring it about that something the patient wishes to discharge in action are disposed if through the work of remembering (1914).

It is true that the analyst's efforts are to convert acting in the motor sphere into awareness in the psychical sphere, but transference may be in the psychical sphere to begin with, albeit disguised. The psychical sphere includes awareness in the transference as well as remembering.

One of the objections one hears, from both analysts and patient, to a heavy emphasis on interpretation of associations about the patients real life primarily in terms of the transference is that it means the analyst is disregarding the importance of what goes on in the patients real life. The criticism is not judiciable. To emphasize the transference meaning is not to deny or belittle other meanings, but to focus on the one of several meanings of the content that is the most important for the analytic process, for the reasons of positing the addition for one coming to any falsifiable conclusion.

Another way in which interpretations of resistance to the transference can be, or at lease appear to the patient to be, a belittling of the importance of the patients outside life is to make the interpretation as though the outside behaviour is primarily an acting out of the transference. The patient may undertake some actions in the outside world as an expression of and resistance to the transference, that is, acting out. But the interpretation of associations about actions in the outside world as having implications for the transference needs mean only that the choice of outside action to figure in the associations is co-determined by the need to express a transference indirectly. It is because of the resistance to awareness of the transference that the transference to be disguised. When the disguise is unmasked by interpretation, it becomes clear that, despite the inevitable differences between the outside situation and the transference situation, the content is the same for the analysis of the necrosis that coincides (Freud wrote that the mastering of the transference neurosis only coincides with getting rid of the illness which was originally brought to the treatment (1917)).

The analytic situation itself fosters the development of attitudes with primary determinants in the past, i.e., transference. The analyst's reserve provides the patient with few and equivocal cues. The purpose of the analytic situation fosters the development of strong emotional responses, and the very fact that the patient has a neurosis means, as Freud said, that' . . . it is a perfectly normal and intelligible thing that the libidinal cathexis [we would now add negative feelings] of someone who is partly unsatisfied, a cathexes which are held ready in anticipation, should be directly as well to the figure of the analyst (1912).

While the analytic setup itself fosters the expansion of the transference within the analytic situation, the interpretation of resistance to the awareness of the transference will further this expansion.

There are important resistances on the part of both patient and analyst to awareness of the transference. On the patient's part, this is because of the difficulty in recognizing erotic and hostile impulses toward the very person to whom they have to be disclosed. On the analyst's part, this is because the patient is likely to attitude the very attitudes to him which are most likely to cause him discomfort. The attitudes the patient believes the analysts has toward him are often the ones the patient is least likely to voice, in a general sense because of a feeling that it is impertinent for him to concern himself with the analyst's feelings, and in a more specific sense because the aptitudes as held by the analyst are often attitudes the patient feels the analyst will be comfortable about having ascribed to him. It is for this reason that the analyst must be especially alert to the attitudes the patient believes he has, not only to the attitudes the patient does have toward him. If the analyst is able to see himself as a participant in an interaction, as he will become much more attuned to this important area of transference, which might otherwise escape him.

The investigations of attitudes are ascribed to the analyst makes easier the subsequent investigation of the intrinsic factors in the patient that played a role in such ascription. For example, the exposure of the fact that the patient ascribes sexual interests in him to the analyst, and generally to the patient, alternatively the subsequent exploration of the patient's sexual wish toward the analyst, and genetically the parent.

The resistance to the awareness of these attitudes is responsible for their appearing in various disguises in the patient's manifested associations and for the analyst's reluctance to unmask the disguise. The most commonly recognized disguise is by displacement, but identification is an equally important one. In displacement, the patient's attitudes are narrated for being toward a third party. In identification, the patient attitudes to himself attitudes he believes the analyst has toward him.

To encourage the expansion of the transference within the analytic situation, the disguises in which the transference appears have to be interpreted in the case of displacement the interpretation will be of allusions to the transference in association not manifestly about the transference. This is a kind of interpretation every analyst often makes. In the case of identifications, the analyst interprets the attitudes that the patient ascribes to himself the identification with which an attitude and subsequently attributed to the analyst. Lipton (1977) has recently described this form of disguise allusion in the transference with illuminating illustration.

In his autobiography, Freud wrote, 'The patient remains under the influence of the analytic situation as hopefully of a latter position or a period of decline, as though he is not directing responsibly for the mental activities onto a particular subject. Justly in assuming that nothing will occur, as not of some reference to the situation (1925). Since associations are obviously often not directed about the analytic situation, the interpretation of Freud's remark rests on what he meant by the 'analytic situation'.

It is believed that Freud's meaning can be clarified by reference to a statement he made in, 'The Interpretation of Dreams'. He said that when the patient is told to say whatever comes into his mind, his associations become directed by the 'purposive ideas inherent in the treatment' and that there are two such inherent regressive themes, one relating to the illness and the other - concerning which, Freud said, the patient has 'no suspicion'; - relating to other analyst's (1900), if the patient has ''no suspicion' of the theme relating to the analyst (1900). If the patient has 'no suspicions' - relating to the analyst (1900). If the patient has 'no suspicions' of the theme relating to the analyst, such that the theme appears only in disguise, the patient 's associations, it is contended that Freud's remark not only specifies the themes inherent in the patient 's identifications', but means that the associations are simultaneously directed by these two purposive ideas, not something by one and sometimes by the other.

One important reason that the early and continuing presence of the transference is not always recognized in that it is considered to be absent in the patient who is talking recognized is that it is considered to be absent in the patient who is talking freely and apparently without resistance. As (Muslin and Gill, 1976) pointed out in a paper on the early interpretation of transference resistance, to the transference is probably present from the beginning, even if the patient is talking apparently freely. The patient may well be talking about issues not manifestingly about the transference which are nevertheless, also allusions to the transference, but the analyst has to be alert to the pervasiveness that sometimes delusion is accepted as true that is actually being false or unreal, to which delusionary deceptions and apparitions of phantom fallacies, of these spurious verifications are judgmental quantification's about them. The analyst should progress on the working assumption, that the patient's associations have transference implications pervasively, that with which this assumption is not to be confused with denial or neglect of the current aspects of the analytic situation. It is theoretically always possible to give precedence to a transference interpretation if one can only discern it through its disguise by resistance. This is not to dispute the desirability of learning as much as one can about the patient, if only to be a position to make more correct interpretations of the transference. One therefore, does not interfere with an apparently free flow of associations, especially early, unless the transference threatens the analytic situation to the point where its interpretation is mandatary rather than optional.

With the recognition that evens apparently freely associating patient may also be showing resistance to awareness of the transference, this formulation should not interfere as long a useful information being gathered should relace Freud's dictum that the transference should not be interpreted until it becomes a resistance (1913).

It can be argued that every transference has some connection to some aspect of the current analytic situation, in the sense that the past can exert an influence only insofar as it exists in the present. Of course, all the determinants of a transference are current in the sense that what I am distinguishing is the current reality of the analytic situation, that is, what actually goes on between patient and analyst in the situation from how the patient is currently constituted as a result of his past.

All analysts would dubiously agree that there are both current and transferential determinants of the analytic situation, and probably no analyst would argue that a transference of the analytic situation, and probably no analyst would argue that a transference idea can be expressed without contamination, as it was, that is, without any connection to anything current in the patient-analyst relationship. Nevertheless, the implications of this fact for technique are often neglected in practice, as my next point is only to argue for the connection.

Several authors, e.g., Kohut 1959 and Loewald 1960, have pointed out that Freud`s early application by the act or practice of using something or the state of being used, this, however, employ of the quality of being appropriate or valuable to some end as to accommodate the accountable or warrant the use of the term transference. In `The Interpretation of Dreams, in a connection not immediately recognizable as related to the present day use of the term, reveals the fallacy of considering that transference can be expressed free of any connection to the present. That early use was to refer to the fact that an unconscious idea cannot be expressed as such, but only as it becomes connected to a preconscious o r conscious content. In the phenomenon with which Freud was then concerned, the dream transference took place from an unconscious wish to a day residue. In `The Interpretation of Dreams, `Freud used the term transference both for the general rule that an unconscious content is expressible only as it becomes transferred to a preconscious or conscious content and for the specific application of this rule to a transference to the analyst. Just as the day residue is the point of attachment of the dream wish, so must there be an analytic-situation residue, though Freud did not use that term, as the point of attachment of the transference.

Analysts have always limited their behaviour, both in variety and intensity, to increase the extent to which the patient's behaviour is determined by his idiosyncratic interpretation of the analyst's behaviour. In fact, analysts unfortunately sometimes limit the behaviour so much as to compare with such an expression or unpiled standard or absolute approximation, that the entire relationship with the patient matter of technique, with no nontechnical personal relation, as Liptop (1977) has pointed out.

But no matter how far the analyst attempts to carry this limitation of his behaviour, the very existence of the analytic situation provides the patient with innumerable cues which can enviably become his rationale for his transference responses. In other words, the current situation cannot be made to disappear - that is, the analytic situation is real. It is easy to forget this truism in one's zeal to diminish the role of the current situation in determining the patient 's responses. One can try to keep past and present determinants relatively perceptible from one another, but one cannot obtain either 'pure culture'. Freud wrote: 'I insist on this procedure [the couch], however, for its purpose and result are to prevent the transference from mingling with the patient's associations imperceptibly, to isolate the transference and to allow it to come forward in due course sharply defined as a resistance' (1913). Even 'isolate' is too strong a word in the light of the inevitable intertwining of the transference with the current situation.

If the analyst remains under the illusion that the current cues he provides to the patient can be reduced to the vanishing point, he may be led into a silent withdrawal, which is not too distant from the caricature of an analyst as someone who does refuse to have any personal relationship with the patient. What happens then is that silence has become a technique rather than merely an indication that the analyst is listening. The patient's responses under such conditions can be mistaken fo uncontaminated transference when they are in fact transference adaptions to the actuality of the silence.

The recognition, from which it takes its point of departure, as it was, has a crucial implications for the technique of interpreting resistance to the awareness of transference, in that, if, the analyst becomes persuaded of the centrality of transference and the importance of encouraging the transference to expand within the analytic situation, he has to find the presenting and plausible interpretation of resistance to the awareness of transference he should make. Is that, his most reliable guide is the cues offered by what is actually going on in the analytic situation? : On the one hand, the events of the situation, such as change in time of session, or an interpretation made by the analyst, and, on the other hand, how the patient is experiencing the situation as reflected in explicit remarks about it, however, fleeting these may be. This is the primary yield for technique of the recognition that any transference must have a link to the actuality of the analytic situation. The cue points to the nature of the transference, just as the day residue for a dream may be a quick pointer of the latent dream thoughts. Attention to the current situation for a transference elaboration will keep the analyst from making mechanical transference interpretation, in which he interprets that there are allusions to the transference in association not manifestly about the transference, but without offering any plausible bias for the interpretation. Attention to the current stimulation offers some degree of protection against the analyst's inevitability whose tendency to project his own views onto the patient, either because of countertransference or because of a preconceived theoretical bias about the content and hierarchical relationships in psychodynamics.

The analyst may be very surprised at what in his behaviour the patient finds important or unimportant, for the patient's responses will be idiosyncratically determined by the transference, the patient's responses may seem to be something the patient as well as the analysts consider trivial, because, as in displacement to a trivial aspect of the day residue of a dream, displacement can better serve resistance when it is to something trivial. Because it is connected to conflict-laden material, the stimulus to the transference may be difficult to find. It may be quickly disavowed, so that its presence in awareness is only transitory. With the discovery of the disavowed, the patient may also gain insight into how it repeats as disavowed earlier in his life. In his search for the present stimuli which the patient is responding transferentially, as the analyst must therefore remain alert to both fleeting and apparently trivial manifested reference to himself as well as in the events of the analytic situation.

If the analyst interprets the patient's attitudes in a spirit of seeing their possible plausibility in the light of what information the patient does have, rather than in the spirit of either affirming or denying the patient's views, the way is open for their further expression and elucidation. The analyst will be respecting the effort to be plausible and realistic, rather than manufacturing his transference attitudes out of whole bodied material.

Importantly, is to make a transference interpretation plausible to the patient in terms of as current stimulus that, if the analyst is persuaded that the manifest content has important implications for the transference but he is unable to see a current stimulus for the attitude, he should explicitly say so if he decides to make the transference interpretation anyway. The patient himself may then be able to say what the current stimulus is.

It is sometimes argued that the analyst's attention to his own behaviour is a precipitant for the transference, will increase the patient's resistance to recognizing the transference. That, on the contrary, that because of the inevitable interrelationship of the current and transferential determinants, it is only through interpretation that they can be disentangled.

It is also argued that one must wait until the transference has reached optimal intensity before it can be advantageously interpreted. It is true that too hasty and interpretation of the transference can serve as a defensive function for the analyst and deny him the information he needs to make a more appropriate transference interpretation. But it is true that delay in interpreting transference interpretation, but it is also true that delay in interpreting runs the risk of allowing an unmanageable transference to develop. It is also true that deliberate delay can be a manipulation in the service of abreaction rather than analysis, and, like silence, can lead to a response to the actual situation which is mistaken for uncontaminated transference. Obviously important, is assumed in the issues of timing are involved, whereas an important clue to when a transference interpretation is apt and which one to makes lies in whether the interpretation can be made plausibly in terms of the determinant, namely, as something in the current analytic situation. Such as, in the approaching transference in the spirit of seeing how it appears plausibly realistic to the patient, it paves the way toward its further elucidation and expression.

Freud's emphasis on remembering as the goal of the analytic work implies that remembering is the principal avenue to the resolution of the transference. But the delineation of the successive steps in the development of the analytic technique (1920) makes clear that he saw this development as a change from an effort to reach memories directly to the utilization of the transference as the necessary intermediacy to reaching the memories.

In contrast to remembering as the way the transference is resolved, Freud also described resistance for beings primarily overcome in the transference, with remembering following relatively easily afterwards, 'From the repetitive reactions which are exhibited in the transference we are led along the familiar paths to the awakening of the memories, which appear without difficulty, as it was, after the resistance has been overcome' (1914), and 'This revision of the process of repetition can be accomplished only in part in connection with the memory traces of the process which led to repression. The decisive part of the work's achieved by creating in the patient's relation to the analyst - in the 'transference' new editions of the old conflicts . . . Thus, the transference becomes the battlefield on which all the mutually struggling forces should meet one another' (1917). This is the primary indication for which Strachey (1934) classified in his seminal paper on the therapeutic action of psychoanalysis.

There are two main ways in which resolution of the transference can take place through work with the transference in the here and now. The first lies in the clarification of what are the clues in the current situation which are the patient's point of departure force a transference elaboration. The exposure of the current point of departure at once raises the question of whether it is adequate to the conclusion drawn from it. The relating of the transference to a current stimulus is, after all, parts of the patient's effort to make, the transference attitude plausibly determined by the present. The reverse and ambiguity of the analyst's behaviour are what increases the ranges of apparently plausible conclusions the patient may draw. If an examination of the basis for the conclusion makes clear that the actual situation to which the patient responds is subject to other meanings than the one the patient has reached, he will more reality consider his pre-existing bias, that is to say, in that of transference.

Another critic of an earlier version of this paper suggested that, in speaking of the current relationship and the relation between the patient's conclusion and the information on which they seem plausibly based, such in some absolute conception of what is real in the analytic situation, of which the analyst is the final arbiter. That is not the case, that what the patient must come to see is that the information he has is subject to other possible interpretations implies the very contrary to an absolute conception of reality. In fact, analyst and patient engage in a dialogue in a spirit of attempting to arrive at a consensus about reality, not about some factious absolute reality.

The second way in which resolution of the transference can take place within the work with the transference in the here and now is that in the very interpretation of the transference the patient had a new experience. He is being treated differently from how he expected to be. Analysts seem reluctant to emphasize his new experience, as though it endangers the role of insight and argue for interpersonal influence as the significant factor in change. Strachey's emphasis on the new experience in the mutative transference interpretation has unfortunately been overshadowed by his views on introjection, which have been mistaken to advocate manipulating the transference. Strachey meant introjection of the more benign superego of the analyst only as a temporary strep on the road toward insight. Not only is the new experience not to be confused with the interpersonal influence of a transference gratification, but the new experience occurs together with insight into both the patient's biassed expectation and the new experience. As Strachey points out, what is unique about the transference interpretation is that insight and the new experience take place in relation to the very person who was expected to behave differently, and it is this which gives the work in the transference, its immediacy and effectiveness. While Freud did stress the effective immediacy of the transference, he did not make the new experience explicit.

It is important to recognize that transference interpretation is not a matter of experience, in contrast to insight, but a joining of the two together, both are needed to bring about and maintain the desired changes in the patient. It is also important to recognize that no new techniques of intervention are required to provide the new experience. It is an inevitable accompaniment of interpretation of the transference in the here and now. It is often overlooked that, although Strachey said that only transference interpretations are outside the transference.

Rosenfeld (1972) has pointed out that clarification of material outside the transference is often necessary to know what is the appropriate transference interpretation, and that both genetic transference interpretations and extratransference interpretation taking to consider an inclination as marked by or indication of notable worth or simply the consequence based upon the role in working through. Strachey said relatively little about working through, but surely nothing against the necessary provision with which every thing needfully is explicitly recognized as the role for the recovery of the past in the resolving dissection of the purposiveness determined by the transference.

In taking positions, as to emphasis the role of the analysis of the transference in here and now, both in interpreting resistance to the awareness of transference and in working toward its resolution by relating to the actuality of the situation. In that of opinion or purpose with the evidence that extratransference and genetic transference interpretation and, of course, working through is important too, that the matter is one of emphasis. Also, interpretation of resistance to awareness of the transference should figure in the majority of sessions, and that if this is done by relating the transference to the actual analytic situation, the very same interpretation is a beginning of work to the resolution of the transference. To justify this view more persuasively would require detailed case material.

The concern and considerations that the Kleinian annalists whom, many analysts feel, are in error in giving the analysis of the transference too great if not even as exclusive role in the analytic process. It is true that Kleinians emphasize the analysis of the transference more, in their writing at least, than does the general run of analysts. As, Anna Freud (1968) complained that the concept of transference has become overexpanded seems to be directed against the Kleinians. One of the reasons the Kleinians consider themselves the true followers of Freud in technique are precisely because of the emphasis they put on the analysis of the transference. Hanna Segal (1967), for example, writes, `Too say that all communications are seen as communications about the patents phantasy as well as current external life is equivalent to saying that all communications contain something relevant to the transference situation. In Kleinian technique, the interpretation of the transference is often more central than in the classical technique.

Affirmly held point of view or way of regarding that Freud and transference had directly connected by simulating observations that we can only offer, that Freud wrote briefly about transference, and did so, to sustain the way in which, is, as a whole, that his actions were justly taken in and around 1917. Another observation which can rarely be made about Freud's works, and which everyone may not agree with, is that, with one or two exceptions, what he did write on transference did not reach the high level of analytical thought which has come to be regarded as standard for him. Some indication of what his contribution consists of is given by the editors of the Standard Edition, who list them in several places. One of the longer lists, in a footnote on page 431 of Volume 16, includes six references: 'Studies of Hysteria' with Breuer (1895), the Dora paper (1905), 'The Dynamics of Transference' (1912), 'Observations on Transference-Love' (1915), the chapter on transference in the Introductory Lectures (1917), and 'Analysis Terminable and Interminable' (1937). Although the editors, in no sense suggest that these six papers include everything Freud wrote on the subject. It does seem evident that, considering the essential importance of transference to analysis, he wrote, 'The Dynamics of Transference', 'Transference-Love', and the transference chapter in the Introductory Lectures, came across, as, perhaps, his least significant contribution.

Freud's first direct mention of transference comes upon the pages ascribed within the 'Studies of Hysteria' (1895), his first significant reference to it, however did not appear until five years later, when, in a letter to Fliess on April 16, 1900, he said (Freud, 1887-1902) he was 'beginning to see that the apparent endlessness of the treatment is something of an inherent feature and is connected with the transference'. In a footnote to this letter the editors said that, 'This was the first insight into the role of transference in psychotherapy.'

Despite these early references, it seems correct to say that yet another five years were to go by before the phenomenon of transference was actually introduced. Even so, the introduction was far from prominent, for it was tacked on like an afterthought as a four-page portion of a postscript to what was perhaps Freud's most fascinating case history to date, the case of Dora (1905).

Using data from Dora's three-month-long, unexpectedly terminated analysis, and especially from her dramatic transference reaction which had taken him quite unawares, Freud now gave to transference its first distinct psychological entity and for the first time indicated its essential role in the analytic process. His account, although in general more than adequate - in the elegant fact and unmistakably 'finished' - was brief, and almost to the point, and perhaps not an entirely worthy introduction so much more a truly great discovery. What was uniquely great was his recognizing the usefulness of transference. In his analysis of Dora he had noted not only that transference feelings existed and were powerful, but, much to his dismay, he had realized what a serious, perhaps, even insurmountable obstacles that objectively would be. Then, in what seems like a creative leap, Freud made the almost unbelievable discoveries that transference was in fact, the key to analysis, that by properly taking the patient's transference and therapeutic force was added to the analytic method.

The impact on analysis of this startling discovery was actually much greater and much more significant than most people seem to appreciate. Although the role of transference as the sine quo non of analysis and is widely accepted, and was stated by Freud from the first, it has almost never been acclaimed for having brought about an entire change in the nature of analysis. The introduction of free association to analysis, a much lesser change, receives and still receives much more recognition.

One of the reasons for the relatively unheralded entry of transference into analysis may have been for circumstances of its discovery. Although Freud's new ideas were recorded as if they arose as sudden inspiration during the Dora analysis, they may in fact have developed somewhat later. In the paper's precatory remarks, for instance, Freud said he had not discussed transference with Dora at all, and in the postscript, he said he had been unaware of her transference feelings. Also, pointing to a later discovery date is the extraordinary delay in the paper's publication. According to the editor's note, the paper had been completed and accepted for publication by late January 1901, but this date was then actually set back more than four and a half years until October 1905. The editors said, 'We have no information as to how it happened that Freud, . . . deferred publication.' It readily seems that for reasons to have been that only during those four and a half years, as a consequence to his own self-analysis, that he came to a better understanding of the relevantly significant as the applicable reason to posit of the transference. Only then may it have been possible for him to turn again to the Dora case, to apply to it of what he had learned in himself, to write this essay as part of the postscript, and at last to release the paper for publication.

Freud's self-analysis has been considered from many angles, but not significantly, as can be of valuing measure, in at least from the standpoint of transference. Opponents of the idea that there is such a thing as definite self-analysis, some of whom say it is impossible, generally an object on grounds that without any analyst there can be no transference neurosis. Freud clearly demonstrated, as, perhaps, that the situation that may be necessary to fill this need: Self-analysis may require that, at least a halfway satisfactory transference object. In Freud's case, the main transference object at this time seems to have been Fliess, who filled the role rather well. As with any analysis, the authenticity as known in the unfeigned design as if existing or having no illusions and facing reality squarely, by which the 'real' impact on Freud was slight, he was essentially a neutral figure, relatively anonymous and physically separates. All of this, and Fliess`s own reciprocal transference reactions, made it possible for Freud to endow Fliess with whatever qualities and whatever feelings were essential to the development of Freud`s transference, and, it should be added, his transference neurosis. In the end, of course, the transference was in part resolved. Freud`s eventual awakening of its self realization in its presence within him of such strange and powerful psychological forces must have come to the conclusion as a stupefied disilluionary dejection toward Fliess, however, his subsequent working out of some of these transference attachments must have been both an intellectual triumph and an immensely healing and releasing of actions, operations or motions involved in the accomplishment of an ending that makes from its process.

In the years following this revolutionary discovery, the central role of transference in analysis increased in remarkable acceptance, and it has easily held this central position ever since. What the substance of this central position distinctfully compose in having or be capable of having within the constructs to which is something of a mystery, for, it seems as nothing about analysis and is, of least to be, the well known than how individual analysis actually uses transference in their day-to-day work with patients. As a guess, as, perhaps of each analysts concept of transference derives variably but significantly from his own inner experience, transference probably means many and varying differentiations to things as to different analysts.

In the same differentiated individuals, as that Freud's own pupils must have differed on this issue, not only from him but from each other. Although some of their differences may have been slight, others, my have contributed significantly to later analytic developments. A question could be raised, for instance, whether differences in handling the transference which at first were the property of one analyst gradually develop into formal clinical methods used by many, and whether these clinical methods, after having been conceptualized, serve as the beginning of variously divergent schools of analysis. Such occurrences, consistent with certain beliefs that analytic ideas do arise in this way, primarily out of transference experiences in the analytic situation, would lead to the question whether the history of the ideological differences in what was actually said and done in response to transference reactions that to any other factor. Whatever the case, many differences and divergencies did occur among the early analysts, and all of that is supposed to have had to do in some major way with differences in the handling of the transference.

Strangely, Freud himself seems to have taken little part in influencing this rapid and divergent period of growth. Usually accused of being too dominating in such matters, Freud seems to have done just the opposite during the development of this most critical aspect of analysis, the process itself, and, for reasons unknown, detached himself from it.

What was needed, one might be inclined to say, was not leadership in the form of domination, but leadership in trying to provide what was lacking, and still lacking, namely an analytical rationale for transference phenomena. The question must be asked, of course, whether in fact this would have been a good thing at that particular time in psychoanalytic history. Perhaps not. The exercise of closure, which Freud's structuring might have amounted to. But although adding to understanding and stability at ceratin theoretical levels, could at another level, so such closures have often done, have placed many obstacles in the way of further analytical developments. Thus, his leaving the matter of transference wide open, even though it led to confusion and uncertainty, may have been just as well.

In many ways the closest Freud ever came to establishing a formal analytical rationale for transference was his first attempt, in the postscript to the case of hysteria (1905). These few pages are and among the most important of all Freud's writings, outweighing by far the paper to which they are appended. Yet, in the case of Dora has always been taught as an entity rather than the ancillary to the essay on transference. In that essay Freud was clear: His ideas revealed tremendous insights and promised more to come, and that, the powers of the neurosis are occupied in creating a new edition of the same disease. Just think of the analytic implications of his saying that this new edition consists of a special class of mental structures, for the most part unconscious, having the peculiar characteristic of being able to replace earlier persons with that of the person of the analyst, and in the fashion applying all components of the original neurosis to the person of the analytical at the present time. Surely as profound a statement as any he ever made.

He then goes on to say that there is no way to avoid transference, that this 'latest creation of the desire must be combatted like all the earlier ones', and that, although this is by far the hardest part of analysis, only after the transference has been resolved can a patient arrive at a sense of conviction of the validity of the connection which have been constructed during analysis.

He concludes by saying, 'In psychoanalysis . . . all the patients' tendencies, including hostile ones, are aroused, they are then turned to account for reasons that explain for the internalization of justification, and by the same measure was to purposively give a sensible reason for the proposed change in the analysis by which of being made conscious. That, in this way, the transference is constantly being put-down, however, transference, which seems ordained to be the greatest obstacle to psychoanalysis, becomes its most powerful . . .

These remarkable observations, in conveying a sense of deep conviction that could arise, one feels, only from Freud's own hard-won inner experience, that nowhere is there a suggestion that transference is a mere technical matter. Far from it, as Freud announces that he has come upon as new and exciting kind of mental function, or, as it is to believe, that a new and exciting kind of ego function.

Very quickly, however, Freud's conviction sees to have failed him. Nothing he wrote afterwards about transference was at this level, and most of his later references were a retreat from it, for instance, he never did develop the promising idea that the mind constantly creates new editions of the original neurosis and meaningfully incline the minded inclusion in them, an ever-changing series of persons. Instead, he tended to become less specific, even referring to transference at times in a broad terms as if it were no more than rapport between patient and analysts, or as if it was an interpersonal or psychosocial relationship, concepts which, of course, a great many analysts have since adopted, but which were not part of Freud's original ideas.

Perhaps his most persistent deviation was an on-and-off tendency to regard transference merely as a technical matter, often writing of it as an asset to analysis when positive and a liability when negative.

Significantly, because it indicated that an active struggle was still going on within him, Freud occasionally expressed once again, even though briefly his earlier insights, particularly his ideas that transference is an essential although unexplored part of mental life. An example of this appears in his alternative obtainments such that is gainfully to appear of as quality of being pleasant or agreeable to a feature that makes for pleasantness or ease, among the amenities of the central geniality, otherwise, the prevailing indifference account for the transference in 'An Autobiographical Study' (1925). Transference, he says, 'is a universal phenomenon of the human mind. And in fact dominated the whole of each person's relations to his human environment. In these few words' Freud again made the point, and in declarative fashion, that transference is a mental structure of the greatest magnitude, but he never really followed it up.

Rather extensive evidence of his departure from the original concept and his continuing struggle with that concept is seen most clearly, wherein, the 'Analysis Terminable and Interminable' is much more than a courageous, brilliant, and pessimistic, appraisal of the difficulties and limitations of analysis, although transference is briefly mentioned in its content, yet a great deal about it comes through, some quite directly, some by easy inference. When looked at in this way, two themes stand out: Freud's personal frustration with the enigmas of transference and his tacit placing of transference in the centre of success and failure in analysis, both as a therapy and as a developing science. What also comes through, is the perplexing realization of how far Freud had, by now, seemingly moved away from his original concepts. Or had he?

All the same, even if it is insufficient for exclusive reliance in relations to the complicated neurosis, for which it would be fallacious to assign to the recall and reconstruction of the past an exclusively explanatory value (in the intellectual sense), important though that functions be, and difficult as its full-blown emotional correlate may be to come by. There is no doubt that, even in complicated neurosis, equivalently complicated transference neurosis, the genuine complex and complicated transference neurosis, the genuinely experienced linking of the past and present can have, at times, a certain uniquely specific dynamic effect of its own, a type of telescoping or merging of common elements in experience, which must be connected with the meaninglessness of time in unconscious life, compared with its stern authority in the life of consciousness and adaptation to everyday reality. Contributing decisively to such experiences as to whatever degree it occurs, is of course, the vivid currency of the transference neurosis, and central in this, the reincarnations of old objects in an actual person, the analyst.

Thus, an allied problem in the general sphere of transference is the fascination and often enigmatic interplay of past and present. If one wishes to view this interplay in terms of a stereotyped formulation, the matter can remain relatively uncomplicated - as a formulation. Unfortunately., This is too often the case. The phenomenon, however, retains some important obscurities, which cannot thoroughly dispel, but to which I would like to call attention. To concentrate on the dimension of time, it seems in reference to the complication and immediate aspects of technique, nonetheless, essential. For example, we can assume that the transference neurosis re-enacts the essential conflicts of the infantile neurosis in a current setting. If a reasonable degree of awareness of transference is established, the next problem is the genetic reduction of the neurosis to its elements in the past, through analysis of the transference resistance and allied intrapsychic resistances, ultimately genetic interpretations, recollections and reconstructions and working through. Such that the transference is related to its genetic origins, the analyst thereby emerges in his true, i.e., real, identity to the patient, the transference is putatively 'resolved'. To the extent that one follows the traditional view that all resistances, including the transference itself, is ultimately directed against the restoration of early memories as such, this is a convincing formulation. Is that, only to say, that in his own right as having to a certain tightly logical quality? However, we know that it this is not so readily accomplished, apart from the special intrapsychic considerations described afterward by Freud in 'Analysis Terminable and Interminable'. Although in a favourable case, much of the cognitive interpretative work can be accomplished, there remains the fact that cognition responsibility, in its bare sense, does not necessarily lead to the subsidence of powerful dynamism, to the withdrawal of 'cathexes' from importantly real objects. For, as mentioned, a short while ago, the analyst is a real and living object, apart from the representations with which the transference invests him, and which are interpretable as such, for which there is no, at any time a seldom, a confusing interrelations and commonly of the emergent responses, due to the same old seeking, and this is directed toward a new individual in his own right, both are important, furthermore, there are large and important ones of overlapping. Apart from such considerations, even the explicitly incestuous transference is currently experienced (as, at least in good part) by a full-grown adult (like the original oedipus), instead of a totally and actually helpless child. To be sure, the latter state is reflected in the emergent transference elements of instinctual striving, but it is subject to analysis, and the residual is something significant, if not totally different. It is these residual sexual wish, presumably directed toward the person of the analyst, as such, which must be displaced to others, if, as generally agreed, the revival of infantile fantasies and strivings in the biologically mature adolescent presents a new and special problem, one must assume distinctiveness of experience for the adult, although it is true that in the majority of instances, adequate solution is favoured by the adult state. There is, in any case, a residual relationship between persons who have worked together in a prolonged, arduous and intimate relationship, which, strictly speaking, are reversibly disconnected or divorced of services, in that the transference merely ushers out the retirement for which its rendering retreat of that state of mind or feeling by an inner avoidance of something usually felt as unpleasant or pronounced for it's adverse but mutual colouration. Blending to some confusion between the two spheres of feeling. The general tendency is that both components are fully gratified to some degree. But, there is the ubiquitous power of the residual primordial transference, yet, argue to cling to an omnipotent partisan to resist the displacement of its 'sublimated' anaclitic aspects, even if the various representation of the wishes for bodily intimacy has been thoroughly analysed and successfully displaced. The outcome is largely the transference of the transference, as mentioned earlier, in a different context. For everyday reality can provide no actual answer to such cravings. In this connection, note, Freud's genial envy of Pfister. If the man of faith finds this gratification in revealing religion, others in a wide range of secular beliefs and 'leaders' the modern rational and sceptical intellectual is less fortunate in this respect. Presumably free, he is prone to invest even intellectual disciplines or the proponents with inappropriate expectations and partisan passions, but, least of mention, that within these fields of analytical and theoretical thought, is not to provide exceptions to this tendency.

Though if one is to maintain and beneficially confine its bothering of reservations about the clarity of conceptualization, the explanatory discussion of Kohut and Seitz, is a very useful contribution to the direct complication or which by some understanding the awareness in one's own self. Both Loewald and Kohut have deliberately associated a special but the different use of one of Freud's three conceptions of transference, i.e., the transference from the unconscious to the preconscious.

Yet, to furthering comments on primordial transference, at least potentially, are largely psychological (mental) component, the concept of 'transference of the transference' would be applicable to this component. For it does appear that certain aspect of the search for the omnipotent and omniscient caretaking parents are implicitly practical as virtually capable for being turned to use or account for its functional practicability for something of a process or the procedure for being all but the essential purpose to come to or tend toward a common point, for which are the knowledgeable information or ideas, is nothing but causative effectuality. As suggested earlier, there are important qualitative and quantitative distinctions in the mode of persistence and such strivings, however, even to the extent that they are detached from the analyst and carried into some reasonably appropriate expression in everyday life, they retain at least a subtle quality which contravenes reality, one which derives from earliest infancy, and remains - to this extent - a transference. 'Santa Claus' lives on, where one might least expect to meet him, whether as a donor of miracle drug or of far more complex panaceas.

If one prescribes to this parasymbiotic transference drive, a true primordial origin, it is necessary to take cognizance of certain important concepts dealing with the earliest period of life. If we assume a powerful original organismic drive toward an original 'object', a striving to nullify separation from the beginning, how does this make something legally valid or operative usually by formal approval or sanctioned with concepts such as 'primary narcissism' or the 'objectless phase' or 'the primary psycho physiological self' (We note in passing that there are those who do not accept these as usually construed in the technique of Balint), for example, or Fairbairn or - conspicuously - Melanie Klein. These are states, variously defined or conceived, which apply to the earliest neonatal period, in which life, to state more simply, exists only as the potential in physiological processes. Since there is (we postulate) no clear awareness of self-withdrawal from the mother, there can be no 'mentally' represented or experienced drive to obliterate the separation (concerning oneself and object, conceiver of as separate, in a continuing sense). There are, of course, discharge phenomena, the precursors of purposive activity, and there are urgent physiological needs, directed toward fulfilment or relief, rather than toward an object as such. However, in relation to these physiological needs as archaistic precursors of object relationships, it must be noted that in all, except respiration and spontaneous sphincter relief (even in these instances, not without exception or reservation), the need fulfilment must be mediated by the primordial object (or her surrogate). There is also, of course, the uniquely important requirement for 'holding', in a literal expression, from the outset. The material partner in human symbiosis which supplies what the neonate cannot seek by 'clinging', as for Bowlty and Murphy, in the sense that must be experienced to the physiological ebb and flow of tension, even if restricted to the kinaesthetic, connected with a peripheral sensory registration, which is the protophase of the recognition of separation from the object or nonpresence of the object, as a painful instance of, her presence in apposition the converse? That the general context may be only in which the sense of unity is preponderant, or, more accurately, that there is no general awareness of 'separation' as such, means that the drive for union does not exist in a general psychological sense. It is, so to speak, satisfied. That object constancy, with its cognate 'longing', is quite a different experience from the urgencies of primitive need fulfilment is true, however, regardless of what may be added by maturational and developmental considerations, instinctual and perceptual, there is no reason to assume other than a core of developmental continuity from the earliest needs and their fulfilment to the later state, and some continuing degree of contingency based on them.

There is a very rough parallel in the way certain analytic patients, before a firm relationship with the analyst is established, signal certain primitive experiences and tendencies in special reactions to the end of the hour, to the nonvisibility of the analyst, to interruption of their association, to failure of the analyst to talk, and similar matters. We must note that in the basic formation of the ego is evident amongst the primitive reactions and beyond to separations, in the form of very early identifications as based on care taking functions. Certainly in the very development of autonomous ego of the mother's investment in the, have a decisive role in the character of the their development. And in the case of object constancy, in its connotation of libidinal cathexis, where is no need whatsoever (emotional or otherwise) is needed for prolonged periods. The importance of the object is, to put it mildly, liable to deteriorate, or to differ complicating aggressive change. Probably the characteristic feature of later developing relations to the object (love and the wish for love), as separate if not always separated from demonstrable primitivity, in the need fulfilment, have a special relationship to those 'ancillary' aspects of neonatal nurture, whose lack has been shown to be an actual threat to life in some instances, not to speak of sound emotional development. So that from the first, regardless of the assumed state of libidinal (and aggressive) economy, or the assumed state of psychological nondifferentiation between self and potential object, there are critical percussive phenomena, objectively observed, and probably prototypic subjective experiences of separation, which are the forerunners of all subsequent experiences of the kind. One may generalize to the effect that, with maturation and development, secondary identifications, and the various other processes of 'internalization' in its broadest sense, the problem of separation and its mastery becomes correspondingly more complex, and changes with the successive phase of life, but never entirely disappears.

In the view of the psychoanalytic situation described earlier, the latent mobilization of experiences of separation stimulated by the situational structure awakens the driving primordial urge to undo or to master the painful separations which it represents, usually embodied in the various forms of clinical transference that which we are familiar. One legitimate gratification which tends to mitigate superfluous transference regression is the transmission of understanding that at times, are thought that by the 'mature transference', in effect, the 'therapeutic alliance' or a group of mature ego functions which enter into such an alliance. Now, there is one blurring and overlapping at the conceptual edges in both instances, but the concept as such is largely distinct from either one, as it is from the primitive transference, which we have been discussing. Whether the concept is thought by others to comprehend a demonstrable actuality, which is a further question. This question, of course, can only follow on conceptual clarity. This in saying, of a nonrational urge, not directly dependent on the perception of immediate clinical purposes, a true transference in the sense that it is displaced (in currently relevant form) from the parent of early childhood to the analyst. Its content is not anti-sensational, but largely non-sensual of sometimes transitional, as the child's pleasure in the assemblages of 'dirty words' and encompasses a special and not minuscule sphere of the object relationship: The wish to understand, and to be understood, the wish to be given understanding, i.e., teaching, specifically by the parent (or later surrogate); the wish to be taught to use ingenuity in making or doing o r achieving an end through the actions in a nonpunitive way, corresponding to the growing perception of hazard and conflict and very likely the implicit wish to be provided with and taught channels of substitutional drive discharge. With this, there may well be a wish, corresponding to that element in Loewald's description of therapeutic process, to be seen in terms of one's developmental potentialities by the analyst. No doubt, the list could be extended into many subtleties, details, and variations. However, one should not omit to specify that, in its peak development, it would include the wish for increasingly accurate interpretations and the wish to facilitate such interpretations by providing adequate material ultimately, of course, by identification, to participate in, or even be the author of the interpretations. The childhood system of wishes which underlies the transference is a correlate of biological maturation, and the latent (i.e., teachable) autonomous ego function, appearing with it, however, there is a drive-like quality in the participation phenomena, which disqualifies any conception of the urge's identical with the functions. No one who has ever watched a child importune a parent with questions, or experiment with new words, or solicit her interests in a new game, or demand a storytelling or reading, can doubt this. That this powerful support and integration in the ego identification with a loved parent is undoubtedly true, just as it is true of the identification with an analyst toward whom a positive relationship has been established. That 'functional pleasure ' inscribes the part, where certain specific ego energies, perhaps very likely the ego's own urge to extend its hegemony in the personality. However, it can be stressed in the derive element, even the special phase configurations and colourations, and with its importance of object relations, libidinal and aggressive, for a specific reason. For just as the primordial transference seeks to undo separation, in a sense to obviate object relationships as we know them, the 'mature transference', tends toward separation and individuation, and increasing contact with the environment, optimally with a large affirmative (increasing neutralized) relationship toward the original object toward whom (or her surrogates) a different dynamic of demands is now increasingly directed. The further considerations which has led to the emphasis that the drive-like element in these attitudes are integrated phenomena, as examples of 'multiple functional' rather than the discrete exorcise of function or functions, is the conviction that there is a continuing dynamic relation of relative interchangeability between the two series, at least based on the response to gratifications in a significant zone of complicated energetic overlap, possibly including the phenomenon of neutralization. That the empirical 'interchangeability' is limited, and that goes without saying, that in no way diminishes its decisive importance. The linguistic communications as in mention, that the excessive transference neurosis regression, which can seriously vitiate the affirmative psychoanalytic process, finds a prototype in the regressive behaviour and demands of certain children, who do not receive their share of teaching, 'attention', play, nonseductive, affectionate demonstration, as to use the quality of being appropriate or valuable to some end, even the act or practice of using something or the state of being used to which of responsible interests in development, and similar matters, from their parents. In the psychnalytic situation, both the gratifications offered by the analyst and the freedom of expression by the patient, are diversely limited and concentrated, practically entirely (in the every day demonstrable sense) in the sphere of linguistic expression, on the analyst's side, further, in the transmission of understanding.

Whereas, the primordial transference exploits the primitive aspects of linguistic communication, by expressing the mature transference as to advocate the seeking mastery of the outer and inner environments, a mastery to which the mature elements in speech contribute importantly, for which these are stressed upon the clear-cut genetic prototype for the free associating its interpretative dialogue is the original learning and teaching of speech, the dialogue between child and mother. It is interesting to note that just as the profundities of interests between people who often include - in the service of the ego - transitory introjection and identifications, of the very word 'communication', representing the central ego function of speech, from which is a closely intimate relation to the etymologically certain, in actual usages, to the word chosen for that major of religious sacrament for that which is the physical ingestion of the body and blood of the Deity. Perhaps, this is just another suggestion that the oldest of individual problems does, after all, continue to seek its solution, in its own terms if only in a minimal sense, and in channels so remote as to be unrecognizable.

The mature transference is a dynamic and integral part of the therapeutic alliance, alone with the tender aspect of the erotic transference, even more attenuated (and more dependable) friendly feeling of adult type, and the ego identification with the analyst. Indispensable, of course, are the genuine adult need for help, the crystallizing rational and intuitive appraisal of the analyst, the adult sense of confidence in him, and innumerable other nuances of adult thought and feeling. With these, giving a driving momentum and power to the analytic process, but always, by its very nature, a potential source of resistance, and always requiring analysis, is the primordial transference and its various appearances in the specific therapeutic transference. That it is, if well managed, not only a reflection of the repetition compulsion in its menacing sense, but a living presentation from the id, seeking new solutions, and trying again, so to speak, to find a place in the patient's conscious and effective life, has important affirmative potentialities. This has been specifically emphasized by Nunberg, Lagache and Loewald among others. Loewald has recently elaborated very effectively the idea of 'ghosts' seeking to become 'ancestors' based on an early figure of speech of Freud. The mature transference, in its own infantile right, provides some of the unique qualities of propulsive force, which comes from the world of feeling, rather than the world of thought. If one views it in a purely figurative sense, that fraction of the mature transference which derives from 'conversion' is somewhat like propulsive fraction as the wind in a boats sailing to windward currents into motion, the strong headwind, the ultimate source of both resistance and propulsion, is the primordial transference. This view, however, should not displace the original and independent, if cognate, a favourable tide or current would also be required. It is not that the mature transference is itself entirely exempt from analytic clarification and interpretation. For one thing, in common with other childhood spheres of experience, there may have been traumas in this sphere, punishments, serious defects or lacks of parental communication, Listening, attention or interest. In general, this is probably far more important than has hitherto appeared in our prevalent paradigmatic approach to adult analysis, even taking into account the considerable changes due to the growing interest in ego psychology. 'Learning' in the analysis can, of course, be a troublesome intellectualizing resistance. Furthermore, both the patient's communications and his receptions and utilization of interpretations may exhibit only too clearly, as sometimes in the case of other ego mechanisms, their origin in and tenacious relation to instinctual or anaclitic dynamism; the longing implement out of silence for which the analyst is to override the uncritical acceptance (or rejection) of interpretations, in that the patient revealingly is to mention the unmindful assimilation, fluently, rich, endlessly detailed associations without spontaneous reflection or integration. In the direct demands for solution of moral and practical probability for an entirely intellectual scope, and a variety of others. It may and always be easy to discriminate between the utilization of speech by an essentially instinctual demand, and an intellectual or linguistic trait or having to be determined by specific factors in their own developmental sphere, however, the underlying and essentially genuine dynamism which have to continue to be placed for a notable time interval or remain arbitrary or conventional character most favoured to the purposes of processes of analysis, as it was to the original processes of maturational development, communication, and benign separation. Lagache, on the desirability of separating the current unqualified usage, 'positive' and 'negative' transference, as based on the patient's immediate state of feeling, from a classification based on the essential effect on analytic processes. Yet, the later of mature transference is, in general, a 'positive transference'.

Concerning considerations in the transference neurosis, and the problem of transference interpretation, may be offered at this point. The whole situational structure of analysis (in contrast with other personal relationships), its dialogue of free association and interpretation, and its deprivations as to most ordinary cognitive and emotional interpersonal drives that tend toward the separation of discrete transferences from their synthesis with one another and with defences in character or symptoms, and with deepening regression, toward a continuative enactment of the essential of the infantile neurosis, in the transference neurosis. In other relationships, the 'give and take' aspects - gratifying aggressive, punitive or otherwise actively responsive, and the open mobility of searching for alternative or greater satisfaction - exert a profound dynamic and economic influence, so that only extraordinary situations, or transference of pathological character, or both, occasion to comparable regression.

It is a curious fact, whereas the dynamic meaning to the importance of the transference neurosis have been well established since Freud gave this the phenomenon a central position in his clinical thinking, the clinical reference, when the term is used, remains variable and somewhat ambiguous. For example, Greenson, in his excellent recent paper, speaks of it as appearing, 'when the analyst and the analysis become the central concern in the patient's life'. However, previous remarks in this connection, for which it is worthwhile to specify certain aspects of Greenson's definition, for the term 'central' is somewhat ambiguous, as to its specific reference. Certainly, the term could apply to the symbolic position of the analyst in relation to the patient's experiencing ego and the symbolically decisive position which he correspondingly assumes in the relation to the other important figures in the patient's current life. However, while the analysis is in any case, and for multiple reasons, exceedingly important the seriously involved patient, there is a free observing portion of is ego, also involved, not in the same sense as that involved in the transference regression and revived in infantile conflicts. And here is here being, of course, always the integrated adult personalty, however diluted in may seem at times, of its rarity, although certainly does occur, that the analysis actually exceeds the quality or state of being of notable worth or influence that the other major concerns, attachments, and responsibilities of the patient's life, nor is it desirable that his should occur, on the other hand, if construed with proper attention to the economic considerations as mentioned, the concept is important, both theoretically and clinically. In the theoretical direction to the assumption that there is a continuing system of object relationships and conflict situations, most important in the unconscious representations, but participating to some degree in all others, deriving in a successive series of transference from the experiences of separation from the original object, the mother. In this sense, the analyst's applicability to a uniquely important portion of the patient's personality, the portion that 'never grew up', to maintain a central figure. In the clinical sense, to call or direct attention especially to a supposed cause, source, or to refer to the importance of the transference neurosis as outlining for the essential and central analytic task, providing by its very currency and demonstrability a relatively secure cognitive base for procedural duties. By its inclusion of the patient's essential psychopathological processes and tendencies, in their original functional connection, it offers, in its resolution or marked reduction, the most formidable lever for analytic cure. Nonetheless, transference neurosis must be seen in its interweaving with the patient's extra-analytic system of personal contacts. The relationship to the analyst may influence the course of relationships to others, in the same sense that the clinical neurosis did, except that the former is alloplastic, relatively exposed, and subject to constant interpretation. It is also an important fact that, except in those rare instances where the original dyadic relationship appears to turn, the analyst, even in the strict transference sphere, cannot be assigned all the transference role simultaneously. Other actors are required. He may at times oscillate with confusing rapidity between the status of mother and father, but he is usually predominantly in one of the roles for long periods, someone else representing the other. Furthermore, apart from 'acting out', complicated and mutually inconsistent attitudes of the anterior apprehensions for realizing often about something not generally realized in the verbalization, may require the seeking of other transference objects, i.e., The husband or wife, friend, another analyst and so forth. Children, even the patient's own children, may be invested with strivings of the patient, displaced from the analysis, even experience the impulses which they would wish to call forth in the analyst. The range is extensive, varied, and complicated, requiring constant alertness. Transference interpretation therefore often has a necessarily paradoxical inclusiveness, which is an important reality of technique. There is another aspect, and that is the dynamic and economic impact of the intimate and actual dramatist personate of the transference neurosis in the progress of the analysis as such, and on the patient 's motivation, as well as his real lifer avenues for recovery. For the persons in his milieu may fulfill their 'positive' or 'negative ' roles in transference drama, which may facilitate or impede interpretative effectiveness, they provide the substantial and dependable real life gratification which ultimately facilitate the analysis of the residual analytic transference, or their capacities or attitudes may occasion overload of the anaclitic and instinctual needs in the transference which renders the same process far more difficultly.

In the most unhappy instances, there can be a serious undercounting of the motivation for basic change.

There is also the fundamental question of the role of the transference interpretation. At the Marienbad Symposium most of Strachey's colleagues appeared to accept the essential import of his contribution and thus unique significance of the transference interpretations, despite the various reservations as to detail and emphasis on other important aspects of the therapeutic process. Nevertheless, there are still many who, if not in doubt regarding the great value of transference interpretations are inclined to doubt their uniqueness, and to stress the importance of economic considerations in determining the choice as to whether transference or extratransference interpretations may be indicated. Now, apart from the realistic considerations mentioned in the preceding passage (in a sense the necessarily 'distributed' character of a variable fraction of transference interpretation). There is in fact that the extra-analytic life of the patent often provides indispensable data fo the understanding of detailed complexities of his psychic functioning, because of the sheer variety of its references, some of which cannot be reproduced in the relationship to the analyst. For example, there is no repartee (in the ordinary sense) in the analysis. The way the patient handles the dialogue with an angry employee may be importantly revealing. The same may be true of the quality of his reaction to a real danger of dismissal. There is not only the realities, but the 'formal' aspects of this responses. These expressions of personality remain important, even though his 'acting out' of the transference (assuming this was this was the case) may have been more important, and, of course, requiring transference interpretation. Furthermore, they remain useful, if discriminatingly and conservatively treated, even if they are inevitably always subject that epistemological reservations, which haunts so much of analytic data. Of course, the 'positive' transference has a role in the utilization of such interpretations that what enables the patent to listen to them and them seriously.

In an operational sense, it would seem that extratransference interpretations cannot set aside, or underestimated in importance, but the unique effectiveness of transference interpretations is not thereby disestablished. No other interpretation is free, within reason, of the doubt introduced by not really knowing the 'other person's' participation in love, or quarrel or criticism or whatever the issue. And no other situation provides the patient the combined sense of cognitive acquisition, with the experience of complete personal tolerance and acceptance, that is implicit in an interpretation by an individual who is an object of the emotion, drive, or even defences, which are active at the time. There is no doubt that such interpretations must not only (in common with all others) include personal tact, but must be offered with special care as to their intellectual reasonability, in relation to the immediate context, lest they defeat their essential purpose. It is not too often likely that a patient who has just been jilted in a long-standing love affair, and suffering exceedingly, will find an immediate interpretation that his suffering is due to the fact that the analyst does not reciprocate his love, even though a dynamism in this general sphere may be ultimately demonstrable, and acceptable to the patient. On the other hand, once the transference neurosis is established, with accompanying subtle (sometime gross) colouration of the patient's life, th n more far-reaching anticipatory, transference interpretations are indicated, for, if all of the patient's libidinal and aggression is not, in fact, invested in the analyst, he has at least an unconscious role in all important emotional transactions, and, if the assumption is correct that the regressive drive, mobilized by the analytic situation, is in the direction of restoration of a single all-encompassing relationship, specified pragmatically in the individual case by the actually attained level of development, then there is a dynamic factor at work, importantly meriting interpretation as such, to the extent that available material supports it. This would be the immediate clinical application on the material regarding the 'cognitive lag' or 'cognitive fall-back'.

Post-Traumatic Stress Disorder, resides in a mental illness that some people develop after experiencing traumatic or life-threatening events. Such events include warfare, rape and other sexual assaults, violent physical attacks, torture, child abuse, natural disasters such as earthquakes and floods, and automobile or aeroplane crashes. People who attest of the traumatic events may also develop the disorder.

Post-traumatic stress disorder in war veterans is sometimes called shell shock or combat fatigue. In victims of sexual or physical abuse, the disorder has been called rape trauma or battered woman syndrome. The American Psychiatric Association (APA) adopted the current name of the disorder in 1980.

In the late 1960's and early 1970's, mass demonstrations erupted throughout the United States protesting US involvement in the Vietnam War (1959-1975). Thousands of veterans joined together in a national organization, Vietnam Veterans Against the War, that supported and influenced the antiwar movement. In this transcript from an April 22, 1971, hearing before the Senate Committee on Foreign Relations, committee chairman Senator J. William Fulbright indicated his sympathy for the antiwar movement. Fulbright's comments were followed by the testimony of Vietnam veteran John Kerry, who called for an end to the war. Kerry also detailed what he believed to be the war's negative effect in both Vietnam and the United States. Kerry became a Democratic senator from Massachusetts in 1985.

People with this disorder relive the traumatic event again and again through nightmares and disturbing memories during the day. They sometimes have flashbacks, in which they suddenly lose touch with reality and relive images, sounds, and other sensations from the trauma. Because of their extreme anxiety and disruptive opposition to events, they try to avoid anything that reminds them of it. They may seem emotionally numb, detached, irritable, and easily startled. They may feel guilty about surviving a traumatic event that killed other people. Other symptoms include trouble concentrating, depression, and sleep difficulties. Symptoms of the disorder usually begin shortly after the traumatic event, although some people may not show symptoms for several years. If left untreated, the disorder can last for years.

Post-traumatic stress disorder can severely disrupt one's life. Besides the emotional pain of reliving the trauma, the symptoms of the disorder may cause a person to think that he or she is "going crazy." In addition, people with this disorder may have unpredictable, angry outbursts at family members. At other times, they may seem to have no affection for their loved ones. Some people try to mask their symptoms by abusing alcohol or drugs. Others work very long hours to prevent any "down" periods when they might relive the trauma. Such actions may delay the onset of the disorder until these individuals retire or become sober.

Studies have set or to bring into a new found control from 1 to 14 percent of people that suffer from post-traumatic stress disorder at some point during their lives. The findings vary widely due to differences in the populations studied and the research methods used. Among people who have survived traumatic events, the prevalence appears to be much higher. The disorder may be particularly prevalent among people who have served in combat. For example, one study of veterans of the Vietnam War (1959-1975) found that veterans exposed to a high level of combat were nine times more likely to have post-traumatic stress disorder than military personnel who did not serve in the war zone of Southeast Asia.

Post-traumatic stress disorder is an extreme reaction to extreme stress. In moments of crisis, people respond in ways that allow them to endure and survive the trauma. Afterward those responses, such as emotional numbing, may persist even though they are no longer necessary.

Not everyone who experiences a traumatic event develops post-traumatic stress disorder. Several factors influence whether people develop the disorder. Those who experience severe and prolonged trauma are more likely to develop the disorder than people who experience less severe trauma. Additionally, those who directly witness or experience death, injury, or attack are more likely to develop symptoms.

People may also have been existing biological and psychological vulnerabilities that make them more likely to develop the disorder. Those with histories of anxiety disorders in their families may have inherited a genetic predisposition to react more severely to stress and trauma than other people. In addition, people's life experiences, especially in childhood, can affect their psychological vulnerability to the disorder. For example, people whose early childhood experiences made them feel that events are unpredictable and uncontrollable have a greater likelihood than others of developing the disorder. Individuals with a strong, supportive social network of friends and family members seem somewhat protected from developing post-traumatic stress disorder.

Treatment of post-traumatic stress disorder may involve psychotherapy, psychoactive drugs, or both. Psychotherapists help individuals confront the traumatic experience, work through their strong negative emotions, and overcome their symptoms. Many people with post-traumatic stress disorder benefit from group therapy with other individuals suffering from the disorder. Physicians may prescribe antidepressants or anxiety-reducing drugs to treat the mood disturbances that sometimes accompany the disorder.

At the arriving considerations that are marked and noted, through which the essence of functional dynamics as based of the transference in the psychoanalytic process or the basic underlying the most basic of beliefs that in politics there is neither good nor evil, however, in that something that forms part of the minimal body, character or structure of that thing predetermines the properties to the good life. Nonetheless, most psychoanalysts maintain that schizophrenic patients cannot be treated psychoanalytically because they are too narcissistic to develop with the psychotherapist as interpersonal relationship that is sufficiently reliable and consistent for psychoanalytic work. Freud, Fenichel and others have recognized that a new technique of approaching patients psychoanalytically must be found if analysts are to work with psychotics. Among those who have worked successfully in recent years with schizophrenics, Sullivan, Hill, and Karl Menninger and his staff have made various modifications of their analytic approach. The techniques that are in use with psychotics is different from our approach to psychoneurotics. This is not a result of the schizophrenic's inability to build up a consistent personal relationship with the therapist but due to his extremely intense and sensitive transference reactions.

Let us see first what the essence of the schizophrenic's transference reactions are and how we try to meet these reactions.

We think of a schizophrenic as a person who has had serious traumatic experiences in early infancy at a time when his ego and its ability to examine reality were not yet developed. These early traumatic experiences seem to furnish the psychological basis for the pathogenic influence of the flustrations of later years. At this early time the infant lives grandiosely in a narcissistic world of his own. His needs and desires seem to be taken care of by something vague and indefinite which he does not yet differentiate. As Ferenczi noted, they are expressed by gestures and movements since speech is as yet undeveloped. Frequently the child's desires are fulfilled without any expression of them, a result that seems to him a product of his magical thinking.

Are a person's characteristics primarily shaped by early influences, remaining relatively stable thereafter throughout life? Or does change spontaneously occur continuously throughout life? Many people believe that early experiences are formative, providing a strong or weak foundation for later psychological growth. This view is expressed in the popular saying "As the twig is bent, so grows the tree." From this perspective, it is crucial to ensure that young children have a good start in life. But many developmental scientists believe that later experiences can modify or even reverse early influences; studies show that even when early experiences are traumatic or abusive, considerable recovery can occur. From this vantage point, early experiences influence, but rarely determine, later characteristics.

Traumatic experiences in this early period of life will damage a personality more seriously than those occurring in later childhood such as are found in the history of psychoneurotics. The infant's mind is more vulnerable the younger and less used it has been, further, the trauma has quickened the infant 's egocentricity. In addition early traumatic experiences shortens the only period in life in which an individual ordinarily enjoys the most security, thus endangering the ability to store up as it were a reasonable supplies of assurance and self-reliance for the individual's later struggles through life. Thus, as such, a child sensitized considerably more toward the frustrations of later like than by later traumatic experiences. hence many experiences in later life which would mean little to a 'healthy' person and not much to a psychoneurotic, mean a great deal of pain and suffering to the schizophrenic. His resistance against frustration is easily exhausted.

Once he reaches his limit of endurance, he escapes the unbearable reality of his present life by attempting to reestablish the autistic, delusional world of the infant, but this is impossible because the content of his delusions and hallucinations are naturally coloured by the experiences of his whole lifetime.

How do these developments influence the patient's attitude toward the analyst and the analyst's approach to him?

Due to the very damage and the succeeding chain of frustrations which the schizophrenic undergoes before finally giving in to illness, he feels extremely suspicious and distrustful of everyone, particularly of the psychotherapist ho approaches him with the intent of intruding into his isolated world and personal life. To him the physician's approach means the threat of being compelled to return to the frustrations of real life and to reveal his inadequacy to meet them or, - still worse – a repetition of the aggressive interference with his initial symptoms and peculiarities which he has encountered in his previous environment.

The difficulty that the patient's dilemma through his frustrations is the product through which is called 'delusion': Delusion itself is a false belief which is firmly held by a person even though other people recognize the belief as obviously untrue. For example, a person who truly believes he is Napoleon Bonaparte is delusional. Religious beliefs or popular conceptions, such as the belief that people have been abducted by aliens, are not delusions because they are widely held beliefs. Delusions are a type of psychotic symptom that indicate a person has lost contact with reality.

There are many different types of delusions. A person with a paranoid delusion believes that others - such as the FBI, or the CIA, even the Mafia as trying to harm or plot against him. A person with a delusion of reference believes that events or people refer specifically to him or her when they do not. For example, a woman with schizophrenia may believe that a television news broadcaster is talking personally to her rather than to the entire viewing audience. A grandiose delusion is a belief that one is extremely famous or that one has special powers, such as the ability to magically heal people.

A delusion of control is a belief that others are able to control one's thoughts, feelings, or actions. For example, a man with this type of delusion may believe that someone has implanted a microchip in his brain that enables other people to control his thoughts. A somatic delusion is a belief that something is wrong with one's body - for example, that one's brain is rotting away - even though no medical evidence supports this belief. A person with an erotic delusion believes that someone is in love with him or her despite a lack of evidence for this belief. In a delusion of jealousy, a person believes that his or her spouse or lover is unfaithful despite evidence to the contrary.

Delusions commonly occur in certain severe mental illnesses, such as schizophrenia, bipolar disorder (also called manic-depressive illness), some cases of major depression, Dissociative disorders, post-traumatic stress disorder, and paranoid personality disorder. In addition, delusions may result from abuse of certain drugs, including alcohol, cocaine, amphetamines, and hallucinogens such as lysergic acid diethylamide (LSD), phencyclidine (PCP), and mescaline. Medical conditions affecting the brain, such as syphilis and brain tumours, may also cause delusions.

Delusional disorder is a relatively uncommon mental illness characterized by delusions. People with this disorder have one or more delusions that persist for at least one month. In addition, they do not suffer from other symptoms of schizophrenia, such as disorganized speech and bizarre behaviour. Usually their delusions are less bizarre than those that occur in schizophrenia and seem merely odd or unsupported by facts. Examples of nonbizarre delusions include beliefs that one is being followed, loved by someone famous, or deceived by one's spouse. Because delusional disorder is relatively rare, little research has systematically examined its treatment. However, doctors most often use Antipsychotic drugs (also called neuroleptics) to treat this disorder. These drugs help reduce or eliminate delusions, hallucinations, and other psychotic symptoms.

In spite of his narcissistic retreat, every schizophrenic has some underlying notion of the unreality and loneliness of his substitute delusionary world. He longs for human contact and understanding, yet is afraid to admit of himself, or his therapist for fear of further frustration.

That is why the patient may take weeks and months to test the analyst before being willing to accept him, however, once he has accepted him. His dependence on the analyst is greater and he is more sensitive about it than is the psychoneurotic because of the schizophrenic's deeply rooted insecurity, the narcissistic seemingly self-righteous attitude is but a defence.

Whenever the analyst fails the patient from reasons to be discussed later - one cannot at times avoid failing one's schizophrenic patients - it will be severe disappointment and a repetition of the chain of frustrations the schizophrenic has previously endured.

The instinctually primitive part of the schizophrenic's mind that does not discriminate between himself and the environment, it may mean the withdrawal of the impersonal supporting forces of his infancy. Severe anxiety will follow this vital deprivation.

In the light of his personal relationship with the analyst it means that the therapist seduced the patient to use him as a bridge over which he might possibly be led from the utter loneliness of his own world to reality and human warmth, only to have him discover that this bridge is not reliable. if so, he will respond helplessly with an outburst of hostility or with renewed withdrawal as may be seen most impressively in catatonic stupor.

The symptoms of mental illness can be very distressing. People who develop schizophrenia may hear voices inside their head that say nasty things about them or command them to act in strange or unpredictable ways. Or they may be paralysed by paranoia—the deep conviction that everyone, including their closest family members, wants to injure or destroy them. People with major depression may feel that nothing brings pleasure and that life is so dreary and unhappy that it is better to be dead. People with panic disorder may experience heart palpitations, rapid breathing, and anxiety so extreme that they may not be able to leave home. People whom experience episodes of mania may engage in reckless sexual behaviour or may spend money indiscriminately, acts that later cause them to feel guilt, shame, and desperation.

Other mental illnesses, while not always debilitating, create certain problems in living. People with personality disorders may experience loneliness and isolation because their personality style interferes with social relations. People with an eating disorder may become so preoccupied with their weight and appearance that they force themselves to vomit or refuse to eat. Individuals who develop post-traumatic stress disorder may become angry easily, experience disturbing memories, and have trouble concentrating.

Experiences of mental illness often interact differently but depends on one's culture or social group, sometimes greatly so. For example, in most of the non-Western world, people with depression complain principally of physical ailments, such as lack of energy, poor sleep, loss of appetite, and various kinds of physical pain. Indeed, even in North America these complaints are commonplace. But in the United States and other Western societies, depressed people and mental health professionals who treat them tend to emphasize psychological problems, such as feelings of sadness, worthlessness, and despair. The experience of schizophrenia also differs by culture. In India, one-third of the new cases of schizophrenia involve catatonia, a behavioural condition in which a person maintains a bizarre statue like pose for hours or days. This condition is rare in Europe and North America.

With appropriate treatment, most people can recover from mental illness and return to normal life. Even those with persistent, long-term mental illnesses can usually learn to manage their symptoms and live productive lives.

By a variety of symptoms, including loss of contact with reality, bizarre behaviour, disorganized thinking and speech, decreased emotional expressiveness, and social withdrawal. Usually only some of these symptoms occur in any one person. The term schizophrenia comes from Greek words meaning "split mind." However, contrary to common belief, schizophrenia does not refer to a person with a split personality or multiple personality. For a description of a mental illness in which a person has multiple personalities. To observers, schizophrenia may seem or appear for being as some sorted kind of madness or a manufacturing insanity.

Perhaps more than any other mental illness, schizophrenia has a debilitating effect on the lives of the people who suffer from it. A person with schizophrenia may have difficulty telling the difference between real and unreal experiences, logical and illogical thoughts, or appropriate and inappropriate behaviour. Schizophrenia seriously impairs a person's ability to work, go to school, enjoy relationships with others, or take care of oneself. In addition, people with schizophrenia frequently require hospitalization because they pose a danger to themselves. About 10 percent of people with schizophrenia commit suicide, and many others attempt suicide. Once people develop schizophrenia, they usually suffer from the illness for the rest of their lives. Although there is no cure, treatment can help many people with schizophrenia lead productive lives.

Schizophrenia also carries an enormous cost to society. People with schizophrenia occupy about one-third of all beds in psychiatric hospitals in the United States. In addition, people with schizophrenia account for at least 10 percent of the homeless population in the United States. The National Institute of Mental Health has estimated that schizophrenia costs the United States tens of billions of dollars each year in direct treatment, social services, and lost productivity.

Approximately 1 percent of people develop schizophrenia at some time during their lives. Experts estimate that about 1.8 million people in the United States have schizophrenia. The prevalence of schizophrenia is the same regardless of sex, race, and culture. Although women are just as likely as men to develop schizophrenia, women tend to experience the illness less severely, with fewer hospitalizations and better social functioning in the community.

Schizophrenia usually develops in late adolescence or early adulthood, between the ages of 15 and 30. Much less commonly, schizophrenia develops later in life. The illness may begin abruptly, but it usually develops slowly over months or years. Mental health professionals diagnose schizophrenia based on an interview with the patient in which they determine whether the person has experienced specific symptoms of the illness.

Symptoms and functioning in people with schizophrenia tend to vary over time, sometimes worsening and other times improving. For many patients the symptoms gradually become less severe as they grow older. About 25 percent of people with schizophrenia become symptom-free later in their lives.

A variety of symptoms characterize schizophrenia. The most prominent include symptoms of psychosis—such as delusions and hallucinations - as well as bizarre behaviour, strange movements, and disorganized thinking and speech. Many people with schizophrenia do not recognize that their mental functioning is disturbed.

Some people with schizophrenia experience delusions of persecution - false beliefs that other people are plotting against them. This interview between a patient with schizophrenia and his therapist illustrates the paranoia that can affect people with this illness.

Delusions are false beliefs that appear obviously untrue to other people. For example, a person with schizophrenia may believe that he is the king of England when he is not. People with schizophrenia may have delusions that others, such as the police or the FBI, are plotting against them or spying on them. They may believe that aliens are controlling their thoughts or that their own thoughts are being broadcast to the world so that other people can hear them.

Research suggests that the genes one inherits strongly influence one's risk of developing schizophrenia. Studies of families have shown that the more close one is related to someone with schizophrenia, the greater the risk one has of developing the illness. For example, the children of one parent with schizophrenia have about a 13 percent chance of developing the illness, and children of two parents with schizophrenia have about a 46 percent chance of eventually developing schizophrenia. This increased risk occurs even when such children are adopted and raised by mentally healthy parents. In comparison, children in the general population have only about a 1 percent chance of developing schizophrenia.

Some evidence suggests that schizophrenia may result from an imbalance of chemicals in the brain called neurotransmitters. These chemicals enable neurons (brain cells) to communicate with each other. Some scientists suggest that schizophrenia results from excess activity of the neurotransmitter dopamine in certain parts of the brain or from an abnormal sensitivity to dopamine. Remedially, antipsychotic drugs reduce psychotic symptoms in schizophrenia by blocking brain receptors for dopamine. In addition, amphetamines, which increase dopamine activity, intensify psychotic symptoms in people with schizophrenia. Despite these findings, many experts believe that excess dopamine activity alone cannot account for schizophrenia. Other neurotransmitters, such as serotonin and norepinephrine, may play important roles as well.

Although scientists favour a biological cause of schizophrenia, stress in the environment may affect the onset and course of the illness. Stressful life circumstances - such as maturing in age and character as for living in poverty, the death of a loved one, an important change in jobs or relationships, or chronic tension and hostility at home—can increase the chances of schizophrenia in a person biologically predisposed to the disease. In addition, stressful events can trigger a relapse of symptoms in a person who already has the illness. Individuals who have effective skills for managing stress may be less susceptible to its negative effects. Psychological and social rehabilitation can help patients develop more effective skills for dealing with stress.

Although there is no cure for schizophrenia, effective treatment exists that can improve the long-term course of the illness. With many years of treatment and rehabilitation, significant numbers of people with schizophrenia experience partial or full remission of their symptoms.

Treatment of schizophrenia usually involves a combination of medication, rehabilitation, and treatment of other problems the person may have. Antipsychotic drugs (also called neuroleptics) are the most frequently used medications for treatment of schizophrenia. Psychological and social rehabilitation programs may help people with schizophrenia function in the community and reduce stress related to their symptoms. Treatment of secondary problems, such as substance abuse and infectious diseases, is also an important part of an overall treatment program.

Antipsychotic medications, developed in the mid-1950s, can dramatically improve the quality of life for people with schizophrenia. The drugs reduce or eliminate psychotic symptoms such as hallucinations and delusions. The medications can also help prevent these symptoms from returning. Common Antipsychotic drugs include risperidone (Risperdal), olanzapine (Zyprexa), clozapine (Clozaril), quetiapine (Seroquel), haloperidol (Haldol), thioridazine (Mellaril), chlorpromazine (Thorazine), fluphenazine (Prolixin), and trifluoperazine (Stelazine). People with schizophrenia usually must take medication for the rest of their lives to control psychotic symptoms. Antipsychotic medications appear to be less effective at treating other symptoms of schizophrenia, such as social withdrawal and apathy.

Because many patients with schizophrenia continue to experience difficulties despite taking medication, psychological and social rehabilitation is often necessary. A variety of methods can be effective. Social skills training helps people with schizophrenia learn specific behaviours for functioning in society, such as making friends, purchasing items at a store, or initiating conversations. Behavioural training methods can also help them learn self-care skills such as personal hygiene, money management, and proper nutrition. In addition, cognitive-behavioural therapy, a type of psychotherapy, can help reduce persistent symptoms such as hallucinations, delusions, and social withdrawal.

Because many patients have difficulty obtaining or keeping jobs, supported employment programs that help patients find and maintain jobs are a helpful part of rehabilitation. In these programs, the patient works alongside people without disabilities and earns competitive wages. An employment specialist (or vocational specialist) helps the person maintain their job by, for example, training the person in specific skills, helping the employer accommodate the person, arranging transportation, and monitoring performance. These programs are most effective when the supported employment is closely integrated with other aspects of treatment, such as medication and monitoring of symptoms.

Some people with schizophrenia are vulnerable to frequent crises because they do not regularly go to mental health centres to receive the treatment they need. These individuals often relapse and face re-hospitalization. To ensure that such patients take their medication and receive appropriate psychological and social rehabilitation, assertive community treatment (ACT) programs have been developed that deliver treatment to patients in natural settings, such as in their homes, in restaurants, or on the street.

People with schizophrenia often have other medical problems, so an effective treatment program must attend to these as well. One of the most generally shared in or participated in things conforming to a type without noteworthy excellence or faults just as common a rule, by ordinary, frequent and ordinarily as an idea or expression deficient in originality or freshness, yet, only of its exchanging the commonplace of the common associated problems is vehemently and usually coarsely expressed condemnation or disapproved, as the interpretative category of an unequalled vocabulary is itself a genuine abuse. Successful treatment of substance abuse inpatients with schizophrenia requires careful coordination with their mental health care, so that the same clinicians are treating both disorders at the same time.

The high rate of substance abuse in patients with schizophrenia contributes to a high prevalence of infectious diseases, including hepatitis B and C and the human immunodeficiency virus (HIV). Assessment, education, and treatment or management of these illnesses is critical for the long-term health of patients.

Other problems frequently associated with schizophrenia include housing instability and homelessness, legal problems, violence, trauma and post-traumatic stress disorder, anxiety, depression, and suicide attempts. Close monitoring and psychotherapeutic interventions are often helpful in addressing these problems.

Several other psychiatric disorders are closely related to schizophrenia. In schizoaffective disorder, a person shows symptoms of schizophrenia combined with either mania or severe depression. Schizophreniform disorder refers to an illness in which a person experiences schizophrenic symptoms for more than one month but fewer than six months. In schizotypal personality disorder, a person engages in odd thinking, speech, and behaviour, but usually does not lose contact with reality. Sometimes mental health professionals refer to these disorders together as schizophrenia-spectrum disorders.

Severe mental illness almost always alters a person's life dramatically. People with severe mental illnesses experience disturbing symptoms that can cause of such difficulties and holding to a job, or go to school, relate to others, or cope with ordinary life demands. Some individuals require hospitalization because they become unable to care for themselves or because they are at risk of committing suicide.

The symptoms of mental illness can be very distressing. People who develop schizophrenia may hear voices inside their head that say nasty things about them or command them to act in strange or unpredictable ways. Or they may be paralysed by paranoia - the deep conviction that everyone, including their closest family members, wants to injure or destroy them. People with major depression may feel that nothing brings pleasure and that life is so dreary and unhappy that it is better to be dead. People with panic disorder may experience heart palpitations, rapid breathing, and anxiety so extreme that they may not be able to leave home. People whom experience episodes of mania may engage in reckless sexual behaviour or may spend money indiscriminately, acts that later cause them to feel guilt, shame, and desperation.

Other mental illnesses, while not always debilitating, create certain problems in living. People with personality disorders may experience loneliness and isolation because their personality style interferes with social relations. People with an eating disorder may become so preoccupied with their weight and appearance that they force themselves to vomit or refuse to eat. Individuals who develop post-traumatic stress disorder may become angry easily, experience disturbing memories, and have trouble concentrating.

Experiences of mental illness often take issue upon its stability for depending on one's culture or social group, sometimes greatly so. For example, in most of the non-Western world, people with depression complain principally of physical ailments, such as lack of energy, poor sleep, loss of appetite, and various kinds of physical pain. Indeed, even in North America these complaints are commonplace. But in the United States and other Western societies, depressed people and mental health professionals who treat them tend to emphasize psychological problems, such as feelings of sadness, worthlessness, and despair. The experience of schizophrenia also differs by culture. In India, one-third of the new cases of schizophrenia involve catatonia, a behavioural condition in which a person maintains a bizarre statue like pose for hours or days. This condition is rare in Europe and North America.

Of furthering issues regarding depersonalization disorder, meaning, in effect, that it is a categorised illness based within its intendment for being an illness, of mind, in which people experience an unwelcome sense of detachment from their own bodies. They may feel as though they are floating above the ground, outside observers of their own mental or physical processes. Other symptoms may include a feeling that they or other people are mechanical or unreal, a feeling of being in a dream, a feeling that their hands or feet are larger or smaller than usual, and a deadening of emotional responses. These symptoms are chronic and severe enough to impede normal functioning in a social, school, or work environment.

Depersonalization disorder is a relatively rare syndrome thought to result from severe psychological stress. It may occur as part of other mental illnesses, especially anxiety disorders. For example, some people with panic disorder feel nervous, have a sense of doom about their future and health, and have a troubling sense of detachment form the lose in the attemptive use in making or doing or achieving a useful regularity as might be expected of the control over their bodies. Depersonalization disorder may also be a component of more severe mental illness, such as schizophrenia. Treatment may include training in relaxation techniques that enhance body perception and control, hypnosis to modify symptoms, and psychotherapy to explore possible stress-related components of the disorder.

Psychiatrists classify depersonalization disorder as one of the Dissociative disorders. Such disorders involve a disruption of consciousness, memory, identity, or perception.

All the while, the schizophrenic responds to altercations in the analyst's defections and understanding by corresponding stormy and dramatic changes from love to hatred, from willingness to leave his delusional world to resistance and renewed withdrawal.

As understandable as these changes are, nevertheless may come as a surprise to the analyst who frequently has not observed their source, this is quite in contrast to his experience with psychoneurosis whose emotional reactions during an interview he can usually predict. These unpredictable changes seem to be the reason for the conception of the unreliability of the schizophrenic's transference reaction, yet they follow the same dynamic rules as the psychoneurotic's oscillations between positive and negative transference and resistance, however, if the schizophrenic's reactions are stormy and seemingly more unpredictable than those of the psychoneurotic, that instances suggested to be due to the inevitable errors in the analyst's approach to the schizophrenic, of which he himself may be unaware, rather than to the unreliability of the patient's emotional response?

Why is it inevitable that the psychoanalyst disappoint his schizophrenic patient time and again?

The schizophrenic withdraws from painful reality and retires to what resembles the early speechless phase of development where consciousness is not yet crystalized. As the expression of his feelings is not hindered by the convention that he has eliminated, as his thinking, feelings, behaviour and speech - when present - obey the working rules of the archaic unconscious. His thinking is magical and does not follow logical rules. It does not admit of the final attempt, but of all others belonging to the ending of 'no', and likewise the no to 'yes': There is no recognition of space and time, I, you, and am, are interchangeable expressions through which of symbols and often by movement and gestures rather than by words.

As the schizophrenic is suspicious, he will distrust the words of his analyst. He will interpret them and incidental gestures and attitudes of the analyst according to his own delusional experience. The analyst may not even be aware of these involuntary manifestations of his attitudes, yet they mean much to the hypersensitive schizophrenic who uses them as a means of orienting himself to the therapist's personality and intentions toward him.

In other words, the schizophrenic patient and the therapist are people living in different worlds and no different levels of personal development with different means of expressing and of orienting themselves. We know little about the language of the unconscious that belongs to the schizophrenic, and our access to it is blocked by the very process of our own adjustment to a world the schizophrenic has relinquished, so, we should not be surprised that errors and misunderstandings occur when we under take to communicate and strive for a rapport with him.

Another source of the schizophrenic's disappointment arises form which the analyser accepts and does not interfere with the behaviour of the schizophrenic, his attitude may lead the patient to expect that the analyst will assist in carrying out all the patient's wishes, even though they may not seem to be in his interest to the analyser's and the hospital's in their relationship to society. This attitude of acceptance so different from the patient's previous experiences readily fosters the anticipation that the analyst will try to carry out the patient's suggestion and take his part, even against conventional society with which it should occasionally arise. Frequently it will be wise for the analyst to agree with the patient's wish to remain unbattled and untidy until he is ready to talk about the reasons for his behaviour or to change spontaneously. At other times, he will unfortunately be unable to take the patient's part without being able to make the patient understand and accept the reasons for the analyst's position.

If the analyst is not able to accept the possibility of misunderstanding the reaction of the schizophrenic patient and in turn of being misunderstood by him, it may shake his security with his patient.

That is to say, that, among other things, the schizophrenic, once he accepts the analyst's insecurity. being helpless and open to himself - in spite of his pretended grandiose isolation - he will feel utterly defeated by the insecurity of his would-be helper. Such disappointment may furnish reasons for outbursts of hatred and are comparable to the negative transference reactions of psychoneurosis, yet more intense than these, since they are not limited by the restrictions of the actual world - that is, it exists in or based on fact, its only problem is a sure-enough externalization for which things are existing in the act of being external in something that has existence, ss if it were an actualization as received in the obtainable enactment for being externalized, such that its problem of in some actual life that proves obtainable achieved, in that of doing something that has an existence for having absolute actuality.

These outbursts are accompanied by anxiety, feelings of guilt, and fear of retaliations which in turn lead to increased hostility. Yet this established a vicious circle: We disappoint the patient, he is afraid that we hate him for his hatred and therefore continues to hate us. If in addition he senses that the analyst is afraid of his aggressiveness, it confirms his fear that he is actually considered as some dangerous and unacceptable, and this augments his hatred.

This establishes that the schizophrenics capable of developing strong relationships of love and hatred toward the analyst. After all, one could not be so hostile if it were not for the background of a very close relationship. In addition, the schizophrenic develops transference reactions on the narrower sense which he can differentiate from the actual interpersonal relationship. For which the schizophrenic's emotional reactions toward the analyst have to be met with extreme care and caution. The love which the sensitive schizophrenic feels as he first emerges, and his cautions acceptance of the analyst's warmth of interest are really most delicate and tender things. If the analyst deals with the transference reactions of a psychoneurotic is bad enough, though as a reparable rule, but if he fails with a schizophrenic in meeting positive feelings by pointing it out for instance before the patient indicates that he is ready to discuss it, he may easily freeze to death what has just begun to grow and so destroy any further possibility of therapy.

Some analysts may feel that the atmosphere of complete acceptance and of strict avoidance of any arbitrary denials which we recommend as a basic rule for the treatment of schizophrenics may not avoid our wish to guide of re-acceptance of reality, nevertheless, Freud says that every science and therapy which accepts his teachings about unconscious, about transference and resistance and about infantile sexuality, may be called psychoanalysis. According in this definition we believe we are practising psychoanalysis with our schizophrenic patients.

Whether we call it analysis or not, it is clear that successful treatment does not depend on technical rules of any special psychiatric school but rather on the basic attitude of individual therapist toward psychologic persons. If he meets them as strangle creatures of another world whose productions are not comprehensible to 'normal' beings, he cannot treat them, if he realizes, however, that the difference between himself and the psychologic is only of degree, and not of kind, he will know better how to meet him. He will not be able to identify himself sufficiently with the patient to understand and accept his emotional reactions without becoming involved in them.

The process of constant and perpetual change is examined and closely matched within the study of philosophical speculations and pointed of a world view which asserts that basic reality is constantly in a process of flux and change. Indeed, reality is identified with pure process. Concepts such as creativity, freedom, novelty, emergence, and growth are fundamental explanatory categories for process philosophy. This metaphysical perspective is to be contrasted with a philosophy of substance, the view that a fixed and permanent reality underlies the changing or fluctuating world of ordinary experience. Whereas substance philosophy emphasizes static being, process philosophy emphasizes dynamically becoming.

Although process philosophy is as old as the 6th-century BC Greek philosopher, Heraclitus, renewed interest in it was stimulated in the 19th century by the theory of evolution. Key figures in the development of modern process philosophy were the British philosophers Herbert Spencer, Samuel Alexander, and Alfred North Whitehead, the American philosophers Charles S. Peirce and William James, and the French philosophers Henri Bergson and Pierre Teilhard de Chardin. Whitehead's Process and Reality: An Essay in Cosmology (1929) is generally considered the most important systematic expression of process philosophy.

Contemporary theology has been strongly influenced by process philosophy. The American theologian Charles Hartshorne, for instance, rather than interpreting God as an unchanging absolute, emphasizes God's sensitive and caring relationship with the world. A personal God enters into relationships in such a way that he is affected by the relationships, and to be affected by relationships is to change. So too is in the process of growth and development. Important contributions to process theology have also been made by such theologians as William Temple, Daniel Day Williams, Schubert Ogden, and John Cobb, Jr.

'Reality' is a difficult word to use to every one's satisfaction or even to one's own satisfaction. In this instance the word reality is used arbitrarily to designate the direct, here-and-now impact of the analyst upon the patient. Reality. In this sense, contrasts with the impact the analyst has through his representation in the patient's fantasy life, neurosis, and transference, since both kinds of impact seem always to coexist and since the former - the analyst's real impact - may be the worst enemy of the transference, the matter of their differentiation is possibly the most challenging aspect of analysis.

The analytic situation, which is set up to shut out ordinary reality intrusions, that cannot . . . neither should not exclude all, but to say, that in the beginning months, for instance, reality inevitably has the upper hand. The analyst, the office, the procedure, are all overwhelmingly real. Everything is strange, frightening and exciting, gratifying and frustrating. Unlike the patient can test it and orient himself to it, the impact of this reality is usually so great that even an ordinary useful transference relationship cannot be expected to develop.

Perhaps the most confusing aspect of this beginning period is the frequent appearance in it of what can be regarded as a false transference relationship. With great intensity and clarity, the patient may reveal, through transference-like references about the analyst, some of the deepest secrets only of his neurosis but of its genesis. The pseudotransference, too good to be true, is almost sure to be nothing more than the patient's attempt to deal with the person of the analyst, the entire spectrum of his various patterns of behaviour. If, it is easy to do, the analyst overlooks the likelihood that the patient's relationship with at this time is really about that almost everything said about it is related, analysis may get off to a very bad start. And if, as is even earlier to do, the analyst's interests the genetic meaning of the openly exposed material, a good transference relationship may be seriously delayed and a workable transference necrosis may never appear. even after initial reality has had time to fade, reality may continue to intrude in ways that are very hard to detect and that are very troublesome.

One of the most serious problems of analysis is the very substantial help which the patient receives directly from the analyst and the analytic situation. For many a patient, the analyst in the analytic situation is in fact the most stable, reasonable, wise and understanding person he has ever met, and the setting in which they meet may actually be the most honest, open, direct and regular relationship he has ever experienced. Added to this is the considerable helpfulness to him of being able to clarify his life storey. confess his guilt, express his ambitions, and explore his confusions. Further real help comes from the learning-about-life accruing from the analyst's skilled questions, observations and interpretations. Taken together, the total real value to the patient of the analytic situation can easily be immense. The trouble with this kind of help is that it goes on and on, it may have such a real, direct and continuing impact upon the patient that he can never get deeply enough involved in transference situation to allow him to resolve or even to become acquainted with his most crippling internal difficulties. The trouble is far too good, the trouble also is that we as analysts apparently cannot resist the seductiveness of being directly helpful, and this, when combined with the compelling assumption that helpfulness is bound to be good, permits us top credit patient improvements to 'analysis' when more properly it should often be recognized for being the amounting result for the patient's using the analytic situation, as the model, for being the preceptors and supporter in the dealing practically within the immediate distractions as holding to some problem.

Perhaps, we can now refer to something in a clear unmistakable manner, and it would be to mention, for being, that one more difficult-to-handle intrusion of reality into the analysis, that by saying, that this is the definitive and final interruption of the transference neurosis by the reality of termination; in the sense, the situation is reversed and the intrusion is analytically desirable, since ideally the impact of reality of impending and certain termination is used to facilitate the resolution of the transference. As with the resolution of earlier episodes of transference neurosis, this final one is brought about principally by the analyst's interpretations and reconstructions. As these take effect, the transference neurosis and, hopefully, along with it the original neurosis is resolved. This final resolution, however, which is much more comprehensive, is usually very different and may not come about at all without the help of the reality of termination. Accordingly, any attenuation of the ending, such as tapering off or causal or tentative stopping, should be expected to stand in the way of an effective resolution of the transference. Yet, it seems that this is what most commonly happens to an ending, and because of this a great many patients may lose the potentially great benefit of a thorough resolution and are forever after left suspended in the net of unresolved transference.

Yet, slurring over a rigorous termination seems understandable, as difficult as transference neurosis may be in the analyst at other times, this ending period, if rigorously carried out, simply has to be the period of his greatest emotional strain. There can surely be no more likely time for an analyst to surrender his analytic position and, responding to his own transference, become personally involved with his patient than during the process of separating from a long and self-restrained relationship. Accordingly, it may be better to slur over the ending lightly than to mishandle it in an attempt to be rigorous.

In considering more broadly the function of the transference in the psychoanalytic process, one is confronted by the apparent naïve, but, nonetheless important questions of the role of the actual (current) object as compared with that of the object representation of the original personage in the past. We recall Freud's paradoxical, somewhat gloomy, but portentous concluding passage in 'The Dynamics of Transference.' This struggle between the doctor and the patient, between intellect and instinctual life, between understanding and seeking to act, is played out almost exclusively in the phenomena of transference. It is on that field that the victory must be won - the victory whose expression is on that field that the victory must be won - the victor y whose expression is the permanent cure of the neuroses. It cannot be disputed that controlling the phenomena of transference presents the psychoanalysis with the greatest difficultly, but it should not be forgotten that they do us the inestimable service of making the patient 's hidden and forgotten erotic impulses of showing their immediate and manifested impossibilities, for when all is said and done, it is impossible to destroy anyone in absentia or in effigies.

Both object and representation are made necessary by the basic phenomenon of original separation. The existence of an image of the object, which persist in the absence of the object, is one of the important beginnings of psychic life in general, certainly an indispensable prerequisite for object relationship. As generally construed. Whether this is viewed as (or a times demonstrably is) something unstable for allotting introjection, s always subject to alternative projection, or an intrapsychic object representation clearly distinguished from the self-representation, or firm identification in the superego, or in the ego itself, these phenomena are in various ways components of the system of mastery of the fact of separation, or separateness, from the original absolutely necessarily anaclitic (in the earliest period) symbiotic 'object'. In the light of clinical observation, it would appear to be that the relative stability (parental) object representation. At which time of varying degree, are to a greater extent for the archaic phenomena. Even in nonpsychotic patients, overwhelmed by them, sometimes resembles the restoration from oedipal identification, which provides the preponderant basis for most demonstrable analytic transferences. That within the necrotic patients, the transference is effectively established when this representation invests the analyst to a degree - depending on intensity of drive and most of ego participation - which ranges in all the, wishing and strivings to remake and analyst to biasses judgements and misinterpretation of data, finally are the actual perceptual distortions.

However, the old object representations as such may be invested, however rigidly established the libidinal or aggressive cathexis of the image may be, this as such can become the actual and exclusive focus of instinctual discharge, or of complicated and intense instinct-defence solutions, only and general energy-sparing quality of strictly intrapsychic processes. For the vast majority of persons, visible to any degree, including those with severe neurosis, character distortions, addictions and certain psychoses, the striving is toward the living and actual object, even at the cost of intense suffering. In a sense, this returns us to the state in which the psychological 'object-to-be'. Has a critical importance never again to be duplicated, except in certain acute life emergencies, even if the object is not firmly perceived as such, in the sense of later object relations? And it does seem that trance impressions from the earliest contacts in the service of life preservation, and the associated instinctual gratifications, and innumerable secondarily associated sensory impressions. Are activated by the specific inborn urges of sexual maturation? These propel the individual to renew many of the earliest modes of actual bodily contact, in connection with seeking for specific instinctual gratification. Or, to look away from clear-cut instinctual matters to the more remote elaborations of human contact: Few regard loneliness as other than a source of suffering, even self-imposed, as an apparent matter of choice, and the forcible imposition of 'solitary confinement ' is surely one of the most cruel of punishments.

Of these few generalizations have some important implications, no reaction to another individual is all transference, just as surely as no relationship is entirely free of it. There is not only the general maturational-developmental drive toward the outer world, but the seeking for a variety of need and pleasure satisfactions, learned or simulated in relation to the primordial object, but necessarily and inevitably transferred from this object the generically related things and persons in the expanding environment. these may be used or enjoyed without penalty, if the distinction between the original and the new is profoundly and genuinely established (with due respect for the quantitative 'relativism' of such concepts). The range of such inevitable displacement (transfers) in endless in all spheres - sexual, aggressive, aesthetic, utilitarian, intellectual. More immediately relevant, in the lives of those whose development has been relatively healthy, are those individuals whose vocations provide similarities or parallels, however, rarefied, to the caretaking functions of the original parents: Teachers, physicians, clergymen, political rulers, occasionally others. Again it must be noted, that such persons perform real functions, that the adult individual's interest in them, his specific need for them, often greatly outweighs similar reactions to parents, who retain their unique place for a complex and variable combination of other reasons. For such surrogate parents perform for the adult what his parents largely performed for him in realist years, and the psychological comparison is with an old object representation, or with an early identification, to which such latter-day parent surrogates may add important layers of elaborations. It is on the basis of such functional resemblances that persons in these roles have a unique transference valence. The analyst is first perceived as a real object, who awakens hope of help in the patients experience at all level of integration, from that of actual and immediate perception, evaluation, and response, to the activation of original parental object representations and their cathexes. That the analyst becomes invested with such representations, in forms ranging from wishes or demands to functional or even perceptual misidentifications, comprises the broad range of phenomena which we know as the therapeutic transference. Thus, the complicate structural phenomena of conflict are activated in relation to a real object, and such activation is uniquely dependent on the participation of this object, in a situation whose realities revive, with the affirmative associations, the memories of old and painful frustrations. In this situation, the continuing and prolonged contact, under strictly controlled conditions, is an important real factor, which has been elaborated previously. Without these actualities, dream life, - or instance of greater energid imbalance between impulses and defence - neurosis, will be the spontaneous solution, while everyday 'give-and-take' object relations are, at least on the surface, maintained as such. Occasionally, neurotic behaviour, where transferences dominate the everyday relationships, will supervene.

Interpretation, recollection or reconstruction, and, of course, working through, are essential for the establishment of effective insight, but they cannot operate mutatively if applied only to memories in the structural sense, whether of higher cathected events or persons. For it is the thrust of wish or impulse, or the elaboration of germane dynamic fantasies, and the corresponding defensive structures and their inadequacies, associated with such memories, which give to neurosis. It is a parallel thrust which creates the transference neurosis. where memories are clear and vivid, through recall, or accepted as much through reconstruction and associated with variable, optional, and adaptive, rather than rigidly structuralized' response patterns, the analytic work has been done.

This view does place somewhat of a weighty emphasis on the horizontal coordinate of procedural operations, the conscious and unconscious relation to the analyst as a living and actual object, which is of investing upon the becoming imagery, traits, and functions of critical objects of the past. The relationship is to be understood in its dynamic, economic, and adaptive meaning, in its current structuralized tenacity, the real and unreal carefully separated from one another. The process of subjective memory or of reconstruction, the indispensable genetic dimension, is, in this sense, involved toward the decisive and specific autobiographic understanding of the living version of old conflict, than with the assumption that the interpretative reduction of the transference neurosis to gross mnemic elements is, in itself and automatically, mutative. At least, this view of the problem would seem appropriate to most chronic neurosis embedded in germane character structures of some plexuity. That neurosis symptoms connected with isolated traumatic events, covered by amnesia, may, at times, disappear on restoration of memories with adequate effective discharge, regardless of technical method, is, of course, indisputably true, even though the details of process, including the role of transference, are probably not yet adequately understood. Psychoanalysis was born in the observation of this type of process. In a thoughtful manner, the role of transference, in the early writings of both Freud and Ferenczi, seemed weighted somewhat in the direction of its resistance function, i.e., as directed against recall, although its affirmative functions were soon adequately appreciated, and placed in the dialectical position, which has obtained to the present day.

Other while, the primal processes of projection ad introjection, being inextricably linked with the infant's emotions and anxieties, initiate object-relations, by projecting, i.e., deflecting libido and aggression onto the mother's breast, the basis for object-relations is established, by introjecting the object, first of all the breast, relations to internal objects come into being. The term 'object-relations' is based on the contention that the infant has from the beginning post-natal life a relation to the mother, although focussing primarily of her breast, which is imbued with the fundamental element's of an object-relation, i.e., love, hatred, phantasies, anxieties, and defences? The introjection of the breast is the beginning of superego formation which extends over years. We have grounds for assuming that from the first feeding experience onwards the infant's introjection, the breast in its various aspects. The core of the superego is thus the mother's breast, both good and bad. Given to the simultaneous operation of introjection and projection, relations to external and internal objects interact. The father too, who soon plays a role in the child's life, early on becomes part of the infant's internal world it is characteristic of the infant's emotional life that there are rapid fluctuations between love and hate, between external and internal situations between perception of reality and the fantasises relating to it, and accordingly, an interplay between prosecutory anxiety and idealization - both referring to the internal and external object's, the idealized object bring a corollary of the prosecutory, extremely bad one.

The ego's growing capacity for integration and synthesis leads more and more, even during these first few months, to states in which love and hatred, and correspondingly the good and bad aspects of objects, for being synthesized. This gives rise to the second form of anxiety - depressive anxiety - for the infant's aggressive impulses and desires toward the bad breast (mother) are now felt to be a danger to the good breast (mother) as well. In the second quarter of the first year these emotions are reinforced, because at this stage the infant increasingly perceives and introjects the mother as a person. Depressive anxiety is intensified, for the infant feels he has destroyed or is destroying a whole object by his greed and uncontrollable aggression. Moreover, owing to the growing synthesis of his emotions, he now feels that these destructive impulses are directed against as a 'loved person'. Similar processes operate in relation to the father and other member s of the family. These anxieties and corresponding defences constitute the 'Depressive position', which comes to a head about the middle of the first year and whose essence is the anxiety and guilt relating to the destruction and loss of the loved internal and external objects.

It is at this stage, and bound up with the depressive position, that the oedipus complex sets in. Anxiety and guilt adds a powerful impetus toward the beginning of the oedipus complex. For anxiety and guilt increase the need to externalize (project) bad figures and to internalize (introject) good ones. There to attaching desires, love, feeling of guilt, and reparative tendencies to internal figures in the external world, however, not only is the search for new objects which dominates the infant's needs, but also, the drive toward new life proposes: Away from the breast toward the penis, i.e., from oral desires toward genital ones. Many factors contribute to these developments, the forward drive of the libido, the growing integration of the ego, physical and mental skills and progressive adaption to the external world. These trends are bound up with the processing of symbol formation, which enables the infant to transfer not only emotions and phantasies, anxiety and guilt, from one object to another.

The processes are linked with another fundamental phenomenon governing its mental life, such that pressures exerted by the earliest anxiety situation, s of the factors through which bring about the repetition compulsion, however, one conclusion about the earliest states of infancy are a continuation of Freud's discoveries; on certain points, nonetheless, the divergencies having to arise of which is very relevant, perhaps, its main contention that object-relations are operative from the beginning of post-natal life.

Nevertheless, the view that autoerotism and narcissism are the young infant contemporaries with the first relation to objects - external and internalized, that hypothetically, autoerotism and narcissism include the love for and relation with the internalized good object which in phantasy forms part of the loved body and self. It is to this internalized object that in autocratic gratification and narcissistic stages a withdrawal takes place. Concurrently, from birth onwards, a relation to objects, primarily the mother (her breasts) is present. This hypothesis contradicts Freud's concept of autoerotic and narcissistic stages which preclude an object-relation. However, the difference between Freud's statement on this issue are equivocal. In various context he explicitly and implicitly expresses opinion which suggested a relation to an object, the mother's breast, preceding autoerotic and narcissism.

In the first instance the oral component instinct finds satisfaction by attaching itself to the sating of the desire for nourishment, and its object in the mother's breast. It then detaches itself, becomes independent and at the same time of autoerotic objectivity is found to an object in the child's own body.

Freud' use of the term object is somewhat different from the context that is used of this term, but Freud is referring the object of an instinctual aim. What it is to mean, that, while, in addition, it is meant as an object-relation involving the infant's emotions, phantasies, anxieties and defences. Nevertheless, in sentence referred to, Freud clearly speaks of a libinal attachment to an object, the mother's breast, which precedes autoerotism and narcissism.

In this context, it is reminded that of Freud's findings about early identification. In "The Ego and the Id," speaking of abandoned object cathexes. He said, ' . . . The effects of the first identification in earliest childhood will be profound and lasting. This leads us back to the origin of the ego-ideal, . . . Freud then defines the first and most important identifications which lie hidden behind the ego-ideal as the identification with the father, or with the parent's, and places them, as he expresses it, in the 'prehistory' of every person'. These formulations come close to the deceptions as described of their resulting of introjected objects, for by definition identifications are the result as such, but that the statement and the passage quoted from the Encyclopaedia article, it can be deduced that Freud, although he did not pursue this line of though t, however, he did assume that in the earliest infancy that both an object and introjective processes play a part.

That is to say, as regards autoerotism and narcissism we meet with an inconsistency in Freud's views. Such inconsistencies which exist on a number of points of theory clearly show, which on these particular of issue s Freud had not yet arrived at a final decision. In respect to the theory of anxiety he stated this explicitly in Inhibitions, Symptoms and Anxiety. His realization that much about the early stages of development was still unknown or obscure to him is also exemplified by his speaking of the first years of a girl's life as, ' . . . lost in a past so dim and shadowy . . .'

As regards to the question of autoerotism and narcissism, Anna Freud - although her views about this aspect of Freud's work remains unknown, but she seems only to have taken into account Freud's conclusions that an autoerotic and a narcissistic stage precede object-relations, and not to be allowed for other possibilities, of which are implied in some of Freud's statements such as the ones inferred above. This is one of the reasons why the divergence between Anna Freud's conception and the immediacy of early infancy is far greater than that between Freud's views, taken as a whole, and those of stating it as the essential to clarify the content and nature of the differences between the two schools of psychoanalytic thought, represented by Anna Freud and those that imply of such clarification is required in the interests of psychoanalytic training and also because it could help to open up fruitful discussions between psychoanalysts and thereby contribute to a greater generality of a better understanding of the fundamental problems of early infancy.

The hypothesis that a time interval extending over several months precedes object-relations implies that - except for the libido attached to the infant's own body - impulses, phantasies, anxieties, and defences either are not present in him, or are not related to an object, that is to say, they would operate in vacua. The analysis of very young children, as to implicate, would show that there is no instinctual urge, no anxiety situation, no mental process which does not involve objects, external or internal, in other words, object-relations are at the centre of emotional life. Furthermore, love and hatred, phantasies, anxiety and defences are also operative from the beginning and are 'ad initio' indivisibly linked with object-relations.

The oedipus complex, in a pragmatic analytic sense, retains its position as the 'nuclear complex' of the neurosis. It is a climactic organization experience of early childhood, apart from its own vicissitudes, It can under favourable circumstances provide certain solutions for pregenital conflicts, or in itself suffer from them. in any case, include them in its structure. Only when the precursor experiences have been of a great severity, for which it is to claim to a shadowy organic determinacy, as the new 'frame of reference', which hardly having the independent and decisive significance of its own. In any case, its attendant phallic conflicts must be resolved in their own right, in the analytic transference. From the analyst, (or his current surrogate in the outer world) thus from the psychic representation of the parent, the literal (i.e., bodily) sexual wishes must be withdrawn, and genuinely displaced to appropriate objects in the outer world. The fraction of such drive elements which can be transmuted to friendly, tender feeling toward the original object. Or too other acceptable (neutralized) variants, will of course, influence the economic problem involved. This genuine displacement is opposed to the sense of 'acting out', while other objects are perceptually different substitutes for the primary object (thus for the analyst). This may be thought to follow automatically on the basic process of coming to terms with (accepting) the childhood incestuous wish and its parricidal connotation. Such assumption does not do justice to the dynamic problem implicit in tenaciously persistent wishes. To the extent that these wishes are to be genuinely disavowed or modified, rather than displaced, a further important step is necessary: The thorough analysis of the functional meaning of the persisting wishes and the special etiologic factors entering into their tenacity, as reflected in the transference neurosis. Thus, in principle, the literal accuracy of the concept phrased by Wilhelm Reich, "transference of the transference," as the final requirement for dissolution of the erotic analytic transference, even though the clinical discussion, which is its context, is useful. This expression would imply that the object representation which largely determine the distinctive erotic interest in the analyst can remain essentially the same, so long as the actual object changes. While a semantic issue may be involved in some degree, it is one which impinges importantly on conceptual clarity. However, such definite conceptualization of one basic element in the phenomenon or transference may be, and should be, subject to the reservations appropriately attaching themselves to any very clear-cut ideas about obscure areas, with the clinical concept of transference, its clinical derivation and its generally accepted place in the psychnalytic process.

The evolution of the reality-relatedness between patient and therapist, over the course of the psychotherapy, is something which has received little more than passing mention in the literature, Hoedemaker (1955), in a paper concerning the therapeutic process in the treatment of schizophrenia, stresses the importance of the schizophrenic patient's forming healthy identifications with the therapist, and Loewald (1960), in his paper concerning the therapeutic action of psychoanalysis in general, repeatedly emphasizes the importance of the real relationship between patient and analyst, but only in the following passage eludes the evolution, the growth, of this relationship over the course of treatment:

> . . . Where repression is lifted and unconscious and preconscious are again in communication, infantile object and contemporary object may be united into one - a truly new object as both unconscious and preconscious are changed by their mutual communication, the object which helps to bring this about in therapy, the analyst, mediates this union. . . .

It has been distinctly impressive that the patient's remembrance of new areas of his past - his manifestation of newly de-repressed transference reactions to the therapist - occurs only hand-in-hand with the reaching of comparable areas of feeling in the evolving reality-relatedness between patient and therapist. For example, he does not come to experiencing fond memories of his mother until the reality-relatedness between himself and the therapist has reached the point where the feelings between them have become, in reality, predominantly positive. Loewald's words, imply that an increment of transference resolution slightly antedates, and makes possible the forming of each successive increment the evolving reality-relationship between patient and analyst. It has been, by contrast, that the evolution of the reality-relatedness proceeds alway ahead of, and makes possible, the progressive evolution and resolution of the transference, although to be sure, the latter insofar as it frees psychological energy and makes it available for reality-relatedness, helping greatly to consolidate the ground just taken over by the advancing reality-relatedness.

It seems that this new object-relationship is more that a potentiality, to be realized with comparative suddenness, toward the end of this treatment with the resolution of the transference. Rather it is, it has seemed as constantly being there, being built up bit by bit, just ahead of the likewise evolving transference relationship. Predeterminates as in Freud's (1922) having pointed out that projection (expressed in the Latin is called 'projectio') which is, after all, so major an aspect of transference - is directed not 'into the sky, so to speak, were there is nothing of the sort already', but rather onto a person who provides some reality-basic for the projection.

In that the patient, schizophrenic or otherwise, becomes one with himself, in the closing phase of psychotherapy. But although the realization may come to him as a sudden one, it is founded on a reality-relatedness which has been building up all along. Loewald (1960) in his magnificent paper to which transference resolution plays in the development of this reality-relatedness. As, perhaps, that the evolution of the 'countertransference' - not counter-transference in the classical sense of the therapist's transference to the patient, but rather in the sense of the therapist's emotional reaction to the patient's transference - forms an equally essential contribution to this reality-relatedness.

It is, nonetheless, but often, that the therapist who sees a new potentiality in the patient, a previously unnoted side of him which heralds a phase of increasing differentiations. And frequently the therapist is the only one who sees it. Even the patient does not see it as ye t, except in the projected form, so that he perceives this as an attribute of the therapist. This situation can make the therapist feel very much inalienable as alone and intensely threatened.

Upon which the transference relationship with the therapist, we find that the patient naturally brings this relationship, just as he brings into the relatedness in which the difficulties concerning differentiation and integration which were engendered by the pathological upbringing upon the advances in differentiation and integration necessarily occur first outside the patient - namely, in the therapist's increasingly well differentiated and well-integrated view of, and consequently, responses to, him - before these can become well established within him.

Because the schizophrenic patient did not experience, in his infancy, the symbolic relatedness with his mother such as each human being needs for the formation of a healthy core in his personality structure, in the emotion of the transference relationship to his therapist he must eventually succeed in establishing such a mode of relatedness.

This means that he must eventually regress, in the transference, to such a level in order to get a fresh start toward a healthier personality differentiation and integration than he had achieved before entering therapy. This is not to say that he must 'act out' the regressive needs in his daily life, to be sure, the schizophrenic patient, whether in therapy or not, inevitably does so to a considerable degree, but to the extent that these needs can be expressed in the transference relationship, they need not seek expression, unconsciously, thorough acting out in daily life.

Focussing now upon the transference relationship with the therapist, we find that the patient naturally brings about the difficulties concerning differentiation in the process of integration which were engendered by the pathological upbringing as for being the one more interruption in the impeding principle of reconstructions of an identifying manufacture of the transference. And the every day, relationships are found in the interplaying form of corresponding advances in differentiated dynamic integrations necessarily occur first outside the patient - namely, in the therapist's increasingly well or acceptably differentiated by the integrated extent or range of vision, that the position or attitude that determine how of the intent of something (as an aim or an end or motive)or by way the mind is directed. Its view of and the consequent response ought to become acknowledgingly established within them.

Because the schizophrenic patient did not experience, in his infancy, the establishment of and later emergence form, a healthy symbiotic relatedness with his mother such as each human bring needs for the formation of a healthy core in his personality structure, in the evolution of the transference relationship to his therapist he must eventually succeed in establishing such a mode of relatedness.

This means that he must eventually regress, in the transference, to such a level, in order to get a fresh start toward a healthier personality differentiation and integration than he had achieved before entering therapy. This is not to say that he must act out the regressive needs in his daily life. To be sure, the schizophrenic patient, whether in therapy or not, inevitably does so to a considerable degree, but to the extent that these needs can be expressed in the transference relationship, they need not seek expression, unconsciously, through acting out in daily life.

This symbiotic mode of relatedness is necessarily mutual, participated in by therapist as well as patient. Thus, the therapist must come to experience not only the oceanic gratification, but also the anxiety involved in his sharing a symbiotic, subjective oneness with the schizophrenic patient. This relationship, with its lack of felt ego-boundaries between the two participants, at times invokes the kind of deep contentment, the kind of felt communion that needs no words, which characterize a loving relatedness between mother and infant. But at other times It involves the therapists feeling unable to experience himself as differentiated from the pathology-ridden personality of the patient. He feels helplessly caught in the patient's deep ambivalence. He feels one with the patient's hatred and despair and thwarted love, and at times he cannot differentiate between his own subjectively harmful effect upon the patient, and the illness with which the patient was to come or go or nearly recede in the achievement afflicting when the therapist first undertook to help him. Thus, at these anxiety-ridden moments in the symbiotic phase, the therapist feels his own personality to be invaded by the patient's pathology, and feels his identity severely threatened, whereas in the more contented moments, part of the contentment resides in both participants enjoying a freedom from any concern with identity.

This same profound lack of differentiation may come to characterize the patient's view of the persons about him, including his therapeutic, and at time's, in line with his need to project a poorly differentiated conglomeration of 'bad' impulses, he may perceive the therapist for being but one head of a hydra-headed monster. The patient's lack of differentiation in this regard, prevailing for month after month of his charging the therapist with saying or doing various things which were actually said or have don e by others amongst the hospitalized presences to its containing of environmental surfaces, or by the family members, can have a formidably eroding effect upon the therapist's sense of personal intensity. but the patient may need to regress to just such a primitivity, poorly differentiated view of the world in order to grow up again, psychologically, in a healthier way this time.

Among the most significant steps in the maturation which occurs in successful psychotherapy are those moments when the therapist suddenly sees the patient in a new light. His image of the patient suddenly changes, because of the entry into his awareness of some potentiality in the patient. Which had not shown itself before? From now on, his responses t o the patient is a response to this new, enriched view, and through such responding he fosters the emergence, and further differentiation, of this new personality area. This is another way of describing the process which Buber and in Friednan, 1955, calls 'making the other person present, seeing in the other persons potentialities of such even presents: Seeing in the other persons potentialities of which even he is not aware of him and helping him, by responding to those potentialities, to realize them.

Schizophrenic patient's feelings start to become differentiated before they have found new and appropriate modes for expressing the new feelings, thus patient's may use the same old stereotyped behaviour or utterance to express nuances of new feelings. This is identical with the situation in those schizophrenics' familiar which are permeated with what Wynne (1958) termed 'pseudo-mutuality' or toward maintaining the sense of reciprocal perceiving expectations. Thus, the expectations are left unexplored, and the old expectations and roles, even though outgrown and inappropriate in one sense, continue to serve as the structure for the relation.

The therapist, through hearing the new emotional connotation, the new meaning, in the stereotyped utterance and responding in accordance with the new connotation, fosters the emerging differentiation. Over the course of months, in therapy, he may find the same verbal stereotype employed in th e expression of a whole gamut of newly emerging feelings. Thus, over a prolonged time-span, the therapist may give as many different responses to a gradually differentiating patient as are simultaneously given by the various members of the surrounding environment, to the patient who shows the contrasting ego-fragmentation (or, in a loose manner of speaking, over-differentiations).

Persistently stereotyped communications from the patient tend to bring from the therapist communications which, over a period of time, become almost equally stereotyped. One can sometimes detect, in recordings playing during supervisory hours, evidence that new emotional connotations are creeping into the patient's verbal stereotypes, and into the therapist's responsive verbal stereotypes, before either of the two participants has noticed this.

What the therapist does, assisting the patient's differentiation often consists in his having the courage and honesty as to differ from whether the patient's expressed feelings or, often most valuable, with the social role into which his sick behaviour tends to fix or transfix the therapist. This may consist in his candid disagreement with some of the patient, and s strongly felt and long-voiced views, or in his flatly declining to try to feel 'sympathy' - such as one would be conventionally expected to feel in response to behaviour, which seems, at first glance, to express the most pitiable suffering but which the therapist is convinced primarily expresses sadism on the patient's part. Such courage to differ with the expected social role is what is needed from the therapist, for closing the symbiotic phase of relatedness which has served, earlier, a necessary and productive function. Through asserting his individuality, and at many later moments in the therapeutic interaction, the therapist fosters the patient's own development of more complete and durable ego-boundaries. At the same time he offers the patient the opportunity to identify with a parent-figure who dares to be an individual-dares to be so in the face of pressures from the working group of which he is part, and from his own reproachful superego, it can be of notice, that of a minor degree a consciously planned and controlled therapeutic technique wherefore, the content descriptions are rather a natural flow of events as in the transference evolution, with which the therapist must have the spontaneity to go along.

The patient, particularly in the symbiotic phase of the therapy but in preceding and succeeding phases as well, is notably intolerant of sudden and marked changes in the therapeutic relationship - that is, of suddenly seeing himself, or feeling that his therapist sees him, through new eyes. He rarely gives the therapist to feel that the latter has made an importantly revealing interpretation, or should be concealed, but when to arrive at by reasoning from evidence or from its premises that we can infer from that which he was derived as to a conclusion, that it conveys of a higher illumination of mind. Methodologically historical information is an approving acceptation by the therapist, he does so causally, he tends to experience important increments of depreciated material, yet not as every bit for reverential abstractions as to make a new, amended, or up-to-date reversion of the many problems involved in revising the earthly shuddering revelations in his development. The things that he has known all along and simply never happened to think of. His experience of an inherent perception of the world as surrounding him is often permeated by 'deja vu' sensations, and misidentification of the emphasizing style at which the expense of thought for taking the rhetorical rhapsody to actions or a single inaction of moving the revolutions of the earth around the sun is mostly familiar an act from his past.

The motional progression in therapy, on the patient's part, occur each time only after a recrudescence in his symptoms. It is as though he has to find reassurance of his personal identity, for being really the same hopeless person he has long felt himself to be, before he can venture into a bit or new and more hopeful identity.

Of what expressions is that object relations exist from th e beginning of life being the mother's breast which it split into a good (gratifying) and bad (frustrating) breast; this splitting results in a division between love and hate. What is more, is that of the relation to the first object implies its introjection and projection, and thus, from the beginning object relations are moulded by an interaction between introjection and projection, between internal and external objects and situation.

. . . .With the introjection of the complete object in about the second quarter of the first year marked steps in integration are made. . . . The loved and hated aspects of the mother are no longer felt to be so widely separated, and the result is an increased fear of loss, a strong feeling of guilt and states akin to mourning, because the aggressive impulses are felt to be divorced against the love object, the depressive position has come to the fore . . .

. . . In th e first few months of life anxiety is predominantly experienced as fear of persecution and . . . this contributes to certain mechanisms and defences which characterize the paranoid and schizoid positions. Outstanding among these defences is the mechanism of splitting internal and external objects, emotions and the ego. These mechanisms and defences are part of normal development and at the same time form the basis for later schizophrenic illness. The descriptive underlying identification by projection, i.e., projective identification, as a combination of splitting off parts of the self and projecting them onto another person . . .

Rosenfeld, a follower of Klein writes that, he presents detailed clinical data which serve to document the implicit point, among others, that whereas, the schizophrenic patient may appear to have regressed to such an objectless autoerotic level of development as was postulated by Freud (1911, 1914) and Abraham (1908), in actuality the patient is involved in object-relatedness with the analyst, object-relatedness of the primitive introjective and projective identification kind.

We find, among the writings of the Kleinian analysts, a number of interesting examples of delusional transference interpretation, in all of which the keynote is the concept of projective (or introjective) identification (1952).

. . . .The patient himself gave the clue to the transference situation, and showed that he had projected his damaged self containing the destroyed world, not only into all the other patients, but into me, and had changed me in this way. But, instead of becoming relieved by this projection he became more anxious, because he was afraid of what I was then putting back into him. Whereupon his introjective processes became severely disturbed. One would therefore expect a severe deterioration in his condition, and in fact his clinical state during the next ten days became very precarious. He began to get more and more suspicious about food, and finally refused to eat and drink anything. . . . everything he took inside seemed to him bad, damaged, and poisonous (like faeces) as there was no point in eating anything. we knew that projection led again into reintroduction, so that also, it had felt as if he had inside himself all the destroyed and bad objects which he had projected into the outer world: And he indicated by coughing, retching and movements of his mouth and fingers that he was preoccupied with this problem, such that he was not only afraid of getting something bad inside him. But that he was also afraid of taking good things, the good orange juice and good interpretations, instead, since he was afraid that these would make him feel guilty again. When l said this, a kind of shock went right through his body; he gave a groan of understanding, and his facial expression changed. By the end of the hour he had emptied the glass of orange juice, the first food or drink he had taken for two days . . .

It now seems that the instances of verbal transference interpretation can be looked upon as one form of intervention, at times effective, which constitutes an appeal for collaboration to the non-psychotic area of the patient's personality, an area of which both Katan (1954) and Bion (1957) have written. But, particularly among long hospitalized chronically schizophrenic persons, we are many a patient who is too ill to be able to register verbal statements, and even in th e foregoing examples from Rosenfeld's and Bion's experiences, it is impossible to know to what extent the patient is helped by an illuminating accurate verbal content in the therapist's words, or to what extent that which is effective springs, rather from the feelings of confidence, firmness, and understanding which accompany these words spoken by a therapist who feels that he has a reliable theoretical value for formulating the clinical phenomena in which he finds himself.

In trying to conceptualize such ego-states in the patient, and such states of relatedness between patient and doctor. Additional value placed the concept presentation by Little in her papers, "On Delusional Transference" (Transference Psychosis) (1958) and "On Basic Unity" (1960).

One of the necessary development, in along-delusional patient's eventual relinquishment of his delusions is for these gradually to become productions which the therapist sees no longer as essentially ominous and the subject for either serious therapeutic investigation, or argumentation, or any other form of opposition, rather, the therapist comes to react to these for being essentially playful, unmaligant, creatively imaginative, and he comes to respond to them with playfully imaginative comments of his own. Nothing helps more finally to detoxicate a patient's previously self-isolating delusional state than to find in his therapist a capacity to engage him in a delightfully crazy playfulness - a kind of relatedness of which the schizophrenic patient had never a chance to have his fill during his childhood. Typically, such early childhood playfulness was subjected to massive repression, because of various intra-familial circumstances.

Innumerable instances of the therapist's uncertainty how to respond to the patient's communication turn upon the question of whether the communication is to be 'taken personally' - to be taken as primarily designed, for instance, toward filling the therapist with perplexity, confusion, anxiety, humiliation, rage, or some other negatively toned affective state; or whether it is to be taken rather as primarily an effort to convey some basically unhostile need on the patient's par. Just as it is often essential that the therapist become able to sense and respond to personal communications in a patient's ostensibly stereotyped behaviour or utterance, so too it is frequently essential that he be able to see, behind the overt 'personal' reference to himself - often a stinging or otherwise emotionally evocative reference - some fundamental need which the patient is hesitantly to communicate openly.

Of the physiological needs, which the schizophrenic manifests, those centring about the oral zone of interaction are usually most prominent, analogous to the predominant place held by nursing in the life of the infant. Desires to be stroked and cuddled, likewise, so characteristic of the very early years of normal development, is prominently held within the schizophrenic. In addition, desires for the relief of genital sexual tensions, even though these have had their advent much later in the life history than have his oral desires, are manifested in much the same level of an early, infantile dependency. That is, such genital hungers are manifested in much the same small-child spirit of, 'you ought to be taking care of this for me' as are the oral hungers.

The psychological needs which are represented among the schizophrenic's dependency processes consist in the desire for the other person to provide him with unvarying love and protection, and to assume a total guidance of his living,

In the course of furthering characterizations of the schizophrenic's dependency processes will be defined much more fully, that is to say, it is to b e emphasized that no of the dependency processes are but described is characteristic only of the schizophrenic, or qualitatively different from processes operative at some level of consciousness in persons with other varieties of psychiatric illness and in normal persons. With regard to dependency processes, we find research in schizophrenia has its greatest potential value in the fact that schizophrenic shows us in a sharply etched form that which is so obscured, by years progressive adaptation to adult interpersonal living, in human beings in general. Wherefore, but in some degree, are about the patient's anxiety about the dependency needs, are (1) As nearly as can be determined, the patient is unaware of pure dependency needs; for him, apparently, they exist in consciousness, if at all, only in the form of a hopelessly conflictual combination of dependency needs plus various defences - defences which render impossible any thoroughgoing sustained gratification of these needs. These defences (which include, grandiosity, hostility, competitiveness, scorn and so forth) have so long ago developed in his personality, as a means of coping with anxiety attendant upon dependency needs, that the experiencing of pure dependency needs it, for him, lost in antiquity and so be achieved only relatively late in therapy after the various defences have been largely relinquished.

Thus it appears to be not only dependency needs 'per se' which arouse anxiety, but rather the dependency needs plus all these various defences (which tend in themselves to be anxiety-provoking) plus the inevitable frustration, to a greater or less degree, of the dependency needs.

Hostility as one of the defences against awareness of 'dependency needs,' that which for certainly repressed dependency needs are one of the most frequent bases of murderous feelings in the schizophrenic, in such instances the murderous feelings may be regarded as a vigorous denial of dependency. What frequently happens in therapy is that both patient and therapist become so anxious about the defensive murderous feelings that the underlying dependency feeling long remain unrecognized.

Every schizophrenic possesses much self-hatred and guilt which may serve as defences against the awareness of dependency feelings ('I am too worthless for anyone possibly to care about me'), and which in any case complicate the matter of dependency. The schizophrenic has generally come to interpret the rejections in his past life as meaning that he is a creature who wants too much and, in fact, a creature who has no legitimate needs. Thus, he can accept gratification of his dependency needs, if at all, only if his needs are rendered acceptable to themselves by reason of his becoming physically ill or in a truly desperate emotional state. It is frequently found that a schizophrenic is more accessible to the gratification of his dependency needs when he is physically ill, or filled with despair, than at other times. In that way, th e presence of self-hatred, and guilt, one ingredient of the patient's overall anxiety about dependancy needs has to do with the fact that these needs connote to him the state of feeling physical illness or despair.

In essence, then, we can see that the patient has a deep-seated conviction that his dependency needs will not be gratified. Further, we see that this conviction is based not alone on the fortunate past expedience of repeated rejection, but also, the fact that his own defences, called forth concomitantly with the dependency desires, make it virtually certain that this dependency needs will not be met. (2) The dependency needs are anxiety-provoking not only because they involve desires to relate in an infantile or small-child fashion (by breast - or penis sucking, being cuddled, and as so forth) which is not generally acceptable behaviour among adult s, but also, and probably more important, because they involve a feeling that the other person is frighteningly important, absolutely indispensable to the patient's survival.

This feeling as to the indispensable of importance of the other person derives from two main sources: (a) the regressed state of the schizophrenic's emotional life, which makes for his perceiving the other as all-important to his survival, just as in infancy the mothering one is all-important to the survival of the infant, and (b) certain additional disabling features of his schizophrenic illness, which render him dependent in various special ways which are not quite comparable with the dependency characteristic of normal infancy or early childhood. Thereof, a number of points in reference to (b) are, first, we can perceive that a schizophrenic who is extremely confused, for example, is utterly dependent on or upon the therapist or, some other relevantly significant person to help him establish a bridge between his incomparable, incongruent, conflicting, conditions in which things are out of their normal or proper places or relationships. Such are the complete mental confusions that the authenticity of a corresponding to known facts are to discover or rediscover the real reason for which such things as having no illusions and facing reality squarely face-to-face, a realistic appraisal of his chances for advancing to the reasonable facts as we can see the factional advent for understanding the absolutizing instinct to fancy of its reality.

Second, we can see also that the patient who is in transition between old, imposed values and not-yet-acquired values of his own, has only the relationship with his therapist to depend upon.

Third, is the concern and consideration that, in many instances, the schizophrenic appears to be what one might call a prisoner in th e present. He is so afraid both of change and of the memories which tend to be called forth by the present that he clings desperately to what in immediate. He is in this sense imprisoned in immediate experience, and looks to the therapist to free him so that he will be able to live in all his life, temporally speaking - present, past and future.

Forth, it might be surmised that an oral type of relatedness to the other person (with the all-importance of the other which this entails) is necessary for the schizophrenic to maintain, partly in order to facilitate his utilization of projection and introjection as defences against anxiety.

Anxiety, is the constructed foundation whose emotional state from which are grounded to the foundation structural called the 'edifice', that an emotional state in which people feel uneasy, apprehensive, or fearful. People usually experience anxiety about events they cannot control or predict, or about events that seem threatening or dangerous. For example, students taking an important test may feel anxious because they cannot predict the test questions or feel certain of a good grade. People often use the words fear and anxiety to describe the same thing. Fear also describes a reaction to immediate danger characterized by a strong desire to escape the situation.

The physical symptoms of anxiety reflect a chronic "readiness" to deal with some future threat. These symptoms may include fidgeting, muscle tension, sleeping problems, and headaches. Higher levels of anxiety may produce such symptoms as rapid heartbeat, sweating, increased blood pressure, nausea, and dizziness.

Bychowski (1952) says, '"The separation between the primitive ego and the external world is closely connected with orality, both form the basis for the mechanism which we call projection," and would add, for introjection., that Starcke (1921) for earlier comments "I might briefly allude to the possibility that in the repeated alternation between becoming one's own and no t one's own, which occurs during lactation . . . the situation of being suckled plays a part in the origin of the mechanism of projection.

The patient has anxiety, and, least of mention, his dependency needs lead him either to take in harmful things, or to lose his identity.

The schizophrenic does not have the ability necessary to tolerate the frustration of his dependency needs, so that he can, once they emerge into awareness, subject them to mature discriminatory judgement before seeking their gratification. Instead, like a voraciously hungry infant, his tendency is to put into his mouth (either literally or figuratively) whatever is at hand, whether nutritious or with a potential of being harmful, this tendency is about th e basis of some of his anxiety concerning his dependency needs, for the fear that they will keep him blindly into receiving harmful medicines, bad advice, electro-shock treatment, lobotomy, and so forth. Schizophrenic patients have been known to beg, in effect, for all these, and many a patients have been known to beg, yet these patients have been 'successful' in his dependency desires. A need for self-punishment is, of course, an additional motivation in such instances.

A statement by Fenichel (1945) indicates that, "The pleasure principle, that is, the need for immediate discharge, is incompatible with correct judgement, which is based on considerable and post postponement of the reaction. The time and energy saved by this postponement are used in the function of sound and stable judgments. That in the early states the weak ego has not yet learned to postpone anything.

In which the symptomatic of one that finds that the extent that the schizophrenic projects onto other persons his own needs too such and to devour, he feels threatened with being devoured by these other persons.

To elaborate now in a somewhat different direction upon this fear of loss of identity. Th e schizophrenic fears that his becoming dependent on another person will lead him into a state of conformity that other person's wishes and life values. A conformer is almost the last sort of person as the schizophrenic wishes to become, since his sense of individuality resides in his very eccentricities. He assumes that the therapist, for example, in the process, requiring him to give up his individuality for the kinds of parental future in his past had e been able to salvage his refuge used to pay the price.

It seems of our apparent need to give the impression of being without necessarily being so in fact that things are not always the way they seem, as things accompanied with action orient of doing whatever is apprehended as having actual, distinct and demonstrateable existence from which there is a place for each thing in the cosmological understanding idea in that something conveys to the mind a rational allotment of the far and near, such of the values and standards moderate the newly proposed to modify as to avoid an extreme or keep within bounds.

For what is to say, in that we need to realize, that the patient is not solely a broken, inert victim of the hostility of persons in his past life. His hebephrenic apathy or his catatonic immobility, for example, represent for one thing an intensely active striving toward unconscious regressive goals, as Greenson (1949, 1953) has for his assistance to make clear in the boredom and apathy in neurotic patients. The patient is, in other words, no inert vehicle which needs to be energized by the therapist; rather, an abundance of energy is locked in him, pressing ceaselessly to be freed, and a hovering 'helpful' orientation on the part of the therapist would only get in the way. We must realize that the patient has made, and is continually making, a contribution to his own illness, however unwittingly, and however obscure the nature of this contribution may long remain.

More than often, it has been found that the histories of schizophrenic patients, whether male or female, describe the father for being by far, the warmer, the more accessible, of the responsive parents, and the patient as having always been very much attached to the father, whereas the mother was always a relatively cold, rejecting, remote figure, but for the repetitive correlative coefficient, that it was to be found that, disguised behind the child's idol or inseparable buddy, is a matter of the father's transference to the child's being a mother-figure that the father, in these instances, is an infantile individual who reacts both to his wife and to his child, as the mother-figure, and who, by striving to be both father and mother to the child, unconsciously seeks to intervene between mother and child, that in such a way as to have each of them to himself, in the considerations that suggest of a number of cases when both are in the transference-development with the patient and the selective prospect of the patient's generalization that limits or qualifies an agreement or other conditions that may contain or depend on a conditioning need for previsional advocates that include the condition that the transference phenomena would effectually raise the needed situational alliance.

The various forms of intense transference on the part of the schizophrenic individual tend forcibly to evoke complementary feeling-responses, comparably intense, in the therapist. Mabel Blake Cohen (1952) has made the extremely valuable observation, for psychoanalysis in general, that, . . . it seems that the patient applies great pressure to the analyst in a variety of non-verbal ways to behave like the significant adults in the patient's earlier life, it is not merely a matter of the patient's seeing the analyst as like his father, but of his actually manipulating the relationship in such away as to elicit the same kind of behaviour from the analyst. . . .

It is no too much to say that, in response to the schizophrenic patient's transference, the therapist not only behaves like the significant adults in the patient's childhood, but experiences most intimately, within himself, activated by the patient's transference the very kind of intense and deeply conflictual feelings which were at work, however repressed, in those adults in the past, as well as experiencing, through the mechanisms of projection and introjection in the relationship between himself and the patient, the comparably intense and conflictual emotion which formed the seed-bed of psychosis in the child himself, years ago.

The accountable explanation in the support for reason to posit for the necessarily deep feeling-involvement on the part of the therapist is inherent in the nature of early ego-formation. The healthy reworking of which is so central to the therapy of schizophrenia. Spitz (1959), in his monograph on the early development of the ego, repeatedly emphasizes that emotion plays a leading role in th e formation of what he described as the 'organizers of the psyche' (which he defines as 'emergent, dominant centres of integration') during the first eighteen months of life. H e says, for example, . . . this integration of isolated functions is built by the infant's object relations, by experiences of an effective nature. Accordingly, the indicator of the organizer of the psyche will be of an effective nature, it is an effective behaviour which clearly precedes development in all other sectors of the personality by several months.

The phases comprising in the over-all course of psychotherapy with chronically schizophrenic persons, is that of recent years it has become increasingly reassuring that it is possible to delineate such phases amongst the complex, individualistic and dynamic events of clinical work. One can be said, that, in this difficult effort at conceptualization, from Freud's delineation of the successive phases of libidinal development in healthy maturation, Erikson's (1956) portrayal of the process of identity formation as gradual unfolding of the personality through phase-specific psycho-social crises of evolution of the reality principle in healthy development - the typical conflicts, the sequence of danger situations, and the ways they are dealt with - can be traced in this process.

The successive phases of which are best characterised, the psychotherapy of chronic schizophrenia, are the 'out-of-contact phases, the phase of ambivalent symbiosis, the phase of pre-ambivalent symbiosis, the phase of resolution of the symbiosis, and the late phase, - that of establishment, and elaboration, of the newly won individuation through selective new identification and repudiation of outmoded identifications.

The sequence of these phases retraces, in reverse, the phases by which the schizophrenic illness was originally formed: The way of thinking, the aetiological roots of schizophrenia are formed when the mother-infant symbiosis fails to resolve into individuation of mother and infant - or, still more harmfully., fails even to become at all firmly established - because of deep ambivalence of the part of the mother which hindered the integration and differentiation of the infant's and young child's ego, the child fails then to proceed through the normative development phases of symbiosis and subsequent individuation. Instead the core of his personality remains uniform, and ego-fragmentation and dedifferentiation become powerful, though deeply primitive and unconscious defences against the awareness of ambivalence in the object and in himself. Even in normal development, one becomes separate person only by becoming able to face, and accept ownership of, one's ambivalence with which he had to cope in his relationship with his mother was too great, and his ego-formation too greatly impeded, for him to be able to integrate his conflictual feeling-states into an individual identity.

Of these, the theoretical concept has been fostered by Mahler's (1956) paper on autistic and symbiotic infantile psychosis and by Balint's (1953, 1955) writings concerning phenomena of early ego-formation which he encountered in the psychoanalysis of neurotic patients. From a purely descriptive viewpoint, schizophrenia can be seen to consist essentially in an impairment of both 'integration' and 'differentiation' - which are but opposite faces of a unitary growth-process. From a psychodynamic view point seems basic to all the bewilderingly complex and varied manifestations of schizophrenia.

Taking in, is the matter of integration; when we assess schizophrenia individual in terms of the classical structural areas of the personality - id, ego, and superego - we discover these to be poorly integrated with one another. The id is experienced by the ego as a Pandora's box, the contents of which will overwhelm one if it is opened. The ego is, as many writers have stated, severely split, sometimes into innumerable islands which are not linked discernibly with one another. And the superego has the nature of a cruel tyrant whose assaults upon the weak and unintegrated ego are, if anything, even more destructive to it than are the assessions of the threatening id-impulses, as Szalita-Pemow (1951), Hill (1955), and others. Moreover, the superego is, like the ego, even in itself not well integrated; it s utterance contain the most glaring inconsistencies from one moment to the next. Jacobson (1954) has shown that there is actually as dissolution of the superego, as an integrated destruction - a regressive transformation back into the threatening parental images whose conglomeration originally formed it.

Differentiation is a process which is essential to integration, and vice versa. For personality structure-functions or psychic contents to become integrated, they must first have emerged as partially differentiated or separate from one another, and differentiation in turn can emerge only out of a foundation of more or less integrated functions or contents. The intertwining mesh upon which is interwoven in the growth precesses of integration and differentiation, such that the impairment of both likewise interlocking. But in the schizophrenic these two processes tend to be out of step with one another, so that at one moment a patient's more urgent need may be for increased integration, whereas at another he may more urgently need increased differentiation. And these are some patients who show for months end, a more urgent need in one of these areas, before the alternate growth-phase on the scene, that type is a modicum of validity in speaking and of two different 'types' of schizophrenic patients.

One comes to realize, upon reasons of how premature have been one's effort to find out what feelings the patient is experiencing or what thoughts he is having; one comes to realize that much of the time he has neither feelings nor thoughts differentiated as such and communicable to us.

Such differentiations as the patient posses an inclining inclination that tend to break down when intense emotion enters his awareness. A paranoid man, for example, may find that when his hatred toward another person reaches a certain degree of intensity, he is flooded with anxiety because he no longer knows whether he hates, or instead 'really loves' the other individual. This is not based, on any line or its course, whereupon the primary mechanism which Freud (1911) outlined in his classical description of the nature of paranoid delusions of persecution, a description in which repressed homosexual love played the central role. The central difficulty is rather than the ego is too poorly differentiated to maintain its structure in the face of such powerful affects, and the patient becomes flooded with what can only be described as 'undifferentiated passion', precisely as one finds an infant to be overwhelmed at times with affect which the observer cannot be specifically identity as any one particular emotion.

As for the feelings with which the therapist himself experiences in working within the variations in the differentiated patient, we find, again, a persistent threat of the therapist's sense of identity. But, whereas in the unitary integration complex manifestations of such of a schizophrenic's sense of identity. But as in the first instance that the threat was felt predominantly as a disturbance of one's personal integration, it seems possible as a weakening of one's sense of differentiation. In this instance, the 'therapeutic symbiosis' which implicate the necessary developments that it tends to occur earlier for which of the patient's predominant mode of relatedness with other persons, at the developmental level at which we find him at the very beginning of our work, is a symbiotic one. Such descriptions, least of mention, agree with the necessary developments, in that it tends to occur for the patient 's predominant mode of relatedness with other persons, the symbiotic relatedness, with its subjective absence of ego-boundaries, involves not only special gratification, but anxiety-provoking disturbances on one's sense of personal identity.

The comparatively rapid development of symbiotic relatedness is facilitated by the patient's characteristically non-verbal, and physically more or less immobile, functioning during the therapeutic sessions. In response, the therapist's own behaviour becomes more and more similar, is that each participant is now offering to the other, saying that over the hours of counselling, a silent, impassive screen which facilitates abundant mutual projecting and introjecting. Thus a symbiotic state is likely to be reached earlier than in one's work with the typically much more verbal type of the patient when described for that instance, the patient's and therapist's more abundant verbalization's tend persistently to stress the ego-boundaries separating the to persons from one another.

The applicability for which the predominantly non-differentiated patient, in that the therapist's sense of identity as a complexly differentiated individual entity becomes further eroded, or undermined, as he finds the patient persistently operating on the unwavering conviction, that the hours of counselling is but an undifferentiated aspect of the whole vague mass of the institution, even in psychodynamic terms, is in actuality the patient's projection of his own poorly differentiated hostility, through which the patient's tenaciously held view, is the way the world around him really is.

Further, since the patient typically verbalizes little but a few maddening monotonous stereotypes, the therapist tends to feel, over the course of time, with so little of his own intellectual content being explicitly tapped in the relationship, that his richness of intellect is progressively rusting away - becoming less differentiated, more stereotyped and rudimentary. Moreover, the patient presents but one of two emotional wave-lengths to which the therapist can himself tune in, rather than a rich spectrum of emotion which calls into response a similarly wide range of feelings from the therapist himself. Thus not only the therapist's intellectual resources, but his emotional capacities too, become subjectively narrowed down and impoverished, as he finds that, over the sessions of counselling, his patient in him neither any wide range of ideas, nor any emotion except, for example, rage, or contempt or dull hopelessness.

The feeling experience on his part, anxiety-provoking and discouraging though he finds it, is a necessary therapeutic development. It is for him thus to experience at first hand something of the patient's own lack of differentiation; for, as in the therapy with the non-integrated patient, as, once, again, the healing process occurs external to the patient, as it were, at an intrapsychic level in the therapist, before it becomes established in the patient himself. That is, the therapist's coming to view the patient, his relationship with the patient, and himself in this relationship, all for being largely non-differentiated, is a development which sets the stage for the patient's gradually increasing differentiation. Now the therapist comes to sense, time and again, newly emerging tendrils of differentiation in the patient, before the latter is himself conscious of them. In responding to these with spontaneity as they show themselves, again, that in the therapist, helps the patient to become aware, as they are a part of him.

To analyst and analytic student alike, the term 'transference psychosis' usually connotes a dramatic but dreaded development in which an analysand, who at the beginning of the analysis was overtly sane but who had in actuality a borderline ego-structure, becomes overtly psychotic, that the course of the evolving transference relationship. We generally blame the analyst for such as development and prefer not to think any more about such matters, because of our own personal fear that we, like the poor misbegotten analysand, might become, or narrowly avoid becoming, psychotic in our own analysis. By contrast, in working with the chronically schizophrenic patient, we are confronted with a person whose transference to us is no harder too identify partly for the very reason that his whole daily life consists in incoherent psychotic transference reactions, for which is to whatever, to everyone about him, including the analyst in the treatment session. Little's comment (1960) that the delusional state 'remains unconscious' until it is uncovered in the analysts' holds true only in the former instance, in the borderline schizophrenic patient; there, it is the fact that the transference is delusional which is the relatively covert, hard-to-discern aspect of the situation, in chronic schizophrenia, by contrast, nearly everything is delusional, and the difficult task to foster the emergence of a coherent transference meaning in the delusional symptomatology. In other words, the difficult thing in the work with the chronically schizophrenic patient is to discover the 'transference reality' in his delusional experience.

The difficultly of discerning the transference aspect of one's relationship with the patient can be traced to his having regressed to a state of ego functioning which is marked by severe impairment in his capacity either to differentiate among, or to integrate, his experiences. He is so incompletely differentiated in his ego functioning that he tends to feel, not that the therapist reminds him of, or is like, his mother or that of his father (or whomever, from his early life) but rather his functioning toward the therapist is couched in the unscrutinised assumption that the therapist is the mother or father. When, for example, in trying to bring to the attention of a paranoid schizophrenic women how much like she seemed to find the persons in her childhood on the one hand, and the person about her in the institution, including myself, on the other, she dismissed this with an impatient retort, "That's what I've been trying to tell you, What difference does it make? For years subsequently in our work together, all the figures in her experience were composite figures, without any clear subjective distinction between past and present experiences, figures from the institutional scene peopled her memories of her past, and figures from what has become known to be her past were experienced by her as blended with the persons she saw about her in current life.

Transference situations in which the psychosis is manifested at a phase in therapy in which the deeply chronically confused patient, who in childhood had been accustomed to a parent's during his thinking for him, is ambivalently (a) trying to perpetuate a symbiotic relationship wherein the therapist to a high degree does the patient's thinking for him, and (b) expressing, by what the therapist feels to be sadistic and castrative and nullifying or undoing the therapist's effort to be helpful, a determination to be a separately thinking, and otherwise separately functioning, individual

Difficult though it is to discern the nature and progressive evolution of the patient's transference to the therapist, it is even more difficult to conceptualize that which is 'new' which the therapist brings into the relationship, and which, as J. M. Rioch (1943) has emphasized, is crucial to the patient's recovery. Rioch is quite right in saying that, "Whether intentionally or not, whether conscious of it or not, the analyst does express, day in and day out, subtle or overt evidences of his own personality in relationship to the patient."

The conjectural considerations for which inadequate evidences in the understanding of questionable intent is that there is a companion evolution of reality relatedness between patient and therapist, concomitant with such a transference evolution as having had the impression that it is only when the reality relatedness between patient and therapist has reached, finally and after many 'real life' vicissitudes between them, a depth of intense fondness that there now emerges, in the form of a transference development, a comparably intense and long-repressed fondness for the mother.

Presumably, a point which Freud (1922) concerning projection also holds true for transference, he stated that projection occurs no 'into the sky, so to speak, where there is nothing of the sort already', but rather the persons who in reality posses an attitude qualitatively like that which the projecting person is attributing to them. So it is with transference, we may presume that when a patient comes to react to us as a loved and loving mother, this phrase - as well as other phrases - of the transference is founded upon our having come to feel, in reality, thus toward him. M. B. Cohen (1952) stresses the importance of the therapist's inevitable feeling response to the patient's transference, and, if only to suggest, that an equally healthy source of the therapist's feeling participation is the evolving reality relatedness which pursues its own course, related to and parallelling, but not fully embraced by, the evolving transference relatedness over the years of person's working together. What is more, is the countertransference which has already been written, but as to indicate, there is a great need for us to become clear about the sequence which the recovery process in the schizophrenic adult, very roughly analogous to the growth process in normal infancy, childhood, and adolescence, tends innately to follow. When we have become clearer and surer about this, and particularly about the validity-relatedness element necessary to it, in that the frequently - though by no means always - various manifestations of feeling regarded as unwanted countertransference will be seen to be inevitable, and utterly essential, components of the recovery process.

Further, the opening view of the personality for being divisible into the areas, id, ego, and superego, tends to shield us from the anxiety-fostering realization that in psychoanalytic change is not merely quantitative and partial - where id was, there will ego be - in Freud's dictum - but qualitative and all-persuasive. That is, that in such passages as the following. Freud gives a picture of personality-structure, and of maturation, which leaves the inaccurate but comforting impression that at least a part of us - namely, as part of the id - is free from change. In his paper entitled "Thoughts for the Times on War and Death" in 1915, saying, . . . the evolution of the mind shows a peculiarity which is present in no other process of development. When a village grows into a town, a child into a man, the village and the child become submerged in the town and the man, . . . it is otherwise with the development of the mind . . . the primitive stages [of mental development] can always be re-established, the primitive mind is, in the fullest meaning of the word, imperishable (Freud, 1915).

In "Introductory Lectures on Psycho-Analysis," Freud says that in psychoanalytic treatment . . . By means of the work of interpretation, which transforms what is unconscious into what is conscious, the ego is enlarged at the cos of this unconscious . . . (Freud, 1915-17)

In "The Ego and the Id" saying that . . . the ego is that part of the id which has been modified by the direct influence of the external world . . . the pleasure-principle . . . reigns unrestricted by the id . . . the ego represents what may be called reason and common sense, in contrast to the id, which contains the passions (Freud, 1923.)

The state of developmental sciences, and about our own individual the individual therapeutic skills, should not cause us to understate the all-embracing extent of human personality-growth in normal maturation at least a few psychoanalysis. It is believed that all encountered, and, at lest a few fortunate instances which have made us wonder whether maturation really leaves any area of the personality untouched, leaves any steel-bound core within which the pleasure principle reigns immutably, or whether, instead, we have seen such a genuine metamorphosis, from an erstwhile hateful and self-seeking orientation to a loving and giving orientation, quite as wonderful and thoroughgoing the metamorphosis of the tadpole into the frog thoroughgoing as the metamorphosis of the tadpole into the frog or that of the caterpillar into the butterfly.

Freud himself, in his emphasis upon the 'negative therapeutic reaction' (1923), the repetition compulsion, and the resistance to analytic insight which he discovered in his work with neurotic patients, has shown the importance, in the neurotic individual, of anxiety concerning change, and he agrees with Jung's statement that 'a peculiar psychic inertia' hostile to change and progress, is the fundamental condition of neurosis (Freud, 1915). This is, as we know, even more true of psychosis - so much as that only in very recent decades have psychotic patients achieved full recovery though modified psycho-analytic therapy. Finding it instructive to explore in detail the psychodynamics of schizophrenia in terms of the anxiety concerning change which one encounters, in a particular intense degree, at work in these patients, and in oneself in the course of treating them. What the therapy of schizophrenia can teach us of the human being's standing concerning change, can broaden and deepen our understanding of the non-psychotic individual also.

Briefly, is to consider countertransference in the history of psychoanalysis are that we meet with a strange fact and striking contrast. The discovery by Freud of countertransference and its great importance in therapeutic work gave to the institution of didactic analysis which became the basis and centre of psychoanalytic training. Yet countertransference received little consideration over the next forty years. Only during the last few years has the situation changed, rather suddenly, and countertransference became a subject examined frequently and with thoroughness. How is one to explain this in initial recognition? This neglect, and the recent change? Is there no reason to question the success of didactic analysis in fulfilling its function, if this very problem, the discovery of which led to the creation of didactic analysis, has had so little scientific elaboration?

These questions are clearly important, and those have personally attested of a great part of the development of psychoanalysis in the last forty years have the best right to answer them. Nonetheless, I will suggest or exemplify on or upon of only one explanation.

The lack of scientific investigation of countertransference must be due to rejection by analyst of their own countertransference - a rejection that represents unresolved struggles with their own primitive anxiety and guilt. These struggles are closely connected with those infantile ideals that survive because of deficiencies the didactic analysis of just those transference problems that latter affect the analyst's countertransference. These deficiencies in the didactic analysis are in turn due to countertransference problems insufficiently solved in the didactic analyst. Thus, we are in a vicious circle, but we can see where a breach must be made. That is to say, that we must begin by revision of our feelings about our own countertransference and try to overcome our infantile ideals more thoroughly, accepting more fully the fact that we are still children and neurotics even when we are adults and analysts. Only in this way - by better overcoming our rejection of countertransference - can we achieve the same result in candidates.

The insufficient dissolution of these idealizations and underlying anxieties and guilt feelings leads to special difficulties when the child becomes an adult and the analysand analyst, for the analyst unconsciously requires of himself that he be fully identified with these ideals, that it is at last, partly for this reason that oedipus complex of the child toward its parents, and of the patient toward his analysand, has been so much more fully considered than that of the parents toward their children and of the analyst toward the analysand. For the same basic reason transference has been dealt with much more than countertransference.

The fact that countertransference conflicts determine the deficiencies in the analysis of transference becomes clear if we recall that transference is the expression of the internal object relations; for understanding of transference will depend on the analyst's capacity to identify himself both with the analysand's impulses and defences, and with his internal object s, and to be conscious of these identification. This ability in the analyst will in turn depend upon the degree to which he accepts his countertransference, fo r his countertransference is likewise based on identification with the patient's id and ego and his internal objects. One might also say that transference is the expression of the patient's relations with the fantasies and real countertransference of the analyst. For just as countertransference is the psychological response to the analysand's real imaginary transference, so also is transference the response to the analyst's imaginary and real countertransference. Analysis of the patient's fantasies out countertransference, which in the widest sense constitute the causes and consequence of the transference, is an essential part of the analysis of the transference. Perception of the patient's fantasies regarding countertransference will depend in turn upon the degree to which the analyst himself perceives his countertransference processes - on the continuity and depth of his conscious constant with himself.

Finally, the repression of countertransference (and other pathological fates that it may meet) necessarily leads to deficiencies in the analysis of transference, which in turn lead to the repression and other mishandling of countertransference soon as the candidate becomes an analyst. It is a heritage from generation to generation, similar to the heritage of idealizations and denials concerning the imagoes of the parents, which continue working even when the child becomes a father or mother. The child's mythology is prolonge in the mythology of the analytic situation, the analyst himself being partially subject to it and collaborating unconsciously in its maintenance in the candidate.

Let us briefly consider one of these ideals in it specifically psychoanalytic expression: The ideal of the analyst's objectivity. No one, of course, denies the existence of subjective factors in th analyst and of countertransference in itself, but there seems to exist an important difference between what is generally acknowledged in practice and the real state of affairs. The first distortion of truth in 'the myth of thee analytic situation' is that analysis is an interaction between two personalities in both of which the ego is under pressure from the id, the superego, and the external world, each personality has its internal and external dependencies, parents, and that of the analyst - responds to every event of the analytic situation. Besides these similarities between the personalities of analyst and analysand, there also exist differences, and one of these is in 'objectivity'. The analyst's objectivity consists mainly in a certain attitude toward his own subjectivity and countertransference. The neurotic (obsessive) ideal of objectivity lead to repression and blocking of subjectivity and so to the apparent fulfilment of the myth of the 'analyst without anxiety or anger'. The other neurotic extreme is that of 'drowning' in the countertransference. True objectivity is based upon a form of internal division that enables the analyst to make himself (his own countertransference and subjectivity) the object of his continuous observations and analysis. This position also enables him to be relatively 'objective' toward the analysand.

The term countertransference has been given various meanings. They may be summarized by the state that for some authors countertransference includes everything that arises in the analysis as psychological response to the analysand, whereas for others not all this should be called countertransference. Some, for example, prefer to reserve the term for what is infantile in the relationship of the analyst with his analysand, while others make different limitation (Annie Reich and Gitelson). Hence efforts to differentiate from each other certain of the complex phenomena of countertransference lead to confusion or to unproductive discussion of terminology. Freud invented the term countertransference in evident analogy to transference, which he defined as 're-impressions' or 're-editions' of childhood experiences, including greater or less modifications of the original experience. hence one frequently uses the term transference for the totality of the psychological attitude of the analysand toward the analyst. We know, to be sure, that real external qualities of the analytic situation in general and of the analyst in particular, have important influences on the relationship of the analysand with the analyst, but we also know that all these present factors are experienced according to the past and the fantasy, - according. That is to say, too a transference predisposition. As determinants of the transference neurosis and, in general, if the psychological situation of the analysand toward the analyst, we have both the transference predisposition and the present real and especially analytic experiences, the transference in its diverse expressions being the resultant of these two factors.

Analogously. In the analyst there are the countertransference predisposition and the present and immediacy or the real, and especially analytic experience and the countertransference is the result. It is precisely this fusion of present immediacy and the past, the continuous and intimate connection of reality and fantasy, of external and internal, conscious and unconscious, that demands a concept embracing the totality of the analyst's psychological response, and renders it advisable, at the same time, to keep for this totality of response the accustomed term 'countertransference'. Where it is necessary for greater clarity one, might say of 'total countertransference' and then differentiated and separate within it one aspect or another. One of its aspects consists precisely in what is transferred in countertransference; this is the part that originates in an earlier time and that is especially the infantile and primitive part within total countertransference. Another of these aspects - closely connected with the previous one - is what is neurotic in countertransference, its main characteristics the unreal anxiety and the pathological defences. Under certain circumstances one might in saying of a countertransference neurosis.

To clarity better the concept of countertransference, on might start from the question of what happens, in general, in the analyst in his relationship with the patient, as one might think that everything happens that can happen in one personality faced with another. But this says so much that it says hardly anything - bearing in mind that in the analyst there is a tendency that normally predominates in his relationship with the patient: Is the tendency pertaining to his function of being an analyst that of understanding what is happening in the patient? Together with the tendency there exist toward the patient virtually all the other possible tendencies, fears, and other feelings that one person may have toward another. The intention to understand creates a certain predisposition, a predisposition to identify oneself with the analysand, which is the basis of comprehension. The analyst may achieve this aim by identifying his ego with the patient's ego, or put it more clearly although a certain terminological inexactitude, by identifying each part of his personality with the corresponding psychological part in the patient - his id with the patient id, his ego with the ego, his superego with the superego, accepting these identifications in his consciousness. But this does not always happen, nor is it all that happens. Apart from these identifications, which might be called concordant (or homologous) identifications, there exist also highly important identifications of the analyst's ego with the patient's internal objects, for example, with the superego. Adapting an expression from Helene Deutsch, they might be called complementary identifications. Such are that follows:

1. The concordant identifications are based on introjection and also projection, or, in other words, on the resonance of the exterior in the interior as justly as the outer is of the inner, on the recognition of what belongs to another as one 's own ('this part of you is I') and on the equation of what is one's own with what belongs to another ('this part of me is you'). The processes inherently in the complementary identifications are the same, but they refer to the patient's objects. The greater the conflicts between the parts of the analyst's personality, the greater are his difficulties in carrying out the concordant identifications in their entirety.
2. The complementary identifications are produced by the fact that the patient treats the analyst as an internal (projected) object, and in consequence the analyst feels treated as such: That is, he identifies himself with the object. The complementary identifications are closely connected with the destiny in the concordant identifications: It seems that to the degree to which the analyst fails in the concordant identifications and rejects them, certain complementary identifications become intensified. It is clear that rejection of a part of tendency in the analyst himself, - his aggressiveness, for instance, - may lead to a rejection of the patient's aggressiveness (whereby this concordant identification fails) and that such a situation leads to a greater complementary identification with the patient's rejecting objects, toward which this aggressive impulse is directed.
3. Current usage applies the term 'countertransference' to the complementary identifications only: This is to say, to those psychological processes in the analysis by which, because he feels treated as and partially identifies himself with an internal object of the patient, the patient becomes an internal (projected) object of the analyst. Usually excluded from the concept countertransference are the concordant identifications, - those psychological content s that arise in the analyst by reason of the empathy achieved with the patient and that really reflect and reproduce the latter's psychological contents. Perhaps it would be best to follow this usage, bu t there are some circumstances that make it unwise to do so. In the first place, some authors include the concordant identifications in the concept of countertransference. One is

thus faced with the choice of entering upon a terminological discussion of accepting the term in this wider sense. Where for various reasons the wider sense is to be preferred. If one considers that the analyst's concordant identifications (his 'understanding') are a sort of reproduction of his own past processes, especially of his own infancy, and that this reproduction or-re-experience is carried out as response to stimuli from the patient, one will b e more read y to include the concordant identifications in the concept of countertransference. Moreover, the concordant identifications are closely connected with the complementary ones (and thus with 'countertransference' in the popular sense), and this fact renders advisable a differentiation but not a total separation of the term. Finally, it should be borne in mind that the disposition to empathy, - this is, to concordant identification, springs largely from the sublimated positive countertransference in the wider sense. All this suggests, then, the acceptance of countertransference as the totality of the analyst's psychological response to the patient. if we accept this broad definition of countertransference, the difference between its two aspects as listed above, must still be defined. On the one hand we have the analyst as subject and the patient as the object of knowledge, which in a certain sense annuls the 'object relationship', such that is said arises in its stead the approximate union of identity between the subject's and the object's parts (experiences, impulses, defences). The aggregate of the processes pertaining to that union might be designed, where necessary, 'concordant countertransference'. However, on the other hand, we have an object relationship like many others, a real 'transference' in which the analyst 'repeats' previous experiences, the patient representing internal objects of the analyst. The aggregate of these experiences, which also exist always and continually, might be termed 'complementary countertransference'.

A brief example can be made if we are to consider in that of patient who threatens the analyst with suicide. In such situations there sometimes occur s rejection of the concordant identifications by the analyst and an identification with the threatened object. The anxiety that such a threat can cause the analyst to lead of various reactions or decence mechanisms within him, for instance, annoyance with the patient. This - his anxiety and annoyance - would be contents of the 'complementary countertransference'. The perception of his annoyance may, in turn, originate guilt feelings in the analyst and these lead to desires for reparation and to intensification of the 'concordant' identification and 'concordant' countertransference.

Moreover, these two aspects of 'total countertransference' have their analogy in transference. sublimated positive transference is the main and indispensable motive force for the patient's work: It does not in itself constitute a technical problem. Transference becomes a 'subject', according to Freud's words, mainly when 'It becomes resistance, when because of resistance, it has become sexual or negative. Analogously, sublimated positive countertransference is the primary and indispensable motive force in the analyst's work (disposing him to the continued concordant identification), and also, countertransference become a technical problem or 'subject' mainly when it becomes sexual or negative, and this occurs (to an intense degree) principally as a resistance - in this case the analyst's - that is to say, as countertransference, in as much as of leading into the problematic function of the dynamics of countertransference.

Every transference situation provokes a countertransference situation, which arises out of the analyst's identification of himself with the analysand's (internal) objects (this is the 'complementary countertransference'). These countertransference situations may be repressed or emotionally blocked, but probably they cannot be avoided; certainly they should not be avoided if full understanding is to be achieved These countertransference reactions are governed by the laws of the general and individual unconscious. Among these the law of talion is especially important. Thus, for example, every positive transference situation is answered by a positive countertransference: To every negative transference there responds, in one part of the analyst, a negative countertransference. It is of great importance that the analyst be conscious of this law, for awareness of it is fundamental to avoid 'drowning' in the countertransference. If he is not aware of it he will not be able to avoid entering into the vicious circle of the analysand's neurosis, which will hinder or even prevent the work of therapy.

A simplified example: If the patient's neurosis centre round a conflict with his introjected father, he will project the latter upon the analyst and treat him as his father. The analyst will feel treated as such - he will feel treated badly - and he will react internally. In part of his personality. In accordance with the treatment he receives. If he fails to be aware of this reaction, his behaviour will inevitably be affected by it, and he will renew the situation that, to a greater or lesser degree, helped to establish the analysand's neurosis. Hence it is of the greatest importance that the analyst develop within himself an ego observer of his countertransference reactions, which are, naturally, continuous. Perception of these countertransference reactions will help him to become conscious of the continuous transference situations of the patient and interpret them rather than unconsciously ruled by these reactions, is not as frequently to happen. A well-known example is the 'revengeful silence' of the analyst. if the analyst is unaware of these interactions there is danger that the patient will have to repeat, in his transference experience, the vicious circle brought about by the projected introjection of 'bad objects' (in reality neurotic ones) and the consequent pathological anxieties and defences, but his transference interpretations made possible by the analyst's of his countertransference expedience making it possible to open important breached in this vicious circle.

To return to the previous example: If the analyst is conscious of his own countertransference, he can more easily make the patient conscious of his projection and the consequent mechanisms. Interpretation of these mechanisms will show the patient that the present reality is not identical with his inner perceptions (for, if it were, the analyst would not interpret and otherwise act as an analyst), the patient then introjects a reality better than his inner world. This sort of rectification does not take place when the analyst is under the sway of his unconscious countertransference.

For some considering applications of these principles one mus t return to the question of what the analyst does during the session and what happens within him, one might say, at first thought, that the analyst liste ns. But this is not completely true, he listens most of the time, or wishes to listen, but variably for doing so. Ferenczi refers to this fact and expresses the opinion that the analyst's distractability is of little importance, for the patient as such moments must certainly be in resistance. Ferenczi's remark (which dates form the year 1918) sounds like an echo from the era when the analyst was mainly interested in the repulses, because now that we attempt to analyze resistance, the patient's manifestations of resistance are a significant as any other of his productions. At any rate, but as Ferenczi refers is the countertransference response and deduces from it the analysand's psychological situation. He says ' . . . we have unconsciously reacted to the emptiness and futility if the associations given a this moment with the withdrawal of the real conscious charge'. The situation might be described as one of mutual withdrawal, however, responses to an imagined or real psychological position in the analyst? If we have withdrawn - if we are not listening but are thinking of something else - we may utilize this event in the service if the analysis, in like any other information we acquire. And the guilt we may feel over such a withdrawal is just as analytically utilizable as any other countertransference reaction. Ferenczi's next words, 'the danger of the doctor's falling asleep . . . need not be regarded as grave because we awake at the first occurrence of any importance for the treatment, are clearly intended to placate this guilt. but better than to allay the analyst's guilt would b e to use it to promote the analysis - and so use the guilt would be the best way of alleviating it. In fact, we encounter a cardinal problem of the relation between transference and countertransference, and of the therapeutic process in general. For the analyst's withdrawal is only an example of how the unconscious of one person responds to the unconscious of another. This response seems in part to be governed, insofar as we identify ourselves with the unconscious objects of the analysand, by the law of talion; and, insofar as this law unconsciously influences the analyst, there is danger of a vicious circle of reactions between them, for the analysand also responds 'talionically' in his turn, and so on without end.

Looking more closely, we see that the 'talionic response' or 'identification with the aggressor' (the frustrating patient) is a complex process. Such a psychological process in the analyst usually starts with a feeling of displeasure or of some anxiety as a response to this aggression (frustration) and, because of this feeling, the analyst identifies himself with the 'aggressor'. By the term 'aggressor' we mus t designate not only the patient but also some internal object of the analyst (especially his own superego or an internal persecutor. Now projected upon the patient, this identification with the aggressor, or persecutor, causes a feeling of guilt; probably it always does so, although awareness of the guilt may be repressed. For what happens is, on a small scale, a process of melancholia, just as Freud described it : The object has to some degree abandoned us, we identify ourselves with the lost object, and then we accuse the introjected 'bad' object- in other words, we have guilt feelings. This may be sensed in Ferenczi's remarks, such of which mechanisms are at work designed to protect the analyst against these guilt feelings; denial or guilt ('the danger is not grave') and a certain accusation against the analysand for the 'emptiness' and 'futility' of his association. In this way a vicious circle - a kind of paranoid ping-pong - has entered into the analytic situation.

Two situations of frequent occurrence illustrate both the complementary and the concordant identifications and the vicious circle these situations may cause.

1. One transference situation of regular occurrence consist s in the patient's seeing in the analyst hi s own superego. The analyst identifies himself with the id and ego of the patient and with the patient's dependence upon his superego, and he also identifies himself with this same superego - a situation in which the patient places him - and experience domination of the superego over the patient's ego. The relation of the ego to the superego of the superego over the patient's ego. The relation of the ego to the superego is, at bottom, a depressive and paranoid situation; the relation of the superego to the ego is, on the same plane, a manioc one insofar as this term may be used to designate the dominating, controlling, and accusing attitude of the superego toward the ego. In this sense we may say, broadly speaking, that to a 'depressive-paranoid' transference in the analysand there corresponds - as regards the complementary identification - a 'manic' countertransference in he analyst. This, in turn, may entail various fears and guilt feelings.
2. When the patient, in defences against this situation, identifies himself with the superego, he may place the analyst in the situation of the dependent and incriminated ego. The analyst will not only identify himself with this position of the patient; he will also experience the situation with the content the patient give it: He will feel subjugated and accused, and may react to some degree with anxiety and guilt. To a 'manic' transference situation (of the type called mania for reproaching) there

corresponds, then - as regards the complementary identification -a 'depressive-paranoid' countertransference situation.

The analyst will normally experience these situations with only a part of his being, leaving another part free to take note of them in a way suitable for the treatment. Perception of such a countertransference situation by the analyst and his understanding of it as a psychological response to certain transference situations will enable him the better to grasp the transference at the precise moment when it is active. It is precisely these situations and the analyst's behaviour regarding them, and in particular his interpretations of them, that are of decisive importance for the process of therapy, fo r they are the moment when the vicious circle within which the neurotic habitually moves - by projecting his inner world outside and reintrojecting his same world is or is not interpreted. Moreover, these decisive points the world - is projecting his inner world outside these decisive points the vicious circle may be-enforced by the analyst, if he is unaware of having entered it.

A brief example: An analysand repeats with the analyst his 'neurosis of failure, closing himself up to every interpretation or representing it at once, reproaching the analyst for the uselessness of the analysis, foreseeing nothing better in the future, continually declaring his complex indifference to everything. The analyst interprets the patient's position toward him, and its origins, in its various aspects. He shows the patient his defences against the danger of becoming too dependent, of being abandoned, or being tricked, or of suffering counter aggression by the analyst, if he abandons his amour and indifference of bad internal objects and his subsequent sado-masochistic behaviour in the transference, his need of punishment, his triumph and 'masochistic-revenge' against the transference patients; his defences against the 'depressive position' by means of schizoid paranoid and manic defences (Melaine Klein) and he interprets the patient's rejection of a bond which is the unconscious has a homosexual significance. But it may happen that all these interpretations, in spite of being directed to the central resistance and connected with the transference situation, suffer the same fate for the same reasons: They fall into the 'whirl in avoid' of the 'neurosis of failure'. Now the decisive moments arrive, the analyst, subdued by the patient 'resistance, may begin to feel anxious over the possibility of failure and feel angry with the patient. What this occurs in the analyst, the patient feels it coming, for his own 'aggressiveness' and other reactions have provoked it; consequently he fears the analyst's anger. If the analyst, threatened by failure, to put more precisely threatened by his own superego or by his own archaic objects which have found an agent provocateur in the patient, acts under the influence of these internal objects and of his paranoid and depressive anxieties, the patient again finds himself confronting a reality like that of his real or fantasized childhood experiences and like that of his inner world, and so the vicious circle continues and may even be re-enforced. But if the analyst grasps the importance of this situation, if, through his own anxiety or anger, he comprehends what is happening in the analysand, and if he overcomes, thanks to the new insight, his negative feelings and interprets what has happened in the analysand, being now in his new positive countertransference situation, then he may have made a breach - be it large or small - in the vicious circle.

Briefly, is to consider countertransference in the history of psychoanalysis are that we meet with a strange fact and striking contrast. The discovery by Freud of countertransference and its great importance in therapeutic work gave to the institution of didactic analysis which became the basis and centre of psychoanalytic training. Yet countertransference received little consideration over the next forty years. Only during the last few years has the situation changed, rather suddenly, and countertransference became a subject examined frequently and with thoroughness. How is one to explain this in initial recognition? This neglect, and the recent change? Is there no reason to question the success of didactic analysis in fulfilling its function, if this very problem, the discovery of which led to the creation of didactic analysis, has had so little scientific elaboration?

These questions are clearly important, and those have personally attested of a great part of the development of psychoanalysis in the last forty years have the best right to answer them. Nonetheless, I will suggest or exemplify on or upon of only one explanation.

The lack of scientific investigation of countertransference must be due to rejection by analyst of their own countertransference - a rejection that represents unresolved struggles with their own primitive anxiety and guilt. These struggles are closely connected with those infantile ideals that survive because of deficiencies the didactic analysis of just those transference problems that latter affect the analyst's countertransference. These deficiencies in the didactic analysis are in turn due to countertransference problems insufficiently solved in the didactic analyst. Thus, we are in a vicious circle, but we can see where a breach must be made. That is to say, that we must begin by revision of our feelings about our own countertransference and try to overcome our infantile ideals more thoroughly, accepting more fully the fact that we are still children and neurotics even when we are adults and analysts. Only in this way - by better overcoming our rejection of countertransference - can we achieve the same result in candidates.

The insufficient dissolution of these idealizations and underlying anxieties and guilt feelings leads to special difficulties when the child becomes an adult and the analysand an analyst, for the analyst unconsciously requires of himself that he be fully identified with these ideals, that it is at last, partly for this reason that oedipus complex of the child toward its parents, and of the patient toward his analysand, has been so much more fully considered than that of the parents toward their children and of the analyst toward the analysand. For the same basic reason transference has been dealt with much more than countertransference.

The fact that countertransference conflicts determine the deficiencies in the analysis of transference becomes clear if we recall that transference is the expression of the internal object relations; for understanding of transference will depend on the analyst's capacity to identify himself both with the analysand's impulses and defences, and with his internal object s, and to be conscious of these identification. This ability in the analyst will in turn depend upon the degree to which he accepts his countertransference, fo r his countertransference is likewise based on identification with the patient's id and ego and his internal objects. One might also say that transference is the expression of the patient's relations with the fantasies and real countertransference of the analyst. For just as countertransference is the psychological response to the analysand's real imaginary transference, so also is transference the response to the analyst's imaginary and real countertransference. Analysis of the patient's fantasies out countertransference, which in the widest sense constitute the causes and consequence of the transference, is an essential part of the analysis of the transference. Perception of the patient's fantasies regarding countertransference will depend in turn upon the degree to which the analyst himself perceives his countertransference processes - on the continuity and depth of his conscious constant with himself.

Finally, the repression of countertransference (and other pathological fates that it may meet) necessarily leads to deficiencies in the analysis of transference, which in turn lead to the repression and other mishandling of countertransference soon as the candidate becomes an analyst. It is a heritage from generation to generation, similar to the heritage of idealizations and denials concerning the imagoes of the parents, which continue working even when the child becomes a father or mother. The child's mythology is prolonge in the mythology of the analytic situation, the analyst himself being partially subject to it and collaborating unconsciously in its maintenance in the candidate.

Let us briefly consider one of these ideals in it specifically psychoanalytic expression: The ideal of the analyst's objectivity. No one, of course, denies the existence of subjective factors in th analyst and of countertransference in itself, but there seems to exist an important difference between what is generally acknowledged in practice and the real state of affairs. The first distortion of truth in 'the myth of thee analytic situation' is that analysis is an interaction between two personalities in both of which the ego is under pressure from the id, the superego, and the external world, each personality has its internal and external dependencies, parents, and that of the analyst - responds to every event of the analytic situation. Besides these similarities between the personalities of analyst and analysand, there also exist differences, and one of these is in 'objectivity'. The analyst's objectivity consists mainly in a certain attitude toward his own subjectivity and countertransference. The neurotic (obsessive) ideal of objectivity lead to repression and blocking of subjectivity and so to the apparent fulfilment of the myth of the 'analyst without anxiety or anger'. The other neurotic extreme is that of 'drowning' in the countertransference. True objectivity is based upon a form of internal division that enables the analyst to make himself (his own countertransference and subjectivity) the object of his continuous observations and analysis. This position also enables him to be relatively 'objective' toward the analysand.

The term countertransference has been given various meanings. They may be summarized by the state that for some authors countertransference includes everything that arises in the analysis as psychological response to the analysand, whereas for others not all this should be called countertransference. Some, for example, prefer to reserve the term for what is infantile in the relationship of the analyst with his analysand, while others make different limitation (Annie Reich and Gitelson). Hence efforts to differentiate from each other certain of the complex phenomena of countertransference lead to confusion or to unproductive discussion of terminology. Freud invented the term countertransference in evident analogy to transference, which he defined as 're-impressions' or 're-editions' of childhood experiences, including greater or less modifications of the original experience. hence one frequently uses the term transference for the totality of the psychological attitude of the analysand toward the analyst. We know, to be sure, that real external qualities of the analytic situation in general and of the analyst in particular, have important influences on the relationship of the analysand with the analyst, but we also know that all these present factors are experienced according to the past and the fantasy, - according. That is to say, too a transference predisposition. As determinants of the transference neurosis and, in general, if the psychological situation of the analysand toward the analyst, we have both the transference predisposition and the present real and especially analytic experiences, the transference in its diverse expressions being the resultant of these two factors.

Analogously. In the analyst there are the countertransference predisposition and the present and immediacy or the real, and especially analytic, experience; and the countertransference is the result. It is precisely this fusion of present immediacy and the past, the continuous and intimate connection of reality and fantasy, of external and internal, conscious and unconscious, that demands a concept embracing the totality of the analyst's psychological response, and renders it advisable, at the same time, to keep for this totality of response the accustomed term 'countertransference'. Where it is necessary for greater clarity one might say of 'total countertransference' and then differentiated and separate within it one aspect or another. One of its aspects consists precisely in what is transferred in countertransference; this is the part that originates in an earlier time and that is especially the infantile and primitive part within total countertransference. Another of these aspects - closely connected with the previous one - is what is neurotic in countertransference, its main characteristics the unreal anxiety and the pathological defences. Under certain circumstances one might in saying of a countertransference neurosis.

To clarity better the concept of countertransference, on might start from the question of what happens, in general, in the analyst in his relationship with the patient, as one might think that everything happens that can happen in one personality faced with another. But this says so much that it says hardly anything - bearing in mind that in the analyst there is a tendency that normally predominates in his relationship with the patient: Is the tendency pertaining to his function of being an analyst that of understanding what is happening in the patient? Together with the tendency there exist toward the patient virtually all the other possible tendencies, fears, and other feelings that one person may have toward another. The intention to understand creates a certain predisposition, a predisposition to identify oneself with the analysand, which is the basis of comprehension. The analyst may achieve this aim by identifying his ego with the patient's ego, or put it more clearly although a certain terminological inexactitude, by identifying each part of his personality with the corresponding psychological part in the patient - his id with the patient id, his ego with the ego, his superego with the superego, accepting these identifications in his consciousness. But this does not always happen, nor is it all that happens. Apart from these identifications, which might be called concordant (or homologous) identifications, there exist also highly important identifications of the analyst's ego with the patient's internal objects, for example, with the superego. Adapting an expression from Helene Deutsch, they might be called complementary identifications. Such are that follows:

1. The concordant identifications are based on introjection and also projection, or, in other words, on the resonance of the exterior in the interior as justly as the outer is of the inner, on the recognition of what belongs to another as one 's own ('this part of you is I') and on the equation of what is one's own with what belongs to another ('this part of me is you'). The processes inherently in the complementary identifications are the same, but they refer to the patient's objects. The greater the conflicts between the parts of the analyst's personality, the greater are his difficulties in carrying out the concordant identifications in their entirety.
2. The complementary identifications are produced by the fact that the patient treats the analyst as an internal (projected) object, and in consequence the analyst feels treated as such: That is, he identifies himself with the object. The complementary identifications are closely connected with the destiny in the concordant identifications: It seems that to

the degree to which the analyst fails in the concordant identifications and rejects them, certain complementary identifications become intensified. It is clear that rejection of a part of tendency in the analyst himself, - his aggressiveness, for instance, - may lead to a rejection of the patient's aggressiveness (whereby this concordant identification fails) and that such a situation leads to a greater complementary identification with the patient's rejecting objects, toward which this aggressive impulse is directed.

3. Current usage applies the term 'countertransference' to the complementary identifications only: This is to say, to those psychological processes in the analysis by which, because he feels treated as and partially identifies himself with an internal object of the patient, the patient becomes an internal (projected) object of the analyst. Usually excluded from the concept countertransference are the concordant identifications, - those psychological content s that arise in the analyst by reason of the empathy achieved with the patient and that really reflect and reproduce the latter's psychological contents. Perhaps it would be best to follow this usage, bu t there are some circumstances that make it unwise to do so. In the first place, some authors include the concordant identifications in the concept of countertransference. One is thus faced with the choice of entering upon a terminological discussion of accepting the term in this wider sense. Where for various reasons the wider sense is to be preferred. If one considers that the analyst's concordant identifications (his 'understanding') are a sort of reproduction of his own past processes, especially of his own infancy, and that this reproduction or-re-experience is carried out as response to stimuli from the patient, one will b e more read y to include the concordant identifications in the concept of countertransference. Moreover, the concordant identifications are closely connected with the complementary ones (and thus with 'countertransference' in the popular sense), and this fact renders advisable a differentiation but not a total separation of the term. Finally, it should be borne in mind that the disposition to empathy, - this is, to concordant identification, springs largely from the sublimated positive countertransference in the wider sense. All this suggests, then, the acceptance of countertransference as the totality of the analyst's psychological response to the patient. if we accept this broad definition of countertransference, the difference between its two aspects as listed above, must still be defined. On the one hand we have the analyst as subject and the patient as the object of knowledge, which in a certain sense annuls the 'object relationship', such that is said arises in its stead the approximate union of identity between the subject's and the object's parts (experiences, impulses, defences). The aggregate of the processes pertaining to that union might be designed, where necessary, 'concordant countertransference'. However, on the other hand, we

have an object relationship like many others, a real 'transference' in which the analyst 'repeats' previous experiences, the patient representing internal objects of the analyst. The aggregate of these experiences, which also exist always and continually, might be termed 'complementary countertransference'.

A brief example can be made if we are to consider in that of patient who threatens the analyst with suicide. In such situations there sometimes occur s rejection of the concordant identifications by the analyst and an identification with the threatened object. The anxiety that such a threat can cause the analyst to lead of various reactions or decence mechanisms within him, for instance, annoyance with the patient. This - his anxiety and annoyance - would be contents of the 'complementary countertransference'. The perception of his annoyance may, in turn, originate guilt feelings in the analyst and these lead to desires for reparation and to intensification of the 'concordant' identification and 'concordant' countertransference.

Moreover, these two aspects of 'total countertransference' have their analogy in transference. sublimated positive transference is the main and indispensable motive force for the patient's work: It does not in itself constitute a technical problem. Transference becomes a 'subject', according to Freud's words, mainly when 'It becomes resistance, when because of resistance, it has become sexual or negative. Analogously, sublimated positive countertransference is the primary and indispensable motive force in the analyst's work (disposing him to the continued concordant identification), and also, countertransference become a technical problem or 'subject' mainly when it becomes sexual or negative, and this occurs (to an intense degree) principally as a resistance - in this case the analyst's - that is to say, as countertransference, in as much as of leading into the problematic function of the dynamics of countertransference.

Every transference situation provokes a countertransference situation, which arises out of the analyst's identification of himself with the analysand's (internal) objects (this is the 'complementary countertransference'). These countertransference situations may be repressed or emotionally blocked, but probably they cannot be avoided; certainly they should not be avoided if full understanding is to be achieved These countertransference reactions are governed by the laws of the general and individual unconscious. Among these the law of talion is especially important. Thus, for example, every positive transference situation is answered by a positive countertransference: To every negative transference there responds, in one part of the analyst, a negative countertransference. It is of great importance that the analyst be conscious of this law, for awareness of it is fundamental to avoid 'drowning' in the countertransference. If he is not aware of it he will not be able to avoid entering into the vicious circle of the analysand's neurosis, which will hinder or even prevent the work of therapy.

A simplified example: If the patient's neurosis centre round a conflict with his introjected father, he will project the latter upon the analyst and treat him as his father. The analyst will feel treated as such - he will feel treated badly - and he will react internally. In part of his personality. In accordance with the treatment he receives. If he fails to be aware of this reaction, his behaviour will inevitably be affected by it, and he will renew the situation that, to a greater or lesser degree, helped to establish the analysand's neurosis. Hence it is of the greatest importance that the analyst develop within himself an ego observer of his countertransference reactions, which are, naturally, continuous. Perception of these countertransference reactions will help him to become conscious of the continuous transference situations of the patient and interpret them rather than unconsciously ruled by these reactions, as not frequently to happen. A well-known example is the 'revengeful silence' of the analyst. if the analyst is unaware of these interactions there is danger that the patient will have to repeat, in his transference experience, the vicious circle brought about by the projected introjection of 'bad objects' (in reality neurotic ones) and the consequent pathological anxieties and defences, but his transference interpretations made possible by the analyst's of his countertransference expedience making it possible to open important breached in this vicious circle.

To return to the previous example: If the analyst is conscious of his own countertransference, he can more easily make the patient conscious of his projection and the consequent mechanisms. Interpretation of these mechanisms will show the patient that the present reality is not identical with his inner perceptions (for, if it were, the analyst would not interpret and otherwise act as an analyst), the patient then introjects a reality better than his inner world. This sort of rectification does not take place when the analyst is under the sway of his unconscious countertransference.

For some considering applications of these principles one mus t return to the question of what the analyst does during the session and what happens within him, one might say, at first thought, that the analyst liste ns. But this is not completely true, he listens most of the time, or wishes to listen, but is variably for doing so. Ferenczi refers to this fact and expresses the opinion that the analyst's distractability is of little importance, for the patient as such moments must certainly be in resistance. Ferenczi's remark (which dates form the year 1918) sounds like an echo from the era when the analyst was mainly interested in the repulses, because now that we attempt to analyze resistance, the patient's manifestations of resistance are a significant as any other of his productions. At any rate, but as Ferenczi refers is the countertransference response and deduces from it the analysand's psychological situation. He says ' . . . we have unconsciously reacted to the emptiness and futility if the associations given a this moment with the withdrawal of the real conscious charge'. The situation might be described as one of mutual withdrawal - which, however. Is are responses to an imagined or real psychological position of th analyst? If we have withdrawn - if we are not listening but are thinking of something else - we may utilize this event in the service if the analysis, in like any other information we acquire. And the guilt we may feel over such a withdrawal is just as analytically utilizable as any other countertransference reaction. Ferenczi's next words, 'the danger of the doctor's falling asleep . . . need not be regarded as grave because we awake at the first occurrence of any importance for the treatment, are clearly intended to placate this guilt. but better than to allay the analyst's guilt would b e to use it to promote the analysis - and so use the guilt would be the best way of alleviating it. In fact, we encounter a cardinal problem of the relation between transference and countertransference, and of the therapeutic process in general. For the analyst's withdrawal is only an example of how the unconscious of one person responds to the unconscious of another. This response seems in part to be governed, insofar as we identify ourselves with the unconscious objects of the analysand, by the law of talion; and, insofar as this law unconsciously influences the analyst, there is danger of a vicious circle of reactions between them, for the analysand also responds 'talionically' in his turn, and so on without end.

Looking more closely, we see that the 'talionic response' or 'identification with the aggressor' (the frustrating patient) is a complex process. Such a psychological process in the analyst usually starts with a feeling of displeasure or of some anxiety as a response to this aggression (frustration) and, because of this feeling, the analyst identifies himself with the 'aggressor'. By the term 'aggressor' we mus t designate not only the patient but also some internal object of the analyst (especially his own superego or an internal persecutor) now projected upon the patient, this identification with the aggressor, or persecutor, causes a feeling of guilt; probably it always does so, although awareness of the guilt may be repressed. For what happens is, on a small scale, a process of melancholia, just as Freud described it : The object has to some degree abandoned us, we identify ourselves with the lost object, and then we accuse the introjected 'bad' object- in other words, we have guilt feelings. This may be sensed in Ferenczi's remarks, such of which mechanisms are at work designed to protect the analyst against these guilt feelings; denial or guilt ('the danger is not grave') and a certain accusation against the analysand for the 'emptiness' and 'futility' of his association. In this way a vicious circle - a kind of paranoid ping-pong - has entered into the analytic situation.

Two situations of frequent occurrence illustrate both the complementary and the concordant identifications and the vicious circle these situations may cause.

1. One transference situation of regular occurrence consist s in the patient's seeing in the analyst hi s own superego. The analyst identifies himself with the id and ego of the patient and with the patient's dependence upon his superego, and he also identifies himself with this same superego - a situation in which the patient places him - and

experience domination of the superego over the patient's ego. The relation of the ego to the superego of the superego over the patient's ego. The relation of the ego to the superego is, at bottom, a depressive and paranoid situation; the relation of the superego to the ego is, on the same plane, a manioc one insofar as this term may be used to designate the dominating, controlling, and accusing attitude of the superego toward the ego. In this sense we may say, broadly speaking, that to a 'depressive-paranoid' transference in the analysand there corresponds - as regards the complementary identification - a 'manic' countertransference in he analyst. This, in turn, may entail various fears and guilt feelings.

2. When the patient, in defences against this situation, identifies himself with the superego, he may place the analyst in the situation of the dependent and incriminated ego. The analyst will not only identify himself with this position of the patient; he will also experience the situation with the content the patient give it: He will feel subjugated and accused, and may react to some degree with anxiety and guilt. To a 'manic' transference situation (of the type called mania for reproaching) there corresponds, then - as regards the complementary identification -a 'depressive-paranoid' countertransference situation.

The analyst will normally experience these situations with only a part of his being, leaving another part free to take note of them in a way suitable for the treatment. Perception of such a countertransference situation by the analyst and his understanding of it as a psychological response to certain transference situations will enable him the better to grasp the transference at the precise moment when it is active. It is precisely these situations and the analyst's behaviour regarding them, and in particular his interpretations of them, that are of decisive importance for the process of therapy, fo r they are the moment when the vicious circle within which the neurotic habitually moves - by projecting his inner world outside and reintrojecting his same world is or is not interpreted. Moreover, these decisive points the world - is projecting his inner world outside these decisive points the vicious circle may be-enforced by the analyst, if he is unaware of having entered it.

A brief example: An analysand repeats with the analyst his 'neurosis of failure', closing himself up to every interpretation or representing it at once, reproaching the analyst for the uselessness of the analysis, foreseeing nothing better in the future, continually declaring his complex indifference to everything. The analyst interprets the patient's position toward him, and its origins, in its various aspects. He shows the patient his defences against the danger of becoming too dependent, of being abandoned, or being tricked, or of suffering counter aggression by the analyst, if he abandons his amour and indifference of bad internal objects and his subsequent sado-masochistic behaviour in the transference, his need of punishment, his triumph and 'masochistic-revenge' against the transference patients; his defences against the 'depressive position' by means of schizoid paranoid and manic defences (Melaine Klein) and he interprets the patient's rejection of a bond which is the unconscious has a homosexual significance. But it may happen that all these interpretations, in spite of being directed to the central resistance and connected with the transference situation, suffer the same fate for the same reasons: They fall into the 'whirl in avoid' of the 'neurosis of failure'. Now the decisive moments arrive, the analyst, subdued by the patient 'resistance, may begin to feel anxious over the possibility of failure and feel angry with the patient. What this occurs in the analyst, the patient feels it coming, for his own 'aggressiveness' and other reactions have provoked it; consequently he fears the analyst's anger. If the analyst, threatened by failure, to put more precisely threatened by his own superego or by his own archaic objects which have found an agent provocateur in the patient, acts under the influence of these internal objects and of his paranoid and depressive anxieties, the patient again finds himself confronting a reality like that of his real or fantasized childhood experiences and like that of his inner world, and so the vicious circle continues and may even be re-enforced. But if the analyst grasps the importance of this situation, if, through his own anxiety or anger, he comprehends what is happening in the analysand, and if he overcomes, thanks to the new insight, his negative feelings and interprets what has happened in the analysand, being now in his new positive countertransference situation, then he may have made a breach - be it large or small - in the vicious circle.

To briefly consider the significance of the transference phenomenon impressed Freud so profoundly that he continued through the years to develop his ideas about it, but his classical observations on the patient Dora formed the basis for his first formulations of this concept. he said, 'What are transferences? They are the new editions or facsimiles of the tendencies and phantasies which are aroused and made conscious during the progress of the analysis: But they have this peculiarity, which is characteristic for their species, that they replace some earlier person by the person of the physician. To put it another way, a whole series of psychological experiences are revived, not as belonging to the past, but as applying to the person of the physician at the present moment.

According to Freud's view, the process of psychoanalytic cure depends mainly upon the patient's ability to remember that which is forgotten and repressed, and thus to gain conviction that the analytical conclusion arrived at being correct. However, 'the unconscious feelings strive to avoid the recognition which the cure demands'. They seek instead, emotional discharge, regardless of the reality of the situation.

Freud believed that these unconscious feelings, which the patient strives to hide, are made up of that part of the libidinal impulse that has turned away from consciousness and reality, due to the frustration of a desirous gratification. Because the attraction of reality has weakened, the libidinal energy is still maintained in a state of regression attached to the original infantile sexual objects, although the reasons for the recoil from reality have disappeared.

Freud stated that in the analytic treatment, the analyst pursued this part of the libido to its hiding place, 'aiming always at unearthing it, making it accessible to consciousness and at last serviceable to reality'. The patient tries to achieve an emotional discharge of this libidinal energy under the pressure of the compulsion to repeat experiences over and again, rather than to become conscious of their origin. He uses the method of transferring to the person of the physician past psychological experiences and reacting to this, at times, with all the power of hallucination. The patient vehemently insists that his impression of the analyst is true for the immediate present, in this way avoiding the recognition of his own unconscious impulses.

Thus, Freud regarded the transference-manifestations as a major problem of the resistance. However, Freud said, 'It must not be forgotten that they (the transference-manifestations) and they only, render the invaluable service of making the patient's buried and forgotten love-emotions actual and manifest.'

Freud regarded the transference-manifestations as having two general aspects - positive and negative. The negative, he at first regarded as having no value in psychoanalytic cure and only something to be 'raised' into consciousness to avoid interference with the progress of the analysis. He later accorded it a place of importance in the therapeutic experience. The positive transference he considered to be ultimately sexual in origin, since Freud said, 'To begin with, we knew none but sexual objects'. However, he divided the positive transference into two components - one, the repressed erotic component, which was used in the service of resistance; the other, the friendly and affectionate component, which, although originally sexual, was the 'unobjectionable' aspect of the positive transference, and was that which 'brings about the successful result in psychoanalysis, as in all other remedial methods' - Freud referred to the element of suggestion in psychoanalytic therapy.

At the moment, I should like to state that it would be a mistake to deny the value and importance of his formulations regarding transference phenomena. Nonetheless, I differ on certain points with Freud, but I do not differ with the formulation that early impressions acquired during childhood are revived in the analytical situation, and are felt as immediate and real - that they form potentially the greatest obstacles to analysis if unnoticed, and, as Freud put it, the greatest ally of the analysis when understood. Wherefore, I agree that the main work of the analysis consists in analyzing the transference phenomena, although I differ somewhat as to how this result is cure. Even so, it is my conviction that the transference is a strictly interpersonal experience. Freud gave the impression that under the stress of the repetition-compulsion the patient was bound to repeat the identical pattern, regardless of the other person, that I believe that the personality of the analyst tends to determine the character of the transference illusions, and especially to determine whether the attempt at analysis will result in cure. Horney has shown that there is no valid reason for assuming that the tendency to repeat past experiences time and again, having that he integrate with any given situation according to the necessities of his character structure.

Yet, among other things, I do want to mention a simple phenomenon, as described by Sherif, connected with the problem of the frame of reference. If you have a completely dark room, with no possibility of any light being seen, and you then turn on a small pinpoint of light, which is kept stationary, this light will soon appear to be moving about. I am sure a good many of you have noticed this phenomenon when gazing upon a single star. The light seems to move, and it does so, apparently because there is no reference point in relation to which one can establish it at a fixed place in space. It just wanders around. If, however, one can at the same time see some other fixed object in the room, the light immediately becomes stationary. A reference point having been established, and there is no longer any uncertainty, and vague wandering of the spot of light? It is fixed. The pinpoint of light wandering in the dark room is symbolic of the original attitude of the person to himself, undetermined, unstructured, with no reference point or points.

The newborn infant probably perceives everything in a vague and uncertain way, including himself. Gradually, reference points that are established that a connection begins to occur between hunger and breast, between a relief if bladder tension and a wet diaper between playing with his genitals and a smack on the hand. The physical boundaries and potentialities of the self are explored. One can observe the baby investigating the extent, shape, and potentialities of his own body, that he can hold his breath and everyone will get excited that he can smile and coo and people will be enchanted, or just the opposite. The nature of the emotional reference points that he determines depends on or upon the environment. By that still unknown quality called 'empathy' he discovers the reference points that help to determine his emotional attitude toward himself. If his mother does not want him, is disgusted with him, treats him with utter disregard, he comes to look upon himself as anything-to-be-disregarded. With the profound human drive to make this rational, he gradually builds up a system of 'reasons why'. Underneath all these reasons is a basic sense of worthlessness, undetermined and undefined, related directly to the original reference frame. Another child discovers that the state of being regarded is dependent upon specific factors all is well as long as one does not act spontaneously, as long as one can be just not of a separate person, as long as one is good, as the state of being good is continuously defined by the parent. Under these conditions, and these only, this child can feel a sense of self-regard.

Other people are encountered with the original reference frame in mind. The child tends to carry over into later situations the patterns he first learned to know. The rigidity with which these original patterns are retained depends upon the hidden nature of the child's experience. If this has been of a traumatic character so that spontaneity has been blocked and further emotional developments has been inhibited, the original orientations will tend to persist. Discrepancies may be rationalized or repressed. Thus, the original impression of the hostile mother may be retained, while the contact with the new person is rationalized to fit the original reference frame. the new person encountered acts differently, but probably that is just a pose. She is just being nice because she does not know me. If she really knew me, she would act differently. Or, the original impressions are out of line with the present actuality, that they remain unconscious, but make themselves apparent in inappropriate behaviour or attitudes, which remain outside the awareness of the person concerned.

The little child who grows more and more negativistic, because of injuries and frustrations, evokes more and more hostility in his environment. However, and this is important, the basic reactions of hostility on the part of the patents, which originally induced his negativism, are still there. Thus, the pattern does not change much in character, but it just gets worse in the same direction. Those persons whose life experience perpetuate the original frames of reference, are more severely injured. Among the children, who has a hostile mother, may then have a hostile teacher. If, by good luck, he got a kind teacher and if his own attitude were not already badly warped, so that he did not induce hostility in this kind teacher, he would be introduced into a startlingly new and pleasant frame of reference, and his personality might not suffer too greatly, especially, if a kindly aunt or uncle happened to be around.

The profoundly sick people have been so early injured, in such a rigid and limited frame of reference, that they are not able to make use of kindliness, decency, or regard when it does come their way. They meet the world as if it were potentially menacing. They have already developed defensive traits entirely appropriate to their original experience, and then carry them out in completely inappropriate situations, rationalizing the discrepancies, but never daring to believe that people are different from the ones they early learned to distrust and hate. By reason of bitter early experience, they learn never to let their guard down, never to permit intimacy, least of mention, the death blow would be dealt to their already partly destroyed sense of self-regard. Despairing of real joy in living, they develop secondary neurotic goals which give a pseud-satisfaction. The secondary gains at first glance might seem to be what the person was really striving for - revenge, power and exclusive possession. Actually, these are but the expressions of the deep injuring sustained by the person. They cannot be fundamentally cured until those interpersonal relationships that caused the original injury are brought back to consciousness in the analytic situation. Step by step, and each phase to the long period of emotional development is exposed, by no means chronologically; the interconnecting, overlapping reference frames are made conscious, those points at which a distortion of reality, or a repression of part of the self had to occur, are uncovered. The reality gradually becomes 'undistorted', the self refound in the personal relationship between the analyst and the patient. This personal relationship with the analyst is the situation in which the transference distortion can be analyzed.

In Freud's view, the transference was either positive or negative, and was related in a rather isolated way to a particular person in the past. Justly, the transference is the experiencing in the analytic situation the entire pattern of the original reference frames, which include at every moment the relationship of the patient to himself, to the important persons, and to others, as he experienced them at that time, in the light of his interrelationships with the important people.

The therapeutic aim in this process is not to uncover childhood memories that will then lend themselves to analytic interpretation. Here, Fromm has pointed out, that psychoanalytic cure is not the amassing of data, either from childhood, or from the study of the present situation. Nor does cure result from repetition of the original injurious experience in the analytic relationship. What is curvature in the process, is that in tending to reconstruct with the analyst that atmosphere which obtained in childhood, the patient actually achieve something new? He discovers that of himself which has to be repressed at the time of the original experience. He can only do this in an interpersonal relationship with the analyst, which is suitable to such a rediscovery. To illustrate this point: If a patient had a hostile parent toward whom he was required to show deference, he has to repress certain of his own spontaneous feelings. In the analytic situation, he tends to carry over his original frame of reference, and again tends to feel himself to be in a similar situation. If the analyst's personality also contains elements of a need for deference that which a want or requirement of some course of action will unconsciously be imparted to the patient, who will, therefore, still repress his spontaneity as he did before. True enough, he may act or try to act as if analyzed, since by definition, that is what the analyst is attempting to accomplish. But he will never have found his repressed self, because the analytic relationship contains for him elements actually identical with his original situation. Only if the analyst provides a genuinely new frame of reference - that is, if he is truly non-hostile, and truly not in need of deference - can this patient discover, and it is a real discovery, the repressed elements of his own personality. Thus, the transference phenomenon is used so that the patient will completely re-experience the original frames of reference, and himself within those frames, in a truly different relationship with the analyst, to the end that he can discover the invalidity of his conclusions about himself and others.

That is to say, by this is not to mean to deny the correctness of Freud's view of transference also acting as a resistance. As a matter of fact, the tendency of the patient to reestablish the original reference frame is precisely because he is afraid to experience the other person in a direct and unreserved way. He has organized his whole system of getting along in the world, bad as that system might be, on the basis of the original distortions of his personality and his subsequent vicissitudes. His capacity for spontaneous feeling and acting has gone into hiding. Now it has to be sought. If some such phrase as the 'capacity for self-realization' is substituted in place of Freud's concept of the repressed libidinal impulse, much is the same conclusions can be reached about the way in which the transference-manifestations appear in the analysis as resistance. It is just in the safest situation, where the spontaneous feelings might come out of hiding, that the patient develops intense feelings, sometimes of a hallucinatory character, that relate to the most dreaded of experience, that of the past. It is at this point that the hidden natures and the use by the patient of the transference distortions have to be understood and correctly interpreted, by the analyst. It is also here that the personality of the analyst modifies the transference reaction, a patient cannot feel close to a detached or hostile analyst and will therefore never display the full intensity of his transference illusions. The plexuity of this process, whereby the transference can be used as the therapeutic instrument and, at the same time, as a resistance may be illustrated by the following example: a patient had developed intense feelings of attachment to a father surrogate in his everyday life. The transference feelings toward this man were of great value in elucidating his original problems with his real father. As the patient became more and more aware of this personal validity, he found this masochistic attachment to be weakening. This occasioned acute feeling of anxiety, since his sense of independence was not ye t fully established. At this point, he developed very disturbing feelings regarding the analyst, believing that she was untrustworthy and hostile, although prior to this, he had successes in establishing a realistically positive relationship to her. The feelings of untrustworthiness precisely reproduced an ancient pattern with his mother. He experienced then at this particular point in the analysis in order to retain and to justify his attachment to the father figure, the weakening of which attachment had threatened him so profoundly. The entire pattern was elucidated when it was seen that he was re-experiencing an ancient triangle, in which he was contentiously driven to a submissive attachment to a dominating father, due to the utter untrustworthiness of his weak mother. If the transference character of this sudden feeling of untrustworthiness of the analyst had not been clarified, he would have turned again, submissively to his father surrogate, which would have further postponed his development of-independence. Nevertheless, the development of this transference to the analyst brought to light a new insight.

Freud felt that personality disorder called schizophrenias or paranoia could not be analyzed because the patient was unable to develop a transference to the analyst. In this view the real difficulty in treating such disorders is that the relationship is essentially nothing but transference illusions. Such persons hallucinate the original frame of reference to the exclusion of reality. Nowhere in the realm of psychoanalysis can one find more complicating and complex proof of the effect of early experience on the person than in attempting to treat these patients. Frieda Fromm Reichmann has shown in her work with schizophrenics the necessity to realize the intensity of the transference reactions, which have become almost completely real to the patient. And yet, if one knows the correct interpretations, by actually feeling the patient's needs, one can over years of time do not the identical thing that is accomplished more quickly and less dramatically with patients suffering a less severe disturbance of their interpersonal relationships.

Another point with which Freud took the position that all subsequent experience in normal life is merely repetition of the original one. Thus love is experienced for someone today in terms of the love felt for someone in the past. As, perhaps, this is not exactly true: Yet the child who has not had to repress certain aspects of his personality enters into a new situation dynamically, not just as a repetition of what he felt, say, with his mother, but as an active continuation of it. That is to say, that there are constitutional differences with respect to the total capacity for emotional experience, just as there are with respect to the total capacity for intellectual experiences. Given this constitutional substratum, the child engages in personal relationships not passively as a lump of clay waiting to be molded, but most dynamically, bringing into play all his emotional potentialities. He may possibly find someone later whose capacity for response is deeper than his mother's. If he is capable of the greater depths, he experiences an expansion of himself. Many later in life have met a 'great' person and have felt a sense of newness in the relationship which is described to others as 'wonderful' and which is regarded with a certain amount of extension of the self to a new horizon.

In considering the process of psychoanalytic cure, Freud very seriously discussed the relationship of analysis to suggestion therapy and hypnosis. He believed, that part of the positive transference could be made use of in the analysis to bring about the successful result. He said, 'In so far we readily admit that the results of psychoanalysis rest upon a basis of suggestion, only by suggestion we must be understood to mean that which we, with Ferenczi, find that it consists of influence on a person through and by means of the transference-manifestations of which he is capable. The eventually independence of the patient is our ultimate object when we use suggestion to bring him into and carry out a mental operation that will necessarily result in a lasting improvement in his mental condition. Freud, elsewhere indicated very clearly, that in hypnosis, the relationship of the patient to the hypnotist was not worked through, whereas in analysis the transference to the analyst was resolved by bringing it entirely into consciousness. He also said, that the patient was protected from the unwitting suggestive influence of the analysis by the awakening of his own unconscious resistance.

We must deal, somewhat more in detail, with one phase of the analysis that can be called the, 'plexuity of analysis' and that preserves an important stage of the amalgamation with academic psychology. The word 'plexuity' was first used by Kosciejew as the simplification of a complicated-complex psychological fact, to designate certain tendencies, characteristic for the person in question, or a related group of affect-coloured conceptions. This interpretation of the word, which is constantly becoming more comprehensive, and had thus come to have almost no meaning, was limited by those who described the unconscious repressed for its part of those group conceptions with its name by the analytical acceptance of 'plexuities'. As the more subtle, labile, fluctuating process of cathexis in the psyche became accessible to research, the acceptance of such inflexible, separate mental components became more and again superfluous. They were to coherent, they could only be excited and displaced in toto, they were much too complicating, as more exact analysis showed to be treated as elements which could not be further reduced. However, in the newer works of Freud, this conception merely figures as the survival of a period since the creation of our meta-psychology.

The most consistent thing would have been to do away entirely with this new useless rudiment of an earlier time, and to give up the terminology, which had become dear to most analysts, in favour of a better understanding. Instead of doing this, the whole of mental life was often regarded as a mosaic of such plexuities, and the analysis then carried out with the object of 'analyzing out' one complex after the other, or the attempt was make of treating the whole personality as a sum total of father-mother, brother and sister complexes. It was naturally easy to collect material for these, since every one has, of course, all the plexuities, that is, every one must, in the course of his development, somehow get on with the persons and object that surround him. The connected recounting of plexuity, or the attributes of these, may have its place in descriptive psychology, but not in the practical analysis of the neurosis, nor does it even belong in the psychoanalytic study of literary or ethno-psychological products, where it must undoubtedly lead to monotony in no way justified by the many-sidelines of the material, and scarcely tempered by giving preference, first to one and then to the other complex.

Although such a flattening out may have to be put up with at times, as unavoidable in a scientific presentation, one should not therefore transfer such a cramped interest into the technique. The analysis of plexuities easily misleads the patient into being pleasing to his analyst, by bringing him 'complex material' as long as he likes, without giving up any of his really unconscious secrets. Thus there came to be histories of illnesses In which the patient recounted memories, evidently fabricating them, in a way that never happens in unprejudiced analyses, and can only be looked upon as the product of such a 'breeding of plexuity'. Such results should naturally not be used subjectively, to show the correctness either of one's own method of interpreting, or as theoretic conclusions, not yet as leading to any sort of evidence.

It happens particularly frequently that the associations of the patient were directed to the sexual factor at the wrong time, or that they remained stuck at this point, if as so often happens - he came to the analysis with the expectation that he must constantly talk exclusively of his actual or infantile sexual life. Aside from the fact that this is not so exclusively the case as our opponents think, permitting such an indulgence in the sexual often gives the patient the opportunity to paralyze the therapeutic effect of the privation he must undergo.

An understanding of the many-sided and important mental contents that underlie the collective name 'castration complex' was also not exactly furthered by bringing the theory of the complexes into the dynamics of the analysis. On the contrary, we are of the opinion that the premature theoretic condensation of the fact under the conception of the complex interfered with the insight into deeper layers of mental life. We believe that the full appreciation of that which the analytic practitioner has accustomed himself to finish off with the label castration complex, is still lacking, so that this attempt at an explanation should not lightly be regarded as the ultimate explanation of such varied mental phenomena and processes of the patient. We can, from the dynamic standpoint which is the only justifiable one in practice, often recognized in the forms of expression of the castration complex, so they manifest themselves in the course of the analysis, only one of the kinds of resistance that the patient erects against his deeper libidinal wishes. In the early stages of some analyses the castration anxiety can often be uncovered as an expression of the dread, transferred onto the analyst, as a protection against further analysis.

Technical difficulties arose also from the analyst's having too much knowledge. thus the importance of the theory of sexual development constructed by Freud, misled some analysts to apply in a mistaken and overly-dogmatic fashion in the therapy of the neuroses, certain systems of organization and autoeroticism, which first gave us an understanding of normal sexual development. In this searching for the constructive elements of the theory of sex, in some cases, the actual analytic task was neglected. These analyses might be compared to psychochemical 'elements analyses'. Here, again, one could see that the theoretical importance did not always correspond to the value in the practical analysis. The technique need not methodically lay bare all the, . . . as it were, prescribed historic phases of the development of the libido, still less should the uncovering of all theoretically established details and gradations be used as a principle of healing in the neuroses. It is also practically superfluous to demonstrate all the original elements of a highly complicated 'connection', while missing the intellectual thread, which combines the few fundamental elements into new and varying phenomena. The same thing holds for the erotogenic zones as for the plexuity, for example the urethral or the anal erotic, and for the stages of organization the oral eroticism anal-sadistic and other pregenital phases, there can be no human development without all of these, but one must not in the analysis attribute to the importance, for the history of the illness, of which the resistance under the pressure of the analytic situation gives the illusion.

On closer observation a certain inner connection between 'element analyses' and 'complex analyses' could be recognized, insofar as the latter, in their attempts to plumb the psychic depths, struck upon the granite of the complexes and thus the work was spread out over the surface instead of going to the bottom. Such analyses then usually tried to make up for the lack of depth in the dynamics of the libido by an excursion into the theory of sex, and united rigid attributes of complexes with equally schematically treated principles of the theory of sex, whereas they missed just the play of forces that takes place between the two.

Such an attitude naturally led to a theoretical overestimation of the factor of quantity, to ascribe everything to a stronger organ - eroticism, a point of view that resembled that of the pre-analytical school of neurologists - who blinded themselves to any insight into actual play of forces of the pathological cayuses by the catch words inheritance, degeneration, and disposition.

Since the theory of the instincts and also the sciences of biology and physiology have been called upon partly as a help in understanding mental phenomena, in particular since the so-called 'pathoneurosen', that is the neurosis on the organic level, the organ-neuroses, and even organic illnesses are treated psychoantically, disputes about border-line cases have taken place between psychoanalysis and physiology. The stereotyped translation of physiological processes into the language of psychoanalysis is incorrect. Insofar as one attempts to approach organic processes analytically the rules of psychoanalysis must be strictly adhered to, as one must try to forget, so to speak, one's organic, medical and physiological knowledge and bear in mind only the mental personality and its reactions.

It was also confusing when simple clinical facts were at once combined with speculations about becoming, being, and duration and such deliberations treated like established rules in practical analysis, whereas Freud himself constantly emphasized the hypothetical character of his last synthetic works. Often enough such a wandering into speculation seems to have been a dodging of uncomfortable technical difficulty. We know how a desire to condense everything prematurely under a speculative principle can wreak vengeance from the point of view of technique (The Jungian theory).

It is also a mistake, while neglecting the individual, in the explanation of the symptoms, to make cultural and phylogenetic analogies at once, no matter how fruitful the latter might be in themselves. The overestimate of the actual factors led to an anagogic prospective interpretation, which was useless so far as the pathologic fixation were concerned. The adherents of the 'anagogic', as well as some of those of the 'genetic' school, in their interest in the future and in the past, neglected the present condition of the patient. and yet almost all of the past, and everything that the unconscious attempts, insofar as it is not directly conscious or remembered (and this occurs extremely seldom), expresses itself in actual reactions in relation to the analyst or to the analysis, in other words, the transference to the analytic situation.

The requirements of the Breuer-Freud catharsis that the affects, displace upon symptoms, should be led back directly to the pathologic memory traces, and at the same time brought to a discharge and bound again proved to be unrealizable, that is, it succeeds only in the case of incompletely repressed, mostly preconscious memory material as in the case of certain derivatives of the actual unconscious. This itself, the uncovering of which is the chief task of the analysis, since it was never 'experienced' it can never be 'remembered', one must let it be produced on the ground of certain indications. The mere communication, something like 'reconstruction', is itself not suited to call forth affect reactions: Such information glides off from the patients without any effect. They can only convince themselves of the reality of the unconscious when they have experienced - mostly after they have frequently experienced - something analogous to it in the actual analytic situation, that is, in the present. The new insight into the topography of mental life and the functions of the separate depth levels gives us the explanation for this state of affairs. The unconscious repressed material has no approach to motility, nor to those motor innervations in the sum total of which the affect discharge consists, the past and the repressed must find their representative factors in the present and the conscious (preconscious) in order that they may be affectively experienced and develop further. In contrast to the stormy abreaction one could designate the unwinding bit by bit of the affects in analysis as a reactional catharsis.

In general that affects in order to work convincingly must first be revived, that is actually present and that what has not affected us directly and actually must remain mentally ineffective.

The analyst must always take into account that almost every expression of his patients springs from several periods, but he must give his chief attention to the present reaction. Only from this point of view can he succeed in uncovering the roots of the actual reaction in the past, which means changing the attempts of the patient to repeat into remembering. In this process be needed pay little attention to the future. One may quietly leave this care to the person himself who has been sufficiently enlightened about his past and present mental strivings. The historic, cultural and phylogenetic analogies also need, for the most part, not be discussed in the analysis. The patient need hardly ever, and the analyst extremely seldom, occupy himself with this early period.

At this place we must consider certain misunderstandings about the enlightenment of people who are being analyzed. There was a phase, in the development of psychoanalysis, in which the goal of the analytic treatment consisted in filling the gaps in the memory of the patient with knowledge. Later recognizes that the neurotic ignorance proceeded from the resistance, which is from not wishing to know, and that it was this resistance that had to be constantly uncovered and made harmless. If one proceeds thus the amnesic gaps in the chain of memories fill themselves in, for the most part automatically, for the other part with the help of sparse interpretations and explanations. The patient therefore learns nothing more and nothing other than what he needs, and in the quantity requisite to allay the predominating disturbances. It was a fatal mistake to believe that no one was completely analyzed who had not been theoretically familiarized with all the separate details of his own abnormality. Naturally it is not easy to set a boundary line up to which the instruction of the patient should be carried. Interruption of the correct analysis by formal courses of instruction may satisfy both the analyst and the patient, but cannot effect any change in the libido-attitude of the sick person. A further result of such instruction was that without noticing it, one pushed the patient into withdrawing himself from the analytical work by means of identifying himself with the analyst. The fact that the desire to learn and to teach creates an unfavourable mental attitude for the analysis is well known but should receive much serious attention.

At times one heard from analysts the complaint that this or that analysis failed on account of 'too great resistances' or a too 'violent transference'. The possibility in principle of such extreme cases is admitted; we do find ourselves at times confronted with quantitative factors, which we, must in no way practically underestimate, since they play an important part in the final; outcome of the analysis, as well as in its causes. But the factor of quantity, so important in itself, can be used as a screen for incomplete insight into the play of forces that finally decide the kind of application and the distribution of those very quantities. Because Freud once uttered the sentence, 'Everything which impedes the analysis work is resistance.' one should not, every time the analysis comes to a standstill, simply say, 'this is a resistance'. This resulted, particularly in patients with an easily aroused sense of guilt, in creating an analytic atmosphere in which th y, so to speak, were fearful of making the 'faux pas' as having a resistance, and the analyst found himself in a helpless situation. One evidently forgot another utterance of Freud's, namely, that the analysis we must be prepared as to meet the same forces, which formerly caused the repression as 'resistance', as soon as one sets to work to release these repressions.

Another analytical situation that one was also in the habit of labeling incorrectly as 'resistance' is the negative transference, which, from its very nature, cannot express itself otherwise than as 'resistance' and the analysis of which is the most important task of the therapeutic activity. One need, of course, not be afraid of the negative reactions of the patient for they constitute, with iron necessity, a part of every analysis. Also the strong positive transference, particularly when it expresses itself in the beginning of the cure, is only a symptom of resistance that requires to be unmasked. In other cases, and particularly in the later stages of an analysis, it is an actual vehicle for bringing to light desires that have remained unconscious.

In this connection an important rule of psychoanalytic technique must be mentioned in regard to the personal relation between the analyst and the patient. The theoretic requirements of avoiding all personal contact outside if the analysis mostly led to an unnatural elimination of all human factors in the analysis, and thus again, to a theorizing of the analytic experience.

From this point of view, some practitioners all too readily failed to attribute that importance to a change in the person of the analyst, which results from the interpretation of the analysis as a mental process, the unity of which is determined by the person of the analyst. A change of analysts may be unavoidable for outer reasons in rare, exceptional cases, but we believe that technical difficulties - in homosexuals, for example - are not simple to be avoided by the choice of an analyst of the opposite sex. For in every correct analysis the analyst plays all possible roles for the unconscious of the patient; it only depends upon him always to recognize this at the proper time and under certain circumstances to make use of it consciously. Particularly important is the role of two parental images - father and mother - in which the analyst actually constantly alternatives (transference and resistance).

It is not an accident that technical mistakes occurred of frequently just in the expression of transference and resistance. One was easily inclined to let oneself be surprised at these elementary experiences in the analysis and strangely enough forgot just here the theory that had been incorrectly pushed into the foreground in the wrong place. This may also be due to subjective factors in the analysis. The narcissism of the analyst seem suited to create a particularly fruitful source of mistakes: Among others the development of a kind of narcissistic counter-transference that provokes the person being analyzed into pushing into the foreground certain things that flatter the analyst and, on the other hand, into suppressing remarks and associations of an unpleasant nature in relation to him. Both are technically incorrect, he first, because it can lead to an apparent improvement of the patient in only intended to bribe the analyst and in this way to win a libidinal counter-interests from him. The second because it keeps the analyst from the necessity of noticing the delicate indications of criticism, which mostly only venture forth hesitantly, and help the patient to express plainly or to abreact them. The anxiety and the sense of guilt of the patient can never be overcome without this self-criticism, requiring a certain overcoming of himself on the part of the analyst; and yet these two emotional factors are the essentials for bringing about and maintaining the repression.

Another form under which technical inaccessibility hid itself was an incidental remark of Freud's to the effect that the narcissism of the patient could set limits to the degrees to which he could be influenced by the analysis. If the analysis did not progress well, one consoled oneself with the thought that the patient was 'too narcissistic'. And since narcissism forms a connecting link between ego and libidinal strivings in all normal, as well as abnormal, mental processes, it is not difficult to find proofs in his behaviour and thoughts of the narcissism of the patient. Particularly one should not handle the narcissistically determined 'castration' or 'masculinity' complexes as they set the limits for analytic solution.

When the analysis struck upon a resistance of the patient one often over-looked extent of pseudo-narcissistic tendencies, as brought into the question. The analyses of people who bring a certain theoretic knowledge a great deal of what one was theoretically inclined to scribe to narcissism, is actually secondary, pseudo-narcissistic and can continue analysis be completely solved in the parental relationship. Naturally it is necessary in doing this to take up analytically the ego-development of the patient, as it is in general, necessary in the analysis of the resistance to consider the up-to-now much-too-neglected analysis of the ego, for which Freud has recently given valuable hints.

The newness of a technical point of view introduced by Ferenczi under the name of 'activity' resulted in some analysts, in order to avoid technical difficulties, overwhelming the patient with commands and prohibitions, which one might characterize as a kind of 'wild activity'. This, however, must be looked upon as a reaction to the other extreme, to holding too fast to an over-looked upon as a reaction to the other extreme, to holding too fast to an overly-right id 'passivity' in the matter of technique. The latter is certainly sufficiently justified by the theoretic attitude of the analyst who must at the same time be an investigator. In practice, however, this easily leads to sparing the patient the pain of necessary intervention, and to allowing him too much initiative in his associations as well as in the interpretation of his ideas.

The moderate, but, when necessary, energetic activity in the analysis consists in the analyst's taking on, and, to a certain extent, really carrying out those rules that the unconscious of the patient and his tendency to flight prescribe. By doing this the tendency to the repetition of earlier traumatic experiences is given an impetus, naturally with the goal of finally overcoming this tendency by revealing its content. When this repetition takes place spontaneously it is superfluous to provoke it and the analyst can simply call forth the transformation of the resistance into remembering (or plausible reconstruction).

These last purely technical remarks lead back to the often-mentioned subject of the reciprocal effect of theory and practice.

I do not mean by this to deny the correctness of Freud's view of transference also acting as a resistance. As a matter of fact, the tendency of the patient to reestablish the original reference frame is precisely because he is afraid to experience the other person in a direct and unreserved way. He has organized his whole system of getting along in the world, bad as that system might be, on the basis of the original distortions of his personality and his subsequent vicissitudes. His capacity for spontaneous feeling and acting has gone into hiding. Now it has to be sought. If some such phase as the 'capacity for self-realization' is substituted in placing Freud's concept of the repressed libidinal impulse, much the same conclusion can be reached about the way in which the transference-manifestations appear in the analysis as resistance. It is just in the satisfactory situation, where the spontaneous feeling might come out of hiding, that the patient develops intense feelings. Sometimes of a hallucinatory character, that relates to most directed experiences of the past. It is at this point that the hidden natures and the use by the patient of the transference distortion have to be understood and correctly interpreted, by the analyst. It is also, that the personality of the analyst modifies the transference reaction. A patient cannot feel close to the character hostile analyst and will therefore never display the full intensity of his transference illusions. The complexity of this process, whereby the transference can because as the therapeutic instrument and, at the same time, as a resistance may be illustrated by the following example, in his everyday life. the transference feelings toward this were of great value and elucidating his origin problems with his real father. As the patient became more and more aware of his own personal+ validity, he found this narcissistic attachment to be weakening. This occasional acute feeling of anxiety, since his sense of independence was not yet fully established. At that point, he developed very disturbing feelings regarding the analyst, believing that she was untrustworthy and hostile, although proof to this, he had succeeded in establishing a realistically positive relationship to her. The feelings of untrustworthiness precisely reproduced an ancient pattern with his mother, but he experienced them at this particular point in the analysis in order to retain and to justify his attachment to his father figure, the weakening of which attachment and threatened him so profoundly. The entire pattern was elucidated as when that which he had driven to a submissive attachment to a dominating father, due to the utter untrustworthiness of his real mother. If the transference character of this sudden feeling of untrustworthiness of the analyst had not been clarified, he would have further postponed his development of independence. Nevertheless, the development of this transference to the analyst brought to light a new insight.

Freud's view of the so-called narcissistic neuroses, was felt that personality disorders called schizophrenia or paranoia could not be analyzed because the patient was unable to develop a transference to the analyst. However, in that the real difficulty in treating such disorders is that the relationship is essentially nothing but transference illusions. Such persons hallucinate the original frame of reference to the exclusion of reality. Nowhere in the realm of psychoanalysis can one find more complete proof of the effect of early experience of the person than in attempting to treat these patients. Frieda Fromm Reichmann has shown in her work with schizophrenics the necessity to realize the intensity of the transferee reactions, which have become almost completely real to the patient. And yet, if one knows the correct interpretation, by actually feeling the patient's needs, one can over years of time do the identical thing that is accomplished more quickly and less dramatically with patients suffering a less severe disturbance of their interpersonal relationship.

Another point of interest is that Freud had taken the position that all subsequent experience in normal life is merely a repetition of the original one. Thus, love is experienced for someone today in terms of the love felt for someone in the past. Perhaps, in believing that this is not exactly true, the child who has not had to repress certain aspects of his personality enters into a new situation dynamically, not just as a repetition of what he felt, say, with his mother, but as an active continuation of it, in that of believing that there are constitutional differences with respect to the total capacity for emotional experience, just as there are with respect on the total capacity for intellectual experiences. Given this constitutional substratum, the child engages in personal relationships not passively as a lump of clay waiting to be molded, but most dynamically, bringing into play all his emotional potentialities. He may possibly find someone later whose capacity for response is deeper than his mother's. If he is capable of a greater depth, he experience s an expansion of himself. Many later in life have met a 'great' person and have felt a sense of newness in the relationship which is described simply as otherwise 'wonderful' and which is regarded with a certain amount of awe. This is not a 'transference' experience, but represents a dynamic extension of the self to a new horizon.

In considering the process of psychoanalytic cure, Freud very seriously discussed the relationship of analysis to suggestion therapy an hypnosis. He believed, that part of the positive transference could be made use of in the analysis to bring about successful result. He said, 'In so far we readily admit that the results of psychoanalysis rest upon a basis of suggestion, only by suggestion we must be understood to mean that which we, with Ferenczi, find that it consists of influence on a person through and by means of the transference-manifestations of which he is capable. The eventual independence of the patient is our ultimate object when we use suggestion to bring him to carry out a mental operation that will necessarily result in a lasting improvement in his mental; condition'. Freud elsewhere indicated very clearly that in hypnosis, the relationship of the patient to the hypnotist was not worked through, whereas in analysis the transference to the analyst was resolved by bringing it entirely into consciousness. He also said that the patient was protected from unwitting suggestive influence of the analyst by the awakening of his own conscious resistance.

Even so, Freud describes transference as both the greatest danger and the best tool for analytic work. He refers to the work of making the repressed past conscious. Besides these two implied meanings of transference, Freud gives it a third meaning: It is in the transference that the analysand may relive the past under better conditions and in the way rectify pathological decisions and destinies. Likewise three meanings of countertransference may be differentiated. It too, may be the greatest danger and at the same time an important tool for understanding, an assistance to the analyst in his function as interpreter. Moreover, it affects the analyst's behaviour. It interferes with his action as object of the patient's re-experience in that new fragment of life that is the analytic situation, in which he found in the reality or fantasy of his childhood.

Briefly, is to consider countertransference in the history of psychoanalysis, that we meet with a strange fact and striking contrast. The discovery by Freud of countertransference and its great importance in therapeutic work gave to the institution of didactic analysis which became the basis and centre of psychoanalytic training. Yet countertransference received little consideration over the next forty years. Only during the last few years has the situation changed, rather suddenly, and countertransference became a subject examined frequently and with thoroughness. How is one to explain this in initial recognition? This neglect, and the recent change? Is there no reason to question the success of didactic analysis in fulfilling its function, if this very problem, the discovery of which led to the creation of didactic analysis, has had so little scientific elaboration?

These questions are clearly important, and those have personally attested of a great part of the development of psychoanalysis in the last forty years have the best right to answer them. Nonetheless, I will suggest or exemplify on or upon of only one explanation.

The lack of scientific investigation of countertransference must be due to rejection by analyst of their own countertransference - a rejection that represents unresolved struggles with their own primitive anxiety and guilt. These struggles are closely connected with those infantile ideals that survive because of deficiencies the didactic analysis of just those transference problems that latter affect the analyst's countertransference. These deficiencies in the didactic analysis are in turn due to countertransference problems insufficiently solved in the didactic analyst. Thus, we are in a vicious circle, but we can see where a breach must be made. That is to say, that we must begin by revision of our feelings about our own countertransference and try to overcome our infantile ideals more thoroughly, accepting more fully the fact that we are still children and neurotics even when we are adults and analysts. Only in this way - by better overcoming our rejection of countertransference - can we achieve the same result in candidates.

The insufficient dissolution of these idealizations and underlying anxieties and guilt feelings leads to special difficulties when the child becomes an adult and the analysand an analyst, for the analyst unconsciously requires of himself that he be fully identified with these ideals, that it is at last, partly for this reason that oedipus complex of the child toward its parents, and of the patient toward his analysand, has been so much more fully considered than that of the parents toward their children and of the analyst toward the analysand. For the same basic reason transference has been dealt with much more than countertransference.

The fact that countertransference conflicts determine the deficiencies in the analysis of transference becomes clear if we recall that transference is the expression of the internal object relations; for understanding of transference will depend on the analyst's capacity to identify himself both with the analysand's impulses and defences, and with his internal object s, and to be conscious of these identification. This ability in the analyst will in turn depend upon the degree to which he accepts his countertransference, fo r his countertransference is likewise based on identification with the patient's id and ego and his internal objects. One might also say that transference is the expression of the patient's relations with the fantasies and real countertransference of the analyst. For just as countertransference is the psychological response to the analysand's real imaginary transference, so also is transference the response to the analyst's imaginary and real countertransference. Analysis of the patient's fantasies out countertransference, which in the widest sense constitute the causes and consequence of the transference, is an essential part of the analysis of the transference. Perception of the patient's fantasies regarding countertransference will depend in turn upon the degree to which the analyst himself perceives his countertransference processes - on the continuity and depth of his conscious constant with himself.

Finally, the repression of countertransference (and other pathological fates that it may meet) necessarily leads to deficiencies in the analysis of transference, which in turn lead to the repression and other mishandling of countertransference soon as the candidate becomes an analyst. It is a heritage from generation to generation, similar to the heritage of idealizations and denials concerning the imagoes of the parents, which continue working even when the child becomes a father or mother. The child's mythology is prolonge in the mythology of the analytic situation, the analyst himself being partially subject to it and collaborating unconsciously in its maintenance in the candidate.

Let us briefly consider one of these ideals in it specifically psychoanalytic expression: The ideal of the analyst's objectivity. No one, of course, denies the existence of subjective factors in th analyst and of countertransference in itself, but there seems to exist an important difference between what is generally acknowledged in practice and the real state of affairs. The first distortion of truth in 'the myth of thee analytic situation' is that analysis is an interaction between two personalities in both of which the ego is under pressure from the id, the superego, and the external world, each personality has its internal and external dependencies, parents, and that of the analyst - responds to every event of the analytic situation. Besides these similarities between the personalities of analyst and analysand, there also exist differences, and one of these is in 'objectivity'. The analyst's objectivity consists mainly in a certain attitude toward his own subjectivity and countertransference. The neurotic (obsessive) ideal of objectivity lead to repression and blocking of subjectivity and so to the apparent fulfilment of the myth of the 'analyst without anxiety or anger'. The other neurotic extreme is that of 'drowning' in the countertransference. True objectivity is based upon a form of internal division that enables the analyst to make himself (his own countertransference and subjectivity) the object of his continuous observations and analysis. This position also enables him to be relatively 'objective' toward the analysand.

The term countertransference has been given various meanings. They may be summarized by the state that for some authors countertransference includes everything that arises in the analysis as psychological response to the analysand, whereas for others not all this should be called countertransference. Some, for example, prefer to reserve the term for what is infantile in the relationship of the analyst with his analysand, while others make different limitation (Annie Reich and Gitelson). Hence efforts to differentiate from each other certain of the complex phenomena of countertransference lead to confusion or to unproductive discussion of terminology. Freud invented the term countertransference in evident analogy to transference, which he defined as 're-mpressions' or 're-editions' of childhood experiences, including greater or less modifications of the original experience. hence one frequently uses the term transference for the totality of the psychological attitude of the analysand toward the analyst. We know, to be sure, that real external qualities of the analytic situation in general and of the analyst in particular, have important influences on the relationship of the analysand with the analyst, but we also know that all these present factors are experienced according to the past and the fantasy, - according. That is to say, too a transference predisposition. As determinants of the transference neurosis and, in general, if the psychological situation of the analysand toward the analyst, we have both the transference predisposition and the present real and especially analytic experiences, the transference in its diverse expressions being the resultant of these two factors.

Analogously. In the analyst there are the countertransference predisposition and the present and immediacy or the real, and especially analytic, experience; and the countertransference is the result. It is precisely this fusion of present immediacy and the past, the continuous and intimate connection of reality and fantasy, of external and internal, conscious and unconscious, that demands a concept embracing the totality of the analyst's psychological response, and renders it advisable, at the same time, to keep for this totality of response the accustomed term 'countertransference'. Where it is necessary for greater clarity one might say of 'total countertransference' and then differentiated and separate within it one aspect or another. One of its aspects consists precisely in what is transferred in countertransference; this is the part that originates in an earlier time and that is especially the infantile and primitive part within total countertransference. Another of these aspects - closely connected with the previous one - is what is neurotic in countertransference, but its main characteristics is the unreal anxiety and the pathological defences. Under certain circumstances one might in saying of a countertransference neurosis.

To clarity better the concept of countertransference, on might start from the question of what happens, in general, in the analyst in his relationship with the patient, as one might think that everything happens that can happen in one personality faced with another. But this says so much that it says hardly anything - bearing in mind that in the analyst there is a tendency that normally predominates in his relationship with the patient: Is the tendency pertaining to his function of being an analyst that of understanding what is happening in the patient? Together with the tendency there exist toward the patient virtually all the other possible tendencies, fears, and other feelings that one person may have toward another. The intention to understand creates a certain predisposition, a predisposition to identify oneself with the analysand, which is the basis of comprehension. The analyst may achieve this aim by identifying his ego with the patient's ego, or put it more clearly although a certain terminological inexactitude, by identifying each part of his personality with the corresponding psychological part in the patient - his id with the patient id, his ego with the ego, his superego with the superego, accepting these identifications in his consciousness. But this does not always happen, nor is it all that happens. Apart from these identifications, which might be called concordant (or homologous) identifications, there exist also highly important identifications of the analyst's ego with the patient's internal objects, for example, with the superego. Adapting an expression from Helene Deutsch, they might be called complementary identifications. Such are that follows:

1. The concordant identifications are based on introjection and also projection, or, in other words, on the resonance of the exterior in the interior as justly as the outer is of the inner, on the recognition of what belongs to another as one 's own ('this part of you is I') and on the equation of what is one's own with what belongs to another ('this part of me is you'). The processes inherently in the complementary identifications are the same, but they refer to the patient's objects. The greater the conflicts between the parts of the analyst's personality, the greater are his difficulties in carrying out the concordant identifications in their entirety.

2. The complementary identifications are produced by the fact that the patient treats the analyst as an internal (projected) object, and in consequence the analyst feels treated as such: That is, he identifies himself with the object. The complementary identifications are closely connected with the destiny in the concordant identifications: It seems that to the

degree to which the analyst fails in the concordant identifications and rejects them, certain complementary identifications become intensified. It is clear that rejection of a part of tendency in the analyst himself, - his aggressiveness, for instance, - may lead to a rejection of the patient's aggressiveness (whereby this concordant identification fails) and that such a situation leads to a greater complementary identification with the patient's rejecting objects, toward which this aggressive impulse is directed.

3. Current usage applies the term 'countertransference' to the complementary identifications only: This is to say, to those psychological processes in the analysis by which, because he feels treated as and partially identifies himself with an internal object of the patient, the patient becomes an internal (projected) object of the analyst. Usually excluded from the concept countertransference are the concordant identifications, - those psychological content s that arise in the analyst by reason of the empathy achieved with the patient and that really reflect and reproduce the latter's psychological contents. Perhaps it would be best to follow this usage, bu t there are some circumstances that make it unwise to do so. In the first place, some authors include the concordant identifications in the concept of countertransference. One is thus faced with the choice of entering upon a terminological discussion of accepting the term in this wider sense. Where for various reasons the wider sense is to be preferred. If one considers that the analyst's concordant identifications (his 'understanding') are a sort of reproduction of his own past processes, especially of his own infancy, and that this reproduction or-re-experience is carried out as response to stimuli from the patient, one will b e more read y to include the concordant identifications in the concept of countertransference. Moreover, the concordant identifications are closely connected with the complementary ones (and thus with 'countertransference' in the popular sense), and this fact renders advisable a differentiation but not a total separation of the term. Finally, it should be borne in mind that the disposition to empathy, - this is, to concordant identification, springs largely from the sublimated positive countertransference in the wider sense. All this suggests, then, the acceptance of countertransference as the totality of the analyst's psychological response to the patient. if we accept this broad definition of countertransference, the difference between its two aspects as listed above, must still be defined. On the one hand we have the analyst as subject and the patient as the object of knowledge, which in a certain sense annuls the 'object relationship', such that is said arises in its stead the approximate union of identity between the subject's and the object's parts (experiences, impulses, defences). The aggregate of the processes pertaining to that union might be designed, where necessary, 'concordant countertransference'. However, on the other hand, we have an object relationship like many others, a real 'transference' in which the analyst 'repeats' previous experiences, the patient representing internal objects of

the analyst. The aggregate of these experiences, which also exist always and continually, might be termed 'complementary countertransference'.

A brief example can be made if we are to consider in that of patient who threatens the analyst with suicide. In such situations there sometimes occur s rejection of the concordant identifications by the analyst and an identification with the threatened object. The anxiety that such a threat can cause the analyst to lead of various reactions or decence mechanisms within him, for instance, annoyance with the patient. This - his anxiety and annoyance - would be contents of the 'complementary countertransference'. The perception of his annoyance may, in turn, originate guilt feelings in the analyst and these lead to desires for reparation and to intensification of the 'concordant' identification and 'concordant' countertransference.

Moreover, these two aspects of 'total countertransference' have their analogy in transference. sublimated positive transference is the main and indispensable motive force for the patient's work: It does not in itself constitute a technical problem. Transference becomes a 'subject', according to Freud's words, mainly when 'It becomes resistance, when because of resistance, it has become sexual or negative. Analogously, sublimated positive countertransference is the primary and indispensable motive force in the analyst's work (disposing him to the continued concordant identification), and also, countertransference become a technical problem or 'subject' mainly when it becomes sexual or negative, and this occurs (to an intense degree) principally as a resistance - in this case the analyst's - that is to say, as countertransference, in as much as of leading into the problematic function of the dynamics of countertransference.

Every transference situation provokes a countertransference situation, which arises out of the analyst's identification of himself with the analysand's (internal) objects (this is the 'complementary countertransference'). These countertransference situations may be repressed or emotionally blocked, but probably they cannot be avoided; certainly they should not be avoided if full understanding is to be achieved These countertransference reactions are governed by the laws of the general and individual unconscious. Among these the law of talion is especially important. Thus, for example, every positive transference situation is answered by a positive countertransference: To every negative transference there responds, in one part of the analyst, a negative countertransference. It is of great importance that the analyst be conscious of this law, for awareness of it is fundamental to avoid 'drowning' in the countertransference. If he is not aware of it he will not be able to avoid entering into the vicious circle of the analysand's neurosis, which will hinder or even prevent the work of therapy.

A simplified example: If the patient's neurosis centre round a conflict with his introjected father, he will project the latter upon the analyst and treat him as his father. The analyst will feel treated as such - he will feel treated badly - and he will react internally. In part of his personality. In accordance with the treatment he receives. If he fails to be aware of this reaction, his behaviour will inevitably be affected by it, and he will renew the situation that, to a greater or lesser degree, helped to establish the analysand's neurosis. Hence it is of the greatest importance that the analyst develop within himself an ego observer of his countertransference reactions, which are, naturally, continuous. Perception of these countertransference reactions will help him to become conscious of the continuous transference situations of the patient and interpret them rather than unconsciously ruled by these reactions, as not as often that happens. A well-known example is the 'revengeful silence' of the analyst. if the analyst is unaware of these interactions there is danger that the patient will have to repeat, in his transference experience, the vicious circle brought about by the projected introjection of 'bad objects' (in reality neurotic ones) and the consequent pathological anxieties and defences, but his transference interpretations made possible by the analyst's of his countertransference expedience making it possible to open important breached in this vicious circle.

To return to the previous example: If the analyst is conscious of his own countertransference, he can more easily make the patient conscious of his projection and the consequent mechanisms. Interpretation of these mechanisms will show the patient that the present reality is not identical with his inner perceptions (for, if it were, the analyst would not interpret and otherwise act as an analyst), the patient then introjects a reality better than his inner world. This sort of rectification does not take place when the analyst is under the sway of his unconscious countertransference.

For some considering applications of these principles one mus t return to the question of what the analyst does during the session and what happens within him, one might say, at first thought, that the analyst liste ns. But this is not completely true, he listens most of the time, or wishes to listen, but is variably doing so. Ferenczi refers to this fact and expresses the opinion that the analyst's distractability is of little importance, for the patient as such moments must certainly be in resistance. Ferenczi's remark (which dates form the year 1918) sounds like an echo from the era when the analyst was mainly interested in the repulses, because now that we attempt to analyze resistance, the patient's manifestations of resistance are a significant as any other of his productions. At any rate, but as Ferenczi refers is the countertransference response and deduces from it the analysand's psychological situation. He says ' . . . we have unconsciously reacted to the emptiness and futility if the associations given a this moment with the withdrawal of the real conscious charge'. The situation might be described as one of mutual withdrawal - which, however. Is are responses to an imagined or real psychological position of the analyst? If we have withdrawn - if we are not listening but are thinking of something else - we may utilize this event in the service if the analysis, in like any other information we acquire. And the guilt we may feel over such a withdrawal is just as analytically utilizable as any other countertransference reaction. Ferenczi's next words, 'the danger of the doctor's falling asleep . . . need not be regarded as grave because we awake at the first occurrence of any importance for the treatment, are clearly intended to placate this guilt. but better than to allay the analyst's guilt would b e to use it to promote the analysis - and so use the guilt would be the best way of alleviating it. In fact, we encounter a cardinal problem of the relation between transference and countertransference, and of the therapeutic process in general. For the analyst's withdrawal is only an example of how the unconscious of one person responds to the unconscious of another. This response seems in part to be governed, insofar as we identify ourselves with the unconscious objects of the analysand, by the law of talion; and, insofar as this law unconsciously influences the analyst, there is danger of a vicious circle of reactions between them, for the analysand also responds 'talionically' in his turn, and so on without end.

Looking more closely, we see that the 'talionic response' or 'identification with the aggressor' (the frustrating patient) is a complex process. Such a psychological process in the analyst usually starts with a feeling of displeasure or of some anxiety as a response to this aggression (frustration) and, because of this feeling, the analyst identifies himself with the 'aggressor'. By the term 'aggressor' we mus t designate not only the patient but also some internal object of the analyst (especially his own superego or an internal persecutor) now projected upon the patient, this identification with the aggressor, or persecutor, causes a feeling of guilt; probably it always does so, although awareness of the guilt may be repressed. For what happens is, on a small scale, a process of melancholia, just as Freud described it : The object has to some degree abandoned us, we identify ourselves with the lost object, and then we accuse the introjected 'bad' object- in other words, we have guilt feelings. This may be sensed in Ferenczi's remarks, such of which mechanisms are at work designed to protect the analyst against these guilt feelings; denial or guilt ('the danger is not grave') and a certain accusation against the analysand for the 'emptiness' and 'futility' of his association. In this way a vicious circle - a kind of paranoid ping-pong - has entered into the analytic situation.

Two situations of frequent occurrence illustrate both the complementary and the concordant identifications and the vicious circle these situations may cause.

1. One transference situation of regular occurrence consist s in the patient's seeing in the analyst hi s own superego. The analyst identifies himself with the id and ego of the patient and with the patient's dependence upon his superego, and he also identifies himself with this same superego - a situation in which the patient places him - and experience domination of the superego over the patient's ego. The relation of the ego to the superego of the superego over the patient's ego. The relation of the ego to the

superego is, at bottom, a depressive and paranoid situation; the relation of the superego to the ego is, on the same plane, a manioc one insofar as this term may be used to designate the dominating, controlling, and accusing attitude of the superego toward the ego. In this sense we may say, broadly speaking, that to a 'depressive-paranoid' transference in the analysand there corresponds - as regards the complementary identification - a 'manic' countertransference in he analyst. This, in turn, may entail various fears and guilt feelings.

2. When the patient, in defences against this situation, identifies himself with the superego, he may place the analyst in the situation of the dependent and incriminated ego. The analyst will not only identify himself with this position of the patient; he will also experience the situation with the content the patient give it : He will also feel subjugated and accused, and may react to some degree with anxiety and guilt. To a 'manic' transference situation (of the type called mania for reproaching) there corresponds, then - as regards the complementary identification -a 'depressive-paranoid' countertransference situation.

The analyst will normally experience these situations with only a part of his being, leaving another part free to take note of them in a way suitable for the treatment. Perception of such a countertransference situation by the analyst and his understanding of it as a psychological response to certain transference situations will enable him the better to grasp the transference at the precise moment when it is active. It is precisely these situations and the analyst's behaviour regarding them, and in particular his interpretations of them, that are of decisive importance for the process of therapy, fo r they are the moment when the vicious circle within which the neurotic habitually moves - by projecting his inner world outside and reintrojecting his same world is or is not interpreted. Moreover, these decisive points the world - is projecting his inner world outside these decisive points the vicious circle may be-enforced by the analyst, if he is unaware of having entered it.

A brief example: An analysand repeats with the analyst his 'neurosis of failure', closing himself up to every interpretation or representing it at once, reproaching the analyst for the uselessness of the analysis, foreseeing nothing better in the future, continually declaring his complex indifference to everything. The analyst interprets the patient's position toward him, and its origins, in its various aspects. He shows the patient his defences against the danger of becoming too dependent, of being abandoned, or being tricked, or of suffering counter aggression by the analyst, if he abandons his amour and indifference of bad internal objects and his subsequent sado-masochistic behaviour in the transference, his need of punishment, his triumph and 'masochistic-revenge' against the transference patients; his defences against the 'depressive position' by means of schizoid paranoid and manic defences (Melaine Klein) and he interprets the patient's rejection of a bond which is the unconscious has a homosexual significance. But it may happen that all these interpretations, in spite of being directed to the central resistance and connected with the transference situation, suffer the same fate for the same reasons: They fall into the 'whirl in avoid' of the 'neurosis of failure'. Now the decisive moments arrive, the analyst, subdued by the patient 'resistance, may begin to feel anxious over the possibility of failure and feel angry with the patient. What this occurs in the analyst, the patient feels it coming, for his own 'aggressiveness' and other reactions have provoked it; consequently he fears the analyst's anger. If the analyst, threatened by failure, to put more precisely threatened by his own superego or by his own archaic objects which have found an agent provocateur in the patient, acts under the influence of these internal objects and of his paranoid and depressive anxieties, the patient again finds himself confronting a reality like that of his real or fantasized childhood experiences and like that of his inner world, and so the vicious circle continues and may even be re-enforced. But if the analyst grasps the importance of this situation, if, through his own anxiety or anger, he comprehends what is happening in the analysand, and if he overcomes, thanks to the new insight, his negative feelings and interprets what has happened in the analysand, being now in his new positive countertransference situation, then he may have made a breach - be it large or small - in the vicious circle.

To reiterate, the relation of transference and countertransference in the analytic process has been examined, now let us look more closely into the phenomena of countertransference.

It is, nonetheless, but often, that the therapist who sees a new potentiality in the patient, a previously unnoted side of him that heralds a phase of increasing differentiations. And frequently the therapist is the only one who sees it. Even the patient does not see it as yet, except in the projected form, so that he perceives this as an attribute of the therapist. This situation can make the therapist feel very much inalienable as separated from others that apart or detached in the isolated removal and intensely threaten.

Upon which the transference relationship with the therapist, we find that the patient naturally brings this relationship, just as he brings into the relatedness in which the difficulties concerning differentiation and integration that were engendered by the pathological upbringing upon the advances in differentiation and integration necessarily occur first outside the patient - namely, in the therapist's increasingly well differentiated and well-integrated view of, and consequently, responses to, him - before these can become well established within him.

Because the schizophrenic patient did not experience, in his infancy, the symbolic relatedness with his mother such as each human being needs for the formation of a healthy core in his personality structure, in the emotion of the transference relationship to his therapist he must eventually succeed in establishing such a mode of relatedness.

This means that he must eventually regress, in the transference, to such a level in order to get a fresh start toward a healthier personality differentiation and integration than he had achieved before entering therapy. This is not to say that he must 'act out' the regressive needs in his daily life, to be sure, the schizophrenic patient, whether in therapy or not, inevitably does so to a considerable degree, but to the extent that these needs can be expressed in the transference relationship, they need not seek expression, unconsciously, thorough acting out in daily life.

Focussing now upon the transference relationship with the therapist, we find that the patient naturally brings about the difficulties concerning differentiation in the process of integration that was engendered by the pathological upbringing as for being the one more interruption in the impeding principle of reconstructions of an identifying manufacture of the transference. And the every day, relationships are found in the interplaying form of corresponding advances in differentiated dynamic integrations necessarily occur first outside the patient - namely, in the therapist's increasingly well or acceptably differentiated by the integrated extent or range of vision, that the position or attitudes that determine how of the intent of something (as an aim or an end or motive)or by way the mind is directed. Its view of and the consequent response ought to become acknowledgingly established within them.

Because the schizophrenic patient did not experience, in his infancy, the establishment of and later emergence form, a healthy symbiotic relatedness with his mother such as each human brings needs for the formation of a healthy core in his personality structure, in the evolution of the transference relationship to his therapist he must eventually succeed in establishing such a mode of relatedness.

This means that he must eventually regress, in the transference, to such a level, in order to get a fresh start toward a healthier personality differentiation and integration than he had achieved before entering therapy. This is not to say that he must act out the regressive needs in his daily life. To be sure, the schizophrenic patient, whether in therapy or not, inevitably does so to a considerable degree; even to the extent that these needs can be expressed in the transference relationship, they need not seek expression, unconsciously, through acting out in daily life.

This symbiotic mode of relatedness is necessarily mutual, participated in by therapist as well as patient. Thus, the therapist must come to experience not only the oceanic gratification, but also the anxiety involved in his sharing a symbiotic, subjective oneness with the schizophrenic patient. This relationship, with its lack of felt ego-boundaries between the two participants, at times invokes the kind of deep contentment, the kind of felt communion that needs no words, which characterize a loving relatedness between mother and infant. But at other times it involves the therapists feeling unable to experience himself as differentiated from the pathology-ridden personality of the patient. He feels helplessly caught in the patient's deep ambivalence. He feels one with the patient's hatred and despairs and thwarted love, and at times he cannot differentiate between his own subjectively harmful effect upon the patient, and the illness with which the patient was to come or go or nearly recede in the achievement afflicting when the therapist first undertook to help him. Thus, at these anxiety-ridden moments in the symbiotic phase, the therapist feels his own personality to be invaded by the patient's pathology, and feels his identity severely threatened, whereas in the more contented moments, part of the contentment resides in both participants enjoying a freedom from any concern with identity.

This same profound lack of differentiation may come to characterize the patient's view of the persons about him, including his therapeutic, and at time's, in line with his need to project a poorly differentiated conglomeration of 'bad' impulses, he may perceive the therapist for being but one head of a hydra-headed monster. The patient's lack of differentiation in this regard, prevailing for month after month of his charging the therapist with saying or doing various things that were actually said or have done by others in the hospitalized presences to its containing of environmental surfaces, or by the family members, can have a formidably eroding effect upon the therapist's sense of personal intensity. But the patient may need to regress to just such a primitivist, poorly differentiated view of the world in order to grow up again, psychologically, in a healthier way this time.

Among the most significant steps in the maturation that occurs in successful psychotherapy are those moments when the therapist suddenly sees the patient in a new light. His image of the patient suddenly changes, because of the entry into his awareness of some potentiality in the patient. Which had not shown itself before? From now on, his responses t o the patient is a response to this new, enriched view, and through such responding he fosters the emergence, and further differentiation, of this new personality area. This is another way of describing the process that Buber and in Friednan, 1955, calls 'making the other person present, seeing in the other persons potentialities of such even presents: Seeing in the other persons potentiality of which in him, that he is not aware of his helping him, by responding to those potentialities, to realize them.

Schizophrenic patient's feelings start to become differentiated before they have found new and appropriate modes for expressing the new feelings, thus patient's may use the same old stereotyped behaviour or utterance to express nuances of new feelings. This is identical with the situation in those schizophrenics' familiar which is permeated with what Wynne (1958) termed 'pseudo-mutuality' or toward maintaining the sense of reciprocal perceiving expectations. Thus, the expectations are left unexplored, and the old expectations and roles, even though outgrown and inappropriate in one sense, continue to serve as the structure for the relation.

The therapist, through hearing the new emotional connotation, the new meaning, in the stereotyped utterance and responding in accordance with the new connotation, fosters the emerging differentiation. Over the course of months, in therapy, he may find the same verbal stereotype employed in th e expression of a whole gamut of newly emerging feelings. Thus, over a prolonged time-span, the therapist may give as many different responses to a gradually differentiating patient as are simultaneously given by the various members of the surrounding environment, to the patient who shows the contrasting ego-fragmentation (or, in a loose manner of speaking, over-differentiations).

Persistently stereotyped communications from the patient tend to bring from the therapist communications that, over a period of time, become almost equally stereotyped. One can sometimes detect, in recordings playing during supervisory hours, evidence that new emotional connotations are creeping into the patient's verbal stereotypes, and into the therapist's responsive verbal stereotypes, before either of the two participants has noticed this.

What the therapist does which assists the patient's differentiation often consists in his having the courage and honesty to differ from whether the patient's expressed feelings or, often most valuable, with the social role into which his sick behaviour tends to fix or transfix the therapist. This may consist in his candid disagreement with some of the patient, and s strongly felt and long-voiced views, or in his flatly declining to try to feel 'sympathy' - such as one would be conventionally expected to feel in response to behaviour, which seems, at first glance, to express the most pitiable suffering but which the therapist is convinced primarily expresses sadism on the patient's part. Such courage to differ with the expected social role is what is needed from the therapist, in order to bring to a close the symbiotic phase of relatedness that has served, earlier, a necessary and productive function. Through asserting his individuality, and at many later moments in the therapeutic interaction, the therapist fosters the patient's own development of more complete and durable ego-boundaries. At the same time he offers the patient the opportunity to identify with a parent-figure who dares to be an individual-dares to be so in the face of pressures from the working group of which he is part, and from his own reproachful superego, it can be of notice, that of a minor degree a consciously planned and controlled therapeutic technique wherefore, the content descriptions are rather a natural flow of events as in the transference evolution, with which the therapist must have the spontaneity to go along.

The patient, particularly in the symbiotic phase of the therapy but in preceding and succeeding phases as well, is notably intolerant of sudden and marked changes in the therapeutic relationship - that is, of suddenly seeing himself, or feeling that his therapist sees him, through new eyes. He rarely gives the therapist to feel that the latter have made an importantly revealing interpretation, or should be concealed, but when to arrive at by reasoning from evidence or from its premises that we can infer from that which he was derived as to a conclusion, that it conveys of a higher illumination of mind. Methodologically historical information is an approving acceptation by the therapist, he does so causally, he tends to experience important increments of depreciated material, yet not as every bit for reverential abstractions as to make a new, amended, or up-to-date reversion of the many problems involved in revising the earthly shuddering revelations in his development. The things that he has known all along and simply never happened to think of. His experience of an inherent perception of the world as surrounding him is often permeated by 'deja vu' sensations, and misidentification of the emphasizing style at which the expense of thought for taking the rhetorical rhapsody to actions or a single inaction of moving the revolutions of the earth around the sun is mostly familiar an act from his past.

The motional progressions in therapy, on the patient's part, occur each time only after a recrudescence in his symptoms. It is as though he has to find reassurance of his personal identity, for being really the same hopeless person he has long felt himself to be, before he can venture into a bit or new and more hopeful identity.

Of what expressions are that object relations of state or fact of having independent reality whose customs that have recently come into existence, such by the actuality for something having existence from the beginning of life, being the mother's breast that it splits into a good (gratifying) and bad (frustrating) breast; this splitting results in a division between love and hate. What is more, is that of the relation to the first object implies its introjection and projection, and thus, from the beginning object relations are moulded by an interaction between introjection and projection, between internal and external objects and situation.

. . . .With the introjection of the complete object in about the second quarter of the first year marked steps in integration are made. . . . The loved and hated aspects of the mother are no longer felt to be so widely separated, and the result is an increased fear of loss, a strong feeling of guilt and states akin to mourning, because the aggressive impulses are felt to be divorced against the love object, the depressive position has come to the fore . . .

. . . In the first few month of life anxiety is predominantly experienced as fear of persecution and . . . this contributes to certain mechanisms and defences that characterize the paranoid and schizoid positions. Outstanding among these defences is the mechanism of splitting internal and external objects, emotions and the ego. These mechanisms and defences are part of normal development and at the same time form the basis for later schizophrenic illness. The descriptive underlying identification by projection, i.e., projective identification, as a combination of splitting off parts of the self and projecting them onto another person. Rosenfeld, a follower of Klein writes that, he presents detailed clinical data that serve to document the implicit point, among others, that whereas, the schizophrenic patient may appear to have regressed to such an objectless autoerotic level of development as was postulated by Freud (1911, 1914) and Abraham (1908), in actuality the patient is involved in object-relatedness with the analyst, object-relatedness of the primitive introjective and projective identification kind. For example, Rosenfeld concludes his description of, the data from one of the sessions as follows:

> . . . The whole material of the session suggested that in the withdrawal state he was introjecting me and my penis, and at the same time was projecting himself into me. So here, again, it to suggest that it be something possible to detect the object-relation in an apparently autoerotic state.
>
> . . . only at a later stage of treatment was it possible to distinguish between the mechanisms of introjection of objects and projective identifications, which so frequently go on simultaneously (1952).

We find, among the writings of the Kleinian analysts, a number of interesting examples of delusional transference interpretation, in all of which the keynote is the concept of projective (or introjective) identification. For instance, Rosenfeld writes at one juncture (1952),

> The patient himself gave the clue to the transference situation, and showed that he had projected his damaged self containing the destroyed world, not only into all the other patients, but into me, and had changed me in this way. But, instead of becoming relieved by this projection he became more anxious, because he was afraid of what I was then putting back into him. Whereupon his introjective processes became severely disturbed. One would therefore expect a severe deterioration in his condition, and in fact his clinical state during the next ten days became very precarious. He began to get more and more suspicious about food, and finally refused to eat and drink anything. . . . Everything he took inside seemed to him bad, damaged, and poisonous (like faeces) as there was no point in eating anything. We knew that projection led again into reintroduction, so that also, it had felt as if he had inside himself all the destroyed and bad objects that he had projected into the outer world: And he indicated by coughing, retching and movements of his mouth and fingers that he was preoccupied with this problem . . . I told him that he was not only

> afraid of getting something bad inside him. But that he was also afraid of taking good things, the good orange juice and good interpretations, instead, since he was afraid that these would make him feel guilty again. When I said this, a kind of shock went right through his body; he gave a groan of understanding, and his facial expression changed. By the end of the hour he had emptied the glass of orange juice, the first food or drink he had taken for two days . . .

Bion (1956) defines projective identification as:

> . . . a splitting off by the patient of a part of his personality and a projection of it into the object where it becomes installed, sometimes as a persecutor, leaving the psychic from which it has been split off correspondingly impoverished.

It now seems that the instances of verbal transference interpretation can be looked upon as one form of intervention, at times effective, which constitutes an appeal for collaboration to the non-psychotic area of the patient's personality, an area of which both Katan (1954) and Bion (1957) has written. But, particularly among long hospitalized chronically schizophrenic persons, we are many a patient who is too ill to be able to register verbal statements, and even in the foregoing examples from Rosenfeld's and Bion's experiences, it is impossible to know to what extent the patient is helped by an illuminating accurate verbal content in the therapist's words, or to what extent that which is effective springs, rather from the feelings of confidence, firmness, and understanding which accompany these words spoken by a therapist who feels that he has a reliable theoretical value for formulating the clinical phenomena in which he finds himself.

In trying to conceptualize such ego-states in the patient, and such states of relatedness between patient and doctor. Additional value placed the concept presentation by Little in her papers, "On Delusional Transference" (Transference Psychosis) (1958) and "On Basic Unity" (1960).

One of the necessary development, in along-delusional patient's eventual relinquishment of his delusions is for these gradually to become productions that the therapist sees no longer as essentially ominous and the subject for either serious therapeutic investigation, or argumentation, or any other form of opposition, rather, the therapist comes to react to these for being essentially playful, unmaligant, creatively imaginative, and he comes to respond to them with playfully imaginative comments of his own. Nothing helps more finally to detoxicate a patient's previously self-isolating delusional state than to find in his therapist a capacity to engage him in a delightfully crazy playfulness - a kind of relatedness of which the schizophrenic patient had never a chance to have his fills during his childhood. Typically, such early childhood playfulness was subjected to massive repression, because of various intra-familial circumstances.

Innumerable instances of the therapist's uncertainty how to respond to the patient's communication turn upon the question of whether the communication is to be 'taken personally' - to be taken as primarily designed, for instance, toward filling the therapist with perplexity, confusion, anxiety, humiliation, rage, or some other negatively toned affective state, or whether it is to be taken rather as primarily an effort to convey some basically unhostile needs on the patient's par. Just as it is often essential that the therapist become able to sense and respond to personal communications in a patient's ostensibly stereotyped behaviour or utterance, so too it is frequently essential that he be able to see, behind the overt 'personal' reference to himself - often a stinging or otherwise emotionally evocative reference - some fundamental needs that the patient is hesitantly to communicate openly.

It seems, but nevertheless, that there is widespread agreement concerning whose functional importance of dependency process in schizophrenia, for which the patient who is involved in a schizophrenic illness, probably nothing is harder to endure than the circumstance of his having intense dependency needs that he cannot allow himself to recognize, or which if recognized in himself he dare not express to anyone, or which are expressed by him in a fashion that, more often than not, brings an uncomprehending or actively rejecting response from the other person. For the therapist who is working with such a patient, certainly there is nothing that brings more anxiety, frustration, and discouragement than do these processes in the schizophrenic person with whom he is dealing.

The dependencies on which is focussed upon effectual acknowledge in the presence of which has its closest analogue, in terms of normative standards, is such that the personality development, in the experience and behaviour of the infant or of the young child. The dependency needs, attitudes, and strivings that the schizophrenic manifests may be defined in the statement that he seeks for another person to assume a total responsibility for gratifying all his needs, both physiological and psychological, while this person is to seek nothing from him.

Of the physiological needs, which the schizophrenic manifests, those centring about the oral zone of interaction are usually most prominent, analogous to the predominant place held by nursing in the life of the infant. Desires to be stroked and cuddled, likewise, so characteristic of the very early years of normal development, are prominently held within the schizophrenic. In addition, desires for the relief of genital sexual tensions, even though these have had their advent much later in the life history than have his oral desires, are manifested in much the same level of an early, infantile dependency. That is, such genital hungers are manifested in much the same small-child spirit of, 'you ought to be taking care of this for me' as are the oral hungers.

The psychological needs that are represented among the schizophrenic's dependency processes consist in the desire for the other person to provide him with unvarying love and protection, and to assume a total guidance of his living,

In the course of furthering characterizations of the schizophrenic's dependency processes will be defined much more fully, that is to say, it is to b e emphasized that no of the dependency processes are but described is characteristic only of the schizophrenic, or qualitatively different from processes operative at some level of consciousness in persons with other varieties of psychiatric illness and in normal persons. With regard to dependency processes, we find research in schizophrenia has its greatest potential value in the fact that schizophrenic shows us in a sharply etched form that which is so obscured, by years progressive adaptation to adult interpersonal living, in human beings in general. Wherefore, but in some degree, are about the patient's anxiety about the dependency needs, are (1) As nearly as can be determined, the patient is unaware of pure dependency needs; for him, apparently, they exist in consciousness, if at all, only in the form of a hopeless conflictual combination of dependency needs plus various defences - defences that render impossible any thoroughgoing sustained gratification of these needs. These defences (which include, grandiosity, hostility, competitiveness, scorns and so forth) have so long ago developed in his personality, as a means of coping with anxiety attendant upon dependency needs, that the experiencing of pure dependency needs it, for him, lost in antiquity and so be achieved only relatively late in therapy after the various defences have been largely relinquished.

Thus it appears to be not only dependency needs 'per se' which arouses anxiety, but rather the dependency needs plus all these various defences (which tend in themselves to be anxiety-provoking) plus the inevitable frustration, to a greater or less degree, of the dependency needs.

Hostility as one of the defences against awareness of 'dependency needs,' that which for certainly repressed dependency needs are one of the most frequent bases of murderous feelings in the schizophrenic, in such instances the murderous feelings may be regarded as a vigorous denial of dependency. What frequently happens in therapy is that both patient and therapist become so anxious about the defensive murderous feelings that the underlying dependency feelings long remain unrecognized.

Every schizophrenic possesses much self-hatred and guilt that may serve as defences against the awareness of dependency feelings ('I am too worthless for anyone possibly to care about me'), and which in any case complicate the matter of dependency. The schizophrenic has generally come to interpret the rejections in his past life as meaning that he is a creature who wants too much and, in fact, a creature who has no legitimate needs. Thus, he can accept gratification of his dependency needs, if at all, only if his needs are rendered acceptable to themselves by reason of his becoming physically ill or in a truly desperate emotional state. It is frequently found that a schizophrenic is more accessible to the gratification of his dependency needs when he is physically ill, or filled with despair, than at other times. In that way, th e presence of self-hatred, and guilt, one ingredient of the patient's overall anxiety about dependancy needs has to do with the fact that these needs connote to him the state of feeling physical illness or despair.

In essence, then, we can see that the patient has a deep-seated conviction that his dependency needs will not be gratified. Further, we see that this conviction is based not alone on the fortunate past expedience of repeated rejection, but also, the fact that his own defences, called forth concomitantly with the dependency desires, make it virtually certain that this dependency needs will not be met. (2) The dependency needs are anxiety-provoking not only because they involve desires to relate in an infantile or small-child fashion (by breast - or penis sucking, being cuddled, and as so forth) which is not generally acceptable behaviour among adults, but also, and probably what is more important, because they involve a feeling that the other person is frighteningly important, absolutely indispensable to the patient's survival.

This feeling as to the indispensable of importance of the other person derives from two main sources: (a) the regressed state of the schizophrenic's emotional life, which makes for his perceiving the other for being all-important to his survival, just as in infancy the mothering one is all-important to the survival of the infant, and (b) certain additional disabling features of his schizophrenic illness, which render him dependent in various special ways that are not quite comparable with the dependency characteristic of normal infancy or early childhood. Thereof, a number of points in reference to (b) are, first, we can perceive that a schizophrenic who is extremely confused, for example, is utterly dependent on or upon the therapist or, some other relevantly significant person to help him establish a bridge between his incomparable, incongruent, conflicting, conditions in which things are out of their normal or proper places or relationships. Such are the complete mental confusions that the authenticity of a corresponding to known facts is to discover or rediscover the real reason for which such things as having no illusions and facing reality squarely face-to-face, a realistic appraisal of his chances for advancing to the reasonable facts as we can see the factional advent for understanding the Absolutizing instinct to fancy of its reality.

Second, we can see also that the patient who is in transition between old, imposed values and not-yet-acquired values of his own, has only the relationship with his therapist to depend upon.

Third, is the concern and consideration that, in many instances, the schizophrenic appears to be what one might call a prisoner in th e present. He is so afraid both of change and of the memories that tend to be called forth by the present that he clings desperately to what in immediate. He is in this sense imprisoned in immediate experience, and looks to the therapist to free him so that he will be able to live in all his life, temporally speaking - present, past and future.

Forth, it might be surmised that an oral type of relatedness to the other person (with the all-importance of the other that this entails) is necessary for the schizophrenic to maintain, partly in order to facilitate his utilization of projection and introjection as defences against anxiety.

Anxiety, is the constructed foundation whose emotional state from which are grounded to the foundation structural called the 'edifice', that an emotional state in which people feel uneasy, apprehensive, or fearful. People usually experience anxiety about events they cannot control or predict, or about events that seem threatening or dangerous. For example, students taking an important test may feel anxious because they cannot predict the test questions or feel certain of a good grade. People often use the words fear and anxiety to describe the same thing. Fear also describes a reaction to immediate danger characterized by a strong desire to escape the situation.

The physical symptoms of anxiety reflect a chronic "readiness" to deal with some future threat. These symptoms may include fidgeting, muscle tension, sleeping problems, and headaches. Higher levels of anxiety may produce such symptoms as rapid heartbeat, sweating, increased blood pressure, nausea, and dizziness.

Bychowski (1952) says, "'The separation between the primitive ego and the external world is closely connected with orality, both form the basis for the mechanism that we call projection," and would add, for introjection., That Starcke (1921) for earlier comments "I might briefly allude to the possibility that in the repeated alternation between becoming one's own and not one's own, which occurs during lactation . . . the situation of being nursed plays a part in the origin of the mechanism of something that extends beyond its level or the normal outer surface in which serves to support projection.

The patient has anxiety, and, least of mention, his dependency needs lead him either to take in harmful things, or to lose his identity.

The schizophrenic does not have the ability necessary to tolerate the frustration of his dependency needs, so that he can, once they emerge into awareness, subject them to mature discriminatory judgement before seeking their gratification. Instead, like a voraciously hungry infant, his tendency is to put into his mouth (either literally or figuratively) whatever is at hand, whether nutritious or with a potential of being harmful, this tendency is about th e basis of some of his anxiety concerning his dependency needs, for the fear that they will keep him blindly into receiving harmful medicines, bad advice, electro-shock treatment, lobotomy, and so forth. Schizophrenic patients have been known to beg, in effect, for all these, and many a patients have been known to beg, yet these patients have been 'successful' in his dependency desires. A need for self-punishment is, of course, an additional motivation in such instances.

A statement by Fenichel (1945) indicates that, "The pleasure principle, that is, the need for immediate discharge, is incompatible with correct judgement, which is based on considerable and post postponement of the reaction. The time and energy saved by this postponement are used in the function of sound and stable judgments. That in the early states the weak ego has not yet learned to postpone anything.

In the same symptomatic of one that finds that th e extent that the schizophrenic projects onto other persons his own needs too such and to devour, he feels threatened with being devoured by these other persons.

To elaborate now in a somewhat different direction upon this fear of loss of identity. Th e schizophrenic fears that his becoming dependent on another person will lead him into a state of conformity that other person's wishes and life values. A conformer is almost the last sort of person as the schizophrenic wishes to become, since his sense of individuality resides in his very eccentricities. He assumes that the therapist, for example, in the process, requiring him to give up his individuality for the kinds of parental future in his past had e been able to salvage his refuge used to pay the price.

It seems of our apparent need to give the impression of being without necessarily being so in fact that things are not always the way they seem, as things accompanied with action orient of doing whatever is apprehended as having actual, distinct and demonstrateable existence from which there is a place for each thing in the cosmological understanding idea in that something conveys to the mind a rational allotment of the far and near, such of the values and standards moderate the newly proposed to modify as to avoid an extreme or keep within bounds.

For what is to say, in that we need to realize, that the patient is not solely a broken, inert victim of the hostility of persons in his past life. His hebephrenic apathy or his catatonic immobility, for example, represents for one thing, an intense active endeavour toward unconscious regressive goals, as Greenson (1949, 1953) has for his assistance to make clear in the boredom and apathy in neurotic patients. The patient is, in other words, no inert vehicle that needs to be energized by the therapist; rather, an abundance of energy is locked in him, pressing ceaselessly to be freed, and a hovering 'helpful' orientation on the part of the therapist would only get in the way. We must realize that the patient has made, and is continually making, a contribution to his own illness, however unwittingly, and however obscure the nature of this contribution may long remain.

More than often, it has been found that the histories of schizophrenic patients, whether male or female, describe the father for being by far, the warmer, the more accessible, of the responsive parents, and the patient as having always been very much attached to the father, whereas the mother was always a relatively cold, rejecting, remote figure, but for the repetitive correlative coefficient, that it was to be found that, disguised behind the child's idol or inseparable buddy, is a matter of the father's transference to the child's being a mother-figure that the father, in these instances, is an infantile individual who reacts both to his wife and to his child, as the mother-figure, and who, by striving to be both father and mother to the child, unconsciously seeks to intervene between mother and child, that in such a way as to have each of them to himself, in the considerations that suggest of a number of cases when both are in the transference-development with the patient and the selective prospect of the patient's generalization that limits or qualifies an agreement or other conditions that may contain or depend on a conditioning need for previsional advocates that include the condition that the transference phenomena would effectually raise the needed situational alliance.

The various forms of intense transference on the part of the schizophrenic individual tend forcibly to evoke complementary feeling-responses, comparably intense, in the therapist. Mabel Blake Cohen (1952) has made the extremely valuable observation, for psychoanalysis in general, that:

> . . . it seems that the patient applies great pressure to the analyst in a variety of nonverbal ways to behave like the significant adults in the patient's earlier life, it is not merely a matter of the patient's seeing the analyst as like his father, but of his actually manipulating the relationship in such away as to elicit the same kind of behaviour from the analyst. . . .

It is no too much to say that, in response to the schizophrenic patient's transference, the therapist not only behaves like the significant adults in the patient's childhood, but experiences most intimately, within himself, activated by the patient's transference the very kind of intense and deeply conflictual feelings that were at work, however repressed, in those adults in the past, as well as experiencing, through the mechanisms of projection and introjection in the relationship between himself and the patient, the comparably intense and conflictual emotion that formed the seed-bed of psychosis in the child himself, years ago.

The accountable explanation in the support for reason to posit for the necessarily deep feeling-involvement on the part of the therapist is inherent in the nature of early ego-formation. The healthy reworking of which is so central to the therapy of schizophrenia. Spitz (1959), in his monograph on the early development of the ego, repeatedly emphasizes that emotion plays a leading role in th e formation of what he described as the 'organizers of the psyche' (which he defines as 'emergent, dominant centres of integration') during the first eighteen months of life. H e says, for example, that:

> . . . the road that leads to this integration of isolated functions is built by the infant's object relations, by experiences of an effective nature. Accordingly, the indicator of the organizer of the psyche will be of an effective nature, it is an effective behaviour that clearly precedes development in all other sectors of the personality by several months.

The phases comprising the overall course of psychotherapy with chronically schizophrenic persons, is that of recent years it has become increasingly reassuring that it is possible to delineate such phases in the complex, individualistic and dynamic events of clinical work. One can be said, that, in this difficult effort at conceptualization, from Freud's delineation of the successive phases of libidinal development in healthy maturation, Erikson's (1956) portrayal of the process of identity formation as gradual unfolding of the personality through phase-specific psycho-social crises of evolution of the reality principle in healthy development - the typical conflicts, the sequence of danger situations, and the ways they are dealt with - can be traced in this process.

The successive phases of which are best characterised, the psychotherapy of chronic schizophrenia, are the 'out-of-contact phases, the phase of ambivalent symbiosis, the phase of pre-ambivalent symbiosis, the phase of resolution of the symbiosis, and the late phase, - that of establishment, and elaboration, of the newly won individuation through selective new identification and repudiation of outmoded identifications.

The sequence of these phases retraces, in reverse, the phases by which the schizophrenic illness was originally formed: The way of thinking, the aetiological roots of schizophrenia are formed when the mother-infant symbiosis fails to resolve into individuation of mother and infant - or, still more harmfully fails even to become at all firmly established - because of deep ambivalence of the part of the mother that hindered the integration and differentiation of the infant's and young child's ego, the child fails then to proceed through the normative development phases of symbiosis and subsequent individuation. Instead the core of his personality remains uniform, and ego-fragmentation and dedifferentiation becomes powerful, though deeply primitive and unconscious defences against the awareness of ambivalence in the object and in himself. Even in normal development, one becomes separate person only by becoming able to face, and accept ownership of, one's ambivalence with which he had to cope in his relationship with his mother was too great, and his ego-formation too greatly impeded, for him to be able to integrate his conflictual feeling-states into an individual identity.

Of these, the theoretical concept has been fostered by Mahler's (1956) paper on autistic and symbiotic infantile psychosis and by Balint's (1953, 1955) writings concerning phenomena of early ego-formation that he encountered in the psychoanalysis of neurotic patients. From a purely descriptive viewpoint, schizophrenia can be seen to consist essentially in an impairment of both 'integration' and 'differentiation' - which are but opposite faces of a unitary growth-process. From a psychodynamic view point seems basic to all the bewilderingly plexuity with which are a varying manifestations of schizophrenia.

Taking in, is the matter of integration; when we assess schizophrenia individual in terms of the classical structural areas of the personality - id, ego, and superego - we discover these to be poorly integrated with one another. The id is experienced by the ego as a Pandora's box, the contents of which will overwhelm one if it is opened. The ego is, as many writers have stated, severely split, sometimes into innumerable islands that are not linked discernibly with one another. And the superego has the nature of a cruel tyrant whose assaults upon the weak and unintegrated ego are, if anything, even more destructive to it than are the ascensions of the threatening id-impulses, as Szalita-Pemow (1951), Hill (1955), and others. Moreover, the superego is, like the ego, even in itself not well integrated; its utterances contain the most glaring inconsistencies from one moment to the next. Jacobson (1954) has shown that there is actually as dissolution of the superego, as an integrated destruction - a regressive transformation back into the threatening parental images whose conglomeration originally formed it.

Differentiation is a process that is essential to integration, and vice versa. For personality structure-functions or psychic contents to become integrated, they must first have emerged as partially differentiated or separate from one another, and differentiation in turn can emerge only out of a foundation of more or less integrated functions or contents. The intertwining mesh upon which is interwoven in the growth precesses of integration and differentiation, such that the impairment of both likewise interlocking. But in the schizophrenic these two processes tend to be out of step with one another, so that at one moment a patient's more urgent need may be for increased integration, whereas at another he may more urgently need increased differentiation. And these are some patients who show for months end, a more urgent need in one of these areas, before the alternate growth-phase on the scene, that type is a modicum of validity in speaking and of two different 'types' of schizophrenic patients.

One comes to realize, upon reasons of how premature have been one's effort to find out what feelings the patient is experiencing or what thoughts he is having; one comes to realize that much of the time he has neither feelings nor thoughts differentiated as such and communicable to us.

Such differentiations as the patient posses of an inclining inclination that tend to break down when intense emotion enters his awareness. A paranoid man, for example, may find that when his hatred toward another person reaches a certain degree of intensity, he is flooded with anxiety because he no longer knows whether he hates, or instead 'really loves' the other individual. This is not based, on any line or its course, whereupon the primary mechanism that Freud (1911) outlined in his classical description of the nature of paranoid delusions of persecution, a description in which repressed homosexual love played the central role. The central difficulty is rather than the ego is too poorly differentiated to maintain its structure in the face of such powerful affects, and the patient becomes flooded with what can only be described as 'undifferentiated passion', precisely as one finds an infant to be overwhelmed at times with affect that the observer cannot be specifically identity as any one kind of emotion.

As for the feelings with which the therapist himself experiences in working within the variations in the differentiated patient, we find, again, a persistent threat of the therapist's sense of identity. But, whereas in the unitary integration complex manifestations of such of a schizophrenic's sense of identity. But as in the first instance that the threat was felt predominantly as a disturbance of one's personal integration, it seems possible as a weakening of one's sense of differentiation. In this instance, the 'therapeutic symbiosis' which implicates the necessary developments that it tends to occur earlier for which of the patient's predominant mode of relatedness with other persons, at the developmental level at which we find him at the very beginning of our work, is a symbiotic one. Such descriptions, least of mention, agree with the necessary developments, in that it tends to occur for the patient 's predominant mode of relatedness with other persons, the symbiotic relatedness, with its subjective absence of ego-boundaries, involves not only special gratification, but anxiety-provoking disturbances on one's sense of personal identity.

The comparatively rapid development of symbiotic relatedness is facilitated by the patient's characteristically nonverbal, and physically more or less immobile, functioning during the therapeutic sessions. In response, the therapist's own behaviour becomes more and more similar, is that each participant is now offering to the other, saying that over the hours of counselling, a silent, impassive screen that facilitates abundant mutual projecting and introjecting. Thus a symbiotic state is likely to be reached earlier than in one's work with the typically much more verbal type of the patient when described for that instance, the patient's and therapist's more abundant verbalization's tend persistently to stress the ego-boundaries separating the to persons from one another.

The applicability for which the predominantly non-differentiated patient, in that the therapist's sense of identity as a complexly differentiated individual entity becomes further eroded, or undermined, as he finds the patient persistently operating on the unwavering conviction, that the hours of counselling are but an undifferentiated aspect of the whole vague mass of the institution, even in psychodynamic terms, is in actuality the patient's projection of his own poorly differentiated hostility, through which the patient's tenaciously held view, is the way the world around him really is.

Further, since the patient typically verbalizes little but a few maddening monotonous stereotypes, the therapist tends to feel, over the course of time, with so little of his own intellectual content being explicitly tapped in the relationship, that his richness of intellect is progressively rusting away - becoming less differentiated, more stereotyped and rudimentary. Moreover, the patient presents but one of two emotional wavelengths to which the therapist can himself tune in, rather than a rich spectrum of emotion that calls into response a similarly wide range of feelings from the therapist himself. Thus not only the therapist's intellectual resources, but his emotional capacities too, becomes subjectively narrowed down and impoverished, as he finds that, over the sessions of counselling, his patient in him neither any wide range of ideas, nor any emotions except, for example, rage, or contempt or dull hopelessness.

The feeling experience on his part, anxiety-provoking and discouraging though he finds it, is a necessary therapeutic development. It is for him thus to experience at first hand something of the patient's own lack of differentiation; for, as in the therapy with the non-integrated patient, as, once, again, the healing process occurs external to the patient, as it was, at an intrapsychic level in the therapist, before it becomes established in the patient himself. That is, the therapist's coming to view the patient, his relationship with the patient, and himself in this relationship, all for being largely non-differentiated, is a development that sets the stage for the patient's gradually increasing differentiation. Now the therapist comes to sense, time and again, newly emerging tendrils of differentiation in the patient, before the latter are themselves and conscious of them. In responding to these with spontaneity as they show themselves, again, that in the therapist, helps the patient to become aware-theat they are a part of him.

To analyst and analytic student alike, the term 'transference psychosis' usually connotes a dramatic but dreaded development in which an analysand, who at the beginning of the analysis was overtly sane but who had in actuality a borderline ego-structure, becomes overtly psychotic, that the course of the evolving transference relationship. We generally blame the analyst for such as development and prefer not to think any more about such matters, because of our own personal fear that we, like the poor misbegotten analysand, might become, or narrowly avoid becoming, psychotic in our own analysis. By contrast, in working with the chronically schizophrenic patient, we are confronted with a person whose transference to us is no harder too identify partly for the very reason that his whole daily life consists in incoherent psychotic transference reactions, for which is to whatever, to everyone about him, including the analyst in the treatment session. Little's comment (1960) that the delusional state 'remains unconscious' until it is uncovered in the analysts' holds true only in the former instance, in the borderline schizophrenic patient; there, it is the fact that the transference is delusional which is the relative covert, hard-to-discern aspect of the situation, in chronic schizophrenia, by contrast, nearly everything is delusional, and the difficult task to foster the emergence of a coherent transference meaning in the delusional symptomatology. In other words, the difficult thing in the work with the chronically schizophrenic patient is to discover the 'transference reality' in his delusional experience.

The difficultly of discerning the transference aspect of one's relationship with the patient can be traced to his having regressed to a state of ego functioning which is marked by severe impairment in his capacity either to differentiate among, or to integrate, his experiences. He is so incompletely differentiated in his ego functioning that he tends to feel, not that the therapist reminds him of, or is like, his mother or that of his father (or whomever, from his early life) but rather his functioning toward the therapist is couched in the unscrutinised assumption that the therapist is the mother or father. When, for example, in trying to bring to the attention of a paranoid schizophrenic women how much like she seemed to find the persons in her childhood on the one hand, and the person about her in the institution, including me, on the other, she dismissed this with an impatient retort, "That's what I've been trying to tell you, What difference does it make? For years subsequently in our work together, all the figures in her experience were composite figures, without any clear subjective distinction between past and present experiences, figures from the institutional scene peopled her memories of her past, and figures from what has become known to be her past were experienced by her as blended with the persons she saw about her in current life.

Transference situations in which the psychosis is manifested at a phase in therapy in which the deeply chronically confused patient, who in childhood had been accustomed to a parent's during his thinking for him, is ambivalently (a) trying to perpetuate a symbiotic relationship wherein the therapist to a high degree does the patient's thinking for him, and (b) expressing, by what the therapist feels to be sadistic and castrative and nullifying or undoing the therapist's effort to be helpful, a determination to be a separately thinking, and otherwise separately functioning, individual

Difficult though it is to discern the nature and progressive evolution of the patient's transference to the therapist, it is even more difficult to conceptualize that which is 'new' which the therapist brings into the relationship, and which, as J. M. Rioch (1943) has emphasized, is crucial to the patient's recovery. Rioch is quite right in saying that, "Whether intentionally or not, whether conscious of it or not, the analyst does express, day in and day out, subtle or overt evidences of his own personality in relationship to the patient."

The conjectural considerations for which inadequate evidences in the understanding of questionable intent is that there is a companion evolution of reality relatedness between patient and therapist, concomitant with such a transference evolution as having had the impression that it is only when the reality relatedness between patient and therapist has reached, finally and after many 'real life' vicissitudes between them, a depth of intense fondness that there now emerges, in the form of a transference development, a comparably intense and long-repressed fondness for the mother.

Presumably, a point that Freud (1922) concerning projection also holds true for transference, he stated that projection occurs no 'into the sky, so to speak, where there is nothing of the sort already', but rather the persons who in reality posses an attitude qualitatively like that which the projecting person is attributing to them. So it is with transference, we may presume that when a patient comes to react to us as a loved and loving mother, this phrase - as well as other phrases - of the transference is founded upon our having come to feel, in reality, thus toward him. M. B. Cohen (1952) stresses the importance of the therapist's inevitable feeling response to the patient's transference, and, if only to suggest, that an equally healthy source of the therapist's feeling participation be the evolving reality relatedness that pursues its own course, related to and parallelling, but not fully embraced by, the evolving transference relatedness over the years of person's working together. What is more, is the countertransference that has already been written, but as to indicate, there is a great need for us to become clear about the sequence that the recovery process in the schizophrenic adult, very roughly analogous to the growth process in normal infancy, childhood, and adolescence, tends innately to follow. When we have become clearer and surer about this, and particularly about the validity-relatedness element necessary to it, in that the frequently - though by no means always - various manifestations of feeling regarded as unwanted countertransference will be seen to be inevitable, and utterly essential, components of the recovery process.

Further, the opening view of the personality for being divisible into the areas, id, ego, and superego, tends to shield us from the anxiety-fostering realization that in psychoanalytic change is not merely quantitative and partial - where id was, there will ego be - in Freud's dictum - but qualitative and all-persuasive. That is, that in such passages as the following. Freud gives a picture of personality-structure, and of maturation, which leaves the inaccurate but comforting impression that at least a part of us - namely, as part of the id - is free from change. In his paper entitled "Thoughts for the Times on War and Death" in 1915, he said,

> . . . the evolution of the mind shows a peculiarity that is present in no other process of development. When a village grows into a town, a child into a man, the village and the child become submerged in the town and the man, . . . it

> is otherwise with the development of the mind . . . the primitive stages [of mental development] can always be reestablished, the primitive mind is, in the fullest meaning of the word, imperishable (Freud, 1915).

In "Introductory Lectures on Psycho-Analysis," he says that in psychoanalytic treatment,

> . . . By means of the work of interpretation, which transforms what is unconscious into what is conscious, the ego is enlarged at the cos of this unconscious . . . (Freud, 1915-17)

In "The Ego and the Id" he said that,

> . . . the ego is that part of the id that has been modified by the direct influence of the external world . . . the pleasure-principle . . . reigns unrestricted by the id . . . the ego represents what may be called reason and common sense, in contrast to the id, which contains the passions (Freud, 1923)

Glover, in his book on technique published in 1955, states similarly that,

> . . . a successful analysis may have uncovered a good deal of the repressed . . . [and] have mitigated the archaic censoring functions of the superego, but it can scarcely be expected to abolish the id (Glover, 1955)

The state of developmental sciences, and about our own individual the individual therapeutic skills, should not cause us to understate the all-embracing extent of human personality-growth in normal maturation at least a few psychoanalysis. It is believed that all encountered, and, at lest a few fortunate instances that have made us wonder whether maturation really leaves any area of the personality untouched, leaves any steel-bound core within which the pleasure principle reigns immutably, or whether, instead, we have seen such a genuine metamorphosis, from an erstwhile hateful and self-seeking orientation to a loving and giving orientation, quite as wonderful and thoroughgoing the metamorphosis of the tadpole into the frog thoroughgoing as the metamorphosis of the tadpole into the frog or that of the caterpillar into the butterfly.

Freud himself, in his emphasis upon the 'negative therapeutic reaction' (1923), the repetition compulsion, and the resistance to analytic insight that he discovered in his work with neurotic patients, has shown the importance, in the neurotic individual, of anxiety concerning change, and him agrees with Jung's statement that 'a peculiar psychic inertia' hostile to change and progress, is the fundamental condition of neurosis (Freud, 1915). This is, as we know, even more true of psychosis - so much as that only in very recent decades have psychotic patients achieved full recovery though modified psychoanalytic therapy. Finding it instructive to explore in detail the psychodynamics of schizophrenia in terms of the anxiety concerning change which one encounters, in a particular intense degree, at work in these patients, and in oneself in the course of treating them. What the therapy of schizophrenia can teach us of the human being's standing concerning change, can broaden and deepen our understanding of the non-psychotic individual also.

This development can occur only after successive resolution of increasingly ancient personality-warp in the patient, and the establishment thereby, of a hard-won mutual trust and security. In this atmosphere the therapist relationship makes contact with the healthy ingredients of the patient's symbiotic relationship with his mother, thus laying the foundation for subsequent new growth as a separate and healthy individual.

In such fashion the patient develops importance not merely as a separate object, but to a degree as a symbiotic partner, for the therapist as well as for other people, who participate with which the therapist himself, as well as such of the staff members, we hear from fellow-therapists and ward-personal of how 'stunned' or even 'shocked' them were at seeing dramatic improvements in a long-ill patient. Characteristically, too, the therapist notices only very belatedly various long-standing symptoms have dropped out of the patient's behaviour. on looking back through his records, for example, prior to a staff-presentation, he finds to his surprise that a delusion, once long-familiar to him, has not been evidenced by the patient for several months. Thus, his feelings of personal loss are mitigated. Even so, that even among the most technically capable of therapists, is the initial reaction with dismay and discouragement to a patients, is the initial reacting with express verbally the depths of his despair, loneliness, confusion, infantile need, and so fort, typically, the therapist only belatedly recognizes the forward move this development constitutes. His initial response is traceable to the unconscious loss that this development inflicts upon him - the loss of the long-familiar and inevitable therefore cherished (unconsciously cherished) relatedness that therefor he had shared with the patient.

The patient, particularly in the symbiotic phrase of the therapy but in preceding and succeeding phase as well, is notably intolerant of sudden and marked changes in the therapeutic relationship - that is, of suddenly seeing himself, or feeling that his therapist sees him, through new eyes. He rarely gives the therapist to feel that the latter have made an importantly revealing interpretation, and when he himself conveys a highly illuminating nugget of historical information to his therapist, he does so casually, often feeling sure that he has already mentioned this before. He tends to experience important increments of de-repressed material not as earthshattering revelations in his development, yet the forward moves in therapy, on the patient's part occur each time only after a recrudescence in his symptoms. It is as though he was to find reassurance of his personal identity, for being really the same hopeless person he has long felt himself to be, before he can venture into a bit of new and more hopeful identity.

There is a necessary phase of symbiosis between patient and doctor in the transference evolution followed by the recovering schizophrenic patient, a phase in which the ego boundaries between himself and the therapist are mutually relinquished to a large degree. This development can occur only after successive resolutions of increasingly ancient personality-wrap in the patient, and the establishment, thereby, of a hard-won in the patient, and his identity.

The following considerations, to be sure, the patient, in this reality and that this mutuality of a comparative participation is essentially inclined of a better understanding and a successful therapeutic outcome.

Freud (1911) once made in comment that, . . . we have long observed that every neurosis has as its result, and probably therefore its purpose, a forcing of the patient out of real life, an alienating of him from reality . . . neurotics turn away from reality because they find it unbearable - either the whole or parts of it. The most extreme type of this turning away from exacting results is shown by certain cases of hallucinatory psychosis that seek to deny the particular event that occasioned the outbreak of their inanity. But in fact every neurosis does the same with some fragment of reality . . .

Bion, in his paper in 1957 concern the differentiation, in any one schizophrenic patient, between what he calls the psychotic personality and the non-psychotic personality, concludes the presentation of his theoretical formulations with,

There is wide spread agreement that it is inherent in therapy that the therapist functions as an auxiliary ego so the patient in the patent's struggle with inner conflicts, until such time as to make this greater strength part of his own ego. To the extent that the schizophrenic patient does not posses an observing ego of sufficient strength to permit the therapist usefully to make transference interpretations, to that degree the therapist must be able to endure - and, eventually, to enjoy - various part-object transference role, until such time as the patient, through increasing ego-integration, becomes of the therapist. Another way of saying this is that the patient develops ego-strength. in the face of his own id impulses and pathogenic superego retaliations, in that, if identification with the therapist who can endure, and integrate into his own larger self, the kind of subjectively nonhuman part-object relatedness that the patient fosters in and needs from him.

Similarly, because the therapist has seen the patient to be, earlier in the therapy, such a deeply fragmented person, he tends to retain a lingering impression of the fragility, an impression that may interfere with his going along at the faster pace that the patient, now a very different and far stronger person, is capable of setting. But even this memory-image of the fragile patient, carried with the therapist, has a natural function in the course of the psychotherapy, for it is only very late in the work that the patient himself is able to realize how very ill, how very fragile, he once was, until he becomes strong enough to integrate his realization into his self-image, the therapist has to be the bearer of this piece of the patient's identity. This process is analogous to the well-known phenomenon in which each major forward stride in the patient's therapeutic growth is accompanied, or presaged, by the therapist's suddenly seeing in the patient a new and healthier person, there, too, the impact of the development falls primarily, for a time, upon the therapist rather than the patient. The patient himself, because his sense of identity is still, during the earlier therapeutic phases to which is easily overwhelming, and relatively tenuous. By the realization of the extent to which he is now changed, even though this change is, in our view, a most beneficial and welcoming one.

More often than not, is that the histories of schizophrenic patients, whether male or female, describe the father for being by far the warmer, and more accessible of the two parents, the father, whereas the mother was always relatively cold, rejecting, remote figure. However, that the disguise behind the child's idol inseparable 'buddy' is a matter of the father's transference to the child for being a mother-figure upon whom he, the father makes insatiable demands. It seems that the father, in these instances, is an infantile individual, who reacts both to his wife and to his child unconscious ly seeks to intervene between mother and child in such a way as to have each of them to himself. The seeming evidence of this by now, in a considerable number of cases, both in the transference-development and interviews with the parents.

The point being made, is that the mother and child allow this interposition by the father to happen, because of their anxiety about their fondness for being a mother-figure who exasperatingly allows as an infantile 'buddy', a kind of father to keep intervening, placing impossible demands for mothering upon the patient; finally comes a phase of th e patient's responding to the therapist as a mother with whom he can share unashamedly fond relatedness, no longer burdened by the father's scornfully and demandingly coming between them.

So it is with transference, we may presume that when a patient comes to react to us as a love and loving mother, this phase - as well as other phases - of the transference is founded upon our having come to feel, in reality, as, M. B. Cohen (1952) stresses the importance of the therapist 's inevitable feeling response to the patient's transference, only to suggest, that of the therapist's feeling participation is the evolving reality relatedness that pursue its own course, related to and parallelling, but not fully embraced by, the evolving transcendence relatedness over which time to occur is, namely introduced as countertransference, nonetheless, in the realm, as situated as one crucial phase of the work - a symbiotic kind of mutual dependency, which he mutually comes to feel toward the patient, his acceptance of a mutual caring which amounts at times to an adoration, and his being able to acknowledge the patient's contribution - inevitable, in successful therapy - to his own personal integration. It must be noted, that the schizophrenic patient responds with great regularity to the therapist's material warmth for being a sure indication that the latter are a homosexual or a lesbian. The younger therapist needs to become quite clear that this is, in actuality, a formidable resistance in the patient again the very kind of loving mother-infant relatedness that offers the patient his only avenue of salvation from his illness. Not to say, that the therapist should depreciate the degree of anxiety, referable to the deep ambivalence of the patient's early relationship with his mother, which is contained within this resistance, perhaps, that the therapist's deep-seated doubts as to his own sexual identity - and what person is totally free of such doubt? - should not make him lose of the fact that the patient's contempt (or revulsion, or what not) is basically a resistance against going ahead and picking up the threads of the loving infant-mother relatedness that were long ago severed.

Upon comment, the patient has in reference to a different person, and is often couched in terms of a different temporal era, that is intended by the preconscious or unconscious impulse striving for expression. The circumstance of the patient's having regressed to a more or less early level of ego-functioning is explanatory of many of the idiosyncrasies of schizophrenic communication. The clinical picture is complicated, in most instances, by the fact that the level of regression varies unceasingly, at times from one moment to the next, and there are even instances where the patient is functioning on more than one developmental level simultaneously.

The fact of the patient's regressed, mode of psychological functioning helps to account for the 'concretization', or contrariwise the seeming oversymbolization, of his communications; these phenomena represent his having regressed, in his thinking (and overall subjective experiencing), to a developmental level comparable with that in the young child who has not yet become able to differentiate between concrete and metaphorical (or similar forms of highly symbolic) thinking.

Similarly, the patient may tittle-tattle in a way that gives us to know that the content of his speech is relatively unimportant to him at the moment he is immersed in the pleasure of saying the words and hearing the sound of them, much like the young child who has not yet learned to talk but loves to babble and to hear the sound of his babbling. A nonverbal patient may usefully be regarded as having regressed even further, to the pre-verbal era of infancy or very early childhood.

The strikingly intense ambivalence, another fundamental aspect of the schizophrenic individual's psychodynamics, contributes to a number of different typical kinds of schizophrenic communications. (1) The indirect communication, (2) Self-contradictory verbal and nonverbal communications, and (3) Verbal communications in which there is a split between content and vocal feeling-tone.

In assessing the meaning of such communications, one soon learns to brush aside the content and attend to the feeling-tone - o r, in still, more complex instances, tones - in which the words are said.

Incidently, a patient sometimes evidences a quite accurate grasp of the true import of such communications that they come from the therapist. at the end of each of the maddening points or the enduring intervals of times of silence. After this had happened several times dawning upon that which he was very accurately expressing the covert message contained in the parting comment to him, as to the (4) No-verbal expression of a feeling contrarily enacted to the one being verbalized? And (5) Expression of contradictory feeling at an entirely nonverbal level.

The archaically harsh, forbidding superego of the patient is another basic factor that helps to account for his heavily disguised and often fragmentary communications.

I can only surmise that there is a companion evolution of reality relatedness between parent and the therapist, concomitant with such a transference evolution, it is only when the real possibilities relatedness between patient and therapist has reached, of a final and after man a depth intensity that there is now emerging, in the form of a transference development a comparable intense and long-represented direction in the fondness for the mother. However, this brings us back to other topics comprising the overall course of psychotherapy as a chronically schizophrenic person, a person preceding in the complex individuality extended to dynamical events of clinical work.

The quality of the transference remittances is to a great extent deepened on the quantity of other remittances. Remittances have the tendency to accumulate wherever there is a favourable opportunity to withstand the analysis. In most cases the transference offers the best opportunity, for example, we see the resistance coming from the conscious repetition, from the unconscious feeling of guilt and from the resistance by repression, takes part of building up the transference resistance. Freud speaks of the transference of resistance into a negative, hostile transference: It is on account of this transformation that the dissolution that transference remittances so often because the chief task of the therapeutics work. In the case of our patient the analysis finally showed the development of anxiety in the transference to b e castration anxiety that had arisen from infantile masturbation with accompanying incestuous wishes toward the mother and the hared and castration wishes toward the father. In the analysis, if the resistance resulting factors in the development of anxiety in the analysis. If the resistance result from this anxiety is analysis the addition of other remittances, then the final resistance in the analysis cannot be considered as an index to the amount of the genuine infantile anxiety for the anxiety resulting from infantile masturbation, on account of the genuine infantile anxiety: For the anxiety resulting from infantile masturbation on account of its anxiety resulting from infantile masturbation, on account of its particular capacity for being used as a resistance in analysis, becomes the nucleus of crystallisation or the basis for the addition of all the other remittances. In a footnote to his paper "The Dynamics of th Transference," this idea was alluded to by Freud, that, 'Over and over again, when one draws near to a pathogenic complex, that part of it that is first thrust forward into consciousness will be some aspect of it that can be transferred, having been so, it will then be defended with the utmost obstinacy by the patient'. The footnote says: 'From which however one need not infer in general any very particular pathogenic importance in the point selected for resistance by transference. In warfare, when a bitter fight is raging over the possession of some little chapel or a single farmhouse, we do not necessarily assume that the church is a national monument, or that the barns contain the military funds. Their value may be merely tactical; in the next onslaught they will very likely be of no importance'.

The dissolution of the transference resistance means then not only the dissolution of the resistance resulting from the genuine infantile castration anxiety but a liberation of the supporting resistance that often can only later be separately dissolved, because during the phase of the violent acting-out in the transference these remittances are not accessible to interpretation and dissolution.

For what is said about the psychology of metaphor is analogous to the transformational aspects of developed transferences and steadfast interpretations that both facilitate and organize them as transferences. Allowing that these transferences and 'remembered' experiences come into existence over a period of time, nothing that is identical with them has ever before been enacted, and nothing identical with them will ever be enacted again. They are creations that may be fully achieved only under specific analytic conditions. For example, at the time of his childhood scene with his father, the young man of the clinical example, could not have had the specific experience as recounted. strictly speaking, he was not reliving that moment. As a bo y, he must have experienced some of the main precursors and constituents of his present mode of experience, but he could not have done so in the present articulated and integrated manner. That present manner was the basis of his anguished outcry. words like re-creating, but re-experiencing and reliving simply do not do justice to the phenomena. In the way he was doing it, he was living that moment for the first time.

By making this claim, there is no constricting some of our well-established ideas about interpretation and insight, for example, disputing point that insight refers to more than the recovery of lost memories, and takes in, as well, a new grasp of the significance and interrelations of events one has always remembered. The latter connections that the analysand will say, as Freud pointed out, "As a matter of fact I've always known it, only I've never thought of" (1914). In fact, it is to develop that points further to say that the young child simply does not have the means of fully defining what we later regard as its own life experiences. It takes an adult to do that, especially with the help of an analyst. It was, after all, Freud's analysis that made it possible to define infantile psychosexuality. in this respect, but without disrespect, child analysis retains a quality of applied psychoanalysis. The adult definition of infantile psychosexuality is 'artificial' in the same way that the interpreting transference neurosis is: Both are ways of describing as true something that was not truer in quite that way as, at the time of its greatest development significance. this apparent paradox about 'remembering' as a form of creating goes a long was, that saying, what it is this distinctive about psychoanalytic interpretation.

In steadfastly and perspicaciously making transference interpretation, the analyst helps constitute new modes of experience and new experiences. This newness characterizes the experience of analytic transference in them. Unlike extra-analytic transference, they can no longer be sheerly repetitive or merely new editions. Instead, they become repetitively new editions understood as such because defined as such by the simplification and steadfast transference interpretation, instead of responding to the analysand in kind, Which would actualize the repetition, the analyst makes an interpretation. This interpretation does not necessarily or regularly match something the analysand does often seem to have always represented often, but he does not seem to have done so at all. To think otherwise about this would, in effect, to claim that, unconsciously, every analysand is Freud or a fully insightful Freudian analyst. And that claim is totally absurd.

It would be closer to the truth to say this: Unconsciously, the analysand already knows or has experienced fragmentary, amorphous, uncoordinated constituents of many of the transference interpretations. Alternatively, one may say that, implicitly, the analysand has been insisting on some as yet unspecified certainties and, in keeping with this, following some set of as yet unspecified rules in his actions, these the transference interpretations now organize explicitly. Each transference interpretation thus refers to many things that have already been defined by the analysand, and it does so in a way that transforms them. That's why one may call it interpretation. Otherwise, it would be mere repeating or sterile paraphrasing. Interpretation is a creative redescription that implicitly has the structure of a simile. It says, "This is like it," Each interpretation does, therefore, add new actions to the life the analysand has already lived.

Technically, redescription in the terms of transference-repetition is necessary. This is so because, up to the time of interpretation and working through, the analysand has been, in one sense unable and, in another sense, unconsciously and desperately unwilling, to conduct his life differently, in and of them, the repetitions cannot after the symptoms, the subjective distress, the wasting of one's possibilities rather they can only perpetuate a static situation by repeatedly confirming its necessity. They prove once again, the unconsciously maintained damaging certainties. But once they get to be viewed as historically grounded actions and subjectively defined situations. As they do upon being interpreted and worked through, they appear as having always been, in crucial respects, inventions of the analysand's making and, so, as his responsibility. in being seen as versions one' past life, they may be changed in significant and beneficial ways. Less of all, are they presented as purely inevitable happenings, as a fixed fate or as the well-established way of the world. However, we encounter a second paradox that goes to the heart of psychoanalysis interpretation, namely, that responsible, insightful change is possible through psychoanalysis just because, as a child the analysand mistakenly assumes and then denied responsibility for much that he encountered in the early formative environment and during maturation.

One major point remains to be made about the logic of viewing transference interpretation as simplifying yet innovative redescription. This point is that the interpretations bring about a coordination of the terms in which to state both the analysand's current problems and their life-historical background. The analysand's symptoms and distress are described as actions and modes of action, with due regard for the principle of multiple function or multiple meaning: In coordination with that description, the decisive developmental situation and conflicts are stated as actions and modes of action. Continuity is established between the childhood constructions of relationships and the self and the present constructions of these interpretations of transference shows who both are part of the same set of practices, that is, how they follow the same set of rules. Past and present are coordinated to show continuity rather than arranged in a definite sequence.

In the same way, the form of analytic behaviour and the content of association are given co-ordinated descriptions, say, for being defiant, devouring, or reparative. Or, in the case of depression, the depressive symptoms, the depressive analytic transference, the themes of present and past loss, destructiveness and helplessness, all will be redescribed under the aspect of one continuously developing self-presentation. And this coordination will be worked out in that hermeneutically circular fashion in which the analyst defines both th facts to be explained and the explanations to be applied to these facts. In the end, as is well known, both the paramount issues of the analysis and the leading explanatory account of them are likely to be significantly different from the provisional versions of them used at the beginning of the analysis.

The increasing influence of the modernist version of transference and its interpretation represents an adaptation to several long-term philosophical, scientific, and cultural shifts we can now recognize. this changing view of transference is also the most visible emblem of the deep changes in psychoanalytic theory that are now quietly taking place, and of their theoretical pluralism that is so prevalent today (Cooper, 1985).

One of these long-term changes in the climate in which psychoanalysis dwells results from a large philosophical debate concerning the nature of history, veridicality, and narrative. Kermode (1985) has written of the change during this century in our modes of understanding and interpreting the past and the present, "Once upon a time it seemed obvious that you could best understand how things are by asking how they got to be that way. Now attention [is] directed to how things are in their immediate plexuities. There is a switch to use the linguistic expressions, from the diachronic to the synchronic view. Diachrony, roughly speaking, studies things in their synchrony to be as they are, synchrony concerns itself with things as they are and ignores the question, how they got that way. This distinction, put forth by de Sasussure (1915), has achieved philosophical dominance today and is the clear source of the hermeneutic view so prevalent in psychoanalysis, proposed by Ricoeur (1970). From here, it is a short distance to Schafer (1981), and Gill (1982), or Spence (1982) who in varying ways adopt the synchronic view. In this view, the analytic task is interpretation, with the patient, of the events of the analytic situation - usually broadly labelled transference - with a construction rather than a reconstruction of the past. In effect, while there is a past of 'there and then' it is knowable only through the filter of the present, of 'here and now'. There is no other past than the one as we construct, and there is no way of understanding the past but through its relation to the present.

Psychoanalysis, like history but unlike fiction, does have anchoring points, for history's anchoring points are the evidences that events really did occur, There was a Roman empire, it did have dates, actual persons lived and died. These 'facts' place a limitation for the narratives an interpretations that may seriously be entertained. Psychoanalysis is anchored in its scientific developmental psychology and in the biology of attachment and affects. Biology confers regularities and limits on possible histories, and our constructions of the past must accord with this scientific knowledge. constructions of childhood that are incompatible with what we know of developmental possibilities may open our eye's to new concepts of development, but more likely they alert us to maimed childhoods that have led our patients to usual narrative constructions in the effort to maintain self-esteem and internal coherence. A second, far less secure, anchorage is the enormous amount of convergent data that accumulate during the course of an analysis, which are likely to give the analyst the impression that he is reconstructing rather than constructing the figures and the circumstances of his patient's past. While a diachronic view may no longer suffice, it may also not be fully dispensable if our patient's histories are to maintain psychoanalytic coherence, rooted in bodily experience, and the loving, hating and terrifying affects accompanying the fantastic world of infantile psychic reality. Not all analysis are yet as ready as Spence, for example, to give up all claim to the truth value explanatory power of the understanding of the past, even if it is limited to knowing past constructions of the past. Nevertheless, the change in philosophical outlook during our century is profound and contributes to our changing view of the analytic process is exemplified in the transference and its interpretation.

Approaching the same issue from an entirely different vantage point, Emde (1981) speaking for the 'baby-watchers' and discusses of two changing models of infancy and early development, details a second source of the major change of climate to which he writes, . . . the models suggest that what we reconstruct, and what may be extraordinarily helpful to the patient in making a biography, may never have happened. The human being, infant child, is understood to be fundamentally active in constructing his experience. Reality is of what exists or is real in that which underlies appearances, but cannot be avoided in conditions of something on which reality is a certain fact, however, it can neither by knowing nor caring of two or more things in the negative, nor is it a given nor necessarily registered in an unmodified form. Perhaps it makes sense, nor is it for the psychoanalysis to place renewed emphasis on recent and current experiences - first, as a context for interpreting early experience - first, as a context for interpreting the potential amelioration, . . . Psychoanalysts are specialists in dealing with the intrapsychic world not only particular with the dynamic unconscious, but we need to pay attention not only to the intrapsychic realm. conflicting-laden and conflict-free, but also to the interpersonal realm. He concludes, . . . we have probably placed far to much an emphasis on early experience itself as opposed to the process by which it is modified or made use of by subsequent experience.

This view of psychic developments, discarding the timeless unconscious and so powerful at odds with the views that were held by psychoanalysts during the time when most of our ideas of transference interpretation were formed, clearly suggests the modernist model of transference interpretation.

A change in the cultural environment of psychoanalysis provides a third source for the changing model of transference interpretation. Valenstein describes oscillations in psychoanalytic outlook between an emphasis on cognition at one end, and on affect at the other. One might see these as differences between old-fashioned scientific and romantic world views. Surely the period of ego psychology, perhaps reflected in the English translation of Freud, and certainly reflected in the effect to insist on the libidinal energetic point of view, represented the attempt to see psychoanalysis as Freud usually did, as an objective science in the nineteenth century style, with hypotheses created out of naïve observations. It accorded with that view to see the transference as an objective reflection of history. We are currently in one of our more romantic periods. It is consonant with that view to see transference as an activity - stormy, romantic, active, affective - a kind of adventure from which the two individuals emerge changed and renewed. In this romantic view, interpretation of the transference are intended to remove obstacles interfering with the heightening and intimacy of the experience, with the implication that self-knowledge and change will result from their encounter. A romantic figure, the patient and analyst set forth on a quest into the unknown, and whether or not one of them returns with a Holy Grail, they return with many new stories to tell and a new life experience - the analysis. Gardner's (1983) book, 'Self Inquiry' epitomizes this romantic view of analyst and patient as a poet-pair engaged in mutual self-inquiry. It is clear that many analysis would rather be artistic than scientist. By contrast, the older, cognitive view of the transference is of an intellectual journey, emotionally loaded of course, but basically a trip back in history, seeking truth and insight.

Psychodynamic therapies are those therapies in some way derived from the work of Austrian physician Sigmund Freud, the founder of psychoanalysis. In general, psychodynamic therapists emphasize the importance of discovering and resolving internal, unconscious conflicts, often through an exploration of one's childhood and past experiences. Although psychoanalysis is the best-known form of psychodynamic therapy, theorists have developed many other psychodynamic therapies, some very different from Freud's original techniques.

Sigmund Freud, the founder of psychoanalysis, compared the human mind to an iceberg. The tip above the water represents consciousness, and the vast region below the surface symbolizes the unconscious mind. Of Freud's three basic personality structures—id, ego, and superego—only the id is totally unconscious.

Freud developed the theory and techniques of psychoanalysis in the 1890s. He believed that much of an individual's personality develops before the age of six. He also proposed that children pass through a series of psychosexual stages, during which they express sexual energy in different ways. For example, during the phallic stage, from about age three to age five, children focus on feelings of pleasure in their genital organs. At this time, according to Freud, boys become sexually attracted to their mothers and feel hostility and jealousy toward their fathers. Similarly, girls develop sexual feelings toward their fathers and feel rage toward their mothers. In Freud's view, such innate sexual and aggressive drives cause feelings and thoughts that the person regards as unacceptable. In response, the individual represses these feelings, driving them into the unconscious mind. In the process, three basic personality structures are formed: the id, the ego, and the superego. The id represents unchecked, instinctual drives; the superego is the voice of social conscience; and the ego is the rational thinking that mediates between the id and superego and deals with reality. These three systems function as a whole, not separately. Id forces are unconscious and often emerge without an individual's awareness, causing fear, anxiety, depression, or other distressing symptoms. Freud used the term neurosis to refer to such symptoms.

In psychoanalysis, Freud sought to eliminate neurotic symptoms by bringing the individual's repressed fantasies, memories, and emotions into consciousness. He placed particular emphasis on helping patients uncover memories about early childhood trauma and conflict, which he regarded as the source of emotional problems in adults. At first, he used hypnosis as a way to gain access to a person's unconscious. Later he developed free association, a method in which patients say whatever thoughts come to their minds about dreams, fantasies, and memories. The analyst's interpretations of this material, Freud believed, could provide patients with insight into their unconscious—insight that would help them become less anxious, less depressed, or better in other ways.

Freud also placed great value on what could be learned from transference, the patient's emotional response to the therapist. Freud believed that during therapy, patients transfer repressed feelings toward their family members to their relationship with the therapist. Transference exposes these repressed feelings and allows the patient to work through them. Free association and transference are still central features of Freudian psychoanalysis.

In contemporary forms of psychoanalysis, the duration of therapy is often shorter - between one and four years - and meetings may take place one or two times a week. Other psychoanalytically oriented therapists work in a brief format of 30 sessions or less. The patient sits on a chair across from the therapist rather than lying on a couch. Modern psychoanalysts tend to focus more on current functioning and make less use of free association techniques.

American psychoanalyst and social philosopher Erich Fromm stressed the importance of social and economic factors on human behaviour. His focus was a departure from traditional psychoanalysis, which emphasized the role of the subconscious. In this 1969 essay for Collier's Year Book, Fromm presents various explanations for human violence. He argues that violence cannot be controlled by imposing stronger legal penalties, but rather by creating a more just society in which people connect with each other as humans and are able to control their own lives.

Several of Freud's followers developed new theories about the causes of psychological disorders. Three important neo-Freudians were Erich Fromm, Karen Horney, and Erik Erikson, who emphasized the role of social and cultural influences in the formation of personality. All three emigrated from Germany to the United States in the 1930s. Their theories have influenced modern psychodynamic therapists.

From believed that the fundamental problem people confront is a sense of isolation deriving from their own separateness. According to Fromm, the goal of therapy is to orient onself and establish roots, and find security by uniting with other people while remaining a separate individual.

Horney talk to each other, the therapist can learn about their communication patterns departed from Freud in her belief in the importance of social forces in personality formation. She asserted that people develop anxiety and other psychological problems because of feelings of isolation during childhood and unmet needs for love and respect from their parents. The goal of therapy, in her view, is to help patients overcome anxiety-driven neurotic needs and move toward a more realistic image of themselves.

Erikson extended Freud's emphasis on childhood development to cover the entire lifespan. Referred to as an ego psychologist, he emphasized the importance of the ego in helping individuals develop healthy ways to deal with their environment. Often working with children, Erikson helped individuals develop the basic trust and confidence needed for the development of a healthy ego.

Other psychoanalytic therapists focussed on how relationships develop between the child and others, especially the mother. British pediatrician Donald Winnicott and Austrian-American pediatrician Margaret Mahler were known as object-relations analysts because of their emphasis on the child's love object (such as the mother or father). They and other object-relations therapists, such as Austrian-born British psychoanalyst Melanie Klein, helped patients deal with problems that arose from being separated inappropriately or at too early an age or from their mothers.

Swiss psychiatrist Carl Jung began his studies of human motivation in the early 1900s and created the school of psychoanalysis known as analytical psychology. A contemporary of Austrian psychoanalyst Sigmund Freud, Jung at first collaborated closely with Freud but eventually moved on to pursue his own theories, including the exploration of personality types. According to Jung, there are two basic personality types, extroverted and introverted, which alternate equally in the completely normal individual. Jung also believed that the unconscious mind is formed by the personal unconscious (the repressed feelings and thoughts developed during an individual's life) and the collective unconscious those inherited feelings, thoughts, and memories and unlike the psychoanalytic therapists, Swiss psychiatrist Carl Jung developed a very different system of therapy. He had worked closely with Freud, but broke away totally from Freud in his own work.

Jung created a school of psychology that he called analytical psychology. He felt that Freud focussed too much on sexual drives and not enough on all of the creative instincts and impulses that motivate individuals. Whereas Freud had described the personal unconscious, which reflected the sum of one person's experience, Jung added the concept of the collective unconscious, which he defined as the reservoir of the experience of the entire human race. The collective unconscious contains images called archetypes that are common to all individuals. They are often expressed in mythological concepts such as good and evil spirits, fairies, dragons, and gods.

In general, Jungian therapists see psychological problems as arising from unconscious conflicts that create disturbances in psychic energy. They treat psychological problems by helping their patients bring material from their personal and collective unconscious into conscious awareness. The therapists do this through a knowledge of symbolism—not only symbols from mythology and folk culture, but also current cultural symbols. By interpreting dreams and other materials, Jungian therapists help their patients become more aware of unconscious processes and become stronger individuals.

Austrian psychologist and psychiatrist Alfred Adler studied under Sigmund Freud, the founder of psychoanalysis, before developing his own theories about human behaviour. Adler's best-known theories stress that individuals are mainly motivated by feelings of inferiority, which he called an inferiority complex.

Like Jung, Austrian physician Alfred Adler believed that Freud overemphasized the importance of sexual and aggressive drives. Adler was particularly interested in sibling relationships, birth order, and relationships with parents. He would ask patients about their early memories and use this information to analyse their attitudes, beliefs, and behaviours. He helped his patients by encouraging them to meet important life goals: love, work, and friendship.

For Adler and modern therapists whose procuring results from persistent endeavours and cultivation are but to acquire from his work, interest in others and participation in society are important goals of therapy. Adlerian therapists see therapy in part as educational, and they use a number of innovative action techniques to help patients change mistaken beliefs and interact more fully with family members and others.

Humanistic therapies focus on the client's present rather than past experiences, and on conscious feelings rather than unconscious thoughts. Therapists try to create a caring, supportive atmosphere and to guide clients toward personal realizations and insights. Clients are encouraged to take responsibility for their lives, to accept themselves, and to recognize their own potential for growth and change.

The length of therapy depends on the severity of the problem and on a client's ability to change and try new behaviours. Because humanistic therapies emphasize the relationship between client and therapist and a gradual development of increased responsibility by the client, these therapies typically take a year or two of the weekly sessions.

Three of the most influential forms of humanistic therapy are existential therapy, person-centred therapy, and Gestalt therapy.

Based on a philosophical approach to people and their existence, existential therapy deals with important life themes. These themes include living and dying, freedom, responsibility to self and others, finding meaning in life, and dealing with a sense of meaninglessness. More than other kinds of therapists, existential therapists examine individuals' awareness of themselves and their ability to look beyond their immediate problems and daily events to problems of human existence.

The first existential therapists were European psychiatrists trained in psychoanalysis who were dissatisfied with Freud's emphasis on biological drives and unconscious processes. Existential therapists help their clients confront and explore anxiety, loneliness, despair, fear of death, and the feeling that life is meaningless. There are few techniques specific to existential therapy. Therapists normally draw on techniques from a variety of therapies. One well-known existential therapy is logotherapy, developed by Austrian psychiatrist Viktor E. Frankl in the 1940s (logos is Greek for meaning).

In the 1940s and 1950s American psychologist Carl Rogers developed a form of psychotherapy known as person-entered therapy. This approach emphasizes that each person has the capacity for self-understanding and self-healing. The therapist tries to demonstrate empathy and true caring for clients, allowing them to reveal their true feelings without fear of being judged.

`Person-centred therapy, originally called client-centred therapy, is perhaps the best-known form of humanistic therapy. American psychologist Carl Rogers developed this type of therapy in the 1940s and 1950s. Rogers believed that people, like other living organisms, are driven by an innate tendency to maintain and enhance themselves, which in turn moves them toward growth, maturity, and life enrichment. Within each person, Rogers believed, is the capacity for self-understanding and constructive change.

Person-centred therapy emphasizes understanding and caring rather than diagnosis, advice, and persuasion. Rogers strongly believed that the quality of the therapist-client relationship influences the success of therapy. He felt that effective therapists must be genuine, accepting, and empathic. A genuine therapist expresses true interest in the client and is open and honest. An accepting therapist cares for the client unconditionally, even if the therapist does not always agree with him or her. An empathic therapist demonstrates a deep understanding of the client's thoughts, ideas, experiences, and feelings and communicates this empathic understanding to the client. Rogers believed that when clients feel unconditional positive regard from a genuine therapist and feel empathically understood, they will be less anxious and more willing to reveal themselves and their weaknesses. By doing so, clients gain a better understanding of their own lives, move toward self-acceptance, and can make progress in resolving a wide variety of personal problems.

Cognitive therapists often give their clients homework assignments designed to help them identify their own irrational patterns of thinking and to reinforce what they learn in therapy. For example, clients often keep a daily log in which they write down distressing emotions, the situation that caused the emotions, their thoughts at the time, whether the thoughts were distorted or not, and alternative ways of thinking about the situation.

Helping individuals change problematic behaviours, thoughts, or feelings is not an easy task. Therapists have tried many creative approaches to help patients, some of which do not fall neatly into the major categories of psychodynamic, humanistic, behavioural, or cognitive. Two such therapies still in use today are transactional analysis and reality therapy.

In the 1950s and 1960s Canadian-American psychiatrist Eric Berne developed a form of therapy he called transactional analysis. Although trained in psychoanalysis, Berne felt that the complexity of psychoanalytic terminology excluded patients from full participation in their own treatment. He developed a theory of personality based on the view that when people interact with each other, they function as either a parent, adult, or child. For example, he would characterize social interactions between two people as parent-adult, parent-child, adult-child, adult-adult, and so forth depending on the situation. He referred to social interactions as transactions and to analysis of these interactions as transactional analysis.

In therapy, which is often conducted in groups, patients learn to recognize when they are assuming one of these roles and to understand when being an authoritarian parent or an impulsive child is appropriate or inappropriate. In addition to identifying these roles, clients learn how to change roles in order to behave in more desirable ways.

American psychiatrist William Glasser developed reality therapy in the 1960s, after working with teenage girls in a correctional institution and observing work with severely disturbed schizophrenic patients in a mental hospital. He observed that psychoanalysis did not help many of his patients change their behaviour, even when they understood the sources of it. Glasser felt it was important to help individuals take responsibility for their own lives and to blame others less. Largely because of this emphasis on personal responsibility, his approach has found widespread acceptance between drug and alcohol-abuse counsellors, corrections workers, school counsellors, and those working with clients who may be disruptive to others.

Reality therapy is based on the premise that all human behaviour is motivated by fundamental needs and specific wants. The reality therapist first seeks to establish a friendly, trusting relationship with clients in which they can express their needs and wants. Then the therapist helps clients explore the behaviours that created problems for them. Clients are encouraged to examine the consequences of their behaviour and to evaluate how well their behaviour helped them fulfill their wants. The therapist does not accept excuses from clients.

Finally, the therapist helps the client formulate a concrete plan of action to change certain behaviours, based on the client's own goals and ability to make choices.

Currently, many therapists describe their approach as eclectic or integrative, meaning that they use ideas and techniques from a variety of therapies. Many therapists like the opportunity to draw from many theories and not limit themselves to one or two. Most therapists who adopt an eclectic approach have a rationale for which techniques they use with specific clients, rather than just choosing an approach randomly or because it suits them at the time.

One of the most influential eclectic approaches is cognitive-behavioural therapy. Other eclectic approaches use other combinations of therapies.

There are almost no pure cognitive or behavioural therapists. Usually therapists combine cognitive and behavioural techniques in an approach known as cognitive-behavioural therapy. For example, to treat a woman with depression, a therapist may help her identify irrational thinking patterns that cause the distressing feelings and to replace these irrational thoughts with new ways of thinking. The therapist may also train her in relaxation techniques and have her try new behaviours that help her become more active and less depressed. The client then reports the results back to the therapist.

Cognitive-behavioural therapy has rapidly become one of the most popular and influential forms of psychotherapy, in part because it takes a relatively short period of time compared to humanistic and psychoanalytic therapies, and also because of its ability to treat a wide range of problems. Sometimes cognitive-behavioural therapy takes only a few sessions, but more often it extends for 20 or 30 sessions more than four to six months. The length of therapy usually depends on the severity and number of the client's problems.

Some therapists have one particular way of understanding clients - that is, they adhere to one theory of personality—but use many techniques from a variety of theories. Other therapists may understand clients using two or three theories of personality and only use techniques to bring about change that are consistent with those theories. Some therapists have combined psychodynamic and behavioural therapies in ways to help their clients deal with fears and anxieties but also understand their causes.

Therapists may use different approaches to treat different problems. For example, a therapist might find that clients who are grieving over the loss of a spouse may respond best to a humanistic approach, in which they can share their grieving and their hurts with the therapist. However, the same therapist may use a cognitive-behavioural approach with a person who reports being anxious most of the time.

All of the individual therapies can also be used with groups. People may choose group therapy for several reasons. First, group therapy is usually less expensive than individual therapy, because group members share the cost. Group therapy also allows a therapist to provide treatment to more people than would be possible otherwise. Aside from cost and efficiency advantages, group therapy allows people to hear and see how others deal with their problems. In addition, group members receive vital support and encouragement from others in the group. They can try out new ways of behaving in a safe, supportive environment and learn how others perceive them.

Groups also have disadvantages. Individuals spend less time talking about their own problems than they would in one-on-one therapy. Also, certain group members may interact with other group members in hurtful ways, such as by yelling at them or criticizing them harshly. Generally, therapists try to intercede when group members act in destructive ways. Another disadvantage of group therapy involves confidentiality. Although group members usually promise to treat all therapy discussions as confidential, some group members may worry that other members will share their secrets outside of the group. Group members who believe this may be less willing to disclose all of their problems, lessening the effectiveness of therapy for them.

Groups vary widely in how they work. The typical group size is from six to ten people with one or two therapists. Often two therapists prefer to work together in a group so that they can respond not only to one person's issues, but also to discussions between group members that may be occurring quickly. Some groups are open or drop-in groups—new clients may join at any time and members may attend or skip whatever sessions they desire. Other groups are closed and admit new members only when all members agree. Regular attendance is usually required in these groups. In closed groups, both the therapist and group members will ask a member to provide an explanation for missing a meeting.

When forming a group, therapists try to make clear to potential participants the goals of the group and for whom it is appropriate. Therapists will often screen potential participants to learn about their problems and decide whether the group is right for them. Sometimes therapists prefer diversity among group members in terms of age, gender, and problem. In other cases, therapists may limit membership in a group to individuals with similar problems and backgrounds. For example, some groups may form specifically for individuals who are grieving the loss of a loved one, individuals who abuse drugs or alcohol, people with eating disorders, people suffering from depression, or troubled elderly individuals.

The techniques used in group therapy depend largely on the theoretical orientation of the therapist. Humanistic therapists tend to respond to the feelings and experiences of other members. They may also interpret or comment on social interactions between group members. In cognitive-behavioural groups, group members try to change their own thoughts and behaviours and support and encourage other members to do the same. Psychoanalytic groups focus on childhood experiences and their impact on participants' current behaviours, thoughts, and feelings.

Psychodrama, the first form of group therapy, was developed in the 1920s by Jacob L. Moreno, an Austrian psychiatrist. Moreno brought his method to the United States in 1925, and its use spread to other parts of the world. Participants in psychodrama act out their problems - often on a real stage and with props - as a means of heightening their awareness of them. The therapist serves as the director, suggesting how participants might act out problems and assigning roles to other group members. For example, a woman might reenact a scene from her childhood with other group members playing her father, mother, brother, or sister. Groups who use psychodrama may do so weekly or simply as a one-time demonstration.

A self-help group or support group involves people with a common problem who convene regularly to acquire or obtain by acquaintance a sharing of experiences, support each other emotionally, and encourage change or recovery. They are usually free of charge to interested participants. Self-help groups are not strictly considered psychotherapy because they are not led by a licensed mental health professional. However, they can serve as an important source of help for people in emotional distress.

There are thousands of self-help and support groups in the United States and Canada. The oldest and best known is Alcoholics Anonymous, which uses a 12-step program to treat alcoholism. Other groups have formed for cancer patients, parents whose children have been murdered, compulsive gamblers, battered women, obese people, and many other types of people.

Family therapy involves the participation of one or more members of the same family who seek help for troubled family relationships or the problems of individual family members. Typical problems that bring families into family therapy are delinquent behaviour by a child or adolescent, a child's poor performance in school, hostilities between a parent and child or between siblings, and severe psychological disturbance or mental illness in a parent or child.

One of the most influential forms of family therapy, family systems therapy, views the family as a single, complex system or unit. Individual members are interdependent parts of the system. Rather than treating one person's symptoms in isolation, therapists try to understand the symptoms in the larger context of the family. For example, a boy who begins picking fights with classmates might do so to get more attention from his busy parents. Therapists work from the rationale that current family relationships profoundly affect, and are affected by, an individual family member's psychological problems. For this reason, most family therapists prefer to work with the entire family during a session, rather than meeting with family members individually.

In most family therapy sessions, the therapist encourages family members to air their feelings, frustrations, and hostilities. By observing how they interact, the therapist can help them recognize their roles and relationships with each other. The therapist tries to avoid assigning blame to any particular family member. Instead, the therapist makes suggestions about how family members might adjust their roles and prevent future conflict.

Couples therapy, also called marital therapy or marriage counselling, is designed to help intimate partners improve their relationship. Therapists treat married couples as well as unmarried couples of the opposite or same sex. Therapists normally hold sessions with both partners present. At certain times during therapy, however, the therapist may choose to see the partners individually.

Couples may seek therapy for a variety of problems, many of which concern a breakdown of communication or trust between the partners. For example, an extramarital affair by one partner may cause the other partner to feel emotional pain, anger, and distrust. Some partners may feel distant from one another or experience sexual problems. In other cases, one or both partners may have psychological problems or alcohol or drug problems that negatively affect their relationship.

The techniques used in therapy vary depending on the theoretical orientation of the therapist and the nature of the couple's problem. Most often, therapists focus on improving communication between partners and on helping them learn to manage conflict. By observing the partners as they and the roles they assume in their relationship. The therapist may then teach the partners new ways of expressing their feelings verbally, how to listen to each other, and how to work together to solve problems. The therapist may also suggest that they try out new roles. For example, if one partner makes all of the decisions in the relationship, the therapist may encourage the couple to try sharing decision-making power.

Because most couples therapists also have trained in family therapy, they often examine the influence of the couple's relationships with parents, children, and siblings. Psychoanalytically oriented therapists may focus on how the partners' childhood experiences affect their current relationship with each other. For couples who cannot work through their differences or reestablish trust and intimacy, separation or divorce may be the best choice. Therapists can help such partners separate in constructive ways.

Some psychotherapists specialize in working with children. Therapists deal with children who are anxious, depressed, or have difficulty getting along with others at home or school. Some children have psychological problems resulting from family issues such as divorce, new stepparents, single-parent homes, death of a parent or sibling, being homeless, or being raised in an alcoholic family. Other children have emotional problems related to physical disabilities, learning disabilities, or attention-deficit hyperactivity disorder.

Play therapy is a special technique that therapists often use with children aged 2 to

12. For children, play is a natural way of learning and relating to others. Play therapy can help therapists both to understand children's problems and to help children deal with their feelings, behaviours, and thoughts. Therapists may use playhouses, puppets, a toy telephone, dolls, bandboxes, food, finger paints, and other toys or objects to help children express their thoughts and feelings. In addition to projecting a caring and gentle manner, therapists who work with children are trained to understand and interpret children's nonverbal and verbal expressions.

For most people, psychotherapy involves a common sequence of events: finding a therapist, assessing the problem, exploring the problem, resolving the problem, and terminating therapy. Sometimes therapy will end prematurely, before the problem is resolved. For example, the therapist or client may move to a new city.

When someone has a personal problem and seeks help from a therapist, the individual may turn to a variety of people to get a referral—a friend, a pastor or rabbi, or a family physician. Phone books list associations of psychologists, psychiatrists, and social workers that can also provide referrals to therapists. As noted earlier, however, some health insurance plans may restrict a person's choice of therapist.

When prospective clients call a therapist for an appointment, they may discuss several aspects of therapy. One concern is availability - is the therapist taking on new patients? Are there hours when both patient and therapist can meet? Another issue is fees. Both therapists in private practice and those in community mental health agencies have to negotiate fees depending in part on the client's health insurance plan. Some agencies do not require health insurance and have very low fees or a sliding scale that sets fees depending on the ability of the client to pay.

During the first meeting, clients try to explain their problems to the therapist. The therapist usually asks about the nature of the problems, what may make the problems better or worse, and how long the problems have existed. For many therapists, hearing details, even small ones, helps them to assess the problems and to decide the best form of treatment. Some therapists collaborate with clients in deciding the goals of therapy and what treatment methods will be used. Assessment does not stop with the first session, but continues through therapy. Occasionally, goals of therapy change upon assessment of new issues or problems.

During therapy, the client sits across from the therapist—except in classical psychoanalysis, in which the client lies on a couch. The specific nature of the discussions between therapist and client differs greatly depending on the therapist's theoretical orientation. Some therapists are interested in unconscious forces and the early childhood years of the client (psychodynamic therapy), others in actions of the client (behavioural therapy), others in the client's thinking patterns (cognitive therapy), and yet others in all or some of these aspects. Therapists often take notes during a session or make notes after the session has ended. Sessions typically last from 45 to 50 minutes, although therapists may hold longer sessions during the initial stages of treatment. Clients typically meet weekly with the therapist, although some may meet twice a week or more.

When does therapy end? Clients and therapists discuss this issue together and determine when it is best to stop. Ideally their decision depends on their judgments about the client's degree of progress and improvement. Some clients may find that therapy does not seem to be making progress, and may decide to change therapists. However, the cost of therapy may also factor in the decision to end therapy. Managed-care companies generally limit the number of sessions they will subsidize to between 15 and 20. Some therapists, especially those in private practice, may arrange to go beyond these limits by negotiating a fee that the client will pay for services. In other cases, the therapist may refer the client to other mental health agencies that have lower fees and do not require insurance. At the end of therapy, the therapist may schedule a follow-up session several months later to check the client's progress. Also, the therapist and client agree on what to do if the client's problems recur.

Almost since the inception of psychotherapy, therapists and their clients have asked, 'Does it work? Does psychotherapy help people resolve their problems, feel better, and change the way they deal with other people?' Therapists and clients are not the only ones asking these questions. In recent years, the agencies that fund mental health services - health insurance companies, health maintenance organizations, and government organizations—have increased their scrutiny of the effectiveness of various psychotherapies in an effort to contain costs.

Measuring the effectiveness of psychotherapy is an extremely complex task. Asking psychotherapists or their clients, 'How helpful has therapy been?' is only a start? The answer does provide some information about how therapists and their clients perceive therapy. However, it does not answer the question of whether psychotherapy is effective because both therapists and clients have vested interests in believing that therapy succeeded. Therapists want to uphold their professional reputation and sense of competence, and clients want to feel that their investment of time and money has been worthwhile. Because of these biases, most studies of effectiveness rely on other evaluations of a client's improvement: Psychological tests given before and after treatment, reports from the client's friends and family, and reports from impartial interviewers who do not know the client or whether the client received any therapy.

In 1952 British psychologist Hans Eysenck reviewed the results of 24 studies of psychotherapy and came to a controversial conclusion: Although two-thirds of the patients who received psychotherapy showed improvement, a roughly equal proportion of patients who had been on a waiting list for therapy improved with no treatment. According to Eysenck, the patients on the waiting list showed spontaneous remission—recovery without treatment. Although researchers soon exposed flaws in his analysis and problems with the original studies, Eysenck's findings touched off hundreds of new studies on the effectiveness of psychotherapy.

In 1980 American researchers statistically combined the results of 475 studies on psychotherapy outcomes using a technique known as meta-analysis. Their study found that the average psychotherapy recipient showed more improvement than 80 percent of untreated individuals. Later studies have confirmed that overall, but psychotherapy is better than no therapy at all. Furthermore, it appears at least as effective as drug treatment for most psychological problems. However, psychotherapy is not effective for everyone. About 10 percent of people who receive psychotherapy show no improvement or actually get worse.

Researchers have also studied how quickly people improve with psychotherapy. One analysis, which reviewed data from more than 2400 psychotherapy patients, found that 50 percent of people receiving once-a-week psychotherapy showed significant improvement after eight sessions, or two months. After six months, or 26 sessions, about 75 percent of people show improvement. However, most people required about a year of psychotherapy for relief from severe symptoms, such as feelings of worthlessness.

Are some types of psychotherapy more effective than others? This question has been hotly debated for decades, and research on this, and issue presents many difficulties. In conducting studies that compare different therapies, researchers seek to make sure that each treatment group is as similar as possible. For example, researchers may limit the groups to people with the same severity of depression. In addition, within each treatment group, researchers try to make sure that therapists are using the same techniques and are trained similarly. However, patients do not come to therapy with simple problems that fit easily into studies. Furthermore, therapists of the same theoretical orientation may vary in their techniques and in the skillfulness with which they apply them.

Because of these problems, there is no conclusive answer about which type of therapy is best. Most studies have failed to demonstrate that anyone approach is superior to another. The meta-analysis of 475 studies mentioned earlier, for example, found that psychodynamic, humanistic, behavioural, and cognitive approaches were all about equally effective. In the 1990s a major study by the National Institute of Mental Health compared the effectiveness of cognitive-behavioural therapy, interpersonal psychotherapy (a form of short-term psychodynamic therapy that focuses on social relations), and drug therapy for people with depression. The study found that all three types of treatment helped individuals become less depressed. Furthermore, no one method was significantly more effective than the others.

Some researchers suggest that all therapies share certain qualities, and that these qualities account for the similar effectiveness of therapies despite quite different techniques. For instance, all therapies offer people hope for recovery. People who begin therapy often expect that therapy will help them, and this expectation alone may lead to some improvement (a phenomenon known as the placebo effect). Also, people in psychotherapy may find that simply being able to talk freely and openly about their problems helps them to feel better. Finally, the support, encouragement, and warmth that clients feel from their therapist lets them know they are mindfully inclined to be aware of the ever-changing complexity of an individual that feels, perceives, thinks, wills, and especially reasons, in whom intentions are shared about and respected, which may positively affect their mental health.

Although different therapeutic approaches may be equally effective on average, mental health researchers agree that some types of therapy are best for particular problems. For panic disorder and phobias, behavioural and cognitive-behavioural therapies seem most effective. Behavioural techniques, often in combination with medication, are also an effective treatment for obsessive-compulsive disorder, post-traumatic stress disorder, generalized anxiety disorder, and sexual dysfunction. Cognitive-behavioural, psychodynamic, and humanistic approaches all provide moderate relief from depression.

Mental health professionals agree that the effectiveness of therapy depends to a large extent on the quality of the relationship between the client and therapist. In general, the better the rapport is between therapist and client, the better the outcome of therapy. If a person does not trust a therapist enough to describe deeply personal problems, the therapist will have trouble helping the person change and improve. For clients, trusting that the therapist can provide help for their problems is essential for making progress.

The founder of person-centred therapy, Carl Rogers, believed that the most important qualities in a therapist are being genuine, accepting, and empathic. Almost all therapists today would agree that these qualities are important. Being genuine means that therapists care for the client and behave toward the client as they really feel. Being accepting means that therapists should appreciate clients for whom they are, despite the things that they may have done. Therapists do not have to agree with clients, but they must accept them. Being empathic means that therapists understand the client's feelings and experiences and convey this understanding back to the client.

In helping their clients, all therapists follow a code of ethics. First, all therapy is confidential. Therapists notify others of a client's disclosures only in exceptional cases, such as when children disclose abuse by parents, parents disclose abuse of children, or clients disclose an intention to harm themselves or others. Also, therapists avoid dual relationships with clients—that is, being friends outside of therapy or maintaining a business relationship. Such relationships may reduce the therapist's objectivity and ability to work with the client. Ethical therapists also do not engage in sexual relationships with clients, and do not accept as clients people with whom they have been sexually intimate.

As more immigrants to the United States and Canada have entered therapy, psychotherapists and counsellors have learned the importance of taking a client's cultural background into account when assessing the problem and determining treatment. Scholars recognize that most psychotherapies are based on Western systems of psychology, which stress the desirability of individualism and independence. However, cultures of Asia and other regions commonly emphasize different values, such as conformity, dependency on others, and obeying one's parents. Thus, techniques that might be effective for someone from North America, Europe, or Australia might be inappropriate for a recent immigrant from Vietnam, Japan, or India. In order to provide effective treatment, therapists must be aware of their own cultural biases and become familiar with their client's ethnic and cultural background.

In his clinical observations Freud found evidence for the mental mechanisms of repression and resistance. He described repression as a device operating unconsciously to make the memory of painful or threatening events inaccessible to the conscious mind. Resistance is defined as the unconscious defence against awareness of repressed experiences in order to avoid the resulting anxiety. He traced the operation of unconscious processes, using the free associations of the patient to guide him in the interpretation of dreams and slips of speech. Dream analysis led to his discoveries of infantile sexuality and of the so-called Oedipus complex, which constitutes the erotic attachment of the child for the parent of the opposite sex, together with hostile feelings toward the other parent. In these years he also developed the theory of transference, the process by which emotional attitudes, established originally toward parental figures in childhood, are transferred in later life to others. The end of this period was marked by the appearance of Freud's most important work, The Interpretation of Dreams (1899). Here Freud analysed many of his own dreams recorded in the 3-year period of his self-analysis, begun in 1897. This work expounds all the fundamental concepts underlying psychoanalytic technique and doctrine.

The Unconscious, in psychology, seems a hypothetical region of the mind containing wishes, memories, fears, feelings, and ideas that are prevented from expression in conscious awareness. They manifest themselves, instead, by their influence on conscious processes and, most strikingly, by such anomalous phenomena as dreams and neurotic symptoms. Not all mental activity of which the subject is unaware belongs to the unconscious; for example, thoughts that may be made conscious by a new focussing of attention are termed foreconscious or preconscious.

The concept of the unconscious was first developed in the period from 1895 to 1900 by Sigmund Freud, who theorized that it consists of survivals of feelings experienced during infantile life, including both instinctual drives or libido and their modifications by the development of the superego. According to the Swiss psychoanalyst Carl Jung, the unconscious also consists of a racial unconscious that contains certain inherited, universal, archaic fantasies belonging to what Jung termed the collective unconscious.

Also, the states of Consciousness. No simple, agreed-upon definition of consciousness exists. Attempted definitions tend to be tautological (for example, consciousness defined as awareness) or merely descriptive (for example, consciousness described as sensations, thoughts, or feelings). Despite this problem of definition, the subject of consciousness has had a remarkable history. At one time the primary subject matter of psychology, consciousness as an area of study suffered an almost total demise, later reemerging to become a topic of current interest.

French thinker René Descartes applied rigorous scientific methods of deduction to his exploration of philosophical questions. Descartes is probably best known for his pioneering work in philosophical skepticism. Author Tom Sorell examines the concepts behind Descartes's work Meditationes de Prima Philosophia (1641; Meditations on First Philosophy), focussing on its unconventional use of logic and the reactions it aroused.

Most of the philosophical discussions of consciousness arose from the mind-body issues posed by the French philosopher and mathematician René Descartes in the 17th century. Descartes asked: Is the mind, or consciousness, independent of matter? Is consciousness extended (physical) or unextended (nonphysical)? Is consciousness determinative, or is it determined? English philosophers such as John Locke equated consciousness with physical sensations and the information they provide, whereas European philosophers such as Gottfried Wilhelm Leibniz and Immanuel Kant gave a more central and active role to consciousness.

The philosopher who most directly influenced subsequent exploration of the subject of consciousness was the 19th-century German educator Johann Friedrich Herbart, who wrote that ideas had quality and intensity and that they may inhibit or facilitate one another. Thus, ideas may pass from 'states of reality' (consciousness) to 'states of tendency' (unconsciousness), with the dividing line between the two states being described as the threshold of consciousness. This formulation of Herbart clearly presages the development, by the German psychologist and physiologist Gustav Theodor Fechner, of the psycho physical measurement of sensation thresholds, and the later development by Sigmund Freud of the concept of the unconscious.

The experimental analysis of consciousness dates from 1879, when the German psychologist Wilhelm Max Wundt started his research laboratory. For Wundt, the task of psychology was the study of the structure of consciousness, which extended well beyond sensations and included feelings, images, memory, attention, duration, and movement. Because early interest focussed on the content and dynamics of consciousness, it is not surprising that the central methodology of such studies was introspection; that is, subjects reported on the mental contents of their own consciousness. This introspective approach was developed most fully by the American psychologist Edward Bradford Titchener at Cornell University. Setting his task as that of describing the structure of the mind, Titchener attempted to detail, from introspective self-reports, the dimensions of the elements of consciousness. For example, taste was 'dimensionalized' into four basic categories: sweet, sour, salt, and bitter. This approach was known as structuralism.

By the 1920s, however, a remarkable revolution had occurred in psychology that was to essentially remove considerations of consciousness from psychological research for some 50 years: Behaviourism captured the field of psychology. The main initiator of this movement was the American psychologist John Broadus Watson. In a 1913 article, Watson stated, 'I believe that we can write a psychology and never use the terms consciousness, mental states, mind . . . imagery and the like.' Psychologists then turned almost exclusively to behaviour, as described in terms of stimulus and response, and consciousness was totally bypassed as a subject. A survey of eight leading introductory psychology texts published between 1930 and the 1950s found no mention of the topic of consciousness in five texts, and in two it was treated as a historical curiosity.

Beginning in the late 1950s, however, interest in the subject of consciousness returned, specifically in those subjects and techniques relating to altered states of consciousness: sleep and dreams, meditation, biofeedback, hypnosis, and drug-induced states. A great deal that can develop or become actual for which of possibilities send forth or come forth abundantly in sleep and dream research was directly fuelled by a discovery relevant to the nature of consciousness. A physiological indicator of the dream state was found: At roughly 90-minute intervals, the eyes of sleepers were observed to move rapidly, and at the same time the sleepers' brain waves would show a pattern resembling the waking state. When people were awakened during these periods of rapid eye movement, they almost always reported dreams, whereas if awakened at other times they did not. This and other research clearly indicated that sleep, once considered a passive state, was instead an active state of consciousness.

During the 1960s, an increased search for 'higher levels' of consciousness through meditation resulted in a growing interest in the practices of Zen Buddhism and Yoga from Eastern cultures. A full flowering of this movement in the United States was seen in the development of training programs, such as Transcendental Meditation, that were self-directed procedures of physical relaxation and focussed attention. Biofeedback techniques also were developed to bring body systems involving factors such as blood pressure or temperature under voluntary control by providing feedback from the body, so that subjects could learn to control their responses. For example, researchers found that persons could control their brain-wave patterns to some extent, particularly the so-called alpha rhythms generally associated with a relaxed, meditative state. This finding was especially relevant to those interested in consciousness and meditation, and a number of 'alpha training' programs emerged.

Another subject that led to increased interest in altered states of consciousness was hypnosis, which involves a transfer of conscious control from the subject to another person. Hypnotism has had a long and intricate history in medicine and folklore and has been intensively studied by psychologists. Much has become known about the hypnotic state, relative to individual suggestibility and personality traits; the subject has now largely been demythologized, and the limitations of the hypnotic state are fairly well known. Despite the increasing use of hypnosis, however, much remains to be learned about this unusual state of focussed attention.

Finally, many people in the 1960s experimented with the psychoactive drugs known as hallucinogens, which produce disorders of consciousness. The most prominent of these drugs are lysergic acid diethylamide, or LSD; mescaline; and psilocybin; the latter two have long been associated with religious ceremonies in various cultures. LSD, because of its radical thought-modifying properties, was initially explored for its so-called mind-expanding potential and for its psychotomimetic effects (imitating psychoses). Little positive use, however, has been found for these drugs, and their use is highly restricted.

Scientists have long considered the nature of consciousness without producing a fully satisfactory definition. In the early 20th century American philosopher and psychologist William James suggested that consciousness is a mental process involving both attention to external stimuli and short-term memory. Later scientific explorations of consciousness mostly expanded upon James's work. In this article from a 1997 special issue of Scientific American, Nobel laureate Francis Crick, who helped determine the structure of DNA, and fellow biophysicist Christof Koch explain how experiments on vision might deepen our understanding of consciousness.

As the concept of a direct, simple linkage between environment and behaviour became unsatisfactory in recent decades, the interest in altered states of consciousness may be taken as a visible sign of renewed interest in the topic of consciousness. That persons are active and intervening participants in their behaviour has become increasingly clear. Environments, rewards, and punishments are not simply defined by their physical character. Memories are organized, not simply stored. An entirely new area called cognitive psychology has emerged that centres on these concerns. In the study of children, increased attention is being paid to how they understand, or perceive, the world at different ages. In the field of animal behaviour, researchers increasingly emphasize the inherent characteristics resulting from the way a species has been shaped to respond adaptively to the environment. Humanistic psychologists, with a concern for self-actualization and growth, have emerged after a long period of silence. Throughout the development of clinical and industrial psychology, the conscious states of persons in terms of their current feelings and thoughts were of obvious importance. The role of consciousness, however, was often de-emphasised in favour of unconscious needs and motivations. Trends can be seen, however, toward a new emphasis on the nature of states of consciousness.

Freud also placed great value on what could be learned from transference, the patient's emotional response to the therapist. Freud believed that during therapy, patients transfer repressed feelings toward their family members to their relationship with the therapist. Transference exposes these repressed feelings and allows the patient to work through them. Free association and transference are still central features of Freudian psychoanalysis

In his clinical observations Freud found evidence for the mental mechanisms of repression and resistance. He described repression as a device operating unconsciously to make the memory of painful or threatening events inaccessible to the conscious mind. Resistance is defined as the unconscious defence against awareness of repressed experiences in order to avoid the resulting anxiety. He traced the operation of unconscious processes, using the free associations of the patient to guide him in the interpretation of dreams and slips of speech. Dream analysis led to his discoveries of infantile sexuality and of the so-called Oedipus complex, which constitutes the erotic attachment of the child for the parent of the opposite sex, together with hostile feelings toward the other parent. In these years he also developed the theory of transference, the process by which emotional attitudes, established originally toward parental figures in childhood, are transferred in later life to others. The end of this period was marked by the appearance of Freud's most important work, The Interpretation of Dreams (1899). Here Freud analysed many of his own dreams recorded in the 3-year period of his self-analysis, begun in 1897. This work expounds all the fundamental concepts underlying psychoanalytic technique and doctrine.

In his clinical observations Freud found evidence for the mental mechanisms of repression and resistance. He described repression as a device operating unconsciously to make the memory of painful or threatening events inaccessible to the conscious mind. Resistance is defined as the unconscious defence against awareness of repressed experiences in order to avoid the resulting anxiety. He traced the operation of unconscious processes, using the free associations of the patient to guide him in the interpretation of dreams and slips of speech. Dream analysis led to his discoveries of infantile sexuality and of the so-called Oedipus complex, which constitutes the erotic attachment of the child for the parent of the opposite sex, together with hostile feelings toward the other parent. In these years he also developed the theory of transference, the process by which emotional attitudes, established originally toward parental figures in childhood, are transferred in later life to others. The end of this period was marked by the appearance of Freud's most important work, The Interpretation of

Dreams (1899). Here Freud analysed many of his own dreams recorded in the 3-year period of his self-analysis, begun in 1897. This work expounds all the fundamental concepts underlying psychoanalytic technique and doctrine.

Freud also placed great value on what could be learned from transference, the patient's emotional response to the therapist. Freud believed that during therapy, patients transfer repressed feelings toward their family members to their relationship with the therapist. Transference exposes these repressed feelings and allows the patient to work through them. Free association and transference are still central features of Freudian psychoanalysis.

We have used the term 'transference' several times, in that we attributed the therapeutic results to the transference without further definition of the word. We will now consider more closely the emotional relationship which is thus designed. During a psychoanalytic treatment, the patient allows the analyst to play a predominating role in his emotional life. This is of great importance in the analytic process. After his treatment is over, this situation is changed. The patient builds up feelings of affection for and resistance to his analyst which, in their ebb and flow, so exceed the normal degree of feeling that the phenomenon has long attracted the theoretical interest of the analyst. Freud studied this phenomenon thoroughly, explained it, and gave it the name 'transference', we most probably will understand the significance of the transference phenomenon impressed Freud so profoundly that he continued through the years to develop his ideas about it.

In all afforded efforts, too refuse to consider the demise of forebears as to merely disdain, that we cannot reproduce of all Freud's research about transference but must it limit to their essentials. When we speak of the transference in connexion with social reeducation, we mean the emotional responses of the education or counsellor or therapist, as the case maybe, without meaning that it takes place in exactly the same way as in an analysis. The 'counter-transference' is emotional aptitude of the teacher toward the pupil, the counsellor toward his charge, the therapist toward the patient. The feeling which the child develops for the mentor is conditioned by a much earlier relationship to someone else. We must take cognisance of this fact in order to understand these relationships. The tender relationship which go to up the child's love life are no longer strange to us. Many of these have already been touched upon in the foregoing literature. We have learned how the small boy takes the father and mother as love objects. We have followed the strivings which arise out of this relationship, the Oedipus situation, we have seen how this runs its course and terminates in an identification with the parents. We have also had opportunity to consider the relationship between brothers and sisters, how their original rivalry is transformed into affection through the pressure of their feeling for the parents. We know that the boy at puberty must give up his first love object within the family and transfers his libido to individuals outside the family.

Why Freud chose the term 'transference' for the emotional relationship between patient and analyst is easy to understand. The feelings which arose long ago in another situation are transferred upon the analyst. Too the counsellor of the child, the knowledge of the transference mechanism is indispensable. In order to influence the dissocial behaviour, he must bring his charge into the transference situation. The study of the transference in the dissocial child shows regularly a love life that has been disturbed in early childhood by a lack of affection or an undue amount of affection. A satisfactory social adjustment depends on certain conditions, among them an adequate constitutional endowment and early love relationships which have been confined within certain limits. Society determines these limitations, just as definitely as the later love life of an individual is determined by early form his libidinal development. The child develops normally and assumes his proper place in society, if he can cultivate in the nursery such relationships as can favourably be carried over into the schools and from there into the ever-broadening world around him. His attitude toward his parents must be such that it can be carried over onto the teacher, and that toward his brothers and sisters must be transferred to his schoolmates. Every new contact, according to the degree of authority or maturity which the person represents, repeats a previous relationship with very little deviation. People whose early adjustment to succeed or supervene from such a normative course have no difficulties in their emotional relations with others, and they are able to form new ties, to deepen them, or to break them off without conflict when the situation demands it.

We can easily see why an attempt to change the present order of society always meets with resistance and where the radical reformer will have to use the greatest leverage. Our attitude to society and its members has a certain standard form. It gets its imprint from the structure of the family and the emotional relationships set up within the family, therefore, the parents, especially the father, assume overwhelming responsibility for the social orientation of the child. The persistent, ineradicable libidinal relationships carried over from childhood are facts with which social reformers must reckon. If the family represents the best preparation for the present social order, which seems to be the case, then the introduction of a new order means that the family must be uprooted and replaced by a different personal world for the child. It is beyond our scope to attempt a solution of this question, which concerns those who strive to build up a new order of society. We are remedial educators and must recognize these sociological relationships. We can ally ourselves with whatever social system will, but we have the path of our present activity well marked out for us, to bring dissocial youth into the line with present-day society.

If the child is harmed through too great disappointment or too great indulgence in his early life, he builds up reaction patterns which are damaged, incomplete, or too delicate to support the wear and tear of life. He is incapable of forming libidinal object relationships which are considered normal by society. His unpreparedness for life, his inability to regulate his conscious and unconscious libidinal striving and to confine his libidinal expectations within normal bounds, create an insecurity in relation to his fellow men and constitute one of the first and most important conditions fo r their development of delinquency. Following this point of view, we look for the primary causes of dissocial behaviour in early childhood, where the abnormal libidinal ties are established. The word 'delinquency' is an expression used to describe a relationship to people and things which is at variance with what society approves in the individual.

It is not immediately clear from the particular form of the delinquency just what libidinal disturbance in childhood had given rise to the dissocial expression. Until we have a psychoanalytically construed scheme for the diagnosis of delinquency, we may content ourselves by separating these forms into two groups: (1) Borderline neurosis cases with dissocial symptoms, and (2) dissocial cases in which that part of the ego giving rise to the dissocial behaviour shows no trace of neurosis. In the first type, the individual finds himself in an inner conflict because of the nature of his love relationships, a part of his own personality forbids the indulgence of libidinal desires and strivings. The dissocial behaviour results from this conflict. In the second type, the individual finds himself in open conflict with his environment, because the outer world has frustrated his childish libidinal desires.

The differences in the forms of dissocial behaviour are important for many reasons. At present, they are significant to us because of the various ways in which the transference is established in these two types, we know that with a normal child the transference takes place of itself through the kindly efforts of the responsible adult. The teacher in his attitude repeats the situations long familiar to the child, and thereby evokes a parental relationship. He does not maintain this relationship at the same level, but continually deepens it as long as he is the parental substitute.

When a neurotic child with symptoms of delinquency comes into the institution, the tendency to transfer his attitude toward his parents to the persons in authority are immediately noticeable. The worker will adopt the same attitude toward the dissocial child as to the normal child, and bring him into a positive transference, if he acts toward him in such a way as to prevent a repetition with the worker of the situation with the parents which led to the conflict. In psychoanalysis, on the other hand, it is of greatest importance to let this situation repeat itself. In a sense the worker becomes the father or the mother, but still not wholly so, he represents their claims, but in the right moment he must let the dissocial child know that he has insight into his difficulties and that he will not interpret the behaviour in the same way as do the parents. He will respond to the child's feeling of a need for punishment, but he will not completely satisfy it.

He will conduct in himself be entirely differently in the case of the child who in open conflict with society. In this instance he must take the child's part, be in agreement with his behaviour, and in the severest cases even give the child to understand that in his place he would behave just the same way. The guilt feelings found so clearly in the neurotic cases with dissocial behaviour are present in these cases also. These feelings do not arise, however, from the dissocial ego, but have another source.

Why does the educator conduct himself differently in dealing with this second type? These children, too, he must draw into a positive transference to him, but what is applicable and appropriate for a normal or a neurotic child would here achieve opposite results. Otherwise the worker would bring onto himself all the hate and aggression which the child bears toward society, thus leading the child into a negative instead of a positive transference, and creating a situation in which the child is not amenable to training.

Nevertheless, what was said about psychoanalysis theory is only a bare outline, that much deeper study of the transference is necessary to anyone interested in re-educational work from the psychoanalytic point of view. The practical application of this theory is not easy, since we deal mostly with mixed types, such that the attitude of the counsellor cannot be as uniform as having enough verbal descriptions for evincing of individual forms of dissociated behaviour to enable us to offer detailed instructions about how to deal with them. At present our psychoanalytic knowledge is such that a correct procedure cannot be stated specifically for each and every dissocial individual.

The necessity for bringing the child into a good relationship to his mentor is of prime importance. The worker cannot leave this to chance, he must deliberately achieve it and he must face the fact thus no effective work is possible without it. It is important for him to grasp the psychic situation of the dissocial child in the very first contact he makes with him, because only this can be known in what attitude to adopt. There is a further difficulty in that the dissocial child takes pains to hide his real nature: He misrepresents himself and lies. This is to be taken for granted, it should not surprise or upset us. Dissocial children do not come to us of their own free will but are brought to us, very often with the threat, 'You'll soon find out what's going to happen to you.' Generally parents resort our help only after every other means, including corporal punishment, has failed. To the child, we are only another form of punishment, an enemy against whom he must be on his guard, not a source of help to him. There is a great difference between this and the psychoanalytic situation, where the patient comes voluntarily for helping. To the dissocial child, we are a menace because we represent society, with which he is in conflict. He must protect himself against this terrible danger and be careful what he says in order not to give himself away. It is hard to make some of these delinquent children talk, remain unresponsive and stubborn. One thing they all have in common: They do not tell the truth. Some lie stupidly, pitiably, others, especially the older ones, show great skill and sophistication. The extremely submissive child, the 'dandly', the very jovial, or the exaggeratedly sincere, some especially hard to reach. This behaviour is so much to be expected that we are not surprised or disarmed by it, the inexperienced teacher or adviser is easily irritated, especially when the lies are transparent, but he must not let the child be aware of this. He must deal with the situation immediately without telling the child that he sees through his behaviour.

There is nothing remarkable in the behaviour of the dissocial, but it differs only quantitatively from normal behaviour. We all hide our real selves and use a great deal of psychic energy to mislead our neighbours. We masquerade more or less, according to necessity. Most of us learn in the nursery the necessity of presenting ourselves in accordance with the environmental demands, and thus we consciously or unconsciously build up a shell around ourselves. Anyone who has had experience with young children must have noticed how they immediately begin to dissimulate when a grown-up comes into the room. Most children succeed in behaving in the manner which they think is expected of them. Thus they lessen the danger to themselves and at the same time they are casting the permanent moulds of their mannerisms and their behaviour. How many parents really bother themselves about the inner life of their children? Is this mask necessarily for life? I do not know, but it often seems that the person on whom childhood experiences have forced the dissocial individual masquerades to a greater extent, and more consciously, then the normal. He is only drawing logical deductions from his unfortunate disagreeable authority? Why should he be sincere with those people who represent disagreeable authority? This is an unfair demand.

We must look further into the differences between the situation of social retraining and the analytic situation. The analyst expects to meet in his patient unconscious remittances which prevent him from being honest or make him silent: But the treatment is in vain when the patient lies persistently. Those who work with dissocial children expect to be lied to. To send this child away because he lies is only giving in to him. We must wait and hope to penetrate this mask which covers the real psychic situation. In the institution it does not matter if this is not achieved immediately, it means merely that the establishment of the transference is postponed. In the clinic, however, we must work more quickly. Taking with the patient does not always suffice, and we must introduce other remedial measures. Generally, we see the delinquent child only a few times, we are forced to take some steps after the first few interviews, to formulate some tentative conception of the difficulty and to establish a positive transference as quickly as possible. This means we must get at least a peep behind the mask. If the child is not put in an institution, he remains in the old situation under the same influences which caused the trouble. In such cases we wish to establish the transference as quickly as possible, to intensify the child`s positive feelings for us that are aroused while the child is with us, and to bring them rapidly to such a pitch that they can no longer be easily disturbed by the old influences. To carry on such work successfully presupposes a long experience.

Let us interrupt our theoretical considerations and see how the analyst and the patient try to grasp upon the situational thoughts for which the transference and to lift the mask, moreover, that it can be understood that feelings and a better understanding astonishes the intentionality that allies with others only because of its need to achieve to some end.

Even so, there are few current problems concerning the problem of transference that Freud did not recognize either implicitly or explicitly in the development of the theoretical and clinical framework. For all essential purposes, moreover, his formulations, in spite of certain shifts in emphasis, remain integral to contemporary psychoanalytic theory and practice. Recent developments mainly concern the impact of an ego-psychological approach, the significance of object relations, both current and infantile, external and internal, the role of aggression in mental life, and the part played by regression and the repetition compulsion in the transference. Nevertheless, analysis of the infantile Oedipal situation in the setting of a genuine transference neurosis is still considered as a primary goal of psychoanalytic procedure.

Originally, transference was ascribed to displacement on the analyst of repressed wishes and fantasies derived from early childhood. The transference neurosis was viewed as a compromise formulation similar to dreams and other neurotic symptoms. Resistance, defined as the clinical manifestation of repression, could be diminished or abolished by interpretation mainly directed toward the content of the repressed. Transference resistance, both positive and negative, was inscribed to the threatened emergence of repressed unconscious material in the analytic situation. Soon, with the development of a structural approach, the superego described as the heir to the genital Oedipal situation was also recognized as playing a leading part in the transference situation. The analysis was subsequently viewed not only as the object by displacement of infantile incestuous fantasies, but also as the substitute by projection for the prohibiting parental figures which had been internalized as the definitive superego. The effect of transference interpretation in mitigating undue severity of the superego has, therefore, been emphasized in many discussions of the concept of transference.

Certain expansions in the structural approach related to increased recognition of the role of early object relations in the development of both ego and superego have affected current concepts of transference. In this connection, the significance of the analytic situation as a repetition of the early mother-child relationship has been stressed from different point of view. Such, are equally important development relates to Freud's revised concept of anxiety which can only lead to theoretical developments in the field of ego psychology, but also bought about related clinical changes in the work of many analysts. As a result, attention was no longer mainly focussed on the content of the unconscious. In addition, increasing importance was attributed to the defence processes by means of which the anxiety which would be engendered if repression and other related mechanisms were broken down, was avoided in the analytic situation. Differences in the interpretation of the role of the analyst and the nature of transference developed from emphasis, on the one hand, on the importance of early object relations, and on the other, from primary attention to the role of the ego and its defences. These defences first emerged clearly in discussion of the technique of child analysis, in which Melanie Klein and Anna Freud, the pioneers in the fields of thought as playing the leading roles.

From a theoretical point of view, discussion foreshadowing the problems which face us today was presented in 1934 in a well-known paper by Richard Sterba and James Strachey, and further elaborated at the Marienbad Symposium at which Edward Bibring made an important contribution. The importance of identification with, or introjection of, the analyst in the transference situation of identification with, or introjection of, the analysts in the transference situation was clearly indicated. The therapeutic results were attributed to the effect of this process In mitigating the need for pathological defences. Strachey, however, considerably influenced by the work of Melanie Klein, regarded transference as essentially a projection onto the analyst of the patient's own superego. The therapeutic process was attributed to subsequent introjection of a modified superego as a result of 'mutative' transference. Sterba and Bibring, on the other hand, intimately involved with development of the ego-psychological approach, reemphasised the central role of the ego, postulating a therapeutic split and identification with the analyst as an essential feature of transference. To some extent, this difference of opinion may be regarded as semantic. If the superego is explicitly defined as the heir of the genital Oedipus conflict, then earlier intra-systematic conflicts within the ego, although they may be related retrospectively to the definite superego, much, nevertheless, be defined as contained within the ego. Later divisions within the ego of the type indicated by Sterba and very much expanded by Edward Bibring in his concept of therapeutic alliance between the analyst and the healthy part of the patient's ego, must also be excluded from superego significance. In contrast, those whom attribute pregenital intra-systemic conflicts within the ego primarily to the introjection of objects, consider that the resultant state of internal conflict resembles in all dynamic respects the situation seen in later conflicts between ego and superego. They, therefore, believe that these structures develop simultaneously and suggest that no sharp distinction should be made between pre-oedipal, oedipal, and post-oedipal superego.

The differences, however, are not entirely verbal, since those whom attribute superego formation to the early months of life tend to attribute a significance to early object relations which differs from the conception of those who stress control and, neutralization of instinctual energy as primary functions of the ego. This theoretical difference necessarily implies some disagreement as how the dynamic situation both in childhood and in adult life, inevitably reflected in the concept of transference and in hypotheses as to the hidden nature of the therapeutic process. From one point of view, the role of the ego is central and crucial at every phase of analysis. A differentiation is made between transference as therapeutic alliance and the transference neurosis, which, on the whole, is considered a manifestation of resistance. Effective analysis depends on a sound and stable therapeutic alliance, a prerequisite for which is the existence, before analysis, of a degree of mature superego functions, the absence of which in certain severely disturbed patients and in young children may preclude traditional psychoanalytic procedure. Whenever indicated, interpretations manifestations, which means, in effect, that the transference must be analysed. The process of analysis, however, is not exclusively ascribed to transference interpretation. Other interpretations of unconscious material, whether related to defence or to early fantasies, will be equally effective provided they are accurately timed and provide a satisfactory therapeutic alliance has been made. Those, in contrast, whom stress the importance of early object relations emphasize the crucial role of transference as an object relationship, distorted though this may be of a variety of defences against primitively unresolved conflicts. The central role of the ego, both in the early stages of development and in the analytic process, is definitely accepted. The hidden natures of the ego is, however, considered at all times to be determined by its external and internal objects. Therapeutic process indicated changes in ego function results, therefore, primarily from a change in object relations though interpretation of the transference situation, finds of a less differentiation as made between transference as for being the therapeutic alliance and transference neurosis as a manifestation of resistance. Therapeutic progress depends almost exclusively on transference interpretation. Other interpretations, although at times, are not, in general, considered an essential feature of the analytic process. From this point of view, the preanalytic maturity of the patient's ego is not stressed as considered potentially suitable for traditional psychoanalytic procedure.

These difference in theoretical orientation are not only reflected in the approach to children and disturbed patients. They may also be recognized in significant variations of technique in respect to all clinical groups, which inevitably affect the opening phases, understanding of the inevitable regressive features of the transference neurosis, and handling of the germinal phases of analysis. By its emphasis as drawn on or upon the main problems, and, by contrast, rather than similarity, our efforts will be to avoid too detailed discussions of controversial theory regarding the hidden nature of early ego development by a somewhat arbitrary differentiation between those who relate ego analysis to the analysis of defences and those who stress the primary significance of object relations both in the transference, and in the development and definitive structure of the ego. Needless to say, this involves some oversimplification, where l hope that it may, at the same time, clarify certain important issues. To take, on or upon the analysis of patients we are generally agreeing to be suitable for classical analytic procedure, the transference neurosis. Those which emphasis the role of the ego and the analysis of defences, not only maintain Freud's conviction that analysis should proceed from surface to depth, but also consider that early materials in the analytic situation derives, that, in general, from defensive processes rather than from displacement onto the analyst of early instinctual fantasies. Deep transference interpretation in the early instinctual fantasies. Deep transference interpretation in the early phases of analysis will, therefore, rather be meaningless to the patient since its unconscious significance is so inaccessible, or, if the defences are precarious, will lead to premature and possibly intolerable anxiety. Premature interpretation of the equally unconscious automatic defensive processes by means of which instinctual fantasy kept unconscious is also ineffective and undesirable. There are, nonetheless, differences of opinion within this group, as to how far analysis of defence can be separated from analysis of content. Waelder, for example, has stressed the impossibility of such separation. Fenichel, however, considered that at least theoretical separation should be made and indicated that, as far as possible, analysis of defence should precede analysis of unconscious fantasy. It is, nevertheless, generally agreed that the transference neurosis develops, as a rule after ego defences have been sufficiently undermined to mobilize previously hidden instinctual conflict. During both the early stages of analysis, and at frequent points after development of the transference neurosis, defences against the transference will become a main feature of the analytic situation.

This approach, has already been indicated, is based on certain definite premises regarding the hidden natures and function of the ego in respect to the control and neutralization of instinctual energy and unconscious fantasies, while the importance of early object relations is not neglected, the conviction that early transference interpretation is ineffective and potentially relations are not neglected, the conviction and unconscious fantasy. The conviction that early transference interpretation is ineffective and potentially dangerous is related to the hypothesis that the instinctual energy available to the mature ego has been neutralized from unconscious fantasies, meaning at the beginning of analysis, for all effective purposes, relatively or absolutely divorced from its unconscious fantasy, as yet, there are a number of analysts of differing theoretical orientation of ego function from unconscious sources, but consider that unconscious fantasy continues to operate in all conscious mental activity. These analysts also make receptive on the whole to emphasize the crucial significance of primitive fantasies in respect to the development of the transference situation. The individual entering analysis will inevitably have unconscious fantasies concerning the analyst derived from primitive sources. This material, although deep in a sense, is, nevertheless, strongly current and accessible to interpretation. Klein, in addition, creates the development and definitive structure of both ego and superego to unconscious fantasy determined by the earliest phases of object relationships. She emphasizes the role of early introjective and projective processes in relation to primitive anxiety ascribed to the death instinct and related aggression drive fantasies. The unresolved difficulties and conflict of the earliest period continue to colour object relations throughout life. Failure to achieve an essentially satisfactory object relationship in this early period, and failure to master relative loss of that object without retaining its good internal representative, will not only affect all object relations and definitive ego function, but more specifically determine the nature of anxiety-provoking fantasies on entering the analytic situation. According to this point of view, therefore, early transference uninterpreted, even thought it may relate to fantasies derived from an early period of life, should result not in an increase, but a decrease of anxiety

In considering next problems of transference in relation to analysis of the transference neurosis, two main points must be kept in mind. First, as already indicated, those who emphasize the analysis of defence tend to make a definite differentiation between transference as therapeutic alliance and the transference neurosis as a compromise formation which serves the purposes of resistance. In contrast, those who emphasize the importance of early object relations view the transference primarily as a revival or repetition, sometimes attributed to symbolic processes of early struggles in respect to objects. Still, there is no sharp differentiation made between the early manifestations of transference and the transference neurosis. In view, moreover, of the weight given to the role of unconscious fantasy and internal objects in every phase of mental life, healthy and pathological functions, though differing in essential respect, do not differ with regard to their direct dependence on unconscious sources.

In the second place, the role of regression in the transference situation is subject to wide differences of opinion. It was, of course, one of Freud's earliest discoveries that regression had of its earliest points of fixation, and is a cardinal feature, not only in the development of neurosis and psychosis, but also in the revival of earlier conflicts in the transference situation. With the development of psychoanalysis and its application to an ever increasing range of received increased attention. The significance of the analytic situation as a means of fostering regression as a prerequisite for the therapeutic work has been emphasized by Ida Macapline in a recent paper. Differing opinions as to the significance, value, and technical handling of regressive manifestoes from the basis of important modifications of analytic technique, which will be considered, however, in respect to the transference neurosis, the view recently expressed by Phyllis Greenacre, that regression, and indispensable features would be generally accepted. It is also a matter of generally based agreement that a prerequisite for successful analysis is revival and repetition in the analytic situation of the struggle of primitive stages of development.

Those who emphasize defence analysis, however, tend to view regression as a manifestation of resistance, as a primitive mechanism of defence employed by the growth sets of the transference neurosis. Analysis of these regressive manifestations with their potential dangers depends on the existing and continued functioning of adequate ego strength to maintain therapeutic alliance at an adult level. Those, in contrast, who stress the significance of transference as a revival of the early mother-child relationship do not emphasize regression as an indication of resistance or defence, the revival of these primitive experiences in the transference situation is, in fact, regarded as can essential prerequisite for satisfactory psychological maturation and true geniality. The Kleinian school, as already indicated features the continued activity of primitive conflicts in determining essential features of the transference at every stage of analysis. Their increasing overt revival in the analytic situation, therefore, signifies a reopening of the analysis, and in general, is regarded as an indication of diminuation rather than increase of resistance. The dangers involved according to this point of view are determined more but failure to mitigate anxiety by suitable transference, an interpretation, than by failure to achieve, in the early phases of analysis, a sound and stabling therapeutic alliance based on the maturity of the patient's essential ego characteristics.

In considering, briefly, the terminal phases of analysis, many unresolved problems concerning the goal of the therapy and definition of a completed psychoanalysis must be kept in mind. Distinction must also be made between the technical problems of the terminal phase and evaluation of transference after the analysis has been terminated, there is widespread agreement as to the frequent revival in the terminal phases of primitive transference manifestations apparently resolved during the early phases of primitive transference manifestation, apparently resolved during the early phase of analysis has been terminated. Balint, and those who accept Ferenczi's concept of primary passive love, suggest that some gratification of primitive passive needs may be essential for successful termination. To Klein, the terminal phases of analysis also represents a repetition of important features of the early mother-child relationship. According to her point of view, this period represents, in essence, a revival of the early weaning situation. Completion depends on a mastery of early depressive struggles culminating in successful introjection of the analysis as a good object. Although, in this connection, emphasis differs considerably, it should be noted that those who stress the importance of identification with the analyst as a basis for therapeutic alliance, also accept the inevitability of some permanent modifications of a similar nature. Those, however, who make a definite differentiation between transference of the transference neurosis as a main prerequisite for successful termination. The identification based on therapeutic alliance must be interpreted and understood, particularly with reference to the reality aspects of the analyst's personality. In spite, therefore, of significant important differences there are, as already indicated in connection with the earlier papers of Sterba and Strachey, important points of agreement in respect to the goal of psychoanalysis.

The differences, already considered indicate some basic current problems of transference. So far, however, discussion has been limited to variations within the framework of a traditional technique. we must consider problems related to overt modifications, so as the essential expanding context of use between variations introduced in respect to certain clinical conditions. Often as a preliminary to classical psychoanalysis, and modifications based on changes on basic approach which lead to significant alterations with regard both to the method and to the aim of therapy. It is generally agreed that some neurosis, borderline patients and the psychosis. The nature and meaning of such changes is, however, viewed differently according to the relative emphasis placed on the ego and its defences, on underlying unconscious conflicts, and on the significance and handling of regression in the therapeutic situation.

There are, nonetheless, a number of therapists, both within and outside the field of psychoanalysis, who consider that the transference situation should not be handled only or mainly as a setting for interpretation even in the treatment or analysis of neurotic patients. Instead, the y advocate utilization of the transference relationship for the manipulation of corrective emotional experience. The theoretical orientation of those utilizing this concept of transference may be closer to, or more distant from the Freudian point of view according to the degree to which current relationships are seen as determined by past events. At one extreme, current aspects and cultural factors are considered of predominant importance, at the other, mental development is viewed in essentially Freudian terms and modifications of technique are ascribed to inherent limitations of the analytic method rather than to essentially changed conceptions of the early phases of mental development. Of this group, Alexander is perhaps the best example. It is thirty years since, in his Salzburg paper, he indicated the tendency for patients to regress, even after apparently successful transference analysis of the oedipus situation to narcissistic dependent pregenital levels which prove stubborn and refractory to transference interpretation. In his more recent work, the role of regression in the transference situation has been increasingly stressed. The emergence and persistence of dependent, pregenital demands in a very wide range of clinical conditions, I t is argued, indicates that the encouragement of a regressive transference situation is undesirable and therapeutically ineffective. The analyst, therefore, should when this threatens adopt a definite role explicitly differing from the behaviour of the parents in early childhood in order to bring about therapeutic results through a corrective emotional experience in the transference situation. This, it is suggested, will obviate the tendency to regression, thus curtailing the length of treatment and improving therapeutic results. Limitations of regressive manifestations by active steps modifying traditional analytic procedure in a variety of ways is also frequently indicated, according to this point of view.

It will be clear that to those who maintain the conviction that interpretation of all transference manifestations remain an essential feature of psychoanalysis, the type of manifestation as described, even though based on a Freudian reconstruction of the early phases of mental developments, and represents a major modification. It is determined by a conviction that psychoanalysis, as a therapeutic method, has limitations related to the tendency to regression, which cannot be resolved by traditional technique. Moreover, the fundamental premise on which, but the conception of corrective emotional experience is based minimizing the significance of insight and recall. It is essentially, suggested that corrective emotional experience alone may bring about qualitative dynamic alterations in mental structure, which can lead to a satisfactory therapeutic goal. This implies a definite modification on the analytic hypothesis that current problems are determined by their defences against instinctual impulses and/or intentional object which had been set up during the decisive periods of early development. An analytic result therefore depends on the revival, repetition and mastery of earlier conflict in the current experience of the transference situation with insight an indispensable feature of an analytic goal.

Since certain important modifications are related t o the concept of regression in the transference situation, it should be considered that this concept is in relation to the repetition compulsion, that transference, essentially is a revival of earlier emotional experience, must be regarded as a manifestation of the repetition compulsion is generally accepted. It is, however, necessary distinguish between repetition compulsion as an attempt to master traumatic experience and repetition compulsion as an attempt too return to a real or fantasized earlier stat e of rest or gratification. Lagache, in a recent paper, has related the repetition compulsion to an inherent need to return to any problem preciously left unsolved. From this point of view, the regressive aspects of the transference situation are to be regarded as a necessary preliminary to the mastery of unresolved conflict, as too, the regressive aspects of transference are mainly attributed to a wish to return to an earlier state of rest or narcissistic gratification, to the maintenance of the status quo in preference to any progressive action, to which Freud's original conception of the death instinct. There is a good deal to suggest that both aspects of the repetition compulsion may bee seen in self-destructive forces tend to be stronger that progressive libidinal impulses, the potentialities of the analytic approach will inevitably appear to be limited. In those, in contrast, in who that regard the reappearance in the transference situation of earlier conflicts as an indication of tendencies to master and progress will continue to feel that the classical analytic method remains the optimal approach to psychological illness wherever it is applicable.

Finally, our newer ideas of transference interpretation come from the rereading and reinterpretations of Freud that necessarily accompany the changes in outlook in the corresponding pendulum of analytic techniques from Freud's actual technique, as reconstructed from his notes and the report s of his patients, to the so-called 'classical' technique that held sway after Freud's death, and again, to the currently changing technical scene. Lipton (1977) has insisted that in the 1940s andv1950s the so-called classical technique replaced Freud's own more personal and relaxed technique, probably in reaction to Alexander's suggestion of the corrective emotional experience. It was Lipton's view that the misnamed 'classical' technique, in contrast to Freud's, emphasized rules for the analyst's behaviour and sacrificed the purpose of the analysis. Eissler's 1953 description of analysis as an activity that ideally uses only interpretations became the paradigm for 'classical' analysis. It was, Lipton, says, a serious and severe distortion of the mature analytic technique developed by Freud. Freud regarded the analyst 's personal behaviour, the personality of the analyst exemplified for Lipton in the case of the Rat Man. The so-called 'classical' (and in his view non-Freudian) techniques attempted to include every aspect of the analytic situation as part of technique and led to the model of the silent, restrained psychoanalyst. Lipton's argument is persuasive.

These two different models of technique have obvious implications concerning the transference and its interpretation. Unless we believe in an extreme version of the historical model, we must expect that the silent, restraint, nonparticipatory psychoanalyst will elicit different responses from his patient than will the vivid, less-hidden, more responsive analyst. The range of personal behaviours available to the analyst before we need be concerned that the analyst is engaging in activities that are excessively self-revelatory or that force the patient into a social relationship is probably much broader than we thought a few years ago. But we also know that almost any behaviour of the analyst, including restraint or silence, immediately influences the patient's responses. In these newer views of the analytic situation it is not easy to know that intrapsychically derived patient behaviours.

It is evident today that psychoanalyst's under the sway of their theories and personalities, differ greatly concerning matters to which they are sensitive, and, of course, we can interpret only the transferences we perceive. Despite this limitation, a review of the literature reveals, along with the usual rigidities, a laudable tendency to describe one's experience as fully as possible, without heed to how it contradicts belief, often blurring over when experience and theory do not match. However, we have always been better at what we do than at what we say we do. This is exemplified in Heimann's (1956) paper. Speaking from a modified Kleinian perspective, and holding the historical theory of transference interpretation, Heimann managed 30 years ago to describe vividly and to support passionately much of what today is under discussion as the modernist version.

Psychoanalysis, since the earliest days of the, Studies on Hysteria (Breuer and Freud, 1993-1905), have always given special attention to the transference and to the interpretation of transference, believing it to be central in our theory and technique. While there, has never been a lack of interest in transference interpreting. It is not clear why this is so, and the reasons may vary in different parts of the international psychoanalytic community. In America, at least, Gill's (1982) recent, and somewhat radical presentation of transference interpretation has surely helped to the grasping upon our developing attentions, nevertheless, of another reasons for our intensified interests in transference interpretation is the opportunity it provided for rhetorically dialectic awareness, in that discussions, have lead us to the diverse analytic theories and techniques that today complete of the global diversities in our lives'. Our attentions and allegiance. In this respect, transference interpretation seems to have replaced self-psychology as the encompassing topic that allows analysts of varied persuasions among many structural and fundamental elements that forge out the shape for taking upon the imparting of instinctual information, as to know, and knowing that you know, however, its concerning contemplations are distinguished by the evolving characterizations that are of knowing that you know is really n1othing whatsoever.

Despite the diversity of the transference and its interpreting in analytic process and cure, differing only in whether transference is everything or almost everything to give a clear-cut definition of what transference is.

Laplanche and Pontalis (1973) had written that, 'The reason it is so difficult to produce a definition of transference is that for many authors the notion has taken on a very broad extension, even coming to connote all the phenomena which constitute the patient's relationship with the psychoanalyst, as a result the concept is burdened down more than any other with each analyst's particular view on the treatment - on its objective, dynamics, tactics, scope, and so forth. The question of the transference is thus beset by a whole series of difficulties which have been the subject of debate in classical psychoanalysis.'

Sandler (1983) has discussed how the terms transference and transference resistance, as well as other terms have undergone profound changes in meaning as new discoveries and new trends of psycho-analytic technique assume ascendency. He said, . . . major changes in technical emphasis brought about the extension of the transference concept, which now has dimensions of meaning which differ from the official definition of the term. I am not sure there has ever been a simplified definition of the term. While a certain flexibility of definition makes conversation possible in a field of diverse views, which we may never be clear on what any two people mean when they use the term is a significant disability to our discourse.

However: with this in mind we might review one of Freud's last comments on transference.

In 'An Outline of Psycho-Analysis' (1940), published posthumously, he wrote on the analytic situation:

The most remarkable thing is this. The patient is not satisfied with regarding the analyst in the light of reality as a helper and advisor who, moreover, is remunerated for the trouble he takes and who would himself be content with some role that of a guide on a different mountain to climb, on the contrary, the patient sees in him, the return, and the reincarnation, of some important figure out of his childhood or past, and consequently transfer onto him, feelings and reactions which undoubtedly apply this prototype. This fact of transference soon proves to be a factor of an undreamt-of importance, on the other hand bud an instrument of irreplaceable value and on the other, that he set out on a different undertaking without any suspicion to the extraordinary power that would be at his command. . . .

Another advantage of transference, too, in that in it the patient produces before us with plastic clarity an important part of his life-story, of which he would, otherwise have probably given us only an insufficient account. He acts it before us, as it were, instead of reporting it to us.

Freud saw the transference interpretation as a method of strengthening the ego against past unconscious wishes and conflicts.

It is the analyst's task constantly to tear the patient out of his menacing illusions and to show him again and again, of what it takes to be or begin of a new life, are the reflections of the past. And least, he should fall into a state in which he is inaccessible to all evidences, the analyst takes that neither the love nor the hostility reaching an extreme height. This is effected, by preparing him in good time for these possibilities and by not overlooking the first signs of them. Careful handling of the transference on these lines is as a role richly rewarded. If we succeed, as we usually can, in enlightenment the patient on the true nature of the phenomena of the transference, we thus have struck a powerful weapon out of the hand of his resistance and will have converted dangers into gains. For a patient never forgets again what he has experienced in the form of transference, it carries a greater force of conviction than anything he can acquire in other ways.

We have used the term 'transference' several times, and in the last, we attributed the therapeutic results to the transference without further definition of the word. As our concerning considerations are more closely intertwined by its emotional relationship, which the word or, perhaps, a combination of words, by which something can be called and by means of which it can be distinguished or identified. During a psychoanalytic treatment, the patient allows the analyst to play a predominating role in his emotional life. This is of great importance in the analytic process. After the treatment for and situation is changed. The patient builds up feelings of affection for the resistance to his analyst which, in their ebb ans flow, so exceed the normal degree of feeling that the phenomenon has long since actuated the theoretical interests of the analyst. Freud studied this phenomenon thoroughly, explained it, and gave it the name 'transference'

I cannot reproduce for you, all of Freud's research about the transference, but must limit myself to essentials, such as the statement of 'counter-transference', is the emotional attitude of the analyst toward the patient, the analyst toward his charge, the therapist toward the patient. The feeling which the child develops for the mentor is conditioned by a much earlier relationship to someone else. We must take cognizance of this fact in order to understand these relationships. The tender relationship which go to make up the child's love life are no longer strange to us. Many of these have already been touched upon in the foregoing contentual frames. We have learned how the small boy takes the father and mother as love objects. We gave in following the strivings which arose in this relationship, the oedipus situation, in that we have seen how this runs its course and terminates in an identification with the parent. We have also had opportunity to consider the relationship between brothers and sisters, how their original rivalry is transformed into affection through the pressure of their feeling for the parent. We know that the boy at puberty must give up his first love objects within the family and transfer his libido to individuals exteriority or outside of the family. not allows the analyst to play a predominating role in his emotional life. This is of great importance in the analytic process, after all the treatment for and situation is changed, as the patient builds up feelings of affection for the resistance to his analyst which, in their ebb and flow, exceed the normal degree of feeling that the phenomenon has long since actuated the theoretical interests of the analyst. Freud studied this phenomenon thoroughly, explained it, and gave it the name 'transference'

I cannot reproduce for you, all of Freud's research about the transference, but must limit myself to essentials, such as the statement of 'counter-transference', is the emotional attitude of the analyst toward the patient, the analyst toward his charge, the therapist toward the patient. The feeling which the child develops for the mentor is conditioned by a much earlier relationship to someone else. We must take cognizance of this fact in order to understand these relationships. The tender relationship which go to make up the child's love life are no longer strange to us. Many of these have already been touched upon in the foregoing contentual frames. We have learned how the small boy takes the father and mother as love objects. We gave in following the strivings which arise in this relationship, the oedipus situation, we have seen how this runs its course and terminates in an identification with the parent. We have also had opportunity to consider the relationship between brothers and sisters, how their original rivalry is transformed into affection through the pressure of their feeling for the parent. We know that the boy at puberty must give up his first love objects within the family and transfer his libido to the individuals exteriority or outside of the family.

The key to understanding the essential pathology as well as the therapeutical impasse was in the failure of the patient to develop a reliable working relation with the analyst. In each case the patient was unable to either establish or maintain a durable working alliance with the analyst and the analyst neglected this fact, pursuing instead the analyst of other transference phenomena, as this error in technique was observable in psychoanalysts with a wide range of clinical experience and to recognize the same shortcomings when resuming the transference interpretations.

In this connection, and, if transference is to be regarded as a significant ego function, a number of inferences are rather obvious. One is that analysis does not 'cause' transference. Yet, although not caused by analysis, transference as it occurs in analysis does seem unique. What is unique, however, may not be transference itself, but rather the effect upon transference of the unique conditions of the analytic situation. These conditions may affect most strongly such things as the choice of content of transference reaction, the intensity of these reactions, their exclusiveness, and their sharp focus on the person of the analyst. Although, as a result of these conditions, transference developments in analysis may differ from those occurring elsewhere, this does not mean that in analysis transference as a function is any different.

Another rather obvious inference, following from the first, is that transference can never be resolved. The content may be, but not the function. Through analysis, the symptomatic, neurotic and historical plexuity have been brought into the transference may be resolved, but not the function itself. The function of transference, like other functions of the ego, may be affected by analysis in many ways, but it never goes away.

Still, another inference is a general one concerning transference and the analyst. If transference is to be regarded as an ever active ego function, then the analyst's transference goes on all the time too, just like the patient's, and despite what he might wish to think. His transference has not been resolved in his own analysis. Admittedly, the impact of the analytic situation upon the analyst is vastly different from what it is upon the patient, but many aspects of that situation do favour development in the analyst of transference relations involving his patient. This does not mean, however, that it would be correct too believe the analyst should attempt to inhibit his transference function, much less disavow it. Yet, what the analyst should do about this transference is a question that has never been significantly pondered over. Aside from any belief that the analyst's transference is remarkably useful in the process of analysing and may be essential for certain aspects of analysis, what can be said?

Would it be wrong, to propose that this ego function be dealt within the same way the analyst deals with his other ego function? Just as the analyst must consciously regulate his responses to the functions in order to create and sustain the analytic situation, should he not also regulate his responses to his transference activity?

This does not mean nor should mean his responses and sustain the analytic situation he not also regulate his responses to his transference activity? This does not mean, not to be thought that the analyst must decide either whether or when a transference reaction to his patient exists. Such an attempt is the point on which has in itself, at least two counts. For one thing, significant transference reactions are usually not conscious, and, fo r another, transference activity in some form is always going on.

In view of these considerations, the simplest position for the analyst to take, and the one most likely to be helped, may be to assume that all feelings and reactions of the analyst concerning the patient are 'prima-facie' evidence of the analyst's transference. Under this arrangement every feeling of warmth, pity, sadness, anger, hope, excitement, even interest, every feeling of coldness, indifference, disinterest, boredom, impatience, discouragement, and every absence of feeling, should be assumed to contain significant elements of the analyst's transference as focussed on the patient. This would mean, essentially, that everything arising in the analyst about his patient assumed to be part of the substance of analysis, that nothing presents merely the analyst's 'real' reaction to his patient, and that especially when something seems most real it can be counted on to contain important aspects of the analyst's transference.

Were the analyst to take this rather imperative view of his own transference potential, he might be much more likely to remain abreast of the personal, neurotic meaning of the myriad but often subtle reactions and attitudes he develops toward his patient. This in turn might make it possible for him, at least to keep his transference out of the patient's way and hopefully to use it to further the analysis.

The final inference from all this is perhaps the most promising. This is that transference, if it belongs to the family of ego functions, can be counted on to posses many of this family 's characteristics. Thus, presently existing knowledge about the ego should provide many ready-made leads as to the nature of transference. The ego's way of reality testing, for instance, its responses to internal and external stimuli, its uses of defence mechanisms, may all reveal much about the basic phenomenology of transference. Similarly, much may be surmised about transference's functional vicissitudes by assuming that transference suffers the same general developmental and neurotic deficiencies, distortions, limitations, and fixations to which various other functions of the ego are susceptible. A particularly important study would seem to be the special strengths of transference functioning, especially its way of joining with other agencies to serve and facilitate the individual's idiosyncratic interests and developments. Such a study, for instance, might centre on the ego's object relations to the reference to the question of whether transference is the ego function mainly responsibly for their development.

Viewing transference in this way as an ego function means, of course, relinquishing certain elements of our existing viewpoint. One prominent feature of these existing viewpoints, no matter what form they take, is how hard they are to define or even to elicit. Another is how unquestioning we seem to be about the viewpoints we grew up with, how easily we assume transference to be, but a therapeutically helpful given, an isolated psychological event having little to do with other psychological event s, and, except in the analytic situation, to be lacking useful purpose. Assigned, without even wondering why, to neither ego nor id, it is usually dropped somewhere in-between. Labelled but rarely described, it is most commonly called a 'projection' or a 'repetition' of the past, neither of them labels of great distinction.

Nevertheless, no matter how inadequate the form in which transference presently exists, it is a form that is deeply entrenched and that does not beg for change. Accordingly, wresting transference from its syntonic limbo is not likely to be easy and may be impossible, but doing so, bringing it out into open view where it can be contemplated as a major member of the ego family, is an utterly fascinating prospect, one that permits one to see transference not only as the best tool clinical analysis has, but possibly the best tool the ego has. It well may be, as Freud suggested, the basis of all human relationship and, as suggested, many may be involved in all the ego's differentiations, integrative and creative capacities. It is these aspects of transference that offer the most exciting questions, and it is with these questions that we will continue.

Without minor exceptions or flaws we are founded against the realm of fact that holds with the distinctive quality of being actual, but, nonetheless, it was from very early times that Freud had called attention to the fact that transference manifested itself in two ways - negatively as well as positively - a good deal less said or known about the negative transference than about the positive. This, of course, corresponds to the circumstance that interest in the destructive and aggressive impulses in general, is only a comparatively recent development. Transference was regarded predominantly as a libidinal phenomena. It was suggested that in everyone there existed a certain number of unsatisfied libidinal impulses, and that whenever some new person came upon the scene these impulses were readily attach themselves to him. This was the account of transferences a universal phenomenon. In neurotics, owing to the abnormally large quantities of unattached libido present in the tendency to transference would be correspondingly greater, and the peculiar circumstances of the analytic situation would further increase it. It was evidently the existence of these feelings of love, thrown by the patient upon the analyst, that provided the necessary y extra force to induce his ego to give up its resistance, undo the repressions and adopt a fresh solution of its ancient problems. This instrument, without which no therapeutic result could be obtained, was at once seen to be no stranger; it was in fact the familiar power of suggestion, which had ostensibly been abandoned long before. Now, however, it was being employed in the very different way, in fact in a contrary direction. In pre-analytic days it had aimed at bringing about an increase in the degree of repression, now it was used to overcome the resistance of the ego, that is to say, to allow the repression to be removed.

But the situation became more and more complicated as more facts about transference came to light. In the first place, the feelings transferred turned out to be of various sorts, besides the loving ones there were the hostile ones, which were naturally far from assisting the analyst's efforts. But, even apart from the hostile transference. The libidinal feelings themselves fell into two groups; friendly and affectionate feeling which were capable of being conscious, and purely erotic ones which has usually too remain unconscious. And these latter feelings, when they became too powerful, stirred up the repressive forces of the ego and thus increased its resistances instead of diminishing them, and in fact produced a state of things that was not easily distinguishable, from a negative transference. And beyond all this there arose the whole question of the lack of permanence of all suggestive treatments. Did not the existence of the transference threaten to leave the analytic patient in the same unending dependence upon the analyst?

All of these difficulties were got over by the discovery that the transference itself could be analysed. Its analysis was soon found to be the most important part of the whole treatment. It was possible to make consciously its roots in the repressed unconscious just as it was possible to make conscious any other repressed material - that is, by inducing the ego to abandon its resistance - and there was nothing self-contradictory in the fact that the forces used for resolving the transference was the transference itself. And once it had been made conscious, its unmanageable, infantile, permanent characteristics disappeared, what was left was like any other 'real' human relationship. But the necessity for constantly analysing the transference became still more apparent from another discovery. It was found that, as work proceeded the transference tended, as, it were, to eat up the entire analysis. More and more of the patient's libido became concentrated upon their relation to the analyst, the patient 's original symptoms were drained of their cathexis, yet and there appeared instead an artificial neurosis to which Freud gave the name of the 'transference neurosis'. This original conflict, which have to the onset of neurosis, began to be re-enacted in the relation to the analyst, now this unexpected event is far from being the misfortune than at first. Sight it might seem to be. In fact, it gives us our great opportunity. Instead, of having to deal as best we may with conflicts of the remote past, Which are concerned with dead circumstances and mummified personalities, and whose outcome is already determined, we find ourselves involved in an actual and immediate situation, in which we and the patient are the principal characters and the development of which is to some re-extent, at least under control. But if we bring it about, that in this revivified transference conflict the patient chooses a new solution instead of the old one, a solution in which the primitive and unadaptable methods of repression is replaced by behaviour more in contact with reality, then, even after his detachment from the analysis, he will never be able to fall back into his former necrosis, the solution of the transference conflict implies as the simultaneous solution of the infantile conflict of which it is a new edition. The 'blame', says Freud in his, 'Introductory Lectures' has been made possible by alterations in the ego's occurring as a consequent of the analyst's suggestion. At the expense of the unconscious, the ego becomes wider by the words of interpretation. In which brings the unconscious material into consciousness; through education it becomes reconciled to the individual and is made willing to grant it a certain degree of satisfaction, and its horror of the claim of its libido is lessoned by the new capacity it acquires to expend a certain amount of the libido in sublimation, the more nearly the course of the treatment corresponds with this ideal description the greater will be the success of the psycho-analytic therapy.

Freud made it clear that the ultimate factor in the therapeutic action of psychoanalysis was suggestion on the part of the analyst acting upon the patient's ego in such a way as to make it more tolerant of the libidinal trends. However, Freud had produced extremely little that bears on the subject, and that little goes to show that he had not altered his views on the main principles involved. In additional lectures which were published last year, he explicitly states that he has nothing to add to the theoretical discussions upon therapy given in the original lectures fifteen years earlier. At the same time, there has in the interval been a considerable further development of his theoretical opinions. And especially in the region of ego-psychology. He had, in particular, formulated the concept of the super-ego. The restatement in super-ego terms of analysis may not involve many changes. But it is reasonable of resistance information about the super-ego will be of special interest from our point of view, and in two ways. In th e first place, it would at first glance seem highly probable that the super-ego should play an important part, direct or indirect, in the setting up and maintaining of the repressions and resistances the demolition of which has been the chief aim of analysis, and is confirmed by an examination of the classification of the various kinds of resistance made by Freud in, 'Hemmung Symptom and Amgst' (1926). Of the five sorts of resistance there mentioned it is true that only one is attributed to the direct intervention of the super-ego, but two of the ego-resistances - the repression resistance and the transference resistance - although actually originally from the ego, as a rule set up by out of fear of the super-ego. It seems likely enough therefore that when Freud wrote the words which, in effect, are the favourable change in the patient. 'Is made possible by alterations in the ego', he was thinking, in part at all events, of that portion of the ego which he subsequently separated off into the super-ego? Quite apart from this, moreover, in another of Freud's more recent works, 'The Group Psychology' (1921), there are passages which suggest a different point - namely, that it may be largely through the patient's super-ego that the analyst on the nature of hypnosis and suggestion. He definitely rejects Bernheim's view that all hypnotic phenomena are traceable to the factor of suggestion, and adopts an alterative theory that suggestion is a partial manifestation of the state of hypnosis. The state of hypnosis, again, is found in certain respects, to resemble the state of being in love. There is, 'the same humble subjection, the same compliance, the same absence of criticism toward the hypnotist as towardly the loved object, has stepped into the place of the subject's ego-ideal'. Now since suggestion is a partial form of hypnosis and since the analyst brings about his changes in the patient's attitude by means of suggestion. It seems to follow that the analyst owes into effectiveness, at all events in some respects, to his having stepped into the place of th e patient's super-ego. Thus, there are two convergent lines of argument which point to the patient's super-ego as occupying a key position in analytic therapy. It is a part of the patient's mind in which a favourable alteration would be likely to lead to general improvement, and it is a part of the patient's mind which is especially subject to the analyst's influence.

Such plausible notions as these were followed up almost immediately after the super-ego made its first début. It has been developed by Ernest Jones, for instance, in his paper on, 'The Nature of Auto-Suggestion'. Soon thereafter, Alexander launches his theory that the principal aim of all psycho-analytic therapy must be the complete demolition of the super-ego and the assumption of its functions by the ego. According to his account, the super-ego are handed over to the analyst, and in the second phase they are passed back again to th e patient, but this time to his ego. The super-ego, according to this view of Alexander's (though he explicitly limits his use of the word to the unconscious parts of the ego-ideal), is a portion of the fundamental apparatuses which is essentially primitive, out of data and out of touch with reality, which is incapable of adapting itself, and which operates automatically, with the monotonous uniformity of a reflex. Any useful functions that it performs can be carried out by the ego. And there is therefore, nothing to be done with it but to discard it. This wholesome attack upon the super-ego seems to be of questionable validity. It seems probable that its abolition, even if that were practical politics, would involve the abolition of a large number off highly desirable mental activities. But the idea that the analyst temporarily takes over the functions of the patient's super-ego during the treatment and by so doing on some way alters it agrees with the tentative literatures.

So, too, do some passages in a paper by Radô upon 'The Economic Principle in Psycho-Analytic Technique'. The second, as such was to have dealt with psych-analysis, that in which has unfortunately never been published, but the first one, on hypnotism and catharsis, contains much that is of interest. It includes a theory that the hypnotic subject introjects the hypnotist in the form of what Radô calls a 'parasitic super-ego', which draw off the energy and takes over the functions of the subject's original super-ego. One feature of the situation brought out by Radô is the unstable and temporary nature of this whole arrangement. If, for instance, the hypnotist gives a command, which is too much in opposition to the subject's original super-ego. The parasite is promptly excluded. And, in any case, when the state of hypnosis comes to an end, the sway of the parasite super-ego also terminates and the original super-ego resumes its functions.

However debatable may be the details of Radô description, it not only emphasizes once again, the notion of the super-ego as the function of psych-therapy, but it draws attention to the important distinction between the effects of hypnosis and analysis in the matter of permanence. Hypnosis acts essentially in a temporary way, and Radô theory of the parasitic super-ego, which does not really replace the original one but merely throws it out of action, gives a very good picture of its apparent workings. Analysis, on the other hand, in so far as it seeks to effect the patient's super-ego, aims at something much more far-reaching and permanent - namely, at an integral change in the nature of the patient's super-ego itself. Some even more recent developments in psych-analytic theory give a hint, so it seems as though it seems as the kind of thing, that along which a cleaver understanding of the question may perhaps be reached.

This latest growth of theory has been very much occupied with the destructive impulses and has brought them for the first time into the centre of interests, and attention has at the same time been concentrated on the correlated problems of guilt and anxiety. That is to say, that in the mind, especially are the ideas upon the formation of the super-ego, recently developed by Melanie Klein and the importance which she attributes to the processes of 'introjection' and 'projection' in the development of the personality. In a schematic outline, the individual, she holds, is perpetually introjecting and projecting the objects of its id-impulses, and the character of the introjected objects depends on the character of the id-impulses, directed toward the external objects. Thus, for instance, during the stage of a child's libidinal development in which it is dominated by feelings of oral aggression, its feelings toward its external object will be orally aggressive; It will then introject the object, and the introjected object will now act (in the manner of a super-ego) in an orally aggressive way toward the child's ego. (The next even will be the projection of this orally aggressive introjected object back onto the external object, which will now in its turn appear to be orally aggressive). The fact of the external object being thus felt as dangerous and destructive once more causes the id-impulses to adopt an even more aggressive and destructive attitude toward the object in self-defences. A vicious circle is thus launched in the celebrations that this process seeks to account for the extreme severity of the super-ego, in that of small children, as well as for their unreasonable fear of outside objects. In the course of the development of the normal individual, his libido eventually reaches the genital stage, at which the positive impulses predominant, and his attitude toward his external objects will thus become more friendly. That according to his introjected object, or super-ego will become less severe and his ego's contact with reality will be less distorted. In the case of the neurotic, however, for various reasons - whether an account of frustration of the destructive components - development to the genital stage does not occur, but the individual remains fixated at a pre-genital level. His ego is thus left exposed to the pressure of a savage id on the one hand and a correspondingly savage super-ego on the other, and the vicious circle is perpetuated.

At the arriving considerations that are marked and noted, through which the essence of functional dynamics as based of the transference in the psychoanalytic process or the basic underlying the most basic of beliefs that in politics there is neither good nor evil, however, in that something that forms part of the minimal body, character or structure of that thing predetermines the properties to the good life. Nonetheless, most psychoanalysts maintain that schizophrenic patients cannot be treated psychoanalytically because they are too narcissistic to develop with the psychotherapist as interpersonal relationship that is sufficiently reliable and consistent for psychoanalytic work. Freud, Fenichel and others have recognized that a new technique of approaching patients psychoanalytically must be found if analysts are to work with psychotics. Among those who have worked successfully in recent years with schizophrenics, Sullivan, Hill, and Karl Menninger and his staffs have made various modifications of their analytic approach. The techniques that are in use with psychotics are different from our approach to psychoneurotics. This is not a result of the schizophrenic's inability to build up a consistent personal relationship with the therapist but due to his extremely intense and sensitive transference reactions.

Let us see first what the essences of the schizophrenic's transference reactions are and how we try to meet these reactions.

We think of a schizophrenic as a person who has had serious traumatic experiences in early infancy at a time when his ego and its ability to examine reality were not yet developed. These early traumatic experiences seem to furnish the psychological basis for the pathogenic influence of the flustrations of later years. At this early time the infant lives grandiosely in a narcissistic world of his own. His needs and desires seem to be taken care of by something vague and indefinite which he does not yet differentiate. As Ferenczi noted, they are expressed by gestures and movements since speech is as yet undeveloped. Frequently the child's desires are fulfilled without any expression of them, a result that seems to him a product of his magical thinking.

Are a person's characteristics primarily shaped by early influences, remaining relatively stable thereafter throughout life? Or does change spontaneously occur continuously throughout life? Many people believe that early experiences are formative, providing a strong or weak foundation for later psychological growth. This view is expressed in the popular saying 'As the twig is bent, so grows the tree.' From this perspective, it is crucial to ensure that young children have a good start in life. But many developmental scientists believe that later experiences can modify or even reverse early influences; studies show that even when early experiences are traumatic or abusive, considerable recovery can occur. From this vantage point, early experiences influence, but rarely determine, later characteristics.

Traumatic experiences in this early period of life will damage a personality more seriously than those occurring in later childhood such as are found in the history of psychoneurotics. The infant's mind is more vulnerable the younger and less used it has been, furthers, the trauma has quickened the infant 's egocentricity. In addition early traumatic experiences shorten the only period in life in which an individual ordinarily enjoys the most security, thus endangering the ability to store up as it was a reasonable supplies of assurance and self-reliance for the individual's later struggles through life. Thus, as such, a child sensitized considerably more toward the frustrations of later like than by later traumatic experiences. hence many experiences in later life which would mean little to a 'healthy' person and not much to a psychoneurotic, mean a great deal of pain and suffering to the schizophrenic. His resistance against frustration is easily exhausted.

Once he reaches his limit of endurance, he escapes the unbearable reality of his present life by attempting to reestablish the autistic, delusional world of the infant, but this is impossible because the content of his delusions and hallucinations are naturally coloured by the experiences of his whole lifetime.

How do these developments influence the patient's attitude toward the analyst and the analyst's approach to him?

Due to the very damage and the succeeding chain of frustrations which the schizophrenic undergoes before finally giving in to illness, he feels extremely suspicious and distrustful of everyone, particularly of the psychotherapist ho approaches him with the intent of intruding into his isolated world and personal life. To him the physician's approach means the threat of being compelled to return to the frustrations of real life and to reveal his inadequacy to meet them or, - still worse – a repetition of the aggressive interference with his initial symptoms and peculiarities which he has encountered in his previous environment.

The difficulty that the patient's dilemma through his frustrations is the product through which is called 'delusion': Delusion itself is a false belief which is firmly held by a person even though other people recognize the belief as obviously untrue. For example, a person who truly believes he is Napoleon Bonaparte is delusional. Religious beliefs or popular conceptions, such as the beliefs that people have been abducted by aliens, are not delusions because they are widely held beliefs. Delusions are a type of psychotic symptom that indicate a person has lost contact with reality.

There are many different types of delusions. A person with a paranoid delusion believes that others - such as the FBI, or the CIA, even the Mafia as trying to harm or plot against him. A person with a delusion of reference believes that events or people refer specifically to him or her when they do not. For example, a woman with schizophrenia may believe that a television news broadcaster is talking personally to her rather than to the entire viewing audience. A grandiose delusion is a belief that one is extremely famous or that one has special powers, such as the ability to magically heal people.

A delusion of control is a belief that others are able to control one's thoughts, feelings, or actions. For example, a man with this type of delusion may believe that someone has implanted a microchip in his brain that enables other people to control his thoughts. A somatic delusion is a belief that something is wrong with one's body - for example, that one's brain is rotting away - even though no medical evidence supports this belief. A person with an erotic delusion believes that someone is in love with him or her despite a lack of evidence for this belief. In a delusion of jealousy, a person believes that his or her spouse or lover is unfaithful despite evidence to the contrary.

Delusions commonly occur in certain severe mental illnesses, such as schizophrenia, bipolar disorder (also called manic-depressive illness), some cases of major depression, Dissociative disorders, post-traumatic stress disorder, and paranoid personality disorder. In addition, delusions may result from abuse of certain drugs, including alcohol, cocaine, amphetamines, and hallucinogens such as lysergic acid diethylamiddlee (LSD), phencyclidine (PCP), and mescaline. Medical conditions affecting the brain, such as syphilis and brain tumours, may also cause delusions.

Delusional disorder is a relatively uncommon mental illness characterized by delusions. People with this disorder have one or more delusions that persist for at least one month. In addition, they do not suffer from other symptoms of schizophrenia, such as disorganized speech and bizarre behaviour. Usually their delusions are less bizarre than those that occur in schizophrenia and seem merely odd or unsupported by facts. Examples of nonbizarre delusions include beliefs that one is being followed, loved by someone famous, or deceived by one's spouse. Because delusional disorder is relatively rare, little research has systematically examined its treatment. However, doctors most often use Antipsychotic drugs (also called neuroleptics) to treat this disorder. These drugs help reduce or eliminate delusions, hallucinations, and other psychotic symptoms.

In spite of his narcissistic retreat, every schizophrenic has some underlying notion of the unreality and loneliness of his substitute delusionary world. He longs for human contact and understanding, yet is afraid to admit of himself, or his therapist for fear of further frustration.

That is why the patient may take weeks and months to test the analyst before being willing to accept him, however, once he has accepted him. His dependence on the analyst is greater and he is more sensitive about it than is the psychoneurotic because of the schizophrenic's deeply rooted insecurity, the narcissistic seemingly self-righteous attitude is but a defence.

Whenever the analyst fails the patient from reasons to be discussed later - one cannot at times avoid failing one's schizophrenic patients - it will be severe disappointment and a repetition of the chain of frustrations the schizophrenic has previously endured.

The instinctually primitive part of the schizophrenic's mind that does not discriminate between himself and the environment, it may mean the withdrawal of the impersonal supporting forces of his infancy. Severe anxiety will follow this vital deprivation.

In the light of his personal relationship with the analyst it means that the therapist seduced the patient to use him as a bridge over which he might possibly be led from the utter loneliness of his own world to reality and human warmth, only to have him discover that this bridge is not reliable. if so, he will respond helplessly with an outburst of hostility or with renewed withdrawal as may be seen most impressively in catatonic stupor.

The symptoms of mental illness can be very distressing. People who develop schizophrenia may hear voices inside their head that say nasty things about them or command them to act in strange or unpredictable ways. Or they may be paralysed by paranoia—the deep conviction that everyone, including their closest family members, wants to injure or destroy them. People with major depression may feel that nothing brings pleasure and that life is so dreary and unhappy that it is better to be dead. People with panic disorder may experience heart palpitations, rapid breathing, and anxiety so extreme that they may not be able to leave home. People whom experience episodes of mania may engage in reckless sexual behaviour or may spend money indiscriminately, acts that later cause them to feel guilt, shame, and desperation.

Other mental illnesses, while not always debilitating, create certain problems in living. People with personality disorders may experience loneliness and isolation because their personality style interferes with social relations. People with an eating disorder may become so preoccupied with their weight and appearance that they force themselves to vomit or refuse to eat. Individuals who develop post-traumatic stress disorder may become angry easily, experience disturbing memories, and have trouble concentrating.

Experiences of mental illness often interact differently but depend on one's culture or social group, sometimes greatly so. For example, in most of the non-Western world, people with depression complain principally of physical ailments, such as lack of energy, poor sleep, loss of appetite, and various kinds of physical pain. Indeed, even in North America these complaints are commonplace. But in the United States and other Western societies, depressed people and mental health professionals who treat them tend to emphasize psychological problems, such as feelings of sadness, worthlessness, and despair. The experience of schizophrenia also differs by culture. In India, one-third of the new cases of schizophrenia involve catatonia, a behavioural condition in which a person maintains a bizarre statue like pose for hours or days. This condition is rare in Europe and North America.

With appropriate treatment, most people can recover from mental illness and return to normal life. Even those with persistent, long-term mental illnesses can usually learn to manage their symptoms and live productive lives.

By a variety of symptoms, including loss of contact with reality, bizarre behaviour, disorganized thinking and speech, decreased emotional expressiveness, and social withdrawal. Usually only some of these symptoms occur in any one person. The term schizophrenia comes from Greek words meaning 'split mind.' However, contrary to common belief, schizophrenia does not refer to a person with a split personality or multiple personality. For a description of a mental illness in which a person has multiple personalities. To observers, schizophrenia may seem or appear for being as some sorted kind of madness or a manufacturing insanity.

Perhaps more than any other mental illness, schizophrenia has a debilitating effect on the lives of the people who suffer from it. A person with schizophrenia may have difficulty telling the difference between real and unreal experiences, logical and illogical thoughts, or appropriate and inappropriate behaviour. Schizophrenia seriously impairs a person's ability to work, go to school, enjoy relationships with others, or take care of oneself. In addition, people with schizophrenia frequently require hospitalization because they pose a danger to themselves. About 10 percent of people with schizophrenia commit suicide, and many others attempt suicide. Once people develop schizophrenia, they usually suffer from the illness for the rest of their lives. Although there is no cure, treatment can help many people with schizophrenia lead productive lives.

Schizophrenia also carries an enormous cost to society. People with schizophrenia occupy about one-third of all beds in psychiatric hospitals in the United States. In addition, people with schizophrenia account for at least 10 percent of the homeless population in the United States. The National Institute of Mental Health has estimated that schizophrenia costs the United States tens of billions of dollars each year in direct treatment, social services, and lost productivity.

Approximately 1 percent of people develop schizophrenia at some time during their lives. Experts estimate that about 1.8 million people in the United States have schizophrenia. The prevalence of schizophrenia is the same regardless of sex, race, and culture. Although women are just as likely as men to develop schizophrenia, women tend to experience the illness less severely, with fewer hospitalizations and better social functioning in the community.

Schizophrenia usually develops in late adolescence or early adulthood, between the ages of 15 and 30. Much less commonly, schizophrenia develops later in life. The illness may begin abruptly, but it usually develops slowly over months or years. Mental health professionals diagnose schizophrenia based on an interview with the patient in which they determine whether the person has experienced specific symptoms of the illness.

Symptoms and functioning in people with schizophrenia tend to vary over time, sometimes worsening and other times improving. For many patients the symptoms gradually become less severe as they grow older. About 25 percent of people with schizophrenia become symptom-free later in their lives.

A variety of symptoms characterize schizophrenia. The most prominent include symptoms of psychosis - such as delusions and hallucinations - as well as bizarre behaviour, strange movements, and disorganized thinking and speech. Many people with schizophrenia do not recognize that their mental functioning is disturbed.

Delusions are false beliefs that appear obviously untrue to other people. For example, a person with schizophrenia may believe that he is the king of England when he is not. People with schizophrenia may have delusions that others, such as the police or the OPP, even the mafia are plotting against them or spying on them. They may believe that aliens are controlling their thoughts or that their own thoughts are being broadcast to the world so that other people can hear them.

Research suggests that the genes one inherits strongly influence one's risk of developing schizophrenia. Studies of families have shown that the more close one is related to someone with schizophrenia, the greater the risk one has of developing the illness. For example, the children of one parent with schizophrenia have about a 13 percent chance of developing the illness, and children of two parents with schizophrenia have about a 46 percent chance of eventually developing schizophrenia. This increased risk occurs even when such children are adopted and raised by mentally healthy parents. In comparison, children in the general population have only about a 1 percent chance of developing schizophrenia.

Some evidence suggests that schizophrenia may result from an imbalance of chemicals in the brain called neurotransmitters. These chemicals enable neurons (brain cells) to communicate with each other. Some scientists suggest that schizophrenia results from excess activity of the neurotransmitter dopamine in certain parts of the brain or from an abnormal sensitivity to dopamine. Support for this hypothesis comes from Antipsychotic drugs, which reduce psychotic symptoms in schizophrenia by blocking brain receptors for dopamine. In addition, amphetamines, which increase dopamine activity, intensify psychotic symptoms in people with schizophrenia. Despite these findings, many experts believe that excess dopamine activity alone cannot account for schizophrenia. Other neurotransmitters, such as serotonin and norepinephrine, may play important roles as well.

Although scientists favour a biological cause of schizophrenia, stress in the environment may affect the onset and course of the illness. Stressful life circumstances - such as maturing in age and character as for living in poverty, the death of a loved one, an important change in jobs or relationships, or chronic tension and hostility at home—can increase the chances of schizophrenia in a person biologically predisposed to the disease. In addition, stressful events can trigger a relapse of symptoms in a person who already has the illness. Individuals who have effective skills for managing stress may be less susceptible to its negative effects. Psychological and social rehabilitation can help patients develop more effective skills for dealing with stress.

Although there is no cure for schizophrenia, effective treatment exists that can improve the long-term course of the illness. With many years of treatment and rehabilitation, significant numbers of people with schizophrenia experience partial or full remission of their symptoms.

Treatment of schizophrenia usually involves a combination of medication, rehabilitation, and treatment of other problems the person may have. Antipsychotic drugs (also called neuroleptics) are the most frequently used medications for treatment of schizophrenia. Psychological and social rehabilitation programs may help people with schizophrenia function in the community and reduce stress related to their symptoms. Treatment of secondary problems, such as substance abuse and infectious diseases, is also an important part of an overall treatment program.

Antipsychotic medications, developed in the middle-1950s, can dramatically improve the quality of life for people with schizophrenia. The drugs reduce or eliminate psychotic symptoms such as hallucinations and delusions. The medications can also help prevent these symptoms from returning. Common Antipsychotic drugs include risperidone (Risperdal), olanzapine (Zyprexa), clozapine (Clozaril), quetiapine (Seroquel), haloperidol (Haldol), thioridazine (Mellaril), chlorpromazine (Thorazine), fluphenazine (Prolixin), and trifluoperazine (Stelazine). People with schizophrenia usually must take medication for the rest of their lives to control psychotic symptoms. Antipsychotic medications appear to be less effective at treating other symptoms of schizophrenia, such as social withdrawal and apathy.

Because many patients with schizophrenia continue to experience difficulties despite taking medication, psychological and social rehabilitation is often necessary. A variety of methods can be effective. Social skills training help people with schizophrenia learn specific behaviours for functioning in society, such as making friends, purchasing items at a store, or initiating conversations. Behavioural training methods can also help them learn self-care skills such as personal hygiene, money management, and proper nutrition. In addition, cognitive-behavioural therapy, a type of psychotherapy, can help reduce persistent symptoms such as hallucinations, delusions, and social withdrawal.

Because many patients have difficulty obtaining or keeping jobs, supported employment programs that help patients find and maintain jobs are a helpful part of rehabilitation. In these programs, the patient works alongside people without disabilities and earns competitive wages. An employment specialist (or vocational specialist) helps the person maintain their job by, for example, training the person in specific skills, helping the employer accommodate the person, arranging transportation, and monitoring performance. These programs are most effective when the supported employment is closely integrated with other aspects of treatment, such as medication and monitoring of symptoms.

Some people with schizophrenia are vulnerable to frequent crises because they do not regularly go to mental health centres to receive the treatment they need. These individuals often relapse and face rehospitalization. To ensure that such patients take their medication and receive appropriate psychological and social rehabilitation, assertive community treatment (ACT) programs have been developed that deliver treatment to patients in natural settings, such as in their homes, in restaurants, or on the street.

People with schizophrenia often have other medical problems, so an effective treatment program must attend to these as well. One of the most generally shared in or participated in things conforming to a type without noteworthy excellence or faults just as common a rule, by ordinary, frequent and ordinarily as an idea or expression deficient in originality or freshness, yet, only of its exchanging the commonplace of the common associated problems is vehemently and usually coarsely expressed condemnation or disapproved, as the interpretative category of an unequalled vocabulary is itself a genuine abuse. Successful treatment of substance abuse inpatients with schizophrenia requires careful coordination with their mental health care, so that the same clinicians are treating both disorders at the same time.

The high rate of substance abuse in patients with schizophrenia contributes to a high prevalence of infectious diseases, including hepatitis B and C and the human immunodeficiency virus (HIV). Assessment, education, and treatment or management of these illnesses is critical for the long-term health of patients.

Other problems frequently associated with schizophrenia include housing instability and homelessness, legal problems, violence, trauma and post-traumatic stress disorder, anxiety, depression, and suicide attempts. Close monitoring and psychotherapeutic interventions are often helpful in addressing these problems.

Several other psychiatric disorders are closely related to schizophrenia. In schizoaffective disorder, a person shows symptoms of schizophrenia combined with either mania or severe depression. Schizophreniform disorder refers to an illness in which a person experiences schizophrenic symptoms for more than one month but fewer than six months. In schizotypal personality disorder, a person engages in odd thinking, speech, and behaviour, but usually does not lose contact with reality. Sometimes mental health professionals refer to these disorders together as schizophrenia-spectrum disorders.

Severe mental illness almost always alters a person's life dramatically. People with severe mental illnesses experience disturbing symptoms that can cause of such difficulties and holding to a job, or go to school, relate to others, or cope with ordinary life demands. Some individuals require hospitalization because they become unable to care for themselves or because they are at risk of committing suicide.

The symptoms of mental illness can be very distressing. People who develop schizophrenia may hear voices inside their head that say nasty things about them or command them to act in strange or unpredictable ways. Or they may be paralysed by paranoia - the deep conviction that everyone, including their closest family members, wants to injure or destroy them. People with major depression may feel that nothing brings pleasure and that life is so dreary and unhappy that it is better to be dead. People with panic disorder may experience heart palpitations, rapid breathing, and anxiety so extreme that they may not be able to leave home. People whom experience episodes of mania may engage in reckless sexual behaviour or may spend money indiscriminately, acts that later cause them to feel guilt, shame, and desperation.

Other mental illnesses, while not always debilitating, create certain problems in living. People with personality disorders may experience loneliness and isolation because their personality style interferes with social relations. People with an eating disorder may become so preoccupied with their weight and appearance that they force themselves to vomit or refuse to eat. Individuals who develop post-traumatic stress disorder may become angry easily, experience disturbing memories, and have trouble concentrating.

Experiences of mental illness often take issue upon its stability for depending on one's culture or social group, sometimes greatly so. For example, in most of the non-Western world, people with depression complain principally of physical ailments, such as lack of energy, poor sleep, loss of appetite, and various kinds of physical pain. Indeed, even in North America these complaints are commonplace. But in the United States and other Western societies, depressed people and mental health professionals who treat them tend to emphasize psychological problems, such as feelings of sadness, worthlessness, and despair. The experience of schizophrenia also differs by culture. In India, one-third of the new cases of schizophrenia involve catatonia, a behavioural condition in which a person maintains a bizarre statue like pose for hours or days. This condition is rare in Europe and North America.

Of furthering issues regarding depersonalization disorder, meaning, in effect, that it is a categorised illness based within its intendment for being an illness, of mind, in which people experience an unwelcome sense of detachment from their own bodies. They may feel as though they are floating above the ground, outside observers of their own mental or physical processes. Other symptoms may include a feeling that they or other people are mechanical or unreal, a feeling of being in a dream, a feeling that their hands or feet are larger or smaller than usual, and a deadening of emotional responses. These symptoms are chronic and severe enough to impede normal functioning in a social, school, or work environment.

Depersonalization disorder is a relatively rare syndrome thought to result from severe psychological stress. It may occur as part of other mental illnesses, especially anxiety disorders. For example, some people with panic disorder feel nervous, have a sense of doom about their future and health, and have a troubling sense of detachment form the lose in the attemptive use in making or doing or achieving a useful regularity as might the quality of being expected of the control over their bodies. Depersonalization disorder may also be a component of more severe mental illness, such as schizophrenia. Treatment may include training in relaxation techniques that enhance body perception and control, hypnosis to modify symptoms, and psychotherapy to explore possible stress-related components of the disorder.

Psychiatrists classify depersonalization disorder as one of the Dissociative disorders. Such disorders involve a disruption of consciousness, memory, identity, or perception.

All the while, the schizophrenic responds to altercations in the analyst's defections and understanding by corresponding stormy and dramatic changes from love to hatred, from willingness to leave his delusional world to resistance and renewed withdrawal.

As understandable as these changes are, nevertheless may come as a surprise to the analyst who frequently has not observed their source, this is quite in contrast to his experience with psychoneurosis whose emotional reactions during an interview he can usually predict. These unpredictable changes seem to be the reason for the conception of the unreliability of the schizophrenic's transference reaction, yet they follow the same dynamic rules as the psychoneurotic's oscillations between positive and negative transference and resistance, however, if the schizophrenic's reactions are stormy and seemingly more unpredictable than those of the psychoneurotic, that instances suggested to be due to the inevitable errors in the analyst's approach to the schizophrenic, of which he himself may be unaware, rather than to the unreliability of the patient's emotional response?

Why is it inevitable that the psychoanalysts disappoint his schizophrenic patient time and again?

The schizophrenic withdraws from painful reality and retires to what resembles the early speechless phase of development where consciousness is not yet crystalized. As the expression of his feelings is not hindered by the convention that he has eliminated, as his thinking, feelings, behaviour and speech - when present - obey the working rules of the archaic unconscious. His thinking is magical and does not follow logical rules. It does not admit to 'no' and likewise the no to 'yes': There is no recognition of space and time, I, you, and these are interchangeable expressions through which of symbols and often by movement and gestures rather than by words.

As the schizophrenic is suspicious, he will distrust the words of his analyst. He will interpret them and incidental gestures and attitudes of the analyst according to his own delusional experience. The analyst may not even be aware of these involuntary manifestations of his attitudes, yet they mean much to the hypersensitive schizophrenic who uses them as a means of orienting himself to the therapist's personality and intentions toward him.

In other words, the schizophrenic patient and the therapist are people living in different worlds and no different levels of personal development with different means of expressing and of orienting themselves. We know little about the language of the unconscious that belongs to the schizophrenic, and our access to it is blocked by the very process of our own adjustment to a world the schizophrenic has relinquished, so, we should not be surprised that errors and misunderstandings occur when we under take to communicate and strive for a rapport with him.

Another source of the schizophrenic's disappointment arises form which the analyser accepts and does not interfere with the behaviour of the schizophrenic, his attitude may lead the patient to expect that the analyst will assist in carrying out all the patient's wishes, even though they may not seem to be in his interest to the analyser's and the hospital's in their relationship to society. This attitude of acceptance so different from the patient's previous experiences readily fosters the anticipation that the analyst will try to carry out the patient's suggestion and take his part, even against conventional society with which it should occasionally arise. Frequently it will be wise for the analyst to agree with the patient's wish to remain unbattled and untidy until he is ready to talk about the reasons for his behaviour or to change spontaneously. At other times, he will unfortunately be unable to take the patient's part without being able to make the patient understand and accept the reasons for the analyst's position.

If the analyst is not able to accept the possibility of misunderstanding the reaction of the schizophrenic patient and in turn of being misunderstood by him, it may shake his security with his patient.

That is to say, that, among other things, the schizophrenic, once he accepts the analyst's insecurity. being helpless and open to himself - in spite of his pretended grandiose isolation - he will feel utterly defeated by the insecurity of his would-be helper. Such disappointment may furnish reasons for outbursts of hatred and are comparable to the negative transference reactions of psychoneurosis, yet more intense than these, since they are not limited by the restrictions of the actual world - that is, it exists in or based on fact, its only problem is a sure-enough externalization for which things are existing in the act of being external in something that has existence, ss if it were an actualization as received in the obtainable enactment for being externalized, such that its problem of in some actual life that proves obtainable achieved, in that of doing something that has an existence for having absolute actuality.

These outbursts are accompanied by anxiety, feelings of guilt, and fear of retaliations which in turn lead to increased hostility. Yet this established a vicious circle: We disappoint the patient, he is afraid that we hate him for his hatred and therefore continues to hate us. If in addition he senses that the analyst is afraid of his aggressiveness, it confirms his fear that he is actually considered as some dangerous and unacceptable, and this augments his hatred.

This establishes that the schizophrenics capable of developing strong relationships of love and hatred toward the analyst. After all, one could not be so hostile if it were not for the background of a very close relationship. In addition, the schizophrenic develops transference reactions on the narrower sense which he can differentiate from the actual interpersonal relationship. For which the schizophrenic's emotional reactions toward the analyst have to be met with extreme care and caution. The love which the sensitive schizophrenic feels as he first emerges, and his cautions acceptances of the analyst's warmth of interest are really most delicate and tender things. If the analyst deals with the transference reactions of a psychoneurotic is bad enough, though as a reparable rule, but if he fails with a schizophrenic in meeting positive feelings by pointing it out for instance before the patient indicates that he is ready to discuss it, he may easily freeze to death what has just begun to grow and so destroy any further possibility of therapy.

Some analysts may feel that the atmosphere of complete acceptance and of strict avoidance of any arbitrary denials which we recommend as a basic rule for the treatment of schizophrenics may not avoid our wish to guide of reacceptance of reality, nevertheless, Freud says that every science and therapy which accept his teachings about unconscious, about transference and resistance and about infantile sexuality, may be called psychoanalysis. According in this definition we believe we are practising psychoanalysis with our schizophrenic patients.

Whether we call it analysis or not, it is clear that successful treatment does not depend on technical rules of any special psychiatric school but rather on the basic attitude of individual therapist toward psychologic persons. If he meets them as strangle creatures of another world whose productions are not comprehensible to 'normal' beings, he cannot treat them, if he realizes, however, that the difference between himself and the psychologic is only of degree, and not of kind, he will know better how to meet him. He will not be able to identify himself sufficiently with the patient to understand and accept his emotional reactions without becoming involved in them.

The process of constant and perpetual change is examined and closely matched within the study of philosophical speculations and pointed of a world view which asserts that basic reality is constantly in a process of flux and change. Indeed, reality is identified with pure process. Concepts such as creativity, freedom, novelty, emergence, and growth are fundamental explanatory categories for process philosophy. This metaphysical perspective is to be contrasted with a philosophy of substance, the view that a fixed and permanent reality underlies the changing or fluctuating world of ordinary experience. Whereas substance philosophy emphasizes static being, process philosophy emphasizes dynamically becoming.

Although process philosophy is as old as the 6th-century BC Greek philosopher, Heraclitus, renewed interest in it was stimulated in the 19th century by the theory of evolution. Key figures in the development of modern process philosophy were the British philosophers Herbert Spencer, Samuel Alexander, and Alfred North Whitehead, the American philosophers Charles S. Peirce and William James, and the French philosophers Henri Bergson and Pierre Teilhard de Chardin. Whitehead's Process and Reality: An Essay in Cosmology (1929) is generally considered the most important systematic expression of process philosophy.

Contemporary theology has been strongly influenced by process philosophy. The American theologian Charles Hartshorne, for instance, rather than interpreting God as an unchanging absolute, emphasizes God's sensitive and caring relationship with the world. A personal God enters into relationships in such a way that he is affected by the relationships, and to be affected by relationships is to change. So too is in the process of growth and development. Important contributions to process theology have also been made by such theologians as William Temple, Daniel Day Williams, Schubert Ogden, and John Cobb, Jr.

'Reality' is a difficult word to use to every one's satisfaction or even to one's own satisfaction. In this instance the word reality is used arbitrarily to designate the direct, here-and-now impact of the analyst upon the patient. Reality. In this sense, contrasts with the impact the analyst has through his representation in the patient's fantasy life, neurosis, and transference, since both kinds of impact seem always to coexist and since the former - the analyst's real impact - may be the worst enemy of the transference, the matter of their differentiation is possibly the most challenging aspect of analysis.

The analytic situation, which is set up to shut out ordinary reality intrusions, that cannot, . . . neither should not exclude all, but to say, that in the beginning months, for instance, reality inevitably has the upper hand. The analyst, the office, the procedure, are all overwhelmingly real. Everything is strange, frightening and exciting, gratifying and frustrating. Unlike the patient can test it and orient himself to it, the impact of this reality is usually so great that even an ordinary useful transference relationship cannot be expected to develop.

Perhaps the most confusing aspect of this beginning period is the frequent appearance in it of what can be regarded as a false transference relationship. With great intensity and clarity, the patient may reveal, through transference-like references about the analyst, some of the deepest secrets only of his neurosis but of its genesis. The pseudotransference, too good to be true, is almost sure to be nothing more than the patient's attempt to deal with the person of the analyst, the entire spectrum of his various patterns of behaviour. If, it is easy to do, the analyst overlooks the likelihood that the patient's relationship with at this time is really about that almost everything said about it is related, analysis may get off to a very bad start. And if, as is even earlier to do, the analyst's interests the genetic meaning of the openly exposed material, a good transference relationship may be seriously delayed and a workable transference neurosis may never appear. even after initial reality has had time to fade, reality may continue to intrude in ways that are very hard to detect and that is very troublesome.

One of the most serious problems of analysis is the very substantial help which the patient receives directly from the analyst and the analytic situation. For many a patient, the analyst in the analytic situation is in fact the most stable, reasonable, wise and understanding person he has ever met, and the setting in which they meet may actually be the most honest, open, direct and regular relationship he has ever experienced. Added to this is the considerable helpfulness to him of being able to clarify his life storey. confess his guilt, express his ambitions, and explore his confusions. Further real help comes from the learning-about-life accruing from the analyst's skilled questions, observations and interpretations. Taken together, the total real value to the patient of the analytic situation can easily be immense. The trouble with this kind of help is that it goes on and on, it may have such a real, direct and continuing impact upon the patient that he can never get deeply enough involved in transference situation to allow him to resolve or even to become acquainted with his most crippling internal difficulties. The trouble is far too good, the trouble also is that we as analysts apparently cannot resist the seductiveness of being directly helpful, and this, when combined with the compelling assumption that helpfulness is bound to be good, permits us top credit patient improvements to 'analysis' when more properly it should often be recognized for being the amounting result for the patient's using the analytic situation, as the model, for being the preceptors and supporter in the dealing practically within the immediate distractions as holding to some problem.

Perhaps, we can now refer to something in a clear unmistakable manner, and it would be to mention, for being, that one more difficult-to-handle intrusion of reality into the analysis, that by saying, that this is the definitive and final interruption of the transference neurosis by the reality of termination; in the sense, the situation is reversed and the intrusion is analytically desirable, since ideally the impact of reality of impending and certain termination is used to facilitate the resolution of the transference. As with the resolution of earlier episodes of transference neurosis, this final one is brought about principally by the analyst's interpretations and reconstructions. As these take effect, the transference neurosis and, hopefully, along with it the original neurosis is resolved. This final resolution, however, which is much more comprehensive, is usually very different and may not come about at all without the help of the reality of termination. Accordingly, any attenuation of the ending, such as tapering off or causal or tentative stopping, should be expected to stand in the way of an effective resolution of the transference. Yet, it seems that this is what most commonly happens to an ending, and because of this a great many patients may lose the potentially great benefit of a thorough resolution and are forever after left suspended in the net of unresolved transference.

Yet, utter indistinctly rigorous termination seems understandable, as difficult as transference neurosis may be in the analyst at other times, this ending period, if rigorously carried out, simply has to be the period of his greatest emotional strain. There can surely be no more likely time for an analyst to surrender his analytic position and, responding to his own transference, become personally involved with his patient than during the process of separating from a long and self-restrained relationship. Accordingly, it may be better to slur over the ending lightly than to mishandle it in an attempt to be rigorous.

In considering more broadly the function of the transference in the psychoanalytic process, one is confronted by the apparent naïve, but, nonetheless important questions of the role of the actual (current) object as compared with that of the object representation of the original personage in the past. We recall Freud's paradoxical, somewhat gloomy, but portentous concluding passage in 'The Dynamics of Transference.' This struggle between the doctor and the patient, between intellect and instinctual life, between understanding and seeking to act, is played out almost exclusively in the phenomena of transference. It is on that field that the victory must be won - the victory whose expression is on that field that the victory must be won - the victory whose expression is the permanent cure of the neuroses. It cannot be disputed that controlling the phenomena of transference presents the psychoanalysis with the greatest difficultly, but it should not be forgotten that they do us the inestimable service of making the patient 's hidden and forgotten erotic impulses of showing their immediate and manifested impossibilities, for when all is said and done, it is impossible to destroy anyone in absentia or in effigies.

Both object and representations are made necessary by the basic phenomenon of original separation. The existence of an image of the object, which persist in the absence of the object, is one of the important beginnings of psychic life in general, certainly an indispensable prerequisite for object relationship. As generally construed. Whether this is viewed as (or a times demonstrably is) something unstable for allotting introjection, s always subject to alternative projection, or an intrapsychic object representation clearly distinguished from the self-representation, or firm identification in the superego, or in the ego itself, these phenomena are in various ways components of the system of mastery of the fact of separation, or separateness, from the original absolutely necessarily anaclitic (in the earliest period) symbiotic 'object'. In the light of clinical observation, it would appear to be that the relative stabilities (parental) object representation. At which time of varying degree, are to a greater extent for the archaic phenomena. Even in nonpsychotic patients, overwhelmed by them, sometimes resembles the restoration from oedipal identification, which provides the preponderant basis for most demonstrable analytic transferences. That within the necrotic patients, the transference is effectively established when this representation invests the analyst to a degree - depending on intensity of drive and most of ego participation - which ranges in all the, wishing and strivings to remake and analyst to biasses judgements and misinterpretation of data, finally are the actual perceptual distortions.

However, the old object representations may be invested, however rigidly established the libidinal or aggressive cathexis of the image may be, this as such can become the actual and exclusive focus of instinctual discharge, or of complicated and intense instinct-defence solutions, only and general energy-sparing quality of strictly intrapsychic processes. For the vast majority of persons, visible to any degree, including those with severe neurosis, character distortions, addictions and certain psychoses, the striving is toward the living and actual object, even at the cost of intense suffering. In a sense, this returns us to the state in which the psychological 'object-to-be'. Has a cr11itical importance never again to be duplicated, except in certain acute life emergencies, even if the object is not firmly perceived as such, in the sense of later object relations? And it does seem that trance impressions from the earliest contacts in the service of life preservation, and the associated instinctual gratifications, and innumerable secondarily associated sensory impressions. Are activated by the specific inborn urges of sexual maturation? These propel the individual to renew many of the earliest modes of actual bodily contact, in connection with seeking for specific instinctual gratification. Or, to look away from clear-cut instinctual matters to the more remote elaborations of human contact: Few regard loneliness as other than a source of suffering, even self-imposed, as an apparent matter of choice, and the forcible imposition of 'solitary confinement ' is surely one of the most cruel of punishments.

In taking to question, we are entering an area of life in which things are other then themselves, where meaning is multifaceted, and where the line between the old and the new is blurred. It should, by, its immediate measure, help develop our recognition or meaning of the pertinent applicability as to the relevance of interrelated aspects of the psychology of 'metaphor'. In the psychology of metaphor we will find a useful analogy to the psychology of transference interpretation. Our's will be newly encountered as good metaphors, those it response to which we say, 'That's it exactly' or 'That really captures it' or 'That says it all'.

Some literary and linguistic analysis, (e.g., Lewis, 1936 and Snell, 1953) and also people in everyday life, believe that there are experiences that can only be expressed metaphorically. And for this achievement that these metaphors, which may be entire poem or as lines or even words highly valued. But how can this be so? Just what in th e 'it' that the metaphor 'is' or 'captures' or 'says'? If this 'is' or this 'experience' can only be rendered metaphorically, when we can know it only as such, that is, as the metaphor itself. Of the position out of which are put forward by, T.S, Eliot (1933) and E.W. Harding (1963) in their discussion of poetry, for in these instances we are granted that there are no known and logically independent version of the experience that can serve to validate the metaphor. Whatever the metaphor makes available to us depends on it and it and so cannot be used to prove its correctness.

It seems justifiably warrantable to consider that the metaphor is a new experience rather than a mere paraphrase of an already fully constituted expedience. The metaphor creates an experience that one has never had before. It is an experience one has not realized by oneself. The metaphor does, of course, suggest certain constituent experiences of which one may have been more or less dimly aware. One may say, therefore, that the metaphor speaks for those constituents, on the existence of which much of its appeal depends. But in its organizing and implicit ly rendering these constituents in its new way, it is a creation rather than a mere paraphrase or anew edition. Paraphrasing and new editions never speak as forcefully as good new metaphors, nor could they facilitate further new experience. One analytically familiar feature of these creations is that they make it safe and pleasing to experience something that otherwise would be considered too threatening and so would be kept in fragmented obscurity through defensive measures.

Thus, when one says, 'That's it exactly' one is implicitly recognizing and announcing that one has found and accepted a new mode of experiencing oneself and one's world, which is to say, asserting a transformation of one's own subjectivity. Something is now said to be true, and in a sense it is true, but it is true for the first time. Nothing of one and the same can ever happen again, for the second time cannot be the same as the first. One can' t step into the same watering point and then step once again into the same spot of that river. A revelatory metaphor re-encountered or repeated later may lose some of its force, alternatively, it may gain some significance, butt it cannot remain exactly the same metaphor or mobilize an experience identical with the first. The point applies as well as to new metaphors that are similar to familiar ones: They have to be judged or experienced through their conventionalized predecessors, as through methods of knowing or already proved instrumentally of perceiving. The audience and the performer, who may be one person, as such that may not have, as yet.

What is to be said about the psychology of metaphor is analogous to the transformational aspects of developed transference and the steadfast interpretation that both facilitate and organize them as transference. Allowing that these transferences and 'remembered' experiences come into existence over a period of time, nothing that is identical with them has ever before been enacted, and nothing will ever be enacted again. They are creations that may be fully achieved only under specific analytic conditions. Such that living was not reliving that moment, words like re-living, re-experiencing and reliving simply do not do justice to the phenomena, that in making this claim. A seeming contradiction over-writes some of our well-establish ideas. - in offering, - I am not contradicting some of our well-established ideas about interpretation and insight, I am, however, disputing the point that insight refers to a greater proportion or in its range of comprehension, which its distance between possible extremes extent and regain former or normal state, such that, for the recovery of lost memories, and takes in as well, a new grasp of the significance and interpretations of events one has always remembered. In point, as, Freud pointed out, 'As a matter of fact I've always known it, only that I've never thought of it; (1914), In fact, it is to develop that point in furthering to say that it takes an adult to do that, especially with the help of an analyst. It was, after all, Freud's analysis of adults that make it possible to define infantile psychosexuality. In this respect, but without disregard, child analysis retains a quality of applied psychoanalysis' in the same way that the interpreted transference neurosis is: Both are always of describing as true something that was not true in quite that way at the time of its greatest developmental significance. This apparent paradox about 'remembering' as a form of creating goes a long way, probably that what it is, is distinctive about psychoanalytic interpretation.

This time, however, to further the discussion on the interpretive technique that surrounds the phase of a mutative interpretation - that in which a portion of the patient's id-relation to the analyst is made conscious in virtue of the latter's positions as auxiliary super-ego - is in itself complex. In the classical model of an interpretation, the patient will first be made aware of a state of tension of an interpretation, will next be made aware that there is repressive factor at work (that his super-ego is threatening him with punishment), and will only then be made aware of the id-impulse which has stirred up the protects of his super-ego and so given to the anxiety in his ego. This is the classical scheme. In actual practice, the analyst finds himself working from all three sides at once, or in irregular successions. At one moment a small portion of the patient's super-ego may be revealed to him in all its savagery, at another the shrinking defencelessness of his ego, at yet another his attention may be directed to the attempts which he is making at restitution - at compensating for his hostility, on some occasions a fraction of id-energy may even be directly encouraged to break its way through the last remains of an already weakened resistance. There is, however, one characteristic which all of these various operations has in common, they are essentially upon a small scale. For the mutative interpretation is inevitably governed by the principle of minimal doses. It is a commonly agreed clinical fact that alternations in a patient under analysis appear almost always to be extremely gradual: We are inclined to suspect sudden and large changes as an indication that suggestive rather than psycho-analyst processes are at work. The gradual nature of the change brought about in psychoanalysis will be explained, as, only to suggest, those changes are the result of the summation of an immense number of minuet steps, each of which correspond to a mutative interpretation. And the smallness of each step is in turn imposed by the very nature of the analytic situation. For each interpretation involves the release of a certain quantity of id-energy, and, if the quantity released is too large, the higher unstable state of equilibrium which enables the analyst to function as the patient's auxiliary super-ego is bound to be upset. The whole analytic situation will thus be imperilled, since it is only in virtue of the analyst's acting as auxiliary super-ego that these released id-energy can occur at all.

The effectuality from which follow the analytic attempt to bring unequalled amounts in the confronting collections of some improper use to a resultant quantity of id-energy into the patient's consciousness all at once. On the one hand, nothing whatever may happen, or on the other hand there may be an unmanageable result, but in neither event will be a mutative interpretation has been effected. The analyst's power as auxiliary super-ego may be for two very different reasons. It may be that the id-impulses were trying to bring out being not in fact sufficiently urgent at the moment: For, after all, the emergence of an id-impulse depends on two factors - not only on the permission of the super-ego, but also on the urgency (the degree of cathaxis) of the id-impulse itself. This, then, may be one cause of an apparently negative response to an interpretation, and evidently a fairly harmless one. but the same apparent result may also be due to something else, in spite of the id-impulse being really urgent, the strength of the patient's own repressive forces (the degree of repression) may have been too great to allow his ego to listen to the persuasive voice of the auxiliary super-ego. Now we have a situation dynamically identical with the next one we have to consider, though economically different. this next situation is one in which the patient accepts the interpretation, that is, allows the id-impulse into his consciousness, but is immediately overwhelmed with anxiety. This may show itself in a number of ways, for instance, the patient may produce a manifest anxiety-attack. Or the may exhibit signs of 'real' anger with the analyst with a complete lack of insight, or he may break off the analysis. In any of these cases the analytic situation will, for the moment, at least, have broken down. The patient will be behaving just as the hypnotic subject behaves when, having been ordered by the hypnotist to perform an action too much at variance with his own consciousness, he breaks off the hypnotic relation and wakes up from his trance. This state of things, which is manifest where the patient responds to an interpretation with an actual outbreak of anxiety or one of its equivalents, may be latent were the patient shows no response, and this latter case may be the more awkward of the two, since it is masked, and it may sometimes be the effect of a greater overdose of interpretation than where manifest anxiety arises (though obviously other factors will be of determining importance, and in particularly the nature of the patient's neurosis). Yet this threatened collapse of the analytic situation to an overdose of interpretation: But it might be more accurate in some ways to ascribe it to an insufficient dose. For what has happened is that the second phase of the interpretation process has not occurred: The phase in which the patient becomes aware that his impulse is directed toward an archaic phantasy object and not toward a real one.

In the second phase of a complete interpretation, therefore, a crucial part is played by the patient's sense of reality: For the successful outcome of that phase depends upon his ability, at the critical moment of the emergence into consciousness of the released quantity of id-energy, to distinguish between his phantasy object and the real analyst. The problem is closely related to one that has been discussed elsewhere, namely that of the extreme liability of the analyst's position as auxiliary super-ego. The analytic situation is all the time threatening to degenerate into a 'real' situation. But this actually means the opposite of what it appears to. It means that the patient is all the time on the brink of turning the really external object (the analyst) into the archaic one; that is to say, he is on the brink of projecting his primitive introjected images onto himself. In so far as the patient actually does this, the analyst becomes like anyone else that he meets in real life - a phantasy object. The analyst then ceases to possess the peculiar advantages derived from the analytic situation, he will be introjected like all other phantasy objects into the analytic situation, he will be introjected like all other phantasy objects into the patient's super-ego, and will no longer be able to function in the peculiar ways which are essential to the effecting of a mutative interpretation. In this difficulty the patient's sense of reality is an essential but a very feeble [-ally]: An improvement in it is one of the things that we hope the analysis will bring about. It is important, therefore, not to submit it to any unnecessary strain, and that is the fundamental reason why the analyst must avoid any real behaviour, that is likely to confirm the patient's view of him as a 'bad' or a 'good' phantasy object. This is perhaps more obvious as regards the 'bad' object. If, for instance, the analyst were to show that he was really shocked or frightened by one of the patient's id-impulses, as the patient would immediately treat him in that respect as a dangerous object and introject him into his archaic severe super-ego. Therefore, on the one hand, there would be a diminuation in the analyst's power to function as an auxiliary super-ego and to allow the patient's to become conscious of his id-impulses - that is to say, in his power to bring about the first phase of a mutative interpretation, and on the other hand, he would, as a real object, become sensibly less distinguishable from the patient's 'bad' phantasy object and to that extent the carrying through of the second phase of a mutative interpretation would also be made more difficult. Or, agin, there is another case. Supposing the analyst behaves in an opposite way and actively urges the patient to give free rein to his id-impulse. There is then a possibility of the patient confusing the analyst with the image of a treacherous parent who, at the beginning, encourages him to seek gratification, and then suddenly turns and punishes him. In such a case the patient's ego may look for defence by itself suddenly turning upon the analyst as though he were his own id-, and treating him with all the severity of which his super-ego is capable. again, the analyst is running a risk of losing his privileged position. But it may be equally unwise for the analyst to act really in such a way as to encourage the patient to project his 'good' introjected object onto him. For the patient will then tend to regard him as a good objective and archaic sense and will incorporate him with his archaic 'good' images and will use him as a protection against his 'bad' ones. In that way, his infantile positive impulses as well as his negative ones may escape analysis, for there may no longer be a possibility for his ego to make a comparison between the phantasy external object and the real one. it will, perhaps, be argued that, with the best of wills in the world, the analyst, however careful he may be, will be unable to prevent the patient from projecting these various images onto him. This is, of course, indisputable, and, the whole effectiveness of analysis depends upon its being so. The lesson of these difficulties is merely to remind us that the patient's sense of reality has the narrowest limits. It is a paradoxical fact that the best way of enuring that his ego will be able to distinguish between phantasy and reality is to withhold reality from him as much as possible. but it is true, his ego is so weak - so much at the mercy of his id and super-ego - that he can only cope with reality if it is administered in minimal doses. And these doses are in fact what the analyst gives him, in the form of interpretations.

A mutative interpretation can only be applied to an id-impulse which is actually on a state of cathexis. This seems self-evident; for the dynamic changes in the patient's mind implied by a mutative interpretation can only be brought about by the operation of a charge of energy originating in the patient himself: The function of the analyst is merely to ensure that the energy should or can flow along one channel rather than along another. It follows that the purely informative 'dictionary' type of interpretation will be non-mutative, but useful it may be a prelude to mutative interpretations. And this leads to a number of practical inferences. Every mutative interpretation must be emotionally 'immediate, but the patient must live through it as something actual or genuine. This requirement, that the interpretation must be 'immediate', may be expressed in another way by saying that interpretation must always be directed to the 'point of urgency'. At any given moment some particular id-impulse will be generated in activity, this is the impulse that is susceptible of mutative interpretation at the time, and no other one. It is, no doubt, neither possible nor desirable to be giving mutative interpretations all the time. as Melanie Klein has pointed out, it is a most precious quality in an analyst to be able at any moment to pick out the point of urgency.

But the fact that every mutative interpretation must deal with an 'urgent' impulse take us back one more to the commonly felt fear of the explosive possibilities of interpretation, and particularly of what is vaguely referred to as 'deep' interpretation. The terminological description is, no doubt, as the interpretation of material which is neither genetically early and historically distant from the patient's actual experience nor under an especially heavy weight of repression – material, in any case, which is in the normal course of things exceedingly inaccessible to his ego and remote from it. There seems reason to believe, moreover, that the anxiety which is liable to be aroused by the approach of such material to consciousness and may be of peculiar severity. The question whether it is 'safe' to interpret such material will, as usual, mainly depend upon whether an interpretation can be carried through, in the ordinary run of the case, as this material which is urgent during the earlier stages of the analysis is not deep. We have to deal at first only with more or less far-going displacements of the deep impulse. And the deep material itself is only reached later and by degrees, so that no sudden appearance of unmanageable quantities of anxiety is to be hesitorially anticipated. In exceptional cases, however, owing to some peculiarities in the structure of the neurosis, deep impulses may be urgent at a very early stage of the analysis. We are then faced by a dilemma. If we give an interpretation of this deep material, the resultant amounts of anxiety produced in the patient may be so great that his sense of reality may not be sufficient to permit of its accomplishment, and the whole analysis may be jeopardised, but, it must not be thought that, in such critical cases as we are now considering, the difficulty can necessarily be avoided simply by not giving any interpretation or by giving more superficial interpretations of non-urgent material or by attempting reassurances. It seems probable, in fact, that these alternative procedures may do little or nothing to obviate the trouble, on the contrary, they may even exacerbate the tension created by the urgency of the deep impulses which are the actual cause of the threatening anxiety. Thus the anxiety may break out in spite of these palliative efforts and, if so, it will be doing so under the most unfavourable conditions, that is to say, outside the mitigating influences afforded by the mechanism of interpretation. It is possible, therefore, that, of these alternative procedures which are open to the analyst faced by such a difficulty. The interpretation of the urgent id-impulses, deep though they may b e, will actually be the safer.

It is, of course, a matter of common experience, that it possible with certain patients to continue indefinitely giving interpretations without producing any apparent effect whatever.

There is an amusing criticism of this kind of 'interpretation-fanaticism' in the excellent historical chapter of Rank and Ferenczi. But it is clear from their words that what they have in mind are essentially extra-transference interpretations, for the burden of their criticism is that such a procedure implies neglect of the analytic situation. This is the simplest case. Where a waste of time and energy is the main result. But there are other occasions, on which a policy of giving strings of extra-transference interpretations is apt to lead the analyst into more positive difficulties. Attention was drawn by Reich a few years back, in the course of some technical discussions in Vienna to a tendency among inexperienced analysts to get into trouble by eliciting from the patient great quantities of material in a disordered and unrelated fashion: This may, be maintained, be carried to such lengths that the analysis is brought to an irremediable state of chaos. He pointe out truly that the material we have to deal with is stratified and that it is highly important in digging it out not to interference, more that we can help with th e arrangement of that state. He had in mind, of course, the analogy of an incompetent archaeologist, whose clumsiness may obliterate for all time the possibility of reconstructing the history of an important site. However, the results in the case of a clumsy analysis do not hold of any pessimistic cause to happen, as it was, re-stratification itself of its own accord if it is given the opportunity; That is to say, in the analytic situation. At the same time, is that of the presence of the risk, and it seems to be particularly likely to occur where extra-transference interpretation is excessively or exclusively restored to. The means of preventing it, and the remedy if it has occurred, lie in returning to transference interpretation at the point of urgency. For if we can discover which of the material is 'immediate' in the sense that the problematic occurrence enabling stratification is automatically solved, and it is a characteristic if most extra-transference material that it has no immediacy and consequently stratification is far more difficult to decipher. The measures suggested by Reich himself for preventing the occurrence of this state of chaos are consistent with those that he stresses the importance of interpreting resistance as opposed to the primary id-impulses themselves - and this, was a policy that was laid down at an early stage in the history of analysis. But it is, of course, one of the characteristics of a resistance that it arises in relation to the analyst. Thus, interpretation of a resistance will almost inevitably be a transference interpretation.

But the most serious risks that arise from the making of extra-transference interpretation are due to the inherent difficulty in completing their interpretation, for a successful outcome as such, depends upon his ability, at which time of the emergence into consciousness and the released quantity of id-energy. They are from their nature unpredictable in their effects. There seems to be a special risk of the patient not carrying through to a competed interpretation, hitherto, namely that the extreme liability of the analyst's position as auxiliary super-ego, is that, the analytic situation is all the time threatening to degenerate into a 'real' situation.

It means that the patient is all the time perched upon the circumference edge-horizon of turning the external object (the analyst) into the archaic one, but of projecting the id-impulse that has been made conscious onto the analyst. This risk, no doubt, applies to some extent to transference interpretations. However, the situation is less likely to arise when the object of the id-impulses is actually present and is moreover the same person as the maker of interpretation. We may, once, more, recall the problem of 'deep' interpretation, and point out that its dangers, even in the most unfavourable circumstances, seem to be greatly diminished if the interpretation in question is a transference interpretation. Even so, there appears to be more of a chance that in this whole process occurring silently and so being overlooked in the case of an extra-transference interpretation, particularly in the earlier stages of an analysis. For this reason, it would seem to be important after giving an extra-transference interpretation to be specially in the 'qui-vive' for transferences complications. This last peculiarity of the extra-transference interpretation is actually one of the most important forms to a practical stand-point of things. For on account of it they can be made to act as 'feeders' for the transference situation, and so to pave the way for mutative interpretations. In other words, by giving an extra-transference interpretation, the analyst can often provide a situation in the transference of which he can then give a mutative interpretation.

Therefore, it is probable that a large majority of our interpretations are outside the transference - though it should be added that it often happens that one is ostensibly giving an extra-transference interpretation one is implicitly giving a transference one. A cake cannot be made of nothing but currants, and, though it is true that extra-transference interpretations, are not for the most part, mutative and do not they bring about the crucial results that involve a permanent change in the patient's mind. They are, nonetheless essential, if taken to an analogy of trench warfare, the acceptance of a transference interpretation corresponds to the capture of a key position, while the extra-transference interpretations correspond to the general advance and to the consolidation of a fresh line of defence, which are made possible by the capture of the key position. But when this general advance goes beyond a certain point, there will be another check, and the capture of a further key position will be necessary before progress can be resumed. An oscillation of this kind between transference and extra-transference interpretations will represent the normative course of events in an analysis.

Although the giving of mutative interpretations may thus only occupy a small portion of psycho-analytic treatment, it will, upon being, that the most important part from the point of view of deeply exerting affective percussions. Do so, because of the influencing characteristic confirmations as drawn upon the spoken-exchange of the patient's mindful knowing, in that the individuals that feel, perceive, think, wills, and especially reasons are all taken into heedful compliance. It may be of interest to consider how a moment through which of such an importance to the patient affects the analyst himself. Mrs. Klein has suggested that there must be some quite special internal difficulty as to involve the analyst in interpretations. This is shown in their avoidance by psycho-therapists of non-analytic schools, but many psycho-analysts will be aware of traces of the same tendency in themselves. It may be rationalized into mutative interpretations. This is shown in the avoidance by psycho-therapists of non-analytic schools, if not many consisting of a psycho-analyst as flown over to passing their flow of emptying space, nonetheless, this dialectic awareness traces of the same tendency as in them. But behind this there is somewhat of a lurking difficulty in the actual giving of the interpretation, for there seems to be a constant temptation for the analyst to do something else instead. Questions may be asked of whether o r not. As given to the reassurances or advice or discourses upon theory, or may give interpretations -but interpretations that are not mutative, extra-transference interpretations, interpretations that are non-immediate, or ambiguous, or in exacting of two or more alternative interpretations simultaneously, or he may, perhaps, give interpretations and at the same time, show his own scepticism about them. All of this strongly suggests that the giving of a mutative interpretation is a crucial act for the analyst as well as for the patient. And this inturn will become intelligible when we reflect that at the moment of interpretation the analyst is in fact deliberately Evoking a quantity of the patients id-energy while it is a live and actual and unambiguous and aimed directly himself. Such a moment must be above all others put to the test his relations with his unconscious impulses.

Interpretation of the transference is central to all psychoanalytic models. Definitions of transference and transference interpretation have changed greatly during the past half-century, influenced by major movements in philosophy, but advances in psycho-analytic research and theory, and changes in our of understanding Freud. Suggestively. The advances in psychnalytic research and theory, and changes in our understanding of Freud. Is that, the historical, relatively simple, concepts of the transference as the reproductions in the presence of significant relationships from therapists do not adequately meet current clinical theoretical demands? Modernist views of the transference emphasize as in additional sources of transference responses, the role of the analytic background of safety, the constant modifications of unconscious fantasy and internal representations, and the interactive nature of transference response, with important interpersonal and intersubjective components. It is suggested that the evolving modernists view of transference and transference interpretation permit a fuller accounting for transference and transference components. Such in a fuller accountability, for which of these issues of psychological 'truth' has open the way for better informed interventions. The issue of psychological 'truth' and 'distortion' as applied to transference phenomena will be presented with clinical vignettes.

Psychoanalysis, since the earliest days of the, Studies on Hysteria (Breuer and Freud,

1993-1905), have always given special attention to the transference and to the interpretation of transference, believing it to be central in our theory and technique. While there, has never been a lack of interest in transference interpreting. It is not clear why this is so, and the reasons may vary in different parts of the international psychoanalytic community. In America, at least, Gill's (1982) recent, and somewhat radical presentation of transference interpretation has surely helped to the grasping upon our developing attentions. Nevertheless, of another reason for our intensified interests in transference interpretation is the opportunity it provides for the rhetorically dialectic awareness, in that discussions, have lead us to the diverse analytic theories and techniques that today complete the diverseness as observed, for which of our attentions and allegiance to which transference interpretation seems to have replaced self-psychology. Thus, the encompassing topic that allows analysts of varied persuasions among many structural and fundamental elements that forge out the shape for taking upon the imparting of instinctual information. As to know, and knowing that you know, is, applied, however, of its concerning contemplations with which is distinguished by the evolving characterizations that are of knowing that you know is really nothing whatsoever.

Despite the diversity of the transference and its interpreting in analytic process and cure, differing only in whether transference is everything or almost everything to give a clear-cut definition of what transference is.

Laplanche and Pontalis (1973) had written that, 'The reason it is so difficult to produce a definition of transference is that for many authors the notion has taken on a very broad extension, even coming to connote all the phenomena which constitute the patient's relationship with the psychoanalyst, as a result the concept is burdened down more than any other with each analyst's particular view on the treatment - on its objective, dynamics, tactics, scope, and so forth. The question of the transference is thus beset by a whole series of difficulties which have been the subject of debate in classical psychoanalysis.'

Sandler (1983) has discussed how the terms transference and transference resistance, as well as other terms have undergone profound changes in meaning as new discoveries and new trends of psycho-analytic technique assume ascendency. He said, . . . major changes in technical emphasis brought about the extension of the transference concept, which now has dimensions of meaning which differ from the official definition of the term. I am not sure there has ever been a simplified definition of the term. While a certain flexibility of definition makes conversation possible in a field of diverse views, which we may never be clear on what any two people mean when they use the term is a significant hindrance to our discourse.

However: with this in mind we might review one of Freud's last comments on transference. In 'An Outline of Psycho-Analysis' (1940), published posthumously, he wrote on the analytic situation:

The most remarkable thing is this. The patient is not satisfied with regarding the analyst in the light of reality as a helper and advisor who, moreover, is remunerated for the trouble he takes and who would himself be content with some role that of a guide on a different mountain to climb, on the contrary, the patient sees in him. the return, and the reincarnation, of some important figure out of his childhood or past, and consequently transfer onto him, feelings and reactions which undoubtedly apply this prototype. This fact of transference soon proves to be a factor of an undreamt-of importance, on the other hand bud an instrument of irreplaceable value and on the other, that he set out on a different undertaking without any suspicion of extraordinary power that would be at his command. . . .

Another advantage of transference, too, in that in it the patient produces before us with plastic clarity an important part of his life-story, of which he would, otherwise have probably given us only an insufficient account. He acts it before us, as it was, instead of reporting it to us.

Freud saw the transference interpretation as a method of strengthening the ego against past unconscious wishes and conflicts.

It is the analyst's task constantly to speak abruptly, and in doing so, the patient may relinquish of his menacing illusions and to show him again and again, of what it takes to be or begin of a new life, are the reflections of the past. And least, he should fall into a state in which he is inaccessible to all evidences, the analyst takes that neither the love nor the hostility reaching an extreme height. This is affected by preparing him in good time for these possibilities and by not overlooking the first signs of them. Careful handling of the transference on these lines is as a role richly rewarded. If we succeed, as we usually can, in enlightenment the patient on the true nature of the phenomena of the transference, we thus have struck a powerful weapon out of the hand of his resistance and will have converted dangers into gains. For a patient never forgets again what he has experienced in the form of transference, it carries a greater force of conviction than anything he can acquire in other ways.

We have used the term 'transference' several times, in that we attributed the therapeutic results to the transference without further definition of the word. We will now consider more closely the emotional relationship which is thus designed. During a psychoanalytic treatment, the patient allows the analyst to play a predominating role in his emotional life. This is of great importance in the analytic process. After his treatment is over, this situation is changed. The patient builds up feelings of affection for and resistance to his analyst which, in their ebb and flow, so exceed the normal degree of feeling that the phenomenon has long attracted the theoretical interest of the analyst. Freud studied this phenomenon thoroughly, explained it, and gave it the name 'transference', we most probably will understand the significance of the transference phenomenon impressed Freud so profoundly that he continued through the years to develop his ideas about it.

In all afforded efforts, to refuse to consider the demise of forebears as too merely disdain, that we cannot reproduce of all Freud's research about transference but for an instance of obligation, would be used to indicate the requirement by the immediate need or purpose upon such condition that might point beyond a normal or acceptable limit, as to an excessive amount of which something does not or cannot to their essentials. When we speak of the transference in connexion with social reeducation, we mean the emotional responses of the education or counsellor or therapist, as the case maybe, without meaning that it takes place in exactly the same way as in an analysis. The 'countertransference' is emotional aptitude of the teacher toward the pupil, the counsellor toward his charge, the therapist toward the patient. The feeling which the child develops for the mentor is conditioned by a much earlier relationship to someone else. We must take cognisance of this fact in order to understand these relationships. The tender relationships which go to up the child's love life are no longer strange to us. Many of these have already been touched upon in the foregoing literature. We have learned how the small boy takes the father and mother as love objects. We have followed the strivings which arise out of this relationship, the Oedipus situation, we have seen how this runs its course and terminates in an identification with the parents. We have also had opportunity to consider the relationship between brothers and sisters, how their original rivalry is transformed into affection through the pressure of their feeling for the parents. We know that the boy at puberty must give up his first love object within the family and transfers his libido to individuals outside the family.

Why Freud chose the term 'transference' for the emotional relationship between patient and analyst is easy to understand. The feelings which arose long ago in another situation are transferred upon the analyst. To the counsellor of the child, the knowledge of the transference mechanism is indispensable. In order to influence the dissocial behaviour, he must bring his charge into the transference situation. The study of the transference in the dissocial child shows regularly a love life that has been disturbed in early childhood by a lack of affection or an undue amount of affection. A satisfactory social adjustment depends on certain conditions, among them an adequate constitutional endowment and early love relationships which have been confined within certain limits. Society determines these limitations, just as definitely as the later love life of an individual is determined by early form his libidinal development. The child develops normally and assumes his proper place in society, if he can cultivate within the privacy to such relationships as can favourably be carried over into the schools and from there into the ever-broadening world around him. His attitude toward his parents must be such that it can be carried over onto the teacher, and that toward his brothers and sisters must be transferred to his schoolmates. Every new contact, according to the degree of authority or maturity which the person represents, repeats a previous relationship with very little deviation. People whose early adjustment to succeed or supervene from such a normative course have no difficulties in their emotional relations with others, and they are able to form new ties, to deepen them, or to break them off without conflict when the situation demands it.

We can easily see why an attempt to change the present order of society always meets with resistance and where the radical reformer will have to use the greatest leverage. Our attitude to society and its members has a certain standard form. It gets its imprint from the structure of the family and the emotional relationships set up within the family, therefore, the parents, especially the father, assume overwhelming responsibility for the social orientation of the child. The persistent, ineradicable libidinal relationships carried over from childhood are facts with which social reformers must reckon. If the family represents the best preparation for the present social order, which seems to be the case, then the introduction of a new order means that the family must be uprooted and replaced by a different personal world for the child. It is beyond our scope to attempt a solution of this question, which concerns those who strive to build up a new order of society. We are remedial educators and must recognize these sociological relationships. We can ally ourselves with whatever social system will, but we have the path of our present activity well marked out for us, to bring dissocial youth into the line with present-day society.

If the child is harmed through too great disappointment or too great indulgence in his early life, he builds up reaction patterns which are damaged, incomplete, or too delicate to support the wear and tear of life. He is incapable of forming libidinal object relationships which are considered normal by society. His unpreparedness for life, his inability to regulate his conscious and unconscious libidinal striving and to confine his libidinal expectations within normal bounds, creates an insecurity in relation to his fellow men and constitute one of the first and most important condition's fo r their development of delinquency. Following this point of view, we look for the primary causes of dissocial behaviour in early childhood, where the abnormal libidinal ties are established. The word 'delinquency' is an expression used to describe a relationship to people and things which are at variance with what society approve in the individual.

It is not immediately clear, from which are pointed from the particular form of the delinquency, just what libidinal disturbances in childhood have given rise to the dissocial expression. Until we have a psychoanalytically construed scheme for the diagnosis of delinquency, we may content ourselves by separating these forms into two groups: (1) Borderline neurosis cases with dissocial symptoms, and (2) dissocial cases for which are in part, the ego giving to develop of the dissocial behaviour, and showing no trace of neurosis.

In the first type, the individual finds himself in an inner conflict because of the nature of his love relationships, a part of his own personality forbids the indulgence of libidinal desires and strivings. The dissocial behaviour results from this conflict. In the second type, the individual finds himself in open conflict with his environment, because the outer world has frustrated his childish libidinal desires.

The differences in the forms of dissocial behaviour are important for many reasons. At present, they are significant to us because of the various ways in which the transference is established in these two types, we know that with a normal child the transference takes place of itself through the kindly efforts of the responsible adult. The teacher in his attitude repeats the situations long familiarly to the child, and thereby evokes a parental relationship. He does not maintain this relationship at the same level, but continually deepens it as long as he is the parental substitute.

When a neurotic child with symptoms of delinquency comes into the institution, the tendencies to transfer his attitude toward his parents to the persons in authority are immediately noticeable. The worker will adopt the same attitude toward the dissocial child as to the normal child, and bring him into positive transference, if he acts toward him in such a way as to prevent a repetition with the worker of the situation with the parents which led to the conflict. In psychoanalysis, on the other hand, it is of greatest importance to let this situation repeat itself. In a sense the worker becomes the father or the mother, but still not wholly so, he represents their claims, but in the right moment he must let the dissocial child know that he has insight into his difficulties and that he will not interpret the behaviour in the same way as do the parents. He will respond to the child's feeling of a need for punishment, but he will not completely satisfy it.

He will conduct in himself be entirely differently in the case of the child who in open conflict with society. In this instance he must take the child's part, be in agreement with his behaviour, and in the severest cases even give the child to understand that in his place he would behave just the same way. The guilt feelings found so clearly in the neurotic cases with dissocial behaviour are present in these cases also. These feelings do not arise, however, from the dissocial ego, but have another source.

Why does the educator conduct himself differently in dealing with this second type? These children, too, he must draw into a positive transference to him, but what is applicable and appropriate for a normal or a neurotic child would achieve opposite results. Otherwise the worker would bring upon himself all the hate and aggression which the child bears toward society, thus leading the child into a negative instead of positive transference, and creating a situation in which the child is not amenable to training.

Nevertheless, what was said about psychoanalysis theory is only a bare outline, that much deeper study of the transference is necessary to anyone interested in re-educational work from the psychoanalytic point of view. The practical application of this theory is not easy, since we deal mostly with mixed types, such that the attitude of the counsellor cannot be as uniform as having enough verbal descriptions for evincing of individual forms of dissociated behaviour to enable us to offer detailed instructions about how to deal with them. At present our psychoanalytic knowledge is such that a correct procedure cannot be stated specifically for each and every dissocial individual.

The necessity for bringing the child into a good relationship to his mentor is of prime importance. The worker cannot leave this to chance, he must deliberately achieve it and he must face the fact thus no effective work is possible without it. It is important for him to grasp the psychic situation of the dissocial child in the very first contact he makes with him, because only this can be known in what attitude to adopt. There is a further difficulty in that the dissocial child takes pains to hide his real nature: He misrepresents himself and lies. This is to be taken for granted, it should not surprise or upset us. Dissocial children do not come to us of their own volition but are brought to us, very often with the threat, 'You'll soon find out what's going to happen to you.' Generally parents resort our help only after every other means, including corporal punishment, have failed. To the child, we are only another form of punishment, an enemy against whom he must be on his guard, not a source of help to him. There is a great difference between this and the psychoanalytic situation, where the patient comes voluntarily for helping. To the dissocial child, we are a menace because we represent society, with which he is in conflict. He must protect himself against this terrible danger and be careful what he says in order not to give himself away. It is hard to make some of these delinquent children talk, remain unresponsive and stubborn. One thing they all have in common: They do not tell the truth. Some lie stupidly, pitiably, others, especially the older ones, show great skill and sophistication. The extremely submissive child, the 'dandily', the very jovial, or the exaggeratedly sincere, some especially hard to reach. This behaviour is so much to be expected that we are not surprised or disarmed by it, the inexperienced teacher or adviser is easily irritated, especially when the lies are transparent, but he must not let the child be aware of this. He must deal with the situation immediately without telling the child that he can see that coming through were attributive values about his attitudinal behaviours.

There is nothing remarkable in the behaviour of the dissocial, but it differs only quantitatively from normal behaviour. We all hide our real selves and use a great deal of psychic energy to mislead our neighbours. We masquerade more or less, according to necessity. Most of us learn in the nursery the necessity of presenting ourselves in accordance with the environmental demands, and thus we consciously or unconsciously build up a shell around ourselves. Anyone who has had experience with young children must have noticed how they immediately begin to dissimulate when a grown-up comes into the room. Most children succeed in behaving in the manner which they think is expected of them. Thus they lessen the danger to themselves and at the same time they are casting the permanent moulds of their mannerisms and their behaviour. How many parents really bother themselves about the inner life of their children? Is this mask necessarily for life? I do not know, but it often seems that the person on whom childhood experiences have forced the dissocial individual masquerades to a greater extent, and more consciously, then the normal. He is only drawing logical deductions from his unfortunate disagreeable authority? Why should he be sincere with those people who represent disagreeable authority? This is an unfair demand.

We must look further into the differences between the situation of social retraining and the analytic situation. The analyst expects to meet in his patient unconscious remittances which prevent him from being honest or make him silent: But the treatment is in vain when the patient lies persistently. Those who work with dissocial children expect to be lied to. To send this child away because he lies are only giving in to him. We must wait and hope to penetrate this mask which covers the really psychic situation. In the institution it does not matter if this is not achieved immediately, it means merely that the establishment of the transference is postponed. In the clinic, however, we must work more quickly. Taking with the patient does not always suffice, and we must introduce other remedial measures. Generally, we see the delinquent child, only, in at least as infrequent to a smattering of times, but we are forced to take some steps after the first few interviews, to formulate some tentative conception of the difficulty and to establish a positive transference as quickly as possible. This means we must get at least a peep behind the mask. If the child is not put in an institution, he remains in the old situation under the same influences which caused the trouble. In such cases we wish to establish the transference as quickly as possible, to intensify the child`s positive feelings for us that are aroused while the child is with us, and to bring them rapidly to such a pitch that they can no longer be easily disturbed by the old influences. To carry on such work successfully presupposes a long experience.

Let us now go against our theoretical concerns and considerations and see how the analyst and the patient seek to grasp upon a try to solve situational thoughts for which the transference, and, moreover, its mask on which can be understood that feelings and a better understanding the differentiation that intentionality that allies with others and exclusively its need to achieve to some end.

Even so, there are few current problems concerning the problem of transference that Freud did not recognize either implicitly or explicitly in the development of the theoretical and clinical framework. For all essential purposes, moreover, his formulations, in spite of certain shifts in emphasis, remain integral to contemporary psychoanalytic theory and practice.

Recent developments mainly concern the impact of an ego-psychological approach, the significance of object relations, both current and infantile, external and internal, the role of aggression in mental life, and the part played by regression and the repetition compulsion in the transference. Nevertheless, analysis of the infantile Oedipal situation in the setting of a genuine transference neurosis is still considered as a primary goal of psychoanalytic procedure.

Originally, transference was ascribed to displacement on the analyst of repressed wishes and fantasies derived from early childhood. The transference neurosis was viewed as a compromise formulation similar to dreams and other neurotic symptoms. Resistance, defined as the clinical manifestation of repression, could be diminished or abolished by interpretation mainly directed toward the content of the repressed. Transference resistance, both positive and negative, was inscribed to the threatened emergence of repressed unconscious material in the analytic situation. Presently, as with the development of a structural approach, the superego had been portrayed as the heir to the genital Oedipal situation, also was the recognition as playing a leading role in the transference situation. The analysis was subsequently viewed not only as the object by displacement of infantile incestuous fantasies, but also as the substitute by projection for the prohibiting parental figures which had been internalized as the definitive superego. The effect of transference interpretation in mitigating undue severity of the superego has, therefore, been emphasized in many discussions of the concept of transference.

Certain expansions in the structural approach related increasingly to the recognition of the role that had earlier objective relations, in the development of the superego. This had affected the current concepts of transference, in that this connection, the significance of the analytic situation as a repetition of the early mother-child relationship has been stressed from different points for viewing to such equally important developments related to Freud's revised concept of anxiety which can only lead to theoretical developments in the field of ego psychology. However, this brought about their related clinical changes in the work of many analysts. As a result, attention was no longer the main attraction that had focussed on the content of the unconscious. In addition, increasing importance was attributed to the defence processes by means of which the anxiety which would be engendered if repression and other related mechanisms were broken down, was avoided in the analytic situation. Differences in the interpretation of the role of the analyst and the nature of transference developed from emphasis, on the one hand, on the importance of early object relations, and on the other, from primary attention to the role of the ego and its defences. These defences first emerged clearly in discussion of the technique of child analysis, in which Melanie Klein and Anna Freud, the pioneers in the fields of thought as playing the leading roles.

From a theoretical point of view, discussion foreshadowing the problems which face us today was presented in 1934 in a well-known paper by Richard Sterba and James Strachey, and further elaborated at the Marienbad Symposium at which Edward Bibring made an important contribution. The importance of identification with, or introjection of, the analyst in the transference situation of identification with, or introjection of, the analysts in the transference situation were clearly indicated. The therapeutic results were attributed to the effect of this process In mitigating the need for pathological defences. Strachey, however, considerably influenced by the work of Melanie Klein, regarded transference as essentially a projection onto the analyst of the patient's own superego. The therapeutic process was attributed to subsequent introjection of a modified superego as a result of 'mutative' transference. Sterba and Bibring, on the other hand, intimately involved with development of the ego-psychological approach, reemphasised the central role of the ego, postulating a therapeutic split and identification with the analyst as an essential feature of transference. To some extent, this difference of opinion may be regarded as semantic. If the superego is explicitly defined as the heir of the genital Oedipus conflict, then earlier intra-systematic conflicts within the ego, although they may be related retrospectively to the definite superego, much, nevertheless, are defined as contained within the ego. Later divisions within the ego of the type indicated by Sterba and very much expanded by Edward Bibring in his concept of therapeutic alliance between the analyst and the healthy part of the patient's ego, must also be excluded from superego significance. In contrast, those whom attribute pregenital intra-systemic conflicts within the ego primarily to the introjection of objects, consider that the resultant state of internal conflict appears like the dynamic idea that something conveys to the mind as having an endless meaning attached to the coherence of the therapeutic situation and seen in the later conflicts between ego and superego. They, therefore, believe that these structures developed simultaneously and suggest that no sharp distinction should be made between pre-oedipal, oedipal, and post-oedipal superego.

The differences, however, are not entirely verbal, since those whom attribute superego formations to the early months of life tend to attribute significantly too early object relation which differs from the conception of those who stress control and, neutralization of instinctual energy as primary functions of the ego. This theoretical difference necessarily implies some disagreement as how the dynamic situation both in childhood and in adult life, inevitably reflected in the concept of transference and in hypotheses as to the hidden nature of the therapeutic process. From one point of view, the role of the ego is central and crucial at every phase of analysis. A differentiation is made between transference as therapeutic alliance and the transference neurosis, which, on the whole, is considered a manifestation of resistance. Effective analysis depends on a sound and stable therapeutic alliance, a prerequisite for which is the existence, before analysis, of a degree of mature superego functions, the absence of which in certain severely disturbed patients and in young children may preclude traditional psychoanalytic procedure. Whenever indicated, interpretation's manifestations, which means, in effect, that the transference must be analysed. The process of analysis, however, is not exclusively ascribed to transference interpretation. Other interpretations of unconscious material, whether related to defence or to early fantasies, will be equally effective provided they are accurately timed and provide a satisfactory therapeutic alliance has been made. Those, in contrast, whom stress the importance of early object relations emphasizes the crucial role of transference as an object relationship, distorted though this may be of a variety of defences against primitively unresolved conflicts. The central role of the ego, both in the early stages of development and in the analytic process, are definitely accepted. The hidden nature of the ego is, however, considered at all times to be determined by its external and internal objects. Therapeutic process indicated changes in ego function results, therefore, primarily from a change in object relations though interpretation of the transference situation, finds of less differentiation as made between transference as for being the therapeutic alliance and transference neurosis as a manifestation of resistance. Therapeutic progress depends almost exclusively on transference interpretation. Other interpretations, although at times, are not, in general, considered an essential feature of the analytic process. From this point of view, the preanalytic maturity of the patient's ego is not stressed as considered potentially suitable for traditional psychoanalytic procedure.

These differences in theoretical orientation are not only reflected in the approach to children and disturbed patients. They may also be recognized in significant variations of technique in respect to all clinical groups, which inevitably affect the opening phases, understanding of the inevitable regressive features of the transference neurosis, and handling of the germinal phases of analysis. By its emphasis as drawn on or upon the main problems, and, by contrast, rather than similarity, our efforts will be to avoid to detailed discussions of controversial theory regarding the hidden nature of early ego development by a somewhat arbitrary differentiation between those who relate ego analysis to the analysis of defences and those who stress the primary significance of object relations both in the transference, and in the development and definitive structure of the ego. Needless to say, this involves some oversimplification, where I hope that it may, at the same time, clarify certain important issues. To take, on or upon the analysis of patients we are generally agreeing to be suitable for classical analytic procedure, the transference neurosis. Those which emphasis the role of the ego and the analysis of defences, not only maintain Freud's conviction that analysis should proceed from surface to depth, but also consider that early material in the analytic situation derives, that, in general, from defensive processes rather than from displacement onto the analyst of early instinctual fantasies. Deep transference interpretation in the early instinctual fantasies. Deep transference interpretation in the early phases of analysis will, therefore, rather be meaningless to the patient since its unconscious significance is so inaccessible, or, if the defences are precarious, will lead to premature and possibly intolerable anxiety. Premature interpretation of the equally unconscious automatic defensive processes by means of which instinctual fantasy kept unconscious is also ineffective and undesirable. There are, nonetheless, differences of opinion within this group, as to how far analysis of defence can be separated from analysis of content. Waelder, for example, has stressed the impossibility of such separation. Fenichel, however, considered that at least theoretical separation should be made and indicated that, as far as possible, analysis of defence should precede analysis of unconscious fantasy. It is, nevertheless, generally agreed that the transference neurosis develops, as a rule after ego defences have been sufficiently undermined to mobilize previously hidden instinctual conflict. During both the early stages of analysis, and at frequent points after development of the transference neurosis, defences against the transference will become a main feature of the analytic situation.

This approach, has already been indicated, is based on certain definite premises regarding the hidden natures and function of the ego in respect to the control and neutralization of instinctual energy and unconscious fantasies, while the importance of early object relations is not neglected, the conviction that early transference interpretation is ineffective and potentially relations are not neglected, the conviction and unconscious fantasy. The conviction that early transference interpretation is ineffective and potentially dangerous is related to the hypothesis that the instinctual energy available to the mature ego has been neutralized from unconscious fantasies, meaning at the beginning of analysis, for all effective purposes, relatively or absolutely divorced from its unconscious fantasy, as yet, there are a number of analysts of differing theoretical orientation of ego function from unconscious sources, but consider that unconscious fantasy continues to operate in all conscious mental activity. The analysts also construct upon the whole of their existing in the emphasis to the crucial significance of primitive fantasies, in respect to the development of the transference situation. The individual entering analysis will inevitably have unconscious fantasies concerning the analyst derived from primitive sources. This material, although deep in a sense, is, nevertheless, strongly current and accessible to interpretation. Klein, in addition, creates the development and definitive structure of the superego to unconscious fantasy determined by the earliest phases of object relationships. She emphasizes the role of early introjective and projective processes in relation to primitive anxiety ascribed to the death instinct and related aggression drive fantasies. The unresolved difficulties and conflict of the earliest period continue to colour object relations throughout life. Failure to achieve an essentially satisfactory object relationship in this early period, and failure to master relative loss of that object without retaining its good internal representative, will not only affect all object relations and definitive ego function, but more specifically determine the nature of anxiety-provoking fantasies on entering the analytic situation. According to this point of view, therefore, early transference uninterpreted, even thought it may relate to fantasies derived from an early period of life, should result not in an increase, but a decrease of anxiety

In considering next problems of transference in relation to analysis of the transference neurosis, two main points must be kept in mind. First, as already indicated, those who emphasize the analysis of defence tend to make a definite differentiation between transference as therapeutic alliance and the transference neurosis as a compromise formation which serves the purposes of resistance. In contrast, those who emphasize the importance of early object relations view the transference primarily as a revival or repetition, sometimes attributed to symbolic processes of early struggles in respect to objects. Still, there is no sharp differentiation made between the early manifestations of transference and the transference neurosis. In view, moreover, of the weight given to the role of unconscious fantasy and internal objects in every phase of mental life, healthy and pathological functions, though differing in essential respect, do not differ with regard to their direct dependence on unconscious sources.

In the second place, the role of regression in the transference situation is subject to wide differences of opinion. It was, of course, one of Freud's earliest discoveries that regression had of its earliest points of fixation, and is a cardinal feature, not only in the development of neurosis and psychosis, but also in the revival of earlier conflicts in the transference situation. With the development of psychoanalysis and its application to an ever increasing range of received increased attention. The significance of the analytic situation as a means of fostering regression as a prerequisite for the therapeutic work has been emphasized by Ida Macapline in a recent paper. Differing opinions as to the significance, value, and technical handling of regressive manifestoes from the basis of important modifications of analytic technique, which will be considered, however, in respect to the transference neurosis, the view recently expressed by Phyllis Greenacre, that regression, and indispensable features would be generally accepted. It is also a matter of generally based agreement that a prerequisite for successful analysis is revival and repetition in the analytic situation of the struggle of primitive stages of development. Those who emphasize defence analysis, however, tend to view regression as a manifestation of resistance, as a primitive mechanism of defence employed by the growth sets of the transference neurosis. Analysis of these regressive manifestations with their potential dangers depends on the existing and continued functioning of adequate ego strength to maintain therapeutic alliance at an adult level. Those, in contrast, who stress the significance of transference as a revival of the early mother-child relationship does not emphasize regression as an indication of resistance or defence, the revival of these primitive experiences in the transference situation is, in fact, regarded as can essential prerequisite for satisfactory psychological maturation and true geniality. The Kleinian school, as already indicated features the continued activity of primitive conflicts in determining essential features of the transference at every stage of analysis. Their increasing overt revival in the analytic situation, therefore, signifies a reopening of the analysis, and in general, is regarded as an indication of diminuation rather than increase of resistance. The dangers involved according to this point of view and are determined more but to the failure to mitigate anxiety by suitable transference interpretation. By this failure to obtainably achieve, in the early phases of analysis, a sound and stabling therapeutic alliance is based on the maturity of the patient's essential ego characteristics.

In considering, briefly, the terminal phases of analysis, many unresolved problems concerning the goal of the therapy and definition of a completed psychoanalysis must be kept in mind. Distinction must also be made between the technical problems of the terminal phase and evaluation of transference after the analysis has been terminated, there is widespread agreement as to the frequent revival in the terminal phases of primitive transference manifestations apparently resolved during the early phases of primitive transference manifestation, apparently resolved during the early phase of analysis has been terminated. Balint, and those who accept Ferenczi's concept of primary passive love, suggest that some gratification of primitive passive needs may be essential for successful termination. To Klein, the terminal phases of analysis also represent a repetition of important features of the early mother-child relationship. According to her point of view, this period represents, in essence, a revival of the early weaning situation. Completion depends on a mastery of early depressive struggles culminating in successful introjection of the analysis as a good object. Although, in this connection, emphasis differs considerably, it should be noted that those who stress the importance of identification with the analyst as a basis for therapeutic alliance, also accept the inevitability of some permanent modifications of a similar nature. Those, however, who make a definite differentiation between transference of the transference neurosis as a main prerequisite for successful termination. The identification based on therapeutic alliance must be interpreted and understood, particularly with reference to the reality aspects of the analyst's personality. In spite, therefore, of significant important differences there are, as already indicated in connection with the earlier papers of Sterba and Strachey, important points of agreement in respect to the goal of psychoanalysis.

The differences already considered indicate some basic current problems of transference. So far, however, discussion has been limited to variations within the framework of a traditional technique. We must consider problems related to overt modifications, so as the essential expanding context of use between variations introduced in respect to certain clinical conditions. Often as a preliminary to classical psychoanalysis, and modifications based on changes on basic approach which lead to significant alterations with regard both to the method and to the aim of therapy. It is generally agreed that some neurosis, borderline patients and the psychosis. The nature and meaning of such changes are, however, viewed differently according to the relative emphasis placed on the ego and its defences, on underlying unconscious conflicts, and on the significance and handling of regression in the therapeutic situation.

In 'Analysis Terminable and Interminable', Freud suggested that certainly inaccessible to psychoanalytic procedure. Hartmann has suggested that in addition to these primary attributes, other ego characteristics, originally develop for defensive purposes, and the related neutralized instinctual energy at the disposal of the ego, may be relatively or absolutely divorced from unconscious fantasy. This not only explains the relative inefficacy of early transference interpretation, but also hints of possible limitations in the potentialities of analysis attributable to secondary autonomy of the ego which is considered to be relatively irreversible. In certain cases, moreover, it is suggested that analysis of precarious or seriously pathological defences - particularly those concerned of aggressive impulses - may be not only ineffective, but dangerous. The relative failure of ego development in such cases not only precludes the development of a genuine therapeutic alliance, but also raises the risk of a serious regressive, often predominantly hostile transference situation. In certain cases, therefore, preliminary period of psychotherapy is recommended in order to explore the capacities of the patient to tolerate traditional psychoanalysis. In others, as Robert Knight in his paper on borderline states, and as many analysts' working with psychotic patients have suggested, psychoanalytic procedure is not considered applicable. Instead, a therapeutic approach based on analytic understanding which, in essence, utilizes an essentially implicit positive transference as a means of reinforcing, rather than analysing the precarious defences of the individual, is advocated. In contrast, Herbert Rosenfeld approached even severely disturbed psychotic patients with minimal modifications of psychoanalytic techniques. Only changes which the severity of the patient's condition enforces are introduced. The dangers of regression in therapy are not emphasized since primitive fantasy is considered to be active under all circumstances. The most primitive period is viewed in terms of early object relations with special stress on prosecutory anxiety related to the death instinct. Interpretation of this primitive fantasy in the transference situation, is best offered the opportunity of strengthening the severity-threatened psychosis mainly to serve traumatic experiences, particularly of deprivation in early infancy. According to this point of view, profound regression offers an opportunity to fulfil, in the transference situation, primitive needs which had not been met at the appropriate level of development. Similar suggestions have been proposed by Margolin and others, in the concept of anaclitic treatment. Serious psychosomatic diseases, that approach the premise that the inevitable regression is shown by certain patients and should be utilized in therapy, as a means for gratifying, in their extremely permissive transference situation. Having distinctive or certain limits in the burdensome instant for demanding to that which has not been met in infancy, as this must, in the connection of being taken to understand that the gratifications recommended in the treatment of severely disturbed patients are determined by their conviction. Of these patients are incapable of developing transference as we understand it, in the connection with neurosis and must therefore be handled by a modified technique.

The opinions so far considered, however, much of them, as mine differ in certain respects, are, nonetheless, all based on the fundamental premise that an essential difference between analysis and other methods of therapy depends on whether or not interpretation of transference is an integral feature of technical procedure. Results based on the effects of suggestions are to be avoided, as far as possible, whenever traditional technique is employed. This goal has, however, tp establish a point by appropriate objective means, that corroborated evidence that proved the need for better a state of being even more difficult to achieve than Freud expected when he first discerned the significance of symptomatic recovery based on positive transference. The importance of suggestion, even in the most strict analytic methods, has been repeatedly stressed by Edward Glover and others. Widespread and increasing emphasis as to the part played by the analyst's personality in determining the nature of the individual transference also implies recognition of unavoidable suggestive tendencies in the therapeutic process. Many analysts today believe that the classical conception of analytic objectivity and anonymity cannot be maintained. Instead, thorough analysis of reality aspects of the therapist's personality and point of view is advocated as an essential feature of transference analysis and an indispensable prerequisite for the dynamic changes already discussed in relation to the termination of analysis. It thus remains the ultimate goal of psychoanalyst's whenever their theoretical orientation, to avoid, as far as is humanly possible, results based on the unrecognized or unanalysed action of suggestion, and to maintain, as a primary goal, the resolution of such results through consistent and careful interpretation.

There are, however, a number of therapists, both within and outside the field of psychoanalysis, who consider that the transference situation should not be handled only or mainly as a setting for interpretation even in the treatment or analysis of neurotic patients. Instead, they advocate utilization of the transference relationship for the manipulation of corrective emotional experience. The theoretical orientation of those utilizing this concept of transference may be closer to, or more distant form, a Freudian point of view according to the degree to which current relationships are seen as determined by past events. At one extreme, current aspects and cultural factors are considered of predominant importance, at the other, mental development is viewed in essentially Freudian terms and modifications of technique are ascribed to inherent limitations of the analytic method rather than to essentially changed conceptions of the early phases of mental development. Of this group, Alexander is perhaps the best example. It is thirty years since, in his Salzburg paper, he indicated the tendency for patients to regress, even after apparently successful transference analysis of the oedipus situation to narcissistic dependent pregenital levels which prove stubborn and refractory to transference interpretation. In his more recent work, the role of regression in the transference situation has been increasingly stressed. The emergence and persistence of dependent, pregenital commands for something as or is if one's right or due requirements are challenged in measuring moderations of a wide range of clinical conditions. It is argued, that its indications that the encouragement of a regressive transference situation is undesirable and therapeutically ineffective. The analyst, therefore, should when this threatens adopt a definite role explicitly differing from the behaviour of the parents in early childhood in order to bring about therapeutic results through a corrective emotional experience in the transference situation. This, it is suggested, will obviate the tendency to regression, thus curtailing the length of treatment and improving therapeutic results. Limitations of regressive manifestations by active steps modifying traditional analytic procedure in a variety of ways are also frequently indicated, according to this point of view.

It will be clear that to those who maintain the conviction that interpretation of all transference manifestations remain an essential feature of psychoanalysis, the type of manifestation as described, even though based on a Freudian reconstruction of the early phases of mental developments, and represent a major modification. It is determined by a conviction that psychoanalysis, as a therapeutic method, has limitations related to the tendency to regression, which cannot be resolved by traditional technique. Moreover, the fundamental premises on which, and the conception of corrective emotional experience is based minimizing the significance of insight and recall. It is essentially, suggested that corrective emotional experience alone may bring about qualitative dynamic alterations in mental structure, which can lead to a satisfactory therapeutic goal. This implies a definite modification on the analytic hypothesis whose current problems are determined by their defences against the direct opposition to the instinctual impulses and the intentional object, to which had been set up during the decisive periods of early development. An analytic result therefore depends on the revival, repetition and mastery of earlier conflict in the current experience of the transference situation with insight an indispensable feature of an analytic goal.

Since certain important modifications are related to the concept of regression in the transference situation, it should be considered that this concept is in relation to the repetition compulsion, that transference, essentially is a revival of earlier emotional experience, must be regarded as a manifestation of the repetition compulsion is generally accepted. It is, however, necessarily to distinguish between repetition compulsion as an attempt to master traumatic experience and repetition compulsion as an attempt to return to a real or fantasized earlier state of rest or gratification. Lagache, in a recent paper, has connected by or as if by the affirming relatedness as associated to the corresponding divergence in the repetition compulsion to an inherent need to appear in the problems that had previously been left unsolved. From this point of view, the regressive aspects of the transference situation are to be regarded as a necessary preliminary to the mastery of unresolved conflict, as too, the regressive aspects of transference are mainly attributed to a wish to return to an earlier state of rest or narcissistic gratification, to the maintenance of the status quo in preference to any progressive action, to which Freud's original conception of the death instinct. There is a good deal to suggest that both aspects of the repetition compulsion may bee seen in self-destructive forces tend to be stronger that progressive libidinal impulses, the potentialities of the analytic approach will inevitably appear to be limited. In those, in contrast, in whom that regard the reappearance in the transference situation of earlier conflicts as an indication of tendencies to master and progress will continue to feel that the classical analytic method remains the optimal approach to psychological illness wherever it is applicable.

Clarifications maintain the position or peculiar state as occupying a spatial point in temporal conditions, with a significant relevance to the amplitude larger in extent or a greater capacity that the average infinitive period has of time. Whereas in absence or termination must reflect on or upon the fearing analysis if the transference, as compelling of a generally acknowledged focal point, this itself may debase the appropriate factor that generates, in every degree. The exemplifying analytic technique that would react upon the discipline needed to utilize the new values, whereby, they can be ascribed as the commonality in holding the services to a suspicious self-direction and comprehensive understanding, in that of whatever is humanly affiliated to the best as can be, and yet, the advocacy to the analysis of the transference is generally acknowledged as the central feature of analytic technique? Freud regarded transference and resistance as facts in the observational conceptuality for which of representing the state of inventions. He writes, . . . that the theory of psychoanalysis in an attempt to account for two striking and unexpected facts of observation which emerge whenever an attempt is made. Evidently the symptoms of a neurotic source, may in his past life, inhabit the sources of experiential recall to the past or the introspective reflections. In the state of affairs, in that for being the latent characterizations announced as the factoring responsibility for the transference and of resistance . . . one which takes the other side of the problem, while accepting as such, to the latencies and the hidden values non-accepting for new interactions as brought through a hypothesis that will hardly escape the charge of misappropriation of properties by attempting endeavour to re-associate the essentially established personalization, that if the pursuit in calling them a psychoanalyst'. Rapaport (1967) argued, in his posthumously published paper on the methodology of psychoanalysis, that transference and resistance inevitably follow from the fact that the analytic situation is interpersonal.

Despite this general agreement on the centrality of transference and resistance in technique, in that, the analysis of transference is not pursued as systematically and comprehensively affirmed, however, it could be and should be. The relative privacy for which psychoanalytic work makes it impossible for one or of that of any-other, to skilfully improve upon the attemptive conceptual representation as comprehended of issues, its assumption to state this view as anything more that impressions, involving on that of what in the analysis of the transference and to states awareness in the number of reasons that an important aspect in the analysis of the transference of the transference, namely in the resistance, by the awareness of the transference is especially, and often adhering to the analytic procedures that interact among cultural inhibitors, but that will be distinguished as such, that its ranging manifold of distancing non-localities as founded of the analyst's.

However, it must first be to distinguish between two types of interpretation of the transference. That one is an interpretation of resistance to the awareness of transference, the other, is an interpretation of resistance to the resolution of transference. The distinction has clearly been best spelled out in the form from which copies or reproductions can be produced, as to cause to make its awareness and yielding values as grounded in the cognisance to Greenson (1967) and Stone (1967). The first kind of resistance may be called decence transference, although this term emphases the terminological characterization by its term is mainly employed to refer to a phrase of analysis and carried within the general resistance to the transference of wishes, it can also be used for a more isolated instance of transference of defence. With some oversimplification, one might say that in resistance to the awareness of transference, the transference, the transference is what does the resisting.

Another connected description of stating this distinction between resistance and the awareness of transference and resistance to the resolution of transference is between implicit and indirect references to the transference and explicitly or directly referential to the transference. The interpretation of resistance to awareness of the transference is intended to make the implicit transference explicit. While the interpretation of resistance to the resolution of transference is intended to make the patient realize that the already explicit transference does indeed include a determinant from the past.

It is also important to distinguish between the general concept of an interpretation of resistance to the resolution of transference and a particular variety of such an interpretation, namely, a genetic transference interpretation - that is, an interpretation of how an attitude in the present is an inappropriate carry-over from the past. While there is a tendency among analysts to deal explicit references to the transference primarily among analyses to deal explicitly the references to the transference as primarily by a genetic transference interpretation, there are other ways of working toward a revolution of the transference. However, this argument does so implicate that not only is not enough emphasis being given to interpretation of the transference in the here and now, that is, to the interpretation of implicit manifestations of the transference, but also that interpretations intended to resolve the transference as manifested in explicit references to the transference should be primarily in the here and now, rather than genetic transference interpretations.

A patient's statement that he feels the analyst is harsh, for example, is, at least to begin with, likely best dealt with not by interpreting that this is a displacement from the patient's feeling that his father was harsh, but by as elucidation of some other aspect of this here and now attitude, such as what has gone on in the analytic situation that seems to the patient to justify his feeling or what was the anxiety that made it so difficult for him to express his feelings. How the patient experiences the actual situation is an example of the role of the actual situation in a manifestation of transference, which will be a major point of relevant significance.

Of course, both interpretations of the transference in the here and now and genetic transference interpretations are valid and constitute a sequence. We presume that a resistance to the transference ultimately rests on the displacement onto the analysts of attitudes from the past.

Because Freud's case histories focus much more on the yield of analysis than on the details of the process, they are readily but perhaps incorrectly construed as emphasizing work outside the transference much more than work within the transference, and, even within the transference, emphasizing genetic transference interpretations much more than work with the transference in the here and now (Muslin and Gill, 1978). The example of Freud's case reports may have played a role in what is to be considered as the common maldistribution of emphasis in these two respects - not enough on the transference and, within the transference, not enough on the here and now.

Transference interpretations in the here and now and genetic transference interpretations are, of course, exemplified in Freud's writings and are in the repertoire of every analyst, but they are not distinguished sharply enough.

Both participants in the analytic situation are motivated to avoid these interactions. Flight away from the transference and to the past can be a relief to both the patient and the analyst.

These aligning measures have been divided into five categorical divisions and placed into the following parts: (1) The principle that the transference should be encouraged to expand as much as possible within the analytic situation because the analytic work is best done within the transference. (2) the interpretation of disguised allusion to the transference as a main technique for encouraging the expansion of the transference within the analytic situation, (3) the principle that all transference has a connection with something in the present actual analysis situation, (4) how the connection between transference and the actual analytic situation is used in interpreting resistance to the awareness of transference, and (5) the resolution of transference within the here and now and the role of genetic transference interpretation.

The importance of transference interpretations will surely be agreeing to by all analysts, the greater effectiveness of transference interpretations than interpretations outside the transference will be agreeing to by many, but what of the relative roles of interpretation of the transference and interpretation outside the transference?

Freud can be interpreted as either of saying that the analysis of the transference in auxiliary to the analysis of the neurosis or that the analysis of the transference is equivalent to the analysis of the neurosis. The first position is stated in his saying (1913) that the disturbance of the transference has to be overcome by the analysis of transference resistance in order to get on with the work of analysing the neurosis. It is also implied in his reiteration that the ultimate task of analysis is to remember the past, to fill in the gap in memory. The second position is stated in his saying that the victory must be won on the field of the transference (1912) and that the mastery of the transference neurosis 'coincides with getting rid of the illness which was originally brought to the neurosis (1917). In this second view, he says that after the resistance is overcome, memories appear relatively without difficulty.

These two different positions also find expression in the two different ways in which Freud speaks of the transference. In `Dynamics of Transference` he refers to the transference, on the one hand, as `the most powerful resistance to the treatment`(1912) but, on the other hand, as doing us the inestimable service of making the patient's . . ., immediate impulses and manifests, when all is said and done, it is impossible to destroy anyone in absentia or in effigie (1912).

It can be agreed that his principal emphasis fails on the second position. He wrote once, in summary, 'Thus our therapeutic work falls into two phases in the first, all the libido is forced from the symptoms into the transference and concentrated there, in the second, the struggle is waged around this new object and the libido is liberated from it`(1912).

The detailed demonstration that he advocated that the transference should be encouraged to expand as much as possible within the analytic situation lies in clarification that resistance is primarily expressed by repetition, and repetition takes place both within and outside the analytic situation, but that the analyst seeks to deal with it primarily within the analytic situation, that repetition can be not only in the motor sphere (acting) but also in the psychical sphere, and that the psychical sphere is not confined to remembering but includes the present, too.

Freud`s emphasis that the purpose of resistance is to prevent remembering can obscure his point that resistance shows itself primarily by repetition, whether inside or outside the analytic situation. `The greater the resistance, the more extensively, and will act out (repetition)replace remembering`. Similarly in `The Dynamics of Transference` Freud said that the main reason that the transference is so well suited to serve the resistance is that the unconscious implies does not want to be remembered . . . but endeavour to reproduce themselves . . . (1918), the transference is a resistance primarily insofar as it is a repetition.

The point can be restated in terms of the relation between transference and resistance. The resistance expresses itself in repetition, that is, in transference both inside and outside the analytic situation. To deal with the transference. Therefore, is equivalent to dealing with the resistance. Freud emphasized transference within the analytic situation so strongly that it has come to mean only repetition within the analytic situation, even though, conceptually speaking, repetition outside the analytic situation is transference too, and Freud once used the term that way. `We soon perceive that the transference is itself only a piece of repetition and that the repetition is a transference of the forgotten past not only onto the analyst but also onto all the other aspects of the current situation. We . . . find . . . the compulsion to repeat, which now replaces the impulsion to remember, not only in his personal attitude to his analyst but also in every other activity and relationship which may occupy his life at the time . . . (1914).

It is important to realize that the expansion of the repetition inside the analytic situation, whether or not in a reciprocal relationship to repetition outside the analytic situation, is the avenue to control the repetition: `The main instrument . . . for curbing the patients compulsion to repeat and for turning it into a motive for remembering lies in the handling of the transference. We render the compulsion harmless, and indeed useful, by giving it the right to assert itself in a definite field`(1914).

Kanzer has discussed this issue well in his paper on 'The Motor Sphere of the Transference' (1966). He writes of a 'double-pronged stick-and-carrot' technique by which the transference is fostered within the analytic situation and discouraged outside the analytic situation. The 'stick' is the principle of abstinence as exemplified in the admonition against making important decisions during treatment, and the 'carrot' is the opportunity afforded the transference to expand within the treatment, 'in almost complete freedom' as in a 'playground' (Freud, 1914). As Freud put it, 'Provided only that the patient shows compliance enough to respect the necessary conditions of the analysis, we regularly succeed in giving all the symptoms of the illness a new transference meaning, and in replacing his ordinary neurosis by a 'transference neurosis' of which he can be cured by the therapeutic work' (1914).

The reason it is desirable for the transference to be expressed within the treatment is that there, it `is at every point accessible to our intervention`(1914). In a later statement he made the same point this way. `We have followed this new edition - the transference-neurosis - of the old disorder from its start, we have observed its origin and growth, and we are especially well able to find our way about in it since, as its object, we are situated at it's very centre, (1917), it is not that the transference is forced into the treatment, but that it is spontaneously but implicitly present and is encouraged to expand there and become explicit

Freud emphasized acting in the transference so strongly that one can overlook the repetition in the transference, but does not of necessity for its enactment or recognition that gives validity to acts of a subordinate conformation as ratified in support of explicit authoritative permission. Repetition need not go as far as motor behaviour, it can also be expressed in attitudes, feelings, and intentions, and, indeed, the repetition often does take such form rather than motor action. The importance of making this clear is that Freud can be mistakenly read to mean that repetition in the psychical sphere can only mean remembering the past, are when he writes that the analyst as prepared for a perpetual struggle with his patient to keep in the psychical sphere all the impulses which the patient would like to direct into the motor sphere, and he celebrates it as a triumph for the treatment if he can bring it about that something the patient wishes to discharge in action are disposed if through the work of remembering (1914).

It is true that the analyst's efforts are to convert acting in the motor sphere into awareness in the psychical sphere, but transference may be in the psychical sphere to begin with, albeit disguised. The psychical sphere includes awareness in the transference as well as remembering.

One of the objections one hears, from both analysts and patient, to a heavy emphasis on interpretation of associations about the patients real life primarily in terms of the transference is that it means the analyst is disregarding the importance of what goes on in the patients real life. The criticism is not judiciable. To emphasize the transference meaning is not to deny or belittle other meanings, but to focus on the one of several meanings of the content that is the most important for the analytic process, for the reasons of positing the addition for one coming to any falsifiable conclusion.

Another way in which interpretations of resistance to the transference can be, or at lease appear to the patient to be, a belittling of the importance of the patients outside life is to make the interpretation as though the outside behaviour is primarily an acting out of the transference. The patient may undertake some actions in the outside world as an expression of and resistance to the transference, that is, acting out. But the interpretation of associations about actions in the outside world as having implications for the transference needs mean only that the choice of outside action to figure in the associations is co-determined by the need to express a transference indirectly. It is because of the resistance to awareness of the transference that the transference to be disguised. When the disguise is unmasked by interpretation, it becomes clear that, despite the inevitable differences between the outside situation and the transference situation, the content is the same for the analysis of the necrosis that coincides (Freud wrote that the mastering of the transference neurosis only coincides with getting rid of the illness which was originally brought to the treatment (1917)).

The analytic situation itself fosters the development of attitudes with primary determinants in the past, i.e., transference. The analyst's reserve provides the patient with few and equivocal cues. The purpose of the analytic situation fosters the development of strong emotional responses, and the very fact that the patient has a neurosis means, as Freud said, that' . . . it is a perfectly normal and intelligible thing that the libidinal cathexis [we would now add negative feelings] of someone who is partly unsatisfied, a cathexes which are held ready in anticipation, should be directly as well to the figure of the analyst (1912).

While the analytic setup itself fosters the expansion of the transference within the analytic situation, the interpretation of resistance to the awareness of transference will further this expansion.

There are important resistances on the part of both patient and analyst to awareness of the transference. On the patient's part, this is because of the difficulty in recognizing erotic and hostile impulses toward the very person to whom they have to be disclosed. On the analyst's part, this is because the patient is likely to attitude the very attitudes to him which are most likely to cause him discomfort. The attitudes the patient believes the analysts has toward him are often the ones the patient is least likely to voice, in a general sense because of a feeling that it is impertinent for him to concern himself with the analyst's feelings, and in a more specific sense because the aptitudes as held by the analyst are often attitudes the patient feels the analyst will be comfortable about having ascribed to him. It is for this reason that the analyst must be especially alert to the attitudes the patient believes he has, not only to the attitudes the patient does have toward him. If the analyst is able to see himself as a participant in an interaction, as he will become much more attuned to this important area of transference, which might otherwise escape him.

The investigations of attitudes are ascribed to the analyst makes easier the subsequent investigation of the intrinsic factors in the patient that played a role in such ascription. For example, the exposure of the fact that the patient ascribes sexual interests in him to the analyst, and generally to the patient, alternatively the subsequent exploration of the patient's sexual wish toward the analyst, and genetically the parent.

The resistance to the awareness of these attitudes is responsible for their appearing in various disguises in the patient's manifested associations and for the analyst's reluctance to unmask the disguise. The most commonly recognized disguise is by displacement, but identification is an equally important one. In displacement, the patient's attitudes are narrated for being toward a third party. In identification, the patient attitudes to himself attitudes he believes the analyst has toward him.

To encourage the expansion of the transference within the analytic situation, the disguises in which the transference appears have to be interpreted in the case of displacement the interpretation will be of allusions to the transference in association not manifestly about the transference. This is a kind of interpretation every analyst often makes. In the case of identifications, the analyst interprets the attitudes that the patient ascribes to himself the identification with which an attitude and subsequently attributed to the analyst. Lipton (1977) has recently described this form of disguise allusion in the transference with illuminating illustration.

In his autobiography, Freud wrote, 'The patient remains under the influence of the analytic situation as hopefully of a latter position or a period of decline, as though he is not directing responsibly for the mental activities onto a particular subject. Justly in assuming that nothing will occur, as not of some reference to the situation (1925). Since associations are obviously often not directed about the analytic situation, the interpretation of Freud's remark rests on what he meant by the 'analytic situation'.

It is believed that Freud's meaning can be clarified by reference to a statement he made in, 'The Interpretation of Dreams'. He said that when the patient is told to say whatever comes into his mind, his associations become directed by the 'purposive ideas inherent in the treatment' and that there are two such inherent regressive themes, one relating to the illness and the other - concerning which, Freud said, the patient has 'no suspicion'; - relating to other analyst's relating to the patient has 'no suspicions' - relating to the analyst (1900). If the patient has 'no suspicions' of the theme relating to the analyst, such that the theme appears only in disguise, the patient 's associations, it is contended that Freud's remark not only specifies the themes inherent in the patient 's identifications', but means that the associations are simultaneously directed by these two purposive ideas, not something by one and sometimes by the other.

The analyst should progress on the working assumption, that the patient's associations have transference implications pervasively, that with which this assumption is not to be confused with denial or neglect of the current aspects of the analytic situation. It is theoretically always possible to give precedence to a transference interpretation if one can only discern it through its disguise by resistance. This is not to dispute the desirability of learning as much as one can about the patient, if only to be a position to make more correct interpretations of the transference. One therefore, does not interfere with an apparently free flow of associations, especially early, unless the transference threatens the analytic situation to the point where its interpretation is mandatory rather than optional.

With the recognition that evens apparently freely associating patient may also be showing resistance to awareness of the transference, this formulation should not interfere as long a useful information being gathered should relace Freud's dictum that the transference should not be interpreted until it becomes a resistance (1913).

It can be argued that every transference has some connection to some aspect of the current analytic situation, in the sense that the past can exert an influence only insofar as it exists in the present. Of course, all the determinants of a transference are current in the sense that what I am distinguishing is the current reality of the analytic situation, that is, what actually goes on between patient and analyst in the situation from how the patient is currently constituted as a result of his past.

All analysts would dubiously agree that there are both current and transferential determinants of the analytic situation, and probably no analyst would argue that a transference of the analytic situation, and probably no analyst would argue that a transference idea can be expressed without contamination, as it was, that is, without any connection to anything current in the patient-analyst relationship. Nevertheless, the implications of this fact for technique are often neglected in practice, as my next point is only to argue for the connection.

Several authors, e.g., Kohut 1959 and Loewald 1960, have pointed out that Freud`s early application by the act or practice of using something or the state of being used, this, however, employ of the quality of being appropriate or valuable to some end as to accommodate the accountable or warrant the use of the term transference. In `The Interpretation of Dreams, in a connection not immediately recognizable as related to the present day use of the term, reveals the fallacy of considering that transference can be expressed free of any connection to the present. That early use was to refer to the fact that an unconscious idea cannot be expressed as such, but only as it becomes connected to a preconscious o r conscious content. In the phenomenon with which Freud was then concerned, the dream transference took place from an unconscious wish to a day residue. In `The Interpretation of Dreams, `Freud used the term transference both for the general rule that an unconscious content is expressible only as it becomes transferred to a preconscious or conscious content and for the specific application of this rule to a transference to the analyst. Just as the day residue is the point of attachment of the dream wish, so must there be an analytic-situation residue, though Freud did not use that term, as the point of attachment of the transference.

Analysts have always limited their behaviour, both in variety and intensity, to increase the extent to which the patient's behaviour is determined by his idiosyncratic interpretation of the analyst's behaviour. In fact, analysts unfortunately sometimes limit the behaviour so much as to compare with such an expression or unpiled standard or absolute approximation, that the entire relationship with the patient matter of technique, with no nontechnical personal relation, as Liptop (1977) has pointed out.

But no matter how far the analyst attempts to carry this limitation of his behaviour, the very existence of the analytic situation provides the patient with innumerable cues which can enviably become his rationale for his transference responses. In other words, the current situation cannot be made to disappear - that is, the analytic situation is real. It is easy to forget this truism in one's zeal to diminish the role of the current situation in determining the patient 's responses. One can try to keep past and present determinants relatively perceptible from one another, but one cannot obtain either 'pure culture'. Freud wrote: 'I insist on this procedure [the couch], however, for its purpose and result are to prevent the transference from mingling with the patient's associations imperceptibly, to isolate the transference and to allow it to come forward in due course sharply defined as a resistance' (1913). Even 'isolate' is too strong a word in the light of the inevitable intertwining of the transference with the current situation.

If the analyst remains under the illusion that the current cues he provides to the patient can be reduced to the vanishing point, he may be led into a silent withdrawal, which is not too distant from the caricature of an analyst as someone who does refuse to have any personal relationship with the patient. What happens then is that silence has become a technique rather than merely an indication that the analyst is listening. The patient's responses under such conditions can be mistaken fo uncontaminated transference when they are in fact transference adaptions to the actuality of the silence.

The recognition, from which it takes its point of departure, as it was, has a crucial implications for the technique of interpreting resistance to the awareness of transference, in that, if, the analyst becomes persuaded of the centrality of transference and the importance of encouraging the transference to expand within the analytic situation, he has to find the presenting and plausible interpretation of resistance to the awareness of transference he should make. Is that, his most reliable guide is the cues offered by what is actually going on in the analytic situation? : On the one hand, the events of the situation, such as change in time of session, or an interpretation made by the analyst, and, on the other hand, how the patient is experiencing the situation as reflected in explicit remarks about it, however, fleeting these may be. This is the primary yield for technique of the recognition that any transference must have a link to the actuality of the analytic situation. The cue points to the nature of the transference, just as the day residue for a dream may be a quick pointer of the latent dream thoughts. Attention to the current situation for a transference elaboration will keep the analyst from making mechanical transference interpretation, in which he interprets that there are allusions to the transference in association not manifestly about the transference, but without offering any plausible bias for the interpretation. Attention to the current stimulation offers some degree of protection against the analyst's inevitability whose tendency to project his own views onto the patient, either because of countertransference or because of a preconceived theoretical bias about the content and hierarchical relationships in psychodynamics.

The analyst may be very surprised at what in his behaviour the patient finds important or unimportant, for the patient's responses will be idiosyncratically determined by the transference, the patient's responses may seem to be something the patient, as well as the analysts consider trivial, because, as in displacement to a trivial aspect of the day residue of a dream, displacement can better serve resistance when it is to something trivial. Because it is connected to conflict-laden material, the stimulus to the transference may be difficult to find. It may be quickly disavowed, so that its presence in awareness is only transitory. With the discovery of the disavowed, the patient may also gain insight into how it repeats as disavowed earlier in his life. In his search for the present stimuli which the patient is responding transferentially, as the analyst must therefore remain alert to both fleeting and apparently trivial manifested reference to himself as well as in the events of the analytic situation.

If the analyst interprets the patient's attitudes in a spirit of seeing their possible plausibility in the light of what information the patient does have, rather than in the spirit of either affirming or denying the patient's views, the way is open for their further expression and elucidation. The analyst will be respecting the effort to be plausible and realistic, rather than manufacturing his transference attitudes out of whole bodied material.

Importantly, is to make a transference interpretation plausible to the patient in terms of as current stimulus that, if the analyst is persuaded that the manifest content has important implications for the transference but he is unable to see a current stimulus for the attitude, he should explicitly say so if he decides to make the transference interpretation anyway. The patient himself may then be able to say what the current stimulus is.

It is sometimes argued that the analyst's attention to his own behaviour is a precipitant for the transference, will increase the patient's resistance to recognizing the transference. That, on the contrary, that because of the inevitable interrelationship of the current and transferential determinants, it is only through interpretation that they can be disentangled.

It is also argued that one must wait until the transference has reached optimal intensity before it can be advantageously interpreted. It is true that too hasty and interpretation of the transference can serve as a defensive function for the analyst and deny him the information he needs to make a more appropriate transference interpretation. But it is true that delay in interpreting transference interpretation, but it is also true that delay in interpreting runs the risk of allowing an unmanageable transference to develop. It is also true that deliberate delay can be a manipulation in the service of abreaction rather than analysis, and, like silence, can lead to a response to the actual situation which is mistaken for uncontaminated transference. Obviously important, is assumed in the issues of timing are involved, whereas an important clue to when a transference interpretation is apt and which one to makes lies in whether the interpretation can be made plausibly in terms of the determinant, namely, as something in the current analytic situation. Such as, in the approaching transference in the spirit of seeing how it appears plausibly realistic to the patient, it paves the way toward its further elucidation and expression.

Freud's emphasis on remembering as the goal of the analytic work implies that remembering is the principal avenue to the resolution of the transference. But the delineation of the successive steps in the development of the analytic technique (1920) makes clear that he saw this development as a change from an effort to reach memories directly to the utilization of the transference as the necessary intermediacy to reaching the memories.

In contrast to remembering as the way the transference is resolved, Freud also described resistance for beings primarily overcome in the transference, with remembering following relatively easily afterwards, 'From the repetitive reactions which are exhibited in the transference we are led along the familiar paths to the awakening of the memories, which appear without difficulty, as it was, after the resistance has been overcome' (1914), and 'This revision of the process of repetition can be accomplished only in part in connection with the memory traces of the process which led to repression. The decisive part of the work's achieved by creating in the patient's relation to the analyst - in the 'transference' new editions of the old conflicts . . . Thus, the transference becomes the battlefield on which all the mutually struggling forces should meet one another' (1917). This is the primary indication for which Strachey (1934) classified in his seminal paper on the therapeutic action of psychoanalysis.

There are two main ways in which resolution of the transference can take place through work with the transference in the here and now. The first lies in the clarification of what are the clues in the current situation which are the patient's point of departure force a transference elaboration. The exposure of the current point of departure at once raises the question of whether it is adequate to the conclusion drawn from it. The relating of the transference to a current stimulus is, after all, parts of the patient's effort to make, the transference attitude plausibly determined by the present. The reverse and ambiguity of the analyst's behaviour are what increases the ranges of apparently plausible conclusions the patient may draw. If an examination of the basis for the conclusion makes clear that the actual situation to which the patient responds is subject to other meanings than the one the patient has reached, he will more reality consider his pre-existing bias, that is to say, in that of transference.

Critically, it is suggested that, in speaking of the current relationship and the relation between the patient's conclusion and the information on which they seem plausibly based, such in some absolute conception of what is real in the analytic situation, of which the analyst is the final arbiter. That is not the case, that what the patient must come to see is that the information he has is subject to other possible interpretations implies the very contrary to an absolute conception of reality. In fact, analyst and patient engage in a dialogue in a spirit of attempting to arrive at a consensus about reality, not about some factious absolute reality.

The second way in which resolution of the transference can take place within the work with the transference in the here and now is that in the very interpretation of the transference the patient had a new experience. He is being treated differently from how he expected to be. Analysts seem reluctant to emphasize his new experience, as though it endangers the role of insight and argue for interpersonal influence as the significant factor in change. Strachey's emphasis on the new experience in the mutative transference interpretation has unfortunately been overshadowed by his views on introjection, which have been mistaken to advocate manipulating the transference. Strachey meant introjection of the more benign superego of the analyst only as a temporary strep on the road toward insight. Not only is the new experience not to be confused with the interpersonal influence of a transference gratification, but the new experience occurs together with insight into both the patient's biassed expectation and the new experience. As Strachey points out, what is unique about the transference interpretation is that insight and the new experience take place in relation to the very person who was expected to behave differently, and it is this which gives the work in the transference, its immediacy and effectiveness. While Freud did stress the effective immediacy of the transference, he did not make the new experience explicit.

It is important to recognize that transference interpretation is not a matter of experience, in contrast to insight, but a joining of the two together, both are needed to bring about and maintain the desired changes in the patient. It is also important to recognize that no new techniques of intervention are required to provide the new experience. It is an inevitable accompaniment of interpretation of the transference in the here and now. It is often overlooked that, although Strachey said that only transference interpretations are outside the transference.

Rosenfeld (1972) has pointed out that clarification of material outside the transference is often necessary to know what is the appropriate transference interpretation, and that both genetic transference interpretations and extratransference interpretation taking to consider an inclination as marked by or indication of notable worth or simply the consequence based upon the role in working through. Strachey said relatively little about working through, but surely nothing against the necessary provision with which every thing needfully is explicitly recognized as the role for the recovery of the past in the resolving dissection of the purposiveness determined by the transference.

In taking positions, as to emphasis the role of the analysis of the transference in the here and now, both in interpreting resistance to the awareness of transference and in working toward its resolution by relating to the actuality of the situation. In that of opinion or purpose with the evidence that extratransference and genetic transference interpretation and, of course, working through is important too, that the matter is one of emphasis. Also, interpretation of resistance to awareness of the transference should figure in the majority of sessions, and that if this is done by relating the transference to the actual analytic situation, the very same interpretation is a beginning of work to the resolution of the transference. To justify this view more persuasively would require detailed case material.

The concern and considerations that the Kleinian annalists whom, many analysts feel, are in error in giving the analysis of the transference too great if not even as exclusive role in the analytic process. It is true that Kleinians emphasize the analysis of the transference more, in their writing at least, than does the general run of analysts. As, Anna Freud (1968) complained that the concept of transference has become overexpanded seems to be directed against the Kleinians. One of the reasons the Kleinians consider themselves the true followers of Freud in technique are precisely because of the emphasis they put on the analysis of the transference. Hanna Segal (1967), for example, writes, `Too say that all communications are seen as communications about the patents phantasy as well as current external life is equivalent to saying that all communications contain something relevant to the transference situation. In Kleinian technique, the interpretation of the transference is often more central than in the classical technique.

Freud's first direct mention of transference comes upon the pages ascribed within the 'Studies of Hysteria' (1895), his first significant reference to it, however did not appear until five years later, when, in a letter to Fliess on April 16, 1900, he said (Freud, 1887-1902) he was 'beginning to see that the apparent endlessness of the treatment is something of an inherent feature and is connected with the transference'. In a footnote to this letter the editors said that, 'This was the first insight into the role of transference in psychotherapy.'

Despite these early references, it seems correct to say that yet another five years were to go by before the phenomenon of transference was actually introduced. Even so, the introduction was far from prominent, for it was tacked on like an afterthought as a four-page portion of a postscript to what was perhaps Freud's most fascinating case history to date, the case of Dora (1905).

Using data from Dora's three-month-long, unexpectedly terminated analysis, and especially from her dramatic transference reaction which had taken him quite unawares, Freud now gave to transference its first distinct psychological entity and for the first time indicated its essential role in the analytic process. His account, although in general more than adequate - in the elegant fact and unmistakably 'finished' - was brief, and almost to the point, and perhaps not an entirely worthy introduction so much more a truly great discovery. What was uniquely great was his recognizing the usefulness of transference. In his analysis of Dora he had noted not only that transference feelings existed and were powerful, but, much to his dismay, he had realized what a serious, perhaps, even insurmountable obstacles that objectively would be. Then, in what seems like a creative leap, Freud made the almost unbelievable discoveries that transference was in fact, the key to analysis, that by properly taking the patient's transference and therapeutic force was added to the analytic method.

The impact on analysis of this startling discovery was actually much greater and much more significant than most people seem to appreciate. Although the role of transference as the sine quo non of analysis and is widely accepted, and was stated by Freud from the first, it has almost never been acclaimed for having brought about an entire change in the nature of analysis. The introduction of free association to analysis, a much lesser change, receives and still receives much more recognition.

One of the reasons for the relatively unheralded entry of transference into analysis may have been for circumstances of its discovery. Although Freud's new ideas were recorded as if they arose as sudden inspiration during the Dora analysis, they may in fact have developed somewhat later. In the paper's precatory remarks, for instance, Freud said he had not discussed transference with Dora at all, and in the postscript, he said he had been unaware of her transference feelings. Also, pointing to a later discovery date is the extraordinary delay in the paper's publication. According to the editor's note, the paper had been completed and accepted for publication by late January 1901, but this date was then actually set back more than four and a half years until October 1905. The editors said, 'We have no information as to how it happened that Freud, . . . deferred publication.' It readily seems that for reasons to have been that only during those four and a half years, as a consequence to his own self-analysis, that he came to a better understanding of the relevantly significant as the applicable reason to posit of the transference. Only then may it have been possible for him to turn again to the Dora case, to apply to it of what he had learned in himself, to write this essay as part of the postscript, and at last to release the paper for publication.

Freud's self-analysis has been considered from many angles, but not significantly, as can be of valuing measure, in at least from the standpoint of transference. Opponents of the idea that there is such a thing as definite self-analysis, some of whom say it is impossible, generally an object on grounds that without any analyst there can be no transference neurosis. Freud clearly demonstrated, as, perhaps, that the situation that may be necessary to fill this need: Self-analysis may require that, at least a halfway satisfactory transference object. In Freud`s case, the main transference object at this time seems to have been Fliess, who filled the role rather well. As with any analysis, the authenticity as known in the unfeigned design as if existing or having no illusions and facing reality squarely, by which the 'real' impact on Freud was slight, he was essentially a neutral figure, relatively anonymous and physically separates. All of this, and Fliess's own reciprocal transference reactions, made it possible for Freud to endow Fliess with whatever qualities and whatever feelings were essential to the development of Freud`s transference, and, it should be added, his transference neurosis. In the end, of course, the transference was in part resolved. Freud`s eventual awakening of its self realization in its presence within him of such strange and powerful psychological forces must have come to the conclusion as a stupefied disilluionary dejection toward Fliess, however, his subsequent working out of some of these transference attachments must have been both an intellectual triumph and an immensely healing and releasing of actions, operations or motions involved in the accomplishment of an ending that makes from its process.

In the years following this revolutionary discovery, the central role of transference in analysis increased in remarkable acceptance, and it has easily held this central position ever since. What the substance of this central position distinctfully compose in having or be capable of having within the constructs to which is something of a mystery, for, it seems as nothing about analysis and is, of least to be, the well known than how individual analysis actually uses transference in their day-to-day work with patients. As a guess, as, perhaps of each analysts concept of transference derives variably but significantly from his own inner experience, transference probably means many and varying differentiations to things as to different analysts.

In the same differentiated individuals, as that Freud's own pupils must have differed on this issue, not only from him but from each other. Although some of their differences may have been slight, others, my have contributed significantly to later analytic developments. A question could be raised, for instance, whether differences in handling the transference which at first were the property of one analyst gradually develop into formal clinical methods used by many, and whether these clinical methods, after having been conceptualized, serve as the beginning of variously divergent schools of analysis. Such occurrences, consistent with certain beliefs that analytic ideas do arise in this way, primarily out of transference experiences in the analytic situation, would lead to the question whether the history of the ideological differences in what was actually said and done in response to transference reactions that to any other factor. Whatever the case, many differences and divergencies did occur among the early analysts, and all of that is supposed to have had to do in some major way with differences in the handling of the transference.

Strangely, Freud himself seems to have taken little part in influencing this rapid and divergent period of growth. Usually accused of being too dominating in such matters, Freud seems to have done just the opposite during the development of this most critical aspect of analysis, the process itself, and, for reasons unknown, detached himself from it.

What was needed, one might be inclined to say, was not leadership in the form of domination, but leadership in trying to provide what was lacking, and still lacking, namely an analytical rationale for transference phenomena. The question must be asked, of course, whether in fact this would have been a good thing at that particular time in psychoanalytic history. Perhaps not. The exercise of closure, which Freud's structuring might have amounted to. But although adding to understanding and stability at ceratin theoretical levels, could at another level, so such closures have often done, have placed many obstacles in the way of further analytical developments. Thus, his leaving the matter of transference wide open, even though it led to confusion and uncertainty, may have been just as well.

In many ways the closest Freud ever came to establishing a formal analytical rationale for transference was his first attempt, in the postscript to the case of hysteria (1905). These few pages are and among the most important of all Freud's writings, outweighing by far the paper to which they are appended. Yet, in the case of Dora has always been taught as an entity rather than the ancillary to the essay on transference. In that essay Freud was clear: His ideas revealed tremendous insights and promised more to come, and that, the powers of the neurosis are occupied in creating a new edition of the same disease. Just think of the analytic implications of his saying that this new edition consists of a special class of mental structures, for the most part unconscious, having the peculiar characteristic of being able to replace earlier persons with that of the person of the analyst, and in the fashion applying all components of the original neurosis to the person of the analytical at the present time. Surely as profound a statement as any he ever made.

He then goes on to say that there is no way to avoid transference, that this 'latest creation of the desire must be combatted like all the earlier ones', and that, although this is by far the hardest part of analysis, only after the transference has been resolved can a patient arrive at a sense of conviction of the validity of the connection which have been constructed during analysis.

He concludes by saying, 'In psychoanalysis . . . all the patients' tendencies, including hostile ones, are aroused, they are then turned to account for reasons to explain or the internalization of justification, and by the same measure was to purposively give a sensible reason for the proposed change in the analysis by which of being made conscious. That, in this way, the transference is constantly being put-down, however, transference, which seems ordained to be the greatest obstacle to psychoanalysis, becomes its most powerfully . . .

These remarkable observations, in conveying a sense of deep conviction that could arise, one feels, only from Freud's own hard-won inner experience, that nowhere is there a suggestion that transference is a mere technical matter. Far from it, as Freud announces that he has come upon as new and exciting kind of mental function, or, as it is to believe, that a new and exciting kind of ego function.

Very quickly, however, Freud's conviction sees to have failed him. Nothing he wrote afterwards about transference was at this level, and most of his later references were a retreat from it, for instance, he never did develop the promising idea that the mind constantly creates new editions of the original neurosis and meaningfully incline the minded inclusion in them, an ever-changing series of persons. Instead, he tended to become less specific, even referring to transference at times in a broad terms as if it were no more than rapport between patient and analysts, or as if it was an interpersonal or psychosocial relationship, concepts which, of course, a great many analysts have since adopted, but which were not part of Freud's original ideas.

Perhaps his most persistent deviation was an on-and-off tendency to regard transference merely as a technical matter, often writing of it as an asset to analysis when positive and a liability when negative.

Significantly, because it indicated that an active struggle was still going on within him, Freud occasionally expressed once again, even though briefly his earlier insights, particularly his ideas that transference is an essential although unexplored part of mental life. An example of this appears in his alternative obtainments such that is gainfully to appear of as quality of being pleasant or agreeable to a feature that makes for pleasantness or ease, among the amenities of the central geniality, otherwise, the prevailing indifference account for the transference in 'An Autobiographical Study' (1925). Transference, he says, 'is a universal phenomenon of the human mind. And in fact dominated the whole of each person's relations to his human environment. In these few words' Freud again made the point, and in declarative fashion, that transference is a mental structure of the greatest magnitude, but he never really followed it up.

Rather extensive evidence of his departure from the original concept and his continuing struggle with that concept is seen most clearly, wherein, the 'Analysis Terminable and Interminable' is much more than a courageous, brilliant, and pessimistic, appraisal of the difficulties and limitations of analysis, although transference is briefly mentioned in its content, yet a great deal about it comes through, some quite directly, some by easy inference. When looked at in this way, two themes stand out: Freud's personal frustration with the enigmas of transference and his tacit placing of transference in the centre of success and failure in analysis, both as a therapy and as a developing science. What also comes through, is the perplexing realization of how far Freud had, by now, seemingly moved away from his original concepts. Or had he?

All the same, even if it is insufficient for exclusive reliance in relations to the complicated neurosis, for which it would be fallacious to assign to the recall and reconstruction of the past an exclusively explanatory value (in the intellectual sense), important though that functions be, and difficult as its full-blown emotional correlate may be to come by. There is no doubt that, even in complicated neurosis, equivalently complicated transference neurosis, the genuine complex and complicated transference neurosis, the genuinely experienced linking of the past and present can have, at times, a certain uniquely specific dynamic effect of its own, a type of telescoping or merging of common elements in experience, which must be connected with the meaninglessness of time in unconscious life, compared with its stern authority in the life of consciousness and adaptation to everyday reality. Contributing decisively to such experiences as to whatever degree it occurs, is of course, the vivid currency of the transference neurosis, and central in this, the reincarnations of old objects in an actual person, the analyst.

Thus, an allied problem in the general sphere of transference is the fascination and often enigmatic interplay of past and present. If one wishes to view this interplay in terms of a stereotyped formulation, the matter can remain relatively uncomplicated - as a formulation. Unfortunately., This is too often the case. The phenomenon, however, retains some important obscurities, which cannot thoroughly dispel, but to which I would like to call attention. To concentrate on the dimension of time, it seems in reference to the complication and immediate aspects of technique, nonetheless, essential. For example, we can assume that the transference neurosis re-enacts the essential conflicts of the infantile neurosis in a current setting. If a reasonable degree of awareness of transference is established, the next problem is the genetic reduction of the neurosis to its elements in the past, through analysis of the transference resistance and allied intrapsychic resistances, ultimately genetic interpretations, recollections and reconstructions and working through. Such that the transference is related to its genetic origins, the analyst thereby emerges in his true, i.e., real, identity to the patient, the transference is putatively 'resolved'. To the extent that one follows the traditional view that all resistances, including the transference itself, is ultimately directed against the restoration of early memories as, this is a convincing formulation. Is that, only to say, that in his own right as such as having to a certain tightly logical quality? However, we know that it this is not so readily accomplished, apart from the special intrapsychic considerations described afterward by Freud in 'Analysis Terminable and Interminable'. Although in a favourable case, much of the cognitive interpretative work can be accomplished, there remains the fact that cognition responsibility, in its bare sense, does not necessarily lead to the subsidence of powerful dynamism, to the withdrawal of 'cathexes' from importantly real objects. For, as mentioned, a short while ago, the analyst is a real and living object, apart from the representations with which the transference invests him, and which are interpretable as such, for which there is no, at any time a seldom, a confusing interrelations and commonly of the emergent responses, due to the same old seeking, and this is directed toward a new individual in his own right, both are important, furthermore, there are large and important ones of overlapping. Apart from such considerations, even the explicitly incestuous transference is currently experienced (as, at least in good part) by a full-grown adult (like the original oedipus), instead of a totally and actually helpless child. To be sure, the latter state is reflected in the emergent transference elements of instinctual striving, but it is subject to analysis, and the residual is something significant, if not totally different. It is these residual sexual wish, presumably directed toward the person of the analyst, as such, which must be displaced to others, if, as generally agreed, the revival of infantile fantasies and strivings in the biologically mature adolescent presents a new and special problem, one must assume distinctiveness of experience for the adult, although it is true that in the majority of instances, adequate solution is favoured by the adult state. There is, in any case, a residual relationship between persons who have worked together in a prolonged, arduous and intimate relationship, which, strictly speaking, are reversibly disconnected or divorced of services, in that the transference merely ushers out the retirement for which its rendering retreat of that state of mind or feeling by an inner avoidance of something usually felt as unpleasant or pronounced for it's adverse but mutual colouration. Blending to some confusion between the two spheres of feeling. The general tendency is that both components are fully gratified to some degree. But, there is the ubiquitous power of the residual primordial transference, yet, argue to cling to an omnipotent partisan to resist the displacement of its 'sublimated' anaclitic aspects, even if the various representation of the wishes for bodily intimacy has been thoroughly analysed and successfully displaced. The outcome is largely the transference of the transference, as mentioned earlier, in a different context. For everyday reality can provide no actual answer to such cravings. In this connection, note, Freud's genial envy of Pfister. If the man of faith finds this gratification in revealing religion, others in a wide range of secular beliefs and 'leaders' the modern rational and sceptical intellectual is less fortunate in this respect. Presumably free, he is prone to invest even intellectual disciplines or the proponents with inappropriate expectations and partisan passions, but, least of mention, that within these fields of analytical and theoretical thought, is not to provide exceptions to this tendency.

Though if one is to maintain and beneficially confine its bothering of reservations about the clarity of conceptualization, the explanatory discussion of Kohut and Seitz, is a very useful contribution to the direct complication or which by some understanding the awkwardness of oneself. Both Loewald and Kohut have deliberately associated a special but the different use of one of Freud's three conceptions of transference, i.e., the transference from the unconscious to the preconscious.

Yet, to furthering comments on primordial transference, at least potentially, are largely psychological (mental) component, the concept of 'transference of the transference' would be applicable to this component. For it does appear that certain aspect of the search for the omnipotent and omniscient caretaking parents are implicitly practical as virtually capable for being turned to use or account for its functional practicability for something of a process or the procedure for being all but the essential purpose to come to or tend toward a common point, for which are the knowledgeable information or ideas, is nothing but causative effectuality. As suggested earlier, there are important qualitative and quantitative distinctions in the mode of persistence and such strivings, however, even to the extent that they are detached from the analyst and carried into some reasonably appropriate expression in everyday life, they retain at least a subtle quality which contravenes reality, one which derives from earliest infancy, and remains - to this extent - a transference. 'Santa Claus' lives on, where one might least expect to meet him, whether as a donor of miracle drug or of far more complex panaceas.

If one prescribes to this parasymbiotic transference drive, a true primordial origin, it is necessary to take cognizance of certain important concepts dealing with the earliest period of life. If we assume a powerful original organismic drive toward an original 'object', a striving to nullify separation from the beginning, how does this make something legally valid or operative usually by formal approval or sanctioned with concepts such as 'primary narcissism' or the 'objectless phase' or 'the primary psycho physiological self' (We note in passing that there are those who do not accept these as usually construed in the technique of Balint), for example, or Fairbairn or - conspicuously - Melanie Klein. These are states, variously defined or conceived, which apply to the earliest neonatal period, in which life, to state more simply, exists only as the potential in physiological processes. Since there is (we postulate) no clear awareness of self-withdrawal from the mother, there can be no 'mentally' represented or experienced drive to obliterate the separation (concerning oneself and object, conceiver of as separate, in a continuing sense). There are, of course, discharge phenomena, the precursors of purposive activity, and there are urgent physiological needs, directed toward fulfilment or relief, rather than toward an object as such. However, in relation to these physiological needs as archaistic precursors of object relationships, it must be noted that in all, except respiration and spontaneous sphincter relief (even in these instances, not without exception or reservation), the need fulfilment must be mediated by the primordial object (or her surrogate). There is also, of course, the uniquely important requirement for 'holding', in a literal expression, from the outset. The material partner in human symbiosis which supplies what the neonate cannot seek by 'clinging', as for Bowlty and Murphy, in the sense that must be experienced to the physiological ebb and flow of tension, even if restricted to the kinaesthetic, connected with a peripheral sensory registration, which is the protophase of the recognition of separation from the object or nonpresence of the object, as a painful instance of, her presence in apposition the converse? That the general context may be only in which the sense of unity is preponderant, or, more accurately, that there is no general awareness of 'separation' as such, means that the drive for union does not exist in a general psychological sense. It is, so to speak, satisfied. That object constancy, with its cognate 'longing', is quite a different experience from the urgencies of primitive need fulfilment is true, however, regardless of what may be added by maturational and developmental considerations, instinctual and perceptual, there is no reason to assume other than a core of developmental continuity from the earliest needs and their fulfilment to the later state, and some continuing degree of contingency based on them.

There is a very rough parallel in the way certain analytic patients, before a firm relationship with the analyst is established, signal certain primitive experiences and tendencies in special reactions to the end of the hour, to the nonvisibility of the analyst, to interruption of their association, to failure of the analyst to talk, and similar matters. We must note that in the basic formation of the ego is evident amongst the primitive reactions and beyond to separations, in the form of very early identifications as based on care taking functions. Certainly in the very development of autonomous ego of the mother's investment in the, have a decisive role in the character of the their development. And in the case of object constancy, in its connotation of libidinal cathexis, where is no need whatsoever (emotional or otherwise) is needed for prolonged periods. The importance of the object is, to put it mildly, liable to deteriorate, or to differ complicating aggressive change. Probably the characteristic feature of later developing relations to the object (love and the wish for love), as separate if not always separated from demonstrable primitivity, in the need fulfilment, have a special relationship to those 'ancillary' aspects of neonatal nurture, whose lack has been shown to be an actual threat to life in some instances, not to speak of sound emotional development. So that from the first, regardless of the assumed state of libidinal (and aggressive) economy, or the assumed state of psychological nondifferentiation between self and potential object, there are critical percussive phenomena, objectively observed, and probably prototypic subjective experiences of separation, which are the forerunners of all subsequent experiences of the kind. One may generalize to the effect that, with maturation and development, secondary identifications, and the various other processes of 'internalization' in its broadest sense, the problem of separation and its mastery becomes correspondingly more complex, and changes with the successive phase of life, but never entirely disappears.

In the view of the psychoanalytic situation described earlier, the latent mobilization of experiences of separation stimulated by the situational structure awakens the driving primordial urge to undo or to master the painful separations which it represents, usually embodied in the various forms of clinical transference that which we are familiar. One legitimate gratification which tends to mitigate superfluous transference regression is the transmission of understanding that at times, are thought that by the 'mature transference', in effect, the 'therapeutic alliance' or a group of mature ego functions which enter into such an alliance. Now, there is one blurring and overlapping at the conceptual edges in both instances, but the concept as such is largely distinct from either one, as it is from the primitive transference, which we have been discussing. Whether the concept is thought by others to comprehend a demonstrable actuality, which is a further question. This question, of course, can only follow on conceptual clarity. This in saying, of a nonrational urge, not directly dependent on the perception of immediate clinical purposes, a true transference in the sense that it is displaced (in currently relevant form) from the parent of early childhood to the analyst. Its content is not anti-sensational, but largely non-sensual of sometimes transitional, as the child's pleasure in the assemblages of 'dirty words' and encompasses a special and not minuscule sphere of the object relationship: The wish to understand, and to be understood, the wish to be given understanding, i.e., teaching, specifically by the parent (or later surrogate); the wish to be taught to use ingenuity in making or doing o r achieving an end through the actions in a nonpunitive way, corresponding to the growing perception of hazard and conflict and very likely the implicit wish to be provided with and taught channels of substitutional drive discharge. With this, there may well be a wish, corresponding to that element in Loewald's description of therapeutic process, to be seen in terms of one's developmental potentialities by the analyst. No doubt, the list could be extended into many subtleties, details, and variations. However, one should not omit to specify that, in its peak development, it would include the wish for increasingly accurate interpretations and the wish to facilitate such interpretations by providing adequate material ultimately, of course, by identification, to participate in, or even be the author of the interpretations. The childhood system of wishes which underlies the transference is a correlate of biological maturation, and the latent (i.e., teachable) autonomous ego function, appearing with it, however, there is a drive-like quality in the participation phenomena, which disqualifies any conception of the urge's identical with the functions. No one who has ever watched a child importune a parent with questions, or experiment with new words, or solicit her interests in a new game, or demand a storytelling or reading, can doubt this. That this powerful support and integration in the ego identification with a loved parent is undoubtedly true, just as it is true of the identification with an analyst toward whom a positive relationship has been established. That 'functional pleasure ' inscribes the part, where certain specific ego energies, perhaps very likely the ego's own urge to extend its hegemony in the personality. However, it can be stressed in the derive element, even the special phase configurations and colourations, and with its importance of object relations, libidinal and aggressive, for a specific reason. For just as the primordial transference seeks to undo separation, in a sense to obviate object relationships as we know them, the 'mature transference', tends toward separation and individuation, and increasing contact with the environment, optimally with a large affirmative (increasing neutralized) relationship toward the original object toward whom (or her surrogates) a different dynamic of demands is now increasingly directed. The further considerations which has led to the emphasis that the drive-like element in these attitudes are integrated phenomena, as examples of 'multiple functional' rather than the discrete exorcise of function or functions, is the conviction that there is a continuing dynamic relation of relative interchangeability between the two series, at least based on the response to gratifications in a significant zone of complicated energetic overlap, possibly including the phenomenon of neutralization. That the empirical 'interchangeability' is limited, and that goes without saying, that in no way diminishes its decisive importance. The linguistic communications as in mention, that the excessive transference neurosis regression, which can seriously vitiate the affirmative psychoanalytic process, finds a prototype in the regressive behaviour and demands of certain children, who do not receive their share of teaching, 'attention', play, nonseductive, affectionate demonstration, as to use the quality of being appropriate or valuable to some end, even the act or practice of using something or the state of being used to which of responsible interests in development, and similar matters, from their parents. In the psychnalytic situation, both the gratifications offered by the analyst and the freedom of expression by the patient, are diversely limited and concentrated, practically entirely (in the every day demonstrable sense) in the sphere of linguistic expression, on the analyst's side, further, in the transmission of understanding.

The mature transference is a dynamic and integral part of the therapeutic alliance, alone with the tender aspect of the erotic transference, even more attenuated (and more dependable) friendly feeling of adult type, and the ego identification with the analyst. Indispensable, of course, are the genuine adult's need for help, the crystallizing rational and intuitive appraisal of the analyst, the adult sense of confidence in him, and innumerable other nuances of adult thought and feeling. With these, giving a driving momentum and power to the analytic process, but always, a potential source of resistance, and always requiring analysis, is the primordial transference and its various appearances in the specific therapeutic transference. That it is, if well managed, not only a reflection of the repetition compulsion in its menacing sense, but a living presentation from the id, seeking new solutions, and trying again, so to speak, to find a place in the patient's conscious and effective life, has important affirmative potentialities. This has been specifically emphasized by Nunberg, Lagache and Loewald among others. Loewald has recently elaborated very effectively the ideas to become 'ancestors' on a bases upon the corpses of times generations. The mature transference, in its own infantile right, provides some of the unique qualities of propulsive force, which comes from the world of feeling, rather than the world of thought. If one views it in a purely figurative sense, that fraction of the mature transference which derives from 'conversion' is somewhat like propulsive fraction as the wind in a boats sailing to windward currents into motion, the strong headwind, the ultimate source of both resistance and propulsion, is the primordial transference. This view, however, should not displace the original and independent, if cognate, a favourable tide or current would also be required. It is not that the mature transference is itself entirely exempt from analytic clarification and interpretation. For one thing, in common with other childhood spheres of experience, there may have been traumas in this sphere, punishments, serious defects or lacks of parental communication, Listening, attention or interest. In general, this is probably far more important than has hitherto appeared in our prevalent paradigmatic approach to adult analysis, even taking into account the considerable changes due to the growing interest in ego psychology. 'Learning' in the analysis can, of course, be a troublesome intellectualizing resistance. Furthermore, both the patient's communications and his receptions and utilization of interpretations may exhibit only too clearly, as sometimes in the case of other ego mechanisms, their origin in and tenacious relation to instinctual or anaclitic dynamism; the longing implement out of silence for which the analyst is to override the uncritical acceptance (or rejection) of interpretations, in that the patient revealingly is to mention the unmindful assimilation, fluently, rich, endlessly detailed associations without spontaneous reflection or integration. In the direct demands for solution of moral and practical probability for an entirely intellectual scope, and a variety of others. It may and always be easy to discriminate between the utilization of speech by an essentially instinctual demand, and an intellectual or linguistic trait or having to be determined by specific factors in their own developmental sphere, however, the underlying and essentially genuine dynamism which have to continue to be placed for a notable time interval or remain to an arbitrary or conventional character most favoured to the purposes of processes of analysis, as it was to the original processes of maturational development, communication, and benign separation. Lagache, on the desirability of separating the current unqualified usage, 'positive' and 'negative' transference, as based on the patient's immediate state of feeling, from a classification based on the essential effect on analytic processes. Yet, the later of mature transference is, in general, a 'positive transference'.

Connecting the considerations in the transference neurosis, and the problem of transference interpretation, may be offered at this point. The whole situational structure of analysis (in contrast with other personal relationships), its dialogue of free association and interpretation, and its deprivations as to most ordinary cognitive and emotional interpersonal drives that tend toward the separation of discrete transferences from their synthesis with one another and with defences in character or symptoms, and with deepening regression, toward a continuative portrayal of the essential of the infantile neurosis, in the transference neurosis. In other relationships, the 'give and take' aspects - gratifying aggressive, punitive or otherwise actively responsive, and the open mobility of searching for alternative or greater satisfaction - exert a profound dynamic and economic influence, so that only extraordinary situations, or transference of pathological character, or both, occasion to comparable regression.

It is a curious fact, whereas the dynamic meaning to the importance of the transference neurosis have been well established since Freud gave this the phenomenon a central position in his clinical thinking, the clinical reference, when the term is used, remains variable and somewhat ambiguous. For example, Greenson, in his excellent recent paper, speaks of it as appearing, 'when the analyst and the analysis become the central concern in the patient's life'. However, previous remarks in this connection, for which it is worthwhile to specify certain aspects of Greenson's definition, for the term 'central' is somewhat ambiguous, as to its specific reference. Certainly, the term could apply to the symbolic position of the analyst in relation to the patient's experiencing ego and the symbolically decisive position which he correspondingly assumes in the relation to the other important figures in the patient's current life. However, while the analysis is in any case, and for multiple reasons, exceedingly important the seriously involved patient, there is a free observing portion of is ego, also involved, not in the same sense as that involved in the transference regression and revived in infantile conflicts. And here is here being, of course, always the integrated adult personalty, however diluted in may seem at times, of its rarity, although certainly does occur, that the analysis actually exceeds the quality or state of being of notable worth or influence that the other major concerns, attachments, and responsibilities of the patient's life, nor is it desirable that his should occur, on the other hand, if construed with proper attention to the economic considerations as mentioned, the concept is important, both theoretically and clinically. In the theoretical direction to the assumption that there is a continuing system of object relationships and conflict situations, most important in the unconscious representations, but participating to some degree in all others, deriving in a successive series of transference from the experiences of separation from the original object, the mother. In this sense, the analyst's applicability to a uniquely important portion of the patient's personality, the portion that 'never grew up', to maintain a central figure. In the clinical sense, to call or direct attention especially to a supposed cause, source, or to refer to the importance of the transference neurosis as outlining for the essential and central analytic task, providing by its very currency and demonstrability a relatively secure cognitive base for procedural duties. By its inclusion of the patient's essential psychopathological processes and tendencies, in their original functional connection, it offers, in its resolution or marked reduction, the most formidable level for analytic cure. Nonetheless, transference neurosis must be seen in its interweaving with the patient's extra-analytic system of personal contacts. The relationship to the analyst may influence the course of relationships to others, in the same sense that the clinical neurosis did, except that the former is alloplastic, relatively exposed, and subject to constant interpretation. It is also an important fact that, except in those rare instances where the original dyadic relationship appears to turn, the analyst, even in the strict transference sphere, cannot be assigned all the transference role simultaneously. Other actors are required. He may at times oscillate with confusing rapidity between the status of mother and father, but he is usually predominantly in one of the roles for long periods, someone else representing the other. Furthermore, apart from 'acting out', complicated and mutually inconsistent attitudes of the anterior apprehensions for realizing often about something not generally realized in the verbalization, may require the seeking of other transference objects, i.e., The husband or wife, friend, another analyst and so forth. Children, even the patient's own children, may be invested with strivings of the patient, displaced from the analysis, even experience the impulses which they would wish to call forth in the analyst. The range is extensive, varied, and complicated, requiring constant alertness. Transference interpretation therefore often has a necessarily paradoxical inclusiveness, which is an important reality of technique. There is another aspect, and that is the dynamic and economic impact of the intimate and actual dramatist personate of the transference neurosis in the progress of the analysis as such, and on the patient 's motivation, as well as his real lifer avenues for recovery. For the persons in his milieu may fulfill their 'positive' or 'negative ' roles in transference drama, which may facilitate or impede interpretative effectiveness, they provide the substantial and dependable real life gratification which ultimately facilitate the analysis of the residual analytic transference, or their capacities or attitudes may occasion overload of the anaclitic and instinctual needs in the transference which renders the same process far more difficultly. In the most unhappy instances, there can be a serious undercounting of the motivation for basic change.

There is also the fundamental question of the role of the transference interpretation. At the Marienbad Symposium most of Strachey's colleagues appeared to accept the essential import of his contribution and thus unique significance of the transference interpretations, despite the various reservations as to detail and emphasis on other important aspects of the therapeutic process. Nevertheless, there are still many who, if not in doubt regarding the great value of transference interpretations are inclined to doubt their uniqueness, and to stress the importance of economic considerations in determining the choice as to whether transference or extratransference interpretations may be indicated. Now, apart from the realistic considerations mentioned in the preceding passage (in a sense the necessarily 'distributed' character of a variable fraction of transference interpretation). There is in fact that the extra-analytic life of the patent often provides indispensable data fo the understanding of detailed complexities of his psychic functioning, because of the sheer variety of its references, some of which cannot be reproduced in the relationship to the analyst. For example, there is no repartee (in the ordinary sense) in the analysis. The way the patient handles the dialogue with an angry employee may be importantly revealing. The same may be true of the quality of his reaction to a real danger of dismissal. There is not only the realities, but the 'formal' aspects of this responses. These expressions of personality remain important, even though his 'acting out' of the transference (assuming this was this was the case) may have been more important, and, of course, requiring transference interpretation. Furthermore, they remain useful, if discriminatingly and conservatively treated, even if they are inevitably always subject that epistemological reservations, which haunts so much of analytic data. Of course, the 'positive' transference has a role in the utilization of such interpretations that what enables the patent to listen to them and them seriously.

In an operational sense, it would seem that extratransference interpretations cannot set aside, or underestimated in importance, but the unique effectiveness of transference interpretations is not thereby disestablished. No other interpretation is free, within reason, of the doubt introduced by not really knowing the 'other person's' participation in love, or quarrel or criticism or whatever the issue. And no other situation provides the patient the combined sense of cognitive acquisition, with the experience of complete personal tolerance and acceptance, that is implicit in an interpretation by an individual who is an object of the emotion, drive, or even defences, which are active at the time. There is no doubt that such interpretations must not only (in common with all others) include personal tact, but must be offered with special care as to their intellectual reasonability, in relation to the immediate context, lest they defeat their essential purpose. It is not too often likely that a patient who has just been jilted in a long-standing love affair, and suffering exceedingly, will find an immediate interpretation that his suffering is due to the fact that the analyst does not reciprocate his love, even though a dynamism in this general sphere may be ultimately demonstrable, and acceptable to the patient. On the other hand, once the transference neurosis is established, with accompanying subtle (sometime gross) colouration of the patient's life, than more far-reaching anticipatory, transference interpretations are indicated, for, if all of the patient's libidinal and aggression is not, in fact, invested in the analyst, he has at least an unconscious role in all important emotional transactions, and, if the assumption is correct that the regressive drive, mobilized by the analytic situation, is in the direction of restoration of a single all-encompassing relationship, specified pragmatically in the individual case by the actually attained level of development, then there is a dynamic factor at work, importantly meriting interpretation as such, to the extent that available material supports it. This would be the immediate clinical application on the material regarding the 'cognitive lag' or 'cognitive fall-back'.

The effectuality from which follow the analytic attempt to bring unequalled amounts in the confronting collections of some improper use too a resultant quantity of id-energy into the patient's consciousness all at once. On the one hand, nothing whatever may happen, or on the other hand there may be an unmanageable result, but in neither event will a mutative interpretation have been effected. The analyst's power as auxiliary super-ego may be for two very different reasons. It may be that the id-impulses was trying to bring out were not in fact sufficiently urgent at the moment: For, after all, the emergence of an id-impulse depends on two factors - not only on the permission of the super-ego, but also on the urgency (the degree of cathaxis) of the id-impulse itself. This, then, may be one cause of an apparently negative response to an interpretation, and evidently a fairly harmless one. but the same apparent result may also be due to something else, in spite of the id-impulse being really urgent, the strength of the patient's own repressive forces (the degree of repression) may have been too great to allow his ego to listen to the persuasive voice of the auxiliary super-ego. Now we have a situation dynamically identical with the next one we have to consider, though economically different. this next situation is one in which the patient accepts the interpretation, that is, allows the id-impulse into his consciousness, but is immediately overwhelmed with anxiety. This may show itself in a number of ways, for instance, the patient may produce a manifest anxiety-attack. Or the may exhibit signs of 'real' anger with the analyst with a complete lack of insight, or he may break off the analysis. In any of these cases the analytic situation will, for the moment, at least, have broken down. The patient will be behaving just as the hypnotic subject behaves when, having been ordered by the hypnotist to perform an action too much at variance with his own consciousness, he breaks off the hypnotic relation and wakes up from his trance. This state of things, which is manifest where the patient responds to an interpretation with an actual outbreak of anxiety or one of its equivalents, may be latent were the patient shows no response, and this latter case may be the more awkward of the two, since it is masked, and it may sometimes be the effect of a greater overdose of interpretation than where manifest anxiety arises (though obviously other factors will be of determining importance, and in particularly the nature of the patient's neurosis). Yet this threatened collapse of the analytic situation to an overdose of interpretation: But it might be more accurate in some ways to ascribe it to an insufficient dose. For what has happened is that the second phase of the interpretation process has not occurred: The phase in which the patient becomes aware that his impulse is directed toward an archaic phantasy object and not toward a real one.

In the second phase of a complete interpretation, therefore, a crucial part is played by the patient's sense of reality: For the successful outcome of that phase depends upon his ability, at the critical moment of the emergence into consciousness of the released quantity of id-energy, to distinguish between his phantasy object and the real analyst. The problem is closely related to one that has been discussed elsewhere, namely that of the extreme liability of the analyst's position as auxiliary super-ego. The analytic situation is all the time threatening to degenerate into a 'real' situation. But this actually means the opposite of what it appears to. It means that the patient is all the time on the brink of turning the real external object (the analyst) into the archaic one; that is to say, he is on the brink of projecting his primitive introjected images onto himself. In so far as the patient actually does this, the analyst becomes like anyone else that he meets in real life - a phantasy object. The analyst then ceases to possess the peculiar advantages derived from the analytic situation, he will be introjected like all other phantasy objects into the analytic situation, he will be introjected like all other phantasy objects into the patient's super-ego, and will no longer be able to function in the peculiar ways which are essential to the effecting of a mutative interpretation. In this difficulty the patient's sense of reality is an essential but a very feeble-ally: An improvement in it is one of the things that we hope the analysis will bring about. It is important, therefore, not to submit it to any unnecessary strain, and that is the fundamental reason why the analyst must avoid any real behaviour, that is likely to confirm the patient's view of him as a 'bad' or a 'good' phantasy object. This is perhaps more obvious as regards the 'bad' object. If, for instance, the analyst were to show that he was really shocked or frightened by one of the patient's id-impulses, as the patient would immediately treat him in that respect as a dangerous object and introject him into his archaic severe super-ego. Therefore, on the one hand, there would be a diminuation in the analyst's power to function as an auxiliary super-ego and to allow the patient's to become conscious of his id-impulses - that is to say, in his power to bring about the first phase of a mutative interpretation, and on the other hand, he would, as a real object, become sensibly less distinguishable from the patient's 'bad' phantasy object and to that extent the carrying through of the second phase of a mutative interpretation would also be made more difficult. Or, agin, there is another case. Supposing the analyst behaves in an opposite way and actively urges the patient to give free rein to his id-impulse. There is then a possibility of the patient confusing the analyst with the image of a treacherous parent who first encourages him to seek gratification, and then suddenly turns and punishes him. In such a case the patient's ego may look for defence by itself suddenly turning upon the analyst as though he were his own id-, and treating him with all the severity of which his super-ego is capable. again, the analyst is running a risk of losing his privileged position. But it may be equally unwise for the analyst to act really in such a way as to encourage the patient to project his 'good' introjected object on to him. For the patient will then tend to regard him as a good objective and archaic sense and will incorporate him with his archaic 'good' images and will use him as a protection against his 'bad' ones. In that way, his infantile positive impulses as well as his negative ones may escape analysis, for there may no longer be a possibility for his ego to make a comparison between the phantasy external object and the real one. it will, perhaps, be argued that, with the best of wills in the world, the analyst, however careful he may be, will be unable to prevent the patient from projecting these various images on to him. This is, of course, indisputable, and, the whole effectiveness of analysis depends upon its being so. The lesson of these difficulties is merely to remind us that the patient's sense of reality has the narrowest limits. It is a paradoxical fact that the best way of enuring that his ego will be able to distinguish between phantasy and reality is to withhold reality from him as much as possible. but it is true, his ego is so weak - in as much at the mercy of his id and super-ego - that he can only cope with reality if it is administered in minimal doses. And these doses are in fact what the analyst gives him, in the form of interpretations.

In the classical conception of transference the patient was really concerned with the major persons in his childhood when addressing the analyst. More recently, the patient has come to be viewed as apt to be unconsciously engaged with the analyst while ostensibly absorbed in somebody else. To be sure, it may then be taken for granted that the analyst, inturn, stands for, say, a parent. But usually that point is not stressed, and the reaction which is interpreted is not one where the reaction does displace toward the analyst, but instead, away from him. Formerly, the perceptiveness of the analyst was to reveal the parent behind himself; now he may discover himself behind the parent or spouse. A typical contemporary case is a patient with 'a disposition to pick quarrels with her husband because of his silence', a conduct which 'diverted a problem from the couch, where she did not verbalize her complaints about the analyst's silence'. The analyst may thus always be present though never in the patient's conscious mind'. 'The quarrels with the husband became . . . the sole preoccupation of the patient's and the sole content of the analytic sessions (Kanzer, 1961). Thus they were filled with what may be called as the 'reactions of disguised transference'.

That in summation, we are found that the significance of the transference phenomenon impressed Freud so profoundly that he continued through the years to develop his ideas about it, his classical observations on the patient Dora formed the basis for his first formulations of this concept. he said, 'What are transferences? They are the new editions or facsimiles of the tendencies and phantasies which are aroused and made conscious during the progress of the analysis: But they have this peculiarity, which is characteristic for their species, that they replace some earlier person by the person of the physician. To put it another way, a whole series of psychological experiences are revived, not as belonging to the past, but as applying to the person of the physician at the present moment.

According to Freud's view, the process of psychoanalytic cure depends mainly upon the patient's ability to remember that which is forgotten and repressed, and thus to gain conviction that the analytical conclusion arrived at are correct. However, 'the unconscious feelings strive to avoid the recognition which the cure demands'. They seek instead, emotional discharge, regardless of the reality of the situation.

Freud believed that these unconscious feelings, which the patient strives to hide, are made up of that part of the libidinal impulse that has turned away from consciousness and reality, due to the frustration of a desirous gratification. Because the attraction of reality has weakened, the libidinal energy is still maintained in a state of regression attached to the original infantile sexual objects, although the reasons for the recoil from reality have disappeared.

Freud stated that in the analytic treatment, the analyst pursued this part of the libido to its hiding place, 'aiming always at unearthing it, making it accessible to consciousness and at last serviceable to reality'. The patient tries to achieve an emotional discharge of this libidinal energy under the pressure of the compulsion to repeat experiences over and again, rather than to become conscious of their origin. He uses the method of transferring to the person of the physician past psychological experiences and reacting to this, at times, with all the power of hallucination. The patient vehemently insists that his impression of the analyst is true for the immediate present, in this way avoiding the recognition of his own unconscious impulses.

Thus, Freud regarded the transference-manifestations as a major problem of the resistance. However, Freud said, 'It must not be forgotten that they (the transference-manifestations) and they only, render the invaluable service of making the patient's buried and forgotten love-emotions actual and manifest.'

Freud regarded the transference-manifestations as having two general aspects - positive and negative. The negative, he at first regarded as having no value in psychoanalytic cure and only something to be 'raised' into consciousness to avoid interference with the progress of the analysis. He later accorded it a place of importance in the therapeutic experience. The positive transference he considered to be ultimately sexual in origin, since Freud said, 'To begin with, we knew none but sexual objects'. However, he divided the positive transference into two components - one, the repressed erotic component, which was used in the service of resistance; the other, the friendly and affectionate component, which, although originally sexual, was the 'unobjectionable' aspect of the positive transference, and was that which 'brings about the successful result in psychoanalysis, as in all other remedial methods' - Freud referred to the element of suggestion in psychoanalytic therapy.

At the moment, I should like to state that it would be a mistake to deny the value and importance of his formulations regarding transference phenomena. Nonetheless, I differ on certain points with Freud, but I do not differ with the formulation that early impressions acquired during childhood are revived in the analytical situation, and are felt as immediate and real - that they form potentially the greatest obstacles to analysis if unnoticed, and, as Freud put it, the greatest ally of the analysis when understood. Wherefore, I agree that the main work of the analysis consists in analyzing the transference phenomena, although I differ somewhat as to how this result is cure. Even so, it is my conviction that the transference is a strictly interpersonal experience. Freud gave the impression that under the stress of the repetition-compulsion the patient was bound to repeat the identical pattern, regardless of the other person, that I believe that the personality of the analyst tends to determine the character of the transference illusions, and especially to determine whether the attempt at analysis will result in cure. Horney has shown that there is no valid reason for assuming that the tendency to repeat past experiences time and again, having that he integrate with any given situation according to the necessities of his character structure.

Yet, among other things, I do want to mention a simple phenomenon, as described by Sherif, connected with the problem of the frame of reference. If you have a completely dark room, with no possibility of any light being seen, and you then turn on a small pinpoint of light, which is kept stationary, this light will soon appear to be moving about. I am sure a good many of you have noticed this phenomenon when gazing upon a single star. The light seems to move, and it does so, apparently because there is no reference point in relation to which one can establish it at a fixed place in space. It just wanders around. If, however, one can at the same time see some other fixed object in the room, the light immediately becomes stationary. Are a reference point having been established, and there is no longer any uncertainty, and vague wandering of the spot of light? It is fixed. The pinpoint of light wandering in the dark room is symbolic of the original attitude of the person to himself, undetermined, unstructured, with no reference point or points.

The newborn infant probably perceives everything in a vague and uncertain way, including himself. Gradually, reference points are established that a connection begins to occur between hunger and breast, between a relief if bladder tension and a wet diaper between playing with his genitals and a smack on the hand. The physical boundaries and potentialities of the self are explored. One can observe the baby investigating the extent, shape, and potentialities of his own body, that he can hold his breath and everyone will get excited that he can smile and coo and people will be enchanted, or just the opposite. The nature of the emotional reference points that he determines depends on or upon the environment. By that still unknown quality called 'empathy' he discovers the reference points that help to determine his emotional attitude toward himself. If his mother does not want him, is disgusted with him, treats him with utter disregard, he comes to look upon himself as anything-to-be-disregarded. With the profound human drive to make this rational, he gradually builds up a system of 'reasons why'. Underneath all these reasons is a basic sense of worthlessness, undetermined and undefined, related directly to the original reference frame. Another child discovers that the state of being regarded is dependent upon specific factor all is well as long as one does not act spontaneously, as long as one can be just not of a separate person, as long as one is good, as the state of being good is continuously defined by the parent. Under these conditions, and these only, this child can feel a sense of self-regard.

Other people are encountered with the original reference frame in mind. The child tends to carry over into later situations the patterns he first learned to know. The rigidity with which these original patterns are retained depends upon the hidden nature of the child's experience. If this has been of a traumatic character so that spontaneity has been blocked and further emotional developments has been inhibited, the original orientations will tend to persist. Discrepancies may be rationalize or repress. Thus, the original impression of the hostile mother may be retained, while the contact with the new person is rationalized to fit the original reference frame. the new person encountered acts differently, but probably that is just a pose. She is just being nice because she does not know me. If she really knew me, she would act differently. Or, the original impressions are out of line with the present actuality, that they remain unconscious, but make themselves apparent in inappropriate behaviour or attitudes, which remain outside the awareness of the person concerned.

The little child who grows more and more negativistic, because of injuries and frustrations, evokes more and more hostility in his environment. However, and this is important, the basic reactions of hostility on the part of the patents, which originally induced his negativism, are still there. Thus, the pattern does not change much in character, but it just gets worse in the same direction. Those persons whose life experience perpetuate the original frames of reference, are more severely injured. Among the children, who has a hostile mother, may then have a hostile teacher. If, by good luck, he got a kind teacher and if his own attitude were not already badly warped, so that he did not induce hostility in this kind teacher, he would be introduced into a startlingly new and pleasant frame of reference, and his personality might not suffer too greatly, especially, if a kindly aunt or uncle happened to be around.

The profoundly sick people have been so early injured, in such a rigid and limited frame of reference, that they are not able to make use of kindliness, decency, or regard when it does come their way. They meet the world as if it were potentially menacing. They have already developed defensive traits entirely appropriate to their original experience, and then carry them out in completely inappropriate situations, rationalizing the discrepancies, but never daring to believe that people are different from the ones they early learned to distrust and hate. By reason of bitter early experience, they learn never to let their guard down, never to permit intimacy, least of mention, the death blow would be dealt to their already partly destroyed sense of self-regard. Despairing of real joy in living, they develop secondary neurotic goals which give a pseud-satisfaction. The secondary gains at first glance might seem to be what the person was really striving for - revenge, power and exclusive possession. Actually, these are but the expressions of the deep injuring sustained by the person. They cannot be fundamentally cured until those interpersonal relationships that caused the original injury are brought back to consciousness in the analytic situation. Step by step, and each phase to the long period of emotional development is exposed, by no means chronologically; the interconnecting, overlapping reference frames are made conscious, those points at which a distortion of reality, or a repression of part of the self had to occur, are uncovered. The reality gradually becomes 'undistorted', the self refound in the personal relationship between the analyst and the patient. This personal relationship with the analyst is the situation in which the transference distortion can be analyzed.

In Freud's view, the transference was either positive or negative, and was related in a rather isolated way to a particular person in the past. Justly, the transference is the experiencing in the analytic situation the entire pattern of the original reference frames, which include at every moment the relationship of the patient to himself, to the important persons, and to others, as he experienced them at that time, in the light of his interrelationships with the important people.

The therapeutic aim in this process is not to uncover childhood memories that will then lend themselves to analytic interpretation. Here, Fromm has pointed out, that psychoanalytic cure is not the amassing of data, either from childhood, or from the study of the present situation. Nor does cure result from repetition of the original injurious experience in the analytic relationship. What is curvature in the process, is that in tending to reconstruct with the analyst that atmosphere which obtained in childhood, the patient actually achieve something new? He discovers that of himself which has to be repressed at the time of the original experience. He can only do this in an interpersonal relationship with the analyst, which is suitable to such a rediscovery. To illustrate this point: If a patient had a hostile parent toward whom he was required to show deference, he has to repress certain of his own spontaneous feelings. In the analytic situation, he tends to carry over his original frame of reference, and again tends to feel himself to be in a similar situation. If the analyst's personality also contains elements of a need for deference that need will unconsciously be imparted to the patient, who will, therefore, still repress his spontaneity as he did before. True enough, he may act or try to act as if analyzed, since by definition, that is what the analyst is attempting to accomplish. But he will never have found his repressed self, because the analytic relationship contains for him elements actually identical with his original situation. Only if the analyst provides a genuinely new frame of reference - that is, if he is truly non-hostile, and truly not in need of deference - can this patient discover, and it is a real discovery, the repressed elements of his own personality. Thus, the transference phenomenon is used so that the patient will completely re-experience the original frames of reference, and himself within those frames, in a truly different relationship with the analyst, to the end that he can discover the invalidity of his conclusions about himself and others.

That is to say, by this is not to mean to deny the correctness of Freud's view of transference also acting as a resistance. As a matter of fact, the tendency of the patient to reestablish the original reference frame is precisely because he is afraid to experience the other person in a direct and unreserved way. He has organized his whole system of getting along in the world, bad as that system might be, on the basis of the original distortions of his personality and his subsequent vicissitudes. His capacity for spontaneous feeling and acting has gone into hiding. Now it has to be sought. If some such phrase as the 'capacity for self-realization' is substituted in place of Freud's concept of the repressed libidinal impulse, much is the same conclusions can be reached about the way in which the transference-manifestations appear in the analysis as resistance. It is just in the safest situation, where the spontaneous feelings might come out of hiding, that the patient develops intense feelings, sometimes of a hallucinatory character, that relate to the most dreaded of experience, that of the past. It is at this point that the hidden natures and the use by the patient of the transference distortions have to be understood and correctly interpreted, by the analyst. It is also here that the personality of the analyst modifies the transference reaction, a patient cannot feel close to a detached or hostile analyst and will therefore never display the full intensity of his transference illusions. The plexuity of this process, whereby the transference can be used as the therapeutic instrument and, at the same time, as a resistance may be illustrated by the following example: a patient had developed intense feelings of attachment to a father surrogate in his everyday life. The transference feelings toward this man were of great value in elucidating his original problems with his real father. As the patient became more and more aware of this personal validity, he found this masochistic attachment to be weakening. This occasioned acute feeling of anxiety, since his sense of independence was not ye t fully established. At this point, he developed very disturbing feelings regarding the analyst, believing that she was untrustworthy and hostile, although prior to this, he had successes in establishing a realistically positive relationship to her. The feelings of untrustworthiness precisely reproduced an ancient pattern with his mother. He experienced then at this particular point in the analysis in order to retain and to justify his attachment to the father figure, the weakening of which attachment had threatened him so profoundly. The entire pattern was elucidated when it was seen that he was re-experiencing an ancient triangle, in which he was contentiously driven to a submissive attachment to a dominating father, due to the utter untrustworthiness of his weak mother. If the transference character of this sudden feeling of untrustworthiness of the analyst had not been clarified, he would have turned again, submissively to his father surrogate, which would have further postponed his development of-independence. Nevertheless, the development of this transference to the analyst brought to light a new insight.

Freud felt that personality disorder called schizophrenias or paranoia could not be analyzed because the patient was unable to develop a transference to the analyst. In this view the real difficulty in treating such disorders is that the relationship is essentially nothing but transference illusions. Such persons hallucinate the original frame of reference to the exclusion of reality. Nowhere in the realm of psychoanalysis can one find more complicating and complex proof of the effect of early experience on the person than in attempting to treat these patients. Frieda Fromm Reichmann has shown in her work with schizophrenics the necessity to realize the intensity of the transference reactions, which have become almost completely real to the patient. And yet, if one knows the correct interpretations, by actually feeling the patient's needs, one can over years of time do not the identical thing that is accomplished more quickly and less dramatically with patients suffering a less severe disturbance of their interpersonal relationships.

Another point with which Freud took the position that all subsequent experience in normal life is merely repetition of the original one. Thus love is experienced for someone today in terms of the love felt for someone in the past. As, perhaps, this is not exactly true: Yet the child who has not had to repress certain aspects of his personality enters into a new situation dynamically, not just as a repetition of what he felt, say, with his mother, but as an active continuation of it. That is to say, that there are constitutional differences with respect to the total capacity for emotional experience, just as there are with respect to the total capacity for intellectual experiences. Given this constitutional substratum, the child engages in personal relationships not passively as a lump of clay waiting to be molded, but most dynamically, bringing into play all his emotional potentialities. He may possibly find someone later whose capacity for response is deeper than his mother's. If he is capable of the greater depths, he experiences an expansion of himself. Many later in life have met a 'great' person and have felt a sense of newness in the relationship which is described to others as 'wonderful' and which is regarded with a certain amount of extension of the self to a new horizon.

In considering the process of psychoanalytic cure, Freud very seriously discussed the relationship of analysis to suggestion therapy and hypnosis. He believed, that part of the positive transference could be made use of in the analysis to bring about the successful result. He said, 'In so far we readily admit that the results of psychoanalysis rest upon a basis of suggestion, only by suggestion we must be understood to mean that which we, with Ferenczi, find that it consists of influence on a person through and by means of the transference-manifestations of which he is capable. The eventually independence of the patient is our ultimate object when we use suggestion to bring him into and carry out a mental operation that will necessarily result in a lasting improvement in his mental condition. Freud, elsewhere indicated very clearly, that in hypnosis, the relationship of the patient to the hypnotist was not worked through, whereas in analysis the transference to the analyst was resolved by bringing it entirely into consciousness. He also said, that the patient was protected from the unwitting suggestive influence of the analysis by the awakening of his own unconscious resistance.

We must deal, somewhat more in detail, with one phase of the analysis that can be called the, 'plexuity of analysis' and that preserves an important stage of the amalgamation with academic psychology. The word 'plexuity' was first used by Kosciejew as the simplification of a complicated-complex psychological fact, to designate certain tendencies, a characteristic for the person in question, or a related group of affect-coloured conceptions. This interpretation of the word, which was constantly becoming more comprehensive, and had thus come to have almost no meaning, was limited by those who described the unconsciously repressed for its part of those group conceptions with its name by the analytical acceptation for 'plexuity'. As the more subtle, labile, fluctuating process of cathexis in the psyche became accessible to research, the acceptance of such inflexible, separate mental components became more and again superfluous. They were to coherent, they could only be excited and displaced in toto, they were much too complicating, as more exact analysis showed to be treated as elements which could not be further reduced. However, in the newer works of Freud, this conception merely figures as the survival of a period since the creation of our meta-psychology.

The most consistent thing would have been to do away entirely with this new useless rudiment of an earlier time, and to give up the terminology, which had become dear to most analysts, in favour of a better understanding. Instead of doing this, the whole of mental life was often regarded as a mosaic of such plexuities, and the analysis then carried out with the object of 'analyzing out' one complex after the other, or the attempt was make of treating the whole personality as a sum total of father-mother, brother and sister complexes. It was naturally easy to collect material for these, since every one has, of course, all the plexuities, that is, every one must, in the course of his development, somehow get on with the persons and object that surround him. The connected recounting of plexuity, or the attributes of these, may have its place in descriptive psychology, but not in the practical analysis of the neurosis, nor does it even belong in the psychoanalytic study of literary or ethno-psychological products, where it must undoubtedly lead to monotony in no way justified by the many-sidelines of the material, and scarcely tempered by giving preference, first to one and then to the other complex.

Although such a flattening out may have to be put up with at times, as unavoidable in a scientific presentation, one should not therefore transfer such a cramped interest into the technique. The analysis of plexuities easily misleads the patient into being pleasing to his analyst, by bringing him 'complex material' as long as he likes, without giving up any of his really unconscious secrets. Thus there came to be histories of illnesses In which the patient recounted memories, evidently fabricating them, in a way that never happens in unprejudiced analyses, and can only be looked upon as the product of such a 'breeding of plexuity'. Such results should naturally not be used subjectively to show the correctness either of one's own method of interpreting, or as theoretic conclusions, not yet as leading to any sort of evidence.

It happens particularly frequently that the associations of the patient were directed to the sexual factor at the wrong time, or that they remained stuck at this point, if as so often happens - he came to the analysis with the expectation that he must constantly talk exclusively of his actual or infantile sexual life. Aside from the fact that this is not so exclusively the case as our opponents think, permitting such an indulgence in the sexual often gives the patient the opportunity to paralyze the therapeutic effect of the privation he must undergo.

An understanding of the many-sided and important mental contents that underlie the collective name 'castration complex' was also not exactly furthered by bringing the theory of the complexes into the dynamics of the analysis. On the contrary, we are of the opinion that the premature theoretic condensation of the fact under the conception of the complex interfered with the insight into deeper layers of mental life. We believe that the full appreciation of that which the analytic practitioner has accustomed himself to finish off with the label castration complex, is still lacking, so that this attempt at an explanation should not lightly be regarded as the ultimate explanation of such varied mental phenomena and processes of the patient. We can, from the dynamic standpoint which is the only justifiable one in practice, often recognized in the forms of expression of the castration complex, so they manifest themselves in the course of the analysis, only one of the kinds of resistance that the patient erects against his deeper libidinal wishes. In the early stages of some analyses the castration anxiety can often be uncovered as an expression of the dread, transferred onto the analyst, as a protection against further analysis.

Technical difficulties arose also from the analyst's having too much knowledge. thus the importance of the theory of sexual development constructed by Freud, misled some analysts to apply in a mistaken and overly-dogmatic fashion in the therapy of the neuroses, certain systems of organization and autoeroticism, which first gave us an understanding of normal sexual development. In this searching for the constructive elements of the theory of sex, in some cases, the actual analytic task was neglected. These analyses might be compared to psychochemical 'elements analyses'. Here, again, one could see that the theoretical importance did not always correspond to the value in the practical analysis. The technique need not methodically lay bare all the, . . . as it were, prescribed historic phases of the development of the libido, still less should the uncovering of all theoretically established details and gradations be used as a principle of healing in the neuroses. It is also practically superfluous to demonstrate all the original elements of a highly complicated 'connection', while missing the intellectual thread, which combines the few fundamental elements into new and varying phenomena. The same thing holds for the erotogenic zones as for the plexuity, for example the urethral or the anal erotic, and for the stages of organization the oral eroticism anal-sadistic and other pregenital phases, there can be no human development without all of these, but one must not in the analysis attribute to the importance, for the history of the illness, of which the resistance under the pressure of the analytic situation gives the illusion.

On closer observation a certain inner connection between 'element analyses' and 'complex analyses' could be recognize, insofar as the latter, in their attempts to plumb the psychic depths, struck upon the granite of the complexes and thus the work was spread out over the surface instead of going to the bottom. Such analyses then usually tried to make up for the lack of depth in the dynamics of the libido by an excursion into the theory of sex, and united rigid attributes of complexes with equally schematically treated principles of the theory of sex, whereas they missed just the play of forces that takes place between the two.

Such an attitude naturally led to a theoretical over-estimation of the factor of quantity, to ascribe everything to a stronger organ - eroticism, a point of view that resembled that of the pre-analytical school of neurologists - who blinded themselves to any insight into actual play of forces of the pathological cayuses by the catch words inheritance, degeneration, and disposition.

Since the theory of the instincts and also the sciences of biology and physiology have been called upon partly as a help in understanding mental phenomena, in particular since the so-called 'pathoneurosen', that is the neurosis on the organic level, the organ-neuroses, and even organic illnesses are treated psychoantically, disputes about border-line cases have taken place between psychoanalysis and physiology. The stereotyped translation of physiological processes into the language of psychoanalysis is incorrect. Insofar as one attempts to approach organic processes of detailed examination of the result of this or in detail constitution of elemental structures that surround of all surfacing processes, as they are proven to be such, though experience also, demonstrated to be effective in a time proven technique/

It was also confusing when simple clinical facts were at once combined with speculations about becoming, being, and duration and such deliberations treated like established rules in practical analysis, whereas Freud himself constantly emphasized the hypothetical character of his last synthetic works. Often enough such a wandering into speculation seems to have been a dodging of uncomfortable technical difficulty. We know how a desire to condense everything prematurely under a speculative principle can wreak vengeance from the point of view of technique (The Jungian theory).

It is also a mistake, while neglecting the individual, in the explanation of the symptoms, to make cultural and phylogenetic analogies at once, no matter how fruitful the latter might be in themselves. The overestimate of the actual factors led to an anagogic prospective interpretation, which was useless so far as the pathologic fixation were concerned. The adherents of the 'anagogic', as well as some of those of the 'genetic' school, in their interest in the future and in the past, neglected the present condition of the patient. and yet almost all of the past, and everything that the unconscious attempts, insofar as it is not directly conscious or remembered (and this occurs extremely seldom), expresses itself in actual reactions in relation to the analyst or to the analysis, in other words, the transference to the analytic situation.

The requirements of the Breuer-Freud catharsis that the affects, displace upon symptoms, should be led back directly to the pathologic memory traces, and at the same time brought to a discharge and bound again proved to be unrealizable, that is, it succeeds only in the case of incompletely repressed, mostly preconscious memory material as in the case of certain derivatives of the actual unconscious. This itself, the uncovering of which is the chief task of the analysis, since it has never been 'experienced' by and sense of exploitation or some stimulant, then it cannot ever be remembered, one must let it be produced on the ground of certain indications. The mere communication, something like 'reconstruction', is itself not suited to call forth affect reactions: Such information glides off from the patients without any effect. They can only convince themselves of the reality of the unconscious when they have experienced - mostly after they have frequently experienced - something analogous to it in the actual analytic situation, that is, in the present. The new insight into the topography of mental life and the functions of the separate depth levels gives us the explanation for this state of affairs. The unconscious repressed material has no approach to motility, nor to those motor innervations in the sum total of which the affect discharge consists, the past and the repressed must find their representative factors in the present and the conscious (preconscious) in order that they may be affectively experienced and develop further. In contrast to the stormy abreaction one could designate the unwinding bit by bit of the affects in analysis as a reactional catharsis.

In general that affects in order to work convincingly must first be revived, that is actually present and that what has not affected us directly and actually must remain mentally ineffective.

The analyst must always take into account that almost every expression of his patients springs from several periods, but he must give his chief attention to the present reaction. Only from this point of view can he succeed in uncovering the roots of the actual reaction in the past, which means changing the attempts of the patient to repeat into remembering. In this process be need pay little attention to the future. One may quietly leave this care to the person himself who has been sufficiently enlightened about his past and present mental strivings. The historic, cultural and phylogenetic analogies also need, for the most part, not be discussed in the analysis. The patient need hardly ever, and the analyst extremely seldom, occupy himself with this early period.

At this place we must consider certain misunderstandings about the enlightenment of people who are being analyzed. There was a phase, in the development of psychoanalysis, in which the goal of the analytic treatment consisted in filling the gaps in the memory of the patient with knowledge. Later recognizes that the neurotic ignorance proceeded from the resistance, which is from not wishing to know, and that it was this resistance that had to be constantly uncovered and made harmless. If one proceeds thus the amnesic gaps in the chain of memories fill themselves in, for the most part automatically, for the other part with the help of sparse interpretations and explanations. The patient therefore learns nothing more and nothing other than what he needs, and in the quantity requisite to allay the predominating disturbances. It was a fatal mistake to believe that no one was completely analyzed who had not been theoretically familiarized with all the separate details of his own abnormality. Naturally it is not easy to set a boundary line up to which the instruction of the patient should be carried. Interruption of the correct analysis by formal courses of instruction may satisfy both the analyst and the patient, but cannot effect any change in the libido-attitude of the sick person. A further result of such instruction was that without noticing it, one pushed the patient into withdrawing himself from the analytical work by means of identifying himself with the analyst. The fact that the desire to learn and to teach creates an unfavourable mental attitude for the analysis is well known but should receive much serious attention.

At times one heard from analysts the complaint that this or that analysis failed on account of 'too great resistances' or a too 'violent transference'. The possibility in principle of such extreme cases is admitted; we do find ourselves at times confronted with quantitative factors, which we, must in no way practically underestimate, since they play an important part in the final; outcome of the analysis, as well as in its causes. But the factor of quantity, so important in itself, can be used as a screen for incomplete insight into the play of forces that finally decide the kind of application and the distribution of those very quantities. Because Freud once uttered the sentence, 'Everything which impedes the analysis work is resistance.' one should not, every time the analysis comes to a standstill, simply say, 'this is a resistance'. This resulted, particularly in patients with an easily aroused sense of guilt, in creating an analytic atmosphere in which th y, so to speak, were fearful of making the 'faux pas' as having a resistance, and the analyst found himself in a helpless situation. One evidently forgot another utterance of Freud's, namely, that the analysis we must be prepared as to meet the same forces, which formerly caused the repression as 'resistance', as soon as one sets to work to release these repressions.

Another analytical situation that one was also in the habit of labeling incorrectly as 'resistance' is the negative transference, which, from its very nature, cannot express itself otherwise than as 'resistance' and the analysis of which is the most important task of the therapeutic activity. One need, of course, not be afraid of the negative reactions of the patient for they constitute, with iron necessity, a part of every analysis. Also the strong positive transference, particularly when it expresses itself in the beginning of the cure, is only a symptom of resistance that requires to be unmasked. In other cases, and particularly in the later stages of an analysis, it is an actual vehicle for bringing to light desires that have remained unconscious.

In this connection an important rule of psychoanalytic technique must be mentioned in regard to the personal relation between the analyst and the patient. The theoretic requirements of avoiding all personal contact outside if the analysis mostly led to an unnatural elimination of all human factors in the analysis, and thus again, to a theorizing of the analytic experience.

From this point of view, some practitioners all too readily failed to attribute that importance to a change in the person of the analyst, which results from the interpretation of the analysis as a mental process, the unity of which is determined by the person of the analyst. A change of analysts may be unavoidable for outer reasons in rare, exceptional cases, but we believe that technical difficulties - in homosexuals, for example - are not simple to be avoided by the choice of an analyst of the opposite sex. For in every correct analysis the analyst plays all possible roles for the unconscious of the patient; it only depends upon him always to recognize this at the proper time and under certain circumstances to make use of it consciously. Particularly important is the role of two parental images - father and mother - in which the analyst actually constantly alternatives (transference and resistance).

It is not an accident that technical mistakes occurred of frequently just in the expression of transference and resistance. One was easily inclined to let oneself be surprised at these elementary experiences in the analysis and strangely enough forgot just here the theory that had been incorrectly pushed into the foreground in the wrong place. This may also be due to subjective factors in the analysis. The narcissism of the analyst seem suited to create a particularly fruitful source of mistakes: Among others the development of a kind of narcissistic counter-transference that provokes the person being analyzed into pushing into the foreground certain things that flatter the analyst and, on the other hand, into suppressing remarks and associations of an unpleasant nature in relation to him. Both are technically incorrect, he first, because it can lead to an apparent improvement of the patient in only intended to bribe the analyst and in this way to win a libidinal counter-interest from him. The second because it keeps the analyst from the necessity of noticing the delicate indications of criticism, which mostly only venture forth hesitantly, and help the patient to express plainly or to abreact them. The anxiety and the sense of guilt of the patient can never be overcome without this self-criticism, requiring a certain overcoming of himself on the part of the analyst; and yet these two emotional factors are the essentials for bringing about and maintaining the repression.

Another form under which technical inaccessibility hid itself was an incidental remark of Freud's to the effect that the narcissism of the patient could set limits to the degrees to which he could be influenced by the analysis. If the analysis did not progress well, one consoled oneself with the thought that the patient was 'too narcissistic'. And since narcissism forms a connecting link between ego and libidinal strivings in all normal, as well as abnormal, mental processes, it is not difficult to find proofs in his behaviour and thoughts of the narcissism of the patient. Particularly one should not handle the narcissistically determined 'castration' or 'masculinity' complexes as they set the limits for analytic solution.

When the analysis struck upon a resistance of the patient one often over-looked to what extent a pseudo-narcissistic tendency was brought into the question. The analyses of people who bring a certain theoretic knowledge a great deal of what one was theoretically inclined to scribe to narcissism, is actually secondary, pseudo-narcissistic and can continue analysis be completely solved in the parental relationship. Naturally it is necessary in doing this to take up analytically the ego-development of the patient, as it is in general, necessary in the analysis of the resistance to consider the up-to-now much-too-neglected analysis of the ego, for which Freud has recently given valuable hints.

The newness of a technical point of view introduced by Ferenczi under the name of 'activity' resulted in some analysts, in order to avoid technical difficulties, overwhelming the patient with commands and prohibitions, which one might characterize as a kind of 'wild activity'. This, however, must be looked upon as a reaction to the other extreme, to holding too fast to an over-looked upon as a reaction to the other extreme, to holding too fast to an overly-rigid 'passivity' in the matter of technique. The latter is certainly sufficiently justified by the theoretic attitude of the analyst who must at the same time be an investigator. In practice, however, this easily leads to sparing the patient the pain of necessary intervention, and to allowing him too much initiative in his associations as well as in the interpretation of his ideas.

The moderate, but, when necessary, energetic activity in the analysis consists in the analyst's taking on, and, to a certain extent, really carrying out those rules that the unconscious of the patient and his tendency to flight prescribe. By doing this the tendency to the repetition of earlier traumatic experiences is given an impetus, naturally with the goal of finally overcoming this tendency by revealing its content. When this repetition takes place spontaneously it is superfluous to provoke it and the analyst can simply call forth the transformation of the resistance into remembering (or plausible reconstruction).

Nevertheless, what was said about psychoanalytic theory is only a bare outline, that much deeper study of the transference is necessary to anyone interested in re-educational work from the psychoanalytic point of view. The practical application of this theory is not easy, since we deal mostly with mixed types, such that the attitude of the counsellor cannot be as uniform as having enough verbal descriptions for evincing of individual forms of dissociated behaviour to enable us to offer detailed instructions about how to deal with them. At present our psychoanalytic knowledge is such that a correct procedure cannot be stated specifically for each and every dissociable individual.

The necessity for bringing the child into a good relationship to his mentor is of prime importance. The worker cannot leave this to chance, he must deliberately achieve it and he must face the fact thus no effective work is possible without it. It is important for him to grasp the psychic situation of the dissociable child in the very first contact he makes with him, because only this can be known in what attitude to adopt. There is a further difficulty in that the dissociable child takes pains to hide his real nature: He misrepresents himself and lies. This is to be taken for granted, it should not surprise or upset us. Dissociable children do not come to us of their own volition but are brought to us, very often with the threat, 'You will soon find out what is going to happen to you.' Generally parents resort our help only after every other means, including corporal punishment, have failed. To the child, we are only another form of punishment, an enemy against whom he must be on his guard, not a source of help to him. There is a great difference between this and the psychoanalytic situation, where the patient comes voluntarily for helping. To the dissociable child, we are a menace because we represent society, with which he is in conflict. He must protect himself against this terrible danger and be careful what he says in order not to give himself away. It is hard to make some of these delinquent children talk, remain unresponsive and stubborn. One thing they all have in common: They do not tell the truth. Some lie stupidly, pitiably, others, especially the older ones, show great skill and sophistication. The extremely submissive child, the 'dandly', the very jovial, or the exaggerated and sincere, but some are especially hard to reach. This behaviour is so much to be expected that we are not surprised or disarmed by it, the inexperienced teacher or adviser is easily irritated, especially when the lies are transparent, but he must not let the child be aware of this. He must deal with the situation immediately without telling the child that he can see that coming through was warrantably attributive value about his attitudinal behaviours.

There is nothing remarkable in the behaviour of the dissociable, but it differs only quantitatively from normal behaviour. We all hide our real selves and use a great deal of psychic energy to mislead our neighbours. We masquerade more or less, according to necessity. Most of us learn in the nursery the necessity of presenting ourselves in accordance with the environmental demands, and thus we consciously or unconsciously build up a shell around ourselves. Anyone who has had experience with young children must have noticed how they immediately begin to dissimulate when a grown-up comes into the room. Most children succeed in behaving in the manner that they think is expected of them. Thus they lessen the danger to themselves and at the same time they are casting the permanent moulds of their mannerisms and their behaviour. How many parents really bother themselves about the inner life of their children? Is this mask necessarily for life? I do not know, but it often seems that the person on whom childhood experiences have forced the dissociable individual masquerades to a greater extent, and more consciously, then the normal. He is only drawing logical deductions from his unfortunate disagreeable authority? Why should he be sincere with those people who represent disagreeable authority? This is an unfair demand.

We must look further into the differences between the situation of social retraining and the analytic situation. The analyst expects to meet in his patient unconscious remittances that prevent him from being honest or make him silent: But the treatment is in vain when the patient lies persistently. Those who work with dissociable children expect to be lied to. To send this child away because he lies are only giving in to him. We must wait and hope to penetrate this mask that covers the really psychic situation. In the institution it does not matter if this is not achieved immediately, it means merely that the establishment of the transference is postponed. In the clinic, however, we must work more quickly. Taking with the patient does not always suffice, and we must introduce other remedial measures. Generally, we see the delinquent child, only, in at least as infrequent to a smattering of times, but we are forced to take some steps after the first few interviews, to formulate some tentative conception of the difficulty and to establish a positive transference as quickly as possible. This simply means that we must get, in at least, a peek behind the mask. If the child is not put in an institution, he remains in the old situation under the same influences that caused the trouble. In such cases we wish to establish the transference as quickly as possible, to intensify of the child`s positive feelings, such that they are stimulated while the child is with us, and to bring them rapidly to such a pitch that they can no longer be easily disturbed by their old influences. To carry on such work successfully presupposes a long and knowing experience.

Even so, there are few current problems concerning the problem of transference that Freud did not recognize either implicitly or explicitly in the development of the theoretical and clinical framework. For all essential purposes, moreover, his formulations, in spite of certain shifts in emphasis, remain integral to contemporary psychoanalytic theory and practice. Recent developments mainly concern the impact of an ego-psychological approach, the significance of object relations, both current and infantile, external and internal, the role of aggression in mental life, and the part played by regression and the repetition compulsion in the transference. Nevertheless, analysis of the infantile Oedipal situation in the setting of a genuine transference neurosis is still considered as a primary goal of psychoanalytic procedure.

Originally, transference was ascribed to displacement on the analyst of repressed wishes and fantasies derived from early childhood. The transference neurosis was viewed as a compromise formulation similar to dreams and other neurotic symptoms. Resistance, defined as the clinical manifestation of repression, could be diminished or abolished by interpretation mainly directed toward the content of the repressed. Transference resistance, both positive and negative, was inscribed to the threatened emergence of repressed unconscious material in the analytic situation. Presently, as with the development of a structural approach, the superego had been portrayed as the heir to the genital Oedipal situation, also was the recognition as playing a leading role in the transference situation. The analysis was subsequently viewed not only as the object by displacement of infantile incestuous fantasies, but also as the substitute by projection for the prohibiting parental figures that had been internalized as the definitive superego. The effect of transference interpretation in mitigating undue severity of the superego has, therefore, been emphasized in many discussions of the concept of transference.

Certain expansions in the structural approach related increasingly to the recognition of the role that had earlier objective relations, in the development of the superego. This had affected the current concepts of transference, in that this connection, the significance of the analytic situation as a repetition of the early mother-child relationship has been stressed from different points for viewing to such equally important developments related to Freud's revised concept of anxiety that can only lead to theoretical developments in the field of ego psychology. However, this brought about their related clinical changes in the work of many analysts. As a result, attention was no longer the main attraction that had focussed on the content of the unconscious. In addition, increasing importance was attributed to the defence processes by means of which the anxiety that would be engendered if repression and other related mechanisms were broken down, was avoided in the analytic situation. Differences in the interpretation of the role of the analyst and the nature of transference developed from emphasis, on the one hand, on the importance of early object relations, and on the other, from primary attention to the role of the ego and its defences. These defences first emerged clearly in discussion of the technique of child analysis, in which Melanie Klein and Anna Freud, the pioneers in the fields of thought as playing the leading roles.

From a theoretical point of view, discussion foreshadowing the problems that face us today was presented in 1934 in a well-known paper by Richard Sterba and James Strachey, and further elaborated at the Marienbad Symposium at which Edward Bibring made an important contribution. The importance of identification with, or introjection of the analyst in the transference situation of identification with, or introjection of, the analysts in the transference situation were clearly indicated. The therapeutic results were attributed to the effect of this process In mitigating the need for pathological defences. Strachey, however, considerably influenced by the work of Melanie Klein, regarded transference as essentially a projection onto the analyst of the patient's own superego. The therapeutic process was attributed to subsequent introjection of a modified superego as a result of 'mutative' transference. Sterba and Bibring, on the other hand, intimately involved with development of the ego-psychological approach, reemphasised the central role of the ego, postulating a therapeutic split and identification with the analyst as an essential feature of transference. To some extent, this difference of opinion may be regarded as semantic. If the superego is explicitly defined as the heir of the genital Oedipus conflict, then earlier intra-systematic conflicts within the ego, although they may be related retrospectively to the definite superego, much, nevertheless, are defined as contained within the ego. Later divisions within the ego of the type indicated by Sterba and very much expanded by Edward Bibring in his concept of therapeutic alliance between the analyst and the healthy part of the patient's ego, must also be excluded from superego significance. In contrast, those whom attribute pregenital intra-systemic conflicts within the ego primarily to the introjection of objects, consider that the resultant state of internal conflict appears like the dynamic idea that something conveys to the mind as having an endless meaning attached to the coherence of the therapeutic situation and seen in the later conflicts between ego and superego. They, therefore, believe that these structures developed simultaneously and suggest that no sharp distinction should be made between pre-oedipal, oedipal, and a post-oedipal superego.

The differences, however, are not entirely verbal, since those whom attribute superego formations to the early months of life tend to attribute significantly too early object relation that differs from the conception of those who stress control and, neutralization of instinctual energy as primary functions of the ego. This theoretical difference necessarily implies some disagreement as how the dynamic situation both in childhood and in adult life, inevitably reflected in the concept of transference and in hypotheses as to the hidden nature of the therapeutic process. From one point of view, the role of the ego is central and crucial at every phase of analysis. A differentiation is made between transference as therapeutic alliance and the transference neurosis, which, on the whole, is considered a manifestation of resistance. Effective analysis depends on a sound and stable therapeutic alliance, a prerequisite for which is the existence, before analysis, of a degree of mature superego functions, the absence of which in certain severely disturbed patients and in young children may preclude traditional psychoanalytic procedure. Whenever indicated, interpretation's manifestations, which means, in effect, that the transference must be analysed. The process of analysis, however, is not exclusively ascribed to transference interpretation. Other interpretations of unconscious material, whether related to defence or to early fantasies, will be equally effective provided they are accurately timed and provide a satisfactory therapeutic alliance has been made. Those, in contrast, whom stress the importance of early object relations emphasizes the crucial role of transference as an object relationship, distorted though this may be of a variety of defences against primitively unresolved conflicts. The central role of the ego, both in the early stages of development and in the analytic process, are definitely accepted. The hidden nature of the ego is, however, considered at all times to be determined by its external and internal objects. Therapeutic process whose changes in ego function results, therefore, primarily from a change in object relations though interpretation of the transference situation, finds of less differentiation as made between transference as for being the therapeutic alliance and transference neurosis as a manifestation of resistance. Therapeutic progress depends almost exclusively on transference interpretation. Other interpretations, although at times, are not, in general, considered an essential feature of the analytic process. From this point of view, the preanalytic maturity of the patient's ego is not stressed as considered potentially suitable for traditional psychoanalytic procedure.

These differences in theoretical orientation are not only reflected in the approach to children and disturbed patients. They may also be recognized in significant variations of technique in respect to all clinical groups, which inevitably affect the opening phases, understanding of the inevitable regressive features of the transference neurosis, and handling of the germinal phases of analysis. By its emphasis as drawn on or upon the main problems, and, by contrast, rather than similarity, our efforts will be to avoid to detailed discussions of controversial theory regarding the hidden nature of early ego development by a somewhat arbitrary differentiation between those who relate ego analysis to the analysis of defences and those who stress the primary significance of object relations both in the transference, and in the development and definitive structure of the ego. Needless to say, this involves some oversimplification, where I hope that it may, at the same time, clarify certain important issues. To take, on or upon the analysis of patients we are generally agreeing to be suitable for classical analytic procedure, the transference neurosis. Those which emphasis the role of the ego and the analysis of defences, not only maintain Freud's conviction that analysis should proceed from the surface to depth, but also consider that early material in the analytic situation derives, that, in general, from defensive processes rather than from displacement onto the analyst of early instinctual fantasies. A Deep transference interpretation, in the early instinctual fantasies, as Deep transference interpretation starts in the early phases of analysis, and will, therefore, be meaningless to the patient since the unconscious significance is so inaccessible, or, if the defences are precarious, will lead to premature and possibly intolerable anxiety. Premature interpretation of the equally unconscious automatic defensive processes by means of which instinctual fantasy kept unconscious is also ineffective and undesirable. There are, nonetheless, differences of opinion within this group, as to how far analysis of defence can be separated from analysis of content. Waelder, for example, has stressed the impossibility of such separation. Fenichel, however, considered that at least theoretical separation should be made and indicated that, as far as possible, analysis of defence should precede analysis of unconscious fantasy. It is, nevertheless, generally agreed that the transference neurosis develops, as a rule after ego defences have been sufficiently undermined to mobilize previously hidden instinctual conflict. During both the early stages of analysis, and at frequent points after development of the transference neurosis, defences against the transference will become a main feature of the analytic situation.

This approach is based on certain definite premises regarding the hidden natures and function of the ego in respect to the control and neutralization of instinctual energy and unconscious fantasies, while the importance of early object relations is not neglected, the conviction that early transference interpretation is ineffective and potentially relations are not neglected, the conviction and unconscious fantasy. The conviction that early transference interpretation is ineffective and potentially dangerous is related to the hypothesis that the instinctual energy available to the mature ego has been neutralized from unconscious fantasies, meaning at the beginning of analysis, for all effective purposes, relatively or absolutely divorced from its unconscious fantasy, as yet, there are a number of analysts of differing theoretical orientation of ego function from unconscious sources, but consider that unconscious fantasy continues to operate in all conscious mental activity. The analyst, moreover, builds on or upon the whole of their existing, in that of an emphasis to the crucial signification of primitive fantasies, in that, if respect to the development of the transference situation. The individual entering analysis will inevitably have unconscious fantasies concerning the analyst derived from primitive sources. This material, although deep in a sense, is, nevertheless, strongly current and accessible to interpretation. Klein, in addition, creates the development and definitive structure of the superego to unconscious fantasy determined by the earliest phases of object relationships. She emphasizes the role of early introjective and projective processes in relation to primitive anxiety ascribed to the death instinct and related aggression drive fantasies. The unresolved difficulties and conflict of the earliest period continue to colour object relations throughout life. Failure to achieve an essentially satisfactory object relationship in this early period, and failure to master relative loss of that object without retaining its good internal representative, will not only affect all object relations and definitive ego function, but more specifically determine the nature of anxiety-provoking fantasies on entering the analytic situation. According to this point of view, therefore, early transference uninterpreted, even thought it may relate to fantasies derived from an early period of life, should result not in an increase, but a decrease of anxiety

In considering next problems of transference in relation to analysis of the transference neurosis, two main points must be kept in mind. First, as already indicated, those who emphasize the analysis of defence tend to make a definite differentiation between transference as therapeutic alliance and the transference neurosis as a compromise formation that serves the purposes of resistance. By contrast, those who emphasize the importance of early object relations view the transference as a primary revival or repetition, and sometimes are attributed to symbolic processes of the earlier struggles in respect to material or immaterial objects. Still, there is no sharp differentiation made between the early manifestations of transference and the transference neurosis. In view, moreover, of the weight given to the role of unconscious fantasy and internal objects in every phase of mental life, healthy and pathological functions, though differing in essential respect, do not differ with regard to their direct dependence on unconscious sources.

In the role of regression in the transference situation is subject to wide differences of opinion. It was, of course, one of Freud's earliest discoveries that regression had of its earliest points of fixation, and is a cardinal feature, not only in the development of neurosis and psychosis, but also in the revival of earlier conflicts in the transference situation. With the development of the psychoanalysis and its practical application by its involving character that an ever increasing range by some extending of increasing attention, whereby the significance of the analytic situation as a means of fostering regression as a prerequisite for the therapeutic work has been emphasized by Ida Macapline in a recent paper. Differing opinions as to the significance, value, and technical handling of regressive manifestoes are the basis of important modifications in the analytic inductance for technique, as will be considered. However, in respect to the transference neurosis, the view recently expressed by Phyllis Greenacre, that regression, and indispensable features would be generally accepted. It is also a matter of generally based agreement that a prerequisite for successful analysis is revival and repetition in the analytic situation of the struggle of primitive stages of development. Those who emphasize defence analysis, however, tend to view regression as a manifestation of resistance, as a primitive mechanism of defence employed by the growth sets of the transference neurosis. Analysis of these regressive manifestations with their potential dangers depends on the existing and continued functioning of adequate ego strength to maintain therapeutic alliance at an adult level. Those, in contrast, who stress the significance of transference as a revival of the early mother-child relationship does not emphasize regression as an indication of resistance or defence, the revival of these primitive experiences in the transference situation is, in fact, regarded as can essential prerequisite for satisfactory psychological maturation and true geniality. The Kleinian school, as already indicated features the continued activity of primitive conflicts in determining essential features of the transference at every stage of analysis. Their increasing overt revival in the analytic situation, therefore, signifies a reopening of the analysis, and in general, is regarded as an indication of diminuation rather than increase of resistance. The dangers involved according to this point of view and are determined more but to the failure to mitigate anxiety by suitable transference interpretation. By this failure to obtainably achieve, in the early phases of analysis, a sound and stabling therapeutic alliance is based on the maturity of the patient's essential ego characteristics.

In considering, briefly, the terminal phases of analysis, many unresolved problems concerning the goal of the therapy and definition of a completed psychoanalysis must be kept in mind. Distinction must also be made between the technical problems of the terminal phase and evaluation of transference after the analysis has been terminated, there is widespread agreement as to the frequent revival in the terminal phases of primitive transference manifestations apparently resolved during the early phases of primitive transference manifestation, apparently resolved during the early phase of analysis has been terminated. Balint, and those who accept Ferenczi's concept of primary passive love, suggest that some gratification of primitive passive needs may be essential for successful termination. To Klein, the terminal phases of analysis also represent a repetition of important features of the early mother-child relationship. According to her point of view, this period represents, in essence, a revival of the early weaning situation. Completion depends on a mastery of early depressive struggles culminating in successful introjection of the analysis as a good object. Although, in this connection, emphasis differs considerably, it should be noted that those who stress the importance of identification with the analyst as a basis for therapeutic alliance, also accept the inevitability of some permanent modifications of a similar nature. Those, however, who make a definite differentiation between transference of the transference neurosis as a main prerequisite for successful termination, will, none the less, be based on therapeutic alliance and must be interpreted and understood, particularly with reference to the reality aspects of the analyst's personality. In spite, therefore, of significant important differences there are, as already indicated in connection with the earlier papers of Sterba and Strachey, important points of agreement in respect to the goal of the psychoanalysis.

The differences already considered indicate some basic current problems of transference. So far, however, discussion has been limited to variations within the framework of a traditional technique. We must consider problems related to overt modifications, so as the essential expanding context of use between variations introduced in respect to certain clinical conditions. Often as a prelude to classical psychoanalysis, and these modifications are based on changes toward their basic approaches that lead to significant alterations with regard to both the method and to the aim of therapy. Yet, It is generally agreed that some neurosis, borderline patients and the psychosis. The nature and meaning of such changes are, however, viewed differently according to the relative emphasis placed on the ego and its defences, on underlying unconscious conflicts, and on the significance and handling of regression in the therapeutic situation.

In 'Analysis Terminable and Interminable', Freud suggested that certainly inaccessible to psychoanalytic procedure. Hartmann has suggested that in addition to these primary attributes, other ego characteristics, originally develop for defensive purposes, and the related neutralized instinctual energy at the disposal of the ego, may be relatively or absolutely divorced from unconscious fantasy. This not only explains the relative inefficacy of early transference interpretation, but also hints of possible limitations in the potentialities of analysis attributable to secondary autonomy of the ego that is considered to be relatively irreversible. In certain cases, moreover, it is suggested that analysis of precarious or seriously pathological defences - particularly those concerned of aggressive impulses - may be not only ineffective, but dangerous. The relative failure of ego development in such cases not only precludes the development of a genuine therapeutic alliance, but also raises the risk of a serious regressive, often predominantly a hostile transference situation. In certain cases, therefore, preliminary period of psychotherapy is recommended in order to explore the capacities of the patient to tolerate a traditional psychoanalysis. In others, as Robert Knight in his paper on borderline states, and as many analysts' working with psychotic patients have suggested, psychoanalytic procedure is not considered applicable. Instead, a therapeutic approach based on analytic understanding that, in essence, utilizes an essentially implicit positive transference as a means of reinforcing, rather than analysing the precarious defences of the individual, is advocated. In contrast, Herbert Rosenfeld approached even severely disturbed psychotic patients with minimal modifications of psychoanalytic techniques. Only changes that the severity of the patient's condition enforces are introduced. The dangers of regression in therapy are not emphasized since primitive fantasy is considered to be active under all circumstances. The most primitive period is viewed in terms of early object relations with special stress on prosecutory anxiety related to the death instinct. Interpretation of this primitive fantasy in the transference situation, is best offered the opportunity of strengthening the severity-threatened psychosis mainly to serve traumatic experiences, particularly of deprivation in early infancy. According to this point of view, profound regression offers an opportunity to fulfil, in the transference situation, primitive needs that had not been met at the appropriate level of development. Similar suggestions have been proposed by Margolin and others, in the concept of anaclitic treatment. Serious psychosomatic diseases, that approach the premise that the inevitable regression is shown by certain patients and should be utilized in therapy, as a means for gratifying, in their extremely permissive transference situation. Having distinctive or certain limits in the burdensome instant for demanding to that which has not been met in infancy, as this must, in the connection of being taken to understand that the gratifications recommended in the treatment of severely disturbed patients are determined by their conviction. Of these patients are incapable of developing transference as we understand it, in the connection with neurosis and must therefore be handled by a modified technique.

The opinions so far considered, however, much of them, as mine differ in certain respects, are, nonetheless, all based on the fundamental premise that an essential difference between analysis and other methods of therapy depends on whether or not interpretation of transference is an integral feature of technical procedure. Results based on the effects of suggestions are to be avoided, as far as possible, whenever traditional technique is employed. This goal has, however, to establish a point by appropriate objective means, that corroborated evidence has proved that the need for a better understanding in which a state for being even more difficult to achieve than Freud expected when he first discerned the significance of symptomatic recovery. This is based on positive transference, as the importance of suggestion, even in the most strict analytic methods, has been repeatedly stressed by Edward Glover and others. Widespread and increasing emphasis as to the part played by the analyst's personality in determining the nature of the individual transference also implies recognition of unavoidable suggestive tendencies in the therapeutic process. Many analysts today believe that the classical conception of analytic objectivity and anonymity cannot be maintained. Instead, thorough analysis of reality aspects of the therapist's personality and point of view is advocated as an essential feature of transference analysis and an indispensable prerequisite for the dynamic changes already discussed in relation to the termination of analysis. It thus remains the ultimate goal of psychoanalysts' whenever their theoretical orientation, to avoid, as far as is humanly possible, results based on the unrecognized or unanalysed action of suggestion, and to maintain, as a primary goal, the resolution of such results through consistent and careful interpretation.

There are, however, a number of therapists, both within and outside the field of the psychoanalysis, who consider that the transference situation should not be handled only or mainly as a setting for interpretation even in the treatment or analysis of neurotic patients. Instead, they advocate utilization of the transference relationship for the manipulation of corrective emotional experience. The theoretical orientation of those utilizing this concept of transference may be closer to, or more distant form, a Freudian point of view according to the degree to which current relationships are seen as determined by past events. At one extreme, current aspects and cultural factors are considered of predominant importance, at the other, mental development is viewed in essentially Freudian terms and modifications of technique are ascribed to inherent limitations of the analytic method rather than to essentially changed conceptions of the early phases of mental development. Of this group, Alexander is perhaps the best example. It is thirty years since, in his Salzburg paper, he indicated the tendency for patients to regress, even after apparently successful transference analysis of the oedipus situation to narcissistic dependent pregenital levels that prove stubborn and refractory to transference interpretation. In his more recent work, the role of regression in the transference situation has been increasingly stressed. The emergence and persistence of dependent, pregenital commands for something as or is if one's right or due requirements are challenged in measuring moderations of a wide range of clinical conditions. It is argued, that its indications that the encouragement of a regressive transference situation is undesirable and therapeutically ineffective. The analyst, therefore, should when this threatens adopt a definite role explicitly differing from the behaviour of the parents in early childhood in order to bring about therapeutic results through a corrective emotional experience in the transference situation. This, it is suggested, will obviate the tendency to regression, thus curtailing the length of treatment and improving therapeutic results. Limitations of regressive manifestations by active steps modifying traditional analytic procedure in a variety of ways are also frequently indicated, according to this point of view.

It will be clear that to those who maintain the conviction that interpretation of all transference manifestations remain an essential feature in the outcome of the psychoanalysis, the type of manifestation as described, even though based on a Freudian reconstruction of the earlier phases of mental development, and represent a major modification. It is determined by a conviction that psychoanalysis, as a therapeutic method, has limitations related to the tendency to regression, which cannot be resolved by traditional technique. Moreover, the fundamental premises on which, and the conception of corrective emotional experience is based minimizing the significance of insight and recall. It is essentially, suggested that corrective emotional experience alone may bring about qualitative dynamic alterations in mental structure, which can lead to a satisfactory therapeutic goal. This implies a definite modification on the analytic hypothesis whose current problems are determined by their defences against the direct opposition to the instinctual impulses and the intentional object, to which had been set up during the decisive periods of early development. An analytic result therefore depends on the revival, repetition and mastery of earlier conflict in the current experience of the transference situation with insight an indispensable feature of an analytic goal.

Since certain important modifications are related to the concept of regression in the transference situation, it should be considered that this concept is in relation to the repetition compulsion, that transference, essentially is a revival of earlier emotional experience, must be regarded as a manifestation of the repetition compulsion is generally accepted. It is, however, necessarily to distinguish between repetition compulsion as an attempt to master traumatic experience and repetition compulsion as an attempt to return to a real or fantasized earlier state of rest or gratification. Lagache, in a recent paper, has connected by or as if by the affirming relatedness as associated to the corresponding divergence in the repetition compulsion to an inherent need to appear in the problems that had previously been left unsolved. From this point of view, the regressive aspects of the transference situation are to be regarded as a necessary preliminary to the mastery of unresolved conflict, as too, the regressive aspects of transference are mainly attributed to a wish to return to an earlier state of rest or narcissistic gratification, to the maintenance of the status quo in preference to any progressive action, to which Freud's original conception of the death instinct. There is a good deal to suggest that both aspects of the repetition compulsion may be seen in self-destructive forces tend to be stronger that progressive libidinal impulses, the potentialities of the analytic approach will inevitably appear to be limited. In those, in contrast, in whom that regard the reappearance in the transference situation of earlier conflicts as an indication of tendencies to master and progress will continue to feel that the classical analytic method remains the optimal approach to psychological illness wherever it is applicable.

Clarifications maintain the position as peculiarly occupying a particular point in space and time. Whereas in absence or termination must reflect on or upon the fearing analysis if the transference, as compelling of a generally acknowledged focal point, this itself may debase the appropriate factor that generates, in every degree. The exemplifying analytic technique that would react upon the discipline needed to utilize the new values, whereby, they can be ascribed as the commonality in holding the services to a suspicious self-direction and comprehensive understanding, in that of whatever is humanly affiliated to the best as can be, and yet, the advocacy to the analysis of the transference is generally acknowledged as the central feature of analytic technique? Freud regarded transference and resistance as facts in the observational conceptuality for which of representing the state of inventions. He writes, . . . that the theory of the psychoanalysis in an attempt to account for two striking and unexpected facts of observation that emerge whenever an attempt is made. Evidently the symptoms of a neurotic source, may in his past life, inhabit the sources of experiential recall to the past or the introspective reflections. In the state of affairs, in that for being the latent characterizations announced as the factoring responsibility for the transference and of resistance . . . one that takes the other side of the problem, while accepting as such, to the latencies and the hidden values non-accepting for new interactions as brought through a hypothesis that will hardly escape the charge of misappropriation of properties by attempting endeavour to re-associate the essentially established personalization, that if the pursuit in calling them a psychoanalyst'. Rapaport (1967) argued, in his posthumously published paper on the methodology of psychoanalysis, that transference and resistance inevitably follow from the fact that the analytic situation is interpersonal.

Despite this general agreement on the centrality of transference and resistance in technique, in that, the analysis of transference is not pursued as systematically and comprehensively affirmed, however, it could be and should be. The relative privacy for which psychoanalytic work makes it impossible for one or of that of any-other, to skilfully improve upon the attemptive conceptual representation as comprehended of issues, its assumption to state this view as anything more that impressions, involving on that of what in the analysis of the transference and to states awareness in the number of reasons that an important aspect in the analysis of the transference of the transference, namely in the resistance, by the awareness of the transference is especially, and often adhering to the analytic procedures that interact among cultural inhibitors, but that will be distinguished as such, that its ranging manifold of distancing non-localities as founded of the analyst's.

However, it must first be to distinguish between two types of interpretation of the transference. That one is an interpretation of resistance to the awareness of transference, the other, is an interpretation of resistance to the resolution of transference. The distinction has clearly been best spelled out in the form from which copies or reproductions can be produced, as to cause to make its awareness and yielding values as grounded in the cognisance to Greenson (1967) and Stone (1967). The first kind of resistance may be called decence transference, although this term emphases the terminological characterization by its term is mainly employed to refer to a phrase of analysis and carried within the general resistance to the transference of wishes, it can also be used for a more isolated instance of transference of defence. With some oversimplification, one might say that in resistance to the awareness of transference, the transference, the transference is what does the resisting.

Another connected description of stating this distinction between resistance and the awareness of transference and resistance to the resolution of transference is between implicit and indirect references to the transference and explicitly or directly referential to the transference. The interpretation of resistance to awareness of the transference is intended to make the implicit transference explicit. While the interpretation of resistance to the resolution of transference is intended to make the patient realize that the already explicit transference does indeed include a determinant from the past.

It is also important to distinguish between the general concept of an interpretation of resistance to the resolution of transference and a particular variety of such an interpretation, namely, a genetic transference interpretation - that is, an interpretation of how an attitude in the present is an inappropriate carry-over from the past. While there is a tendency among analysts to deal explicit references to the transference primarily among analyses to deal explicitly the references to the transference as primarily by a genetic transference interpretation, there are other ways of working toward a revolution of the transference. However, this argument does so implicate that not only is not enough emphasis being given to interpretation of the transference in the therapeutic attentions to the existing instant of here and now, that is, to the interpretation of implicit manifestations of the transference, but also that interpretations intended to resolve the transference as manifested in explicit references to the transference should be primarily of having independent reality in actuality within here and now, rather than genetic transference interpretation.

A patient's statement that he feels the analyst is harsh, for example, is, at least to begin with, likely best dealt with not by interpreting that this is a displacement from the patient's feeling that his father was harsh, but by as elucidation of another aspect of this here and now attitude, such as what has gone on in the analytic situation that seems to the patient to justify his feeling or what was the anxiety that made it so difficult for him to express his feelings. How the patient experiences the actual situation as found in its state of affairs, that is, that the applicability of an example of the characteristics of the actual situation in a manifestation of transference, which will be a major point for issuing forth their significant meaning.

Of course, both interpretations of the transference of here and now and genetic transference interpretations are valid and constitute a sequence. We presume that a resistance to the transference ultimately rests on the displacement onto the analysts of attitudes from the past.

Because Freud's case histories focus much more on the yield of analysis than on the details of the process, they are readily but perhaps incorrectly construed as emphasizing work outside the transference much more than work within the transference, and, even within the transference, emphasizing genetic transference interpretations much more than work with the transference in here and now (Muslin and Gill, 1978). The example of Freud's case reports may have played a role in what is to be considered as the common maldistribution of emphasis in these two respects - not enough on the transference and, within the transference, not enough in here and now.

Transference interpretations in here and now and genetic transference interpretations are, of course, exemplified in Freud's writings and are in the repertoire of every analyst, but they are not distinguished sharply enough.

Both participants in the analytic situation are motivated to avoid these interactions. Flight away from the transference and to the past can be a relief to both the patient and the analyst.

These aligning measures have been divided into five categorical divisions and placed into the following parts: (1) The principle that the transference should be encouraged to expand as much as possible within the analytic situation because the analytic work is best done within the transference. (2) the interpretation of disguised allusion to the transference as a main technique for encouraging the expansion of the transference within the analytic situation, (3) the principle that all transference has a connection with something in the present actual analysis situation, (4) how the connection between transference and the actual analytic situation is used in interpreting resistance to the awareness of transference, and (5) the resolution of transference within here and now and the role of genetic transference interpretation.

The importance of transference interpretations will surely be agreeing to by all analysts, the greater effectiveness of transference interpretations than interpretations outside the transference will be agreeing to by many, but what of the relative roles of interpretation of the transference and interpretation outside the transference?

Freud can be interpreted as either of saying that the analysis of the transference in auxiliary to the analysis of the neurosis or that the analysis of the transference is equivalent to the analysis of the neurosis. The first position is stated in his saying (1913) that the disturbance of the transference has to be overcome by the analysis of transference resistance in order to get on with the work of analysing the neurosis. It is also implied in his reiteration that the ultimate task of analysis is to remember the past, to fill in the gap in memory. The second position is stated in his saying that the victory must be won on the field of the transference (1912) and that the mastery of the transference neurosis 'coincides with getting rid of the illness which was originally brought to the neurosis (1917). In this second view, he says that after the resistance is overcome, memories appear relatively without difficulty.

These two different positions also find expression in the two different ways in which Freud speaks of the transference. In `Dynamics of Transference` he refers to the transference, on the one hand, as `the most powerful resistance to the treatment`(1912) but, on the other hand, as doing us the inestimable service of making the patient's . . ., immediate impulses and manifests, when all is said and done, it is impossible to destroy anyone in absentia or in effigy (1912).

It can be agreed that his principal emphasis fails on the second position. He wrote once, in summary, 'Thus our therapeutic work falls into two phases in the first, all the 'libido' is forced from the symptoms into the transference and concentrated there, in the second, the struggle is waged around this new object and the libido is liberated from it`(1912).

The detailed demonstration that he advocated that the transference should be encouraged to expand as much as possible within the analytic situation lies in clarification that resistance is primarily expressed by repetition, and repetition takes place both within and outside the analytic situation, but that the analyst seeks to deal with it primarily within the analytic situation, that repetition can be not only in the motor sphere (acting) but also in the psychical sphere, and that the psychical sphere is not confined to remembering but includes the present, too.

Freud`s emphasis that the purpose of resistance is to prevent remembering can obscure his point that resistance shows itself primarily by repetition, whether inside or outside the analytic situation. `The greater the resistance, to a greater or higher degree of widely ranging differentiating comprehension, as do, the application whose attentions are extensively but will act out (repetition)replace remembering`. Similarly in `The Dynamics of Transference` Freud said that the main reason that the transference is so well suited to serve the resistance is that the unconscious implies does not want to be remembered . . . but endeavour to reproduce themselves . . . (1918), the transference is a resistance primarily insofar as it is a repetition.

The point can be restated in terms of the relation between transference and resistance. The resistance expresses itself in repetition, that is, in transference both inside and outside the analytic situation. But to deal with the transference, is, therefore, is equivalent to dealing with the resistance. Freud emphasized transference within the analytic situation so strongly that it has come to mean only repetition within the analytic situation, even though, conceptually speaking, repetition outside the analytic situation is transference too, and Freud once used the term that way. `We soon perceive that the transference is itself only a piece of repetition and that the repetition is a transference of the forgotten past not only onto the analyst but also onto all the other aspects of the current situation. We . . . find . . . the compulsion to repeat, which now replaces the impulsion to remember, not only in his personal attitude to his analyst but also in every other activity and relationship which may occupy his life at the time . . . (1914).

It is important to realize that the expansion of the repetition inside the analytic situation, whether or not in a reciprocal relationship to repetition outside the analytic situation, is the avenue to control the repetition: `The main instrument . . . for curbing the patient's compulsion to repeat and for turning it into a motive for remembering lies in the handling of the transference. We render the compulsion harmless, and indeed useful, by giving it the right to assert itself in a definite field`(1914).

Kanzer has discussed this issue well in his paper on 'The Motor Sphere of the Transference' (1966). He writes of a 'double-pronged stick-and-carrot' technique by which the transference is fostered within the analytic situation and discouraged outside the analytic situation. The 'stick' is the principle of abstinence as exemplified in the admonition against making important decisions during treatment, and the 'carrot' is the opportunity afforded the transference to expand within the treatment, 'in almost complete freedom' as in a 'playground' (Freud, 1914). As Freud put it, 'Provided only that the patient shows compliance enough to respect the necessary conditions of the analysis, we regularly succeed in giving all the symptoms of the illness a new transference meaning, and in replacing his ordinary neurosis by a 'transference neurosis' of which he can be cured by the therapeutic work' (1914).

The reason it is desirable for the transference to be expressed within the treatment is that there, it `is at every point accessible to our intervention`(1914). In a later statement he made the same point this way. `We have followed this new edition - the transference-neurosis - of the old disorder from its start, we have observed its origin and growth, and we are especially well able to find our way about in it since, as its object, we are situated at it's very centre, (1917), it is not that the transference is forced into the treatment, but that it is spontaneously but implicitly present and is encouraged to expand there and become explicit

Freud emphasized acting in the transference so strongly that one can overlook the repetition in the transference, but does not of necessity for its enactment or recognition that gives validity to acts of a subordinate conformation as ratified in support of explicit authoritative permission. Repetition need not go as far as motor behaviour, it can also be expressed in attitudes, feelings, and intentions, and, indeed, the repetition often does take such form rather than motor action. The importance of making this clear is that Freud can be mistakenly read to mean that repetition in the psychical sphere can only mean remembering the past, is when he writes that the analyst as prepared for a perpetual struggle with his patient to keep in the psychical sphere all the impulse that the patient would like to direct into the motor sphere, and he celebrates it as a triumph for the treatment if he can bring it about that something the patient wishes to discharge in action are disposed if through the work of remembering (1914).

It is true that the analyst's efforts are to convert acting in the motor sphere into awareness in the psychical sphere, but transference may be in the psychical sphere to begin with, even if disguised. The psychical sphere includes awareness in the transference as well as remembering.

One of the objections one hears, from both analysts and patient, to a heavy emphasis on interpretation of associations about the patients real life primarily in terms of the transference is that it means the analyst is disregarding the importance of what goes on in the patients real life. The criticism is not judiciable. To emphasize the transference meaning is not to deny or belittle other meanings, but to focus on the one of several meanings of the content that is the most important for the analytic process, for the reasons of positing the addition for one coming to any falsifiable conclusion.

Another way in which interpretations of resistance to the transference can be, or at lease appear to the patient to be, a belittling of the importance of the patients outside life is to make the interpretation as though the outside behaviour is primarily of acting out in the transference. The patient may undertake some actions in the outside world as an expression of and resistance to the transference, that is, acting out. But the interpretation of associations about actions in the outside world as having implications for the transference needs mean only that the choice of outside action to figure in the associations is co-determined by the need to express of transference indirectly. It is because of the resistance to awareness of the transference that the transference to be disguised. When the disguise is unmasked by interpretation, it becomes clear that, despite the inevitable differences between the outside situation and the transference situation, the content is the same for the analysis of the necrosis that coincides (Freud wrote that the mastering of the transference neurosis only coincides with getting rid of the illness that was originally brought to the treatment (1917)).

The analytic situation itself fosters the development of attitudes with primary determinants in the past, i.e., transference. The analyst's reserve provides the patient with few and equivocal cues. The purpose of the analytic situation fosters the development of strong emotional responses, and the very fact that the patient has a neurosis means, as Freud said, that' . . . it is a perfectly normal and intelligible thing that the libidinal cathexes [we would now add negative feelings] of someone who is partly unsatisfied cathexis, of which are held of readies in anticipation, should be directly as well to the figure of the analyst (1912).

While the analytic setup itself fosters the expansion of the transference within the analytic situation, the interpretation of resistance to the awareness of transference will further this expansion.

There are important resistances on the part of both patient and analyst to awareness of the transference. On the patient's part, this is because of the difficulty in recognizing erotic and hostile impulses toward the very person to whom they have to be disclosed. On the analyst's part, this is because the patient is likely to attitude the very attitudes to him that are most likely to cause him discomfort. The attitudes the patient believes the analysts have toward him are often the ones the patient is least likely to voice, in a general sense because of a feeling that it is impertinent for him to concern himself with the analyst's feelings, and in a more specific sense because the aptitudes as held by the analyst are often attitudes the patient feels the analyst will be comfortable about having ascribed to him. It is for this reason that the analyst must be especially alert to the attitudes the patient believes he has, not only to the attitudes the patient does have toward him. If the analyst is able to see himself as a participant in an interaction, as he will become much more attuned to this important area of transference, which might otherwise escape him.

The investigations of attitudes are ascribed to the analyst makes easier the subsequent investigation of the intrinsic factors in the patient that played a role in such ascription. For example, the exposure and the appearances of fact are that the patient ascribes sexual interests in him to the analyst, and generally to the patient, alternatively the subsequent exploration of the patient's sexual wish toward the analyst, and genetically the parent.

The resistance to the awareness of these attitudes is responsible for their appearing in various disguises in the patient's manifested associations and for the analyst's reluctance to unmask the disguise. The most commonly recognized disguise is by displacement, but identification is an equally important one. In displacement, the patient's attitudes are narrated for being toward a third party. In identification, the patient attitudes to himself attitudes he believes the analyst has toward him.

To encourage the expansion of the transference within the analytic situation, the disguises in which the transference appears have to be interpreted in the case of displacement the interpretation will be of allusions to the transference in association not manifestly about the transference. This is a kind of interpretation every analyst often makes. In the case of identifications, the analyst interprets the attitudes that the patient ascribes to himself the identification with which an attitude and subsequently attributed to the analyst. Lipton (1977) has recently described this form of disguise allusion in the transference with illuminating illustration.

In his autobiography, Freud wrote, 'The patient remains under the influence of the analytic situation as hopefully of a latter position or a period of decline, as though he is not directing responsibly for the mental activities onto a particular subject. This instant we are of assuming that nothing will occur, as not of some reference to the situation (1925), since associations are obviously and oftentimes not directed about the analytic situation, the interpretation of Freud's remark rests on what he meant by the 'analytic situation'.

It is believed that Freud's meaning can be clarified by reference to a statement he made in, 'The Interpretation of Dreams'. He said that when the patient is told to say whatever comes into his mind, his associations become directed by the 'purposive ideas inherent in the treatment' and that there are two such inherent regressive themes, one relating to the illness and the other - concerning which, Freud said, the patient has 'no suspicion'; - relating to other analyst's (1900), if the patient has ''no suspicion' of the theme relating to the analyst (1900). If the patient has 'no suspicions' - relating to the analyst (1900). If the patient has 'no suspicions' of the theme relating to the analyst, such that the theme appears only in disguise, the patient 's associations, it is contended that Freud's remark not only specifies the themes inherent in the patient 's identifications', but means that the associations are simultaneously directed by these two purposive ideas, not something by one and sometimes by the other.

One important reason that the early and continuing presence of the transference is not always recognized in that it is considered to be absent in the patient who is talking recognized is that it is considered to be absent in the patient who is talking freely and apparently without resistance. As (Muslin and Gill, 1976) pointed out in a paper on the early interpretation of transference resistance, to the transference is probably present from the beginning, even if the patient is talking apparently freely. The patient may be talking about issues not manifesting about the transference that are nevertheless, also allusions to the transference, but the analyst has to be alert to the pervasiveness of such illusionary discernment about them.

The analyst should progress on the working assumption, that the patient's associations have transference implications pervasively, that with which this assumption is not to be confused with denial or neglect of the current aspects of the analytic situation. It is theoretically always possible to give precedence to a transference interpretation if one can only discern it through its disguise by resistance. This is not to dispute the desirability of learning as much as one can about the patient, if only to be a position to make correct interpretations of the transference. One therefore, does not interfere with an apparently free flow of associations, especially early, unless the transference threatens the analytic situation to the point where its interpretation is mandatary rather than optional.

With the recognition that evens apparently freely associating patient may also be showing resistance to awareness of the transference, this formulation should not interfere as long a useful information being gathered should relace Freud's dictum that the transference should not be interpreted until it becomes a resistance (1913).

It can be argued that most transferences induce to come into being with some interconnection to some aspect of the immediate analytic situation, in the sense that the past can exert an influence only insofar as it exists in the present. Of course, all the determinants of transference are current in the sense that what I am distinguishing is the current reality of the analytic situation, that is, what actually goes on between patient and analyst in the situation from how the patient is currently constituted as a result of his past.

All analysts would dubiously agree that there are both current and transferential determinants of the analytic situation, and probably no analyst would argue that a transference of the analytic situation, and probably no analyst would argue that a transference idea can be expressed without contamination, as it was, that is, without any connection to anything current in the patient-analyst relationship. Nevertheless, the implications of this fact for technique are often neglected in practice, as my next point is only to argue for the connection.

Several authors, e.g., Kohut 1959 and Loewald 1960, have pointed out that Freud`s early application by the act or practice of using something or the state of being used, this, however, employ of the quality of being appropriate or valuable to some end as to accommodate the accountable or warrant the use of the term transference. In `The Interpretation of Dreams, in a connection not immediately recognizable as related to the present day use of the term, reveals the fallacy of considering that transference can be expressed free of any connection to the present. That early use was to refer to the fact that an unconscious idea cannot be expressed as such, but only as it becomes connected to a preconscious or conscious content. In the phenomenon with which Freud was then concerned, the dream transference took place from an unconscious wish to a day residue. In `The Interpretation of Dreams, `Freud used the term transference both for the general rule that an unconscious content is expressible only as it becomes transferred to a preconscious or conscious content and for the specific application of this rule to a transference to the analyst. Just as the day residue is the point of attachment of the dream wish, so must there be an analytic-situation residue, though Freud did not use that term, as the point of attachment of the transference.

Analysts have always limited their behaviour, both in variety and intensity, to increase the extent to which the patient's behaviour is determined by his idiosyncratic interpretation of the analyst's behaviour. In fact, analysts unfortunately sometimes limit the behaviour so much as to compare with such an expression or unpiled standard or absolute approximation, that the entire relationship with the patient matter of technique, with no nontechnical personal relation, as Liptop (1977) has pointed out.

But no matter how far the analyst attempts to carry this limitation of his behaviour, the very existence of the analytic situation provides the patient with innumerable cues that can enviably become his rationale for his transference responses. In other words, the current situation cannot be made to disappear - that is, the analytic situation is real. It is easy to forget this truism in one's zeal to diminish the role of the current situation in determining the patient 's responses. One can try to keep past and present determinants relatively perceptible from one and the other, however, one cannot obtain either 'pure culture'. Freud wrote: 'I insist on this procedure [the couch], however, for its purpose and result are to prevent the transference from mingling with the patient's associations imperceptibly, to isolate the transference and to allow it to come forward in due course sharply defined as a resistance' (1913). Even 'isolate' is too strong a word in the light of the inevitable intertwining of the transference with the current situation.

If the analyst remains under the illusion that the current cues he provides to the patient can be reduced to the vanishing point, he may be led into a silent withdrawal, which is not too distant from the caricature of an analyst as someone who does refuse to have any personal relationship with the patient. What happens then is that silence has become a technique rather than merely an indication that the analyst is listening. The patient's responses under such conditions can be mistaken fo uncontaminated transference when they are in fact transference adaptions to the actuality of the silence.

The recognition, from which it takes its point of departure, as it was, has a crucial implication for the technique of interpreting resistance to the awareness of transference, in that, if, the analyst becomes persuaded of the centrality of transference and the importance of encouraging the transference to expand within the analytic situation, he has to find the presenting and plausible interpretation of resistance to the awareness of transference he should make. Is that, his most reliable guide is the cues offered by what is actually going on in the analytic situation? : On the one hand, the events of the situation, such as change in time of session, or an interpretation made by the analyst, and, on the other hand, how the patient is experiencing the situation as reflected in explicit remarks about it, however, fleeting these may be. This is the primary yield for technique of the recognition that any transference must have a link to the actuality of the analytic situation. The cue points to the nature of the transference, just as the day residue for a dream may be a quick pointer of the latent dream thoughts. Attention to the current situation for a transference elaboration will keep the analyst from making mechanical transference interpretation, in which he interprets that there are allusions to the transference in association not manifestly about the transference, but without offering any plausible bias for the interpretation. Attention to the current stimulation offers some degree of protection against the analyst's inevitability whose tendency to project his own views onto the patient, either because of countertransference or because of a preconceived theoretical bias about the content and hierarchical relationships in psychodynamics.

The analyst may be very surprised at what in his behaviour the patient finds important or unimportant, for the patient's responses will be idiosyncratically determined by the transference, the patient's responses may seem to be something the patient as well as the analysts consider trivial, because, as in displacement to a trivial aspect of the day residue of a dream, displacement can better serve resistance when it is to something trivial. Because it is connected to conflict-laden material, the stimulus to the transference may be difficult to find. It may be quickly disavowed, so that its presence in awareness is only transitory. With the discovery of the disavowed, the patient may also gain insight into how it repeats as disavowed earlier in his life. In his search for the present stimuli that the patient is responding transferentially, as the analyst must therefore remain alert to both fleeting and apparently trivial manifested reference to himself as well as in the events of the analytic situation.

If the analyst interprets the patient's attitudes in a spirit of seeing their possible plausibility in the light of what information the patient does have, rather than in the spirit of either affirming or denying the patient's views, the way is open for their further expression and elucidation. The analyst will be respecting the effort to be plausible and realistic, rather than manufacturing his transference attitudes out of whole bodied material.

Importantly, is to make a transference interpretation plausible to the patient in terms of as current stimulus that, if the analyst is persuaded that the manifest content has important implications for the transference but he is unable to see a current stimulus for the attitude, he should explicitly say so if he decides to make the transference interpretation anyway. The patient himself may then be able to say what the current stimulus is.

It is sometimes argued that the analyst's attention to his own behaviour is a precipitant for the transference, will increase the patient's resistance to recognizing the transference. That, on the contrary, that because of the inevitable interrelationship of the current and transferential determinants, it is only through interpretation that they can be disentangled.

It is also argued that one must wait until the transference has reached optimal intensity before it can be advantageously interpreted. It is true that too hasty and interpretation of the transference can serve as a defensive function for the analyst and deny him the information he needs to make a more appropriate transference interpretation. But it is true that delay in interpreting transference interpretation, but it is also true that delay in interpreting runs the risk of allowing an unmanageable transference to develop. It is also true that deliberate delay can be a manipulation in the service of abreaction rather than analysis, and, like silence, can lead to a response to the actual situation that is mistaken for uncontaminated transference. Obviously important, is assumed in the issues of timing are involved, whereas an important clue to when a transference interpretation is apt and which one to makes lies in whether the interpretation can be made plausibly in terms of the determinant, namely, as something in the current analytic situation. Such as, in the approaching transference in the spirit of seeing how it appears plausibly realistic to the patient, it paves the way toward its further elucidation and expression.

Freud's emphasis on remembering as the goal of the analytic work implies that remembering is the principal avenue to the resolution of the transference. But the delineation of the successive steps in the development of the analytic technique (1920) makes clear that he saw this development as a change from an effort to reach memories directly to the utilization of the transference as the necessary intermediacy to reaching the memories.

In contrast to remembering as the way the transference is resolved, Freud also described resistance for beings primarily overcome in the transference, with remembering following relatively easily afterwards, 'From the repetitive reactions that are exhibited in the transference we are led along the familiar paths to the awakening of the memories, which appear without difficulty, as it was, after the resistance has been overcome' (1914), and 'This revision of the process of repetition can be accomplished only in part in connection with the memory traces of the process that led to repression. The decisive part of the work's achieved by creating in the patient's relation to the analyst - in the 'transference' new editions of the old conflicts . . . Thus, the transference becomes the battlefield on which all the mutually struggling forces should meet one and the other' (1917). This is the primary indication for which Strachey (1934) classified in his seminal paper on the therapeutic action of psychoanalysis.

There are two main ways in which resolution of the transference can take place through work with the transference in here and now. The first lies in the clarification of what are the clues in the current situation that are the patient's point of departure force a transference elaboration. The exposure of the current point of departure at once raises the question of whether it is adequate to the conclusion drawn from it. The relating of the transference to a current stimulus is, after all, parts of the patient's effort to make, the transference attitude plausibly determined by the present. The reverse and ambiguity of the analyst's behaviour are what increases the ranges of apparently plausible conclusions the patient may draw. If an examination of the basis for the conclusion makes clear that the actual situation to which the patient responds is subject to other meanings than the one the patient has reached, he will more reality consider his pre-existing bias, that is to say, in that of transference.

Another critic of an earlier version of this paper suggested that, in speaking of the current relationship and the relation between the patient's conclusion and the information on which they seem plausibly based, such in some absolute conception of what is real in the analytic situation, of which the analyst is the final arbiter. That is not the case, that what the patient must come to see is that the information he has is subject to other possible interpretations implies the very contrary to an absolute conception of reality. In fact, analyst and patient engage in a dialogue in a spirit of attempting to arrive at a consensus about reality, not about some factious absolute reality.

The second way in which resolution of the transference can take place within the work with the transference in here and now is that in the very interpretation of the transference the patient had a new experience. He is being treated differently from how he expected to be. Analysts seem reluctant to emphasize his new experience, as though it endangers the role of insight and argue for interpersonal influence as the significant factor in change. Strachey's emphasis on the new experience in the mutative transference interpretation has unfortunately been overshadowed by his views on introjection, which have been mistaken to advocate manipulating the transference. Strachey meant introjection of the more benign superego of the analyst only as a temporary strep on the road toward insight. Not only is the new experience not to be confused with the interpersonal influence of a transference gratification, but the new experience occurs together with insight into both the patient's biassed expectation and the new experience. As Strachey points out, what is unique about the transference interpretation is that insight and the new experience take place in relation to the very person who was expected to behave differently, and it is this that gives the work in the transference, its immediacy and effectiveness. While Freud did stress the effective immediacy of the transference, he did not make the new experience explicit.

It is important to recognize that transference interpretation is not a matter of experience, in contrast to insight, but a joining of the two together, both are needed to bring about and maintain the desired changes in the patient. It is also important to recognize that no new techniques of intervention are required to provide the new experience. It is an inevitable accompaniment of interpretation of the transference in here and now. It is often overlooked that, although Strachey said that only transference interpretations are outside the transference.

Rosenfeld (1972) has pointed out that clarification of material outside the transference is often necessary to know what is the appropriate transference interpretation, and that both genetic transference interpretations and extratransference interpretation taking to consider an inclination as marked by or indication of notable worth or simply the consequence based upon the role in working through. Strachey said relatively little about working through, but surely nothing against the necessary provision with which every thing needfully is explicitly recognized as the role for the recovery of the past in the resolving dissection of the purposiveness determined by the transference.

In the infilling absorption to the role as played in the transference, the analysis of the transference in here and now, however, both in interpreting resistance to the awareness of transference and in working toward its resolution by relating to the actuality of the situation, it is to be found that with the evidence that extratransference and genetic transference interpretation and, of course, working through are importantly the matter is one of emphasis. Also, interpretation of resistance to awareness of the transference should figure in the majority of sessions, and that if this is done by relating the transference to the actual analytic situation, the very same interpretation is a beginning of work to the resolution of the transference. To warrant this view more convincingly would require detailed case material, but, nonetheless, the concerning fact in the considerations that the Kleinian analyst's, and among others, are by the many who feel, are in error in giving the analysis or thought taken into account or judging agreements. That something given of the transference too great if not even as in excursions in the analytic process. It is true that Kleinians emphasize the analysis of the transference more, in their writing at least, than does the general run of analysts. As, Anna Freud (1968) complained that the concept of transference has become overexpanded seems to be directed against the Kleinians. One of the reasons the Kleinians consider themselves the true followers of Freud in technique are precisely because of the emphasis they put on the analysis of the transference. Hanna Segal (1967), for example, writes, `Too say that all communications are seen as communications about the patent's phantasy as well as current external life is equivalent to saying that all communications contain something relevant to the transference situation. In Kleinian technique, the interpretation of the transference is often more central than in the classical technique.

As an affirmingly held point of view or way of regarding that Freud and transference had connected by simulating observations that we can only offer, that Freud wrote briefly about transference, and did so, to sustain the way in which, is, as a whole, that his actions were justly taken in and around 1917. Another observation that can rarely be made about Freud's works, and which everyone may not agree with, is that, with one or two exceptions, what he did write on transference did not reach the high level of analytical thought that has come to be regarded as standard for him. Some indication of what his contribution consists of is given by the editors of the Standard Edition, who list them in several places. One of the longer lists, in a footnote on page 431 of Volume 16, includes six references: 'Studies of Hysteria' with Breuer (1895), the Dora paper (1905), 'The Dynamics of Transference' (1912), 'Observations on Transference-Love' (1915), the chapter on transference in the Introductory Lectures (1917), and 'Analysis Terminable and Interminable' (1937). Although the editors, in no sense suggest that these six papers include everything Freud wrote on the subject. It does seem evident that, considering the essential importance of transference to analysis, he wrote, 'The Dynamics of Transference', 'Transference-Love', and the transference chapter in the Introductory Lectures, came across, as, perhaps, his least significant contribution.

Freud's first direct mention of transference comes upon the pages ascribed within the 'Studies of Hysteria' (1895), his first significant reference to it, however did not appear until five years later, when, in a letter to Fliess on April 16, 1900, he said (Freud, 1887-1902) he was 'beginning to see that the apparent endlessness of the treatment is something of an inherent feature and is connected with the transference'. In a footnote to this letter the editors said that, 'This was the first insight into the role of transference in psychotherapy.'

Despite these early references, it seems correct to say that yet another five years were to go by before the phenomenon of transference was actually introduced. Even so, the introduction was far from prominent, for it was tacked on like an afterthought as a four-page portion of a postscript to what was perhaps Freud's most fascinating case history to date, the case of Dora (1905).

Using data from Dora's three-month-long, unexpectedly terminated analysis, and especially from her dramatic transference reaction that had taken him quite unawares, Freud now gave to transference its first distinct psychological entity and for the first time indicated its essential role in the analytic process. His account, although in general more than adequate - in the elegant fact and unmistakably 'finished' - was brief, and almost to the point, and perhaps not an entirely worthy introduction so much more a truly great discovery. What was uniquely great was his recognizing the usefulness of transference. In his analysis of Dora he had noted not only that transference feelings existed and were powerful, but, much to his dismay, he had realized what a serious, perhaps, even insurmountable obstacles that objectively would be. Then, in what seems like a creative leap, Freud made the almost unbelievable discoveries that transference was in fact, the key to analysis, that by properly taking the patient's transference and therapeutic force was added to the analytic method.

The impact on analysis of this startling discovery was actually much greater and much more significant than most people seem to appreciate. Although the role of transference as the sine quo non of analysis and widely accepted, and was stated by Freud from the first, it has almost never been acclaimed for having brought about an entire change in the nature of analysis. The introduction of free association to analysis, a much lesser change, receives and still receives much more recognition.

One of the reasons for the relatively unheralded entry of transference into analysis may have been for circumstances of its discovery. Although Freud's new ideas were recorded as if they arose as sudden inspiration during the Dora analysis, they may in fact have developed somewhat later. In the paper's precatory remarks, for instance, Freud said he had not discussed transference with Dora at all, and in the postscript, he said he had been unaware of her transference feelings. Also, pointing to a later discovery date is the extraordinary delay in the paper's publication. According to the editor's note, the paper had been completed and accepted for publication by late January 1901, but this date was then actually set back more than four and a half years until October 1905. The editors said, 'We have no information as to how it happened that Freud, . . . deferred publication.' It readily seems that for reasons to have been that only during those four and a half years, as a consequence to his own self-analysis, that he came to a better understanding of the relevantly significant as the applicable reason to posit of the transference. Only then may it have been possible for him to turn again to the Dora case, to apply to it of what he had learned in himself, to write this essay as part of the postscript, and at last to release the paper for publication.

Freud's self-analysis has been considered from many angles, but not significantly, as can be of valuing measure, in at least from the standpoint of transference. Opponents of the idea that there is such a thing as definite self-analysis, some of whom say it is impossible, generally an object on grounds that without any analyst there can be no transference neurosis. Freud clearly demonstrated, as, perhaps, that the situation that may be necessary to fill this need: Self-analysis may require that, at least a halfway satisfactory transference object. In Freud`s case, the main transference object at this time seems to have been Fliess, who filled the role rather well. As with any analysis, the authenticity as known in the unfeigned design as if existing or having no illusions and facing reality squarely, by which the 'real' impact on Freud was slight, he was essentially a neutral figure, relatively anonymous and physically separates. All of this, and Fliess`s own reciprocal transference reactions, made it possible for Freud to endow Fliess with whatever qualities and whatever feelings were essential to the development of Freud`s transference, and, it should be added, his transference neurosis. In the end, of course, the transference was in part resolved. Freud`s eventual awakening of its self realization in its presence within him of such strange and powerful psychological forces must have come to the conclusion as a stupefied disilluionary dejection toward Fliess, however, his subsequent working out of some of these transference attachments must have been both an intellectual triumph and an immensely healing and releasing of actions, operations or motions involved in the accomplishment of an ending that makes from its process.

In the years following this revolutionary discovery, the central role of transference in analysis increased in remarkable acceptance, and it has easily held this central position ever since. What the substance of this central position distinctfully composes in having or be capable of having within the constructs to which is something of a mystery, for, it seems as nothing about analysis and is, of least to be, the well known than how individual analysis actually uses transference in their day-to-day work with patients. As a guess, as, perhaps of each analysts concept of transference derives variably but significantly from his own inner experience, transference probably means many and varying differentiations to things as to different analysts.

In the same differentiated individuals, such that Freud's own pupils must have differed on this issue, not only from him but from each other, although some of their differences may have been slight, others, my have contributed significantly to the later analytic developments. A question could be raised, for instance, whether differences in handling the transference that at first were the property of one analyst gradually develop into formal clinical methods used by many, and whether these clinical methods, after having been conceptualized, serve as the beginning of variously divergent schools of analysis. Such occurrences, consistent with certain beliefs that analytic ideas do arise in this way, primarily out of transference experiences in the analytic situation, would lead to the question whether the history of the ideological differences in what was actually said and done in response to transference reactions that to any other factor. Whatever the case, many differences and divergencies did occur among the early analysts, and all of that is supposed to have had to do in some major way with differences in the handling of the transference.

Strangely, Freud himself seems to have taken little part in influencing this rapid and divergent period of growth. Usually accused of being too dominating in such matters, Freud seems to have done just the opposite during the development of this most critical aspect of analysis, the process itself, and, for reasons unknown, detached himself from it.

What was needed, one might be inclined to say, was not leadership in the form of domination, but leadership in trying to provide what was lacking, and still lacking, namely an analytical rationale for transference phenomena. The question must be asked, of course, whether in fact this would have been a good thing at that particular time in psychoanalytic history. Perhaps, not. The exercise of closure, to which Freud's structuring might have amounted. But although adding to understanding and stability at ceratin theoretical levels, could at another level, so such closures have often done, have placed many obstacles in the way of further analytical developments. Thus, his leaving the matter of transference wide open, even though it led to confusion and uncertainty, may have been just as well.

In many ways the closest Freud ever came to establishing a formal analytical rationale for transference was his first attempt, in the postscript to the case of hysteria (1905). These few pages are and among the most important of all Freud's writings, outweighing by far the paper to which they are appended. Yet, in the case of Dora has always been taught as an entity rather than the ancillary to the essay on transference. In that essay Freud was clear: His ideas revealed tremendous insights and promised more to come, and that, the powers of the neurosis are occupied in creating a new edition of the same disease. Just think of the analytic implications of his saying that this new edition consists of a special class of mental structures, for the most part unconscious, having the peculiar characteristic of being able to replace earlier persons with that of the person of the analyst, and in the fashion applying all components of the original neurosis to the person of the analytical at the present time. Surely as profound a statement as any he ever made.

He then goes on to say that there is no way to avoid transference, that this 'latest creation of the desire must be combatted like all the earlier ones', and that, although this is by far the hardest part of analysis, only after the transference has been resolved can a patient arrive at a sense of conviction of the validity of the connection that have been constructed during analysis.

He concludes by saying, 'In psychoanalysis . . . all the patients' tendencies, including hostile ones, are aroused, they are then turned to account for reasons to explain or the internalization of justification, and by the same measure was to purposively give a sensible reason for the proposed change in the analysis by which of being made conscious. That, in this way, the transference is constantly being put-down, however, transference, which seems ordained to be the greatest obstacle to psychoanalysis, becomes its most powerful . . .

These remarkable observations, in conveying a sense of deep conviction that could arise, one feels, only from Freud's own hard-won inner experience, that nowhere is there a suggestion that transference is a mere technical matter. Far from it, as Freud announces that he has come upon as new and exciting kind of mental function, or, as it is to believe, that a new and exciting kind of ego function.

Very quickly, however, Freud's conviction sees to have failed him. Nothing he wrote afterwards about transference was at this level, and most of his later references were a retreat from it, for instance, he never did develop the promising idea that the mind constantly creates new editions of the original neurosis and meaningfully inclines the minded inclusion in them, an ever-changing series of persons. Instead, he tended to become less specific, even referring to transference at times in a broad terms as if it were no more than rapport between patient and analysts, or as if it was an interpersonal or psychosocial relationship, concepts that, of course, a great many analysts have since adopted, but which were not part of Freud's original ideas.

Perhaps his most persistent deviation was an on-and-off tendency to regard transference merely as a technical matter, often writing of it as an asset to analysis when positive and a liability when negative.

Significantly, because it indicated that an active struggle was still going on within him, Freud occasionally expressed once again, even though briefly his earlier insights, particularly his ideas that transference is an essential although unexplored part of mental life. An example of this appears in his alternative obtainments such that is gainfully to appear of as quality of being pleasant or agreeable to a feature that makes for pleasantness or ease, among the amenities of the central geniality, otherwise, the prevailing indifference account for the transference in 'An Autobiographical Study' (1925). Transference, he says, 'is a universal phenomenon of the human mind. And in fact dominated the whole of each person's relations to his human environment. In these few words' Freud again made the point, and in declarative fashion, that transference is a mental structure of the greatest magnitude, but he never really followed it up.

Rather extensive evidence of his departure from the original concept and his continuing struggle with that concept is seen most clearly, wherein, the 'Analysis Terminable and Interminable' is much more than a courageous, brilliant, and pessimistic, appraisal of the difficulties and limitations of analysis, although transference is briefly mentioned in its content, yet a great deal about it comes through, some quite directly, some by easy inference. When looked at in this way, two themes stand out: Freud's personal frustration with the enigmas of transference and his tacit placing of transference in the centre of success and failure in analysis, both as a therapy and as a developing science. What also comes through, is the perplexing realization of how far Freud had, by now, seemingly moved away from his original concepts. Or had he?

All the same, even if it is insufficient for exclusive reliance in relations to the complicated neurosis, for which it would be fallacious to assign to the recall and reconstruction of the past an exclusively explanatory value (in the intellectual sense), important though that functions be, and difficult as its full-blown emotional correlate may be to come by. There is no doubt that, even in complicated neurosis, equivalently complicated transference neurosis, the genuine complex and complicated transference neurosis, the genuinely experienced linking of the past and present can have, at times, a certain uniquely specific dynamic effect of its own, a type of telescoping or merging of common elements in experience, which must be connected with the meaninglessness of time in unconscious life, compared with its stern authority in the life of consciousness and adaptation to everyday reality. Contributing decisively to such experiences as to whatever degree it occurs, is of course, the vivid currency of the transference neurosis, and central in this, the reincarnations of old objects in an actual person, the analyst.

Thus, an allied problem in the general sphere of transference is the fascination and often enigmatic interplay of past and present. If one wishes to view this interplay in terms of a stereotyped formulation, the matter can remain relatively uncomplicated - as a formulation. Unfortunately., This is too often the case. The phenomenon, however, retains some important obscurities, which cannot thoroughly dispel, but to which I would like to call attention. To concentrate on the dimension of time, it seems in reference to the complication and immediate aspects of technique, nonetheless, essential. For example, we can assume that the transference neurosis re-enacts the essential conflicts of the infantile neurosis in a current setting. If a reasonable degree of awareness of transference is established, the next problem is the genetic reduction of the neurosis to its elements in the past, through analysis of the transference resistance and allied intrapsychic resistances, ultimately genetic interpretations, recollections and reconstructions and working through. Such that the transference is related to its genetic origins, the analyst thereby emerges in his true, i.e., real, identity to the patient, the transference is putatively 'resolved'. To the extent that one follows the traditional view that all resistances, including the transference itself, is ultimately directed against the restoration of early memories as such, this is a convincing formulation. Is that, only to say, that in his own right as having to a certain tightly logical quality? However, we know that it this is not so readily accomplished, apart from the special intrapsychic considerations described afterward by Freud in 'Analysis Terminable and Interminable'. Although in a favourable case, much of the cognitive interpretative work can be accomplished, there remains the fact that cognition responsibility, in its bare sense, does not necessarily lead to the subsidence of powerful dynamism, to the withdrawal of 'cathexes' from importantly real objects. For, as mentioned, a short while ago, the analyst is a real and living object, apart from the representations with which the transference invests him, and which are interpretable as such, for which there is no, at any time a seldom, a confusing interrelations and commonly of the emergent responses, due to the same old seeking, and this is directed toward a new individual in his own right, both are important, furthermore, there are large and important ones of overlapping. Apart from such considerations, even the explicitly incestuous transference is currently experienced (as, at least in good part) by a full-grown adult (like the original oedipus), instead of a totally and actually helpless child. To be sure, the latter state is reflected in the emergent transference elements of instinctual striving, but it is subject to analysis, and the residual is something significant, if not totally different. It is these residual sexual wish, presumably directed toward the person of the analyst, as such, which must be displaced to others, if, as generally agreed, the revival of infantile fantasies and striving in the biologically mature adolescent presents a new and special problem, one must assume distinctiveness of experience for the adult, although it is true that in the majority of instances, adequate solution is favoured by the adult state. There is, in any case, a residual relationship between persons who have worked together in a prolonged, arduous and intimate relationship, which, strictly speaking, are reversibly disconnected or divorced of services, in that the transference merely ushers out the retirement for which its rendering retreat of that state of mind or feeling by an inner avoidance of something usually felt as unpleasant or pronounced for it's adverse but mutual colouration. An amalgamation of some confusion between the two spheres of feeling that was generally the tendency or course having a particular direction and character as of a growing tendency to underestimate the potentialities as based upon inclination. The general tendency is that both components are fully gratified to some degree. But, there is the ubiquitous power of the residual primordial transference, yet, argue to cling to an omnipotent partisan to resist the displacement of its 'sublimated' anaclitic aspects, even if the various representation of the wishes for bodily intimacy has been thoroughly analysed and successfully displaced. The outcome is largely the transference of the transference, as mentioned earlier, in a different context. For everyday reality can provide no actual answer to such cravings. Nevertheless, by this connection, we are to convene by the pivotal affliction as fundamentally as the burdened or disquieted state of mind, a mind filled of care and sadness. However the state of mind in which is free from doubt and must take note by answering with complete certainty, yet, the central occupying dominance or supremely important position can be significantly over riding. Freud's genial envy of Pfister; that if the man of faith finds this gratification in revealing religion, others in a wide range of secular beliefs and 'leaders' the modern rational and sceptical intellectual is less fortunate in this respect. Presumably free, he is prone to invest even intellectual disciplines or the proponents with inappropriate expectations and partisan passions, but, least of mention, that within these fields of analytical and theoretical thought, is not to provide exceptions to this tendency.

Though if one is to maintain and beneficially confine its bothering of reservations about the clarity of conceptualization, the explanatory discussion with Kohut and Seitz, is a very useful contribution to the direct complication or which of some understanding the awkwardness of one's intuitiveness and placement within the world, especially in or of itself, that is, as accorded to a spatial temporality. Both Loewald and Kohut have deliberately associated a special but the different use of one of Freud's three conceptions of transference, i.e., the transference from the unconscious to the preconscious.

Yet, to furthering comments on primordial transference, at least potentially, are largely psychological (mental) component, the concept of 'transference of the transference' would be applicable to this component. For it does appear that certain aspect of the search for the omnipotent and omniscient caretaking parents are implicitly practical as virtually capable for being turned to use or account for its functional practicability for something of a process or the procedure for being all but the essential purpose to come to or tend toward a common point, for which are the knowledgeable information or ideas, is nothing but causative effectuality. As suggested earlier, there are important qualitative and quantitative distinctions in the mode of persistence and such striving, however, even to the extent that they are detached from the analyst and carried into some reasonably appropriate expression in everyday life, they retain at least a subtle quality that contravenes reality, one that derives from earliest infancy, and remains - to this extent - a transference. 'Santa Claus' lives on, where one might least expect to meet him, whether as a donor of miracle drug or of far more complex panaceas.

If one prescribes to this parasymbiotic transference drive, a true primordial origin, it is necessary to take cognizance of certain important concepts dealing with the earliest period of life. If we assume a powerful original organismic drive toward an original 'object', a striving to nullify separation from the beginning, how does this make something legally valid or operative usually by formal approval or sanctioned with concepts such as 'primary narcissism' or the 'objectless phase' or 'the primary psycho physiological self' (We note in passing that there are those who do not accept these as usually construed in the technique of Balint), for example, or Fairbairn or - conspicuously - Melanie Klein. These are states, variously defined or conceived, which apply to the earliest neonatal period, in which life, to state more simply, exists only as the potential in physiological processes. Since there is (we postulate) no clear awareness of self-withdrawal from the mother, there can be no 'mentally' represented or experienced drive to obliterate the separation (concerning oneself and object, conceiver of a conventional orientation where it's separately in a continuing sense). There are, of course, discharge phenomena, the precursors of purposive activity, and there are urgent physiological needs, directed toward fulfilment or relief, rather than toward an object as such. However, in relation to these physiological needs as archaistic precursors of object relationships, it must be noted that in all, except respiration and spontaneous sphincter relief (even in these instances, not without exception or reservation), the need fulfilment must be mediated by the primordial object (or her surrogate). There is also, of course, the uniquely important requirement for 'holding', in a literal expression, from the outset. The material partner in human symbiosis that supplies what the neonate cannot seek by 'clinging', as for Bowlty and Murphy, in the sense that must be experienced to the physiological ebb and flow of tension, even if restricted to the kinaesthetic, connected with a peripheral sensory registration, which is the protophase of the recognition of separation from the object or nonpresence of the object, as a painful instance of, her presence in apposition the converse? That the general context may be only in which the sense of unity is preponderant, or, more accurately, that there is no general awareness of 'separation' as such, means that the drive for union does not exist in a general psychological sense. It is, so to speak, satisfied. That object constancy, with its cognate 'longing', is quite a different experience from the urgencies of primitive need fulfilment is true, however, regardless of what may be added by maturational and developmental considerations, instinctual and perceptual, there is no reason to assume other than a core of developmental continuity from the earliest needs and their fulfilment to the later state, and some continuing degree of contingency based on them.

There is a very rough parallel in the way certain analytic patients, before a firm relationship with the analyst is established, signal certain primitive experiences and tendencies in special reactions to the end of the hour, to the nonvisibility of the analyst, to interruption of their association, to failure of the analyst to talk, and similar matters. We must note that in the basic formation of the ego is evident between the primitive reactions and beyond to separations, in the form of very early identifications as based on care taking functions. Certainly in the very development of autonomous ego of the mother's investment in a decisive role in the character of the their development. And in the case of object constancy, in its connotation of libidinal cathexis, where is no need whatsoever (emotional or otherwise) is needed for prolonged periods. The importance of the object is, to put it mildly, liable to deteriorate, or to differ complicating aggressive change. Probably the characteristic feature of later developing relations to the object (love and the wish for love), as separate if not always separated from demonstrable primitivity, in the need fulfilment, have a special relationship to those 'ancillary' aspects of neonatal nurture, whose lack has been shown to be an actual threat to life in some instances, not to speak of sound emotional development. So that from the first, regardless of the assumed state of libidinal (and aggressive) economy, or the assumed state of psychological nondifferentiation between self and potential object, there are critical percussive phenomena, objectively observed, and probably prototypic subjective experiences of separation, which are the forerunners of all subsequent experiences of the kind. One may generalize to the effect that, with maturation and development, secondary identifications, and the various other processes of 'internalization' in its broadest sense, the problem of separation and its mastery becomes correspondingly more complex, and changes with the successive phase of life, but never entirely disappears.

In the view of the psychoanalytic situation the latent mobilization of experiences of separation stimulated by the situational structure awakens the driving primordial urge to undo or to master the painful separations that it represents, usually embodied in the various forms of clinical transference that which we are familiar. One legitimate gratification that tends to mitigate superfluous transference regression is the transmission of understanding that at times, are thought that by the 'mature transference', in effect, the 'therapeutic alliance' or a group of mature ego functions that enter such an alliance. However, there are one obscuring and overlapping conceptual edge, in both instances, the concept as such, is to a greater extent as distinct from either one, as it is from the primitive transference, which we have been discussing. Whether the concept is thought by others to comprehend a demonstrable actuality, which is a further question. This question, of course, can only follow on conceptual clarity, saying., That of a nonrational urge, not directly dependent on the perception of immediate clinical purposes, a true transference in the sense that it is displaced (in currently relevant form) from the parent of early childhood to the analyst. Its content is not anti-sensational, but largely non-sensual of sometimes transitional, as the child's pleasure in the assemblages of 'dirty words' and encompasses a special and not minuscule sphere of the object relationship: The wish to understand, and to be understood, the wish to be given understanding, i.e., teaching, specifically by the parent (or later surrogate); the wish to be taught to use ingenuity in making or doing o r achieving an end through the actions in a nonpunitive way, corresponding to the growing perception of hazard and conflict and very likely the implicit wish to be provided with and taught channels of substitutional drive discharge. With this, there may be a wish, corresponding to that element in Loewald's description of therapeutic process, to be seen in terms of one's developmental potentialities by the analyst. No doubt, the list could be extended into many subtleties, details, and variations. However, one should not omit to specify that, in its peak development, it would include the wish for increasingly accurate interpretations and the wish to facilitate such interpretations by providing adequate material ultimately, of course, by identification, to participate in, or even be the author of the interpretations. The childhood system of wishes that underlie the transference is a correlate of biological maturation, and the latent (i.e., teachable) autonomous ego function, appearing with it, however, there is a drive-like quality in the participation phenomena, which disqualifies any conception of the urge's identical with the functions. No one who has ever watched a child importunes a parent with questions, or experiment with new words, or solicit her interests in a new game, or demand a storytelling or reading, can doubt this. That this powerful support and integration in the ego identification with a loved parent are undoubtedly true, just as it is true of the identification with an analyst toward whom a positive relationship has been established. That 'functional pleasure ' inscribes the part, where certain ego energies, perhaps very likely the ego's own urge to extend its hegemony in the personality. However, it can be stressed in the derive element, even the special phase configurations and colourations, and with its importance of object relations, libidinal and aggressive, for a specific reason. For just as the primordial transference seeks to undo separation, in a sense to obviate object relationships as we know them, the 'mature transference', tends toward separation and individuation, and increasing contact with the environment, optimally with a large affirmative (increasing neutralized) relationship toward the original object toward whom (or her surrogates) a different dynamic of demands is now increasingly directed. The further consideration that has led to the emphasis that the drive-like elements in these attitudes are integrated phenomena, as examples of 'multiple functional' rather than the discrete exorcise of function or functions, are the conviction that there is a continuing dynamic relation of relative interchangeability between the two series, at least based on the response to gratifications in a significant zone of complicated energetic overlap, possibly including the phenomenon of neutralization. That the empirical 'interchangeability' is limited, and that goes without saying, that in no way diminishes its decisive importance. The linguistic communications as in mention, that the excessive transference neurosis regression, which can seriously vitiate the affirmative psychoanalytic process, finds a prototype in the regressive behaviour and demands of certain children, who do not receive their share of teaching, 'attention', play, nonseductive, affectionate demonstration, as to use the quality of being appropriate or valuable to some end, even the act or practice of using something or the state of being used to which of responsible interests in development, and similar matters, from their parents. In the psychoanalytic situation, both the gratifications offered by the analyst and the freedom of expression by the patient, are diversely limited and concentrated, practically entirely (in the every day demonstrable sense) in the sphere of linguistic expression, on the analyst's side, further, in the transmission of understanding.

Whereas, the primordial transference exploits the primitive aspects of linguistic communication, by expressing the mature transference as to advocate the seeking mastery of the outer and inner environments, a mastery to which the mature elements in speech contribute importantly, for which these are stressed upon the clear-cut genetic prototype for the free associating its interpretative dialogue is the original learning and teaching of speech, the dialogue between child and mother. It is interesting to note that just as the profundities of interests between people who often include - in the service of the ego - transitory introjection and identifications, of the very word 'communication', representing the central ego function of speech, from which are a closely intimate relation to the etymologically certain, in actual usages, to the word chosen for that major of religious sacrament for that which is the physical ingestion of the body and blood of the Deity. Perhaps, this is just another suggestion that the oldest of individual problems does, after all, continue to seek its solution, in its own terms if only in a minimal sense, and in channels so remote as to be unrecognizable.

The mature transference is a dynamic and integral part of the therapeutic alliance, alone with the tender aspect of the erotic transference, evens more attenuated (and more dependable) friendly feeling of adult type, and the ego identification with the analyst. Indispensable, of course, are the genuine adult need for help, the crystallizing rational and intuitive appraisal of the analyst, the adult sense of confidence in him, and innumerable other nuances of adult thought and feeling. With these, giving a driving momentum and power to the analytic process, but always, by it's very nature, a potential source of resistance, and always requiring analysis, is the primordial transference and its various appearances in the specific therapeutic transference. That it is, if well managed, not only a reflection of the repetition compulsion in its menacing sense, but a living presentation from the id, seeking new solutions, and trying again, so to speak, to find a place in the patient's conscious and effective life, has important affirmative potentialities. This has been specifically emphasized by Nunberg, Lagache and Loewald among others. Loewald has recently elaborated very effectively the idea of 'ghosts' seeking to become 'ancestors' based on an early figure of speech of Freud. The mature transference, in its own infantile right, provides some of the unique qualities of propulsive force, which comes from the world of feeling, rather than the world of thought. If one views it in a purely figurative sense, that fraction of the mature transference that derives from 'conversion' is somewhat like propulsive fraction as the wind in a boats sailing to windward currents into motion, the strong headwind, the ultimate source of both resistance and propulsion, is the primordial transference. This view, however, should not displace the original and independent, if cognate, a favourable tide or current would also be required. It is not that the mature transference is itself entirely exempt from analytic clarification and interpretation. For one thing, in common with other childhood spheres of experience, there may have been traumas in this sphere, punishments, serious defects or lacks of parental communication, Listening, attention or interest. In general, this is probably far more important than has hitherto appeared in our prevalent paradigmatic approach to adult analysis, even taking into account the considerable changes due to the growing interest in ego psychology. 'Learning' in the analysis can, of course, be a troublesome intellectualizing resistance. Furthermore, both the patient's communications and his receptions and utilization of interpretations may exhibit only too clearly, as sometimes in the case of other ego mechanisms, their origin in and tenacious relation to instinctual or anaclitic dynamism; the longing implement outside of silence, for which the analyst is to override such as the uncritical acceptance (or rejection) of interpretation, in that the patient revealingly is to mention the unmindful assimilation, fluently, rich, endlessly detailed associations without spontaneous reflection or integration. In the direct demands for solution as the moral and practical probability for an entirely intellectual scope, and a variety of others. It may and always be easy to discriminate between the utilization of speech by an essentially instinctual demand, and an intellectual or linguistic trait or having to be determined by specific factors in their own developmental sphere, in at least, the underlying and essentially genuine dynamism that have to continue to be placed for a notable interval or remain arbitrary or conventional character most favoured to the purposes of processes of analysis, as it was to the original processes of maturational development, communication, and benign separation. Lagache, on the desirability of separating the current unqualified usage, 'positive' and 'negative' transference, as based on the patient's immediate state of feeling, from a classification based on the essential effect on analytic processes. Yet, the later of mature transference is, in general, a 'positive transference'.

Concerning considerations in the transference neurosis, and the problem of transference interpretation, may be offered at this point. The whole situational structure of analysis (in contrast with other personal relationships), its dialogue of free association and interpretation, and its deprivations as to most ordinary cognitive and emotional interpersonal drives that tend toward the separation of discrete transferences from their synthesis with one another and with defences in character or symptoms, and with deepening regression, toward a continuative enactment of the essential of the infantile neurosis, in the transference neurosis. In other relationships, the 'give and take' aspects - gratifying aggressive, punitive or otherwise actively responsive, and the open mobility of searching for alternative or greater satisfaction - exert a profound dynamic and economic influence, so that only extraordinary situations, or transference of pathological character, or both, occasion to comparable regression.

It is a curious fact, whereas the dynamic meaning to the importance of the transference neurosis has been well established since Freud gave this the phenomenon a central position in his clinical thinking, the clinical reference, when the term is used, remains variable and somewhat ambiguous. For example, Greenson, in his excellent recent paper, speaks of it as appearing, 'when the analyst and the analysis become the central concern in the patient's life'. However, previous remarks in this connection, for which it is worthwhile to specify certain aspects of Greenson's definition, for the term 'central' is somewhat ambiguous, as to its specific reference. Certainly, the term could apply to the symbolic position of the analyst in relation to the patient's experiencing ego and the symbolically decisive position that he correspondingly assumes in the relation to the other important figures in the patient's current life. However, while the analysis is in any case, and for multiple reasons, exceedingly important the seriously involved patient, there is a free observing portion of is ego, also involved, not in the same sense as that involved in the transference regression and revived in infantile conflicts. And here is here being, of course, always the integrated adult personalty, however diluted in may seem at times, of its rarity, although certainly does occur, that the analysis actually exceeds the quality or state of being of notable worth or influence that the other major concerns, attachments, and responsibilities of the patient's life, nor is it desirable that his should occur, on the other hand, if construed with proper attention to the economic considerations as mentioned, the concept is important, both theoretically and clinically. In the theoretical direction to the assumption that there is a continuing system of object relationships and conflict situations, most important in the unconscious representations, but participating to some degree in all others, deriving in a successive series of transference from the experiences of separation from the original object, the mother. In this sense, the analyst's applicability to a uniquely important portion of the patient's personality, the portion that 'never grew up', to maintain a central figure. In the clinical sense, to call or direct attention especially to a supposed cause, source, or to refer to the importance of the transference neurosis as outlining for the essential and central analytic task, providing by it's very currency and demonstrability a relatively secure cognitive base for procedural duties. By its inclusion of the patient's essential psychopathological processes and tendencies, in their original functional connection, it offers, in its resolution or marked reduction, the most formidable lever for analytic cure. Nonetheless, transference neurosis must be seen in its interweaving with the patient's extra-analytic system of personal contacts. The relationship to the analyst may influence the course of relationships to others, in the same sense that the clinical neurosis did, except that the former is alloplastic, relatively exposed, and subject to constant interpretation. It is also an important fact that, except in those rare instances where the original dyadic relationship appears to turn, the analyst, even in the strict transference sphere, cannot be assigned all the transference role simultaneously. Other actors are required. He may at times oscillate with confusing rapidity between the status of mother and father, but he is usually predominantly in one of the roles for long periods, someone else representing the other. Furthermore, apart from 'acting out', complicated and mutually inconsistent attitudes of the anterior apprehensions for realizing often about something not generally realized in the verbalization, may require the seeking of other transference objects, i.e., The husband or wife, friend, another analyst and so forth. Children, even the patient's own children, may be invested with striving of the patient, displaced from the analysis, even experience the impulses that they would wish to call forth in the analyst. The range is extensive, varied, and complicated, requiring constant alertness. Transference interpretation therefore often has a necessarily paradoxical inclusiveness, which is an important reality of technique. There is another aspect, and that is the dynamic and economic impact of the intimate and actual dramatist personate of the transference neurosis in the progress of the analysis as such, and on the patient 's motivation, as well as his real lifer avenues for recovery. For the persons in his milieu may fulfill their 'positive' or 'negative ' roles in transference drama, which may facilitate or impede interpretative effectiveness, they provide the substantial and dependable real life gratification that ultimately facilitates the analysis of the residual analytic transference, or their capacities or attitudes may occasion overload of the anaclitic and instinctual needs in the transference that renders the same process far more difficultly. In the most unhappy instances, there can be a serious undercounting of the motivation for basic change.

There is also the fundamental question of the role of the transference interpretation. At the Marienbad Symposium most of Strachey's colleagues appeared to accept the essential import of his contribution and thus unique significance of the transference interpretations, despite the various reservations as to detail and emphasis on other important aspects of the therapeutic process. Nevertheless, there are still many who, if not in doubt regarding the great value of transference interpretations are inclined to doubt their uniqueness, and to stress the importance of economic considerations in determining the choice as to whether transference or extratransference interpretations may be indicated. Now, apart from the realistic considerations mentioned in the preceding passage (in a sense the necessarily 'distributed' character of a variable fraction of transference interpretation). There is in fact that the extra-analytic life of the patent often provides indispensable data fo the understanding of detailed complexities of his psychic functioning, because of the sheer variety of its references, some of which cannot be reproduced in the relationship to the analyst. For example, there is no repartee (in the ordinary sense) in the analysis. The way the patient handles the dialogue with an angry employee may be importantly revealing. The same may be true of the quality of his reaction to a real danger of dismissal. There are not only the realities, but the 'formal' aspects of this responses. These expressions of personality remain important, even though his 'acting out' of the transference (assuming this was this was the case) may have been more important, and, of course, requiring transference interpretation. Furthermore, they remain useful, if discriminatingly and conservatively treated, even if they are inevitably always subject that epistemological reservations, which haunts so much of analytic data. Of course, the 'positive' transference has a role in the utilization of such interpretations that what enables the patent to listen to them and them seriously.

In an operational sense, it would seem that extratransference interpretations cannot set aside, or underestimated in importance, but the unique effectiveness of transference interpretations is not thereby disestablished. No other interpretation is free, within reason, of the doubt introduced by not really knowing the 'other person's' participation in love, or quarrel or criticism or whatever the issue. And no other situation provides the patient the combined sense of cognitive acquisition, with the experience of complete personal tolerance and acceptance, that is implicit in an interpretation by an individual who is an object of the emotion, drive, or even defences, which are active at the time. There is no doubt that such interpretations must not only (in common with all others) include personal tact, but must be offered with special care as to their intellectual reasonability, in relation to the immediate context, lest they defeat their essential purpose. It is not too often likely that a patient who has just been jilted in a long-standing love affair, and suffering exceedingly, will find an immediate interpretation that his suffering is due to the fact that the analyst does not reciprocate his love, even though a dynamism in this general sphere may be ultimately demonstrable, and acceptable to the patient. On the other hand, once the transference neurosis is established, with accompanying subtle (sometime gross) colouration of the patient's life, th n more far-reaching anticipatory, transference interpretations are indicated, for, if all of the patient's libidinal and aggression are not, in fact, invested in the analyst, he has at least an unconscious role in all important emotional transactions, and, if the assumption is correct that the regressive drive, mobilized by the analytic situation, is in the direction of restoration of a single all-encompassing relationship, specified pragmatically in the individual case by the actually attained level of development, then there is a dynamic factor at work, importantly meriting interpretation as such, to the extent that available material supports it. This would be the immediate clinical application on the material regarding the 'cognitive lag' or 'cognitive fall-back'.

Post-Traumatic Stress Disorder, resides in a mental illness that some people develop after experiencing traumatic or life-threatening events. Such events include warfare, rape and other sexual assaults, violent physical attacks, torture, child abuse, natural disasters such as earthquakes and floods, and automobile or aeroplane crashes. People who attest of the traumatic events may also develop the disorder.

Post-traumatic stress disorder in war veterans is sometimes called shell shock or combat fatigue. In victims of sexual or physical abuse, the disorder has been called rape trauma or battered woman syndrome. The American Psychiatric Association (APA) adopted the current name of the disorder in 1980.

In the late 1960's and early 1970's, mass demonstrations erupted throughout the United States protesting US involvement in the Vietnam War (1959-1975). Thousands of veterans joined in a national organization, Vietnam Veterans Against the War, that supported and influenced the antiwar movement. In this transcript from an April 22, 1971, hearing before the Senate Committee on Foreign Relations, committee chairman Senator J. William Fulbright indicated his sympathy for the antiwar movement. Fulbright's comments were followed by the testimony of Vietnam veteran John Kerry, who called for an end to the war. Kerry also detailed what he believed to be the war's negative effect in both Vietnam and the United States. Kerry became a Democratic senator from Massachusetts in 1985.

People with this disorder relive the traumatic event again and again through nightmares and disturbing memories during the day. They sometimes have flashbacks, in which they suddenly lose touch with reality and relive images, sounds, and other sensations from the trauma. Because of their extreme anxiety and disruptive opposition to events, they try to avoid anything that reminds them of it. They may seem emotionally numb, detached, irritable, and easily startled. They may feel guilty about surviving a traumatic event that killed other people. Other symptoms include trouble concentrating, depression, and sleep difficulties. Symptoms of the disorder usually begin shortly after the traumatic event, although some people may not show symptoms for several years. If left untreated, the disorder can last for years.

Post-traumatic stress disorder can severely disrupt one's life. Besides the emotional pain of reliving the trauma, the symptoms of the disorder may cause a person to think that he or she is "going crazy." In addition, people with this disorder may have unpredictable, angry outbursts at family members. At other times, they may seem to have no affection for their loved ones. Some people try to mask their symptoms by abusing alcohol or drugs. Others work very long hours to prevent any "down" periods when they might relive the trauma. Such actions may delay the onset of the disorder until these individuals retire or become sober.

Studies have set or to bring into a new found control from 1 to 14 percent of people that suffer from post-traumatic stress disorder at some point during their lives. The findings vary widely due to differences in the populations studied and the research methods used. Among people who have survived traumatic events, the prevalence appears to be much higher. The disorder may be particularly prevalent among people who have served in combat. For example, one study of veterans of the Vietnam War (1959-1975) found that veterans exposed to a high level of combat were nine times more likely to have post-traumatic stress disorder than military personnel who did not serve in the war zone of Southeast Asia.

Post-traumatic stress disorder is an extreme reaction to extreme stress. In moments of crisis, people respond in ways that allow them to endure and survive the trauma. Afterward those responses, such as emotional numbing, may persist even though they are no longer necessary.

Not everyone who experiences a traumatic event develops post-traumatic stress disorder. Several factors influence whether people develop the disorder. Those who experience severe and prolonged traumas are more likely to develop the disorder than people who experience less severe trauma. Additionally, those who directly witness or experience death, injury, or attack is more likely to develop symptoms.

People may also have been existing biological and psychological vulnerabilities that make them more likely to develop the disorder. Those with histories of anxiety disorders in their families may have inherited a genetic predisposition to react more severely to stress and trauma than other people. In addition, people's life experiences, especially in childhood, can affect their psychological vulnerability to the disorder. For example, people whose early childhood experiences made them feel that events are unpredictable and uncontrollable have a greater likelihood than others of developing the disorder. Individuals with a strong, supportive social network of friends and family members seem somewhat protected from developing post-traumatic stress disorder.

Treatment of post-traumatic stress disorder may involve psychotherapy, psychoactive drugs, or both. Psychotherapists help individuals confront the traumatic experience, work through their strong negative emotions, and overcome their symptoms. Many people with post-traumatic stress disorder benefit from group therapy with other individuals suffering from the disorder. Physicians may prescribe antidepressants or anxiety-reducing drugs to treat the mood disturbances that sometimes accompany the disorder.

At the arriving considerations that are marked and noted, through which the essence of functional dynamics as based of the transference in the psychoanalytic process or the basic underlying the most basic of beliefs that in politics there is neither good nor evil, however, in that something that forms part of the minimal body, character or structure of that thing predetermines the properties to the good life. Nonetheless, most psychoanalysts maintain that schizophrenic patients cannot be treated psychoanalytically because they are too narcissistic to develop with the psychotherapist as interpersonal relationship that is sufficiently reliable and consistent for psychoanalytic work. Freud, Fenichel and others have recognized that a new technique of approaching patients psychoanalytically must be found if analysts are to work with psychotics. Among those who have worked successfully in recent years with schizophrenics, Sullivan, Hill, and Karl Menninger and his staff has made various modifications of their analytic approach. The techniques that are in use with psychotics are different from our approach to psychoneurotics. This is not a result of the schizophrenic's inability to build up a consistent personal relationship with the therapist but due to his extremely intense and sensitive transference reactions.

Let us see first what the essences of the schizophrenic's transference reactions are and how we try to meet these reactions.

We think of a schizophrenic as a person who has had serious traumatic experiences in early infancy at a time when his ego and its ability to examine reality were not yet developed. These early traumatic experiences seem to furnish the psychological basis for the pathogenic influence of the flustrations of later years. At this early time the infant lives grandiosely in a narcissistic world of his own. His needs and desires seem to be taken care of by something vague and indefinite which he does not yet differentiate. As Ferenczi noted, they are expressed by gestures and movements since speech is as yet undeveloped. Frequently the child's desires are fulfilled without any expression of them, a result that seems to him a product of his magical thinking.

Are a person's characteristics primarily shaped by early influences, remaining relatively stable thereafter throughout life? Or does change spontaneously occur continuously throughout life? Many people believe that early experiences are formative, providing a strong or weak foundation for later psychological growth. This view is expressed in the popular saying "As the twig is bent, so grows the tree." From this perspective, it is crucial to ensure that young children have a good start in life. But many developmental scientists believe that later experiences can modify or even reverse early influences; studies show that even when early experiences are traumatic or abusive, considerable recovery can occur. From this vantage point, early experiences influence, but rarely determine, later characteristics.

Traumatic experiences in this early period of life will damage a personality more seriously than those occurring in later childhood such as are found in the history of psychoneurotics. The infant's mind is more vulnerable the younger and less used it has been, furthers, the trauma has quickened the infant 's egocentricity. In addition early traumatic experiences shorten the only period in life in which an individual ordinarily enjoys the most security, thus endangering the ability to store up as it was a reasonable supply of assurance and self-reliance for the individual's later struggles through life. Thus, as such, a child sensitized considerably more toward the frustrations of later like than by later traumatic experiences. Hence many experiences in later life that would mean little to a 'healthy' person and not much to a psychoneurotic, mean a great deal of pain and suffering to the schizophrenic. His resistance against frustration is easily exhausted.

Once he reaches his limit of endurance, he escapes the unbearable reality of his present life by attempting to reestablish the autistic, delusional world of the infant, but this is impossible because the content of his delusions and hallucinations are naturally coloured by the experiences of his whole lifetime.

How do these developments influence the patient's attitude toward the analyst and the analyst's approach to him?

Due to the very damage and the succeeding chain of frustrations that the schizophrenic undergoes before finally giving in to illness, he feels extremely suspicious and distrustful of everyone, particularly of the psychotherapist ho approaches him with the intent of intruding into his isolated world and personal life. To him the physician's approach means the threat of being compelled to return to the frustrations of real life and to reveal his inadequacy to meet them or, - still worse – a repetition of the aggressive interference with his initial symptoms and peculiarities that he has encountered in his previous environment.

The difficulty that the patient's dilemma through his frustrations is the product through which is called 'delusion': Delusion itself is a false belief that is firmly held by a person even though other people recognize the belief as obviously untrue. For example, a person who truly believes he is Napoleon Bonaparte is delusional. Religious beliefs or popular conceptions, such as the beliefs that people have been abducted by aliens, are not delusions because they are widely held beliefs. Delusions are a type of psychotic symptom that indicate a person has lost contact with reality.

There are many different types of delusions. A person with a paranoid delusion believes that others - such as the local police, or the OPP, even the Mafia as trying to harm or plot against him. A person with a delusion of reference believes that events or people refer specifically to him or her when they do not. For example, a woman with schizophrenia may believe that a television news broadcaster is talking personally to her rather than to the entire viewing audience. A grandiose delusion is a belief that one is extremely famous or that one has special powers, such as the ability to magically heal people.

A delusion of control is a belief that others are able to control one's thoughts, feelings, or actions. For example, a man with this type of delusion may believe that someone has implanted a microchip in his brain that enables other people to control his thoughts. A somatic delusion is a belief that something is wrong with one's body - for example, that one's brain is rotting away - even though no medical evidence supports this belief. A person with an erotic delusion believes that someone is in love with him or her despite a lack of evidence for this belief. In a delusion of jealousy, a person believes that his or her spouse or lover is unfaithful despite evidence to the contrary.

Delusions commonly occur in certain severe mental illnesses, such as schizophrenia, bipolar disorder (also called manic-depressive illness), some cases of major depression, Dissocialise disorders, post-traumatic stress disorder, and paranoid personality disorder. In addition, delusions may result from abuse of certain drugs, including alcohol, cocaine, amphetamines, and hallucinogens such as lysergic acid diethylamide (LSD), phencyclidine (PCP), and mescaline. Medical conditions affecting the brain, such as syphilis and brain tumours, may also cause delusions.

Delusional disorder is a relatively uncommon mental illness characterized by delusions. People with this disorder have one or more delusions that persist for at least one month. In addition, they do not suffer from other symptoms of schizophrenia, such as disorganized speech and bizarre behaviour. Usually their delusions are less bizarre than those that occur in schizophrenia and seem merely odd or unsupported by facts. Examples of nonbizarre delusions include beliefs that one is being followed, loved by someone famous, or deceived by one's spouse. Because delusional disorder is relatively rare, little research has systematically examined its treatment. However, doctors most often use Antipsychotic drugs (also called neuroleptics) to treat this disorder. These drugs help reduce or eliminate delusions, hallucinations, and other psychotic symptoms.

In spite of his narcissistic retreat, every schizophrenic has some underlying notion of the unreality and loneliness of his substitute psychotic beliefs for the world. He longs for human contact and understanding, yet is afraid to admit of himself, or his therapist for fear of further frustration.

That is why the patient may take weeks and months to test the analyst before being willing to accept him, however, once he has accepted him. His dependence on the analyst is greater and he is more sensitive about it than is the psychoneurotic because of the schizophrenic's deeply rooted insecurity, the narcissistic seemingly self-righteous attitude is but a defence.

Whenever the analyst fails the patient from reasons to be discussed later - one cannot at times avoid failing one's schizophrenic patients - it will be severe disappointment and a repetition of the chain of frustrations the schizophrenic has previously endured.

The instinctually primitive part of the schizophrenic's mind that does not discriminate between himself and the environment, it may mean the withdrawal of the impersonal supporting forces of his infancy. Severe anxiety will follow this vital deprivation.

In the light of his personal relationship with the analyst it means that the therapist seduced the patient to use him as a bridge over which he might be led from the utter loneliness of his own world to reality and human warmth, only to have him discover that this bridge is not reliable. If so, he will respond helplessly with an outburst of hostility or with renewed withdrawal as may be seen most impressively in catatonic stupor.

The symptoms of mental illness can be very distressing. People who develop schizophrenia may hear voices inside their head that say nasty things about them or command them to act in strange or unpredictable ways. Or they may be paralysed by paranoia—the deep conviction that everyone, including their closest family members, wants to injure or destroy them. People with major depression may feel that nothing brings pleasure and that life is so dreary and unhappy that it is better to be dead. People with panic disorder may experience heart palpitations, rapid breathing, and anxiety so extreme that they may not be able to leave home. People whom experience episodes of mania may engage in reckless sexual behaviour or may spend money indiscriminately, acts that later cause them to feel guilt, shame, and desperation.

Other mental illnesses, while not always debilitating, create certain problems in living. People with personality disorders may experience loneliness and isolation because their personality style interferes with social relations. People with an eating disorder may become so preoccupied with their weight and appearance that they force themselves to vomit or refuse to eat. Individuals who develop post-traumatic stress disorder may become angry easily, experience disturbing memories, and have trouble concentrating.

Experiences of mental illness often interact differently but depend on one's culture or social group, sometimes greatly so. For example, in most of the non-Western world, people with depression complain principally of physical ailments, such as lack of energy, poor sleep, loss of appetite, and various kinds of physical pain. Indeed, even in North America these complaints are commonplace. But in the United States and other Western societies, depressed people and mental health professionals who treat them tend to emphasize psychological problems, such as feelings of sadness, worthlessness, and despair. The experience of schizophrenia also differs by culture. In India, one-third of the new cases of schizophrenia involve catatonia, a Behavioural condition in which a person maintains a bizarre statue like pose for hours or days. This condition is rare in Europe and North America.

With appropriate treatment, most people can recover from mental illness and return to normal life. Even those with persistent, long-term mental illnesses can usually learn to manage their symptoms and live productive lives.

By a variety of symptoms, including loss of contact with reality, bizarre behaviour, disorganized thinking and speech, decreased emotional expressiveness, and social withdrawal. Usually only some of these symptoms occur in any one person. The term schizophrenia comes from Greek words meaning "split mind." However, contrary to common belief, schizophrenia does not refer to a person with a split personality or multiple personality. For a description of a mental illness in which a person has multiple personalities. To observers, schizophrenia may seem or appear for being as some sorted kind of madness or a manufacturing insanity.

Perhaps more than any other mental illness, schizophrenia has a debilitating effect on the lives of the people who suffer from it. A person with schizophrenia may have difficulty telling the difference between real and unreal experiences, logical and illogical thoughts, or appropriate and inappropriate behaviour. Schizophrenia seriously impairs a person's ability to work, go to school, enjoy relationships with others, or take care of oneself. In addition, people with schizophrenia frequently require hospitalization because they pose a danger to themselves. About 10 percent of people with schizophrenia commit suicide, and many others attempt suicide. Once people develop schizophrenia, they usually suffer from the illness for the rest of their lives. Although there is no cure, treatment can help many people with schizophrenia lead productive lives.

Schizophrenia also carries an enormous cost to society. People with schizophrenia occupy about one-third of all beds in psychiatric hospitals in the United States. In addition, people with schizophrenia account for at least 10 percent of the homeless population in the United States. The National Institute of Mental Health has estimated that schizophrenia costs the United States tens of billions of dollars each year in direct treatment, social services, and lost productivity.

Approximately 1 percent of people develop schizophrenia at some time during their lives. Experts estimate that about 1.8 million people in the United States have schizophrenia. The prevalence of schizophrenia is the same regardless of sex, race, and culture. Although women are just as likely as men to develop schizophrenia, women tend to experience the illness less severely, with fewer hospitalizations and better social functioning in the community.

Schizophrenia usually develops in late adolescence or early adulthood, between the ages of 15 and 30. Much less commonly, schizophrenia develops later in life. The illness may begin abruptly, but it usually develops slowly over months or years. Mental health professionals diagnose schizophrenia based on an interview with the patient in which they determine whether the person has experienced specific symptoms of the illness.

Symptoms and functioning in people with schizophrenia tend to vary over time, sometimes worsening and other times improving. For many patients the symptoms gradually become less severe as they grow older. About 25 percent of people with schizophrenia become symptom-free later in their lives.

A variety of symptoms characterize schizophrenia. The most prominent include symptoms of psychosis—such as delusions and hallucinations - as well as bizarre behaviour, strange movements, and disorganized thinking and speech. Many people with schizophrenia do not recognize that their mental functioning is disturbed.

Some people with schizophrenia experience delusions of persecution - false beliefs that other people are plotting against them. This interview between a patient with schizophrenia and his therapist illustrates the paranoia that can affect people with this illness.

Delusions are false beliefs that appear obviously untrue to other people. For example, a person with schizophrenia may believe that he is the king of England when he is not. People with schizophrenia may have delusions that others, such as the police or the FBI, are plotting against them or spying on them. They may believe that aliens are controlling their thoughts or that their own thoughts are being broadcast to the world so that other people can hear them.

Research suggests that the gene's one inherit strongly influence one's risk of developing schizophrenia. Studies of families have shown that the more close one is related to someone with schizophrenia, the greater the risk one has of developing the illness. For example, the children of one parent with schizophrenia have about a 13 percent chance of developing the illness, and children of two parents with schizophrenia have about a 46 percent chance of eventually developing schizophrenia. This increased risk occurs even when such children are adopted and raised by mentally healthy parents. In comparison, children in the general population have only about a 1 percent chance of developing schizophrenia.

Some evidence suggests that schizophrenia may result from an imbalance of chemicals in the brain called neurotransmitters. These chemicals enable neurons (brain cells) to communicate with each other. Some scientists suggest that schizophrenia results from excess activity of the neurotransmitter dopamine in certain parts of the brain or from an abnormal sensitivity to dopamine. Support for this hypothesis comes from Antipsychotic drugs, which reduce psychotic symptoms in schizophrenia by blocking brain receptors for dopamine. In addition, amphetamines, which increase dopamine activity, intensify psychotic symptoms in people with schizophrenia. Despite these findings, many experts believe that excess dopamine activity alone cannot account for schizophrenia. Other neurotransmitters, such as serotonin and norepinephrine, may play important roles as well.

Although scientists favour a biological cause of schizophrenia, stress in the environment may affect the onset and course of the illness. Stressful life circumstances - such as maturing in age and character as for living in poverty, the death of a loved one, an important change in jobs or relationships, or chronic tension and hostility at home—can increase the chances of schizophrenia in a person biologically predisposed to the disease. In addition, stressful events can trigger a relapse of symptoms in a person who already has the illness. Individuals who have effective skills for managing stress may be less susceptible to its negative effects. Psychological and social rehabilitation can help patients develop more effective skills for dealing with stress.

Although there is no cure for schizophrenia, effective treatment exists that can improve the long-term course of the illness. With many years of treatment and rehabilitation, significant numbers of people with schizophrenia experience partial or full remission of their symptoms.

Treatment of schizophrenia usually involves a combination of medication, rehabilitation, and treatment of other problems the person may have. Antipsychotic drugs (also called neuroleptics) are the most frequently used medications for treatment of schizophrenia. Psychological and social rehabilitation programs may help people with schizophrenia function in the community and reduce stress related to their symptoms. Treatment of secondary problems, such as substance abuse and infectious diseases, is also an important part of an overall treatment program.

Antipsychotic medications, developed in the mid-1950s, can dramatically improve the quality of life for people with schizophrenia. The drugs reduce or eliminate psychotic symptoms such as hallucinations and delusions. The medications can also help prevent these symptoms from returning. Common Antipsychotic drugs include risperidone (Risperdal), olanzapine (Zyprexa), clozapine (Clozaril), quetiapine (Seroquel), haloperidol (Haldol), thioridazine (Mellaril), chlorpromazine (Thorazine), fluphenazine (Prolixin), and trifluoperazine (Stelazine). People with schizophrenia must usually take medication for the rest of their lives to control psychotic symptoms. Antipsychotic medications appear to be less effective at treating other symptoms of schizophrenia, such as social withdrawal and apathy.

Because many patients with schizophrenia continue to experience difficulties despite taking medication, psychological and social rehabilitation is often necessary. A variety of methods can be effective. Social skills training help people with schizophrenia learn specific behaviours for functioning in society, such as making friends, purchasing items at a store, or initiating conversations. Behavioural training methods can also help them learn self-care skills such as personal hygiene, money management, and proper nutrition. In addition, cognitive-Behavioural therapy, a type of psychotherapy, can help reduce persistent symptoms such as hallucinations, delusions, and social withdrawal.

Because many patients have difficulty obtaining or keeping jobs, supported employment programs that help patients find and maintain jobs are a helpful part of rehabilitation. In these programs, the patient works alongside people without disabilities and earns competitive wages. An employment specialist (or vocational specialist) helps the person maintain their job by, for example, training the person in specific skills, helping the employer accommodate the person, arranging transportation, and monitoring performance. These programs are most effective when the supported employment is closely integrated with other aspects of treatment, such as medication and monitoring of symptoms.

Some people with schizophrenia are vulnerable to frequent crises because they do not regularly go to mental health centres to receive the treatment they need. These individuals often relapse and face rehospitalization. To ensure that such patients take their medication and receive appropriate psychological and social rehabilitation, assertive community treatment (ACT) programs have been developed that deliver treatment to patients in natural settings, such as in their homes, in restaurants, or on the street.

People with schizophrenia often have other medical problems, so an effective treatment program must attend to these as well. One of the most generally shared in or participated in things conforming to a type without noteworthy excellence or faults just as common a rule, by ordinary, frequent and ordinarily as an idea or expression deficient in originality or freshness, yet, only of its exchanging the commonplace of the common associated problems is vehemently and usually coarsely expressed condemnation or disapproved, as the interpretative category of an unequalled vocabulary is itself a genuine abuse. Successful treatment of substance abuse inpatients with schizophrenia requires careful coordination with their mental health care, so that the same clinicians are treating both disorders at the same time.

The high rate of substance abuse in patients with schizophrenia contributes to a high prevalence of infectious diseases, including hepatitis B and C and the human immunodeficiency virus (HIV). Assessment, education, and treatment or management of these illnesses is critical for the long-term health of patients.

Other problems frequently associated with schizophrenia include housing instability and homelessness, legal problems, violence, trauma and post-traumatic stress disorder, anxiety, depression, and suicide attempts. Close monitoring and psychotherapeutic interventions are often helpful in addressing these problems.

Several other psychiatric disorders are closely related to schizophrenia. In schizoaffective disorder, a person shows symptoms of schizophrenia combined with either mania or severe depression. Schizophreniform disorder refers to an illness in which a person experiences schizophrenic symptoms for more than one month but fewer than six months. In schizotypal personality disorder, a person engages in odd thinking, speech, and behaviour, but usually does not lose contact with reality. Sometimes mental health professionals refer to these disorders together as schizophrenia-spectrum disorders.

Severe mental illness almost always alters a person's life dramatically. People with severe mental illnesses experience disturbing symptoms that can cause of such difficulties and holding to a job, or go to school, relate to others, or cope with ordinary life demands. Some individuals require hospitalization because they become unable to care for themselves or because they are at risk of committing suicide.

The symptoms of mental illness can be very distressing. People who develop schizophrenia may hear voices inside their head that say nasty things about them or command them to act in strange or unpredictable ways. Or they may be paralysed by paranoia - the deep conviction that everyone, including their closest family members, wants to injure or destroy them. People with major depression may feel that nothing brings pleasure and that life is so dreary and unhappy that it is better to be dead. People with panic disorder may experience heart palpitations, rapid breathing, and anxiety so extreme that they may not be able to leave home. People whom experience episodes of mania may engage in reckless sexual behaviour or may spend money indiscriminately, acts that later cause them to feel guilt, shame, and desperation.

Other mental illnesses, while not always debilitating, create certain problems in living. People with personality disorders may experience loneliness and isolation because their personality style interferes with social relations. People with an eating disorder may become so preoccupied with their weight and appearance that they force themselves to vomit or refuse to eat. Individuals who develop post-traumatic stress disorder may become angry easily, experience disturbing memories, and have trouble concentrating.

Experiences of mental illness often take issue upon its stability for depending on one's culture or social group, sometimes greatly so. For example, in most of the non-Western world, people with depression complain principally of physical ailments, such as lack of energy, poor sleep, loss of appetite, and various kinds of physical pain. Indeed, even in North America these complaints are commonplace. But in the United States and other Western societies, depressed people and mental health professionals who treat them tend to emphasize psychological problems, such as feelings of sadness, worthlessness, and despair. The experience of schizophrenia also differs by culture. In India, one-third of the new cases of schizophrenia involve catatonia, a Behavioural condition in which a person maintains a bizarre statue like pose for hours or days. This condition is rare in Europe and North America.

Of furthering issues regarding depersonalization disorder, meaning, in effect, that it is a categorised illness based within its intendment for being an illness, of mind, in which people experience an unwelcome sense of detachment from their own bodies. They may feel as though they are floating above the ground, outside observers of their own mental or physical processes. Other symptoms may include a feeling that they or other people are mechanical or unreal, a feeling of being in a dream, a feeling that their hands or feet are larger or smaller than usual, and a deadening of emotional responses. These symptoms are chronic and severe enough to impede normal functioning in a social, school, or work environment.

Depersonalization disorder is a relatively rare syndrome thought to result from severe psychological stress. It may occur as part of other mental illnesses, especially anxiety disorders. For example, some people with panic disorder feel nervous, have a sense of doom about their future and health, and have a troubling sense of detachment form the lose in the attemptive use in making or doing or achieving a useful regularity, as every bit as to be expected in having power over their bodies. Depersonalization disorder may also be a component of more severe mental illness, such as schizophrenia. Treatment may include training in relaxation techniques that enhance body perception and control, hypnosis to modify symptoms, and psychotherapy to explore possible stress-related components of the disorder.

Psychiatrists classify depersonalization disorder as one of the Dissocialise disorders. Such disorders involve a disruption of consciousness, memory, identity, or perception.

All the while, the schizophrenic responds to altercations in the analyst's defections and understanding by corresponding stormy and dramatic changes from love to hatred, from willingness to leave his delusional world to resistance and renewed withdrawal.

As understandable as these changes are, nevertheless may come as a surprise to the analyst who frequently has not observed their source, this is quite in contrast to his experience with psychoneurosis whose emotional reactions during an interview he can usually predict. These unpredictable changes seem to be the reason for the conception of the unreliability of the schizophrenic's transference reaction, yet they follow the same dynamic rules as the psychoneurotic's oscillations between positive and negative transference and resistance, however, if the schizophrenic's reactions are stormy and seemingly more unpredictable than those of the psychoneurotic, that instances suggested to be due to the inevitable errors in the analyst's approach to the schizophrenic, of which he himself may be unaware, rather than to the unreliability of the patient's emotional response?

Why is it inevitable that the psychoanalysts disappoint his schizophrenic patient time and again?

The schizophrenic withdraws from painful reality and retires to what resembles the early speechless phase of development where consciousness is not yet crystalized. As the expression of his feelings is not hindered by the convention that he has eliminated, as his thinking, feelings, behaviour and speech - when present - obey the working rules of the archaic unconscious. His thinking is magical and does not follow logical rules. It does not admit by 'no' and likewise the 'no' to 'yes': There is no recognition of space and time, I, you, they, and am, that each interchangeable expression through which of symbols and often by movement and gestures rather than by words.

As the schizophrenic is suspicious, he will distrust the words of his analyst. He will interpret them and incidental gestures and attitudes of the analyst according to his own delusional experience. The analyst may not even be aware of these involuntary manifestations of his attitudes, yet they mean much to the hypersensitive schizophrenic who uses them as a means of orienting himself to the therapist's personality and intentions toward him.

In other words, the schizophrenic patient and the therapist are people living in different worlds and no different levels of personal development with different means of expressing and of orienting themselves. We know little about the language of the unconscious that belongs to the schizophrenic, and our access to it is blocked by the very process of our own adjustment to a world the schizophrenic has relinquished, so, we should not be surprised that errors and misunderstandings occur when we under take to communicate and strive for a rapport with him.

Another source of the schizophrenic's disappointment arises form that the analyser accepts and does not interfere with the behaviour of the schizophrenic, his attitude may lead the patient to expect that the analyst will assist in carrying out all the patients' wishes, even though they may not seem to be in his interest to the analyser's and the hospital's in their relationship to society. This attitude of acceptance so different from the patient's experiences readily fosters the anticipation that the analyst will try to carry out the patient's suggestion and take his part, even against conventional society with which it should occasionally arise. Frequently it will be wise for the analyst to agree with the patient's wish to remain unbattled and untidy until he is ready to talk about the reasons for his behaviour or to change spontaneously. At other times, he will unfortunately be unable to take the patient's part without being able to make the patient understand and accept the reasons for the analyst's position.

If the analyst is not able to accept the possibility of misunderstanding the reaction of the schizophrenic patient and in turn of being misunderstood by him, it may shake his security with his patient.

That is to say, that, among other things, the schizophrenic, once he accepts the analyst's insecurity. Being helpless and open to himself - in spite of his pretended grandiose isolation - he will feel utterly defeated by the insecurity of his would-be helper. Such disappointment may furnish reasons for outbursts of hatred and are comparable to the negative transference reactions of psychoneurosis, yet more intense than these, since they are not limited by the restrictions of the actual world - that is, it exists in or based on fact, its only problem is a sure-enough externalization for which things are existing in the act of being external in something that has existence, ss if it were an actualization as received in the obtainable enactment for being externalized, such that its problem of in some actual life that proves obtainable achieved, in that of doing something that has an existence for having absolute actuality.

These outbursts are accompanied by anxiety, feelings of guilt, and fear of retaliations that in turn lead to increased hostility. Yet this established a vicious circle: We disappoint the patient, he is afraid that we hate him for his hatred and therefore continues to hate us. If in addition he senses that the analyst is afraid of his aggressiveness, it confirms his fear that he is actually considered as some dangerous and unacceptable, and this augments his hatred.

This establishes that the schizophrenics capable of developing strong relationships of love and hatred toward the analyst. After all, one could not be so hostile if it were not for the background of a very close relationship. In addition, the schizophrenic develops transference reactions on the narrower sense that he can differentiate from the actual interpersonal relationship. For which the schizophrenic's emotional reactions toward the analyst have to be met with extreme care and caution. The love that the sensitive schizophrenic feels as he first emerges, and his caution's acceptance of the analyst's warmth of interest is really most delicate and tender things. If the analyst deals with the transference reactions of a psychoneurotic is bad enough, though as a reparable rule, but if he fails with a schizophrenic in meeting positive feelings by pointing it out for instance before the patient indicates that he is ready to discuss it, he may easily freeze to death what has just begun to grow and so destroy any further possibility of therapy.

Some analysts may feel that the atmosphere of complete acceptance and of strict avoidance of any arbitrary denials that we recommend as a basic rule for the treatment of schizophrenics may not avoid our wish to guide to the reacceptance of reality, nevertheless, Freud says that every science and therapy that accept his teachings about unconscious, about transference and resistance and about infantile sexuality, may be called psychoanalysis. According in this definition we believe we are practising psychoanalysis with our schizophrenic patients.

Whether we call it analysis or not, it is clear that successful treatment does not depend on technical rules of any special psychiatric school but rather on the basic attitude of individual therapist toward psychologic persons. If he meets them as strangle creatures of another world whose productions are not comprehensible to 'normal' beings, he cannot treat them, if he realizes, however, that the difference between himself and the psychologic is only of degree, and not of kind, he will know better how to meet him. He will not be able to identify himself sufficiently with the patient to understand and accept his emotional reactions without becoming involved in them.

The process of constant and perpetual change is examined and closely matched within the study of philosophical speculations and pointed of a world view that asserts that basic reality is constantly in a process of flux and change. Indeed, reality is identified with pure process. Concepts such as creativity, freedom, novelty, emergence, and growth are fundamental explanatory categories for process philosophy. This metaphysical perspective is to be contrasted with a philosophy of substance, the view that a fixed and permanent reality underlies the changing or fluctuating world of ordinary experience. Whereas substance philosophy emphasizes static being, process philosophy emphasizes dynamically becoming.

Although process philosophy is as old as the 6th-century Bc Greek philosopher, Heraclitus, renewed interest in it was stimulated in the 19th century by the theory of evolution. Key figures in the development of modern process philosophy were the British philosopher's Herbert Spencer, Samuel Alexander, and Alfred North Whitehead, the American philosopher's Charles S. Peirce and William James, and the French philosopher's Henri Bergson and Pierre Teilhard de Chardin. Whitehead's Process and Reality: An Essay in Cosmology (1929) is generally considered the most important systematic expression of process philosophy.

Contemporary theology has been strongly influenced by process philosophy. The American theologian Charles Hartshorne, for instance, rather than interpreting God as an unchanging absolute, emphasizes God's sensitive and caring relationship with the world. A personal God enters relationships in such a way that he is affected by the relationships, and to be affected by relationships is to change. So too is in the process of growth and development. Important contributions to process theology have also been made by such theologians as William Temple, Daniel Day Williams, Schubert Ogden, and John Cobb, Jr.

'Reality' is a difficult word to use to every one's satisfaction or even to one's own satisfaction. In this instance the word reality is used arbitrarily to designate the direct, here-and-now impact of the analyst upon the patient. Reality. In this sense, contrasts with the impact the analyst has through his representation in the patient's fantasy life, neurosis, and transference, since both kinds of impact seem always to coexist and since the former - the analyst's real impact - may be the worst enemy of the transference, the matter of their differentiation is possibly the most challenging aspect of analysis.

The analytic situation, which is set up to shut out ordinary reality intrusions, that cannot . . . neither should not exclude all, but to say, that in the beginning months, for instance, reality inevitably has the upper hand. The analyst, the office, the procedure, are all overwhelmingly real. Everything is strange, frightening and exciting, gratifying and frustrating. Unlike the patient can test it and orient himself to it, the impact of this reality is usually so great that even an ordinary useful transference relationship cannot be expected to develop.

Perhaps the most confusing aspect of this beginning period is the frequent appearance in it of what can be regarded as a false transference relationship. With great intensity and clarity, the patient may reveal, through transference-like references about the analyst, some of the deepest secrets only of his neurosis but of its genesis. The pseudotransference, too good to be true, is almost sure to be nothing more than the patient's attempt to deal with the person of the analyst, the entire spectrum of his various patterns of behaviour. If, it is easy to do, the analyst overlooks the likelihood that the patient's relationship with at this time is really about that almost everything said about it is related, analysis may get off to a very bad start. And if, as is even earlier to do, the analyst's interests the genetic meaning of the openly exposed material, a good transference relationship may be seriously delayed and a workable transference necrosis may never appear. Even after initial reality has had time to fade, reality may continue to intrude in ways that are very hard to detect and that is very troublesome.

One of the most serious problems of analysis is the very substantial help that the patient receives directly from the analyst and the analytic situation. For many a patient, the analyst in the analytic situation is in fact the most stable, reasonable, wise and understanding person he has ever met, and the setting in which they meet may actually be the most honest, open, direct and regular relationship he has ever experienced. Added to this is the considerable helpfulness to him of being able to clarify his life storey. Confess his guilt, express his ambitions, and explore his confusions. Further real help comes from the learning-about-life accruing from the analyst's skilled questions, observations and interpretations. Taken together, the total real value to the patient of the analytic situation can easily be immense. The trouble with this kind of help is that it goes on and on, it may have such a real, direct and continuing impact upon the patient that he can never get deeply enough involved in transference situation to allow him to resolve or even to become acquainted with his most crippling internal difficulties. The trouble is far too good, the trouble also is that we as analysts apparently cannot resist the seductiveness of being directly helpful, and this, when combined with the compelling assumption that helpfulness is bound to be good, permits us top credit patient improvements to 'analysis' when more properly it should often be recognized for being the amounting result for the patient's using the analytic situation, as the model, for being the preceptors and supporter in the dealing practically within the immediate distractions as holding to some problem.

Perhaps, we can now refer to something in a clear unmistakable manner, and it would be to mention, for being, that one more difficult-to-handle intrusion of reality into the analysis, that by saying, that this is the definitive and final interruption of the transference neurosis by the reality of termination; in the sense, the situation is reversed and the intrusion is analytically desirable, since ideally the impact of reality of impending and certain termination is used to facilitate the resolution of the transference. As with the resolution of earlier episodes of transference neurosis, this final one is brought about principally by the analyst's interpretations and reconstructions. As these take effect, the transference neurosis and, hopefully, along with it the original neurosis is resolved. This final resolution, however, which is much more comprehensive, is usually very different and may not come about at all without the help of the reality of termination. Accordingly, any attenuation of the ending, such as tapering off or causal or tentative stopping, should be expected to stand in the way of an effective resolution of the transference. Yet, it seems that this is what most commonly happens to an ending, and because of this a great many patients may lose the potentially great benefit of a thorough resolution and are forever after left suspended in the net of unresolved transference.

Yet, slurring over a rigorous termination seems understandable, as difficult as transference neurosis may be in the analyst at other times, this ending period, if rigorously carried out, simply has to be the period of his greatest emotional strain. There can surely be no more likely time for an analyst to surrender his analytic position and, responding to his own transference, become personally involved with his patient than during the process of separating from a long and self-restrained relationship. Accordingly, it may be better to slur over the ending lightly than to mishandle it in an attempt to be rigorous.

In considering more broadly the function of the transference in the psychoanalytic process, one is confronted by the apparent naïve, but, nonetheless important questions of the role of the actual (current) object as compared with that of the object representation of the original personage in the past. We recall Freud's paradoxical, somewhat gloomy, but portentous concluding passage in 'The Dynamics of Transference.' This struggle between the doctor and the patient, between intellect and instinctual life, between understanding and seeking to act, is played out almost exclusively in the phenomena of transference. It is on that field that the victory must be won - the victory whose expression is on that field that the victory must be won - the victor y whose expression is the permanent cure of the neuroses. It cannot be disputed that controlling the phenomena of transference presents the psychoanalysis with the greatest difficultly, but it should not be forgotten that they do us the inestimable service of making the patient 's hidden and forgotten erotic impulses of showing their immediate and manifested impossibilities, for when all is said and done, it is impossible to destroy anyone in absentia or in effigies.

Both object and representation is made necessary by the basic phenomenon of original separation. The existence of an image of the object, which persist in the absence of the object, is one of the important beginnings of psychic life in general, certainly an indispensable prerequisite for object relationship. As generally construed. Whether this is viewed as (or a times demonstrably is) something unstable for allotting introjection, s always subject to alternative projection, or an intrapsychic object representation clearly distinguished from the self-representation, or firm identification in the superego, or in the ego itself, these phenomena are in various ways components of the system of mastery of the fact of separation, or separateness, from the original absolutely necessarily anaclitic (in the earliest period) symbiotic 'object'. In the light of clinical observation, it would appear to be that the relative stability (parental) objects representation. At which time of varying degree, are to a greater extent for the archaic phenomena. Even in nonpsychotic patients, overwhelmed by them, sometimes resembles the restoration from oedipal identification, which provides the preponderant basis for most demonstrable analytic transferences. That within the necrotic patients, the transference is effectively established when this representation invests the analyst to a degree - depending on intensity of drive and most of ego participation - which ranges in all the, wishing and striving to remake and analyst to biasses judgements and misinterpretation of data, are finally the actual perceptual distortions.

However, the old object representations as such may be invested, however rigidly established the libidinal or aggressive cathexis of the image may be, this as such can become the actual and exclusive focus of instinctual discharge, or of complicated and intense instinct-defence solutions, only and general energy-sparing quality of strictly intrapsychic processes. For the vast majority of persons, visible to any degree, including those with severe neurosis, character distortions, addictions and certain psychoses, the striving is toward the living and actual object, even at the cost of intense suffering. In a sense, this returns us to the state in which the psychological 'object-to-be'. Has a critical importance never again to be duplicated, except in certain acute life emergencies, even if the object is not firmly perceived as such, in the sense of later object relations? And it does seem that trance impressions from the earliest contacts in the service of life preservation, and the associated instinctual gratifications, and innumerable secondarily associated sensory impressions. Are activated by the specific inborn urges of sexual maturation? These propel the individual to renew many of the earliest modes of actual bodily contact, in connection with seeking for specific instinctual gratification. Or, to look away from clear-cut instinctual matters to the more remote elaborations of human contact: Few regard loneliness as other than a source of suffering, even self-imposed, as an apparent matter of choice, and the forcible imposition of 'solitary confinement ' is surely one of the most cruel of punishments.

Of these few generalizations have some important implications, no reaction to another individual is all transference, just as surely as no relationship is entirely free of it. There is not only the general maturational-developmental drive toward the outer world, but the seeking for a variety of need and pleasure satisfactions, learned or simulated in relation to the primordial object, but necessarily and inevitably transferred from this object the generically related things and persons in the expanding environment. These may be used or enjoyed without penalty, if the distinction between the original and the new is profoundly and genuinely established (with due respect for the quantitative 'relativism' of such concepts). The range of such inevitable displacement (transfers) in endless in all spheres - sexual, aggressive, aesthetic, utilitarian, intellectual. More immediately relevant, in the lives of those whose development has been relatively healthy, are those individuals whose vocations provide similarities or parallels, however, rarefied, to the caretaking functions of the original parents: Teachers, physicians, clergymen, political rulers, occasionally others. Again it must be noted, that such persons perform real functions, that the adult individual's interest in them, his specific need for them, often greatly outweighs similar reactions to parents, who retain their unique place for a complex and variable combination of other reasons. For such surrogate parents perform for the adult what his parents largely performed for him in realist years, and the psychological comparison is with an old object representation, or with an early identification, to which such latter-day parent surrogates may add important layers of elaborations. It is on the basis of such functional resemblances that persons in these roles have a unique transference valence. The analyst is first perceived as a real object, who awakens hope of help in the patient's experience at all level of integration, from that of actual and immediate perception, evaluation, and response, to the activation of original parental object representations and their cathexes. That the analyst becomes invested with such representations, in forms ranging from wishes or demands to functional or even perceptual misidentifications, comprises the broad range of phenomena that we know as the therapeutic transference. Thus, the complicate structural phenomena of conflict are activated in relation to a real object, and such activation is uniquely dependent on the participation of this object, in a situation whose realities revive, with the affirmative associations, the memories of old and painful frustrations. In this situation, the continuing and prolonged contact, under strictly controlled conditions, is an important real factor, which has been elaborated previously. Without these actualities, dream life, - or instance of greater energid imbalance between impulses and defence - neurosis, will be the spontaneous solution, while everyday 'give-and-take' object relations are, at least on the surface, maintained as such. Occasionally, neurotic behaviour, where transferences dominate the everyday relationships, will supervene.

Interpretation, recollection or reconstruction, and, of course, working through, is essential for the establishment of effective insight, but they cannot operate mutatively if applied only to memories in the structural sense, whether of higher cathected events or persons. For it is the thrust of wish or impulse, or the elaboration of germane dynamic fantasies, and the corresponding defensive structures and their inadequacies, associated with such memories, which give to neurosis. It is a parallel thrust that creates the transference neurosis. Where memories are clear and vivid, through recall, or accepted as much through reconstruction and associated with variable, optional, and adaptive, rather than rigidly structuralized' response patterns, the analytic work has been done.

This view does place somewhat of a weighty emphasis on the horizontal coordinate of procedural operations, the conscious and unconscious relation to the analyst as a living and actual object, which is of investing upon the becoming imagery, traits, and functions of critical objects of the past. The relationship is to be understood in its dynamic, economic, and adaptive meaning, in its current structuralized tenacity, the real and unreal carefully separated from one another. The process of subjective memory or of reconstruction, the indispensable genetic dimension, is, in this sense, involved toward the decisive and specific autobiographic understanding of the living version of old conflict, than with the assumption that the interpretative reduction of the transference neurosis to gross mnemic elements is, in itself and automatically, mutative. At least, this view of the problem would seem appropriate to most chronic neurosis embedded in germane character structures of some plexuity. That neurosis symptoms connected with isolated traumatic events, covered by amnesia, may, at times, disappear on restoration of memories with adequate effective discharge, regardless of technical method, is, of course, indisputably true, even though the details of process, including the role of transference, are probably not yet adequately understood. Psychoanalysis was born in the observation of this type of process. In a thoughtful manner, the role of transference, in the early writings of both Freud and Ferenczi, seemed weighted somewhat in the direction of its resistance function, i.e., as directed against recall, although its affirmative functions were soon adequately appreciated, and placed in the dialectical position, which has obtained to the present day.

Other while, the primal processes of projection ad introjection, being inextricably linked with the infant's emotions and anxieties, initiate object-relations, by projecting, i.e., deflecting libido and aggression onto the mother's breast, the basis for object-relations is established, by introjecting the object, first of all the breast, relations to internal objects comes into being. The term 'object-relations' are based on the contention that the infant has from the beginning post-natal life a relation to the mother, although focussing primarily of her breast, which is imbued with the fundamental element's of an object-relation, i.e., loves, hatred, phantasies, anxieties, and defences? The introjection of the breast is the beginning of superego formation that extends over years. We have grounds for assuming that from the first feeding experience onwards the infant's introjection, the breast in its various aspects. The core of the superego is thus the mother's breast, both good and bad. Given to the simultaneous operation of introjection and projection, relations to external and internal objects interact. The father too, who soon plays a role in the child's life, early on becomes part of the infant's internal world it is characteristic of the infant's emotional life that there are rapid fluctuations between love and hate, between external and internal situations between perception of reality and the fantasises relating to it, and accordingly, an interplay between prosecutory anxiety and idealization - both referring to the internal and external object's, the idealized object brings a corollary of the prosecutory, extremely bad one.

The ego's growing capacity for integration and synthesis leads more and more, even during these first few months, to states in which love and hatred, and correspondingly the good and bad aspects of objects, for being synthesized. This gives rise to the second form of anxiety - depressive anxiety - for the infant's aggressive impulses and desires toward the bad breast (mother) are now felt to be a danger to the good breast (mother) as well. In the second quarter of the first year these emotions are reinforced, because at this stage the infant increasingly perceives and introjects the mother as a person. Depressive anxiety is intensified, for the infant feels he has destroyed or is destroying a whole object by his greed and uncontrollable aggression. Moreover, owing to the growing synthesis of his emotions, he now feels that these destructive impulses are directed against as a 'loved person'. Similar processes operate in relation to the father and other members of the family. These anxieties and corresponding defences constitute the 'Depressive position', which comes to a head about the middle of the first year and whose essence is the anxiety and guilt relating to the destruction and loss of the loved internal and external objects.

It is at this stage, and bound up with the depressive position, that the oedipus complex sets in. Anxiety and guilt add a powerful impetus toward the beginning of the oedipus complex. For anxiety and guilt increase the need to externalize (project) bad figures and to internalize (introject) good ones. There to attaching desires, love, feeling of guilt, and reparative tendencies to internal figures in the external world, however, not only is the search for new objects that dominates the infant's needs, but also, the drive toward new life proposes: Away from the breast toward the penis, i.e., from oral desires toward genital ones. Many factors contribute to these developments, the forward drive of the libido, the growing integration of the ego, physical and mental skills and progressive adaption to the external world. These trends are bound up with the processing of symbol formation, which enables the infant to transfer not only emotions and phantasies, anxiety and guilt, from one object to another.

The processes are linked with another fundamental phenomenon governing its mental life, such that pressures exerted by the earliest anxiety situation are factors through which bring about the repetition compulsion, however, one conclusion about the earliest states of infancy is a continuation of Freud's discoveries; on certain points, nonetheless, the divergencies having to arise of which are very relevant, perhaps, its main contention that object-relations are operative from the beginning of post-natal life.

Nevertheless, the view that autoerotism and narcissism are the young infant contemporaries with the first relation to objects - external and internalized, that hypothetically, autoerotism and narcissism include the love for and relation with the internalized good object that in phantasy forms part of the loved body and self. It is to this internalized object that in autocratic gratification and narcissistic stages a withdrawal takes place. Concurrently, from birth onwards, a relation to objects, primarily the mother (her breasts) is present. This hypothesis contradicts Freud's concept of autoerotic and narcissistic stages that preclude an object-relation. However, the difference between Freud's statement on this issue is equivocal. In various context he explicitly and implicitly expresses opinion that suggested a relation to an object, the mother's breast, preceding autoerotic and narcissism.

In the first instance the oral component instinct finds satisfaction by attaching itself to the sating of the desire for nourishment, and its object in the mother's breast. It then detaches itself, becomes independent and at the same time of autoerotic objectivity is found to an object in the child's own body.

The act or practice for which Freud' of using something or the state of being used is found in the applications availing to the term object is somewhat different from the context that is used of this term, but Freud is referring the object of an instinctual aim. What it is to mean, that, while, in addition, it is meant as an object-relation involving the infant's emotions, phantasies, anxieties and defences. Nevertheless, in sentence referred to, Freud clearly speaks of a libinal attachment to an object, the mother's breast, which precedes autoerotism and narcissism.

In this context, it is reminded that of Freud's findings about early identification. In "The Ego and the Id," speaking of abandoned object cathexes. He said, . . . The effects of the first identification in earliest childhood will be profound and lasting. This leads us back to the origin of the ego-ideal, . . . Freud then defines the first and most important identifications that lie hidden behind the ego-ideal as the identification with the father, or with the parent's, and places them, as he expresses it, in the 'prehistory' of every person'. These formulations come close to the deceptions as described of their resulting of introjected objects, for by definition identifications are the result as such, but that the statement and the passage quoted from the Encyclopaedia article, it can be deduced that Freud, although he did not pursue this line of though t, however, he did assume that in the earliest infancy that both an object and introjective processes play a part.

That is to say, as regards autoerotism and narcissism we meet with an inconsistency in Freud's views. Such inconsistencies that exist on a number of points of theory clearly show, which on these particular of issue s Freud had not yet arrived at a final decision. In respect to the theory of anxiety he stated this explicitly in Inhibitions, Symptoms and Anxiety. His realization that much about the early stages of development was still unknown or obscure to him is also exemplified by his speaking of the first years of a girl's life as, ' . . . lost in a past so dim and shadowy . . .'

As regards to the question of autoerotism and narcissism, Anna Freud - although her views about this aspect of Freud's work remains unknown, but she seems only to have taken into account Freud's conclusions that an autoerotic and a narcissistic stage precede object-relations, and not to be allowed for other possibilities, of which are implied in some of Freud's statements such as the ones inferred above. This is one of the reasons why the divergence between Anna Freud's conception and the immediacy of early infancy is far greater than that between Freud's views, taken as a whole, and those of stating it as the essential to clarify the content and nature of the differences between the two schools of psychoanalytic thought, represented by Anna Freud and those that imply of such clarification is required in the interests of psychoanalytic training and also because it could help to open up fruitful discussions between psychoanalysts and thereby contribute to a greater generality of a better understanding of the fundamental problems of early infancy.

The hypothesis that a time interval extending over several months precedes object-relations implies that - except for the libido attached to the infant's own body - impulses, phantasies, anxieties, and defences either are not present in him, or are not related to an object, that is to say, they would operate in vacua. The analysis of very young children, as to implicate, would show that there is no instinctual urge, no anxiety situation, no mental process that does not involve objects, external or internal, in other words, object-relations are at the centre of emotional life. Furthermore, love and hatred, phantasies, anxiety and defences are also operative from the beginning and are 'ad initio' indivisibly linked with object-relations.

The oedipus complex, in a pragmatic analytic sense, retains its position as the 'nuclear complex' of the neurosis. It is a climactic organization experience of early childhood, apart from its own vicissitudes, It can under favourable circumstances provide certain solutions for pregenital conflicts, or in itself suffer from them. In any case, include them in its structure. Only when the precursor experiences have been of a great severity, for which it is to claim to a shadowy organic determinacy, as the new 'frame of reference', which hardly having the independent and decisive significance of its own. In any case, its attendant phallic conflicts must be resolved in their own right, in the analytic transference. From the analyst, (or his current surrogate in the outer world) thus from the psychic representation of the parent, the literal (i.e., bodily) sexual wishes must be withdrawn, and genuinely displaced to appropriate objects in the outer world. The fraction of such drive elements that can be transmuted to friendly, tender feeling toward the original object. Or too other acceptable (neutralized) variants, will of course, influence the economic problem involved. This genuine displacement is opposed to the sense of 'acting out', while other objects are perceptually different substitutes for the primary object (thus for the analyst). This may be thought to follow automatically on the basic process of coming to terms with (accepting) the childhood incestuous wish and its parricidal connotation. Such assumption does not do justice to the dynamic problem implicit in tenaciously persistent wishes. To the extent that these wishes are to be genuinely disavowed or modified, rather than displaced, a further important step is necessary: The thorough analysis of the functional meaning of the persisting wishes and the special etiologic factors entering into their tenacity, as reflected in the transference neurosis. Thus, in principle, the literal accuracy of the concept phrased by Wilhelm Reich, "transference of the transference," as the final requirement for dissolution of the erotic analytic transference, even though the clinical discussion, which is its context, is useful. This expression would imply that the object representation that largely determines the distinctive erotic interest in the analyst can remain essentially the same, so long as the actual object changes. While a semantic issue may be involved in some degree, it is one that impinges importantly on conceptual clarity. However, such definite conceptualization of one basic element in the phenomenon or transference may be, and should be, subject to the reservations appropriately attaching themselves to any very clear-cut ideas about obscure areas, with the clinical concept of transference, its clinical derivation and its generally accepted place in the psychoanalytic process.

The evolution of the reality-relatedness between patient and therapist, over the course of the psychotherapy, is something that has received little more than passing mention in the literature, Hoedemaker (1955), in a paper concerning the therapeutic process in the treatment of schizophrenia, stresses the importance of the schizophrenic patient's forming healthy identifications with the therapist, and Loewald (1960), his concerns and considerations to the therapeutic action of psychoanalysis in general, repeatedly emphasizes the importance of the real relationship between patient and analyst, but only in the following passage eludes the evolution, the growth, of this relationship over the course of treatment:

> . . . Where repression is lifted and unconscious and preconscious are again in communication, infantile object and contemporary object may be united into one - a truly new object as both unconscious and preconscious are changed by their mutual communication, the object that helps to bring this about in therapy, the analyst, mediates this union. . . .

It has been distinctly impressive that the patient's remembrance of new areas of his past - his manifestation of newly de-repressed transference reactions to the therapist - occurs only hand-in-hand with the reaching of comparable areas of feeling in the evolving reality-relatedness between patient and therapist. For example, he does not come to experiencing fond memories of his mother until the reality-relatedness between himself and the therapist has reached the point where the feelings between them have become, in reality, predominantly positive. Loewald's words, imply that an increment of transference resolution slightly comes slightly before in time or that in arrangements that go before as to go before time, hence, the all-out precede, since that many are the cause to be preceded, which makes it possible in the forming of each successive increment the evolving reality-relationship seems taken between patent and analyst, in that it has been, by contrast, that the evolutionary principles preceded its oriented set advantage to set points of reality, -in that of a relatedness that proceeds alway a bit ahead of, and makes possibly, the progressive evolution and resolution of the transference. Although to be sure of the latter, in so far as it liberates of a psychological energy and makes it available for reality-relatedness, such that it helps greatly to consolidate the grounds as justly of the possibilities as taken over by the advancing reality-relatedness. Loewald (1960) thinks that:

> . . . The patient can dare to take the plunge into the regressive crises of the transference neurosis that brings him face to face again with his childhood anxieties and conflicts, if he can hold on to the potentialities of a new object-relationship, represented by the analyst.

It seems that this new object-relationship is more that a potentiality, to be realized with comparative suddenness, toward the end of this treatment with the resolution of the transference. Rather it is, it has seemed as constantly being there, being built up bit by bit, just ahead of the likewise evolving transference relationship. Predeterminates as in Freud's (1922) having pointed out that projection (expressed in the Latin is called 'projectio') which is, after all, so major an aspect of transference - is directed not 'into the sky, so to speak, were there is nothing of the sort already', but rather onto a person who provides some reality-basic for the projection.

In the final months of the therapy, the therapist clearly sees that extent to which the patient's transferences to him as representing a succession of figures from the latter's earlier years have all been in the service the patient's unconscious successively decreasing extent, fro experiencing the full and complex reality of the immediate relatedness with the therapist in the present. The patent at last comes to realize that the relationship with a single other human being - in this instance, the therapist - is so rich as to comprise all these earlier relationships - so rich as to evoke all the myriad feelings that have been parcelled out and crystallized, wherefore, in the transference that have now been resolved. This is a province most beautifully described by the Swiss novelist, Herman Hesse (1951) winner of the Nobel Prize in 1946,in his little novel. Siddhartha. The protagonist in a lifelong quest for the ultimate answer to the enigma of man's role on earth, finally discovers a basic underlying or constituting entity, substance or the form as a face of his beloved friend of all the myriad persons, things, and events that he has known, but incoherently before, during the vicissitudes of his many years of searching.

It is thus that the patient, schizophrenic or otherwise, becoming as one with himself, in the closing phase of psychotherapy. But although the realization may come to him as a sudden one, it is founded on a reality-relatedness that has been building up all along. Loewald (1960) in his magnificent paper to which transference resolution plays in the development of this reality-relatedness. As, perhaps, that the evolution of the 'countertransference' - not countertransference in the classical sense of the therapist's transference to the patient, but rather in the sense of the therapist's emotional reaction to the patient's transference - forms an equally essential contribution to this reality-relatedness.

It is, nonetheless, but often, that the therapist who sees a new potentiality in the patient, a previously unnoted side of him that heralds a phase of increasing differentiations. And frequently the therapist is the only one who sees it. Even the patient does not see it as yet, except in the projected form, so that he perceives this as an attribute of the therapist. This situation can make the therapist feel very much inalienable as separated from others that apart or detached in the isolated removal and intensely threaten.

Upon which the transference relationship with the therapist, we find that the patient naturally brings this relationship, just as he brings into the relatedness in which the difficulties concerning differentiation and integration that were engendered by the pathological upbringing upon the advances in differentiation and integration necessarily occur first outside the patient - namely, in the therapist's increasingly well differentiated and well-integrated view of, and consequently, responses to, him - before these can become well established within him.

Because the schizophrenic patient did not experience, in his infancy, the symbolic relatedness with his mother such as each human being needs for the formation of a healthy core in his personality structure, in the emotion of the transference relationship to his therapist he must eventually succeed in establishing such a mode of relatedness.

This means that he must eventually regress, in the transference, to such a level in order to get a fresh start toward a healthier personality differentiation and integration than he had achieved before entering therapy. This is not to say that he must 'act out' the regressive needs in his daily life, to be sure, the schizophrenic patient, whether in therapy or not, inevitably does so to a considerable degree, but to the extent that these needs can be expressed in the transference relationship, they need not seek expression, unconsciously, thorough acting out in daily life.

Focussing now upon the transference relationship with the therapist, we find that the patient naturally brings about the difficulties concerning differentiation in the process of integration that was engendered by the pathological upbringing as for being the one more interruption in the impeding principle of reconstructions of an identifying manufacture of the transference. And the every day, relationships are found in the interplaying form of corresponding advances in differentiated dynamic integrations necessarily occur first outside the patient - namely, in the therapist's increasingly well or acceptably differentiated by the integrated extent or range of vision, that the position or attitudes that determine how of the intent of something (as an aim or an end or motive)or by way the mind is directed. Its view of and the consequent response ought to become acknowledged as to be established within them.

Because the schizophrenic patient did not experience, in his infancy, the establishment of and later emergence form, a healthy symbiotic relatedness with his mother such as each human brings needs for the formation of a healthy core in his personality structure, in the evolution of the transference relationship to his therapist he must eventually succeed in establishing such a mode of relatedness.

This means that he must eventually regress, in the transference, to such a level, in order to get a fresh start toward a healthier personality differentiation and integration than he had achieved before entering therapy. This is not to say that he must act out the regressive needs in his daily life. To be sure, the schizophrenic patient, whether in therapy or not, inevitably does so to a considerable degree; even to the extent that these needs can be expressed in the transference relationship, they need not seek expression, unconsciously, through acting out in daily life.

This symbiotic mode of relatedness is necessarily mutual, participated in by therapist as well as patient. Thus, the therapist must come to experience not only the oceanic gratification, but also the anxiety involved in his sharing a symbiotic, subjective oneness with the schizophrenic patient. This relationship, with its lack of felt ego-boundaries between the two participants, at times invokes the kind of deep contentment, the kind of felt communion that needs no words, which characterize a loving relatedness between mother and infant. But at other times it involves the therapists feeling unable to experience himself as differentiated from the pathology-ridden personality of the patient. He feels helplessly caught in the patient's deep ambivalence. He feels one with the patient's hatred and despairs and thwarted love, and at times he cannot differentiate between his own subjectively harmful effect upon the patient, and the illness with which the patient was to come or go or nearly recede in the achievement afflicting when the therapist first undertook to help him. Thus, at these anxiety-ridden moments in the symbiotic phase, the therapist feels his own personality to be invaded by the patient's pathology, and feels his identity severely threatened, whereas in the more contented moments, part of the contentment resides in both participants enjoying a freedom from any concern with identity.

This same profound lack of differentiation may come to characterize the patient's view of the persons about him, including his therapeutic, and at time's, in line with his need to project a poorly differentiated conglomeration of 'bad' impulses, he may perceive the therapist for being but one head of a hydra-headed monster. The patient's lack of differentiation in this regard, prevailing for month after month of his charging the therapist with saying or doing various things that were actually said or have done by others in the hospitalized presences to its containing of environmental surfaces, or by the family members, can have a formidably eroding effect upon the therapist's sense of personal intensity. But the patient may need to regress to just such a primitivity, poorly differentiated view of the world in order to grow up again, psychologically, in a healthier way this time.

Among the most significant steps in the maturation that occurs in successful psychotherapy are those moments when the therapist suddenly sees the patient in a new light. His image of the patient suddenly changes, because of the entry into his awareness of some potentiality in the patient. Which had not shown itself before? From now on, his responses to the patient are a response to this new, enriched view, and through such responding he fosters the emergence, and further differentiation, of this new personality area. This is another way of describing the process that Buber and in Friednan, 1955, calls 'making the other person present, seeing in the other persons potentialities of such even presents: Seeing that in the other persons potential which is of a possible, yet conceivable that something as existing is possible and that something that can develop or become actual of seemed within the realm, or range of possibility that he, in some mannerlifashion, that it was he, that he is not aware of his helping him, by responding to those potentialities, even so, but, to realize them.

Schizophrenic patient's feelings start to become differentiated before they have found new and appropriate modes for expressing the new feelings, thus patient's may use the same old stereotyped behaviour or utterance to express nuances of new feelings. This is identical with the situation in those schizophrenics' familiar which is permeated with what Wynne (1958) termed 'pseudo-mutuality' or toward maintaining the sense of reciprocal perceiving expectations. Thus, the expectations are left unexplored, and the old expectations and roles, even though outgrown and inappropriate in one sense, continue to serve as the structure for the relation.

The therapist, through hearing the new emotional connotation, the new meaning, in the stereotyped utterance and responding in accordance with the new connotation, fosters the emerging differentiation. Over the course of months, in therapy, he may find the same verbal stereotype employed in th e expression of a whole gamut of newly emerging feelings.

Thus, over a prolonged time-span, the therapist may give as many different responses to a gradually differentiating patient as are simultaneously given by the various members of the surrounding environment, to the patient who shows the contrasting ego-fragmentation (or, in a loose manner of speaking, over-differentiation).

Persistently stereotyped communications from the patient tend to bring from the therapist communications that, over a period of time, become almost equally stereotyped. One can sometimes detect, in recordings playing during supervisory hours, evidence that new emotional connotations are creeping into the patient's verbal stereotypes, and into the therapist's responsive verbal stereotypes, before either of the two participants has noticed this.

What the therapist does which assists the patient's differentiation often consists in his courage and honesty to differ from whether the patient's expressed feelings or, often most valuable, with the social role into which his sick behaviour tends to fix or transfix the therapist. This may consist in his candid disagreement with some of the patient, and s strongly felt and long-voiced views, or in his flatly declining to try to feel 'sympathy' - such as one would be conventionally expected to feel in response to behaviour, which seems, at first glance, to express the most pitiable suffering but which the therapist is convinced primarily expresses sadism on the patient's part. Such courage to differ with the expected social role is what is needed from the therapist, in order to bring of a closed condition the symbiotic phase of relatedness that has served, earlier, a necessary and productive function. Through asserting his individuality, and at many later moments in the therapeutic interaction, the therapist fosters the patient's own development of more complete and durable ego-boundaries. At the same time he offers the patient the opportunity to identify with a parent-figure who dares to be an individual-dares to be so in the face of pressures from the working group of which he is part, and from his own reproachful superego, it can be of notice, that of a minor degree a consciously planned and controlled therapeutic technique wherefore, the content descriptions are rather a natural flow of events as in the transference evolution, with which the therapist must have the spontaneity to go along.

The patient, particularly in the symbiotic phase of the therapy but in preceding and succeeding phases as well, is notably intolerant of sudden and marked changes in the therapeutic relationship - that is, of suddenly seeing himself, or feeling that his therapist sees him, through new eyes. He rarely gives the therapist to feel that the latter have made an importantly revealing interpretation, or should be concealed, but when to arrive at by reasoning from evidence or from its premises that we can infer from that which he was derived as to a conclusion, that it conveys of a higher illumination of mind. Methodologically historical information is an approving acceptation by the therapist, he does so causally, he tends to experience important increments of depreciated material, yet not as every bit for reverential abstractions as to make a new, amended, or up-to-date reversion of the many problems involved in revising the earthly shuddering revelations in his development. The things that he has known all along and simply never happened to think of. His experience of an inherent perception of the world as surrounding him is often permeated by 'deja vu' sensations, and misidentification of the emphasizing style at which the expense of thought for taking the rhetorical rhapsody to actions or a single inaction of moving the revolutions of the earth around the sun is mostly familiar an act from his past.

The motional progressions in therapy, on the patient's part, occur each time only after a recrudescence in his symptoms. It is as though he has to find reassurance of his personal identity, for being really the same hopeless person he has long felt himself to be, before he can venture into a bit or new and more hopeful identity.

Of what expressions are that objects relational states or fact for having independent reality and whose customs that have recently come into existence, such by the actuality for something having existence from the beginning of life, being the mother's breast that it splits into a good (gratifying) and bad (frustrating) The breast becomes this splitting of dual results in a division between love and hate. What is more, is that of the relation to the first object implies its introjection and projection, and thus, from the beginning object relations are moulded by an interaction between introjection and projection, between internal and external objects and situation.

. . . .With the introjection of the complete object in about the second quarter of the first year marked steps in integration are made. . . . The loved and hated aspects of the mother are no longer felt to be so widely separated, and the result is an increased fear of loss, a strong feeling of guilt and states akin to mourning, because the aggressive impulses are felt to be divorced against the love object, the depressive position has come to the fore . . .

. . . In the first few month of life anxiety is predominantly experienced as fear of persecution and . . . this contributes to certain mechanisms and defences that characterize the paranoid and schizoid positions. Outstanding among these defences is the mechanism of splitting internal and external objects, emotions and the ego. These mechanisms and defences are part of normal development and at the same time form the basis for later schizophrenic illness. The descriptive underlying identification by projection, i.e., projective identification, as a combination of splitting off parts of the self and projecting them onto another person . . .

Rosenfeld, a follower of Klein writes that, he presents detailed clinical data that serve to document the implicit point, among others, that whereas, the schizophrenic patient may appear to have regressed to such an objectless autoerotic level of development as was postulated by Freud (1911, 1914) and Abraham (1908), in actuality the patient is involved in object-relatedness with the analyst, object-relatedness of the primitive introjective and projective identification kind. For example, Rosenfeld concludes his description of, the data from one of the sessions as follows:

> . . . The whole material of the session suggested that in the withdrawal state he was introjecting me and my penis, and at the same time was projecting himself into me. So here, again, it to suggest that it be something possible to detect the object-relation in an apparently autoerotic state.
>
> . . . only at a later stage of treatment was it possible to distinguish between the mechanisms of introjection of objects and projective identifications, which so frequently go on simultaneously (1952).

We find, among the writings of the Kleinian analysts, a number of interesting examples of delusional transference interpretation, in all of which the keynote is the concept of projective (or introjective) identification. For instance, Rosenfeld writes at one juncture (1952),

> The patient himself gave the clue to the transference situation, and showed that he had projected his damaged self containing the destroyed world, not only into all the other patients, but into me, and had changed me in this way. But, instead of becoming relieved by this projection he became more anxious, because he was afraid of what I was then putting back into him. Whereupon his introjective processes became severely disturbed. One would therefore expect a severe deterioration in his condition, and in fact his clinical state during the next ten days became very precarious. He began to get more and more suspicious about food, and finally refused to eat and drink anything. . . . Everything he took inside seemed to him bad, damaged, and poisonous (like faeces) as there was no point in eating anything. We knew that projection led again into reintroduction, so that also, it had felt as if he had a direct passage inside himself all the destroyed and bad objects that he had projected into the outer world: And he indicated by coughing, retching and movements of his mouth and fingers that he was preoccupied with this problem . . . I told him that he was not only afraid of getting something bad inside him. But that he was also afraid of taking good things, the good orange juice and good interpretations, instead, since he was afraid that these would make him feel guilty again. When l said this, a kind of shock went right through his body; he gave a groan of understanding, and his facial expression changed. By the end

> of the hour he had emptied the glass of orange juice, the first food or drink he had taken for two days . . .

Bion (1956) defines projective identification as:

> . . . a splitting off by the patient of a part of his personality and a projection of it into the object where it becomes installed, sometimes as a persecutor, leaving the psychic from which it has been split off correspondingly impoverished.

It now seems that the instances of verbal transference interpretation can be looked upon as one form of intervention, at times effective, which constitutes an appeal for collaboration to the non-psychotic area of the patient's personality, an area of which both Katan (1954) and Bion (1957) has written. But, particularly among long hospitalized chronically schizophrenic persons, we are many a patient who is too ill to be able to register verbal statements, and even in th e foregoing examples from Rosenfeld and Bion's experiences, it is impossible to know to what extent the patient is helped by an illuminating accurate verbal content in the therapist's words, or to what extent that which is effective springs, rather from the feelings of confidence, firmness, and understanding which accompany these words spoken by a therapist who feels that he has a reliable theoretical value for formulating the clinical phenomena in which he finds himself.

In trying to conceptualize such ego-states in the patient, and such states of relatedness between patient and doctor. Additional value placed the concept presentation by Little in her papers, "On Delusional Transference" (Transference Psychosis) (1958) and "On Basic Unity" (1960).

One of the necessary development, in along-delusional patient's eventual relinquishment of his delusions is for these gradually to become productions that the therapist sees no longer as essentially ominous and the subject for either serious therapeutic investigation, or argumentation, or any other form of opposition, rather, the therapist comes to react to these for being essentially playful, unmaligant, creatively imaginative, and he comes to respond to them with playfully imaginative comments of his own. Nothing helps more finally to detoxicate a patient's previously self-isolating delusional state than to find in his therapist a capacity to engage him in a delightfully crazy playfulness - a kind of relatedness of which the schizophrenic patient had never a chance to have his fills during his childhood. Typically, such early childhood playfulness was subjected to massive repression, because of various intra-familial circumstances.

Innumerable instances of the therapist's uncertainty how to respond to the patient's communication turn upon the question of whether the communication is to be 'taken personally' - to be taken as primarily designed, for instance, toward filling the therapist with perplexity, confusion, anxiety, humiliation, rage, or some other negatively toned affective state, or whether it is to be taken rather as primarily an effort to convey some basically unhostile needs on the patient's par. Just as it is often essential that the therapist become able to sense and respond to personal communications in a patient's ostensibly stereotyped behaviour or utterance, so too it is frequently essential that he be able to see, behind the overt 'personal' reference to himself - often a stinging or otherwise emotionally evocative reference - some fundamental needs that the patient is hesitantly to communicate openly.

Some comments by Ruesch, although concerned primarily with nonverbal communication, are beautifully descriptive of the process that occurs in such patients as the transference evolves over the course of the therapy:

> . . . .The primitive and uncoordinated movements of patient at the peak of severe functional psychosis . . . may be viewed as attempts to reestablish the infantile system of communication through action. It is as if these were frustrating in early childhood, with the hope that this time there will be another person who will understand and reply in nonverbal terms. This thesis is supported by observations of the behaviour of psychotic children who tend to play with their fingers, make grimaces or assume bizarre body position. Their movements are rarely directed at other people but rather at themselves, something to the point of producing serious injuries. As therapy proceeds, interpersonal movements gradually replace the solipsistic movements, and stimulus becomes marching to response. Once these children have been satisfied in a nonverbal ways, they become willing to learn verbal forms of codification and begin to acquire mastery of discursive language.

It seems, but nevertheless, that there is widespread agreement concerning whose functional importance of dependency process in schizophrenia, for which the patient who is involved in a schizophrenic illness, probably nothing is harder to endure than the circumstance of his having intense dependency needs that he cannot allow himself to recognize, or which if recognized in himself he dare not express to anyone, or which are expressed by him in a fashion that, more often than not, brings an uncomprehending or actively rejecting response from the other person. For the therapist who is working with such a patient, certainly there is nothing that brings more anxiety, frustration, and discouragement than do these processes in the schizophrenic person with whom he is dealing.

The dependencies on which is focussed upon effectual acknowledge in the presence of which has its closest analogue, in terms of normative standards, is such that the personality development, in the experience and behaviour of the infant or of the young child. The dependency needs, attitudes, and striving that the schizophrenic manifests may be defined in the statement that he seeks for another person to assume a total responsibility for gratifying all his needs, both physiological and psychological, while this person is to seek nothing from him.

Of the physiological needs, which the schizophrenic manifests, those centring about the oral zone of interaction are usually most prominent, analogous to the predominant place held by nursing in the life of the infant. Desires to be stroked and cuddled, likewise, so characteristic of the very early years of normal development, are prominently held within the schizophrenic. In addition, desires for the relief of genital sexual tensions, even though these have had their advent much later in the life history than have his oral desires, are manifested in much the same level of an early, infantile dependency. That is, such genital hungers are manifested in much the same small-child spirit of, 'you ought to be taking care of this for me' as are the oral hungers.

The psychological needs that are represented among the schizophrenic's dependency processes consist in the desire for the other person to provide him with unvarying love and protection, and to assume a total guidance of his living,

In the course of furthering characterizations of the schizophrenic's dependency processes will be defined much more fully, that is to say, it is to b e emphasized that no of the dependency processes are but described is characteristic only of the schizophrenic, or qualitatively different from processes operative at some level of consciousness in persons with other varieties of psychiatric illness and in normal persons. With regard to dependency processes, we find research in schizophrenia has its greatest potential value in the fact that schizophrenic shows us in a sharply etched form that which is so obscured, by years progressive adaptation to adult interpersonal living, in human beings in general. Wherefore, but in some degree, are about the patient's anxiety about the dependency needs, are (1) As nearly as can be determined, the patient is unaware of pure dependency needs; for him, apparently, they exist in consciousness, if at all, only in the form of a hopeless conflictual combination of dependency needs plus various defences - defences that render impossible any thoroughgoing sustained gratification of these needs. These defences (which include, grandiosity, hostility, competitiveness, scornful and so forth) have so long ago developed in his personality, as a means of coping with anxiety attendant upon dependency needs, that the experiencing of pure dependency needs it, for him, lost in antiquity and so be achieved only relatively late in therapy after the various defences have been largely relinquished.

Thus it appears to be not only dependency needs 'per se' which arouses anxiety, but rather the dependency on itself that needs plus all these various defences (which tend in themselves to be anxiety-provoking) plus the inevitable frustration, to a greater or less degree, of the dependency needs.

Hostility as one of the defences against awareness of 'dependency needs,' that which for certainly repressed dependency needs is one of the most frequent bases of murderous feelings in the schizophrenic, in such instances the murderous feelings may be regarded as a vigorous denial of dependency. What frequently happens in therapy is that both patient and therapist become so anxious about the defensive murderous feelings that the underlying dependency feelings long remain unrecognized.

Every schizophrenic possesses much self-hatred and guilt that may serve as defences against the awareness of dependency feelings ('I am too worthless for anyone possibly to care about me'), and which in any case complicate the matter of dependency. The schizophrenic has generally come to interpret the rejections in his past life as meaning that he is a creature who wants too much and, in fact, a creature who has no legitimate needs. Thus, he can accept gratification of his dependency needs, if at all, only if his needs are rendered acceptable to themselves by reason of his becoming physically ill or in a truly desperate emotional state. It is frequently found that a schizophrenic is more accessible to the gratification of his dependency needs when he is physically ill, or filled with despair, than at other times. In that way, th e presence of self-hatred, and guilt, one ingredient of the patient's overall anxiety about dependancy needs has to do with the fact that these needs of exemplifications connoted as having applied in their communication to him, that the states of feeling physical illness or despair are certain to lose all hope or confidence. Its voice gave to imply, that, I said to my to lie still, and be without hope, for hope would be hope for the wrong thing.

In essence, then, we can see that the patient has a deep-seated conviction that his dependency needs will not be gratified. Further, we see that this conviction is based not alone on the fortunate past expedience of repeated rejection, but also, the fact that his own defences, called forth concomitantly with the dependency desires, make it virtually certain that this dependency needs will not be met. (2) The dependency needs are anxiety-provoking not only because they involve desires to relate in an infantile or small-child fashion (by breast - or penis sucking, being cuddled, and as so forth) which is not generally acceptable behaviour among adults, but also, and probably what is more important, because they involve a feeling that the other person is frighteningly important, absolutely indispensable to the patient's survival.

This feeling as to the indispensable of importance of the other person derives from two main sources: (a) the regressive state of the schizophrenic's emotional life, which makes for his perceiving the other for being all-important to his survival, just as in infancy the mothering one is all-important to the survival of the infant, and (b) certain additional disabling features of his schizophrenic illness, which render him dependent in various special ways that are not quite comparable with the dependency characteristic of normal infancy or early childhood. Thereof, a number of points in reference to (b) are, first, we can perceive that a schizophrenic who is extremely confused, for example, is utterly dependent on or upon the therapist or, some other relevantly significant person to help him establish a bridge between his incomparable, incongruent, conflicting, conditions in which things are out of their normal or proper places or relationships. Such are the complete mental confusions that the authenticity of a corresponding to known facts is to discover or rediscover the real reason for which such things as having no illusions and facing reality squarely face-to-face, a realistic appraisal of his chances for advancing to the reasonable facts as we can see the factional advent for understanding the Absolutizing instinct to fancies of its reality.

Second, we can see also that the patient who is in transition between old, imposed values and not-yet-acquired values of his own, has only the relationship with his therapist to depend upon.

Third, are the concern and consideration that, in many instances, the schizophrenic appears to be what one might call a prisoner in th e present. He is so afraid both of change and of the memories that tend to be called forth by their presence in that he clings desperately to what is immediate. He is in this sense imprisoned in immediate experience, and looks to the therapist to free him so that he will be able to live in all his life, temporally speaking - present, past and future.

Forth, it might be surmised that an oral type of relatedness to the other person (with the all-importance of the other that this entails) is necessary for the schizophrenic to maintain, partly in order to facilitate his utilization of projection and introjection as defences against anxiety.

Anxiety, is the constructed foundation whose emotional state from which are grounded to the foundation structural called the 'edifice', that an emotional state in which people feel uneasy, apprehensive, or fearful. People usually experience anxiety about events they cannot control or predict, or about events that seem threatening or dangerous. For example, students taking an important test may feel anxious because they cannot predict the test questions or feel certain of a good grade. People often use the word's fear and anxiety to describe the same thing. Fear also describes a reaction to immediate danger characterized by a strong desire to escape the situation.

The physical symptoms of anxiety reflect a chronic "readiness" to deal with some future threat. These symptoms may include fidgeting, muscle tension, sleeping problems, and headaches. Higher levels of anxiety may produce such symptoms as rapid heartbeat, sweating, increased blood pressure, nausea, and dizziness.

Bychowski (1952) says, '"The separation between the primitive ego and the external world is closely connected with orality, both form the basis for the mechanism that we call projection," and would add, for introjection. That, Starcke (1921) made in earlier comments, that, "I might briefly allude to the possibility that in the repeated alternation between becoming one's own and not one's own, which occurs during lactation . . . the situation of being nursed plays a part in the origin of the mechanism of something that extends beyond its level or the normal outer surface in which serves to support projection."

The patient is under the vexation of his anxiety, meaning a concurrent as derived from the distributive contributions as anxieties afflictions and regretfully burdened or disquieted state of mind, a mind full of care and sadness, however, its grieving of sorrow is much to distress in the mind to feel or express deep distress, as grieving at the loss of so many lives, that such as insanity is alterably held within the madness for which the unbalanced compositions leave the distracted if agitation, with doubt or mental conflict distraught over the health if those perturbed in the state of being in serious trouble or in mental or physical anguish, as causing pain or suffering of a death for which of structures we are in trouble. This lamentable agitation of doubt or mental conflict, in the greater amounts of distress seem as afflicted by or manifesting unsoundness of mind or an inability to control one's rational processes. This account of an estranging disorder of mind that impairs one's capacity to function safely of a normal order in society. In that his dependency as leaning toward some destination, is that he either takes in harmful things, or to lose his identity.

The schizophrenic does not have the ability necessary to tolerate the frustration of his dependency needs, so that he can, once they emerge into awareness, subject them to mature discriminatory judgement before seeking their gratification. Instead, like a voraciously hungry infant, his tendency is to put into his mouth (either literally or figuratively) whatever is at hand, whether nutritious or with a potential of being harmful, this tendency is about th e basis of some of his anxiety concerning his dependency needs, for the fear that they will keep him blindly into receiving harmful medicines, bad advice, electro-shock treatment, lobotomy, and so forth. Schizophrenic patients have been known to beg, in effect, for all these, and many a patients have been known to beg, yet these patients have been 'successful' in his dependency desires. A need for self-punishment is, of course, an additional motivation in such instances.

A statement by Fenichel (1945) indicates that, "The pleasure principle, that is, the need for immediate discharge, is incompatible with correct judgement, which is based on considerable and post postponement of the reaction. The time and energy saved by this postponement are used in the function of sound and stable judgments. That in the early states the weak ego has not yet learned to postpone anything.

In the same symptomatic of one that finds that th e extent that the schizophrenic projects onto other persons his own needs too such and to devour, he feels threatened with being devoured by these other persons.

To elaborate now in a somewhat different direction upon this fear of loss of identity. Th e schizophrenic fears that his becoming dependent on another person will lead him into a state of conformity that other person's wishes and life value. A conformer is almost the last sort of person as the schizophrenic wishes to become, since his sense of individuality resides in his very eccentricities. He assumes that the therapist, for example, in the process, requiring him to give up his individuality for the kinds of parental future in his past had e been able to salvage his refuge used to pay the price.

It seems of our apparent need to give the impression of being without necessarily being so in fact that things are not always the way they seem, as things accompanied with action orient of doing whatever is apprehended as having actual, distinct and demonstrateable existence from which there is a place for each thing in the cosmological understanding idea in that something conveys to the mind a rational allotment of the far and near, such of the values and standards moderate the newly proposed to modify as to avoid an extreme or keep within bounds.

For what is to say, in that we need to realize, that the patient is not solely a broken, inert victim of the hostility of persons in his past life. His hebephrenic apathy or his catatonic immobility, for example, representation for one thing, an intense active a forwarded endeavour toward unconscious regressive goals, as Greenson (1949, 1953) has for his assistance to make clear in the boredom and apathy in neurotic patients. That the patient, is, in other words, no inert vehicle that needs to be energized by the therapist; rather, an abundance of energy is locked in him, pressing ceaselessly to be freed, and a hovering 'helpful' orientation on the part of the therapist would only get in the way. We must realize that the patient has made, and is continually making, a contribution to his own illness, however unwittingly, and however obscure the nature of this contribution may long remain.

More than often, it has been found that the histories of schizophrenic patients, whether male or female, describe the father for being by far, the warmer, the more accessible, of the responsive parents, and the patient as having always been very much attached to the father, whereas the mother was always a relatively cold, rejecting, remote figure, but for the repetitive correlative coefficient, that it was to be found that, disguised behind the child's idol or inseparable buddy, is a matter of the father's transference to the child's being a mother-figure that the father, in these instances, is an infantile individual who reacts both to his wife and to his child, as the mother-figure, and who, by striving to be both father and mother To the child, unconsciously seeks to intervene between mother and child, that in such a way as to have each of them to himself, in the considerations that suggest of a number of cases when both are in the transference-development with the patient and the selective prospect of the patient's generalization that limits or qualifies an agreement or other conditions that may contain or depend on a conditioning need for previsional advocates that include the condition that the transference phenomena would effectually raise the needed situational alliance.

The various forms of intense transference on the part of the schizophrenic individual tend forcibly to evoke complementary feeling-responses, comparably intense, in the therapist. Mabel Blake Cohen (1952) has made the extremely valuable observation, for psychoanalysis in general, that:

> . . . it seems that the patient applies great pressure to the analyst in a variety of nonverbal ways to behave like the significant adults in the patient's earlier life, it is not merely a matter of the patient's seeing the analyst as like his father, but of his actually manipulating the relationship in such away as to elicit the same kind of behaviour from the analyst. . . .

It is no too much to say that, in response to the schizophrenic patient's transference, the therapist not only behaves like the significant adults in the patient's childhood, but experiences most intimately, within himself, activated by the patient's transference the very kind of intense and deeply conflictual feelings that were at work, however repressed, in those adults in the past, as well as experiencing, through the mechanisms of projection and introjection in the relationship between himself and the patient, the comparably intense and conflictual emotion that formed the seed-bed of psychosis in the child himself, years ago.

The accountable explanation in the support for reason to posit for the necessarily deep feeling-involvement on the part of the therapist is inherent in the nature of early ego-formation. The healthy reworking of which is so central to the therapy of schizophrenia. Spitz (1959), in his monograph on the early development of the ego, repeatedly emphasizes that emotion plays a leading role in th e formation of what he described as the 'organizers of the psyche' (which he defines as 'emergent, dominant centres of integration') during the first eighteen months of life. H e says, for example, that:

> . . . the road that leads to this integration of isolated functions is built by the infant's object relations, by experiences of an effective nature. Accordingly, the indicator of the organizer of the psyche will be of an effective nature, it is an effective behaviour that clearly precedes development in all other sectors of the personality by several months.

The phases comprising the overall course of psychotherapy with chronically schizophrenic persons, is that of recent years it has become increasingly reassuring that it is possible to delineate such phases in the complex, individualistic and dynamic events of clinical work. One can be said, that, in this difficult effort at conceptualization, from Freud's delineation of the successive phases of libidinal development in healthy maturation, Erikson's (1956) portrayal of the process of identity formation as gradual unfolding of the personality through phase-specific psycho-social crises of evolution of the reality principle in healthy development - the typical conflicts, the sequence of danger situations, and the ways they are dealt with - can be traced in this process.

The successive phases of which are best characterised, the psychotherapy of chronic schizophrenia, are the 'out-of-contact phases, the phase of ambivalent symbiosis, the phase of pre-ambivalent symbiosis, the phase of resolution of the symbiosis, and the late phase, - that of establishment, and elaboration, of the newly won individuation through selective new identification and repudiation of outmoded identifications.

The sequence of these phases retraces, in reverse, the phases by which the schizophrenic illness was originally formed: The way of thinking, the aetiological roots of schizophrenia are formed when the mother-infant symbiosis fails to resolve into individuation of mother and infant - or, still more harmfully and fails even to become and at all firmly established - for accountable reasons of deep ambivalence of the part that intersects of the mother that hindered the integration and differentiation of the infant's and young of a child's ego, the child fails then to proceed through the normative development phases of symbiosis and subsequent individuation. Instead the core of his personality remains uniform, and ego-fragmentation and dedifferentiation becomes powerful, though deeply primitive and unconscious defences against the awareness of ambivalence in the object and in himself. Even in normal development, one becomes separate person only by becoming able to face, and accept ownership of, one's ambivalence with which he had to cope in his relationship with his mother was too great, and his ego-formation too greatly impeded, for him to be able to integrate his conflictual feeling-states into an individual identity.

Of these, the theoretical concept has been fostered by Mahler's (1956) paper on autistic and symbiotic infantile psychosis and by Balint's (1953, 1955) writing concerning phenomena of early ego-formation that he encountered in the psychoanalysis of neurotic patients. From a purely descriptive viewpoint, schizophrenia can be seen to consist essentially in an impairment of both 'integration' and 'differentiation' - which are but opposite faces of a unitary growth-process. From a psychodynamic point of view, seeming to points as to the basic oft all the reprehensible confusion, with which is a varying manifestations of schizophrenia.

Taking in, is the matter of integration; when we assess schizophrenia individual in terms of the classical structural areas of the personality - id, ego, and superego - we discover these to be poorly integrated with one another. The id is experienced by the ego as a Pandora's box, the contents of which will overwhelm one if it is opened. The ego is, as many writers have stated, severely split, sometimes into innumerable islands that are not linked discernibly with one another. And the superego has the nature of a cruel tyrant whose assaults upon the weak and unintegrated ego are, if anything, even more destructive to it than are the assessions of the threatening id-impulses, as Szalita-Pemow (1951), Hill (1955), and others. Moreover, the superego is, like the ego, even in itself not well integrated; its utterances contain the most glaring inconsistencies from one moment to the next. Jacobson (1954) has shown that there is actually as dissolution of the superego, as an integrated destruction - a regressive transformation back into the threatening parental images whose conglomeration originally formed it.

Differentiation is a process that is essential to integration, and vice versa. For personality structure-functions or psychic contents to become integrated, they must first have emerged as partially differentiated or separate from one another, and differentiation in turn can emerge only out of a foundation of more or less integrated functions or contents. The intertwining mesh upon which is interwoven in the growth precesses of integration and differentiation, such that the impairment of both likewise interlocking. But in the schizophrenic these two processes tend to be out of step with one another, so that at one moment a patient's more urgent need may be for increased integration, whereas at another he may more urgently need increased differentiation. And these are some patients who show for months end, a more urgent need in one of these areas, before the alternate growth-phase on the scene, that type is a modicum of validity in speaking and of two different 'types' of schizophrenic patients.

One comes to realize, upon reasons of how premature have been one's effort to find out what feelings the patient is experiencing or what thoughts he is having; one comes to realize that much of the time he has neither feelings nor thoughts differentiated as such and communicable to us.

Such differentiations as the patient posses of an inclining inclination that tend to break down when intense emotion enters his awareness. A paranoid man, for example, may find that when his hatred toward another person reaches a certain degree of intensity, he is flooded with anxiety because he no longer knows whether he hates, or instead 'really loves' the other individual. This is not based, on any line or its course, whereupon the primary mechanism that Freud (1911) outlined in his classical description of the nature of paranoid delusions of persecution, a description in which repressed homosexual love played the central role. The central difficulty is rather than the ego is too poorly differentiated to maintain its structure in the face of such powerful effects, and the patient becomes flooded with what can only be described as 'undifferentiated passion', precisely as one finds an infant to be overwhelmed at times with effects that the observer cannot be specifically identified as any a kind of emotion.

As for the feelings with which the therapist himself experiences in working within the variations in the differentiated patient, we find, again, a persistent threat of the therapist's sense of identity. But, whereas in the unitary integration complex manifestations of such of a schizophrenic's sense of identity. But as in the first instance that the threat was felt predominantly as a disturbance of one's personal integration, it seems possible as a weakening of one's sense of differentiation. In this instance, the 'therapeutic symbiosis' which implicates the necessary developments that it tends to occur earlier for which of the patient's predominant mode of relatedness with other persons, at the developmental level at which we find him at the very beginning of our work, is a symbiotic one. Such descriptions, least of mention, agree with the necessary developments, in that it tends to occur for the patient 's predominant mode of relatedness with other persons, the symbiotic relatedness, with its subjective absence of ego-boundaries, involves not only special gratification, but anxiety-provoking disturbances on one's sense of personal identity.

The comparatively rapid development of symbiotic relatedness is facilitated by the patient's characteristically nonverbal, and physically more or less immobile, functioning during the therapeutic sessions. In response, the therapist's own behaviour becomes more and more similar, is that each participant is now offering to the other, saying that over the hours of counselling, a silent, impassive screen that facilitates abundant mutual projecting and introjecting. Thus a symbiotic state is likely to be reached earlier than in one's work with the typically much more verbal type of the patient when described as the uncomplaining patient that example, in that of the patient and therapist's additionally abundant linguistic comprehension tend persistently to stress the ego-boundaries separating to persons from one and of the other.

The overall applicability for which is generally the predominantly mutually exclusive-differentiated distinction of the patient, though, unlike in kind or character the therapist's sense of identity as a complexly differentiated individual entity becomes further eroded, or undermined, as he finds the patient persistently operating on the unwavering conviction, that the hours of counselling are but an undifferentiated aspect of the whole vague mass of the institution, even in Psychodynamical terms, is in actuality the patient's projection of his own poorly differentiated hostility, through which the patient's tenaciously held view, is the way the world around him really is.

Further, since the patient typically verbalizes little but a few maddening monotonous stereotypes, the therapist tends to feel, over the course of time, with so little of his own intellectual content being explicitly tapped in the relationship, that his richness of intellect is progressively rusting away - becoming less differentiated, more stereotyped and rudimentary. Moreover, the patient presents but one of two emotional wavelengths to which the therapist can himself tune in, rather than a rich spectrum of emotion that calls into response a similarly wide range of feelings from the therapist himself. Thus not only the therapist's intellectual resources, but his emotional capacities too, becomes subjectively narrowed down and impoverished, as he finds that, over the sessions of counselling, his patient in him, has neither any wide range of ideas, nor any emotions with the or exception of any other condition than that, however, excluding that something that seriously hampers action or progress, e.g., lack of education is an obstacle to advancement.

The feeling experience on his part, anxiety-provoking and discouraging though he finds it, is a necessary therapeutic development. It is for him thus to experience at first hand something of the patient's own lack of differentiation; for, as in the therapy with the non-integrated patient, as, once, again, the healing process occurs external to the patient, as it was, at an intrapsychic level in the therapist, before it becomes established in the patient himself. That is, the therapist's coming to view the patient, his relationship with the patient, and himself in this relationship, all for being largely the act in opposition to-differentiated development that sets the stage for the patient's gradually increasing differentiation. Now the therapist comes to sense, time and again, newly emerging tendrils of differentiation in the patient, before the latter are themselves and conscious of them. In responding to these with spontaneity as they show themselves, again, that in the therapist, helps the patient to become aware-theat they are a part of him.

To analyst and analytic student alike, the term 'transference psychosis' usually connotes a dramatic but dreaded development in which an analysand, who at the beginning of the analysis was overtly sane but who had in actuality a borderline ego-structure, becomes overtly psychotic, that the course of the evolving transference relationship. We generally blame the analyst for such as development and prefer not to think any more about such matters, because of our own personal fear that we, like the poor misbegotten analysand, might become, or narrowly avoid becoming, psychotic in our own analysis. By contrast, in working with the chronically schizophrenic patient, we are confronted with a person whose transference to us is no harder to identify partly for the very reason that his whole daily life consists in incoherent psychotic transference reactions, for which is to whatever, to everyone about him, including the analyst in the treatment session. Little's comment (1960) that the delusional state 'remains unconscious' until it is uncovered in the analysts' holds true only in the former instance, in the borderline schizophrenic patient; there, it is the fact that the transference is delusional which is the relative covert, hard-to-discern aspect of the situation, in chronic schizophrenia, by contrast, nearly everything is delusional, and the difficult task to foster the emergence of a coherent transference meaning in the delusional symptomatology. In other words, the difficult thing in the work with the chronically schizophrenic patient is to discover the 'transference reality' in his delusional experience.

The difficultly of discerning the transference aspect of one's relationship with the patient can be traced to his having regressed to a state of ego functioning which is marked by severe impairment in his capacity either to differentiate among, or to integrate, his experiences. He is so incompletely differentiated in his ego functioning that he tends to feel, not that the therapist reminds him of, or is like, his mother or that of his father (or whomever, from his early life) but rather his functioning toward the therapist is couched in the unscrutinised assumption that the therapist is the mother or father. When, for example, in trying to bring to the attention of a paranoid schizophrenic women how much like she seemed to find the persons in her childhood on the one hand, and the person about her in the institution, including me, on the other, she dismissed this with an impatient retort, "That's what I've been trying to tell you, What difference does it make? For years subsequently in our work together, all the figures in her experience were composite figures, without any clear subjective distinction between past and present experiences, figures from the institutional scene peopled her memories of her past, and figures from what has become known to be her past was experienced by her as blended with the persons she saw about her in current life.

Transference situations in which the psychosis is manifested at a phase in therapy in which the deeply chronically confused patient, who in childhood had been accustomed to a parent's during his thinking for him, is ambivalently (a) trying to perpetuate a symbiotic relationship wherein the therapist to a high degree does the patient's thinking for him, and (b) expressing, by what the therapist feels to be sadistic and castrative and nullifying or undoing the therapist's effort to be helpful, a determination to be a separately thinking, and otherwise separately functioning, individual

Difficult though it is to discern the nature and progressive evolution of the patient's transference to the therapist, it is even more difficult to conceptualize that which is 'new' which the therapist brings into the relationship, and which, as J. M. Rioch (1943) has emphasized, is crucial to the patient's recovery. Rioch is quite right in saying that, "Whether intentionally or not, whether conscious of it or not, the analyst does express, day in and day out, subtle or overt evidences of his own personality in relationship to the patient."

The conjectural considerations for which inadequate evidences in the understanding of questionable intent is that there is a companion evolution of reality relatedness between patient and therapist, concomitant with such a transference evolution as having had the impression that it is only when the reality relatedness between patient and therapist has reached, finally and after many 'real life' vicissitudes between them, a depth of intense fondness that there now emerges, in the form of a transference development, a comparably intense and long-repressed fondness for the mother.

Presumably, a point that Freud (1922) concerning projection also holds true for transference, he stated that projection occurs no 'into the sky, so to speak, where there is nothing of the sort already', but rather the persons who in reality posses an attitude qualitatively like that which the projecting person is attributing to them. So it is with transference, we may presume that when a patient comes to react to us as a loved and loving mother, this phrase - as well as other phrases - of the transference is founded upon our having come to feel, in reality, thus toward him. M. B. Cohen (1952) stresses the importance of the therapist's inevitable feeling response to the patient's transference, and, if only to suggest, that an equally healthy source of the therapist's feeling participation be the evolving reality relatedness that pursues its own course, related to and parallelling, but not fully embraced by, the evolving transference relatedness over the years of person's working together. What is more, is the countertransference that has already been written, but as to indicate, there is a great need for us to become clear about the sequence that the recovery process in the schizophrenic adult, very roughly analogous to the growth process in normal infancy, childhood, and adolescence, tends innately to follow. When we have become clearer and surer about this, and particularly about the validity-relatedness element necessary to it, in that the frequently - though by no means always - various manifestations of feeling regarded as unwanted countertransference will be seen to be inevitable, and utterly essential, components of the recovery process.

Further, the opening view of the personality for being divisible into the areas, id, ego, and superego, tends to shield us from the anxiety-fostering realization that in psychoanalytic change is not merely quantitative and partial - where id was, there will ego be - in Freud's dictum - but qualitative and all-persuasive. That is, that in such passages as the following. Freud gives a picture of personality-structure, and of maturation, which leaves the inaccurate but comforting impression that at least a part of us - namely, as part of the id - is free from change. In his paper entitled "Thoughts for the Times on War and Death" in 1915, he said, that, . . . 'the evolution of the mind shows a peculiarity that is present in no other process of development. When a village grows into a town, a child into a man, the village and the child become submerged in the town and the man, . . . it is otherwise with the development of the mind . . . the primitive stages [of mental development] can always be reestablished, the primitive mind is, in the fullest meaning of the word, imperishable' (Freud, 1915).

In "Introductory Lectures on Psycho-Analysis," also saying that in psychoanalytic treatment,. . . .By means of the work of interpretation, which transforms what is unconscious into what is conscious, the ego is enlarged at the cost of this unconscious . . . (Freud, 1915-17) In "The Ego and the Id" he said that . . . the ego is that part of the id that has been modified by the direct influence of the external world . . . the pleasure-principle . . . reigns unrestricted by the id . . . the ego represents what may be called reason and common sense, in contrast to the id, which contains the passions (Freud, 1923).

The state of developmental sciences, and about our own individual the individual therapeutic skills, should not cause us to understate the all-embracing extent of human personality-growth in normal maturation at least a few psychoanalysis. It is believed that all encountered, and, at lest a few fortunate instances that have made us wonder whether maturation really leaves any area of the untouched personality, leaves any steel-bound core within which the pleasure principle reigns immutably, or whether, instead, we have seen such a genuine metamorphosis, from an erstwhile hateful and self-seeking orientation to a loving and giving orientation, quite as wonderful and thoroughgoing the metamorphosis of the tadpole into the frog thoroughgoing as the metamorphosis of the tadpole into the frog or that of the caterpillar into the butterfly.

Freud himself, in his emphasis upon the 'negative therapeutic reaction' (1923), the repetition compulsion, and the resistance to analytic insight that he discovered in his work with neurotic patients, has shown the importance, in the neurotic individual, of anxiety concerning change, and him agrees with Jung's statement that 'a peculiar psychic inertia' hostile to change and progress, is the fundamental condition of neurosis (Freud, 1915). This is, as we know, even more true of psychosis - so much as that only in very recent decades have psychotic patients achieved full recovery though modified psychoanalytic therapy. Finding it instructive to explore in detail the psychodynamics of schizophrenia in terms of the anxiety concerning change which one encounters, in a particular, an intense degree, at work in these patients, and especially the work involving the depths within the 'self', the difficulty is, of course, in treating them. What the therapy of schizophrenia can teach us of the human being's standing concerning change, can broaden and deepen our understanding of the non-psychotic individual also.

This development can occur only after successive resolution of increasingly ancient personality-warp in the patient, and the establishment thereby, of a hard-won mutual trust and security. In this atmosphere the therapist relationship makes contact with the healthy ingredients of the patient's symbiotic relationship with his mother, thus laying the foundation for subsequent new growth as a separate and healthy individual.

In such fashion the patient develops importance not merely as a separate object, but to a degree as a symbiotic partner, for the therapist as well as for other people, who participate with which the therapist himself, as well as such of the staff members, we hear from fellow-therapists and ward-personal of how 'stunned' or even 'shocked' them were at seeing dramatic improvements in a long-ill patient. Characteristically, too, the therapist notices only very belatedly various long-standing symptoms have dropped out of the patient's behaviour. On looking back through his records, for example, prior to a staff-presentation, he finds to his surprise that a delusion, once long-familiar to him, has not been evidenced by the patient for several months. Thus, his feelings of personal loss are mitigated. Even so, that even among the most technically capable of therapists, is the initial reaction with dismay and discouragement to a patients, is the initial reacting with express verbally the depths of his despair, loneliness, confusion, infantile need, and so fort, typically, the therapist only belatedly recognizes the forward move this development constitutes. His initial response is traceable to the unconscious loss that this development inflicts upon him - the loss of the long-familiar and inevitable therefore cherished (unconsciously cherished) relatedness that therefor he had shared with the patient.

The patient, particularly in the symbiotic phrase of the therapy but in preceding and succeeding phase as well, is notably intolerant of sudden and marked changes in the therapeutic relationship - that is, of suddenly seeing himself, or feeling that his therapist sees him, through new eyes. He rarely gives the therapist to feel that the latter have made an importantly revealing interpretation, and when he of himself conveys a highly illuminating nugget of historical information to his therapist, he does so casually, often feeling sure that he has already mentioned this before. He tends to experience important increments of de-repressed material not as earthshattering revelations in his development, yet the forward moves in therapy, on the patient's part occur each time only after a recrudescence in his symptoms. It is as though he was to find reassurance of his personal identity, for being really the same hopeless person he has long felt himself to be, before he can venture into a bit of new and more hopeful identity.

There is a necessary phase of symbiosis between patient and doctor in the transference evolution followed by the recovering schizophrenic patient, a phase in which the ego boundaries between himself and the therapist are mutually relinquished to a large degree. This development can occur only after successive resolutions of increasingly ancient personality-wrap in the patient, and the establishment, thereby, of a hard-won in the patient, and his identity.

The following considerations, to be sure, the patient, in this reality and that this mutuality of a comparative participation is essentially inclined of a better understanding and a successful therapeutic outcome: Freud (1911) made the comment that:

'We have long observed that every neurosis has as its result, and probably therefore its purpose, a forcing of the patient out of real life, an alienating of him from reality . . . neurotics turn away from reality because they find it unbearable - either the whole or parts of it. The most extreme type of this 'turning away from', is a resulting amount on which certain cases of hallucinatory psychosis that seek to deny the particular event that occasioned of the outbreak of their inanity. But in fact every neurosis does the same with some fragment of reality' . . .

Bion, in his paper in 1957 concerning the differentiation, in that a theory of probability simulates, that any schizophrenic patient, between what he calls the psychotic personality and the non-psychotic personality, concludes the presentation of his theoretical formulations with:

> . . . Further, I consider that this holds true for the severe neurotic, in those who believe there is a psychotic personality concealed by neurosis as the neurotic personality is screened by psychosis in the psychotic, that has to be laid bare and dealt with.

Bion conveys in his paper entitled "Language d the Schizophrenic" (1955) a warning of the patient's tendency to project his own sanity upon the analyst and of the massive regression that follows if this is condoned by the analyst. He says:

> . . . I have no doubt whatever that the analyst should always insist, by the way in which he conducts the case, that he is addressing himself to a sane person and is entitled to expect some sane reception . . .,

There is wide spread agreement that it is inherent in therapy that the therapist functions as an auxiliary ego so the patient in the patent's struggle with inner conflicts, until such time as to make this greater strength part of his own ego. To the extent that the schizophrenic patient does not posses an observing ego of sufficient strength to permit the therapist usefully to make transference interpretations, to that degree the therapist must be able to endure - and, eventually, to enjoy - various part-object transference characteristics, until such time as the patient, through increasing ego-integration, becomes of the therapist. Another way of saying this is that the patient develops ego-strength. In the face of his own id impulses and pathogenic superego retaliations, in that, if identification with the therapist who can endure, and integrate into his own larger self, the kind of subjectively nonhuman part-object relatedness that the patient fosters in and needs from him.

Similarly, because the therapist has seen the patient to be, earlier in the therapy, such a deeply fragmented person, he tends to retain a lingering impression of the fragility, an impression that may interfere with his going along at the faster pace that the patient, now a very different and far stronger person, is capable of setting. But even this memory-image of the fragile patient, carried with the therapist, has a natural function in the course of the psychotherapy, for it is only very late in the work that the patient himself is able to realize how very ill, how very fragile, he once was, until he becomes strong enough to integrate his realization into his self-image, the therapist has to be the bearer of this piece of the patient's identity. This process is analogous to the well-known phenomenon in which each major forward stride in the patient's therapeutic growth is accompanied, or presaged, by the therapist's suddenly seeing in the patient a new and healthier person, there, too, the impact of the development falls primarily, for a time, upon the therapist rather than the patient. The patient himself, because his sense of identity is still, during the earlier therapeutic phases to which is easily overwhelming, and relatively tenuous. By the realization of the extent to which he is now changed, even though this change is, in our view, a most beneficial and welcoming one.

More often than not, that the histories of schizophrenic patients, whether male or female, describe the father for being by far the warmer, and more accessible of the two parents, the father, whereas the mother was always relatively cold, rejecting, remote figure. However, that the disguise behind the child's idol inseparable 'buddy' is a matter of the father's transference to the child for being a mother-figure upon whom he, the father makes insatiable demands. It seems that the father, in these instances, is an infantile individual, who reacts both to his wife and to his child's unconscious ly seeks to intervene between mother and child in such a way as to have each of them to himself. The seeming evidence of this by now, in a considerable number of cases, both in the transference-development and interviews with the parents.

The point being made, is that the mother and child allow this interposition by the father to happen, because of their anxiety about their fondness for being a mother-figure who exasperatingly allows as an infantile 'buddy', a kind of father to keep intervening, placing impossible demands for mothering upon the patient; finally comes a phase of th e patient's responding to the therapist as a mother with whom he can share unashamedly fond relatedness, no longer burdened by the father's scornfully and demandingly coming between them.

So it is with transference, we may presume that when a patient comes to react to us as a love and loving mother, this phase - as well as other phases - of the transference is founded upon our having come to feel, in reality, as, M. B. Cohen (1952) stresses the importance of the therapist 's inevitable feeling response to the patient's transference, only to suggest, that of the therapist's feeling participation is the evolving reality relatedness that pursue its own course, related to and parallelling, but not fully embraced by, the evolving transcendence relatedness over which time to occur is, namely introduced as countertransference, nonetheless, in the realm, as situated as one crucial phase of the work - a symbiotic kind of mutual dependency, Which he mutually comes to feel toward the patient, his acceptance regarding the commonality, from which are in and of the same thing that events that occurring events are simultaneous, where in the caring which amount at times to an adoration, and his being able to acknowledge the patient's contribution - inevitable, in successful therapy - to his own personal integration. It must be noted, that the schizophrenic patient responds with great regularity to the therapist's material warmth for being a sure indication that the latter are a homosexual or a lesbian. The younger therapist needs to become quite clear that this is, in actuality, a formidable resistance in the patient again the very kind of loving mother-infant relatedness that offers the patient his only avenue of salvation from his illness. Not to say, that the therapist should depreciate the degree of anxiety, referable to the deep ambivalence of the patient's early relationship with his mother, which is contained within this resistance, perhaps, that the therapist's deep-seated doubts as to his own sexual identity - and what person is totally free of such doubt? - should not make him lose of the fact that the patient's contempt (or revulsion, or what not) is basically a resistance against going ahead and picking up the threads of the loving infant-mother relatedness that were long ago severed.

Upon comment, the patient has in reference to a different person, and is often couched in terms of a different temporal era, that is intended by the preconscious or unconscious impulse striving for expression. The circumstance of the patient's having regressed to a more or less early level of ego-functioning is explanatory of many of the idiosyncrasies of schizophrenic communication. The clinical picture is complicated, in most instances, by the fact that the level of regression varies unceasingly, at times from one moment to the next, and there are even instances where the patient is functioning on more than one developmental level simultaneously.

The fact of the patient's regressed, mode of psychological functioning helps to account for the 'concretization', or contrariwise the seeming oversymbolization, of his communications; these phenomena represent his having regressed, in his thinking (and overall subjective experiencing), to a developmental level comparable with that in the young child who has not yet become able to differentiate between concrete and metaphorical (or similar forms of highly symbolic) thinking.

Similarly, the patient may tittle-tattle in a way that gives us to know that the content of his speech is relatively unimportant to him at the moment he is immersed in the pleasure of saying the words and hearing the sound of them, much like the young child who has not yet learned to talk but loves to babble and to hear the sound of his babbling. A nonverbal patient may usefully be regarded as having regressed even further, to the pre-verbal era of infancy or very early childhood.

The strikingly intense ambivalence, another fundamental aspect of the schizophrenic individual's psychodynamics, contributions to a number of different typical kinds of schizophrenic communications. (1) The indirect communication, (2) Self-contradictory verbal and nonverbal communications, and (3) Verbal communications in which there is a split between content and vocal feeling-tone.

In assessing the meaning of such communications, one soon learns to brush aside the content and attend to the feeling-tone - o r, in still, more complex instances, tones - in which the words are said.

Incidently, a patient sometimes evidences a quite accurate grasp of the true import of such communications that they come from the therapist. At the end of each of the maddening points or the enduring intervals of times of silence. After this had happened several times dawning upon that which he was very accurately expressing the covert message contained in the parting comment to him, as to the (4) No-verbal expression of a feeling contrarily enacted to the one being verbalized? And (5) Expression of contradictory feeling at an entirely nonverbal level.

The archaically harsh, forbidding superego of the patient is another basic factor that helps to account for his heavily disguised and often fragmentary communications.

I can only surmise that there is a companion evolution of reality relatedness between parent and the therapist, concomitant with such a transference evolution, it is only when the really possible relatedness enters between patient and the therapists have reached, of a final and aftermath, containing a depthful intensity that there is now emerging, in the form of a transference development a comparable intense and long-represented direction in the fondness for the mother. However, this brings us back to other topics comprising the overall course of psychotherapy as a chronically schizophrenic person, a person preceding in the complex individuality extended to dynamical events of clinical work.

The quality of the transference resistances is to a greater extent as deepened by the quantity of other resistances. Resistances have the tendency to accumulate wherever there is a favourable opportunity to withstand the analysis. In most cases the transference offers the best opportunity, for example, we see the resistance coming from the conscious repetition, from the unconscious feeling of guilt and from the resistance by repression, takes part of building up the transference resistance. Freud speaks of the transference of resistance into a negative, hostile transference: It is on account of this transformation that the dissolution that transference resistances so often because the chief task of the therapeutics work. In the case of our patient the analysis finally showed the development of anxiety in the transference to b e castration anxiety that had arisen from infantile masturbation with accompanying incestuous wishes toward the mother and the hared and castration wishes toward the father. In the analysis, if the resistance resulting factors in the development of anxiety in the analysis. If the resistance result from this anxiety is analysis the addition of other resistances, then the final resistance in the analysis cannot be considered as an index to the amount of the genuine infantile anxiety for the anxiety resulting from infantile masturbation, on account of the genuine infantile anxiety: For the anxiety resulting from infantile masturbation on account of its anxiety resulting from infantile masturbation, on account of its particular capacity for being used as a resistance in analysis, becomes the nucleus of crystallisation or the basis for the addition of all the other resistances. In a footnote to his paper "The Dynamics of th Transference," this idea was alluded to by Freud, that, 'Over and over again, when one draws near to a pathogenic complex, that part of it that is first thrust forward into consciousness will be some aspect of it that can be transferred, having been so, it will then be defended with the utmost obstinacy by the patient'. The footnote says: 'From which however one need not infer in general any very particular pathogenic importance in the point selected for resistance by transference. In warfare, when a bitter fight is raging over the possession of some little chapel or a single farmhouse, we do not necessarily assume that the church is a national monument, or that the barns contain the military funds. Their value may be merely tactical; in the next onslaught they will very likely be of no importance'.

The dissolution of the transference resistance means then not only the dissolution of the resistance resulting from the genuine infantile castration anxiety but a liberation of the supporting resistance that often can only later be separately dissolved, because during the phase of the violent acting-out in the transference these resistances are not accessible to interpretation and dissolution.

For what is said about the psychology of metaphor is analogous to the transformational aspects of developed transferences and steadfast interpretations that both facilitate and organize them as transferences. Allowing that these transferences and 'remembered' experiences come into existence over a period of time, nothing that is identical with them has ever before been enacted, and nothing identical with them will ever be enacted again. They are creations that may be fully achieved only under specific analytic conditions. For example, at the time of his childhood scene with his father, the young man of the clinical example, could not have had the specific experience as recounted. Strictly speaking, he was not reliving that moment. As a bo y, he must have experienced some of the main precursors and constituents of his present mode of experience, but he could not have done so in the present articulated and integrated manner. That present manner was the basis of his anguished outcry. Words like re-creating, but re-experiencing and reliving simply do not do justice to the phenomena. In the way he was doing it, he was living that moment for the first time.

By making this claim, there is no constricting some of our well-established ideas about interpretation and insight, for example, disputing point that insight refers to more than the recovery of lost memories, and takes in, as well, a new grasp of the significance and interrelations of events one has always remembered. The latter connections that the analysand will say, as Freud pointed out, "As a matter of fact I've always known it, only I've never thought of" (1914). In fact, it is to develop that points further to say that the young child simply does not have the means of fully defining what we later regard as its own life experiences. It takes an adult to do that, especially with the help of an analyst. It was, after all, Freud's analysis that made it possible to define infantile psychosexuality. In this respect, but without disrespect, child analysis retains a quality of applied psychoanalysis. The adult definition of infantile psychosexuality is 'artificial' in the same way that the interpreting transference neurosis is: Both are ways of describing as true something that was not truer in quite that way as, at the time of its greatest development significance. This apparent paradox about 'remembering' as a form of creating goes the distance, that saying, what it is this distinctive about psychoanalytic renditions that implicate the interpretation steadfastly and perspicaciously making transference interpretation, the analyst helps constitute new modes of experience and new experiences. This newness characterizes the experience of analytic transference in them. Unlike extra-analytic transference, they can no longer be sheerly repetitive or merely new editions. Instead, they become repetitively new editions understood as such because defined as such by the simplification and steadfast transference interpretation, instead of responding to the analysand in kind, Which would actualize the repetition, the analyst makes an interpretation. This interpretation does not necessarily or regularly match something the analysand does often seem to have always represented often, but he does not seem to have done so at all. To think otherwise about this would, in effect, to claim that, unconsciously, every analysand is Freud or a fully insightful Freudian analyst. And that claim is totally absurd.

It would be closer to the truth to say this: Unconsciously, the analysand already knows or has experienced fragmentary, amorphous, uncoordinated constituents of many of the transference interpretations. Alternatively, one may say that, implicitly, the analysand has been insisting on some as yet unspecified certainties and, in keeping with this, following some set of as yet unspecified rules in his actions, these the transference interpretations now organize explicitly. Each transference interpretation thus refers to many things that have already been defined by the analysand, and it does so in a way that transforms them. That's why one may call it interpretation. Otherwise, it would be mere repeating or sterile paraphrasing. Interpretation is a creative redescription that implicitly has the structure of a simile. It says, "This is like it," Each interpretation does, therefore, add new actions to the life the analysand has already lived.

Technically, redescription in the terms of transference-repetition is necessary. This is so because, up to the time of interpretation and working through, the analysand has been, in one sensory faculty that of enabling in another sense, unconsciously and desperately unwilling, to conduct his life differently, in and of them, the repetitions cannot after the symptoms, the subjective distress, the wasting of one's possibilities rather they can only perpetuate a static situation by repeatedly confirming its necessity. They prove once again, the unconsciously maintained damaging certainties. But once they get to be viewed as historically grounded actions and subjectively defined situations. As they do upon being interpreted and worked through, they appear as having always been, in crucial respects, inventions of the analysand's making and, so, as his responsibility. In being seen as versions one' past life, they may be changed in significant and beneficial ways. Less of all, are they presented as purely inevitable happenings, as a fixed fate or as the well-established way of the world. However, we encounter a second paradox that goes to the heart of psychoanalysis interpretation, namely, that responsible, insightful change is possible through psychoanalysis just because, as a child the analysand mistakenly assumes and then denied responsibility for much that he encountered in the early formative environment and during maturation.

One major point remains to be made about the logic of viewing transference interpretation as simplifying yet innovative redescription. This point is that the interpretations bring about a coordination of the terms in which to state both the analysand's current problems and their life-historical background. The analysand's symptoms and distress are described as actions and modes of action, with due regard for the principle of multiple function or multiple meaning: In coordination with that description, the decisive developmental situation and conflicts are stated as actions and modes of action. Continuity is established between the childhood constructions of relationships and the self and the present constructions of these interpretations of transference show who both are part of the same set of practices, that is, how they follow the same set of rules. Past and present are coordinated to show continuity rather than arranged in a definite sequence.

In the same way, the form of analytic behaviour and the content of association are given co-ordinated descriptions, say, for being defiant, devouring, or reparative. Or, in the case of depression, the depressive symptoms, the depressive analytic transference, the themes of present and past loss, destructiveness and helplessness, all will be redescribed under the aspect of one continuously developing self-presentation. And this coordination will be worked out in that hermeneutically circular fashion in which the analyst defines both th facts to be explained and the explanations to be applied to these facts. In the end, as is well known, both the paramount issues of the analysis and the leading explanatory account of them are likely to be significantly different from the provisional versions of them used at the beginning of the analysis.

The increasing influence of the modernist version of transference and its interpretation represents an adaptation to several long-term philosophical, scientific, and cultural shifts we can now recognize. This changing view of transference is also the most visible emblem of the deep changes in psychoanalytic theory that are now quietly taking place, and of their theoretical pluralism that is so prevalent today (Cooper, 1985).

One of these long-term changes in the climate in which psychoanalysis dwells results from a large philosophical debate concerning the nature of history, veridicality, and narrative. Kermode (1985) has written of the change during this century in our modes of understanding and interpreting the past and the present, "Once upon a time it seemed obvious that you could best understand how things are by asking how they got to be that way. Now attention [is] directed to how things are in their immediate plexuities. There is a switch to use the linguistic expressions, from the diachronic to the synchronic view. Diachrony, roughly speaking, studies things in their synchrony to be as they are, synchrony concerns itself with things as they are and ignores the question, how they got that way. This distinction, put forth by de Sasussure (1915), has achieved philosophical dominance today and is the clear source of the hermeneutic view so prevalent in psychoanalysis, proposed by Ricoeur (1970). From here, it is a short distance to Schafer (1981), and Gill (1982), or Spence (1982) who in varying ways adopt the synchronic view. In this view, the analytic task is interpretation, with the patient, of the events of the analytic situation - usually broadly labelled transference - with a construction rather than a reconstruction of the past. In effect, while there is a past of 'there and then' it is knowable only through the filter of the present, of 'here and now'. There is no other past than the one as we construct, and there is no way of understanding the past but through its relation to the present.

Psychoanalysis, like history but unlike fiction, does have anchoring points, for history's anchoring points are the evidences that events really did occur, There was a Roman empire, it did have dates, actual persons lived and died. These 'facts' place a limitation for the narratives an interpretations that may seriously be entertained. Psychoanalysis is anchored in its scientific developmental psychology and in the biology of attachment and affects. Biology confers regularities and limits on possible histories, and our constructions of the past must accord with this scientific knowledge. Constructions of childhood that are incompatible with what we know of developmental possibilities may open our eye's to new concepts of development, but more likely they alert us to maimed childhoods that have led our patients to usual narrative constructions in the effort to maintain self-esteem and internal coherence. A second, far less secure, anchorage is the enormous amount of convergent data that accumulate during the course of an analysis, which are likely to give the analyst the impression that he is reconstructing rather than constructing the figures and the circumstances of his patient's past. While a diachronic view may no longer suffice, it may also not be fully dispensable if our patient's histories are to maintain psychoanalytic coherence, rooted in bodily experience, and the loving, hating and terrifying affects accompanying the fantastic world of infantile psychic reality. Not all analysts are yet as ready as Spence, for example, to give up all claim to the truth value explanatory power of the understanding of the past, even if it is limited to knowing past constructions of the past. Nevertheless, the change in philosophical outlook during our century is profound and contributes to our changing view of the analytic process is exemplified in the transference and its interpretation.

Approaching the same issue from an entirely different vantage point, Emde (1981) speaking for the 'baby-watchers' and discussing changing models of infancy and early development, details a second source of the major change of climate to which he writes, The models suggest that what we reconstruct, and what may be extraordinarily helpful to the patient in making a biography, may never have happened. The human being, infant child, is understood to be fundamentally active in constructing his experience. The realm of fact is distinct from fancy, as something that has actual existence, of such stubborn facts that cannot be confused, however, appearing for considerations is other that seems the care, yet are apparently evident by the actualization of a demonstrable existence. Of any genuine corresponding to know facts are discoverable facts, as true and undeniable. For Reality either is not given or is it necessarily registered in any unmodified form. Discovering the real, as having no illusions and to face reality squarely. Perhaps it makes sense for the psychoanalysis to place renewed emphasis on recent and current experiences - first, as a context for interpreting early experience - as a context for interpreting the potential amelioration, . . . Psychoanalysts are specialists in dealing with the intrapsychic world not only particular with the dynamic unconscious, but we need to pay attention not only to the intrapsychic realm. Conflicting-laden and conflict-free, but also to the interpersonal realm. He concludes, . . . we have probably placed far to much an emphasis on early experience itself as opposed to the process by which it is modified or made use of by subsequent experience.

This view of psychic developments, discarding the timeless unconscious and so powerful at odds with the views that were held by psychoanalysts during the time when most of our ideas of transference interpretation were formed, clearly suggests the modernist model of transference interpretation.

A change in the cultural environment of psychoanalysis provides a third source for the changing model of transference interpretation. Valenstein describes oscillations in psychoanalytic outlook between an emphasis on cognition at one end, and on affect at the other. One might see these as differences between old-fashioned scientific and romantic world views. Surely the period of ego psychology, perhaps reflected in the English translation of Freud, and certainly reflected in the effect to insist on the energetic libidinal as a point of view, represented in the attempt to see psychoanalysis as Freud usually did, as an objective science in the nineteenth century style, with hypotheses created out of naïve observations. It is accorded with that view to see the transference as an objective reflection of history. We are currently in one of our more romantic periods. It is consonant with that view to see transference as an activity - stormy, romantic, active, affective - a kind of adventure from which the two individuals emerge changed and renewed. In this romantic view, interpretations of the transference are intended to remove obstacles interfering with the heightening and intimacy of the experience, with the implication that self-knowledge and change will result from their encounter. A romantic figure, the patient and analyst set forth on a quest into the unknown, and whether or not one of them returns with a Holy Grail, they return with many new stories to tell and a new life experience - the analysis. Gardner's (1983) book, 'Self Inquiry' epitomizes this romantic view of analyst and patient as a poet-pair engaged in mutual self-inquiry. It is clear that many analysis would rather be artistic than scientist. By contrast, the older, cognitive view of the transference is of an intellectual journey, emotionally loaded of course, but basically a trip back in history, seeking truth and insight.

Finally, our newer ideas of transference interpretation come from the rereading and reinterpretations of Freud that necessarily accompany the changes in outlook in the corresponding pendulum of analytic techniques from Freud's actual technique, as reconstructed from his notes and the report s of his patients, to the so-called 'classical' technique that held sway after Freud's death, and again, to the currently changing technical scene. Lipton (1977) has insisted that in the 1940s andv1950s the so-called classical technique replaced Freud's own more personal and relaxed technique, probably in reaction to Alexander's suggestion of the corrective emotional experience. It was Lipton's view that the misnamed 'classical' technique, in contrast to Freud's, emphasized rules for the analyst's behaviour and sacrificed the purpose of the analysis. Eissler's 1953 description of analysis as an activity that ideally uses only interpretations became the paradigm for 'classical' analysis. It was, Lipton, says, a serious and severe distortion of the mature analytic technique developed by Freud. Freud regarded the analyst 's personal behaviour, the personality of the analyst exemplified for Lipton in the case of the Rat Man. The so-called 'classical' (and in his view non-Freudian) techniques attempted to include every aspect of the analytic situation as part of technique and led to the model of the silent, restrained psychoanalyst. Lipton's argument is persuasive.

These two different models of technique have obvious implications concerning the transference and its interpretation. Unless we believe in an extreme version of the historical model, we must expect that the silent, restraint, nonparticipatory psychoanalyst will elicit different responses from his patient than will the vivid, less-hidden, more responsive analyst. The range of personal behaviours available to the analyst before we need be concerned that the analyst is engaging in activities that are excessively self-revelatory or that force the patient into a social relationship is probably much broader than we thought a few years ago. But we also know that almost any behaviour of the analyst, including restraint or silence, immediately influences the patient's responses. In these newer views of the analytic situation it is not easy to know that intrapsychically derived patient behaviours.

It is evident today that psychoanalyst's under the sway of their theories and personalities differ greatly concerning matters which they are sensitive about, and, of course, we can interpret only the transferences that we perceive. Despite this limitation, a review of the literature reveals, along with the usual rigidities, a laudable tendencies to describe one's experience as fully as possible, without heed to how it contradicts belief, often blurring over when experience and theory do not match. However, we have always been better at what we do than at what we say we do. This is exemplified in Heimann's (1956) paper. Speaking from a modified Kleinian perspective, and holding the historical theory of transference interpretation, Heimann managed 30 years ago to describe vividly and to support passionately much of what today is under discussion as the modernist version. That her positions were contradictory bothered her not at all. While many of us prefer to think we are following our theories, like all good scientists, good psychoanalysts, beginning with Freud, have always seen and responded to far more than our theories admit. When we have seen too much, we change our theories.

Overall, during the last half of this century, these trends, as well as our ever-increasing knowledge of our increasing distance from Freud's authority have led to specific theoretical developments (Cooper, 1984, 1985), many of them inferred in the newer transference model. Our current pluralistic theoretical world, in which almost all analysts are working, wittingly or not, with individual amalgams of Freud's drive theory, ego psychology, interpersonal Sullivanian psychoanalysis, object-relationship theory, Bowlbyan or Mahlerian attachment theory, and usually smuggled-in versions of self-psychology, lies at the base of the newer ideas and disagreements concerning transference interpretation.

Although the historical definitions of transference and transference interpretation have the merit of seeming precision and limited scope, they are based on a psychoanalytical theory that no longer stands alone and has lost ground in at least, subsumed, by modernist conceptions that are more attuned to the theories that abound today.

As a prefatory remark about Freud and transference, the observations can be offered that Freud wrote briefly about transference and did so, in the main, before 1917. Another observation which can rarely be made about Freud's work, what he did write on transference and did not reach the high level of analytical thought which has come to be regarded as standard for him. Some indication of what his contribution consists of is given by the editors of the Standard Edition, who list them in several places. One of the longer lists, in a footnote includes six reference 'Studies on Hysteria', with Breuer (1895), the Dora paper (1905), The Dynamics of Transference' (1912), Observations on Transference-Love' (1915), the chapter on transference in the Introductory Lectures (1917), and Analysis Terminable and Interminable (1937). Although the editors in no sense suggest that these six papers include everything Freud wrote on the subject that these six papers include everything Freud wrote on the subject, it does seem evident that, considering the essential importance of transference to analysis, he wrote little. Moreover, the three papers in which transference is the specific theme. `The Dynamics of Transference and transference-love and the transference chapter in the Introductory Lectures, come across as his least significant of contributions.

Freud's first direct mention of transference occurs in "Studies on Hysteria" (1895), His first significant reference to it, however, did not appear until five years later when, in a lecture to Fliess on April 16, 1900, he said (Freud 1887-1902) he was 'beginning to see that the apparent endlessness of the treatment is something of an inherent feature and is connected with transference. In a footnote to his letter the editors state that, 'this is the first insight into the role of transference in psychoanalytic therapy'.

Despite these early references, it seems correct to say that yet another five yea s was to go by before the phenomenon of transference was actually introduced. Even then the introduction was far from prominent, for it was tacked like an afterthought as a four-page portion of a postscript to what was perhaps Freud's most fascinating case history to date, the case of Dora (1905).

Using data from Dora's three-month-long, unexpected terminated analysis, and especially from her dramatic transference reactions which had taken him quite unaware. Freud now gave to transference, and its first distinct psychological entity for th first time indicated its essential role in the analytic process. His account, although in general more than adequate - in fact elegant and remarkable 'finished' - was brief, almost Iaconic, and perhaps not an entirely worthy introduction to such a truly great discovery. What was uniquely great was his recognizing the usefulness of transference. In his analysis of Dora h e had noted not only that transference feelings existed and were powerful, but much to his dismay, he had realized that as serious, perhaps, even insurmountable, obstacle they could be. Then, in what seems like a creative leap, Freud made the almost und unbelievable discovery that transference was in fact the key to analysis, that by properly taking the patient's transference into account, an entirely new, essential and immensely effective heuristic and therapeutic force was added to the analytic method.

The impact on analysis of this startling discovery was actually much greater and much more significant than most people seem to appreciate. Although the role of transference as the 'sine quo non' of analysis was and is widely accepted, and was so stated by Freud from the first, It has almost never been acclaimed for having brought about an entire change in the nature of analysis. The introduction of free association to analysis, a much lesser change, received and still received much more recognition.

One of the reasons for the relatively unheralded entry of transference into analysis my have been the circumstances of its discovery. Although Freud's new ideas were recorded as if they arose as a sudden inspiration during the Dora analysis, they may in fact have developed somewhat later. In the paper's prefatory remarks, for instance, Freud said he had no t discussed transference with Dora at all, and in the postscript, he said he had been unaware of her transference feelings. Also, pointing to a later discovery date is the extraordinary delay in the paper's publication. According to the editors' note, the paper had been completed and accepted for publication by late January 1901, but this date was actually set back more than four and half years until October 1905. The editor's said: 'We have no information as to how it happened that Freud . . . deferred publication'. As, perhaps, that this reason may have been that only during those four and half years, as a consequence to his own self-analysis, did he or not, really come to an understanding of the significance of the transference. Only then may it have been possible for him to turn again to the Dora case, to apply to it what he had learned in himself, to write his essay as part of the postscript, and, at last, to release the paper for publication.

Freud's self-analysis has been considered from many angles, but not significantly, is that from the standpoint of transference. Opponents of the idea that there is such a thing as definitive self-analysis, some of whom say it is impossible, generally object on grounds that without an analyst there can be no transference neurosis. Freud clearly demonstrated, such as the situation that may be necessary to fill this need, self-analysis may require at least a half-way satisfactory transference object. In Freud's case, the transference at this times seems to have been Fliess, who filled the role rather well. As with any analyst, this, 'real' impact on Freud was slight. He was essentially a neutral figure, relatively anonymous and physically separates. All of this, and Fliess's own reciprocal transference reactions, makes it possible for Freud to endow Fliess with whatever qualities and whatever feelings were essential to the development of Freud's transference, and it should be added. His transference neurosis, in the end, of course, the transference was in part resolved. Freud's eventual awakening to realization about its presence within him such strange and powerful psychological forces must have come as a stupendous disillusionment, directed not only toward Fliess but toward him, and yet his subsequent working out of some of these transference attachments must have been both an intellectual triumph and an immensely healing and process of free spoken and unrecompensed as to be free and in no hurry to fall in love again, not having the affections fixed on a particular object for which to relieve from constraint or restraint.

It was this event, the development, the discovery, and then the resolution within himself of the complexities of the transference neurosis, that constitute the actual centre of his self-analysis, and it was this event that was the beginning of analysis as we know it.

In the years following this revolutionary discovery, the central role of transference in analysis gained remarkably wide acceptance, and it has, long since of becoming to change from a closed to an open condition, as something of a mystery, there is nothing about analysis that is less known than how individual analysts actually use transference in their day-to-day handling in the work with patients. Ast first glance, because each analyst's conception of transference derives variously, but significantly from the analysts own inner experience, Transference probably means many different things to many different analysts.

The significance of the transference phenomenon impressed Freud so profoundly that he continued through the years to develop his ideas about it, but his classical observations on the patient Dora formed the basis for his first formulations of this concept. He said, 'What is transference? They are the new editions or facsimiles of the tendencies and phantasies which are aroused and made conscious during the progress of the analysis: But they have this peculiarity, which is characteristic for their species, that they replace some earlier person by the person of the physician. To put it another way, a whole series of psychological experiences is revived, not as belonging to the past, but as applying to the person of the physician at the present moment.

According to Freud's view, the process of a psychoanalytic cure depends mainly upon the patient's ability to remember that which is forgotten and repressed, and thus to gain conviction that the analytical conclusion arrived at being correct. However, 'the unconscious feelings strive to avoid the recognition which the cure demands'. They seek instead, emotional discharge, regardless of the reality of the situation.

Freud believed that these unconscious feelings, which the patient strives to hide, are made up of that part of the libidinal impulse that has turned away from consciousness and reality, due to the frustration of a desirous gratification. Because the attraction of reality has weakened, the libidinal energy is still maintained in a state of regression attached to the original infantile sexual objects, although the reasons for the recoil from reality have disappeared.

Freud stated that in the analytic treatment, the analyst pursued this part of the libido to its hiding place, 'aiming always at unearthing it, making it accessible to consciousness and at last serviceable to reality'. The patient tries to achieve an emotional discharge of this libidinal energy under the pressure of the compulsion to repeat experiences over and again, rather than to become conscious of their origin. He uses the method of transferring to the person of the physician past psychological experiences and reacting to this, at times, with all the power of hallucination. The patient vehemently insists that his impression of the analyst is true for the immediate present, in this way avoiding the recognition of his own unconscious impulses.

Thus, Freud regarded the transference-manifestations as a major problem of the resistance. However, Freud said, 'It must not be forgotten that they (the transference-manifestations) and they only, render the invaluable service of making the patient's buried and forgotten to loves-emotions, as endlessly existent and manifesting evidenced.

Freud considered the transference-manifestations as having two general aspects - positive and negative. The negative, he at first took to be, as having no value in a psychoanalytic cure and only something to be 'raised' into consciousness to avoid interference with the progress of the analysis. He later accorded it a place of importance in the therapeutic experience. The positive transference he considered to be ultimately sexual in origin, since Freud said, 'To begin with, we knew none but sexual objects'. However, he divided the positive transference into two components - one, the repressed erotic component, which was used in the service of resistance; the other, the friendly and affectionate component, which, although originally sexual, was the 'unobjectionable' aspect of the positive transference, and was that which 'brings about the successful result in the psychoanalysis, as in all other remedial methods' - Freud referred to the element of suggestion in psychoanalytic therapy.

At the moment, I should like to state that it would be a mistake to deny the value and importance of his formulations regarding transference phenomena. Nonetheless, I differ on certain points with Freud, but I do not differ with the formulation that early impressions acquired during childhood are revived in the analytical situation, and are felt as immediate and real - that they form potentially the greatest obstacles to analysis if unnoticed, and, as Freud put it, the greatest ally of the analysis when understood. Wherefore, I agree that the main work of the analysis consists in analyzing the transference phenomena, although I differ somewhat as to how this result is a cure. Even so, it is my conviction that the transference is a strictly interpersonal experience. Freud gave the impression that under the stress of the repetition-compulsion the patient was bound to repeat the identical pattern, regardless of the other person, that I believe that the personality of the analyst tends to determine the character of the transference illusions, and especially to determine whether the attempt at analysis will be a result of some remedial curative. Horney has shown that there is no valid reason for assuming that the tendency to repeat past experiences time and again, having integration between them with any given situation as accorded to the necessities of his character reference and foundational structure.

Yet, among other things, I do want to mention a simple phenomenon, as described by Sherif, connected with the problem of the frame of reference. If you have a completely dark room, with no possibility of any light being seen, and you then turn on a small pinpoint of light, which is kept stationary, this light will soon appear to be moving about. I am sure a good many of you have noticed this phenomenon when gazing upon a single star. The light seems to move, and it does so, apparently because there is no reference point in relation to which one can establish it at a fixed place in space. It just wanders around. If, however, one can at the same time see some other fixed object in the room, the light immediately becomes stationary. As ast point reference, as having been illuminated, and there are no longer any uncertainty, and vague wandering of the spot of light? It is fixed firmly. The pinpoint of light wandering in the dark room is symbolic of the original attitude of the person to himself, undetermined, unstructured, with no reference point or points.

The newborn infant probably perceives everything in a vague and uncertain way, including himself. Gradually, reference points are established that a connection begins to occur between hunger and breast, between a relief if bladder tension and a wet diaper between playing with his genitals and a smack on the hand. The physical boundaries and potentialities of the self are explored. One can observe the baby investigating the extent, shape, and potentialities of his own body, that he can hold his breath and everyone will get excited that he can smile and coo and people will be enchanted, or just the opposite. The nature of the emotional reference points that he determines depends on or upon the environment. By that still unknown quality called 'empathy' he discovers the reference points that help to determine his emotional attitude toward himself. If his mother does not want him, is disgusted with him, treats him with utter disregard, he comes to look upon himself as anything-to-be-disregarded. With the profound human drive to carry out this equilibrium or as such, for being rational, it gradually builds up a situated arrangement of an integrated whole, made up of diverse but interrelated and interdependent parts of 'reasons why' expressions of an act, process, or instance if expressing in words, whereas a statement conveying something that is said or a pronounceable sound or combination of sounds that expresses and symbolizes an idea. Wherefore a statement whose weight or worth depends on the truthfulness or authority of its maker, but, underneath all these reasons is a basic sense of worthlessness, undetermined and undefined, related directly to the original reference frame. Another child discovers that the state of being regarded is dependent upon specific factors all is well as long as one does not act spontaneously, as long as one can be just not of a separate person, as long as one is good, as the state of being good is continuously defined by the parent. Under these conditions, and these only, this child can feel a sense of self-regard.

Other people are encountered with the original reference frame in mind. The child tends to carry over into later situations the patterns he first learned to know. The rigidity with which these original patterns are retained depends upon the hidden nature of the child's experience. If this has been of a traumatic character so that spontaneity has been blocked and further emotional developments have been inhibited, the original orientations will tend to persist. Discrepancies may be rationalized or repressed. Thus, the original impression of the hostile mother may be retained, while the contact with the new person is rationalized to fit the original reference frame. The new person encountered acts differently, but probably that is just a pose. She is just being nice because she does not know me. If she really knew me, she would act differently. Or, the original impressions are out of line with the present actuality, that they remain unconscious, but make themselves apparent in inappropriate behaviour or attitudes, which remain outside the awareness of the person concerned.

The little child who grows more and more negativistic, because of injuries and frustrations, evokes more and more hostility in his environment. However, and this is important, the basic reactions of hostility on the part of the patents, which originally induced his negativism, are still there. Thus, the pattern does not change much in character, but it just gets worse in the same direction. Those persons whose life experiences perpetuate the original frames of reference, are more severely injured. Among the children, who has a hostile mother, may then have a hostile teacher. If, by good luck, he got a kind teacher and if his own attitude were not already badly warped, so that he did not induce hostility in this kind teacher, he would be introduced into a startlingly new and pleasant frame of reference, and his personality might not suffer too greatly, especially, if a kindly aunt or uncle happened to be around.

The profoundly sick people have been so early injured, in such a rigid and limited frame of reference, that they are not able to make use of kindliness, decency, or regard when it does come their way. They meet the world as if it were potentially menacing. They have already developed defensive traits entirely appropriate to their original experience, and then carry them out in completely inappropriate situations, rationalizing the discrepancies, but never daring to believe that people are different from the ones they early learned to distrust and hate. By reason of bitter early experience, they learn never to let their guard down, never to permit intimacy, least of mention, the death blow would be dealt to their already partly destroyed sense of self-regard. Despairing of real joy in living, they develop secondary neurotic goals which give a pseud-satisfaction. The secondary gains at first glance might seem as what the person was really attempting to achieve - revenge, power and individual possession for thing one owns usually excluding real property and intangibles. Actually, these are but the expressions of the deep injuring sustained by the person. They cannot be fundamentally cured until those interpersonal relationships that caused the original injury are brought back to consciousness in the analytic situation. Step by step, and each phase to the long period of emotional development is exposed, by no means chronologically; the interconnecting, overlapping reference frames are made conscious, those points at which a distortion of reality, or a repression of part of the self had to occur, are uncovered. The reality gradually becomes 'undistorted', the self refound in the personal relationship between the analyst and the patient.

This personal relationship with the analyst is the situation in which the transference distortion can be analyzed.

In Freud's view, the transference was either positive or negative, and was related in a rather isolated way to a particular person in the past. Justly, the transference is the experiencing in the analytic situation the entire pattern of the original reference frames, that in addition may include at every moment, of what posses as an integral part of a whole, such inclination in the relationship of the patient to himself, it is noted, that the important persons, and to others, as he experienced them at that time, in the light of his interrelationships with the important people.

The therapeutic aim in this process is not to uncover childhood memories that will then lend themselves to analytic interpretation. Here, Fromm has pointed out, that psychoanalytic cure is not the amassing of data, either from childhood, or from the study of the present situation. Nor causes to any remedial curative for the purposes of the cure, as the result from repetition of the original injurious experience in the analytic relationship, but, the curvature in the process, are that for willing if a desire to act in a particular way or have a particular thing, such that supports of the mindful inclination to be aware. The element or complex of elements in an individual that, feels, perceives, thinks, wills, and especially reasons, supposedly has chosen or decided whether of controlling one's actions, impulses, or emotions, for these are formidably mind-bending interactions for being so as having or exhibiting the inclination or tendency, such that as movements on course for having a particular direction and character growing potential, yet up to the time when the analyst and the patient have mutually capitulated upon some insightful gratifications as for launching the areas inhibited by the patient's free-associations of his childhood. The patient, as if by conquest, obtainably achieves in the discoveries that he himself has to be repressed of the original experience. He can only do this in an interpersonal relationship with the analyst, which is suitable to such a rediscovery. To illustrate this point, is that, of a patient had a hostile parent toward whom he was required to show deference, he has to repress certain of his own spontaneous feelings. In the analytic situation, he tends to carry over his original frame of reference, and again tends to feel himself to be in a similar situation. If the analyst's personality also contains elements of a need for deference that need will unconsciously be imparted to the patient, who will, therefore, still repress his spontaneity as he did before. True enough, he may act or try to act as if analyzed, since by definition, that is what the analyst is attempting to accomplish. But he will never have found his repressed self, because the analytic relationship contains a lengthy interval through which time and spaces have no equaling measure for any contrasting of situational constitutions for objective reality of separate things, especially with his original situation. Only if the analyst provides a genuinely new frame of reference - that is, if he is truly non-hostile, and noticeably attracting or compelling notice of attention as taken on note of or concerning oneself with something in opposition and truly not in need of deference - can this patient discover, and something as really to discovery, the repressed elements of his own personality. Thus, the transference phenomenon is used so that the patient will completely re-experience the original frames of reference, and himself within those frames, in a truly different relationship with the analyst, to the end that he can discover the invalidity of his conclusions about himself and others.

That is to say, by this is not to mean to deny the correctness of Freud's view of transference also acting as a resistance. As a matter of fact, the tendency of the patient to reestablish the original reference frame is precisely because he is afraid to experience the other person in a direct and unreserved way. He has organized his whole system of getting along in the world, bad as that system might be, on the basis of the original distortions of his personality and his subsequent vicissitudes. His capacity for spontaneous feeling and acting has gone into hiding. Now it has to be sought. If some such phrase as the 'capacity for self-realization' is substituted in place of Freud's concept of the repressed libidinal impulse, much is the same conclusions can be reached about the way in which the transference-manifestations appear in the analysis as resistance. It is just in the safest situation, where the spontaneous feelings might come out of hiding, that the patient develops intense feelings, sometimes of a hallucinatory character, that relate to the most dreaded of experience, that of the past. It is at this point that the hidden natures and the use by the patient of the transference distortions have to be understood and correctly interpreted, by the analyst. It is also here that the personality of the analyst modifies the transference reaction, a patient cannot feel close to a detached or hostile analyst and will therefore never display the full intensity of his transference illusions. The plexuity of this process, whereby the transference can be used as the therapeutic instrument and, at the same time, as a resistance may be illustrated by the following example: a patient had developed intense feelings of attachment to a father surrogate in his everyday life. The transference feelings toward this man were of great value in elucidating his original problems with his real father. As the patient became more and more aware of this personal validity, he found this masochistic attachment to be weakening. This occasioned acute feeling of anxiety, since his sense of independence was not ye t fully established. At this point, he developed very disturbing feelings regarding the analyst, believing that she was untrustworthy and hostile, although prior to this, he had successes in establishing a realistically positive relationship to her. The feelings of untrustworthiness precisely reproduced an ancient pattern with his mother. He then experienced of this particular point, in that which the analysis in order to retain and to justify his attachment to the father figure, the weakening of which attachments had threatened him so profoundly. The entire pattern was elucidated when it was seen that he was re-experiencing an ancient triangle, from which he was contentiously driven to a submissive attachment for his dominating father, due to the utter untrustworthiness of his weak mother. If the transference character of this sudden feeling of untrustworthiness of the analyst had not been clarified, he would have turned again, submissively to his father surrogate, which would have further postponed his development of-independence. Nevertheless, the development of this transference to the analyst brought to light a new insightful quality of an utterance that arouses interest and produces an effect.

Freud felt that personality disorder called schizophrenias or paranoia could not be analyzed because the patient was unable to develop a transference to the analyst. In this view the real difficulty in treating such disorders is that the relationship is essentially nothing but transference illusions. Such persons hallucinate exteriorly on or upon the original-set frame of reference to the exclusion of reality, however, in the realm of psychoanalysis one can find more complicating and complex proof of the effect of early experiences on the person than attempting to treat these same peoples. Frieda Fromm Reichmann has shown in her work with schizophrenics the necessity to realize the intensity of the transference reactions, which have become almost completely real to the patient. And yet, if one knows the correct interpretations, by actually feeling the patient's needs, one can over years of time do not the identical thing that is accomplished more quickly and less dramatical within the patients suffering with fewer but still severe disturbances, as attribute by their interpersonal relationships.

Another point with which Freud took the position that all subsequent experiences of a normal life is merely repetition, in that of the original one. Thus, love is experienced for someone today in terms of the love felt for someone in the past. As, perhaps, this is not exactly true: Yet the child who has not had to repress certain aspects of his personality enters into a new situation dynamically, not just as a repetition of what he felt, such on saying, with his mother, but as an active continuation of it. Again to say, that there are constitutional differences with respect to the total capacity for emotional experience, just as there are with respect to the total capacity for intellectual experiences. Given this constitutional substratum, the child engages in personal relationships not passively as a lump of clay waiting to be molded, but most dynamically, bringing from the corpses of times generations of all his emotional potentialities. He may possibly find someone later whose capacity for response is deeper than his mother's. If he is capable of the greater depths, he experiences an expansion of himself. Many later in life have met a 'great' person and have felt a sense of newness in the relationship which is described to others as 'wonderful' and which is regarded with a certain amount of extension of the self to a new horizon.

In considering the process of a psychoanalytic cure, Freud very seriously discussed the relationship of analysis to suggestion therapy and hypnosis. He believed, that part of the positive transference could be made use of in the analysis to bring about the successful result. He said, 'In so far that the realities, within which are sustained that we readily admit that the results of psychoanalysis rest upon a fundamental basis of suggestion, only by suggestion can we communicatively be understood, in meaning that with which, we concede to Ferenczi, in the finding that it consists to have existence or a place of persuasive influences especially on a person through and by means of the transference-manifestations, in that, we are adequately capable. The eventual independence as awaiting in the presence toward which is the future, as the patient is our ultimate object when we use suggestion to bring him into and carry out from the mental operation that will necessitate in the resulting of a lasting improvement in his mental condition. Freud, elsewhere indicated very clearly, that in hypnosis, the relationship of the patient to the hypnotist was not worked through, whereas in analysis the transference to the analyst was resolved by bringing it entirely into consciousness. He also said, that the patient was protected from the unwitting suggestive influence of the analysis by the awakening of his own unconscious resistance.

The most consistent thing would have been to do away entirely with this new useless rudiment of an earlier time, and to give up the terminology, which had become dear to most analysts, in favour of a better understanding. Instead of doing this, the whole of mental life was often regarded as a mosaic of such plexuities, and the analysis then carried out with the object of 'analyzing out' one complex after the other, or the attempt was made for treating the whole personality as a sum total of father-mother, brother and sister complexes. It was naturally easy to collect material for these, since everyone has, of course, all the plexuities, that is, everyone must, in the course of his development, somehow get on with the persons and object that surround him. The connected recounting of plexuity, or the attributes of these, may have its place in descriptive psychology, but not in the practical analysis of the neurosis, nor does it even belong in the psychoanalytic study of literary or ethno-psychological products, where it must undoubtedly lead to monotony in no way justified by the many-sidelines of the material, and scarcely tempered by giving preference, first to one and then to the other complex.

Although such a flattening universe may have to be put up with at times, but as unavoidable to the scientific presentation, one should not therefore transfer such a cramped interest into the technique. The analysis of plexuities easily misleads the patient into being pleasing to his analyst, by bringing him 'complex material' as long as he likes, without giving up any of his really unconscious secrets. Thus there came to be histories of illnesses In which the patient recounted memories, evidently fabricating them, in a way that never happens in unprejudiced analyses, and can only be looked upon as the product of such a 'breeding of plexuity'. Such results should naturally not be used subjectively to show the correctness either of one's own methods of interpreting, or as theoretic conclusions, not yet as leading to any sort of evidence.

It happens particularly frequently that the associations of the patient were directed to the sexual factor at the wrong time, or that they remained stuck at this point, if as so often happens - he came to the analysis with the expectation that he must constantly talk exclusively of his actual or infantile sexual life. Aside from the fact that this is not so exclusively the case as our opponents think, permitting such an indulgence in the sexual often gives the patient the opportunity to paralyze the therapeutic effect of the privation he must undergo.

An understanding of the many-sided and important mental contents that underlie the collective name 'castration complex' was also not exactly furthered by bringing the theory of the complexes into the dynamics of the analysis. On the contrary, we are of the opinion that the premature theoretic condensation of the fact under the conception of the complex interfered with the insight into deeper layers of mental life. We believe that the full appreciation of which the analytic practitioner has habituated of an accustomed spatiality, as to finish off with the label castration complex, is still lacking of this attempt of an accountable explanation, this, nonetheless, should not lightly be considered as the ultimate explanation of such a varied mental phenomenon, as the protocol for procedural processes that include the patient. We can, from the dynamic standpoint which is the only justifiable one in practice, often recognized in the forms of expression of the castration complex, so they manifest themselves in the course of the analysis, only one of the kinds of resistance that the patient erects against his deeper libidinal wishes. In the early stages of some analyses the castration anxiety can often be uncovered as an expression of the dread, transferred onto the analyst, as a protection against further analysis.

Technical difficulties arose also from the analyst's having too much knowledge. Thus the importance of the theory of sexual development constructed by Freud, misled some analysts to apply in a mistaken and overly dogmatic fashion in the therapy of the neuroses, certain systems of organization and autoeroticism, first to which had given us an understanding to a normally sexual development. In this searching for the constructive elements of the theory of sex, in some cases, the actual analytic task was neglected. These analyses might be compared to psychochemical 'elements analyses'. Here, again, one could see that the theoretical importance did not always correspond to the value in the practical analysis. The technique need not methodically lay bare all, . . . as it was, prescribed historic phases of the development of the libido, still less should the uncovering of all theoretically established details and gradations are used as a principle of healing in the neuroses. It is also practically superfluous to demonstrate all the original elements of a highly complicated 'connection', while missing the intellectual thread, which combines the few fundamental elements into new and varying phenomena. The same thing holds for the erotogenic zones as for the plexuity, for example the urethral or the anal erotic, and for the stages of organization the oral eroticism anal-sadistic and other pregenital phases, there can be no human development without all of these, but one must not in the analysis attribute to the importance, for the history of the illness, of which the resistance under the pressure of the analytic situation gives the illusion.

On closer observation a certain inner connection between 'element analyses' and 'complex analyses' could be recognized, insofar as the latter, in their attempts to plummet the psychic abstrusity, struck upon the granite of plexuity and thus the work was spread out over the surface instead of going to the bottom. Such analyses then usually trying to make up for the lack of depth in the dynamics of the libido by an excursion into the theory of sex, and unified attributions of complexes with equally schematically treated principles, is that the theory of sex, whereas they overlooked the forces of concerned considerations that takes place between the two.

Despite the diversity of the transference and its interpreting in analytic process and cure, differing only in whether transference is everything or almost everything to give a clear-cut definition of what transference is.

Laplanche and Pontalis (1973) had written that, 'The reason it is so difficult to produce a definition of transference is that for many authors the notion has taken on a very broad extension, even coming to connote all the phenomena which constitute the patient's relationship with the psychoanalyst, as a result the concept is burdened down more than any other with each analyst's particular view on the treatment - on its objective, dynamics, tactics, scope, and so forth. The question of the transference is thus beset by a whole series of difficulties which have been the subject of debate in a classical psychoanalysis.'

Sandler (1983) has discussed how the term's transference and transference resistance, as well as other terms have undergone profound changes in meaning as new discoveries and new trends of psychoanalytic technique assume ascendency. He said, . . . major changes in technical emphasis brought about the extension of the transference concept, which now has dimensions of meaning which differ from the official definition of the term. I am not sure there has ever been a simplified definition of the term. While a certain flexibility of definition makes conversation possible in a field of diverse views, which we may never be clear on what any two people mean when they use the term is a significant disability to our discourse.

However: with this in mind we might review one of Freud's last comments on transference. In 'An Outline of Psycho-Analysis' (1940), published posthumously, he wrote on the analytic situation:

The most remarkable thing is this. The patient is not satisfied with regarding the analyst in the light of reality as a helper and advisor who, moreover, is remunerated for the trouble he takes and who would himself be content with some role that of a guide on a different mountain to climb, on the contrary, the patient sees in him, the return, and the reincarnation, of some important figure out of his childhood or past, and consequently transfer onto him, feelings and reactions which undoubtedly apply this prototype. This fact of transference soon proves to be a factor of undreamed importance, on the other hand bud an instrument of irreplaceable value and on the other, that he set out on a different undertaking without any suspicion to the extraordinary power that would be at his command.

Another advantage of transference, too, in that in it the patient produces before us with plastic clarity an important part of his life-story, of which he would, otherwise have probably given us only an insufficient account. He acts it before us, as it was, instead of reporting it to us.

Freud saw the transference interpretation as a method of strengthening the ego against past unconscious wishes and conflicts.

It is the analyst's task constantly to tear the patient out of his menacing illusions and to show him again and again, of what it takes to be or begin of a new life, are the reflections of the past. And least, he should fall into a state in which he is inaccessible to all evidences, the analyst takes that neither the love nor the hostility reaching an extreme height. This is affected, by preparing him in good time for these possibilities and by not overlooking the first signs of them. Careful handling of the transference on these lines is as a role richly rewarded. If we succeed, as we usually can, in enlightenment the patient on the true nature of the phenomena of the transference, we thus have struck a powerful weapon out of the hand of his resistance and will have converted dangers into gains. For a patient never forgets again what he has experienced in the form of transference, it carries a greater force of conviction than anything he can acquire in other ways.

We have used the term 'transference' several times, and in the last, we attributed the therapeutic results to the transference without further definition of the word. As our concerning considerations are more closely intertwined by its emotional relationship, which the word or, perhaps, a combination of words, by which something can be called and by means of which it can be distinguished or identified. During a psychoanalytic treatment, the patient allows the analyst to play a predominating role in his emotional life. This is of great importance in the analytic process. After the treatment for and the situation is changed. The patient builds up feelings of affection for the resistance to his analyst which, in their ebb and flow, so exceed the normal degree of feeling that the phenomenon has long since actuated the theoretical interests of the analyst. Freud studied this phenomenon thoroughly, explained it, and gave it the name 'transference'

I cannot reproduce for you, all of Freud's research about the transference, but must limit myself to essentials, such as the statement of 'counter-transference', is the emotional attitude of the analyst toward the patient, the analyst toward his charge, the therapist toward the patient. The feeling which the child develops for the mentor is conditioned by a much earlier relationship to someone else. We must take cognizance of this fact in order to understand these relationships. The tender relationship which goes to make up the child's love life is no longer strange to us. Many of these have already been touched upon in the foregoing contentual frames. We have learned how the small boy takes the father and mother as love objects. We gave in following the striving which arose in this relationship, the oedipus situation, in that we have seen how this runs its course and terminates in an identification with the parent. We have also had opportunity to consider the relationship between brothers and sisters, how their original rivalry is transformed into affection through the pressure of their feeling for the parent. We know that the boy at puberty must give up his first love objects within the family and transfer his libido to individuals' exteriority or outside of the family. Not allows the analyst to play a predominating role in his emotional life. This is of great importance in the analytic process, after all the treatment for and the situation is changed, as the patient builds up feelings of affection for the resistance to his analyst which, in their ebb and flow, exceeds the normal degree of feeling that the phenomenon has long since actuated the theoretical interests of the analyst. Freud studied this phenomenon thoroughly, explained it, and gave it the name 'transference'

I cannot reproduce for you, all of Freud's research about the transference, but must limit myself to essentials, such as the statement of 'counter-transference', is the emotional attitude of the analyst toward the patient, the analyst toward his charge, the therapist toward the patient. The feeling which the child develops for the mentor is conditioned by a much earlier relationship to someone else. We must take cognizance of this fact in order to understand these relationships. The tender relationship which goes to make up the child's love life is no longer strange to us. Many of these have already been touched upon in the foregoing contentual frames. We have learned how the small boy takes the father and mother as love objects. We gave in following the striving which arise in this relationship, the oedipus situation, we have seen how this runs its course and terminates in an identification with the parent. We have also had opportunity to consider the relationship between brothers and sisters, how their original rivalry is transformed into affection through the pressure of their feeling for the parent. We know that the boy at puberty must give up his first love objects within the family and transfer his libido to the individual's exteriority or outside of the family.

The key to understanding the essential pathology as well as the therapeutical impasse was in the failure of the patient to develop a reliable working relation with the analyst. In each case the patient was unable to either establish or maintain a durable working alliance with the analyst and the analyst neglected this fact, pursuing instead the analyst of other transference phenomena, as this error in technique was observable in psychoanalysts with a wide range of clinical experience and to recognize the same shortcomings when resuming the transference interpretations.

In this connection, and, if transference is to be regarded as a significant ego function, a number of inferences are rather obvious. One is that analysis does not 'cause' transference. Yet, although not caused by analysis, transference as it occurs in analysis does seem unique. What is unique, however, may not be transference itself, but rather the effect upon transference of the unique conditions of the analytic situation. These conditions may affect most strongly such things as the choice of content of transference reaction, the intensity of these reactions, their exclusiveness, and their sharp focus on the person of the analyst. Although, as a result of these conditions, transference developments in analysis may differ from those occurring elsewhere, this does not mean that in analysis transference as a function is any different.

Another rather obvious inference, following from the first, is that transference can never be resolved. The content may be, but not the function. Through analysis, the symptomatic, neurotic and historical plexuity have been brought into the transference may be resolved, but not the function itself. The function of transference, like other functions of the ego, may be affected by analysis in many ways, but it never goes away.

Still, another inference is a general one concerning transference and the analyst. If transference is to be regarded as an ever active ego function, then the analyst's transference goes on all the time too, just like the patient's, and despite what he might wish to think. His transference has not been resolved in his own analysis. Admittedly, the impact of the analytic situation upon the analyst is vastly different from what it is upon the patient, but many aspects of that situation do favour development in the analyst of transference relations involving his patient. This does not mean, however, that it would be correct to believe the analyst should attempt to inhibit his transference function, much less disavows it. Yet, what the analyst should do about this transference is a question that has never been significantly pondered over. Aside from any belief that the analyst's transference is remarkably useful in the process of analysing and may be essential for certain aspects of analysis, what can be said?

Would it be wrong, to propose that this ego function be dealt within the same way the analyst deals with his other ego function? Just as the analyst must consciously regulate his responses to the functions in order to create and sustain the analytic situation, should he not also regulate his responses to his transference activity?

This does not mean nor should it mean his responses and sustain the analytic situation does not also regulate his responses to his transference activity? This does not mean, not to be thought that the analyst must decide either whether or when a transference reaction to his patient exists. Such an attempt is the point on which has in itself, at least two counts.

For one thing, significant transference reactions are usually not conscious, and, fo r another, transference activity in some form is always going on.

In view of these considerations, the simplest position for the analyst to take, and the one most likely to be helped, may be to assume that all feelings and reactions of the analyst concerning the patient are 'prima-facie' evidence of the analyst's transference. Under this arrangement every feeling of warmth, pity, sadness, anger, hope, excitement, even interest, every feeling of coldness, indifference, disinterest, boredom, impatience, discouragement, and every absence of feeling, should be assumed to contain significant elements of the analyst's transference as focussed on the patient. This would mean, essentially, that everything arising in the analyst about his patient assumed to be part of the substance of analysis, that nothing presents merely the analyst's 'real' reaction to his patient, and that especially when something seems most real it can be counted on to contain important aspects of the analyst's transference.

Were the analysts to take this rather imperative view of his own transference potential, he might be much more likely to remain abreast of the personal, neurotic meaning of the myriad but often subtle reactions and attitudes he develops toward his patient. This in turn might make it possible for him, at least to keep his transference out of the patient's way and hopefully to use it to further the analysis.

The final inference from all this is perhaps the most promising. This is that transference, if it belongs to the family of ego functions, can be counted onto posses many of this family 's characteristics. Thus, presently existing knowledge about the ego should provide many ready-made leads as to the nature of transference. The ego's way of reality testing, for instance, its responses to internal and external stimuli, its uses of defence mechanisms, may all reveal much about the basic phenomenology of transference. Similarly, much may be surmised about transference's functional vicissitudes by assuming that transference suffers the same general developmental and neurotic deficiencies, distortions, limitations, and fixations to which various other functions of the ego are susceptible. A particularly important study would seem to be the special strength of transference functioning, especially its way of joining with other agencies to serve and facilitate the individual's idiosyncratic interests and developments. Such a study, for instance, might centre on the ego's object relations to the reference to the question of whether transference is the ego function mainly responsibly for their development.

Viewing transference in this way as an ego function means, of course, relinquishing certain elements of our existing viewpoint. One prominent feature of these existing viewpoints, no matter what form they take, is how hard they are to define or even to elicit. Another is how unquestioning we seem to be, about the viewpoints we grew up with, how easily we assume transference to be, but a therapeutically helpful given, an isolated psychological event having little to do with other psychological events, except in the analytic situation, to be lacking a useful purpose, and assigned without even wondering why, not either ego or id, it is usually dropped somewhere between. Labelled but rarely described, it is most commonly called 'projection' or a 'repetition' of the past, neither of them pronounce of the greater distinction.

Nevertheless, no matter how inadequate the form in which transference presently exists, it is a form that is deeply entrenched and that does not beg for change. Accordingly, wresting transference from its syntonic limbo is not likely to be easy and may be impossible, but doing so, bringing it out into open view where it can be contemplated as a major member of the ego family, is an utterly fascinating prospect, one that permits one to see transference not only as the best tool clinical analysis has, but possibly the best tool the ego has. It well may be, as Freud suggested, the basis of all human relationship and, as suggested, many may be involved in all the ego's differentiations, integrative and creative capacities. These aspects of transference offer the most exciting questions, and it is with these questions that we will continue.

Without minor exceptions or flaws we are founded against the realm of fact that holds with the distinctive quality of being actual, but, nonetheless, it was from very early times that Freud had called attention to the fact that transference manifested itself in two ways - negatively as well as positively - a good deal less said or known about the negative transference than about the positive. This, of course, corresponds to the circumstance that interest in the destructive and aggressive impulses in general, is only a comparatively recent development. Transference was regarded predominantly as a libidinal phenomenon. It was suggested that in everyone there existed a certain number of unsatisfied libidinal impulses, and that whenever some new person came upon the scene these impulses were readily attach them to him. This is the account for which of the transferences stands as a universal phenomenon. In neurotics, owing to the abnormally large quantities of an unattached libido present in the tendency to transference would be correspondingly greater, and the peculiar circumstances of the analytic situation would further increase it. It was evidently the existence of these feelings of love, thrown by the patient upon the analyst, that provided the necessary y extra force to induce his ego to give up its resistance, undo the repressions and adopt a fresh solution of its ancient problems. This instrument, without which no therapeutic result could be obtained, was at once seen to be no stranger; it was in fact the familiar power of suggestion, which had ostensibly been abandoned long before. Now, however, it was being employed in the very different way, in fact in a contrary direction. In pre-analytic days it had aimed at bringing about an increase in the degree of repression, now it was used to overcome the resistance of the ego, that is to say, to allow the repression to be removed.

But the situation became more and more complicated as more facts about transference came to light. In the first place, the feelings transferred turned out to be of various sorts, besides the loving ones there were the hostile ones, which were naturally far from assisting the analyst's efforts. But, even apart from the hostile transference. The libidinal feelings themselves fell into two groups; friendly and affectionate feelings which were capable of being conscious, and purely erotic ones which have usually too remain unconscious. And these latter feelings, when they became too powerful, stirred up the repressive forces of the ego and thus increased of its resistances are, instead of diminishing them and in fact, are produced on a state of things that were not easily distinguishable for being the negative transference. And beyond all this, there accented in the whole question of the lack of permanence of all suggestive treatments. Did not the existence of the transference threaten to leave the analytic patient in the same unending dependence upon the analyst?

All of these difficulties were got over by the discovery that the transference itself could be analyzed. Its analysis was soon found to be the most important part of the whole treatment. It was possible to make consciously its roots in the repressed unconscious just as it was possible to make conscious any other repressed material - that is, inducing the ego to abandon its resistance - and there was nothing self-contradictory in the fact that the forces used for resolving the transference was the transference itself. And once it had been made conscious, its unmanageable, infantile, permanent characteristics disappeared, what was left was like any other 'real' human relationship. But the necessity for constantly analysing the transference became still more apparent from another discovery. It was found that, as work proceeded the transference tended, as, it was, to eat up the entire analysis. More and more of the patient's libido became concentrated upon their relation to the analyst, the patient 's original symptoms were drained of their cathexis, yet and there appeared instead an artificial neurosis to which Freud gave the name of the 'transference neurosis'. These original conflicts, which have to the onset of neurosis, began to be re-enacted in the relation to the analyst, now this unexpected event is far from being the misfortune than at first. Sight it might seem to be. In fact, it gives us our great opportunity. Instead, of having to deal as best we may with conflicts of the remote past, Which are concerned with dead circumstances and mummified personalities, and whose outcome is already determined, we find ourselves involved in an actual and immediate situation, in which we and the patient are the principal characters and the development of which is to some re-extent, at least under control. But if we bring it about, that in this revivified transference conflict the patient chooses a new solution instead of the old one, a solution in which the primitive and unadaptable methods of repression are replaced by behaviour more in contact with reality, then, even after his detachment from the analysis, he will never be able to fall back into his former necrosis, the solution of the transference conflict implies as the simultaneous solution of the infantile conflict of which it is a new edition. The 'blame', says Freud in his, 'Introductory Lectures' has been made possible by alterations in the ego's occurring as a consequent of the analyst's suggestion. At the expense of the unconscious, the ego becomes wider by the words of interpretation. In which brings the unconscious material into consciousness; through education it becomes reconciled to the individual and is made willing to grant it a certain degree of satisfaction, and its horror of the claim of its libido is lessoned by the new capacity it acquires to expend a certain amount of libido sublimation, in more that is near the course of the treatment that corresponds with this ideal description in the greater, will be the success of the psychoanalytical therapy.

Freud made it clear that the ultimate factor in the therapeutic action of the psychoanalysis was suggestion on the part of the analyst acting upon the patient's ego in such a way as to make it more tolerant of the libidinal trends. However, Freud had produced extremely little that bear on the subject, and that little goes to show that he had not altered his views on the main principles involved. In additional lectures which were published last year, he explicitly states that he has nothing to add to the theoretical discussions upon therapy given in the original lectures fifteen years earlier. At the same time, there has in the interval been a considerable further development of his theoretical opinions. And especially in the region of ego-psychology. He had, in particular, formulated the concept of the superego. The restatement in superego terms of analysis may not involve many changes. But it is reasonable of resistance information about the superego will be of special interest from our point of view, and in two ways. In th e first place, it would at first glance seem highly probable that the superego should play an important part, direct or indirect, in the setting up and maintaining of the repressions and resistance, the demolition of which has been the chief aim of analysis, and is confirmed by an examination of the classification of the various kinds of resistance made by Freud in, 'Hemmung Symptom and Amgst' (1926). Of the five sorts of resistance there mentioned it is true that only one is attributed to the direct intervention of the superego, but two of the ego-resistance - the repression resistance and the transference resistance - although actually originally from the ego, as a rule set up by out of fear of the superego. It seems likely enough therefore that when Freud wrote the words which, in effect, is the favourable change in the patient. 'Is made possible by alterations in the ego', he was thinking, in part at all events, of that portion of the ego which he subsequently separated off into the superego? Quite apart from this, moreover, in another of Freud's more recent works, 'The Group Psychology' (1921), there are passages which suggest a different point - namely, that it may be largely through the patient's superego that the analyst on the nature of hypnosis and suggestion. He definitely rejects Bernheim's view that all hypnotic phenomena are traceable to the factor of suggestion, and adopts an alterative theory that suggestion is a partial manifestation of the state of hypnosis. The state of hypnosis, again, is found in certain respects, to resemble the state of being in love. There is, 'the same humble subjection, the same compliance, the same absence of criticism toward the hypnotist as towardly the loved object, has stepped into the place of the subject's ego-ideal'. Now since suggestion is a partial form of hypnosis and since the analyst brings about his changes in the patient's attitude by means of suggestion. It seems to follow that the analyst has a debt into the effectiveness, at all events in some respects, to his having stepped into the place of th e patients' superego. Thus, there are two convergent lines of argument which point to the patient's superego as occupying a key position in analytic therapy. It is a part of the patient's mind in which a favourable alteration would be likely to lead to general improvement, and it is a part of the patient's mind which is especially subject to the analyst's influence.

Such plausible notions as these were followed up almost immediately after the superego made its first début. It has been developed by Ernest Jones, for instance, in his paper on, 'The Nature of Auto-Suggestion'. Soon thereafter, Alexander launches his theory that the principal aim of all psychoanalytic therapy must be the complete demolition of the superego and the assumption of its functions by the ego. According to his account, the superego is handed over to the analyst, and in the second phase they are passed back again to th e patient, but this time to his ego. The superego, according to this view of Alexander's (though he explicitly limits his use of the word to the unconscious parts of the ego-ideal), is a portion of the fundamental apparatus which is essentially primitive, out of data and out of touch with reality, which is incapable of adapting itself, and which operates automatically, with the monotonous uniformity of a reflex. Any useful functions that it performs can be carried out by the ego. And there is therefore, nothing to be done with it but to discard it. This wholesome attack upon the superego seems to be of questionable validity. It seems probable that its abolition, even if that were practical politics, would involve the abolition of a large number off highly desirable mental activities. But the idea that the analyst temporarily takes over the functions of the patient's superego during the treatment and by so doing on some way alters it agrees with the tentative literatures.

So, too, do some passages in a paper by Radô upon 'The Economic Principle in Psycho-Analytic Technique'. The second, as such was to have dealt with psych-analysis, that in which has unfortunately never been published, but the first one, on hypnotism and catharsis, contains much that is of interest. It includes a theory that the hypnotic subject introjects the hypnotist in the form of what Radô calls a 'parasitic superego', which draw off the energy and takes over the functions of the subject's original superego. One feature of the situation brought out by Radô is the unstable and temporary nature of this whole arrangement. If, for instance, the hypnotist gives a command, which is too much in opposition to the subject's original superego. The parasite is promptly excluded. And, in any case, when the state of hypnosis comes to an end, the sway of the parasite superego also terminates and the original superego resumes its functions.

However debatable may be the details of Radô description, it not only emphasizes once again, the notion of the superego as the function of psych-therapy, but it draws attention to the important distinction between the effects of hypnosis and analysis in the matter of permanence. Hypnosis acts essentially in a temporary way, and Radô theory of the parasitic superego, which does not really replace the original one but merely throws it out of action, gives a very good picture of its apparent workings. Analysis, on the other hand, in so far as it seeks to effect the patient's superego, takes aim at something much more far-reaching and permanent than of an integral change in the nature of the patient's superego itself. Some even more recent developments in psych-analytic theory give a hint, so it seems as though it seems as the kind of thing, that along which a cleaver understanding of the question may perhaps be reached.

This latest growth of theory has been very much occupied with the destructive impulses and has brought them for the first time into the centre of interests, and attention has at the same time been concentrated on the correlated problems of guilt and anxiety. That is to say, that in the mind, especially are the ideas upon the formation of the superego, recently developed by Melanie Klein and the importance which she attributes are the processes of 'introjection' and 'projection', in the development of the personality. In a schematic outline, the individual, she holds, is perpetually introjecting and projecting the objects of its id-impulses, and the character of the introjected objects depends on the character of the id-impulses, directed toward the external objects. Thus, for instance, during the stage of a child's libidinal development in which it is dominated by feelings of oral aggression, its feelings toward its external object will be orally aggressive; It will then introject the object, and the introjected object will now act (in the manner of a superego) in an orally aggressive way toward the child's ego. (The next even will be the projection of this orally aggressive introjected object back onto the external object, which will now in its turn appear to be orally aggressive). The fact of the external object being thus felt as dangerous and destructive once more causes the id-impulses to adopt an even more aggressive and destructive attitude toward the object in self-defences. A vicious circle is thus launched in the celebrations that this process seeks to account for the extreme severity of the superego, in that of small children, as well as for their unreasonable fear of outside objects. In the course of the development of the normal individual, his libido eventually reaches the genital stage, at which the positive impulses predominant, and his attitude toward his external objects will thus become more friendly. That according to his introjected object, or super-ego will become less severe and his ego's contact with reality will be less distorted. In the case of the neurotic, however, for various reasons - whether an account of frustration of the destructive components - development to the genital stage does not occur, but the individual remains fixated at a pre-genital level. His ego is thus left exposed to the pressure of a savage id on the one hand and a correspondingly savage super-ego on the other, and the vicious circle is perpetuated.

At the arriving considerations that are marked and noted, through which the essence of functional dynamics as based of the transference in the psychoanalytic process or the basic underlying the most basic of beliefs that in politics there is neither good nor evil, however, in that something that forms part of the minimal body, character or structure of that thing predetermines the properties to the good life. Nonetheless, most psychoanalysts maintain that schizophrenic patients cannot be treated psychoanalytically because they are too narcissistic to develop with the psychotherapist as interpersonal relationship that is sufficiently reliable and consistent for psychoanalytic work. Freud, Fenichel and others have recognized that a new technique of approaching patients psychoanalytically must be found if analysts are to work with psychotics. Among those who have worked successfully in recent years with schizophrenics, Sullivan, Hill, and Karl Menninger and his staffs have made various modifications of their analytic approach. The techniques that are in use with psychotics are different from our approach to psychoneurotics. This is not a result of the schizophrenic's inability to build up a consistent personal relationship with the therapist but due to his extremely intense and sensitive transference reactions.

Let us see first what the essences of the schizophrenic's transference reactions are and how we try to meet these reactions.

We think of a schizophrenic as a person who has had serious traumatic experiences in early infancy at a time when his ego and its ability to examine reality were not yet developed. These early traumatic experiences seem to furnish the psychological basis for the pathogenic influence of the flustrations of later years. At this early time the infant lives grandiosely in a narcissistic world of his own. His needs and desires seem to be taken care of by something vague and indefinite which he does not yet differentiate. As Ferenczi noted, they are expressed by gestures and movements since speech is as yet undeveloped. Frequently the child's desires are fulfilled without any expression of them, a result that seems to him a product of his magical thinking.

Are a person's characteristics primarily shaped by early influences, remaining relatively stable thereafter throughout life? Or does change spontaneously occur continuously throughout life? Many people believe that early experiences are formative, providing a strong or weak foundation for later psychological growth. This view is expressed in the popular saying 'As the twig is bent, so grows the tree.' From this perspective, it is crucial to ensure that young children have a good start in life. But many developmental scientists believe that later experiences can modify or even reverse early influences; studies show that even when early experiences are traumatic or abusive, considerable recovery can occur. From this vantage point, early experiences influence, but rarely determine, later characteristics.

Traumatic experiences in this early period of life will damage a personality more seriously than those occurring in later childhood such as are found in the history of psychoneurotics. The infant's mind is more vulnerable the younger and less used it has been, furthers, the trauma has quickened the infant 's egocentricity. In addition early traumatic experiences shorten the only period in life in which an individual ordinarily enjoys the most security, thus endangering the ability to store up as it was a reasonable supply of assurance and self-reliance for the individual's later struggles through life. Thus, as such, a child sensitized considerably more toward the frustrations of later like than by later traumatic experiences. Hence many experiences in later life which would mean little to a 'healthy' person and not much to a psychoneurotic, mean a great deal of pain and suffering to the schizophrenic. His resistance against frustration is easily exhausted.

Once he reaches his limit of endurance, he escapes the unbearable reality of his present life by attempting to reestablish the autistic, delusional world of the infant, but this is impossible because the content of his delusions and hallucinations are naturally coloured by the experiences of his whole lifetime.

How do these developments influence the patient's attitude toward the analyst and the analyst's approach to him?

Due to the very damage and the succeeding chain of frustrations which the schizophrenic undergoes before finally giving in to illness, he feels extremely suspicious and distrustful of everyone, particularly of the psychotherapist ho approaches him with the intent of intruding into his isolated world and personal life. To him the physician's approach means the threat of being compelled to return to the frustrations of real life and to reveal his inadequacy to meet them or, - still worse – a repetition of the aggressive interference with his initial symptoms and peculiarities which he has encountered in his previous environment.

The difficulty that the patient's dilemma through his frustrations is the product through which is called 'delusion': Delusion itself is a false belief which is firmly held by a person even though other people recognize the belief as obviously untrue. For example, a person who truly believes he is Napoleon Blonaparte is delusional. Religious beliefs or popular conceptions, such as the beliefs that people have been abducted by aliens, are not delusions because they are widely held beliefs. Delusions are a type of psychotic symptom that indicate a person has lost contact with reality.

There are many different types of delusions. A person with a paranoid delusion believes that others - such as the FBI, or the CIA, even the Mafia as trying to harm or plot against him. A person with a delusion of reference believes that events or people refer specifically to him or her when they do not. For example, a woman with schizophrenia may believe that a television news broadcaster is talking personally to her rather than to the entire viewing audience. A grandiose delusion is a belief that one is extremely famous or that one has special powers, such as the ability to magically heal people.

A delusion of control is a belief that others are able to control one's thoughts, feelings, or actions. For example, a man with this type of delusion may believe that someone has implanted a microchip in his brain that enables other people to control his thoughts. A somatic delusion is a belief that something is wrong with one's body - for example, that one's brain is rotting away - even though no medical evidence supports this belief. A person with an erotic delusion believes that someone is in love with him or her despite a lack of evidence for this belief. In a delusion of jealousy, a person believes that his or her spouse or lover is unfaithful despite evidence to the contrary.

Delusions commonly occur in certain severe mental illnesses, such as schizophrenia, bipolar disorder (also called manic-depressive illness), some cases of major depression, Dissociative disorders, post-traumatic stress disorder, and paranoid personality disorder. In addition, delusions may result from abuse of certain drugs, including alcohol, cocaine, amphetamines, and hallucinogens such as lysergic acid diethylamide (LSD), phencyclidine (PCP), and mescaline. Medical conditions affecting the brain, such as syphilis and brain tumours, may also cause delusions.

Delusional disorder is a relatively uncommon mental illness characterized by delusions. People with this disorder have one or more delusions that persist for at least one month. In addition, they do not suffer from other symptoms of schizophrenia, such as disorganized speech and bizarre behaviour. Usually their delusions are less bizarre than those that occur in schizophrenia and seem merely odd or unsupported by facts. Examples of nonbizarre delusions include beliefs that one is being followed, loved by someone famous, or deceived by one's spouse. Because delusional disorder is relatively rare, little research has systematically examined its treatment. However, doctors most often use Antipsychotic drugs (also called neuroleptics) to treat this disorder. These drugs help reduce or eliminate delusions, hallucinations, and other psychotic symptoms.

In spite of his narcissistic retreat, every schizophrenic has some underlying notion of the unreality and loneliness of his substitute delusionary world. He longs for human contact and understanding, yet is afraid to admit of himself, or his therapist for fear of further frustration.

That is why the patient may take weeks and months to test the analyst before being willing to accept him, however, once he has accepted him. His dependence on the analyst is greater and he is more sensitive about it than is the psychoneurotic because of the schizophrenic's deeply rooted insecurity, the narcissistic seemingly self-righteous attitude is but a defence.

Whenever the analyst fails the patient from reasons to be discussed later - one cannot at times avoid failing one's schizophrenic patients - it will be severe disappointment and a repetition of the chain of frustrations the schizophrenic has previously endured.

The instinctually primitive part of the schizophrenic's mind that does not discriminate between himself and the environment, it may mean the withdrawal of the impersonal supporting forces of his infancy. Severe anxiety will follow this vital deprivation.

In the light of his personal relationship with the analyst it means that the therapist seduced the patient to use him as a bridge over which he might possibly be led from the utter loneliness of his own world to reality and human warmth, only to have him discover that this bridge is not reliable. If so, he will respond helplessly with an outburst of hostility or with renewed withdrawal and may be seen most impressively in catatonic stupors.

The symptoms of mental illness can be very distressing. People who develop schizophrenia may hear voices inside their head that say nasty things about them or command them to act in strange or unpredictable ways. Or they may be paralysed by paranoia—the deep conviction that everyone, including their closest family members, wants to injure or destroy them. People with major depression may feel that nothing brings pleasure and that life is so dreary and unhappy that it is better to be dead. People with panic disorder may experience heart palpitations, rapid breathing, and anxiety so extreme that they may not be able to leave home. People whom experience episodes of mania may engage in reckless sexual behaviour or may spend money indiscriminately, acts that later cause them to feel guilt, shame, and desperation.

Other mental illnesses, while not always debilitating, create certain problems in living. People with personality disorders may experience loneliness and isolation because their personality style interferes with social relations. People with an eating disorder may become so preoccupied with their weight and appearance that they force themselves to vomit or refuse to eat. Individuals who develop post-traumatic stress disorder may become angry easily, experience disturbing memories, and have trouble concentrating.

Experiences of mental illness often interact differently but depend on one's culture or social group, sometimes greatly so. For example, in most of the non-Western world, people with depression complain principally of physical ailments, such as lack of energy, poor sleep, loss of appetite, and various kinds of physical pain. Indeed, even in North America these complaints are commonplace. But in the United States and other Western societies, depressed people and mental health professionals who treat them tend to emphasize psychological problems, such as feelings of sadness, worthlessness, and despair. The experience of schizophrenia also differs by culture. In India, one-third of the new cases of schizophrenia involve catatonia, a behaviourial condition in which a person maintains a bizarre statue like pose for hours or days. This condition is rare in Europe and North America.

With appropriate treatment, most people can recover from mental illness and return to normal life. Even those with persistent, long-term mental illnesses can usually learn to manage their symptoms and live productive lives.

By a variety of symptoms, including loss of contact with reality, bizarre behaviour, disorganized thinking and speech, decreased emotional expressiveness, and social withdrawal. Usually only some of these symptoms occur in any one person. The term schizophrenia comes from Greek words meaning 'split mind.' However, contrary to common belief, schizophrenia does not refer to a person with a split personality or multiple personality. For a description of a mental illness in which a person has multiple personalities. To observers, schizophrenia may seem or appear for being as some sorted kind of insanity or the manufacture of madness.

Perhaps more than any other mental illness, schizophrenia has a debilitating effect on the lives of the people who suffer from it. A person with schizophrenia may have difficulty telling the difference between real and unreal experiences, logical and illogical thoughts, or appropriate and inappropriate behaviour. Schizophrenia seriously impairs a person's ability to work, go to school, enjoy relationships with others, or take care of oneself. In addition, people with schizophrenia frequently require hospitalization because they pose a danger to themselves. About 10 percent of people with schizophrenia commit suicide, and many others attempt suicide. Once people develop schizophrenia, they usually suffer from the illness for the rest of their lives. Although there is no cure, treatment can help many people with schizophrenia lead productive lives.

Schizophrenia also carries an enormous cost to society. People with schizophrenia occupy about one-third of all beds in psychiatric hospitals in the United States. In addition, people with schizophrenia account for at least 10 percent of the homeless population in the United States. The National Institute of Mental Health has estimated that schizophrenia costs the United States tens of billions of dollars each year in direct treatment, social services, and lost productivity.

Approximately 1 percent of people develop schizophrenia at some time during their lives. Experts estimate that about 1.8 million people in the United States have schizophrenia. The prevalence of schizophrenia is the same regardless of sex, race, and culture. Although women are just as likely as men to develop schizophrenia, women tend to experience the illness less severely, with fewer hospitalizations and better social functioning in the community.

Schizophrenia usually develops in late adolescence or early adulthood, between the ages of 15 and 30. Much less commonly, schizophrenia develops later in life. The illness may begin abruptly, but it usually develops slowly over months or years. Mental health professionals diagnose schizophrenia based on an interview with the patient in which they determine whether the person has experienced specific symptoms of the illness.

Symptoms and functioning in people with schizophrenia tend to vary over time, sometimes worsening and other times improving. For many patients the symptoms gradually become less severe as they grow older. About 25 percent of people with schizophrenia become symptom-free later in their lives.

A variety of symptoms characterize schizophrenia. The most prominent include symptoms of psychosis—such as delusions and hallucinations - as well as bizarre behaviour, strange movements, and disorganized thinking and speech. Many people with schizophrenia do not recognize that their mental functioning is disturbed.

Delusions are false beliefs that appear obviously untrue to other people. For example, a person with schizophrenia may believe that he is the king of England when he is not. People with schizophrenia may have delusions that others, such as the police or the FBI, are plotting against them or spying on them. They may believe that aliens are controlling their thoughts or that their own thoughts are being broadcast to the world so that other people can hear them.

Research suggests that the genes one inherits strongly influence one's risk of developing schizophrenia. Studies of families have shown that the more close one is related to someone with schizophrenia, the greater the risk one has of developing the illness. For example, the children of one parent with schizophrenia have about a 13 percent chance of developing the illness, and children of two parents with schizophrenia have about a 46 percent chance of eventually developing schizophrenia. This increased risk occurs even when such children are adopted and raised by mentally healthy parents. In comparison, children in the general population have only about a 1 percent chance of developing schizophrenia.

Some evidence suggests that schizophrenia may result from an imbalance of chemicals in the brain called neurotransmitters. These chemicals enable neurons (brain cells) to communicate with each other. Some scientists suggest that schizophrenia results from excess activity of the neurotransmitter dopamine in certain parts of the brain or from an abnormal sensitivity to dopamine. Support for this hypothesis comes from Antipsychotic drugs, which reduce psychotic symptoms in schizophrenia by blocking brain receptors for dopamine. In addition, amphetamines, which increase dopamine activity, intensify psychotic symptoms in people with schizophrenia. Despite these findings, many experts believe that excess dopamine activity alone cannot account for schizophrenia. Other neurotransmitters, such as serotonin and norepinephrine, may play important roles as well.

Although scientists favour a biological cause of schizophrenia, stress in the environment may affect the onset and course of the illness. Stressful life circumstances - such as maturing in age and character as for living in poverty, the death of a loved one, an important change in jobs or relationships, or chronic tension and hostility at home—can increase the chances of schizophrenia in a person biologically predisposed to the disease. In addition, stressful events can trigger a relapse of symptoms in a person who already has the illness. Individuals who have effective skills for managing stress may be less susceptible to its negative effects. Psychological and social rehabilitation can help patients develop more effective skills for dealing with stress.

Although there is no cure for schizophrenia, effective treatment exists that can improve the long-term course of the illness. With many years of treatment and rehabilitation, significant numbers of people with schizophrenia experience partial or full remission of their symptoms.

Treatment of schizophrenia usually involves a combination of medication, rehabilitation, and treatment of other problems the person may have. Antipsychotic drugs (also called neuroleptics) are the most frequently used medications for treatment of schizophrenia. Psychological and social rehabilitation programs may help people with schizophrenia function in the community and reduce stress related to their symptoms. Treatment of secondary problems, such as substance abuse and infectious diseases, is also an important part of an overall treatment program.

Antipsychotic medications, developed in the mid-1950s, can dramatically improve the quality of life for people with schizophrenia. The drugs reduce or eliminate psychotic symptoms such as hallucinations and delusions. The medications can also help prevent these symptoms from returning. Common Antipsychotic drugs include risperidone (Risperdal), olanzapine (Zyprexa), clozapine (Clozaril), quetiapine (Seroquel), haloperidol (Haldol), thioridazine (Mellaril), chlorpromazine (Thorazine), fluphenazine (Prolixin), and trifluoperazine (Stelazine). People with schizophrenia usually must take medication for the rest of their lives to control psychotic symptoms. Antipsychotic medications appear to be less effective at treating other symptoms of schizophrenia, such as social withdrawal and apathy.

Because many patients with schizophrenia continue to experience difficulties despite taking medication, psychological and social rehabilitation is often necessary. A variety of methods can be effective. Social skills training help people with schizophrenia learn specific behaviours for functioning in society, such as making friends, purchasing items at a store, or initiating conversations. Behaviourial training methods can also help them learn self-care skills such as personal hygiene, money management, and proper nutrition. In addition, cognitive-behaviourial therapy, a type of psychotherapy, can help reduce persistent symptoms such as hallucinations, delusions, and social withdrawal.

Because many patients have difficulty obtaining or keeping jobs, supported employment programs that help patients find and maintain jobs are a helpful part of rehabilitation. In these programs, the patient works alongside people without disabilities and earns competitive wages. An employment specialist (or vocational specialist) helps the person maintain their job by, for example, training the person in specific skills, helping the employer accommodate the person, arranging transportation, and monitoring performance. These programs are most effective when the supported employment is closely integrated with other aspects of treatment, such as medication and monitoring of symptoms.

Some people with schizophrenia are vulnerable to frequent crises because they do not regularly go to mental health centres to receive the treatment they need. These individuals often relapse and face rehospitalization. To ensure that such patients take their medication and receive appropriate psychological and social rehabilitation, assertive community treatment (ACT) programs have been developed that deliver treatment to patients in natural settings, such as in their homes, in restaurants, or on the street.

People with schizophrenia often have other medical problems, so an effective treatment program must attend to these as well. One of the most generally shared in or participated in things conforming to a type without noteworthy excellence or faults just as common a rule, by ordinary, frequent and ordinarily as an idea or expression deficient in originality or freshness, yet, only of its exchanging the commonplace of the common associated problems is vehemently and usually coarsely expressed condemnation or disapproved, as the interpretative category of an unequalled vocabulary is itself a genuine abuse. Successful treatment of substance abuse inpatients with schizophrenia requires careful coordination with their mental health care, so that the same clinicians are treating both disorders at the same time.

The high rate of substance abuse in patients with schizophrenia contributes to a high prevalence of infectious diseases, including hepatitis B and C and the human immunodeficiency virus (HIV). Assessment, education, and treatment or management of these illnesses is critical for the long-term health of patients.

Other problems frequently associated with schizophrenia include housing instability and homelessness, legal problems, violence, trauma and post-traumatic stress disorder, anxiety, depression, and suicide attempts. Close monitoring and psychotherapeutic interventions are often helpful in addressing these problems.

Several other psychiatric disorders are closely related to schizophrenia. In schizoaffective disorder, a person shows symptoms of schizophrenia combined with either mania or severe depression. Schizophreniform disorder refers to an illness in which a person experiences schizophrenic symptoms for more than one month but fewer than six months. In schizotypal personality disorder, a person engages in odd thinking, speech, and behaviour, but usually does not lose contact with reality. Sometimes mental health professionals refer to these disorders together as schizophrenia-spectrum disorders.

Severe mental illness almost always alters a person's life dramatically. People with severe mental illnesses experience disturbing symptoms that can cause of such difficulties and holding to a job, or go to school, relate to others, or cope with ordinary life demands. Some individuals require hospitalization because they become unable to care for themselves or because they are at risk of committing suicide.

The symptoms of mental illness can be very distressing. People who develop schizophrenia may hear voices inside their head that say nasty things about them or command them to act in strange or unpredictable ways. Or they may be paralysed by paranoia - the deep conviction that everyone, including their closest family members, wants to injure or destroy them. People with major depression may feel that nothing brings pleasure and that life is so dreary and unhappy that it is better to be dead. People with panic disorder may experience heart palpitations, rapid breathing, and anxiety so extreme that they may not be able to leave home. People whom experience episodes of mania may engage in reckless sexual behaviour or may spend money indiscriminately, acts that later cause them to feel guilt, shame, and desperation.

Other mental illnesses, while not always debilitating, create certain problems in living. People with personality disorders may experience loneliness and isolation because their personality style interferes with social relations. People with an eating disorder may become so preoccupied with their weight and appearance that they force themselves to vomit or refuse to eat. Individuals who develop post-traumatic stress disorder may become angry easily, experience disturbing memories, and have trouble concentrating.

Experiences of mental illness often take issue upon its stability for depending on one's culture or social group, sometimes greatly so. For example, in most of the non-Western world, people with depression complain principally of physical ailments, such as lack of energy, poor sleep, loss of appetite, and various kinds of physical pain. Indeed, even in North America these complaints are commonplace. But in the United States and other Western societies, depressed people and mental health professionals who treat them tend to emphasize psychological problems, such as feelings of sadness, worthlessness, and despair. The experience of schizophrenia also differs by culture. In India, one-third of the new cases of schizophrenia involve catatonia, a behaviourial condition in which a person maintains a bizarre statue like pose for hours or days. This condition is rare in Europe and North America.

Of furthering issues regarding depersonalization disorder, meaning, in effect, that it is a categorised illness based within its intendment for being an illness, of mind, in which people experience an unwelcome sense of detachment from their own bodies. They may feel as though they are floating above the ground, outside observers of their own mental or physical processes. Other symptoms may include a feeling that they or other people are mechanical or unreal, a feeling of being in a dream, a feeling that their hands or feet are larger or smaller than usual, and a deadening of emotional responses. These symptoms are chronic and severe enough to impede normal functioning in a social, school, or work environment.

Depersonalization disorder is a relatively rare syndrome thought to result from severe psychological stress. It may occur as part of other mental illnesses, especially anxiety disorders. For example, some people with panic disorder feel nervous, have a sense of doom about their future and health, and have a troubling sense of detachment form the lose in the attemptive use in making or doing or achieving a useful regularity as might the quality of being expected of the control over their bodies. Depersonalization disorder may also be a component of more severe mental illness, such as schizophrenia. Treatment may include training in relaxation techniques that enhance body perception and control, hypnosis to modify symptoms, and psychotherapy to explore possible stress-related components of the disorder.

Psychiatrists classify depersonalization disorder as one of the Dissociative disorders. Such disorders involve a disruption of consciousness, memory, identity, or perception.

All the while, the schizophrenic responds to altercations in the analyst's defections and understanding by corresponding stormy and dramatic changes from love to hatred, from willingness to leave his delusional world to resistance and renewed withdrawal.

As understandable as these changes are, nevertheless may come as a surprise to the analyst who frequently has not observed their source, this is quite in contrast to his experience with psychoneurosis whose emotional reactions during an interview he can usually predict. These unpredictable changes seem to be the reason for the conception of the unreliability of the schizophrenic's transference reaction, yet they follow the same dynamic rules as the psychoneurotic's oscillations between positive and negative transference and resistance, however, if the schizophrenic's reactions are stormy and seemingly more unpredictable than those of the psychoneurotic, that instances suggested to be due to the inevitable errors in the analyst's approach to the schizophrenic, of which he himself may be unaware, rather than to the unreliability of the patient's emotional response?

Why is it inevitable that the psychoanalysts disappoint his schizophrenic patient time and again?

The schizophrenic withdraws from painful reality and retires to what resembles the early speechless phase of development where consciousness is not yet crystalized. As the expression of his feelings is not hindered by the convention that he has eliminated, as his thinking, feelings, behaviour and speech - when present - obey the working rules of the archaic unconscious. His thinking is magical and does not follow logical rules. It does not admit to every last 'no' and likewise the no to 'yes': There is no recognition of space and time, I, you, and they, am interchangeable expression through which of symbols and often by movement and gestures rather than by words.

As the schizophrenic is suspicious, he will distrust the words of his analyst. He will interpret them and incidental gestures and attitudes of the analyst according to his own delusional experience. The analyst may not even be aware of these involuntary manifestations of his attitudes, yet they mean much to the hypersensitive schizophrenic who uses them as a means of orienting himself to the therapist's personality and intentions toward him.

In other words, the schizophrenic patient and the therapist are people living in different worlds and no different levels of personal development with different means of expressing and of orienting themselves. We know little about the language of the unconscious that belongs to the schizophrenic, and our access to it is blocked by the very process of our own adjustment to a world the schizophrenic has relinquished, so, we should not be surprised that errors and misunderstandings occur when we under take to communicate and strive for a rapport with him.

Another source of the schizophrenic's disappointment arises form which the analyser accepts and does not interfere with the behaviour of the schizophrenic, his attitude may lead the patient to expect that the analyst will assist in carrying out all the patient's wishes, even though they may not seem to be in his interest to the analyser's and the hospital's in their relationship to society. This attitude of acceptance so different from the patient's previous experiences readily fosters the anticipation that the analyst will try to carry out the patient's suggestion and take his part, even against conventional society with which it should occasionally arise. Frequently it will be wise for the analyst to agree with the patient's wish to remain unbattled and untidy until he is ready to talk about the reasons for his behaviour or to change spontaneously. At other times, he will unfortunately be unable to take the patient's part without being able to make the patient understand and accept the reasons for the analyst's position.

If the analyst is not able to accept the possibility of misunderstanding the reaction of the schizophrenic patient and in turn of being misunderstood by him, it may shake his security with his patient.

That is to say, that, among other things, the schizophrenic, once he accepts the analyst's insecurity. being helpless and open to himself - in spite of his pretended grandiose isolation - he will feel utterly defeated by the insecurity of his would-be helper. Such disappointment may furnish reasons for outbursts of hatred and are comparable to the negative transference reactions of psychoneurosis, yet more intense than these, since they are not limited by the restrictions of the actual world - that is, it exists in or based on fact, its only problem is a sure-enough externalization for which things are existing in the act of being external in something that has existence, ss if it were an actualization as received in the obtainable enactment for being externalized, such that its problem of in some actual life that proves obtainable achieved, in that of doing something that has an existence for having absolute actuality.

These outbursts are accompanied by anxiety, feelings of guilt, and fear of retaliations which in turn lead to increased hostility. Yet this established a vicious circle: We disappoint the patient, he is afraid that we hate him for his hatred and therefore continues to hate us. If in addition he senses that the analyst is afraid of his aggressiveness, it confirms his fear that he is actually considered as some dangerous and unacceptable, and this augments his hatred.

This establishes that the schizophrenics capable of developing strong relationships of love and hatred toward the analyst. After all, one could not be so hostile if it were not for the background of a very close relationship. In addition, the schizophrenic develops transference reactions on the narrower sense which he can differentiate from the actual interpersonal relationship. For which the schizophrenic's emotional reactions toward the analyst have to be met with extreme care and caution. The love which the sensitive schizophrenic feels as he first emerges, and his cautions acceptances of the analyst's warmth of interest are really most delicate and tender things. If the analyst deals with the transference reactions of a psychoneurotic is bad enough, though as a reparable rule, but if he fails with a schizophrenic in meeting positive feelings by pointing it out for instance before the patient indicates that he is ready to discuss it, he may easily freeze to death what has just begun to grow and so destroy any further possibility of therapy.

Some analysts may feel that the atmosphere of complete acceptance and of strict avoidance of any arbitrary denials which we recommend as a basic rule for the treatment of schizophrenics may not avoid our wish to guide of reacceptance of reality, nevertheless, Freud says that every science and therapy which accept his teachings about unconscious, about transference and resistance and about infantile sexuality, may be called psychoanalysis. According in this definition we believe we are practising psychoanalysis with our schizophrenic patients.

Whether we call it analysis or not, it is clear that successful treatment does not depend on technical rules of any special psychiatric school but rather on the basic attitude of individual therapist toward psychologic persons. If he meets them as strangle creatures of another world whose productions are not comprehensible to 'normal' beings, he cannot treat them, if he realizes, however, that the difference between himself and the psychologic is only of degree, and not of kind, he will know better how to meet him. He will not be able to identify himself sufficiently with the patient to understand and accept his emotional reactions without becoming involved in them.

The process of constant and perpetual change is examined and closely matched within the study of philosophical speculations and pointed of a world view which asserts that basic reality is constantly in a process of flux and change. Indeed, reality is identified with pure process. Concepts such as creativity, freedom, novelty, emergence, and growth are fundamental explanatory categories for process philosophy. This metaphysical perspective is to be contrasted with a philosophy of substance, the view that a fixed and permanent reality underlies the changing or fluctuating world of ordinary experience. Whereas substance philosophy emphasizes static being, process philosophy emphasizes dynamically becoming.

Although process philosophy is as old as the 6th-century Bc Greek philosopher, Heraclitus, renewed interest in it was stimulated in the 19th century by the theory of evolution. Key figures in the development of modern process philosophy were the British philosophers Herbert Spencer, Samuel Alexander, and Alfred North Whitehead, the American philosophers Charles S. Peirce and William James, and the French philosophers Henri Bergson and Pierre Teilhard de Chardin. Whitehead's Process and Reality: An Essay in Cosmology (1929) is generally considered the most important systematic expression of process philosophy.

Contemporary theology has been strongly influenced by process philosophy. The American theologian Charles Hartshorne, for instance, rather than interpreting God as an unchanging absolute, emphasizes God's sensitive and caring relationship with the world. A personal God enters into relationships in such a way that he is affected by the relationships, and to be affected by relationships is to change. So too is in the process of growth and development. Important contributions to process theology have also been made by such theologians as William Temple, Daniel Day Williams, Schubert Ogden, and John Cobb, Jr.

'Reality' is a difficult word to use to every one's satisfaction or even to one's own satisfaction. In this instance the word reality is used arbitrarily to designate the direct, here-and-now impact of the analyst upon the patient. Reality. In this sense, contrasts with the impact the analyst has through his representation in the patient's fantasy life, neurosis, and transference, since both kinds of impact seem always to coexist and since the former - the analyst's real impact - may be the worst enemy of the transference, the matter of their differentiation is possibly the most challenging aspect of analysis.

The analytic situation, which is set up to shut out ordinary reality intrusions, that cannot, . . . neither should not exclude all, but to say, that in the beginning months, for instance, reality inevitably has the upper hand. The analyst, the office, the procedure, are all overwhelmingly real. Everything is strange, frightening and exciting, gratifying and frustrating. Unlike the patient can test it and orient himself to it, the impact of this reality is usually so great that even an ordinary useful transference relationship cannot be expected to develop.

Perhaps the most confusing aspect of this beginning period is the frequent appearance in it of what can be regarded as a false transference relationship. With great intensity and clarity, the patient may reveal, through transference-like references about the analyst, some of the deepest secrets only of his neurosis but of its genesis. The pseudotransference, too good to be true, is almost sure to be nothing more than the patient's attempt to deal with the person of the analyst, the entire spectrum of his various patterns of behaviour. If, it is easy to do, the analyst overlooks the likelihood that the patient's relationship with at this time is really about that almost everything said about it is related, analysis may get off to a very bad start. And if, as is even earlier to do, the analyst's interests the genetic meaning of the openly exposed material, a good transference relationship may be seriously delayed and a workable transference neurosis may never appear. even after initial reality has had time to fade, reality may continue to intrude in ways that are very hard to detect and that is very troublesome.

One of the most serious problems of analysis is the very substantial help which the patient receives directly from the analyst and the analytic situation. For many a patient, the analyst in the analytic situation is in fact the most stable, reasonable, wise and understanding person he has ever met, and the setting in which they meet may actually be the most honest, open, direct and regular relationship he has ever experienced. Added to this is the considerable helpfulness to him of being able to clarify his life storey. confess his guilt, express his ambitions, and explore his confusions. Further real help comes from the learning-about-life accruing from the analyst's skilled questions, observations and interpretations. Taken together, the total real value to the patient of the analytic situation can easily be immense. The trouble with this kind of help is that it goes on and on, it may have such a real, direct and continuing impact upon the patient that he can never get deeply enough involved in transference situation to allow him to resolve or even to become acquainted with his most crippling internal difficulties. The trouble is far too good, the trouble also is that we as analysts apparently cannot resist the seductiveness of being directly helpful, and this, when combined with the compelling assumption that helpfulness is bound to be good, permits us top credit patient improvements to 'analysis' when more properly it should often be recognized for being the amounting result for the patient's using the analytic situation, as the model, for being the preceptors and supporter in the dealing practically within the immediate distractions as holding to some problem.

Perhaps, we can now refer to something in a clear unmistakable manner, and it would be to mention, for being, that one more difficult-to-handle intrusion of reality into the analysis, that by saying, that this is the definitive and final interruption of the transference neurosis by the reality of termination; in the sense, the situation is reversed and the intrusion is analytically desirable, since ideally the impact of reality of impending and certain termination is used to facilitate the resolution of the transference. As with the resolution of earlier episodes of transference neurosis, this final one is brought about principally by the analyst's interpretations and reconstructions. As these take effect, the transference neurosis and, hopefully, along with it the original neurosis is resolved. This final resolution, however, which is much more comprehensive, is usually very different and may not come about at all without the help of the reality of termination. Accordingly, any attenuation of the ending, such as tapering off or causal or tentative stopping, should be expected to stand in the way of an effective resolution of the transference. Yet, it seems that this is what most commonly happens to an ending, and because of this a great many patients may lose the potentially great benefit of a thorough resolution and are forever after left suspended in the net of unresolved transference.

Yet, utter indistinctly rigorous termination seems understandable, as difficult as transference neurosis may be in the analyst at other times, this ending period, if rigorously carried out, simply has to be the period of his greatest emotional strain. There can surely be no more likely time for an analyst to surrender his analytic position and, responding to his own transference, become personally involved with his patient than during the process of separating from a long and self-restrained relationship. Accordingly, it may be better to slur over the ending lightly than to mishandle it in an attempt to be rigorous.

In considering more broadly the function of the transference in the psychoanalytic process, one is confronted by the apparent naïve, but, nonetheless important questions of the role of the actual (current) object as compared with that of the object representation of the original personage in the past. We recall Freud's paradoxical, somewhat gloomy, but portentous concluding passage in 'The Dynamics of Transference.' This struggle between the doctor and the patient, between intellect and instinctual life, between understanding and seeking to act, is played out almost exclusively in the phenomena of transference. It is on that field that the victory must be won - the victory whose expression is on that field that the victory must be won - the victory whose expression is the permanent cure of the neuroses. It cannot be disputed that controlling the phenomena of transference presents the psychoanalysis with the greatest difficultly, but it should not be forgotten that they do us the inestimable service of making the patient 's hidden and forgotten erotic impulses of showing their immediate and manifested impossibilities, for when all is said and done, it is impossible to destroy anyone in absentia or in effigies.

Both object and representations are made necessary by the basic phenomenon of original separation. The existence of an image of the object, which persist in the absence of the object, is one of the important beginnings of psychic life in general, certainly an indispensable prerequisite for object relationship. As generally construed. Whether this is viewed as (or a times demonstrably is) something unstable for allotting introjection, s always subject to alternative projection, or an intrapsychic object representation clearly distinguished from the self-representation, or firm identification in the superego, or in the ego itself, these phenomena are in various ways components of the system of mastery of the fact of separation, or separateness, from the original absolutely necessarily anaclitic (in the earliest period) symbiotic 'object'. In the light of clinical observation, it would appear to be that the relative stabilities (parental) object representation. At which time of varying degree, are to a greater extent for the archaic phenomena. Even in nonpsychotic patients, overwhelmed by them, sometimes resembles the restoration from oedipal identification, which provides the preponderant basis for most demonstrable analytic transferences. That within the necrotic patients, the transference is effectively established when this representation invests the analyst to a degree - depending on intensity of drive and most of ego participation - which ranges in all the, wishing and strives to remake and analyst to biasses judgements and misinterpretation of data, finally are the actual perceptual distortions.

However, the old object representations may be invested, however rigidly established the libidinal or aggressive cathexis of the image may be, this as such can become the actual and exclusive focus of instinctual discharge, or of complicated and intense instinct-defence solutions, only and general energy-sparing quality of strictly intrapsychic processes. For the vast majority of persons, visible to any degree, including those with severe neurosis, character distortions, addictions and certain psychoses, the striving is toward the living and actual object, even at the cost of intense suffering. In a sense, this returns us to the state in which the psychological 'object-to-be'. Has a cr11itical importance never again to be duplicated, except in certain acute life emergencies, even if the object is not firmly perceived as such, in the sense of later object relations? And it does seem that trance impressions from the earliest contacts in the service of life preservation, and the associated instinctual gratifications, and innumerable secondarily associated sensory impressions. Are activated by the specific inborn urges of sexual maturation? These propel the individual to renew many of the earliest modes of actual bodily contact, in connection with seeking for specific instinctual gratification. Or, to look away from clear-cut instinctual matters to the more remote elaborations of human contact: Few regard loneliness as other than a source of suffering, even self-imposed, as an apparent matter of choice, and the forcible imposition of 'solitary confinement ' is surely one of the most cruel of punishments.

In taking to question, we are entering an area of life in which things are other then themselves, where meaning is multifaceted, and where the line between the old and the new is blurred. It should, by, its immediate measure, help develop our recognition or meaning of the pertinent applicability as to the relevance of interrelated aspects of the psychology of 'metaphor'. In the psychology of metaphor we will find a useful analogy to the psychology of transference interpretation. Our's will be newly encountered as good metaphors, those it response to which we say, 'That's it exactly' or 'That really captures it' or 'That says it all'.

Some literary and linguistic analysis, (e.g., Lewis, 1936 and Snell, 1953) and also people in everyday life, believe that there are experiences that can only be expressed metaphorically. And for this achievement that these metaphors, which may be entire poem or as lines or even words highly valued. But how can this be so? Just what in th e 'it' that the metaphor 'is' or 'captures' or 'says'? If this 'is' or this 'experience' can only be rendered metaphorically, when we can know it only as such, that is, as the metaphor itself. Of the position out of which are put forward by, T.S, Eliot (1933) and E.W. Harding (1963) in their discussion of poetry, for in these instances we are granted that there are no known and logically independent version of the experience that can serve to validate the metaphor. Whatever the metaphor makes available to us depends on it and it and so cannot be used to prove its correctness.

It seems justifiably warrantable to consider that the metaphor is a new experience rather than a mere paraphrase of an already fully constituted expedience. The metaphor creates an experience that one has never had before. It is an experience one has not realized by oneself. The metaphor does, of course, suggest certain constituent experiences of which one may have been more or less dimly aware. One may say, therefore, that the metaphor speaks for those constituents, on the existence of which much of its appeal depends. But in its organizing and implicit ly rendering these constituents in its new way, it is a creation rather than a mere paraphrase or anew edition. Paraphrasing and new editions never speak as forcefully as good new metaphors, nor could they facilitate further new experience. One analytically familiar feature of these creations is that they make it safe and pleasing to experience something that otherwise would be considered too threatening and so would be kept in fragmented obscurity through defensive measures.

Thus, when one says, 'That's it exactly' one is implicitly recognizing and announcing that one has found and accepted a new mode of experiencing oneself and one's world, which is to say, asserting a transformation of one's own subjectivity. Something is now said to be true, and in a sense it is true, but it is true for the first time. Nothing of one and the same can ever happen again, for the second time cannot be the same as the first. One can' t step into the same watering point and then step once again into the same spot of that river. A revelatory metaphor re-encountered or repeated later may lose some of its force, alternatively, it may gain some significance, butt it cannot remain exactly the same metaphor or mobilize an experience identical with the first. The point applies as well as to new metaphors that are similar to familiar ones: They have to be judged or experienced through their conventionalized predecessors, as through methods of knowing or already proved instrumentally of perceiving. The audience and the performer, who may be one person, as such that may not have, as yet.

What is to be said about the psychology of metaphor is analogous to the transformational aspects of developed transference and the steadfast interpretation that both facilitate and organize them as transference. Allowing that these transferences and 'remembered' experiences come into existence over a period of time, nothing that is identical with them has ever before been enacted, and nothing will ever be enacted again. They are creations that may be fully achieved only under specific analytic conditions. Such that living was not reliving that moment, words like re-living, re-experiencing and reliving simply do not do justice to the phenomena, that in making this claim. A seeming contradiction over-writes some of our well-establish ideas. - in offering, - I am not contradicting some of our well-established ideas about interpretation and insight, I am, however, disputing the point that insight refers to a greater proportion or in its range of comprehension, which its distance between possible extremes extent and regain former or normal state, such that, for the recovery of lost memories, and takes in as well, a new grasp of the significance and interpretations of events one has always remembered. In point, as, Freud pointed out, 'As a matter of fact I've always known it, only that I've never thought of it; (1914), In fact, it is to develop that point in furthering to say that it takes an adult to do that, especially with the help of an analyst. It was, after all, Freud's analysis of adults that make it possible to define infantile psychosexuality. In this respect, but without disregard, child analysis retains a quality of applied psychoanalysis' in the same way that the interpreted transference neurosis is: Both are always of describing as true something that was not true in quite that way at the time of its greatest developmental significance. This apparent paradox about 'remembering' as a form of creating goes a long way, probably that what it is, is distinctive about psychoanalytic interpretation.

This time, however, to further the discussion on the interpretive technique that surrounds the phase of a mutative interpretation - that in which a portion of the patient's id-relation to the analyst is made conscious in virtue of the latter's positions as auxiliary super-ego - is in itself complex. In the classical model of an interpretation, the patient will first be made aware of a state of tension of an interpretation, will next be made aware that there is repressive factor at work (that his super-ego is threatening him with punishment), and will only then be made aware of the id-impulse which has stirred up the protects of his super-ego and so given to the anxiety in his ego. This is the classical scheme. In actual practice, the analyst finds himself working from all three sides at once, or in irregular successions. At one moment a small portion of the patient's super-ego may be revealed to him in all its savagery, at another the shrinking defencelessness of his ego, at yet another his attention may be directed to the attempts which he is making at restitution - at compensating for his hostility, on some occasions a fraction of id-energy may even be directly encouraged to break its way through the last remains of an already weakened resistance. There is, however, one characteristic which all of these various operations has in common, they are essentially upon a small scale. For the mutative interpretation is inevitably governed by the principle of minimal doses. It is a commonly agreed clinical fact that alternations in a patient under analysis appear almost always to be extremely gradual: We are inclined to suspect sudden and large changes as an indication that suggestive rather than psycho-analyst processes are at work. The gradual nature of the change brought about in psychoanalysis will be explained, as, only to suggest, those changes are the result of the summation of an immense number of minuet steps, each of which correspond to a mutative interpretation. And the smallness of each step is in turn imposed by the very nature of the analytic situation. For each interpretation involves the release of a certain quantity of id-energy, and, if the quantity released is too large, the higher unstable state of equilibrium which enables the analyst to function as the patient's auxiliary super-ego is bound to be upset. The whole analytic situation will thus be imperilled, since it is only in virtue of the analyst's acting as auxiliary super-ego that these released id-energy can occur at all.

The effectuality from which follow the analytic attempt to bring unequalled amounts in the confronting collections of some improper use to a resultant quantity of id-energy into the patient's consciousness all at once. On the one hand, nothing whatever may happen, or on the other hand there may be an unmanageable result, but in neither event will be a mutative interpretation has been effected. The analyst's power as auxiliary super-ego may be for two very different reasons. It may be that the id-impulses were trying to bring out being not in fact sufficiently urgent at the moment: For, after all, the emergence of an id-impulse depends on two factors - not only on the permission of the super-ego, but also on the urgency (the degree of cathaxis) of the id-impulse itself. This, then, may be one cause of an apparently negative response to an interpretation, and evidently a fairly harmless one. but the same apparent result may also be due to something else, in spite of the id-impulse being really urgent, the strength of the patient's own repressive forces (the degree of repression) may have been too great to allow his ego to listen to the persuasive voice of the auxiliary super-ego. Now we have a situation dynamically identical with the next one we have to consider, though economically different. this next situation is one in which the patient accepts the interpretation, that is, allows the id-impulse into his consciousness, but is immediately overwhelmed with anxiety. This may show itself in a number of ways, for instance, the patient may produce a manifest anxiety-attack. Or the may exhibit signs of 'real' anger with the analyst with a complete lack of insight, or he may break off the analysis. In any of these cases the analytic situation will, for the moment, at least, have broken down. The patient will be behaving just as the hypnotic subject behaves when, having been ordered by the hypnotist to perform an action too much at variance with his own consciousness, he breaks off the hypnotic relation and wakes up from his trance. This state of things, which is manifest where the patient responds to an interpretation with an actual outbreak of anxiety or one of its equivalents, may be latent were the patient shows no response, and this latter case may be the more awkward of the two, since it is masked, and it may sometimes be the effect of a greater overdose of interpretation than where manifest anxiety arises (though obviously other factors will be of determining importance, and in particularly the nature of the patient's neurosis). Yet this threatened collapse of the analytic situation to an overdose of interpretation: But it might be more accurate in some ways to ascribe it to an insufficient dose. For what has happened is that the second phase of the interpretation process has not occurred: The phase in which the patient becomes aware that his impulse is directed toward an archaic phantasy object and not toward a real one.

In the second phase of a complete interpretation, therefore, a crucial part is played by the patient's sense of reality: For the successful outcome of that phase depends upon his ability, at the critical moment of the emergence into consciousness of the released quantity of id-energy, to distinguish between his phantasy object and the real analyst. The problem is closely related to one that has been discussed elsewhere, namely that of the extreme liability of the analyst's position as auxiliary super-ego. The analytic situation is all the time threatening to degenerate into a 'real' situation. But this actually means the opposite of what it appears to. It means that the patient is all the time on the brink of turning the really external object (the analyst) into the archaic one; that is to say, he is on the brink of projecting his primitive introjected images onto himself. In so far as the patient actually does this, the analyst becomes like anyone else that he meets in real life - a phantasy object. The analyst then ceases to possess the peculiar advantages derived from the analytic situation, he will be introjected like all other phantasy objects into the analytic situation, he will be introjected like all other phantasy objects into the patient's super-ego, and will no longer be able to function in the peculiar ways which are essential to the effecting of a mutative interpretation. In this difficulty the patient's sense of reality is an essential but a very feeble [-ally]: An improvement in it is one of the things that we hope the analysis will bring about. It is important, therefore, not to submit it to any unnecessary strain, and that is the fundamental reason why the analyst must avoid any real behaviour, that is likely to confirm the patient's view of him as a 'bad' or a 'good' phantasy object. This is perhaps more obvious as regards the 'bad' object. If, for instance, the analyst were to show that he was really shocked or frightened by one of the patient's id-impulses, as the patient would immediately treat him in that respect as a dangerous object and introject him into his archaic severe super-ego. Therefore, on the one hand, there would be a diminuation in the analyst's power to function as an auxiliary super-ego and to allow the patient's to become conscious of his id-impulses - that is to say, in his power to bring about the first phase of a mutative interpretation, and on the other hand, he would, as a real object, become sensibly less distinguishable from the patient's 'bad' phantasy object and to that extent the carrying through of the second phase of a mutative interpretation would also be made more difficult. Or, agin, there is another case. Supposing the analyst behaves in an opposite way and actively urges the patient to give free rein to his id-impulse. There is then a possibility of the patient confusing the analyst with the image of a treacherous parent who, at the beginning, encourages him to seek gratification, and then suddenly turns and punishes him. In such a case the patient's ego may look for defence by itself suddenly turning upon the analyst as though he were his own id-, and treating him with all the severity of which his super-ego is capable. again, the analyst is running a risk of losing his privileged position. But it may be equally unwise for the analyst to act really in such a way as to encourage the patient to project his 'good' introjected object onto him. For the patient will then tend to regard him as a good objective and archaic sense and will incorporate him with his archaic 'good' images and will use him as a protection against his 'bad' ones. In that way, his infantile positive impulses as well as his negative ones may escape analysis, for there may no longer be a possibility for his ego to make a comparison between the phantasy external object and the real one. it will, perhaps, be argued that, with the best of wills in the world, the analyst, however careful he may be, will be unable to prevent the patient from projecting these various images onto him. This is, of course, indisputable, and, the whole effectiveness of analysis depends upon its being so. The lesson of these difficulties is merely to remind us that the patient's sense of reality has the narrowest limits. It is a paradoxical fact that the best way of enuring that his ego will be able to distinguish between phantasy and reality is to withhold reality from him as much as possible. but it is true, his ego is so weak - so much at the mercy of his id and super-ego - that he can only cope with reality if it is administered in minimal doses. And these doses are in fact what the analyst gives him, in the form of interpretations.

A mutative interpretation can only be applied to an id-impulse which is actually on a state of cathexis. This seems self-evident; for the dynamic changes in the patient's mind implied by a mutative interpretation can only be brought about by the operation of a charge of energy originating in the patient himself: The function of the analyst is merely to ensure that the energy should or can flow along one channel rather than along another. It follows that the purely informative 'dictionary' type of interpretation will be non-mutative, but useful it may be a prelude to mutative interpretations. And this leads to a number of practical inferences. Every mutative interpretation must be emotionally 'immediate, but the patient must live through it as something actual or genuine. This requirement, that the interpretation must be 'immediate', may be expressed in another way by saying that interpretation must always be directed to the 'point of urgency'. At any given moment some particular id-impulse will be generated in activity, this is the impulse that is susceptible of mutative interpretation at the time, and no other one. It is, no doubt, neither possible nor desirable to be giving mutative interpretations all the time. as Melanie Klein has pointed out, it is a most precious quality in an analyst to be able at any moment to pick out the point of urgency.

But the fact that every mutative interpretation must deal with an 'urgent' impulse take us back one more to the commonly felt fear of the explosive possibilities of interpretation, and particularly of what is vaguely referred to as 'deep' interpretation. The terminological description is, no doubt, as the interpretation of material which is neither genetically early and historically distant from the patient's actual experience nor under an especially heavy weight of repression – material, in any case, which is in the normal course of things exceedingly inaccessible to his ego and remote from it. There seems reason to believe, moreover, that the anxiety which is liable to be aroused by the approach of such material to consciousness and may be of peculiar severity. The question whether it is 'safe' to interpret such material will, as usual, mainly depend upon whether an interpretation can be carried through, in the ordinary run of the case, as this material which is urgent during the earlier stages of the analysis is not deep. We have to deal at first only with more or less far-going displacements of the deep impulse. And the deep material itself is only reached later and by degrees, so that no sudden appearance of unmanageable quantities of anxiety is to be hesitorially anticipated. In exceptional cases, however, owing to some peculiarities in the structure of the neurosis, deep impulses may be urgent at a very early stage of the analysis. We are then faced by a dilemma. If we give an interpretation of this deep material, the resultant amounts of anxiety produced in the patient may be so great that his sense of reality may not be sufficient to permit of its accomplishment, and the whole analysis may be jeopardised, but, it must not be thought that, in such critical cases as we are now considering, the difficulty can necessarily be avoided simply by not giving any interpretation or by giving more superficial interpretations of non-urgent material or by attempting reassurances. It seems probable, in fact, that these alternative procedures may do little or nothing to obviate the trouble, on the contrary, they may even exacerbate the tension created by the urgency of the deep impulses which are the actual cause of the threatening anxiety. Thus the anxiety may break out in spite of these palliative efforts and, if so, it will be doing so under the most unfavourable conditions, that is to say, outside the mitigating influences afforded by the mechanism of interpretation. It is possible, therefore, that, of these alternative procedures which are open to the analyst faced by such a difficulty. The interpretation of the urgent id-impulses, deep though they may b e, will actually be the safer.

It is, of course, a matter of common experience, that it possible with certain patients to continue indefinitely giving interpretations without producing any apparent effect whatever. There is an amusing criticism of this kind of 'interpretation-fanaticism' in the excellent historical chapter of Rank and Ferenczi. But it is clear from their words that what they have in mind are essentially extra-transference interpretations, for the burden of their criticism is that such a procedure implies neglect of the analytic situation. This is the simplest case. Where a waste of time and energy is the main result. But there are other occasions, on which a policy of giving strings of extra-transference interpretations is apt to lead the analyst into more positive difficulties. Attention was drawn by Reich a few years back, in the course of some technical discussions in Vienna to a tendency among inexperienced analysts to get into trouble by eliciting from the patient great quantities of material in a disordered and unrelated fashion: This may, be maintained, be carried to such lengths that the analysis is brought to an irremediable state of chaos. He pointe out truly that the material we have to deal with is stratified and that it is highly important in digging it out not to interference, more that we can help with th e arrangement of that state. He had in mind, of course, the analogy of an incompetent archaeologist, whose clumsiness may obliterate for all time the possibility of reconstructing the history of an important site. However, the results in the case of a clumsy analysis do not hold of any pessimistic cause to happen, as it was, re-stratification itself of its own accord if it is given the opportunity; That is to say, in the analytic situation. At the same time, is that of the presence of the risk, and it seems to be particularly likely to occur where extra-transference interpretation is excessively or exclusively restored to. The means of preventing it, and the remedy if it has occurred, lie in returning to transference interpretation at the point of urgency. For if we can discover which of the material is 'immediate' in the sense that the problematic occurrence enabling stratification is automatically solved, and it is a characteristic if most extra-transference material that it has no immediacy and consequently stratification is far more difficult to decipher. The measures suggested by Reich himself for preventing the occurrence of this state of chaos are consistent with those that he stresses the importance of interpreting resistance as opposed to the primary id-impulses themselves - and this, was a policy that was laid down at an early stage in the history of analysis. But it is, of course, one of the characteristics of a resistance that it arises in relation to the analyst. Thus, interpretation of a resistance will almost inevitably be a transference interpretation.

But the most serious risks that arise from the making of extra-transference interpretation are due to the inherent difficulty in completing their interpretation, for a successful outcome as such, depends upon his ability, at which time of the emergence into consciousness and the released quantity of id-energy. They are from their nature unpredictable in their effects. There seems to be a special risk of the patient not carrying through to a competed interpretation, hitherto, namely that the extreme liability of the analyst's position as auxiliary super-ego, is that, the analytic situation is all the time threatening to degenerate into a 'real' situation. It means that the patient is all the time perched upon the circumference edge-horizon of turning the external object (the analyst) into the archaic one, but of projecting the id-impulse that has been made conscious onto the analyst. This risk, no doubt, applies to some extent to transference interpretations. However, the situation is less likely to arise when the object of the id-impulses is actually present and is moreover the same person as the maker of interpretation. We may, once, more, recall the problem of 'deep' interpretation, and point out that its dangers, even in the most unfavourable circumstances, seem to be greatly diminished if the interpretation in question is a transference interpretation. Even so, there appears to be more of a chance that in this whole process occurring silently and so being overlooked in the case of an extra-transference interpretation, particularly in the earlier stages of an analysis. For this reason, it would seem to be important after giving an extra-transference interpretation to be specially in the 'qui-vive' for transferences complications. This last peculiarity of the extra-transference interpretation is actually one of the most important forms to a practical standpoint of things. For on account of it they can be made to act as 'feeders' for the transference situation, and so to pave the way for mutative interpretations. In other words, by giving an extra-transference interpretation, the analyst can often provide a situation in the transference of which he can then give a mutative interpretation.

Therefore, it is probable that a large majority of our interpretations are outside the transference - though it should be added that it often happens that one is ostensibly giving an extra-transference interpretation one is implicitly giving a transference one. A cake cannot be made of nothing but currants, and, though it is true that extra-transference interpretations, are not for the most part, mutative and do not they bring about the crucial results that involve a permanent change in the patient's mind. They are, nonetheless essential, if taken to an analogy of trench warfare, the acceptance of a transference interpretation corresponds to the capture of a key position, while the extra-transference interpretations correspond to the general advance and to the consolidation of a fresh line of defence, which are made possible by the capture of the key position. But when this general advance goes beyond a certain point, there will be another check, and the capture of a further key position will be necessary before progress can be resumed. An oscillation of this kind between transference and extra-transference interpretations will represent the normative course of events in an analysis.

Although the giving of mutative interpretations may thus only occupy a small portion of psycho-analytic treatment, it will, upon being, that the most important part from the point of view of deeply exerting affective percussions. Do so, because of the influencing characteristic confirmations as drawn upon the spoken-exchange of the patient's mindful knowing, in that the individuals that feel, perceive, think, wills, and especially reasons are all taken into heedful compliance. It may be of interest to consider how a moment through which of such an importance to the patient affects the analyst himself. Mrs. Klein has suggested that there must be some quite special internal difficulty as to involve the analyst in interpretations. This is shown in their avoidance by psycho-therapists of non-analytic schools, but many psycho-analysts will be aware of traces of the same tendency in themselves. It may be rationalized into mutative interpretations. This is shown in the avoidance by psycho-therapists of non-analytic schools, if not many consisting of a psycho-analyst as flown over to passing their flow of emptying space, nonetheless, this dialectic awareness traces of the same tendency as in them. But behind this there is somewhat of a lurking difficulty in the actual giving of the interpretation, for there seems to be a constant temptation for the analyst to do something else instead. Questions may be asked of whether o r not. As given to the reassurances or advice or discourses upon theory, or may give interpretations -but interpretations that are not mutative, extra-transference interpretations, interpretations that are non-immediate, or ambiguous, or in exacting of two or more alternative interpretations simultaneously, or he may, perhaps, give interpretations and at the same time, show his own scepticism about them. All of this strongly suggests that the giving of a mutative interpretation is a crucial act for the analyst as well as for the patient. And this inturn will become intelligible when we reflect that at the moment of interpretation the analyst is in fact deliberately Evoking a quantity of the patients id-energy while it is a live and actual and unambiguous and aimed directly himself. Such a moment must be above all others put to the test his relations with his unconscious impulses.

Interpretation of the transference is central to all psychoanalytic models. Definitions of transference and transference interpretation have changed greatly during the past half-century, influenced by major movements in philosophy, but advances in psycho-analytic research and theory, and changes in our of understanding Freud. Suggestively. The advances in psychoanalytic research and theory, and changes in our understanding of Freud. Is that, the historical, relatively simple, concepts of the transference as the reproductions in the presence of significant relationships from therapists do not adequately meet current clinical theoretical demands? Modernist views of the transference emphasize as in additional sources of transference responses, the role of the analytic background of safety, the constant modifications of unconscious fantasy and internal representations, and the interactive nature of transference response, with important interpersonal and intersubjective components. It is suggested that the evolving modernists view of transference and transference interpretation permit a fuller accounting for transference and transference components. Such in a fuller accountability, for which of these issues of psychological 'truth' has open the way for better informed interventions. The issue of psychological 'truth' and 'distortion' as applied to transference phenomena will be presented with clinical vignettes.

Psychoanalysis, since the earliest days of the, Studies on Hysteria (Breuer and Freud, 1993-1905), have always given special attention to the transference and to the interpretation of transference, believing it to be central in our theory and technique. While there, has never been a lack of interest in transference interpreting. It is not clear why this is so, and the reasons may vary in different parts of the international psychoanalytic community. In America, at least, Gill's (1982) recent, and somewhat radical presentation of transference interpretation has surely helped to the grasping upon our developing attentions. Nevertheless, of another reason for our intensified interests in transference interpretation is the opportunity it provides for the rhetorically dialectic awareness, in that discussions, have lead us to the diverse analytic theories and techniques that today complete the diverseness as observed, for which of our attentions and allegiance to which transference interpretation seems to have replaced self-psychology. Thus, the encompassing topic that allows analysts of varied persuasions among many structural and fundamental elements that forge out the shape for taking upon the imparting of instinctual information. As to know, and knowing that you know, is, applied, however, of its depthful concerning contemplations with which is distinguished by the evolving characterizations that are of knowing that you know is really nothing whatsoever.

Despite the diversity of the transference and its interpreting in analytic process and cure, differing only in whether transference is everything or almost everything to give a clear-cut definition of what transference is.

Laplanche and Pontalis (1973) had written that, 'The reason it is so difficult to produce a definition of transference is that for many authors the notion has taken on a very broad extension, even coming to connote all the phenomena which constitute the patient's relationship with the psychoanalyst, as a result the concept is burdened down more than any other with each analyst's particular view on the treatment - on its objective, dynamics, tactics, scope, and so forth. The question of the transference is thus beset by a whole series of difficulties which have been the subject of debate in classical psychoanalysis.'

Sandler (1983) has discussed how the terms transference and transference resistance, as well as other terms have undergone profound changes in meaning as new discoveries and new trends of psycho-analytic technique assume ascendency. He said, . . . major changes in technical emphasis brought about the extension of the transference concept, which now has dimensions of meaning which differ from the official definition of the term. I am not sure there has ever been a simplified definition of the term. While a certain flexibility of definition makes conversation possible in a field of diverse views, which we may never be clear on what any two people mean when they use the term is a significant hindrance to our discourse.

However: with this in mind we might review one of Freud's last comments on transference. In 'An Outline of Psycho-Analysis' (1940), published posthumously, he wrote on the analytic situation:

The most remarkable thing is this. The patient is not satisfied with regarding the analyst in the light of reality as a helper and advisor who, moreover, is remunerated for the trouble he takes and who would himself be content with some role that of a guide on a different mountain to climb, on the contrary, the patient sees in him. the return, and the reincarnation, of some important figure out of his childhood or past, and consequently transfer onto him, feelings and reactions which undoubtedly apply this prototype. This fact of transference soon proves to be a factor of an undreamt-of importance, on the other hand bud an instrument of irreplaceable value and on the other, that he set out on a different undertaking without any suspicion of extraordinary power that would be at his command. . . .

Another advantage of transference, too, in that in it the patient produces before us with plastic clarity an important part of his life-story, of which he would, otherwise have probably given us only an insufficient account. He acts it before us, as it was, instead of reporting it to us. Freud saw the transference interpretation as a method of strengthening the ego against past unconscious wishes and conflicts.

It is the analyst's task constantly to speak abruptly, and in doing so, the patient may relinquish of his menacing illusions and to show him again and again, of what it takes to be or begin of a new life, are the reflections of the past. And least, he should fall into a state in which he is inaccessible to all evidences, the analyst takes that neither the love nor the hostility reaching an extreme height. This is affected by preparing him in good time for these possibilities and by not overlooking the first signs of them. Careful handling of the transference on these lines is as a role richly rewarded. If we succeed, as we usually can, in enlightenment the patient on the true nature of the phenomena of the transference, we thus have struck a powerful weapon out of the hand of his resistance and will have converted dangers into gains. For a patient never forgets again what he has experienced in the form of transference, it carries a greater force of conviction than anything he can acquire in other ways.

Alzheimer's Disease, a progressive brain disorders that causes a gradual and irreversible decline in memory, language skills, perception of time and space, and, eventually, the inability to care for them. First described by German psychiatrist Alois Alzheimer in 1906, Alzheimer's disease was initially thought to be a rare condition affecting only young people, and was referred to as prehensile dementia. Today late-onset Alzheimer's disease is recognized as the most common cause of the loss of mental function in those aged 65 and over. Alzheimer's in people in their 30s, 40s, and 50s, called early-onset Alzheimer's disease, inhabits less frequently, accountings for less than 10 percent of the estimated 4 million Alzheimer's cases in the United States.

Although Alzheimer's disease is not a normal part of the aging process, the risk of developing the disease increases as people grow older. About 10 percent of the United States population over the age of 65 is affected by Alzheimer's disease, and nearly 50 percent of those over age 85 may have the disease.

Alzheimer's disease takes a devastating toll, not only on the patients, but also on those who love and care for them. Some patients experience immense fear and frustration as they struggle with once commonplace tasks and slowly lose their independence. Family, friends, and especially those who provide daily care suffer immeasurable pain and stress as they witness Alzheimer's disease slowly and apprehensively take their loved one from them.

The onset of Alzheimer's disease is usually very gradual. In the early stages, Alzheimer's patients have relatively mild problems learning new information and remembering where they have left common objects, such as keys or a wallet. In time, they begin to have trouble recollecting recent events and finding the right words to express themselves. As the disease progresses, patients may have difficulty remembering what day or month it is, or finding their way around familiar surroundings. They may develop a tendency to wander off and then be unable to find their way back. Patients often become irritable or withdrawn as they struggle with fear and frustration when once commonplace tasks become unfamiliar and intimidating. Behavioural changes may become more pronounced as patients become paranoid or delusional and unable to engage in normal conversation.

Eventually Alzheimer's patients become completely incapacitated and unable to take care of their most basic life functions, such as eating and using the bathroom. Alzheimer's patients may live many years with the disease, usually dying from other disorders that may develop, such as pneumonia. Typically the time from initial diagnosis until death is seven to ten years, but this is quite variable and can range from three to twenty years, depending on the age of the onset, other medical conditions present, and the care patients receive.

The brains of patients with Alzheimer's have distinctive formations - abnormally shaped proteins called tangles and plaques - that are recognized as the hallmark of the disease. Not all brain regions show these characteristic formations. The areas most prominently affected are those related to memory.

Tangles are long, slender tendrils found inside nerve cells, or neurons. Scientists have learned that when a protein-called tau becomes altered, it may cause the characteristic tangles in the brain of the Alzheimer's patient. In healthy brains provides structural support for neurons, but in Alzheimer's patients this structural support collapses.

Plaques, or clumps of fibres, form outside the neurons in the adjacent brain tissue. Scientists found that a type of protein, called amyloid precursor protein, forms toxic plaques when it is cut in two places. Researchers have isolated the enzyme beta-secretes, which is believed to make one of the cuts in the amyloid precursor protein. Researchers also identified another enzyme, called gamma secretes, that makes the second cut in the amyloid precursor protein. These two enzymes snip the amyloid precursor protein into fragments that then accumulate to form plaques that are toxic to neurons.

Scientists have found that tangles and plaques cause neurons in the brains of Alzheimer's patients to shrink and eventually die, first in the memory and language centres and finally throughout the brain. This widespread neuron degeneration leaves gaps in the brain's messaging network that may interfere with communication between cells, causing some of the symptoms of Alzheimer's disease.

Alzheimer's patients have lower levels of neurotransmitters, chemicals that carry complex messages back and forth between the nerve cells. For instance, Alzheimer's disease seems to decrease the level of the neurotransmitter acetylcholine, which is known to influence memory. A deficiency in other neurotransmitters, including somatostatin and corticotropin-releasing factor, and, particularly in younger patients, serotonin and norepinephrine, are seemed as obstacles within the normal communication between brain cells.

The causes of Alzheimer's disease remain a mystery, but researchers have found that particular groups of people have risk factors that make them more likely to develop the disease than the general population. For example, people with a family history of Alzheimer's are more likely to develop Alzheimer's disease.

Some of the most promising Alzheimer's research is being conducted in the field of genetics to learn the role a family history of the disease has in its development. Scientists have learned that people who are carriers of a specific version of the apolipoprotein E gene (apoE genes), found on chromosome 19, are several times more likely to develop Alzheimer's than carriers of other versions of the apoE gene. The most common version of this gene in the general population is apoE3. Nearly half of all late-onset Alzheimer's patients have the fewer in common apoE4 versions, however, and research has shown that this gene plays a role in Alzheimer's disease. Scientists have also found evidence that variations in one or more genes located on chromosomes 1, 10, and 14 may increase a person's risk for Alzheimer's disease. Scientists have identified the gene variations on chromosomes 1 and 14 and learned that these genes produce mutations in proteins called presenilins. These mutated proteins apparently trigger the activity of the enzyme gamma secretes, which splices the amyloid precursor protein.

Researchers have made similar strides in the investigation of early-onset of Alzheimer's disease, as to a series of genetic mutations in patients with an early-grip upon the onset of Alzheimer's has been linked to the production of amyloid precursor protein, the protein in plaques that may be implicated in the destruction of neurons. One mutation is particularly interesting to geneticists because it occurs on a gene involved in the genetic disorder Down syndrome. People with Down syndrome usually develop plaques and tangles in their brains as they get older, and researchers believe that learning more about the similarities between Down syndrome and Alzheimer's may further our understanding of the genetic elements of the disease.

Some studies suggest that one or more factors other than heredity may determine whether people develop the disease. One study published in February 2001 compared residents of Ibadan, Nigeria, who eat a mostly low-fat vegetarian diet, with African Americans living in Indianapolis, Indiana, whose diet included a variety of high-fat foods. The Nigerians were less likely to develop Alzheimer's disease compared to their US counterparts. Some researchers suspect that health imposes on high blood pressure, atherosclerosis (arteries clogged by fatty deposits), high cholesterol levels, or other cardiovascular problems may play a role in the development of the disease.

Other studies have suggested that environmental agents may be a possible cause of Alzheimer's disease; for example, one study suggested that high levels of aluminum in the brain may be a risk factor. Several scientists initiated research projects to further investigate this connection, but no conclusive evidence has been found linking aluminum with Alzheimer's disease. Similarly, investigations into other potential environmental causes, such as zinc exposure, viral agents, and food-borne poisons, while initially promising, have generally turned up inconclusive results.

Some studies indicate that brain trauma can trigger a degenerative process that results in Alzheimer's disease. In one study, an analysis of the medical records scribed upon veterans of World War II (1939-1945) linked serious head injury in early adulthood with Alzheimer's disease in later life. The study also looked at other factors that could possibly influence the development of the disease among the veterans, such as the presence of the apoE gene, but no other factors were identified.

Alzheimer's disease is only positively diagnosed by examining brain tissue under a microscope to see the hallmark plaques and tangles, and this is only possible after a patient dies. As a result, physicians rely on a series of other techniques to diagnose probable Alzheimer's disease in living patients. Diagnosis begins by ruling out other problems that cause memory loss, such as stroke, depression, alcoholism, and the use of certain prescription drugs. The patient undergoes a thorough examination, including specialized brain scans, to eliminate other disorders. The patient may be given a detailed evaluation called a neuropsychological examination, which is designed to evaluate a patient's ability to perform specific mental tasks. This helps the physician determine whether the patient is showing the characteristic symptoms of Alzheimer's disease - progressively worsening memory problems, language difficulties, and trouble with spatial direction and time. The physician also asks about the patient's family medical history to learn about any past serious illnesses, which may give a hint about the patient's current symptoms.

Evidence shows that there is inflammation in the brains of Alzheimer's patients, which may be associated with the production of amyloid precursor protein. Studies are underway to find drugs that prevent this inflammation, to possibly slow or even halt the progress of the disease. Other promising approaches centre on mechanisms that manipulate amyloid precursor protein production or accumulation. Drugs are in development that may block the activity of the enzymes that cut the amyloid precursor protein, halting amyloid production.

Other studies in mice suggest those vaccinating animals with amyloid precursor protein can produce a reaction that clears amyloid precursor protein from the brain. Physicians have started vaccination studies in humans to determine if the same potentially beneficial effects can be obtained. There is still much to be learned, but as scientists better understand the genetic components of Alzheimer's, the roles of the amyloid precursor protein and the tau protein in the disease, and the mechanisms of nerve cell degeneration, the possibility that a treatment will be developed is more likely.

The responsibility for caring for Alzheimer's patients generally falls on their spouses and children. Care givers must constantly be on guard for the possibility of Alzheimer's patients wandering away or becoming agitated or confused in a manner that jeopardizes the patient or others. Coping with a loved one's decline and inability to recognize familiar face causes enormous pain.

The increased burden faced by families is intense, and the life of the Alzheimer's care giver is often called a 36-hour day. Not surprisingly, care givers often develop health and psychological problems of their own as a result of this stress. The Alzheimer's Association, a national organization with local chapters throughout the United States, was formed in 1980 in large measure to provide support for Alzheimer's care givers. Today, national and local chapters are a valuable source for information, referral, and advice.

Of which is to say, that Roderick MacKinnon, born in 1956, is the American biomedical researcher and co-winner of the 2003 Nobel Prize in chemistry for his discoveries involving ion channels. The pores that govern the passage of molecules into and out of cells, in that of every second in each of the billions of cells in the human body, millions of ions, such as potassium and sodium, shuttles back and forth through these special portals in the cellular membrane. This action underlies a range of physiological processes, including muscle contraction and the communication of impulses between nerve cells. MacKinnon and his colleagues were the first to show the detailed structure of one type of ion channel.

Born in 1956, MacKinnon grew up in Burlington, Massachusetts, outside Boston. He earned his bachelor's degree in biochemistry from Brandeis University in Waltham, Massachusetts, in 1978, and his medical degree from Tufts University School of Medicine in Boston in 1982. After beginning a career in medicine, MacKinnon turned to biomedical research. Postdoctoral fellowships at Harvard University in Cambridge, Massachusetts, and Brandeis ultimately led to a professorship in the Department of Neurobiology at Harvard Medical School in 1989. In 1996 MacKinnon moved to Rockefeller University in New York City, where he became a professor of molecular Neurobiology and biophysics.

To study an ion channel - in this case, a particular cellular protein involved in the transport of potassium - MacKinnon chose a difficult method known as X-ray crystallography. This method involves forming the protein into a crystal and then using X rays to determine the protein's structure. Many scientists doubted that the approach would work, but in 1998 MacKinnon and his team achieved success, presenting a detailed three-dimensional picture of the potassium channel.

In subsequent research, MacKinnon and his colleagues discovered more about the chemical workings of ion channels. This work helped to explain, for example, how such a pore permits the passage of millions of potassium ions per second while largely blocking the passage of sodium ions. Increased knowledge of these protein pores will be important for the design of future drugs because the malfunctioning of ion channels has been linked to heart disease and cystic fibrosis, among other illnesses.

In addition to the Nobel Prize, MacKinnon has been honoured with the 1999 Albert Lasker Basic Medical Research Award. He shared the Nobel Prize with American biologist Peter Agre, who, in separate research, discovered the molecular channel through which cells transport water.

When a neuron is in its resting state, its voltage is about -70 millivolts. An excitatory neurotransmitter alters the membrane of the postsynaptic neuron, making it possible for ions (electrically charged molecules) to move back and forth across the neuron's membranes. This flow of ions makes the neuron's voltage rise toward zero. At one end of a nerve cell to the other by means of an electrical impulse, when it reaches the terminal end of a nerve cell, the impulse trigger's tiny sacs called presynaptic vessicles to release their contents, chemical messengers called neurotransmitters. The neurotransmitters float across the synapse, or gap between adjacent nerve cells. When they reach the neighbouring nerve cell, the neurotransmitters fit into specialized receptor sites much as a key fits into a lock, causing that nerve cell to 'fire,' or generate an electric message-carrying impulse. As the message continues through the nervous system, the presynaptic cell absorbs the excess neurotransmitters, and repackages them in presynaptic vessicles in a process called neurotransmitter reuptake. If enough excitatory receptors have been activated, the postsynaptic neuron responds by firing, generating a nerve impulse that causes its own neurotransmitter to be released into the next synapse. An inhibitory neurotransmitter causes different ions to pass back and forth across the postsynaptic neuron's membrane, lowering the nerve cell's voltage to -80 or -90 millivolts. The drop in voltage makes it less likely that the postsynaptic cell will fire.

If the postsynaptic cell is a muscle cell rather than a neuron, an excitatory neurotransmitter will cause the muscle to contract. If the postsynaptic cell is a gland cell, an excitatory neurotransmitter will cause the cell to secrete its contents.

While most neurotransmitters interact with their receptors to create new electrical nerve impulses that energize or inhibit the adjoining cell, some neurotransmitter interactions do not generate or suppress nerve impulses. Instead, they interact with a second type of receptor that changes the internal chemistry of the postsynaptic cell by either causing or blocking the formation of chemicals called second messenger molecules. These second messengers regulate the postsynaptic cell's biochemical processes and enable it to conduct the maintenance necessary to continue synthesizing neurotransmitters and conducting nerve impulses. Examples of second messengers, which are formed and entirely contained within the postsynaptic cell, include cyclic adenosine monophosphate, diacylglycerol, and inositol phosphates.

Once neurotransmitters have been secreted into synapses and have passed on their chemical signals, the presynaptic neuron clears the synapse of neurotransmitter molecules. For example, acetylcholine is broken down by the enzyme acetylcholinesterase into choline and acetate. Neurotransmitters like dopamine, serotonin, and GABA is removed by a physical process called reuptake. In reuptake, a protein in the presynaptic membrane acts as a sort of sponge, causing the neurotransmitters to reenter the presynaptic neuron, where they can be broken down by enzymes or repackaged for reuse.

Neurotransmitters are known to be involved in a number of disorders, including Alzheimer's disease. Victims of Alzheimer's disease suffer from loss of intellectual capacity, disintegration of personality, mental confusion, hallucinations, and aggressive - even violent - behaviour. These symptoms are the result of progressive degeneration in many types of neurons in the brain. Forgetfulness, one of the earliest symptoms of Alzheimer's disease, is partly caused by the destruction of neurons that normally release the neurotransmitter acetylcholine. Medications that increase brain levels of acetylcholine have helped restore short-term memory and reduce mood swings in some Alzheimer's patients.

Neurotransmitters also play a role in Parkinson disease, which slowly attacks the nervous system, causing symptoms that worsen over time. Fatigue, mental confusion, a mask-like facial expression, stooping posture, shuffling gait, and problems with and speaking is among the difficulties suffered by Parkinson victims. These symptoms have been partly linked to the deterioration and eventual death of neurons that run from the base of the brain to the basal ganglia, a collection of nerve cells that manufacture the neurotransmitter dopamine. The reasons why such neurons die are yet to be understood, but the related symptoms can be alleviated. L-dopa, or levodopa, widely used to treat Parkinson disease, acts as a supplementary precursor for dopamine. It causes the surviving neurons in the basal ganglia to increase their production of dopamine, thereby compensating to some extent for the disabled neurons.

Many other effective drugs have been shown to act by influencing neurotransmitter behaviour. Some drugs work by interfering with the interactions between neurotransmitters and intestinal receptors. For example, belladonna decreases intestinal cramps in such disorders as irritable bowel syndrome by blocking acetylcholine from combining with receptors. This process reduces nerve signals to the bowel wall, which prevents painful spasms.

Other drugs block the reuptake process. One well-known example is the drug Fluoxetine (Prozac), which blocks the reuptake of serotonin. Serotonin then remains in the synapse for a longer time, and its ability to act as a signal is prolonged, which contributes to the relief of depression and the control of obsessive-compulsive behaviours.

Neurotransmitters are released into a microscopic gap, called a synapse, that separates the transmitting neuron from the cell receiving the chemical signal. The cell that generates the signal is called the presynaptic cell, while the receiving cell is termed the postsynaptic cell.

After their release into the synapse, neurotransmitters combine chemically with highly specific protein molecules, termed receptors, that are embedded in the surface membranes of the postsynaptic cell. When this combination occurs, the voltage, or electrical force, of the postsynaptic cell is either increased (excited) or decreased (inhibited).

When a neuron is in its resting state, its voltage is about -70 millivolts. An excitatory neurotransmitter alters the membrane of the postsynaptic neuron, making it possible for ions (electrically charged molecules) to move back and forth across the neuron's membranes. This flow of ions makes the neuron's voltage rise toward zero. If enough excitatory receptors have been activated, the postsynaptic neuron responds by firing, generating a nerve impulse that causes its own neurotransmitter to be released into the next synapse. An inhibitory neurotransmitter causes different ions to pass back and forth across the postsynaptic neuron's membrane, lowering the nerve cell's voltage to -80 or -90 millivolts. The drop in voltage makes it less likely that the postsynaptic cell will fire.

If the postsynaptic cell is a muscle cell rather than a neuron, an excitatory neurotransmitter will cause the muscle to contract. If the postsynaptic cell is a gland cell, an excitatory neurotransmitter will cause the cell to secrete its contents.

While most neurotransmitters interact with their receptors to create new electrical nerve impulses that energize or inhibit the adjoining cell, some neurotransmitter interactions do not generate or suppress nerve impulses. Instead, they interact with a second type of receptor that changes the internal chemistry of the postsynaptic cell by either causing or blocking the formation of chemicals called second messenger molecules. These second messengers regulate the postsynaptic cell's biochemical processes and enable it to conduct the maintenance necessary to continue synthesizing neurotransmitters and conducting nerve impulses. Examples of second messengers, which are formed and entirely contained within the postsynaptic cell, include cyclic adenosine monophosphate, diacylglycerol, and inositol phosphates.

Once neurotransmitters have been secreted into synapses and have passed on their chemical signals, the presynaptic neuron clears the synapse of neurotransmitter molecules. For example, acetylcholine is broken down by the enzyme acetylcholinesterase into choline and acetate. Neurotransmitters like dopamine, serotonin, and GABA is removed by a physical process called reuptake. In reuptake, a protein in the presynaptic membrane acts as a sort of sponge, causing the neurotransmitters to reenter the presynaptic neuron, where they can be broken down by enzymes or repackaged for reuse.

Severe mental illness almost always alters a person's life dramatically. People with severe mental illnesses experience disturbing symptoms that can make it difficult in holding down a job, or go to school, relate to others, or cope with ordinary life demands. Some individuals require hospitalization because they become unable to care for themselves or because they are at risk of committing suicide.

The symptoms of mental illness can be very distressing. People who develop schizophrenia may hear voices inside their head that say nasty things about them or command them to act in strange or unpredictable ways. Or they may be paralysed by paranoia - the deep conviction that everyone, including their closest family members, wants to injure or destroy them. People with major depression may feel that nothing brings pleasure and that life is so dreary and unhappy that it is better to be dead. People with panic disorder may experience heart palpitations, rapid breathing, and anxiety so extreme that they may not be able to leave home. People whom experience episodes of mania may engage in reckless sexual behaviour or may spend money indiscriminately, acts that later cause them to feel guilt, shame, and desperation.

Other mental illnesses, while not always debilitating, create certain problems in living. People with personality disorders may experience loneliness and isolation because their personality style interferes with social relations. People with an eating disorder may become so preoccupied with their weight and appearance that they force themselves to vomit or refuse to eat. Individuals who develop post-traumatic stress disorder may become angry easily, experience disturbing memories, and have trouble concentrating.

Experiences of mental illness often differ to be unlike or distinct in nature as it depends on one's culture or social group, sometimes greatly so. For example, in most of the non-Western world, people with depression complain principally of physical ailments, such as lack of energy, poor sleep, loss of appetite, and various kinds of physical pain. And yet, even in North America these complaints are commonplace. But in the United States and other Western societies, depressed people and mental health professionals who treat them tend to emphasize psychological problems, such as feelings of sadness, worthlessness, and despair. The experience of schizophrenia also differs by culture. In India, one-third of the new cases of schizophrenia involve catatonia, a behaviourial condition in which a person maintains a bizarre statue-like posture for hours or days. This condition is rare in Europe and North America.

Schizophrenia, is a very severe mental illness characterized by a variety of symptoms, including loss of contact with reality, bizarre behaviour, disorganized thinking and speech, decreased emotional expressiveness, and social withdrawal. Usually only some of these symptoms occur in any one person. The term schizophrenia comes from Greek words meaning 'split mind.' However, contrary to common belief, schizophrenia does not refer to a person with a split personality or multiple personality. For a description of a mental illness in which a person has multiple personalities, to observers, schizophrenia may seem like madness or insanity, but persons with schizophrenia have disturbed, frightening thoughts and may have trouble telling the difference between real and unreal experiences.

Perhaps more than any other mental illness, schizophrenia has a debilitating effect on the lives of the people who suffer from it. A person with schizophrenia may have difficulty telling the difference between real and unreal experiences, logical and illogical thoughts, or appropriate and inappropriate behaviourial interactions whose appropriations are to express of the objectifying descriptions upon the cases to act of having or having to carry of a definite direction, resisting upon those forms that exploit the contribution in weights of others, or sustain without the adequate issues for which exists or going together without conflict or incongruity, which are accorded to the agreeing conditions, that are disinherently limited. Schizophrenia seriously impairs a person's ability to work, go to school, enjoy relationships with others, or take care of oneself. In addition, people with schizophrenia frequently require hospitalization because they pose a danger to themselves. About 10 percent of people with schizophrenia commit suicide, and many others attempt suicide. Once people develop schizophrenia, they usually suffer from the illness for the rest of their lives. Although there is no cure, treatment can help many people with schizophrenia lead productive lives.

Schizophrenia also carries an enormous cost to society. People with schizophrenia occupy about one-third of all beds in psychiatric hospitals in the United States. In addition, people with schizophrenia account for at least 10 percent of the homeless population in the United States. The National Institute of Mental Health has estimated that schizophrenia costs the United States tens of billions of dollars each year in direct treatment, social services, and lost productivity.

Approximately 1 percent of people develop schizophrenia at some time during their lives. Experts estimate that about 1.8 million people in the United States have schizophrenia. The prevalence of schizophrenia is rather being one than another or more, regardless of sex, race, and culture. Although women are just as likely as men to develop schizophrenia, women tend to experience the illness to a lesser extent than is severely, with fewer hospitalizations and better social functioning in the community.

Schizophrenia usually develops in late adolescence or early adulthood, between the ages of 15 and 30. Much less common, schizophrenia develops later in life. The illness may begin abruptly, but it usually develops slowly over months or years. Mental health professionals diagnose schizophrenia based on an interview with the patient in which they determine whether the person has experienced specific symptoms of the illness.

Symptoms and functioning in people with schizophrenia tend to vary over time, sometimes worsening and other times improving. For many patients the symptoms gradually become less severe as they grow older. About 25 percent of people with schizophrenia become symptom-free later in their lives.

A variety of symptoms characterize schizophrenia. The most prominent include symptoms of psychosis - such as delusions and hallucinations - as well as bizarre behaviour, strange movements, and disorganized thinking and speech. Many people with schizophrenia do not recognize that their mental functioning is disturbed.

Delusions are false beliefs that appear obviously untrue to other people. For example, a person with schizophrenia may believe that he is the king of England when he is not. People with schizophrenia may have delusions that others, such as the local police or the FBI are plotting against them or spying on them. They may believe that aliens are controlling their thoughts or that their own thoughts are being broadcast to the world so that other people can hear them.

People with schizophrenia may also experience hallucinations (false sensory perceptions). People with hallucinations see, hear, smell, feel, or taste things that are not really there. Auditory hallucinations, such as hearing voices when no one else is around, are especially common in schizophrenia. These hallucinations may include, in and around two or more voices conversing with other, voices that continually comment on the person's life, or voices that command the person to do something.

People with schizophrenia often behave bizarrely. They may talk to themselves, walk backward, laugh suddenly without explanation, make funny faces, or masturbate in public. In rare cases, they maintain a rigid, bizarre pose for hours on end. Alternately, they may engage in constant random or repetitive movement, such that the actions justified, the dynamical situation has proven current to the motional services in moderation that include the primary presence of its operateness.

People with schizophrenia sometimes talk in incoherent or nonsensical ways, which may commonly suggest of an impounding distinction the impact to cause confused or disorganized thinking? In conversation they may eradicably jump from subject to subject or string together loosely associated phrases. They may combine words and phrases in meaningless ways or make up new words. In addition, they may show poverty of speech, in which they talk less and more slowly than other people, fail to answer questions or reply only briefly, or suddenly stop talking in the middle of speech.

Another common characteristic of schizophrenia is social withdrawal. People with schizophrenia may avoid others or act as though others do not exist. They often show decreased emotional expressiveness. For example, they may talk in a low, monotonous voice, avoid eye contact with others, and display a blank facial expression. They may also have difficulties experiencing pleasure and may lack interest in participating in activities.

Other symptoms of schizophrenia include difficulties with memory, attention span, abstract thinking, and planning ahead. People with schizophrenia commonly have problems with anxiety, depression, and suicidal thoughts. In addition, people with schizophrenia are much more likely to abuse or become dependent upon drugs or alcohol than other people. The use of alcohol and drugs often worsens the symptoms of schizophrenia, resulting in relapses and hospitalizations.

Schizophrenia appears to result not from a single cause, but from a variety of factors. Most scientists believe that schizophrenia is a biological disease caused by genetic factors, an imbalance of chemicals in the brain, structural brain abnormalities, or abnormalities in the prenatal environment. In addition, stressful life events may contribute to the development of schizophrenia in those who are predisposed to the illness.

Research shows that the more genetically related a person is to someone with schizophrenia, the greater the risk that person has of developing the illness. For example, children of one parent with schizophrenia have a 13 percent chance of developing the illness, whereas children of two parents with schizophrenia have a 46 percent chance of developing the disorder.

Mental health professionals do not rely on psychotherapy to treat schizophrenia, a severe mental illness. Drugs are used to treat this disorder. However, some psychotherapeutic techniques may help people with schizophrenia learn appropriate social skills and skills for managing anxiety. Another severe mental illness, bipolar disorder (popularly called manic depression), is treated with drugs or a combination of drugs and psychotherapy.

Some evidence suggests that schizophrenia may result from an imbalance of chemicals in the brain called neurotransmitters. These chemicals enable neurons (brain cells) to communicate with other. Some scientists suggest that schizophrenia result from excess activity of the neurotransmitter dopamine in certain parts of the brain or from an abnormal sensitivity to dopamine. Support for this hypothesis comes from Antipsychotic drugs, which reduce psychotic symptoms in schizophrenia by blocking brain receptors for dopamine. In addition, amphetamines, which increase dopamine activity, intensify psychotic symptoms in people with schizophrenia. Despite these findings, many experts believe that excess dopamine activity alone cannot account for schizophrenia. Other neurotransmitters, such as serotonin and norepinephrine, may play important roles as well.

Brain imaging techniques, such as magnetic resonance imaging and positron-emission tomography, have led researchers to discover specific structural abnormalities in the brains of people with schizophrenia. For example, people with chronic schizophrenia tend to have enlarged brain ventricles (cavities in the brain that contains cerebrospinal fluid). They also have a smaller overall volume of brain tissue compared to mentally healthy people. Other people with schizophrenia show abnormally low activity in the frontal lobe of the brain, which governs abstract thought, planning, and judgment. Research has identified possible abnormalities in many other parts of the brain, including the temporal lobes, basal ganglia, thalamus, hippocampus, and superior temporal gyrus. These defects may partially explain the abnormal thoughts, perceptions, and behaviours that characterize schizophrenia.

Evidence suggests those factors in the prenatal environment and during birth can increase the risk of a person later developing schizophrenia. These events are believed to affect the brain development of the fetus during a critical period. For example, pregnant women who have been exposed to the influenza virus or who have poor nutrition have a slightly increased chance of giving birth to a child who later develops schizophrenia. In addition, obstetric complications during the birth of a child - for example, delivery with forceps - can slightly increase the chances of the child later developing schizophrenia.

Although scientists favour a biological cause of schizophrenia, stress in the environment may affect the onset and course of the illness. Stressful life circumstances - such as growing up and living in poverty, the death of a loved one, an important change in jobs or relationships, or chronic tension and hostility at home - can increase the chances of schizophrenia in a person biologically predisposed to the disease. In addition, stressful events can trigger a relapse of symptoms in a person who already has the illness. Individuals who have effective skills for managing stress may be less susceptible to its negative effects. Psychological and social rehabilitation can help patients develop more effective skills for dealing with stress.

Although there is no cure for schizophrenia, effective treatment exists that can improve the long-term course of the illness. With many years of treatment and rehabilitation, significant numbers of people with schizophrenia experience partial or full remission of their symptoms.

Treatment of schizophrenia usually involves a combination of medication, rehabilitation, and treatment of other problems the person may have. Antipsychotic drugs (also called neuroleptics) are the most frequently used medications for treatment of schizophrenia. Psychological and social rehabilitation programs may help people with schizophrenia function in the community and reduce stress related to their symptoms. Treatment of secondary problems, such as substance abuse and infectious diseases, is also an important part of an overall treatment program.

Serotonin, neurotransmitter, or chemical that transmits messages across the synapses, or gaps, between adjacent cells, in among the many functions, serotonin is released from blood cells called platelets to activate blood vessel constriction and blood clotting. In the gastrointestinal tract, serotonin inhibits gastric acid production and stimulates muscle contraction in the intestinal wall. Its functions in the central nervous system and effects on human behaviour - including mood, memory, and appetite control - have been the subject of a great deal of research. This intensive study of serotonin has revealed important knowledge about the serotonin-related cause and treatment of many illnesses.

Serotonin is produced in the brain from the amino acid tryptophan, which is derived from foods high in protein, such as meat and dairy products. Tryptophan is transported to the brain, where it is broken down by enzymes to produce serotonin. In the process of neurotransmission, serotonin is transferred from one nerve cell, or neuron, to another, triggering an electrical impulse that stimulates or inhibits cell activity as needed. Serotonin is then reabsorbed by the first neuron, in a process known as reuptake, where it is recycled and used again or converted into an inactive chemical form and excreted.

While the complete picture of serotonin's function in the body is still being investigated, many disorders are known to be associated with an imbalance of serotonin in the brain. Drugs that manipulate serotonin levels have been used to alleviate the symptoms of serotonin imbalances. Some of these drugs, known as selective serotonin reuptake inhibitors (SSRIs), block or inhibit the reuptake of serotonin into neurons, enabling serotonin to remain active in the synapses for a longer period of time. These medications are used to treat such psychiatric disorders as depression; obsessive-compulsive disorder, in which repetitive and disturbing thoughts trigger bizarre, ritualistic behaviours; and impulsive aggressive behaviours. Fluoxetine (more commonly known by the brand name Prozac), is a widely prescribed SSRI used to treat depression, and more recently, obsessive-compulsive disorder.

Drugs that affect serotonin levels may prove beneficial in the treatment of nonpsychiatric disorders as well, including diabetic neuropathy (degeneration of nerves outside the central nervous system in diabetics) and premenstrual syndrome. Recently the serotonin-releasing agent dexfenfluramine has been approved for patients who are 30 percent or more over their ideal body weight. By preventing serotonin reuptake, dexfenfluramine promotes satiety, or fullness, after eating less food.

Other drugs serve as agonists that react with neurons to produce effects similar to those of serotonin. Serotonin agonists have been used to treat migraine headaches, in which low levels of serotonin cause arteries in the brain to swell, resulting in a headache. Sumatriptan is an agonist drug that mimics the effects of serotonin in the brain, constricting blood vessels and alleviating pain.

Drugs known as antagonists bind with neurons to prevent serotonin neurotransmission. Some antagonists have been found effective in treating the nausea that typically accompanies radiation and chemotherapy in cancer treatment. Antagonists are also being tested to treat high blood pressure and other cardiovascular disorders by blocking serotonin's ability to constrict blood vessels. Other antagonists may produce an effect on learning and memory in age-associated memory impairment.

Antipsychotic medications, developed in the mid-1950's, can dramatically improve the quality of life for people with schizophrenia. The drugs reduce or eliminate psychotic symptoms such as hallucinations and delusions. The medications can also help prevent these symptoms from returning. Common Antipsychotic drugs include risperidone (Risperdal), olanzapine (Zyprexa), clozapine (Clozaril), quetiapine (Seroquel), haloperidol (Haldol), thioridazine (Mellaril), chlorpromazine (Thorazine), fluphenazine (Prolixin), and trifluoperazine (Stelazine). People with schizophrenia usually must take medication for the rest of their lives to control psychotic symptoms. Antipsychotic medications appear to be less effective at treating other symptoms of schizophrenia, such as social withdrawal and apathy.

Antipsychotic drugs help reduce symptoms in 80 to 90 percent of people with schizophrenia. However, those who benefit often stop taking medication because they do not understand that they are ill or because of unpleasant side effects. Minor side effects include weight gain, dry mouth, blurred vision, restlessness, constipation, dizziness, and drowsiness. Other side effects are more serious and debilitating. These may include muscle spasms or cramps, tremors, and tardive dyskinesia. Newer drugs, such as clozapine, olanzapine, risperidone, and quetiapine, tend to produce fewer of these side effects. However, clozapine can cause agranulocytosis, a significant reduction in white blood cells necessary to fight infections. This condition can be fatal if not detected early enough. For this reason, people taking clozapine must have weekly tests to monitor their blood.

Because many patients with schizophrenia continue to experience difficulties despite taking medication, psychological and social rehabilitation is often necessary. A variety of methods can be effective. Social skills training help people with schizophrenia learn specific behaviours for functioning in society, such as making friends, purchasing items at a store, or initiating conversations. Behaviourial training methods can also help them learn self-care skills such as personal hygiene, money management, and proper nutrition. In addition, cognitive-behaviourial therapy, a type of psychotherapy, can help reduce persistent symptoms such as hallucinations, delusions, and social withdrawal.

Family intervention programs can also benefit people with schizophrenia. These programs focus on helping family members understand the nature and treatment of schizophrenia, how to monitor the illness, and how to help the patient make progress toward personal goals and greater independence. They can also lower the stress experienced by everyone in the family and help prevent the patient from relapsing or being re-hospitalized.

Because many patients have difficulty obtaining or keeping jobs, supported employment programs that help patients find and maintain jobs are a helpful part of rehabilitation. In these programs, the patient works alongside people without disabilities and earns competitive wages. An employment specialist (or a vocational specialist) helps the person maintain their job by, for example, training the person in specific skills, helping the employer accommodate the person, arranging transportation, and monitoring performance. These programs are most effective when the supported employment is closely integrated with other aspects of treatment, such as medication and monitoring of symptoms.

Some people with schizophrenia are vulnerable to frequent crises because they do not regularly go to mental health centres to receive the treatment they need. These individuals often relapse and face rehospitalization. To ensure that such patients take their medication and receive appropriate psychological and social rehabilitation, assertive community treatment (ACT) programs have been developed that deliver treatment to patients in natural settings, such as in their homes, in restaurants, or on the street.

People with schizophrenia often have other medical problems, so an effective treatment program must attend to these as well. One of the most commonly associated problems is substance abuse. Successful treatment of substance abuse in patients with schizophrenia requires careful coordination with their mental health care, so that the same clinicians are treating both disorders at the same time.

The high rate of substance abuse in patients with schizophrenia contributes to a high prevalence of infectious diseases, including hepatitis B and C and the human immunodeficiency virus (HIV). Assessment, education, and treatment or management of these illnesses is critical for the long-term health of patients.

Other problems frequently associated with schizophrenia include housing instability and homelessness, legal problems, violence, trauma and post-traumatic stress disorder, anxiety, depression, and suicide attempts. Close monitoring and psychotherapeutic interventions are often helpful in addressing these problems.

Certain personality traits may also directively lead to stress-related disorders. The so-called Type A personality, characterized by competitive, hard-driving intensity, is common in American society. Although early studies suggested a link between Type A behaviour and coronary heart disease, most studies since the 1980s have failed to find such a relationship. However, research has consistently demonstrated that people who show a high level of hostility, anger, and cynicism - often components of Type A behaviour - have a higher risk of coronary heart disease than people without these traits.

Several other psychiatric disorders are closely related to schizophrenia. In schizoaffective disorder, a person shows symptoms of schizophrenia combined whether mania or severe depression. Schizophreniform disorder refers to an illness in which a person experiences schizophrenic symptoms for more than one month but fewer than six months. In schizotypal personality disorder, a person engages in odd thinking, speech, and behaviour, but usually does not lose contact with reality

The occurring personality disorders, disorders in which one's personality results in personal state of being agitated with doubt or mental conflict as unconcerning a crazed derangement or significantly inflicting something that gives rise to the defragmentation of the social or working function, such that of every person has a personality — that is to say, a characteristic way of thinking, feeling, behaving, and relating to others. Most people experience at least some difficulties and problems that result from their personality. The specific point at which those problems justify the diagnosis of a personality disorder is controversial. To some extent the definition of a personality disorder is arbitrary, reflecting as well as professional judgments about the person's degree of dysfunction, needs for change, and motivation for change.

The occurring personality disorders involve behaviour that deviates from the norms or expectations of one's culture. However, people who digress from cultural norms are not necessarily dysfunctional, nor are people who conform to cultural norms necessarily healthy. Many personality disorders represent extreme variants of behaviour patterns that people usually value and encourage. For example, most people value confidence but not arrogance, agreeableness but not submissiveness, and conscientiousness but not perfectionism.

Because no clear line exists between healthy and unhealthy functioning, critics question the reliability of personality disorder diagnoses. A behaviour that seems deviant to one person may seem normal to another depending on one's gender, ethnicity, and cultural background. The personal and cultural biases of mental health professionals may influence their diagnoses of personality disorders.

An estimated 20 percent of people in the general population have one or more personality disorders. Some people with personality disorders have other mental illnesses as well. About 50 percent of people who are treated for any psychiatric disorder have a personality disorder.

Mental health professionals rarely diagnose personality disorders in children because their manner of thinking, feeling, and relating to others does not usually stabilize until young adulthood. Thereafter, personality traits usually remain stable. Personality disorders often decrease in severity as some person ages.

People with antisocial personality disorder act in a way that disregards the feelings and rights of other people. Antisocial personalities often break the law, and they may use or exploit other people for their own gain. They may lie repeatedly, act impulsively, and get into physical fights. They may mistreat their spouses, neglect or abuse their children, and exploit their employees. They may even kill other people. People with this disorder are also sometimes called sociopaths or psychopaths. Antisocial behaviour in people less than 18 years old is called conduct disorder.

Antisocial personalities usually fail to understand that their behaviour is dysfunctional because their ability to feel guilty, remorseful, and anxious is impaired. Guilt, remorse, shame, and anxiety are unpleasant feelings, but they are also necessary for social functioning and even physical survival. For example, people who are found in their deficiency, such as their ability to feel anxious will often fail to anticipate actual dangers and risks. They may take chances that other people would not take.

Antisocial personality disorder affects about 3 percent of males and 1 percent of females. This is the most heavily researched personality disorder, in part because it costs society the most. People with this disorder are at high risk for premature and violent death, injury, imprisonment, loss of employment, bankruptcy, alcoholism, drug dependence, and failed personal relationships.

People with borderline personality disorder experience intense emotional instability, particularly in relationships with others. They may make frantic efforts to avoid real or imagined abandonment by others. They may experience minor problems as major crises. They may also express their anger, frustration, and dismay through suicidal gestures, self-mutilation, and other self-destructive acts. They tend to have an unstable self-image or sense of self.

As children, most people with this disorder were emotionally unstable, impulsive, and often bitter or angry, although their chaotic impulsiveness and intense emotions may have made them popular at school. At first they may impress people as stimulating and exciting, but their relationships tend to be unstable and explosive.

About 2 percent of all people have borderline personality disorder. About 75 percent of people with this disorder are female. Borderline personalities are at high risk for developing depression, alcoholism, drug dependence, bulimia, Dissociative disorders, and post-traumatic stress disorder. As many as 10 percent of people with this disorder commit suicide by the age of 30. People with borderline personality disorder are among the most difficult to treat with psychotherapy, in part because their relationship with their therapist may become as intense and unstable as their other personal relationships.

Avoidant personality disorder is social withdrawal due to intense, anxious shyness. People with Avoidant personalities are reluctant to interact with others unless they feel certain of the likened impact, which they fear for being criticized or rejected. Often they view themselves as socially inept and inferior to others.

Dependent personality disorder involves severe and disabling emotional dependency on others. People with this disorder have difficulty making decisions without a great deal of advice and reassurance from others. They urgently seek out another relationship when a close relationship ends. They feel uncomfortable by themselves.

People with histrionic personality disorder constantly strive to be the centres of attention. They may act overly flirtatious or dress in ways that draw attention. They may also talk in a dramatic or theatrical style and display exaggerated emotional reactions.

People with narcissistic personality disorder have a grandiose sense of a self-importance. They seek excessive admiration from others and fantasize about unlimited success or power. They believe they are special, unique, or superior to others. However, they often have very fragile self-esteem.

Obsessive-compulsive personality disorder is characterized by a preoccupation with details, orderliness, perfection, and control. People with this disorder often devote excessive amounts of time toward working and individual productivity and fail to take time for leisure activities and friendships. They tend to be rigid, formal, stubborn, and serious. This disorder differs from obsessive-compulsive disorder, which often includes more bizarre behaviour and rituals.

People with paranoid personality disorder feel constant suspicion and distrust toward other people. They believe that others are against them and constantly look for evidence to support their suspicions. They are hostile toward others and react angrily to perceived insults.

Schizoid personality disorder involves social isolation and a lack of desire for close personal relationships. People with this disorder prefer to be alone and seem withdrawn and emotionally detached. They seem indifferent to felicitation or criticism from other people.

People with schizotypal personality disorder engage in odd thinking, speech, and behaviour. They may ramble or use words and phrases in unusual ways, and they may believe they have magical control over others. They feel very uncomfortable with close personal relationships and tend to be suspicious of others. Some research indications to bare procedures in the disorder which is less severe form of schizophrenia.

Many psychiatrists and psychologists use two additional diagnoses. Depressive personality disorder is characterized by chronic pessimism, gloominess, and cheerlessness. In passive-aggressive personality disorder, a person passively resists completing tasks and chores, criticizes and scorns authority figures, and seems negative and sullen.

Personality disorders result from a complex interaction of inherited traits and life experience, not from a single cause. For example, some cases of antisocial personality disorder may result from a combination of a genetic predisposition to impulsiveness and violence, very inconsistent or erratic parenting, and a harsh environment that discourage feelings of empathy and warmth but rewards exploitation and aggressiveness. Borderline personality disorder may result from a genetic predisposition to impulsiveness and emotional instability combined with parental neglect, intense marital conflicts between parents, and repeated episodes of severe emotional or sexual abuse. Dependent personality disorder may result from genetically based anxiety, an inhibited temperament, and overly protective, clinging, or neglectful parenting.

The pervasive and chronic nature of personality disorders makes them difficult to treat. People with these disorders often fail to recognize that their personality has contributed to their social, occupational, and personal problems. They may not think they have any real problems despite a history of drug abuse, failed relationships, and irregular employment. Thus, therapists must first focuses on helping the person understand and become aware of the significance of their personality traits.

People with personality disorders sometimes feel that they can never change their dysfunctional behaviour because they have always acted the same way. Although personality change is exceedingly difficult, sometimes people can change the most dysfunctional aspects of their feelings and behaviour.

Therapists use a variety of methods to treat personality disorders, depending on the specific disorder. For example, cognitive and behaviourial techniques, such as role playing and logical argument, may help alter a person's irrational perceptions and assumptions about himself or herself. Certain psychoactive drugs may help control feelings of anxiety, depression, or severe distortions of thought. Psychotherapy may help people to understand the impact of experiences and responsibilities. These programs appear to help some people, but it is unclear how long their beneficial effects last.

The appropriate treatment, most people can recover from mental illness and return to normal life. Even those with persistent, long-term mental illnesses can usually learn to manage their symptoms and live productive lives.

In most societies mental illness carries a substantial stigma, or mark of shame. The mentally ill, were at most, blamed for their own ill's, blamed for bringing it upon their own illnesses, and others may see them as victims of bad fate, religious and moral transgression, or witchcraft. Such stigmas may keep families from acknowledging that a family member is ill. Some families may hide or overprotect a member with mental illness - keeping the person from receiving potentially effective care - or they may reject the person from the family. When magnified from individuals to a whole society, such attitudes lead to under-funding of mental health services and terribly inadequate care. In much of the world, even today, the mentally ill, were chained, shackled and caged, or hospitalized in filthy, brutal institutions. Yet attitudes toward mental illness have improved in many areas, especially owing to a heralded breed and advocacy for the mentally ill.

Mental illness creates enormous social and economic costs. Depression, for example, affects some 500 million people in the world and results in more time lost to disability than such chronic diseases as diabetes mellitus and arthritis. Estimating the economic cost of mental illness is complex because there are direct costs (actual medical expenditures), indirect costs (the cost to individuals and society due to reduced or lost productivity, for example), and support costs (time lost to care of family members with mental illnesses).

Another method of estimating the cost of mental illness to society measures the impact of premature deaths and disablements. Research by the World Health Organization and the World Bank estimated that in 1990, among the world's population aged 15 to 44 years, depression accounted for more than 10 percent of the total burden attributable to all diseases. Two other illnesses, bipolar disorder and schizophrenia, accounted for another 6 percent of the burden. This research has helped governments recognize that mental illnesses constitute a far greater challenge to public health systems than previously realized.

No universally accepted definition of mental illness exists. In general, the definition of mental illness depends on a society's norms, or rules of behaviour. Behaviours that violate these norms are considered signs of deviance or, in some cases, of mental illness.

The variation in behaviourial norms does not mean, however, that definitions of mental illness are necessarily incompatible across cultures. Many behaviours are recognized throughout the world for being indicative of mental illness. These include extreme social withdrawal, violence to oneself, hallucinations (false sensory perceptions), and delusions (fixed, false ideas).

Another way of defining mental illness is based on whether a person's behaviours are maladaptive - that is, whether they cause a person to experience problems in coping with common life demands. For example, people with social phobias may avoid interacting with other people and experience problems at work as a result. Critics note that under this definition, political dissidents could be considered mentally ill for refusing to accept the dictates of their government.

Mental illness affects people of all ages, races, cultures, and socioeconomic classes. The prevalence of mental illness refers to what degree or to the greater extent do peoples experience of a mental illness during a specified time period.

Psychosomatic Illness, illness that has no basic physical or organic cause but appears to be the result of psychological conditions, such as stress, anxiety, and depression. Such illnesses reflect the general belief that the mind is capable of strongly affecting bodily reactions, and that a person's mental condition can actually cause changes in the chemistry of the body, thereby creating physical illness. In cases of psychosomatic illness, a marked change in the body can often be readily detected.

The most effective treatment for psychosomatic disorders takes account into both the physical and the emotional aspects of the disease. The physical symptoms usually cannot be cured until the person's psychological environment has improved. For instance, a business executive working under severe pressure may develop ulcers. Although medicine and a special diet can improve this condition, if the person fails to cut down on work or learn relaxation techniques, he or she will probably continue to suffer from the disease and may even develop additional psychosomatic illnesses. In more serious cases of psychosomatic illness, doctors may recommend that the patient undergo some form of psychotherapy in addition to treatment for the physical aspects of the illness.

Depression can take several other forms. In bipolar disorder, sometimes called manic-depressive illness, a person's mood swings back and forth between depression and mania. People with seasonal affective disorder typically suffer from depression only during autumn and winter, when there are fewer hours of daylight. In dysthymia, people feel depressed, have low self-esteem, and concentrate poorly most of the time - often for a period of years - but their symptoms are milder than in major depression. Some people with dysthymia experience occasional episodes of major depression. Mental health professionals use the term clinical depression to refer to any of the above forms of depression.

Major depression, the most severe form of depression, affects from 1 to 2 percent of people aged 65 or older who are living in the community (rather than in nursing homes or other institutions). The prevalence of depression and other mental illnesses is much higher among elderly residents of nursing homes. Although most older people with depression respond to treatment, many cases of depression among the elderly go undetected or untreated. Research indicates that depression is a major risk factor for suicide among the elderly in the United States. People over age 65 in the United States have the highest suicide rate of any age group.

Generally, the overall prevalence rates of mental illnesses between men and women are similar. However, men have much higher rates of antisocial personality disorder and substance abuse. In the United States, women suffer from depression and anxiety disorders at about twice the rate of men. The gender gap is even wider in some countries. For example, in China, women suffer from depression at nine times the rate of men.

Mental illness is becoming an increasing problem for two reasons. First, increases in life expectancy have brought increased numbers of certain chronic mental illnesses. For example, because more people are living into old age, more people are suffering from dementia. Second, a number of studies provide evidence that rates of depression are rising throughout the world. The reasons may be related to such factors as economic change, political and social violence, and cultural disruptions. While some have questioned these findings, dramatic increases in the numbers of refugees and people dislocated from their homes by economic forces or civil strife are associated with great increases in a variety of mental illnesses for those populations. According to the United Nations High Commissioner for Refugees, the number of refugees worldwide increased from 2.5 million in 1971 to 13.2 million in 1996, peaking at 17 million in 1991.

A number of mental illnesses - such as depression, anxiety disorders, schizophrenia, and bipolar disorder - occur worldwide. Others seem to occur only in particular cultures. For example, eating disorders, such as anorexia nervosa (compulsive dieting associated with unrealistic fears of fatness), occurs mostly between girls and women in Europe, North America, and Westernized areas of Asia, whose cultures view thinness as an essential component of female beauty. In Latin America, people who are met with directly (as through participation or observation) in having known the intimacy or inward practices that are acquainted or familiar with or versed of something based on the personal exposure seem as been awarded of an experience, perhaps, an experience overwhelming of some causal reason to fright after a dangerous or traumatic event is said to have sustained (fright), an illness in which their soul has been frightened away. In some societies of West Africa and elsewhere, brain fatigue describes individuals (usually students) who experience difficulties in concentrating and thinking, as well as physical symptoms of pain and wearing out.

Most mental health professionals in the United States use the Diagnostic and Statistical Manual of Mental Disorders(DSM), a reference book published by the American Psychiatric Association, as a guide to the different kinds of mental illnesses. The foundation, known as DSM-IV, describes more than 300 mental disorders, behaviourial disorders, addictive disorders, and other psychological problems and groups them into broad categories. This describes some of the major categories, including anxiety disorders, mood disorders, schizophrenia and other psychotic disorders, personality disorders, cognitive disorders, Dissociative disorders, somatoform disorders, factitious disorders, substance-related disorders, eating disorders, and impulse-control disorders. Mental health professionals in many other parts of the world use a different classification system, the International Classification of Diseases (ICD), published by the World Health Organization.

The DSM and ICD are both categorical systems of classification, in which each mental illness is defined by its own unique set of symptoms and characteristics. In theory, each disorder should possess diagnostic criteria that are independent of from each one and another, just as tuberculosis and lung cancer are discrete diseases. Yet symptoms of many mental disorders overlap, and many people - such as those who experience both depression and severe anxiety - show symptoms of more than one disorder at the same time. For these reasons, some mental health professionals advocate a dimensional system of classification. In contrast to the categorical approach, which sees mental disorders as qualitatively distinct from normal behaviour, a dimensional system views behaviour as falling along a continuum of normality, with some behaviours considered more abnormally than others. In a dimensional system, diagnoses do not describe discrete diseases but rather portray the relative importance of an array of symptoms.

Mood disorders, also called affective disorders, create disturbances in a person's emotional life. Depression, mania, and bipolar disorder are examples of mood disorders. Symptoms of depression may include feelings of sadness, hopelessness, and worthlessness, as well as complaints of physical pain and changes in appetite, sleep patterns, and energy level. In mania, on the other hand, an individual experiences an abnormally elevated mood, often marked by exaggerated self-importance, irritability, agitation, and a decreased need for sleep. In bipolar disorder, also called manic-depressive illness, a person's mood alternates between extremes of mania and depression.

Bipolar disorder is a mental illness that causes mood swings. In the manic phase, a person might feel ecstatic, self-important, and energetic. But when the person becomes depressed, the mood shifts to extreme sadness, negative thinking, and apathy. Some studies indicate that the disease occurs at unusually high rates in creative people, such as artists, writers, and musicians. But some researchers contend that the methodology of these studies was flawed and their results were misleading. In the October 1996 Discover Magazine article, anthropologist Jo Ann C. Gutin presents the results of several studies that explore the link between creativity and mental illness.

People with schizophrenia and other psychotic disorders lose contact with reality. Symptoms may include delusions and hallucinations, disorganized thinking and speech, bizarre behaviour, a diminished range of emotional responsiveness, and social withdrawal. In addition, people who suffer from these illnesses experience and inability function operates in one or more important areas of life, such as social relations, work, or school.

Personality disorders are mental illnesses in which one's personality results in personal distress or a significant impairment in social or work functioning. In general, people with personality disorders have poor perceptions of themselves or others. They may have low self-esteem or overwhelming narcissism, poor impulse control, troubled social relationships, and inappropriate emotional responses. Considerable controversy exists over where to draw the distinction between a normal personality and a personality disorder.

Cognitive disorders, such as delirium and dementia, involve a significant loss of mental functioning. Dementia, for example, is characterized by impaired memory and difficulties in such functions as speaking, abstract thinking, and the ability to identify familiar objects. The conditions in this category usually result from a medical condition, substance abuse, or adverse reactions to medication or poisonous substances.

Dissociative disorders involve disturbances in a person's consciousness, memories, identity, and perception of the environment. Dissociative disorders include amnesia that has no physical cause; Dissociative identity disorders, in which a person has what more is less, such are the considerations in having two or more distinct personalities that alternate in their control of the person's behaviour; depersonalization disorder, characterized by a chronic feeling of being detached from one's body or mental processes; and Dissociative fugues, an episode of sudden departure from home or work with an accompanying loss of memory. In some parts of the world people experience Dissociative states as 'possession', is that by a god or ghost instead of separate personalities, insofar as many societies, a trance and possession states are normal parts of cultural and religious practices, as well as, to what they are, and not too considered for Dissociative disorders.

Somatoform disorders are characterized by the presence of physical symptoms that cannot be explained by a medical condition or another mental illness. Thus, physicians often judge that such symptoms result from psychological conflicts or distress. For example, in conversion disorder, also called hysteria, a person may experience blindness, deafness, or seizures, but a physician cannot find anything wrong with the person. People with another somatoform disorder, hypochondriasis, constantly fear that they will develop a serious disease and misinterpret minor physical symptoms as evidence of illness.

Substance-related disorders result from the abuse of drugs, side effects of medications, or exposure to toxic substances. Many mental health professionals regard these disorders as behaviourial or addictive disorders rather than as mental illnesses, although substance-related disorders commonly occur in people with mental illnesses. Common substance-related disorders include alcoholism and other forms of drug dependence. In addition, drug use can contribute to symptoms of other mental disorders, such as depression, anxiety, and psychosis. Drugs associated with substance-related disorders include alcohol, caffeine, nicotine, cocaine, heroin, amphetamines, hallucinogens, and sedatives.

Eating disorders are conditions in which an individual experience severe disturbances in eating behaviours. People with anorexia nervosa have an intense fear about gaining weight and refuse to eat adequately or maintain a normal body weight. People with bulimia nervosa repeatedly engage in episodes of binge eating, usually followed by self-induced vomiting or the use of laxatives, diuretics, or other medications to prevent weight gain. Eating disorders occur mostly among young women in Western societies and certain parts of Asia.

People with impulse-control disorders cannot control an impulse to engage in harmful behaviours, such as explosive anger, stealing (kleptomania), setting fires (pyromania), gambling, or pulling out their own hair (trichotillomania). Some mental illnesses - such as mania, schizophrenia, and antisocial personality disorder - may include symptoms of impulsive behaviour.

People have tried to understand the causes of mental illness for thousands of years. The modern era of psychiatry, which began in the late 19th and early 20th centuries, has witnessed a sharp debate between biological and psychological perspectives of mental illness. The biological perspective views mental illness in terms of bodily processes, whereas psychological perspectives emphasize the roles of a person's upbringing and environment.

These two perspectives are exemplified in the work of German psychiatrist Emil Kraepelin and Austrian psychoanalyst Sigmund Freud. Kraepelin, influenced by the work in the mid-1800's of German psychiatrist Wilhelm Griesinger, believed that psychiatric disorders were disease entities that could be classified like physical illnesses. That is, Kraepelin believed that the fundamental causes of mental illness lay in the physiology and biochemistry of the human brain. His classification system of mental disorders, first published in 1883, formed the basis for later diagnostic systems. Freud, on the other hand, argued that the source of mental illness lay in unconscious conflicts originating in early childhood experiences. Freud found evidence for this idea through the analysis of dreams, free association, and slips of speech.

This debate has continued into the late 20th century. Beginning in the 1960's, the biological perspective became dominant, supported by numerous breakthroughs in psychopharmacology, genetics, neurophysiology, and brain research. For example, scientists discovered many medications that helped to relieve symptoms of certain mental illnesses and demonstrated that people can inherit a vulnerability to some mental illnesses. Psychological perspectives also remain influential, including the psychodynamic perspective, the humanistic and existential perspectives, the behaviourial perspective, the cognitive perspective, and the Sociocultural perspective.

Psychiatry has increasingly emphasized a biological basis for the causes of mental illness. Studies suggest a genetic influence in some mental illnesses, such as schizophrenia and bipolar disorder, although the evidence is not conclusive.

Clinical depression is one of the most common forms of mental illness. Although depression can be treated with psychotherapy, many scientists believe there are biological causes for the disease. In the June 1998 Scientific American article, neurobiologist Charles B. Nemeroff reports upon the connection between biochemical changes in the brain and depression.

Scientists have identified a number of neurotransmitters, or chemical substances that enable brain cells to communicate with other, that appears important in regulating a person's emotions and behaviour. These include dopamine, serotonin, norepinephrine, gamma-amino butyric acid (GABA), and acetylcholine. Excesses and deficiencies in levels of these neurotransmitters have been associated with depression, anxiety, and schizophrenia, but scientists have yet to determine the exact mechanisms involved.

Research shows that the more genetically related a person is to someone with schizophrenia, the greater the risk that person has of developing the illness. For example, children of one parent with schizophrenia have a 13 percent chance of developing the illness, whereas children of two parents with schizophrenia have a 46 percent chance of developing the disorder.

Advances in brain imaging techniques, such as magnetic resonance imaging (MRI) and positron emission tomography (PET), have enabled scientists to study the role of brain structure in mental illness. Some studies have revealed structural brain abnormalities in certain mental illnesses. For example, some people with schizophrenia have enlarged brain ventricles (cavities in the brain that contains cerebrospinal fluid). However, this may be a result of schizophrenia rather than a cause, and not all people with schizophrenia show this abnormality.

A variety of medical conditions can cause mental illness. Brain damage and strokes can cause loss of memory, impaired concentration and speech, and unusual changes in behaviour. In addition, brain tumours, if left to grow, can cause psychosis and personality changes. Other possible biological factors in mental illness include an imbalance of hormones, deficiencies in diet, and infections from viruses.

In the late 19th century Viennese neurologist Sigmund Freud developed a theory of personality and a system of psychotherapy known as psychoanalysis. According to this theory, people are strongly influenced by unconscious forces, including innate sexual and aggressive drives.

The psychodynamic perspective views mental illness Psychodynamic caused by unconscious and unresolved conflicts in the mind. As stated by Freud, these conflicts arise in early childhood and may cause mental illness by impeding the balanced development of the three systems that constitute the human psyche: the id, which comprises innate sexual and aggressive drives; the ego, the conscious portion of the mind that mediates between the unconscious and reality; the superego, which controls the primitive impulses of the id and represents moral ideals. In this view, generalized anxiety disorder stems from a signal of unconscious danger whose source can only be identified through a thorough analysis of the person's personality and life experiences. Present Psychodynamic theorists tend to emphasize sexuality less than Freud did and focus more on problems in the individual's relationships with others.

Both the humanistic and existential perspectives view abnormal behaviour as resulting from a person's failure to find meaning in life and fulfill his or her potential. The humanistic school of psychology, as represented in the work of American psychologist Carl Rogers, views mental health and personal growth as the natural conditions of human life. In Rogers's view, every person possesses a drive toward self-actualization, the fulfilment of one's greatest potential. Mental illness develops when a person's condition by some circumstantial environment interferes with this drive. The existential perspective sees emotional disturbances as the result of a person's failure to act authentically - that is, to behave in accordance with one's own goals and values, rather than the goals and values of others.

The pioneers of behaviourism, American psychologists' John B. Watson and B. F. Skinner, maintained that psychology should confine itself to the study of observable behaviour, rather than explore a person's unconscious feelings. The behaviourial perspective explains mental illness, as well as all of human behaviour, as a learned response to, malaria, and infection's stimuli. In this view, rewards and punishments in a person's environment shape that person's behaviour, for example, a person involved in a serious car accident may develop a phobia of cars or the generalized fear to all forms of transportation.

The cognitive perspective holds that mental illness result from problems in cognition - that is, problems in how a person reasons, perceives events, and solves problems. American psychiatrist Aaron Beck proposed that some mental illnesses - such as depression, anxiety disorders, and personality disorders - result from a way of thinking learned in childhood that is not consistent with reality. For example, people with depression tend to see themselves in a negative light, exaggerate the importance of minor flaws or failures, and misinterpret the behaviour of others in negative ways. It remains unclear, however, whether these kinds of cognitive problems actually cause mental illness or merely represent symptoms of the illnesses themselves.

The Sociocultural perspective regards mental illness as the result of social, economic, and cultural factors. Evidence for this view comes from research that has demonstrated an increased risk of mental illness among people living in poverty. In addition, the incidence of mental illness rises in times of high unemployment. The shift in the world population from rural areas to cities - with their crowding, noise, pollution, decay, and social isolation - and, has also, been implicated in causing relatively high rates of mental illness. Furthermore, rapid social change, which has particularly affected indigenous peoples throughout the world, brings about high rates of suicide and alcoholism. Refugees and victims of social disasters - warfare, displacement, genocide, violence - have a higher risk of mental illness, especially depression, anxiety, and post-traumatic stress disorder.

Social scientists emphasize that the link between social ills and mental illness is correlational rather than causal. For example, although societies undergoing rapid social change often have high rates of suicide the specific causes have not been identified. Social and cultural factors may create relative risks for a population or class of people, but it is unclear how such factors raise the risk of mental illness for an individual.

There are no blood tests, imaging techniques, or other laboratory procedures that can reliably diagnose a mental illness. Thus, the diagnosis of mental illness is always a judgment or an interpretation by an observer based on the spoken exchange, ideas, behaviours, and experiences of the patient.

For the most part, mental health professionals determine the presence of mental illness in an individual by conducting an interview intended to reveal symptoms of abnormal behaviour. That is, the professional asks the patient questions about their mental state: 'Do you hear voices of people who are not with you?' 'Have you felt depressed or lost interest in most activities?' 'Have you experienced a marked increase or decrease in your appetite?' 'Have you been sleeping less than normal?' 'Are you easily distracted?' The answers to these questions will suggest other questions. Eventually, the clinician will feel that he or she has enough information to determine whether the patient is suffering from a mental illness and, if so, to make a diagnosis.

The process of diagnosis is not as simple as it might seem. Patients often have difficulty remembering symptoms or feel reluctant to talk about their fantasies, sex life, or use of drugs and alcohol. Many patients suffer in forms that are more than there is one disorder at a time - for example, depression and anxiety, or schizophrenia and depression - and determining which symptoms constitute the primary problem is complex. In addition, symptoms may not be specific to mental illnesses. For example, brain tumours of the central nervous system can produce symptoms that mimic those of the Psychotic disorders.

Another problem in diagnosis is that mental health professionals may interpret symptoms differently based on their personal or cultural biases. One study examined this effect by showing 300 American and British psychiatrists videotaped interviews of eight patients with mental illnesses. Although the psychiatrists' diagnoses substantially agreed for patients with 'textbook' cases of schizophrenia, their diagnoses varied widely for patients who had symptoms of both schizophrenia and other disorders, depending on whether the psychiatrist was American or British. The risk of misdiagnosis is even greater when the mental health professional and the patient come from different cultural groups.

Mental health professionals use a number of methods to treat people with mental illnesses. The two most common treatments by far are drug therapy and psychotherapy. In drug therapy, a person takes regular doses of a prescription medication intended to reduce symptoms of mental illness. Psychotherapy is the treatment of mental illness through verbal and nonverbal communication between the patient and a trained professional. A person can receive psychotherapy individually or in a group setting.

The type of treatment administered depends on the type and severity of the disorder. For example, doctors usually treat schizophrenia primarily with drugs, but specialized forms of psychotherapy may more effectively relieve phobias. For some mental illnesses, such as depression, the most effective treatment seems to be a combination of drug therapy and psychotherapy. Although some people with severe mental illnesses may never fully recover, most people with mental illnesses improve with treatment and can resume normal lives. Despite the availability of effective treatments, only about 40 percent of people with mental illnesses ever seek professional help.

A variety of mental health professionals offer treatment for mental illness. These include psychiatrists, psychologists, psychotherapists, psychiatric social workers, and psychiatric nurses.

Drugs introduced by the mid-1950's had enabled many people who otherwise would have spent years in mental institutions to return to the community and live productive lives. Since then, advances in psychopharmacology have led to the development of drugs of even greater effectiveness. These drugs often relieve symptoms of schizophrenia, depression, anxiety, and other disorders. However, they may produce undesirable and sometimes serious side effects. In addition, relapses may occur when they are discontinued, so long-term use may be required. Drugs that control symptoms of mental illness are called psychotherapeutic substance or preparation, in that a substance used by itself or in a mixture in the treatment of or the dependence on drugs, if only to make it bearable. The major categories of psychotherapeutic drugs include Antipsychotic drugs, Antianxiety drugs, antidepressant drugs, and antimanic drugs.

Antipsychotic drugs, also called neuroleptics and major tranquillizers, control symptoms of psychosis, such as hallucinations and delusions, which characterize schizophrenia and related disorders. They can also prevent such symptoms from returning. Antipsychotic drugs may produce side effects ranging from dry mouth and blurred vision to a tardive dyskinesia. The occasioning of Panic Disorders, is a mental illness in which a person experiences repeated, unexpected panic attacks and persistent anxiety about the possibility that the panic attacks will recur. A panic attack is a period of intense fear, apprehension, or discomfort. In panic disorder, the attacks usually occur without warning. Symptoms include a racing heart, shortness of breath, trembling, choking or smothering sensations, and fears of 'going crazy,' losing control, or dying from a heart attack. Panic attacks may last from a few seconds to several hours. Most peak within 10 minutes and render of their potentialities or peak, within 20 or 30 minutes.

About 2 percent of people in the United States suffer from panic disorder during any given year, and the condition affects more than twice as many women as men. People with panic disorder may experience panic attacks frequently, such as daily or weekly, or more sporadically. Additionally, panic attacks may occur as part of other anxiety disorders, such as phobias - in which a specific object or situation triggers the attack - and, more rarely, post-traumatic stress disorder.

People with panic disorder frequently develop agoraphobia, a fear of being in places or situations from which escape might be difficult if a panic attack occurs. People with agoraphobia typically fear situations such as travelling in a bus, train, car, or aeroplane, shopping at malls, going to theatres, crossing over bridges or through tunnels, and being alone in unfamiliar places. Therefore, they avoid these situations and may eventually become reluctant to leave their home. In addition, people with panic disorder appear to have an increased risk of alcoholism and drug dependence. Some studies indicate they also have a higher risk of depression and suicide.

Panic disorder, and both with and without agoraphobia, result from a combination of biological and psychological factors. Some individuals may inherit a vulnerability to accentuation and the availing of anxiety and an increased risk of experiencing panic attacks. In addition, certain physiological cues may trigger a panic attack. For example, if a person experiences a racing heart during a panic attack, he or she may begin to associate this sensation with panic attacks. An accelerated heart beat can be addictive and may impair movement and concentration in some people. Some antidepressant drugs, such as imipramine (Tofranil), also reduce panic symptoms in some people but can produce side effects such as dizziness or dry mouths. Another class of drugs, selective serotonin reuptake inhibitors (SSRIs), appears to reduce panic symptoms with fewer side effects. SSRIs used to treat panic disorder, would remedially need paroxetine (Paxil) and fluvoxamine (Luvox). Medication eliminates panic symptoms in 50 to 60 percent of patients. For many patients, however, panic attacks return when they stop taking the medication.

Research has shown that cognitive-behaviourial therapy, a type of psychotherapy, eliminates panic attacks in 80 to 100 percent of patients. In this method, therapists help patients re-create the physical symptoms of a panic attack, teach them coping skills, and help them to alter their beliefs about the danger of these sensations. Patients with agoraphobia face their feared situations under the therapist's supervision, using coping skills to overcome their strong anxiety. These coping skills may include physical relaxation techniques, such as deep breathing and muscle relaxation, as well as cognitive techniques that help people think rationally about anxiety-provoking situations. About 70 percent of panic disorders patients who also have moderate to severe agoraphobia benefit from this type of treatment.

Antianxiety drugs, also called minor tranquillizers, reduce high levels of anxiety. They may help people with generalized anxiety disorder, panic disorder, and other anxiety disorders. Benzodiazepines, a class of drugs that includes diazepam (Valium), are the most widely prescribed Antianxiety drugs. Benzodiazepines can be addictive and may cause drowsiness and impaired coordination during the day.

Antidepressant drugs help relieve symptoms of depression. Some antidepressant drugs can relieve symptoms of other disorders as well, such as panic disorder and obsessive-compulsive disorder.

Antidepressant drugs comprise three major classes: tricyclics, monoamine oxidase inhibitors (MAO inhibitors), and selective serotonin reuptake inhibitors (SSRIs). Side effects of tricyclics may include dizziness upon standing, blurred vision, dry mouth, difficulty urinating, constipation, and drowsiness. People who take MAO inhibitors may experience some of the same side effects, and must follow a special diet that excludes certain foods. SSRIs generally produce fewer side effects, although these may include anxiety, drowsiness, and sexual dysfunction. One type of SSRI, Fluoxetine (Prozac), is the most widely prescribed antidepressant drug.

Antimanic drugs help control the mania that occurs as part of bipolar disorder. One of the most effective antimanic drugs is lithium carBlonate, a natural mineral salt. Common side effects include nausea, stomach upset, vertigo, and increased thirst and urination. In addition, long-term use of lithium can damage the kidneys.

Psychotherapy can be an effective treatment for many mental illnesses. Unlike drug therapy, psychotherapy produces no physical side effects, although it can cause psychological damage when improperly administered. On the other hand, psychotherapy may take longer than drugs to produce benefits. In addition, sessions may be expensive and time-consuming. In response to this complaint and demands from insurance companies to reduce the costs of mental health treatment, many therapists have started providing therapy of shorter duration.

Psychotherapy encompasses a wide range of techniques and practices. Some forms of psychotherapy, such as psychodynamic therapy and humanistic therapy, focus on helping people understand the internal motivations for their problematic behaviour. Other forms of therapy, such as behaviourial therapy and cognitive therapy, focus one's actions in general or on a particular occasion, should, in the manner of recognizing the controversial behaviour communicative impact, which to cause to acquire knowledge for which of people skills are essential to set right in that as wrong must be corrected. The majority of therapists today incorporate treatment techniques from a number of theoretical perspectives. For example, cognitive-behaviourial therapy combines aspects of cognitive therapy and behaviourial therapy.

Psychodynamic therapy is one of the most common forms of psychotherapy. The therapist focuses on a person's past experiences as a source of internal, unconscious conflicts and tries to help the person resolve those conflicts. Some therapists may use hypnosis to uncover repressed memories. Psychoanalysis, a technique developed by Freud, is one kind of psychodynamic therapy. In psychoanalysis, the person lies on a couch and says whatever comes to mind, a process called free association. The therapist interprets these thoughts along with the person's dreams and memories. Classical psychoanalysis, which requires years of intensive treatment, is not as widely practised today as in previous years.

Both humanistic therapy and existential therapy treat mental illnesses by helping people achieve personal growth and attain meaning in life. The best-known humanistic therapy is client-centred therapy, developed by Carl Rogers in the 1950's. In this technique, the therapist provides no advice but restates the observations and insights of the client (the person in treatment) in nonjudgmental terms. In addition, the therapist offers the person unconditional empathy and acceptance. Existential therapists help people confront basic questions about the meaning of their lives and guide them toward discovery of their own uniqueness.

Psychotherapists whom practice behaviourial therapies do not focus on a person's past experiences or inner life, instead, they help the person to change their conduct behaviourial, and patterns of abnormal behaviour by applying established principles of conditioning and of learning. Behaviourial therapy has proven effective in the treatment of phobias, obsessive-compulsive disorder, and other disorders.

The Obsessive-Compulsive Disorder categorized the mental illness in which a person experiences recurrent, intrusive thoughts (obsessions) and feels compelled to perform certain behaviours (compulsions) again and again. Most people have experienced bizarre or inappropriate thoughts and have engaged in repetitive behaviours at times. However, people with obsessive-compulsive disorder find that their disturbing thoughts and behaviours consume large amounts of time, cause them anxiety and distress, and interfere with their ability to function at work and in social activities. Most people with this disorder recognize that their obsessions and compulsions are irrational but cannot suppress them.

Obsessive-compulsive disorder usually begins in adolescence or early adulthood. It effects from 1.5 to 2 percent of people in the United States, as the disorder affects that are slightly more prominent in women than men.

Obsessions can include a variety of thoughts, images, and impulses. Common obsessions include fears of contamination from germs, doubts about whether doors are locked or appliances are turned off, nonsensical impulses such as shouting in public, sexual thoughts that are disturbing to the individual, and thoughts of accidentally and unknowingly harming someone. People with obsessions may avoid shaking hands with other people because they fear contamination, or they may avoid driving because they fear they will injure someone in a traffic accident.

People usually perform compulsions to relieve the anxiety produced by their obsessions, although not all people with obsessions perform compulsions. The most common compulsions involve cleaning rituals and checking rituals. For example, people with obsessions about germs may wash their hand's dozens of times each day until their skin becomes raw. People with obsessions about neatness and symmetry may constantly rearrange or straighten objects on their desk. People with checking compulsions must repeatedly check to make sure they locked doors and windows or turned off water faucets. Other compulsions include counting objects, hoarding vast amounts of useless materials, and repeating words or prayers internally.

Obsessive-compulsive disorder can have disabling effects on people's lives. People with severe cases of this disorder may need hospitalization to help treat the compulsions. In fewer extreme instances, individuals with compulsions often must allow a great deal of extra time to complete seemingly routine tasks, such as preparing to leave the house in the morning. Individuals may avoid going to certain places or engaging in certain activities because they feel embarrassed about their behaviour.

In addition, family members of someone with this disorder may feel angry at the person because the compulsive behaviours intrude on their time together or interfere with the family's functioning. For instance, some individuals hoard things, such as newspapers or magazines, because they believe they may someday need certain pieces of information. The piles of newspapers may cover the living areas and make other family members feel embarrassed to have guests in the home.

Like many other mental illnesses, obsessive-compulsive disorder appears to result from a combination of biological and psychological influences. Some people may have a biological predisposition to experience anxiety. Research also suggests that abnormal levels of the neurotransmitter serotonin may play a role in obsessive-compulsive disorder. Brain scans of people with obsessive-compulsive disorder have revealed abnormalities in the activity level of the orbital cortex, cingulate cortex, and caudate nucleus, a brain circuit that helps control movements of the limbs.

The disorder may develop when these biological influences combine with a psychological vulnerability to anxiety. Some people may develop a psychological vulnerability to anxiety in childhood. They may come to believe that the world is a potentially dangerous place over which one has little control. People seem to develop obsessive-compulsive disorder specifically when they learn that some thoughts are dangerous or unacceptable and, while attempting to suppress these thoughts, develop anxiety about the recurrence of the thoughts and about the perceived dangerousness and intrusiveness of the thoughts.

Treatment for obsessive-compulsive disorder includes psychotherapy, psychoactive drugs, or both. Mental health professionals consider exposure and response prevention, a type of cognitive-behaviourial therapy, to be the most effective form of psychotherapy for this disorder. In this technique, the therapist exposes the patient to feared thoughts or situations and prevents the patient from acting on their own compulsion. For example, a therapist might have patients with cleaning compulsions touch something dirty and then prevent them from washing their hands. This technique helps 60 to 70 percent of people with obsessive-compulsive disorder.

Medications to treat obsessive-compulsive disorder are made up of selective serotonin reuptake inhibitors, such as Fluoxetine (Prozac) and fluvoxamine (Luvox). A tricyclic antidepressant, clomipramine (Anafranil), also helps relieve symptoms of the disorder. About 80 percent of people with the disorder show some improvement with a combined treatment of medication and behaviourial therapy. However, many patients relapse when they stop taking the medication.

The goal of cognitive therapy is to identify patterns of irrational thinking that cause a person to behave abnormally. The therapist teaches skills that enable the person to recognize the irrationality of the thoughts. The person eventually learns to perceive people, situations, and himself or herself in a more realistic way and develops improved problem-solving and coping skills. Psychotherapists use cognitive therapy to treat depression, panic disorder, and some personality disorders.

Rehabilitation programs assist people with severe mental illnesses in learning independent living skills and in obtaining community services. Counsellors may teach them personal hygiene skills, home cleaning and maintenance, meal preparation, social skills, and employment skills. In addition, case managers or social workers may help people with mental illnesses obtain employment, medical care, housing, education, and social services. Some intensive rehabilitation programs strive to provide active follow-up and social support to prevent hospitalization.

Therapists often use play therapy to treat young children with depression, anxiety disorders, and problems stemming from child abuse and neglect. The therapist spends time with the child in a playroom filled with dolls, puppets, and drawing materials, which the child may use to act out personal and family conflicts. The therapist helps the child recognize and confront their own feelings.

In group therapy, a number of people gather together to discuss problems under the guidance of a therapist. By sharing their feelings and experiences with others, group members learn their problems are not unique, receive emotional support, and learn ways to cope with their problems. Psychodrama is a type of group therapy in which participants act out emotional conflicts, often on a stage, with the goals of increasing their understanding of their behaviours and resolving conflicts. Group therapy generally costs less per person than individual psychotherapy.

Family intervention programs help families learn to cope with and manage a family member's chronic mental illness, such as schizophrenia. Family members learn to monitor the illness, help with daily life problems, ensure adherence to medication, and cope with stigma.

Electroconvulsive therapy (ECT) is a treatment for severe depression in which an electrical current is passed through the patient's brain for one or two seconds to induce a controlled seizure. The treatments are repeated over a period of several weeks. For unknown reasons, ECT often relieves severe depression even when drug therapy and psychotherapy have failed. The treatment has created controversy because its side effects may include confusion and memory loss. Both of these effects, however, are usually temporary.

Seeking a treatment for extreme cases of mental illness, Portuguese neurologist António Egas Moniz invented the lobotomy, a surgical technique that destroys tissue in the frontal lobe of the brain. The procedures, widely performed in the 1940s and 1950s, often leaving the person in a vegetative state or caused drastic changes in personality and behaviour.

Even more controversial than ECT is Psychosurgery, the surgical removal or destruction of sections of the brain in order to reduce severe and chronic psychiatric symptoms. The best-known example of Psychosurgery is the lobotomy, a procedure developed by Portuguese neurologist António Egas Moniz that was widely performed in the 1940's and early 1950's. Psychosurgery is now rarely performed because no research has proven it effective and because it can produce drastic changes in personality and behaviour.

A significant portion of the homeless population in the United States suffers from a chronic mental illness, such as schizophrenia. The shortage of mental health treatment centres in many cities may partly account for the large number of mentally ill people who are homeless or in jail.

Treatment for mental illness takes places in a number of settings. Mental hospitals or psychiatric wards in general hospitals are used to treat patients in acute phases of their illnesses and when the severity of their symptoms requires constant supervision. Most individuals who suffer from severe mental illness, however, do not require such close attention, and they can usually receive treatment in community settings.

Often, patients who have just completed a period of hospitalization go to group homes or halfway houses before returning to independent living. These facilities offer patients the opportunity to take part in group activities and to receive training in social and job skills. In supportive housing, mentally ill individuals can live independently in an environment that offers an array of mental health and social services. Some people with chronic and severe mental illnesses require care in long-term facilities, such as nursing homes, where they can receive close supervision.

Not all ancient scholars agreed with this theory of mental illness. The Greek physician Hippocrates believed that all illnesses, including mental illnesses, had natural origins. For example, he rejected the prevailing notion that epilepsy had its origins in the divine or sacred, viewing it as a disease of the brain. Hippocrates categorically considered mental illnesses as itemized positions, in that to include mania, melancholia (depression), and phrenitis (brain fever), and he advocated humane treatment that included rest, bathing, exercise, and dieting.

The Greek philosopher Plato, although adhering to a somewhat supernatural view of mental illness, believed that childhood experiences shaped adult behaviours, anticipating modern psychodynamic theories by more than 2000 years.

The Middle Ages in Europe, from the fall of the Roman empire in the 5th century ad too about the 15th century, was a period in which religious beliefs, specifically Christianity, dominated concepts of mental illness. Much of the society believed that mentally ill people were possessed by the devil or demons, or accused them of being witches and infecting others with madness. Thus, instead of receiving care from physicians, the mentally ill became objects of religious inquisition and barbaric treatment. On the other hand, some historians of medicine cite evidence that evens in the Middle Ages, many people believed mental illness to have its basis in physical and psychological disturbances, such as imbalances in the four bodily humours (blood, black bile, yellow bile, and phlegm), poor diet, and grief.

The Islamic world of North Africa, Spain, and the Middle East generally held far more humane attitudes toward people with mental illnesses. Following the belief that God loved insane people, communities began establishing asylums beginning in the 8th century ad, first in Baghdad and later in Cairo, Damascus, and Fez. The asylums offered patients special diets, baths, drugs, music, and pleasant surroundings.

The Renaissance, which began in Italy in the 14th century and spread throughout Europe in the 16th and 17th century, brought both deterioration and progress in perceptions of mental illness. On the one hand, witch-hunts and executions escalated throughout Europe, as of relating to the mind, the mental aspects of the problem, is that the mentally ill, and among them were in vengeance a reprisal for they're merciless persecuted. The infamous Malleus Maleficarum (The Witches Hammer or, Hammer of the Witch) which served as a handbook for inquisitors, claimed that witches could be identified by delusions, hallucinations, or other peculiar behaviours. To make matters worse, many of the most eminent physicians of the time fervently advocated these beliefs.

On the other hand, some scholars vigorously protested these supernatural views and called renewed attention to more rational explanations of behaviour. In the early 16th century, for example, the Swiss physician Paracelsus returned to the views of Hippocrates, asserting that mental illnesses were due to natural causes. Later in the century, German physician Johann Weyer argued that witches were actually mentally disturbed people in need of humane medical treatment.

French physician Philippe Pinel supervises the unshackling of mentally ill patients in 1794 at La Salpêtrière, a large hospital in Paris. Pinel believed in treating mentally ill people with compassion and patience, rather than with cruelty and violence.

During the Age of Enlightenment, in the 18th and early 19th centuries, people with mental illnesses continued to suffer from poor treatment. For the most part, they were left to wander the countryside or committed to institutions. In either case, conditions were generally wretched. One mental hospital, the Hospital of Saint Mary of Bethlehem in London, England, became notorious for its noisy, chaotic conditions and cruel treatment of patients.

Yet as the public's awareness of such conditions grew, improvements in care and treatment began to appear. In 1789 Vincenzo Chiarugi, superintendent of a mental hospital in Florence, Italy, introduced hospital regulations that provided patients with high standards of hygiene, recreation and work opportunities, and minimal restraint. At nearly the same time, Jean-Baptiste Pussin, superintendent of a ward for 'incurable' mental patients at La Bicêtre hospital in Paris, France, forbade staff to beat patients and released patients from chains. Philippe Pinel continued these reforms upon becoming chief physician of La Bicêtre's ward for the mentally ill in 1793. Pinel began to keep case histories of patients and developed the concept of 'moral treatment,' which involved treating patients with kindness and sensitivity, and without cruelty or violence. In 1796, a Quaker named William Tuke who had laid the groundwork for the York Retreat in rural England, which became a model of compassionate care. The retreat enabled people with mental illnesses to rest peacefully, talk about their problems, and work. Eventually these humane techniques became widespread in Europe.

In 1908, after his release from an asylum for the mentally ill, Clifford Whittingham Beers wrote, 'A Mind That Found Itself,' which exposed the poor conditions he had suffered while confined. He went on to establish several organizations dedicated to the promotion of mental health reforms in the United States.

People living in the colonies of North America in the 17th and 18th century generally explained bizarre or deviant behaviour as God's will or the obstacle working as of the devil. Some people with mental illnesses received care from their families, but most were jailed or confined in almshouses with the poor and infirm. By the mid-18th century, however, American physicians came to view mental illnesses as diseases of the brain, and advocated specialized facilities to treat the mentally ill. The Pennsylvania Hospital in Philadelphia, which opened in 1752, became the first hospital in the American colonies to admit people with mental illnesses, housing them in a separate ward. However, in the hospital's early years, mentally ill patients were chained to the walls of dark, cold cells.

In the 1780s American physician Benjamin Rush instituted changes at the Pennsylvania Hospital that greatly improved conditions for mentally ill patients. Although he endorsed the continued use of restraints, punishment, and bleeding, he also arranged for heat and better ventilation in the wards, separation of violent patients from other patients, and programs that offered work, exercise, and recreation to patients. Between the years 1817 and 1828, following the examples of Tuke and Pinel, a number of institutions opened that devoted themselves exclusively to the care of mentally ill people. The first private mental hospital in the United States was the Asylum for the Relief of Persons Deprived of the Use of Their Reason (now Friends Hospital), opened by Quakers in 1817 in what is now Philadelphia. Other privately established institutions soon followed, and state-sponsored hospitals - in Kentucky, New York, Virginia, and South Carolina - opened beginning in 1824.

American reformer Dorothea Dix championed the causes of prison inmates, the mentally ill, and the destitute. Horrified by the conditions provided for the mentally ill in Massachusetts. Dix successfully petitioned the state government for improvements in 1843. She was directly responsible for building or enlarging 32 mental hospitals in North America, Europe, and Japan.

Nevertheless, circumstances for most mentally ill people in the United States, especially those who were poor, remained dreadful. In 1841 Dorothea Dix, a Boston schoolteacher, began a campaign to make the public aware of the plight of mentally ill people. By 1880, as a direct result of her efforts, 32 psychiatric hospitals for the poor had opened. Increasingly, society viewed psychiatric institutions as the most appropriate form of care for people with mental illnesses. However, by the late 19th century, conditions in these institutions had deteriorated. Overcrowded and understaffed, psychiatric hospitals had shifted their treatment approach from moral therapy to warehousing and punishment. In 1908 Clifford Whittingham Beers aroused new concern for mentally ill individuals with the publication of A Mind That Found Itself, an account of his experiences as a mental patient. In 1909 Beers founded the National Committee for Mental Hygiene, which worked to prevent mental illness and ensure humane treatment of the mentally ill.

Following World War II (1939-1945), a movement emerged in the United States to reform the system of psychiatric hospitals, in which hundreds of thousands of mentally ill persons lived in isolation for years or decades. Many mental health professionals - seeing that large state institutions caused as much, if not more, harm to patients than mental illnesses themselves - came to believe that only patients with severe symptoms should be hospitalized. In addition, the development in the 1950s of Antipsychotic drugs, which helped to control bizarre and violent behaviour, allowed more patients to be treated in the community. In combination, these factors led to the deinstitutionalisation movement: the release, over the next four decades, of hundreds of thousands of patients from state mental hospitals. In 1950, 513,000 patients resided in these institutions. By 1965 there were 475,000, and 1990 states' mental hospitals housed only 92,000 patients on any given night. Many patients who were released returned to their families, although many were transferred to questionable conditions in nursing homes or board-and-care homes. Many patients had no place to go and began to live on the streets.

The National Mental Health Act of 1946 created the National Institute of Mental Health as a centre for research and funding of research on mental illness. In 1955 Congress created a commission to investigate the state of mental health care, treatment, and prevention. In 1963, as a result of the commission's findings, Congress passed the Community Mental Health Centres Act, had authorized the construction of community mental health centres throughout the country. Implementation of these centres was not as extensive as originally planned, and many people with severe mental illnesses failed to receive care of any kind.

One of the most important developments in the field of mental health in the United States has been the establishment of advocacy and support groups. The National Alliance for the Mentally ill (NAMI), one of the most influential of these groups, was founded in 1972. NAMI's goal is to improve the lives of people with severe mental illnesses and their families by eliminating discrimination in housing and employment and by improving access to essential treatments and programs.

During the 1980's, all levels of government in the United States cut back on funding for social services. For example, the Social Security Administration discontinued benefits for approximately 300,000 people between 1981 and 1983. Of these, an estimated 100,000 were people with mental illnesses. Although the government eventually restored Social Security benefits to many of these people, the interruption of services caused widespread hardship.

The emergence of managed care in the 1990's as a way to contain health care costs had a tremendous impact on mental health care in the United States. Health insurance companies and health maintenance organizations increasingly scrutinized the effectiveness of various psychotherapies and drug treatments and put stricter limits on mental health care. In response to these restrictions, but congress passed the Mental Health Parity Act of 1996. This law required private medical plans that offer mental health coverage to set equal yearly and lifetime payment limits for coverage of both mental and physical illnesses.

In 1997 the US Equal Employment Opportunity Commission issued new guidelines intended to prevent discrimination against people with mental illnesses in the workplace. The rules, based on the Americans with Disabilities Act of 1990, prohibit employers from asking job applicants if they have a history of mental illness and require employers to provide reasonable accommodations to workers with mental illnesses.

In recent years international agencies, led by the World Health Organization (WHO) of the United Nations (UN) have developed mental health policies that seek to reduce the huge burden of mental illness worldwide. These agencies are working to improve the quality of mental health services in Africa, Asia, Latin America, the Middle East, and elsewhere by educating governments on prevention and treatment of mental illness and on the rights of the mentally ill.

Psychiatry, is the branch of medicine specializing in mental illnesses. Psychiatrists not only diagnose and treat these disorders but also conduct research directed at understanding and preventing them.

A psychiatrist is a doctor of medicine who has had four years of postgraduate training in psychiatry. Many psychiatrists take further training in psychoanalysis, child psychiatry, or other subspecialties. Psychiatrists treat patients in private practice, in general hospitals, or in specialized facilities for the mentally ill (psychiatric hospitals, outpatient clinics, or community mental health centres). Some spend part or all of their time doing research or administering mental health programs. By contrast, psychologists, who often work closely with psychiatrists and treat many of the same kinds of patients, are not trained in medicine; consequently, they neither diagnose physical illness nor administer drugs.

The province of psychiatry is unusually broad for a medical specialty. Mental disorders may affect most aspects of a patient's life, including physical functioning, behaviour, emotions, thought, perception, interpersonal relationships, sexuality, work, and play. These disorders are caused by a poorly understood combination of biological, psychological, and social determinants. Psychiatry's task is to account for the diverse sources and manifestations of mental illness.

Physicians in the Western world began specializing in the treatment of the mentally ill in the 19th century. Known as alienists, psychiatrists of that era worked in large asylums, practising what was then called moral treatment, a humane approach aimed at quieting mental turmoil and restoring reason. During the second half of the century, psychiatrists abandoned this mode of treatment and, with it, the tacit recognition that mental illness is caused by both psychological and social influences. For a while, their attention focussed almost exclusively on biological factors. Drugs and other forms of somatic (physical) treatment was common. The German psychiatrist Emil Kraepelin identified and classified mental disorders into a system that is the foundation for modern diagnostic practices. Another important figure was the Swiss psychiatrist Eugen Bleuler, who coined the word schizophrenia and described its characteristics.

The discovery of unconscious sources of behaviour - an insight dominated by the psychoanalytic writings of Sigmund Freud in the early 20th century - enriched psychiatric thought and changed the direction of its practice. Attention shifted to processes within the individual psyche, and psychoanalysis came to be regarded as the preferred mode of treatment for most mental disorders. In the years 1940 and the 1950s emphasis shifted again: This time to the social and physical environment. Many psychiatrists had all but ignored biological influences, but others were studying those involved in mental illness and were using somatic forms of treatment such as electroconvulsive therapy (electric shock) and Psychosurgery.

Dramatic changes in the treatment of the mentally ill in the United States began in the mid-1950's with the introduction of the first effective drugs for treating psychotic symptoms. Along with drug treatment, new, more liberal and humane policies and treatment strategies were introduced into mental hospitals. More and more patients were treated in community settings in the 1960s and 1970s. Support for mental health research led to significant new discoveries, especially in the understanding of genetic and biochemical determinants in mental illness and the functioning of the brain. Thus, by the 1980's, psychiatry had once again shifted in emphasis to the biological, to the relative neglect of psychosocial influences in mental health and illness.

Psychiatrists use a variety of methods to detect specific disorders in their patients. The most fundamental is the psychiatric interview, during which the patient's psychiatric history is taken and mental status is evaluated. The psychiatric history is a picture of the patient's personality characteristics, relationships with others, and past and present experience with psychiatric problems - all told in the patient's words (sometimes supplemented by comments from other family members). Psychiatrists use mental-status examinations much as internists use physical examinations. They elicit and classify aspects of the patient's mental functioning.

Some diagnostic methods rely on testing by other specialists. Psychologists administer intelligence and personality tests, as well as tests designed to detect damage to the brain or other parts of the central nervous system. Neurologists also test psychiatric patients for evidence of impairment of the nervous system. Other physicians sometimes examine patients who complain of physical symptoms. Psychiatric social workers explore family and community problems. The psychiatrist integrates all this information in making a diagnosis according to criteria established by the psychiatric profession.

Psychiatric treatments fall into two classes: organic and nonorganic forms. Organic treatments, such as drugs, are those that affect the body directly. Nonorganic types of treatment improve the patient's functioning by psychological means, such as psychotherapy, or by altering the social environment.

Psychotropic drugs are by far the most commonly used organic treatment. The first to be discovered were the antipsychotics, used primarily to treat schizophrenia. The phenothiazine is the most frequently prescribed class of Antipsychotic drugs. Others are the thioxanthenes, butyrophenones, and indoles. All Antipsychotic drugs diminish such symptoms as delusions, hallucinations, and thought disorder. Because they can reduce agitation, they are sometimes used to control manic excitement in manic-depressive patients and to calm geriatric patients. Some childhood behaviour disorders respond to these drugs.

Despite their value, the Antipsychotic drugs have drawbacks. The most serious is the neurological condition tardive dyskinesia, which occurs in patients who have taken the drugs over extended periods. The condition is characterized by abnormal movements of the tongue, mouth, and body. It is especially serious because its symptoms do not always disappear when the drug is stopped, and no known treatment for it has been developed.

Most Psychotropic drugs are chemically synthesized. Lithium carBlonate, however, is a naturally occurring element used to prevent, or at least reduce, the severity of shifts of mood in manic-depression. It is especially effective in controlling mania. Psychiatrists must monitor lithium dosages carefully, because only a small margin exists between an effective dose and a toxic one.

Three major classes of antidepressant drugs are used. The tricyclic and tetracyclic antidepressants, the most frequently prescribed, are used for the most common form of serious depression. Monoamine oxidase (MAO) inhibitors are used for so-called atypical depressions. Serotonin-selective reuptake inhibitors (SSRIs) are effective against both typical and atypical depressions. Although all three classes are quite effective in relieving depression in correctly matched patients, they also have disadvantages. The tricyclics and tetracyclics can take two to five weeks to become effective and can cause such side effects as oversedation and cardiac problems. MAO inhibitors can cause severe hypertension in patients who ingest certain types of food (such as cheese, beer, and wine) or drugs (such as cold medicines). SSRI drugs, such as Fluoxetine (Prozac), take 2 to 12 weeks to become effective and can cause headaches, nausea, insomnia, and nervousness.

Anxiety, tension and insomnia are often treated with drugs that are commonly called minor tranquillizers. Barbiturates have been used for the longest time, but they produce more severe side effects and are more often abused than the newer classes of Antianxiety drugs. Of the new drugs, the benzodiazepines are the most frequently prescribed, very often in nonpsychiatric settings.

The stimulant drugs, such as amphetamine - a drug that is often abused - have legitimate uses in psychiatry. They help to control overactivity and lack of concentration in hyperactive children and to stimulate the victims of narcolepsy, a disorder characterized by sudden, uncontrollable episodes of sleep.

Another organic treatment is electroconvulsive therapy, or ECT, in which seizures similar to those of epilepsy are produced by a current of electricity passed through the forehead. ECT is most commonly used to treat severe depressions that have not responded to drug treatment. It is also sometimes used to treat schizophrenia. Other forms of organic treatment are much less frequently used than drugs and ETC. They include the controversial technique Psychosurgery, in which fibres in the brain are severed; this technique is now used very rarely.

The most common nonorganic treatment is psychotherapy. Most psychotherapies conducted by psychiatrists are psychodynamic in orientation - that is, they focus on internal psychic conflict and its resolution as a means of restoring mental health. The prototypical psychodynamic therapy is psychoanalysis, which is aimed at untangling the sources of unconscious conflict in the past and restructuring the patient's personality. Psychoanalysis is the treatment in which the patient lies on a couch, with the psychoanalyst out of sight, and says whatever comes to mind. The patient relates dreams, fantasies, and memories, along with thoughts and feelings associated with them. The analyst helps the patient interpret these associations and the meaning of the patient's relationship to the analyst. Because it is lengthy and expensive, often several years in duration, classical psychoanalysis is now infrequently used.

More common are shorter forms of psychotherapy that supplement psychoanalytic principles with other theoretical ideas and scientifically derived information. In these types of therapy, psychiatrists are more likely to give the patient advice and try to influence behaviour. Some use techniques derived from behaviour therapy, which is based on learning theory (although these methods are more commonly used by psychologists).

Besides psychotherapy, the other major form of nonorganic treatment used in psychiatry is milieu therapy. Usually carried out in psychiatric wards, milieu therapy directs social relations between patients and staff toward therapeutic ends. Ward activities, too, are planned to serve specific therapeutic goals.

In general, psychotherapy is relied on more heavily for the treatment of neuroses and other nonpsychotic conditions than it is for psychoses. In psychotic patients, who usually receive psychoactive drugs, psychotherapy is used to improve social and vocational functioning. Milieu therapy is limited to hospitalized patients. Increasingly, psychiatrists use a combination of organic and nonorganic techniques for all patients, depending on their diagnosis and response to treatment.

Bipolar Disorder, is consistent of a mental illness in which a person's mood alternates between extreme mania and depression, even that Bipolar disorder is also called manic-depressive illness. When manic, people with bipolar disorder feel intensely elated, self-important, energetic, and irritable. When depressed, they experience painful sadness, negative thinking, and indifference to things that used to bring them happiness.

Bipolar disorder is much less common than depression. In North America and Europe, about 1 percent of people experience bipolar disorder during their lives. Rates of bipolar disorder are similar throughout the world. In comparison, at least 8 percent of people experience serious depression during their lives. Bipolar disorder affects men and women about equally and is somewhat more common in higher socioeconomic classes. At least 15 percent of people with bipolar disorder commit suicide. This rate roughly equals the rate for people with major depression, the most severe form of depression.

Bipolar disorder is a mental illness that causes mood swings. In the manic phase, a person might feel ecstatic, self-important, and energetic. But when the person becomes depressed, the mood shifts to extreme sadness, negative thinking, and apathy. Some studies indicate that the disease occurs at unusually high rates in creative people, such as artists, writers, and musicians. But some researchers contend that the methodology of these studies was flawed and their results were misleading. In the October 1996 Discover magazine article, anthropologist Jo Ann C. Gutin presents the results of several studies that explore the link between creativity and mental illness.

Bipolar disorder usually begins in a person's late teens or 20's. Men usually experience mania as the first mood episode, whereas women typically experience depression first. Episodes of mania and depression usually last from several weeks to several months. On average, people with untreated bipolar disorder experience four episodes of mania or depression throughout any ten-year period, that many people with bipolar disorder function normally between episodes. In 'rapid-cycling' bipolar disorder, however, which represents 5 to 15 percent of all cases, a person experiences four or more mood episodes within a year and may have little or no normal functioning in between episodes. In rare cases, swings between mania and depression occur over a period of days.

In another type of bipolar disorder, a person experiences major depression and hypomanic episodes, or episodes of milder mania. In a related disorder called cyclothymic disorder, a person's mood alternates between mild depression and mild mania. Some people with cyclothymic disorder later develop full-blown bipolar disorder. Bipolar disorder may also follow a seasonal pattern, with a person typically experiencing depression in the fall and winter and mania in the spring or summer.

People, encompassed within the depressive point of bipolar disorder, experience the intensely sad or profoundly transferring formation showing the indifference to work, activities, and people that once brought them pleasure. They think slowly, concentrate poorly, feel tired, and experience changes - usually an increase - in their appetite and sleep. They often feel a sense of worthlessness or helplessness. In addition, they may feel pessimistic or hopeless about the future and may think about or attempt suicide. In some cases of severe depression, people may experience psychotic symptoms, such as delusions (false beliefs) or hallucinations (false sensory perceptions).

In the manic phase of bipolar disorder, people feel intensely and inappropriately happy, self-important, and irritable. In this highly energized state they sleep less, have racing thoughts, and talk in rapid-fire speech that goes off in many directions. They have inflated self-esteem and confidence and may even have delusions of grandeur. Mania may make people impatient and abrasive, and when frustrated, physically abusive. They often behave in socially inappropriate ways, think irrationally, and show impaired judgment. For example, they may take aeroplane trips all over the country, make indecent sexual advances, and formulate grandiose plans involving indiscriminate investments of money. The self-destructive behaviour of mania includes excessive gambling, buying outrageously expensive gifts, abusing alcohol or other drugs, and provoking confrontations with obnoxious or combative behaviour.

Clinical depression is one of the most common forms of mental illness. Although depression can be treated with psychotherapy, many scientists believe there are biological causes for the disease. The June 1998 publication, of the Scientific American, in the article that neurobiologist Charles B. Nemeroff exchanges views about something in order to arrive at the truth or to convince others that the connection concerning to considerations that are differentiated between biochemical changes in the brain and the finding of depression.

The genes that a person inherits seem to have a strong influence on whether the person will develop bipolar disorder. Studies of twins provide evidence for this genetic influence. Among genetically identical twins where one twin has bipolar disorder, the other twin has the disorder in more than 70 percent of cases. But among pairs of fraternal twins, who have about half their genes in common, both twins have bipolar disorder in less than 15 percent of cases in which one twin has the disorder. The degree of genetic similarity seems to account for the difference between identical and fraternal twins. Further evidence for a genetic influence comes from studies of adopted children with bipolar disorder. These studies show that biological relatives of the children have a higher incidence of bipolar disorder than do people in the general population. Thus, bipolar disorder seems to run in families for genetic reasons.

Owing or relating to, or affecting a particular person, over which a personal allegiance about the concerns and considerations or work-related stress can trigger a manic episode, but this usually occurs in people with genetic vulnerabilities, other factors - such as prenatal development, childhood experiences, and social conditions - seem to have relatively little influence in causing bipolar disorder. One study examined the children of identical twins in which only one member of each pair of twins had bipolar disorder. The study found that regardless of whether the parent had bipolar disorder or not, all of the children had the same high 10-percent rate of bipolar disorder. This observation clearly suggests that risk for bipolar illness comes from genetic influence, not from exposure to a parent's bipolar illness or from family problems caused by that illness.

Different therapies may shorten, delay, or even prevent the extreme moods caused by bipolar disorder. Lithium carBlonate, a natural mineral salt, can help control both mania and depression in bipolar disorder. The drug generally takes two to three weeks to become effective. People with bipolar disorder may take lithium during periods of relatively normal mood to delay or prevent subsequent episodes of mania or depression. Common side effects of lithium include nausea, increased thirst and urination, vertigo, loss of appetite, and muscle weakness. In addition, long-term use can impair functioning of the kidneys. For this reason, doctors do not prescribe lithium to bipolar patients with kidney disease. Many people find the side effects so unpleasant that they stop taking the medication, which often results in relapse.

From 20 to 40 percent of people do not respond to lithium therapy. For these people, two anticonvulsant drugs may help dampen severe manic episodes: carbamazepine (Tegretol) and valproate (Depakene). The use of traditional antidepressants to treat bipolar disorder carries risks of triggering a manic episode or a rapid-cycling pattern.

A psychiatrist is a doctor of medicine who has had four years of postgraduate training in psychiatry. Many psychiatrists take further training in psychoanalysis, child psychiatry, or other subspecialties. Psychiatrists treat patients in private practice, in general hospitals, or in specialized facilities for the mentally ill (psychiatric hospitals, outpatient clinics, or community mental health centres). Some spend part or all of their time doing research or administering mental health programs. By contrast, psychologists, who often work closely with psychiatrists and treat many of the same kinds of patients, are not trained in medicine; consequently, they neither diagnose physical illness nor administer drugs.

The province of psychiatry is unusually broad for a medical specialty. Mental disorders may affect most aspects of a patient's life, including physical functioning, behaviour, emotions, thought, perception, interpersonal relationships, sexuality, work, and play. These disorders are caused by a poorly understood combination of biological, psychological, and social determinants. Psychiatry's task is to account for the diverse sources and manifestations of mental illness.

Physicians in the Western world began specializing in the treatment of the mentally ill in the 19th century. Known as alienists, psychiatrists of that era worked in large asylums, practising what was then called moral treatment, a humane approach aimed at quieting mental turmoil and restoring reason. During the second half of the century, psychiatrists abandoned this mode of treatment and, with it, the tacit recognition that mental illness is caused by both psychological and social influences. For a while, their attention focussed almost exclusively on biological factors. Drugs and other forms of somatic (physical) treatments were common. The German psychiatrist Emil Kraepelin identified and classified mental disorders into a system that is the foundation for modern diagnostic practices. Another important figure was the Swiss psychiatrist Eugen Bleuler, who coined the word schizophrenia and described its characteristics.

The discovery of unconscious sources of behaviour - an insight dominated by the psychoanalytic writings of Sigmund Freud in the early 20th century - enriched psychiatric thought and changed the direction of its practice. Attention shifted to processes within the individual psyche, and psychoanalysis came to be regarded as the preferred mode of treatment for most mental disorders. In the 1940s and 1950s emphasis shifted again: this time to the social and physical environment. Many psychiatrists had all but ignored biological influences, but others were studying those involved in mental illness and were using somatic forms of treatment such as electroconvulsive therapy (electric shock) and Psychosurgery.

Dramatic changes in the treatment of the mentally ill in the United States began in the mid-1950's with the introduction of the first effective drugs for treating psychotic symptoms. Along with drug treatment, new, more liberal and humane policies and treatment strategies were introduced into mental hospitals. More and more patients were treated in community settings in the 1960s and 1970s. Support for mental health research led to significant new discoveries, especially in the understanding of genetic and biochemical determinants in mental illness and the functioning of the brain. Thus, by the 1980s, psychiatry had once again shifted in emphasis to the biological, to the relative neglect of psychosocial influences in mental health and illness.

Psychiatrists use a variety of methods to detect specific disorders in their patients. The most fundamental is the psychiatric interview, during which the patient's psychiatric history is taken and mental status is evaluated. The psychiatric history is a picture of the patient's personality characteristics, relationships with others, and past and present experience with psychiatric problems - all told in the patient's words (sometimes supplemented by comments from other family members). Psychiatrists use mental-status examinations much as internists use physical examinations. They elicit and classify aspects of the patient's mental functioning.

Some diagnostic methods rely on testing by other specialists. Psychologists administer intelligence and personality tests, as well as tests designed to detect damage to the brain or other parts of the central nervous system. Neurologists also test psychiatric patients for evidence of impairment of the nervous system. Other physicians sometimes examine patients who complain of physical symptoms. Psychiatric social workers explore family and community problems. The psychiatrist integrates all this information in making a diagnosis according to criteria established by the psychiatric profession.

Psychotropic drugs are by far the most commonly used organic treatment. The first to be discovered were the antipsychotics, used primarily to treat schizophrenia. The phenothiazine is the most frequently prescribed class of Antipsychotic drugs. Others are the thioxanthenes, butyrophenones, and indoles. All Antipsychotic drugs diminish such symptoms as delusions, hallucinations, and thought disorder. Because they can reduce agitation, they are sometimes used to control manic excitement in manic-depressive patients and to calm geriatric patients. Some childhood behaviour disorders respond to these drugs.

The general goal of Gestalt therapy is awareness of self, others, and the environment that bring about growth, wholeness, and integration of one's thoughts, feelings, and actions. Gestalt therapists use a wide variety of techniques to make clients more aware of themselves, and they often invent or experiment with techniques that might help to accomplish this goal. One of the best-known Gestalt techniques is the empty-chair technique, in which an empty chair represents another person or another part of the client's self. For example, if a client is angry at herself for not being kinder to her mother, the client may pretend her mother is sitting in an empty chair. The client may then express her feelings by speaking in the direction of the chair. Alternatively, the client might play the role of the understanding daughter while sitting in one chair and the angry daughter while sitting in another. As she talks to different parts of herself, differences may be resolved. The empty-chair technique reflects Gestalt therapy's strong emphasis on dealing with problems in the present.

Behaviourial therapies differ dramatically from psychodynamic and humanistic therapies. Behaviourial therapists do not explore an individual's thoughts, feelings, dreams, or past experiences. Rather, they focus on the behaviour that is causing distress for their clients. They believe that behaviour of all kinds, both normal and abnormal, is the product of learning. By applying the principles of learning, they help individuals replace distressing behaviours with more appropriate ones.

Typical problems treated with behaviourial therapy include alcohol or drug addiction, phobias (such as a fear of heights), and anxiety. Modern behaviourial therapists work with other problems, such as depression, by having clients develop specific behaviourial goals - such as returning to work, talking with others, or cooking a meal. Because behaviourial therapy can work through nonverbal means, it can also help people who would not respond to other forms of therapy. For example, behaviourial therapists can teach social and self-care skills to children with severe learning disabilities and to individuals with schizophrenia who are out of touch with reality.

Some researchers suggest that all therapies share certain qualities, and that these qualities account for the similar effectiveness of therapies despite quite different techniques. For instance, all therapies offer people hope for recovery. People who begin therapy often expect that therapy will help them, and this expectation alone may lead to some improvement (a phenomenon known as the placebo effect). Also, people in psychotherapy may find that simply being able to talk freely and openly about their problems helps them to feel better. Finally, the support, encouragement, and cared about, that clients feel from their therapist let them know they are care about and respected, which may positively affect their mental health.

Although different therapeutic approaches may be equally effective on average, mental health researchers agree that some types of therapy are best for particular problems. For panic disorder and phobias, behaviourial and cognitive-behaviourial therapies seem most effective.

Behaviourial techniques, often in combination with medication, are also an effective treatment for obsessive-compulsive disorder, post-traumatic stress disorder, generalized anxiety disorder, and sexual dysfunction. Cognitive-behaviourial, psychodynamic, and humanistic approaches all provide moderate relief from depression.

Mental health professionals agree that the effectiveness of therapy depends to a large extent on the quality of the relationship between the client and therapist. In general, the better the rapport is between therapist and client, the better the outcome of therapy. If a person does not trust a therapist enough to describe deeply personal problems, the therapist will have trouble helping the person change and improve. For clients, trusting that the therapist can provide help for their problems is essential for making progress.

The founder of person-centred therapy, Carl Rogers, believed that the most important qualities in a therapist are being genuine, accepting, and empathic. Almost all therapists today would agree that these qualities are important. Being genuine means that therapists care for the client and behave toward the client as they really feel. Being accepting means that therapists should appreciate clients for whom they are, despite the things that they may have done. Therapists do not have to agree with clients, but they must accept them. Being empathic means that therapists understand the client's feelings and experiences and convey this understanding back to the client.

In helping their clients, all therapists follow a code of ethics. First, all therapy is confidential. Therapists notify others of a client's disclosures only in exceptional cases, such as when children disclose abuse by parents, parents disclose abuse of children, or clients disclose an intention to harm themselves or others. Also, therapists avoid dual relationships with clients - that is, being friends outside of therapy or maintaining a business relationship. Such relationships may reduce the therapist's objectivity and ability to work with the client. Ethical therapists also do not engage in sexual relationships with clients, and do not accept as clients people with whom they have been sexually intimate.

As more immigrants to the United States and Canada have entered therapy, psychotherapists and Counsellors have learned the importance of taking a client's cultural background into account when assessing the problem and determining treatment. Scholars recognize that most psychotherapies are based on Western systems of psychology, which stress the desirability of individualism and independence. However, cultures of Asia and other regions commonly emphasize different values, such as conformity, dependency on others, and obeying one's parents. Thus, techniques that might be effective for someone from North America, Europe, or Australia might be inappropriate for a recent immigrant from Vietnam, Japan, or India. In order to provide effective treatment, therapists must be aware of their own cultural biases and become familiar with their client's ethnic and cultural background.

Anxiety, is the emotional state in which people feel uneasy, apprehensive, or fearful. People usually experience anxiety about events they cannot control or predict, or about events that seem threatening or dangerous. For example, students taking an important test may feel anxious because they cannot predict the test questions or feel certain of a good grade. People often use the word's fear and anxiety to describe the same thing. Fear also describes a reaction to immediate danger characterized by a strong desire to escape the situation.

The physical symptoms of anxiety reflect chronic 'readiness' to deal with some future threat. These symptoms may include fidgeting, muscle tension, sleeping problems, and headaches. Higher levels of anxiety may produce such symptoms as rapid heartbeat, sweating, increased blood pressure, nausea, and dizziness.

All people experience anxiety to some degree. Most people feel anxious when faced with a new situation, such as a first date, or when trying to do something well, such as give a public speech. A mild to moderate amount of anxiety in these situations is normal and even beneficial. Anxiety can motivate people to prepare for an upcoming event and can help keep them focussed on the task at hand.

However, too little anxiety or too much anxiety can cause problems. Individuals who feel no anxiety when faced with an important situation may lack alertness and focus. On the other hand, individuals who experience an abnormally high amount of anxiety often feel overwhelmed, immobilized, and unable to accomplish the task at hand. People with too much anxiety often suffer from one of the anxiety disorders, a group of mental illnesses. In fact, more people experience anxiety disorders than any other type of mental illness. A survey of people aged 15 to 54 in the United States found that about 17 percent of this population suffers from an anxiety disorder during any given year.

The Foundation of the Diagnostic and Statistical Manual of Mental Disorders, a handbook for mental health professionals, describes a variety of anxiety disorders. These include generalized anxiety disorder, phobias, panic disorder, obsessive-compulsive disorder, and post-traumatic stress disorder.

People with generalized anxiety disorder feel anxious most of the time. They worry excessively about routine events or circumstances in their lives. Their worries often relate to finances, family, personal health, and relationships with others. Although they recognize their anxiety as irrational or out of proportion to actual events, they feel unable to control their worrying. For example, they may worry uncontrollably and intensely about money despite evidence that their financial situation is stable. Children with this disorder typically worry about their performance at school or about catastrophic events, such as tornadoes, earthquakes, and nuclear war.

People with generalized anxiety disorder often find that their worries interfere with their ability to function at work or concentrate on tasks. Physical symptoms, such as disturbed sleep, irritability, muscle aches, and tension, may accompany the anxiety. To receive a diagnosis of this disorder, individuals must have experienced its symptoms for at least six months.

Generalized anxiety disorder affects about 3 percent of people in the general population in any given year. From 55 to 66 percent of people with this disorder are female.

A phobia is an excessive, enduring fear of clearly defined objects or situations that interferes with a person's normal functioning. Although they know their fear is irrational, people with phobias always try to avoid the source of their fear. Common phobias include fear of heights (acrophobia), fear of enclosed places (claustrophobia), fear of insects, snakes, or other animals, and fear of air travel. Social phobias involve a fear of performing, of critical evaluation, or of being embarrassed in front of other people.

Panic is an intense, overpowering surge of fear. People with panic disorder experience panic attacks - periods of quickly escalating, intense fear and discomfort accompanied by such physical symptoms as rapid heartbeat, trembling, shortness of breath, dizziness, and nausea. Because people with this disorder cannot predict when these attacks will strike, they develop anxiety about having additional panic attacks and may limit their activities outside the home.

In obsessive-compulsive disorder, people persistently experience certain intrusive thoughts or images (obsessions) or feel compelled to perform certain behaviours (compulsions). Obsessions may include unwanted thoughts about inadvertently poisoning others or injuring a pedestrian while driving. Common compulsions include repetitive hand washing or such mental acts as repeated counting. People with this disorder often perform compulsions to reduce the anxiety produced by their obsessions. The obsessions and compulsions significantly interfere with their ability to function and may consume a great deal of time.

Post-traumatic stress disorder sometimes occurs after people experience traumatic or catastrophic events, such as physical or sexual assaults, natural disasters, accidents, and wars. People with this disorder relive the traumatic event through recurrent dreams or intrusive memories called flashbacks. They avoid things or places associated with the trauma and may feel emotionally detached or estranged from others. Other symptoms may include difficulty sleeping, irritability, and trouble concentrating.

Most anxiety disorders do not have an obvious cause. They result from a combination of biological, psychological, and social factors.

Studies suggest that anxiety disorders run in families. That is, children and close relatives of people with disorders are more likely than most to develop anxiety disorders. Some people may inherit genes that make them particularly vulnerable to anxiety. These genes do not necessarily cause people to be anxious, but the genes may increase the risk of anxiety disorders when certain psychological and social factors are also present.

Anxiety also appears to be related to certain brain functions. Chemicals in the brain called neurotransmitters enable neurons, or brain cells, to communicate with other. One neurotransmitter, gamma-amino butyric acid (GABA), appears to play a role in regulating one's level of anxiety. Lower levels of GABA are associated with higher levels of anxiety. Some studies suggest that the neurotransmitter's norepinephrine and serotonin play a role in panic disorder.

Psychologists have proposed a variety of models to explain anxiety. Austrian psychoanalyst Sigmund Freud suggested that anxiety result from internal, unconscious conflicts. He believed that a person's mind represses wishes and fantasies about which the person feels uncomfortable. This repression, Freud believed, results in anxiety disorders, which he called neuroses.

More recently, behaviourial researchers have challenged Freud's model of anxiety. They believe one's anxiety level relates to how much a person believes events can be predicted or controlled. Children who have little control over events, perhaps because of overprotective parents, may have little confidence in their ability to handle problems as adults. This lack of confidence can lead to increased anxiety.

Behaviourial theorists also believe that children may learn anxiety from a role model, such as a parent. By observing their parent's anxious response to difficult situations, the child may learn a similar anxious response. A child may also learn anxiety as a conditioned response. For example, an infant often startled by a loud noise while playing with a toy may become anxious just at the sight of the toy. Some experts suggest that people with a high level of anxiety misinterpret normal events as threatening. For instance, they may believe their rapid heartbeat indicates they are experiencing a panic attack when in reality it may be the result of exercise.

While some people may be biologically and psychologically predisposed to feel anxious, most anxiety is triggered by social factors. Many people feel anxious in response to stress, such as a divorce, starting a new job, or moving. Also, how a person expresses anxiety appears to be shaped by social factors. For example, many cultures accept the expression of anxiety and emotion in women, but expect more reserved emotional displays from men.

Mental health professionals use a variety of methods to help people overcome anxiety disorders. These include psychoactive drugs and psychotherapy, particularly behaviour therapy. Other techniques, such as exercise, hypnosis, meditation, and biofeedback, may also prove helpful.

Psychiatrists often prescribe benzodiazepines, a group of tranquillizing drugs, to reduce anxiety in people with high levels of anxiety. Benzodiazepines help to reduce anxiety by stimulating the GABA neurotransmitter system. Common benzodiazepines include alprazolam (Xanax), clonazepam (Klonopin), and diazepam (Valium). Two classes of antidepressant drugs—tricyclics and selective serotonin reuptake inhibitors (SSRIs) - also have proven effective in treating certain anxiety disorders.

Benzodiazepines can work quickly with few unpleasant side effects, but they can also be addictive. In addition, benzodiazepines can slow down or impair motor behaviour or thinking and must be used with caution, particularly in elderly persons. SSRIs take longer to work than the benzodiazepines but are not addictive. Some people experience anxiety symptoms again when they stop taking the medications.

Therapists who attribute the cause of anxiety to unconscious, internal conflicts may use psychoanalysis to assist in filling the 'gap' with which people and their added understanding and resolve their conflicts, other types of psychotherapy, such as cognitive-behaviourial therapy, have proven effective in treating anxiety disorders. In cognitive-behaviourial therapy, the therapist often educates the person about the nature of their particular anxiety disorder. Then, the therapist may help the person challenge, but irrational thoughts that lead to anxiety. For example, to treat a person with a snake phobia, a therapist might gradually expose the person to snakes, beginning with pictures of snakes and progressing to rubber snakes and real snakes. The patient can use relaxation techniques acquired in therapy to overcome the fear of snakes.

Research has shown psychotherapy to be as effective or more effective than medications in treating many anxiety disorders. Psychotherapy may also provide more lasting benefits than medications when patients discontinue treatment.

Unconscious, in psychology, hypothetical region of the mind containing wishes, memories, fears, feelings, and ideas that are prevented from expression in conscious awareness. They manifest themselves, instead, by their influence on conscious processes and, most strikingly, by such anomalous phenomena as dreams and neurotic symptoms. Not all mental activity of which the subject is unaware belongs to the unconscious; for example, thoughts that may be made conscious by a new focussing of attention are termed foreconscious or preconscious.

The concept of the unconscious was first developed in the period from 1895 to 1900 by Sigmund Freud, who theorized that it consists of survivals of feelings experienced during infantile life, including both instinctual drives or libido and their modifications by the development of the superego. According to the Swiss psychoanalyst Carl Jung, the unconscious also consists of a racial unconscious that contains certain inherited, universal, archaic fantasies belonging to what Jung termed the collective unconscious.

A defining understanding of the states of consciousness is not at all simple, is agreed-upon definition of consciousness exists. Attempted definitions tend to be tautological (for example, consciousness defined as awareness) or merely descriptive (for example, consciousness described as sensations, thoughts, or feelings). Despite this problem of definition, the subject of consciousness has had a remarkable history. At one time the primary subject matter of psychology, consciousness as an area of study, that the idea that something conveys to the mind, from which of critics has endlessly debated the meaning of the ascribing interactions that otherwise to ascertain the quality, mass, extent or degree of terminological statements that its standard unit or mixed distributive analysis, is such, that a conceptualized form of its reasons to posit of a direct interpretation whose interference became of the total demise, even so, there is the result reemerging to become a topic of current interests.

Most of the philosophical discussions of consciousness arose from the mind-body issues posed by the French philosopher and mathematician René Descartes in the 17th century. Descartes asked: Is the mind, or consciousness, independent of matter? Is consciousness extended (physical) or unextended (nonphysical)? Is consciousness determinative, or is it determined? English philosophers such as John Locke equated consciousness with physical sensations and the information they provide, whereas European philosophers such as Gottfried Wilhelm Leibniz and Immanuel Kant gave a more central and active role to consciousness.

The philosopher who most directly influenced subsequent exploration of the subject of consciousness was the 19th-century German educator Johann Friedrich Herbart, who wrote that ideas had quality and intensity and that they may suppress or may facilitate or place of one another. Thus, ideas may pass from 'states of reality' (consciousness) to 'states of tendency' (unconsciousness), with the dividing line between the two states being described as the threshold of consciousness. This formulation of Herbart clearly presages the development, by the German psychologist and physiologist Gustav Theodor Fechner, of the psychophysical measurement of sensation thresholds, and the later development by Sigmund Freud of the concept of the unconscious.

The experimental analysis of consciousness dates from 1879, when the German psychologist Wilhelm Max Wundt started his research laboratory. For Wundt, the task of psychology was the study of the structure of consciousness, which ed well beyond sensations and included feelings, images, memory, attention, duration, and movement. Because early interest focussed on the content and dynamics of consciousness, it is not surprising that the central methodology of such studies was introspection; that is, subjects reported on the mental contents of their own consciousness. This introspective approach was developed most fully by the American psychologist Edward Bradford Titchener at Cornell University. Setting his task as that of describing the structure of the mind, Titchener attempted to detail, from introspective self-reports, the dimensions of the elements of consciousness. For example, taste was 'dimensionalized' into four basic categories: sweet, sour, salt, and bitter. This approach was known as structuralism.

By the 1920's, however, a remarkable revolution had occurred in psychology that was to essentially remove considerations of consciousness from psychological research for some 50 years: Behaviourism captured the field of psychology. The main initiator of this movement was the American psychologist John Broadus Watson. In a 1913 article, Watson stated, 'I believe that we can write of some psychology and never use the term's consciousness, mental states, mind . . . imagery and the like.' Psychologists then turned almost exclusively to behaviour, as described in terms of stimulus and response, and consciousness was totally bypassed as a subject. A survey of eight leading introductory psychology texts published between 1930 and the 1950's found no mention of the topic of consciousness in five texts, and in two it was treated as a historical curiosity.

Beginning in the later part of the 1950s, are, however, the grounded interests in the foundational subject of consciousness, for returning from its absence were subjects and techniques relating to altered states of consciousness: sleep and dreams, meditation, biofeedback, hypnosis, and drug-induced states. Much in the surge in sleep and dream research was directly fuelled by a discovery relevant to the nature of consciousness. A physiological indicator of the dream state was found: At roughly 90-minute intervals, the eyes of sleepers were observed to move rapidly, and at the same time the sleepers' brain waves would show a pattern resembling the waking state. When people were awakened during these periods of rapid eye movement, they almost always reported dreams, whereas if awakened at other times they did not. This and other research clearly indicated that sleep, once considered a passive state, were instead an active state of consciousness.

American psychiatrist William Glasser developed reality therapy in the 1960s, after working with teenage girls in a correctional institution and observing work with severely disturbed schizophrenic patients in a mental hospital. He observed that psychoanalysis did not help many of his patients change their behaviour, even when they understood the sources of it. Glasser felt it was important to help individuals take responsibility for their own lives and to blame others less. Largely because of this emphasis on personal responsibility, his approach has found widespread acceptance among drugs - and alcohol-abuse counsellor's, correction's workers, school counsellors, and those working with clients who may be disruptive to others.

Reality therapy is based on the premise that all human behaviour is motivated by fundamental needs and specific wants. The reality therapist first seeks to establish a friendly, trusting relationship with clients in which they can express their needs and wants. Then the therapist helps clients explore the behaviours that created problems for them. Clients are encouraged to examine the consequences of their behaviour and to evaluate how well their behaviour helped them fulfill their wants. The therapist does not accept excuses from clients. Finally, the therapist helps the client formulate a concrete plan of action to change certain behaviours, based on the client's own goals and ability to make choices.

During the 1960's, an increased search for 'higher levels' of consciousness through meditation resulted in a growing interest in the practices of Zen Buddhism and Yoga from Eastern cultures. A full flowering of this movement in the United States was seen in the development of training programs, such as Transcendental Meditation, that were self-directed procedures of physical relaxation and focussed attention. Biofeedback techniques also were developed to bring body systems involving factors such as blood pressure or temperature under voluntary control by providing feedback from the body, so that subjects could learn to control their responses. For example, researchers found that persons could control their brain-wave patterns to some extent, particularly the so-called alpha rhythms generally associated with a relaxed, meditative state. This finding was especially relevant to those interested in consciousness and meditation, and a number of 'alpha training' programs emerged.

Another subject that led to increased interest in altered states of consciousness was hypnosis, which involves a transfer of conscious control from the character interpretation belonging in the dependent sector, whose occasions, as basic of an idea or the principal object of attention, in the course of its immediate composition, and like the substance to a particular individual finds to the subject that the modification as when of transferring to that of another person. Hypnotism has had a long and intricate history in medicine and folklore and has been intensively studied by psychologists. Much has become known about the hypnotic state, relative to individual suggestibility and personality traits; the subject has now largely been demythologized, and the limitations of the hypnotic state are fairly well known. Despite the increasing use of hypnosis, however, much remains to be learned about this unusual state of focussed attention.

Finally, many people in the 1960's experimented with the psychoactive drugs known as hallucinogens, which produce deranging disorder of consciousness. The most prominent of these drugs is lysergic acid diethylamide, or LSD; mescaline; and psilocybin; the latter two have long been associated with religious ceremonies in various cultures. LSD, because of its radical thought-modifying properties, was initially explored for its so-called mind-expanding potential and for its psychotomimetic effects (imitating psychoses). Little positive use, however, has been found for these drugs, and their use is highly restricted.

Scientists have long considered the nature of consciousness without producing a fully satisfactory definition. In the early 20th century American philosopher and psychologist William James suggested that consciousness is a mental process involving both attention to external stimuli and short-term memory. Later scientific explorations of consciousness mostly expanded upon James's work. In the article from a 1997 special issue of Scientific American, Nobel laureate Francis Crick, who helped determine the structure of DNA, and fellow biophysicist Christof Koch explains how experiments on vision might deepen our understanding of consciousness.

As the concept of a direct simple linkage between environment and behaviour became unsatisfactory in recent decades, the interest in altered states of consciousness may be taken as a visible sign of renewed interest in the topic of consciousness. That persons are active and intervening participants in their behaviour has become increasingly clear. Environments, rewards, and punishments are not simply defined by their physical character. Memories are organized, not simply stored, an entirely new area called cognitive psychology has emerged that centre on these concerns. In the study of children, increased attention is being paid to how they understand, or perceive, the world at different ages. In the field of animal behaviour, researchers increasingly emphasize the inherent characteristics resulting from the way a species has been shaped to respond adaptively to the environment. Humanistic psychologists, with a concern for self-actualization and growth, have emerged after a long period of silence. Throughout the development of clinical and industrial psychology, the conscious states of persons in terms of their current feelings and thoughts were of obvious importance. The role of consciousness, however, was often de-emphasised in favour of unconscious needs and motivations. Trends can be seen, however, toward a new emphasis on the nature of states of consciousness.

We have used the term 'transference' several times, in that we attributed the therapeutic results to the transference without further definition of the word. We will now consider more closely the emotional relationship which is thus designed. During a psychoanalytic treatment, the patient allows the analyst to play a predominating role in his emotional life. This is of great importance in the analytic process. After his treatment is over, this situation is changed. The patient builds up feelings of affection for and resistance to his analyst which, in their ebb and flow, so exceed the normal degree of feeling that the phenomenon has long attracted the theoretical interest of the analyst. Freud studied this phenomenon thoroughly, explained it, and gave it the name 'transference', we most probably will understand the significance of the transference phenomenon impressed Freud so profoundly that he continued through the years to develop his ideas about it.

In all afforded efforts, to refuse to consider the demise of forebears as too merely disdain, that we cannot reproduce of all Freud's research about transference but for an instance of obligation, would be used to indicate the requirement by the immediate need or purpose upon such condition that might point beyond a normal or acceptable limit, as to an excessive amount of which something does not or cannot to their essentials. When we speak of the transference in connexion with social reeducation, we mean the emotional responses of the education or counsellor or therapist, as the case maybe, without meaning that it takes place in exactly the same way as in an analysis. The 'countertransference' is emotional aptitude of the teacher toward the pupil, the counsellor toward his charge, the therapist toward the patient. The feeling which the child develops for the mentor is conditioned by a much earlier relationship to someone else. We must take cognisance of this fact in order to understand these relationships. The tender relationships which go to up the child's love life are no longer strange to us. Many of these have already been touched upon in the foregoing literature. We have learned how the small boy takes the father and mother as love objects. We have followed the striving which arise out of this relationship, the Oedipus situation, we have seen how this runs its course and terminates in an identification with the parents. We have also had opportunity to consider the relationship between brothers and sisters, how their original rivalry is transformed into affection through the pressure of their feeling for the parents. We know that the boy at puberty must give up his first love object within the family and transfers his libido to individuals outside the family.

Our present purpose is to consider the effects of these first experiences from a certain angle. The child's attachment to the family, the continuance and the subsequent dissolution of these love relationships within the family, not only leave a deep effect on the child through the resulting identifications, they determine at the same the actual forms of this love relationships in the future. Freud compares these forms, without implying too great a rigidity, to copper plates for engraving. He has shown that in the emotional relationships of our later life we can do nothing but make an imprint from one or another of these patterns which we have established in early childhood.

Why Freud chose the term 'transference' for the emotional relationship between patient and analyst is easy to understand. The feelings which arose long ago in another situation are transferred upon the analyst. To the counsellor of the child, the knowledge of the transference mechanism is indispensable. In order to influence the dissociable behaviour, he must bring his charge into the transference situation. The study of the transference in the dissociable child shows regularly a love life that has been disturbed in early childhood by a lack of affection or an undue amount of affection. A satisfactory social adjustment depends on certain conditions, among them an adequate constitutional endowment and early love relationships which have been confined within certain limits. Society determines these limitations, just as definitely as the later love life of an individual is determined by early form his libidinal development. The child develops normally and assumes his proper place in society, if he can cultivate within the privacy to such relationships as can favourably be carried over into the schools and from there into the ever-broadening world around him. His attitude toward his parents must be such that it can be carried over onto the teacher, and that toward his brothers and sisters must be transferred to his schoolmates. Every new contact, according to the degree of authority or maturity which the person represents, repeats a previous relationship with very little deviation. People whose early adjustment to succeed or supervene from such a normative course have no difficulties in their emotional relations with others, and they are able to form new ties, to deepen them, or to break them off without conflict when the situation demands it.

We can easily see why an attempt to change the present order of society always meets with resistance and where the radical reformer will have to use the greatest leverage. Our attitude to society and its members has a certain standard form. It gets its imprint from the structure of the family and the emotional relationships set up within the family, therefore, the parents, especially the father, assume overwhelming responsibility for the social orientation of the child. The persistent, ineradicable libidinal relationships carried over from childhood are facts with which social reformers must reckon. If the family represents the best preparation for the present social order, which seems to be the case, then the introduction of a new order means that the family must be uprooted and replaced by a different personal world for the child. It is beyond our scope to attempt a solution of this question, which concerns those who strive to build up a new order of society. We are remedial educators and must recognize these sociological relationships. We can ally ourselves with whatever social system will, but we have the path of our present activity well marked out for us, to bring dissociable youth into the line with present-day society.

If the child is harmed through too great disappointment or too great indulgence in his early life, he builds up reaction patterns which are damaged, incomplete, or too delicate to support the wear and tear of life. He is incapable of forming libidinal object relationships which are considered normal by society. His unpreparedness for life, his inability to regulate his conscious and unconscious libidinal striving and to confine his libidinal expectations within normal bounds, creates an insecurity in relation to his fellow men and constitute one of the first and most important condition's fo r their development of delinquency. Following this point of view, we look for the primary causes of dissociable behaviour in early childhood, where the abnormal libidinal ties are established. The word 'delinquency' is an expression used to describe a relationship to people and things which are at variance with what society approve in the individual.

It is not immediately clear, from which are pointed from the particular form of the delinquency, just what libidinal disturbances in childhood have given rise to the dissociable expression. Until we have a psychoanalytically construed scheme for the diagnosis of delinquency, we may content ourselves by separating these forms into two groups: (1) Borderline neurosis cases with dissociable symptoms, and (2) dissociable cases for which are in part, the ego giving to develop of the dissociable behaviour, and showing no trace of neurosis. In the first type, the individual finds himself in an inner conflict because of the nature of his love relationships, a part of his own personality forbids the indulgence of libidinal desires and strives. The dissociable behaviour results from this conflict. In the second type, the individual finds himself in open conflict with his environment, because the outer world has frustrated his childish libidinal desires.

The differences in the forms of dissociable behaviour are important for many reasons. At present, they are significant to us because of the various ways in which the transference is established in these two types, we know that with a normal child the transference takes place of itself through the kindly efforts of the responsible adult. The teacher in his attitude repeats the situations long familiarly to the child, and thereby evokes a parental relationship. He does not maintain this relationship at the same level, but continually deepens it as long as he is the parental substitute.

When a neurotic child with symptoms of delinquency comes into the institution, the tendencies to transfer his attitude toward his parents to the persons in authority are immediately noticeable. The worker will adopt the same attitude toward the dissociable child as to the normal child, and bring him into positive transference, if he acts toward him in such a way as to prevent a repetition with the worker of the situation with the parents which led to the conflict. In psychoanalysis, on the other hand, it is of greatest importance to let this situation repeat itself. In a sense the worker becomes the father or the mother, but still not wholly so, he represents their claims, but in the right moment he must let the dissociable child know that he has insight into his difficulties and that he will not interpret the behaviour in the same way as do the parents. He will respond to the child's feeling of a need for punishment, but he will not completely satisfy it.

He will conduct in himself be entirely differently in the case of the child who in open conflict with society. In this instance he must take the child's part, be in agreement with his behaviour, and in the severest cases even give the child to understand that in his place he would behave just the same way. The guilt feelings found so clearly in the neurotic cases with dissociable behaviour are present in these cases also. These feelings do not arise, however, from the dissociable ego, but have another source.

Why does the educator conduct himself differently in dealing with this second type? These children, too, he must draw into a positive transference to him, but what is applicable and appropriate for a normal or a neurotic child would achieve opposite results. Otherwise the worker would bring upon himself all the hate and aggression which the child bears toward society, thus leading the child into a negative instead of positive transference, and creating a situation in which the child is not amenable to training.

Nevertheless, what was said about psychoanalysis theory is only a bare outline, that much deeper study of the transference is necessary to anyone interested in re-educational work from the psychoanalytic point of view. The practical application of this theory is not easy, since we deal mostly with mixed types, such that the attitude of the counsellor cannot be as uniform as having enough verbal descriptions for evincing of individual forms of dissociated behaviour to enable us to offer detailed instructions about how to deal with them. At present our psychoanalytic knowledge is such that a correct procedure cannot be stated specifically for each and every dissociable individual.

The necessity for bringing the child into a good relationship to his mentor is of prime importance. The worker cannot leave this to chance, he must deliberately achieve it and he must face the fact thus no effective work is possible without it. It is important for him to grasp the psychic situation of the dissociable child in the very first contact he makes with him, because only this can be known in what attitude to adopt. There is a further difficulty in that the dissociable child takes pains to hide his real nature: He misrepresents himself and lies. This is to be taken for granted, it should not surprise or upset us. Dissociable children do not come to us of their own volition but are brought to us, very often with the threat, 'You'll soon find out what's going to happen to you.' Generally parents resort our help only after every other means, including corporal punishment, have failed. To the child, we are only another form of punishment, an enemy against whom he must be on his guard, not a source of help to him. There is a great difference between this and the psychoanalytic situation, where the patient comes voluntarily for helping. To the dissociable child, we are a menace because we represent society, with which he is in conflict. He must protect himself against this terrible danger and be careful what he says in order not to give himself away. It is hard to make some of these delinquent children talk, remain unresponsive and stubborn. One thing they all have in common: They do not tell the truth. Some lie stupidly, pitiably, others, especially the older ones, show great skill and sophistication. The extremely submissive child, the 'dandily', the very jovial, or the exaggeratedly sincere, some especially hard to reach. This behaviour is so much to be expected that we are not surprised or disarmed by it, the inexperienced teacher or adviser is easily irritated, especially when the lies are transparent, but he must not let the child be aware of this. He must deal with the situation immediately without telling the child that he can see that coming through was attributive values about his attitudinal behaviours.

There is nothing remarkable in the behaviour of the dissociable, but it differs only quantitatively from normal behaviour. We all hide our real selves and use a great deal of psychic energy to mislead our neighbours. We masquerade more or less, according to necessity. Most of us learn in the nursery the necessity of presenting ourselves in accordance with the environmental demands, and thus we consciously or unconsciously build up a shell around ourselves. Anyone who has had experience with young children must have noticed how they immediately begin to dissimulate when a grown-up comes into the room. Most children succeed in behaving in the manner which they think is expected of them. Thus they lessen the danger to themselves and at the same time they are casting the permanent moulds of their mannerisms and their behaviour. How many parents really bother themselves about the inner life of their children? Is this mask necessarily for life? I do not know, but it often seems that the person on whom childhood experiences have forced the dissociable individual masquerades to a greater extent, and more consciously, then the normal. He is only drawing logical deductions from his unfortunate disagreeable authority? Why should he be sincere with those people who represent disagreeable authority? This is an unfair demand.

We must look further into the differences between the situation of social retraining and the analytic situation. The analyst expects to meet in his patient unconscious remittances which prevent him from being honest or make him silent: But the treatment is in vain when the patient lies persistently. Those who work with dissociable children expect to be lied to. To send this child away because he lies are only giving in to him. We must wait and hope to penetrate this mask which covers the really psychic situation. In the institution it does not matter if this is not achieved immediately, it means merely that the establishment of the transference is postponed. In the clinic, however, we must work more quickly. Taking with the patient does not always suffice, and we must introduce other remedial measures. Generally, we see the delinquent child, only, in at least as infrequent to a smattering of times, but we are forced to take some steps after the first few interviews, to formulate some tentative conception of the difficulty and to establish a positive transference as quickly as possible. This means we must get at least a peep behind the mask. If the child is not put in an institution, he remains in the old situation under the same influences which caused the trouble. In such cases we wish to establish the transference as quickly as possible, to intensify the child`s positive feelings for us that are aroused while the child is with us, and to bring them rapidly to such a pitch that they can no longer be easily disturbed by the old influences. To carry on such work successfully presupposes a long experience.

Even so, there are few current problems concerning the problem of transference that Freud did not recognize either implicitly or explicitly in the development of the theoretical and clinical framework. For all essential purposes, moreover, his formulations, in spite of certain shifts in emphasis, remain integral to contemporary psychoanalytic theory and practice. Recent developments mainly concern the impact of an ego-psychological approach, the significance of object relations, both current and infantile, external and internal, the role of aggression in mental life, and the part played by regression and the repetition compulsion in the transference. Nevertheless, analysis of the infantile Oedipal situation in the setting of a genuine transference neurosis is still considered as a primary goal of psychoanalytic procedure.

Originally, transference was ascribed to displacement on the analyst of repressed wishes and fantasies derived from early childhood. The transference neurosis was viewed as a compromise formulation similar to dreams and other neurotic symptoms. Resistance, defined as the clinical manifestation of repression, could be diminished or abolished by interpretation mainly directed toward the content of the repressed. Transference resistance, both positive and negative, was inscribed to the threatened emergence of repressed unconscious material in the analytic situation. Presently, as with the development of a structural approach, the superego had been portrayed as the heir to the genital Oedipal situation, also was the recognition as playing a leading role in the transference situation. The analysis was subsequently viewed not only as the object by displacement of infantile incestuous fantasies, but also as the substitute by projection for the prohibiting parental figures which had been internalized as the definitive superego. The effect of transference interpretation in mitigating undue severity of the superego has, therefore, been emphasized in many discussions of the concept of transference.

Certain expansions in the structural approach related increasingly to the recognition of the role that had earlier objective relations, in the development of the superego. This had affected the current concepts of transference, in that this connection, the significance of the analytic situation as a repetition of the early mother-child relationship has been stressed from different points for viewing to such equally important developments related to Freud's revised concept of anxiety which can only lead to theoretical developments in the field of ego psychology. However, this brought about their related clinical changes in the work of many analysts. As a result, attention was no longer the main attraction that had focussed on the content of the unconscious. In addition, increasing importance was attributed to the defence processes by means of which the anxiety which would be engendered if repression and other related mechanisms were broken down, was avoided in the analytic situation. Differences in the interpretation of the role of the analyst and the nature of transference developed from emphasis, on the one hand, on the importance of early object relations, and on the other, from primary attention to the role of the ego and its defences. These defences first emerged clearly in discussion of the technique of child analysis, in which Melanie Klein and Anna Freud, the pioneers in the fields of thought as playing the leading roles.

From a theoretical point of view, discussion foreshadowing the problems which face us today was presented in 1934 in a well-known paper by Richard Sterba and James Strachey, and further elaborated at the Marienbad Symposium at which Edward Bibring made an important contribution. The importance of identification with, or introjection of, the analyst in the transference situation of identification with, or introjection of, the analysts in the transference situation were clearly indicated. The therapeutic results were attributed to the effect of this process In mitigating the need for pathological defences. Strachey, however, considerably influenced by the work of Melanie Klein, regarded transference as essentially a projection onto the analyst of the patient's own superego. The therapeutic process was attributed to subsequent introjection of a modified superego as a result of 'mutative' transference. Sterba and Bibring, on the other hand, intimately involved with development of the ego-psychological approach, reemphasised the central role of the ego, postulating a therapeutic split and identification with the analyst as an essential feature of transference. To some extent, this difference of opinion may be regarded as semantic. If the superego is explicitly defined as the heir of the genital Oedipus conflict, then earlier intra-systematic conflicts within the ego, although they may be related retrospectively to the definite superego, much, nevertheless, are defined as contained within the ego. Later divisions within the ego of the type indicated by Sterba and very much expanded by Edward Bibring in his concept of therapeutic alliance between the analyst and the healthy part of the patient's ego, must also be excluded from superego significance. In contrast, those whom attribute pregenital intra-systemic conflicts within the ego primarily to the introjection of objects, consider that the resultant state of internal conflict appears like the dynamic idea that something conveys to the mind as having an endless meaning attached to the coherence of the therapeutic situation and seen in the later conflicts between ego and superego. They, therefore, believe that these structures developed simultaneously and suggest that no sharp distinction should be made between pre-oedipal, oedipal, and post-oedipal superego.

The differences, however, are not entirely verbal, since those whom attribute superego formations to the early months of life tend to attribute significantly too early object relation which differs from the conception of those who stress control and, neutralization of instinctual energy as primary functions of the ego. This theoretical difference necessarily implies some disagreement as how the dynamic situation both in childhood and in adult life, inevitably reflected in the concept of transference and in hypotheses as to the hidden nature of the therapeutic process. From one point of view, the role of the ego is central and crucial at every phase of analysis. A differentiation is made between transference as therapeutic alliance and the transference neurosis, which, on the whole, is considered a manifestation of resistance. Effective analysis depends on a sound and stable therapeutic alliance, a prerequisite for which is the existence, before analysis, of a degree of mature superego functions, the absence of which in certain severely disturbed patients and in young children may preclude traditional psychoanalytic procedure. Whenever indicated, interpretation's manifestations, which means, in effect, that the transference must be analyzed. The process of analysis, however, is not exclusively ascribed to transference interpretation. Other interpretations of unconscious material, whether related to defence or to early fantasies, will be equally effective provided they are accurately timed and provide a satisfactory therapeutic alliance has been made. Those, in contrast, whom stress the importance of early object relations emphasizes the crucial role of transference as an object relationship, distorted though this may be of a variety of defences against primitively unresolved conflicts. The central role of the ego, both in the early stages of development and in the analytic process, are definitely accepted. The hidden nature of the ego is, however, considered at all times to be determined by its external and internal objects. Therapeutic process indicated changes in ego function results, therefore, primarily from a change in object relations though interpretation of the transference situation, finds of less differentiation as made between transference as for being the therapeutic alliance and transference neurosis as a manifestation of resistance. Therapeutic progress depends almost exclusively on transference interpretation. Other interpretations, although at times, are not, in general, considered an essential feature of the analytic process. From this point of view, the preanalytic maturity of the patient's ego is not stressed as considered potentially suitable for traditional psychoanalytic procedure.

These differences in theoretical orientation are not only reflected in the approach to children and disturbed patients. They may also be recognized in significant variations of technique in respect to all clinical groups, which inevitably affect the opening phases, understanding of the inevitable regressive features of the transference neurosis, and handling of the germinal phases of analysis. By its emphasis as drawn on or upon the main problems, and, by contrast, rather than similarity, our efforts will be to avoid to detailed discussions of controversial theory regarding the hidden nature of early ego development by a somewhat arbitrary differentiation between those who relate ego analysis to the analysis of defences and those who stress the primary significance of object relations both in the transference, and in the development and definitive structure of the ego. Needless to say, this involves some oversimplification, where I hope that it may, at the same time, clarify certain important issues. To take, on or upon the analysis of patients we are generally agreeing to be suitable for classical analytic procedure, the transference neurosis. Those which emphasis the role of the ego and the analysis of defences, not only maintain Freud's conviction that analysis should proceed from surface to depth, but also consider that early material in the analytic situation derives, that, in general, from defensive processes rather than from displacement onto the analyst of early instinctual fantasies. Deep transference interpretation in the early instinctual fantasies. Deep transference interpretation in the early phases of analysis will, therefore, rather be meaningless to the patient since its unconscious significance is so inaccessible, or, if the defences are precarious, will lead to premature and possibly intolerable anxiety. Premature interpretation of the equally unconscious automatic defensive processes by means of which instinctual fantasy kept unconscious is also ineffective and undesirable. There are, nonetheless, differences of opinion within this group, as to how far analysis of defence can be separated from analysis of content. Waelder, for example, has stressed the impossibility of such separation. Fenichel, however, considered that at least theoretical separation should be made and indicated that, as far as possible, analysis of defence should precede analysis of unconscious fantasy. It is, nevertheless, generally agreed that the transference neurosis develops, as a rule after ego defences have been sufficiently undermined to mobilize previously hidden instinctual conflict. During both the early stages of analysis, and at frequent points after development of the transference neurosis, defences against the transference will become a main feature of the analytic situation.

This approach, has already been indicated, is based on certain definite premises regarding the hidden natures and function of the ego in respect to the control and neutralization of instinctual energy and unconscious fantasies, while the importance of early object relations is not neglected, the conviction that early transference interpretation is ineffective and potentially relations are not neglected, the conviction and unconscious fantasy. The conviction that early transference interpretation is ineffective and potentially dangerous is related to the hypothesis that the instinctual energy available to the mature ego has been neutralized from unconscious fantasies, meaning at the beginning of analysis, for all effective purposes, relatively or absolutely divorced from its unconscious fantasy, as yet, there are a number of analysts of differing theoretical orientation of ego function from unconscious sources, but consider that unconscious fantasy continues to operate in all conscious mental activity. The analysts also construct upon the whole of their existing in the emphasis to the crucial significance of primitive fantasies, in respect to the development of the transference situation. The individual entering analysis will inevitably have unconscious fantasies concerning the analyst derived from primitive sources. This material, although deep in a sense, is, nevertheless, strongly current and accessible to interpretation. Klein, in addition, creates the development and definitive structure of the superego to unconscious fantasy determined by the earliest phases of object relationships. She emphasizes the role of early introjective and projective processes in relation to primitive anxiety ascribed to the death instinct and related aggression drive fantasies. The unresolved difficulties and conflict of the earliest period continue to colour object relations throughout life. Failure to achieve an essentially satisfactory object relationship in this early period, and failure to master relative loss of that object without retaining its good internal representative, will not only affect all object relations and definitive ego function, but more specifically determine the nature of anxiety-provoking fantasies on entering the analytic situation. According to this point of view, therefore, early transference uninterpreted, even thought it may relate to fantasies derived from an early period of life, should result not in an increase, but a decrease of anxiety

In considering next problems of transference in relation to analysis of the transference neurosis, two main points must be kept in mind. First, as already indicated, those who emphasize the analysis of defence tend to make a definite differentiation between transference as therapeutic alliance and the transference neurosis as a compromise formation which serves the purposes of resistance. In contrast, those who emphasize the importance of early object relations view the transference primarily as a revival or repetition, sometimes attributed to symbolic processes of early struggles in respect to objects. Still, there is no sharp differentiation made between the early manifestations of transference and the transference neurosis. In view, moreover, of the weight given to the role of unconscious fantasy and internal objects in every phase of mental life, healthy and pathological functions, though differing in essential respect, do not differ with regard to their direct dependence on unconscious sources.

In the second place, the role of regression in the transference situation is subject to wide differences of opinion. It was, of course, one of Freud's earliest discoveries that regression had of its earliest points of fixation, and is a cardinal feature, not only in the development of neurosis and psychosis, but also in the revival of earlier conflicts in the transference situation. With the development of psychoanalysis and its application to an ever increasing range of received increased attention. The significance of the analytic situation as a means of fostering regression as a prerequisite for the therapeutic work has been emphasized by Ida Macapline in a recent paper. Differing opinions as to the significance, value, and technical handling of regressive manifestoes from the basis of important modifications of analytic technique, which will be considered, however, in respect to the transference neurosis, the view recently expressed by Phyllis Greenacre, that regression, and indispensable features would be generally accepted. It is also a matter of generally based agreement that a prerequisite for successful analysis is revival and repetition in the analytic situation of the struggle of primitive stages of development. Those who emphasize defence analysis, however, tend to view regression as a manifestation of resistance, as a primitive mechanism of defence employed by the growth sets of the transference neurosis. Analysis of these regressive manifestations with their potential dangers depends on the existing and continued functioning of adequate ego strength to maintain therapeutic alliance at an adult level. Those, in contrast, who stress the significance of transference as a revival of the early mother-child relationship does not emphasize regression as an indication of resistance or defence, the revival of these primitive experiences in the transference situation is, in fact, regarded as can essential prerequisite for satisfactory psychological maturation and true geniality. The Kleinian school, as already indicated features the continued activity of primitive conflicts in determining essential features of the transference at every stage of analysis. Their increasing overt revival in the analytic situation, therefore, signifies a reopening of the analysis, and in general, is regarded as an indication of diminuation rather than increase of resistance. The dangers involved according to this point of view and are determined more but to the failure to mitigate anxiety by suitable transference interpretation. By this failure to obtainably achieve, in the early phases of analysis, a sound and stabling therapeutic alliance is based on the maturity of the patient's essential ego characteristics.

In considering, briefly, the terminal phases of analysis, many unresolved problems concerning the goal of the therapy and definition of a completed psychoanalysis must be kept in mind. Distinction must also be made between the technical problems of the terminal phase and evaluation of transference after the analysis has been terminated, there is widespread agreement as to the frequent revival in the terminal phases of primitive transference manifestations apparently resolved during the early phases of primitive transference manifestation, apparently resolved during the early phase of analysis has been terminated. Balint, and those who accept Ferenczi's concept of primary passive love, suggest that some gratification of primitive passive needs may be essential for successful termination. To Klein, the terminal phases of analysis also represent a repetition of important features of the early mother-child relationship. According to her point of view, this period represents, in essence, a revival of the early weaning situation. Completion depends on a mastery of early depressive struggles culminating in successful introjection of the analysis as a good object. Although, in this connection, emphasis differs considerably, it should be noted that those who stress the importance of identification with the analyst as a basis for therapeutic alliance, also accept the inevitability of some permanent modifications of a similar nature. Those, however, who make a definite differentiation between transference of the transference neurosis as a main prerequisite for successful termination. The identification based on therapeutic alliance must be interpreted and understood, particularly with reference to the reality aspects of the analyst's personality. In spite, therefore, of significant important differences there are, as already indicated in connection with the earlier papers of Sterba and Strachey, important points of agreement in respect to the goal of psychoanalysis.

The differences already considered indicate some basic current problems of transference. So far, however, discussion has been limited to variations within the framework of a traditional technique. We must consider problems related to overt modifications, so as the essential expanding context of use between variations introduced in respect to certain clinical conditions. Often as a preliminary to classical psychoanalysis, and modifications based on changes on basic approach which lead to significant alterations with regard both to the method and to the aim of therapy. It is generally agreed that some neurosis, borderline patients and the psychosis. The nature and meaning of such changes are, however, viewed differently according to the relative emphasis placed on the ego and its defences, on underlying unconscious conflicts, and on the significance and handling of regression in the therapeutic situation.

In 'Analysis Terminable and Interminable', Freud suggested that certainly inaccessible to psychoanalytic procedure. Hartmann has suggested that in addition to these primary attributes, other ego characteristics, originally develop for defensive purposes, and the related neutralized instinctual energy at the disposal of the ego, may be relatively or absolutely divorced from unconscious fantasy. This not only explains the relative inefficacy of early transference interpretation, but also hints of possible limitations in the potentialities of analysis attributable to secondary autonomy of the ego which is considered to be relatively irreversible. In certain cases, moreover, it is suggested that analysis of precarious or seriously pathological defences - particularly those concerned of aggressive impulses - may be not only ineffective, but dangerous. The relative failure of ego development in such cases not only precludes the development of a genuine therapeutic alliance, but also raises the risk of a serious regressive, often predominantly hostile transference situation. In certain cases, therefore, preliminary period of psychotherapy is recommended in order to explore the capacities of the patient to tolerate traditional psychoanalysis. In others, as Robert Knight in his paper on borderline states, and as many analysts' working with psychotic patients have suggested, psychoanalytic procedure is not considered applicable. Instead, a therapeutic approach based on analytic understanding which, in essence, utilizes an essentially implicit positive transference as a means of reinforcing, rather than analysing the precarious defences of the individual, is advocated. In contrast, Herbert Rosenfeld approached even severely disturbed psychotic patients with minimal modifications of psychoanalytic techniques. Only changes which the severity of the patient's condition enforces are introduced. The dangers of regression in therapy are not emphasized since primitive fantasy is considered to be active under all circumstances. The most primitive period is viewed in terms of early object relations with special stress on prosecutory anxiety related to the death instinct. Interpretation of this primitive fantasy in the transference situation, is best offered the opportunity of strengthening the severity-threatened psychosis mainly to serve traumatic experiences, particularly of deprivation in early infancy. According to this point of view, profound regression offers an opportunity to fulfil, in the transference situation, primitive needs which had not been met at the appropriate level of development. Similar suggestions have been proposed by Margolin and others, in the concept of anaclitic treatment. Serious psychosomatic diseases, that approach the premise that the inevitable regression is shown by certain patients and should be utilized in therapy, as a means for gratifying, in their extremely permissive transference situation. Having distinctive or certain limits in the burdensome instant for demanding to that which has not been met in infancy, as this must, in the connection of being taken to understand that the gratifications recommended in the treatment of severely disturbed patients are determined by their conviction. Of these patients are incapable of developing transference as we understand it, in the connection with neurosis and must therefore be handled by a modified technique.

The opinions so far considered, however, much of them, as mine differ in certain respects, are, nonetheless, all based on the fundamental premise that an essential difference between analysis and other methods of therapy depends on whether or not interpretation of transference is an integral feature of technical procedure. Results based on the effects of suggestions are to be avoided, as far as possible, whenever traditional technique is employed. This goal has, however, to establish a point by appropriate objective means, that corroborated evidence that proved the need for better a state of being even more difficult to achieve than Freud expected when he first discerned the significance of symptomatic recovery based on positive transference. The importance of suggestion, even in the most strict analytic methods, has been repeatedly stressed by Edward Glover and others. Widespread and increasing emphasis as to the part played by the analyst's personality in determining the nature of the individual transference also implies recognition of unavoidable suggestive tendencies in the therapeutic process. Many analysts today believe that the classical conception of analytic objectivity and anonymity cannot be maintained. Instead, thorough analysis of reality aspects of the therapist's personality and point of view is advocated as an essential feature of transference analysis and an indispensable prerequisite for the dynamic changes already discussed in relation to the termination of analysis. It thus remains the ultimate goal of psychoanalyst's whenever their theoretical orientation, to avoid, as far as is humanly possible, results based on the unrecognized or unanalyzed action of suggestion, and to maintain, as a primary goal, the resolution of such results through consistent and careful interpretation.

There are, however, a number of therapists, both within and outside the field of psychoanalysis, who consider that the transference situation should not be handled only or mainly as a setting for interpretation even in the treatment or analysis of neurotic patients. Instead, they advocate utilization of the transference relationship for the manipulation of corrective emotional experience. The theoretical orientation of those utilizing this concept of transference may be closer to, or more distant from, a Freudian point of view according to the degree to which current relationships are seen as determined by past events. At one extreme, current aspects and cultural factors are considered of predominant importance, at the other, mental development is viewed in essentially Freudian terms and modifications of technique are ascribed to inherent limitations of the analytic method rather than to essentially changed conceptions of the early phases of mental development. Of this group, Alexander is perhaps the best example. It is thirty years since, in his Salzburg paper, he indicated the tendency for patients to regress, even after apparently successful transference analysis of the oedipus situation to narcissistic dependent pregenital levels which prove stubborn and refractory to transference interpretation. In his more recent work, the role of regression in the transference situation has been increasingly stressed. The emergence and persistence of dependent, pregenital commands for something as or is if one's right or due requirements are challenged in measuring moderations of a wide range of clinical conditions. It is argued, that its indications that the encouragement of a regressive transference situation is undesirable and therapeutically ineffective. The analyst, therefore, should when this threatens adopt a definite role explicitly differing from the behaviour of the parents in early childhood in order to bring about therapeutic results through a corrective emotional experience in the transference situation. This, it is suggested, will obviate the tendency to regression, thus curtailing the length of treatment and improving therapeutic results. Limitations of regressive manifestations by active steps modifying traditional analytic procedure in a variety of ways are also frequently indicated, according to this point of view.

It will be clear that to those who maintain the conviction that interpretation of all transference manifestations remain an essential feature of psychoanalysis, the type of manifestation as described, even though based on a Freudian reconstruction of the early phases of mental developments, and represent a major modification. It is determined by a conviction that psychoanalysis, as a therapeutic method, has limitations related to the tendency to regression, which cannot be resolved by traditional technique. Moreover, the fundamental premises on which, and the conception of corrective emotional experience is based minimizing the significance of insight and recall. It is essentially, suggested that corrective emotional experience alone may bring about qualitative dynamic alterations in mental structure, which can lead to a satisfactory therapeutic goal. This implies a definite modification on the analytic hypothesis whose current problems are determined by their defences against the direct opposition to the instinctual impulses and the intentional object, to which had been set up during the decisive periods of early development. An analytic result therefore depends on the revival, repetition and mastery of earlier conflict in the current experience of the transference situation with insight an indispensable feature of an analytic goal.

Since certain important modifications are related to the concept of regression in the transference situation, it should be considered that this concept is in relation to the repetition compulsion, that transference, essentially is a revival of earlier emotional experience, must be regarded as a manifestation of the repetition compulsion is generally accepted. It is, however, necessarily to distinguish between repetition compulsion as an attempt to master traumatic experience and repetition compulsion as an attempt to return to a real or fantasized earlier state of rest or gratification. Lagache, in a recent paper, has connected by or as if by the affirming relatedness as associated to the corresponding divergence in the repetition compulsion to an inherent need to appear in the problems that had previously been left unsolved. From this point of view, the regressive aspects of the transference situation are to be regarded as a necessary preliminary to the mastery of unresolved conflict, as too, the regressive aspects of transference are mainly attributed to a wish to return to an earlier state of rest or narcissistic gratification, to the maintenance of the status quo in preference to any progressive action, to which Freud's original conception of the death instinct. There is a good deal to suggest that both aspects of the repetition compulsion may bee seen in self-destructive forces tend to be stronger that progressive libidinal impulses, the potentialities of the analytic approach will inevitably appear to be limited. In those, in contrast, in whom that regard the reappearance in the transference situation of earlier conflicts as an indication of tendencies to master and progress will continue to feel that the classical analytic method remains the optimal approach to psychological illness wherever it is applicable.

Clarifications maintain the position or peculiar state as occupying a spatial point in temporal conditions, with a significant relevance to the amplitude larger in extent or a greater capacity that the average infinitive period has of time. Whereas in absence or termination must reflect on or upon the fearing analysis if the transference, as compelling of a generally acknowledged focal point, this itself may debase the appropriate factor that generates, in every degree. The exemplifying analytic technique that would react upon the discipline needed to utilize the new values, whereby, they can be ascribed as the commonality in holding the services to a suspicious self-direction and comprehensive understanding, in that of whatever is humanly affiliated to the best as can be, and yet, the advocacy to the analysis of the transference is generally acknowledged as the central feature of analytic technique? Freud regarded transference and resistance as facts in the observational conceptuality for which of representing the state of inventions. He writes, . . . that the theory of psychoanalysis in an attempt to account for two striking and unexpected facts of observation which emerge whenever an attempt is made. Evidently the symptoms of a neurotic source, may in his past life, inhabit the sources of experiential recall to the past or the introspective reflections. In the state of affairs, in that for being the latent characterizations announced as the factoring responsibility for the transference and of resistance . . . one which takes the other side of the problem, while accepting as such, to the latencies and the hidden values non-accepting for new interactions as brought through a hypothesis that will hardly escape the charge of misappropriation of properties by attempting endeavour to re-associate the essentially established personalization, that if the pursuit in calling them a psychoanalyst'. Rapaport (1967) argued, in his posthumously published paper on the methodology of psychoanalysis, that transference and resistance inevitably follow from the fact that the analytic situation is interpersonal.

Despite this general agreement on the centrality of transference and resistance in technique, in that, the analysis of transference is not pursued as systematically and comprehensively affirmed, however, it could be and should be. The relative privacy for which psychoanalytic work makes it impossible for one or of that of any-other, to skilfully improve upon the attemptive conceptual representation as comprehended of issues, its assumption to state this view as anything more that impressions, involving on that of what in the analysis of the transference and to states awareness in the number of reasons that an important aspect in the analysis of the transference of the transference, namely in the resistance, by the awareness of the transference is especially, and often adhering to the analytic procedures that interact among cultural inhibitors, but that will be distinguished as such, that its ranging manifold of distancing non-localities as founded of the analyst's.

However, it must first be to distinguish between two types of interpretation of the transference. That one is an interpretation of resistance to the awareness of transference, the other, is an interpretation of resistance to the resolution of transference. The distinction has clearly been best spelled out in the form from which copies or reproductions can be produced, as to cause to make its awareness and yielding values as grounded in the cognisance to Greenson (1967) and Stone (1967). The first kind of resistance may be called decence transference, although this term emphasis, wherefore is the terminological characterization by its term is mainly employed to refer to a phrase of analysis and carried within the general resistance to the transference of wishes, it can also be used for a more isolated instance of transference of defence. With some oversimplification, one might say that in resistance to the awareness of transference, the transference, the transference is what does the resisting.

Another connected description of stating this distinction between resistance and the awareness of transference and resistance to the resolution of transference is between implicit and indirect references to the transference and explicitly or directly referential to the transference. The interpretation of resistance to awareness of the transference is intended to make the implicit transference explicit. While the interpretation of resistance to the resolution of transference is intended to make the patient realize that the already explicit transference does indeed include a determinant from the past.

It is also important to distinguish between the general concept of an interpretation of resistance to the resolution of transference and a particular variety of such an interpretation, namely, a genetic transference interpretation - that is, an interpretation of how an attitude in the present is an inappropriate carry-over from the past. While there is a tendency among analysts to deal explicit references to the transference primarily among analyses to deal explicitly the references to the transference as primarily by a genetic transference interpretation, there are other ways of working toward a revolution of the transference. However, this argument does so implicate that not only is not enough emphasis being given to interpretation of the transference in the here and now, that is, to the interpretation of implicit manifestations of the transference, but also that interpretations intended to resolve the transference as manifested in explicit references to the transference should be primarily in the here and now, rather than genetic transference interpretations.

A patient's statement that he feels the analyst is harsh, for example, is, at least to begin with, likely best dealt with not by interpreting that this is a displacement from the patient's feeling that his father was harsh, but by as elucidation of some other aspect of this here and now attitude, such as what has gone on in the analytic situation that seems to the patient to justify his feeling or what was the anxiety that made it so difficult for him to express his feelings. How the patient experiences the actual situation is an example of the role of the actual situation in a manifestation of transference, which will be a major point of relevant significance.

Of course, both interpretations of the transference in the here and now and genetic transference interpretations are valid and constitute a sequence. We presume that a resistance to the transference ultimately rests on the displacement onto the analysts of attitudes from the past.

Because Freud's case histories focus much more on the yield of analysis than on the details of the process, they are readily but perhaps incorrectly construed as emphasizing work outside the transference much more than work within the transference, and, even within the transference, emphasizing genetic transference interpretations much more than work with the transference in the here and now (Muslin and Gill, 1978). The example of Freud's case reports may have played a role in what is to be considered as the common maldistribution of emphasis in these two respects - not enough on the transference and, within the transference, not enough on the here and now.

Transference interpretations in the here and now and genetic transference interpretations are, of course, exemplified in Freud's writings and are in the repertoire of every analyst, but they are not distinguished sharply enough.

Both participants in the analytic situation are motivated to avoid these interactions. Flight away from the transference and to the past can be a relief to both the patient and the analyst.

These aligning measures have been divided into five categorical divisions and placed into the following parts: (1) The principle that the transference should be encouraged to expand as much as possible within the analytic situation because the analytic work is best done within the transference. (2) the interpretation of disguised allusion to the transference as a main technique for encouraging the expansion of the transference within the analytic situation, (3) the principle that all transference has a connection with something in the present actual analysis situation, (4) how the connection between transference and the actual analytic situation is used in interpreting resistance to the awareness of transference, and (5) the resolution of transference within the here and now and the role of genetic transference interpretation.

The importance of transference interpretations will surely be agreeing to by all analysts, the greater effectiveness of transference interpretations than interpretations outside the transference will be agreeing to by many, but what of the relative roles of interpretation of the transference and interpretation outside the transference?

Freud can be interpreted as either of saying that the analysis of the transference in auxiliary to the analysis of the neurosis or that the analysis of the transference is equivalent to the analysis of the neurosis. The first position is stated in his saying (1913) that the disturbance of the transference has to be overcome by the analysis of transference resistance in order to get on with the work of analysing the neurosis. It is also implied in his reiteration that the ultimate task of analysis is to remember the past, to fill in the gap in memory. The second position is stated in his saying that the victory must be won on the field of the transference (1912) and that the mastery of the transference neurosis 'coincides with getting rid of the illness which was originally brought to the neurosis (1917). In this second view, he says that after the resistance is overcome, memories appear relatively without difficulty.

These two different positions also find expression in the two different ways in which Freud speaks of the transference. In `Dynamics of Transference` he refers to the transference, on the one hand, as `the most powerful resistance to the treatment`(1912) but, on the other hand, as doing us the inestimable service of making the patient's . . ., immediate impulses and manifests, when all is said and done, it is impossible to destroy anyone in absentia or in effigie (1912).

It can be agreed that his principal emphasis fails on the second position. He wrote once, in summary, 'Thus our therapeutic work falls into two phases in the first, all the libido is forced from the symptoms into the transference and concentrated there, in the second, the struggle is waged around this new object and the libido is liberated from it`(1912).

The detailed demonstration that he advocated that the transference should be encouraged to expand as much as possible within the analytic situation lies in clarification that resistance is primarily expressed by repetition, and repetition takes place both within and outside the analytic situation, but that the analyst seeks to deal with it primarily within the analytic situation, that repetition can be not only in the motor sphere (acting) but also in the psychical sphere, and that the psychical sphere is not confined to remembering but includes the present, too.

Freud`s emphasis that the purpose of resistance is to prevent remembering can obscure his point that resistance shows itself primarily by repetition, whether inside or outside the analytic situation. `The greater the resistance, the more extensively, and will act out (repetition)replace remembering`. Similarly in `The Dynamics of Transference` Freud said that the main reason that the transference is so well suited to serve the resistance is that the unconscious implies does not want to be remembered . . . but endeavour to reproduce themselves . . . (1918), the transference is a resistance primarily insofar as it is a repetition.

The point can be restated in terms of the relation between transference and resistance. The resistance expresses itself in repetition, that is, in transference both inside and outside the analytic situation. To deal with the transference. Therefore, is equivalent to dealing with the resistance. Freud emphasized transference within the analytic situation so strongly that it has come to mean only repetition within the analytic situation, even though, conceptually speaking, repetition outside the analytic situation is transference too, and Freud once used the term that way. `We soon perceive that the transference is itself only a piece of repetition and that the repetition is a transference of the forgotten past not only onto the analyst but also onto all the other aspects of the current situation. We . . . find . . . the compulsion to repeat, which now replaces the impulsion to remember, not only in his personal attitude to his analyst but also in every other activity and relationship which may occupy his life at the time . . . (1914).

It is important to realize that the expansion of the repetition inside the analytic situation, whether or not in a reciprocal relationship to repetition outside the analytic situation, is the avenue to control the repetition: `The main instrument . . . for curbing the patients compulsion to repeat and for turning it into a motive for remembering lies in the handling of the transference. We render the compulsion harmless, and indeed useful, by giving it the right to assert itself in a definite field`(1914).

Kanzer has discussed this issue well in his paper on 'The Motor Sphere of the Transference' (1966). He writes of a 'double-pronged stick-and-carrot' technique by which the transference is fostered within the analytic situation and discouraged outside the analytic situation. The 'stick' is the principle of abstinence as exemplified in the admonition against making important decisions during treatment, and the 'carrot' is the opportunity afforded the transference to expand within the treatment, 'in almost complete freedom' as in a 'playground' (Freud, 1914). As Freud put it, 'Provided only that the patient shows compliance enough to respect the necessary conditions of the analysis, we regularly succeed in giving all the symptoms of the illness a new transference meaning, and in replacing his ordinary neurosis by a 'transference neurosis' of which he can be cured by the therapeutic work' (1914).

The reason it is desirable for the transference to be expressed within the treatment is that there, it `is at every point accessible to our intervention`(1914). In a later statement he made the same point this way. `We have followed this new edition - the transference-neurosis - of the old disorder from its start, we have observed its origin and growth, and we are especially well able to find our way about in it since, as its object, we are situated at it's very centre,

(1917), it is not that the transference is forced into the treatment, but that it is spontaneously but implicitly present and is encouraged to expand there and become explicit

Freud emphasized acting in the transference so strongly that one can overlook the repetition in the transference, but does not of necessity for its enactment or recognition that gives validity to acts of a subordinate conformation as ratified in support of explicit authoritative permission. Repetition need not go as far as motor behaviour, it can also be expressed in attitudes, feelings, and intentions, and, indeed, the repetition often does take such form rather than motor action. The importance of making this clear is that Freud can be mistakenly read to mean that repetition in the psychical sphere can only mean remembering the past, is when he writes that the analyst as prepared for a perpetual struggle with his patient to keep in the psychical sphere all the impulses which the patient would like to direct into the motor sphere, and he celebrates it as a triumph for the treatment if he can bring it about that something the patient wishes to discharge in action are disposed if through the work of remembering (1914).

It is true that the analyst's efforts are to convert acting in the motor sphere into awareness in the psychical sphere, but transference may be in the psychical sphere to begin with, albeit disguised. The psychical sphere includes awareness in the transference as well as remembering.

One of the objections one hears, from both analysts and patient, to a heavy emphasis on interpretation of associations about the patients real life primarily in terms of the transference is that it means the analyst is disregarding the importance of what goes on in the patients real life. The criticism is not judiciable. To emphasize the transference meaning is not to deny or belittle other meanings, but to focus on the one of several meanings of the content that is the most important for the analytic process, for the reasons of positing the addition for one coming to any falsifiable conclusion.

Another way in which interpretations of resistance to the transference can be, or at lease appear to the patient to be, a belittling of the importance of the patients outside life is to make the interpretation as though the outside behaviour is primarily an acting out of the transference. The patient may undertake some actions in the outside world as an expression of and resistance to the transference, that is, acting out. But the interpretation of associations about actions in the outside world as having implications for the transference needs mean only that the choice of outside action to figure in the associations is co-determined by the need to express a transference indirectly. It is because of the resistance to awareness of the transference that the transference to be disguised. When the disguise is unmasked by interpretation, it becomes clear that, despite the inevitable differences between the outside situation and the transference situation, the content is the same for the analysis of the necrosis that coincides (Freud wrote that the mastering of the transference neurosis only coincides with getting rid of the illness which was originally brought to the treatment (1917)).

The analytic situation itself fosters the development of attitudes with primary determinants in the past, i.e., transference. The analyst's reserve provides the patient with few and equivocal cues. The purpose of the analytic situation fosters the development of strong emotional responses, and the very fact that the patient has a neurosis means, as Freud said, that' . . . it is a perfectly normal and intelligible thing that the libidinal cathexis [we would now add negative feelings] of someone who is partly unsatisfied, a cathexes which are held ready in anticipation, should be directly as well to the figure of the analyst (1912).

While the analytic setup itself fosters the expansion of the transference within the analytic situation, the interpretation of resistance to the awareness of transference will further this expansion.

There are important resistance on the part of both patient and analyst to awareness of the transference. On the patient's part, this is because of the difficulty in recognizing erotic and hostile impulses toward the very person to whom they have to be disclosed. On the analyst's part, this is because the patient is likely to attitude the very attitudes to him which are most likely to cause him discomfort. The attitudes the patient believes the analysts have toward him are often the ones the patient is least likely to voice, in a general sense because of a feeling that it is impertinent for him to concern himself with the analyst's feelings, and in a more specific sense because the aptitudes as held by the analyst are often attitudes the patient feels the analyst will be comfortable about having ascribed to him. It is for this reason that the analyst must be especially alert to the attitudes the patient believes he has, not only to the attitudes the patient does have toward him. If the analyst is able to see himself as a participant in an interaction, as he will become much more attuned to this important area of transference, which might otherwise escape him.

The investigations of attitudes are ascribed to the analyst makes easier the subsequent investigation of the intrinsic factors in the patient that played a role in such ascription. For example, the exposure of the fact that the patient ascribes sexual interests in him to the analyst, and generally to the patient, alternatively the subsequent exploration of the patient's sexual wish toward the analyst, and genetically the parent.

The resistance to the awareness of these attitudes is responsible for their appearing in various disguises in the patient's manifested associations and for the analyst's reluctance to unmask the disguise. The most commonly recognized disguise is by displacement, but identification is an equally important one. In displacement, the patient's attitudes are narrated for being toward a third party. In identification, the patient attitudes to himself attitudes he believes the analyst has toward him.

To encourage the expansion of the transference within the analytic situation, the disguises in which the transference appears have to be interpreted in the case of displacement the interpretation will be of allusions to the transference in association not manifestly about the transference. This is a kind of interpretation every analyst often makes. In the case of identifications, the analyst interprets the attitudes that the patient ascribes to himself the identification with which an attitude and subsequently attributed to the analyst. Lipton (1977) has recently described this form of disguise allusion in the transference with illuminating illustration.

In his autobiography, Freud wrote, 'The patient remains under the influence of the analytic situation as hopefully of a latter position or a period of decline, as though he is not directing responsibly for the mental activities onto a particular subject. Justly in assuming that nothing will occur, as not of some reference to the situation (1925). Since associations are obviously often not directed about the analytic situation, the interpretation of Freud's remark rests on what he meant by the 'analytic situation'.

It is believed that Freud's meaning can be clarified by reference to a statement he made in, 'The Interpretation of Dreams'. He said that when the patient is told to say whatever comes into his mind, his associations become directed by the 'purposive ideas inherent in the treatment' and that there are two such inherent regressive themes, one relating to the illness and the other - concerning which, Freud said, the patient has 'no suspicion'; - relating to other analyst's relating to the patient has 'no suspicions' - relating to the analyst (1900). If the patient has 'no suspicions' of the theme relating to the analyst, such that the theme appears only in disguise, the patient 's associations, it is contended that Freud's remark not only specifies the themes inherent in the patient 's identifications', but means that the associations are simultaneously directed by these two purposive ideas, not something by one and sometimes by the other.

The analyst should progress on the working assumption, that the patient's associations have transference implications pervasively, that with which this assumption is not to be confused with denial or neglect of the current aspects of the analytic situation. It is theoretically always possible to give precedence to a transference interpretation if one can only discern it through its disguise by resistance. This is not to dispute the desirability of learning as much as one can about the patient, if only to be a position to make more correct interpretations of the transference. One therefore, does not interfere with an apparently free flow of associations, especially early, unless the transference threatens the analytic situation to the point where its interpretation is mandatory rather than optional.

With the recognition that evens apparently freely associating patient may also be showing resistance to awareness of the transference, this formulation should not interfere as long a useful information being gathered should relace Freud's dictum that the transference should not be interpreted until it becomes a resistance (1913).

It can be argued that every transference has some connection to some aspect of the current analytic situation, in the sense that the past can exert an influence only insofar as it exists in the present. Of course, all the determinants of a transference are current in the sense that what I am distinguishing is the current reality of the analytic situation, that is, what actually goes on between patient and analyst in the situation from how the patient is currently constituted as a result of his past.

All analysts would dubiously agree that there are both current and transferential determinants of the analytic situation, and probably no analyst would argue that a transference of the analytic situation, and probably no analyst would argue that a transference idea can be expressed without contamination, as it was, that is, without any connection to anything current in the patient-analyst relationship. Nevertheless, the implications of this fact for technique are often neglected in practice, as my next point is only to argue for the connection.

Several authors, e.g., Kohut 1959 and Loewald 1960, have pointed out that Freud`s early application by the act or practice of using something or the state of being used, this, however, employ of the quality of being appropriate or valuable to some end as to accommodate the accountable or warrant the use of the term transference. In `The Interpretation of Dreams, in a connection not immediately recognizable as related to the present day use of the term, reveals the fallacy of considering that transference can be expressed free of any connection to the present. That early use was to refer to the fact that an unconscious idea cannot be expressed as such, but only as it becomes connected to a preconscious o r conscious content. In the phenomenon with which Freud was then concerned, the dream transference took place from an unconscious wish to a day residue. In `The Interpretation of Dreams, `Freud used the term transference both for the general rule that an unconscious content is expressible only as it becomes transferred to a preconscious or conscious content and for the specific application of this rule to a transference to the analyst. Just as the day residue is the point of attachment of the dream wish, so must there be an analytic-situation residue, though Freud did not use that term, as the point of attachment of the transference.

Analysts have always limited their behaviour, both in variety and intensity, to increase the extent to which the patient's behaviour is determined by his idiosyncratic interpretation of the analyst's behaviour. In fact, analysts unfortunately sometimes limit the behaviour so much as to compare with such an expression or unpiled standard or absolute approximation, that the entire relationship with the patient matter of technique, with no nontechnical personal relation, as Liptop (1977) has pointed out.

But no matter how far the analyst attempts to carry this limitation of his behaviour, the very existence of the analytic situation provides the patient with innumerable cues which can enviably become his rationale for his transference responses. In other words, the current situation cannot be made to disappear - that is, the analytic situation is real. It is easy to forget this truism in one's zeal to diminish the role of the current situation in determining the patient 's responses. One can try to keep past and present determinants relatively perceptible from one another, but one cannot obtain either 'pure culture'. Freud wrote: 'I insist on this procedure [the couch], however, for its purpose and result are to prevent the transference from mingling with the patient's associations imperceptibly, to isolate the transference and to allow it to come forward in due course sharply defined as a resistance' (1913). Even 'isolate' is too strong a word in the light of the inevitable intertwining of the transference with the current situation.

If the analyst remains under the illusion that the current cues he provides to the patient can be reduced to the vanishing point, he may be led into a silent withdrawal, which is not too distant from the caricature of an analyst as someone who does refuse to have any personal relationship with the patient. What happens then is that silence has become a technique rather than merely an indication that the analyst is listening. The patient's responses under such conditions can be mistaken for uncontaminated transference when they are in fact transference adaptions to the actuality of the silence.

The recognition, from which it takes its point of departure, as it was, has a crucial implications for the technique of interpreting resistance to the awareness of transference, in that, if, the analyst becomes persuaded of the centrality of transference and the importance of encouraging the transference to expand within the analytic situation, he has to find the presenting and plausible interpretation of resistance to the awareness of transference he should make. Is that, his most reliable guide is the cues offered by what is actually going on in the analytic situation? : On the one hand, the events of the situation, such as change in time of session, or an interpretation made by the analyst, and, on the other hand, how the patient is experiencing the situation as reflected in explicit remarks about it, however, fleeting these may be. This is the primary yield for technique of the recognition that any transference must have a link to the actuality of the analytic situation. The cue points to the nature of the transference, just as the day residue for a dream may be a quick pointer of the latent dream thoughts. Attention to the current situation for a transference elaboration will keep the analyst from making mechanical transference interpretation, in which he interprets that there are allusions to the transference in association not manifestly about the transference, but without offering any plausible bias for the interpretation. Attention to the current stimulation offers some degree of protection against the analyst's inevitability whose tendency to project his own views onto the patient, either because of countertransference or because of a preconceived theoretical bias about the content and hierarchical relationships in psychodynamics.

The analyst may be very surprised at what in his behaviour the patient finds important or unimportant, for the patient's responses will be idiosyncratically determined by the transference, the patient's responses may seem to be something the patient as well as the analysts consider trivial, because, as in displacement to a trivial aspect of the day residue of a dream, displacement can better serve resistance when it is to something trivial. Because it is connected to conflict-laden material, the stimulus to the transference may be difficult to find. It may be quickly disavowed, so that its presence in awareness is only transitory. With the discovery of the disavowed, the patient may also gain insight into how it repeats as disavowed earlier in his life. In his search for the present stimuli which the patient is responding transferentially, as the analyst must therefore remain alert to both fleeting and apparently trivial manifested reference to himself as well as in the events of the analytic situation.

If the analyst interprets the patient's attitudes in a spirit of seeing their possible plausibility in the light of what information the patient does have, rather than in the spirit of either affirming or denying the patient's views, the way is open for their further expression and elucidation. The analyst will be respecting the effort to be plausible and realistic, rather than manufacturing his transference attitudes out of whole bodied material.

Importantly, is to make a transference interpretation plausible to the patient in terms of as current stimulus that, if the analyst is persuaded that the manifest content has important implications for the transference but he is unable to see a current stimulus for the attitude, he should explicitly say so if he decides to make the transference interpretation anyway. The patient himself may then be able to say what the current stimulus is.

It is sometimes argued that the analyst's attention to his own behaviour is a precipitant for the transference, will increase the patient's resistance to recognizing the transference. That, on the contrary, that because of the inevitable interrelationship of the current and transferential determinants, it is only through interpretation that they can be disentangled.

It is also argued that one must wait until the transference has reached optimal intensity before it can be advantageously interpreted. It is true that too hasty and interpretation of the transference can serve as a defensive function for the analyst and deny him the information he needs to make a more appropriate transference interpretation. But it is true that delay in interpreting transference interpretation, but it is also true that delay in interpreting runs the risk of allowing an unmanageable transference to develop. It is also true that deliberate delay can be a manipulation in the service of abreaction rather than analysis, and, like silence, can lead to a response to the actual situation which is mistaken for uncontaminated transference. Obviously important, is assumed in the issues of timing are involved, whereas an important clue to when a transference interpretation is apt and which one to makes lies in whether the interpretation can be made plausibly in terms of the determinant, namely, as something in the current analytic situation. Such as, in the approaching transference in the spirit of seeing how it appears plausibly realistic to the patient, it paves the way toward its further elucidation and expression.

Freud's emphasis on remembering as the goal of the analytic work implies that remembering is the principal avenue to the resolution of the transference. But the delineation of the successive steps in the development of the analytic technique (1920) makes clear that he saw this development as a change from an effort to reach memories directly to the utilization of the transference as the necessary intermediacy to reaching the memories.

In contrast to remembering as the way the transference is resolved, Freud also described resistance for beings primarily overcome in the transference, with remembering following relatively easily afterwards, 'From the repetitive reactions which are exhibited in the transference we are led along the familiar paths to the awakening of the memories, which appear without difficulty, as it was, after the resistance has been overcome' (1914), and 'This revision of the process of repetition can be accomplished only in part in connection with the memory traces of the process which led to repression. The decisive part of the work's achieved by creating in the patient's relation to the analyst - in the 'transference' new editions of the old conflicts . . . Thus, the transference becomes the battlefield on which all the mutually struggling forces should meet one another' (1917). This is the primary indication for which Strachey (1934) classified in his seminal paper on the therapeutic action of psychoanalysis.

There are two main ways in which resolution of the transference can take place through work with the transference in the here and now. The first lies in the clarification of what are the clues in the current situation which are the patient's point of departure force a transference elaboration. The exposure of the current point of departure at once raises the question of whether it is adequate to the conclusion drawn from it. The relating of the transference to a current stimulus is, after all, parts of the patient's effort to make, the transference attitude plausibly determined by the present. The reverse and ambiguity of the analyst's behaviour are what increases the ranges of apparently plausible conclusions the patient may draw. If an examination of the basis for the conclusion makes clear that the actual situation to which the patient responds is subject to other meanings than the one the patient has reached, he will more reality consider his pre-existing bias, that is to say, in that of transference.

Critically, it is suggested that, in speaking of the current relationship and the relation between the patient's conclusion and the information on which they seem plausibly based, such in some absolute conception of what is real in the analytic situation, of which the analyst is the final arbiter. That is not the case, that what the patient must come to see is that the information he has is subject to other possible interpretations implies the very contrary to an absolute conception of reality. In fact, analyst and patient engage in a dialogue in a spirit of attempting to arrive at a consensus about reality, not about some factious absolute reality.

The second way in which resolution of the transference can take place within the work with the transference in the here and now is that in the very interpretation of the transference the patient had a new experience. He is being treated differently from how he expected to be. Analysts seem reluctant to emphasize his new experience, as though it endangers the role of insight and argue for interpersonal influence as the significant factor in change. Strachey's emphasis on the new experience in the mutative transference interpretation has unfortunately been overshadowed by his views on introjection, which have been mistaken to advocate manipulating the transference. Strachey meant introjection of the more benign superego of the analyst only as a temporary strep on the road toward insight. Not only is the new experience not to be confused with the interpersonal influence of a transference gratification, but the new experience occurs together with insight into both the patient's biassed expectation and the new experience. As Strachey points out, what is unique about the transference interpretation is that insight and the new experience take place in relation to the very person who was expected to behave differently, and it is this which gives the work in the transference, its immediacy and effectiveness. While Freud did stress the effective immediacy of the transference, he did not make the new experience explicit.

It is important to recognize that transference interpretation is not a matter of experience, in contrast to insight, but a joining of the two together, both are needed to bring about and maintain the desired changes in the patient. It is also important to recognize that no new techniques of intervention are required to provide the new experience. It is an inevitable accompaniment of interpretation of the transference in the here and now. It is often overlooked that, although Strachey said that only transference interpretations are outside the transference.

Rosenfeld (1972) has pointed out that clarification of material outside the transference is often necessary to know what is the appropriate transference interpretation, and that both genetic transference interpretations and extratransference interpretation taking to consider an inclination as marked by or indication of notable worth or simply the consequence based upon the role in working through. Strachey said relatively little about working through, but surely nothing against the necessary provision with which every thing needfully is explicitly recognized as the role for the recovery of the past in the resolving dissection of the purposiveness determined by the transference.

In taking positions, as to emphasis the role of the analysis of the transference in the here and now, both in interpreting resistance to the awareness of transference and in working toward its resolution by relating to the actuality of the situation. In that of opinion or purpose with the evidence that extratransference and genetic transference interpretation and, of course, working through is important too, that the matter is one of emphasis. Also, interpretation of resistance to awareness of the transference should figure in the majority of sessions, and that if this is done by relating the transference to the actual analytic situation, the very same interpretation is a beginning of work to the resolution of the transference. To justify this view more persuasively would require detailed case material.

The concern and considerations that the Kleinian annalists whom, many analysts feel, are in error in giving the analysis of the transference too great if not even as exclusive role in the analytic process. It is true that Kleinians emphasize the analysis of the transference more, in their writing at least, than does the general run of analysts. As, Anna Freud (1968) complained that the concept of transference has become overexpanded seems to be directed against the Kleinians. One of the reasons the Kleinians consider themselves the true followers of Freud in technique are precisely because of the emphasis they put on the analysis of the transference. Hanna Segal (1967), for example, writes, `Too say that all communications are seen as communications about the patents phantasy as well as current external life is equivalent to saying that all communications contain something relevant to the transference situation. In Kleinian technique, the interpretation of the transference is often more central than in the classical technique.

Freud's first direct mention of transference comes upon the pages ascribed within the 'Studies of Hysteria' (1895), his first significant reference to it, however did not appear until five years later, when, in a letter to Fliess on April 16, 1900, he said (Freud, 1887-1902) he was 'beginning to see that the apparent endlessness of the treatment is something of an inherent feature and is connected with the transference'. In a footnote to this letter the editors said that, 'This was the first insight into the role of transference in psychotherapy.'

Despite these early references, it seems correct to say that yet another five years were to go by before the phenomenon of transference was actually introduced. Even so, the introduction was far from prominent, for it was tacked on like an afterthought as a four-page portion of a postscript to what was perhaps Freud's most fascinating case history to date, the case of Dora (1905).

Using data from Dora's three-month-long, unexpectedly terminated analysis, and especially from her dramatic transference reaction which had taken him quite unawares, Freud now gave to transference its first distinct psychological entity and for the first time indicated its essential role in the analytic process. His account, although in general more than adequate - in the elegant fact and unmistakably 'finished' - was brief, and almost to the point, and perhaps not an entirely worthy introduction so much more a truly great discovery. What was uniquely great was his recognizing the usefulness of transference. In his analysis of Dora he had noted not only that transference feelings existed and were powerful, but, much to his dismay, he had realized what a serious, perhaps, even insurmountable obstacles that objectively would be. Then, in what seems like a creative leap, Freud made the almost unbelievable discoveries that transference was in fact, the key to analysis, that by properly taking the patient's transference and therapeutic force was added to the analytic method.

The impact on analysis of this startling discovery was actually much greater and much more significant than most people seem to appreciate. Although the role of transference as the sine quo non of analysis and is widely accepted, and was stated by Freud from the first, it has almost never been acclaimed for having brought about an entire change in the nature of analysis. The introduction of free association to analysis, a much lesser change, receives and still receives much more recognition.

One of the reasons for the relatively unheralded entry of transference into analysis may have been for circumstances of its discovery. Although Freud's new ideas were recorded as if they arose as sudden inspiration during the Dora analysis, they may in fact have developed somewhat later. In the paper's precatory remarks, for instance, Freud said he had not discussed transference with Dora at all, and in the postscript, he said he had been unaware of her transference feelings. Also, pointing to a later discovery date is the extraordinary delay in the paper's publication. According to the editor's note, the paper had been completed and accepted for publication by late January 1901, but this date was then actually set back more than four and a half years until October 1905. The editors said, 'We have no information as to how it happened that Freud, . . . deferred publication.' It readily seems that for reasons to have been that only during those four and a half years, as a consequence to his own self-analysis, that he came to a better understanding of the relevantly significant as the applicable reason to posit of the transference. Only then may it have been possible for him to turn again to the Dora case, to apply to it of what he had learned in himself, to write this essay as part of the postscript, and at last to release the paper for publication.

Freud's self-analysis has been considered from many angles, but not significantly, as can be of valuing measure, in at least from the standpoint of transference. Opponents of the idea that there is such a thing as definite self-analysis, some of whom say it is impossible, generally an object on grounds that without any analyst there can be no transference neurosis. Freud clearly demonstrated, as, perhaps, that the situation that may be necessary to fill this need: Self-analysis may require that, at least a halfway satisfactory transference object. In Freud`s case, the main transference object at this time seems to have been Fliess, who filled the role rather well. As with any analysis, the authenticity as known in the unfeigned design as if existing or having no illusions and facing reality squarely, by which the 'real' impact on Freud was slight, he was essentially a neutral figure, relatively anonymous and physically separates. All of this, and Fliess`s own reciprocal transference reactions, made it possible for Freud to endow Fliess with whatever qualities and whatever feelings were essential to the development of Freud`s transference, and, it should be added, his transference neurosis. In the end, of course, the transference was in part resolved. Freud`s eventual awakening of its self realization in its presence within him of such strange and powerful psychological forces must have come to the conclusion as a stupefied disilluionary dejection toward Fliess, however, his subsequent working out of some of these transference attachments must have been both an intellectual triumph and an immensely healing and releasing of actions, operations or motions involved in the accomplishment of an ending that makes from its process.

In the years following this revolutionary discovery, the central role of transference in analysis increased in remarkable acceptance, and it has easily held this central position ever since. What the substance of this central position distinctfully composes in having or be capable of having within the constructs to which is something of a mystery, for, it seems as nothing about analysis and is, of least to be, the well known than how individual analysis actually uses transference in their day-to-day work with patients. As a guess, as, perhaps of each analysts concept of transference derives variably but significantly from his own inner experience, transference probably means many and varying differentiations to things as to different analysts.

In the same differentiated individuals, as that Freud's own pupils must have differed on this issue, not only from him but from each other. Although some of their differences may have been slight, others, my have contributed significantly to later analytic developments. A question could be raised, for instance, whether differences in handling the transference which at first were the property of one analyst gradually develop into formal clinical methods used by many, and whether these clinical methods, after having been conceptualized, serve as the beginning of variously divergent schools of analysis. Such occurrences, consistent with certain beliefs that analytic ideas do arise in this way, primarily out of transference experiences in the analytic situation, would lead to the question whether the history of the ideological differences in what was actually said and done in response to transference reactions that to any other factor. Whatever the case, many differences and divergencies did occur among the early analysts, and all of that is supposed to have had to do in some major way with differences in the handling of the transference.

Strangely, Freud himself seems to have taken little part in influencing this rapid and divergent period of growth. Usually accused of being too dominating in such matters, Freud seems to have done just the opposite during the development of this most critical aspect of analysis, the process itself, and, for reasons unknown, detached himself from it.

What was needed, one might be inclined to say, was not leadership in the form of domination, but leadership in trying to provide what was lacking, and still lacking, namely an analytical rationale for transference phenomena. The question must be asked, of course, whether in fact this would have been a good thing at that particular time in psychoanalytic history. Perhaps not. The exercise of closure, which Freud's structuring might have amounted to. But although adding to understanding and stability at ceratin theoretical levels, could at another level, so such closures have often done, have placed many obstacles in the way of further analytical developments. Thus, his leaving the matter of transference wide open, even though it led to confusion and uncertainty, may have been just as well.

In many ways the closest Freud ever came to establishing a formal analytical rationale for transference was his first attempt, in the postscript to the case of hysteria (1905). These few pages are and among the most important of all Freud's writings, outweighing by far the paper to which they are appended. Yet, in the case of Dora has always been taught as an entity rather than the ancillary to the essay on transference. In that essay Freud was clear: His ideas revealed tremendous insights and promised more to come, and that, the powers of the neurosis are occupied in creating a new edition of the same disease. Just think of the analytic implications of his saying that this new edition consists of a special class of mental structures, for the most part unconscious, having the peculiar characteristic of being able to replace earlier persons with that of the person of the analyst, and in the fashion applying all components of the original neurosis to the person of the analytical at the present time. Surely as profound a statement as any he ever made.

He then goes on to say that there is no way to avoid transference, that this 'latest creation of the desire must be combatted like all the earlier ones', and that, although this is by far the hardest part of analysis, only after the transference has been resolved can a patient arrive at a sense of conviction of the validity of the connection which have been constructed during analysis.

He concludes by saying, 'In psychoanalysis . . . all the patients' tendencies, including hostile ones, are aroused, they are then turned to account for reasons to explain or the internalization of justification, and by the same measure was to purposively give a sensible reason for the proposed change in the analysis by which of being made conscious. That, in this way, the transference is constantly being put-down, however, transference, which seems ordained to be the greatest obstacle to psychoanalysis, becomes its most powerfully . . .

These remarkable observations, in conveying a sense of deep conviction that could arise, one feels, only from Freud's own hard-won inner experience, that nowhere is there a suggestion that transference is a mere technical matter. Far from it, as Freud announces that he has come upon as new and exciting kind of mental function, or, as it is to believe, that a new and exciting kind of ego function.

Very quickly, however, Freud's conviction sees to have failed him. Nothing he wrote afterwards about transference was at this level, and most of his later references were a retreat from it, for instance, he never did develop the promising idea that the mind constantly creates new editions of the original neurosis and meaningfully inclines the minded inclusion in them, an ever-changing series of persons. Instead, he tended to become less specific, even referring to transference at times in a broad terms as if it were no more than rapport between patient and analysts, or as if it was an interpersonal or psychosocial relationship, concepts which, of course, a great many analysts have since adopted, but which were not part of Freud's original ideas.

Perhaps his most persistent deviation was an on-and-off tendency to regard transference merely as a technical matter, often writing of it as an asset to analysis when positive and a liability when negative.

Significantly, because it indicated that an active struggle was still going on within him, Freud occasionally expressed once again, even though briefly his earlier insights, particularly his ideas that transference is an essential although unexplored part of mental life. An example of this appears in his alternative obtainments such that is gainfully to appear of as quality of being pleasant or agreeable to a feature that makes for pleasantness or ease, among the amenities of the central geniality, otherwise, the prevailing indifference account for the transference in 'An Autobiographical Study' (1925). Transference, he says, 'is a universal phenomenon of the human mind. And in fact dominated the whole of each person's relations to his human environment. In these few words' Freud again made the point, and in declarative fashion, that transference is a mental structure of the greatest magnitude, but he never really followed it up.

Rather extensive evidence of his departure from the original concept and his continuing struggle with that concept is seen most clearly, wherein, the 'Analysis Terminable and Interminable' is much more than a courageous, brilliant, and pessimistic, appraisal of the difficulties and limitations of analysis, although transference is briefly mentioned in its content, yet a great deal about it comes through, some quite directly, some by easy inference. When looked at in this way, two themes stand out: Freud's personal frustration with the enigmas of transference and his tacit placing of transference in the centre of success and failure in analysis, both as a therapy and as a developing science. What also comes through, is the perplexing realization of how far Freud had, by now, seemingly moved away from his original concepts. Or had he?

All the same, even if it is insufficient for exclusive reliance in relations to the complicated neurosis, for which it would be fallacious to assign to the recall and reconstruction of the past an exclusively explanatory value (in the intellectual sense), important though that functions be, and difficult as its full-blown emotional correlate may be to come by. There is no doubt that, even in complicated neurosis, equivalently complicated transference neurosis, the genuine complex and complicated transference neurosis, the genuinely experienced linking of the past and present can have, at times, a certain uniquely specific dynamic effect of its own, a type of telescoping or merging of common elements in experience, which must be connected with the meaninglessness of time in unconscious life, compared with its stern authority in the life of consciousness and adaptation to everyday reality. Contributing decisively to such experiences as to whatever degree it occurs, is of course, the vivid currency of the transference neurosis, and central in this, the reincarnations of old objects in an actual person, the analyst.

Thus, an allied problem in the general sphere of transference is the fascination and often enigmatic interplay of past and present. If one wishes to view this interplay in terms of a stereotyped formulation, the matter can remain relatively uncomplicated - as a formulation. Unfortunately., This is too often the case. The phenomenon, however, retains some important obscurities, which cannot thoroughly dispel, but to which I would like to call attention. To concentrate on the dimension of time, it seems in reference to the complication and immediate aspects of technique, nonetheless, essential. For example, we can assume that the transference neurosis re-enacts the essential conflicts of the infantile neurosis in a current setting. If a reasonable degree of awareness of transference is established, the next problem is the genetic reduction of the neurosis to its elements in the past, through analysis of the transference resistance and allied intrapsychic resistance, ultimately genetic interpretations, recollections and reconstructions and working through. Such that the transference is related to its genetic origins, the analyst thereby emerges in his true, i.e., real, identity to the patient, the transference is putatively 'resolved'. To the extent that one follows the traditional view that all resistance, including the transference itself, is ultimately directed against the restoration of early memories as, this is a convincing formulation. Is that, only to say, that in his own right as such as having to a certain tightly logical quality? However, we know that it this is not so readily accomplished, apart from the special intrapsychic considerations described afterward by Freud in 'Analysis Terminable and Interminable'. Although in a favourable case, much of the cognitive interpretative work can be accomplished, there remains the fact that cognition responsibility, in its bare sense, does not necessarily lead to the subsidence of powerful dynamism, to the withdrawal of 'cathexes' from importantly real objects. For, as mentioned, a short while ago, the analyst is a real and living object, apart from the representations with which the transference invests him, and which are interpretable as such, for which there is no, at any time a seldom, a confusing interrelations and commonly of the emergent responses, due to the same old seeking, and this is directed toward a new individual in his own right, both are important, furthermore, there are large and important ones of overlapping. Apart from such considerations, even the explicitly incestuous transference is currently experienced (as, at least in good part) by a full-grown adult (like the original oedipus), instead of a totally and actually helpless child. To be sure, the latter state is reflected in the emergent transference elements of instinctual striving, but it is subject to analysis, and the residual is something significant, if not totally different. It is these residual sexual wish, presumably directed toward the person of the analyst, as such, which must be displaced to others, if, as generally agreed, the revival of infantile fantasies and strives in the biologically mature adolescent presents a new and special problem, one must assume distinctiveness of experience for the adult, although it is true that in the majority of instances, adequate solution is favoured by the adult state. There is, in any case, a residual relationship between persons who have worked together in a prolonged, arduous and intimate relationship, which, strictly speaking, are reversibly disconnected or divorced of services, in that the transference merely ushers out the retirement for which its rendering retreat of that state of mind or feeling by an inner avoidance of something usually felt as unpleasant or pronounced for it's adverse but mutual colouration. Blending to some confusion between the two spheres of feeling. The general tendency is that both components are fully gratified to some degree. But, there is the ubiquitous power of the residual primordial transference, yet, argue to cling to an omnipotent partisan to resist the displacement of its 'sublimated' anaclitic aspects, even if the various representation of the wishes for bodily intimacy has been thoroughly analyzed and successfully displaced. The outcome is largely the transference of the transference, as mentioned earlier, in a different context. For everyday reality can provide no actual answer to such cravings. In this connection, note, Freud's genial envy of Pfister. If the man of faith finds this gratification in revealing religion, others in a wide range of secular beliefs and 'leaders' the modern rational and sceptical intellectual is less fortunate in this respect. Presumably free, he is prone to invest even intellectual disciplines or the proponents with inappropriate expectations and partisan passions, but, least of mention, that within these fields of analytical and theoretical thought, is not to provide exceptions to this tendency.

Though if one is to maintain and beneficially confine its bothering of reservations about the clarity of conceptualization, the explanatory discussion of Kohut and Seitz, is a very useful contribution to the direct complication or which by some understanding the awkwardness of oneself. Both Loewald and Kohut have deliberately associated a special but the different use of one of Freud's three conceptions of transference, i.e., the transference from the unconscious to the preconscious.

Yet, to furthering comments on primordial transference, at least potentially, are largely psychological (mental) component, the concept of 'transference of the transference' would be applicable to this component. For it does appear that certain aspect of the search for the omnipotent and omniscient caretaking parents are implicitly practical as virtually capable for being turned to use or account for its functional practicability for something of a process or the procedure for being all but the essential purpose to come to or tend toward a common point, for which are the knowledgeable information or ideas, is nothing but causative effectuality. As suggested earlier, there are important qualitative and quantitative distinctions in the mode of persistence and such striving, however, even to the extent that they are detached from the analyst and carried into some reasonably appropriate expression in everyday life, they retain at least a subtle quality which contravenes reality, one which derives from earliest infancy, and remains - to this extent - a transference. 'Santa Claus' lives on, where one might least expect to meet him, whether as a donor of miracle drug or of far more complex panaceas.

If one prescribes to this parasymbiotic transference drive, a true primordial origin, it is necessary to take cognizance of certain important concepts dealing with the earliest period of life. If we assume a powerful original organismic drive toward an original 'object', a striving to nullify separation from the beginning, how does this make something legally valid or operative usually by formal approval or sanctioned with concepts such as 'primary narcissism' or the 'objectless phase' or 'the primary psycho physiological self' (We note in passing that there are those who do not accept these as usually construed in the technique of Balint), for example, or Fairbairn or - conspicuously - Melanie Klein. These are states, variously defined or conceived, which apply to the earliest neonatal period, in which life, to state more simply, exists only as the potential in physiological processes. Since there is (we postulate) no clear awareness of self-withdrawal from the mother, there can be no 'mentally' represented or experienced drive to obliterate the separation (concerning oneself and object, conceivers of as separate, in a continuing sense). There are, of course, discharge phenomena, the precursors of purposive activity, and there are urgent physiological needs, directed toward fulfilment or relief, rather than toward an object as such. However, in relation to these physiological needs as archaistic precursors of object relationships, it must be noted that in all, except respiration and spontaneous sphincter relief (even in these instances, not without exception or reservation), the need fulfilment must be mediated by the primordial object (or her surrogate). There is also, of course, the uniquely important requirement for 'holding', in a literal expression, from the outset. The material partner in human symbiosis which supplies what the neonate cannot seek by 'clinging', as for Bowlty and Murphy, in the sense that must be experienced to the physiological ebb and flow of tension, even if restricted to the kinaesthetic, connected with a peripheral sensory registration, which is the protophase of the recognition of separation from the object or nonpresence of the object, as a painful instance of, her presence in apposition the converse? That the general context may be only in which the sense of unity is preponderant, or, more accurately, that there is no general awareness of 'separation' as such, means that the drive for union does not exist in a general psychological sense. It is, so to speak, satisfied. That object constancy, with its cognate 'longing', is quite a different experience from the urgencies of primitive need fulfilment is true, however, regardless of what may be added by maturational and developmental considerations, instinctual and perceptual, there is no reason to assume other than a core of developmental continuity from the earliest needs and their fulfilment to the later state, and some continuing degree of contingency based on them.

There is a very rough parallel in the way certain analytic patients, before a firm relationship with the analyst is established, signal certain primitive experiences and tendencies in special reactions to the end of the hour, to the nonvisibility of the analyst, to interruption of their association, to failure of the analyst to talk, and similar matters. We must note that in the basic formation of the ego is evident amongst the primitive reactions and beyond to separations, in the form of very early identifications as based on care taking functions. Certainly in the very development of autonomous ego of the mother's investment in the, have a decisive role in the character of the their development. And in the case of object constancy, in its connotation of libidinal cathexis, where is no need whatsoever (emotional or otherwise) is needed for prolonged periods. The importance of the object is, to put it mildly, liable to deteriorate, or to differ complicating aggressive change. Probably the characteristic feature of later developing relations to the object (love and the wish for love), as separate if not always separated from demonstrable primitivity, in the need fulfilment, have a special relationship to those 'ancillary' aspects of neonatal nurture, whose lack has been shown to be an actual threat to life in some instances, not to speak of sound emotional development. So that from the first, regardless of the assumed state of libidinal (and aggressive) economy, or the assumed state of psychological nondifferentiation between self and potential object, there are critical percussive phenomena, objectively observed, and probably prototypic subjective experiences of separation, which are the forerunners of all subsequent experiences of the kind. One may generalize to the effect that, with maturation and development, secondary identifications, and the various other processes of 'internalization' in its broadest sense, the problem of separation and its mastery becomes correspondingly more complex, and changes with the successive phase of life, but never entirely disappears.

In the view of the psychoanalytic situation described earlier, the latent mobilization of experiences of separation stimulated by the situational structure awakens the driving primordial urge to undo or to master the painful separations which it represents, usually embodied in the various forms of clinical transference that which we are familiar. One legitimate gratification which tends to mitigate superfluous transference regression is the transmission of understanding that at times, are thought that by the 'mature transference', in effect, the 'therapeutic alliance' or a group of mature ego functions which enter into such an alliance. Now, there are one blurring and overlapping at the conceptual edges in both instances, but the concept as such is largely distinct from either one, as it is from the primitive transference, which we have been discussing. Whether the concept is thought by others to comprehend a demonstrable actuality, which is a further question. This question, of course, can only follow on conceptual clarity. This in saying, of a nonrational urge, not directly dependent on the perception of immediate clinical purposes, a true transference in the sense that it is displaced (in currently relevant form) from the parent of early childhood to the analyst. Its content is not anti-sensational, but largely non-sensual of sometimes transitional, as the child's pleasure in the assemblages of 'dirty words' and encompasses a special and not minuscule sphere of the object relationship: The wish to understand, and to be understood, the wish to be given understanding, i.e., teaching, specifically by the parent (or later surrogate); the wish to be taught to use ingenuity in making or doing o r achieving an end through the actions in a nonpunitive way, corresponding to the growing perception of hazard and conflict and very likely the implicit wish to be provided with and taught channels of substitutional drive discharge. With this, there may well be a wish, corresponding to that element in Loewald's description of therapeutic process, to be seen in terms of one's developmental potentialities by the analyst. No doubt, the list could be extended into many subtleties, details, and variations. However, one should not omit to specify that, in its peak development, it would include the wish for increasingly accurate interpretations and the wish to facilitate such interpretations by providing adequate material ultimately, of course, by identification, to participate in, or even be the author of the interpretations. The childhood system of wishes which underlie the transference is a correlate of biological maturation, and the latent (i.e., teachable) autonomous ego function, appearing with it, however, there is a drive-like quality in the participation phenomena, which disqualifies any conception of the urge's identical with the functions. No one who has ever watched a child importunes a parent with questions, or experiment with new words, or solicit her interests in a new game, or demand a storytelling or reading, can doubt this. That this powerful support and integration in the ego identification with a loved parent are undoubtedly true, just as it is true of the identification with an analyst toward whom a positive relationship has been established. That 'functional pleasure ' inscribes the part, where certain specific ego energies, perhaps very likely the ego's own urge to extend its hegemony in the personality. However, it can be stressed in the derive element, even the special phase configurations and colourations, and with its importance of object relations, libidinal and aggressive, for a specific reason. For just as the primordial transference seeks to undo separation, in a sense to obviate object relationships as we know them, the 'mature transference', tends toward separation and individuation, and increasing contact with the environment, optimally with a large affirmative (increasing neutralized) relationship toward the original object toward whom (or her surrogates) a different dynamic of demands is now increasingly directed. The further considerations which have led to the emphasis that the drive-like elements in these attitudes are integrated phenomena, as example of 'multiple functional' rather than the discrete exorcise of function or functions, is the conviction that there is a continuing dynamic relation of relative interchangeability between the two series, at least based on the response to gratifications in a significant zone of complicated energetic overlap, possibly including the phenomenon of neutralization. That the empirical 'interchangeability' is limited, and that goes without saying, that in no way diminishes its decisive importance. The linguistic communications as in mention, that the excessive transference neurosis regression, which can seriously vitiate the affirmative psychoanalytic process, finds a prototype in the regressive behaviour and demands of certain children, who do not receive their share of teaching, 'attention', play, nonseductive, affectionate demonstration, as to use the quality of being appropriate or valuable to some end, even the act or practice of using something or the state of being used to which of responsible interests in development, and similar matters, from their parents. In the psychoanalytic situation, both the gratifications offered by the analyst and the freedom of expression by the patient, are diversely limited and concentrated, practically entirely (in the every day demonstrable sense) in the sphere of linguistic expression, on the analyst's side, further, in the transmission of understanding.

Whereas, the primordial transference exploits the primitive aspects of linguistic communication, by expressing the mature transference as to advocate the seeking mastery of the outer and inner environments, a mastery to which the mature elements in speech contribute importantly, for which these are stressed upon the clear-cut genetic prototype for the free associating its interpretative dialogue is the original learning and teaching of speech, the dialogue between child and mother. It is interesting to note that just as the profundities of interests between people who often include - in the service of the ego - transitory introjection and identifications, of the very word 'communication', representing the central ego function of speech, from which are a closely intimate relation to the etymologically certain, in actual usages, to the word chosen for that major of religious sacrament for that which is the physical ingestion of the body and blood of the Deity. Perhaps, this is just another suggestion that the oldest of individual problems does, after all, continue to seek its solution, in its own terms if only in a minimal sense, and in channels so remote as to be unrecognizable.

The mature transference is a dynamic and integral part of the therapeutic alliance, alone with the tender aspect of the erotic transference, evens more attenuated (and more dependable) friendly feeling of adult type, and the ego identification with the analyst. Indispensable, of course, are the genuine adult need for help, the crystallizing rational and intuitive appraisal of the analyst, the adult sense of confidence in him, and innumerable other nuances of adult thought and feeling. With these, giving a driving momentum and power to the analytic process, but always, by its very nature, a potential source of resistance, and always requiring analysis, is the primordial transference and its various appearances in the specific therapeutic transference. That it is, if well managed, not only a reflection of the repetition compulsion in its menacing sense, but a living presentation from the id, seeking new solutions, and trying again, so to speak, to find a place in the patient's conscious and effective life, has important affirmative potentialities. This has been specifically emphasized by Nunberg, Lagache and Loewald among others. Loewald has recently elaborated very effectively the idea of 'ghosts' seeking to become 'ancestors' based on an early figure of speech of Freud. The mature transference, in its own infantile right, provides some of the unique qualities of propulsive force, which comes from the world of feeling, rather than the world of thought. If one views it in a purely figurative sense, that fraction of the mature transference which derives from 'conversion' is somewhat like propulsive fraction as the wind in a boats sailing to windward currents into motion, the strong headwind, the ultimate source of both resistance and propulsion, is the primordial transference. This view, however, should not displace the original and independent, if cognate, a favourable tide or current would also be required. It is not that the mature transference is itself entirely exempt from analytic clarification and interpretation. For one thing, in common with other childhood spheres of experience, there may have been traumas in this sphere, punishments, serious defects or lacks of parental communication, Listening, attention or interest. In general, this is probably far more important than has hitherto appeared in our prevalent paradigmatic approach to adult analysis, even taking into account the considerable changes due to the growing interest in ego psychology. 'Learning' in the analysis can, of course, be a troublesome intellectualizing resistance. Furthermore, both the patient's communications and his receptions and utilization of interpretations may exhibit only too clearly, as sometimes in the case of other ego mechanisms, their origin in and tenacious relation to instinctual or anaclitic dynamism; the longing implement out of silence for which the analyst is to override the uncritical acceptance (or rejection) of interpretations, in that the patient revealingly is to mention the unmindful assimilation, fluently, rich, endlessly detailed associations without spontaneous reflection or integration. In the direct demands for solution of moral and practical probability for an entirely intellectual scope, and a variety of others. It may and always be easy to discriminate between the utilization of speech by an essentially instinctual demand, and an intellectual or linguistic trait or having to be determined by specific factors in their own developmental sphere, however, the underlying and essentially genuine dynamism which have to continue to be placed for a notable time interval or remain arbitrary or the conventional character most favoured to the purposes of processes of analysis, as it was to the original processes of maturational development, communication, and benign separation. Lagache, on the desirability of separating the current unqualified usage, 'positive' and 'negative' transference, as based on the patient's immediate state of feeling, from a classification based on the essential effect on analytic processes. Yet, the later of mature transference is, in general, a 'positive transference'.

It is a curious fact, whereas the dynamic meaning to the importance of the transference neurosis has been well established since Freud gave this the phenomenon a central position in his clinical thinking, the clinical reference, when the term is used, remains variable and somewhat ambiguous. For example, Greenson, in his excellent recent paper, speaks of it as appearing, 'when the analyst and the analysis become the central concern in the patient's life'. However, previous remarks in this connection, for which it is worthwhile to specify certain aspects of Greenson's definition, for the term 'central' is somewhat ambiguous, as to its specific reference. Certainly, the term could apply to the symbolic position of the analyst in relation to the patient's experiencing ego and the symbolically decisive position which he correspondingly assumes in the relation to the other important figures in the patient's current life. However, while the analysis is in any case, and for multiple reasons, exceedingly important the seriously involved patient, there is a free observing portion of is ego, also involved, not in the same sense as that involved in the transference regression and revived in infantile conflicts. And here is here being, of course, always the integrated adult personalty, however diluted in may seem at times, of its rarity, although certainly does occur, that the analysis actually exceeds the quality or state of being of notable worth or influence that the other major concerns, attachments, and responsibilities of the patient's life, nor is it desirable that his should occur, on the other hand, if construed with proper attention to the economic considerations as mentioned, the concept is important, both theoretically and clinically. In the theoretical direction to the assumption that there is a continuing system of object relationships and conflict situations, most important in the unconscious representations, but participating to some degree in all others, deriving in a successive series of transference from the experiences of separation from the original object, the mother. In this sense, the analyst's applicability to a uniquely important portion of the patient's personality, the portion that 'never grew up', to maintain a central figure. In the clinical sense, to call or direct attention especially to a supposed cause, source, or to refer to the importance of the transference neurosis as outlining for the essential and central analytic task, providing by its very currency and demonstrability a relatively secure cognitive base for procedural duties. By its inclusion of the patient's essential psychopathological processes and tendencies, in their original functional connection, it offers, in its resolution or marked reduction, the most formidable lever for analytic cure. Nonetheless, transference neurosis must be seen in its interweaving with the patient's extra-analytic system of personal contacts. The relationship to the analyst may influence the course of relationships to others, in the same sense that the clinical neurosis did, except that the former is alloplastic, relatively exposed, and subject to constant interpretation. It is also an important fact that, except in those rare instances where the original dyadic relationship appears to turn, the analyst, even in the strict transference sphere, cannot be assigned all the transference role simultaneously. Other actors are required. He may at times oscillate with confusing rapidity between the status of mother and father, but he is usually predominantly in one of the roles for long periods, someone else representing the other. Furthermore, apart from 'acting out', complicated and mutually inconsistent attitudes of the anterior apprehensions for realizing often about something not generally realized in the verbalization, may require the seeking of other transference objects, i.e., The husband or wife, friend, another analyst and so forth. Children, even the patient's own children, may be invested with striving of the patient, displaced from the analysis, even experience the impulses which they would wish to call forth in the analyst. The range is extensive, varied, and complicated, requiring constant alertness. Transference interpretation therefore often has a necessarily paradoxical inclusiveness, which is an important reality of technique. There is another aspect, and that is the dynamic and economic impact of the intimate and actual dramatist personate of the transference neurosis in the progress of the analysis as such, and on the patient 's motivation, as well as his real lifer avenues for recovery. For the persons in his milieu may fulfill their 'positive' or 'negative ' roles in transference drama, which may facilitate or impede interpretative effectiveness, they provide the substantial and dependable real life gratifications which ultimately facilitate the analysis of the residual analytic transference, or their capacities or attitudes may occasion overload of the anaclitic and instinctual needs in the transference which renders the same process far more difficultly. In the most unhappy instances, there can be a serious undercounting of the motivation for basic change.

There is also the fundamental question of the role of the transference interpretation. At the Marienbad Symposium most of Strachey's colleagues appeared to accept the essential import of his contribution and thus unique significance of the transference interpretations, despite the various reservations as to detail and emphasis on other important aspects of the therapeutic process. Nevertheless, there are still many who, if not in doubt regarding the great value of transference interpretations are inclined to doubt their uniqueness, and to stress the importance of economic considerations in determining the choice as to whether transference or extratransference interpretations may be indicated. Now, apart from the realistic considerations mentioned in the preceding passage (in a sense the necessarily 'distributed' character of a variable fraction of transference interpretation). There is in fact that the extra-analytic life of the patent often provides indispensable data fo the understanding of detailed complexities of his psychic functioning, because of the sheer variety of its references, some of which cannot be reproduced in the relationship to the analyst. For example, there is no repartee (in the ordinary sense) in the analysis. The way the patient handles the dialogue with an angry employee may be importantly revealing. The same may be true of the quality of his reaction to a real danger of dismissal. There are not only the realities, but the 'formal' aspects of this responses. These expressions of personality remain important, even though his 'acting out' of the transference (assuming this was this was the case) may have been more important, and, of course, requiring transference interpretation. Furthermore, they remain useful, if discriminatingly and conservatively treated, even if they are inevitably always subject that epistemological reservations, which haunts so much of analytic data. Of course, the 'positive' transference has a role in the utilization of such interpretations that what enables the patent to listen to them and them seriously.

In an operational sense, it would seem that extratransference interpretations cannot set aside, or underestimated in importance, but the unique effectiveness of transference interpretations is not thereby disestablished. No other interpretation is free, within reason, of the doubt introduced by not really knowing the 'other person's' participation in love, or quarrel or criticism or whatever the issue. And no other situation provides the patient the combined sense of cognitive acquisition, with the experience of complete personal tolerance and acceptance, that is implicit in an interpretation by an individual who is an object of the emotion, drive, or even defences, which are active at the time. There is no doubt that such interpretations must not only (in common with all others) include personal tact, but must be offered with special care as to their intellectual reasonability, in relation to the immediate context, lest they defeat their essential purpose. It is not too often likely that a patient who has just been jilted in a long-standing love affair, and suffering exceedingly, will find an immediate interpretation that his suffering is due to the fact that the analyst does not reciprocate his love, even though a dynamism in this general sphere may be ultimately demonstrable, and acceptable to the patient. On the other hand, once the transference neurosis is established, with accompanying subtle (sometime gross) colouration of the patient's life, th n more far-reaching anticipatory, transference interpretations are indicated, for, if all of the patient's libidinal and aggression are not, in fact, invested in the analyst, he has at least an unconscious role in all important emotional transactions, and, if the assumption is correct that the regressive drive, mobilized by the analytic situation, is in the direction of restoration of a single all-encompassing relationship, specified pragmatically in the individual case by the actually attained level of development, then there is a dynamic factor at work, importantly meriting interpretation as such, to the extent that available material supports it. This would be the immediate clinical application on the material regarding the 'cognitive lag' or 'cognitive fall-back'.

Post-Traumatic Stress Disorder, resides in a mental illness that some people develop after experiencing traumatic or life-threatening events. Such events include warfare, rape and other sexual assaults, violent physical attacks, torture, child abuse, natural disasters such as earthquakes and floods, and automobile or aeroplane crashes. People who attest of the traumatic events may also develop the disorder.

Post-traumatic stress disorder in war veterans is sometimes called shell shock or combat fatigue. In victims of sexual or physical abuse, the disorder has been called rape trauma or battered woman syndrome. The American Psychiatric Association (APA) adopted the current name of the disorder in 1980.

In the late 1960's and early 1970's, mass demonstrations erupted throughout the United States protesting US involvement in the Vietnam War (1959-1975). Thousands of veterans joined together in a national organization, Vietnam Veterans Against the War, that supported and influenced the antiwar movement. In this transcript from an April 22, 1971, hearing before the Senate Committee on Foreign Relations, committee chairman Senator J. William Fulbright indicated his sympathy for the antiwar movement. Fulbright's comments were followed by the testimony of Vietnam veteran John Kerry, who called for an end to the war. Kerry also detailed what he believed to be the war's negative effect in both Vietnam and the United States. Kerry became a Democratic senator from Massachusetts in 1985.

People with this disorder relive the traumatic event again and again through nightmares and disturbing memories during the day. They sometimes have flashbacks, in which they suddenly lose touch with reality and relive images, sounds, and other sensations from the trauma. Because of their extreme anxiety and disruptive opposition to events, they try to avoid anything that reminds them of it. They may seem emotionally numb, detached, irritable, and easily startled. They may feel guilty about surviving a traumatic event that killed other people. Other symptoms include trouble concentrating, depression, and sleep difficulties. Symptoms of the disorder usually begin shortly after the traumatic event, although some people may not show symptoms for several years. If left untreated, the disorder can last for years.

Post-traumatic stress disorder can severely disrupt one's life. Besides the emotional pain of reliving the trauma, the symptoms of the disorder may cause a person to think that he or she is 'going crazy.' In addition, people with this disorder may have unpredictable, angry outbursts at family members. At other times, they may seem to have no affection for their loved ones. Some people try to mask their symptoms by abusing alcohol or drugs. Others work very long hours to prevent any 'down' periods when they might relive the trauma. Such actions may delay the onset of the disorder until these individuals retire or become sober.

Studies have set or to bring into a new found control from 1 to 14 percent of people that suffer from post-traumatic stress disorder at some point during their lives. The findings vary widely due to differences in the populations studied and the research methods used. Among people who have survived traumatic events, the prevalence appears to be much higher. The disorder may be particularly prevalent among people who have served in combat. For example, one study of veterans of the Vietnam War (1959-1975) found that veterans exposed to a high level of combat were nine times more likely to have post-traumatic stress disorder than military personnel who did not serve in the war zone of Southeast Asia.

Post-traumatic stress disorder is an extreme reaction to extreme stress. In moments of crisis, people respond in ways that allow them to endure and survive the trauma. Afterward those responses, such as emotional numbing, may persist even though they are no longer necessary.

Not everyone who experiences a traumatic event develops post-traumatic stress disorder. Several factors influence whether people develop the disorder. Those who experience severe and prolonged traumas are more likely to develop the disorder than people who experience less severe trauma. Additionally, those who directly witness or experience death, injury, or attacks are more likely to develop symptoms.

People may also have been existing biological and psychological vulnerabilities that make them more likely to develop the disorder. Those with histories of anxiety disorders in their families may have inherited a genetic predisposition to react more severely to stress and trauma than other people. In addition, people's life experiences, especially in childhood, can affect their psychological vulnerability to the disorder. For example, people whose early childhood experiences made them feel that events are unpredictable and uncontrollable have a greater likelihood than others of developing the disorder. Individuals with a strong, supportive social network of friends and family members seem somewhat protected from developing post-traumatic stress disorder.

Treatment of post-traumatic stress disorder may involve psychotherapy, psychoactive drugs, or both. Psychotherapists help individuals confront the traumatic experience, work through their strong negative emotions, and overcome their symptoms. Many people with post-traumatic stress disorder benefit from group therapy with other individuals suffering from the disorder. Physicians may prescribe antidepressants or anxiety-reducing drugs to treat the mood disturbances that sometimes accompany the disorder.

At the arriving considerations that are marked and noted, through which the essence of functional dynamics as based of the transference in the psychoanalytic process or the basic underlying the most basic of beliefs that in politics there is neither good nor evil, however, in that something that forms part of the minimal body, character or structure of that thing predetermines the properties to the good life. Nonetheless, most psychoanalysts maintain that schizophrenic patients cannot be treated psychoanalytically because they are too narcissistic to develop with the psychotherapist as interpersonal relationship that is sufficiently reliable and consistent for psychoanalytic work. Freud, Fenichel and others have recognized that a new technique of approaching patients psychoanalytically must be found if analysts are to work with psychotics. Among those who have worked successfully in recent years with schizophrenics, Sullivan, Hill, and Karl Menninger and his staffs have made various modifications of their analytic approach. The techniques that are in use with psychotics are different from our approach to psychoneurotics. This is not a result of the schizophrenic's inability to build up a consistent personal relationship with the therapist but due to his extremely intense and sensitive transference reactions.

Let us see first what the essences of the schizophrenic's transference reactions are and how we try to meet these reactions.

We think of a schizophrenic as a person who has had serious traumatic experiences in early infancy at a time when his ego and its ability to examine reality were not yet developed. These early traumatic experiences seem to furnish the psychological basis for the pathogenic influence of the flustrations of later years. At this early time the infant lives grandiosely in a narcissistic world of his own. His needs and desires seem to be taken care of by something vague and indefinite which he does not yet differentiate. As Ferenczi noted, they are expressed by gestures and movements since speech is as yet undeveloped. Frequently the child's desires are fulfilled without any expression of them, a result that seems to him a product of his magical thinking.

Are a person's characteristics primarily shaped by early influences, remaining relatively stable thereafter throughout life? Or does change spontaneously occur continuously throughout life? Many people believe that early experiences are formative, providing a strong or weak foundation for later psychological growth. This view is expressed in the popular saying 'As the twig is bent, so grows the tree.' From this perspective, it is crucial to ensure that young children have a good start in life. But many developmental scientists believe that later experiences can modify or even reverse early influences; studies show that even when early experiences are traumatic or abusive, considerable recovery can occur. From this vantage point, early experiences influence, but rarely determine, later characteristics.

Traumatic experiences in this early period of life will damage a personality more seriously than those occurring in later childhood such as are found in the history of psychoneurotics. The infant's mind is more vulnerable the younger and less used it has been, furthers, the trauma has quickened the infant 's egocentricity. In addition early traumatic experiences shorten the only period in life in which an individual ordinarily enjoys the most security, thus endangering the ability to store up as it was a reasonable supplies of assurance and self-reliance for the individual's later struggles through life. Thus, as such, a child sensitized considerably more toward the frustrations of later like than by later traumatic experiences. hence many experiences in later life which would mean little to a 'healthy' person and not much to a psychoneurotic, mean a great deal of pain and suffering to the schizophrenic. His resistance against frustration is easily exhausted.

Once he reaches his limit of endurance, he escapes the unbearable reality of his present life by attempting to reestablish the autistic, delusional world of the infant, but this is impossible because the content of his delusions and hallucinations are naturally coloured by the experiences of his whole lifetime.

How do these developments influence the patient's attitude toward the analyst and the analyst's approach to him?

Due to the very damage and the succeeding chain of frustrations which the schizophrenic undergoes before finally giving in to illness, he feels extremely suspicious and distrustful of everyone, particularly of the psychotherapist ho approaches him with the intent of intruding into his isolated world and personal life. To him the physician's approach means the threat of being compelled to return to the frustrations of real life and to reveal his inadequacy to meet them or, - still worse – a repetition of the aggressive interference with his initial symptoms and peculiarities which he has encountered in his previous environment.

The difficulty that the patient's dilemma through his frustrations is the product through which is called 'delusion': Delusion itself is a false belief which is firmly held by a person even though other people recognize the belief as obviously untrue. For example, a person who truly believes he is Napoleon Blonaparte is delusional. Religious beliefs or popular conceptions, such as the beliefs that people have been abducted by aliens, are not delusions because they are widely held beliefs. Delusions are a type of psychotic symptom that indicate a person has lost contact with reality.

There are many different types of delusions. A person with a paranoid delusion believes that others - such as the FBI, or the CIA, even the Mafia as trying to harm or plot against him. A person with a delusion of reference believes that events or people refer specifically to him or her when they do not. For example, a woman with schizophrenia may believe that a television news broadcaster is talking personally to her rather than to the entire viewing audience. A grandiose delusion is a belief that one is extremely famous or that one has special powers, such as the ability to magically heal people.

A delusion of control is a belief that others are able to control one's thoughts, feelings, or actions. For example, a man with this type of delusion may believe that someone has implanted a microchip in his brain that enables other people to control his thoughts. A somatic delusion is a belief that something is wrong with one's body - for example, that one's brain is rotting away - even though no medical evidence supports this belief. A person with an erotic delusion believes that someone is in love with him or her despite a lack of evidence for this belief. In a delusion of jealousy, a person believes that his or her spouse or lover is unfaithful despite evidence to the contrary.

Delusions commonly occur in certain severe mental illnesses, such as schizophrenia, bipolar disorder (also called manic-depressive illness), some cases of major depression, Dissociative disorders, post-traumatic stress disorder, and paranoid personality disorder. In addition, delusions may result from abuse of certain drugs, including alcohol, cocaine, amphetamines, and hallucinogens such as lysergic acid diethylamide (LSD), phencyclidine (PCP), and mescaline. Medical conditions affecting the brain, such as syphilis and brain tumours, may also cause delusions.

Delusional disorder is a relatively uncommon mental illness characterized by delusions. People with this disorder have one or more delusions that persist for at least one month. In addition, they do not suffer from other symptoms of schizophrenia, such as disorganized speech and bizarre behaviour. Usually their delusions are less bizarre than those that occur in schizophrenia and seem merely odd or unsupported by facts. Examples of nonbizarre delusions include beliefs that one is being followed, loved by someone famous, or deceived by one's spouse. Because delusional disorder is relatively rare, little research has systematically examined its treatment. However, doctors most often use Antipsychotic drugs (also called neuroleptics) to treat this disorder. These drugs help reduce or eliminate delusions, hallucinations, and other psychotic symptoms.

In spite of his narcissistic retreat, every schizophrenic has some underlying notion of the unreality and loneliness of his substitute delusionary world. He longs for human contact and understanding, yet is afraid to admit of himself, or his therapist for fear of further frustration.

That is why the patient may take weeks and months to test the analyst before being willing to accept him, however, once he has accepted him. His dependence on the analyst is greater and he is more sensitive about it than is the psychoneurotic because of the schizophrenic's deeply rooted insecurity, the narcissistic seemingly self-righteous attitude is but a defence.

Whenever the analyst fails the patient from reasons to be discussed later - one cannot at times avoid failing one's schizophrenic patients - it will be severe disappointment and a repetition of the chain of frustrations the schizophrenic has previously endured.

The instinctually primitive part of the schizophrenic's mind that does not discriminate between himself and the environment, it may mean the withdrawal of the impersonal supporting forces of his infancy. Severe anxiety will follow this vital deprivation.

In the light of his personal relationship with the analyst it means that the therapist seduced the patient to use him as a bridge over which he might possibly be led from the utter loneliness of his own world to reality and human warmth, only to have him discover that this bridge is not reliable. if so, he will respond helplessly with an outburst of hostility or with renewed withdrawal as may be seen most impressively in catatonic stupor.

The symptoms of mental illness can be very distressing. People who develop schizophrenia may hear voices inside their head that say nasty things about them or command them to act in strange or unpredictable ways. Or they may be paralysed by paranoia—the deep conviction that everyone, including their closest family members, wants to injure or destroy them. People with major depression may feel that nothing brings pleasure and that life is so dreary and unhappy that it is better to be dead. People with panic disorder may experience heart palpitations, rapid breathing, and anxiety so extreme that they may not be able to leave home. People whom experience episodes of mania may engage in reckless sexual behaviour or may spend money indiscriminately, acts that later cause them to feel guilt, shame, and desperation.

Other mental illnesses, while not always debilitating, create certain problems in living. People with personality disorders may experience loneliness and isolation because their personality style interferes with social relations. People with an eating disorder may become so preoccupied with their weight and appearance that they force themselves to vomit or refuse to eat. Individuals who develop post-traumatic stress disorder may become angry easily, experience disturbing memories, and have trouble concentrating.

Experiences of mental illness often interact differently but depend on one's culture or social group, sometimes greatly so. For example, in most of the non-Western world, people with depression complain principally of physical ailments, such as lack of energy, poor sleep, loss of appetite, and various kinds of physical pain. Indeed, even in North America these complaints are commonplace. But in the United States and other Western societies, depressed people and mental health professionals who treat them tend to emphasize psychological problems, such as feelings of sadness, worthlessness, and despair. The experience of schizophrenia also differs by culture. In India, one-third of the new cases of schizophrenia involve catatonia, a behaviourial condition in which a person maintains a bizarre statue like pose for hours or days. This condition is rare in Europe and North America.

With appropriate treatment, most people can recover from mental illness and return to normal life. Even those with persistent, long-term mental illnesses can usually learn to manage their symptoms and live productive lives.

By a variety of symptoms, including loss of contact with reality, bizarre behaviour, disorganized thinking and speech, decreased emotional expressiveness, and social withdrawal. Usually only some of these symptoms occur in any one person. The term schizophrenia comes from Greek words meaning 'split mind.' However, contrary to common belief, schizophrenia does not refer to a person with a split personality or multiple personality. For a description of a mental illness in which a person has multiple personalities. To observers, schizophrenia may seem or appear for being as some sorted kind of madness or a manufacturing insanity.

Perhaps more than any other mental illness, schizophrenia has a debilitating effect on the lives of the people who suffer from it. A person with schizophrenia may have difficulty telling the difference between real and unreal experiences, logical and illogical thoughts, or appropriate and inappropriate behaviour. Schizophrenia seriously impairs a person's ability to work, go to school, enjoy relationships with others, or take care of oneself. In addition, people with schizophrenia frequently require hospitalization because they pose a danger to themselves. About 10 percent of people with schizophrenia commit suicide, and many others attempt suicide. Once people develop schizophrenia, they usually suffer from the illness for the rest of their lives. Although there is no cure, treatment can help many people with schizophrenia lead productive lives.

Schizophrenia also carries an enormous cost to society. People with schizophrenia occupy about one-third of all beds in psychiatric hospitals in the United States. In addition, people with schizophrenia account for at least 10 percent of the homeless population in the United States. The National Institute of Mental Health has estimated that schizophrenia costs the United States tens of billions of dollars each year in direct treatment, social services, and lost productivity.

Approximately 1 percent of people develop schizophrenia at some time during their lives. Experts estimate that about 1.8 million people in the United States have schizophrenia. The prevalence of schizophrenia is the same regardless of sex, race, and culture. Although women are just as likely as men to develop schizophrenia, women tend to experience the illness less severely, with fewer hospitalizations and better social functioning in the community.

Schizophrenia usually develops in late adolescence or early adulthood, between the ages of 15 and 30. Much less commonly, schizophrenia develops later in life. The illness may begin abruptly, but it usually develops slowly over months or years. Mental health professionals diagnose schizophrenia based on an interview with the patient in which they determine whether the person has experienced specific symptoms of the illness.

Symptoms and functioning in people with schizophrenia tend to vary over time, sometimes worsening and other times improving. For many patients the symptoms gradually become less severe as they grow older. About 25 percent of people with schizophrenia become symptom-free later in their lives.

A variety of symptoms characterize schizophrenia. The most prominent include symptoms of psychosis—such as delusions and hallucinations - as well as bizarre behaviour, strange movements, and disorganized thinking and speech. Many people with schizophrenia do not recognize that their mental functioning is disturbed.

Delusions are false beliefs that appear obviously untrue to other people. For example, a person with schizophrenia may believe that he is the king of England when he is not. People with schizophrenia may have delusions that others, such as the police or the FBI, are plotting against them or spying on them. They may believe that aliens are controlling their thoughts or that their own thoughts are being broadcast to the world so that other people can hear them.

Research suggests that the genes one inherits strongly influence one's risk of developing schizophrenia. Studies of families have shown that the more close one is related to someone with schizophrenia, the greater the risk one has of developing the illness. For example, the children of one parent with schizophrenia have about a 13 percent chance of developing the illness, and children of two parents with schizophrenia have about a 46 percent chance of eventually developing schizophrenia. This increased risk occurs even when such children are adopted and raised by mentally healthy parents. In comparison, children in the general population have only about a 1 percent chance of developing schizophrenia.

Some evidence suggests that schizophrenia may result from an imbalance of chemicals in the brain called neurotransmitters. These chemicals enable neurons (brain cells) to communicate with each other. Some scientists suggest that schizophrenia results from excess activity of the neurotransmitter dopamine in certain parts of the brain or from an abnormal sensitivity to dopamine. Support for this hypothesis comes from Antipsychotic drugs, which reduce psychotic symptoms in schizophrenia by blocking brain receptors for dopamine. In addition, amphetamines, which increase dopamine activity, intensify psychotic symptoms in people with schizophrenia. Despite these findings, many experts believe that excess dopamine activity alone cannot account for schizophrenia. Other neurotransmitters, such as serotonin and norepinephrine, may play important roles as well.

Although scientists favour a biological cause of schizophrenia, stress in the environment may affect the onset and course of the illness. Stressful life circumstances - such as maturing in age and character as for living in poverty, the death of a loved one, an important change in jobs or relationships, or chronic tension and hostility at home—can increase the chances of schizophrenia in a person biologically predisposed to the disease. In addition, stressful events can trigger a relapse of symptoms in a person who already has the illness. Individuals who have effective skills for managing stress may be less susceptible to its negative effects. Psychological and social rehabilitation can help patients develop more effective skills for dealing with stress.

Although there is no cure for schizophrenia, effective treatment exists that can improve the long-term course of the illness. With many years of treatment and rehabilitation, significant numbers of people with schizophrenia experience partial or full remission of their symptoms.

Treatment of schizophrenia usually involves a combination of medication, rehabilitation, and treatment of other problems the person may have. Antipsychotic drugs (also called neuroleptics) are the most frequently used medications for treatment of schizophrenia. Psychological and social rehabilitation programs may help people with schizophrenia function in the community and reduce stress related to their symptoms. Treatment of secondary problems, such as substance abuse and infectious diseases, is also an important part of an overall treatment program.

Antipsychotic medications, developed in the mid-1950s, can dramatically improve the quality of life for people with schizophrenia. The drugs reduce or eliminate psychotic symptoms such as hallucinations and delusions. The medications can also help prevent these symptoms from returning. Common Antipsychotic drugs include risperidone (Risperdal), olanzapine (Zyprexa), clozapine (Clozaril), quetiapine (Seroquel), haloperidol (Haldol), thioridazine (Mellaril), chlorpromazine (Thorazine), fluphenazine (Prolixin), and trifluoperazine (Stelazine). People with schizophrenia usually must take medication for the rest of their lives to control psychotic symptoms. Antipsychotic medications appear to be less effective at treating other symptoms of schizophrenia, such as social withdrawal and apathy.

Because many patients with schizophrenia continue to experience difficulties despite taking medication, psychological and social rehabilitation is often necessary. A variety of methods can be effective. Social skills training help people with schizophrenia learn specific behaviours for functioning in society, such as making friends, purchasing items at a store, or initiating conversations. Behaviourial training methods can also help them learn self-care skills such as personal hygiene, money management, and proper nutrition. In addition, cognitive-behaviourial therapy, a type of psychotherapy, can help reduce persistent symptoms such as hallucinations, delusions, and social withdrawal.

Because many patients have difficulty obtaining or keeping jobs, supported employment programs that help patients find and maintain jobs are a helpful part of rehabilitation. In these programs, the patient works alongside people without disabilities and earns competitive wages. An employment specialist (or vocational specialist) helps the person maintain their job by, for example, training the person in specific skills, helping the employer accommodate the person, arranging transportation, and monitoring performance. These programs are most effective when the supported employment is closely integrated with other aspects of treatment, such as medication and monitoring of symptoms.

Some people with schizophrenia are vulnerable to frequent crises because they do not regularly go to mental health centres to receive the treatment they need. These individuals often relapse and face rehospitalization. To ensure that such patients take their medication and receive appropriate psychological and social rehabilitation, assertive community treatment (ACT) programs have been developed that deliver treatment to patients in natural settings, such as in their homes, in restaurants, or on the street.

People with schizophrenia often have other medical problems, so an effective treatment program must attend to these as well. One of the most generally shared in or participated in things conforming to a type without noteworthy excellence or faults just as common a rule, by ordinary, frequent and ordinarily as an idea or expression deficient in originality or freshness, yet, only of its exchanging the commonplace of the common associated problems is vehemently and usually coarsely expressed condemnation or disapproved, as the interpretative category of an unequalled vocabulary is itself a genuine abuse. Successful treatment of substance abuse inpatients with schizophrenia requires careful coordination with their mental health care, so that the same clinicians are treating both disorders at the same time.

The high rate of substance abuse in patients with schizophrenia contributes to a high prevalence of infectious diseases, including hepatitis B and C and the human immunodeficiency virus (HIV). Assessment, education, and treatment or management of these illnesses is critical for the long-term health of patients.

Other problems frequently associated with schizophrenia include housing instability and homelessness, legal problems, violence, trauma and post-traumatic stress disorder, anxiety, depression, and suicide attempts. Close monitoring and psychotherapeutic interventions are often helpful in addressing these problems.

Several other psychiatric disorders are closely related to schizophrenia. In schizoaffective disorder, a person shows symptoms of schizophrenia combined with either mania or severe depression. Schizophreniform disorder refers to an illness in which a person experiences schizophrenic symptoms for more than one month but fewer than six months. In schizotypal personality disorder, a person engages in odd thinking, speech, and behaviour, but usually does not lose contact with reality. Sometimes mental health professionals refer to these disorders together as schizophrenia-spectrum disorders.

Severe mental illness almost always alters a person's life dramatically. People with severe mental illnesses experience disturbing symptoms that can cause of such difficulties and holding to a job, or go to school, relate to others, or cope with ordinary life demands. Some individuals require hospitalization because they become unable to care for themselves or because they are at risk of committing suicide.

The symptoms of mental illness can be very distressing. People who develop schizophrenia may hear voices inside their head that say nasty things about them or command them to act in strange or unpredictable ways. Or they may be paralysed by paranoia - the deep conviction that everyone, including their closest family members, wants to injure or destroy them. People with major depression may feel that nothing brings pleasure and that life is so dreary and unhappy that it is better to be dead. People with panic disorder may experience heart palpitations, rapid breathing, and anxiety so extreme that they may not be able to leave home.

People whom experience episodes of mania may engage in reckless sexual behaviour or may spend money indiscriminately, acts that later cause them to feel guilt, shame, and desperation.

Other mental illnesses, while not always debilitating, create certain problems in living. People with personality disorders may experience loneliness and isolation because their personality style interferes with social relations. People with an eating disorder may become so preoccupied with their weight and appearance that they force themselves to vomit or refuse to eat. Individuals who develop post-traumatic stress disorder may become angry easily, experience disturbing memories, and have trouble concentrating.

Experiences of mental illness often take issue upon its stability for depending on one's culture or social group, sometimes greatly so. For example, in most of the non-Western world, people with depression complain principally of physical ailments, such as lack of energy, poor sleep, loss of appetite, and various kinds of physical pain. Indeed, even in North America these complaints are commonplace. But in the United States and other Western societies, depressed people and mental health professionals who treat them tend to emphasize psychological problems, such as feelings of sadness, worthlessness, and despair. The experience of schizophrenia also differs by culture. In India, one-third of the new cases of schizophrenia involve catatonia, a behaviourial condition in which a person maintains a bizarre statue like pose for hours or days. This condition is rare in Europe and North America.

Of furthering issues regarding depersonalization disorder, meaning, in effect, that it is a categorised illness based within its intendment for being an illness, of mind, in which people experience an unwelcome sense of detachment from their own bodies. They may feel as though they are floating above the ground, outside observers of their own mental or physical processes. Other symptoms may include a feeling that they or other people are mechanical or unreal, a feeling of being in a dream, a feeling that their hands or feet are larger or smaller than usual, and a deadening of emotional responses. These symptoms are chronic and severe enough to impede normal functioning in a social, school, or work environment.

Depersonalization disorder is a relatively rare syndrome thought to result from severe psychological stress. It may occur as part of other mental illnesses, especially anxiety disorders. For example, some people with panic disorder feel nervous, have a sense of doom about their future and health, and have a troubling sense of detachment form the lose in the attemptive use in making or doing or achieving a useful regularity as might beg to ask for something equally expected of the control over their bodies. Depersonalization disorder may also be a component of more severe mental illness, such as schizophrenia. Treatment may include training in relaxation techniques that enhance body perception and control, hypnosis to modify symptoms, and psychotherapy to explore possible stress-related components of the disorder.

Psychiatrists classify depersonalization disorder as one of the Dissociative disorders. Such disorders involve a disruption of consciousness, memory, identity, or perception.

All the while, the schizophrenic responds to altercations in the analyst's defections and understanding by corresponding stormy and dramatic changes from love to hatred, from willingness to leave his delusional world to resistance and renewed withdrawal.

As understandable as these changes are, nevertheless may come as a surprise to the analyst who frequently has not observed their source, this is quite in contrast to his experience with psychoneurosis whose emotional reactions during an interview he can usually predict. These unpredictable changes seem to be the reason for the conception of the unreliability of the schizophrenic's transference reaction, yet they follow the same dynamic rules as the psychoneurotic's oscillations between positive and negative transference and resistance, however, if the schizophrenic's reactions are stormy and seemingly more unpredictable than those of the psychoneurotic, that instances suggested to be due to the inevitable errors in the analyst's approach to the schizophrenic, of which he himself may be unaware, rather than to the unreliability of the patient's emotional response?

Why is it inevitable that the psychoanalysts disappoint his schizophrenic patient time and again?

The schizophrenic withdraws from painful reality and retires to what resembles the early speechless phase of development where consciousness is not yet crystalized. As the expression of his feelings is not hindered by the convention that he has eliminated, as his thinking, feelings, behaviour and speech - when present - obey the working rules of the archaic unconscious. His thinking is magical and does not follow logical rules. It does not admit to every last saying of 'no', but likewise nor the positive expression in the no to 'yes': There is no recognition of space and time, I, you, and they, are interchangeable expression through which of symbols and often by movement and gestures rather than by words.

As the schizophrenic is suspicious, he will distrust the words of his analyst. He will interpret them and incidental gestures and attitudes of the according to his own delusional experience. The analyst may not even be aware of these involuntary manifestations of his attitudes, yet they mean much to the hypersensitive schizophrenic who uses them as a means of orienting himself to the therapist's personality and intentions toward him.

In other words, the schizophrenic patient and the therapist are people living in different worlds and no different levels of personal development with different means of expressing and of orienting themselves. We know little about the language of the unconscious that belongs to the schizophrenic, and our access to it is blocked by the very process of our own adjustment to a world the schizophrenic has relinquished, so, we should not be surprised that errors and misunderstandings occur when we under take to communicate and strive for a rapport with him.

Another source of the schizophrenic's disappointment arises form which the analyser accepts and does not interfere with the behaviour of the schizophrenic, his attitude may lead the patient to expect that the analyst will assist in carrying out all the patient's wishes, even though they may not seem to be in his interest to the analyser's and the hospital's in their relationship to society. This attitude of acceptance so different from the patient's previous experiences readily fosters the anticipation that the analyst will try to carry out the patient's suggestion and take his part, even against conventional society with which it should occasionally arise. Frequently it will be wise for the analyst to agree with the patient's wish to remain unbattled and untidy until he is ready to talk about the reasons for his behaviour or to change spontaneously. At other times, he will unfortunately be unable to take the patient's part without being able to make the patient understand and accept the reasons for the analyst's position.

If the analyst is not able to accept the possibility of misunderstanding the reaction of the schizophrenic patient and in turn of being misunderstood by him, it may shake his security with his patient.

That is to say, that, among other things, the schizophrenic, once he accepts the analyst's insecurity. being helpless and open to himself - in spite of his pretended grandiose isolation - he will feel utterly defeated by the insecurity of his would-be helper. Such disappointment may furnish reasons for outbursts of hatred and are comparable to the negative transference reactions of psychoneurosis, yet more intense than these, since they are not limited by the restrictions of the actual world - that is, it exists in or based on fact, its only problem is a sure-enough externalization for which things are existing in the act of being external in something that has existence, ss if it were an actualization as received in the obtainable enactment for being externalized, such that its problem of in some actual life that proves obtainable achieved, in that of doing something that has an existence for having absolute actuality.

These outbursts are accompanied by anxiety, feelings of guilt, and fear of retaliations which in turn lead to increased hostility. Yet this established a vicious circle: We disappoint the patient, he is afraid that we hate him for his hatred and therefore continues to hate us. If in addition he senses that the analyst is afraid of his aggressiveness, it confirms his fear that he is actually considered as some dangerous and unacceptable, and this augments his hatred.

This establishes that the schizophrenics capable of developing strong relationships of love and hatred toward the analyst. After all, one could not be so hostile if it were not for the background of a very close relationship. In addition, the schizophrenic develops transference reactions on the narrower sense which he can differentiate from the actual interpersonal relationship. For which the schizophrenic's emotional reactions toward the analyst have to be met with extreme care and caution. The love which the sensitive schizophrenic feels as he first emerges, and his cautions acceptances of the analyst's warmth of interest are really most delicate and tender things. If the analyst deals with the transference reactions of a psychoneurotic is bad enough, though as a reparable rule, but if he fails with a schizophrenic in meeting positive feelings by pointing it out for instance before the patient indicates that he is ready to discuss it, he may easily freeze to death what has just begun to grow and so destroy any further possibility of therapy.

Some analysts may feel that the atmosphere of complete acceptance and of strict avoidance of any arbitrary denials which we recommend as a basic rule for the treatment of schizophrenics may not avoid our wish to guide of reacceptance of reality, nevertheless, Freud says that every science and therapy which accept his teachings about unconscious, about transference and resistance and about infantile sexuality, may be called psychoanalysis. According in this definition we believe we are practising psychoanalysis with our schizophrenic patients.

Whether we call it analysis or not, it is clear that successful treatment does not depend on technical rules of any special psychiatric school but rather on the basic attitude of individual therapist toward psychologic persons. If he meets them as strangle creatures of another world whose productions are not comprehensible to 'normal' beings, he cannot treat them, if he realizes, however, that the difference between himself and the psychologic is only of degree, and not of kind, he will know better how to meet him. He will not be able to identify himself sufficiently with the patient to understand and accept his emotional reactions without becoming involved in them.

The process of constant and perpetual change is examined and closely matched within the study of philosophical speculations and pointed of a world view which asserts that basic reality is constantly in a process of flux and change. Indeed, reality is identified with pure process. Concepts such as creativity, freedom, novelty, emergence, and growth are fundamental explanatory categories for process philosophy. This metaphysical perspective is to be contrasted with a philosophy of substance, the view that a fixed and permanent reality underlies the changing or fluctuating world of ordinary experience. Whereas substance philosophy emphasizes static being, process philosophy emphasizes dynamically becoming.

Although process philosophy is as old as the 6th-century BC Greek philosopher, Heraclitus, renewed interest in it was stimulated in the 19th century by the theory of evolution. Key figures in the development of modern process philosophy were the British philosophers Herbert Spencer, Samuel Alexander, and Alfred North Whitehead, the American philosophers Charles S. Peirce and William James, and the French philosophers Henri Bergson and Pierre

Teilhard de Chardin. Whitehead's Process and Reality: An Essay in Cosmology (1929) is generally considered the most important systematic expression of process philosophy.

Contemporary theology has been strongly influenced by process philosophy. The American theologian Charles Hartshorne, for instance, rather than interpreting God as an unchanging absolute, emphasizes God's sensitive and caring relationship with the world. A personal God enters into relationships in such a way that he is affected by the relationships, and to be affected by relationships is to change. So too is in the process of growth and development. Important contributions to process theology have also been made by such theologians as William Temple, Daniel Day Williams, Schubert Ogden, and John Cobb, Jr.

'Reality' is a difficult word to use to every one's satisfaction or even to one's own satisfaction. In this instance the word reality is used arbitrarily to designate the direct, here-and-now impact of the analyst upon the patient. Reality. In this sense, contrasts with the impact the analyst has through his representation in the patient's fantasy life, neurosis, and transference, since both kinds of impact seem always to coexist and since the former - the analyst's real impact - may be the worst enemy of the transference, the matter of their differentiation is possibly the most challenging aspect of analysis.

The analytic situation, which is set up to shut out ordinary reality intrusions, that cannot, . . . neither should not exclude all, but to say, that in the beginning months, for instance, reality inevitably has the upper hand. The analyst, the office, the procedure, are all overwhelmingly real. Everything is strange, frightening and exciting, gratifying and frustrating. Unlike the patient can test it and orient himself to it, the impact of this reality is usually so great that even an ordinary useful transference relationship cannot be expected to develop.

Perhaps the most confusing aspect of this beginning period is the frequent appearance in it of what can be regarded as a false transference relationship. With great intensity and clarity, the patient may reveal, through transference-like references about the analyst, some of the deepest secrets only of his neurosis but of its genesis. The pseudotransference, too good to be true, is almost sure to be nothing more than the patient's attempt to deal with the person of the analyst, the entire spectrum of his various patterns of behaviour. If, it is easy to do, the analyst overlooks the likelihood that the patient's relationship with at this time is really about that almost everything said about it is related, analysis may get off to a very bad start. And if, as is even earlier to do, the analyst's interests the genetic meaning of the openly exposed material, a good transference relationship may be seriously delayed and a workable transference neurosis may never appear. even after initial reality has had time to fade, reality may continue to intrude in ways that are very hard to detect and that is very troublesome.

One of the most serious problems of analysis is the very substantial help which the patient receives directly from the analyst and the analytic situation. For many a patient, the analyst in the analytic situation is in fact the most stable, reasonable, wise and understanding person he has ever met, and the setting in which they meet may actually be the most honest, open, direct and regular relationship he has ever experienced. Added to this is the considerable helpfulness to him of being able to clarify his life storey. confess his guilt, express his ambitions, and explore his confusions. Further real help comes from the learning-about-life accruing from the analyst's skilled questions, observations and interpretations. Taken together, the total real value to the patient of the analytic situation can easily be immense. The trouble with this kind of help is that it goes on and on, it may have such a real, direct and continuing impact upon the patient that he can never get deeply enough involved in transference situation to allow him to resolve or even to become acquainted with his most crippling internal difficulties. The trouble is far too good, the trouble also is that we as analysts apparently cannot resist the seductiveness of being directly helpful, and this, when combined with the compelling assumption that helpfulness is bound to be good, permits us top credit patient improvements to 'analysis' when more properly it should often be recognized for being the amounting result for the patient's using the analytic situation, as the model, for being the preceptors and supporter in the dealing practically within the immediate distractions as holding to some problem.

Perhaps, we can now refer to something in a clear unmistakable manner, and it would be to mention, for being, that one more difficult-to-handle intrusion of reality into the analysis, that by saying, that this is the definitive and final interruption of the transference neurosis by the reality of termination; in the sense, the situation is reversed and the intrusion is analytically desirable, since ideally the impact of reality of impending and certain termination is used to facilitate the resolution of the transference. As with the resolution of earlier episodes of transference neurosis, this final one is brought about principally by the analyst's interpretations and reconstructions. As these take effect, the transference neurosis and, hopefully, along with it the original neurosis is resolved. This final resolution, however, which is much more comprehensive, is usually very different and may not come about at all without the help of the reality of termination. Accordingly, any attenuation of the ending, such as tapering off or causal or tentative stopping, should be expected to stand in the way of an effective resolution of the transference. Yet, it seems that this is what most commonly happens to an ending, and because of this a great many patients may lose the potentially great benefit of a thorough resolution and are forever after left suspended in the net of unresolved transference.

Yet, utter indistinctly rigorous termination seems understandable, as difficult as transference neurosis may be in the analyst at other times, this ending period, if rigorously carried out, simply has to be the period of his greatest emotional strain. There can surely be no more likely time for an analyst to surrender his analytic position and, responding to his own transference, become personally involved with his patient than during the process of separating from a long and self-restrained relationship. Accordingly, it may be better to slur over the ending lightly than to mishandle it in an attempt to be rigorous.

In considering more broadly the function of the transference in the psychoanalytic process, one is confronted by the apparent naïve, but, nonetheless important questions of the role of the actual (current) object as compared with that of the object representation of the original personage in the past. We recall Freud's paradoxical, somewhat gloomy, but portentous concluding passage in 'The Dynamics of Transference.' This struggle between the doctor and the patient, between intellect and instinctual life, between understanding and seeking to act, is played out almost exclusively in the phenomena of transference. It is on that field that the victory must be won - the victory whose expression is on that field that the victory must be won - the victory whose expression is the permanent cure of the neuroses. It cannot be disputed that controlling the phenomena of transference presents the psychoanalysis with the greatest difficultly, but it should not be forgotten that they do us the inestimable service of making the patient 's hidden and forgotten erotic impulses of showing their immediate and manifested impossibilities, for when all is said and done, it is impossible to destroy anyone in absentia or in effigies.

Both object and representations are made necessary by the basic phenomenon of original separation. The existence of an image of the object, which persist in the absence of the object, is one of the important beginnings of psychic life in general, certainly an indispensable prerequisite for object relationship. As generally construed. Whether this is viewed as (or a times demonstrably is) something unstable for allotting introjection, s always subject to alternative projection, or an intrapsychic object representation clearly distinguished from the self-representation, or firm identification in the superego, or in the ego itself, these phenomena are in various ways components of the system of mastery of the fact of separation, or separateness, from the original absolutely necessarily anaclitic (in the earliest period) symbiotic 'object'. In the light of clinical observation, it would appear to be that the relative stabilities (parental) object representation. At which time of varying degree, are to a greater extent for the archaic phenomena. Even in nonpsychotic patients, overwhelmed by them, sometimes resembles the restoration from oedipal identification, which provides the preponderant basis for most demonstrable analytic transferences. That within the necrotic patients, the transference is effectively established when this representation invests the analyst to a degree - depending on intensity of drive and most of ego participation - which ranges in all the, wishing and striving to remake and analyst to biasses judgements and misinterpretation of data, finally are the actual perceptual distortions.

However, the old object representations may be invested, however rigidly established the libidinal or aggressive cathexis of the image may be, this as such can become the actual and exclusive focus of instinctual discharge, or of complicated and intense instinct-defence solutions, only and general energy-sparing quality of strictly intrapsychic processes. For the vast majority of persons, visible to any degree, including those with severe neurosis, character distortions, addictions and certain psychoses, the striving is toward the living and actual object, even at the cost of intense suffering. In a sense, this returns us to the state in which the psychological 'object-to-be'. Has a cr11itical importance never again to be duplicated, except in certain acute life emergencies, even if the object is not firmly perceived as such, in the sense of later object relations? And it does seem that trance impressions from the earliest contacts in the service of life preservation, and the associated instinctual gratifications, and innumerable secondarily associated sensory impressions. Are activated by the specific inborn urges of sexual maturation? These propel the individual to renew many of the earliest modes of actual bodily contact, in connection with seeking for specific instinctual gratification. Or, to look away from clear-cut instinctual matters to the more remote elaborations of human contact: Few regard loneliness as other than a source of suffering, even self-imposed, as an apparent matter of choice, and the forcible imposition of 'solitary confinement ' is surely one of the most cruel of punishments.

In taking to question, we are entering an area of life in which things are other then themselves, where meaning is multifaceted, and where the line between the old and the new is blurred. It should, by, its immediate measure, help develop our recognition or meaning of the pertinent applicability as to the relevance of interrelated aspects of the psychology of 'metaphor'. In the psychology of metaphor we will find a useful analogy to the psychology of transference interpretation. Our's will be newly encountered as good metaphors, those it response to which we say, 'That's it exactly' or 'That really captures it' or 'That says it all'.

Some literary and linguistic analysis, (e.g., Lewis, 1936 and Snell, 1953) and also people in everyday life, believe that there are experiences that can only be expressed metaphorically. And for this achievement that these metaphors, which may be entire poem or as lines or even words highly valued. But how can this be so? Just what in th e 'it' that the metaphor 'is' or 'captures' or 'says'? If this 'is' or this 'experience' can only be rendered metaphorically, when we can know it only as such, that is, as the metaphor itself. Of the position out of which are put forward by, T.S, Eliot (1933) and E.W. Harding (1963) in their discussion of poetry, for in these instances we are granted that there are no known and logically independent version of the experience that can serve to validate the metaphor. Whatever the metaphor makes available to us depends on it and it and so cannot be used to prove its correctness.

It seems justifiably warrantable to consider that the metaphor is a new experience rather than a mere paraphrase of an already fully constituted expedience. The metaphor creates an experience that one has never had before. It is an experience one has not realized by oneself. The metaphor does, of course, suggest certain constituent experiences of which one may have been more or less dimly aware. One may say, therefore, that the metaphor speaks for those constituents, on the existence of which much of its appeal depends. But in its organizing and implicit ly rendering these constituents in its new way, it is a creation rather than a mere paraphrase or anew edition. Paraphrasing and new editions never speak as forcefully as good new metaphors, nor could they facilitate further new experience. One analytically familiar feature of these creations is that they make it safe and pleasing to experience something that otherwise would be considered too threatening and so would be kept in fragmented obscurity through defensive measures.

Thus, when one says, 'That's it exactly' one is implicitly recognizing and announcing that one has found and accepted a new mode of experiencing oneself and one's world, which is to say, asserting a transformation of one's own subjectivity. Something is now said to be true, and in a sense it is true, but it is true for the first time. Nothing of one and the same can ever happen again, for the second time cannot be the same as the first. One can' t step into the same watering point and then step once again into the same spot of that river. A revelatory metaphor re-encountered or repeated later may lose some of its force, alternatively, it may gain some significance, butt it cannot remain exactly the same metaphor or mobilize an experience identical with the first. The point applies as well as to new metaphors that are similar to familiar ones: They have to be judged or experienced through their conventionalized predecessors, as through methods of knowing or already proved instrumentally of perceiving. The audience and the performer, who may be one person, as such that may not have, as yet.

What is to be said about the psychology of metaphor is analogous to the transformational aspects of developed transference and the steadfast interpretation that both facilitate and organize them as transference. Allowing that these transferences and 'remembered' experiences come into existence over a period of time, nothing that is identical with them has ever before been enacted, and nothing will ever be enacted again. They are creations that may be fully achieved only under specific analytic conditions. Such that living was not reliving that moment, words like re-living, re-experiencing and reliving simply do not do justice to the phenomena, that in making this claim. A seeming contradiction over-writes some of our well-establish ideas. - in offering, - I am not contradicting some of our well-established ideas about interpretation and insight, I am, however, disputing the point that insight refers to a greater proportion or in its range of comprehension, which its distance between possible extremes extent and regain former or normal state, such that, for the recovery of lost memories, and takes in as well, a new grasp of the significance and interpretations of events one has always remembered. In point, as, Freud pointed out, 'As a matter of fact I've always known it, only that I've never thought of it; (1914), In fact, it is to develop that point in furthering to say that it takes an adult to do that, especially with the help of an analyst. It was, after all, Freud's analysis of adults that make it possible to define infantile psychosexuality. In this respect, but without disregard, child analysis retains a quality of applied psychoanalysis' in the same way that the interpreted transference neurosis is: Both are always of describing as true something that was not true in quite that way at the time of its greatest developmental significance. This apparent paradox about 'remembering' as a form of creating goes a long way, probably that what it is, is distinctive about psychoanalytic interpretation.

This time, however, to further the discussion on the interpretive technique that surrounds the phase of a mutative interpretation - that in which a portion of the patient's id-relation to the analyst is made conscious in virtue of the latter's positions as auxiliary super-ego - is in itself complex. In the classical model of an interpretation, the patient will first be made aware of a state of tension of an interpretation, will next be made aware that there is repressive factor at work (that his super-ego is threatening him with punishment), and will only then be made aware of the id-impulse which has stirred up the protects of his super-ego and so given to the anxiety in his ego. This is the classical scheme. In actual practice, the analyst finds himself working from all three sides at once, or in irregular successions. At one moment a small portion of the patient's super-ego may be revealed to him in all its savagery, at another the shrinking defencelessness of his ego, at yet another his attention may be directed to the attempts which he is making at restitution - at compensating for his hostility, on some occasions a fraction of id-energy may even be directly encouraged to break its way through the last remains of an already weakened resistance. There is, however, one characteristic which all of these various operations has in common, they are essentially upon a small scale. For the mutative interpretation is inevitably governed by the principle of minimal doses. It is a commonly agreed clinical fact that alternations in a patient under analysis appear almost always to be extremely gradual: We are inclined to suspect sudden and large changes as an indication that suggestive rather than psycho-analyst processes are at work. The gradual nature of the change brought about in psychoanalysis will be explained, as, only to suggest, those changes are the result of the summation of an immense number of minuet steps, each of which correspond to a mutative interpretation. And the smallness of each step is in turn imposed by the very nature of the analytic situation. For each interpretation involves the release of a certain quantity of id-energy, and, if the quantity released is too large, the higher unstable state of equilibrium which enables the analyst to function as the patient's auxiliary super-ego is bound to be upset. The whole analytic situation will thus be imperilled, since it is only in virtue of the analyst's acting as auxiliary super-ego that these released id-energy can occur at all.

The effectuality from which follow the analytic attempt to bring unequalled amounts in the confronting collections of some improper use too a resultant quantity of id-energy into the patient's consciousness all at once. On the one hand, nothing whatever may happen, or on the other hand there may be an unmanageable result, but in neither event will be a mutative interpretation has been effected. The analyst's power as auxiliary super-ego may be for two very different reasons. It may be that the id-impulses were trying to bring out being not in fact sufficiently urgent at the moment: For, after all, the emergence of an id-impulse depends on two factors - not only on the permission of the super-ego, but also on the urgency (the degree of cathaxis) of the id-impulse itself. This, then, may be one cause of an apparently negative response to an interpretation, and evidently a fairly harmless one. but the same apparent result may also be due to something else, in spite of the id-impulse being really urgent, the strength of the patient's own repressive forces (the degree of repression) may have been too great to allow his ego to listen to the persuasive voice of the auxiliary super-ego. Now we have a situation dynamically identical with the next one we have to consider, though economically different. this next situation is one in which the patient accepts the interpretation, that is, allows the id-impulse into his consciousness, but is immediately overwhelmed with anxiety. This may show itself in a number of ways, for instance, the patient may produce a manifest anxiety-attack. Or the may exhibit signs of 'real' anger with the analyst with a complete lack of insight, or he may break off the analysis. In any of these cases the analytic situation will, for the moment, at least, have broken down. The patient will be behaving just as the hypnotic subject behaves when, having been ordered by the hypnotist to perform an action too much at variance with his own consciousness, he breaks off the hypnotic relation and wakes up from his trance. This state of things, which is manifest where the patient responds to an interpretation with an actual outbreak of anxiety or one of its equivalents, may be latent were the patient shows no response, and this latter case may be the more awkward of the two, since it is masked, and it may sometimes be the effect of a greater overdose of interpretation than where manifest anxiety arises (though obviously other factors will be of determining importance, and in particularly the nature of the patient's neurosis). Yet this threatened collapse of the analytic situation to an overdose of interpretation: But it might be more accurate in some ways to ascribe it to an insufficient dose. For what has happened is that the second phase of the interpretation process has not occurred: The phase in which the patient becomes aware that his impulse is directed toward an archaic phantasy object and not toward a real one.

In the second phase of a complete interpretation, therefore, a crucial part is played by the patient's sense of reality: For the successful outcome of that phase depends upon his ability, at the critical moment of the emergence into consciousness of the released quantity of id-energy, to distinguish between his phantasy object and the real analyst. The problem is closely related to one that has been discussed elsewhere, namely that of the extreme liability of the analyst's position as auxiliary super-ego. The analytic situation is all the time threatening to degenerate into a 'real' situation. But this actually means the opposite of what it appears to. It means that the patient is all the time on the brink of turning the really external object (the analyst) into the archaic one; that is to say, he is on the brink of projecting his primitive introjected images onto himself. In so far as the patient actually does this, the analyst becomes like anyone else that he meets in real life - a phantasy object. The analyst then ceases to possess the peculiar advantages derived from the analytic situation, he will be introjected like all other phantasy objects into the analytic situation, he will be introjected like all other phantasy objects into the patient's super-ego, and will no longer be able to function in the peculiar ways which are essential to the effecting of a mutative interpretation. In this difficulty the patient's sense of reality is an essential but a very feeble [-ally]: An improvement in it is one of the things that we hope the analysis will bring about. It is important, therefore, not to submit it to any unnecessary strain, and that is the fundamental reason why the analyst must avoid any real behaviour, that is likely to confirm the patient's view of him as a 'bad' or a 'good' phantasy object. This is perhaps more obvious as regards the 'bad' object. If, for instance, the analyst were to show that he was really shocked or frightened by one of the patient's id-impulses, as the patient would immediately treat him in that respect as a dangerous object and introject him into his archaic severe super-ego. Therefore, on the one hand, there would be a diminuation in the analyst's power to function as an auxiliary super-ego and to allow the patient's to become conscious of his id-impulses - that is to say, in his power to bring about the first phase of a mutative interpretation, and on the other hand, he would, as a real object, become sensibly less distinguishable from the patient's 'bad' phantasy object and to that extent the carrying through of the second phase of a mutative interpretation would also be made more difficult. Or, agin, there is another case. Supposing the analyst behaves in an opposite way and actively urges the patient to give free rein to his id-impulse. There is then a possibility of the patient confusing the analyst with the image of a treacherous parent who, at the beginning, encourage him to seek gratification, and then suddenly turns and punishes him. In such a case the patient's ego may look for defence by itself suddenly turning upon the analyst as though he were his own id-, and treating him with all the severity of which his super-ego is capable. again, the analyst is running a risk of losing his privileged position. But it may be equally unwise for the analyst to act really in such a way as to encourage the patient to project his 'good' introjected object on to him. For the patient will then tend to regard him as a good objective and archaic sense and will incorporate him with his archaic 'good' images and will use him as a protection against his 'bad' ones. In that way, his infantile positive impulses as well as his negative ones may escape analysis, for there may no longer be a possibility for his ego to make a comparison between the phantasy external object and the real one. it will, perhaps, be argued that, with the best of wills in the world, the analyst, however careful he may be, will be unable to prevent the patient from projecting these various images on to him. This is, of course, indisputable, and, the whole effectiveness of analysis depends upon its being so. The lesson of these difficulties is merely to remind us that the patient's sense of reality has the narrowest limits. It is a paradoxical fact that the best way of enuring that his ego will be able to distinguish between phantasy and reality is to withhold reality from him as much as possible. but it is true, his ego is so weak - so much at the mercy of his id and super-ego - that he can only cope with reality if it is administered in minimal doses. And these doses are in fact what the analyst gives him, in the form of interpretations.

A mutative interpretation can only be applied to an id-impulse which is actually on a state of cathexis. This seems self-evident; for the dynamic changes in the patient's mind implied by a mutative interpretation can only be brought about by the operation of a charge of energy originating in the patient himself: The function of the analyst is merely to ensure that the energy should or can flow along one channel rather than along another. It follows that the purely informative 'dictionary' type of interpretation will be non-mutative, but useful it may be a prelude to mutative interpretations. And this leads to a number of practical inferences. Every mutative interpretation must be emotionally 'immediate, but the patient must live through it as something actual or genuine. This requirement, that the interpretation must be 'immediate', may be expressed in another way by saying that interpretation must always be directed to the 'point of urgency'. At any given moment some particular id-impulse will be generated in activity, this is the impulse that is susceptible of mutative interpretation at the time, and no other one. It is, no doubt, neither possible nor desirable to be giving mutative interpretations all the time. as Melanie Klein has pointed out, it is a most precious quality in an analyst to be able at any moment to pick out the point of urgency.

But the fact that every mutative interpretation must deal with an 'urgent' impulse takes us back one more to the commonly felt fear of the explosive possibilities of interpretation, and particularly of what is vaguely referred to as 'deep' interpretation. The terminological description is, no doubt, as the interpretation of material which is neither genetically early and historically distant from the patient's actual experience nor under an especially heavy weight of repression – material, in any case, which is in the normal course of things exceedingly inaccessible to his ego and remote from it. There seems reason to believe, moreover, that the anxiety which is liable to be aroused by the approach of such material to consciousness and may be of peculiar severity. The question whether it is 'safe' to interpret such material will, as usual, mainly depend upon whether an interpretation can be carried through, in the ordinary run of the case, as this material which is urgent during the earlier stages of the analysis is not deep. We have to deal at first only with more or less far-going displacements of the deep impulse. And the deep material itself is only reached later and by degrees, so that no sudden appearance of unmanageable quantities of anxiety is to be hesitorially anticipated. In exceptional cases, however, owing to some peculiarities in the structure of the neurosis, deep impulses may be urgent at a very early stage of the analysis. We are then faced by a dilemma. If we give an interpretation of this deep material, the resultant amounts of anxiety produced in the patient may be so great that his sense of reality may not be sufficient to permit of its accomplishment, and the whole analysis may be jeopardised, but, it must not be thought that, in such critical cases as we are now considering, the difficulty can necessarily be avoided simply by not giving any interpretation or by giving more superficial interpretations of non-urgent material or by attempting reassurances. It seems probable, in fact, that these alternative procedures may do little or nothing to obviate the trouble, on the contrary, they may even exacerbate the tension created by the urgency of the deep impulses which are the actual cause of the threatening anxiety. Thus the anxiety may break out in spite of these palliative efforts and, if so, it will be doing so under the most unfavourable conditions, that is to say, outside the mitigating influences afforded by the mechanism of interpretation. It is possible, therefore, that, of these alternative procedures which are open to the analyst faced by such a difficulty. The interpretation of the urgent id-impulses, deep though they may b e, will actually be the safer.

It is, of course, a matter of common experience, that it possible with certain patients to continue indefinitely giving interpretations without producing any apparent effect whatever. There is an amusing criticism of this kind of 'interpretation-fanaticism' in the excellent historical chapter of Rank and Ferenczi. But it is clear from their words that what they have in mind are essentially extra-transference interpretations, for the burden of their criticism is that such a procedure implies neglect of the analytic situation. This is the simplest case. Where a waste of time and energy is the main result. But there are other occasions, on which a policy of giving strings of extra-transference interpretations is apt to lead the analyst into more positive difficulties. Attention was drawn by Reich a few years back, in the course of some technical discussions in Vienna too a tendency among inexperienced analysts to get into trouble by eliciting from the patient great quantities of material in a disordered and unrelated fashion: This may, be maintained, be carried to such lengths that the analysis is brought to an irremediable state of chaos. He pointe out truly that the material we have to deal with is stratified and that it is highly important in digging it out not to interference, more that we can help with th e arrangement of that state. He had in mind, of course, the analogy of an incompetent archaeologist, whose clumsiness may obliterate for all time the possibility of reconstructing the history of an important site. However, the results in the case of a clumsy analysis do not hold of any pessimistic cause to happen, as it were, re-stratification itself of its own accord if it is given the opportunity; That is to say, in the analytic situation. At the same time, is that of the presence of the risk, and it seems to be particularly likely to occur where extra-transference interpretation is excessively or exclusively restored to. The means of preventing it, and the remedy if it has occurred, lie in returning to transference interpretation at the point of urgency. For if we can discover which of the material is 'immediate' in the sense that the problematic occurrence enabling stratification is automatically solved, and it is a characteristic if most extra-transference material that it has no immediacy and consequently stratification is far more difficult to decipher. The measures suggested by Reich himself for preventing the occurrence of this state of chaos are consistent with those that he stresses the importance of interpreting resistance as opposed to the primary id-impulses themselves - and this, was a policy that was laid down at an early stage in the history of analysis. But it is, of course, one of the characteristics of a resistance that it arises in relation to the analyst. Thus, interpretation of a resistance will almost inevitably be a transference interpretation.

But the most serious risks that arise from the making of extra-transference interpretation are due to the inherent difficulty in completing their interpretation, for a successful outcome as such, depends upon his ability, at which time of the emergence into consciousness and the released quantity of id-energy. They are from their nature unpredictable in their effects. There seems to be a special risk of the patient not carrying through to a competed interpretation, hitherto, namely that the extreme liability of the analyst's position as auxiliary super-ego, is that, the analytic situation is all the time threatening to degenerate into a 'real' situation. It means that the patient is all the time perched upon the circumference edge-horizon of turning the external object (the analyst) into the archaic one, but of projecting the id-impulse that has been made conscious on to the analyst. This risk, no doubt, applies to some extent to transference interpretations. However, the situation is less likely to arise when the object of the id-impulses is actually present and is moreover the same person as the maker of interpretation. We may, once, more, recall the problem of 'deep' interpretation, and point out that its dangers, even in the most unfavourable circumstances, seem to be greatly diminished if the interpretation in question is a transference interpretation. Even so, there appears to be more of a chance that in this whole process occurring silently and so being overlooked in the case of an extra-transference interpretation, particularly in the earlier stages of an analysis. For this reason, it would seem to be important after giving an extra-transference interpretation to be specially in the 'qui-vive' for transferences complications. This last peculiarity of the extra-transference interpretation is actually one of their most important from a practical stand-point. For on account of it they can be made to act as 'feeders' for the transference situation, and so to pave the way for mutative interpretations. In other words, by giving an extra-transference interpretation, the analyst can often provide a situation in the transference of which he can then give a mutative interpretation.

Therefore, it is probable that a large majority of our interpretations are outside the transference - though it should be added that it often happens that one is ostensibly giving an extra-transference interpretation one is implicitly giving a transference one. A cake cannot be made of nothing but currants, and, though it is true that extra-transference interpretations, are not for the most part, mutative and do not they bring about the crucial results that involve a permanent change in the patient's mind. They are, nonetheless essential, if taken to an analogy of trench warfare, the acceptance of a transference interpretation corresponds to the capture of a key position, while the extra-transference interpretations correspond to the general advance and to the consolidation of a fresh line of defence, which are made possible by the capture of the key position. But when this general advance goes beyond a certain point, there will be another check, and the capture of a further key position will be necessary before progress can be resumed. An oscillation of this kind between transference and extra-transference interpretations will represent the normative course of events in an analysis.

Although the giving of mutative interpretations may thus only occupy a small portion of psycho-analytic treatment, it will, upon being, that the most important part from the point of view of deeply exerting affective percussions. Do so, because of the influencing characteristic confirmations as drawn upon the spoken-exchange of the patient's mindful knowing, in that the individuals that feel, perceive, think, wills, and especially reasons are all taken into heedful compliance. It may be of interest to consider how a moment which is such importance to th e patient affects the analyst himself. Mrs. Klein has suggested that there must be some quite special internal difficulty as to involve the analyst in interpretations. This is shown in their avoidance by psycho-therapists of non-analytic schools, but many psycho-analysts will be aware of traces of the same tendency in themselves. It may be rationalized into mutative interpretations. This is shown in the avoidance by psycho-therapists of non-analytic schools, in that, are not many consisting of a psycho-analyst flow of some passing over the peculiarity of empty space or the nothingness to themselves, nonetheless, this dialectic awareness traces of the same tendency as 1in themselves. But behind this there is somewhat of a lurking difficulty in the actual giving of the interpretation, for there seems to be a constant temptation for the analyst to do something else instead. Questions may be asked of whether o r not. As given to the reassurances or advice or discourses upon theory, or may give interpretations -but interpretations that are not mutative, extra-transference interpretations, interpretations that are non-immediate, or ambiguous, or in exacting of two or more alternative interpretations simultaneously, or he may, perhaps, give interpretations and at the same time, show his own scepticism about them. All of this strongly suggests that the giving of a mutative interpretation is a crucial act for the analyst as well as for the patient. And this inturn will become intelligible when we reflect that at the moment of interpretation the analyst is in fact deliberately Evoking a quantity of the patients id-energy while it is a live and actual and unambiguous and aimed directly himself. Such a moment must be above all others put to the test his relations with his unconscious impulses.

Psychoanalysis, since the earliest days of the, Studies on Hysteria (Breuer and Freud, 1993-1905), have always given special attention to the transference and to the interpretation of transference, believing it to be central in our theory and technique. While there, has never been a lack of interest in transference interpreting. It is not clear why this is so, and the reasons may vary in different parts of the international psychoanalytic community. In America, at least, Gill's (1982) recent, and somewhat radical presentation of transference interpretation has surely helped to the grasping upon our developing attentions, nevertheless, of another reasons for our intensified interests in transference interpretation is the opportunity it provided for rhetorically dialectic awareness, in that discussions, have lead us to the diverse analytic theories and techniques that today complete of the global diversities in our lives'. Our attentions and allegiance. In this respect, transference interpretation seems to have replaced self-psychology as the encompassing topic that allows analysts of varied persuasions among many structural and fundamental elements that forge out the shape for taking upon the imparting of instinctual information, as to know, and knowing that you know, however, its depthful concerning contemplations are distinguished by the evolving characterizations that are of knowing that you know is really n1othing whatsoever.

Despite the diversity of the transference and its interpreting in analytic process and cure, differing only in whether transference is everything or almost everything to give a clear-cut definition of what transference is.

Laplanche and Pontalis (1973) had written that, 'The reason it is so difficult to produce a definition of transference is that for many authors the notion has taken on a very broad extension, even coming to connote all the phenomena which constitute the patient's relationship with the psychoanalyst, as a result the concept is burdened down more than any other with each analyst's particular view on the treatment - on its objective, dynamics, tactics, scope, and so forth. The question of the transference is thus beset by a whole series of difficulties which have been the subject of debate in classical psychoanalysis.'

Sandler (1983) has discussed how the terms transference and transference resistance, as well as other terms have undergone profound changes in meaning as new discoveries and new trends of psycho-analytic technique assume ascendency. He said, . . . major changes in technical emphasis brought about the extension of the transference concept, which now has dimensions of meaning which differ from the official definition of the term. I am not sure there has ever been a simplified definition of the term. While a certain flexibility of definition makes conversation possible in a field of diverse views, which we may never be clear on what any two people mean when they use the term is a significant disability to our discourse.

However: with this in mind we might review one of Freud's last comments on transference. In 'An Outline of Psycho-Analysis' (1940), published posthumously, he wrote on the analytic situation:

The most remarkable thing is this. The patient is not satisfied with regarding the analyst in the light of reality as a helper and advisor who, moreover, is remunerated for the trouble he takes and who would himself be content with some role that of a guide on a different mountain to climb, on the contrary, the patient sees in him, the return, and the reincarnation, of some important figure out of his childhood or past, and consequently transfer onto him, feelings and reactions which undoubtedly apply this prototype. This fact of transference soon proves to be a factor of an undreamt-of importance, on the other hand bud an instrument of irreplaceable value and on the other, that he set out on a different undertaking without any suspicion to the extraordinary power that would be at his command. . . .

Another advantage of transference, too, in that in it the patient produces before us with plastic clarity an important part of his life-story, of which he would, otherwise have probably given us only an insufficient account. He acts it before us, as it were, instead of reporting it to us.

Freud saw the transference interpretation as a method of strengthening the ego against past unconscious wishes and conflicts.

It is the analyst's task constantly to tear the patient out of his menacing illusions and to show him again and again, of what it takes to be or begin of a new life, are the reflections of the past. And least, he should fall into a state in which he is inaccessible to all evidences, the analyst takes that neither the love nor the hostility reaching an extreme height. This is effected, by preparing him in good time for these possibilities and by not overlooking the first signs of them. Careful handling of the transference on these lines is as a role richly rewarded. If we succeed, as we usually can, in enlightenment the patient on the true nature of the phenomena of the transference, we thus have struck a powerful weapon out of the hand of his resistance and will have converted dangers into gains. For a patient never forgets again what he has experienced in the form of transference, it carries a greater force of conviction than anything he can acquire in other ways.

We have used the term 'transference' several times, and in the last, we attributed the therapeutic results to the transference without further definition of the word. As our concerning considerations are more closely intertwined by its emotional relationship, which the word or, perhaps, a combination of words, by which something can be called and by means of which it can be distinguished or identified. During a psychoanalytic treatment, the patient allows the analyst to play a predominating role in his emotional life. This is of great importance in the analytic process. After the treatment for and situation is changed. The patient builds up feelings of affection for the resistance to his analyst which, in their ebb ans flow, so exceed the normal degree of feeling that the phenomenon has long since actuated the theoretical interests of the analyst. Freud studied this phenomenon thoroughly, explained it, and gave it the name 'transference'

I cannot reproduce for you, all of Freud's research about the transference, bu t must limit myself to essentials, such as the statement of 'counter-transference', is the emotional attitude of the analyst toward the patient, the analyst toward his charge, the therapist toward the patient. The feeling which the child develops for the mentor is conditioned by a much earlier relationship to someone else. We must take cognizance of this fact in order to understand these relationships. The tender relationship which go to make up the child's love life are no longer strange to us. Many of these have already been touched upon in the foregoing contentual frames. We have learned how the small boy takes the father and mother as love objects. We gave in following the striving which arose in this relationship, the oedipus situation, in that we have seen how this runs its course and terminates in an identification with the parent. We have also had opportunity to consider the relationship between brothers and sisters, how their original rivalry is transformed into affection through the pressure of their feeling for the parent. We know that the boy at puberty must give up his first love objects within the family and transfer his libido to individuals exteriority or outside of the family. not allows the analyst to play a predominating role in his emotional life. This is of great importance in the analytic process, after all the treatment for and situation is changed, as the patient builds up feelings of affection for the resistance to his analyst which, in their ebb and flow, exceed the normal degree of feeling that the phenomenon has long since actuated the theoretical interests of the analyst. Freud studied this phenomenon thoroughly, explained it, and gave it the name 'transference'

I cannot reproduce for you, all of Freud's research about the transference, but must limit myself to essentials, such as the statement of 'counter-transference', is the emotional attitude of the analyst toward the patient, the analyst toward his charge, the therapist toward the patient. The feeling which the child develops for the mentor is conditioned by a much earlier relationship to someone else. We must take cognizance of this fact in order to understand these relationships. The tender relationship which go to make up the child's love life are no longer strange to us. Many of these have already been touched upon in the foregoing contentual frames. We have learned how the small boy takes the father and mother as love objects. We gave in following the striving which arise in this relationship, the oedipus situation, we have seen how this runs its course and terminates in an identification with the parent. We have also had opportunity to consider the relationship between brothers and sisters, how their original rivalry is transformed into affection through the pressure of their feeling for the parent. We know that the boy at puberty must give up his first love objects within the family and transfer his libido to the individuals exteriority or outside of the family.

The key to understanding the essential pathology as well as the therapeutical impasse was in the failure of the patient to develop a reliable working relation with the analyst. In each case the patient was unable to either establish or maintain a durable working alliance with the analyst and the analyst neglected this fact, pursuing instead the analyst of other transference phenomena, as this error in technique was observable in psychoanalysts with a wide range of clinical experience and to recognize the same shortcomings when resuming the transference interpretations.

In this connection, and, if transference is to be regarded as a significant ego function, a number of inferences are rather obvious. One is that analysis does not 'cause' transference. Yet, although not caused by analysis, transference as it occurs in analysis does seem unique. What is unique, however, may not be transference itself, but rather the effect upon transference of the unique conditions of the analytic situation. These conditions may affect most strongly such things as the choice of content of transference reaction, the intensity of these reactions, their exclusiveness, and their sharp focus on the person of the analyst. Although, as a result of these conditions, transference developments in analysis may differ from those occurring elsewhere, this does not mean that in analysis transference as a function is any different.

Another rather obvious inference, following from the first, is that transference can never be resolved. The content may be, but not the function. Through analysis, the symptomatic, neurotic and historical plexuity have been brought into the transference may be resolved, but not the function itself. The function of transference, like other functions of the ego, may be affected by analysis in many ways, but it never goes away.

Still, another inference is a general one concerning transference and the analyst. If transference is to be regarded as an ever active ego function, then the analyst's transference goes on all the time too, just like the patient's, and despite what he might wish to think. His transference has not been resolved in his own analysis. Admittedly, the impact of the analytic situation upon the analyst is vastly different from what it is upon the patient, but many aspects of that situation do favour development in the analyst of transference relations involving his patient. This does not mean, however, that it would be correct too believe the analyst should attempt to inhibit his transference function, much less disavow it. Yet, what the analyst should do about this transference is a question that has never been significantly pondered over. Aside from any belief that the analyst's transference is remarkably useful in the process of analysing and may be essential for certain aspects of analysis, what can be said?

Would it be wrong, to propose that this ego function be dealt within the same way the analyst deals with his other ego function? Just as the analyst must consciously regulate his responses to the functions in order to create and sustain the analytic situation, should he not also regulate his responses to his transference activity?

This does not mean nor should mean his responses and sustain the analytic situation he not also regulate his responses to his transference activity? This does not mean, not to be thought that the analyst must decide either whether or when a transference reaction to his patient exists. Such an attempt is the point on which has in itself, at least two counts. For one thing, significant transference reactions are usually not conscious, and, fo r another, transference activity in some form is always going on.

In view of these considerations, the simplest position for the analyst to take, and the one most likely to be helped, may be to assume that all feelings and reactions of the analyst concerning the patient are 'prima-facie' evidence of the analyst's transference. Under this arrangement every feeling of warmth, pity, sadness, anger, hope, excitement, even interest, every feeling of coldness, indifference, disinterest, boredom, impatience, discouragement, and every absence of feeling, should be assumed to contain significant elements of the analyst's transference as focussed on the patient. This would mean, essentially, that everything arising in the analyst about his patient assumed to be part of the substance of analysis, that nothing presents merely the analyst's 'real' reaction to his patient, and that especially when something seems most real it can be counted on to contain important aspects of the analyst's transference.

Were the analyst to take this rather imperative view of his own transference potential, he might be much more likely to remain abreast of the personal, neurotic meaning of the myriad but often subtle reactions and attitudes he develops toward his patient. This in turn might make it possible for him, at least to keep his transference out of the patient's way and hopefully to use it to further the analysis.

Th e final inference from all this is perhaps the most promising. This is that transference, if it belongs to the family of ego functions, can be counted on to posses many of this family 's characteristics. Thus, presently existing knowledge about the ego should provide many ready-made leads as to the nature of transference. The ego's way of reality testing, for instance, its responses to internal and external stimuli, its uses of defence mechanisms, may all reveal much about the basic phenomenology of transference. Similarly, much may be surmised about transference's functional vicissitudes by assuming that transference suffers the same general developmental and neurotic deficiencies, distortions, limitations, and fixations to which various other functions of the ego are susceptible. A particularly important study would seem to be the special strengths of transference functioning, especially its way of joining with other agencies to serve and facilitate the individual's idiosyncratic interests and developments. Such a study, for instance, might centre on the ego's object relations to the reference to the question of whether transference is the ego function mainly responsibly for their development.

Viewing transference in this way as an ego function means, of course, relinquishing certain elements of our existing viewpoint. One prominent feature of these existing viewpoints, no matter what form they take, is how hard they are to define or even to elicit. Another is how unquestioning we seem to be about the viewpoints we grew up with, how easily we assume transference to be, but a therapeutically helpful given, an isolated psychological event having little to do with other psychological event s, and, except in the analytic situation, to be lacking useful purpose. Assigned, without even wondering why, to neither ego nor id, it is usually dropped somewhere in-between. Labelled but rarely described, it is most commonly called a 'projection' or a 'repetition' of the past, neither of them labels of great distinction.

Nevertheless, no matter how inadequate the form in which transference presently exists, it is a form that is deeply entrenched and that does not beg for change. Accordingly, wresting transference from its syntonic limbo is not likely to be easy and may be impossible, but doing so, bringing it out into open view where it can be contemplated as a major member of the ego family, is an utterly fascinating prospect, one that permits one to see transference not only as the best tool clinical analysis has, but possibly the best tool the ego has. It well may be, as Freud suggested, the basis of all human relationship and, as suggested, many may be involved in all the ego's differentiations, integrative and creative capacities. It is these aspects of transference that offer the most exciting questions, and it is with these questions that we will continue.

Without minor exceptions or flaws we are founded against the realm of fact that holds with the distinctive quality of being actual, but, nonetheless, it was from very early times that Freud had called attention to the fact that transference manifested itself in two ways - negatively as well as positively - a good deal less said or known about the negative transference than about the positive. This, of course, corresponds to the circumstance that interest in the destructive and aggressive impulses in general, is only a comparatively recent development. Transference was regarded predominantly as a libidinal phenomena. It was suggested that in everyone there existed a certain number of unsatisfied libidinal impulses, and that whenever some new person came upon the scene these impulses were readily attach themselves to him. This was the account of transferences a universal phenomenon. In neurotics, owing to the abnormally large quantities of unattached libido present in the tendency to transference would be correspondingly greater, and the peculiar circumstances of the analytic situation would further increase it. It was evidently the existence of these feelings of love, thrown by the patient upon the analyst, that provided the necessary y extra force to induce his ego to give up its resistance, undo the repressions and adopt a fresh solution of its ancient problems. This instrument, without which no therapeutic result could be obtained, was at once seen to be no stranger; it was in fact the familiar power of suggestion, which had ostensibly been abandoned long before. Now, however, it was being employed in the very different way, in fact in a contrary direction. In pre-analytic days it had aimed at bringing about an increase in the degree of repression, now it was used to overcome the resistance of the ego, that is to say, to allow the repression to be removed.

But the situation became more and more complicated as more facts about transference came to light. In the first place, the feelings transferred turned out to be of various sorts, besides the loving ones there were the hostile ones, which were naturally far from assisting the analyst's efforts. But, even apart from the hostile transference. The libidinal feelings themselves fell into two groups; friendly and affectionate feeling which were capable of being conscious, and purely erotic ones which has usually too remain unconscious. And these latter feelings, when they became too powerful, stirred up the repressive forces of the ego and thus increased its resistance instead of diminishing them, and in fact produced a state of things that was not easily distinguishable, from a negative transference. And beyond all this there arose the whole question of the lack of permanence of all suggestive treatments. Did not the existence of the transference threaten to leave the analytic patient in the same unending dependence upon the analyst?

All of these difficulties were got over by the discovery that the transference itself could be analyzed. Its analysis was soon found to be the most important part of the whole treatment. It was possible to make consciously its roots in the repressed unconscious just as it was possible to make conscious any other repressed material - that is, by inducing the ego to abandon its resistance - and there was nothing self-contradictory in the fact that the forces used for resolving the transference was the transference itself. And once it had been made conscious, its unmanageable, infantile, permanent characteristics disappeared, what was left was like any other 'real' human relationship. But the necessity for constantly analysing the transference became still more apparent from another discovery. It was found that, as work proceeded the transference tended, as, it were, to eat up the entire analysis. More and more of the patient's libido became concentrated upon their relation to the analyst, the patient 's original symptoms were drained of their cathexis, yet and there appeared instead an artificial neurosis to which Freud gave the name of the 'transference neurosis'. This original conflict, which have to the onset of neurosis, began to be re-enacted in the relation to the analyst, now this unexpected event is far from being the misfortune than at first. Sight it might seem to be. In fact, it gives us our great opportunity. Instead, of having to deal as best we may with conflicts of the remote past, Which are concerned with dead circumstances and mummified personalities, and whose outcome is already determined, we find ourselves involved in an actual and immediate situation, in which we and the patient are the principal characters and the development of which is to some re-extent, at least under control. But if we bring it about, that in this revivified transference conflict the patient chooses a new solution instead of the old one, a solution in which the primitive and unadaptable methods of repression is replaced by behaviour more in contact with reality, then, even after his detachment from the analysis, he will never be able to fall back into his former necrosis, the solution of the transference conflict implies as the simultaneous solution of the infantile conflict of which it is a new edition. The 'blame', says Freud in his, 'Introductory Lectures' has been made possible by alterations in the ego's occurring as a consequent of the analyst's suggestion. At the expense of the unconscious, the ego becomes wider by the words of interpretation. In which brings the unconscious material into consciousness; through education it becomes reconciled to the individual and is made willing to grant it a certain degree of satisfaction, and its horror of the claim of its libido is lessoned by the new capacity it acquires to expend a certain amount of the libido in sublimation, the more nearly the course of the treatment corresponds with this ideal description the greater will be the success of the psycho-analytic therapy.

Freud made it clear that the ultimate factor in the therapeutic action of psychoanalysis was suggestion on the part of the analyst acting upon the patient's ego in such a way as to make it more tolerant of the libidinal trends. However, Freud had produced extremely little that bears on the subject, and that little goes to show that he had not altered his views on the main principles involved. In additional lectures which were published last year, he explicitly states that he has nothing to add to the theoretical discussions upon therapy given in the original lectures fifteen years earlier. At the same time, there has in the interval been a considerable further development of his theoretical opinions. And especially in the region of ego-psychology. He had, in particular, formulated the concept of the super-ego. The restatement in super-ego terms of analysis may not involve many changes. But it is reasonable of resistance information about the super-ego will be of special interest from our point of view, and in two ways. In th e first place, it would at first glance seem highly probable that the super-ego should play an important part, direct or indirect, in the setting up and maintaining of the repressions and resistance the demolition of which has been the chief aim of analysis, and is confirmed by an examination of the classification of the various kinds of resistance made by Freud in, 'Hemmung Symptom and Amgst' (1926). Of the five sorts of resistance there mentioned it is true that only one is attributed to the direct intervention of the super-ego, but two of the ego-resistance - the repression resistance and the transference resistance - although actually originally from the ego, as a rule set up by out of fear of the super-ego. It seems likely enough therefore that when Freud wrote the words which, in effect, are the favourable change in the patient. 'Is made possible by alterations in the ego', he was thinking, in part at all events, of that portion of the ego which he subsequently separated off into the super-ego? Quite apart from this, moreover, in another of Freud's more recent works, 'The Group Psychology' (1921), there are passages which suggest a different point - namely, that it may be largely through the patient's super-ego that the analyst on the nature of hypnosis and suggestion. He definitely rejects Bernheim's view that all hypnotic phenomena are traceable to the factor of suggestion, and adopts an alterative theory that suggestion is a partial manifestation of the state of hypnosis. The state of hypnosis, again, is found in certain respects, to resemble the state of being in love. There is, 'the same humble subjection, the same compliance, the same absence of criticism toward the hypnotist as towardly the loved object, has stepped into the place of the subject's ego-ideal'. Now since suggestion is a partial form of hypnosis and since the analyst brings about his changes in the patient's attitude by means of suggestion. It seems to follow that the analyst owes into effectiveness, at all events in some respects, to his having stepped into the place of th e patient's super-ego. Thus, there are two convergent lines of argument which point to the patient's super-ego as occupying a key position in analytic therapy. It is a part of the patient's mind in which a favourable alteration would be likely to lead to general improvement, and it is a part of the patient's mind which is especially subject to the analyst's influence.

Such plausible notions as these were followed up almost immediately after the super-ego made its first début. It has been developed by Ernest Jones, for instance, in his paper on, 'The Nature of Auto-Suggestion'. Soon thereafter, Alexander launches his theory that the principal aim of all psycho-analytic therapy must be the complete demolition of the super-ego and the assumption of its functions by the ego. According to his account, the super-ego are handed over to the analyst, and in the second phase they are passed back again to th e patient, but this time to his ego. The super-ego, according to this view of Alexander's (though he explicitly limits his use of the word to the unconscious parts of the ego-ideal), is a portion of the fundamental apparatuses which is essentially primitive, out of data and out of touch with reality, which is incapable of adapting itself, and which operates automatically, with the monotonous uniformity of a reflex. Any useful functions that it performs can be carried out by the ego. And there is therefore, nothing to be done with it but to discard it. This wholesome attack upon the super-ego seems to be of questionable validity. It seems probable that its abolition, even if that were practical politics, would involve the abolition of a large number off highly desirable mental activities. But the idea that the analyst temporarily takes over the functions of the patient's super-ego during the treatment and by so doing on some way alters it agrees with the tentative literatures.

So, too, do some passages in a paper by Radô upon 'The Economic Principle in

Psycho-Analytic Technique'. The second, as such was to have dealt with psych-analysis, that in which has unfortunately never been published, but the first one, on hypnotism and catharsis, contains much that is of interest. It includes a theory that the hypnotic subject introjects the hypnotist in the form of what Radô calls a 'parasitic super-ego', which draw off the energy and takes over the functions of the subject's original super-ego. One feature of the situation brought out by Radô is the unstable and temporary nature of this whole arrangement. If, for instance, the hypnotist gives a command, which is too much in opposition to the subject's original super-ego. The parasite is promptly excluded. And, in any case, when the state of hypnosis comes to an end, the sway of the parasite super-ego also terminates and the original super-ego resumes its functions.

However debatable may be the details of Radô description, it not only emphasizes once again, the notion of the super-ego as the function of psych-therapy, but it draws attention to the important distinction between the effects of hypnosis and analysis in the matter of permanence. Hypnosis acts essentially in a temporary way, and Radô theory of the parasitic super-ego, which does not really replace the original one but merely throws it out of action, gives a very good picture of its apparent workings. Analysis, on the other hand, in so far as it seeks to effect the patient's super-ego, aims at something much more far-reaching and permanent - namely, at an integral change in the nature of the patient's super-ego itself. Some even more recent developments in psych-analytic theory give a hint, so it seems as though it seems as the kind of thing, that along which a cleaver understanding of the question may perhaps be reached.

This latest growth of theory has been very much occupied with the destructive impulses and has brought them for the first time into the centre of interests, and attention has at the same time been concentrated on the correlated problems of guilt and anxiety. That is to say, that in the mind, especially are the ideas upon the formation of the super-ego, recently developed by Melanie Klein and the importance which she attributes to the processes of 'introjection' and 'projection' in the development of the personality. In a schematic outline, the individual, she holds, is perpetually introjecting and projecting the objects of its id-impulses, and the character of the introjected objects depends on the character of the id-impulses, directed toward the external objects. Thus, for instance, during the stage of a child's libidinal development in which it is dominated by feelings of oral aggression, its feelings toward its external object will be orally aggressive; It will then introject the object, and the introjected object will now act (in the manner of a super-ego) in an orally aggressive way toward the child's ego. (The next even will be the projection of this orally aggressive introjected object back onto the external object, which will now in its turn appear to be orally aggressive). The fact of the external object being thus felt as dangerous and destructive once more causes the id-impulses to adopt an even more aggressive and destructive attitude toward the object in self-defences. A vicious circle is thus launched in the celebrations that this process seeks to account for the extreme severity of the super-ego, in that of small children, as well as for their unreasonable fear of outside objects. In the course of the development of the normal individual, his libido eventually reaches the genital stage, at which the positive impulses predominant, and his attitude toward his external objects will thus become more friendly. That according to his introjected object, or super-ego will become less severe and his ego's contact with reality will be less distorted. In the case of the neurotic, however, for various reasons - whether an account of frustration of the destructive components - development to the genital stage does not occur, but the individual remains fixated at a pre-genital level. His ego is thus left exposed to the pressure of a savage id on the one hand and a correspondingly savage super-ego on the other, and the vicious circle is perpetuated.

At the arriving considerations that are marked and noted, through which the essence of functional dynamics as based of the transference in the psychoanalytic process or the basic underlying the most basic of beliefs that in politics there is neither good nor evil, however, in that something that forms part of the minimal body, character or structure of that thing predetermines the properties to the good life. Nonetheless, most psychoanalysts maintain that schizophrenic patients cannot be treated psychoanalytically because they are too narcissistic to develop with the psychotherapist as interpersonal relationship that is sufficiently reliable and consistent for psychoanalytic work. Freud, Fenichel and others have recognized that a new technique of approaching patients psychoanalytically must be found if analysts are to work with psychotics. Among those who have worked successfully in recent years with schizophrenics, Sullivan, Hill, and Karl Menninger and his staffs have made various modifications of their analytic approach. The techniques that are in use with psychotics are different from our approach to psychoneurotics. This is not a result of the schizophrenic's inability to build up a consistent personal relationship with the therapist but due to his extremely intense and sensitive transference reactions.

Let us see first what the essences of the schizophrenic's transference reactions are and how we try to meet these reactions.

We think of a schizophrenic as a person who has had serious traumatic experiences in early infancy at a time when his ego and its ability to examine reality were not yet developed. These early traumatic experiences seem to furnish the psychological basis for the pathogenic influence of the flustrations of later years. At this early time the infant lives grandiosely in a narcissistic world of his own. His needs and desires seem to be taken care of by something vague and indefinite which he does not yet differentiate. As Ferenczi noted, they are expressed by gestures and movements since speech is as yet undeveloped. Frequently the child's desires are fulfilled without any expression of them, a result that seems to him a product of his magical thinking.

Are a person's characteristics primarily shaped by early influences, remaining relatively stable thereafter throughout life? Or does change spontaneously occur continuously throughout life? Many people believe that early experiences are formative, providing a strong or weak foundation for later psychological growth. This view is expressed in the popular saying 'As the twig is bent, so grows the tree.' From this perspective, it is crucial to ensure that young children have a good start in life. But many developmental scientists believe that later experiences can modify or even reverse early influences; studies show that even when early experiences are traumatic or abusive, considerable recovery can occur. From this vantage point, early experiences influence, but rarely determine, later characteristics.

Traumatic experiences in this early period of life will damage a personality more seriously than those occurring in later childhood such as are found in the history of psychoneurotics. The infant's mind is more vulnerable the younger and less used it has been, furthers, the trauma has quickened the infant 's egocentricity. In addition early traumatic experiences shorten the only period in life in which an individual ordinarily enjoys the most security, thus endangering the ability to store up as it was a reasonable supplies of assurance and self-reliance for the individual's later struggles through life. Thus, as such, a child sensitized considerably more toward the frustrations of later like than by later traumatic experiences. hence many experiences in later life which would mean little to a 'healthy' person and not much to a psychoneurotic, mean a great deal of pain and suffering to the schizophrenic. His resistance against frustration is easily exhausted.

Once he reaches his limit of endurance, he escapes the unbearable reality of his present life by attempting to reestablish the autistic, delusional world of the infant, but this is impossible because the content of his delusions and hallucinations are naturally coloured by the experiences of his whole lifetime.

How do these developments influence the patient's attitude toward the analyst and the analyst's approach to him?

Due to the very damage and the succeeding chain of frustrations which the schizophrenic undergoes before finally giving in to illness, he feels extremely suspicious and distrustful of everyone, particularly of the psychotherapist ho approaches him with the intent of intruding into his isolated world and personal life. To him the physician's approach means the threat of being compelled to return to the frustrations of real life and to reveal his inadequacy to meet them or, - still worse – a repetition of the aggressive interference with his initial symptoms and peculiarities which he has encountered in his previous environment.

The difficulty that the patient's dilemma through his frustrations is the product through which is called 'delusion': Delusion itself is a false belief which is firmly held by a person even though other people recognize the belief as obviously untrue. For example, a person who truly believes he is Napoleon Blonaparte is delusional. Religious beliefs or popular conceptions, such as the beliefs that people have been abducted by aliens, are not delusions because they are widely held beliefs. Delusions are a type of psychotic symptom that indicate a person has lost contact with reality.

There are many different types of delusions. A person with a paranoid delusion believes that others - such as the FBI, or the CIA, even the Mafia as trying to harm or plot against him. A person with a delusion of reference believes that events or people refer specifically to him or her when they do not. For example, a woman with schizophrenia may believe that a television news broadcaster is talking personally to her rather than to the entire viewing audience. A grandiose delusion is a belief that one is extremely famous or that one has special powers, such as the ability to magically heal people.

A delusion of control is a belief that others are able to control one's thoughts, feelings, or actions. For example, a man with this type of delusion may believe that someone has implanted a microchip in his brain that enables other people to control his thoughts. A somatic delusion is a belief that something is wrong with one's body - for example, that one's brain is rotting away - even though no medical evidence supports this belief. A person with an erotic delusion believes that someone is in love with him or her despite a lack of evidence for this belief. In a delusion of jealousy, a person believes that his or her spouse or lover is unfaithful despite evidence to the contrary.

Delusions commonly occur in certain severe mental illnesses, such as schizophrenia, bipolar disorder (also called manic-depressive illness), some cases of major depression, Dissociative disorders, post-traumatic stress disorder, and paranoid personality disorder. In addition, delusions may result from abuse of certain drugs, including alcohol, cocaine, amphetamines, and hallucinogens such as lysergic acid diethylamide (LSD), phencyclidine (PCP), and mescaline. Medical conditions affecting the brain, such as syphilis and brain tumours, may also cause delusions.

Delusional disorder is a relatively uncommon mental illness characterized by delusions. People with this disorder have one or more delusions that persist for at least one month. In addition, they do not suffer from other symptoms of schizophrenia, such as disorganized speech and bizarre behaviour. Usually their delusions are less bizarre than those that occur in schizophrenia and seem merely odd or unsupported by facts. Examples of nonbizarre delusions include beliefs that one is being followed, loved by someone famous, or deceived by one's spouse. Because delusional disorder is relatively rare, little research has systematically examined its treatment. However, doctors most often use Antipsychotic drugs (also called neuroleptics) to treat this disorder. These drugs help reduce or eliminate delusions, hallucinations, and other psychotic symptoms.

In spite of his narcissistic retreat, every schizophrenic has some underlying notion of the unreality and loneliness of his substitute delusionary world. He longs for human contact and understanding, yet is afraid to admit of himself, or his therapist for fear of further frustration.

That is why the patient may take weeks and months to test the analyst before being willing to accept him, however, once he has accepted him. His dependence on the analyst is greater and he is more sensitive about it than is the psychoneurotic because of the schizophrenic's deeply rooted insecurity, the narcissistic seemingly self-righteous attitude is but a defence.

Whenever the analyst fails the patient from reasons to be discussed later - one cannot at times avoid failing one's schizophrenic patients - it will be severe disappointment and a repetition of the chain of frustrations the schizophrenic has previously endured.

The instinctually primitive part of the schizophrenic's mind that does not discriminate between himself and the environment, it may mean the withdrawal of the impersonal supporting forces of his infancy. Severe anxiety will follow this vital deprivation.

In the light of his personal relationship with the analyst it means that the therapist seduced the patient to use him as a bridge over which he might possibly be led from the utter loneliness of his own world to reality and human warmth, only to have him discover that this bridge is not reliable. if so, he will respond helplessly with an outburst of hostility or with renewed withdrawal as may be seen most impressively in catatonic stupor.

The symptoms of mental illness can be very distressing. People who develop schizophrenia may hear voices inside their head that say nasty things about them or command them to act in strange or unpredictable ways. Or they may be paralysed by paranoia—the deep conviction that everyone, including their closest family members, wants to injure or destroy them. People with major depression may feel that nothing brings pleasure and that life is so dreary and unhappy that it is better to be dead. People with panic disorder may experience heart palpitations, rapid breathing, and anxiety so extreme that they may not be able to leave home. People whom experience episodes of mania may engage in reckless sexual behaviour or may spend money indiscriminately, acts that later cause them to feel guilt, shame, and desperation.

Other mental illnesses, while not always debilitating, create certain problems in living. People with personality disorders may experience loneliness and isolation because their personality style interferes with social relations. People with an eating disorder may become so preoccupied with their weight and appearance that they force themselves to vomit or refuse to eat. Individuals who develop post-traumatic stress disorder may become angry easily, experience disturbing memories, and have trouble concentrating.

Experiences of mental illness often interact differently but depend on one's culture or social group, sometimes greatly so. For example, in most of the non-Western world, people with depression complain principally of physical ailments, such as lack of energy, poor sleep, loss of appetite, and various kinds of physical pain. Indeed, even in North America these complaints are commonplace. But in the United States and other Western societies, depressed people and mental health professionals who treat them tend to emphasize psychological problems, such as feelings of sadness, worthlessness, and despair. The experience of schizophrenia also differs by culture. In India, one-third of the new cases of schizophrenia involve catatonia, a behaviourial condition in which a person maintains a bizarre statue like pose for hours or days. This condition is rare in Europe and North America.

With appropriate treatment, most people can recover from mental illness and return to normal life. Even those with persistent, long-term mental illnesses can usually learn to manage their symptoms and live productive lives.

By a variety of symptoms, including loss of contact with reality, bizarre behaviour, disorganized thinking and speech, decreased emotional expressiveness, and social withdrawal. Usually only some of these symptoms occur in any one person. The term schizophrenia comes from Greek words meaning 'split mind.' However, contrary to common belief, schizophrenia does not refer to a person with a split personality or multiple personality. For a description of a mental illness in which a person has multiple personalities. To observers, schizophrenia may seem or appear for being as some sorted kind of madness or a manufacturing insanity.

Perhaps more than any other mental illness, schizophrenia has a debilitating effect on the lives of the people who suffer from it. A person with schizophrenia may have difficulty telling the difference between real and unreal experiences, logical and illogical thoughts, or appropriate and inappropriate behaviour. Schizophrenia seriously impairs a person's ability to work, go to school, enjoy relationships with others, or take care of oneself. In addition, people with schizophrenia frequently require hospitalization because they pose a danger to themselves. About 10 percent of people with schizophrenia commit suicide, and many others attempt suicide. Once people develop schizophrenia, they usually suffer from the illness for the rest of their lives. Although there is no cure, treatment can help many people with schizophrenia lead productive lives.

Schizophrenia also carries an enormous cost to society. People with schizophrenia occupy about one-third of all beds in psychiatric hospitals in the United States. In addition, people with schizophrenia account for at least 10 percent of the homeless population in the United States. The National Institute of Mental Health has estimated that schizophrenia costs the United States tens of billions of dollars each year in direct treatment, social services, and lost productivity.

Approximately 1 percent of people develop schizophrenia at some time during their lives.

Experts estimate that about 1.8 million people in the United States have schizophrenia. The prevalence of schizophrenia is the same regardless of sex, race, and culture. Although women are just as likely as men to develop schizophrenia, women tend to experience the illness less severely, with fewer hospitalizations and better social functioning in the community.

Schizophrenia usually develops in late adolescence or early adulthood, between the ages of 15 and 30. Much less commonly, schizophrenia develops later in life. The illness may begin abruptly, but it usually develops slowly over months or years. Mental health professionals diagnose schizophrenia based on an interview with the patient in which they determine whether the person has experienced specific symptoms of the illness.

Symptoms and functioning in people with schizophrenia tend to vary over time, sometimes worsening and other times improving. For many patients the symptoms gradually become less severe as they grow older. About 25 percent of people with schizophrenia become symptom-free later in their lives.

A variety of symptoms characterize schizophrenia. The most prominent include symptoms of psychosis—such as delusions and hallucinations - as well as bizarre behaviour, strange movements, and disorganized thinking and speech. Many people with schizophrenia do not recognize that their mental functioning is disturbed.

Delusions are false beliefs that appear obviously untrue to other people. For example, a person with schizophrenia may believe that he is the king of England when he is not. People with schizophrenia may have delusions that others, such as the police or the FBI, are plotting against them or spying on them. They may believe that aliens are controlling their thoughts or that their own thoughts are being broadcast to the world so that other people can hear them.

Research suggests that the genes one inherits strongly influence one's risk of developing schizophrenia. Studies of families have shown that the more close one is related to someone with schizophrenia, the greater the risk one has of developing the illness. For example, the children of one parent with schizophrenia have about a 13 percent chance of developing the illness, and children of two parents with schizophrenia have about a 46 percent chance of eventually developing schizophrenia. This increased risk occurs even when such children are adopted and raised by mentally healthy parents. In comparison, children in the general population have only about a 1 percent chance of developing schizophrenia.

Some evidence suggests that schizophrenia may result from an imbalance of chemicals in the brain called neurotransmitters. These chemicals enable neurons (brain cells) to communicate with each other. Some scientists suggest that schizophrenia results from excess activity of the neurotransmitter dopamine in certain parts of the brain or from an abnormal sensitivity to dopamine. Support for this hypothesis comes from Antipsychotic drugs, which reduce psychotic symptoms in schizophrenia by blocking brain receptors for dopamine. In addition, amphetamines, which increase dopamine activity, intensify psychotic symptoms in people with schizophrenia. Despite these findings, many experts believe that excess dopamine activity alone cannot account for schizophrenia. Other neurotransmitters, such as serotonin and norepinephrine, may play important roles as well.

Although scientists favour a biological cause of schizophrenia, stress in the environment may affect the onset and course of the illness. Stressful life circumstances - such as maturing in age and character as for living in poverty, the death of a loved one, an important change in jobs or relationships, or chronic tension and hostility at home—can increase the chances of schizophrenia in a person biologically predisposed to the disease. In addition, stressful events can trigger a relapse of symptoms in a person who already has the illness. Individuals who have effective skills for managing stress may be less susceptible to its negative effects. Psychological and social rehabilitation can help patients develop more effective skills for dealing with stress.

Although there is no cure for schizophrenia, effective treatment exists that can improve the long-term course of the illness. With many years of treatment and rehabilitation, significant numbers of people with schizophrenia experience partial or full remission of their symptoms.

Treatment of schizophrenia usually involves a combination of medication, rehabilitation, and treatment of other problems the person may have. Antipsychotic drugs (also called neuroleptics) are the most frequently used medications for treatment of schizophrenia. Psychological and social rehabilitation programs may help people with schizophrenia function in the community and reduce stress related to their symptoms. Treatment of secondary problems, such as substance abuse and infectious diseases, is also an important part of an overall treatment program.

Antipsychotic medications, developed in the mid-1950s, can dramatically improve the quality of life for people with schizophrenia. The drugs reduce or eliminate psychotic symptoms such as hallucinations and delusions. The medications can also help prevent these symptoms from returning. Common Antipsychotic drugs include risperidone (Risperdal), olanzapine (Zyprexa), clozapine (Clozaril), quetiapine (Seroquel), haloperidol (Haldol), thioridazine (Mellaril), chlorpromazine (Thorazine), fluphenazine (Prolixin), and trifluoperazine (Stelazine). People with schizophrenia usually must take medication for the rest of their lives to control psychotic symptoms. Antipsychotic medications appear to be less effective at treating other symptoms of schizophrenia, such as social withdrawal and apathy.

Because many patients with schizophrenia continue to experience difficulties despite taking medication, psychological and social rehabilitation is often necessary. A variety of methods can be effective. Social skills training help people with schizophrenia learn specific behaviours for functioning in society, such as making friends, purchasing items at a store, or initiating conversations. Behaviourial training methods can also help them learn self-care skills such as personal hygiene, money management, and proper nutrition. In addition, cognitive-behaviourial therapy, a type of psychotherapy, can help reduce persistent symptoms such as hallucinations, delusions, and social withdrawal.

Because many patients have difficulty obtaining or keeping jobs, supported employment programs that help patients find and maintain jobs are a helpful part of rehabilitation. In these programs, the patient works alongside people without disabilities and earns competitive wages. An employment specialist (or vocational specialist) helps the person maintain their job by, for example, training the person in specific skills, helping the employer accommodate the person, arranging transportation, and monitoring performance. These programs are most effective when the supported employment is closely integrated with other aspects of treatment, such as medication and monitoring of symptoms.

Some people with schizophrenia are vulnerable to frequent crises because they do not regularly go to mental health centres to receive the treatment they need. These individuals often relapse and face rehospitalization. To ensure that such patients take their medication and receive appropriate psychological and social rehabilitation, assertive community treatment (ACT) programs have been developed that deliver treatment to patients in natural settings, such as in their homes, in restaurants, or on the street.

People with schizophrenia often have other medical problems, so an effective treatment program must attend to these as well. One of the most generally shared in or participated in things conforming to a type without noteworthy excellence or faults just as common a rule, by ordinary, frequent and ordinarily as an idea or expression deficient in originality or freshness, yet, only of its exchanging the commonplace of the common associated problems is vehemently and usually coarsely expressed condemnation or disapproved, as the interpretative category of an unequalled vocabulary is itself a genuine abuse. Successful treatment of substance abuse inpatients with schizophrenia requires careful coordination with their mental health care, so that the same clinicians are treating both disorders at the same time.

The high rate of substance abuse in patients with schizophrenia contributes to a high prevalence of infectious diseases, including hepatitis B and C and the human immunodeficiency virus (HIV). Assessment, education, and treatment or management of these illnesses is critical for the long-term health of patients.

Other problems frequently associated with schizophrenia include housing instability and homelessness, legal problems, violence, trauma and post-traumatic stress disorder, anxiety, depression, and suicide attempts. Close monitoring and psychotherapeutic interventions are often helpful in addressing these problems.

Several other psychiatric disorders are closely related to schizophrenia. In schizoaffective disorder, a person shows symptoms of schizophrenia combined with either mania or severe depression. Schizophreniform disorder refers to an illness in which a person experiences schizophrenic symptoms for more than one month but fewer than six months. In schizotypal personality disorder, a person engages in odd thinking, speech, and behaviour, but usually does not lose contact with reality. Sometimes mental health professionals refer to these disorders together as schizophrenia-spectrum disorders.

Severe mental illness almost always alters a person's life dramatically. People with severe mental illnesses experience disturbing symptoms that can cause of such difficulties and holding to a job, or go to school, relate to others, or cope with ordinary life demands. Some individuals require hospitalization because they become unable to care for themselves or because they are at risk of committing suicide.

The symptoms of mental illness can be very distressing. People who develop schizophrenia may hear voices inside their head that say nasty things about them or command them to act in strange or unpredictable ways. Or they may be paralysed by paranoia - the deep conviction that everyone, including their closest family members, wants to injure or destroy them. People with major depression may feel that nothing brings pleasure and that life is so dreary and unhappy that it is better to be dead. People with panic disorder may experience heart palpitations, rapid breathing, and anxiety so extreme that they may not be able to leave home. People whom experience episodes of mania may engage in reckless sexual behaviour or may spend money indiscriminately, acts that later cause them to feel guilt, shame, and desperation.

Other mental illnesses, while not always debilitating, create certain problems in living. People with personality disorders may experience loneliness and isolation because their personality style interferes with social relations. People with an eating disorder may become so preoccupied with their weight and appearance that they force themselves to vomit or refuse to eat. Individuals who develop post-traumatic stress disorder may become angry easily, experience disturbing memories, and have trouble concentrating.

Experiences of mental illness often take issue upon its stability for depending on one's culture or social group, sometimes greatly so. For example, in most of the non-Western world, people with depression complain principally of physical ailments, such as lack of energy, poor sleep, loss of appetite, and various kinds of physical pain. Indeed, even in North America these complaints are commonplace. But in the United States and other Western societies, depressed people and mental health professionals who treat them tend to emphasize psychological problems, such as feelings of sadness, worthlessness, and despair. The experience of schizophrenia also differs by culture. In India, one-third of the new cases of schizophrenia involve catatonia, a behaviourial condition in which a person maintains a bizarre statue like pose for hours or days. This condition is rare in Europe and North America.

Of furthering issues regarding depersonalization disorder, meaning, in effect, that it is a categorised illness based within its intendment for being an illness, of mind, in which people experience an unwelcome sense of detachment from their own bodies. They may feel as though they are floating above the ground, outside observers of their own mental or physical processes. Other symptoms may include a feeling that they or other people are mechanical or unreal, a feeling of being in a dream, a feeling that their hands or feet are larger or smaller than usual, and a deadening of emotional responses. These symptoms are chronic and severe enough to impede normal functioning in a social, school, or work environment.

Depersonalization disorder is a relatively rare syndrome thought to result from severe psychological stress. It may occur as part of other mental illnesses, especially anxiety disorders. For example, some people with panic disorder feel nervous, have a sense of doom about their future and health, and have a troubling sense of detachment form the lose in the attemptive use in making or doing or achieving a useful regularity as might the quality of being expected of the control over their bodies. Depersonalization disorder may also be a component of more severe mental illness, such as schizophrenia. Treatment may include training in relaxation techniques that enhance body perception and control, hypnosis to modify symptoms, and psychotherapy to explore possible stress-related components of the disorder.

Psychiatrists classify depersonalization disorder as one of the Dissociative disorders. Such disorders involve a disruption of consciousness, memory, identity, or perception.

All the while, the schizophrenic responds to altercations in the analyst's defections and understanding by corresponding stormy and dramatic changes from love to hatred, from willingness to leave his delusional world to resistance and renewed withdrawal.

As understandable as these changes are, nevertheless may come as a surprise to the analyst who frequently has not observed their source, this is quite in contrast to his experience with psychoneurosis whose emotional reactions during an interview he can usually predict. These unpredictable changes seem to be the reason for the conception of the unreliability of the schizophrenic's transference reaction, yet they follow the same dynamic rules as the psychoneurotic's oscillations between positive and negative transference and resistance, however, if the schizophrenic's reactions are stormy and seemingly more unpredictable than those of the psychoneurotic, that instances suggested to be due to the inevitable errors in the analyst's approach to the schizophrenic, of which he himself may be unaware, rather than to the unreliability of the patient's emotional response?

Why is it inevitable that the psychoanalysts disappoint his schizophrenic patient time and again?

The schizophrenic withdraws from painful reality and retires to what resembles the early speechless phase of development where consciousness is not yet crystalized. As the expression of his feelings is not hindered by the convention that he has eliminated, as his thinking, feelings, behaviour and speech - when present - obey the working rules of the archaic unconscious. His thinking is magical and does not follow logical rules. It does not admit to every last 'no' and likewise the no to 'yes': There is no recognition of space and time, I, you, and they, am interchangeable expression through which of symbols and often by movement and gestures rather than by words.

As the schizophrenic is suspicious, he will distrust the words of his analyst. He will interpret them and incidental gestures and attitudes of the analyst according to his own delusional experience. The analyst may not even be aware of these involuntary manifestations of his attitudes, yet they mean much to the hypersensitive schizophrenic who uses them as a means of orienting himself to the therapist's personality and intentions toward him.

In other words, the schizophrenic patient and the therapist are people living in different worlds and no different levels of personal development with different means of expressing and of orienting themselves. We know little about the language of the unconscious that belongs to the schizophrenic, and our access to it is blocked by the very process of our own adjustment to a world the schizophrenic has relinquished, so, we should not be surprised that errors and misunderstandings occur when we under take to communicate and strive for a rapport with him.

Another source of the schizophrenic's disappointment arises form which the analyser accepts and does not interfere with the behaviour of the schizophrenic, his attitude may lead the patient to expect that the analyst will assist in carrying out all the patient's wishes, even though they may not seem to be in his interest to the analyser's and the hospital's in their relationship to society. This attitude of acceptance so different from the patient's previous experiences readily fosters the anticipation that the analyst will try to carry out the patient's suggestion and take his part, even against conventional society with which it should occasionally arise. Frequently it will be wise for the analyst to agree with the patient's wish to remain unbattled and untidy until he is ready to talk about the reasons for his behaviour or to change spontaneously. At other times, he will unfortunately be unable to take the patient's part without being able to make the patient understand and accept the reasons for the analyst's position.

If the analyst is not able to accept the possibility of misunderstanding the reaction of the schizophrenic patient and in turn of being misunderstood by him, it may shake his security with his patient.

That is to say, that, among other things, the schizophrenic, once he accepts the analyst's insecurity. being helpless and open to himself - in spite of his pretended grandiose isolation - he will feel utterly defeated by the insecurity of his would-be helper. Such disappointment may furnish reasons for outbursts of hatred and are comparable to the negative transference reactions of psychoneurosis, yet more intense than these, since they are not limited by the restrictions of the actual world - that is, it exists in or based on fact, its only problem is a sure-enough externalization for which things are existing in the act of being external in something that has existence, ss if it were an actualization as received in the obtainable enactment for being externalized, such that its problem of in some actual life that proves obtainable achieved, in that of doing something that has an existence for having absolute actuality.

These outbursts are accompanied by anxiety, feelings of guilt, and fear of retaliations which in turn lead to increased hostility. Yet this established a vicious circle: We disappoint the patient, he is afraid that we hate him for his hatred and therefore continues to hate us. If in addition he senses that the analyst is afraid of his aggressiveness, it confirms his fear that he is actually considered as some dangerous and unacceptable, and this augments his hatred.

This establishes that the schizophrenics capable of developing strong relationships of love and hatred toward the analyst. After all, one could not be so hostile if it were not for the background of a very close relationship. In addition, the schizophrenic develops transference reactions on the narrower sense which he can differentiate from the actual interpersonal relationship. For which the schizophrenic's emotional reactions toward the analyst have to be met with extreme care and caution. The love which the sensitive schizophrenic feels as he first emerges, and his cautions acceptances of the analyst's warmth of interest are really most delicate and tender things. If the analyst deals with the transference reactions of a psychoneurotic is bad enough, though as a reparable rule, but if he fails with a schizophrenic in meeting positive feelings by pointing it out for instance before the patient indicates that he is ready to discuss it, he may easily freeze to death what has just begun to grow and so destroy any further possibility of therapy.

Some analysts may feel that the atmosphere of complete acceptance and of strict avoidance of any arbitrary denials which we recommend as a basic rule for the treatment of schizophrenics may not avoid our wish to guide of reacceptance of reality, nevertheless, Freud says that every science and therapy which accept his teachings about unconscious, about transference and resistance and about infantile sexuality, may be called psychoanalysis. According in this definition we believe we are practising psychoanalysis with our schizophrenic patients.

Whether we call it analysis or not, it is clear that successful treatment does not depend on technical rules of any special psychiatric school but rather on the basic attitude of individual therapist toward psychologic persons. If he meets them as strangle creatures of another world whose productions are not comprehensible to 'normal' beings, he cannot treat them, if he realizes, however, that the difference between himself and the psychologic is only of degree, and not of kind, he will know better how to meet him. He will not be able to identify himself sufficiently with the patient to understand and accept his emotional reactions without becoming involved in them.

The process of constant and perpetual change is examined and closely matched within the study of philosophical speculations and pointed of a world view which asserts that basic reality is constantly in a process of flux and change. Indeed, reality is identified with pure process. Concepts such as creativity, freedom, novelty, emergence, and growth are fundamental explanatory categories for process philosophy. This metaphysical perspective is to be contrasted with a philosophy of substance, the view that a fixed and permanent reality underlies the changing or fluctuating world of ordinary experience. Whereas substance philosophy emphasizes static being, process philosophy emphasizes dynamically becoming.

Although process philosophy is as old as the 6th-century Bc Greek philosopher, Heraclitus, renewed interest in it was stimulated in the 19th century by the theory of evolution. Key figures in the development of modern process philosophy were the British philosophers Herbert Spencer, Samuel Alexander, and Alfred North Whitehead, the American philosophers Charles S. Peirce and William James, and the French philosophers Henri Bergson and Pierre Teilhard de Chardin. Whitehead's Process and Reality: An Essay in Cosmology (1929) is generally considered the most important systematic expression of process philosophy.

Contemporary theology has been strongly influenced by process philosophy. The American theologian Charles Hartshorne, for instance, rather than interpreting God as an unchanging absolute, emphasizes God's sensitive and caring relationship with the world. A personal God enters into relationships in such a way that he is affected by the relationships, and to be affected by relationships is to change. So too is in the process of growth and development. Important contributions to process theology have also been made by such theologians as William Temple, Daniel Day Williams, Schubert Ogden, and John Cobb, Jr.

'Reality' is a difficult word to use to every one's satisfaction or even to one's own satisfaction. In this instance the word reality is used arbitrarily to designate the direct, here-and-now impact of the analyst upon the patient. Reality. In this sense, contrasts with the impact the analyst has through his representation in the patient's fantasy life, neurosis, and transference, since both kinds of impact seem always to coexist and since the former - the analyst's real impact - may be the worst enemy of the transference, the matter of their differentiation is possibly the most challenging aspect of analysis.

The analytic situation, which is set up to shut out ordinary reality intrusions, that cannot, . . . neither should not exclude all, but to say, that in the beginning months, for instance, reality inevitably has the upper hand. The analyst, the office, the procedure, are all overwhelmingly real. Everything is strange, frightening and exciting, gratifying and frustrating. Unlike the patient can test it and orient himself to it, the impact of this reality is usually so great that even an ordinary useful transference relationship cannot be expected to develop.

Perhaps the most confusing aspect of this beginning period is the frequent appearance in it of what can be regarded as a false transference relationship. With great intensity and clarity, the patient may reveal, through transference-like references about the analyst, some of the deepest secrets only of his neurosis but of its genesis. The pseudotransference, too good to be true, is almost sure to be nothing more than the patient's attempt to deal with the person of the analyst, the entire spectrum of his various patterns of behaviour. If, it is easy to do, the analyst overlooks the likelihood that the patient's relationship with at this time is really about that almost everything said about it is related, analysis may get off to a very bad start. And if, as is even earlier to do, the analyst's interests the genetic meaning of the openly exposed material, a good transference relationship may be seriously delayed and a workable transference neurosis may never appear. even after initial reality has had time to fade, reality may continue to intrude in ways that are very hard to detect and that is very troublesome.

One of the most serious problems of analysis is the very substantial help which the patient receives directly from the analyst and the analytic situation. For many a patient, the analyst in the analytic situation is in fact the most stable, reasonable, wise and understanding person he has ever met, and the setting in which they meet may actually be the most honest, open, direct and regular relationship he has ever experienced. Added to this is the considerable helpfulness to him of being able to clarify his life storey. confess his guilt, express his ambitions, and explore his confusions. Further real help comes from the learning-about-life accruing from the analyst's skilled questions, observations and interpretations. Taken together, the total real value to the patient of the analytic situation can easily be immense. The trouble with this kind of help is that it goes on and on, it may have such a real, direct and continuing impact upon the patient that he can never get deeply enough involved in transference situation to allow him to resolve or even to become acquainted with his most crippling internal difficulties. The trouble is far too good, the trouble also is that we as analysts apparently cannot resist the seductiveness of being directly helpful, and this, when combined with the compelling assumption that helpfulness is bound to be good, permits us top credit patient improvements to 'analysis' when more properly it should often be recognized for being the amounting result for the patient's using the analytic situation, as the model, for being the preceptors and supporter in the dealing practically within the immediate distractions as holding to some problem.

Perhaps, we can now refer to something in a clear unmistakable manner, and it would be to mention, for being, that one more difficult-to-handle intrusion of reality into the analysis, that by saying, that this is the definitive and final interruption of the transference neurosis by the reality of termination; in the sense, the situation is reversed and the intrusion is analytically desirable, since ideally the impact of reality of impending and certain termination is used to facilitate the resolution of the transference. As with the resolution of earlier episodes of transference neurosis, this final one is brought about principally by the analyst's interpretations and reconstructions. As these take effect, the transference neurosis and, hopefully, along with it the original neurosis is resolved. This final resolution, however, which is much more comprehensive, is usually very different and may not come about at all without the help of the reality of termination. Accordingly, any attenuation of the ending, such as tapering off or causal or tentative stopping, should be expected to stand in the way of an effective resolution of the transference. Yet, it seems that this is what most commonly happens to an ending, and because of this a great many patients may lose the potentially great benefit of a thorough resolution and are forever after left suspended in the net of unresolved transference.

Yet, utter indistinctly rigorous termination seems understandable, as difficult as transference neurosis may be in the analyst at other times, this ending period, if rigorously carried out, simply has to be the period of his greatest emotional strain. There can surely be no more likely time for an analyst to surrender his analytic position and, responding to his own transference, become personally involved with his patient than during the process of separating from a long and self-restrained relationship. Accordingly, it may be better to slur over the ending lightly than to mishandle it in an attempt to be rigorous.

In considering more broadly the function of the transference in the psychoanalytic process, one is confronted by the apparent naïve, but, nonetheless important questions of the role of the actual (current) object as compared with that of the object representation of the original personage in the past. We recall Freud's paradoxical, somewhat gloomy, but portentous concluding passage in 'The Dynamics of Transference.' This struggle between the doctor and the patient, between intellect and instinctual life, between understanding and seeking to act, is played out almost exclusively in the phenomena of transference. It is on that field that the victory must be won - the victory whose expression is on that field that the victory must be won - the victory whose expression is the permanent cure of the neuroses. It cannot be disputed that controlling the phenomena of transference presents the psychoanalysis with the greatest difficultly, but it should not be forgotten that they do us the inestimable service of making the patient 's hidden and forgotten erotic impulses of showing their immediate and manifested impossibilities, for when all is said and done, it is impossible to destroy anyone in absentia or in effigies.

Both object and representations are made necessary by the basic phenomenon of original separation. The existence of an image of the object, which persist in the absence of the object, is one of the important beginnings of psychic life in general, certainly an indispensable prerequisite for object relationship. As generally construed. Whether this is viewed as (or a times demonstrably is) something unstable for allotting introjection, s always subject to alternative projection, or an intrapsychic object representation clearly distinguished from the self-representation, or firm identification in the superego, or in the ego itself, these phenomena are in various ways components of the system of mastery of the fact of separation, or separateness, from the original absolutely necessarily anaclitic (in the earliest period) symbiotic 'object'. In the light of clinical observation, it would appear to be that the relative stabilities (parental) object representation. At which time of varying degree, are to a greater extent for the archaic phenomena. Even in nonpsychotic patients, overwhelmed by them, sometimes resembles the restoration from oedipal identification, which provides the preponderant basis for most demonstrable analytic transferences. That within the necrotic patients, the transference is effectively established when this representation invests the analyst to a degree - depending on intensity of drive and most of ego participation - which ranges in all the, wishing and striving to remake and analyst to biasses judgements and misinterpretation of data, finally are the actual perceptual distortions.

However, the old object representations may be invested, however rigidly established the libidinal or aggressive cathexis of the image may be, this as such can become the actual and exclusive focus of instinctual discharge, or of complicated and intense instinct-defence solutions, only and general energy-sparing quality of strictly intrapsychic processes. For the vast majority of persons, visible to any degree, including those with severe neurosis, character distortions, addictions and certain psychoses, the striving is toward the living and actual object, even at the cost of intense suffering. In a sense, this returns us to the state in which the psychological 'object-to-be'. Has a cr11itical importance never again to be duplicated, except in certain acute life emergencies, even if the object is not firmly perceived as such, in the sense of later object relations? And it does seem that trance impressions from the earliest contacts in the service of life preservation, and the associated instinctual gratifications, and innumerable secondarily associated sensory impressions. Are activated by the specific inborn urges of sexual maturation? These propel the individual to renew many of the earliest modes of actual bodily contact, in connection with seeking for specific instinctual gratification. Or, to look away from clear-cut instinctual matters to the more remote elaborations of human contact: Few regard loneliness as other than a source of suffering, even self-imposed, as an apparent matter of choice, and the forcible imposition of 'solitary confinement ' is surely one of the most cruel of punishments.

In taking to question, we are entering an area of life in which things are other then themselves, where meaning is multifaceted, and where the line between the old and the new is blurred. It should, by, its immediate measure, help develop our recognition or meaning of the pertinent applicability as to the relevance of interrelated aspects of the psychology of 'metaphor'. In the psychology of metaphor we will find a useful analogy to the psychology of transference interpretation. Our's will be newly encountered as good metaphors, those it response to which we say, 'That's it exactly' or 'That really captures it' or 'That says it all'.

Some literary and linguistic analysis, (e.g., Lewis, 1936 and Snell, 1953) and also people in everyday life, believe that there are experiences that can only be expressed metaphorically. And for this achievement that these metaphors, which may be entire poem or as lines or even words highly valued. But how can this be so? Just what in th e 'it' that the metaphor 'is' or 'captures' or 'says'? If this 'is' or this 'experience' can only be rendered metaphorically, when we can know it only as such, that is, as the metaphor itself. Of the position out of which are put forward by, T.S, Eliot (1933) and E.W. Harding (1963) in their discussion of poetry, for in these instances we are granted that there are no known and logically independent version of the experience that can serve to validate the metaphor. Whatever the metaphor makes available to us depends on it and it and so cannot be used to prove its correctness.

It seems justifiably warrantable to consider that the metaphor is a new experience rather than a mere paraphrase of an already fully constituted expedience. The metaphor creates an experience that one has never had before. It is an experience one has not realized by oneself. The metaphor does, of course, suggest certain constituent experiences of which one may have been more or less dimly aware. One may say, therefore, that the metaphor speaks for those constituents, on the existence of which much of its appeal depends. But in its organizing and implicit ly rendering these constituents in its new way, it is a creation rather than a mere paraphrase or anew edition. Paraphrasing and new editions never speak as forcefully as good new metaphors, nor could they facilitate further new experience. One analytically familiar feature of these creations is that they make it safe and pleasing to experience something that otherwise would be considered too threatening and so would be kept in fragmented obscurity through defensive measures.

Thus, when one says, 'That's it exactly' one is implicitly recognizing and announcing that one has found and accepted a new mode of experiencing oneself and one's world, which is to say, asserting a transformation of one's own subjectivity. Something is now said to be true, and in a sense it is true, but it is true for the first time. Nothing of one and the same can ever happen again, for the second time cannot be the same as the first. One can't step into the same spot of a river and feel its same waters. A revelatory metaphor re-encountered or repeated later may lose some of its force, alternatively, it may gain some significance, butt it cannot remain exactly the same metaphor or mobilize an experience identical with the first. The point applies as well as to new metaphors that are similar to familiar ones: They have to be judged or experienced through their conventionalized predecessors, as through methods of knowing or already proved instrumentally of perceiving. The audience and the performer, who may be one person, as such that may not have, as yet.

What is to be said about the psychology of metaphor is analogous to the transformational aspects of developed transference and the steadfast interpretation that both facilitate and organize them as transference. Allowing that these transferences and 'remembered' experiences come into existence over a period of time, nothing that is identical with them has ever before been enacted, and nothing will ever be enacted again. They are creations that may be fully achieved only under specific analytic conditions. Such that living was not reliving that moment, words like re-living, re-experiencing and reliving simply do not do justice to the phenomena, that in making this claim. A seeming contradiction over-writes some of our well-establish ideas. - in offering, - I am not contradicting some of our well-established ideas about interpretation and insight, I am, however, disputing the point that insight refers to a greater proportion or in its range of comprehension, which its distance between possible extremes extent and regain former or normal state, such that, for the recovery of lost memories, and takes in as well, a new grasp of the significance and interpretations of events one has always remembered. In point, as, Freud pointed out, 'As a matter of fact I've always known it, only that I've never thought of it; (1914), In fact, it is to develop that point in furthering to say that it takes an adult to do that, especially with the help of an analyst. It was, after all, Freud's analysis of adults that make it possible to define infantile psychosexuality. In this respect, but without disregard, child analysis retains a quality of applied psychoanalysis' in the same way that the interpreted transference neurosis is: Both are always of describing as true something that was not true in quite that way at the time of its greatest developmental significance. This apparent paradox about 'remembering' as a form of creating goes a long way, probably that what it is, is distinctive about psychoanalytic interpretation.

This time, however, to further the discussion on the interpretive technique that surrounds the phase of a mutative interpretation - that in which a portion of the patient's id-relation to the analyst is made conscious in virtue of the latter's positions as auxiliary super-ego - is in itself complex. In the classical model of an interpretation, the patient will first be made aware of a state of tension of an interpretation, will next be made aware that there is repressive factor at work (that his super-ego is threatening him with punishment), and will only then be made aware of the id-impulse which has stirred up the protects of his super-ego and so given to the anxiety in his ego. This is the classical scheme. In actual practice, the analyst finds himself working from all three sides at once, or in irregular successions. At one moment a small portion of the patient's super-ego may be revealed to him in all its savagery, at another the shrinking defencelessness of his ego, at yet another his attention may be directed to the attempts which he is making at restitution - at compensating for his hostility, on some occasions a fraction of id-energy may even be directly encouraged to break its way through the last remains of an already weakened resistance. There is, however, one characteristic which all of these various operations has in common, they are essentially upon a small scale. For the mutative interpretation is inevitably governed by the principle of minimal doses. It is a commonly agreed clinical fact that alternations in a patient under analysis appear almost always to be extremely gradual: We are inclined to suspect sudden and large changes as an indication that suggestive rather than psycho-analyst processes are at work. The gradual nature of the change brought about in psychoanalysis will be explained, as, only to suggest, those changes are the result of the summation of an immense number of minuet steps, each of which correspond to a mutative interpretation. And the smallness of each step is in turn imposed by the very nature of the analytic situation. For each interpretation involves the release of a certain quantity of id-energy, and, if the quantity released is too large, the higher unstable state of equilibrium which enables the analyst to function as the patient's auxiliary super-ego is bound to be upset. The whole analytic situation will thus be imperilled, since it is only in virtue of the analyst's acting as auxiliary super-ego that these released id-energy can occur at all.

The effectuality from which follow the analytic attempt to bring unequalled amounts in the confronting collections of some improper use to a resultant quantity of id-energy into the patient's consciousness all at once. On the one hand, nothing whatever may happen, or on the other hand there may be an unmanageable result, but in neither event will be a mutative interpretation has been effected. The analyst's power as auxiliary super-ego may be for two very different reasons. It may be that the id-impulses were trying to bring out being not in fact sufficiently urgent at the moment: For, after all, the emergence of an id-impulse depends on two factors - not only on the permission of the super-ego, but also on the urgency (the degree of cathaxis) of the id-impulse itself. This, then, may be one cause of an apparently negative response to an interpretation, and evidently a fairly harmless one. but the same apparent result may also be due to something else, in spite of the id-impulse being really urgent, the strength of the patient's own repressive forces (the degree of repression) may have been too great to allow his ego to listen to the persuasive voice of the auxiliary super-ego. Now we have a situation dynamically identical with the next one we have to consider, though economically different. this next situation is one in which the patient accepts the interpretation, that is, allows the id-impulse into his consciousness, but is immediately overwhelmed with anxiety. This may show itself in a number of ways, for instance, the patient may produce a manifest anxiety-attack. Or the may exhibit signs of 'real' anger with the analyst with a complete lack of insight, or he may break off the analysis. In any of these cases the analytic situation will, for the moment, at least, have broken down. The patient will be behaving just as the hypnotic subject behaves when, having been ordered by the hypnotist to perform an action too much at variance with his own consciousness, he breaks off the hypnotic relation and wakes up from his trance. This state of things, which is manifest where the patient responds to an interpretation with an actual outbreak of anxiety or one of its equivalents, may be latent were the patient shows no response, and this latter case may be the more awkward of the two, since it is masked, and it may sometimes be the effect of a greater overdose of interpretation than where manifest anxiety arises (though obviously other factors will be of determining importance, and in particularly the nature of the patient's neurosis). Yet this threatened collapse of the analytic situation to an overdose of interpretation: But it might be more accurate in some ways to ascribe it to an insufficient dose. For what has happened is that the second phase of the interpretation process has not occurred: The phase in which the patient becomes aware that his impulse is directed toward an archaic phantasy object and not toward a real one.

In the second phase of a complete interpretation, therefore, a crucial part is played by the patient's sense of reality: For the successful outcome of that phase depends upon his ability, at the critical moment of the emergence into consciousness of the released quantity of id-energy, to distinguish between his phantasy object and the real analyst. The problem is closely related to one that has been discussed elsewhere, namely that of the extreme liability of the analyst's position as auxiliary super-ego. The analytic situation is all the time threatening to degenerate into a 'real' situation. But this actually means the opposite of what it appears to. It means that the patient is all the time on the brink of turning the really external object (the analyst) into the archaic one; that is to say, he is on the brink of projecting his primitive introjected images onto himself. In so far as the patient actually does this, the analyst becomes like anyone else that he meets in real life - a phantasy object. The analyst then ceases to possess the peculiar advantages derived from the analytic situation, he will be introjected like all other phantasy objects into the analytic situation, he will be introjected like all other phantasy objects into the patient's super-ego, and will no longer be able to function in the peculiar ways which are essential to the effecting of a mutative interpretation. In this difficulty the patient's sense of reality is an essential but a very feeble [-ally]: An improvement in it is one of the things that we hope the analysis will bring about. It is important, therefore, not to submit it to any unnecessary strain, and that is the fundamental reason why the analyst must avoid any real behaviour, that is likely to confirm the patient's view of him as a 'bad' or a 'good' phantasy object. This is perhaps more obvious as regards the 'bad' object. If, for instance, the analyst were to show that he was really shocked or frightened by one of the patient's id-impulses, as the patient would immediately treat him in that respect as a dangerous object and introject him into his archaic severe super-ego. Therefore, on the one hand, there would be a diminuation in the analyst's power to function as an auxiliary super-ego and to allow the patient's to become conscious of his id-impulses - that is to say, in his power to bring about the first phase of a mutative interpretation, and on the other hand, he would, as a real object, become sensibly less distinguishable from the patient's 'bad' phantasy object and to that extent the carrying through of the second phase of a mutative interpretation would also be made more difficult. Or, agin, there is another case. Supposing the analyst behaves in an opposite way and actively urges the patient to give free rein to his id-impulse. There is then a possibility of the patient confusing the analyst with the image of a treacherous parent who, at the beginning, encourages him to seek gratification, and then suddenly turns and punishes him. In such a case the patient's ego may look for defence by itself suddenly turning upon the analyst as though he were his own id-, and treating him with all the severity of which his super-ego is capable. again, the analyst is running a risk of losing his privileged position. But it may be equally unwise for the analyst to act really in such a way as to encourage the patient to project his 'good' introjected object onto him. For the patient will then tend to regard him as a good objective and archaic sense and will incorporate him with his archaic 'good' images and will use him as a protection against his 'bad' ones. In that way, his infantile positive impulses as well as his negative ones may escape analysis, for there may no longer be a possibility for his ego to make a comparison between the phantasy external object and the real one. it will, perhaps, be argued that, with the best of wills in the world, the analyst, however careful he may be, will be unable to prevent the patient from projecting these various images onto him. This is, of course, indisputable, and, the whole effectiveness of analysis depends upon its being so. The lesson of these difficulties is merely to remind us that the patient's sense of reality has the narrowest limits. It is a paradoxical fact that the best way of enuring that his ego will be able to distinguish between phantasy and reality is to withhold reality from him as much as possible. but it is true, his ego is so weak - so much at the mercy of his id and super-ego - that he can only cope with reality if it is administered in minimal doses. And these doses are in fact what the analyst gives him, in the form of interpretations.

A mutative interpretation can only be applied to an id-impulse which is actually on a state of cathexis. This seems self-evident; for the dynamic changes in the patient's mind implied by a mutative interpretation can only be brought about by the operation of a charge of energy originating in the patient himself: The function of the analyst is merely to ensure that the energy should or can flow along one channel rather than along another. It follows that the purely informative 'dictionary' type of interpretation will be non-mutative, but useful it may be a prelude to mutative interpretations. And this leads to a number of practical inferences. Every mutative interpretation must be emotionally 'immediate, but the patient must live through it as something actual or genuine. This requirement, that the interpretation must be 'immediate', may be expressed in another way by saying that interpretation must always be directed to the 'point of urgency'. At any given moment some particular id-impulse will be generated in activity, this is the impulse that is susceptible of mutative interpretation at the time, and no other one. It is, no doubt, neither possible nor desirable to be giving mutative interpretations all the time. as Melanie Klein has pointed out, it is a most precious quality in an analyst to be able at any moment to pick out the point of urgency.

But the fact that every mutative interpretation must deal with an 'urgent' impulse take us back one more to the commonly felt fear of the explosive possibilities of interpretation, and particularly of what is vaguely referred to as 'deep' interpretation. The terminological description is, no doubt, as the interpretation of material which is neither genetically early and historically distant from the patient's actual experience nor under an especially heavy weight of repression – material, in any case, which is in the normal course of things exceedingly inaccessible to his ego and remote from it. There seems reason to believe, moreover, that the anxiety which is liable to be aroused by the approach of such material to consciousness and may be of peculiar severity. The question whether it is 'safe' to interpret such material will, as usual, mainly depend upon whether an interpretation can be carried through, in the ordinary run of the case, as this material which is urgent during the earlier stages of the analysis is not deep. We have to deal at first only with more or less far-going displacements of the deep impulse. And the deep material itself is only reached later and by degrees, so that no sudden appearance of unmanageable quantities of anxiety is to be hesitorially anticipated. In exceptional cases, however, owing to some peculiarities in the structure of the neurosis, deep impulses may be urgent at a very early stage of the analysis. We are then faced by a dilemma. If we give an interpretation of this deep material, the resultant amounts of anxiety produced in the patient may be so great that his sense of reality may not be sufficient to permit of its accomplishment, and the whole analysis may be jeopardised, but, it must not be thought that, in such critical cases as we are now considering, the difficulty can necessarily be avoided simply by not giving any interpretation or by giving more superficial interpretations of non-urgent material or by attempting reassurances. It seems probable, in fact, that these alternative procedures may do little or nothing to obviate the trouble, on the contrary, they may even exacerbate the tension created by the urgency of the deep impulses which are the actual cause of the threatening anxiety. Thus the anxiety may break out in spite of these palliative efforts and, if so, it will be doing so under the most unfavourable conditions, that is to say, outside the mitigating influences afforded by the mechanism of interpretation. It is possible, therefore, that, of these alternative procedures which are open to the analyst faced by such a difficulty. The interpretation of the urgent id-impulses, deep though they may b e, will actually be the safer.

It is, of course, a matter of common experience, that it possible with certain patients to continue indefinitely giving interpretations without producing any apparent effect whatever. There is an amusing criticism of this kind of 'interpretation-fanaticism' in the excellent historical chapter of Rank and Ferenczi. But it is clear from their words that what they have in mind are essentially extra-transference interpretations, for the burden of their criticism is that such a procedure implies neglect of the analytic situation. This is the simplest case. Where a waste of time and energy is the main result. But there are other occasions, on which a policy of giving strings of extra-transference interpretations is apt to lead the analyst into more positive difficulties. Attention was drawn by Reich a few years back, in the course of some technical discussions in Vienna to a tendency among inexperienced analysts to get into trouble by eliciting from the patient great quantities of material in a disordered and unrelated fashion: This may, be maintained, be carried to such lengths that the analysis is brought to an irremediable state of chaos. He pointe out truly that the material we have to deal with is stratified and that it is highly important in digging it out not to interference, more that we can help with th e arrangement of that state. He had in mind, of course, the analogy of an incompetent archaeologist, whose clumsiness may obliterate for all time the possibility of reconstructing the history of an important site. However, the results in the case of a clumsy analysis do not hold of any pessimistic cause to happen, as it was, re-stratification itself of its own accord if it is given the opportunity; That is to say, in the analytic situation. At the same time, is that of the presence of the risk, and it seems to be particularly likely to occur where extra-transference interpretation is excessively or exclusively restored to. The means of preventing it, and the remedy if it has occurred, lie in returning to transference interpretation at the point of urgency. For if we can discover which of the material is 'immediate' in the sense that the problematic occurrence enabling stratification is automatically solved, and it is a characteristic if most extra-transference material that it has no immediacy and consequently stratification is far more difficult to decipher. The measures suggested by Reich himself for preventing the occurrence of this state of chaos are consistent with those that he stresses the importance of interpreting resistance as opposed to the primary id-impulses themselves - and this, was a policy that was laid down at an early stage in the history of analysis. But it is, of course, one of the characteristics of a resistance that it arises in relation to the analyst. Thus, interpretation of a resistance will almost inevitably be a transference interpretation.

But the most serious risks that arise from the making of extra-transference interpretation are due to the inherent difficulty in completing their interpretation, for a successful outcome as such, depends upon his ability, at which time of the emergence into consciousness and the released quantity of id-energy. They are from their nature unpredictable in their effects. There seems to be a special risk of the patient not carrying through to a competed interpretation, hitherto, namely that the extreme liability of the analyst's position as auxiliary super-ego, is that, the analytic situation is all the time threatening to degenerate into a 'real' situation. It means that the patient is all the time perched upon the circumference edge-horizon of turning the external object (the analyst) into the archaic one, but of projecting the id-impulse that has been made conscious onto the analyst. This risk, no doubt, applies to some extent to transference interpretations. However, the situation is less likely to arise when the object of the id-impulses is actually present and is moreover the same person as the maker of interpretation. We may, once, more, recall the problem of 'deep' interpretation, and point out that its dangers, even in the most unfavourable circumstances, seem to be greatly diminished if the interpretation in question is a transference interpretation. Even so, there appears to be more of a chance that in this whole process occurring silently and so being overlooked in the case of an extra-transference interpretation, particularly in the earlier stages of an analysis. For this reason, it would seem to be important after giving an extra-transference interpretation to be specially in the 'qui-vive' for transferences complications. This last peculiarity of the extra-transference interpretation is actually one of the most important forms to a practical stand-point of things. For on account of it they can be made to act as 'feeders' for the transference situation, and so to pave the way for mutative interpretations. In other words, by giving an extra-transference interpretation, the analyst can often provide a situation in the transference of which he can then give a mutative interpretation.

Therefore, it is probable that a large majority of our interpretations are outside the transference - though it should be added that it often happens that one is ostensibly giving an extra-transference interpretation one is implicitly giving a transference one. A cake cannot be made of nothing but currants, and, though it is true that extra-transference interpretations, are not for the most part, mutative and do not they bring about the crucial results that involve a permanent change in the patient's mind. They are, nonetheless essential, if taken to an analogy of trench warfare, the acceptance of a transference interpretation corresponds to the capture of a key position, while the extra-transference interpretations correspond to the general advance and to the consolidation of a fresh line of defence, which are made possible by the capture of the key position. But when this general advance goes beyond a certain point, there will be another check, and the capture of a further key position will be necessary before progress can be resumed. An oscillation of this kind between transference and extra-transference interpretations will represent the normative course of events in an analysis.

Although the giving of mutative interpretations may thus only occupy a small portion of psycho-analytic treatment, it will, upon being, that the most important part from the point of view of deeply exerting affective percussions. Do so, because of the influencing characteristic confirmations as drawn upon the spoken-exchange of the patient's mindful knowing, in that the individuals that feel, perceive, think, wills, and especially reasons are all taken into heedful compliance. It may be of interest to consider how a moment through which of such an importance to the patient affects the analyst himself. Mrs. Klein has suggested that there must be some quite special internal difficulty as to involve the analyst in interpretations. This is shown in their avoidance by psycho-therapists of non-analytic schools, but many psycho-analysts will be aware of traces of the same tendency in themselves. It may be rationalized into mutative interpretations. This is shown in the avoidance by psycho-therapists of non-analytic schools, if not many consisting of a psycho-analyst as flown over to passing their flow of emptying space, nonetheless, this dialectic awareness traces of the same tendency as in them. But behind this there is somewhat of a lurking difficulty in the actual giving of the interpretation, for there seems to be a constant temptation for the analyst to do something else instead. Questions may be asked of whether o r not. As given to the reassurances or advice or discourses upon theory, or may give interpretations -but interpretations that are not mutative, extra-transference interpretations, interpretations that are non-immediate, or ambiguous, or in exacting of two or more alternative interpretations simultaneously, or he may, perhaps, give interpretations and at the same time, show his own scepticism about them. All of this strongly suggests that the giving of a mutative interpretation is a crucial act for the analyst as well as for the patient. And this inturn will become intelligible when we reflect that at the moment of interpretation the analyst is in fact deliberately evoking a quantity of the patients id-energy while it is a live and actual and unambiguous and aimed directly himself. Such a moment must be above all others put to the test his relations with his unconscious impulses.

Interpretation of the transference is central to all psychoanalytic models. Definitions of transference and transference interpretation have changed greatly during the past half-century, influenced by major movements in philosophy, but advances in psycho-analytic research and theory, and changes in our of understanding Freud. Suggestively. The advances in psychoanalytic research and theory, and changes in our understanding of Freud. Is that, the historical, relatively simple, concepts of the transference as the reproductions in the presence of significant relationships from therapists do not adequately meet current clinical theoretical demands? Modernist views of the transference emphasize as in additional sources of transference responses, the role of the analytic background of safety, the constant modifications of unconscious fantasy and internal representations, and the interactive nature of transference response, with important interpersonal and intersubjective components. It is suggested that the evolving modernists view of transference and transference interpretation permit a fuller accounting for transference and transference components. Such in a fuller accountability, for which of these issues of psychological 'truth' has open the way for better informed interventions. The issue of psychological 'truth' and 'distortion' as applied to transference phenomena will be presented with clinical vignettes.

Psychoanalysis, since the earliest days of the, Studies on Hysteria (Breuer and Freud, 1993-1905), have always given special attention to the transference and to the interpretation of transference, believing it to be central in our theory and technique. While there, has never been a lack of interest in transference interpreting. It is not clear why this is so, and the reasons may vary in different parts of the international psychoanalytic community. In America, at least, Gill's (1982) recent, and somewhat radical presentation of transference interpretation has surely helped to the grasping upon our developing attentions. Nevertheless, of another reason for our intensified interests in transference interpretation is the opportunity it provides for the rhetorically dialectic awareness, in that discussions, have lead us to the diverse analytic theories and techniques that today complete the diverseness as observed, for which of our attentions and allegiance to which transference interpretation seems to have replaced self-psychology. Thus, the encompassing topic that allows analysts of varied persuasions among many structural and fundamental elements that forge out the shape for taking upon the imparting of instinctual information. As to know, and knowing that you know, is, applied, however, of its depthful concerning contemplations with which is distinguished by the evolving characterizations that are of knowing that you know is really nothing whatsoever.

Despite the diversity of the transference and its interpreting in analytic process and cure, differing only in whether transference is everything or almost everything to give a clear-cut definition of what transference is.

Laplanche and Pontalis (1973) had written that, 'The reason it is so difficult to produce a definition of transference is that for many authors the notion has taken on a very broad extension, even coming to connote all the phenomena which constitute the patient's relationship with the psychoanalyst, as a result the concept is burdened down more than any other with each analyst's particular view on the treatment - on its objective, dynamics, tactics, scope, and so forth. The question of the transference is thus beset by a whole series of difficulties which have been the subject of debate in classical psychoanalysis.'

Sandler (1983) has discussed how the terms transference and transference resistance, as well as other terms have undergone profound changes in meaning as new discoveries and new trends of psycho-analytic technique assume ascendency. He said, . . . major changes in technical emphasis brought about the extension of the transference concept, which now has dimensions of meaning which differ from the official definition of the term. I am not sure there has ever been a simplified definition of the term. While a certain flexibility of definition makes conversation possible in a field of diverse views, which we may never be clear on what any two people mean when they use the term is a significant hindrance to our discourse.

However: with this in mind we might review one of Freud's last comments on transference. In 'An Outline of Psycho-Analysis' (1940), published posthumously, he wrote on the analytic situation:

The most remarkable thing is this. The patient is not satisfied with regarding the analyst in the light of reality as a helper and advisor who, moreover, is remunerated for the trouble he takes and who would himself be content with some role that of a guide on a different mountain to climb, on the contrary, the patient sees in him. the return, and the reincarnation, of some important figure out of his childhood or past, and consequently transfer onto him, feelings and reactions which undoubtedly apply this prototype. This fact of transference soon proves to be a factor of an undreamt-of importance, on the other hand bud an instrument of irreplaceable value and on the other, that he set out on a different undertaking without any suspicion of extraordinary power that would be at his command. . . .

Another advantage of transference, too, in that in it the patient produces before us with plastic clarity an important part of his life-story, of which he would, otherwise have probably given us only an insufficient account. He acts it before us, as it was, instead of reporting it to us.

Freud saw the transference interpretation as a method of strengthening the ego against past unconscious wishes and conflicts.

It is the analyst's task constantly to speak abruptly, and in doing so, the patient may relinquish of his menacing illusions and to show him again and again, of what it takes to be or begin of a new life, are the reflections of the past. And least, he should fall into a state in which he is inaccessible to all evidences, the analyst takes that neither the love nor the hostility reaching an extreme height. This is affected by preparing him in good time for these possibilities and by not overlooking the first signs of them. Careful handling of the transference on these lines is as a role richly rewarded. If we succeed, as we usually can, in enlightenment the patient on the true nature of the phenomena of the transference, we thus have struck a powerful weapon out of the hand of his resistance and will have converted dangers into gains. For a patient never forgets again what he has experienced in the form of transference, it carries a greater force of conviction than anything he can acquire in other ways.

In considering more broadly the function of the transference in the psychoanalytic process, one is confronted by the apparent naïve, but, nonetheless important questions of the role of the actual (current) object as compared with that of the object representation of the original personage in the past. We recall Freud's paradoxical, somewhat gloomy, but portentous concluding passage in 'The Dynamics of Transference.' This struggle between the doctor and the patient, between intellect and instinctual life, between understanding and seeking to act, is played out almost exclusively in the phenomena of transference. It is on that field that the victory must be won - the victory whose expression is on that field that the victory must be won - the victory whose expression is the permanent cure of the neuroses. It cannot be disputed that controlling the phenomena of transference presents the psychoanalysis with the greatest difficultly, but it should not be forgotten that they do us the inestimable service of making the patient 's hidden and forgotten erotic impulses of showing their immediate and manifested impossibilities, for when all is said and done, it is impossible to destroy anyone in absentia or in effigies.

Both object and representation are made necessary by the basic phenomenon of original separation. The existence of an image of the object, which persist in the absence of the object, is one of the important beginnings of psychic life in general, certainly an indispensable prerequisite for object relationship. As generally construed. Whether this is viewed as (or a times demonstrably is) something unstable for allotting introjection, s always subject to alternative projection, or an intrapsychic object representation clearly distinguished from the self-representation, or firm identification in the superego, or in the ego itself, these phenomena are in various ways components of the system of mastery of the fact of separation, or separateness, from the original absolutely necessarily anaclitic (in the earliest period) symbiotic 'object'. In the light of clinical observation, it would appear to be that the relative stability (parental) object representation. At which time of varying degree, are to a greater extent for the archaic phenomena. Even in nonpsychotic patients, overwhelmed by them, sometimes resembles the restoration from oedipal identification, which provides the preponderant basis for most demonstrable analytic transferences. That within the necrotic patients, the transference is effectively established when this representation invests the analyst to a degree - depending on intensity of drive and most of ego participation - which ranges in all the, wishing and striving to remake and analyst to biasses judgements and misinterpretation of data, finally are the actual perceptual distortions.

However, the old object representations as such may be invested, however rigidly established the libidinal or aggressive cathexis of the image may be, this as such can become the actual and exclusive focus of instinctual discharge, or of complicated and intense instinct-defence solutions, only and general energy-sparing quality of strictly intrapsychic processes. For the vast majority of persons, visible to any degree, including those with severe neurosis, character distortions, addictions and certain psychoses, the striving is toward the living and actual object, even at the cost of intense suffering. In a sense, this returns us to the state in which the psychological 'object-to-be'. Has a critical importance never again to be duplicated, except in certain acute life emergencies, even if the object is not firmly perceived as such, in the sense of later object relations? And it does seem that trance impressions from the earliest contacts in the service of life preservation, and the associated instinctual gratifications, and innumerable secondarily associated sensory impressions. Are activated by the specific inborn urges of sexual maturation? These propel the individual to renew many of the earliest modes of actual bodily contact, in connection with seeking for specific instinctual gratification. Or, to look away from clear-cut instinctual matters to the more remote elaborations of human contact: Few regard loneliness as other than a source of suffering, even self-imposed, as an apparent matter of choice, and the forcible imposition of 'solitary confinement ' is surely one of the most cruel of punishments.

In taking to question, we are entering an area of life in which things are other then themselves, where meaning is multifaceted, and where the line between the old and the new is blurred. It should, by, its immediate measure, help develop our recognition or meaning of the pertinent applicability as to the relevance of interrelated aspects of the psychology of 'metaphor'. In the psychology of metaphor we will find a useful analogy to the psychology of transference interpretation. Our's will be newly encountered as good metaphors, those it response to which we say, 'That's it exactly' or 'That really captures it' or 'That says it all'.

Some literary and linguistic analysis, (e.g., Lewis, 1936 and Snell, 1953) and also people in everyday life, believe that there are experiences that can only be expressed metaphorically. And it is for this achievement that these metaphors, which may be entire poem or as lines or even words highly valued. But how can this be so? Just what in th e 'it' that the metaphor 'is' or 'captures' or 'says'? If this 'is' or this 'experience' can only be rendered metaphorically, when we can know it only as such, that is, as the metaphor itself. Of the position out of which are put forward by, T.S, Eliot (1933) and E.W. Harding (1963) in their discussion of poetry, for in these instances we are granted that there is no known and logically independent version of the experience that can serve to validate the metaphor. Whatever the metaphor makes available to us depends on it and it and so cannot be used to prove its correctness.

It seems justifiable to conclude that the metaphor is a new experience rather than a mere paraphrase of an already fully constituted expedience. The metaphor creates an experience that one has never had before. It is an experience one has not realized by oneself. The metaphor does, of course, suggest certain constituent experiences of which one may have been more or less dimly aware. One may say, therefore, that the metaphor speaks for those constituents, on the existence of which much of its appeal depends. But in its organizing and implicit ly rendering these constituents in its new way, it is a creation rather than a mere paraphrase or anew edition. Paraphrasing and new editions never speak as forcefully as good new metaphors, nor could they facilitate further new experience. One analytically familiar feature of these creations is that they make it safe and pleasing to experience something that otherwise would be considered too threatening and so would be kept in fragmented obscurity through defensive measures.

Thus, when one says, 'That's it exactly' one is implicitly recognizing and announcing that one has found and accepted a new mode of experiencing oneself and one's world, which is to say, asserting a transformation of one's own subjectivity. Something is now said to be true, and in a sense it is true, but it is true for the first time. Where this quality or state of being, is that there is nothing just like it, or can ever happen again, for the second time cannot be the same as the first. One can' t step into a stream of the same watering point and then step once again into the same spot. A revelatory metaphor re-encountered or repeated later may lose some of its force, alternatively, it may gain some significance, but it cannot remain exactly the same metaphor or mobilize an experience identical with the first. The point applies as well as to new metaphors that are similar to familiar ones: They have to be judged or experienced through their conventionalized predecessors, as through methods of knowing or already proved instrumentally of perceiving. The audience and the performer, who may be one person, as such that may not have, as yet.

What is to be said about the psychology of metaphor is analogous to the transformational aspects of developed transference and the steadfast interpretation that both facilitate and organize them as transference. Allowing that these transferences and 'remembered' experiences come into existence over a period of time, nothing that is identical with them has ever before been enacted, and nothing will ever be enacted again. They are creations that may be fully achieved only under specific analytic conditions. Such that living was not reliving that moment, words like re-living, re-experiencing and reliving simply do not do justice to the phenomena, that in making this claim. A seeming contradiction over-writes some of our well-establish ideas. - in offering, - I am not contradicting some of our well-established ideas about interpretation and insight, I am, however, disputing the point that insight refers to much than the recovery of lost memories, and takes in as well, a new grasp of the significance and interpretations of events one has always remembered. In point, as, Freud pointed out, 'As a matter of fact I've always known it, only that I've never thought of it; (1914), In fact, it is to develop that point in furthering to say that it takes an adult to do that, especially with the help of an analyst. It was, after all, Freud's analysis of adults that make it possible to define infantile psychosexuality. In this respect, but without disregard, child analysis retains a quality of applied psychoanalysis' in the same way that the interpreted transference neurosis is: Both are always of describing as true something that was not true in quite that way at the time of its greatest developmental significance. This apparent paradox about 'remembering' as a form of creating goes a long way, probably that what it is, is distinctive about psychoanalytic interpretation.

In steadfastly and perspicaciously making transference interpretation. This newness characterizes the experience of analytic transference themselves. Unlike extra-analytic transferences, they can no longer be sheerly repetitive or merely new editions. Instead, they become repetitive new editions understood as such because defined as such by the simplifying and steadfast transference interpretations. Instead of responding to the analysand in kind, which would actualize the repetition, the analyst makes an interpretation. This interpretation does not necessarily or regularly match something the analysand already knows or has experienced unconsciously. Although, the analysand does often seem to have already represented some things unconsciously in the very terms of the interpretation. Equally often he does not seem to have done so at all. To think otherwise about this would be, in effect, to claim that, unconsciously, every analysand is Freud or a fully insightful Freudian. And that claim is absurd.

It would be closer to the truth to say this: Unconsciously, the analysand already knows or has experienced fragmentary, amorphous, uncoordinated constituents of many of the transference interpretations. Alternatively, one may say that, implicitly, the analysand has been insisting on some as yet unspecified certainties and, in keeping with this, following some set of as yet unspecified rules in his actions, these transference interpretations now organize explicitly. Each transference interpretation refers to many things that have already been defined by the analysand, and it does so in a way that transforms them. That's why one may call it interpretation, but it would be mere repeating or sterile paraphrasing. Interpretation is a creative redescription that implicitly has the structure of a simile. It says, 'This is like that', Each interpretation does, therefore, add new actions to the life and analysand had already lived.

Technically, redescription in the terms of transference-repetition is necessary. This is so because, up to the time of interpretation and working through, the analysand has been, in one sense, unable and, in another sense, unconsciously and desperately unwilling, to conduct his life differently. in and of themselves, the repetitions cannot alter the symptoms, the subjective distress, and wasting of one's possibilities, rather, they can only perpetuate state situation by repeatedly confirming its necessity. They prove once again, the unconsciously maintained, damaging certainties. But once they get to be viewed as historically grounded actions and subjectively defined situations, as they do upon being interpreted and worked through, they appear as having always been, in crucial respects, inventions of the analysand's making and, so, as his responsibility. in being seen as versions of one's past life. As they may be significantly different, as the subject of change in favouring - as something that is desirable or beneficial - within the common ability to make intelligent choices and to reach intelligent conclusions or decisions in understanding ways. Less and less are they presented as purely inevitable happenings, as a fixed state or as the well-established way of the world. As, here, we encounter a second paradox that goes to the heart of psychoanalytic interpretation, namely, that responsible, insightful change is possible thorough psychoanalysis just because, as a child, the analysand mistakenly assumed and then denied responsibility for much that he encountered in the early formative environment and during maturation.

One major point remains to be made about the logic of viewing transference interpretation as simplifying yet innovative redescription. This point is that the interpretation bring about a coordination of the terms in which to state both the analysand's current problems and their life-historical background. The analysand's symptoms and desires are described as actions and, modes of action, with due regard for the principle of multiple function or multiple meaning, in coordination with that description, the decisive developmental situations and conflicts are stated as actions and modes of action. Continuity is established between the childhood constructions of relationships and self and the present constructions of these. Interpretation of transferences shows how both are part of the same set of practice, that is, how they follow the same set of rules. Past and present are coordinated to show continuity rather than arranged in a definite causal sequence.

In the same way, the form of analytic behaviour and the content of associations are given coordinate descriptions, say, for being defiant, devouring, or reparative. Or, in the case of depression, the depressive symptoms, the depressive analytic transference, the themes of present and past loss destructiveness and helplessness, all will be redescribed under the aspect of one continuously developing self-presentation. And this coordination will be worked out in the hermeneutically circular fashion in which the analyst defines both the facts to be explained and the explanations to be applied to these facts. In the end, as is well known, Both the paramount issues of the analysis and the leading explanatory account of them are likely to be significantly different from the provisional versions of them used at the beginning of the analysis.

This is the sophisticated cognitive simplification that promotes the convincing development and recognition of transference and the emotional experiencing of the past as it is now remembered. The coordination of terms is the only way to break into the vicious circle of the neurosis disturbance and reduce its unconsciously self-confirming character. New meaning is established by steadfast interpretation of transference and the condition for loving of which they are enactments.

That this kind of analytic work is not simply intellectual but shown in the analytic presentations that analysand was now operating according to rules which, through previous transference interpretations and coordination of terms, had changed. The changed rules were implicit in this hitherto-avoided experiencing of the past. It was not re-experiencing, or not mainly that: In its special way, it was experiencing that past for the first time.

It should take to be marked and noted, and, if not only to mention of two implications of which (1) The transference phenomena that finally constitute the transference e neurosis and to be taken as regressive in only some of their aspects. This is so because, viewed as achievements of the analysis, they have never existed before as such, rather, they constitute a creation achieved through a novel relationship into which one has entered by conscious and rational design. The analytic definition of the conditions for loving has never been arrived at before: They have never been simplified, organized, intensified, and transparent as they get to be in the analytically circumscribed and identified transference neurosis. It seems a more adequate or balanced view of transference neurosis. It seems a more adequate or balanced view of transference phenomena to regard them as multidirectional in meaning rather than as simply regressive or repetitive. This would be to look at them in as ways that are analogous to the way we look at creative works of art. We would see the transference as creating the past in the present, in a special analytic way and under favourable conditions. Essentially, they represent movement forward, and not backward.

And, (2) It is wrong to think that interpretation deals only in what is concealed or disguised or, what is its correlate, that 'the unconscious' is omniscient. In particular, it cannot be the case that 'the unconscious' knows all about transference and repetition, By establishing new connections, comprehensive context, and coordinated perspectives on familiar actions, interpretation creates new meanings or new actions. Not everything that has yet been organized has been actively kept apart by defensive measures, not everything that has not yet been recognized has been denied. This point is obvious, but it is often obscured by formulation, some of Freud's among them, which suggest that interpretation is only just uncovering (Fingarette, 1963).

What, then, is interpretation? And how does it work? Extremely little seems to be known about it, but this does not prevent an almost universal belief in its remarkable efficacy as a weapon. Interpretation has, it must be confessed, many of the qualities of a magic weapon. It is, of course, felt as such by many patients. Some of them spend hours at a time in providing interpretations of their own - often ingenious, illuminating, correct. others, again, derive a direct libidinal gratification from being given interpretations and may even circulate interpretation is usually either scoffed at as something indicated or develop something parallel to a drug-addition to them. In some non-analytical circles interpretation is usually either scoffed at as something ludicrous or dreaded as a frightful danger. This last attitude is shared, as more than is often realized, by a certain number of analysts. This was particularly revealed by the reactions shown in many quarters when the idea of giving interpretations to small children was first mooted by Melanie Klein. However, it is believed that it would be true in general to say, that analysts are incline to feel interpretation as something extremely powerful whether for good or ill. And there might seem to be a good many grounds for thinking that our feelings on the subject tend to distort our beliefs, at all events, many of these beliefs seem superficially to be contradictory, and the contradictions do not always spring from different schools of though, but are apparently sometimes held simultaneously by one individual. Thus, we are told that if we interpret too soon or too rashly, we hazardously risk of losing a patient: That interpretation may give rise to intolerable and unmanageable outbreaks of anxiety by 'liberating' it. That interpretation is the only way of enabling a patient to cope with an unmanageable outbreak of anxiety by 'resolving' it. That interpretation must always refer to material on the very point of emerging into consciousness, that the most useful interpretations are rally deep ones. Be cautious with your interpretations;, says one voice, 'When in doubt, interpret' says another. Nevertheless, although there is enviably a good deal of confusion in all of this. Do not think these views are necessarily incompatible: The various pieces of advice may turn out to refer to different circumstances and different cases and to imply unlike moderations of differently more or less kinds of applicable character uses of the word 'interpretation'.

For the word is evidently used in more than on sense. It is, after all, perhaps, only a synonym for the old phrase we have already come across - 'making what unconscious conscious and it shares all of the phrase's ambiguities. For in one sense, if you give a German-English dictionary to someone who knows no German, you will be giving him a collection of interpretations, what is more, is the kind of sense in which the nature of interpretation has been discussed in a recent paper by Bernfield. Such descriptive interpretations have no relevance to our present topic, nonetheless, in proceeding, the actuality as dispensed among the ultimate instrumentations of psychoanalytic therapy. In that which for its convenience the name 'mutative' interpretation is so that is, given a schematized outline of what is understood by a view to clarify of expositional instances for which the interpretation of hostile impulses are by virtue of this power (his strictly limited power) as auxiliary superego, that the analyst gives permission for a certain small quantity of the patient's id-energy (in our instance, in the form of an aggressive impulse), the object of the patient's id-impulses, the quality of these impulses which is now released into consciousness will become consciously directed toward the analyst. This is the critical point. If all goes well, the patient's ego will become aware of the contrast between the aggressive character of his feelings and the real nature of the analyst, who does not behave like the patient's 'good' or 'bad' archaic objects. The patient, which is to say, will become aware of a distinction between his archaic phantasy object and the dimensionality of an actualized external object. The interpretation has now become a mutative one, since it has produced a breach in the neurotic vicious circle. For the patient, having become aware of the lack of aggressiveness of actuality that is potentially realized of the existing external object, will be able to diminish his own aggressiveness; the new object which he introjects will be less aggressive, and consequently, the aggressiveness of his superego will also diminish, as, too, the further corollary of these events. And with them the patient will obtain access to the infantile material which is being re-experienced by him in his relation to the analyst.

Something as taken or advanced as fact, which is in having the quality of becoming actual and not confuted in being of such a comparison with an expressed or implied standard or absolute, that we are now found to embark upon a description of the successive phases of therapy with the chronically schizophrenic adult patient. The 'Out-of-contact' phase', is not properly or sufficiently attended to or in progress of any measurable extent over which of something exists, however, the term is phraseologically accessible to meaning, such that I do not term this the 'autistic phase', for the reason that the word 'autistic' has come to have a certain connotation, in psychodynamic theory, which is regarded as invalid and therefore do not advocate. Specifically, the term 'autistic', as generally used, conjures up Freud's (1911) psychodynamic formulation of schizophrenia as involving withdrawal of libido from the outer world and its subsequent investment in the self-as involving of a regression into narcissism. Instead, however, is that there occurs in schizophrenia, a regressive dedifferentiation toward an early level of ego-development which has its prototype in the experience of a young infant for whom the inner and outer worlds have not yet become clearly distinguishable, as an amount of anxiety which is related to the unfamiliarity as found to be the major sources of anxiety in individuals suffering from [paranoid] schizophrenia. Where the sources of such anxiety is variously ego-defensive by phenomena. We well know that to any psychiatric patient himself, the threatening affects present themselves not undistortedly, but in forms modified by ego-defences which, although intently protective, at the same time distortions that may appear as something experiential in a strange and frightening way.

He finds himself unable to renounce any concern with that of the other patients. Exceptions are those patients whose projections attach not to any real-life figure at all, but to quite pure-culture alter-ego. And reach their of peace about the matter. For in actuality this would be tantamount to repudiating important components of himself, moreover, the other person is necessary to him as the bearer of these externalized (e.g., projected) emotions. Bu t, cannot find peace through a friendly acceptance of the prosecutory figure, for this would b e unsurmountable to accept, however, his own picture of himself, various qualities abhorrent to him. So an uneasy equilibrium is maintained, with his experiencing a gnawing, threatened, absorbing concern with the prosecutory figure whom he cannot rid from his mind (this is in line with the formulation of Werner (1940) and Loewald (1960)).

It leaves to appear with great interest that which Mahler and Furer (1960) emphasize that 'Our first therapeutic endeavour in both types of infantile psychosis (i.e., both autistic and symbiotic) is to engage the child in a 'corrective symbiotic experience' . . . Loewald (1960) too, report that what a symbiotic relatedness occurs in the schizophrenic patient's transference to the therapist: As he puts it, . . . If ego and objects are not clearly differentiated, if ego boundaries and object boundaries are not clearly established, the character of transference also is different, In as much as ego and objects are still largely merged. . . .

Such that the therapist, operating from this basic-orientation can meet usefully a wide variety of typical problem-situations, that which is in response to the patient's manifestation of delusional thinking, he will be aware that, for the patient, the delusions represent years of arduous and subjectively constructive thought, and are therefore most deeply cherished. He will not forget that obscured that obscures them is an indispensable nucleus of reality-perception. Likewise, when a patient is having vigorously to disavow any feeling about a clearly affect -laden matter, the therapist will remain in tune with the patient's own feeling experience, by remarking, "I gather you don' t find yourself having any particular feeling about this" - or. Better, will make no mention of feeling - rather than try to overcome the unconscious denial by asserting: But ' surely this must make you very angry (or hurt, or whatever). Similarly, in response to the expressions of an archaic, harsh, superego in the patient, rather than set himself up as the spokesman, the personification, of the repressed id-impulses, he will realize that it is in the superego that the patient's conscious self-his personal identity-mainly resides: Thus, he will seldom urge the patient to recognize sexual or aggressive feelings within, and will more often acknowledge how strong a sense of protest or outrage the patient feels upon perceiving these in others.

To the extent that the therapist is free from a compulsion to rescue the suffering patient, he can remain sufficiently extricated from that suffering to be able to note significant sequence in the appearance of such symptoms as hallucinations, verbalized delusions, and so forth, and thus be in a position to be genuinely helpful. Even when on a car ride with a patient, or grappling with the latter's physical assault, the therapist may on occasion be able to allow himself enough detachment to help the patient situations from earlier life, such 'action interpretations' may be especially important to the patient whose memory and whose capacity for abstract thinking are severely impaired.

Thus, one places in the long run a minimum of pressure on the patient who is already paralysed with pressure, and keeps oneself in a comparatively unanimous and receptive state which, better than anything else, helps eventually to relieve the patient's anxiety and unlock his tongue. Sooner or later, like a bright dawn pushing back a long night, the patient will put his rusty vocalization capacities to work in venting reproach, contempt, and fury upon the therapist for doing, as the patient sees it, nothing to help him.

The therapist learns to take fewer and fewer things for grantee in his work, to question more and more of his long-held assumptions and discard many of them. He learns that one does not set a ceiling upon human beings' potential growth. He finds recurrent delight in the creative spontaneity with which the schizophrenic patient pierces the sober and constructing wrapping of our culture's conventions, and he discovers that humour is present in his work in rich abundance, leaving the genuine tragedy and helping to make it supportable. While developing a deep confidence in his intuitive ability, when working with the severely fragmented or differentiated patient he will not jump too quickly to attempted communicated 'closure' (in the Gestalt sense), but will leave it in the patient's hands to do, no matter how slowly and painfully, the parts of the communicational work which only he can do. Meanwhile, he will not need no shield himself, through the maintenance of an urgently and actively 'helpful' or 'rescuing' attitude, from feeling at a deep level the impact of the fragmented and differentiated world, with its attendment feelings, in which the patient exists. The unfolding of such feeling experiences, the therapist of the next phase of the therapy, the 'urgently helpful' therapist attitude is unconsciously designed to avert, comparable to the defensive function. In the patient, of the latter's schizophrenic delusions.

From a purely descriptive viewpoint, schizophrenia an be seen to consist essentially in an impairment of both 'integration' and 'differentiation' - which are but opposite faces of a unitary growth process. From a psychodynamic viewpoint as well, this malfunctioning of integration-and-differentiation seems basic to all the bewilderingly complex and varied manifestations of schizophrenia.

Taking first the matter of integration: When we assess the schizophrenic individual in terms of the classically structural areas of the personality - id, ego, and superego - we discover these to be poorly integrated with one another. The id is experienced by the ego as a Pandora's box, the contents of which will overwhelm one if it is opened. The ego is, as many writers have stated, severely split, sometimes into innumerable islands which are not linked discernibly with one another. And the superego unintegrated ego are, if anything, even more destructive to it than are the accessions of the threatening id-impulses, as Szalita-Pemow (1951), Hill (1955) and others have emphasized. Moreover, the superego is, like the ego, even in itself not well integrated, its utterances contain the most glaring inconsistencies from one moment to the next. Jacobson (1954) has shown that there is actually a dissolution of the superego, as an integral structure - a regressive transformation back into the threatening parental images whose conglomeration originally formed it.

Differentiation is a process which is essentially to integration, and vice versa, for personality structure-functions or psychic contents to become integrated, they must first have emerged as partially differentiated or separated from one another, and differentiation in turn can emerge only out of a foundation of more or less integrated function or contents.

When we look at this process of differentiation in the schizophrenic person, we find it to be, similarly, severely impaired. It is difficult or impossible for him to differentiate between himself and the outer world. He often cannot distinguish between memories and present perceptions, memories experienced with hallucinatory vividness and immediacy are sensed as perceptions of present events. And perceptions of present events may be experienced as memories from the past. He may be unable to distinguish between emotions and somatic sensations, feelings from the emotional sphere often come through to him as somatic sensations, or even variations in his somatic structure (changes in the size, colour and so forth, of bodily parts).

He cannot distinguish between thoughts and feelings on the one hand, and action on the other: Thus, if the therapist encourages him to explore thoughts and feelings of a sexual or murderous nature, for example, he feels that the therapist is trying to invite him into sexual activity, or incite him to murder. He may be unable to differentiate, perceptually, one person from another, so that he is prone to misidentify them.

In the conduct of his daily life and in his communicating with other persons, he is unable, as Bateson et al. has reported, to distinguish between the symbolic and the concrete. If his therapist uses symbolic language, he may experience this in literal terms, and, on the other hand, the affairs of daily life (eating, dressing, sleeping and so on) which we think of as literal and concrete, he may react to as possessing a unique symbolic significance which completely obscures their 'practical' importance in his life for being part of the untold story for being human.

However, in the schizophrenic these two processes, that is to say, that of integration and differentiation, that tend to be out of step with one another, so that at one moment a patient's more urgent need may be for increased integration, whereas at another he may more urgently need increased differentiation. And there are some patients who show for months on end a more urgent need in one of these areas, before the alternate growth-phase comes on the scene. Thus, there is a modicum of validity in speaking of two different 'types' of schizophrenic patients. This distinction is largely artificial, but it is useful for purposes of serving to explain of something that makes clear what is obscure bu t not readily understood or grasped from the main centres of human activity.

One comes to realize, how premature have been one's efforts to find out what feelings the patient is experiencing or what thoughts he is having: One comes to realize that much of the time he has neither feelings nor thoughts differentiated as such and communicable to us.

Such differentiation as the patient possess tends to crumble when intense emotion enters his awareness. A paranoid man, for example, may find that when his hatred toward another person reaches a certain degree of intensity, he is flooded with anxiety because he no longer knows whether he hates, or instead, 'really loves' the other individual. This is not based, as primarily upon the mechanism which Freud (1911) outlined in his classical description of the nature of paranoid delusions of persecution, a description in which repressed homosexual love played the central role. the central difficulty is rather that the ego is too poorly differentiated to maintain its structure in the face of such powerful affects, and the patient becomes overwhelmed with what can only be described as 'undifferentiated passion', precisely as one finds an infant to be overwhelmed at times with affect which the observer cannot specifically identify as any one kind of emotion.

As for the feelings which the therapist himself experiences in working with the 'non-differentiated type' of patient, we fund, again, a persistent threat of the therapist's sense of identity. But whereas, in the instance the threat was felt predominantly as a disturbance of one's personal integration, it is felt predominantly as a weakening of one's sense of differentiation. In this instance, the 'therapeutic symbiosis' which a necessary development, tends to occur earlier, for this patient's predominant mode of relatedness with other persons, at the developmental level at which point we find him at the very beginning of a symbiotic relatedness among others, that is to say, with its subjective absence of ego-boundaries, involves not only special gratification but anxiety-provoking disturbances of one's sense of personal identity.

The comparatively rapid development of symbiotic relatedness is facilitated by the patient's characteristically non-verbal, therapeutic sessions. In response, the therapist's own behaviour becomes more and more similar, so that each participant is now offering to the other, the intermittence over which of times are silent, impassive screen which facilitates abundant mutual projecting and introjecting. Thus a symbiotic state is likely to be reached earlier than in one's work with the typically much more verbal type of patient whom, for instance, that the patient's and the therapist's more abundant verbalizations tend persistently to stress the ego-boundaries separating the two persons from one another.

With the predominantly non-differentiated patient, the therapist's sense of identity as a complexly differentiated individual entity becomes further eroded, or undermined, as he finds the patient persistently operating on the unwavering conviction, that, time after time, that the therapist is but an undifferentiated aspect of the whole vague mass of which his own poorly differentiated hostility, but which in the patient's tenaciously held view, is the way the world around him really is.

Further, since the patient typically verbalized little but a few maddeningly monotonous stereotypes, the therapist tends to feel over the course of time, with so little of his own intellectual content being explicitly tapped in the relationship, that his richness of intellect is progressively rusting away - becoming less differentiated, more stereotyped and rudimentary. Moreover, the patient presents but one of two emotional wavelengths to which the therapist can himself tune in. Rather than a rich spectrum of emotion which calls into resource a similarly wide range of feelings from the therapist himself. Thus not only the therapist's intellectual resources, but his emotional capacities too, become subjectively narrowed down and impoverished, as he finds that his patient evokes in him neither any wide range of ideas, nor any emotion except, for example, rage, or contempt, or dull hopelessness.

This feeling experience on his part, anxiety-provoking and discouraging though he finds it, is a necessary therapeutic development. it is necessary, that is, for him thus to experience at first hand something of the patient's own lack of differentiation, for, as in the therapy with the non-integrated patient, that, again, the healing process occurs external to the patient, as it were, at an intrapsychic level in the therapist, before it becomes established in the patient himself. That is, the therapist's coming to view the patient, his relationship with the patient, and himself in this relationship, all for being largely non-differentiated, is a development which sets the stage for the patient's gradually increasing differentiation. Now the therapist comes too sense, time after time, newly emerging tendrils of differentiation in the patient, before the latter is himself conscious of them. In responding to these with spontaneity as they show themselves, time and again, that the therapist helps the patient to become aware that they are a part of him. But there are times when a therapist can only say that he feels a new response in himself in reaction to behaviour which objectively seems as stereotyped as ever.

Thus a heavy reliance upon one's intuition is a technical point, although a second point concerns the relatively sparing use of transference interpretation - perhaps, more sparing than in one's work with the predominantly non-integrated, or fragmented, patient. in the instance of that first 'type' of patient, such that transference interpretations may have a specific value in fostering the patient's wholeness, his integration, by focussing his disparate personality fragments into the context of the patient-therapist relationship. But the predominantly non-differentiated patient, who is, above all trying to branch out, in his interpersonal relationships and in his intrapsychic content, beyond the immediate, symbiotic situation with the therapist, premature transference interpretations which tend to bring it all back to the relationship with his therapist - which tend, that is, to reduce divergent ramifications of meaning to this one idea that something conveys to the mind as the one purpose to accomplish or do, as such is the intention of meaning.

The third and last technical point is, like the others, a function of the growth process of a process which involves both patient and the therapist. The patient's differentiation is fostered not only by the therapist's sensing, and responding to, an increasingly differentiated person in him, but also by the therapist's permitting his own personality differentiation, his own complex individuality which was to a greater extent, already firmly established before beginning work with this patient, to come more and more freely into play in the therapeutic relationship. At a crucial point is, for example, he must have the courage to act upon the course that his own intuition directs, in deferring sharply from the patient - to be the person he knows himself to be and to address the person he knows to inhabit the patient's body, no matter how sharply this conflicts with the patient's own image of himself and of his therapist. Whereas, it was essential earlier to allow the anxiety-arousing symbiosis to develop, now the therapist must find similar courage to help determinedly in its resolution. In asserting increasingly his own complex individuality, he provides the patient with an increasingly clearly differentiated person with whom to identify and over against whom to become conscious of his own separate self.

That the states of what are called non-integration and non-differentiation should be thought of as not merely rather fixed levels of maturation or regression at which a patient exists over a long period of time, but as flexible defences of the ego against overwhelming anxiety. Thus, from noticing at what moments in the theopathic session, or at what junctures over the long course of treatment, a patient's characteristic non-integration or non-differentiation notably increases or notably lessons, we can tell when areas of particularity severe anxiety have been encountered in his personality investigation, and chart the resolution of this anxiety as growth proceeds.

Reality is a difficult word to use to every one's satisfaction or even to one's own satisfaction. In this instance the word reality is used arbitrarily to designate the direct, here-and-now impact of the analyst upon the patient. Reality. In this sense, contrasts with the impact the analyst has through his representation in the patient's fantasy life, neurosis, and transference, since both kinds of impact seem always to coexist and since the former - the analyst's real impact - may be the worst enemy of the transference, the matter of their differentiation is possibly the most challenging aspect of analysis.

The analytic situation, which is set up to shut out ordinary reality intrusions, that cannot, . . . neither should not exclude all, but to say, that in the beginning months, for instance, reality inevitably has the upper hand. The analyst, the office, the procedure, are all overwhelmingly real. Everything is strange, frightening and exciting, gratifying and frustrating. Unlike the patient can test it and orient himself to it, the impact of this reality is usually so great that even an ordinary useful transference relationship cannot be expected to develop.

Perhaps the most confusing aspect of this beginning period is the frequent appearance in it of what can be regarded as a false transference relationship. With great intensity and clarity, the patient may reveal, through transference-like references about the analyst, some of the deepest secrets only of his neurosis but of its genesis. The pseudotransference, too good to be true, is almost sure to be nothing more than the patient's attempt to deal with the person of the analyst, the entire spectrum of his various patterns of behaviour. If, it is easy to do, the analyst overlooks the likelihood that the patient's relationship with at this time is really about that almost everything said about it is related, analysis may get off to a very bad start. And if, as is even earlier to do, the analyst's interests the genetic meaning of the openly exposed material, a good transference relationship may be seriously delayed and a workable transference neurosis may never appear. even after initial reality has had time to fade, reality may continue to intrude in ways that are very hard to detect and that is very troublesome.

One of the most serious problems of analysis is the very substantial help which the patient receives directly from the analyst and the analytic situation. For many a patient, the analyst in the analytic situation is in fact the most stable, reasonable, wise and understanding person he has ever met, and the setting in which they meet may actually be the most honest, open, direct and regular relationship he has ever experienced. Added to this is the considerable helpfulness to him of being able to clarify his life storey. confess his guilt, express his ambitions, and explore his confusions. Further real help comes from the learning-about-life accruing from the analyst's skilled questions, observations and interpretations. Taken together, the total real value to the patient of the analytic situation can easily be immense. The trouble with this kind of help is that it goes on and on, it may have such a real, direct and continuing impact upon the patient that he can never get deeply enough involved in transference situation to allow him to resolve or even to become acquainted with his most crippling internal difficulties. The trouble is far too good, the trouble also is that we as analysts apparently cannot resist the seductiveness of being directly helpful, and this, when combined with the compelling assumption that helpfulness is bound to be good, permits us top credit patient improvements to 'analysis' when more properly it should often be recognized for being the amounting result for the patient's using the analytic situation, as the model, for being the preceptors and supporter in the dealing practically within the immediate distractions as holding to some problem.

Perhaps, we can now refer to something in a clear unmistakable manner, and it would be to mention, for being, that one more difficult-to-handle intrusion of reality into the analysis, that by saying, that this is the definitive and final interruption of the transference neurosis by the reality of termination; in the sense, the situation is reversed and the intrusion is analytically desirable, since ideally the impact of reality of impending and certain termination is used to facilitate the resolution of the transference. As with the resolution of earlier episodes of transference neurosis, this final one is brought about principally by the analyst's interpretations and reconstructions. As these take effect, the transference neurosis and, hopefully, along with it the original neurosis is resolved. This final resolution, however, which is much more comprehensive, is usually very different and may not come about at all without the help of the reality of termination. Accordingly, any attenuation of the ending, such as tapering off or causal or tentative stopping, should be expected to stand in the way of an effective resolution of the transference. Yet, it seems that this is what most commonly happens to an ending, and because of this a great many patients may lose the potentially great benefit of a thorough resolution and are forever after left suspended in the net of unresolved transference.

Yet, utter indistinctly rigorous termination seems understandable, as difficult as transference neurosis may be in the analyst at other times, this ending period, if rigorously carried out, simply has to be the period of his greatest emotional strain. There can surely be no more likely time for an analyst to surrender his analytic position and, responding to his own transference, become personally involved with his patient than during the process of separating from a long and self-restrained relationship. Accordingly, it may be better to slur over the ending lightly than to mishandle it in an attempt to be rigorous.

In considering more broadly the function of the transference in the psychoanalytic process, one is confronted by the apparent naïve, but, nonetheless important questions of the role of the actual (current) object as compared with that of the object representation of the original personage in the past. We recall Freud's paradoxical, somewhat gloomy, but portentous concluding passage in 'The Dynamics of Transference.' This struggle between the doctor and the patient, between intellect and instinctual life, between understanding and seeking to act, is played out almost exclusively in the phenomena of transference. It is on that field that the victory must be won - the victory whose expression is on that field that the victory must be won - the victory whose expression is the permanent cure of the neuroses. It cannot be disputed that controlling the phenomena of transference presents the psychoanalysis with the greatest difficultly, but it should not be forgotten that they do us the inestimable service of making the patient 's hidden and forgotten erotic impulses of showing their immediate and manifested impossibilities, for when all is said and done, it is impossible to destroy anyone in absentia or in effigies.

Both object and representations are made necessary by the basic phenomenon of original separation. The existence of an image of the object, which persist in the absence of the object, is one of the important beginnings of psychic life in general, certainly an indispensable prerequisite for object relationship. As generally construed. Whether this is viewed as (or a times demonstrably is) something unstable for allotting introjection, s always subject to alternative projection, or an intrapsychic object representation clearly distinguished from the self-representation, or firm identification in the superego, or in the ego itself, these phenomena are in various ways components of the system of mastery of the fact of separation, or separateness, from the original absolutely necessarily anaclitic (in the earliest period) symbiotic 'object'. In the light of clinical observation, it would appear to be that the relative stabilities (parental) object representation. At which time of varying degree, are to a greater extent for the archaic phenomena. Even in nonpsychotic patients, overwhelmed by them, sometimes resembles the restoration from oedipal identification, which provides the preponderant basis for most demonstrable analytic transferences. That within the necrotic patients, the transference is effectively established when this representation invests the analyst to a degree - depending on intensity of drive and most of ego participation - which ranges in all the wishing and contending attempts of striving to remake and analyst to biasses judgements and misinterpretation of data, finally are the actual perceptual distortions.

However, the old object representations may be invested, however rigidly established the libidinal or aggressive cathexis of the image may be, this as such can become the actual and exclusive focus of instinctual discharge, or of complicated and intense instinct-defence solutions, only and general energy-sparing quality of strictly intrapsychic processes. For the vast majority of persons, visible to any degree, including those with severe neurosis, character distortions, addictions and certain psychoses, the striving is toward the living and actual object, even at the cost of intense suffering. In a sense, this returns us to the state in which the psychological 'object-to-be'. Has a cr11itical importance never again to be duplicated, except in certain acute life emergencies, even if the object is not firmly perceived as such, in the sense of later object relations? And it does seem that trance impressions from the earliest contacts in the service of life preservation, and the associated instinctual gratifications, and innumerable secondarily associated sensory impressions. Are activated by the specific inborn urges of sexual maturation? These propel the individual to renew many of the earliest modes of actual bodily contact, in connection with seeking for specific instinctual gratification. Or, to look away from clear-cut instinctual matters to the more remote elaborations of human contact: Few regard loneliness as other than a source of suffering, even self-imposed, as an apparent matter of choice, and the forcible imposition of 'solitary confinement ' is surely one of the most cruel of punishments.

In taking to question, we are entering an area of life in which things are other then themselves, where meaning is multifaceted, and where the line between the old and the new is blurred. It should, by, its immediate measure, help develop our recognition or meaning of the pertinent applicability as to the relevance of interrelated aspects of the psychology of 'metaphor'. In the psychology of metaphor we will find a useful analogy to the psychology of transference interpretation. Our's will be newly encountered as good metaphors, those it response to which we say, 'That's it exactly' or 'That really captures it' or 'That says it all'.

Some literary and linguistic analysis, (e.g., Lewis, 1936 and Snell, 1953) and also people in everyday life, believe that there are experiences that can only be expressed metaphorically. And for this achievement that these metaphors, which may be entire poem or as lines or even words highly valued. But how can this be so? Just what in th e 'it' that the metaphor 'is' or 'captures' or 'says'? If this 'is' or this 'experience' can only be rendered metaphorically, when we can know it only as such, that is, as the metaphor itself. Of the position out of which are put forward by, T.S, Eliot (1933) and E.W. Harding (1963) in their discussion of poetry, for in these instances we are granted that there are no known and logically independent version of the experience that can serve to validate the metaphor. Whatever the metaphor makes available to us depends on it and it and so cannot be used to prove its correctness.

It seems justifiable warrantable to consider that the metaphor is a new experience rather than a mere paraphrase of an already fully constituted expedience. The metaphor creates an experience that one has never had before. It is an experience one has not realized by oneself. The metaphor does, of course, suggest certain constituent experiences of which one may have been more or less dimly aware. One may say, therefore, that the metaphor speaks for those constituents, on the existence of which much of its appeal depends. But in its organizing and implicit ly rendering these constituents in its new way, it is a creation rather than a mere paraphrase or anew edition. Paraphrasing and new editions never speak as forcefully as good new metaphors, nor could they facilitate further new experience. One analytically familiar feature of these creations is that they make it safe and pleasing to experience something that otherwise would be considered too threatening and so would be kept in fragmented obscurity through defensive measures.

Thus, when one says, 'That's it exactly' one is implicitly recognizing and announcing that one has found and accepted a new mode of experiencing oneself and one's world, which is to say, asserting a transformation of one's own subjectivity. Something is now said to be true, and in a sense it is true, but it is true for the first time. Nothing of one and the same can ever happen again, for the second time cannot be the same as the first. One can' t step into the same watering point and then step once again into the same spot of that river. A revelatory metaphor re-encountered or repeated later may lose some of its force, alternatively, it may gain some significance, butt it cannot remain exactly the same metaphor or mobilize an experience identical with the first. The point applies as well as to new metaphors that are similar to familiar ones: They have to be judged or experienced through their conventionalized predecessors, as through methods of knowing or already proved instrumentally of perceiving. The audience and the performer, who may be one person, as such that may not have, as yet.

What is to be said about the psychology of metaphor is analogous to the transformational aspects of developed transference and the steadfast interpretation that both facilitate and organize them as transference. Allowing that these transferences and 'remembered' experiences come into existence over a period of time, nothing that is identical with them has ever before been enacted, and nothing will ever be enacted again. They are creations that may be fully achieved only under specific analytic conditions. Such that living was not reliving that moment, words like re-living, re-experiencing and reliving simply do not do justice to the phenomena, that in making this claim. A seeming contradiction over-writes some of our well-establish ideas. - in offering, - I am not contradicting some of our well-established ideas about interpretation and insight, I am, however, disputing the point that insight refers to a greater proportion or in its range of comprehension, which its distance between possible extremes extent and regain former or normal state, such that, for the recovery of lost memories, and takes in as well, a new grasp of the significance and interpretations of events one has always remembered. In point, as, Freud pointed out, 'As a matter of fact I've always known it, only that I've never thought of it; (1914), In fact, it is to develop that point in furthering to say that it takes an adult to do that, especially with the help of an analyst. It was, after all, Freud's analysis of adults that make it possible to define infantile psychosexuality. In this respect, but without disregard, child analysis retains a quality of applied psychoanalysis' in the same way that the interpreted transference neurosis is: Both are always of describing as true something that was not true in quite that way at the time of its greatest developmental significance. This apparent paradox about 'remembering' as a form of creating goes a long way, probably that what it is, is distinctive about psychoanalytic interpretation.

This time, however, to further the discussion on the interpretive technique that surrounds the phase of a mutative interpretation - that in which a portion of the patient's id-relation to the analyst is made conscious in virtue of the latter's positions as auxiliary superego - is in itself complex. In the classical model of an interpretation, the patient will first be made aware of a state of tension of an interpretation, will next be made aware that there is repressive factor at work (that his superego is threatening him with punishment), and will only then be made aware of the id-impulse which has stirred up the protects of his superego and so given to the anxiety in his ego. This is the classical scheme. In actual practice, the analyst finds himself working from all three sides at once, or in irregular successions. At one moment a small portion of the patient's superego may be revealed to him in all its savagery, at another the shrinking defencelessness of his ego, at yet another his attention may be directed to the attempts which he is making at restitution - at compensating for his hostility, on some occasions a fraction of id-energy may even be directly encouraged to break its way through the last remains of an already weakened resistance. There is, however, one characteristic which all of these various operations has in common, they are essentially upon a small scale. For the mutative interpretation is inevitably governed by the principle of minimal doses. It is a commonly agreed clinical fact that alternations in a patient under analysis appear almost always to be extremely gradual: We are inclined to suspect sudden and large changes as an indication that suggestive rather than psycho-analyst processes are at work. The gradual nature of the change brought about in psychoanalysis will be explained, as, only to suggest, those changes are the result of the summation of an immense number of minuet steps, each of which correspond to a mutative interpretation. And the smallness of each step is in turn imposed by the very nature of the analytic situation. For each interpretation involves the release of a certain quantity of id-energy, and, if the quantity released is too large, the higher unstable state of equilibrium which enables the analyst to function as the patient's auxiliary superego is bound to be upset. The whole analytic situation will thus be imperilled, since it is only in virtue of the analyst's acting as auxiliary superego that these released id-energy can occur at all.

The effectuality from which follow the analytic attempt to bring unequalled amounts in the confronting collections of some improper use too a resultant quantity of id-energy into the patient's consciousness all at once. On the one hand, nothing whatever may happen, or on the other hand there may be an unmanageable result, but in neither event will be a mutative interpretation has been effected. The analyst's power as auxiliary superego may be for two very different reasons. It may be that the id-impulses were trying to bring out being not in fact sufficiently urgent at the moment: For, after all, the emergence of an id-impulse depends on two factors - not only on the permission of the superego, but also on the urgency (the degree of cathaxis) of the id-impulse itself. This, then, may be one cause of an apparently negative response to an interpretation, and evidently a fairly harmless one. but the same apparent result may also be due to something else, in spite of the id-impulse being really urgent, the strength of the patient's own repressive forces (the degree of repression) may have been too great to allow his ego to listen to the persuasive voice of the auxiliary superego. Now we have a situation dynamically identical with the next one we have to consider, though economically different. this next situation is one in which the patient accepts the interpretation, that is, allows the id-impulse into his consciousness, but is immediately overwhelmed with anxiety. This may show itself in a number of ways, for instance, the patient may produce a manifest anxiety-attack. Or the may exhibit signs of 'real' anger with the analyst with a complete lack of insight, or he may break off the analysis. In any of these cases the analytic situation will, for the moment, at least, have broken down. The patient will be behaving just as the hypnotic subject behaves when, having been ordered by the hypnotist to perform an action too much at variance with his own consciousness, he breaks off the hypnotic relation and wakes up from his trance. This state of things, which is manifest where the patient responds to an interpretation with an actual outbreak of anxiety or one of its equivalents, may be latent were the patient shows no response, and this latter case may be the more awkward of the two, since it is masked, and it may sometimes be the effect of a greater overdose of interpretation than where manifest anxiety arises (though obviously other factors will be of determining importance, and in particularly the nature of the patient's neurosis). Yet this threatened collapse of the analytic situation to an overdose of interpretation: But it might be more accurate in some ways to ascribe it to an insufficient dose. For what has happened is that the second phase of the interpretation process has not occurred: The phase in which the patient becomes aware that his impulse is directed toward an archaic phantasy object and not toward a real one.

In the second phase of a complete interpretation, therefore, a crucial part is played by the patient's sense of reality: For the successful outcome of that phase depends upon his ability, at the critical moment of the emergence into consciousness of the released quantity of id-energy, to distinguish between his phantasy object and the real analyst. The problem is closely related to one that has been discussed elsewhere, namely that of the extreme liability of the analyst's position as auxiliary superego. The analytic situation is all the time threatening to degenerate into a 'real' situation. But this actually means the opposite of what it appears to. It means that the patient is all the time on the brink of turning the really external object (the analyst) into the archaic one; that is to say, he is on the brink of projecting his primitive introjected images onto himself. In so far as the patient actually does this, the analyst becomes like anyone else that he meets in real life - a phantasy object. The analyst then ceases to possess the peculiar advantages derived from the analytic situation, he will be introjected like all other phantasy objects into the analytic situation, he will be introjected like all other phantasy objects into the patient's superego, and will no longer be able to function in the peculiar ways which are essential to the effecting of a mutative interpretation. In this difficulty the patient's sense of reality is an essential but a very feeble [-ally]: An improvement in it is one of the things that we hope the analysis will bring about. It is important, therefore, not to submit it to any unnecessary strain, and that is the fundamental reason why the analyst must avoid any real behaviour, that is likely to confirm the patient's view of him as a 'bad' or a 'good' phantasy object. This is perhaps more obvious as regards the 'bad' object. If, for instance, the analyst were to show that he was really shocked or frightened by one of the patient's id-impulses, as the patient would immediately treat him in that respect as a dangerous object and introject him into his archaic severe superego. Therefore, on the one hand, there would be a diminuation in the analyst's power to function as an auxiliary superego and to allow the patient's to become conscious of his id-impulses - that is to say, in his power to bring about the first phase of a mutative interpretation, and on the other hand, he would, as a real object, become sensibly less distinguishable from the patient's 'bad' phantasy object and to that extent the carrying through of the second phase of a mutative interpretation would also be made more difficult. Or, agin, there is another case. Supposing the analyst behaves in an opposite way and actively urges the patient to give free rein to his id-impulse. There is then a possibility of the patient confusing the analyst with the image of a treacherous parent who, at the beginning, encourage him to seek gratification, and then suddenly turns and punishes him. In such a case the patient's ego may look for defence by itself suddenly turning upon the analyst as though he were his own id-, and treating him with all the severity of which his superego is capable. again, the analyst is running a risk of losing his privileged position. But it may be equally unwise for the analyst to act really in such a way as to encourage the patient to project his 'good' introjected object on to him. For the patient will then tend to regard him as a good objective and archaic sense and will incorporate him with his archaic 'good' images and will use him as a protection against his 'bad' ones. In that way, his infantile positive impulses as well as his negative ones may escape analysis, for there may no longer be a possibility for his ego to make a comparison between the phantasy external object and the real one. it will, perhaps, be argued that, with the best of wills in the world, the analyst, however careful he may be, will be unable to prevent the patient from projecting these various images on to him. This is, of course, indisputable, and, the whole effectiveness of analysis depends upon its being so. The lesson of these difficulties is merely to remind us that the patient's sense of reality has the narrowest limits. It is a paradoxical fact that the best way of enuring that his ego will be able to distinguish between phantasy and reality is to withhold reality from him as much as possible. but it is true, his ego is so weak - so much at the mercy of his id and superego - that he can only cope with reality if it is administered in minimal doses. And these doses are in fact what the analyst gives him, in the form of interpretations.

A mutative interpretation can only be applied to an id-impulse which is actually on a state of cathexis. This seems self-evident; for the dynamic changes in the patient's mind implied by a mutative interpretation can only be brought about by the operation of a charge of energy originating in the patient himself: The function of the analyst is merely to ensure that the energy should or can flow along one channel rather than along another. It follows that the purely informative 'dictionary' type of interpretation will be non-mutative, but useful it may be a prelude to mutative interpretations. And this leads to a number of practical inferences. Every mutative interpretation must be emotionally 'immediate, but the patient must live through it as something actual or genuine. This requirement, that the interpretation must be 'immediate', may be expressed in another way by saying that interpretation must always be directed to the 'point of urgency'. At any given moment some particular id-impulse will be generated in activity, this is the impulse that is susceptible of mutative interpretation at the time, and no other one. It is, no doubt, neither possible nor desirable to be giving mutative interpretations all the time. as Melanie Klein has pointed out, it is a most precious quality in an analyst to be able at any moment to pick out the point of urgency.

But the fact that every mutative interpretation must deal with an 'urgent' impulse takes us back one more to the commonly felt fear of the explosive possibilities of interpretation, and particularly of what is vaguely referred to as 'deep' interpretation. The terminological description is, no doubt, as the interpretation of material which is neither genetically early and historically distant from the patient's actual experience nor under an especially heavy weight of repression – material, in any case, which is in the normal course of things exceedingly inaccessible to his ego and remote from it. There seems reason to believe, moreover, that the anxiety which is liable to be aroused by the approach of such material to consciousness and may be of peculiar severity. The question whether it is 'safe' to interpret such material will, as usual, mainly depend upon whether an interpretation can be carried through, in the ordinary run of the case, as this material which is urgent during the earlier stages of the analysis is not deep. We have to deal at first only with more or less far-going displacements of the deep impulse. And the deep material itself is only reached later and by degrees, so that no sudden appearance of unmanageable quantities of anxiety is to be hesitorially anticipated. In exceptional cases, however, owing to some peculiarities in the structure of the neurosis, deep impulses may be urgent at a very early stage of the analysis. We are then faced by a dilemma. If we give an interpretation of this deep material, the resultant amounts of anxiety produced in the patient may be so great that his sense of reality may not be sufficient to permit of its accomplishment, and the whole analysis may be jeopardised, but, it must not be thought that, in such critical cases as we are now considering, the difficulty can necessarily be avoided simply by not giving any interpretation or by giving more superficial interpretations of non-urgent material or by attempting reassurances. It seems probable, in fact, that these alternative procedures may do little or nothing to obviate the trouble, on the contrary, they may even exacerbate the tension created by the urgency of the deep impulses which are the actual cause of the threatening anxiety. Thus the anxiety may break out in spite of these palliative efforts and, if so, it will be doing so under the most unfavourable conditions, that is to say, outside the mitigating influences afforded by the mechanism of interpretation. It is possible, therefore, that, of these alternative procedures which are open to the analyst faced by such a difficulty. The interpretation of the urgent id-impulses, deep though they may b e, will actually be the safer.

It is, of course, a matter of common experience, that it possible with certain patients to continue indefinitely giving interpretations without producing any apparent effect whatever. There is an amusing criticism of this kind of 'interpretation-fanaticism' in the excellent historical chapter of Rank and Ferenczi. But it is clear from their words that what they have in mind are essentially extra-transference interpretations, for the burden of their criticism is that such a procedure implies neglect of the analytic situation. This is the simplest case. Where a waste of time and energy is the main result. But there are other occasions, on which a policy of giving strings of extra-transference interpretations is apt to lead the analyst into more positive difficulties. Attention was drawn by Reich a few years back, in the course of some technical discussions in Vienna too a tendency among inexperienced analysts to get into trouble by eliciting from the patient great quantities of material in a disordered and unrelated fashion: This may, be maintained, be carried to such lengths that the analysis is brought to an irremediable state of chaos. He pointe out truly that the material we have to deal with is stratified and that it is highly important in digging it out not to interference, more that we can help with th e arrangement of that state. He had in mind, of course, the analogy of an incompetent archaeologist, whose clumsiness may obliterate for all time the possibility of reconstructing the history of an important site. However, the results in the case of a clumsy analysis do not hold of any pessimistic cause to happen, as it were, re-stratification itself of its own accord if it is given the opportunity; That is to say, in the analytic situation. At the same time, is that of the presence of the risk, and it seems to be particularly likely to occur where extra-transference interpretation is excessively or exclusively restored to. The means of preventing it, and the remedy if it has occurred, lie in returning to transference interpretation at the point of urgency. For if we can discover which of the material is 'immediate' in the sense that the problematic occurrence enabling stratification is automatically solved, and it is a characteristic if most extra-transference material that it has no immediacy and consequently stratification is far more difficult to decipher. The measures suggested by Reich himself for preventing the occurrence of this state of chaos are not inconsistent with those that he stresses the importance of interpreting resistance as opposed to the primary id-impulses themselves - and this, was a policy that was laid down at an early stage in the history of analysis. But it is, of course, one of the characteristics of a resistance that it arises in relation to the analyst. Thus, interpretation of a resistance will almost inevitably be a transference interpretation.

But the most serious risks that arise from the making of extra-transference interpretation are due to the inherent difficulty in completing their interpretation, for a successful outcome as such, depends upon his ability, at which time of the emergence into consciousness and the released quantity of id-energy. They are from their nature unpredictable in their effects. There seems to be a special risk of the patient not carrying through to a competed interpretation, hitherto, namely that the extreme liability of the analyst's position as auxiliary superego, is that, the analytic situation is all the time threatening to degenerate into a 'real' situation. It means that the patient is all the time perched upon the circumference edge-horizon of turning the external object (the analyst) into the archaic one, but of projecting the id-impulse that has been made conscious on to the analyst. This risk, no doubt, applies to some extent to transference interpretations. However, the situation is less likely to arise when the object of the id-impulses is actually present and is moreover the same person as the maker of interpretation. We may, once, more, recall the problem of 'deep' interpretation, and point out that its dangers, even in the most unfavourable circumstances, seem to be greatly diminished if the interpretation in question is a transference interpretation. Even so, there appears to be more of a chance that in this whole process occurring silently and so being overlooked in the case of an extra-transference interpretation, particularly in the earlier stages of an analysis. For this reason, it would seem to be important after giving an extra-transference interpretation to be specially in the 'qui-vive' for transferences complications. This last peculiarity of the extra-transference interpretation is actually one of their most important from a practical stand-point. For on account of it they can be made to act as 'feeders' for the transference situation, and so to pave the way for mutative interpretations. In other words, by giving an extra-transference interpretation, the analyst can often provide a situation in the transference of which he can then give a mutative interpretation.

Therefore, it is probable that a large majority of our interpretations are outside the transference - though it should be added that it often happens that one is ostensibly giving an extra-transference interpretation one is implicitly giving a transference one. A cake cannot be made of nothing but currants, and, though it is true that extra-transference interpretations, are not for the most part, mutative and do not they bring about the crucial results that involve a permanent change in the patient's mind. They are, nonetheless essential, if taken to an analogy of trench warfare, the acceptance of a transference interpretation corresponds to the capture of a key position, while the extra-transference interpretations correspond to the general advance and to the consolidation of a fresh line of defence, which are made possible by the capture of the key position. But when this general advance goes beyond a certain point, there will be another check, and the capture of a further key position will be necessary before progress can be resumed. An oscillation of this kind between transference and extra-transference interpretations will represent the normative course of events in an analysis.

Although the giving of mutative interpretations may thus only occupy a small portion of psychoanalytic treatment, it will, upon be, that the most important part from the point of view of deeply exerting affective percussions. Do so, because of the influencing characteristic confirmations as drawn upon the spoken-exchange of the patient's mindful knowing, in that the individuals that feel, perceive, think, wills, and especially reasons are all taken into heedful compliance. It may be of interest to consider how a moment which is such importance to th e patient affects the analyst himself. Mrs. Klein has suggested that there must be some quite special internal difficulty as to involve the analyst in interpretations. This is shown in their avoidance by psycho-therapists of non-analytic schools, but many psycho-analysts will be aware of traces of the same tendency in themselves. It may be rationalized into mutative interpretations. This is shown in the avoidance by psycho-therapists of non-analytic schools, yet not many consisting of a psycho-analyst flow of some flowing emptiness, nonetheless, this dialectic awareness traces of the same tendency as in themselves. But behind this there is somewhat of a lurking difficulty in the actual giving of the interpretation, for there seems to be a constant temptation for the analyst to do something else instead. Questions may be asked of whether o r not. As given to the reassurances or advice or discourses upon theory, or may give interpretations -but interpretations that are not mutative, extra-transference interpretations, interpretations that are non-immediate, or ambiguous, or in exacting of two or more alternative interpretations simultaneously, or he may, perhaps, give interpretations and at the same time, show his own scepticism about them. All of this strongly suggests that the giving of a mutative interpretation is a crucial act for the analyst as well as for the patient. And this inturn will become intelligible when we reflect that at the moment of interpretation the analyst is in fact deliberately evoking a quantity of the patients id-energy while it is a live and actual and unambiguous and aimed directly himself. Such a moment must be above all others put to the test his relations with his unconscious impulses.

One of the most serious problems of analysis is the very substantial help that the patient receives directly from the analyst and the analytic situation. For many a patient, the analyst in the analytic situation is in fact the most stable, reasonable, wise and understanding person he has ever met, and the setting in which they meet may actually be the most honest, open, direct and regular relationship he has ever experienced. Added to this is the considerable helpfulness to him of being able to clarify his life storey. Confess his guilt, express his ambitions, and explore his confusions. Further real help comes from the learning-about-life accruing from the analyst's skilled questions, observations and interpretations. Taken together, the total real value to the patient of the analytic situation can easily be immense. The trouble with this kind of help is that it goes on and on, it may have such a real, direct and continuing impact upon the patient that he can never get deeply enough involved in transference situation to allow him to resolve or even to become acquainted with his most crippling internal difficulties. The trouble is far too good, the trouble also is that we as analysts apparently cannot resist the seductiveness of being directly helpful, and this, when combined with the compelling assumption that helpfulness is bound to be good, permits us top credit patient improvements to 'analysis' when more properly it should often be recognized for being the amounting result for the patient's using the analytic situation, as the model, for being the preceptors and supporter in the dealing practically within the immediate distractions as holding to some problem.

Perhaps, we can now refer to something in a clear unmistakable manner, and it would be to mention, for being, that one more difficult-to-handle intrusion of reality into the analysis, that by saying, that this is the definitive and final interruption of the transference neurosis by the reality of termination; in the sense, the situation is reversed and the intrusion is analytically desirable, since ideally the impact of reality of impending and certain termination is used to facilitate the resolution of the transference. As with the resolution of earlier episodes of transference neurosis, this final one is brought about principally by the analyst's interpretations and reconstructions. As these take effect, the transference neurosis and, hopefully, along with it the original neurosis is resolved. This final resolution, however, which is much more comprehensive, is usually very different and may not come about at all without the help of the reality of termination. Accordingly, any attenuation of the ending, such as tapering off or causal or tentative stopping, should be expected to stand in the way of an effective resolution of the transference. Yet, it seems that this is what most commonly happens to an ending, and because of this a great many patients may lose the potentially great benefit of a thorough resolution and are forever after left suspended in the net of unresolved transference.

Yet, slurring over a rigorous termination seems understandable, as difficult as transference neurosis may be in the analyst at other times, this ending period, if rigorously carried out, simply has to be the period of his greatest emotional strain. There can surely be no more likely time for an analyst to surrender his analytic position and, responding to his own transference, become personally involved with his patient than during the process of separating from a long and self-restrained relationship. Accordingly, it may be better to slur over the ending lightly than to mishandle it in an attempt to be rigorous.

In considering more broadly the function of the transference in the psychoanalytic process, one is confronted by the apparent naïve, but, nonetheless important questions of the role of the actual (current) object as compared with that of the object representation of the original personage in the past. We recall Freud's paradoxical, somewhat gloomy, but portentous concluding passage in 'The Dynamics of Transference.' This struggle between the doctor and the patient, between intellect and instinctual life, between understanding and seeking to act, is played out almost exclusively in the phenomena of transference. It is on that field that the victory must be won - the victory whose expression is on that field that the victory must be won - the victor y whose expression is the permanent cure of the neuroses. It cannot be disputed that controlling the phenomena of transference presents the psychoanalysis with the greatest difficultly, but it should not be forgotten that they do us the inestimable service of making the patient 's hidden and forgotten erotic impulses of showing their immediate and manifested impossibilities, for when all is said and done, it is impossible to destroy anyone in absentia or in effigies.

Both object and representation is made necessary by the basic phenomenon of original separation. The existence of an image of the object, which persist in the absence of the object, is one of the important beginnings of psychic life in general, certainly an indispensable prerequisite for object relationship. As generally construed. Whether this is viewed as (or a times demonstrably is) something unstable for allotting introjection, s always subject to alternative projection, or an intrapsychic object representation clearly distinguished from the self-representation, or firm identification in the superego, or in the ego itself, these phenomena are in various ways components of the system of mastery of the fact of separation, or separateness, from the original absolutely necessarily anaclitic (in the earliest period) symbiotic 'object'. In the light of clinical observation, it would appear to be that the relative stability (parental) objects representation. At which time of varying degree, are to a greater extent for the archaic phenomena. Even in nonpsychotic patients, overwhelmed by them, sometimes resembles the restoration from oedipal identification, which provides the preponderant basis for most demonstrable analytic transferences. That within the necrotic patients, the transference is effectively established when this representation invests the analyst to a degree - depending on intensity of drive and most of ego participation - which ranges in all the, wishing and striving to remake and analyst to biasses judgements and misinterpretation of data, are finally the actual perceptual distortions.

However, the old object representations as such may be invested, however rigidly established the libidinal or aggressive cathexis of the image may be, this as such can become the actual and exclusive focus of instinctual discharge, or of complicated and intense instinct-defence solutions, only and general energy-sparing quality of strictly intrapsychic processes. For the vast majority of persons, visible to any degree, including those with severe neurosis, character distortions, addictions and certain psychoses, the striving is toward the living and actual object, even at the cost of intense suffering. In a sense, this returns us to the state in which the psychological 'object-to-be'. Has a critical importance never again to be duplicated, except in certain acute life emergencies, even if the object is not firmly perceived as such, in the sense of later object relations? And it does seem that trance impressions from the earliest contacts in the service of life preservation, and the associated instinctual gratifications, and innumerable secondarily associated sensory impressions. Are activated by the specific inborn urges of sexual maturation? These propel the individual to renew many of the earliest modes of actual bodily contact, in connection with seeking for specific instinctual gratification. Or, to look away from clear-cut instinctual matters to the more remote elaborations of human contact: Few regard loneliness as other than a source of suffering, even self-imposed, as an apparent matter of choice, and the forcible imposition of 'solitary confinement ' is surely one of the most cruel of punishments.

Of these few generalizations have some important implications, no reaction to another individual is all transference, just as surely as no relationship is entirely free of it. There is not only the general maturational-developmental drive toward the outer world, but the seeking for a variety of need and pleasure satisfactions, learned or simulated in relation to the primordial object, but necessarily and inevitably transferred from this object the generically related things and persons in the expanding environment. These may be used or enjoyed without penalty, if the distinction between the original and the new is profoundly and genuinely established (with due respect for the quantitative 'relativism' of such concepts). The range of such inevitable displacement (transfers) in endless in all spheres - sexual, aggressive, aesthetic, utilitarian, intellectual. More immediately relevant, in the lives of those whose development has been relatively healthy, are those individuals whose vocations provide similarities or parallels, however, rarefied, to the caretaking functions of the original parents: Teachers, physicians, clergymen, political rulers, occasionally others. Again it must be noted, that such persons perform real functions, that the adult individual's interest in them, his specific need for them, often greatly outweighs similar reactions to parents, who retain their unique place for a complex and variable combination of other reasons. For such surrogate parents perform for the adult what his parents largely performed for him in realist years, and the psychological comparison is with an old object representation, or with an early identification, to which such latter-day parent surrogates may add important layers of elaborations. It is on the basis of such functional resemblances that persons in these roles have a unique transference valence. The analyst is first perceived as a real object, who awakens hope of help in the patients experience at all level of integration, from that of actual and immediate perception, evaluation, and response, to the activation of original parental object representations and their cathexes. That the analyst becomes invested with such representations, in forms ranging from wishes or demands to functional or even perceptual misidentifications, comprises the broad range of phenomena that we know as the therapeutic transference. Thus, the complicate structural phenomena of conflict are activated in relation to a real object, and such activation is uniquely dependent on the participation of this object, in a situation whose realities revive, with the affirmative associations, the memories of old and painful frustrations. In this situation, the continuing and prolonged contact, under strictly controlled conditions, is an important real factor, which has been elaborated previously. Without these actualities, dream life, - or instance of greater energid imbalance between impulses and defence - neurosis, will be the spontaneous solution, while everyday 'give-and-take' object relations are, at least on the surface, maintained as such. Occasionally, neurotic behaviour, where transferences dominate the everyday relationships, will supervene.

Interpretation, recollection or reconstruction, and, of course, working through, is essential for the establishment of effective insight, but they cannot operate mutatively if applied only to memories in the structural sense, whether of higher cathected events or persons. For it is the thrust of wish or impulse, or the elaboration of germane dynamic fantasies, and the corresponding defensive structures and their inadequacies, associated with such memories, which give to neurosis. It is a parallel thrust that creates the transference neurosis. Where memories are clear and vivid, through recall, or accepted as much through reconstruction and associated with variable, optional, and adaptive, rather than rigidly structuralized' response patterns, the analytic work has been done.

This view does place somewhat of a weighty emphasis on the horizontal coordinate of procedural operations, the conscious and unconscious relation to the analyst as a living and actual object, which is of investing upon the becoming imagery, traits, and functions of critical objects of the past. The relationship is to be understood in its dynamic, economic, and adaptive meaning, in its current structuralized tenacity, the real and unreal carefully separated from one another. The process of subjective memory or of reconstruction, the indispensable genetic dimension, is, in this sense, involved toward the decisive and specific autobiographic understanding of the living version of old conflict, than with the assumption that the interpretative reduction of the transference neurosis to gross mnemic elements is, in itself and automatically, mutative. At least, this view of the problem would seem appropriate to most chronic neurosis embedded in germane character structures of some plexuity. That neurosis symptoms connected with isolated traumatic events, covered by amnesia, may, at times, disappear on restoration of memories with adequate effective discharge, regardless of technical method, is, of course, indisputably true, even though the details of process, including the role of transference, are probably not yet adequately understood. Psychoanalysis was born in the observation of this type of process. In a thoughtful manner, the role of transference, in the early writings of both Freud and Ferenczi, seemed weighted somewhat in the direction of its resistance function, i.e., as directed against recall, although its affirmative functions were soon adequately appreciated, and placed in the dialectical position, which has obtained to the present day.

Other while, the primal processes of projection ad introjection, being inextricably linked with the infant's emotions and anxieties, initiate object-relations, by projecting, i.e., deflecting libido and aggression onto the mother's breast, the basis for object-relations is established, by introjecting the object, first of all the breast, relations to internal objects comes into being. The term 'object-relations' are based on the contention that the infant has from the beginning post-natal life a relation to the mother, although focussing primarily of her breast, which is imbued with the fundamental element's of an object-relation, i.e., loves, hatred, phantasies, anxieties, and defences? The introjection of the breast is the beginning of superego formation that extends over years. We have grounds for assuming that from the first feeding experience onwards the infant's introjection, the breast in its various aspects. The core of the superego is thus the mother's breast, both good and bad. Given to the simultaneous operation of introjection and projection, relations to external and internal objects interact. The father too, who soon plays a role in the child's life, early on becomes part of the infant's internal world it is characteristic of the infant's emotional life that there are rapid fluctuations between love and hate, between external and internal situations between perception of reality and the fantasises relating to it, and accordingly, an interplay between prosecutory anxiety and idealization - both referring to the internal and external object's, the idealized object brings a corollary of the prosecutory, extremely bad one.

The ego's growing capacity for integration and synthesis leads more and more, even during these first few months, to states in which love and hatred, and correspondingly the good and bad aspects of objects, for being synthesized. This gives rise to the second form of anxiety - depressive anxiety - for the infant's aggressive impulses and desires toward the bad breast (mother) are now felt to be a danger to the good breast (mother) as well. In the second quarter of the first year these emotions are reinforced, because at this stage the infant increasingly perceives and introjects the mother as a person. Depressive anxiety is intensified, for the infant feels he has destroyed or is destroying a whole object by his greed and uncontrollable aggression. Moreover, owing to the growing synthesis of his emotions, he now feels that these destructive impulses are directed against as a 'loved person'. Similar processes operate in relation to the father and other member s of the family. These anxieties and corresponding defences constitute the 'Depressive position', which comes to a head about the middle of the first year and whose essence is the anxiety and guilt relating to the destruction and loss of the loved internal and external objects.

It is at this stage, and bound up with the depressive position, that the oedipus complex sets in. Anxiety and guilt add a powerful impetus toward the beginning of the oedipus complex. For anxiety and guilt increase the need to externalize (project) bad figures and to internalize (introject) good ones. There to attaching desires, love, feeling of guilt, and reparative tendencies to internal figures in the external world, however, not only is the search for new objects that dominates the infant's needs, but also, the drive toward new life proposes: Away from the breast toward the penis, i.e., from oral desires toward genital ones. Many factors contribute to these developments, the forward drive of the libido, the growing integration of the ego, physical and mental skills and progressive adaption to the external world. These trends are bound up with the processing of symbol formation, which enables the infant to transfer not only emotions and phantasies, anxiety and guilt, from one object to another.

The processes are linked with another fundamental phenomenon governing its mental life, such that pressures exerted by the earliest anxiety situation are factors through which bring about the repetition compulsion, however, one conclusion about the earliest states of infancy are a continuation of Freud's discoveries; on certain points, nonetheless, the divergencies having to arise of which are very relevant, perhaps, its main contention that object-relations are operative from the beginning of post-natal life.

Nevertheless, the view that autoerotism and narcissism are the young infant contemporaries with the first relation to objects - external and internalized, that hypothetically, autoerotism and narcissism include the love for and relation with the internalized good object that in phantasy forms part of the loved body and self. It is to this internalized object that in autocratic gratification and narcissistic stages a withdrawal takes place. Concurrently, from birth onwards, a relation to objects, primarily the mother (her breasts) is present. This hypothesis contradicts Freud's concept of autoerotic and narcissistic stages that preclude an object-relation. However, the difference between Freud's statement on this issue is equivocal. In various context he explicitly and implicitly expresses opinion that suggested a relation to an object, the mother's breast, preceding autoerotic and narcissism.

> In the first instance the oral component instinct finds satisfaction by attaching itself to the sating of the desire for nourishment, and its object in the mother's breast. It then detaches itself, becomes independent and at the same time of autoerotic objectivity is found to an object in the child's own body.

The act or practice for which Freud' of using something or the state of being used is found in the applications availing to the term object is somewhat different from the context that is used of this term, but Freud is referring the object of an instinctual aim. What it is to mean, that, while, in addition, it is meant as an object-relation involving the infant's emotions, phantasies, anxieties and defences. Nevertheless, in sentence referred to, Freud clearly speaks of a libidinal attachment to an object, the mother's breast, which precedes autoerotism and narcissism.

In this context, it is reminded that of Freud's findings about early identification. In "The Ego and the Id," speaking of abandoned object cathexes. He said, ' . . . The effects of the first identification in earliest childhood will be profound and lasting. This leads us back to the origin of the ego-ideal, . . . Freud then defines the first and most important identifications that lie hidden behind the ego-ideal as the identification with the father, or with the parent's, and places them, as he expresses it, in the 'prehistory' of every person'. These formulations come close to the deceptions as described of their resulting of introjected objects, for by definition identifications are the result as such, but that the statement and the passage quoted from the Encyclopaedia article, it can be deduced that Freud, although he did not pursue this line of though t, however, he did assume that in the earliest infancy that both an object and introjective processes play a part.

That is to say, as regards autoerotism and narcissism we meet with an inconsistency in Freud's views. Such inconsistencies that exist on a number of points of theory clearly show, which on these particular of issue s Freud had not yet arrived at a final decision. In respect to the theory of anxiety he stated this explicitly in Inhibitions, Symptoms and Anxiety. His realization that much about the early stages of development was still unknown or obscure to him is also exemplified by his speaking of the first years of a girl's life as, ' . . . lost in a past so dim and shadowy . . .'

As regards to the question of autoerotism and narcissism, Anna Freud - although her views about this aspect of Freud's work remains unknown, but she seems only to have taken into account Freud's conclusions that an autoerotic and a narcissistic stage precede object-relations, and not to be allowed for other possibilities, of which are implied in some of Freud's statements such as the ones inferred above. This is one of the reasons why the divergence between Anna Freud's conception and the immediacy of early infancy is far greater than that between Freud's views, taken as a whole, and those of stating it as the essential to clarify the content and nature of the differences between the two schools of psychoanalytic thought, represented by Anna Freud and those that imply of such clarification is required in the interests of psychoanalytic training and also because it could help to open up fruitful discussions between psychoanalysts and thereby contribute to a greater generality of a better understanding of the fundamental problems of early infancy.

The hypothesis that a time interval extending over several months precedes object-relations implies that - except for the libido attached to the infant's own body - impulses, phantasies, anxieties, and defences either are not present in him, or are not related to an object, that is to say, they would operate in vacua. The analysis of very young children, as to implicate, would show that there is no instinctual urge, no anxiety situation, no mental process that does not involve objects, external or internal, in other words, object-relations are at the centre of emotional life. Furthermore, love and hatred, phantasies, anxiety and defences are also operative from the beginning and are 'ad initio' indivisibly linked with object-relations.

The oedipus complex, in a pragmatic analytic sense, retains its position as the 'nuclear complex' of the neurosis. It is a climactic organization experience of early childhood, apart from its own vicissitudes, It can under favourable circumstances provide certain solutions for pregenital conflicts, or in itself suffer from them. In any case, include them in its structure. Only when the precursor experiences have been of a great severity, for which it is to claim to a shadowy organic determinacy, as the new 'frame of reference', which hardly having the independent and decisive significance of its own. In any case, its attendant phallic conflicts must be resolved in their own right, in the analytic transference. From the analyst, (or his current surrogate in the outer world) thus from the psychic representation of the parent, the literal (i.e., bodily) sexual wishes must be withdrawn, and genuinely displaced to appropriate objects in the outer world. The fraction of such drive elements that can be transmuted to friendly, tender feeling toward the original object. Or too other acceptable (neutralized) variants, will of course, influence the economic problem involved. This genuine displacement is opposed to the sense of 'acting out', while other objects are perceptually different substitutes for the primary object (thus for the analyst). This may be thought to follow automatically on the basic process of coming to terms with (accepting) the childhood incestuous wish and its parricidal connotation. Such assumption does not do justice to the dynamic problem implicit in tenaciously persistent wishes. To the extent that these wishes are to be genuinely disavowed or modified, rather than displaced, a further important step is necessary: The thorough analysis of the functional meaning of the persisting wishes and the special etiologic factors entering into their tenacity, as reflected in the transference neurosis. Thus, in principle, the literal accuracy of the concept phrased by Wilhelm Reich, "transference of the transference," as the final requirement for dissolution of the erotic analytic transference, even though the clinical discussion, which is its context, is useful. This expression would imply that the object representation that largely determines the distinctive erotic interest in the analyst can remain essentially the same, so long as the actual object changes. While a semantic issue may be involved in some degree, it is one that impinges importantly on conceptual clarity. However, such definite conceptualization of one basic element in the phenomenon or transference may be, and should be, subject to the reservations appropriately attaching themselves to any very clear-cut ideas about obscure areas, with the clinical concept of transference, its clinical derivation and its generally accepted place in the psychoanalytic process.

The evolution of the reality-relatedness between patient and therapist, over the course of the psychotherapy, is something that has received little more than passing mention in the literature, Hoedemaker (1955), in a paper concerning the therapeutic process in the treatment of schizophrenia, stresses the importance of the schizophrenic patient's forming healthy identifications with the therapist, and Loewald (1960), his concerns and considerations to the therapeutic action of psychoanalysis in general, repeatedly emphasizes the importance of the real relationship between patient and analyst, but only in the following passage eludes the evolution, the growth, of this relationship over the course of treatment:

> . . . Where repression is lifted and unconscious and preconscious are again in communication, infantile object and contemporary object may be united into one - a truly new object as both unconscious and preconscious are changed by their mutual communication, the object that helps to bring this about in therapy, the analyst, mediates this union. . . .

It has been distinctly impressive that the patient's remembrance of new areas of his past - his manifestation of newly de-repressed transference reactions to the therapist - occurs only hand-in-hand with the reaching of comparable areas of feeling in the evolving reality-relatedness between patient and therapist. For example, he does not come to experiencing fond memories of his mother until the reality-relatedness between himself and the therapist has reached the point where the feelings between them have become, in reality, predominantly positive. Loewald's words, imply that an increment of transference resolution slightly preceding in time or in arrangement to go before as to go before time, the all-out preceding that many are the cause to be preceded, which makes it possible in the forming of each successive increment the evolving reality-relationship between patent and analyst. It has been, by contrast, that the evolution of the reality-relatedness proceeds alway a bi t ahead of, and makes possibly, the progressive evolution and resolution of the transference, although to be sure the latter, in so far as it frees psychological energy and makes it available for reality-relatedness, helps greatly to consolidate the ground just taken over by the advancing reality-relatedness. Loewald (1960) thinks of it that

> . . . The patient can dare to take the plunge into the regressive crises of the transference neurosis that brings him face to face again with his childhood anxieties and conflicts, if he can hold on to the potentialities of a new object-relationship, represented by thc analyst.

It seems that this new object-relationship is more that a potentiality, to be realized with comparative suddenness, toward the end of this treatment with the resolution of the transference. Rather it is, it has seemed as constantly being there, being built up bit by bit, just ahead of the likewise evolving transference relationship. Predeterminates as in Freud's (1922) having pointed out that projection (expressed in the Latin from 'projectio') which is, after all, so major an aspect of transference - is directed not 'into the sky, so to speak, were there is nothing of the sort already', but rather onto a person who provides some reality-basic for the projection.

In the final months of the therapy, the therapist clearly sees that extent to which the patient's transferences to him as representing a succession of figures from the latter's earlier years have all been in the service the patient's unconscious successively decreasing extent, fro experiencing the full and complex reality of the immediate relatedness with the therapist in the present. The patent at last comes to realize that the relationship with a single other human being - in this instance, the therapist - is so rich as to comprise all these earlier relationships - so rich as to evoke all the myriad feelings that have been parcelled out and crystallized, wherefore, in the transference that have now been resolved. This is a province most beautifully described by the Swiss novelist, Herman Hesse (1951) winner of the Nobel Prize in 1946,in his little novel. Siddhartha. The protagonist in a lifelong quest for the ultimate answer to the enigma of man's role on earth, finally discovers in the face of his beloved friend all the myriad persons, things, and events that he has known, but incoherently before, during the vicissitudes of his many years of searching.

It is thus that the patient, schizophrenic or otherwise, becomes at one with himself, in the closing phase of psychotherapy. But although the realization may come to him as a sudden one, it is founded on a reality-relatedness that has been building up all along. Loewald (1960) in his magnificent paper to which transference resolution plays in the development of this reality-relatedness. As, perhaps, that the evolution of the 'countertransference' - not countertransference in the classical sense of the therapist's transference to the patient, but rather in the sense of the therapist's emotional reaction to the patient's transference - forms an equally essential contribution to this reality-relatedness.

It is, nonetheless, but often, that the therapist who sees a new potentiality in the patient, a previously unnoted side of him that heralds a phase of increasing differentiations. And frequently the therapist is the only one who sees it. Even the patient does not see it as yet, except in the projected form, so that he perceives this as an attribute of the therapist. This situation can make the therapist feel very much inalienable as separated from others that apart or detached in the isolated removal and intensely threaten.

Upon which the transference relationship with the therapist, we find that the patient naturally brings this relationship, just as he brings into the relatedness in which the difficulties concerning differentiation and integration that were engendered by the pathological upbringing upon the advances in differentiation and integration necessarily occur first outside the patient - namely, in the therapist's increasingly well differentiated and well-integrated view of, and consequently, responses to, him - before these can become well established within him.

Because the schizophrenic patient did not experience, in his infancy, the symbolic relatedness with his mother such as each human being needs for the formation of a healthy core in his personality structure, in the emotion of the transference relationship to his therapist he must eventually succeed in establishing such a mode of relatedness.

This means that he must eventually regress, in the transference, to such a level in order to get a fresh start toward a healthier personality differentiation and integration than he had achieved before entering therapy. This is not to say that he must 'act out' the regressive needs in his daily life, to be sure, the schizophrenic patient, whether in therapy or not, inevitably does so to a considerable degree, but to the extent that these needs can be expressed in the transference relationship, they need not seek expression, unconsciously, thorough acting out in daily life.

Focussing now upon the transference relationship with the therapist, we find that the patient naturally brings about the difficulties concerning differentiation in the process of integration that was engendered by the pathological upbringing as for being the one more interruption in the impeding principle of reconstructions of an identifying manufacture of the transference. And the every day, relationships are found in the interplaying form of corresponding advances in differentiated dynamic integrations necessarily occur first outside the patient - namely, in the therapist's increasingly well or acceptably differentiated by the integrated extent or range of vision, that the position or attitudes that determine how of the intent of something (as an aim or an end or motive)or by way the mind is directed. Because the schizophrenic patient did not experience, in his infancy, the establishment of and later emergence form, a healthy symbiotic relatedness with his mother such as each human brings needs for the formation of a healthy core in his personality structure, in the evolution of the transference relationship to his therapist he must eventually succeed in establishing such a mode of relatedness.

This means that he must eventually regress, in the transference, to such a level, in order to get a fresh start toward a healthier personality differentiation and integration than he had achieved before entering therapy. This is not to say that he must act out the regressive needs in his daily life. To be sure, the schizophrenic patient, whether in therapy or not, inevitably does so to a considerable degree; even to the extent that these needs can be expressed in the transference relationship, they need not seek expression, unconsciously, through acting out in daily life.

This symbiotic mode of relatedness is necessarily mutual, participated in by therapist as well as patient. Thus, the therapist must come to experience not only the oceanic gratification, but also the anxiety involved in his sharing a symbiotic, subjective oneness with the schizophrenic patient. This relationship, with its lack of felt ego-boundaries between the two participants, at times invokes the kind of deep contentment, the kind of felt communion that needs no words, which characterize a loving relatedness between mother and infant. But at other times it involves the therapists feeling unable to experience himself as differentiated from the pathology-ridden personality of the patient. He feels helplessly caught in the patient's deep ambivalence. He feels one with the patient's hatred and despairs and thwarted love, and at times he cannot differentiate between his own subjectively harmful effect upon the patient, and the illness with which the patient was to come or go or nearly recede in the achievement afflicting when the therapist first undertook to help him. Thus, at these anxiety-ridden moments in the symbiotic phase, the therapist feels his own personality to be invaded by the patient's pathology, and feels his identity severely threatened, whereas in the more contented moments, part of the contentment resides in both participants enjoying a freedom from any concern with identity.

This same profound lack of differentiation may come to characterize the patient's view of the persons about him, including his therapeutic, and at time's, in line with his need to project a poorly differentiated conglomeration of 'bad' impulses, he may perceive the therapist for being but one head of a hydra-headed monster. The patient's lack of differentiation in this regard, prevailing for month after month of his charging the therapist with saying or doing various things that were actually said or have done by others in the hospitalized presences to its containing of environmental surfaces, or by the family members, can have a formidably eroding effect upon the therapist's sense of personal intensity. But the patient may need to regress to just such a primitivity, poorly differentiated view of the world in order to grow up again, psychologically, in a healthier way this time.

Among the most significant steps in the maturation that occurs in successful psychotherapy are those moments when the therapist suddenly sees the patient in a new light. His image of the patient suddenly changes, because of the entry into his awareness of some potentiality in the patient. Which had not shown itself before? From now on, his responses t o the patient is a response to this new, enriched view, and through such responding he fosters the emergence, and further differentiation, of this new personality area. This is another way of describing the process that Buber and in Friednan, 1955, calls 'making the other person present, seeing in the other persons potentialities of such even presents: Seeing in the other persons potentiality of which in him, that he is not aware of his helping him, by responding to those potentialities, to realize them.

Schizophrenic patient's feelings start to become differentiated before they have found new and appropriate modes for expressing the new feelings, thus patient's may use the same old stereotyped behaviour or utterance to express nuances of new feelings. This is identical with the situation in those schizophrenics' familiar which is permeated with what Wynne (1958) termed 'pseudo-mutuality' or toward maintaining the sense of reciprocal perceiving expectations. Thus, the expectations are left unexplored, and the old expectations and roles, even though outgrown and inappropriate in one sense, continue to serve as the structure for the relation.

The therapist, through hearing the new emotional connotation, the new meaning, in the stereotyped utterance and responding in accordance with the new connotation, fosters the emerging differentiation. Over the course of months, in therapy, he may find the same verbal stereotype employed in th e expression of a whole gamut of newly emerging feelings. Thus, over a prolonged time-span, the therapist may give as many different responses to a gradually differentiating patient as are simultaneously given by the various members of the surrounding environment, to the patient who shows the contrasting ego-fragmentation (or, in a loose manner of speaking, over-differentiations).

Persistently stereotyped communications from the patient tend to bring from the therapist communications that, over a period of time, become almost equally stereotyped. One can sometimes detect, in recordings playing during supervisory hours, evidence that new emotional connotations are creeping into the patient's verbal stereotypes, and into the therapist's responsive verbal stereotypes, before either of the two participants has noticed this.

What the therapist does which assists the patient's differentiation often consists in his having the courage and honesty to differ from whether the patient's expressed feelings or, often most valuable, with the social role into which his sick behaviour tends to fix or transfix the therapist. This may consist in his candid disagreement with some of the patient, and s strongly felt and long-voiced views, or in his flatly declining to try to feel 'sympathy' - such as one would be conventionally expected to feel in response to behaviour, which seems, at first glance, to express the most pitiable suffering but which the therapist is convinced primarily expresses sadism on the patient's part. Such courage to differ with the expected social role is what is needed from the therapist, in order to bring to a close the symbiotic phase of relatedness that has served, earlier, a necessary and productive function. Through asserting his individuality, and at many later moments in the therapeutic interaction, the therapist fosters the patient's own development of more complete and durable ego-boundaries. At the same time he offers the patient the opportunity to identify with a parent-figure who dares to be an individual-dares to be so in the face of pressures from the working group of which he is part, and from his own reproachful superego, it can be of notice, that of a minor degree a consciously planned and controlled therapeutic technique wherefore, the content descriptions are rather a natural flow of events as in the transference evolution, with which the therapist must have the spontaneity to go along.

The patient, particularly in the symbiotic phase of the therapy but in preceding and succeeding phases as well, is notably intolerant of sudden and marked changes in the therapeutic relationship - that is, of suddenly seeing himself, or feeling that his therapist sees him, through new eyes. He rarely gives the therapist to feel that the latter have made an importantly revealing interpretation, or should be concealed, but when to arrive at by reasoning from evidence or from its premises that we can infer from that which he was derived as to a conclusion, that it conveys of a higher illumination of mind. Methodologically historical information is an approving acceptation by the therapist, he does so causally, he tends to experience important increments of depreciated material, yet not as every bit for reverential abstractions as to make a new, amended, or up-to-date reversion of the many problems involved in revising the earthly shuddering revelations in his development. The things that he has known all along and simply never happened to think of. His experience of an inherent perception of the world as surrounding him is often permeated by 'deja vu' sensations, and misidentification of the emphasizing style at which the expense of thought for taking the rhetorical rhapsody to actions or a single inaction of moving the revolutions of the earth around the sun is mostly familiar an act from his past.

The motional progressions in therapy, on the patient's part, occur each time only after a recrudescence in his symptoms. It is as though he has to find reassurance of his personal identity, for being really the same hopeless person he has long felt himself to be, before he can venture into a bit or new and more hopeful identity.

Of what expressions are that object relations of state or fact of having independent reality whose customs that have recently come into existence, such by the actuality for something having existence from the beginning of life, being the mother's breast that it splits into a good (gratifying) and bad (frustrating) breast; this splitting results in a division between love and hate. What is more, is that of the relation to the first object implies its introjection and projection, and thus, from the beginning object relations are moulded by an interaction between introjection and projection, between internal and external objects and situation.

. . . .With the introjection of the complete object in about the second quarter of the first year marked steps in integration are made. . . . The loved and hated aspects of the mother are no longer felt to be so widely separated, and the result is an increased fear of loss, a strong feeling of guilt and states akin to mourning, because the aggressive impulses are felt to be divorced against the love object, the depressive position has come to the fore . . .

. . . In the first few month of life anxiety is predominantly experienced as fear of persecution and . . . this contributes to certain mechanisms and defences that characterize the paranoid and schizoid positions. Outstanding among these defences is the mechanism of splitting internal and external objects, emotions and the ego. These mechanisms and defences are part of normal development and at the same time form the basis for later schizophrenic illness. The descriptive underlying identification by projection, i.e., projective identification, as a combination of splitting off parts of the self and projecting them onto another person . . .

Rosenfeld, a follower of Klein writes that, he presents detailed clinical data that serve to document the implicit point, among others, that whereas, the schizophrenic patient may appear to have regressed to such an objectless autoerotic level of development as was postulated by Freud (1911, 1914) and Abraham (1908), in actuality the patient is involved in object-relatedness with the analyst, object-relatedness of the primitive introjective and projective identification kind. (1952). We find, among the writings of the Kleinian analysts, a number of interesting examples of delusional transference interpretation, in all of which the keynote is the concept of projective (or introjective) identification.

The dependencies on which is focussed upon effectual acknowledge in the presence of which has its closest analogue, in terms of normative standards, is such that the personality development, in the experience and behaviour of the infant or of the young child. The dependency needs, attitudes, and the striving that the schizophrenic manifests may be defined in the statement that he seeks for another person to assume a total responsibility for gratifying all his needs, both physiological and psychological, while this person is to seek nothing from him.

Of the physiological needs, which the schizophrenic manifests, those centring about the oral zone of interaction are usually most prominent, analogous to the predominant place held by nursing in the life of the infant. Desires to be stroked and cuddled, likewise, so characteristic of the very early years of normal development, are prominently held within the schizophrenic. In addition, desires for the relief of genital sexual tensions, even though these have had their advent much later in the life history than have his oral desires, are manifested in much the same level of an early, infantile dependency. That is, such genital hungers are manifested in much the same small-child spirit of, 'you ought to be taking care of this for me' as are the oral hungers.

The psychological needs that are represented among the schizophrenic's dependency processes consist in the desire for the other person to provide him with unvarying love and protection, and to assume a total guidance of his living,

In the course of furthering characterizations of the schizophrenic's dependency processes will be defined much more fully, that is to say, it is to b e emphasized that no of the dependency processes are but described is characteristic only of the schizophrenic, or qualitatively different from processes operative at some level of consciousness in persons with other varieties of psychiatric illness and in normal persons. With regard to dependency processes, we find research in schizophrenia has its greatest potential value in the fact that schizophrenic shows us in a sharply etched form that which is so obscured, by years progressive adaptation to adult interpersonal living, in human beings in general. Wherefore, but in some degree, are about the patient's anxiety about the dependency needs, are (1) As nearly as can be determined, the patient is unaware of pure dependency needs; for him, apparently, they exist in consciousness, if at all, only in the form of a hopeless conflictual combinations of dependency needs plus various defences - defences that render impossible any thoroughgoing sustained gratification of these needs. These defences (which include, grandiosity, hostility, competitiveness, scorns and so forth) have so long ago developed in his personality, as a means of coping with anxiety attendant upon dependency needs, that the experiencing of pure dependency needs it, for him, lost in antiquity and so be achieved only relatively late in therapy after the various defences have been largely relinquished.

Thus it appears to be not only dependency needs 'per se' which arouses anxiety, but rather the dependency needs plus all these various defences (which tend in themselves to be anxiety-provoking) plus the inevitable frustration, to a greater or less degree, of the dependency needs.

Hostility as one of the defences against awareness of 'dependency needs,' that which for certainly repressed dependency needs are one of the most frequent bases of murderous feelings in the schizophrenic, in such instances the murderous feelings may be regarded as a vigorous denial of dependency. What frequently happens in therapy is that both patient and therapist become so anxious about the defensive murderous feelings that the underlying dependency feelings long remain unrecognized.

Every schizophrenic possesses much self-hatred and guilt that may serve as defences against the awareness of dependency feelings ('I am too worthless for anyone possibly to care about me'), and which in any case complicate the matter of dependency. The schizophrenic has generally come to interpret the rejections in his past life as meaning that he is a creature who wants too much and, in fact, a creature who has no legitimate needs. Thus, he can accept gratification of his dependency needs, if at all, only if his needs are rendered acceptable to themselves by reason of his becoming physically ill or in a truly desperate emotional state. It is frequently found that a schizophrenic is more accessible to the gratification of his dependency needs when he is physically ill, or filled with despair, than at other times. In that way, th e presence of self-hatred, and guilt, one ingredient of the patient's overall anxiety about dependancy needs has to do with the fact that these needs connote to him the state of feeling physical illness or despair.

In essence, then, we can see that the patient has a deep-seated conviction that his dependency needs will not be gratified. Further, we see that this conviction is based not alone on the fortunate past expedience of repeated rejection, but also, the fact that his own defences, called forth concomitantly with the dependency desires, make it virtually certain that this dependency needs will not be met. (2) The dependency needs are anxiety-provoking not only because they involve desires to relate in an infantile or small-child fashion (by breast - or penis sucking, being cuddled, and as so forth) which is not generally acceptable behaviour among adults, but also, and probably what is more important, because they involve a feeling that the other person is frighteningly important, absolutely indispensable to the patient's survival.

This feeling as to the indispensable of importance of the other person derives from two main sources: (a) the regressed state of the schizophrenic's emotional life, which makes for his perceiving the other for being all-important to his survival, just as in infancy the mothering one is all-important to the survival of the infant, and (b) certain additional disabling features of his schizophrenic illness, which render him dependent in various special ways that are not quite comparable with the dependency characteristic of normal infancy or early childhood. Thereof, a number of points in reference to (b) are, first, we can perceive that a schizophrenic who is extremely confused, for example, is utterly dependent on or upon the therapist or, some other relevantly significant person to help him establish a bridge between his incomparable, incongruent, conflicting, conditions in which things are out of their normal or proper places or relationships. Such are the complete mental confusions that the authenticity of a corresponding to known facts is to discover or rediscover the real reason for which such things as having no illusions and facing reality squarely face-to-face, a realistic appraisal of his chances for advancing to the reasonable facts as we can see the factional advent for understanding the Absolutizing instinct to fancy of its reality.

Second, we can see also that the patient who is in transition between old, imposed values and not-yet-acquired values of his own, has only the relationship with his therapist to depend upon.

Third, is the concern and consideration that, in many instances, the schizophrenic appears to be what one might call a prisoner in th e present. He is so afraid both of change and of the memories that tend to be called forth by the present that he clings desperately to what in immediate. He is in this sense imprisoned in immediate experience, and looks to the therapist to free him so that he will be able to live in all his life, temporally speaking - present, past and future.

Forth, it might be surmised that an oral type of relatedness to the other person (with the all-importance of the other that this entails) is necessary for the schizophrenic to maintain, partly in order to facilitate his utilization of projection and introjection as defences against anxiety.

Anxiety, is the constructed foundation whose emotional state from which are grounded to the foundation structural called the 'edifice', that an emotional state in which people feel uneasy, apprehensive, or fearful. People usually experience anxiety about events they cannot control or predict, or about events that seem threatening or dangerous. For example, students taking an important test may feel anxious because they cannot predict the test questions or feel certain of a good grade. People often use the words fear and anxiety to describe the same thing. Fear also describes a reaction to immediate danger characterized by a strong desire to escape the situation.

The physical symptoms of anxiety reflect a chronic "readiness" to deal with some future threat. These symptoms may include fidgeting, muscle tension, sleeping problems, and headaches. Higher levels of anxiety may produce such symptoms as rapid heartbeat, sweating, increased blood pressure, nausea, and dizziness.

Bychowski (1952) says, '"The separation between the primitive ego and the external world is closely connected with orality, both form the basis for the mechanism that we call projection," and would add, for introjection., That Starcke (1921) for earlier comments "I might briefly allude to the possibility that in the repeated alternation between becoming one's own and not one's own, which occurs during lactation . . . the situation of being nursed plays a part in the origin of the mechanism of something that extends beyond its level or the normal outer surface in which serves to support projection.

The patient has anxiety, and, least of mention, his dependency needs lead him either to take in harmful things, or to lose his identity.

The schizophrenic does not have the ability necessary to tolerate the frustration of his dependency needs, so that he can, once they emerge into awareness, subject them to mature discriminatory judgement before seeking their gratification. Instead, like a voraciously hungry infant, his tendency is to put into his mouth (either literally or figuratively) whatever is at hand, whether nutritious or with a potential of being harmful, this tendency is about th e basis of some of his anxiety concerning his dependency needs, for the fear that they will keep him blindly into receiving harmful medicines, bad advice, electro-shock treatment, lobotomy, and so forth. Schizophrenic patients have been known to beg, in effect, for all these, and many a patients have been known to beg, yet these patients have been 'successful' in his dependency desires. A need for self-punishment is, of course, an additional motivation in such instances.

A statement by Fenichel (1945) indicates that, "The pleasure principle, that is, the need for immediate discharge, is incompatible with correct judgement, which is based on considerable and post postponement of the reaction. The time and energy saved by this postponement are used in the function of sound and stable judgments. That in the early states the weak ego has not yet learned to postpone anything.

In the same symptomatic of one that finds that th e extent that the schizophrenic projects onto other persons his own needs too such and to devour, he feels threatened with being devoured by these other persons.

To elaborate now in a somewhat different direction upon this fear of loss of identity. Th e schizophrenic fears that his becoming dependent on another person will lead him into a state of conformity that other person's wishes and life values. A conformer is almost the last sort of person as the schizophrenic wishes to become, since his sense of individuality resides in his very eccentricities. He assumes that the therapist, for example, in the process, requiring him to give up his individuality for the kinds of parental future in his past had e been able to salvage his refuge used to pay the price.

It seems of our apparent need to give the impression of being without necessarily being so in fact that things are not always the way they seem, as things accompanied with action orient of doing whatever is apprehended as having actual, distinct and demonstrateable existence from which there is a place for each thing in the cosmological understanding idea in that something conveys to the mind a rational allotment of the far and near, such of the values and standards moderate the newly proposed to modify as to avoid an extreme or keep within bounds.

For what is to say, in that we need to realize, that the patient is not solely a broken, inert victim of the hostility of persons in his past life. His hebephrenic apathy or his catatonic immobility, for example, represents for one thing, an intense active endeavour toward unconscious regressive goals, as Greenson (1949, 1953) has for his assistance to make clear in the boredom and apathy in neurotic patients. The patient is, in other words, no inert vehicle that needs to be energized by the therapist; rather, an abundance of energy is locked in him, pressing ceaselessly to be freed, and a hovering 'helpful' orientation on the part of the therapist would only get in the way. We must realize that the patient has made, and is continually making, a contribution to his own illness, however unwittingly, and however obscure the nature of this contribution may long remain.

More than often, it has been found that the histories of schizophrenic patients, whether male or female, describe the father for being by far, the warmer, the more accessible, of the responsive parents, and the patient as having always been very much attached to the father, whereas the mother was always a relatively cold, rejecting, remote figure, but for the repetitive correlative coefficient, that it was to be found that, disguised behind the child's idol or inseparable buddy, is a matter of the father's transference to the child's being a mother-figure that the father, in these instances, is an infantile individual who reacts both to his wife and to his child, as the mother-figure, and who, by striving to be both father and mother to the child, unconsciously seeks to intervene between mother and child, that in such a way as to have each of them to himself, in the considerations that suggest of a number of cases when both are in the transference-development with the patient and the selective prospect of the patient's generalization that limits or qualifies an agreement or other conditions that may contain or depend on a conditioning need for previsional advocates that include the condition that the transference phenomena would effectually raise the needed situational alliance.

The various forms of intense transference on the part of the schizophrenic individual tend forcibly to evoke complementary feeling-responses, comparably intense, in the therapist. Mabel Blake Cohen (1952) has made the extremely valuable observation, for psychoanalysis in general, that:

> . . . it seems that the patient applies great pressure to the analyst in a variety of nonverbal ways to behave like the significant adults in the patient's earlier life, it is not merely a matter of the patient's seeing the analyst as like his father, but of his actually manipulating the relationship in such away as to elicit the same kind of behaviour from the analyst. . . .

It is no too much to say that, in response to the schizophrenic patient's transference, the therapist not only behaves like the significant adults in the patient's childhood, but experiences most intimately, within himself, activated by the patient's transference the very kind of intense and deeply conflictual feelings that were at work, however repressed, in those adults in the past, as well as experiencing, through the mechanisms of projection and introjection in the relationship between himself and the patient, the comparably intense and conflictual emotion that formed the seed-bed of psychosis in the child himself, years ago.

The accountable explanation in the support for reason to posit for the necessarily deep feeling-involvement on the part of the therapist is inherent in the nature of early ego-formation. The healthy reworking of which is so central to the therapy of schizophrenia. Spitz (1959), in his monograph on the early development of the ego, repeatedly emphasizes that emotion plays a leading role in th e formation of what he described as the 'organizers of the psyche' (which he defines as 'emergent, dominant centres of integration') during the first eighteen months of life. H e says, for example, that:

> . . . the road that leads to this integration of isolated functions is built by the infant's object relations, by experiences of an effective nature. Accordingly, the indicator of the organizer of the psyche will be of an effective nature, it is an effective behaviour that clearly precedes development in all other sectors of the personality by several months.

The phases comprising the overall course of psychotherapy with chronically schizophrenic persons, is that of recent years it has become increasingly reassuring that it is possible to delineate such phases in the complex, individualistic and dynamic events of clinical work. One can be said, that, in this difficult effort at conceptualization, from Freud's delineation of the successive phases of libidinal development in healthy maturation, Erikson's (1956) portrayal of the process of identity formation as gradual unfolding of the personality through phase-specific psycho-social crises of evolution of the reality principle in healthy development - the typical conflicts, the sequence of danger situations, and the ways they are dealt with - can be traced in this process.

The successive phases of which are best characterised, the psychotherapy of chronic schizophrenia, are the 'out-of-contact phases, the phase of ambivalent symbiosis, the phase of pre-ambivalent symbiosis, the phase of resolution of the symbiosis, and the late phase, - that of establishment, and elaboration, of the newly won individuation through selective new identification and repudiation of outmoded identifications.

The sequence of these phases retraces, in reverse, the phases by which the schizophrenic illness was originally formed: The way of thinking, the aetiological roots of schizophrenia are formed when the mother-infant symbiosis fails to resolve into individuation of mother and infant - or, still more harmfully fails even to become at all firmly established - because of deep ambivalence of the part of the mother that hindered the integration and differentiation of the infant's and young child's ego, the child fails then to proceed through the normative development phases of symbiosis and subsequent individuation. Instead the core of his personality remains uniform, and ego-fragmentation and dedifferentiation becomes powerful, though deeply primitive and unconscious defences against the awareness of ambivalence in the object and in himself. Even in normal development, one becomes separate person only by becoming able to face, and accept ownership of, one's ambivalence with which he had to cope in his relationship with his mother was too great, and his ego-formation too greatly impeded, for him to be able to integrate his conflictual feeling-states into an individual identity.

Of these, the theoretical concept has been fostered by Mahler's (1956) paper on autistic and symbiotic infantile psychosis and by Balint's (1953, 1955) writings concerning phenomena of early ego-formation that he encountered in the psychoanalysis of neurotic patients. From a purely descriptive viewpoint, schizophrenia can be seen to consist essentially in an impairment of both 'integration' and 'differentiation' - which are but opposite faces of a unitary growth-process. From a psychodynamic view point seems basic to all the bewilderingly plexuity with which are a varying manifestations of schizophrenia.

Taking in, is the matter of integration; when we assess schizophrenia individual in terms of the classical structural areas of the personality - id, ego, and superego - we discover these to be poorly integrated with one another. The id is experienced by the ego as a Pandora's box, the contents of which will overwhelm one if it is opened. The ego is, as many writers have stated, severely split, sometimes into innumerable islands that are not linked discernibly with one another. And the superego has the nature of a cruel tyrant whose assaults upon the weak and unintegrated ego are, if anything, even more destructive to it than are the ascensions of the threatening id-impulses, as Szalita-Pemow (1951), Hill (1955), and others. Moreover, the superego is, like the ego, even in itself not well integrated; its utterances contain the most glaring inconsistencies from one moment to the next. Jacobson (1954) has shown that there is actually as dissolution of the superego, as an integrated destruction - a regressive transformation back into the threatening parental images whose conglomeration originally formed it.

Differentiation is a process that is essential to integration, and vice versa. For personality structure-functions or psychic contents to become integrated, they must first have emerged as partially differentiated or separate from one another, and differentiation in turn can emerge only out of a foundation of more or less integrated functions or contents. The intertwining mesh upon which is interwoven in the growth precesses of integration and differentiation, such that the impairment of both likewise interlocking. But in the schizophrenic these two processes tend to be out of step with one another, so that at one moment a patient's more urgent need may be for increased integration, whereas at another he may more urgently need increased differentiation. And these are some patients who show for months end, a more urgent need in one of these areas, before the alternate growth-phase on the scene, that type is a modicum of validity in speaking and of two different 'types' of schizophrenic patients.

One comes to realize, upon reasons of how premature have been one's effort to find out what feelings the patient is experiencing or what thoughts he is having; one comes to realize that much of the time he has neither feelings nor thoughts differentiated as such and communicable to us.

Such differentiations as the patient posses of an inclining inclination that tend to break down when intense emotion enters his awareness. A paranoid man, for example, may find that when his hatred toward another person reaches a certain degree of intensity, he is flooded with anxiety because he no longer knows whether he hates, or instead 'really loves' the other individual. This is not based, on any line or its course, whereupon the primary mechanism that Freud (1911) outlined in his classical description of the nature of paranoid delusions of persecution, a description in which repressed homosexual love played the central role. The central difficulty is rather than the ego is too poorly differentiated to maintain its structure in the face of such powerful affects, and the patient becomes flooded with what can only be described as 'undifferentiated passion', precisely as one finds an infant to be overwhelmed at times with affect that the observer cannot be specifically identity as any one kind of emotion.

As for the feelings with which the therapist himself experiences in working within the variations in the differentiated patient, we find, again, a persistent threat of the therapist's sense of identity. But, whereas in the unitary integration complex manifestations of such of a schizophrenic's sense of identity. But as in the first instance that the threat was felt predominantly as a disturbance of one's personal integration, it seems possible as a weakening of one's sense of differentiation. In this instance, the 'therapeutic symbiosis' which implicates the necessary developments that it tends to occur earlier for which of the patient's predominant mode of relatedness with other persons, at the developmental level at which we find him at the very beginning of our work, is a symbiotic one. Such descriptions, least of mention, agree with the necessary developments, in that it tends to occur for the patient 's predominant mode of relatedness with other persons, the symbiotic relatedness, with its subjective absence of ego-boundaries, involves not only special gratification, but anxiety-provoking disturbances on one's sense of personal identity.

The comparatively rapid development of symbiotic relatedness is facilitated by the patient's characteristically nonverbal, and physically more or less immobile, functioning during the therapeutic sessions. In response, the therapist's own behaviour becomes more and more similar, is that each participant is now offering to the other, saying that over the hours of counselling, a silent, impassive screen that facilitates abundant mutual projecting and introjecting. Thus a symbiotic state is likely to be reached earlier than in one's work with the typically much more verbal type of the patient when described for that instance, the patient's and therapist's more abundant verbalization's tend persistently to stress the ego-boundaries separating the to persons from one another.

The applicability for which the predominantly non-differentiated patient, in that the therapist's sense of identity as a complexly differentiated individual entity becomes further eroded, or undermined, as he finds the patient persistently operating on the unwavering conviction, that the hours of counselling are but an undifferentiated aspect of the whole vague mass of the institution, even in psychodynamic terms, is in actuality the patient's projection of his own poorly differentiated hostility, through which the patient's tenaciously held view, is the way the world around him really is.

Further, since the patient typically verbalizes little but a few maddening monotonous stereotypes, the therapist tends to feel, over the course of time, with so little of his own intellectual content being explicitly tapped in the relationship, that his richness of intellect is progressively rusting away - becoming less differentiated, more stereotyped and rudimentary. Moreover, the patient presents but one of two emotional wavelengths to which the therapist can himself tune in, rather than a rich spectrum of emotion that calls into response a similarly wide range of feelings from the therapist himself. Thus not only the therapist's intellectual resources, but his emotional capacities too, becomes subjectively narrowed down and impoverished, as he finds that, over the sessions of counselling, his patient in him neither any wide range of ideas, nor any emotions except, for example, rage, or contempt or dull hopelessness.

The feeling experience on his part, anxiety-provoking and discouraging though he finds it, is a necessary therapeutic development. It is for him thus to experience at first hand something of the patient's own lack of differentiation; for, as in the therapy with the non-integrated patient, as, once, again, the healing process occurs external to the patient, as it was, at an intrapsychic level in the therapist, before it becomes established in the patient himself. That is, the therapist's coming to view the patient, his relationship with the patient, and himself in this relationship, all for being largely non-differentiated, is a development that sets the stage for the patient's gradually increasing differentiation. Now the therapist comes to sense, time and again, newly emerging tendrils of differentiation in the patient, before the latter are themselves and conscious of them. In responding to these with spontaneity as they show themselves, again, that in the therapist, helps the patient to become aware-theat they are a part of him.

To analyst and analytic student alike, the term 'transference psychosis' usually connotes a dramatic but dreaded development in which an analysand, who at the beginning of the analysis was overtly sane but who had in actuality a borderline ego-structure, becomes overtly psychotic, that the course of the evolving transference relationship. We generally blame the analyst for such as development and prefer not to think any more about such matters, because of our own personal fear that we, like the poor misbegotten analysand, might become, or narrowly avoid becoming, psychotic in our own analysis. By contrast, in working with the chronically schizophrenic patient, we are confronted with a person whose transference to us is no harder too identify partly for the very reason that his whole daily life consists in incoherent psychotic transference reactions, for which is to whatever, to everyone about him, including the analyst in the treatment session. Little's comment (1960) that the delusional state 'remains unconscious' until it is uncovered in the analysts' holds true only in the former instance, in the borderline schizophrenic patient; there, it is the fact that the transference is delusional which is the relative covert, hard-to-discern aspect of the situation, in chronic schizophrenia, by contrast, nearly everything is delusional, and the difficult task to foster the emergence of a coherent transference meaning in the delusional symptomatology. In other words, the difficult thing in the work with the chronically schizophrenic patient is to discover the 'transference reality' in his delusional experience.

The difficultly of discerning the transference aspect of one's relationship with the patient can be traced to his having regressed to a state of ego functioning which is marked by severe impairment in his capacity either to differentiate among, or to integrate, his experiences. He is so incompletely differentiated in his ego functioning that he tends to feel, not that the therapist reminds him of, or is like, his mother or that of his father (or whomever, from his early life) but rather his functioning toward the therapist is couched in the unscrutinised assumption that the therapist is the mother or father. When, for example, in trying to bring to the attention of a paranoid schizophrenic women how much like she seemed to find the persons in her childhood on the one hand, and the person about her in the institution, including me, on the other, she dismissed this with an impatient retort, "That's what I've been trying to tell you, What difference does it make? For years subsequently in our work together, all the figures in her experience were composite figures, without any clear subjective distinction between past and present experiences, figures from the institutional scene peopled her memories of her past, and figures from what has become known to be her past were experienced by her as blended with the persons she saw about her in current life.

Transference situations in which the psychosis is manifested at a phase in therapy in which the deeply chronically confused patient, who in childhood had been accustomed to a parent's during his thinking for him, is ambivalently (a) trying to perpetuate a symbiotic relationship wherein the therapist to a high degree does the patient's thinking for him, and (b) expressing, by what the therapist feels to be sadistic and castrative and nullifying or undoing the therapist's effort to be helpful, a determination to be a separately thinking, and otherwise separately functioning, individual

Difficult though it is to discern the nature and progressive evolution of the patient's transference to the therapist, it is even more difficult to conceptualize that which is 'new' which the therapist brings into the relationship, and which, as J. M. Rioch (1943) has emphasized, is crucial to the patient's recovery. Rioch is quite right in saying that, "Whether intentionally or not, whether conscious of it or not, the analyst does express, day in and day out, subtle or overt evidences of his own personality in relationship to the patient."

The conjectural considerations for which inadequate evidences in the understanding of questionable intent is that there is a companion evolution of reality relatedness between patient and therapist, concomitant with such a transference evolution as having had the impression that it is only when the reality relatedness between patient and therapist has reached, finally and after many 'real life' vicissitudes between them, a depth of intense fondness that there now emerges, in the form of a transference development, a comparably intense and long-repressed fondness for the mother.

Presumably, a point that Freud (1922) concerning projection also holds true for transference, he stated that projection occurs no 'into the sky, so to speak, where there is nothing of the sort already', but rather the persons who in reality posses an attitude qualitatively like that which the projecting person is attributing to them. So it is with transference, we may presume that when a patient comes to react to us as a loved and loving mother, this phrase - as well as other phrases - of the transference is founded upon our having come to feel, in reality, thus toward him. M. B. Cohen (1952) stresses the importance of the therapist's inevitable feeling response to the patient's transference, and, if only to suggest, that an equally healthy source of the therapist's feeling participation be the evolving reality relatedness that pursues its own course, related to and parallelling, but not fully embraced by, the evolving transference relatedness over the years of person's working together. What is more, is the countertransference that has already been written, but as to indicate, there is a great need for us to become clear about the sequence that the recovery process in the schizophrenic adult, very roughly analogous to the growth process in normal infancy, childhood, and adolescence, tends innately to follow. When we have become clearer and surer about this, and particularly about the validity-relatedness element necessary to it, in that the frequently - though by no means always - various manifestations of feeling regarded as unwanted countertransference will be seen to be inevitable, and utterly essential, components of the recovery process.

Further, the opening view of the personality for being divisible into the areas, id, ego, and superego, tends to shield us from the anxiety-fostering realization that in psychoanalytic change is not merely quantitative and partial - where id was, there shall ego be - in Freud's dictum - but qualitative and all-persuasive. That is, that in such passages as the following. Freud gives a picture of personality-structure, and of maturation, which leaves the inaccurate but comforting impression that at least a part of us - namely, as part of the id - is free from change. In his paper entitled "Thoughts for the Times on War and Death" in 1915, he said,

> . . . the evolution of the mind shows a peculiarity that is present in no other process of development. When a village grows into a town, a child into a man, the village and the child become submerged in the town and the man, . . . it is otherwise with the development of the mind . . . the primitive stages [of mental development] can always be reestablished, the primitive mind is, in the fullest meaning of the word, imperishable (Freud, 1915).

In "Introductory Lectures on Psycho-Analysis," he says that in psychoanalytic treatment,

> . . . By means of the work of interpretation, which transforms what is unconscious into what is conscious, the ego is enlarged at the cos of this unconscious . . . (Freud, 1915-17)

In "The Ego and the Id" he said that,

> . . . the ego is that part of the id that has been modified by the direct influence of the external world . . . the pleasure-principle . . . reigns unrestricted by the id . . . the ego represents what may be called reason and common sense, in contrast to the id, which contains the passions (Freud, 1923)

Glover, in his book on technique published in 1955, states similarly that,

> . . . a successful analysis may have uncovered a good deal of the repressed . . . [and] have mitigated the archaic censoring functions of the superego, but it can scarcely be expected to abolish the id (Glover, 1955)

The state of developmental sciences, and about our own individual the individual therapeutic skills, should not cause us to understate the all-embracing extent of human personality-growth in normal maturation at least a few psychoanalysis. It is believed that all encountered, and, at lest a few fortunate instances that have made us wonder whether maturation really leaves any area of the personality untouched, leaves any steel-bound core within which the pleasure principle reigns immutably, or whether, instead, we have seen such a genuine metamorphosis, from an erstwhile hateful and self-seeking orientation to a loving and giving orientation, quite as wonderful and thoroughgoing the metamorphosis of the tadpole into the frog thoroughgoing as the metamorphosis of the tadpole into the frog or that of the caterpillar into the butterfly.

Freud himself, in his emphasis upon the 'negative therapeutic reaction' (1923), the repetition compulsion, and the resistance to analytic insight that he discovered in his work with neurotic patients, has shown the importance, in the neurotic individual, of anxiety concerning change, and him agrees with Jung's statement that 'a peculiar psychic inertia' hostile to change and progress, is the fundamental condition of neurosis (Freud, 1915). This is, as we know, even more true of psychosis - so much as that only in very recent decades have psychotic patients achieved full recovery though modified psychoanalytic therapy. Finding it instructive to explore in detail the psychodynamics of schizophrenia in terms of the anxiety concerning change which one encounters, in a particular intense degree, at work in these patients, and in oneself in the course of treating them. What the therapy of schizophrenia can teach us of the human being's standing concerning change, can broaden and deepen our understanding of the non-psychotic individual also.

This development can occur only after successive resolution of increasingly ancient personality-warp in the patient, and the establishment thereby, of a hard-won mutual trust and security. In this atmosphere the therapist relationship makes contact with the healthy ingredients of the patient's symbiotic relationship with his mother, thus laying the foundation for subsequent new growth as a separate and healthy individual.

In such fashion the patient develops importance not merely as a separate object, but to a degree as a symbiotic partner, for the therapist as well as for other people, who participate with which the therapist himself, as well as such of the staff members, we hear from fellow-therapists and ward-personal of how 'stunned' or even 'shocked' them were at seeing dramatic improvements in a long-ill patient. Characteristically, too, the therapist notices only very belatedly various long-standing symptoms have dropped out of the patient's behaviour. on looking back through his records, for example, prior to a staff-presentation, he finds to his surprise that a delusion, once long-familiar to him, has not been evidenced by the patient for several months. Thus, his feelings of personal loss are mitigated. Even so, that even among the most technically capable of therapists, is the initial reaction with dismay and discouragement to a patients, is the initial reacting with express verbally the depths of his despair, loneliness, confusion, infantile need, and so fort, typically, the therapist only belatedly recognizes the forward move this development constitutes. His initial response is traceable to the unconscious loss that this development inflicts upon him - the loss of the long-familiar and inevitable therefore cherished (unconsciously cherished) relatedness that therefor he had shared with the patient.

The patient, particularly in the symbiotic phrase of the therapy but in preceding and succeeding phase as well, is notably intolerant of sudden and marked changes in the therapeutic relationship - that is, of suddenly seeing himself, or feeling that his therapist sees him, through new eyes. He rarely gives the therapist to feel that the latter have made an importantly revealing interpretation, and when he himself conveys a highly illuminating nugget of historical information to his therapist, he does so casually, often feeling sure that he has already mentioned this before. He tends to experience important increments of de-repressed material not as earthshattering revelations in his development, yet the forward moves in therapy, on the patient's part occur each time only after a recrudescence in his symptoms. It is as though he was to find reassurance of his personal identity, for being really the same hopeless person he has long felt himself to be, before he can venture into a bit of new and more hopeful identity.

There is a necessary phase of symbiosis between patient and doctor in the transference evolution followed by the recovering schizophrenic patient, a phase in which the ego boundaries between himself and the therapist are mutually relinquished to a large degree. This development can occur only after successive resolutions of increasingly ancient personality-wrap in the patient, and the establishment, thereby, of a hard-won in the patient, and his identity.

The following considerations, to be sure, the patient, in this reality and that this mutuality of a comparative participation is essentially inclined of a better understanding and a successful therapeutic outcome.

Freud (1911) made the comment that:

> We have long observed that every neurosis has as its result, and probably therefore its purpose, a forcing of the patient out of real life, an alienating of him from reality . . . neurotics turn away from reality because they find it unbearable - either the whole or parts of it. The most extreme type of this turning away from result is shown by certain cases of hallucinatory psychosis that seek to deny the particular event that occasioned the outbreak of their inanity. But in fact every neurosis does the same with some fragment of reality . . .

Bion, in his paper in 1957 concern the differentiation, in any one schizophrenic patient, between what he calls the psychotic personality and the non-psychotic personality, concludes the presentation of his theoretical formulations with. . . . Further, I consider that this holds true for the severe neurotic, in whom believe there is a [psychotic personality concealed by neurosis as the neurotic personality is screened by psychosis in the psychotic, that has to be laid bare and dealt with0.

Bion conveys in his paper entitled "Language d the Schizophrenic" (1955) a warning of the patient's tendency to project his own sanity upon the analyst and of the massive regression that follows if this is condoned by the analyst. He says:

> . . . I have no doubt whatever that the analyst should always insist, by the way in which he conducts the case, that he is addressing himself to a sane person and is entitled to expect some sane reception . . .

There is wide spread agreement that it is inherent in therapy that the therapist functions as an auxiliary ego so the patient in the patent's struggle with inner conflicts, until such time as to make this greater strength part of his own ego. To the extent that the schizophrenic patient does not posses an observing ego of sufficient strength to permit the therapist usefully to make transference interpretations, to that degree the therapist must be able to endure - and, eventually, to enjoy - various part-object transference role, until such time as the patient, through increasing ego-integration, becomes of the therapist. Another way of saying this is that the patient develops ego-strength. in the face of his own id impulses and pathogenic superego retaliations, in that, if identification with the therapist who can endure, and integrate into his own larger self, the kind of subjectively nonhuman part-object relatedness that the patient fosters in and needs from him.

Similarly, because the therapist has seen the patient to be, earlier in the therapy, such a deeply fragmented person, he tends to retain a lingering impression of the fragility, an impression that may interfere with his going along at the faster pace that the patient, now a very different and far stronger person, is capable of setting. But even this memory-image of the fragile patient, carried with the therapist, has a natural function in the course of the psychotherapy, for it is only very late in the work that the patient himself is able to realize how very ill, how very fragile, he once was, until he becomes strong enough to integrate his realization into his self-image, the therapist has to be the bearer of this piece of the patient's identity. This process is analogous to the well-known phenomenon in which each major forward stride in the patient's therapeutic growth is accompanied, or presaged, by the therapist's suddenly seeing in the patient a new and healthier person, there, too, the impact of the development falls primarily, for a time, upon the therapist rather than the patient. The patient himself, because his sense of identity is still, during the earlier therapeutic phases to which is easily overwhelming, and relatively tenuous. By the realization of the extent to which he is now changed, even though this change is, in our view, a most beneficial and welcoming one.

More often than not, is that the histories of schizophrenic patients, whether male or female, describe the father for being by far the warmer, and more accessible of the two parents, the father, whereas the mother was always relatively cold, rejecting, remote figure. However, that the disguise behind the child's idol inseparable 'buddy' is a matter of the father's transference to the child for being a mother-figure upon whom he, the father makes insatiable demands. It seems that the father, in these instances, is an infantile individual, who reacts both to his wife and to his child unconscious ly seeks to intervene between mother and child in such a way as to have each of them to himself. The seeming evidence of this by now, in a considerable number of cases, both in the transference-development and interviews with the parents.

The point being made, is that the mother and child allow this interposition by the father to happen, because of their anxiety about their fondness for being a mother-figure who exasperatingly allows as an infantile 'buddy', a kind of father to keep intervening, placing impossible demands for mothering upon the patient; finally comes a phase of th e patient's responding to the therapist as a mother with whom he can share unashamedly fond relatedness, no longer burdened by the father's scornfully and demandingly coming between them.

So it is with transference, we may presume that when a patient comes to react to us as a love and loving mother, this phase - as well as other phases - of the transference is founded upon our having come to feel, in reality, as, M. B. Cohen (1952) stresses the importance of the therapist 's inevitable feeling response to the patient's transference, only to suggest, that of the therapist's feeling participation is the evolving reality relatedness that pursue its own course, related to and parallelling, but not fully embraced by, the evolving transcendence relatedness over which time to occur is, namely introduced as countertransference, nonetheless, in the realm, as situated as one crucial phase of the work - a symbiotic kind of mutual dependency, which he mutually comes to feel toward the patient, his acceptance of a mutual caring which amounts at times to an adoration, and his being able to acknowledge the patient's contribution - inevitable, in successful therapy - to his own personal integration. It must be noted, that the schizophrenic patient responds with great regularity to the therapist's material warmth for being a sure indication that the latter are a homosexual or a lesbian. The younger therapist needs to become quite clear that this is, in actuality, a formidable resistance in the patient again the very kind of loving mother-infant relatedness that offers the patient his only avenue of salvation from his illness. Not to say, that the therapist should depreciate the degree of anxiety, referable to the deep ambivalence of the patient's early relationship with his mother, which is contained within this resistance, perhaps, that the therapist's deep-seated doubts as to his own sexual identity - and what person is totally free of such doubt? - should not make him lose of the fact that the patient's contempt (or revulsion, or what not) is basically a resistance against going ahead and picking up the threads of the loving infant-mother relatedness that were long ago severed.

Upon comment, the patient has in reference to a different person, and is often couched in terms of a different temporal era, that is intended by the preconscious or unconscious impulse striving for expression. The circumstance of the patient's having regressed to a more or less early level of ego-functioning is explanatory of many of the idiosyncrasies of schizophrenic communication. The clinical picture is complicated, in most instances, by the fact that the level of regression varies unceasingly, at times from one moment to the next, and there are even instances where the patient is functioning on more than one developmental level simultaneously.

The fact of the patient's regressed, mode of psychological functioning helps to account for the 'concretization', or contrariwise the seeming oversymbolization, of his communications; these phenomena represent his having regressed, in his thinking (and overall subjective experiencing), to a developmental level comparable with that in the young child who has not yet become able to differentiate between concrete and metaphorical (or similar forms of highly symbolic) thinking.

Similarly, the patient may tittle-tattle in a way that gives us to know that the content of his speech is relatively unimportant to him at the moment he is immersed in the pleasure of saying the words and hearing the sound of them, much like the young child who has not yet learned to talk but loves to babble and to hear the sound of his babbling. A nonverbal patient may usefully be regarded as having regressed even further, to the pre-verbal era of infancy or very early childhood.

The strikingly intense ambivalence, another fundamental aspect of the schizophrenic individual's psychodynamics, contributes to a number of different typical kinds of schizophrenic communications. (1) The indirect communication, (2) Self-contradictory verbal and nonverbal communications, and (3) Verbal communications in which there is a split between content and vocal feeling-tone.

In assessing the meaning of such communications, one soon learns to brush aside the content and attend to the feeling-tone - o r, in still, more complex instances, tones - in which the words are said.

Incidently, a patient sometimes evidences a quite accurate grasp of the true import of such communications that they come from the therapist. at the end of each of the maddening points or the enduring intervals of times of silence. After this had happened several times dawning upon that which he was very accurately expressing the covert message contained in the parting comment to him, as to the (4) No-verbal expression of a feeling contrarily enacted to the one being verbalized? And (5) Expression of contradictory feeling at an entirely nonverbal level.

The archaically harsh, forbidding superego of the patient is another basic factor that helps to account for his heavily disguised and often fragmentary communications.

I can only surmise that there is a companion evolution of reality relatedness between parent and the therapist, concomitant with such a transference evolution, it is only when the real possibilities relatedness between patient and therapist has reached, of a final and after man a depth intensity that there is now emerging, in the form of a transference development a comparable intense and long-represented direction in the fondness for the mother. However, this brings us back to other topics comprising the overall course of psychotherapy as a chronically schizophrenic person, a person preceding in the complex individuality extended to dynamical events of clinical work.

The quality of the transference resistance is to a great extent deepened on the quantity of other resistance. Resistance have the tendency to accumulate wherever there is a favourable opportunity to withstand the analysis. In most cases the transference offers the best opportunity, for example, we see the resistance coming from the conscious repetition, from the unconscious feeling of guilt and from the resistance by repression, takes part of building up the transference resistance. Freud speaks of the transference of resistance into a negative, hostile transference: It is on account of this transformation that the dissolution that transference resistance so often because the chief task of the therapeutics work. In the case of our patient the analysis finally showed the development of anxiety in the transference to b e castration anxiety that had arisen from infantile masturbation with accompanying incestuous wishes toward the mother and the hared and castration wishes toward the father. In the analysis, if the resistance resulting factors in the development of anxiety in the analysis. If the resistance result from this anxiety is analysis the addition of other resistance, then the final resistance in the analysis cannot be considered as an index to the amount of the genuine infantile anxiety for the anxiety resulting from infantile masturbation, on account of the genuine infantile anxiety: For the anxiety resulting from infantile masturbation on account of its anxiety resulting from infantile masturbation, on account of its particular capacity for being used as a resistance in analysis, becomes the nucleus of crystallisation or the basis for the addition of all the other resistance. In a footnote to his paper "The Dynamics of th Transference," this idea was alluded to by Freud, that, 'Over and over again, when one draws near to a pathogenic complex, that part of it that is first thrust forward into consciousness will be some aspect of it that can be transferred, having been so, it will then be defended with the utmost obstinacy by the patient'.

The footnote says: 'From which however one need not infer in general any very particular pathogenic importance in the point selected for resistance by transference. In warfare, when a bitter fight is raging over the possession of some little chapel or a single farmhouse, we do not necessarily assume that the church is a national monument, or that the barns contain the military funds. Their value may be merely tactical; in the next onslaught they will very likely be of no importance'.

The dissolution of the transference resistance means then not only the dissolution of the resistance resulting from the genuine infantile castration anxiety but a liberation of the supporting resistance that often can only later be separately dissolved, because during the phase of the violent acting-out in the transference these resistance are not accessible to interpretation and dissolution.

For what is said about the psychology of metaphor is analogous to the transformational aspects of developed transferences and steadfast interpretations that both facilitate and organize them as transferences. Allowing that these transferences and 'remembered' experiences come into existence over a period of time, nothing that is identical with them has ever before been enacted, and nothing identical with them will ever be enacted again. They are creations that may be fully achieved only under specific analytic conditions. For example, at the time of his childhood scene with his father, the young man of the clinical example, could not have had the specific experience as recounted. strictly speaking, he was not reliving that moment. As a bo y, he must have experienced some of the main precursors and constituents of his present mode of experience, but he could not have done so in the present articulated and integrated manner. That present manner was the basis of his anguished outcry. words like re-creating, but re-experiencing and reliving simply do not do justice to the phenomena. In the way he was doing it, he was living that moment for the first time.

By making this claim, there is no constricting some of our well-established ideas about interpretation and insight, for example, disputing point that insight refers to more than the recovery of lost memories, and takes in, as well, a new grasp of the significance and interrelations of events one has always remembered. The latter connections that the analysand will say, as Freud pointed out, "As a matter of fact I've always known it, only I've never thought of" (1914). In fact, it is to develop that points further to say that the young child simply does not have the means of fully defining what we later regard as its own life experiences. It takes an adult to do that, especially with the help of an analyst. It was, after all, Freud's analysis that made it possible to define infantile psychosexuality. in this respect, but without disrespect, child analysis retains a quality of applied psychoanalysis. The adult definition of infantile psychosexuality is 'artificial' in the same way that the interpreting transference neurosis is: Both are ways of describing as true something that was not truer in quite that way as, at the time of its greatest development significance. this apparent paradox about 'remembering' as a form of creating goes a long was, that saying, what it is this distinctive about psychoanalytic interpretation.

In steadfastly and perspicaciously making transference interpretation, the analyst helps constitute new modes of experience and new experiences. This newness characterizes the experience of analytic transference in them. Unlike extra-analytic transference, they can no longer be sheerly repetitive or merely new editions. Instead, they become repetitively new editions understood as such because defined as such by the simplification and steadfast transference interpretation, instead of responding to the analysand in kind, Which would actualize the repetition, the analyst makes an interpretation. This interpretation does not necessarily or regularly match something the analysand does often seem to have always represented often, but he does not seem to have done so at all. To think otherwise about this would, in effect, to claim that, unconsciously, every analysand is Freud or a fully insightful Freudian analyst. And that claim is totally absurd.

It would be closer to the truth to say this: Unconsciously, the analysand already knows or has experienced fragmentary, amorphous, uncoordinated constituents of many of the transference interpretations. Alternatively, one may say that, implicitly, the analysand has been insisting on some as yet unspecified certainties and, in keeping with this, following some set of as yet unspecified rules in his actions, these the transference interpretations now organize explicitly. Each transference interpretation thus refers to many things that have already been defined by the analysand, and it does so in a way that transforms them. That's why one may call it interpretation. Otherwise, it would be mere repeating or sterile paraphrasing. Interpretation is a creative redescription that implicitly has the structure of a simile. It says, "This is like it," Each interpretation does, therefore, add new actions to the life the analysand has already lived.

Technically, redescription in the terms of transference-repetition is necessary. This is so because, up to the time of interpretation and working through, the analysand has been, in one sense unable and, in another sense, unconsciously and desperately unwilling, to conduct his life differently, in and of them, the repetitions cannot after the symptoms, the subjective distress, the wasting of one's possibilities rather they can only perpetuate a static situation by repeatedly confirming its necessity. They prove once again, the unconsciously maintained damaging certainties. But once they get to be viewed as historically grounded actions and subjectively defined situations. As they do upon being interpreted and worked through, they appear as having always been, in crucial respects, inventions of the analysand's making and, so, as his responsibility. in being seen as versions one' past life, they may be changed in significant and beneficial ways. Less of all, are they presented as purely inevitable happenings, as a fixed fate or as the well-established way of the world. However, we encounter a second paradox that goes to the heart of psychoanalysis interpretation, namely, that responsible, insightful change is possible through psychoanalysis just because, as a child the analysand mistakenly assumes and then denied responsibility for much that he encountered in the early formative environment and during maturation.

One major point remains to be made about the logic of viewing transference interpretation as simplifying yet innovative redescription. This point is that the interpretations bring about a coordination of the terms in which to state both the analysand's current problems and their life-historical background. The analysand's symptoms and distress are described as actions and modes of action, with due regard for the principle of multiple function or multiple meaning: In coordination with that description, the decisive developmental situation and conflicts are stated as actions and modes of action. Continuity is established between the childhood constructions of relationships and the self and the present constructions of these interpretations of transference shows who both are part of the same set of practices, that is, how they follow the same set of rules. Past and present are coordinated to show continuity rather than arranged in a definite sequence.

In the same way, the form of analytic behaviour and the content of association are given co-ordinated descriptions, say, as being defiant, devouring, or reparative. Or, in the case of depression, the depressive symptoms, the depressive analytic transference, the themes of present and past loss, destructiveness and helplessness, all will be redescribed under the aspect of one continuously developing self-presentation. And this coordination will be worked out in that hermeneutically circular fashion in which the analyst defines both th facts to be explained and the explanations to be applied to these facts. In the end, as is well known, both the paramount issues of the analysis and the leading explanatory account of them are likely to be significantly different from the provisional versions of them used at the beginning of the analysis.

The increasing influence of the modernist version of transference and its interpretation represents an adaptation to several long-term philosophical, scientific, and cultural shifts we can now recognize. this changing view of transference is also the most visible emblem of the deep changes in psychoanalytic theory that are now quietly taking place, and of their theoretical pluralism that is so prevalent today (Cooper, 1985).

One of these long-term changes in the climate in which psychoanalysis dwells results from a large philosophical debate concerning the nature of history, veridicality, and narrative. Kermode (1985) has written of the change during this century in our modes of understanding and interpreting the past and the present, "Once upon a time it seemed obvious that you could best understand how things are by asking how they got to be that way. Now attention [is] directed to how things are in their immediate plexuities. There is a switch to use the linguistic expressions, from the diachronic to the synchronic view. Diachrony, roughly speaking, studies things in their synchrony to be as they are, synchrony concerns itself with things as they are and ignores the question, how they got that way. This distinction, put forth by de Sasussure (1915), has achieved philosophical dominance today and is the clear source of the hermeneutic view so prevalent in psychoanalysis, proposed by Ricoeur (1970). From here, it is a short distance to Schafer (1981), and Gill (1982), or Spence (1982) who in varying ways adopt the synchronic view. In this view, the analytic task is interpretation, with the patient, of the events of the analytic situation - usually broadly labelled transference - with a construction rather than a reconstruction of the past. In effect, while there is a past of 'there and then' it is knowable only through the filter of the present, of 'here and now'. There is no other past than the one as we construct, and there is no way of understanding the past but through its relation to the present.

Psychoanalysis, like history but unlike fiction, does have anchoring points, for history's anchoring points are the evidences that events really did occur, There was a Roman empire, it did have dates, actual persons lived and died. These 'facts' place a limitation for the narratives an interpretations that may seriously be entertained. Psychoanalysis is anchored in its scientific developmental psychology and in the biology of attachment and affects. Biology confers regularities and limits on possible histories, and our constructions of the past must accord with this scientific knowledge. constructions of childhood that are incompatible with what we know of developmental possibilities may open our eye's to new concepts of development, but more likely they alert us to maimed childhoods that have led our patients to usual narrative constructions in the effort to maintain self-esteem and internal coherence. A second, far less secure, anchorage is the enormous amount of convergent data that accumulate during the course of an analysis, which are likely to give the analyst the impression that he is reconstructing rather than constructing the figures and the circumstances of his patient's past. While a diachronic view may no longer suffice, it may also not be fully dispensable if our patient's histories are to maintain psychoanalytic coherence, rooted in bodily experience, and the loving, hating and terrifying affects accompanying the fantastic world of infantile psychic reality. Not all analysis are yet as ready as Spence, for example, to give up all claim to the truth value explanatory power of the understanding of the past, even if it is limited to knowing past constructions of the past. Nevertheless, the change in philosophical outlook during our century is profound and contributes to our changing view of the analytic process is exemplified in the transference and its interpretation.

Approaching the same issue from an entirely different vantage point, Emde (1981) speaking for the 'baby-watchers' and discussing changing models of infancy and early development, details a second source of the major change of climate to which he writes, The models suggest that what we reconstruct, and what may be extraordinarily helpful to the patient in making a biography, may never have happened. The human being, infant child, is understood to be fundamentally active in constructing his experience. Reality not a given nor necessarily registered in an unmodified form. Perhaps it makes sense for the psychoanalysis to place renewed emphasis on recent and current experiences - first, as a context for interpreting early experience - first, as a context for interpreting the potential amelioration, . . . Psychoanalysts are specialists in dealing with the intrapsychic world not only particular with the dynamic unconscious, but we need to pay attention not only to the intrapsychic realm. conflicting-laden and conflict-free, but also to the interpersonal realm. He concludes, . . . we have probably placed far to much an emphasis on early experience itself as opposed to the process by which it is modified or made use of by subsequent experience.

This view of psychic developments, discarding the timeless unconscious and so powerful at odds with the views that were held by psychoanalysts during the time when most of our ideas of transference interpretation were formed, clearly suggests the modernist model of transference interpretation.

A change in the cultural environment of psychoanalysis provides a third source for the changing model of transference interpretation. Valenstein describes oscillations in psychoanalytic outlook between an emphasis on cognition at one end, and on affect at the other. One might see these as differences between old-fashioned scientific and romantic world views. Surely the period of ego psychology, perhaps reflected in the English translation of Freud, and certainly reflected in the effect to insist on the libidinal energetic point of view, represented the attempt to see psychoanalysis as Freud usually did, as an objective science in the nineteenth century style, with hypotheses created out of naïve observations. It accorded with that view to see the transference as an objective reflection of history. We are currently in one of our more romantic periods. It is consonant with that view to see transference as an activity - stormy, romantic, active, affective - a kind of adventure from which the two individuals emerge changed and renewed. In this romantic view, interpretation of the transference are intended to remove obstacles interfering with the heightening and intimacy of the experience, with the implication that self-knowledge and change will result from their encounter. A romantic figure, the patient and analyst set forth on a quest into the unknown, and whether or not one of them returns with a Holy Grail, they return with many new stories to tell and a new life experience - the analysis. Gardner's (1983) book, 'Self Inquiry' epitomizes this romantic view of analyst and patient as a poet-pair engaged in mutual self-inquiry. It is clear that many analysis would rather be artistic than scientist. By contrast, the older, cognitive view of the transference is of an intellectual journey, emotionally loaded of course, but basically a trip back in history, seeking truth and insight.

Finally, our newer ideas of transference interpretation come from the rereading and reinterpretations of Freud that necessarily accompany the changes in outlook in the corresponding pendulum of analytic techniques from Freud's actual technique, as reconstructed from his notes and the report s of his patients, to the so-called 'classical' technique that held sway after Freud's death, and again, to the currently changing technical scene. Lipton (1977) has insisted that in the 1940s andv1950s the so-called classical technique replaced Freud's own more personal and relaxed technique, probably in reaction to Alexander's suggestion of the corrective emotional experience. It was Lipton's view that the misnamed 'classical' technique, in contrast to Freud's, emphasized rules for the analyst's behaviour and sacrificed the purpose of the analysis. Eissler's 1953 description of analysis as an activity that ideally uses only interpretations became the paradigm for 'classical' analysis. It was, Lipton, says, a serious and severe distortion of the mature analytic technique developed by Freud. Freud regarded the analyst 's personal behaviour, the personality of the analyst exemplified for Lipton in the case of the Rat Man. The so-called 'classical' (and in his view non-Freudian) techniques attempted to include every aspect of the analytic situation as part of technique and led to the model of the silent, restrained psychoanalyst. Lipton's argument is persuasive.

These two different models of technique have obvious implications concerning the transference and its interpretation. Unless we believe in an extreme version of the historical model, we must expect that the silent, restraint, nonparticipatory psychoanalyst will elicit different responses from his patient than will the vivid, less-hidden, more responsive analyst. The range of personal behaviours available to the analyst before we need be concerned that the analyst is engaging in activities that are excessively self-revelatory or that force the patient into a social relationship is probably much broader than we thought a few years ago. But we also know that almost any behaviour of the analyst, including restraint or silence, immediately influences the patient's responses. In these newer views of the analytic situation it is not easy to know that intrapsychically derived patient behaviours.

It is evident today that psychoanalyst's under the sway of their theories and personalities, differ greatly concerning matters to which they are sensitive, and, of course, we can interpret only the transferences we perceive. Despite this limitation, a review of the literature reveals, along with the usual rigidities, a laudable tendency to describe one's experience as fully as possible, without heed to how it contradicts belief, often blurring over when experience and theory do not match. However, we have always been better at what we do than at what we say we do. This is exemplified in Heimann's (1956) paper. Speaking from a modified Kleinian perspective, and holding the historical theory of transference interpretation, Heimann managed 30 years ago to describe vividly and to support passionately much of what today is under discussion as the modernist version. That her position were contradictory bothered her not at all. While many of us prefer to think we are following our theories, like all good scientists, good psychoanalysts, beginning with Freud, have always seen and responded to far more than our theories admit. when we have seen too much, we change our theories.

Overall, during the last half of this century, these trends, as well as our ever-increasing knowledge of our increasing distance from Freud's authority have led to specific theoretical developments (Cooper, 1984, 1985), many of them inferred in the newer transference model. Our current pluralistic theoretical world, in which almost all analysts are working, wittingly or not, with individual amalgams of Freud's drive theory, ego psychology, interpersonal Sullivanian psychoanalysis, object-relationship theory, Bowlbyan or Mahlerian attachment theory, and usually smuggled-in versions of self-psychology, lies at the base of the newer ideas and disagreements concerning transference interpretation.

Although the historical definitions of transference and transference interpretation have the merit of seeming precision and limited scope, they are based on a psychoanalytical theory that no longer stands alone and has lost ground in at least, subsumed, by modernist conceptions that are more attuned to the theories that abound today.

Asa prefatory remark about Freud and transference, the observations can be offered that Freud wrote briefly about transference and did so, in the main, before 1917. Another observation which can rarely be made about Freud's work, what he did write on transference and did not reach the high level of analytical thought which has come to be regarded as standard for him. Some indication of what his contribution consist of is given by the editors of the Standard Edition, who list them in several places. One of the longer lists, in a footnote includes six reference 'Studies on Hysteria', with Breuer (1895),the Dora paper (1905), The Dynamics of Transference' (1912), Observations on Transference-Love' (1915), the chapter on transference in the Introductory Lectures (1917), and Analysis Terminable and Interminable (1937). Although the editors in no sense suggest that these six papers include everything Freud wrote on the subject that these six papers include everything Freud wrote on the subject, it does seem evident that, considering the essential importance of transference to analysis, he wrote little. moreover, the three papers in which transference is the specific theme. `The Dynamics of Transference,`Transference-Love ; and the transference chapter in the Introductory Lectures, come across as perhaps his least significant contributions.

Freud's first direct mention of transference occurs in "Studies on Hysteria" (1895), His first significant reference to it, however, did not appear until five years later when, in a lecture to Fliess on April 16, 1900, he said (Freud 1887-1902) he was 'beginning to see that the apparent endlessness of the treatment is something of an inherent feature and is connected with transference. In a footnote to his letter the editors state that, 'this is the first insight into the role of transference in psychoanalytic therapy'.

Despite these early references, it seems correct to say that yet another five yea s was to go by before the phenomenon of transference was actually introduced. Even then the introduction was far from prominent, for it was tacked like an afterthought as a four-page portion of a postscript to what was perhaps Freud's most fascinating case history to date, the case of Dora (1905).

Using data from Dora's three-month-long, unexpected terminated analysis, and especially from her dramatic transference reactions which had taken him quite unaware. Freud now gave to the transference its first distinct psychological entity, for the first time indicated its essential role in the analytic process. His account, although in general more than adequate - in fact elegant and remarkable 'finished' - was brief, almost Iaconic, and perhaps not an entirely worthy introduction to such a truly great discovery. What was uniquely great was his recognizing the usefulness of transference. In his analysis of Dora h e had noted not only that transference feelings existed and were powerful, but much to his dismay, he had realized that as serious, perhaps, even insurmountable, obstacle they could be,. Then, in what seems like a creative leap, Freud made the almost und unbelievable discovery that transference was in fact the key to analysis, that by properly taking the patient's transference into account, an entirely new, essential and immensely effective heuristic and therapeutic force was added to the analytic method.

Treatment of schizophrenia usually involves a combination of medication, rehabilitation, and treatment of other problems the person may have. Antipsychotic drugs (also called neuroleptics) are the most frequently used medications for treatment of schizophrenia. Psychological and social rehabilitation programs may help people with schizophrenia function in the community and reduce stress related to their symptoms. Treatment of secondary problems, such as substance abuse and infectious diseases, is also an important part of an overall treatment program.

Antipsychotic medications, developed in the mid-1950s, can dramatically improve the quality of life for people with schizophrenia. The drugs reduce or eliminate psychotic symptoms such as hallucinations and delusions. The medications can also help prevent these symptoms from returning. Common Antipsychotic drugs include risperidone (Risperdal), olanzapine (Zyprexa), clozapine (Clozaril), quetiapine (Seroquel), haloperidol (Haldol), thioridazine (Mellaril), chlorpromazine (Thorazine), fluphenazine (Prolixin), and trifluoperazine (Stelazine). People with schizophrenia usually must take medication for the rest of their lives to control psychotic symptoms. Antipsychotic medications appear to be less effective at treating other symptoms of schizophrenia, such as social withdrawal and apathy.

Because many patients with schizophrenia continue to experience difficulties despite taking medication, psychological and social rehabilitation is often necessary. A variety of methods can be effective. Social skills training helps people with schizophrenia learn specific behaviours for functioning in society, such as making friends, purchasing items at a store, or initiating conversations. Behaviourial training methods can also help them learn self-care skills such as personal hygiene, money management, and proper nutrition. In addition, cognitive-behaviourial therapy, a type of psychotherapy, can help reduce persistent symptoms such as hallucinations, delusions, and social withdrawal.

Because many patients have difficulty obtaining or keeping jobs, supported employment programs that help patients find and maintain jobs are a helpful part of rehabilitation. In these programs, the patient works alongside people without disabilities and earns competitive wages. An employment specialist (or vocational specialist) helps the person maintain their job by, for example, training the person in specific skills, helping the employer accommodate the person, arranging transportation, and monitoring performance. These programs are most effective when the supported employment is closely integrated with other aspects of treatment, such as medication and monitoring of symptoms.

Some people with schizophrenia are vulnerable to frequent crises because they do not regularly go to mental health centres to receive the treatment they need. These individuals often relapse and face rehospitalization. To ensure that such patients take their medication and receive appropriate psychological and social rehabilitation, assertive community treatment (ACT) programs have been developed that deliver treatment to patients in natural settings, such as in their homes, in restaurants, or on the street.

People with schizophrenia often have other medical problems, so an effective treatment program must attend to these as well. One of the most generally shared in or participated in things conforming to a type without noteworthy excellence or faults just as common a rule, by ordinary, frequent and ordinarily as an idea or expression deficient in originality or freshness, yet, only of its exchanging the commonplace of the common associated problems is vehemently and usually coarsely expressed condemnation or disapproved, as the interpretative category of an unequalled vocabulary is itself a genuine abuse. Successful treatment of substance abuse inpatients with schizophrenia requires careful coordination with their mental health care, so that the same clinicians are treating both disorders at the same time.

The high rate of substance abuse in patients with schizophrenia contributes to a high prevalence of infectious diseases, including hepatitis B and C and the human immunodeficiency virus (HIV). Assessment, education, and treatment or management of these illnesses is critical for the long-term health of patients.

Other problems frequently associated with schizophrenia include housing instability and homelessness, legal problems, violence, trauma and post-traumatic stress disorder, anxiety, depression, and suicide attempts. Close monitoring and psychotherapeutic interventions are often helpful in addressing these problems.

Several other psychiatric disorders are closely related to schizophrenia. In schizoaffective disorder, a person shows symptoms of schizophrenia combined with either mania or severe depression. Schizophreniform disorder refers to an illness in which a person experiences schizophrenic symptoms for more than one month but fewer than six months. In schizotypal personality disorder, a person engages in odd thinking, speech, and behaviour, but usually does not lose contact with reality. Sometimes mental health professionals refer to these disorders together as schizophrenia-spectrum disorders.

Severe mental illness almost always alters a person's life dramatically. People with severe mental illnesses experience disturbing symptoms that can cause of such difficulties and holding to a job, or go to school, relate to others, or cope with ordinary life demands. Some individuals require hospitalization because they become unable to care for themselves or because they are at risk of committing suicide.

The symptoms of mental illness can be very distressing. People who develop schizophrenia may hear voices inside their head that say nasty things about them or command them to act in strange or unpredictable ways. Or they may be paralysed by paranoia - the deep conviction that everyone, including their closest family members, wants to injure or destroy them. People with major depression may feel that nothing brings pleasure and that life is so dreary and unhappy that it is better to be dead. People with panic disorder may experience heart palpitations, rapid breathing, and anxiety so extreme that they may not be able to leave home. People whom experience episodes of mania may engage in reckless sexual behaviour or may spend money indiscriminately, acts that later cause them to feel guilt, shame, and desperation.

Other mental illnesses, while not always debilitating, create certain problems in living. People with personality disorders may experience loneliness and isolation because their personality style interferes with social relations. People with an eating disorder may become so preoccupied with their weight and appearance that they force themselves to vomit or refuse to eat. Individuals who develop post-traumatic stress disorder may become angry easily, experience disturbing memories, and have trouble concentrating.

Experiences of mental illness often take issue upon its stability for depending on one's culture or social group, sometimes greatly so. For example, in most of the non-Western world, people with depression complain principally of physical ailments, such as lack of energy, poor sleep, loss of appetite, and various kinds of physical pain. Indeed, even in North America these complaints are commonplace. But in the United States and other Western societies, depressed people and mental health professionals who treat them tend to emphasize psychological problems, such as feelings of sadness, worthlessness, and despair. The experience of schizophrenia also differs by culture. In India, one-third of the new cases of schizophrenia involve catatonia, a behaviourial condition in which a person maintains a bizarre statue like pose for hours or days. This condition is rare in Europe and North America.

Of furthering issues regarding depersonalization disorder, meaning, in effect, that it is a categorised illness based within its intendment for being an illness, of mind, in which people experience an unwelcome sense of detachment from their own bodies. They may feel as though they are floating above the ground, outside observers of their own mental or physical processes. Other symptoms may include a feeling that they or other people are mechanical or unreal, a feeling of being in a dream, a feeling that their hands or feet are larger or smaller than usual, and a deadening of emotional responses. These symptoms are chronic and severe enough to impede normal functioning in a social, school, or work environment.

Depersonalization disorder is a relatively rare syndrome thought to result from severe psychological stress. It may occur as part of other mental illnesses, especially anxiety disorders. For example, some people with panic disorder feel nervous, have a sense of doom about their future and health, and have a troubling sense of detachment form the lose in the attemptive use in making or doing or achieving a useful regularity as might be expected of the control over their bodies. Depersonalization disorder may also be a component of more severe mental illness, such as schizophrenia. Treatment may include training in relaxation techniques that enhance body perception and control, hypnosis to modify symptoms, and psychotherapy to explore possible stress-related components of the disorder.

Psychiatrists classify depersonalization disorder as one of the Dissociative disorders. Such disorders involve a disruption of consciousness, memory, identity, or perception.

All the while, the schizophrenic responds to altercations in the analyst's defections and understanding by corresponding stormy and dramatic changes from love to hatred, from willingness to leave his delusional world to resistance and renewed withdrawal.

As understandable as these changes are, nevertheless may come as a surprise to the analyst who frequently has not observed their source, this is quite in contrast to his experience with psychoneurosis whose emotional reactions during an interview he can usually predict. These unpredictable changes seem to be the reason for the conception of the unreliability of the schizophrenic's transference reaction, yet they follow the same dynamic rules as the psychoneurotic's oscillations between positive and negative transference and resistance, however, if the schizophrenic's reactions are stormy and seemingly more unpredictable than those of the psychoneurotic, that instances suggested to be due to the inevitable errors in the analyst's approach to the schizophrenic, of which he himself may be unaware, rather than to the unreliability of the patient's emotional response?

Why is it inevitable that the psychoanalyst disappoint his schizophrenic patient time and again?

The schizophrenic withdraws from painful reality and retires to what resembles the early speechless phase of development where consciousness is not yet crystalized. As the expression of his feelings is not hindered by the convention that he has eliminated, as his thinking, feelings, behaviour and speech - when present - obey the working rules of the archaic unconscious. His thinking is magical and does not follow logical rules. It does not admit to every last 'no', and likewise the no to 'yes': There is no recognition of space and time, I, you, and they, are interchangeable expression through which of symbols and often by movement and gestures rather than by words.

As the schizophrenic is suspicious, he will distrust the words of his analyst. He will interpret them and incidental gestures and attitudes of the analyst according to his own delusional experience. The analyst may not even be aware of these involuntary manifestations of his attitudes, yet they mean much to the hypersensitive schizophrenic who uses them as a means of orienting himself to the therapist's personality and intentions toward him.

In other words, the schizophrenic patient and the therapist are people living in different worlds and no different levels of personal development with different means of expressing and of orienting themselves. We know little about the language of the unconscious that belongs to the schizophrenic, and our access to it is blocked by the very process of our own adjustment to a world the schizophrenic has relinquished, so, we should not be surprised that errors and misunderstandings occur when we under take to communicate and strive for a rapport with him.

Another source of the schizophrenic's disappointment arises form which the analyser accepts and does not interfere with the behaviour of the schizophrenic, his attitude may lead the patient to expect that the analyst will assist in carrying out all the patient's wishes, even though they may not seem to be in his interest to the analyser's and the hospital's in their relationship to society. This attitude of acceptance so different from the patient's previous experiences readily fosters the anticipation that the analyst will try to carry out the patient's suggestion and take his part, even against conventional society with which it should occasionally arise. Frequently it will be wise for the analyst to agree with the patient's wish to remain unbattled and untidy until he is ready to talk about the reasons for his behaviour or to change spontaneously. At other times, he will unfortunately be unable to take the patient's part without being able to make the patient understand and accept the reasons for the analyst's position.

If the analyst is not able to accept the possibility of misunderstanding the reaction of the schizophrenic patient and in turn of being misunderstood by him, it may shake his security with his patient.

That is to say, that, among other things, the schizophrenic, once he accepts the analyst's insecurity. being helpless and open to himself - in spite of his pretended grandiose isolation - he will feel utterly defeated by the insecurity of his would-be helper. Such disappointment may furnish reasons for outbursts of hatred and are comparable to the negative transference reactions of psychoneurosis, yet more intense than these, since they are not limited by the restrictions of the actual world - that is, it exists in or based on fact, its only problem is a sure-enough externalization for which things are existing in the act of being external in something that has existence, ss if it were an actualization as received in the obtainable enactment for being externalized, such that its problem of in some actual life that proves obtainable achieved, in that of doing something that has an existence for having absolute actuality.

These outbursts are accompanied by anxiety, feelings of guilt, and fear of retaliations which in turn lead to increased hostility. Yet this established a vicious circle: We disappoint the patient, he is afraid that we hate him for his hatred and therefore continues to hate us. If in addition he senses that the analyst is afraid of his aggressiveness, it confirms his fear that he is actually considered as some dangerous and unacceptable, and this augments his hatred.

This establishes that the schizophrenics capable of developing strong relationships of love and hatred toward the analyst. After all, one could not be so hostile if it were not for the background of a very close relationship. In addition, the schizophrenic develops transference reactions on the narrower sense which he can differentiate from the actual interpersonal relationship. For which the schizophrenic's emotional reactions toward the analyst have to be met with extreme care and caution. The love which the sensitive schizophrenic feels as he first emerges, and his cautions acceptance of the analyst's warmth of interest are really most delicate and tender things. If the analyst deals with the transference reactions of a psychoneurotic is bad enough, though as a reparable rule, but if he fails with a schizophrenic in meeting positive feelings by pointing it out for instance before the patient indicates that he is ready to discuss it, he may easily freeze to death what has just begun to grow and so destroy any further possibility of therapy.

Some analysts may feel that the atmosphere of complete acceptance and of strict avoidance of any arbitrary denials which we recommend as a basic rule for the treatment of schizophrenics may not avoid our wish to guide of reacceptance of reality, nevertheless, Freud says that every science and therapy which accepts his teachings about unconscious, about transference and resistance and about infantile sexuality, may be called psychoanalysis. According in this definition we believe we are practising psychoanalysis with our schizophrenic patients.

Whether we call it analysis or not, it is clear that successful treatment does not depend on technical rules of any special psychiatric school but rather on the basic attitude of individual therapist toward psychologic persons. If he meets them as strangle creatures of another world whose productions are not comprehensible to 'normal' beings, he cannot treat them, if he realizes, however, that the difference between himself and the psychologic is only of degree, and not of kind, he will know better how to meet him. He will not be able to identify himself sufficiently with the patient to understand and accept his emotional reactions without becoming involved in them.

The process of constant and perpetual change is examined and closely matched within the study of philosophical speculations and pointed of a world view which asserts that basic reality is constantly in a process of flux and change. Indeed, reality is identified with pure process. Concepts such as creativity, freedom, novelty, emergence, and growth are fundamental explanatory categories for process philosophy. This metaphysical perspective is to be contrasted with a philosophy of substance, the view that a fixed and permanent reality underlies the changing or fluctuating world of ordinary experience. Whereas substance philosophy emphasizes static being, process philosophy emphasizes dynamically becoming.

Although process philosophy is as old as the 6th-century Bc Greek philosopher, Heraclitus, renewed interest in it was stimulated in the 19th century by the theory of evolution. Key figures in the development of modern process philosophy were the British philosophers Herbert Spencer, Samuel Alexander, and Alfred North Whitehead, the American philosophers Charles S. Peirce and William James, and the French philosophers Henri Bergson and Pierre Teilhard de Chardin. Whitehead's Process and Reality: An Essay in Cosmology (1929) is generally considered the most important systematic expression of process philosophy.

Contemporary theology has been strongly influenced by process philosophy. The American theologian Charles Hartshorne, for instance, rather than interpreting God as an unchanging absolute, emphasizes God's sensitive and caring relationship with the world. A personal God enters into relationships in such a way that he is affected by the relationships, and to be affected by relationships is to change. So too is in the process of growth and development. Important contributions to process theology have also been made by such theologians as William Temple, Daniel Day Williams, Schubert Ogden, and John Cobb, Jr.

'Reality' is a difficult word to use to every one's satisfaction or even to one's own satisfaction. In this instance the word reality is used arbitrarily to designate the direct, here-and-now impact of the analyst upon the patient. Reality. In this sense, contrasts with the impact the analyst has through his representation in the patient's fantasy life, neurosis, and transference, since both kinds of impact seem always to coexist and since the former - the analyst's real impact - may be the worst enemy of the transference, the matter of their differentiation is possibly the most challenging aspect of analysis.

The analytic situation, which is set up to shut out ordinary reality intrusions, that cannot nor should not exclude all, but to say, that in the beginning months, for instance, reality inevitably has the upper hand. The analyst, the office, the procedure, are all overwhelmingly real. Everything is strange, frightening and exciting, gratifying and frustrating. Unlike the patient can test it and orient himself to it, the impact of this reality is usually so great that even an ordinary useful transference relationship cannot be expected to develop.

Perhaps the most confusing aspect of this beginning period is the frequent appearance in it of what can be regarded as a false transference relationship. With great intensity and clarity, the patient may reveal, through transference-like references about the analyst, some of the deepest secrets only of his neurosis but of its genesis. The pseudotransference, too good to be true, is almost sure to be nothing more than the patient's attempt to deal with the person of the analyst, the entire spectrum of his various patterns of behaviour. If, it is easy to do, the analyst overlooks the likelihood that the patient's relationship with at this time is really about that almost everything said about it is related, analysis may get off to a very bad start. And if, as is even earlier to do, the analyst's interests the genetic meaning of the openly exposed material, a good transference relationship may be seriously delayed and a workable transference neurosis may never appear. even after initial reality has had time to fade, reality may continue to intrude in ways that are very hard to detect and that are very troublesome.

One of the most serious problems of analysis is the very substantial help which the patient receives directly from the analyst and the analytic situation. For many a patient, the analyst in the analytic situation is in fact the most stable, reasonable, wise and understanding person he has ever met, and the setting in which they meet may actually be the most honest, open, direct and regular relationship he has ever experienced. Added to this is the considerable helpfulness to him of being able to clarify his life storey. confess his guilt, express his ambitions, and explore his confusions. Further real help comes from the learning-about-life accruing from the analyst's skilled questions, observations and interpretations. Taken together, the total real value to the patient of the analytic situation can easily be immense. The trouble with this kind of help is that it goes on and on, it may have such a real, direct and continuing impact upon the patient that he can never get deeply enough involved in transference situation to allow him to resolve or even to become acquainted with his most crippling internal difficulties. The trouble is far too good, the trouble also is that we as analysts apparently cannot resist the seductiveness of being directly helpful, and this, when combined with the compelling assumption that helpfulness is bound to be good, permits us top credit patient improvements to 'analysis' when more properly it should often be recognized for being the amounting result for the patient's using the analytic situation, as the model, for being the preceptors and supporter in the dealing practically within the immediate distractions as holding to some problem.

Perhaps, we can now refer to something in a clear unmistakable manner, and it would be to mention, for being, that one more difficult-to-handle intrusion of reality into the analysis, that by saying, that this is the definitive and final interruption of the transference neurosis by the reality of termination; in the sense, the situation is reversed and the intrusion is analytically desirable, since ideally the impact of reality of impending and certain termination is used to facilitate the resolution of the transference. As with the resolution of earlier episodes of transference neurosis, this final one is brought about principally by the analyst's interpretations and reconstructions. As these take effect, the transference neurosis and, hopefully, along with it the original neurosis is resolved. This final resolution, however, which is much more comprehensive, is usually very different and may not come about at all without the help of the reality of termination. Accordingly, any attenuation of the ending, such as tapering off or causal or tentative stopping, should be expected to stand in the way of an effective resolution of the transference. Yet, it seems that this is what most commonly happens to an ending, and because of this a great many patients may lose the potentially great benefit of a thorough resolution and are forever after left suspended in the net of unresolved transference.

Yet, utter indistinctly rigorous termination seems understandable, as difficult as transference neurosis may be in the analyst at other times, this ending period, if rigorously carried out, simply has to be the period of his greatest emotional strain. There can surely be no more likely time for an analyst to surrender his analytic position and, responding to his own transference, become personally involved with his patient than during the process of separating from a long and self-restrained relationship. Accordingly, it may be better to slur over the ending lightly than to mishandle it in an attempt to be rigorous.

In considering more broadly the function of the transference in the psychoanalytic process, one is confronted by the apparent naïve, but, nonetheless important questions of the role of the actual (current) object as compared with that of the object representation of the original personage in the past. We recall Freud's paradoxical, somewhat gloomy, but portentous concluding passage in 'The Dynamics of Transference.' This struggle between the doctor and the patient, between intellect and instinctual life, between understanding and seeking to act, is played out almost exclusively in the phenomena of transference. It is on that field that the victory must be won - the victory whose expression is on that field that the victory must be won - the victory whose expression is the permanent cure of the neuroses. It cannot be disputed that controlling the phenomena of transference presents the psychoanalysis with the greatest difficultly, but it should not be forgotten that they do us the inestimable service of making the patient 's hidden and forgotten erotic impulses of showing their immediate and manifested impossibilities, for when all is said and done, it is impossible to destroy anyone in absentia or in effigies.

Both object and representation are made necessary by the basic phenomenon of original separation. The existence of an image of the object, which persist in the absence of the object, is one of the important beginnings of psychic life in general, certainly an indispensable prerequisite for object relationship. As generally construed. Whether this is viewed as (or a times demonstrably is) something unstable for allotting introjection, s always subject to alternative projection, or an intrapsychic object representation clearly distinguished from the self-representation, or firm identification in the superego, or in the ego itself, these phenomena are in various ways components of the system of mastery of the fact of separation, or separateness, from the original absolutely necessarily anaclitic (in the earliest period) symbiotic 'object'. In the light of clinical observation, it would appear to be that the relative stability (parental) object representation. At which time of varying degree, are to a greater extent for the archaic phenomena. Even in nonpsychotic patients, overwhelmed by them, sometimes resembles the restoration from oedipal identification, which provides the preponderant basis for most demonstrable analytic transferences. That within the necrotic patients, the transference is effectively established when this representation invests the analyst to a degree - depending on intensity of drive and most of ego participation - which ranges in all the, wishing and the striving to remake and analyst to biasses judgements and misinterpretation of data, finally are the actual perceptual distortions.

However, the old object representations may be invested, however rigidly established the libidinal or aggressive cathexis of the image may be, this as such can become the actual and exclusive focus of instinctual discharge, or of complicated and intense instinct-defence solutions, only and general energy-sparing quality of strictly intrapsychic processes. For the vast majority of persons, visible to any degree, including those with severe neurosis, character distortions, addictions and certain psychoses, the striving is toward the living and actual object, even at the cost of intense suffering. In a sense, this returns us to the state in which the psychological 'object-to-be'. Has a cr11itical importance never again to be duplicated, except in certain acute life emergencies, even if the object is not firmly perceived as such, in the sense of later object relations? And it does seem that trance impressions from the earliest contacts in the service of life preservation, and the associated instinctual gratifications, and innumerable secondarily associated sensory impressions. Are activated by the specific inborn urges of sexual maturation? These propel the individual to renew many of the earliest modes of actual bodily contact, in connection with seeking for specific instinctual gratification. Or, to look away from clear-cut instinctual matters to the more remote elaborations of human contact: Few regard loneliness as other than a source of suffering, even self-imposed, as an apparent matter of choice, and the forcible imposition of 'solitary confinement ' is surely one of the most cruel of punishments.

In taking to question, we are entering an area of life in which things are other then themselves, where meaning is multifaceted, and where the line between the old and the new is blurred. It should, by, its immediate measure, help develop our recognition or meaning of the pertinent applicability as to the relevance of interrelated aspects of the psychology of 'metaphor'. In the psychology of metaphor we will find a useful analogy to the psychology of transference interpretation. Our';s will be newly encountered as good metaphors, those it response to which we say, 'That's it exactly' or 'That really captures it' or 'That says it all'.

Some literary and linguistic analysis, (e.g., Lewis, 1936 and Snell, 1953) and also people in everyday life, believe that there are experiences that can only be expressed metaphorically. And it is for this achievement that these metaphors, which may be entire poem or as lines or even words highly valued. But how can this be so? Just what in th e 'it' that the metaphor 'is' or 'captures' or 'says'? If this 'is' or this 'experience' can only be rendered metaphorically, when we can know it only as such, that is, as the metaphor itself. Of the position out of which are put forward by, T.S, Eliot (1933) and E.W. Harding (1963) in their discussion of poetry, for in these instances we are granted that there is no known and logically independent version of the experience that can serve to validate the metaphor. Whatever the metaphor makes available to us depends on it and it and so cannot be used to prove its correctness.

It seems justifiable conclude that the metaphor is a new experience rather than a mere paraphrase of an already fully constituted expedience. The metaphor creates an experience that one has never had before. It is an experience one has not realized by oneself. The metaphor does, of course, suggest certain constituent experiences of which one may have been more or less dimly aware. One may say, therefore, that the metaphor speaks for those constituents, on the existence of which much of its appeal depends. But in its organizing and implicit ly rendering these constituents in its new way, it is a creation rather than a mere paraphrase or anew edition. Paraphrasing and new editions never speak as forcefully as good new metaphors, nor could they facilitate further new experience. One analytically familiar feature of these creations is that they make it safe and pleasing to experience something that otherwise would be considered too threatening and so would be kept in fragmented obscurity through defensive measures.

Thus, when one says, 'That's it exactly' one is implicitly recognizing and announcing that one has found and accepted a new mode of experiencing one's self and one's world, which is to say, asserting a transformation of one's own subjectivity. Something is now said to be true, and in a sense it is true, but it is true for the first time. Nothing just like it can ever happen again, for the second time cannot be the same as the first. One can' t step into the same watering point and then step once again into the same spot of that river. A revelatory metaphor re-encountered or repeated later may lose some of its force, alternatively, it may gain some significance, butt it cannot remain exactly the same metaphor or mobilize an experience identical with the first. The point applies as well as to new metaphors that are similar to familiar ones: They have to be judged or experienced through their conventionalized predecessors, as through methods of knowing or already proved instrumentally of perceiving. The audience and the performer, who may be one person, as such that may not have, as yet.

What is to be said about the psychology of metaphor is analogous to the transformational aspects of developed transference and the steadfast interpretation that both facilitate and organize them as transference. Allowing that these transferences and 'remembered' experiences come into existence over a period of time, nothing that is identical with them has ever before been enacted, and nothing will ever be enacted again. They are creations that may be fully achieved only under specific analytic conditions. Such that living was not reliving that moment, words like re-living, re-experiencing and reliving simply do not do justice to the phenomena, that in making this claim. A seeming contradiction over-writes some of our well-establish ideas. - in offering, - I am not contradicting some of our well-established ideas about interpretation and insight, I am, however, disputing the point that insight refers to much than the recovery of lost memories, and takes in as well, a new grasp of the significance and interpretations of events one has always remembered. In point, as, Freud pointed out, 'As a matter of fact I've always known it, only that I've never thought of it; (1914), In fact, it is to develop that point in furthering to say that it takes an adult to do that, especially with the help of an analyst. It was, after all, Freud's analysis of adults that make it possible to define infantile psychosexuality. In this respect, but without disregard, child analysis retains a quality of applied psychoanalysis' in the same way that the interpreted transference neurosis is: Both are always of describing as true something that was not true in quite that way at the time of its greatest developmental significance. This apparent paradox about 'remembering' as a form of creating goes a long way, probably that what it is, is distinctive about psychoanalytic interpretation.

This time, however, to further the discussion on the interpretive technique that surrounds the phase of a mutative interpretation - that in which a portion of the patient's id-relation to the analyst is made conscious in virtue of the latter's position as auxiliary superego - is in itself complex. In the classical model of an interpretation, the patient will first be made aware of a state of tension of an interpretation, will next be made aware that there is repressive factor at work (that his superego is threatening him with punishment), and will only then be made aware of the id-impulse which has stirred up the protects of his superego and so given to the anxiety in his ego. This is the classical scheme. In actual practice, the analyst finds himself working from all three sides at once, or in irregular successions. At one moment a small portion of the patient's superego may be revealed to him in all its savagery, at another the shrinking defencelessness of his ego, at yet another his attention may be directed to the attempts which he is making at restitution - at compensating for his hostility, on some occasions a fraction of id-energy may even be directly encouraged to break its way through the last remains of an already weakened resistance. There is, however, one characteristic which all of these various operations have in common, they are essentially upon a small scale. For the mutative interpretation is inevitably governed by the principle of minimal doses. It is a commonly agreed clinical fact that alternations in a patient under analysis appear almost always to be extremely gradual: We are inclined to suspect sudden and large changes as an indication that suggestive rather than psycho-analyst processes are at work. The gradual nature of the change brought about in psychoanalysis will be explained, as, only to suggest, those changes are the result of the summation of an immense number of minuet steps, each of which correspond to a mutative interpretation. And the smallness of each step is in turn imposed by the very nature of the analytic situation. For each interpretation involves the release of a certain quantity of id-energy, and, if the quantity released is too large, the higher unstable state of equilibrium which enables the analyst to function as the patient's auxiliary superego is bound to be upset. The whole analytic situation will thus be imperilled, since it is only in virtue of the analyst's acting as auxiliary superego that these released id-energy can occur at all.

The effectuality from which follow the analytic attempt to bring unequalled amounts in the confronting collections of some improper use too a resultant quantity of id-energy into the patient's consciousness all at once. On the one hand, nothing whatever may happen, or on the other hand there may be an unmanageable result, but in neither event will a mutative interpretation have been effected. The analyst's power as auxiliary superego may be for two very different reasons. It may be that the id-impulses was trying to bring out were not in fact sufficiently urgent at the moment: For, after all, the emergence of an id-impulse depends on two factors - not only on the permission of the superego, but also on the urgency (the degree of cathaxis) of the id-impulse itself. This, then, may be one cause of an apparently negative response to an interpretation, and evidently a fairly harmless one. but the same apparent result may also be due to something else, in spite of the id-impulse being really urgent, the strength of the patient's own repressive forces (the degree of repression) may have been too great to allow his ego to listen to the persuasive voice of the auxiliary superego. Now we have a situation dynamically identical with the next one we have to consider, though economically different. this next situation is one in which the patient accepts the interpretation, that is, allows the id-impulse into his consciousness, but is immediately overwhelmed with anxiety. This may show itself in a number of ways, for instance, the patient may produce a manifest anxiety-attack. Or the may exhibit signs of 'real' anger with the analyst with a complete lack of insight, or he may break off the analysis. In any of these cases the analytic situation will, for the moment, at least, have broken down. The patient will be behaving just as the hypnotic subject behaves when, having been ordered by the hypnotist to perform an action too much at variance with his own consciousness, he breaks off the hypnotic relation and wakes up from his trance. This state of things, which is manifest where the patient responds to an interpretation with an actual outbreak of anxiety or one of its equivalents, may be latent were the patient shows no response, and this latter case may be the more awkward of the two, since it is masked, and it may sometimes be the effect of a greater overdose of interpretation than where manifest anxiety arises (though obviously other factors will be of determining importance, and in particularly the nature of the patient's neurosis). Yet this threatened collapse of the analytic situation to an overdose of interpretation: But it might be more accurate in some ways to ascribe it to an insufficient dose. For what has happened is that the second phase of the interpretation process has not occurred: The phase in which the patient becomes aware that his impulse is directed toward an archaic phantasy object and not toward a real one.

In the second phase of a complete interpretation, therefore, a crucial part is played by the patient's sense of reality: For the successful outcome of that phase depends upon his ability, at the critical moment of the emergence into consciousness of the released quantity of id-energy, to distinguish between his phantasy object and the real analyst. The problem is closely related to one that has been discussed elsewhere, namely that of the extreme liability of the analyst's position as auxiliary superego. The analytic situation is all the time threatening to degenerate into a 'real' situation. But this actually means the opposite of what it appears to. It means that the patient is all the time on the brink of turning the real external object (the analyst) into the archaic one; that is to say, he is on the brink of projecting his primitive introjected images onto himself. In so far as the patient actually does this, the analyst becomes like anyone else that he meets in real life - a phantasy object. The analyst then ceases to possess the peculiar advantages derived from the analytic situation, he will be introjected like all other phantasy objects into the analytic situation, he will be introjected like all other phantasy objects into the patient's superego, and will no longer be able to function in the peculiar ways which are essential to the effecting of a mutative interpretation. In this difficulty the patient's sense of reality is an essential but a very feeble-ally: An improvement in it is one of the things that we hope the analysis will bring about. It is important, therefore, not to submit it to any unnecessary strain, and that is the fundamental reason why the analyst must avoid any real behaviour, that is likely to confirm the patient's view of him as a 'bad' or a 'good' phantasy object. This is perhaps more obvious as regards the 'bad' object. If, for instance, the analyst were to show that he was really shocked or frightened by one of the patient's id-impulses, as the patient would immediately treat him in that respect as a dangerous object and introject him into his archaic severe superego. Therefore, on the one hand, there would be a diminuation in the analyst's power to function as an auxiliary superego and to allow the patient's to become conscious of his id-impulses - that is to say, in his power to bring about the first phase of a mutative interpretation, and on the other hand, he would, as a real object, become sensibly less distinguishable from the patient's 'bad' phantasy object and to that extent the carrying through of the second phase of a mutative interpretation would also be made more difficult. Or, agin, there is another case. Supposing the analyst behaves in an opposite way and actively urges the patient to give free rein to his id-impulse. There is then a possibility of the patient confusing the analyst with the image of a treacherous parent who first encourages him to seek gratification, and then suddenly turns and punishes him. In such a case the patient's ego may look for defence by itself suddenly turning upon the analyst as though he were his own id-, and treating him with all the severity of which his superego is capable. again, the analyst is running a risk of losing his privileged position. But it may be equally unwise for the analyst to act really in such a way as to encourage the patient to project his 'good' introjected object on to him. For the patient will then tend to regard him as a good objective and archaic sense and will incorporate him with his archaic 'good' images and will use him as a protection against his 'bad' ones. In that way, his infantile positive impulses as well as his negative ones may escape analysis, for there may no longer be a possibility for his ego to make a comparison between the phantasy external object and the real one. it will, perhaps, be argued that, with the best of wills in the world, the analyst, however careful he may be, will be unable to prevent the patient from projecting these various images on to him. This is, of course, indisputable, and, the whole effectiveness of analysis depends upon its being so. The lesson of these difficulties is merely to remind us that the patient's sense of reality has the narrowest limits. It is a paradoxical fact that the best way of enuring that his ego shall be able to distinguish between phantasy and reality is to withhold reality from him as much as possible. but it is true, his ego is so weak - in as much at the mercy of his id and superego - that he can only cope with reality if it is administered in minimal doses. And these doses are in fact what the analyst gives him, in the form of interpretations.

In the classical conception of transference the patient was really concerned with the major persons in his childhood when addressing the analyst. More recently, the patient has come to be viewed as apt to be unconsciously engaged with the analyst while ostensibly absorbed in somebody else. To be sure, it may then be taken for granted that the analyst, inturn, stands for, say, a parent. But usually that point is not stressed, and the reaction which is interpreted is not one where the reaction does displace toward the analyst, but instead, away from him. Formerly, the perceptiveness of the analyst was to reveal the parent behind himself; now he may discover himself behind the parent or spouse. A typical contemporary case is a patient with 'a disposition to pick quarrels with her husband because of his silence', a conduct which 'diverted a problem from the couch, where she did not verbalize her complaints about the analyst's silence'. The analyst may thus always be present though never in the patient's conscious mind'. 'The quarrels with the husband became . . . the sole preoccupation of the patient's and the sole content of the analytic sessions (Kanzer, 1961). Thus they were filled with what may be called as the 'reactions of disguised transference'.

That no standard word already exists for this, and, of course, important relationship, indicating how little awareness there has been that 'transference' has, to a substantial extent, reversed in its direction. That is, it travels more only from parent to analyst, but also from the analyst to a person of the patient's past or present. The very magnitude of the shift - putting the analyst where the parent was seems to have militated against lucidity about it.

Sandler and his colleagues recalling 'The Ego and the Mechanisms of Defence' (1936) Anna Freud had distinguished different types of transference phenomena according to the degree of their plexuities. These are (1) transference of libidinal impulses, in which . . . wishes attached to infantile objects . . . attempt to break through toward . . . the analyst: (2) transference of defence, in which former defensive measures . . . are repeated, and (3) acting in the transference, on which the transference . . . spills over into the patient's life (Sandler et al. 1969).

In taking to question, we are entering an area of life in which things are other then themselves, where meaning is multifaceted, and where the line between the old and the new is blurred. It should, by, its immediate measure, help develop our recognition or meaning of the pertinent applicability as to the relevance of interrelated aspects of the psychology of 'metaphor'. In the psychology of metaphor we will find a useful analogy to the psychology of transference interpretation. Our's will be newly encountered as good metaphors, those it response to which we say, 'That's it exactly' or 'That really captures it' or 'That says it all'.

Some literary and linguistic analysis, (e.g., Lewis, 1936 and Snell, 1953) and also people in everyday life, believe that there are experiences that can only be expressed metaphorically. And for this achievement that these metaphors, which may be entire poem or as lines or even words highly valued. But how can this be so? Just what in th e 'it' that the metaphor 'is' or 'captures' or 'says'? If this 'is' or this 'experience' can only be rendered metaphorically, when we can know it only as such, that is, as the metaphor itself. Of the position out of which are put forward by, T.S, Eliot (1933) and E.W. Harding (1963) in their discussion of poetry, for in these instances we are granted that there are no known and logically independent version of the experience that can serve to validate the metaphor. Whatever the metaphor makes available to us depends on it and it and so cannot be used to prove its correctness.

It seems justifiably warrantable to consider that the metaphor is a new experience rather than a mere paraphrase of an already fully constituted expedience. The metaphor creates an experience that one has never had before. It is an experience one has not realized by oneself. The metaphor does, of course, suggest certain constituent experiences of which one may have been more or less dimly aware. One may say, therefore, that the metaphor speaks for those constituents, on the existence of which much of its appeal depends. But in its organizing and implicit ly rendering these constituents in its new way, it is a creation rather than a mere paraphrase or anew edition. Paraphrasing and new editions never speak as forcefully as good new metaphors, nor could they facilitate further new experience. One analytically familiar feature of these creations is that they make it safe and pleasing to experience something that otherwise would be considered too threatening and so would be kept in fragmented obscurity through defensive measures.

Thus, when one says, 'That's it exactly' one is implicitly recognizing and announcing that one has found and accepted a new mode of experiencing oneself and one's world, which is to say, asserting a transformation of one's own subjectivity. Something is now said to be true, and in a sense it is true, but it is true for the first time. Nothing of one and the same can ever happen again, for the second time cannot be the same as the first. One can' t step into the same watering point and then step once again into the same spot of that river. A revelatory metaphor re-encountered or repeated later may lose some of its force, alternatively, it may gain some significance, butt it cannot remain exactly the same metaphor or mobilize an experience identical with the first. The point applies as well as to new metaphors that are similar to familiar ones: They have to be judged or experienced through their conventionalized predecessors, as through methods of knowing or already proved instrumentally of perceiving. The audience and the performer, who may be one person, as such that may not have, as yet.

What is to be said about the psychology of metaphor is analogous to the transformational aspects of developed transference and the steadfast interpretation that both facilitate and organize them as transference. Allowing that these transferences and 'remembered' experiences come into existence over a period of time, nothing that is identical with them has ever before been enacted, and nothing will ever be enacted again. They are creations that may be fully achieved only under specific analytic conditions. Such that living was not reliving that moment, words like re-living, re-experiencing and reliving simply do not do justice to the phenomena, that in making this claim. A seeming contradiction over-writes some of our well-establish ideas. - in offering, - I am not contradicting some of our well-established ideas about interpretation and insight, I am, however, disputing the point that insight refers to a greater proportion or in its range of comprehension, which its distance between possible extremes extent and regain former or normal state, such that, for the recovery of lost memories, and takes in as well, a new grasp of the significance and interpretations of events one has always remembered. In point, as, Freud pointed out, 'As a matter of fact I've always known it, only that I've never thought of it; (1914), In fact, it is to develop that point in furthering to say that it takes an adult to do that, especially with the help of an analyst. It was, after all, Freud's analysis of adults that make it possible to define infantile psychosexuality. In this respect, but without disregard, child analysis retains a quality of applied psychoanalysis' in the same way that the interpreted transference neurosis is: Both are always of describing as true something that was not true in quite that way at the time of its greatest developmental significance. This apparent paradox about 'remembering' as a form of creating goes a long way, probably that what it is, is distinctive about psychoanalytic interpretation.

This time, however, to further the discussion on the interpretive technique that surrounds the phase of a mutative interpretation - that in which a portion of the patient's id-relation to the analyst is made conscious in virtue of the latter's positions as auxiliary super-ego - is in itself complex. In the classical model of an interpretation, the patient will first be made aware of a state of tension of an interpretation, will next be made aware that there is repressive factor at work (that his super-ego is threatening him with punishment), and will only then be made aware of the id-impulse which has stirred up the protects of his super-ego and so given to the anxiety in his ego. This is the classical scheme. In actual practice, the analyst finds himself working from all three sides at once, or in irregular successions. At one moment a small portion of the patient's super-ego may be revealed to him in all its savagery, at another the shrinking defencelessness of his ego, at yet another his attention may be directed to the attempts which he is making at restitution - at compensating for his hostility, on some occasions a fraction of id-energy may even be directly encouraged to break its way through the last remains of an already weakened resistance. There is, however, one characteristic which all of these various operations has in common, they are essentially upon a small scale. For the mutative interpretation is inevitably governed by the principle of minimal doses. It is a commonly agreed clinical fact that alternations in a patient under analysis appear almost always to be extremely gradual: We are inclined to suspect sudden and large changes as an indication that suggestive rather than psycho-analyst processes are at work. The gradual nature of the change brought about in psychoanalysis will be explained, as, only to suggest, those changes are the result of the summation of an immense number of minuet steps, each of which correspond to a mutative interpretation. And the smallness of each step is in turn imposed by the very nature of the analytic situation. For each interpretation involves the release of a certain quantity of id-energy, and, if the quantity released is too large, the higher unstable state of equilibrium which enables the analyst to function as the patient's auxiliary super-ego is bound to be upset. The whole analytic situation will thus be imperilled, since it is only in virtue of the analyst's acting as auxiliary super-ego that these released id-energy can occur at all.

The effectuality from which follow the analytic attempt to bring unequalled amounts in the confronting collections of some improper use to a resultant quantity of id-energy into the patient's consciousness all at once. On the one hand, nothing whatever may happen, or on the other hand there may be an unmanageable result, but in neither event will be a mutative interpretation has been effected. The analyst's power as auxiliary super-ego may be for two very different reasons. It may be that the id-impulses were trying to bring out being not in fact sufficiently urgent at the moment: For, after all, the emergence of an id-impulse depends on two factors - not only on the permission of the super-ego, but also on the urgency (the degree of cathaxis) of the id-impulse itself. This, then, may be one cause of an apparently negative response to an interpretation, and evidently a fairly harmless one. but the same apparent result may also be due to something else, in spite of the id-impulse being really urgent, the strength of the patient's own repressive forces (the degree of repression) may have been too great to allow his ego to listen to the persuasive voice of the auxiliary super-ego. Now we have a situation dynamically identical with the next one we have to consider, though economically different. this next situation is one in which the patient accepts the interpretation, that is, allows the id-impulse into his consciousness, but is immediately overwhelmed with anxiety. This may show itself in a number of ways, for instance, the patient may produce a manifest anxiety-attack. Or the may exhibit signs of 'real' anger with the analyst with a complete lack of insight, or he may break off the analysis. In any of these cases the analytic situation will, for the moment, at least, have broken down. The patient will be behaving just as the hypnotic subject behaves when, having been ordered by the hypnotist to perform an action too much at variance with his own consciousness, he breaks off the hypnotic relation and wakes up from his trance. This state of things, which is manifest where the patient responds to an interpretation with an actual outbreak of anxiety or one of its equivalents, may be latent were the patient shows no response, and this latter case may be the more awkward of the two, since it is masked, and it may sometimes be the effect of a greater overdose of interpretation than where manifest anxiety arises (though obviously other factors will be of determining importance, and in particularly the nature of the patient's neurosis). Yet this threatened collapse of the analytic situation to an overdose of interpretation: But it might be more accurate in some ways to ascribe it to an insufficient dose. For what has happened is that the second phase of the interpretation process has not occurred: The phase in which the patient becomes aware that his impulse is directed toward an archaic phantasy object and not toward a real one.

In the second phase of a complete interpretation, therefore, a crucial part is played by the patient's sense of reality: For the successful outcome of that phase depends upon his ability, at the critical moment of the emergence into consciousness of the released quantity of id-energy, to distinguish between his phantasy object and the real analyst. The problem is closely related to one that has been discussed elsewhere, namely that of the extreme liability of the analyst's position as auxiliary super-ego. The analytic situation is all the time threatening to degenerate into a 'real' situation. But this actually means the opposite of what it appears to. It means that the patient is all the time on the brink of turning the really external object (the analyst) into the archaic one; that is to say, he is on the brink of projecting his primitive introjected images onto himself. In so far as the patient actually does this, the analyst becomes like anyone else that he meets in real life - a phantasy object. The analyst then ceases to possess the peculiar advantages derived from the analytic situation, he will be introjected like all other phantasy objects into the analytic situation, he will be introjected like all other phantasy objects into the patient's super-ego, and will no longer be able to function in the peculiar ways which are essential to the effecting of a mutative interpretation. In this difficulty the patient's sense of reality is an essential but a very feeble [-ally]: An improvement in it is one of the things that we hope the analysis will bring about. It is important, therefore, not to submit it to any unnecessary strain, and that is the fundamental reason why the analyst must avoid any real behaviour, that is likely to confirm the patient's view of him as a 'bad' or a 'good' phantasy object. This is perhaps more obvious as regards the 'bad' object. If, for instance, the analyst were to show that he was really shocked or frightened by one of the patient's id-impulses, as the patient would immediately treat him in that respect as a dangerous object and introject him into his archaic severe super-ego. Therefore, on the one hand, there would be a diminuation in the analyst's power to function as an auxiliary super-ego and to allow the patient's to become conscious of his id-impulses - that is to say, in his power to bring about the first phase of a mutative interpretation, and on the other hand, he would, as a real object, become sensibly less distinguishable from the patient's 'bad' phantasy object and to that extent the carrying through of the second phase of a mutative interpretation would also be made more difficult. Or, agin, there is another case. Supposing the analyst behaves in an opposite way and actively urges the patient to give free rein to his id-impulse. There is then a possibility of the patient confusing the analyst with the image of a treacherous parent who, at the beginning, encourages him to seek gratification, and then suddenly turns and punishes him. In such a case the patient's ego may look for defence by itself suddenly turning upon the analyst as though he were his own id-, and treating him with all the severity of which his super-ego is capable. again, the analyst is running a risk of losing his privileged position. But it may be equally unwise for the analyst to act really in such a way as to encourage the patient to project his 'good' introjected object onto him. For the patient will then tend to regard him as a good objective and archaic sense and will incorporate him with his archaic 'good' images and will use him as a protection against his 'bad' ones. In that way, his infantile positive impulses as well as his negative ones may escape analysis, for there may no longer be a possibility for his ego to make a comparison between the phantasy external object and the real one. it will, perhaps, be argued that, with the best of wills in the world, the analyst, however careful he may be, will be unable to prevent the patient from projecting these various images onto him. This is, of course, indisputable, and, the whole effectiveness of analysis depends upon its being so. The lesson of these difficulties is merely to remind us that the patient's sense of reality has the narrowest limits. It is a paradoxical fact that the best way of enuring that his ego will be able to distinguish between phantasy and reality is to withhold reality from him as much as possible. but it is true, his ego is so weak - so much at the mercy of his id and super-ego - that he can only cope with reality if it is administered in minimal doses. And these doses are in fact what the analyst gives him, in the form of interpretations.

A mutative interpretation can only be applied to an id-impulse which is actually on a state of cathexis. This seems self-evident; for the dynamic changes in the patient's mind implied by a mutative interpretation can only be brought about by the operation of a charge of energy originating in the patient himself: The function of the analyst is merely to ensure that the energy should or can flow along one channel rather than along another. It follows that the purely informative 'dictionary' type of interpretation will be non-mutative, but useful it may be a prelude to mutative interpretations. And this leads to a number of practical inferences. Every mutative interpretation must be emotionally 'immediate, but the patient must live through it as something actual or genuine. This requirement, that the interpretation must be 'immediate', may be expressed in another way by saying that interpretation must always be directed to the 'point of urgency'. At any given moment some particular id-impulse will be generated in activity, this is the impulse that is susceptible of mutative interpretation at the time, and no other one. It is, no doubt, neither possible nor desirable to be giving mutative interpretations all the time. as Melanie Klein has pointed out, it is a most precious quality in an analyst to be able at any moment to pick out the point of urgency.

But the fact that every mutative interpretation must deal with an 'urgent' impulse take us back one more to the commonly felt fear of the explosive possibilities of interpretation, and particularly of what is vaguely referred to as 'deep' interpretation. The terminological description is, no doubt, as the interpretation of material which is neither genetically early and historically distant from the patient's actual experience nor under an especially heavy weight of repression – material, in any case, which is in the normal course of things exceedingly inaccessible to his ego and remote from it. There seems reason to believe, moreover, that the anxiety which is liable to be aroused by the approach of such material to consciousness and may be of peculiar severity. The question whether it is 'safe' to interpret such material will, as usual, mainly depend upon whether an interpretation can be carried through, in the ordinary run of the case, as this material which is urgent during the earlier stages of the analysis is not deep. We have to deal at first only with more or less far-going displacements of the deep impulse. And the deep material itself is only reached later and by degrees, so that no sudden appearance of unmanageable quantities of anxiety is to be hesitorially anticipated. In exceptional cases, however, owing to some peculiarities in the structure of the neurosis, deep impulses may be urgent at a very early stage of the analysis. We are then faced by a dilemma. If we give an interpretation of this deep material, the resultant amounts of anxiety produced in the patient may be so great that his sense of reality may not be sufficient to permit of its accomplishment, and the whole analysis may be jeopardised, but, it must not be thought that, in such critical cases as we are now considering, the difficulty can necessarily be avoided simply by not giving any interpretation or by giving more superficial interpretations of non-urgent material or by attempting reassurances. It seems probable, in fact, that these alternative procedures may do little or nothing to obviate the trouble, on the contrary, they may even exacerbate the tension created by the urgency of the deep impulses which are the actual cause of the threatening anxiety. Thus the anxiety may break out in spite of these palliative efforts and, if so, it will be doing so under the most unfavourable conditions, that is to say, outside the mitigating influences afforded by the mechanism of interpretation. It is possible, therefore, that, of these alternative procedures which are open to the analyst faced by such a difficulty. The interpretation of the urgent id-impulses, deep though they may b e, will actually be the safer.

It is, of course, a matter of common experience, that it possible with certain patients to continue indefinitely giving interpretations without producing any apparent effect whatever. There is an amusing criticism of this kind of 'interpretation-fanaticism' in the excellent historical chapter of Rank and Ferenczi. But it is clear from their words that what they have in mind are essentially extra-transference interpretations, for the burden of their criticism is that such a procedure implies neglect of the analytic situation. This is the simplest case. Where a waste of time and energy is the main result. But there are other occasions, on which a policy of giving strings of extra-transference interpretations is apt to lead the analyst into more positive difficulties. Attention was drawn by Reich a few years back, in the course of some technical discussions in Vienna to a tendency among inexperienced analysts to get into trouble by eliciting from the patient great quantities of material in a disordered and unrelated fashion: This may, be maintained, be carried to such lengths that the analysis is brought to an irremediable state of chaos. He pointe out truly that the material we have to deal with is stratified and that it is highly important in digging it out not to interference, more that we can help with th e arrangement of that state. He had in mind, of course, the analogy of an incompetent archaeologist, whose clumsiness may obliterate for all time the possibility of reconstructing the history of an important site. However, the results in the case of a clumsy analysis do not hold of any pessimistic cause to happen, as it was, re-stratification itself of its own accord if it is given the opportunity; That is to say, in the analytic situation. At the same time, is that of the presence of the risk, and it seems to be particularly likely to occur where extra-transference interpretation is excessively or exclusively restored to. The means of preventing it, and the remedy if it has occurred, lie in returning to transference interpretation at the point of urgency. For if we can discover which of the material is 'immediate' in the sense that the problematic occurrence enabling stratification is automatically solved, and it is a characteristic if most extra-transference material that it has no immediacy and consequently stratification is far more difficult to decipher. The measures suggested by Reich himself for preventing the occurrence of this state of chaos are consistent with those that he stresses the importance of interpreting resistance as opposed to the primary id-impulses themselves - and this, was a policy that was laid down at an early stage in the history of analysis. But it is, of course, one of the characteristics of a resistance that it arises in relation to the analyst. Thus, interpretation of a resistance will almost inevitably be a transference interpretation.

But the most serious risks that arise from the making of extra-transference interpretation are due to the inherent difficulty in completing their interpretation, for a successful outcome as such, depends upon his ability, at which time of the emergence into consciousness and the released quantity of id-energy. They are from their nature unpredictable in their effects. There seems to be a special risk of the patient not carrying through to a competed interpretation, hitherto, namely that the extreme liability of the analyst's position as auxiliary super-ego, is that, the analytic situation is all the time threatening to degenerate into a 'real' situation. It means that the patient is all the time perched upon the circumference edge-horizon of turning the external object (the analyst) into the archaic one, but of projecting the id-impulse that has been made conscious onto the analyst. This risk, no doubt, applies to some extent to transference interpretations. However, the situation is less likely to arise when the object of the id-impulses is actually present and is moreover the same person as the maker of interpretation. We may, once, more, recall the problem of 'deep' interpretation, and point out that its dangers, even in the most unfavourable circumstances, seem to be greatly diminished if the interpretation in question is a transference interpretation. Even so, there appears to be more of a chance that in this whole process occurring silently and so being overlooked in the case of an extra-transference interpretation, particularly in the earlier stages of an analysis. For this reason, it would seem to be important after giving an extra-transference interpretation to be specially in the 'qui-vive' for transferences complications. This last peculiarity of the extra-transference interpretation is actually one of the most important forms to a practical stand-point of things. For on account of it they can be made to act as 'feeders' for the transference situation, and so to pave the way for mutative interpretations. In other words, by giving an extra-transference interpretation, the analyst can often provide a situation in the transference of which he can then give a mutative interpretation.

Therefore, it is probable that a large majority of our interpretations are outside the transference - though it should be added that it often happens that one is ostensibly giving an extra-transference interpretation one is implicitly giving a transference one. A cake cannot be made of nothing but currants, and, though it is true that extra-transference interpretations, are not for the most part, mutative and do not they bring about the crucial results that involve a permanent change in the patient's mind. They are, nonetheless essential, if taken to an analogy of trench warfare, the acceptance of a transference interpretation corresponds to the capture of a key position, while the extra-transference interpretations correspond to the general advance and to the consolidation of a fresh line of defence, which are made possible by the capture of the key position. But when this general advance goes beyond a certain point, there will be another check, and the capture of a further key position will be necessary before progress can be resumed. An oscillation of this kind between transference and extra-transference interpretations will represent the normative course of events in an analysis.

Although the giving of mutative interpretations may thus only occupy a small portion of psycho-analytic treatment, it will, upon being, that the most important part from the point of view of deeply exerting affective percussions. Do so, because of the influencing characteristic confirmations as drawn upon the spoken-exchange of the patient's mindful knowing, in that the individuals that feel, perceive, think, wills, and especially reasons are all taken into heedful compliance. It may be of interest to consider how a moment through which of such an importance to the patient affects the analyst himself. Mrs. Klein has suggested that there must be some quite special internal difficulty as to involve the analyst in interpretations. This is shown in their avoidance by psycho-therapists of non-analytic schools, but many psycho-analysts will be aware of traces of the same tendency in themselves. It may be rationalized into mutative interpretations. This is shown in the avoidance by psycho-therapists of non-analytic schools, if not many consisting of a psycho-analyst as flown over to passing their flow of emptying space, nonetheless, this dialectic awareness traces of the same tendency as in them. But behind this there is somewhat of a lurking difficulty in the actual giving of the interpretation, for there seems to be a constant temptation for the analyst to do something else instead. Questions may be asked of whether o r not. As given to the reassurances or advice or discourses upon theory, or may give interpretations -but interpretations that are not mutative, extra-transference interpretations, interpretations that are non-immediate, or ambiguous, or in exacting of two or more alternative interpretations simultaneously, or he may, perhaps, give interpretations and at the same time, show his own scepticism about them. All of this strongly suggests that the giving of a mutative interpretation is a crucial act for the analyst as well as for the patient. And this inturn will become intelligible when we reflect that at the moment of interpretation the analyst is in fact deliberately Evoking a quantity of the patients id-energy while it is a live and actual and unambiguous and aimed directly himself. Such a moment must be above all others put to the test his relations with his unconscious impulses.

Interpretation of the transference is central to all psychoanalytic models. Definitions of transference and transference interpretation have changed greatly during the past half-century, influenced by major movements in philosophy, but advances in psycho-analytic research and theory, and changes in our of understanding Freud. Suggestively. The advances in psychoanalytic research and theory, and changes in our understanding of Freud. Is that, the historical, relatively simple, concepts of the transference as the reproductions in the presence of significant relationships from therapists do not adequately meet current clinical theoretical demands? Modernist views of the transference emphasize as in additional sources of transference responses, the role of the analytic background of safety, the constant modifications of unconscious fantasy and internal representations, and the interactive nature of transference response, with important interpersonal and intersubjective components. It is suggested that the evolving modernists view of transference and transference interpretation permit a fuller accounting for transference and transference components. Such in a fuller accountability, for which of these issues of psychological 'truth' has open the way for better informed interventions. The issue of psychological 'truth' and 'distortion' as applied to transference phenomena will be presented with clinical vignettes.

Psychoanalysis, since the earliest days of the, Studies on Hysteria (Breuer and Freud, 1993-1905), have always given special attention to the transference and to the interpretation of transference, believing it to be central in our theory and technique. While there, has never been a lack of interest in transference interpreting. It is not clear why this is so, and the reasons may vary in different parts of the international psychoanalytic community. In America, at least, Gill's (1982) recent, and somewhat radical presentation of transference interpretation has surely helped to the grasping upon our developing attentions. Nevertheless, of another reason for our intensified interests in transference interpretation is the opportunity it provides for the rhetorically dialectic awareness, in that discussions, have lead us to the diverse analytic theories and techniques that today complete the diverseness as observed, for which of our attentions and allegiance to which transference interpretation seems to have replaced self-psychology. Thus, the encompassing topic that allows analysts of varied persuasions among many structural and fundamental elements that forge out the shape for taking upon the imparting of instinctual information. As to know, and knowing that you know, is, applied, however, of its depthful concerning contemplations with which is distinguished by the evolving characterizations that are of knowing that you know is really nothing whatsoever.

Despite the diversity of the transference and its interpreting in analytic process and cure, differing only in whether transference is everything or almost everything to give a clear-cut definition of what transference is.

Laplanche and Pontalis (1973) had written that, "The reason it is so difficult to produce a definition of transference is that for many authors the notion has taken on a very broad extension, even coming to connote all the phenomena which constitute the patient's relationship with the psychoanalyst, as a result the concept is burdened down more than any other with each analyst's particular view on the treatment - on its objective, dynamics, tactics, scope, and so forth. The question of the transference is thus beset by a whole series of difficulties which have been the subject of debate in classical psychoanalysis."

Sandler (1983) has discussed how the terms transference and transference resistance, as well as other terms have undergone profound changes in meaning as new discoveries and new trends of psycho-analytic technique assume ascendency. He said, . . . major changes in technical emphasis brought about the extension of the transference concept, which now has dimensions of meaning which differ from the official definition of the term. I am not sure there has ever been a simplified definition of the term. While a certain flexibility of definition makes conversation possible in a field of diverse views, which we may never be clear on what any two people mean when they use the term is a significant hindrance to our discourse.

However: with this in mind we might review one of Freud's last comments on transference. In "An Outline of Psycho-Analysis" (1940), published posthumously, he wrote on the analytic situation:

The most remarkable thing is this. The patient is not satisfied with regarding the analyst in the light of reality as a helper and advisor who, moreover, is remunerated for the trouble he takes and who would himself be content with some role that of a guide on a different mountain to climb, on the contrary, the patient sees in him. the return, and the reincarnation, of some important figure out of his childhood or past, and consequently transfer onto him, feelings and reactions which undoubtedly apply this prototype. This fact of transference soon proves to be a factor of an undreamt-of importance, on the other hand bud an instrument of irreplaceable value and on the other, that he set out on a different undertaking without any suspicion of extraordinary power that would be at his command. . . .

Another advantage of transference, too, in that in it the patient produces before us with plastic clarity an important part of his life-story, of which he would, otherwise have probably given us only an insufficient account. He acts it before us, as it was, instead of reporting it to us.

Freud saw the transference interpretation as a method of strengthening the ego against past unconscious wishes and conflicts.

It is the analyst's task constantly to speak abruptly, and in doing so, the patient may relinquish of his menacing illusions and to show him again and again, of what it takes to be or begin of a new life, are the reflections of the past. And least, he should fall into a state in which he is inaccessible to all evidences, the analyst takes that neither the love nor the hostility reaching an extreme height. This is affected by preparing him in good time for these possibilities and by not overlooking the first signs of them. Careful handling of the transference on these lines is as a role richly rewarded. If we succeed, as we usually can, in enlightenment the patient on the true nature of the phenomena of the transference, we thus have struck a powerful weapon out of the hand of his resistance and will have converted dangers into gains. For a patient never forgets again what he has experienced in the form of transference, it carries a greater force of conviction than anything he can acquire in other ways.

The theories advanced by Austrian physician Sigmund Freud were among the first attempts to understand malfunctioning of the mind, but the methods of psychoanalysis advocated by Freud and modified by his followers proved ineffective for treating certain serious mental illnesses. Two early attempts to treat psychotic illness were the destruction of parts of the brain in a procedure-called lobotomy, introduced in 1935, and electroconvulsive therapy, devised in 1938. Lobotomy and less severe forms of psychosurgery are now used only rarely, and electroconvulsive therapy is primarily a treatment for depressive illness that has not responded to

A new era in treatment of schizophrenia, a severe form of mental illness, began in the early 1950s with the introduction of phenothiazine drugs. These drugs led to a new trend, deinstitutionalisation, in which patients were released from mental hospitals and treated in the community. Valium and other benzodiazepine drugs went into wide use in the 1970s for treating anxiety and other emotional illness. Late in the century, there was growing awareness about the importance of diagnosing and treating clinical depression, a leading cause of suicide. Advanced imaging techniques that show the structural and functional differences in the brains of people with certain mental illnesses have opened the door for new treatment options.

R. D. Lange (1927-1989), is the Scottish psychiatrist and social critic. Lange is best known for his controversial analyses of communication patterns in dysfunctional families, especially families in which one member has been diagnosed as having schizophrenia. Lange analyzed power relations in family interactions and viewed the schizophrenic patient as a victim of those power relations.

Lange came to believe that schizophrenia is a social disorder, rather than a biochemical disease. In his attempt to identify and empathize more closely with his patients, Lange rejected standard forms of treatment. He developed unorthodox methods of treating the disease and founded a communal treatment centre for schizophrenic patients. Lange strengthened the movement for mental patients' rights and had a hand in changing the medical model of mental illness in general and of schizophrenia in particular.

In his early writings, such as the widely read The Divided Self (1960), Lange proposed the theories that would underlie his life's work. Above all, he called schizophrenia a social problem, rather than a medical ailment. Although he accepted the idea that schizophrenia could be identified by symptoms such as deranged speech and bizarre behaviour, he argued that these symptoms were intelligible when viewed in a family context. Thus, schizophrenic patients were seen not as "crazy" but as coping with a bad situation. Lange saw the family unit as deranged and the patient as merely a victim of the family's conflicting, hypocritical messages. The patient's self was split between his or her true needs and feelings and a false front erected to please the family. Lange called this facade a "false self system."

In the mid-1960s Lange began to write and lecture about the possible positive aspects of psychotic experience. Normal adjustment to a dysfunctional family and to modern society, he asserted, often requires hypocrisy, repression of feelings, splitting of the self, and cruelty to others. A psychotic person, in Lange's view, deserves praise for being sensitive enough to disintegrate under the pressure and seek a more honest, unified organization of the self. Unlike most psychiatric researchers and theorists, Lange was an advocate of patients' rights. He attempted to convey the experiences and feelings of his patients in order to empathize with them and to describe their world.

Lange and his associates experimented with untraditional forms of treatment for mental illness. They criticized standard mental hospitals, which treated patients' experiences as something to be eliminated - by methods such as electric shock - rather than experienced and resolved. Lange's positions attracted attention during the 1960s, partly because they corresponded closely to counterculture attacks upon traditional institutions, such as the family, and also because he often experimented with the therapeutic use of hallucinogens.

To provide a place for schizophrenics to live free of subjection to invasive treatment, Lange and his associates opened a communal treatment centre called Kingsley Hall in 1965. There, the staff, including Lange, lived on equal status with patients, in keeping with Lange's desire to empathize fully with mentally ill people. The patients were not drugged with traditional anti-schizophrenia drugs or otherwise inhibited from fully experiencing and expressing their feelings. Kingsley Hall was considered revolutionary, and it was admired and discussed by many professionals of the time. Although some of Lange's patients persisted in bizarre, regressive behaviour, others, such as a schizophrenic nurse named Mary Barnes, purportedly regained their mental health and left Kingsley Hall. Barnes and her psychoanalyst, Joseph Burke, gave an account of Barnes's Kingsley Hall experience in their book Mary Barnes: Two Accounts of a Journey Through Madness (1972).

In addition to The Divided Self, Lange wrote and co-wrote several other major works. These include Reason and Violence (with David Cooper, 1964); Sanity, Madness, and the Family (with Aaron Esterson, 1964); Interpersonal Perception (with H. Phillipson and A. R. Lee, 1966); The Politics of Experience (1967); The Politics of the Family; (1969; revised and retitled The Politics of the Family and Other Essays, 1971); Self and Others (1969); and The Facts of Life (1976). His autobiography, Wisdom, Madness and Folly, was published in 1985. Lange has been the subject of several biographies.

While these matters under discussion should enhance our understanding and conditions in terms through which the past and present are to be understood. Despite their brevity, these discussions, to a better kind, as their discerning intendment would not only make in agreement of an acceptation in meaning but understood by their endeavour upon undertaking of our present concerns and considerations, that in issues regarding the transference and the conditions for loving, with which Freud's views may be best approached through his introduction of the idea of conditions for loving that project the analysis of transferences. For example, Freud says, in this context that, . . . each individual, . . . has acquired a specific method of his own in this conduct of his erotic life - that is, in the precondition of falling in love which he lays down, in the instincts he satisfies and the aim he sets himself in the course of it'. In another place, Freud is advising the analyst to adopt a special attitude toward erotic transference; this is the attitude that combines attentiveness, neutrality, non-gratification, and insistence on analysing the erotic feelings as 'unreal' but necessary features of the treatment. he goes on to describe the consequence of maintaining this attitude in the following words: 'The patient, whose sexual repression is of course not yet removed but merely pushed into the back-ground, will then feel safe enough to allow all her preconditions for loving, all the phantasies springing from her sexual desires, all the detailed characteristics of her state of being in love, to come to light, and from these she will herself open up the way to the infantile roots of her love (1915). And, in a number of papers dating from about the same time, that is between the years of 1910 and 1922, he describes particular conditions for loving. Among these are the man's condition that the woman he loves sexually must somehow be degraded or in need of rescue or that there be an injured third party in the interpersonal configuration, also. In the instance of male homosexuality, in addition to the partner's possessing a penis, there is the condition that the young man who is loved be the same age that the lover was when he developed his dominant identification with his mother (1922).

Freud described many such conditions throughout his writings. Although he was obviously intent on particularizing the conditions for loving, nothing stands in the way of our including under that designation the general or universal conditions for loving on which we now put so much emphasis, especially on our analysis of the preoedipal phase of development and their sequelae. Freud set forth a general outline of development (e.g., in the "Three Essays on the Theory of Sexuality" [1905], that easily accommodates this general extension of the idea of conditions for loving.

In the end, as is well known, both the paramount issues of the analysis and the leading explanatory account of them are likely to be significantly different from the provisional versions of them used at the beginning of the analysis.

The increasing influence of the modernist version of transference and its interpretation represents an adaptation to several long-term philosophical, scientific, and cultural shifts we can now recognize. this changing view of transference is also the most visible emblem of the deep changes in psychoanalytic theory that are now quietly taking place, and of their theoretical pluralism that is so prevalent today (Cooper, 1985).

One of these long-term changes in the climate in which psychoanalysis dwells results from a large philosophical debate concerning the nature of history, veridicality, and narrative. Kermode (1985) has written of the change during this century in our modes of understanding and interpreting the past and the present, "Once upon a time it seemed obvious that you could best understand how things are by asking how they got to be that way. Now attention [is] directed to how things are in their immediate plexuities. There is a switch to use the linguistic expressions, from the diachronic to the synchronic view. Diachrony, roughly speaking, studies things in their synchrony to be as they are, synchrony concerns itself with things as they are and ignores the question, how they got that way. This distinction, put forth by de Sasussure (1915), has achieved philosophical dominance today and is the clear source of the hermeneutic view so prevalent in psychoanalysis, proposed by Ricoeur (1970). From here, it is a short distance to Schafer (1981), and Gill (1982), or Spence (1982) who in varying ways adopt the synchronic view. In this view, the analytic task is interpretation, with the patient, of the events of the analytic situation - usually broadly labelled transference - with a construction rather than a reconstruction of the past. In effect, while there is a past of 'there and then' it is knowable only through the filter of the present, of 'here and now'. There is no other past than the one as we construct, and there is no way of understanding the past but through its relation to the present.

Psychoanalysis, like history but unlike fiction, does have anchoring points, for history's anchoring points are the evidences that events really did occur, There was a Roman empire, it did have dates, actual persons lived and died. These 'facts' place a limitation for the narratives an interpretations that may seriously be entertained. Psychoanalysis is anchored in its scientific developmental psychology and in the biology of attachment and affects. Biology confers regularities and limits on possible histories, and our constructions of the past must accord with this scientific knowledge. constructions of childhood that are incompatible with what we know of developmental possibilities may open our eye's to new concepts of development, but more likely they alert us to maimed childhoods that have led our patients to usual narrative constructions in the effort to maintain self-esteem and internal coherence. A second, far less secure, anchorage is the enormous amount of convergent data that accumulate during the course of an analysis, which are likely to give the analyst the impression that he is reconstructing rather than constructing the figures and the circumstances of his patient's past. While a diachronic view may no longer suffice, it may also not be fully dispensable if our patient's histories are to maintain psychoanalytic coherence, rooted in bodily experience, and the loving, hating and terrifying affects accompanying the fantastic world of infantile psychic reality. Not all analysis are yet as ready as Spence, for example, to give up all claim to the truth value explanatory power of the understanding of the past, even if it is limited to knowing past constructions of the past. Nevertheless, the change in philosophical outlook during our century is profound and contributes to our changing view of the analytic process is exemplified in the transference and its interpretation.

Approaching the same issue from an entirely different vantage point, Emde (1981) speaking for the 'baby-watchers' and discussing changing models of infancy and early development, details a second source of the major change of climate to which he writes, The models suggest that what we reconstruct, and what may be extraordinarily helpful to the patient in making a biography, may never have happened. The human being, infant child, is understood to be fundamentally active in constructing his experience. Perhaps it makes sense for the psychoanalysis to place renewed emphasis on recent and current experiences - first, as a context for interpreting early experience - first, as a context for interpreting the potential amelioration, . . . Psychoanalysts are specialists in dealing with the intrapsychic world not only particular with the dynamic unconscious, but we need to pay attention not only to the intrapsychic realm. conflicting-laden and conflict-free, but also to the interpersonal realm. He concludes, . . . we have probably placed far to much an emphasis on early experience itself as opposed to the process by which it is modified or made use of by subsequent experience.

This view of psychic developments, discarding the timeless unconscious and so powerful at odds with the views that were held by psychoanalysts during the time when most of our ideas of transference interpretation were formed, clearly suggests the modernist model of transference interpretation.

A change in the cultural environment of psychoanalysis provides a third source for the changing model of transference interpretation. Valenstein describes oscillations in psychoanalytic outlook between an emphasis on cognition at one end, and on affect at the other. One might see these as differences between old-fashioned scientific and romantic world views. Surely the period of ego psychology, perhaps reflected in the English translation of Freud, and certainly reflected in the effect to insist on the libidinal energetic point of view, represented the attempt to see psychoanalysis as Freud usually did, as an objective science in the nineteenth century style, with hypotheses created out of naïve observations. It accorded with that view to see the transference as an objective reflection of history. We are currently in one of our more romantic periods. It is consonant with that view to see transference as an activity - stormy, romantic, active, affective - a kind of adventure from which the two individuals emerge changed and renewed. In this romantic view, interpretation of the transference are intended to remove obstacles interfering with the heightening and intimacy of the experience, with the implication that self-knowledge and change will result from their encounter. A romantic figure, the patient and analyst set forth on a quest into the unknown, and whether or not one of them returns with a Holy Grail, they return with many new stories to tell and a new life experience - the analysis. Gardner's (1983) book, 'Self Inquiry' epitomizes this romantic view of analyst and patient as a poet-pair engaged in mutual self-inquiry. It is clear that many analysis would rather be artistic than scientist. By contrast, the older, cognitive view of the transference is of an intellectual journey, emotionally loaded of course, but basically a trip back in history, seeking truth and insight.

Finally, our newer ideas of transference interpretation come from the rereading and reinterpretations of Freud that necessarily accompany the changes in outlook in the corresponding pendulum of analytic techniques from Freud's actual technique, as reconstructed from his notes and the report s of his patients, to the so-called 'classical' technique that held sway after Freud's death, and again, to the currently changing technical scene. Lipton (1977) has insisted that in the 1940s andv1950s the so-called classical technique replaced Freud's own more personal and relaxed technique, probably in reaction to Alexander's suggestion of the corrective emotional experience. It was Lipton's view that the misnamed 'classical' technique, in contrast to Freud's, emphasized rules for the analyst's behaviour and sacrificed the purpose of the analysis. Eissler's 1953 description of analysis as an activity that ideally uses only interpretations became the paradigm for 'classical' analysis. It was, Lipton, says, a serious and severe distortion of the mature analytic technique developed by Freud. Freud regarded the analyst 's personal behaviour, the personality of the analyst exemplified for Lipton in the case of the Rat Man. The so-called 'classical' (and in his view non-Freudian) techniques attempted to include every aspect of the analytic situation as part of technique and led to the model of the silent, restrained psychoanalyst. Lipton's argument is persuasive.

These two different models of technique have obvious implications concerning the transference and its interpretation. Unless we believe in an extreme version of the historical model, we must expect that the silent, restraint, nonparticipatory psychoanalyst will elicit different responses from his patient than will the vivid, less-hidden, more responsive analyst. The range of personal behaviours available to the analyst before we need be concerned that the analyst is engaging in activities that are excessively self-revelatory or that force the patient into a social relationship is probably much broader than we thought a few years ago. But we also know that almost any behaviour of the analyst, including restraint or silence, immediately influences the patient's responses. In these newer views of the analytic situation it is not easy to know that intrapsychically derived patient behaviours

It is evident today that psychoanalyst's under the sway of their theories and personalities, differ greatly concerning matters to which they are sensitive, and, of course, we can interpret only the transferences we perceive. Despite this limitation, a review of the literature reveals, along with the usual rigidities, a laudable tendency to describe one's experience as fully as possible, without heed to how it contradicts belief, often blurring over when experience and theory do not match. However, we have always been better at what we do than at what we say we do. This is exemplified in Heimann's (1956) paper. Speaking from a modified Kleinian perspective, and holding the historical theory of transference interpretation, Heimann managed 30 years ago to describe vividly and to support passionately much of what today is under discussion as the modernist version. That her position were contradictory bothered her not at all. While many of us prefer to think we are following our theories, like all good scientists, good psychoanalysts, beginning with Freud, have always seen and responded to far more than our theories admit. when we have seen too much, we change our theories.

Overall, during the last half of this century, these trends, as well as our ever-increasing knowledge of our increasing distance from Freud's authority have led to specific theoretical developments (Cooper, 1984, 1985), many of them inferred in the newer transference model. Our current pluralistic theoretical world, in which almost all analysts are working, wittingly or not, with individual amalgams of Freud's drive theory, ego psychology, interpersonal Sullivanian psychoanalysis, object-relationship theory, Bowlbyan or Mahlerian attachment theory, and usually smuggled-in versions of self-psychology, lies at the base of the newer ideas and disagreements concerning transference interpretation.

Although the historical definitions of transference and transference interpretation have the merit of seeming precision and limited scope, they are based on a psychoanalytical theory that no longer stands alone and has lost ground in at least, subsumed, by modernist conceptions that are more attuned to the theories that abound today.

CPSIA information can be obtained
at www.ICGtesting.com
Printed in the USA
BVHW011103030720
582914BV00009B/505